Sunday Express

GUIDE TO
GOLF
COURSES
—— 1997 ——

*"Every golfer should have a copy of
this comprehensive, beautifully-organised
compendium"* Golf Weekly

Produced by the Automobile Association

PRODUCED BY AA PUBLISHING

Maps prepared by the Cartographic Department of The
Automobile Association

Maps © The Automobile Association 1996

Directory generated by the AA Establishment Database,
Information Research, Hotel and Touring Services

Editor: David Hancock

Cover photograph by Peter Dazeley

Editorial contributors: John Ingham, writer for *Golf
Monthly* and Charlie Mulqueen of the *Cork Examiner*

Illustrations by Alan Roe and Tessa Lecomber

Head of Advertisement Sales
Christopher Heard: Tel 01256 20123 (ext 21544)

Advertisement Production
Karen Weeks: Tel 01256 20123 (ext 21545)

Typeset by Avonset, Midsomer Norton, Nr Bath

Printed and bound in Great Britain by Bemrose Security
Printing, Derby

A CIP catalogue record for this book is available from the
British Library

Published by AA Publishing, which is a trading name
of Automobile Association Developments Limited
whose registered office is Norfolk House, Priestley
Road, Basingstoke, Hampshire RG24 9NY, Registered
number 1878835.

ISBN 0 7495 1386 1

CONTENTS

LOOKING FOR SOMEWHERE DIFFERENT TO STAY OR EAT?

Try one of the 4000 inspected hotels on offer in

AA The Hotel Guide

- Country house hotels, town houses, busy city hotels or cliff-top seaside hotels

- Whatever you fancy – whether you are on holiday or on business the wide range of hotels has something for everyone

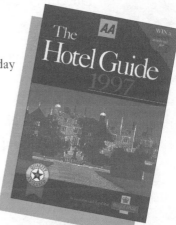

You can be sure of a delicious meal if you use

AA Best Restaurants in Britain

- The Abbey Well guide to AA recommended restaurants

- With 1500 AA Rosette-awarded restaurants, the excellence of the food is assured

- With over 20 national cuisines represented, there should be something for every palate

HOW TO USE THIS
GUIDE

This guide contains about 2800 golf courses in Britain and Ireland most of which welcome visiting golfers. This includes many newly-built courses.

ALL YOU NEED TO KNOW

We have endeavoured to supply all the information you need to know before your visit by telling you what kind of course you can expect, what club facilities are available, including catering, any leisure facilities and the green fees you can expect to pay. We have also included AA-recommended accommodation - whether it be at the course itself or slightly further away.

ARRANGING A VISIT

Some courses want advance notice of any visit, and possibly a letter of introduction from your own club. They may also require a handicap certificate. If this is the case the directory will include this information. However, it is always a good idea to check with any course in advance as **details in the directory can change**, particularly green fees, during the currency of the guide.

COURSES OF NOTE

Courses that are considered to be of particular merit or interest have been placed within a shaded box. They may be very historic clubs or they may have been chosen because their courses are particularly testing or enjoyable to play. Some have been included because they are in holiday areas and have proved popular with visiting golfers. Such a selection cannot be either exhaustive or totally objective, and these courses do not represent any formal category on quality or other grounds.

Major Championship courses have special treatment with a full page entry, including a selection of places at which to eat as well as to stay.

THE DIRECTORY

The directory is arranged in countries: England, Northern Ireland and the Republic of Ireland are listed in alphabetical location within each county. Scotland and Wales are listed in alphabetical location within regions - the counties that comprise each region are listed below the region heading. If you are not sure where your chosen course may be, there is an alphabetical index of courses at the end of the directory. The maps at the end of the book will also help to locate any golf course.

MAP REFERENCES

Should you be travelling in an unfamiliar part of the country and want to know the choice of courses available to you, consult the atlas at the end of the book. In its directory entry, each course has a map number and National Grid reference and there are directions to the course giving the nearest place located on the map. The grid references for the Irish Republic are unique to the atlas at the back of this book.

SYMBOLS AND ABBREVIATIONS

In order to maximise the space available, we have used certain symbols and abbreviations within the directory entries and these are explained in the panel below.

04 TQ21	atlas page and National Grid reference
☎	telephone number
IR£	Irish Punts (Republic only - the rates of exchange between Punts and pounds sterling are liable to fluctuate)
⊗	lunch
〗Ⅲ	dinner
🍴	bar snacks
☕	tea/coffee
♀	bar open midday and evenings
🛏	accommodation at club
👗	changing rooms
🏚	well-stocked shop
⌐	clubs for hire
ſ	professional at club
★	hotel classification
✿	restaurant classification (applicable to championship course entry only)
Q	Guest house classification
B	AA Branded group hotels
TH	Town House hotels

5

ENTRIES IN BOLD ITALICS

NB Although we make every effort to obtain up-to-date information from golf clubs, in some cases we have been unable to verify details with the club's management. Where this is the case the course name is shown in bold italics and you would be strongly advised to check with the club in advance of your visit

TELEPHONE CODES

The area codes shown against telephone numbers under Republic of Ireland courses are applicable within the Republic only. Similarly the area codes shown for entries in Great Britain and Northern Ireland cannot be used direct from the Republic. Check your telephone directory for details.

ACCOMMODATION

For each course listed, we recommend a nearby AA-appointed hotel, giving its classification, full name and address, telephone number and total number of bedrooms, including the number with private bath or shower. In some cases the hotel will be within the grounds of the golf course itself. The hotels recommended in the Golf Guide are mostly in the ★★, ★★★, and ★★★★ star categories. Where there is no AA-appointed hotel nearby, we have recommended an AA-inspected Listed Establishment These are classified by a quality assessment, or Q rating, of 1-5 Q's.

CLUB ACCOMMODATION

Some courses offer accommodation at their club. Where this facility exists, the 'bed' symbol (🛏) will appear in the entry under club facilities. This has been listed as a further option for those who might wish to stay at the course. However, unless the club accommodation has an AA star-rating, the only accommodation recommended by the AA is the star-rated hotel that appears at the foot of each entry.

KEY TO HOTEL CLASSIFICATION

The AA system of star rating from one to five stars is the market leader in hotel classifications and has long been universally recognised as an accurate, objective indication of the facilities one can expect to find at any hotel in the AA scheme.

★ Black stars indicate the level of facilities and services available at a hotel. One-star hotels are generally small hotels and inns, with good but often simple furnishings, facilities and food.

★★ Small to medium-sized hotels offering more facilities(telephones and televisions etc), and at least half the bedrooms will have en-suite bath or shower.

★★★ Medium-sized hotels with more spacious accommodation and a greater range of facilities and services; all rooms have en-suite bath or shower.

★★★★ Large hotels with spacious accommodation and high standards od comfort, service and food; all rooms have full en suite facilities.

★★★★★ Large luxury hotels offering the highest international standards of accommodation, facilities, services and cuisine.

⚘ This denotes an AA Country House hotel with a relaxed informal atmosphere and offering a personal welcome. Often secluded, they are not always rurally situated but are quiet.

Branded Hotels Hotels belonging to large groups do not carry star ratings as they reach a common level of comfort and facilities. They are indicated by a B prior to the hotel name.

PERCENTAGE RATINGS FOR QUALITY

Our inspectors give percentage scores to hotels with black stars as a way of comparing hotels of the same star rating in terms of quality. This covers all aspects of a hotel's operation, including hospitality, service, cleanliness, food, and overall presentation of bedrooms and public areas. A high percentage score indicates superior standards within the star rating.

RED STARS

The AA recognises hotels that consistently provide outstanding levels of hospitality, service, food and comfort through its prestigious red-star award scheme. These are given to a select group of hotels considered to be of the very best within their star rating. In such cases, a percentage score for quality is considered unnecessary. Red-star hotels in this guide are indicated by the word 'red' after the star classification.

ROSETTES

🏵 Rosettes are awarded to hotels and restaurants achieving notable excellence for quality of cuisine, from one rosette – indicating carefully prepared food reflecting a high level of culinary skill – to a maximum of five rosettes, indicating outstanding cuisine reaching the highest international standards.

STUFF of DREAMS

From any viewpoint, the United Kingdom is a golfing jewel, set among wild seas, created by nature, basic and pure and often oblivious to modern trends. Some of the great links, famed throughout the world, remain mercifully undisturbed and unspoiled. The passage of time has, obviously, produced 'modifications' but we ordinary mortals can still walk old gems, sinking our shoes into the spike-marks of champions long gone. These classic tests are available to the traveller who makes an early request for admission. But there can be problems!

Our golfing kingdom is divided into four quite different countries - but all of them speak the same language. However, it is true that knocking on the door of an exclusive club does not guarantee a round. A well-written letter of introduction can work wonders, particularly if you stress that a game at an off-peak time is what you have in mind. It is important to bear in mind though that famous courses near big cities usually refuse casual visitors.

Britain's golf population is guessed at almost 4 million people and I am assured by Bernard Pendry, Chief Executive of the Golf Club Great Britain, that there are 1.3 million players who belong to no club, being nomads of a huge sporting fraternity.

So let's grasp the nettle and name Britain's clubs that must be played. A daunting task, I'm sure you'll agree.

ENGLAND

'Seek out England's golf heritage. Those stretches are the old established classics with no artificial lakes, or whopping clubhouses.......'

Where better to start than at the headquarters of the English Golf Union which bases itself at one of the finest inland courses you'll ever find, at Woodhall Spa in Lincolnshire. Without doubt this test is one of my top 10 favourites in England. Play it, you must!

Many of the classic English courses are close to the seaside. These links are selected by the R&A for the Open, and not just because they have sufficient space to park thousands of cars! Raw and basic, exposed to the elements and close to the ancient town of Sandwich in Kent, any American visitor accustomed to manicured excellences at Augusta will find the whopping, breezey links course of Royal St George's a culture shock. Nearby, ships heave their way through the choppy seas of the English Channel in winter, while on a still, summer day, high-climbing skylarks accompany your every shot with an unforgettable chorus. Arnold Palmer won a professional event here in 1970s and I bought him the champagne, while Greg Norman collected an Open Championship here, as did Sandy Lyle, Harry Vardon, Walter Hagen, Sir Henry Cotton - and many other legendary names.

If you wish to join those at the 19th hole talking about the qualities of English golf, your entry ticket must include the Sandwich experience. But there are others, of course!

HERE'S A HIDDEN GEM

Moving inland, nearer London, one finds world class stretches like West Sussex (Pulborough) and Sunningdale (both Old and New), not to mention the splendid Berkshire course, near Ascot. Playing the marvellous and expansive Walton Heath courses is a joy and, also in Surrey, Hankley Common is a hidden gem while Woking, West Hill, Swinley Forest and Worplesdon are all 5-star. I also rate the North Hants course at Fleet and usually enjoy Wentworth, although I once competed in the English Amateur Championship there with no distinction as, from the back tees, it is designed with the Toyota World Match-Play Championship, and Ernie Els in mind!

Heading cross country, try the 18-holes of Royal West Norfolk at Brancaster before the tide claims it, and sink to your knees to beg to play Royal Worlington, the home of Cambridge University golfers and a challenge accepted as the best 9-holer in Europe. Mentioning excellent golf courses by name is fatal because of the ones you leave out, including my own home course at Royal Wimbledon, designed by the great Colt.

But travel north and tackle three other 'Royal' courses - Birkdale, Liverpool and Lytham St Anne's. These Lancashire challenges are known far and wide. However, if you are in that neck of the woods, also seek out and enjoy Formby and Hillside which I know to be good from personal experience. And in Yorkshire, I boast about shots hit across the Moortown course (Leeds), and the sporty Pannal test near Harrogate.

IMPORTED COPIES

But what, you cry, about the new and wondrous courses, such as the ones constructed recently alongside castles, in the parkland grounds belonging to some Lord who has fallen on hard times - aren't they worthy? And why leave out newish tests like East Sussex National, or the huge Oxfordshire, built with no Japanese money spared? These have magnificent facilities, the greens are automatically watered and the artificial lakes are certainly not dyed. They fulfil everything their millionaire designers intended. But are they, I ask, what you call English courses, or imported copies of some stretch that is forever un-English?

On this subject, you are the jury and finding out will provide years of endless pleasure. Believe me, I know........

ENGLAND

BEDFORDSHIRE

ASPLEY GUISE   Map 04 SP93

Aspley Guise & Woburn Sands West Hill MK17 8DX
☎ 01908 583596
A fine undulating course in expansive heathland
interspersed with many attractive clumps of gorse, broom
and bracken. Some well-established silver birch are a
feature. The 7th, 8th and 9th are really tough holes to
complete the first half.
18 holes, 6135yds, Par 71, SSS 70, Course record 67.
Club membership 600.
Visitors   with member only at weekends.
Societies   normally booked 12 mths ahead.
Green Fees   £28 per day; £22 per round.
Facilities   ⊗ ⅏ ⓛ ➋ ♀ ⚑ 🛆 ⓕ David Marsden.
Leisure   trolley for hire, putting green, practice area.
Location   2m W of M1 junc 13
Hotel   ★★★ 69% Moore Place Hotel, The Square,
                  ASPLEY GUISE
                  ☎ 01908 282000 39 ⇆ ⓕAnnexe15 ⇆ ⓕ

BEDFORD   Map 04 TL04

Bedford & County Green Ln, Clapham MK41 6ET
☎ 01234 352617
Pleasant parkland course with views over Bedford and
surrounding countryside. The 15th is a testing par 4.
18 holes, 6347yds, Par 70, SSS 70.
Club membership 600.
Visitors   handicap certificate required, weekends with
                  member only.
Societies   welcome Mon,Tue,Thu & Fri, telephone in
                  advance.
Green Fees   not confirmed.
Facilities   ♀ 🛆 ⚑ ⓕ E Bullock.
Location   2m N off A6
Hotel   ★★★ 72% Woodlands Manor Hotel, Green Ln,
                  Clapham, BEDFORD
                  ☎ 01234 363281 22 ⇆ ⓕAnnexe3 ⇆ ⓕ

Bedfordshire Bromham Rd, Biddenham MK40 4AF
☎ 01234 261669
An easy walking, parkland course with tree hazards.
18 holes, 6196yds, Par 70, SSS 69, Course record 63.
Club membership 700.
Visitors   may not play at weekends except with member.
Societies   must telephone in advance/confirm in writing.
Green Fees   not confirmed.
Facilities   ♀ 🛆 ⚑ ⓕ
Leisure   putting green, practice area, trolley hire.
Location   1m W on A428
Hotel   ★★★ 72% Woodlands Manor Hotel, Green Ln,
                  Clapham, BEDFORD
                  ☎ 01234 363281 22 ⇆ ⓕAnnexe3 ⇆ ⓕ

Mowsbury Cleat Hill, Kimbolton Rd MK41 8DQ
☎ 01234 771041 & 216374
Parkland municipal course in rural surroundings. Long and
testing 14-bay driving range and squash facilities.
18 holes, 6514yds, Par 72, SSS 71, Course record 66.
Club membership 800.
Visitors   no restrictions.
Societies   apply in writing.
Green Fees   not confirmed.
Facilities   ♀ 🛆 ⚑ ⓣ ⓕ Malcolm Summers.
Leisure   squash, driving range.
Location   2m N of town centre on B660
Hotel   ★★★ 72% Woodlands Manor Hotel, Green Ln,
                  Clapham, BEDFORD
                  ☎ 01234 363281 22 ⇆ ⓕAnnexe3 ⇆ ⓕ

COLMWORTH   Map 04 TL15

Colmworth & North Bedfordshire New Rd MK44 2BY
☎ 01234 378181
An easy walking course with well-bunkered greens, opened
in 1991. The course is often windy and plays longer than the
yardage suggests. Water comes into play on 3 holes.
18 holes, 6459yds, Par 71, SSS 71, Course record 69.
9 holes, 611yds, Par 27.
Club membership 230.
Visitors   advisable to contact in advance, tee reserved for
                  members Sat & Sun until 9.30 am & between
                  12.30 & 2pm.
Societies   telephone in advance.
Green Fees   £10 per 18 holes (£15 weekends); £6 per 9 holes
                  (£8 weekends).
Facilities   ⊗ ⅏ ⓛ ➋ ♀ 🛆 ⚑ ⓣ ⓕ Steve Brydon.
Leisure   fishing, trolley for hire, putting green, practice
                  area, snooker.
Location   7m NE of Bedford, off B660
Hotel   ★★★ 68% The Barns Hotel, Cardington Rd,
                  BEDFORD ☎ 01234 270044 49 ⇆ ⓕ

DUNSTABLE   Map 04 TL02

Dunstable Downs Whipsnade Rd LU6 2NB
☎ 01582 604472
A fine downland course set on two levels with far-
reaching views and frequent sightings of graceful gliders.
The 9th hole is one of the best short holes in the country.
There is a modernised clubhouse.
18 holes, 6255yds, Par 70, SSS 70, Course record 64.
Club membership 600.
Visitors   weekends with member only. Handicap
                  certificate required.
Societies   apply in advance.
Green Fees   £28 per round/day.
Facilities   ⊗ ⅏ ⓛ ➋ ♀ 🛆 ⚑ ⓕ Michael Weldon.
Leisure   trolley for hire, putting green, practice area.
Location   2m S off B4541
Hotel   ★★★ 66% Old Palace Lodge Hotel,
                  Church St, DUNSTABLE
                  ☎ 01582 662201 50 ⇆ ⓕ

Griffin Chaul End Rd, Caddington LU1 4AX
☎ 01582 415573
A new challenging 18-hole course with a SSS of 69.
18 holes, 6161yds, Par 71, SSS 69.
Club membership 450.
                                                                                      ▶

Visitors with member only after 3pm & at weekends.
Societies apply in writing.
Green Fees not confirmed.
Facilities ♀ ♣ 🖼
Location Off A505 Luton/Dunstable
Hotel ★★★ 60% Luton Gateway, Dunstable Rd, LUTON ☎ 01582 575955 117 ➡ ♠

LEIGHTON BUZZARD   Map 04 SP92

Leighton Buzzard Plantation Rd LU7 7JF
☎ 01525 373811/2
Parkland course with easy walking. The 17th and 18th holes are challenging tree-lined finishing holes with tight fairways.
18 holes, 6101yds, Par 71, SSS 70, Course record 66.
Club membership 700.
Visitors may not play Tue (Ladies Day). May only play with member weekends and bank holidays. Handicap certificate required. Must contact in advance and have an introduction from own club.
Societies prior booking required.
Green Fees £27 per day; £20 per round.
Facilities ⊗ ⫚ ▟ ♣ ♀ ♣ 🖼 ♟ ᚖ Lee Scarbrow.
Leisure trolley for hire, putting green, practice area.
Location 1.5m N of town centre off A4146
Hotel ★★★ 58% Swan Hotel, High St, LEIGHTON BUZZARD ☎ 01525 372148 38 ➡ ♠

LOWER STONDON   Map 04 TL13

Mount Pleasant Station Rd SG16 6JL ☎ 01462 850999
A 9-hole course which, when played over 18 totals some 5644 yards. The course is undulating meadowland and there is a significant ditch in play on 2,7,8,9th holes. The 5th hole plays long in a prevailing West wind. Alternative tees for all holes are planned for the end of 1996 which will change the par and SSS.
9 holes, 3086yds, Par 72, SSS 69, Course record 70.
Club membership 300.
Visitors no restrictions, can book 1 day in advance, booking advisable weekends & evenings May-Sep.
Societies telephone or apply in writing.
Green Fees not confirmed.
Facilities ♀ ♣ 🖼 ᚖ ᚖ Zac Thompson.
Location 0.75m W of A600
Hotel ★★★ 75% Flitwick Manor Hotel, Church Rd, FLITWICK ☎ 01525 712242 15 ➡ ♠

LUTON   Map 04 TL02

South Beds Warden Hill LU2 7AA ☎ 01582 591500
27-hole downland course, slightly undulating.
Galley Course: 18 holes, 6389yds, Par 71, SSS 71, Course record 64.
Warden Course: 9 holes, 2500yds, Par 32.
Club membership 1000.
Visitors must contact in advance.
Societies telephone for details.
Green Fees Galley Course; £28 per day; £18 per round (£36.50/£25 weekends & bank holidays). Warden Course; £7 (£10 weekends & bank holidays).
Facilities ⊗ ⫚ ▟ ♣ ♀ ♣ 🖼 ᚖ Eddie Cogle.

Leisure trolley for hire, putting green, practice area.
Location 2m N of Luton on A6
Hotel ★★★ 71% Strathmore Thistle, Arndale Centre, LUTON ☎ 01582 34199 150 ➡ ♠

Stockwood Park London Rd LU1 4LX ☎ 01582 413704
Well laid out municipal parkland course with established trees and several challenging holes.
18 holes, 6049yds, Par 69, SSS 69, Course record 67.
Club membership 800.
Visitors no restrictions.
Societies Mon, Tue & Thu only, telephone for application.
Green Fees £7.30 per round (£9.60 weekends).
Facilities ⊗ ⫚ ▟ ♣ ♀ ♣ 🖼 ᚖ Glyn McCarthy.
Leisure motorised carts for hire, buggies for hire, trolley for hire, driving range, putting green, practice area.
Location 1m S
Hotel ★★★ 62% The Chiltern, Waller Av, Dunstable Rd, LUTON ☎ 01582 575911 91 ➡ ♠

MILLBROOK   Map 04 TL03

Millbrook Millbrook Village MK45 2JB ☎ 01525 840252
Long parkland course, on rolling countryside high above the Bedfordshire plains, with several water hazards. Laid out on well-drained sandy soil with many fairways lined with silver birch, pine and larch.
18 holes, 7100yds, Par 74, SSS 73, Course record 68.
Club membership 550.
Visitors must contact in advance, may not play after 11am on Thu.
Societies telephone for details.
Green Fees £15 (£25 weekends & bank holidays).
Facilities ⊗ ⫚ ▟ ♣ ♀ ♣ 🖼 ᚖ David Armour.
Leisure trolley for hire, practice area.
Location E side of village off A507
Hotel ★★★ 75% Flitwick Manor Hotel, Church Rd, FLITWICK ☎ 01525 712242 15 ➡ ♠

SANDY   Map 04 TL14

John O'Gaunt Sutton Park SG19 2LY ☎ 01767 260360
Two magnificent parkland courses - John O'Gaunt and Carthagena - covering a gently undulating and tree-lined terrain. The John O'Gaunt course makes the most of numerous natural features, including a river which crosses the fairways of four holes. The Carthagena course has larger greens, longer tees and from the back tees is a challenging course. Fine clubhouse.
John O'Gaunt Course: 18 holes, 6513yds, Par 71, SSS 71, Course record 64.
Carthagena Course: 18 holes, 5869yds, Par 69, SSS 69, Course record 62.
Club membership 1500.
Visitors must contact in advance.
Societies must pre-book.
Green Fees £42 per day/round (£50 weekends & bank holidays).
Facilities ⊗ ⫚ ▟ ♣ ♀ ♣ 🖼 ᚖ Peter Round.
Leisure motorised carts for hire, buggies for hire, trolley for hire, putting green, practice area.
Location 3m NE of Biggleswade on B1040
Hotel ★★ 65% Abbotsley Golf Hotel, Eynesbury Hardwicke, ST NEOTS ☎ 01480 474000 15 ➡ ♠

SHEFFORD
Map 04 TL13

Beadlow Manor Hotel & Golf & Country Club SG17 5PH
☎ 01525 861292 & 860800 Hotel
A 36-hole golf and leisure complex. The Baroness Manhattan and the Baron Manhattan golf courses are undulating with water hazards on numerous holes. The parkland course are good challenging gourses of the beginner and low handicap player.
Baroness Course: 18 holes, 6072yds, Par 71, SSS 69, Course record 67.
Baron Course: 18 holes, 6619yds, Par 73, SSS 72, Course record 66.
Club membership 600.
Visitors must adhere to dress code.
Societies apply in writing or telephone in advance.
Green Fees not confirmed.
Facilities ♀ ⚞ 🏌 🍴 ⌷ ℓ Dale Brightman.
Leisure sauna, solarium, gymnasium, range, putting, motor cart/trolley hire.
Location 2m W on A507
Hotel ★★★ 75% Flitwick Manor Hotel, Church Rd, FLITWICK ☎ 01525 712242 15 ⇌ 𝆑

TILSWORTH
Map 04 SP92

Tilsworth Dunstable Rd LU7 9PU ☎ 01525 210721/2
An undulating parkland course upgraded from 9 to 18 holes in 1992. 30-bay floodlit driving range.
18 holes, 5306yds, Par 69, SSS 66, Course record 66.
Club membership 400.
Visitors may book up to 7 days in advance.
Societies apply in advance.
Green Fees £8 per 18 holes; £5 per 9 holes (£10/£6 weekends & bank holidays).
Facilities ⊗ 🍴 🏌 🍺 ♀ ⚞ 🍴 ℓ Nick Webb.
Leisure buggies for hire, trolley for hire, floodlit driving range, practice area.
Location 0.5m NE off A5
Hotel ★★★ 66% Old Palace Lodge Hotel, Church St, DUNSTABLE ☎ 01582 662201 50 ⇌ 𝆑

WHIPSNADE
Map 04 TL01

Whipsnade Park Studham Ln, Dagnall HP4 1RH
☎ 01442 842330 & 842310
Parkland course situated on downs overlooking the Chilterns adjoining Whipsnade Zoo. Easy walking, good views.
18 holes, 6800yds, Par 73, SSS 72, Course record 69.
Club membership 600.
Visitors with member only at weekends. Must contact in advance.
Societies by prior arrangement.
Green Fees Weekdays: £32 per 36 holes; £21 per 18 holes.
Facilities ⊗ 🍴 🏌 🍺 ♀ ⚞ 🍴 ℓ Michael Lewendon.
Leisure motorised carts for hire, buggies for hire, trolley for hire, putting green, practice area.
Location 1m E off B4506
Hotel ★★★ 66% Old Palace Lodge Hotel, Church St, DUNSTABLE ☎ 01582 662201 50 ⇌ 𝆑

WOBURN
Map 04 SP93

For Woburn Golf Course see Bow Brickhill, Buckinghamshire.

WYBOSTON
Map 04 TL15

Wyboston Lakes MK44 3AL ☎ 01480 223004
Parkland course, with narrow fairways, small greens, set around four lakes and a river which provide the biggest challenge on this very scenic course.
18 holes, 5803yds, Par 69, SSS 69, Course record 65.
Club membership 300.
Visitors a booking system is in operation at weekends, book no more than 8 days in advance.
Societies telephone in advance.
Green Fees £10 per 18 holes; £5 per 9 holes (£14/£7 weekends & bank holidays) Twilight round £7.
Facilities ⊗ 🍴 🏌 🍺 ♀ ⚞ 🍴 ℓ
Leisure fishing, motorised carts for hire, buggies for hire, trolley for hire, driving range, putting green, practice area.
Location NE side of village off A1
Hotel ★★★ 72% Woodlands Manor Hotel, Green Ln, Clapham, BEDFORD ☎ 01234 363281 22 ⇌ 𝆑Annexe3 ⇌ 𝆑

BERKSHIRE

ASCOT
Map 04 SU96

Berkshire Swinley Rd SL5 8AY ☎ 01344 21496
Two heathland courses with splendid tree-lined fairways.
Red Course: 18 holes, 6369yds, Par 72, SSS 71.
Blue Course: 18 holes, 6260yds, Par 71, SSS 71.
Club membership 1000.
Visitors weekdays only on application to secretary.
Societies applications in writing only.
Green Fees £65 per day; £50 per round.
Facilities ⊗ 🏌 🍺 ♀ ⚞ 🍴 ℓ P Anderson.
Leisure motorised carts for hire, buggies for hire, trolley for hire, putting green, practice area.
Location 2.5m NW of M3 jct 3 on A332
Hotel ★★★★ 68% The Berystede, Bagshot Rd, Sunninghill, ASCOT ☎ 01344 23311 91 ⇌ 𝆑

Lavender Park Swinley Rd SL5 8BD
☎ 01344 890940 & 886096
Public parkland course, ideal for the short game featuring challenging narrow fairways. Driving range with 9-hole par 3 course, floodlit until 22.30 hrs.
9 holes, 1102yds, Par 27, SSS 28.
Visitors no restrictions.
Societies welcome, notice prefered.
Green Fees £4.50 per 18 holes; £3.25 per 9 holes (£7/£4.50 weekends & bank holidays).
Facilities 🍺 ♀ ⚞ 🍴 ℓ Wayne Ower/Andy Piper.
Leisure floodlit driving range, snooker hall.
Location 3.5m SW of Ascot, on A332 ▶

Hotel   ★★★★ 68% The Berystede, Bagshot Rd,
Sunninghill, ASCOT
☎ 01344 23311 91 ⇥ ๏

Mill Ride Mill Ride Estate SL5 8LT ☎ 01344 886777
Opened for play in 1991, this 18-hole course combines good
golfing country and attractive surroundings with a
challenging design. The holes require as much thinking as
playing.
18 holes, 6752yds, Par 72, SSS 72, Course record 64.
Club membership 400.
Visitors   must contact in advance.
Societies   apply in advance.
Green Fees prices on application.
Facilities ⊗ ⫘ ⓚ ♥ ♀ ⅄ ⋔ ⋔ ⌤ Mark Palmer.
Leisure   sauna, trolley for hire, driving range, putting
green, practice area.
Location   2m W of Ascot
Hotel   ★★★★ 68% The Berystede, Bagshot Rd,
Sunninghill, ASCOT ☎ 01344 23311 91 ⇥ ๏

Royal Ascot Winkfield Rd SL5 7LJ ☎ 01344 25175
Heathland course inside Ascot racecourse and exposed to
weather.
18 holes, 5716yds, Par 68, SSS 68, Course record 65.
Club membership 620.
Visitors   must be guest of member.
Societies   telephone for provisional booking.
Green Fees on request.
Facilities ⊗ ⫘ ⓚ ♥ ♀ ⅄ ⌂ ⌤ Garry Malia.
Leisure   trolley for hire, putting green, practice area.
Location   0.5m N on A330
Hotel   ★★★★ 68% The Berystede, Bagshot Rd,
Sunninghill, ASCOT ☎ 01344 23311 91 ⇥ ๏

Swinley Forest Coronation Rd SL5 9LE
☎ 01344 874979 (Secretary) & 874811 (Pro)
An attractive and immaculate course of heather and pine
situated in the heart of Swinley Forest. The 17th is as
good a short hole as will be found, with a bunkered
plateau green and the 12th hole is one of the most
challenging par 4's.
18 holes, 6100yds, Par 68, SSS 69, Course record 62.
Club membership 275.
Visitors   by invitation only.
Societies   must contact in writing.
Green Fees £60 per day.
Facilities ⊗ ⓚ ♥ ♀ ⅄ ⌂ ⋔ ⌤ R C Parker.
Leisure   motorised carts for hire, buggies for hire,
trolley for hire, putting green.
Location   1.5m S, off A330
Hotel   ★★★★ 68% The Berystede, Bagshot Rd,
Sunninghill, ASCOT
☎ 01344 23311 91 ⇥ ๏

Blue Mountain Golf Centre Wood Ln RG42 4EX
☎ 01344 300200
An 18-hole Pay and Play course with many testing holes with
water hazards. Greens are large, undulating and strategically
placed bunkers provide a fair challenge.
18 holes, 6097yds, Par 70, SSS 70, Course record 63.
Club membership 1250.
Visitors   tee times bookable in person at the Golf Shop up
to 9 days in advance.

Societies   must contact in advance.
Green Fees £14 per 18 holes; £7 per 9 holes (£18/£9
weekends).
Facilities ⊗ ⫘ ⓚ ♥ ♀ ⅄ ⌂ ⋔ ⌤ Neil Dainton.
Leisure   motorised carts for hire, trolley for hire, driving
range, putting green, practice area.
Location   2m from junct 10 of the M4
Hotel   ★★★★ 64% Reading Moat House, Mill Ln,
Sindlesham, WOKINGHAM
☎ 01734 499988 96 ⇥ ๏

West Berkshire RG16 0HS ☎ 01488 638574 & 638851
Challenging and interesting downland course with testing 635
yds 5th hole, one of the longest par 5's in southern England.
18 holes, 7059yds, Par 73, SSS 74.
Club membership 650.
Visitors   must contact in advance, may play weekends pm
only.
Societies   telephone in advance
Green Fees £24 per day; £16 per round (£20 per round
weekends pm only).
Facilities ⊗ ⫘ ⓚ ♥ ♀ ⅄ ⌂ ⋔ ⌤ Wraith Grant.
Leisure   buggies for hire, trolley for hire, putting green,
practice area.
Location   1m S of village off A338
Hotel   ★★★ 62% The Chequers, Oxford St,
NEWBURY
☎ 01635 38000 45 ⇥ ๏Annexe11 ⇥ ๏

Winter Hill Grange Ln SL6 9RP
☎ 01628 527613 (Secretary) 527610 (Pro)
Parkland course set in a curve of the Thames with wonderful
views across the river to Cliveden.
18 holes, 6408yds, Par 72, SSS 71, Course record 69.
Club membership 850.
Visitors   not permitted weekends.
Societies   welcome Wed & Fri, telephone initially.
Green Fees £25 per day; summer £15 after 2pm; winter £12
after noon..
Facilities ⊗ ⓚ ♥ ♀ ⅄ ⌂ ⋔ ⌤ David Hart.
Leisure   trolley for hire, driving range, putting green,
practice area.
Location   1m NW off B4447
Hotel   ★★★★ 72% The Compleat Angler, Marlow
Bridge, MARLOW ☎ 01628 484444 62 ⇥ ๏

East Berkshire Ravenswood Ave RG45 6BD
☎ 01344 772041
An attractive heathland course with an abundance of
heather and pine trees. Walking is easy and the greens are
exceptionally good. Some fairways become tight where
the heather encroaches on the line of play. The course is
testing and demands great accuracy.
18 holes, 6344yds, Par 69, SSS 70.
Club membership 766.
Visitors   must contact in advance and have a
handicap certificate; must play with member
at weekends & bank holidays.

Societies   telephone for availability.
Green Fees   £35 per day.
Facilities   ⊗ ⅏ ᛤ 🗜 ♀ ᐃ 🏠 ⵏ 𝘭 Arthur Roe.
Leisure   trolley for hire, putting green, practice area.
Location   W side of town centre off B3348
Hotel   ★★★★(red)♨ Pennyhill Park Hotel,
              London Rd, BAGSHOT
              ☎ 01276 471774 22 ⇆ 🖣Annexe54 ⇆ 🖣

DATCHET   Map 04 SU97

Datchet Buccleuch Rd SL3 9BP
☎ 01753 543887 & 541872
Meadowland course, easy walking.
9 holes, 5978yds, Par 70, SSS 69, Course record 63.
Club membership 405.
Visitors   may play weekdays before 3pm.
Societies   Tue only.
Green Fees   not confirmed.
Facilities   ♀ ᐃ 🏠 𝘭 Bill Mainwaring.
Leisure   trolleys.
Location   NW side of Datchet off B470
Hotel   ★★★ 69% The Castle, High St, WINDSOR
              ☎ 01753 851011 104 ⇆ 🖣

MAIDENHEAD   Map 04 SU88

Bird Hills Drift Rd, Hawthorn Hill SL6 3ST
☎ 01628 771030
A gently undulating course with easy walking and many
water hazards. Some challenging holes are the Par 5 6th
dogleg, Par 3 9th surrounded by water and bunkers, and the
16th which is a long uphill Par 4 and a two-tier green.
18 holes, 6176yds, Par 72, SSS 69, Course record 65.
Club membership 400.
Visitors   to book ring 7 days in advance.
Societies   write or telephone in advance.
Green Fees   not confirmed.
Facilities   ♀ ᐃ 🏠 ⵏ 𝘭 Nick Slimming/Adam Bishop.
Location   4m SW of Bray on A330
Hotel   ★★★ 70% Stirrups Country House, Maidens
              Green, BRACKNELL ☎ 01344 882284 24 ⇆

Castle Royle Golf & Country Club Knowl Hill RG10 9XA
☎ 01628 829252
Designed by Neil Coles to championship standard, Castle
Royle has six lakes and is well drained and irrigated. In
attractive countryside with views of Windsor Castle, the
course is very well bunkered with wide fairways and there are
Par 3's with all four aspects to the prevailing wind as each
faces a different direction. Visitors are usually only permitted
as a guest of a member but it is suitable for low or high
handicappers.
18 holes, 6828yds, Par 72, SSS 73.
Club membership 400.
Visitors   with member only.
Green Fees   Members Guests: £20 per round.
Facilities   ⊗ ⅏ ᛤ 🗜 ♀ ᐃ 🏠 ⵏ 𝘭 Paul Stanwick.
Leisure   fishing, trolley for hire, putting green, practice
              area.
Location   Bath road A4
Hotel   ★★★★ 78% Fredrick's Hotel, Shoppenhangers
              Rd, MAIDENHEAD ☎ 01628 35934 37 ⇆ 🖣

Maidenhead Shoppenhangers Rd SL6 2PZ
☎ 01628 24693 & 24067
A pleasant parkland course on level ground with easy
walking to good greens. Perhaps a little short but there
are many natural features and some first-rate short holes.
18 holes, 6364yds, Par 70, SSS 70.
Club membership 650.
Visitors   may not play after noon on Fri or at
              weekends. Must contact in advance and
              have a handicap certificate.
Societies   must contact in writing.
Green Fees   not confirmed.
Facilities   ♀ ᐃ 🏠 ⵏ 𝘭 Steve Geary.
Leisure   putting green,carts,trolley hire.
Location   S side of town centre off A308
Hotel   ★★★★ 78% Fredrick's Hotel,
              Shoppenhangers Rd, MAIDENHEAD
              ☎ 01628 35934 37 ⇆ 🖣

Temple Henley Rd, Hurley SL6 5LH
☎ 01628 824795
An open parkland course with many excellent, fast
greens relying on natural slopes rather than heavy
bunkering. On one 'blind' punchbowl hole there is
actually a bunker on the green. Good drainage assures
play when many other courses are closed.
18 holes, 6207yds, Par 70, SSS 70, Course record 63.
Club membership 480.
Visitors   must contact in advance, limited weekend
              access.
Societies   apply in writing for formal bookings.
Green Fees   £40 per 36 holes; £25 per 18 holes (£40 Sun
              & bank holidays).
Facilities   ⊗ ⅏ ᛤ 🗜 ♀ ᐃ 🏠 ⵏ 𝘭 James Whiteley.
Leisure   squash, motorised carts for hire, buggies for
              hire, trolley for hire, putting green, practice
              area.
Location   Exit M4 junct 8/9 and take A404 and then
              A423
Hotel   ★★★★ 72% The Compleat Angler,
              Marlow Bridge, MARLOW
              ☎ 01628 484444 62 ⇆ 🖣

NEWBURY   Map 04 SU46

Donnington Valley Old Oxford Rd, Donnington RG14 3AG
☎ 01635 551199
Undulating, short, but testing course with mature trees and
elevated greens, some protected by water.
18 holes, 4000yds, Par 61, SSS 60, Course record 59.
Club membership 500.
Visitors   booking system up to 7 days in advance,
              members have priority weekends.
Societies   write or telephone in advance.
Green Fees   £13 per round (£17 weekends).
Facilities   ⊗ ⅏ ᛤ 🗜 ♀ ᐃ 🏠 ⵏ ⋈ 𝘭 Nick Mitchell.
Leisure   hard tennis courts, trolley for hire, putting green,
              practice area.
Location   2m N of Newbury
Hotel   ★★★★ 76% Donnington Valley Hotel & Golf
              Course, Old Oxford Rd, Donnington,
              NEWBURY
              ☎ 01635 551199 58 ⇆ 🖣

Newbury & Crookham Bury's Bank Rd, Greenham RG19 8BZ ☎ 01635 40035
A well-laid out, attractive course running mostly through woodland, and giving more of a challenge than its length suggests.
18 holes, 5880yds, Par 68, SSS 68.
Club membership 800.

Visitors	must play with member on weekends & bank holidays. Handicap certificate required.
Societies	must contact in advance.
Green Fees	not confirmed.
Facilities	♀♣☎ℓ David Harris.
Leisure	putting,trolley hire,practice area.
Location	2m SE off A34
Hotel	★★★ 62% The Chequers, Oxford St, NEWBURY ☎ 01635 38000 45 ⇆ ℝ Annexe11 ⇆ ℝ

READING   Map 04 SU77

Calcot Park Bath Rd, Calcot RG31 7RN
☎ 01734 427124
A delightfully sporting parkland course just outside the town. Hazards include a lake and many trees. The 6th is the longest, 497 yard par 5, with the tee-shot hit downhill over cross-bunkers to a well-guarded green. The 13th (188 yards) requires a big carry over a gully to a plateau green.
18 holes, 6283yds, Par 70, SSS 70, Course record 65.
Club membership 730.

Visitors	must have handicap certificate or letter of introduction from club. May play weekdays only, excluding bank holidays.
Societies	must apply in writing.
Green Fees	£33 per day/round; £20 after 4pm Apr-Sep, noon Oct to Mar.
Facilities	⊗🏮🏠💺♀♣☎🚩 ℓ Albert MacKenzie.
Leisure	motorised carts for hire, trolley for hire, putting green, practice area.
Location	1.5m from M4 junct 4 on A4 towards Reading
Hotel	★★★ 55% The Copper Inn, Church Rd, PANGBOURNE ☎ 01734 842244 14 ⇆ ℝ Annexe8 ⇆ ℝ

Hennerton Crazies Hill Rd, Wargrave RG10 8LT
☎ 01734 401000
Overlooking the Thames Valley, this Par 68 course has many of existing natural features and an good number of hazards such as bunker, mature trees and two small lakes. The most memorable hole is probably the 7th which is a par 3, 183 yards crossing a sharp valley to the green from which there are spectacular views of the whole course.
9 holes, 5460yds, Par 68, SSS 67, Course record 66.
Club membership 430.

Visitors	telephone in advance.
Societies	telephone or write for information.
Green Fees	£12 per 18 holes; £9 per 9 holes (£18/£14 weekends).
Facilities	⊗🏮💺♀♣☎🚩ℓ William Farrow.
Leisure	trolley for hire, floodlit driving range, putting green, practice area.
Hotel	★★★ 66% Red Lion Hotel, Hart St, HENLEY-ON-THAMES ☎ 01491 572161 26rm(23 ⇆ ℝ)

Mapledurham Chazey Heath, Mapledurham RG4 7UD
☎ 01734 463353
18-hole course designed by Bob Sandow. Flanked by hedgerows and mature woods, it is testing for players of all levels.
18 holes, 5750yds, Par 69, SSS 68 or 57 holes.
Club membership 600.

Visitors	no restrictions.
Societies	must contact in advance.
Green Fees	£19 per day; £14 per 18 holes (£23/£17 weekends).
Facilities	⊗🏮💺♀♣☎🚩ℓ Symon O'Keefe.
Leisure	trolley for hire, putting green, practice area, video tuition.
Location	On A4074 to Oxford
Hotel	★★★★ 61% Holiday Inn, Caversham Bridge, Richfield Av, READING ☎ 01734 259988 111 ⇆ ℝ

Reading 17 Kidmore End Rd, Emmer Green RG4 8SG
☎ 01734 472909 (Manager) & 476115 (Pro)
Pleasant tree-lined parkland course, part hilly and part flat with interesting views and several challenging par 3's.
18 holes, 6212yds, Par 70, SSS 70, Course record 67.
Club membership 700.

Visitors	contact the professional. With member only weekends.
Societies	apply by telephone.
Green Fees	£27 per day.
Facilities	⊗🏮💺♀♣☎ℓ Andrew Wild.
Leisure	trolley for hire, putting green, practice area.
Location	2m N off B481
Hotel	★★★ 61% Ship Hotel, 4-8 Duke St, READING ☎ 01734 583455 31rm(21 ⇆ ℝ)

SINDLESHAM   Map 04 SU76

Bearwood Mole Rd RG41 5DB ☎ 01734 760060
Flat parkland course with one water hazard, the 40 lake which features on the challenging 6th and 7th holes. Also 9-hole pitch and putt.
9 holes, 5610yds, Par 70, SSS 68, Course record 66.
Club membership 500.

Visitors	with member only on weekends.
Societies	apply in writing.
Green Fees	£15 per 18 holes; £8 per 9 holes.
Facilities	⊗🏮💺♀♣☎
Leisure	trolley for hire, putting green, practice area, pitch & putt.
Location	1m SW on B3030
Hotel	★★★★ 64% Reading Moat House, Mill Ln, Sindlesham, WOKINGHAM ☎ 01734 499988 96 ⇆ ℝ

SONNING   Map 04 SU77

Sonning Duffield Rd RG4 6GJ ☎ 01734 693332
A quality parkland course and the scene of many county championships. Wide fairways, not overbunkered, and very good greens. Holes of changing character through wooded belts.
18 holes, 6366yds, Par 70, SSS 70, Course record 65.

Visitors	weekdays only. Handicap certificate required.
Societies	must apply in writing. ▶

SUNNINGDALE

SUNNINGDALE *Berks* ☎ 01344 21681   Map 04 SU96

*J*ohn Ingham writes: Many famous golfers maintain that Sunningdale, on the borders of Berkshire, is the most attractive inland course in Britain. The great Bobby Jones once played the 'perfect' round of 66 made up of threes and fours on the Old Course. Later, Norman von Nida of Australia shot a 63 while the then professional at the club, Arthur Lees, scored a 62 to win a huge wager.

To become a member of this club takes years of waiting. Maybe it is the quality of the courses, maybe the clubhouse atmosphere and perhaps the excellence of the professionals shop has something to do with it; but added up, it has to be the most desirable place to spend a day.

Founded just over ninety years ago, the Old Course was designed by Willie Park, while H.S. Colt created the New Course in 1923. Most golfers will agree that there isn't one indifferent hole on either course. While the Old Course, with silver birch, heather and perfect turf, is lovely to behold, the New Course alongside is considered by many to be its equal. But just as golfers want to play the Old Course at St Andrews, and miss the redesigned Jubilee, so visitors to Sunningdale opt for the Old, and fail to realise what they are overlooking by not playing the New.

The classic Old Course is not long, measuring just 6341 yards, and because the greens are normally in excellent condition, anyone with a 'hot' putter can have an exciting day, providing they keep teeshots on the fairway and don't stray into the gorse and the pine trees that lie in wait. On a sunny day, if you had to be anywhere in the world playing well, then we opt for the elevated 10th tee on the Old. What bliss!

Visitors	May not play Fri, Sat, Sun or public holidays. Must contact in advance and have a handicap certificate and letter of introduction
Societies	Tue, Wed, Thu by arrangement.
Green fees	£88 per day
Facilities	⊗ ⓛ 🍷 🍸 ⚑ 🏠 🏌 ℓ (Keith Maxwell) practice area, trolleys
Location	Ridgemount Rd Sunningdale, Ascot SL5 9RR (1m S of Sunningdale, off A30)

36 holes. **Old Course: 18 holes, 6341yds, Par 70, SSS 70, Course record 62 (Nick Faldo)**
New Course: 18 holes 6703yds, Par 70, SSS 72, Course record 62 (C. Challen)

WHERE TO STAY AND EAT NEARBY

HOTELS:

ASCOT
★★★★⚜ 68% The Berystede, Bagshot Rd, Sunninghill. ☎ 01344 23311.
91 (1 🐾 90 ⇆ 🐾)

★★ 71% Highclere, 19 Kings Rd, Sunninghill. ☎ 01344 25220. 11 ⇆ 🐾

BAGSHOT
★★★★(Red)⚜⚜⚜ ♨ Pennyhill Park, London Rd. ☎ 01276 471774
22 ⇆ 🐾 Annexe 54 ⇆ 🐾

RESTAURANTS:

BRAY
⚜⚜⚜⚜ Waterside Inn, River Cottage, Ferry Road. ☎ 01628 20691.

Green Fees not confirmed.
Facilities ⚲⚑☎𝄞 R McDougall.
Location 1m S off A4
Hotel ★★★ 68% The French Horn, SONNING
☎ 01734 692204 12 ⇄ 🐾Annexe4 ⇄ 🐾

STREATLEY   Map 04 SU58

Goring & Streatley RG8 9QA
☎ 01491 873229 & 873715
A parkland/moorland course that requires 'negotiating'.
Four well-known first holes lead up to the heights of the
5th tee, to which there is a 300ft climb. Wide fairways,
not overbunkered, with nice rewards on the way home
down the last few holes.
18 holes, 6320yds, Par 71, SSS 70, Course record 65.
Club membership 740.
Visitors must contact in advance, with member only
at weekends.
Societies must telephone in advance.
Green Fees £30 per day; £20 per round.
Facilities ⊗ �🏑 🍴 ⚑ ⚲⚑☎𝄞 Roy Mason.
Leisure trolley for hire, putting green, practice area.
Location N of village off A417
Hotel ★★★★ 66% Swan Diplomat Hotel, High St,
STREATLEY ☎ 01491 873737 46 ⇄ 🐾

SUNNINGDALE   Map 04 SU96

SUNNINGDALE See page 15

Sunningdale Ladies Cross Rd SL5 9RX ☎ 01344 20507
A short 18-hole course with a typical Surrey heathland
layout. A very tight course, making for a challenging game.
18 holes, 3616yds, Par 60, SSS 60.
Club membership 350.
Visitors telephone in advance.
Societies Ladies societies only.
Green Fees not confirmed.
Facilities ⚲⚑
Location 1m S off A30
Hotel ★★★★ 68% The Berystede, Bagshot Rd,
Sunninghill, ASCOT ☎ 01344 23311 91 ⇄ 🐾

WOKINGHAM   Map 04 SU86

Downshire Easthampstead Park RG40 3DH
☎ 01344 302030
Beautiful municipal parkland course with mature trees. Water
hazards come into play on the 14th and 18th holes, and
especially on the short 7th, a testing downhill 169 yards over
the lake. Pleasant easy walking. Challenging holes: 7th (par
4), 15th (par 4), 16th (par 3).
18 holes, 6383yds, Par 73, SSS 70.
Club membership 1000.
Visitors must book six days in advance by telephone or
seven days in person, weekend times available.
Societies must telephone in advance.
Green Fees £12.50 per 18 holes (£15.50 weekends).
Facilities ⊗ �🏑 🍴 ⚑ ⚲⚑☎𝄞 Warren Humphries.
Leisure motorised carts for hire, buggies for hire, trolley
for hire, floodlit driving range, putting green,
practice area.

Location 3m SW of Bracknell
Hotel ★★★★ 75% Coppid Beech, John Nike Way,
BRACKNELL
☎ 01344 303333 205 ⇄ 🐾

Sand Martins Finchampstead Rd RG40 3RQ
☎ 01734 770265 & 792711
Two different 9-hole loops: the front nine is mostly tree-lined
with ponds and the back nine is similar to a links course.
18 holes, 6204yards, Par 70, SSS 70, Course record 65.
Club membership 750.
Visitors no restrictions, but with member only at
weekends.
Societies prior arrangement by telephone.
Green Fees £35 per day (£20 per 18 holes).
Facilities ⊗ �🏑 🍴 ⚑ ⚲⚑☎𝄞 Andrew Hall.
Leisure motorised carts for hire, buggies for hire, trolley
for hire, driving range, putting green.
Location 1m S of Wokingham
Hotel ★★★★ 64% Reading Moat House, Mill Ln,
Sindlesham, WOKINGHAM
☎ 01734 499988 96 ⇄ 🐾

BRISTOL

BRISTOL   Map 03 ST57

Bristol and Clifton Beggar Bush Ln, Failand BS8 3TH
☎ 01275 393474
A downland course with splendid turf and fine tree-lined
fairways. The 222-yard (par 3) 13th with the green well
below, and the par 4 16th, with its second shot across an
old quarry, are outstanding. There are splendid views
over the Bristol Channel towards Wales.
18 holes, 6316yds, Par 70, SSS 70, Course record 65.
Club membership 968.
Visitors must contact in advance & have a handicap
certificate. Weekends restricted.
Societies telephone to enquire.
Green Fees £30 per day (£38 weekends).
Facilities ⊗ 🍴 ⚑ ⚲⚑☎𝄞 Peter Mawson.
Leisure trolley for hire, putting green, practice area.
Location 4m W on B3129 off A369
Hotel ★★★ 66% Redwood Lodge Hotel, Country
Club Resort, Beggar Bush Ln, Failand,
BRISTOL ☎ 01275 393901 108 ⇄ 🐾

Filton Golf Course Ln, Filton BS12 7QS ☎ 0117 969 4169
Challenging parkland course situated on high ground in a
pleasant suburb to the north of the city. Extensive views can
be enjoyed from the course, especially from the second tee
and the clubhouse, where on a clear day the Cotswold Hills
and the Brecon Beacons can be seen. Good par 4 testing hole
'dog-leg' 383 yds.
18 holes, 6310yds, Par 70, SSS 70, Course record 68.
Club membership 730.
Visitors advisable to contact in advance for availability,
may not play at weekends unless with member.
Societies apply in writing Nov/Dec for following year.
Green Fees £25 per day; £20 per round.
Facilities ⊗ ⼒🏑 🍴 ⚑ ⚲⚑☎𝄞 J C N Lumb.

Leisure motorised carts for hire, buggies for hire, trolley for hire, putting green, practice area.
Location 5m NW off A38
Hotel B Forte Posthouse Bristol, Filton Rd, Hambrook, BRISTOL ☎ 0117 956 4242 197 ⇌ ⁣

Henbury Henbury Hill, Westbury-on-Trym BS10 7QB
☎ 0117 950 0044
A parkland course tree-lined and on two levels. The River Trym comes into play on the 7th drop-hole with its green set just over the stream. The last nine holes have the beautiful Blaise Castle woods for company.
18 holes, 6039yds, Par 70, SSS 70, Course record 64.
Club membership 760.
Visitors with member only weekends. Advisable to contact in advance for availability.
Societies apply in writing or telephone well in advance.
Green Fees £21 per round; £28 per 18+ holes.
Facilities ⊗ ⥿ ⅃ ♨ ♀ ♨ ⌂ ⚐ ⌣ Nick Riley.
Leisure trolley for hire, putting green, practice area.
Location 3m NW of city centre on B4055 off A4018
Hotel ★★★ 65% Henbury Lodge Hotel, Station Rd, Henbury, BRISTOL
☎ 0117 950 2615 11 ⇌ ⁣Annexe8 ⇌ ⁣

Knowle West Town Ln, Brislington BS4 5DF
☎ 0117 977 0660
A parkland course with nice turf. The first five holes climb up and down hill but the remainder are on a more even plane.
18 holes, 6016yds, Par 69, SSS 69.
Club membership 700.
Visitors must have handicap certificate. Must play with member at weekends.
Societies Thu only, apply in writing.
Green Fees £27 per day; £22 per round.
Facilities ⊗ ⥿ by prior arrangement ⅃ ♀ ♀ ⌂ ⚐ ⌣ Gordon Brand Snr.
Leisure buggies for hire, trolley for hire, putting green, practice area.
Location 3m SE of city centre off A37
Hotel ★★★(red)♨ Hunstrete House Hotel, CHELWOOD ☎ 01761 490490 13 ⇌ ⁣Annexe11 ⇌ ⁣

Mangotsfield Carsons Rd, Mangotsfield BS17 3LW
☎ 0117 956 5501
An easy hilly parkland course. Caravan site.
18 holes, 5337yds, Par 68, SSS 66, Course record 61.
Club membership 400.
Visitors no restrictions.
Societies bookings in advance to Craig Trewin.
Green Fees £9 (£11 weekends & bank holidays).
Facilities ⊗ ⅃ ♀ ♀ ⌂ ⚐ ⌣ Craig Trewin.
Leisure sauna, motorised carts for hire, buggies for hire, trolley for hire, putting green, practice area.
Location 6m NE of city centre off B4465
Hotel B Forte Posthouse Bristol, Filton Rd, Hambrook, BRISTOL ☎ 0117 956 4242 197 ⇌ ⁣

Shirehampton Park Park Hill, Shirehampton BS11 0UL
☎ 0117 982 2083
A lovely course in undulating parkland comprising two loops. There are views over the Portway beside the River Avon,

where sliced balls at the opening hole are irretrievable.
18 holes, 5600yds, Par 67, SSS 68.
Club membership 600.
Visitors with member only at weekends.
Societies Mon (if booked).
Green Fees not confirmed.
Facilities ♀ ♨ ⌂ ⚐ ⌣ Brent Ellis.
Location 4m NW of city centre on A4
Hotel ★★★ 66% Redwood Lodge Hotel, Country Club Resort, Beggar Bush Ln, Failand, BRISTOL ☎ 01275 393901 108 ⇌ ⁣

Woodlands Woodlands Ln, Almondsbury BS12 4JZ
☎ 01454 619319 & 618121
Situated on the edge of the Severn Valley, bordered by Hortham Brook and Shepherds Wood this interesting parkland course, features five testing par 3's set around the course's five lakes, notably the 206 yd 5th hole which extends over water.
18 holes, 6068yds, Par 69, SSS 67.
Club membership 101.
Visitors no restrictions.
Societies telephone in advance.
Green Fees £12 per round (£15 weekends & bank holidays).
Facilities ⊗ ⅃ ♀ ♀ ⌂ ⚐
Leisure fishing, trolley for hire, putting green, practice area.
Location N of Bristol off A38
Hotel B Forte Posthouse Bristol, Filton Rd, Hambrook, BRISTOL ☎ 0117 956 4242 197 ⇌ ⁣

BUCKINGHAMSHIRE

Aylesbury

Map 04 SP81

Aylesbury Golf Centre Hulcott Ln, Bierton HP22 5GA
☎ 01296 393644
A parkland course with magnificent views to the Chiltern Hills. The course is tight with out of bounds coming into play on the 1st, 2nd, 6th 7th and 8th.
9 holes, 2744yds, Par 68, SSS 67.
Visitors no restrictions, but booking advisable.
Societies telephone for details.
Green Fees £9 per 18 holes; £6 per 9 holes (£10/£7 weekends).
Facilities ⊗ ⥿ ⅃ ♀ ♀ ⌂ ⚐ ⌣ Mitch Kierstenson.
Leisure trolley for hire, driving range, putting green, practice area.
Location 1m N of Aylesbury on A418
Hotel B Forte Posthouse Aylesbury, Aston Clinton Rd, AYLESBURY ☎ 01296 393388 94 ⇌ ⁣

Ellesborough Butlers Cross HP17 0TZ
☎ 01296 622114
Once part of the property of Chequers, and under the shadow of the famous monument at the Wendover end of the Chilterns. A downland course, it is rather hilly with most holes enhanced by far-ranging views over the Aylesbury countryside.
18 holes, 6283yds, Par 71, SSS 71, Course record 64.
Club membership 700. ▶

Visitors	contact for details.
Societies	Wed & Thu only, by prior arrangement with General Manager.
Green Fees	fees on application.
Facilities	⊗ ⍂ ⓑ ⛳ ♀ ⚲ ⌂ ℓ Mike Squires.
Leisure	trolley for hire, putting green, practice area.
Location	1m E of Ellesborough on B4010
Hotel	★★★ 75% The Bell Inn, ASTON CLINTON
	☎ 01296 630252 6 ⇄ ☞Annexe15 ⇄ ☞

BEACONSFIELD　　　　　　　　　　　Map 04 SU99

Beaconsfield Seer Green HP9 2UR ☎ 01494 676545
An interesting and, at times, testing tree-lined and
parkland course which frequently plays longer than
appears on the card! Each hole differs to a considerable
degree and here lies the charm. Walking is easy, except
perhaps to the 6th and 8th. Well bunkered.
18 holes, 6487yds, Par 72, SSS 71, Course record 63.
Club membership 850.

Visitors	must contact in advance and have a handicap certificate. May not play weekends.
Societies	phone for details
Green Fees	£48 per day; £36 per round.
Facilities	⊗ ⍂ by prior arrangement ⓑ ⛳ ♀ ⚲ ⌂ ♈ ℓ Michael Brothers.
Leisure	trolley for hire, driving range, putting.
Location	2m E,S of Seer Green
Hotel	★★★★ 62% Bellhouse Hotel, Oxford Rd, BEACONSFIELD
	☎ 01753 887211 136 ⇄ ☞

The Bell Inn
Woburn

★★
69%

Bedford Street, Woburn, Beds MK17 9QD
Telephone: 01525 290280 Fax: 01525 290017

This friendly Inn is a mixture of Tudor, Georgian
and Victorian architecture. The beamed
Elizabethan restaurant serves excellent food and
wine or try real ale and bar food with the locals
in our pub. Bedrooms are individual with tasteful
fabrics and furnishings. Woburn Abbey with its
beautiful park is close by, as is Woburn Golf
Club. Special rates for golfing breaks.

Egon Ronay listed

BLETCHLEY　　　　　　　　　　　Map 04 SP83

Windmill Hill Tattenhoe Ln MK3 7RB ☎ 01908 378623
Long, open-parkland course designed by Henry Cotton and
opened in 1972. Municipal.
18 holes, 6773yds, Par 73, SSS 72, Course record 68.
Club membership 400.

Visitors	booking system in operation up to 7 days in advance.
Societies	packages available, contact for details.
Green Fees	£8.50 per 18 holes (£11.85 weekends).
Facilities	⊗ ⍂ ⓑ ⛳ ♀ ⚲ ⌂ ℓ Colin Clingan.
Leisure	buggies for hire, trolley for hire, driving range, putting green.
Location	W side of town centre on A421
Hotel	★★ 71% Shenley Church Inn, Burchard Crescent, Shenley Church End, MILTON KEYNES ☎ 01908 505467 50 ⇄ ☞

BOW BRICKHILL　　　　　　　　　　　Map 04 SP93

BOW BRICKHILL See page 19

BUCKINGHAM　　　　　　　　　　　Map 04 SP63

Buckingham Tingewick Rd MK18 4AE
☎ 01280 815566 & 815210
Undulating parkland course with a stream and river affecting
8 holes.
18 holes, 6082yds, Par 70, SSS 69, Course record 67.
Club membership 690.

Visitors	welcome Mon-Fri, with member only at weekends.
Societies	by prior arrangement.
Green Fees	£28 (weekdays).
Facilities	⊗ ⍂ ⓑ ⛳ ♀ ⚲ ⌂ ℓ Tom Gates.
Leisure	trolley for hire, putting green, practice area.
Location	1.5m W on A421
Hotel	★★★ 66% Buckingham Four Pillars Hotel, Ring Rd South, BUCKINGHAM ☎ 01280 822622 70 ⇄ ☞

BURNHAM　　　　　　　　　　　Map 04 SU98

Burnham Beeches Green Ln SL1 8EG
☎ 01628 661448
In the centre of the lovely Burnham Beeches countryside.
Wide fairways, carefully maintained greens, some hills,
and some devious routes to a few holes. A good finish.
18 holes, 6449yds, Par 70, SSS 71.
Club membership 670.

Visitors	must contact in advance. May play on weekdays only.
Societies	welcome Apr-Oct, write or telephone for information.
Green Fees	£42 per day; £28 per round (£37.50/£25 in winter).
Facilities	⊗ ⍂ ⓑ ⛳ ♀ ⚲ ⌂ ♈ ℓ Ronnie Bolton.
Leisure	motorised carts for hire, buggies for hire, trolley for hire, putting green, practice area.
Location	0.5m NE of Burnham　　　　　　　　▶

WOBURN

BOW BRICKHILL *Bucks* ☎ 01908 370756   Map O4 SP93

*J*ohn Ingham writes: Come off the M1 motorway at Junction 13 and you are quickly at Woburn, with its magnificent stately home, wildlife safari park and surrounding echoes of Henry VIII and the Dukes of Bedford. Within the last 20 years two new attractions have been added - two golf courses designed by the famed Charles Lawrie of Cotton Pennink.

To create these beautiful courses, the bulldozers got among pine and chestnut and literally cut fairways through some of the most picturesque country in all England - but it had been country seen by very few. From the very back tees, both courses are somewhat long for the weekend amateur. The Duke's measures 69461 yards and makes for a stiff test for any class of golfer, while the 'easier' Duchess, measuring a very respectable 6651 yards, requires a high degree of skill on its fairways guarded by towering pines.

Today, under the direction of Alex Hay, a Scottish TV golf commentator, the Dukes course has become the home of the increasingly popular Weetabix Women's British Open. It has been held at Woburn since 1990.

The town of Woburn and the Abbey are both within Bedfordshire, while the golf and country club actually lie over the border in Buckinghamshire. Although just 45 miles from London, you will feel very much in the wilds and the local pubs and people, plus some wonderful countryside, make this area an excellent place to stay for a few days.

And, if you can hit the ball straight, you might get near the course record of 63 achieved by Peter Baker and Ian Woosnam!

Visitors	must play with a member at weekends. Must contact in advance and have an introduction from own club
Societies	must telephone in advance
Green fees	on application
Facilities	⊗ 〲 by prior arrangement (groups only) 🍴 ♀ ⚒ 🏠 ⛳ Ր driving range, putting green. (Luther Blacklock) motor carts, buggies, trolleys,practice area
Leisure	outdoor swimming pool (heated)
Location	Bow Brickhill,nr Milton Keynes MK17 9LJ. 0.5miles SE of Bow Brickhill

36 holes. Dukes Course: 18 holes, 6961 yds,Par 72 , SSS 74
Duchess Course: 18 holes, 6651yds, Par 72, SSS 72

WHERE TO STAY AND EAT NEARBY

HOTELS:

ASPLEY GUISE
★★★69% Moore Place, The Square ☎ 01908 282000, 39 ⇌ Ր Annexe 15 ⇌ Ր

Flitwick
★★★ ❀❀❀ 75% Flitwick Manor, Church Rd. ☎ 01525 712242. 15 (2 Ր.12 ⇌ 1 ⇌ Ր)

WOBURN
★★ ❀ 69% The Bell Inn, 34 Bedford St ☎ 01525 290280 21 (3 Ր 18 ⇌) Annexe 6 (1 Ր 3 ⇌)

RESTAURANTS:
WOBURN
❀❀Paris House, Woburn Park ☎ 01525 290692.

| Hotel | ★★★ 68% Burnham Beeches Hotel, Grove Rd, BURNHAM ☎ 01628 429955 75 ➡ ▮ |

Lambourne Dropmore Rd SL1 8NF
☎ 01628 666755 & 662936
A championship standard 18-hole parkland course. Undulating terrain with many trees and several lakes, notably on the tricky 7th hole which has a tightly guarded green reached via a shot over a lake.
18 holes, 6764yds, Par 72, SSS 72.
Club membership 600.
Visitors must contact in advance.
Green Fees £30 per day (£40 weekends).
Facilities ⊗ ⊪ ⓑ ⬤ ♀ ♨ 🏠 ▾ ♪ David Mart.
Leisure sauna, motorised carts for hire, buggies for hire, trolley for hire, driving range, putting green, practice area.
Hotel ★★ 66% Chequers Inn, Kiln Ln, Woobum, WOOBURN COMMON ☎ 01628 529575 17 ➡ ▮

CHALFONT ST GILES   Map 04 SU99

Harewood Downs Cokes Ln HP8 4TA
☎ 01494 762308 & 762184
A testing undulating parkland course with sloping greens and plenty of trees.
18 holes, 5958yds, Par 69, SSS 69, Course record 64.
Visitors must contact in advance.
Societies apply in writing or telephone.
Green Fees £25 (£30 weekends & bank holidays).
Facilities ⊗ ⊪ ⓑ ⬤ ♀ ♨ 🏠 ♪ G C Morris.
Leisure trolley for hire, putting green, practice area.
Location 2m E of Amersham on A413
Hotel ★★★★ 62% Bellhouse Hotel, Oxford Rd, BEACONSFIELD ☎ 01753 887211 136 ➡ ▮

CHARTRIDGE   Map 04 SP90

Chartridge Park HP5 2TF ☎ 01494 791772
A family, easy walking parkland course set high in the beautiful Chiltern Hills, affording breathtaking views.
18 holes, 5516yds, Par 69, SSS 67.
Club membership 600.
Visitors no restrictions.
Societies must telephone in advance.
Green Fees £20 per 18/36 holes (£25 per round weekends and bank holidays).
Facilities ⊗ ⊪ ⓑ ⬤ ♀ ♨ ▾ ♪ Peter Gibbins.
Leisure motorised carts for hire, buggies for hire, trolley for hire.
Location 3m NW of Chesham
Hotel ★★★ 62% The Crown Hotel, High St, AMERSHAM ☎ 01494 721541 19 ➡ ▮Annexe4 ➡ ▮

CHESHAM   Map 04 SP90

Chesham & Ley Hill Ley Hill Common HP5 1UZ
☎ 01494 784541
Heathland course on hilltop with easy walking. Subject to wind.
9 holes, 5296yds, Par 66, SSS 65, Course record 62.
Club membership 400.

Visitors may play Mon & Thu all day, Wed after noon, Fri up to 4pm.
Societies subject to approval, Thu only.
Green Fees £12 per 18 holes.
Facilities ⊗ ⊪ ⓑ ⬤ ♀ ♨
Leisure putting green.
Location 2m E of Chesham
Hotel ★★★ 62% The Crown Hotel, High St, AMERSHAM ☎ 01494 721541 19 ➡ ▮Annexe4 ➡ ▮

DENHAM   Map 04 TQ08

Buckinghamshire Denham Court Dr UB9 5BG
☎ 01895 835777
A John Jacobs designed championship-standard course. Visitors only welcome as guests of members to this beautiful course in 269 acres of lovely grounds including mature trees, five lakes and two rivers. The testing 7th hole requires a 185 yd carry over a stream, followed by a second shot over a river to a green guarded by a lake.
18 holes, 6880yds, Par 72, SSS 73, Course record 70.
Club membership 500.
Visitors with member only or introduced by member. Weekdays only.
Societies must contact in advance.
Green Fees on application.
Facilities ⊗ ⊪ ⓑ ⬤ ♀ ♨ 🏠 ▾ ♪ John O'Leary.
Leisure sauna, trolley for hire, driving range, putting green, practice area.
Hotel ★★★★ 62% Bellhouse Hotel, Oxford Rd, BEACONSFIELD ☎ 01753 887211 136 ➡ ▮

| **Denham** Tilehouse Ln UB9 5DE ☎ 01895 832022 A beautifully maintained parkland/heathland course, home of many county champions. Slightly hilly and calling for good judgement of distance in the wooded areas. *18 holes, 6440yds, Par 70, SSS 71, Course record 66.* *Club membership 550.* **Visitors** must contact in advance & have handicap certificate. Must play with member Fri-Sun. **Societies** must book in advance. **Green Fees** not confirmed. **Facilities** ♀ ♨ 🏠 ▾ ♪ John Sheridan. **Location** 2m NW **Hotel** ★★★★ 62% Bellhouse Hotel, Oxford Rd, BEACONSFIELD ☎ 01753 887211 136 ➡ ▮ |

FLACKWELL HEATH   Map 04 SU89

Flackwell Heath Treadaway Rd, High Wycombe HP10 9PE
☎ 01628 520929
Open sloping heath and tree-lined course on hills overlooking Loudwater and the M40. Some good challenging par 3's and a several testing small greens.
18 holes, 6207yds, Par 71, SSS 70, Course record 63.
Club membership 800.
Visitors with member only at weekends.
Societies Wed & Thu only, by prior booking.
Green Fees £27 per day.
Facilities ⊗ ⊪ by prior arrangement ⓑ ⬤ ♀ ♨ 🏠 ♪ Paul Watson.
Leisure trolley for hire, putting green, practice area.

Location	NE side of town centre
Hotel	★★★★ 62% Bellhouse Hotel, Oxford Rd, BEACONSFIELD ☎ 01753 887211 136 ⇋ ↾

GERRARDS CROSS
Map 04 TQ08

Gerrards Cross Chalfont Park SL9 0QA
☎ 01753 883263
A wooded parkland course which has been modernised in recent years and is now a very pleasant circuit with infinite variety. The best part lies on the plateau above the clubhouse where there are some testing holes.
18 holes, 6295yds, Par 69, SSS 70, Course record 65. Club membership 773.

Visitors	must contact professional in advance, a handicap certificate is required, may not play Tuesday, weekends or public holidays.
Societies	booking well in advance necessary, handicap certicates required, packages to suit.
Green Fees	£36 per day; £29 per round.
Facilities	⊗ ℳ by prior arrangement ⓑ ♥ ♀ ⚑ 🏠 ↾ ⚐ Matthew Barr.
Leisure	trolley for hire, putting green, practice area.
Location	NE side of town centre off A413
Hotel	★★★★ 62% Bellhouse Hotel, Oxford Rd, BEACONSFIELD ☎ 01753 887211 136 ⇋ ↾

HALTON
Map 04 SP81

Chiltern Forest Aston Hill HP22 5NQ
☎ 01296 630899 & 631817
Extended to 18 holes in 1992, this very hilly wooded parkland course is on two levels. It is a true test of skill to the low handicap golfer, as well as being a fair challenge to higher handicap golfers. The surrounding woodland makes the course very scenic.
18 holes, 5765yds, Par 70, SSS 70, Course record 69. Club membership 600.

Visitors	must play with member at weekends.
Societies	contact in advance for booking form.
Green Fees	£23 per day weekdays only.
Facilities	⊗ ℳ ⓑ ♥ ♀ ⚑ 🏠 ⚐ C Skeet.
Leisure	trolley for hire, putting green.
Location	1m NE off A4011
Hotel	★★★ 64% Rose & Crown Hotel & Restaurant, High St, TRING ☎ 01442 824071 27 ⇋ ↾

HIGH WYCOMBE
Map 04 SU89

Hazlemere Golf & Country Club Penn Rd, Hazlemere HP15 7LR ☎ 01494 714722 & 718298
Undulating parkland course in beautiful countryside with water hazards in play on some holes. Two long par 5s and a fine par 4 closing hole.
18 holes, 5873yds, Par 70, SSS 68, Course record 62. Club membership 700.

Visitors	weekdays all day. Weekends in the afternoon by prior arrangement through Pro. shop telephone 01494 718298.
Societies	by prior telephone arrangement.
Green Fees	£35 per day; £26 per round (£40 per round subject to availability at weekends).

Facilities	⊗ ℳ ⓑ ♥ ♀ ⚑ 🏠 ⚐ ⚐ Steve Morvell.
Leisure	motorised carts for hire, buggies for hire, trolley for hire, putting green, practice area.
Location	2m NE, A404 towards Amersham
Hotel	★★★ 62% The Crown Hotel, High St, AMERSHAM ☎ 01494 721541 19 ⇋ ↾Annexe4 ⇋ ↾

IVER
Map 04 TQ08

Iver Hollow Hill Ln, Langley Park Rd SL0 0JJ
☎ 01753 655615
Fairly flat, pay and play parkland course with challenging par 5s, plenty of hazards - water and ditches - and strong crosswinds to contend with.
9 holes, 6288yds, Par 72, SSS 72, Course record 68. Club membership 200.

Visitors	competitions at weekends, telephone to pre book tee times.
Societies	telephone in advance.
Green Fees	£9 per 18 holes; £5.30 per 9 holes (£12.50/£7 weekends).
Facilities	⊗ ⓑ ♥ ♀ ⚑ 🏠 ⚐ ⚐ Karl Teschner.
Leisure	trolley for hire, driving range, putting green, practice area.
Location	1.5m SW off B470
Hotel	B Marriott Hotel, Ditton Road, Langley, SLOUGH ☎ 01753 544244 350 ⇋ ↾

IVINGHOE
Map 04 SP91

Ivinghoe Wellcroft LU7 9EF ☎ 01296 668696
Testing parkland course with water on three holes. Easy walking on rolling countryside.
9 holes, 4508yds, Par 62, SSS 62, Course record 57. Club membership 250.

Visitors	may only play after 8am.
Societies	must contact in advance.
Green Fees	not confirmed.
Facilities	♀ ⚑ 🏠 ⚐ ⚐ Bill Garrad.
Leisure	putting, bunker practice, trolley hire.
Location	N side of village
Hotel	★★★ 75% The Bell Inn, ASTON CLINTON ☎ 01296 630252 6 ⇋ ↾Annexe15 ⇋ ↾

LITTLE CHALFONT
Map 04 SU99

Little Chalfont Lodge Ln HP8 4AJ
☎ 01494 764877
Gently undulating flat course surrounded by woods.
9 holes, 5852yds, Par 68, SSS 68, Course record 66. Club membership 300.

Visitors	no restrictions, please phone to ensure there are no competitions in progress.
Societies	please telephone in advance.
Green Fees	£10 per 18 holes (£12 weekends).
Facilities	⊗ ℳ ⓑ ♥ ♀ ⚑ 🏠 ⚐ ⚐ David Hawes.
Leisure	trolley for hire, putting green, practice area, one motorised cart for hire by arrangement.
Location	Between Little Chalfont & Chorleywood
Hotel	★★★ 62% The Crown Hotel, High St, AMERSHAM ☎ 01494 721541 19 ⇋ ↾Annexe4 ⇋ ↾

LOUDWATER

Map 04 SU89

Wycombe Heights Golf Centre Rayners Ave HP10 9SW
☎ 01494 816686
Opened in 1991 and designed by the John Jacobs Partnership.
The golf centre includes a 24-bay driving range.
18 holes, 6253yds, Par 70, SSS 72, Course record 69.
Club membership 1070.
Visitors   booking advisable 6 days in advance.
Societies   telephone in advance & confirm in writing.
Green Fees   £17.95 per day; £10.95 per round (£14.35 per
                 round weekends) Twilight fee available.
Facilities   ⊗ ⅢⅢ ⅃ ♥ ♀ ♨ 🖭 🍴 ⎰ Adam Bishop.
Leisure   motorised carts for hire, buggies for hire, trolley
                 for hire, driving range, putting green, 18 hole par
                 3 course.
Hotel   B Forte Posthouse High Wycombe, Handy
                 Cross, HIGH WYCOMBE
                 ☎ 01494 442100 106 ⇌ ⚑

MENTMORE

Map 04 SP91

Mentmore Golf & Country Club LU7 0UA
☎ 01296 662020
Two 18-hole courses - Roseberry and Rothschild - set within
the wooded estate grounds of Mentmore Towers. Gently
rolling parkland course with mature trees and lakes and two
interesting feature holes; the long par 5 (606 yds) 9th on the
Roseberry course with fine views of the Chilterns and the par
4 (340yd) 5th on the Rothschild course, in front of the hall.
Roseberry Course: 18 holes, 6777yds, Par 72, SSS 72.
Rothschild Course: 18 holes, 6763yds, Par 72, SSS 72.
Club membership 1100.
Visitors   must contact in advance, may not play weekends
                 before 11am.
Societies   by prior arrangement.
Green Fees   £45 per day; £30 per round (£45/35 weekends).
Facilities   ⊗ ⅢⅢ ⅃ ♥ ♀ ♨ 🖭 🍴 ⎰ ⎰ Pip Elson.
Leisure   hard tennis courts, heated indoor swimming
                 pool, fishing, sauna, gymnasium, motorised carts
                 for hire, buggies for hire, trolley for hire, driving
                 range, putting green, practice area, jacuzzi.
Location   4m S of Leighton Buzzard
Hotel   ★★★ 58% Swan Hotel, High St, LEIGHTON
                 BUZZARD ☎ 01525 372148 38 ⇌ ⚑

MILTON KEYNES

Map 04 SP83

Abbey Hill Two Mile Ash MK8 8AA ☎ 01908 563845
Undulating municipal course within the new city. Tight
fairways and well-placed bunkers. Stream comes into play on
five holes. Also Par 3 course.
18 holes, 6177yds, Par 68, SSS 69.
Club membership 600.
Visitors   no restrictions.
Societies   must telephone (01908) 562408 in advance.
Green Fees   not confirmed.
Facilities   ♀ ♨ 🖭 🍴 ⎰ Gary George.
Leisure   pool table, darts.
Location   2m W of new town centre off A5
Hotel   ★★★ 62% Quality Friendly Hotel, Monks
                 Way, Two Mile Ash, MILTON KEYNES
                 ☎ 01908 561666 88 ⇌ ⚑

Three Locks Great Brickhill MK17 9BH
☎ 01525 270470 & 270050
Parkland course offering a challenge to beginners and
experienced golfers, with water coming into play on ten
holes. Magnificent views.
18 holes, 5850yds, Par 69, SSS 68, Course record 69.
Club membership 350.
Visitors   telephone 01525 270050 to book tee times.
Societies   write or telephone for details.
Green Fees   £16 per day; £10 per round; £7.50 twilight
                 (£20/£12.50/£8 weekends).
Facilities   ⊗ ⅃ ♥ ♀ ♨ 🖭 🍴 ⎰
Leisure   fishing, motorised carts for hire, buggies for hire,
                 trolley for hire, putting green, practice area.
Location   A4146 between Leighton Buzzard/Bletchley
Hotel   ★★ 71% Shenley Church Inn, Burchard
                 Crescent, Shenley Church End, MILTON
                 KEYNES ☎ 01908 505467 50 ⇌ ⚑

PRINCES RISBOROUGH

Map 04 SP80

Whiteleaf Whiteleaf HP27 0LY
☎ 01844 343097 & 274058
Short, hilly and tricky 9-hole parkland course, requiring great
accuracy, set high in the Chilterns with beautiful views.
9 holes, 5391yds, Par 66, SSS 66, Course record 64.
Club membership 400.
Visitors   advisable to contact in advance, with member
                 only at weekends.
Societies   on Thu only, must contact the secretary in
                 advance.
Green Fees   £25 per day; £18 per round.
Facilities   ⊗ ⅢⅢ ⅃ ♥ ♀ ♨ 🖭 🍴 ⎰ Ken Ward.
Leisure   trolley for hire, putting green, practice area.
Location   1m NE off A4010
Hotel   ★★★ 75% The Bell Inn, ASTON CLINTON
                 ☎ 01296 630252 6 ⇌ ⚑Annexe15 ⇌ ⚑

STOKE POGES

Map 04 SU98

Farnham Park Park Rd SL2 4PJ ☎ 01753 643332
Fine, public parkland course in pleasing setting.
18 holes, 6172yds, Par 71, SSS 70, Course record 68.
Club membership 600.
Visitors   telephone in advance for tee times.
Societies   apply in writing.
Green Fees   £8 per round (£11 weekends and bank holidays).
Facilities   ⊗ ⅢⅢ ⅃ ♥ ♀ ♨ 🖭 🍴 ⎰ Paul Warner.
Leisure   trolley for hire, putting green.
Location   W side of village off B416
Hotel   B Marriott Hotel, Ditton Road, Langley,
                 SLOUGH ☎ 01753 544244 350 ⇌ ⚑

Stoke Poges Stoke Park, North Dr SL2 4PG
☎ 01753 717171
Judgement of the distance from the tee is all important on
this first-class parkland course. There are 8 outstanding
par 4's of around 440 yards, several calling for much
thought. Fairways are wide and the challenge seemingly
innocuous.
18 holes, 6654yds, Par 71, SSS 72, Course record 65.
Club membership 564.
Visitors   must contact in advance.
Societies   apply in writing or telephone in advance.

Green Fees £65 per day; £45 per round; £30 after 5pm
(£100 per round; £50 after 4pm weekends).
Facilities ⊗ ⅷ ┗ ☕ ♀ ♨ ☎ ⓣ ⓒ Tim Morrison.
Leisure hard and grass tennis courts, sauna,
motorised carts for hire, buggies for hire,
trolley for hire, driving range, putting green,
practice area, snooker room,croquet lawn.
Location 2m N of Slough
Hotel B Marriott Hotel, Ditton Road, Langley,
SLOUGH ☎ 01753 544244 350 ⇄ ⓡ

WAVENDON   Map 04 SP93

Wavendon Golf Centre Lower End Rd MK17 8DA
☎ 01908 281811
Pleasant parkland course set within mature oak and lime trees
and incorporating several small lakes as water hazards. Easy
walking.
18 holes, 5540yds, Par 67, SSS 67.
Club membership 300.
Visitors must book 3 days in advance.
Societies must contact in advance by telephone.
Green Fees £10 per 18 holes (£13.50 weekends). Par3 £3.75
(£4.75 weekends).
Facilities ⊗ ⅷ ┗ ☕ ♀ ♨ ☎ ⓣ ⓒ Greg Iron.
Leisure trolley for hire, driving range, 9 hole Par 3
course, putting green, practice area.
Location Just off A421
Hotel ★★★ 69% Moore Place Hotel, The Square,
ASPLEY GUISE
☎ 01908 282000 39 ⇄ ⓡAnnexe15 ⇄ ⓡ

WESTON TURVILLE   Map 04 SP81

Weston Turville Golf & Squash Club New Rd HP22 5QT
☎ 01296 24084 & 25949
Parkland course situated at the foot of the Chiltern Hills and
providing an excellent challenge for the accomplished golfer,
yet not too daunting for the higher handicap player. Flat easy
walking with water hazards and many interesting holes,
notably the testing dog-leg 5th (418yds).
18 holes, 6008yds, Par 69, SSS 69, Course record 71.
Club membership 600.
Visitors no restrictions.
Societies must contact in advance.
Green Fees £15 per round (£20 weekends & bank holidays).
Facilities ⊗ ⅷ by prior arrangement ┗ ☕ ♀ ♨ ☎ ⓣ
ⓒ Gary George.
Leisure squash, buggies for hire, trolley for hire, putting
green.
Location 2m SE of Aylesbury, off A41
Hotel ★★★ 75% The Bell Inn, ASTON CLINTON
☎ 01296 630252 6 ⇄ ⓡAnnexe15 ⇄ ⓡ

WEXHAM STREET   Map 04 SU98

Wexham Park SL3 6ND ☎ 01753 663271
Gently undulating parkland course. Two courses.
*18 holes, 5836yds, Par 69, SSS 68 or 9 holes, 2283yds, Par
32, SSS 32.*
Club membership 500.
Visitors no restrictions
Societies may not play at weekends; must contact in
advance.

Green Fees not confirmed.
Facilities ♀ ♨ ☎ ⓣ ⓒ
Location 0.5m S
Hotel B Marriott Hotel, Ditton Road, Langley,
SLOUGH ☎ 01753 544244 350 ⇄ ⓡ

WING   Map 04 SP82

Aylesbury Vale Stewkley Rd LU7 0UJ ☎ 01525 240196
The course, which is gently undulating and played over
water, was opened in the autumn of 1991. There are five
ponds to add interest, notably on the par 4 420 yd 13th -
unlucky for some - where the second shot is all downhill with
an inviting pond spanning the approach to the green. In
addition there is a 10-bay driving range, a practice fairway
and practice putting green as well as an In-Golf Simulator.
18 holes, 6622yds, Par 72, SSS 72, Course record 65.
Club membership 545.
Visitors must adhere to dress regulations. Must contact in
advance.
Societies telephone to book in advance.
Green Fees £16 per day; £10 per round; £6 per 9 holes
(£28/£18.50/£10 weekends and bank holidays).
Facilities ⊗ ⅷ ┗ ☕ ♀ ♨ ☎ ⓣ ⓒ Richard Hodgson.
Leisure trolley for hire, covered driving range, putting
green.
Location 2m NW on unclassified Stewkley road
Hotel ★★★ 58% Swan Hotel, High St, LEIGHTON
BUZZARD ☎ 01525 372148 38 ⇄ ⓡ

CAMBRIDGESHIRE

BAR HILL   Map 05 TL36

Cambridgeshire Moat House Moat House Hotel
CB3 8EU ☎ 01954 780098 & 780555
Undulating parkland course with lake and water hazards,
easy walking. Many leisure facilities. Course record
holders, Paul Way and Peter Townsend.
18 holes, 6734yds, Par 72, SSS 72.
Club membership 500.
Visitors must book in advance.
Societies must telephone in advance.
Green Fees not confirmed.
Facilities ♀ ♨ ☎ ⓣ ⇄ ⓒ David Vernon.
Leisure hard tennis courts, heated indoor swimming
pool, squash, sauna, solarium, gymnasium,
buggies.
Location 5m NW of Cambridge on A604
Hotel ★★★ 64% Cambridgeshire Moat House,
BAR HILL ☎ 01954 249988 99 ⇄ ⓡ

BRAMPTON   Map 04 TL27

Brampton Park Buckden Rd PE18 8NF ☎ 01480 434700
Set in truly attractive countryside, bounded by the River
Great Ouse and bisected by the River Lane. Great variety
with mature trees, lakes and water hazards. One of the most
difficult holes is the 4th, a Par 3 island green, named
'Fowler's Folly'.   ▶

18 holes, 6403yds, Par 72, SSS 73, Course record 69.
Club membership 700.

Visitors	must contact in advance.
Societies	apply in advance.
Green Fees	£24 per day; £18 per round (£36 per day weekend, includes meal voucher); Nov-Mar £15 day (including light lunch).
Facilities	⊗ 洲 ﻟ ⌧ ♚ ♀ △ 숍 ﻭﻝ ﻝ Alisdair Currie.
Leisure	fishing, trolley for hire, putting green, practice area.
Hotel	★★ 64% Grange Hotel, 115 High St, Brampton, HUNTINGDON ☎ 01480 459516 9rm(1 ⇔7 ⋔)

CAMBRIDGE Map 05 TL45

Gog Magog Shelford Bottom CB2 4AB
☎ 01223 247626
Situated just outside the centre of the university town, Gog Magog, established in 1901, is known as the nursery of Cambridge undergraduate golf. The course is on high ground, and it is said that if you stand on the highest point and could see far enough to the east the next highest ground would be the Ural Mountains! The courses (there are two of them) are open but there are enough trees and other hazards to provide plenty of problems. Views from the high parts are superb. The nature of the ground ensures good winter golf.
Old Course: 18 holes, 6400yds, Par 70, SSS 70, Course record 64.
New Course: 9 holes, 2979yds, Par 69, SSS 68.
Club membership 1130.

Visitors	must contact in advance.
Societies	Tue & Thu by reservation.
Green Fees	Old Course: £37.50 per day; £30 per round. New Course £19 per day/round.
Facilities	⊗ 洲 ﻟ ⌧ ♚ ♀ △ 숍 ﻭﻝ ﻝ Ian Bamborough.
Leisure	trolley for hire, putting green, practice area.
Location	3m SE on A1307
Hotel	★★★ 71% Gonville Hotel, Gonville Place, CAMBRIDGE ☎ 01223 366611 64 ⇔ ⋔

ELY Map 05 TL58

Ely City Cambridge Rd CB7 4HX
☎ 01353 662751 (Office) & 663317 (Pro)
Parkland course slightly undulating with water hazards formed by lakes and natural dykes. Demanding par 4 5th hole (467yds), often into a headwind, and a testing par 3 2nd hole (160yds) played over 2 ponds Magnificent views of Cathedral. Lee Trevino is the professional record holder.
18 holes, 6627yds, Par 72, SSS 72, Course record 66.
Club membership 850.

Visitors	advisable to contact the club in advance.
Societies	Tue to Fri, advisable to contact club well in advance.
Green Fees	£25 per day; £20 per round (£32/£25 weekends & bank holidays).
Facilities	⊗ 洲 ﻟ ⌧ ♚ ♀ △ 숍 ﻭﻝ ﻝ Andrew George.
Leisure	trolley for hire, putting green, practice area.
Location	SW side of city centre on A10
Hotel	★★ 64% Lamb Hotel, 2 Lynn Rd, ELY ☎ 01353 663574 32 ⇔ ⋔

GIRTON Map 05 TL46

Girton Dodford Ln CB3 0QE ☎ 01223 276169
Flat, open parkland course with many trees and ditches. Easy walking.
18 holes, 6085yds, Par 69, SSS 69, Course record 66.
Club membership 800.

Visitors	with member only at weekends. Contact professional in advance (01223 276991).
Societies	apply writing.
Green Fees	£16 per day.
Facilities	⊗ 洲 ﻟ ⌧ ♚ ♀ △ 숍 ﻭﻝ ﻝ Scott Thomson.
Leisure	trolley for hire, putting green, practice area.
Location	NW side of village
Hotel	B Forte Posthouse Cambridge, Lakeview, Bridge Rd, Impington, CAMBRIDGE ☎ 01223 237000 118 ⇔ ⋔

HEMINGFORD ABBOTS Map 04 TL27

Hemingford Abbots Cambridge Rd PE18 9HQ
☎ 01480 495000 & 493900
Interesting 9-hole course featuring a par 5 dog-leg 4th with a testing tapering fairway, two ponds at the entrance to the 8th green and an island green on the 9th.
9 holes, 5468yds, Par 68, SSS 68.
Club membership 170.

Visitors	advisable to phone in advance, particularly for weekends.
Societies	advise in writing or telephone.
Green Fees	not confirmed.
Facilities	⊗ 洲 ﻟ ⌧ ♚ ♀ △ 숍 ﻭﻝ ﻝ Craig Watson.
Leisure	trolley for hire, driving range, putting green.
Location	A14 Hemingford Abbots turning
Hotel	★★★ 73% The Old Bridge Hotel, HUNTINGDON ☎ 01480 052681 26 ⇔ ⋔

MARCH Map 05 TL49

March Frogs Abbey, Grange Rd PE15 0YH
☎ 01354 52364
Nine-hole parkland course with a particularly challenging par 3 9th hole, with out of bounds on the left and high hedges to the right.
9 holes, 6204yds, Par 70, SSS 70, Course record 65.
Club membership 413.

Visitors	contact in advance, with member only at weekends.
Societies	apply in writing.
Green Fees	£15 per day.
Facilities	⊗ 洲 ⌧ ♚ ♀ △ 숍 ﻝ Jason Hadland.
Leisure	trolley for hire, putting green, practice area.
Location	0.5m off A141, March bypass
Hotel	★★ 66% Olde Griffin Hotel, High St, MARCH ☎ 01354 52517 20rm(19 ⇔ ⋔)

PETERBOROUGH Map 04 TL19

Elton Furze Bullock Rd, Haddon PE7 3TT
☎ 01832 280189
A new course opened in 1993. Wooded parkland 18-hole course in lovely surroundings.
18 holes, 6289yds, Par 70, SSS 70, Course record 69.
Club membership 388.

Visitors weekends only with prior permission.
Societies by prior arrangement telephone for details.
Green Fees not confirmed.
Facilities ⊗ ⅏ ⓫ ♥ ♀ ⅄ 🏠 ⌇ Frank Kiddie.
Leisure sauna, trolley for hire, putting green, practice area.
Location 4m SW of Peterborough, off A605
Hotel ★★★★ 65% Swallow Hotel, Peterborough Business Park, Lynchwood, PETERBOROUGH ☎ 01733 371111 163 ⇌ ⌊

Orton Meadows Ham Ln, Orton Waterville PE2 0UU
☎ 01733 237478
Pretty municipal parkland course set within the Nene Valley Country Park with large lakes and water hazards. Challenging 3rd hole (616yards from white tee) incorporating lots of water and 'out of bounds' areas. Also 12-hole pitch and putt course.
18 holes, 5664yds, Par 67, SSS 68, Course record 71.
Club membership 520.
Visitors no restrictions.
Societies apply in advance.
Green Fees £9 per round (£11.50 weekends & bank holidays).
Facilities ♥ ⅄ 🏠 ⌇ Neil Grant.
Leisure trolley for hire, putting green, practice area.
Location 3m W of town on A605
Hotel ★★★ 68% Orton Hall Hotel, Orton Longueville, PETERBOROUGH ☎ 01733 391111 49 ⇌ ⌊

Peterborough Milton Milton Ferry PE6 7AG
☎ 01733 380489 & 380793
Designed by James Braid, this well-bunkered parkland course is set in the grounds of the Earl Fitzwilliam's estate, many of the holes being played in full view of Milton Hall. Challenging holes are the difficult dog-leg 10th and 15th. Easy walking.
18 holes, 6198yds, Par 71, SSS 70.
Club membership 800.
Visitors must contact in advance.
Societies bookings in writing to secretary.
Green Fees £30 per day; £20 per round (£25 per round weekends).
Facilities ⊗ ⅏ ⓫ ♥ ♀ ⅄ 🏠 ⌇ Michael Gallagher.
Leisure motorised carts for hire, buggies for hire, trolley for hire, driving range, putting green, practice area.
Location 2m W of Peterborough on A47
Hotel ★★★ 66% Butterfly Hotel, Thorpe Meadows, Off Longthorpe Parkway, PETERBOROUGH ☎ 01733 64240 70 ⇌ ⌊

Thorpe Wood Thorpe Wood, Nene Parkway PE3 6SE
☎ 01733 267701
Gently undulating, municipal parkland course designed by Peter Alliss and Dave Thomas. Challenging holes include the 5th, the longest hole usually played with prevailing wind and the 14th, entailing a difficult approach shot over water to a two-tier green.
18 holes, 7086yds, Par 73, SSS 74, Course record 71.
Club membership 750.
Visitors phone for reservations.
Societies must telephone in advance, bookings taken up to year ahead.
Green Fees £9 per round (£11.50 weekends & bank holidays).

Facilities ⊗ ⅏ ⓫ ♥ ♀ ⅄ 🏠 ⌇ Dennis & Roger Fitton.
Leisure trolley for hire, putting green, practice area.
Location 3m W of city centre on A47
Hotel ★★★ 67% Peterborough Moat House, Thorpe Wood, PETERBOROUGH ☎ 01733 260000 125 ⇌ ⌊

PIDLEY
Map 05 TL37

Lakeside Lodge Fen Rd PE17 3DD
☎ 01487 740540 & 741541
A well designed, spacious course incorporating eight lakes, 12,000 trees and a modern clubhouse. The 9th and 18th holes both finish dramatically alongside a lake in front of the clubhouse. Also 9-hole Par 3 and 25-bay driving range.
18 holes, 6821yds, Par 72, SSS 73, Course record 72.
Club membership 350.
Visitors no restrictions.
Societies must telephone in advance.
Green Fees £9 per 18 holes (£15 weekends).
Facilities ⊗ ⅏ ⓫ ♥ ♀ ⅄ 🏠 ⌇ Alistair Headley.
Leisure fishing, motorised carts for hire, buggies for hire, trolley for hire, driving range, par 3 course, hot-air ballooning, bowling.
Hotel ★★★ 64% Slepe Hall Hotel, Ramsey Rd, ST IVES ☎ 01480 463122 16rm(15 ⇌ ⌊)

RAMSEY
Map 04 TL28

Old Nene Golf & Country Club Muchwood Ln, Bodsey PE17 1XQ ☎ 01487 813519
A flat well-drained course with water hazards and boundaries. There are excellent greens and the 8th and 9th holes are challenging across water in either a head wind or cross wind.
9 holes, 2762yds, Par 68, SSS 67, Course record 66.
Club membership 200.
Visitors book in advance especially evenings & weekends.
Societies arrange in advance with Secretary.
Green Fees £10 per 18 holes; £7 per 9 holes (£13/£9 weekends & bank holidays).
Facilities ⊗ ⅏ by prior arrangement ⓫ ♥ ♀ ⅄ 🏠 ⌇ Ken McKechnie.
Leisure fishing, motorised carts for hire, buggies for hire, trolley for hire, driving range, practice area.
Location 0.75m N of Ramsey
Hotel ★★★ 73% The Old Bridge Hotel, HUNTINGDON ☎ 01480 052681 26 ⇌ ⌊

Ramsey 4 Abbey Ter PE17 1DD ☎ 01487 812600
Flat, parkland course with water hazards.
18 holes, 6123yds, Par 71, SSS 70, Course record 66.
Club membership 750.
Visitors contact professional in advance (01487 813022), may only play with member at weekends & bank holidays.
Societies apply in writing.
Green Fees £22 per day/round.
Facilities ⊗ ⅏ ⓫ ♥ ♀ ⅄ 🏠 ⌇ Stuart Scott.
Leisure trolley for hire, putting green, practice area.
Location 12m SE of Peterborough on B1040
Hotel ★★★ 73% The Old Bridge Hotel, HUNTINGDON ☎ 01480 052681 26 ⇌ ⌊

St Ives
Map 05 TL37

St Ives (Cambs) Westwood Rd PE17 4RS
☎ 01480 468392
Picturesque parkland course.
9 holes, 6100yds, Par 70, SSS 69.
Club membership 500.
Visitors   must contact in advance, may not play
     weekends.
Societies   welcome Wednesday & Fridays.
Green Fees £20 per day.
Facilities   ⊗ ⅲ � ♥ ♀ ♨ 🖕 ⚑ ℓ Darren Glasby.
Leisure   trolley for hire, putting green, practice area.
Location   W side of town centre off A1123
Hotel   ★★★ 64% Slepe Hall Hotel, Ramsey Rd,
     ST IVES
     ☎ 01480 463122 16rm(15 ⇆ ↾)

St Neots
Map 04 TL16

Abbotsley Golf & Squash Club PE19 4XN
☎ 01480 474000 & 215153
Two courses - main Abbotsley course featuring mature
parkland with tree-lined fairways, plenty of water hazards and
a particularly testing par 3 2nd hole - the 'Mousehole'.
Cromwell course, opened in 1991, is less demanding with
tricky driving holes and sloping greens. Courses surround
moated country house and hotel. Residential golf schools 30
weeks of the year plus floodlit, covered driving range.
*Abbotsley Course: 18 holes, 6311yds, Par 73, SSS 71, Course
record 69.*
Cromwell Course: 18 holes, 6087yds, Par 70, SSS 69.
Club membership 500.
Visitors   welcome all times advisable to book weekends.
Societies   prior booking for large parties.
Green Fees Abbotsley: £20 per round (£25 weekends).
     Cromwell: £9 per round (£13 weekends).
Facilities   ⊗ ⅲ � ♥ ♀ ♨ 🖕 ⚑ ℓ Vivien Saunders.
Leisure   squash, motorised carts for hire, buggies for hire,
     trolley for hire, driving range, putting green,
     practice area.
Location   2m SE off B1046
Hotel   ★★ 65% Abbotsley Golf Hotel, Eynesbury
     Hardwicke, ST NEOTS
     ☎ 01480 474000 15 ⇆ ↾

St Neots Crosshall Rd PE19 4AE
☎ 01480 472363
Undulating and very picturesque parkland course with lake
and water hazards and exceptional greens, close to the Kym
and Great Ouse rivers. Easy, level walking.
18 holes, 6074yds, Par 69, SSS 69, Course record 64.
Club membership 630.
Visitors   must book in advance. with member only at
     weekends.
Societies   must contact in advance.
Green Fees £30 per day; £20 per round.
Facilities   ⊗ ⅲ � ♥ ♀ ♨ 🖕 ⚑ ℓ Graham Bithrey.
Leisure   motorised carts for hire, buggies for hire, trolley
     for hire, putting green, practice area.
Location   W side of town centre on A428
Hotel   ★★ 64% Grange Hotel, 115 High St, Brampton,
     HUNTINGDON
     ☎ 01480 459516 9rm(1 ⇆7 ↾)

Thorney
Map 04 TF20

Thorney English Drove, Thorney PE6 0TJ
☎ 01733 270570
The 18-hole Fen course is ideal for the beginner, while the
Lakes course, opened in June 1995, has a challenging links-
style layout with eight holes around water.
*Fen Course: 18 holes, 6104yds, Par 70, SSS 69, Course
record 66.*
*Lakes Course: 18 holes, 6400yds, Par 71, SSS 71, Course
record 72 or 9 holes, 990yds, Par 27.*
Club membership 400.
Visitors   book in advance for Fen course, limited
     weekend play Lakes course.
Societies   contact in advance.
Green Fees Fen: £5.75 (£7.75 weekends & bank holidays).
     Lakes: £10 (£16 weekends & bank holidays).
     Day tickets available.
Facilities   ⊗ ⅲ � ♥ ♀ ♨ 🖕 ⚑ ℓ Mark Templeman.
Leisure   motorised carts for hire, buggies for hire, trolley
     for hire, driving range, par 3 course, putting
     green, practice area.
Location   Off A47, 7m NE of Peterborough
Hotel   ★★★ 66% Butterfly Hotel, Thorpe Meadows,
     Off Longthorpe Parkway, PETERBOROUGH
     ☎ 01733 64240 70 ⇆ ↾

Toft
Map 05 TL35

Cambridge Meridian Comberton Rd CB3 7RY
☎ 01223 264700
Opened in 1993. Set in 207 acres to a Peter Allis/Clive Clark
design with sweeping fairways, lakes and well bunkered
greens. The 4th hole has bunker complexes, a sharp dog-leg
and a river with the green heavily guarded by bunkers.
18 holes, 6651yds, Par 73, SSS 72, Course record 72.
Club membership 600.
Visitors   must contact in advance.
Societies   telephone for provisional booking
Green Fees £25 per day; £16 per round (£30/£18 weekends).
Facilities   ⊗ ⅲ � ♥ ♀ ♨ 🖕 ⚑ ℓ Michael Clemons.
Leisure   motorised carts for hire, buggies for hire, trolley
     for hire, putting green, practice area.
Location   3m W of Cambridge, on B1046
Hotel   ★★ 65% Abbotsley Golf Hotel, Eynesbury
     Hardwicke, ST NEOTS
     ☎ 01480 474000 15 ⇆ ↾

CHESHIRE

Alderley Edge
Map 07 SJ87

Alderley Edge Brook Ln SK9 7RU
☎ 01625 585583
Well-wooded, undulating pastureland course. A stream
crosses 7 of the 9 holes.
9 holes, 5823yds, Par 68, SSS 68, Course record 62.
Club membership 400.
Visitors   by arrangement on Thu.
Societies   Thu only, apply in writing or telephone.

Green Fees £18 per day; (£22 weekends).
Facilities ⊗ Ⅲ ⅼ ♥ ♀ ♣ 📷 ℂ Peter Bowring.
Leisure trolley for hire, putting green, small practice area.
Location 1m NW on B5085
Hotel ★★★ 70% Alderley Edge Hotel, Macclesfield Rd, ALDERLEY EDGE
☎ 01625 583033 32 ⇆ ℟

ALSAGER — Map 07 SJ75

Alsager Golf & Country Club Audley Rd ST7 2UR
☎ 01270 875700
An 18-hole parkland course situated in rolling Cheshire countryside and offering a challenge to all golfers whatever their standard. Clubhouse is well appointed with good facilities and a friendly atmosphere.
18 holes, 6200yds, Par 70, SSS 70.
Club membership 640.
Visitors must contact in advance, can only play with member at weekends.
Societies must contact in advance.
Green Fees £25 per round Mon-Fri.
Facilities ⊗ Ⅲⅼ ♥ ♀ ♣ 📷 ℂ Paul Preston.
Leisure motorised carts for hire, buggies for hire, trolley for hire, putting green, practice area, bowls, snooker.
Location 2m NE of M6 junct 16
Hotel ★★★ 66% Manor House Hotel, Audley Rd, ALSAGER
☎ 01270 884000 57 ⇆ ℟

CHESTER — Map 07 SJ46

Carden Park Hotel Carden Park CH3 9DQ
☎ 01829 731000
Currently under construction and scheduled to open in May 1997, this championship course, designed by Jack and Steve Nicklaus, will enjoy a splendid setting within a magnificent country estate. Teaching Academy headed by the former Ryder Cup player John Garner. Excellent leisure facilities at adjacent Country Club.
18 holes, 6775yds, Par 72, SSS 73, Course record 74.
Visitors must contact in advance.
Societies contact for details.
Green Fees £25 per 18 holes (£30 weekends).
Facilities ⊗ Ⅲⅼ ♥ ♀ ♣ ⅏ ⇅

Chester Curzon Park CH4 8AR
☎ 01244 677760
Meadowland course on two levels contained within a loop of the River Dee. The car park overlooks the racecourse across the river.
18 holes, 6500yds, Par 72, SSS 71, Course record 66.
Club membership 820.
Visitors must contact in advance.
Societies must telephone or write in advance.
Green Fees £23 per day (£26 weekends).
Facilities ⊗ Ⅲⅼ ♥ ♀ ♣ 📷 ℂ George Parton.
Leisure trolley for hire, putting green, practice area.
Location 1m W of city centre
Hotel ★★★★ 65% Chester Moat House, Trinity St, CHESTER
☎ 01244 899988 150 ⇆

Upton-by-Chester Upton Ln, Upton-by-Chester CH2 1EE
☎ 01244 381183
Pleasant, tree-lined, parkland course. Not easy for low-handicap players to score well. Testing holes are 2nd (par 4), 14th (par 4) and 15th (par 3).
18 holes, 5808yds, Par 69, SSS 68, Course record 63.
Club membership 800.
Visitors must contact in advance.
Societies apply in writing.
Green Fees £20 per day (£25 per round weekends).
Facilities ⊗ Ⅲⅼ ♥ ♀ ♣ 📷 ℂ P A Gardner.
Leisure motorised carts for hire, buggies for hire, trolley for hire, putting green.
Location N side off A5116
Hotel ★★★★ 65% Mollington Banastre Hotel, Parkgate Rd, CHESTER
☎ 01244 851471 63 ⇆

Vicars Cross Tarvin Rd, Great Barrow CH3 7HN
☎ 01244 335174
Tree-lined parkland course, with undulating terrain.
18 holes, 6243yds, Par 72, SSS 70, Course record 64.
Club membership 750.
Visitors advisable to contact in advance, visitors may not play competition days.
Societies Tue & Thu only.
Green Fees £22 per day.
Facilities ⊗ Ⅲⅼ ♥ ♀ ♣ 📷 ℂ J A Forsythe.
Leisure buggies for hire, trolley for hire, putting green, practice area.
Location 4m E on A51
Hotel ★★★ 66% Rowton Hall Hotel, Whitchurch Road,Rowton, CHESTER
☎ 01244 335262 42 ⇆ ℟

CONGLETON — Map 07 SJ86

Astbury Peel Ln, Astbury CW12 4RE ☎ 01260 272772
Parkland course in open countryside, bisected by a canal. The testing 12th hole involves a long carry over a tree-filled ravine. Large practice area.
18 holes, 6296yds, Par 71, SSS 70.
Visitors with member only at weekends, contact for further details.
Societies contact for details.
Green Fees £25 per day.
Facilities ⊗ Ⅲ ♥ ♀ ♣ 📷 ℂ Ashley Salt.
Leisure trolley for hire, putting green, practice area.
Location 1.5m S between A34 and A527
Hotel ★★★ 65% Lion & Swan Hotel, Swan Bank, CONGLETON ☎ 01260 273115 21 ⇆ ℟

Congleton Biddulph Rd CW12 3LZ ☎ 01260 273540
Superbly-manicured parkland course with views over three counties from the balcony of the clubhouse.
9 holes, 5103yds, Par 68, SSS 65.
Club membership 400.
Visitors may not play during competitions.
Societies must apply in writing to Secretary.
Green Fees not confirmed.
Facilities ♀ ♣ 📷 ℂ John Colclough.
Location 1.5m SE on A527
Hotel ★★★ 65% Lion & Swan Hotel, Swan Bank, CONGLETON
☎ 01260 273115 21 ⇆ ℟

CREWE
Map 07 SJ75

Crewe Fields Rd, Haslington CW1 1TB ☎ 01270 584099
Undulating parkland course.
18 holes, 6259yds, Par 70, SSS 69, Course record 65.
Club membership 674.
Visitors contact for details.
Societies Tue only, prior arrangement with the secretary.
Green Fees not confirmed.
Facilities ⊗ ⅢⅢ ⅃⅃ ⅃⅃ ⅃ ℓ Mike Booker.
Leisure trolley for hire, putting green, practice area.
Location 2.25m NE off A534
Hotel ★★★ 64% Hunters Lodge Hotel, Sydney Rd,
Sydney, CREWE
☎ 01270 583440 & 588216 42 ⇥ ℟

Queen's Park Queen's Park Dr CW2 7SB ☎ 01270 666724
A short but testing municipal course, the 9 holes are
highlighted by the tight dogleg 4th holes and 450yard Par 4
7th hole. There is a testing Par 4 on finishing hole with a
bomb crater on left and outerbounds on the right.
9 holes, 4920yds, Par 68, SSS 64, Course record 67.
Club membership 400.
Visitors booking for weekends, cannot play Wed or Sun
before 10.30am.
Societies must book at least 2 weeks in advance.
Green Fees £4.60 per 18 holes; £3.60 per per 9 holes
(£6.10/£4.60 weekends & bank holidays).
Facilities ⊗ ⅢⅢ ⅃⅃ ⅃ ⅃ ⅃
Leisure hard tennis courts, putting green, bowling green.
Hotel ★★★ 64% Hunters Lodge Hotel, Sydney Rd,
Sydney, CREWE
☎ 01270 583440 & 588216 42 ⇥ ℟

DELAMERE
Map 07 SJ56

Delamere Forest Station Rd CW8 2JE
☎ 01606 883264 & 883307
Played mostly on undulating open heath there is great
charm in the way this course drops down into the
occasional pine sheltered valley. Six of the first testing
nine hole are between 420 and 455 yards in length.
18 holes, 6305yds, Par 69, SSS 70, Course record 63.
Visitors must contact in advance.
Societies apply in writing.
Green Fees £35 per day; £25 per round (£30 per round
weekends and bank holidays).
Facilities ⊗ by prior arrangement Ⅲ by prior
arrangement ⅃⅃ ⅃ ⅃ ⅃ ℓ Ellis B Jones.
Leisure motorised carts for hire, buggies for hire,
trolley for hire, putting green, practice area.
Location 1.5m NE, off B5152
Hotel ★★★(red)▲▲ Nunsmere Hall Country
House Hotel, Tarporley Rd, Oakmere,
SANDIWAY ☎ 01606 889100 32 ⇥ ℟

DISLEY
Map 07 SJ98

Disley Stanley Hall Ln, Jacksons Edge SK12 2JX
☎ 01663 762071
Parkland/moorland course with trees. Often breezy. Good
views. Testing hole: 3rd (par 5).
18 holes, 6015yds, Par 71, SSS 69, Course record 63.
Club membership 500.

Visitors contact in advance, may not normally play at
weekends.
Societies by prior arrangement.
Green Fees £25 per day (£30 weekends).
Facilities ⊗ ⅃⅃ ⅃ ⅃ ⅃ ⅃ ℓ Andrew Esplin.
Leisure trolley for hire, putting green, practice area.
Location NW side of village off A6
Hotel ★★★ 67% Bramhall Moat House, Bramhall Ln
South, BRAMHALL
☎ 0161 439 8116 65 ⇥ ℟

ELLESMERE PORT
Map 07 SJ47

Ellesmere Port Chester Rd, Hooton L66 1QF
☎ 0151 339 7689
Municipal parkland course with natural hazards of woods,
brook and ponds.
18 holes, 6432yds, Par 71, SSS 71, Course record 66.
Club membership 300.
Visitors must book with professional & send a deposit.
Societies by arrangement with professional.
Green Fees not confirmed.
Facilities ⅃ ⅃ ⅃ ⅃ ℓ David Yates.
Leisure squash, putting green, practice area, trolley hire.
Location NW side of town centre on A41
Hotel ★★★ 66% Woodhey Hotel, Welsh Rd, Little
Sutton, WIRRAL ☎ 0151 339 5121 53 ⇥ ℟

FRODSHAM
Map 07 SJ57

Frodsham Simons Ln WA6 6HE ☎ 01928 732159
Undulating parkland course with pleasant views from all
parts. Emphasis on accuracy over the whole course, the long
and difficult par 5 18th necessitating a drive across water to
the green. Crossed by two footpaths so extreme care needed.
18 holes, 6298yds, Par 70, SSS 70.
Club membership 600.
Visitors must contact in advance.
Societies telephone for bookings.
Green Fees £18 per day (£25/£20 weekends & bank
holidays).
Facilities ⊗ ⅢⅢ ⅃⅃ ⅃ ⅃ ⅃ ⅃ ℓ Graham Tonge.
Leisure motorised carts for hire, buggies for hire, trolley
for hire, putting green, practice area.
Location 1.5m SW
Hotel ★★★ 66% Forest Hills Hotel & Leisure
Complex, Bellemonte Rd, Overton Hill,
FRODSHAM ☎ 01928 735255 57 ⇥ ℟

HELSBY
Map 07 SJ47

Helsby Towers Ln WA6 0JB ☎ 01928 722021
Quiet parkland course with many trees, natural hazards and a
very challenging final three holes.
18 holes, 6229yds, Par 70, SSS 70.
Club membership 590.
Visitors weekends and bank holidays with member only.
Societies Tue & Thu. Booking through Hon Secretary.
Green Fees £27 per day; £20 per round.
Facilities ⊗ ⅢⅢ ⅃⅃ ⅃ ⅃ ⅃ ⅃ ℓ Matthew Jones.
Leisure trolley for hire, putting green, practice area.
Location 1m S off A56
Hotel ★★★★(red) The Chester Grosvenor Hotel,
Eastgate, CHESTER
☎ 01244 324024 86 ⇥ ℟

KNUTSFORD
Map 07 SJ77

Heyrose Budworth Rd, Tabley WA16 0HY
☎ 01565 733664
An 18-hole course in wooded and gently undulating terrain.
The par 3 16th (237yrds), bounded by a small river in a
wooded valley, is an interesting and testing hole - one of the
toughest par 3s in Cheshire. Both the course and the
comfortable clubhouse have attractive views.
18 holes, 6510yds, Par 73, SSS 71, Course record 66.
Club membership 600.
Visitors   not before 3pm Sat, ladies priority Wed and
                 seniors priority Thu am.
Societies   must contact in advance.
Green Fees   £24 per day; £19 per round (£29/£24 weekends
                 & bank holidays).
Facilities   ⊗ ⓑ ♥ ♀ ⚲ 🖻 ⌔ Martin Redrup.
Leisure   trolley for hire, putting green, practice area &
                 bunker.
Location   1.5m from junc 19 on M6
Hotel   ★★★★ 64% Cottons Hotel, Manchester Rd,
                 KNUTSFORD ☎ 01565 650333 82 ⇆ ⓚ

Knutsford Mereheath Ln WA16 6HS ☎ 01565 633355
Parkland course set in a beautiful old deer park. It demands
some precise iron play.
9 holes, 6288yds, Par 70, SSS 70.
Club membership 600.
Visitors   are not permitted weekends and restricted Wed.
                 Must contact in advance.
Green Fees   not confirmed.
Facilities   ♀ ⚲
Location   N side of town centre off A50
Hotel   ★★★★ 64% Cottons Hotel, Manchester Rd,
                 KNUTSFORD ☎ 01565 650333 82 ⇆ ⓚ

Mere Golf & Country Club Chester Rd, Mere
WA16 6LJ ☎ 01565 830155
A gracious parkland championship course designed by
James Braid in the Cheshire sand belt, with several holes
close to a lake. The round has a tight finish with four
testing holes.
18 holes, 6817yds, Par 71, SSS 73, Course record 64.
Club membership 540.
Visitors   must contact in advance.
Societies   Mon,Tue & Thu only by prior arrangement.
Green Fees   not confirmed.
Facilities   ♀ ⚲ 🖻 ⌔ Peter Eyre.
Leisure   hard tennis courts, heated indoor swimming
                 pool, squash, fishing, sauna, solarium,
                 gymnasium, floating ball drive range, petrol
                 buggies.
Location   1m E of junc 19 of M6
Hotel   ★★★★ 64% Cottons Hotel, Manchester Rd,
                 KNUTSFORD ☎ 01565 650333 82 ⇆ ⓚ

LYMM
Map 07 SJ68

Lymm Whitbarrow Rd WA13 9AN
☎ 01925 752177 & 755020
First ten holes are gently undulating with the Manchester
Ship Canal running alongside the 9th hole. The remaining
holes are comparatively flat.
18 holes, 6304yds, Par 71, SSS 70.
Club membership 650.

Visitors   may not play at weekends except with member.
                 Must contact in advance.
Societies   Wed only, must contact in advance.
Green Fees   £20 per day.
Facilities   ⊗ ⓜ ⓑ ♥ ♀ ⚲ 🖻 ⌔ Steve McCarthy.
Leisure   trolley for hire, putting green, practice area.
Location   0.5m N off A6144
Hotel   ★★★ 61% Lymm Hotel, Whitbarrow Rd,
                 LYMM
                 ☎ 01925 752233 22 ⇆ ⓚAnnexe47 ⇆ ⓚ

MACCLESFIELD
Map 07 SJ97

Macclesfield The Hollins SK11 7EA
☎ 01625 615845 (Secretary) & 616952 (Pro)
Very hilly heathland course situated on the edge of the
Pennines with excellent views across the Cheshire Plain. A
pleasant course providing a good test for players of all
abilities..
18 holes, 5769yds, Par 70, SSS 68.
Club membership 620.
Visitors   apply in advance.
Societies   telephone initially.
Green Fees   £17 per day (£20 weekends & bank holidays).
Facilities   ⊗ ⓜ ⓑ ♥ ♀ ⚲ 🖻 ⌔ ⌔ Tony Taylor.
Leisure   motorised carts for hire, trolley for hire, putting
                 green, practice area.
Location   SE side of town centre off A523
Hotel   ★★★ 63% Belgrade Hotel & Restaurant,
                 Jackson Ln, Kerridge, Bollington,
                 MACCLESFIELD ☎ 01625 573246 54 ⇆ ⓚ

Tytherington Dorchester Way, Tytherington SK10 2JP
☎ 01625 434562
Modern championship course in beautiful, mature
parkland setting with numerous water features. Testing
holes, notably the signature 12th hole (par 5), played
from an elevated tee with adjacent snaking ditch and a
lake guarding the green. Headquarters of the Women's
European Tour and venue of the WPGET English Open
and County matches. Country club facilities.
18 holes, 6750yds, Par 72, SSS 72.
Club membership 3100.
Visitors   advisable to contact in advance and be of
                 handicap standard.
Societies   weekdays only by prior arrangement.
Green Fees   £35 per day; £25 per 18 hole (£40/£30
                 weekends). Prices under review.
Facilities   ⊗ ⓜ ⓑ ♥ ♀ ⚲ 🖻 ⌔ ⌔ John Garner.
Leisure   motorised carts for hire, buggies for hire,
                 trolley for hire, driving range, putting green,
                 practice area.
Location   1m N of Macclesfield off A523
Hotel   ★★★★ 60% Shrigley Hall Golf & Country
                 Club, Shrigley Park, POTT SHRIGLEY
                 ☎ 01625 575757 156 ⇆ ⓚ

NANTWICH
Map 07 SJ65

Reaseheath Research Course Reaseheath College CW5 6DF
☎ 01270 625131
The course at Reaseheath is attached to Reaseheath College,
which is one of the major centres of greenkeeper training in
the UK. It is a short 9-hole which can only be played with a
member. ▶

9 holes, 1618yds, Par 60, SSS 55, Course record 62.
Club membership 250.
Societies by prior arrangement, apply in writing.
Location 1.5m NE of Nantwich, off A51

POTT SHRIGLEY Map 07 SJ97

Shrigley Hall Hotel Shrigley Park SK10 5SB
☎ 01625 575755 & 575757
Parkland course set in 262-acre estate with breathtaking views
over the Peak District and Cheshire Plain. Designed by Donald
Steel, this championship standard course provides a
real sporting challenge while the magnificent hotel provides a
wealth of sporting facilities as well as accommodation and food.
18 holes, 6305yds, Par 71, SSS 71, Course record 68.
Visitors must contact in advance by telephone.
Societies contact in advance.
Green Fees not confirmed.
Facilities ♀ ♨ 🏌 ⚑ 🍴 Granville Ogden.
Leisure hard tennis courts, heated indoor swimming pool,
squash, fishing, sauna, solarium, gymnasium.
Hotel ★★★★ 60% Shrigley Hall Golf & Country
Club, Shrigley Park, POTT SHRIGLEY
☎ 01625 575757 156 ⇄ ♞

POYNTON Map 07 SJ98

Davenport Worth Hall, Middlewood Rd SK12 1TS
☎ 01625 876951
Undulating parkland course. Extensive view over Cheshire
Plain from elevated 5th tee. Testing 17th hole, par 4.
18 holes, 6027yds, Par 69, SSS 69, Course record 64.
Club membership 700.
Visitors contact professional in advance (01625 858387).
May not play Wed or Sat.
Societies Tue and Thu only. Must apply in advance.
Green Fees £24 (£30 weekends).
Facilities ⊗ 🍺 🛥 ♥ ♀ ♨ 🏌 🍴 Wyn Harris.
Leisure trolley for hire, putting green, practice area.
Location 1m E off A523
Hotel ★★★ 67% Bramhall Moat House, Bramhall Ln
South, BRAMHALL ☎ 0161 439 8116 65 ⇄ ♞

PRESTBURY Map 07 SJ97

Prestbury Macclesfield Rd SK10 4BJ
☎ 01625 828241 & 829388
Rather strenuous parkland course, undulating hills, with
many plateau greens looked after by one of only 7 Master
Greenkeepers in the world. The 9th hole has a
challenging uphill 3-tier green and the 17th is over a
valley. Host to county and inter-county championships as
well as England v USA competitions.
18 holes, 6359yds, Par 71, SSS 71, Course record 64.
Club membership 702.
Visitors must contact in advance and have an
introduction from own club, with member
only at weekends.
Societies apply in writing, Thu only.
Green Fees £32 per day.
Facilities ⊗ 🍺 🛥 ♥ ♀ ♨ 🏌
🍴 Nick Summerfield.
Leisure motorised carts for hire, trolley for hire,
driving range, putting green, practice area.

Location S side of village off A538
Hotel ★★★★ 64% Mottram Hall Hotel,
Wilmslow Rd, Prestbury, WILMSLOW
☎ 01625 828135 133 ⇄ ♞

RUNCORN Map 07 SJ58

Runcorn Clifton Rd WA7 4SU ☎ 01928 574214
Parkland course with tree-lined fairways and easy walking.
Fine views over Mersey and Weaver valleys. Testing holes:
7th par 5; 14th par 5; 17th par 4.
18 holes, 6035yds, Par 69, SSS 69, Course record 58.
Club membership 570.
Visitors weekends restricted to playing with member
only.
Societies telephone in advance.
Green Fees £18 per day.
Facilities ⊗ 🍺 🛥 ♥ ♀ ♨ 🏌 🍴 Steve Dooley.
Leisure putting green.
Location 1.25m S of Runcorn Station
Hotel B Forte Posthouse Warrington/Runcorn, Wood
Ln, Beechwood, RUNCORN
☎ 01928 714000 135 ⇄ ♞

SANDBACH Map 07 SJ76

Malkins Bank Betchton Rd, Malkins Bank CW11 0XN
☎ 01270 765931
Parkland course. Tight 13th hole with stream running through.
18 holes, 6071yds, Par 70, SSS 69, Course record 65.
Club membership 500.
Visitors no restrictions. Advisable to book in advance.
Societies apply for booking form to course professional
Green Fees not confirmed.
Facilities ♀ ♨ 🏌 🍴 David Wheeler.
Leisure practice area, putting green, trolley hire.
Location 1.5m SE off A533
Hotel ★★★ 63% Saxon Cross Hotel, Holmes Chapel
Rd, SANDBACH ☎ 01270 763281 52 ⇄ ♞

Sandbach Middlewich Rd CW11 9BT ☎ 01270 762117
Meadowland, undulating course with easy walking. Limited
facilities.
9 holes, 5598yds, Par 68, SSS 67.
Club membership 570.
Visitors weekdays except Tue, and with member only
weekends & bank holidays. Must contact in
advance.
Societies apply by letter.
Green Fees not confirmed.
Facilities ♀ ♨
Location 0.5m W on A533
Hotel ★★★ 63% Saxon Cross Hotel, Holmes Chapel
Rd, SANDBACH ☎ 01270 763281 52 ⇄ ♞

SANDIWAY Map 07 SJ67

Sandiway Chester Rd CW8 2DJ
☎ 01606 883247 (Secretary) & 883180 (Pro)
Delightful undulating woodland and heath golf with long
hills up to the 8th, 16th and 17th holes. Many dog-legged
and tree-lined holes give opportunities for the deliberate
fade or draw.

18 holes, 6435yds, Par 70, SSS 72, Course record 65.
Club membership 700.

Visitors	book through professional, members have reserved tees 8.30-9.30 and 12.30-1.30 (11.30-12.30 winter).
Societies	book in advance through Secretary/Manager.
Green Fees	£35 per day; £30 per round (£40/£35 weekends and bank holidays).
Facilities	⊗ ⅲ ᕮ ⬛ ♀ ⚥ 🏠 🛈 ℓ William Laird.
Leisure	trolley for hire, putting green, practice area.
Location	1m E on A556
Hotel	★★★ 64% Hartford Hall Hotel, School Ln, Hartford, NORTHWICH ☎ 01606 75711 20 ⇆

TARPORLEY   Map 07 SJ56

Portal Golf & Country Club Cobbler's Cross Ln CW6 0DJ
☎ 01829 733933 & 733884
Opened in 1991, there are two 18-hole courses here - Championship and Premier - and one 9-hole course - Arderne. They are set in mature, wooded parkland. There are fine views over the Cheshire Plain and numerous water hazards. The Championship 13th is just a short iron through trees, but its green is virtually an island surrounded by water.
Championship Course: 18 holes, 7037yds, Par 73, SSS 74, Course record 64.
Premier Course: 18 holes, 6508yds, Par 71, SSS 72.
Arderne Course: 9 holes, 1724yds, Par 30.
Club membership 250.

Visitors	must contact in advance.
Societies	must pre-book.
Green Fees	Championship: £30 per round Mon-Sun. Premier: £22 per round (£25 weekends).
Facilities	⊗ ⅲ ᕮ ⬛ ♀ ⚥ 🏠 🛈 ℓ David Clare.
Leisure	hard tennis courts, motorised carts for hire, buggies for hire, trolley for hire, driving range, putting green, practice area.
Location	Off A49
Hotel	★★★ 67% The Wild Boar, Whitchurch Rd, Beeston, TARPORLEY ☎ 01829 260309 37 ⇆ 📷

WARRINGTON   Map 07 SJ68

Birchwood Kelvin Close, Birchwood WA3 7PB
☎ 01925 818819 & 816574
Very testing parkland course with many natural water hazards and the prevailing wind creating a problem on each hole. The 11th hole is particularly challenging.
18 holes, 6727yds, Par 71, SSS 73, Course record 67.
Club membership 675.

Visitors	advisable to check with the professional to determine if course is being used.
Societies	Mon, Wed & Thu. Apply in writing, or telephone.
Green Fees	£26 per day; £19 per round (£34 Sat and bank holidays).
Facilities	⊗ ⅲ ᕮ ⬛ ♀ ⚥ 🏠 🛈 ℓ Paul McEwan.
Leisure	sauna, trolley for hire, putting green, practice area.
Location	4m NE on A574

Hotel	B Forte Posthouse Haydock, Lodge Ln, Newton-Le-Willows, HAYDOCK ☎ 01942 717878 136 ⇆ 📷

Leigh Kenyon Hall, Broseley Ln, Culcheth WA3 4BG
☎ 01925 762943 (Secretary) & 762013 (Pro)
A pleasant, well-wooded parkland course. Any discrepancy in length is compensated by the wide variety of golf offered here. The course is well maintained and there is a comfortable clubhouse.
18 holes, 5853yds, Par 69, SSS 68, Course record 64.
Club membership 550.

Visitors	contact professional for details.
Societies	Mon (ex bank holidays) & Tue, apply by telephone.
Green Fees	£26 per day/round (£33 weekends & bank holidays).
Facilities	⊗ ⅲ ᕮ ⬛ ♀ ⚥ 🏠 ℓ Andrew Baguley.
Leisure	trolley for hire, putting green, practice area.
Location	5m NE off A579
Hotel	★★★ 65% Fir Grove Hotel, Knutsford Old Rd, WARRINGTON ☎ 01925 267471 40 ⇆ 📷

Poulton Park Dig Ln, Cinnamon Brow, Padgate WA2 0SH
☎ 01925 822802
Tight, flat parkland course with good greens and many trees. A straight drive off each tee is important. The 4/13th has a fairway curving to the left with water and out-of-bounds on left and trees on right.
9 holes, 4978metres, Par 68, SSS 66, Course record 66.
Club membership 350.

Visitors	contact professional for details (01925 825220).
Societies	apply in advance.
Green Fees	£17 per day (£19 weekends).
Facilities	⊗ ⅲ ᕮ ⬛ ♀ ⚥ 🏠 ℓ Darren Newing.
Leisure	practice area, putting green.
Location	3m from Warrington on A574
Hotel	★★★ 65% Fir Grove Hotel, Knutsford Old Rd, WARRINGTON ☎ 01925 267471 40 ⇆ 📷

Walton Hall Warrington Rd, Higher Walton WA4 5LU
☎ 01925 263061
A quiet, wooded, municipal parkland course on Walton Hall estate.
18 holes, 6801yds, Par 72, SSS 73, Course record 70.
Club membership 400.

Visitors	must book 6 days in advance.
Societies	must contact in writing.
Green Fees	not confirmed.
Facilities	♀ ⚥ 🏠 🛈 ℓ Peter Maton.
Leisure	putting, trolley hire, driving range.
Location	2m from junct 11 of M56
Hotel	★★★ 65% Fir Grove Hotel, Knutsford Old Rd, WARRINGTON ☎ 01925 267471 40 ⇆ 📷

Warrington Hill Warren, London Rd, Appleton WA4 5HR
☎ 01925 261775 (Secretary) & 265431 (Pro)
Meadowland, with varied terrain and natural hazards. Major work has recently been carried out on both the clubhouse and the course to ensure high standards. The course is a constant challenge with with ponds, trees and bunkers threatening the errant shot!
18 holes, 6305yds, Par 72, SSS 70, Course record 61.
Club membership 840.   ▶

Visitors contact in advance.
Societies by prior arrangement with Secretary.
Green Fees £25 per day (£38 weekends & bank holidays).
Facilities ⊗ ⅢⅡ ⅃ ⅃ ♀ ⅄ 🕮 ⅙ ⅃ Reay Mackay.
Leisure trolley for hire, putting green, practice area.
Location 2.5m S on A49
Hotel ★★ 70% Rockfield Hotel, Alexandra Rd,
Grappenhall, WARRINGTON
☎ 01925 262898 6 ⇔ ⅙Annexe6 ⇔ ⅙

WAVERTON   Map 07 SJ46

Eaton Guy Ln CH3 7PH ☎ 01244 335885 & 335826
Eaton Golf Club has moved to a new course. Designed by
Donald Steel, the course was opened in 1993 and is parkland
with a liberal covering of both mature trees and new planting
enhanced by natural water hazards. The old course at
Eccleston has been returned to nature.
18 holes, 6562yds, Par 72, SSS 71, Course record 69.
Club membership 550.
Visitors must contact in advance particularly for
weekends.
Societies must contact in advance. May not play weekends
or Wednesdays.
Green Fees £21 per round/day (£27 weekends & bank
holidays).
Facilities ⊗ ⅢⅡ ⅃ ⅃ ♀ ⅄ 🕮 ⅙ ⅃ Neil Dunroe.
Leisure motorised carts for hire, buggies for hire, trolley
for hire, putting, practice area.
Location 3m SE of Chester off A41
Hotel ★★★★(red) The Chester Grosvenor Hotel,
Eastgate, CHESTER
☎ 01244 324024 86 ⇔ ⅙

WIDNES   Map 07 SJ58

St Michael Jubilee Dunalk Rd WA8 8BS
☎ 0151 424 6230
Municipal parkland course dominated by the 'Stewards
Brook'. It is divided into two sections which are split by the
main road and joined by an underpass.
18 holes, 2648yds, Par 69, SSS 68.
Visitors must be accompanied by member, contact in
advance and have an introduction from own
club.
Societies must contact in writing.
Green Fees not confirmed.
Facilities ♀ ⅄ 🕮 ⅃
Location W side of town centre off A562
Hotel ★★★ 61% Everglades Park Hotel, Derby Rd,
WIDNES ☎ 0151 495 2040 32 ⇔ ⅙

Widnes Highfield Rd WA8 7DT ☎ 0151 424 2440
Parkland course, easy walking.
18 holes, 5719yds, Par 69, SSS 68.
Visitors may play after 9am & after 4pm on competition
days. Must contact in advance.
Societies must contact in writing.
Green Fees not confirmed.
Facilities ♀ ⅄ 🕮 ⅃ S Forster.
Hotel ★★★ 61% Everglades Park Hotel, Derby Rd,
WIDNES
☎ 0151 495 2040 32 ⇔ ⅙

WILMSLOW   Map 07 SJ88

Mottram Hall Wilmslow Rd, Mottram St Andrew SK10
4QT ☎ 01625 828135
Championship standard course with flat meadowland on the
front nine and undulating woodland on the back with well
guarded greens. The course was designed in 1989 and opened
in May 1991. The course is unusual as each half opens and
closes with Par 5's. The hotel offers many leisure facilities.
18 holes, 7006yds, Par 72, SSS 74, Course record 65.
Club membership 500.
Visitors must contact in advance.
Societies must contact in advance.
Green Fees £35 (£40 weekends).
Facilities ⊗ ⅢⅡ ⅃ ⅃ ♀ ⅄ 🕮 ⅙ ⅃ ⅙ ⅃ Tim Rastall.
Leisure hard tennis courts, heated indoor swimming
pool, squash, sauna, solarium, gymnasium,
motorised carts for hire, buggies for hire, trolley
for hire, driving range, putting green, practice
area, clay pigeon shooting.
Location On A538 between Wilmslow and Preston
Hotel ★★★★ 64% Mottram Hall Hotel, Wilmslow
Rd, Prestbury, WILMSLOW
☎ 01625 828135 133 ⇔ ⅙

Wilmslow Great Warford, Mobberley WA16 7AY
☎ 01565 872148
A fine parkland championship course, of middle length,
fair to all classes of player and almost in perfect
condition.
18 holes, 6607yds, Par 72, SSS 72, Course record 62.
Club membership 800.
Visitors must contact in advance.
Societies Tue & Thu only application in writing.
Green Fees £40 per day; £30 per round (£50/£40
weekends).
Facilities ⊗ ⅢⅡ ⅃ ⅃ ♀ ⅄ 🕮 ⅙ ⅃ John Nowicki.
Leisure trolley for hire, putting green, practice area.
Location 2m SW off B5058
Hotel ★★★ 70% Alderley Edge Hotel,
Macclesfield Rd, ALDERLEY EDGE
☎ 01625 583033 32 ⇔ ⅙

WINSFORD   Map 07 SJ66

Knights Grange Grange Ln CW7 2PT
☎ 01606 552780
Municipal parkland course with water hazards.
9 holes, 2719yds, Par 33, SSS 68.
Visitors 24 hr booking system for weekly play, after
10am Wed for weekend bookings.
Societies apply in writing.
Green Fees £3.50 per 18 holes; £2.70 per 9 holes
(£5.10/£3.95 weekends). Prices under review..
Facilities ⅃ ⅄ ⅙ ⅃ Graham Moore.
Leisure hard and grass tennis courts, trolley for hire,
putting green, practice area, bowls.
Location N side of town off A54
Hotel ★★★ 64% Hartford Hall Hotel, School Ln,
Hartford, NORTHWICH
☎ 01606 75711 20 ⇔

CORNWALL & ISLES OF SCILLY

BODMIN
Map 02 SX06

Lanhydrock Lostwithiel Rd, Lanhydrock PL30 5AQ
☎ 01208 73600
Championship standard parkland/moorland course adjacent to the National Trust property Lanhydrock house. Nestling in a picturesque wooded valley of oak and birch, this undulating course provides an exciting and enjoyable challenge to all abilities with discreet use of water and bunkers.
18 holes, 6185yds, Par 71, SSS 69.
Club membership 300.
Visitors   no restrictions.
Societies   please telephone in advance.
Green Fees £33 per 36 holes; £23 per 18 holes. 7 Day ticket £100.
Facilities   ⊗ ⅢⓁ ▆ ♀ ⚲ 📷 ⫟ 𝄖 𝘍 Jason Broadway.
Leisure   motorised carts for hire, buggies for hire, trolley for hire, putting green, practice area.
Location   1m S of Bodmin from B3268
Hotel   ★★★ 65% Restormel Lodge Hotel, Hillside Gardens, LOSTWITHIEL
                     ☎ 01208 872223 21 ⇆ 𝘍Annexe12 ⇆

BUDE
Map 02 SS20

Bude & North Cornwall Burn View EX23 8DA
☎ 01288 352006
Seaside links course with natural sand bunkers, superb greens and breathtaking views. Club established in 1893.
18 holes, 6205yds, Par 71, SSS 70.
Club membership 1000.
Visitors   book by telephone 6 days in advance for starting time - or before 6 days with a deposit.
Societies   apply in writing or telephone.
Green Fees £20 per day (£25 per round weekends & bank holidays).
Facilities   ⊗ Ⅲ Ⓛ ▆ ♀ ⚲ 📷 𝘍 John Yeo.
Leisure   trolley for hire, putting green, practice area.
Location   N side of town
Hotel   ★★ 66% Camelot Hotel, Downs View, BUDE
                     ☎ 01288 352361 21 ⇆ 𝘗

BUDOCK VEAN
Map 02 SW73

Budock Vean Golf & Country House Hotel Mawnan Smith TR11 5LG ☎ 01326 250288
Set in 65 acres of mature grounds with a private foreshore to the Helford River, this undulating parkland course has a tough par 4 5th hole (456yds) which dog-legs at halfway around an oak tree.
9 holes, 2657yds, Par 68, SSS 65, Course record 61.
Club membership 200.
Visitors   must contact in advance.
Societies   apply in writing or telephone in advance.
Green Fees £14 per day (£18 Sun & bank holidays).
Facilities   ⊗ Ⅲ Ⓛ ▆ ♀ ⚲ 📷 ⫟ 𝄖
Leisure   hard tennis courts, heated indoor swimming pool, motorised carts for hire, buggies for hire, trolley for hire, putting green, practice area.
Location   1.5m SW

Hotel   ★★★ 73% Budock Vean Hotel, MAWNAN SMITH ☎ 01326 250288 58 ⇆ 𝘗

CAMBORNE
Map 02 SW64

Tehidy Park TR14 0HH ☎ 01209 842208
A well-maintained parkland course providing good holiday golf.
18 holes, 6241yds, Par 72, SSS 71, Course record 65.
Club membership 850.
Visitors   must contact in advance and have a handicap certificate.
Societies   telephone followed by letter.
Green Fees £22 per day; £16 per round (£32/£27 weekends).
Facilities   ⊗ Ⅲ Ⓛ ▆ ♀ ⚲ 📷 ⫟ 𝄖 James Dumbreck.
Leisure   motorised carts for hire, trolley for hire, putting green, practice area.
Location   On Portreath/Pool road, 2m S of Camborne
Hotel   ★★★ 66% Penventon Hotel, REDRUTH
                     ☎ 01209 214141 50 ⇆ 𝘗

CARLYON BAY
Map 02 SX05

Carlyon Bay Hotel Sea Rd PL25 3RD
☎ 01726 814250
Championship-length, cliff-top course moving into parkland. Magnificent views surpassed only by the quality of the course. The 230-yard (par 3) 18th with railway and road out-of-bounds, holds the player's interest to the end.
18 holes, 6549yds, Par 72, SSS 71, Course record 66.
Club membership 500.
Visitors   no restrictions.
Societies   must contact in advance.
Green Fees £20 per round £5 per extra round.
Facilities   ⊗ Ⅲ by prior arrangement Ⓛ ▆ ♀ ⚲ 📷 ⫟ 𝄖 Nigel Sears.
Leisure   hard tennis courts, outdoor and indoor heated swimming pools, sauna, solarium, motorised carts for hire, buggies for hire, trolley for hire, putting green, practice area.
Hotel   ★★★★ 73% Carlyon Bay Hotel, Sea Rd, Carlyon Bay, ST AUSTELL
                     ☎ 01726 812304 73 ⇆ 𝘗

CONSTANTINE BAY
Map 02 SW87

Trevose PL28 8JB ☎ 01841 520208
A pleasant holiday seaside course with early holes close to the sea on excellent springy turf. A championship course affording varying degrees of difficulty appealing to both the professional and higher handicap player. It is a good test with well-positioned bunkers, and a meandering stream, and the wind playing a decisive role in preventing low scoring. Self-catering accommodation is available at the club.
Championship Course: 18 holes, 6461yds, Par 71, SSS 71, Course record 67.
Short Course: 9 holes, 1360yds, Par 29, SSS 29.
New Course: 9 holes, 3031yds, Par 35, SSS 35.
Club membership 1200.
Visitors   must contact in advance.
Societies   telephone or write to the secretary.
Green Fees contact for details.
Facilities   ⊗ Ⅲ Ⓛ ▆ ♀ ⚲ 📷 ⫟ 𝄖 Gary Alliss. ▶

Leisure hard tennis courts, heated outdoor swimming pool, motorised carts for hire, buggies for hire, trolley for hire, putting green, practice area.
Location N of Constantine Bay, off B3276
Hotel ★★★ 77% Treglos Hotel, CONSTANTINE BAY ☎ 01841 520727 44 ⇔ ⚑

FALMOUTH
Map 02 SW83

Falmouth Swanpool Rd TR11 5BQ ☎ 01326 311262
Seaside/parkland course with outstanding coastal views. Sufficiently bunkered to punish any inaccurate shots. Five acres of practice grounds.
18 holes, 5680yds, Par 70, SSS 68, Course record 61.
Club membership 600.
Visitors restricted play on competition days. Must contact in advance.
Societies must contact in advance.
Green Fees not confirmed.
Facilities ♀ ⚲ 🏠 ⚐ ⟋ David J Short.
Leisure practice fields, putting green,trolleys.
Location SW side of town centre
Hotel ★★★🏊 76% Penmere Manor, Mongleath Rd, FALMOUTH ☎ 01326 211411 38 ⇔ ⚑

HOLYWELL BAY
Map 02 SW75

Holywell Bay TR8 5PW ☎ 01637 830095
Holywell Golf Club is situated beside a family fun park with many amenities. The course is an 18 hole Par 3 with excellent sea views. Fresh Atlantic winds make the course hard to play and there are several tricky holes, particularly the 18th over the trout pond. The site also has and excellent 18 hole Pitch & Putt course for the whole family.
18 holes, 2784yds, Par 61, Course record 58.
Club membership 100.
Visitors no restrictions.
Societies telephone in advance.
Green Fees £7, £3.90 pitch & putt.
Facilities ⊗ ⚲ 🍺 ♀ 🏠 ⚐
Leisure hard tennis courts, heated outdoor swimming pool, fishing, putting green, practice area, 18 hole pitch & putt, fun park.
Location Off A3075 Newquay/Perranporth road
Hotel ★★ 67% Crantock Bay Hotel, West Pentire, CRANTOCK ☎ 01637 830229 34 ⇔ ⚑

LAUNCESTON
Map 02 SX38

Launceston St Stephens PL15 8HF ☎ 01566 773442
Undulating parkland course with views over Tamar Valley to Dartmoor and Bodmin Moor. Dominated by the 'The Hill' up which the 8th and 11th fairways rise, and on which the 8th, 9th, 11th and 12th greens sit.
18 holes, 6407yds, Par 70, SSS 71, Course record 65.
Club membership 800.
Visitors must contact in advance, may not play weekends Apr-Oct.
Societies telephone in first instance.
Green Fees £20 per day.
Facilities ⊗ ⚲ 🍺 ♀ ⚲ 🏠 ⚐ ⟋ John Tozer.
Leisure trolley for hire, putting green.

Location NW side of town centre on B3254
Hotel ★★ 60% Eagle House, Castle St, LAUNCESTON ☎ 01566 772036 14 ⇔ ⚑

LELANT
Map 02 SW53

West Cornwall TR26 3DZ ☎ 01736 753319 753401
A seaside links with sandhills and lovely turf adjacent to the Hayle estuary and St Ives Bay. A real test of the player's skill, especially 'Calamity Corner' starting at the 5th on the lower land by the River Hayle. A small (3 hole) course is available for practice.
18 holes, 5884yds, Par 69, SSS 69, Course record 63.
Club membership 748.
Societies must apply in writing.
Green Fees £20 per day (£25 weekends and bank holidays).
Facilities ⊗ ⚲ 🍺 ♀ ⚲ 🏠 ⚐ ⟋ Paul Atherton.
Leisure trolley for hire, putting green, practice area.
Location N side of village off A3074
Hotel ★★ 66% Boskerris Hotel, Boskerris Rd, Carbis Bay, ST IVES ☎ 01736 795295 13rm(11 ⇔ ⚑)Annexe5 ⇔ ⚑

LOOE
Map 02 SX25

Looe Widegates PL13 1PX ☎ 01503 240239
Exposed and somewhat windy course on high moorland; designed by Harry Vardon in 1935. Easy walking. Fine views over Looe coastline.
18 holes, 5940yds, Par 70, SSS 68.
Club membership 600.
Visitors booking must be made in advance, no limitations subject to availability.
Societies telephone in advance, booking to be confirmed in writing.
Green Fees £24 per 36/27 holes; £18 per 18 holes.
Facilities 🍺 ♀ ⚲ 🏠 ⚐ ⟋ Alistair Macdonald.
Leisure motorised carts for hire, buggies for hire, trolley for hire, putting green, practice area.
Location 3.5m NE off B3253
Hotel ★★ 68% Commonwood Manor Hotel, St Martin's Rd, LOOE ☎ 01503 262929 11 ⇔ ⚑

LOSTWITHIEL
Map 02 SX15

Lostwithiel Golf & Country Club Lower Polscoe PL22 0HQ ☎ 01208 873550
An undulating, parkland course with water hazards. Overlooked by Restormel Castle and the Rover Fowey flows alongside the course. Driving range.
18 holes, 5984yds, Par 72, SSS 71.
Club membership 500.
Visitors must contact in advance.
Societies contact in advance.
Green Fees summer £18 per round (£20 weekend).
Facilities ⊗ ⚲ 🍺 ♀ ⚲ 🏠 ⚐ ⟋ Tony Nash.
Leisure hard tennis courts, heated indoor swimming pool, fishing, sauna, gymnasium, trolley for hire, driving range, putting green, practice area.
Location 1m outside Lostwithiel off A390
Hotel ★★ 66% Lostwithiel Golf & Country Club, Lower Polscoe, LOSTWITHIEL ☎ 01208 873550 18 ⇔ ⚑

MAWGAN PORTH   Map 02 SW86

Merlin TR8 4AD ☎ 01841 540222
A heathland course. The most challenging hole is the Par 5 3rd with out of bounds along the lefthand side.
18 holes, 5227yds, Par 67, SSS 67.
Visitors   no restrictions.
Societies   telephone in advance.
Green Fees £10 per day.
Facilities   ⊗ ⅷ ㄴ 🝙 ☲ ♀ ♋ 🖻 ⚐
Leisure   motorised carts for hire, trolley for hire, driving range, putting green, practice area.
Hotel   ★★ 66% Tredragon Hotel, MAWGAN PORTH ☎ 01637 860213 27 ⇌ 🝰

MAWNAN SMITH   See **Budock Vean**

MULLION   Map 02 SW61

Mullion Cury TR12 7BP ☎ 01326 240685
Founded in 1895, a clifftop and links course with panoramic views over Mounts Bay. A steep downhill slope on 6th and the 10th descends to the beach with a deep ravine alongside the green. Most southerly course in the British Isles.
18 holes, 6022yds, Par 69, SSS 69, Course record 69.
Club membership 654.
Visitors   preferable to contact in advance, restricted during club competitions.
Societies   must contact in advance.

Green Fees £20 per day/round.
Facilities   ⊗ ⅷ ㄴ 🝙 ☲ ♀ ♋ 🖻 ⚐ ⚑ Phil Blundell.
Leisure   motorised carts for hire, buggies for hire, trolley for hire, putting green, practice area.
Location   1.5m NW of Mullion, off A3083
Hotel   ★★★ 74% Polurrian Hotel, MULLION ☎ 01326 240421 39 ⇌ 🝰

NEWQUAY   Map 02 SW86

Newquay Tower Rd TR7 1LT
☎ 01637 874354 & 872091
Gently undulating seaside course running parallel to the beach and open to wind. Breathtaking views.
18 holes, 6140yds, Par 69, SSS 69, Course record 63.
Club membership 700.
Visitors   please telephone in advance.
Societies   apply in writing or telephone.
Green Fees £20 per round/day.
Facilities   ⊗ ⅷ ㄴ 🝙 ☲ ♀ ♋ 🖻 ⚐ ⚑ Anfrew J Cullen.
Leisure   hard tennis courts, trolley for hire, putting green, practice area.
Location   W side of town
Hotel   ★★ 63% Philema Hotel, 1 Esplanade Rd, Pentire, NEWQUAY ☎ 01637 872571 27 ⇌ 🝰

Treloy TR8 4JN ☎ 01637 878554
An Executive course constructed in 1991 to American specifications with large contoured and mounded greens. Offers an interesting round for all categories of player.
9 holes, 2143yds, Par 32, SSS 31.
Visitors   no restrictions.
Societies   telephone in advance.
Green Fees £11.50 per 18 holes; £7.50 per 9 holes.
Facilities   ㄴ 🝙 ♀ ♋ 🖻 ⚐
Location   On A3059 Newquay to St Columb Major Road
Hotel   ★★ 70% Whipsiderry Hotel, Trevelgue Road, Porth, NEWQUAY ☎ 01637 874777 24rm(5 ⇌14 🝰)

PADSTOW   See **Constantine Bay**

PERRANPORTH   Map 02 SW75

Perranporth Budnick Hill TR6 0AB ☎ 01872 573701
There are three testing par 5 holes on the links course (2nd, 5th, 11th) and a fine view over Perranporth Beach from all holes.
18 holes, 6288yds, Par 72, SSS 72, Course record 63.
Club membership 618.
Visitors   no reserved tee times.
Societies   by prior arrangement.
Green Fees £20 per day (£25 weekends & bank holidays).
Facilities   ⊗ ⅷ ㄴ 🝙 ☲ ♀ ♋ 🖻 ⚐ ⚑ D Michell.
Leisure   trolley for hire, putting green, practice area.
Location   0.75m NE on B3285
Hotel   ★★ 63% Beach Dunes Hotel, Ramoth Way, Reen Sands, PERRANPORTH ☎ 01872 572263 6rm(5 ⇌ 🝰)Annexe3 ⇌ 🝰

PRAA SANDS Map 02 SW52

Praa Sands Germoe Cross Roads TR20 9TQ
☎ 01736 763445
A beautiful parkland course with outstanding sea views from every tee and green.
9 holes, 4104yds, Par 62, SSS 60, Course record 59.
Club membership 220.
Visitors   restricted Sun 8-12.30pm.
Societies   telephone for details.
Green Fees £14 per 18 holes.
Facilities   ⊗ ⊪ ⓑ ⬛ ♀ ♣ ☎ ⚲
Leisure   trolley for hire, putting green, practice area.
Location   (A394 midway between Penzance/Helston)
Hotel   ★★♨ 76% Nansloe Manor Hotel, Meneage Rd, HELSTON ☎ 01326 574691 7rm(6 ⇆ ℞)

ROCK Map 02 SW97

St Enodoc PL27 6LB ☎ 01208 863216
Classic links courses with huge sand hills and rolling fairways. James Braid laid out the original 18 holes in 1907 and changes were made in 1922 and 1935. English County Final and English Ladies Closed Amateur Championships held recently. On the Church, the 10th is the toughest par 4 on the course and on the 6th is a truly enormous sand hill known as the Himalayas.
Church Course: 18 holes, 6207yds, Par 69, SSS 70, Course record 65.
Holywell Course: 18 holes, 4142yds, Par 63, SSS 61.
Club membership 1500.
Visitors   may not play on bank holidays. Must have a handicap certificate of 24 or below for Church Course. Must contact in advance.
Societies   must contact in writing.
Green Fees not confirmed.
Facilities   ♀ ♣ ☎ ⚲ ℓ Nick Williams.
Leisure   putting, buggies/trolleys hire.
Location   W side of village
Hotel   ★★ 63% St Enodoc Hotel, ROCK ☎ 01208 863394 13 ⇆ ℞

ST AUSTELL Map 02 SX05

Porthpean Porthpean PL26 6AY ☎ 01726 64613
A challenging 9-hole course which plays out at over 6500 yards. There are spectacular views over St Austell Bay. There is also an 8-bay covered and floodlit driving range.
9 holes, 3266yds, Par 37, SSS 37.
Club membership 180.
Visitors   no restrictions
Societies   telephone in advance.
Green Fees not confirmed.
Facilities   ♀ ♣ ☎ ⚲
Leisure   8 bay covered & floodlit driving range.
Location   1.5m from St Austell by-pass
Hotel   ★★ 66% The Pier House, Harbour Front, Charlestown, ST AUSTELL ☎ 01726 67955 12 ⇆ ℞Annexe13 ℞

St Austell Tregongeeves Ln PL26 7DS ☎ 01726 72649
Very interesting inland parkland course designed by James Braid and offering glorious views of the surrounding countryside. Undulating, well-covered with tree plantations

and well-bunkered. Notable holes are 8th (par 4) and 16th (par 3).
18 holes, 6089yds, Par 69, SSS 69, Course record 67.
Club membership 700.
Visitors   advisable to contact in advance, weekend play is limited.
Societies   must apply in writing.
Green Fees £15 per round (£18 weekends & bank holidays).
Facilities   ⊗ ⊪ ⓑ ⬛ ♀ ♣ ☎ ⚲ Mark Rowe.
Leisure   trolley for hire, putting green, practice area.
Location   1m W of St Austell on A390
Hotel   ★★★ 65% Porth Avallen Hotel, Sea Rd, Carlyon Bay, ST AUSTELL ☎ 01726 812802 24 ⇆ ℞

ST IVES Map 02 SW54

Tregenna Castle Hotel, Golf & Country Club TR26 2DE
☎ 01736 797381
Parkland course surrounding a castellated hotel and overlooking St Ives Bay and harbour.
18 holes, 3464, Par 59, SSS 57.
Club membership 150.
Visitors   no booking needed.
Societies   telephone for details.
Green Fees £17.50 per day; £12.50 per round.
Facilities   ⊗ ⊪ by prior arrangement ⬛ ♀ ☎ ⚲ ⊨
Leisure   trolley for hire.
Location   From A30 Penzance road turn off just past Hayle onto A3074
Hotel   ★★★ 69% Carbis Bay Hotel, Carbis Bay, ST IVES ☎ 01736 795311 30 ⇆ ℞

ST JUST (NEAR LAND'S END) Map 02 SW33

Cape Cornwall Golf & Country Club Cape Cornwall TR19 7NL ☎ 01736 788611
Coastal parkland, walled course. The walls are an integral part of its design. Country club facilities.
18 holes, 5650yds, Par 70, SSS 68, Course record 69.
Club membership 700.
Visitors   may not play before 11.30am at weekends.
Societies   must contact in advance.
Green Fees not confirmed.
Facilities   ♀ ♣ ☎ ⚲ ⊨ ℓ Bob Hamilton.
Leisure   heated indoor swimming pool, sauna, solarium, gymnasium, trolley for hire, driving range, children's area.
Location   1m W of St Just
Hotel   ★★★♨ 61% Higher Faugan Hotel, Newlyn, PENZANCE ☎ 01736 62076 11 ⇆ ℞

ST MARY'S

Isles of Scilly TR21 0NF ☎ 01720 422692
Links course, glorious views.
9 holes, 6001yds, Par 73, SSS 69.
Club membership 300.
Visitors   only with member on Sun.
Societies   must apply in writing
Green Fees not confirmed.
Facilities   ♀ ♣ ☎ ⚲
Leisure   putting,trolley hire,practice area.
Location   1m N of Hugh Town   ▶

ST MELLION

ST MELLION *Cornwall*
☎ **01579 351351**   Map 02 SX36

John Ingham writes: Five miles north west of Saltash, St Mellion is set in Sherlock Holmes country, not far from the famous moor. Opened in 1986, the big course was created by two farming brothers, Martin and Hermon Bond who decided the Tamar Valley, not far from Plymouth, deserved a golf course – and they were prepared to sacrifice their farm to achieve that end.

The first problem was to get hold of an architect who would not be overwhelmed by the problem of converting the rugged countryside into eighteen holes. They had set their hearts on a Jack Nicklaus layout and to ensure he would take on the task, they sent him a letter and a cheque, said to be for £1 million and their determination concentrated the mind of Nicklaus comprehensively!

I have known Tony Moore, the one-time professional here, for thirty odd years and he suggested I play the course, with his long-hitting son Bobby. But first we were to enjoy a dinner at the heart of this St Mellion International Golf & Country Club, which they thought, would be the ideal preparation for the task of facing a course with four holes in excess of 500 yards!

Tony's son Bobby was one of those strapping lads who lashed the ball miles. But in the first few holes he was missing the fairway, and lost four balls fairly quickly, putting me in what I thought was an unbeatable position. But his erratic play did not last, neither did my lead despite a birdie two at the short 11th, a delightful hole across water from a tee almost overlooked by the ancient church in the background. The two courses are both rugged tests. and St Mellion is home of the Benson & Hedges tournament.

When Jack Nicklaus played here he said: 'I knew it was going to be good, but not this good – it's everything I had hoped for and more ... St Mellion is potentially the finest course in Europe'. This may be true. But it is a tough one, and for some it's too severe a challenge.

Visitors	no restrictions but dress code to be observed
Societies	please apply in writing
Green fees	on application; telephone 01579 351182
Facilities	⊗ ⅺ 🍴 ♦ 🏌 ♀ 🎣 ⚓ 🏌 ᐟ driving range, putting green, ↻ (Andrew Milton/David Moon) motor carts, buggies, trolleys, caddy cars, practice area
Leisure	tennis courts, indoor swimming (heated), squash, snooker, health spa
Location	Saltash PL12 6SD 0.5m NW off A388

36 holes. Nicklaus Course: 18 holes, 6651yds, Par72 SSS 72 Course record 63 (Carl Mason)
The Old Course: 18 holes, 5782yds, Par 68 SSS 68 Course record 64 (David Russell)

WHERE TO STAY AND EAT NEARBY

HOTELS:
ST MELLION
★★★ 65% St Mellion Hotel,
☎ 01579 351351. Annexe 24 🛏 🥢

LISKEARD
★★ (Red)🌸🌸🌸 ≗ Well House, St Keyne ☎ 01579 342001. 7 🛏 🥢

RESTAURANTS:
CALSTOCK
🌸🌸 Danescombe Valley, Lower Kelly
☎ 01822 832414

Hotel ★★ 73% Tregarthens Hotel, Hugh Town, ST
MARY'S
☎ 01720 422540 28 ⇄ ⚑Annexe1 ⇄ ⚑

St Mellion   Map 02 SX36

St Mellion   See page 37

Saltash   Map 02 SX45

China Fleet Country Club PL12 6LJ ☎ 01752 848668
A parkland course with river views. The 14th tee shot has to
carry a lake of approximately 150yards.
18 holes, 6551yds, Par 72, SSS 72, Course record 69.
Club membership 550.
Visitors may play anytime and can book up to 7 days in
advance.
Societies telephone for provisional booking.
Green Fees £20 per day (£25 weekends).
Facilities ⊗ ⅢⓀ ⬛ ♀ ⚡ ⛿ ⚑ ⚑ ⚑ Robert Moore.
Leisure hard tennis courts, heated indoor swimming
pool, squash, sauna, solarium, gymnasium,
trolley for hire, driving range, putting green,
practice area.
Location 1m from the Tamar Bridge
Hotel B Granada Lodge, Callington Rd, Carkeel,
SALTASH
☎ Central Res 0800 555300 32 ⇄ ⚑

Torpoint   Map 02 SX45

Whitsand Bay Hotel Golf & Country Club Portwrinkle
PL11 3BU ☎ 01503 230276 & 230900
Testing seaside course laid-out on cliffs overlooking
Whitsand Bay. Easy walking after 1st hole. The par 3 (3rd)
hole is acknowledged as one of the most attractive holes in
Cornwall.
18 holes, 5796yds, Par 69, SSS 68, Course record 62.
Club membership 400.
Visitors visitors welcome.
Societies must contact in advance.
Green Fees £15 per day/round (£17.50 weekends & bank
holidays).
Facilities ⊗ Ⅲ Ⓚ ⬛ ♀ ⚡ ⛿ ⚑ ⚑ Stephen Poole.
Leisure heated indoor swimming pool, sauna, solarium,
motorised carts for hire, buggies for hire, trolley
for hire, putting green, practice area.
Location 5m W off B3247
Hotel ★★ 64% Whitsand Bay Hotel, Golf & Country
Club, Portwrinkle, TORPOINT
☎ 01503 230276 34rm(32 ⇄ ⚑)

Truro   Map 02 SW84

Killiow Park Killiow, Kea TR3 6AG ☎ 01872 70246
Picturesque parkland course with mature oaks and woodland
and five holes played across or around water hazards.
Floodlit, all-weather driving range.
18 holes, 3542yds, Par 60.
Club membership 500.
Visitors may not play until after 10.30am at weekends.
Societies apply in writing, limited catering facilities at
present.

Green Fees not confirmed.
Facilities ⚡ ⛿ ⚑
Location 3m SW of Truro, off A39
Hotel ★★★ 66% Brookdale Hotel, Tregolls Rd,
TRURO ☎ 01872 73513 & 79305 22 ⇄

Truro Treliske TR1 3LG ☎ 01872 78684
Undulating parkland course with small greens requiring
accurate play. Lovely views over the cathedral city of Truro.
18 holes, 5306yds, Par 66, SSS 66.
Club membership 900.
Visitors must have handicap certificate.
Societies telephone for details.
Green Fees £18 per day (£22 weekends & bank holidays).
Facilities ⊗ Ⅲ Ⓚ ⬛ ♀ ⚡ ⛿ ⚑ ⚑ Nigel Bicknell.
Leisure motorised carts for hire, buggies for hire, trolley
for hire, putting green, small practice area.
Location 1.5m W on A390
Hotel ★★★ 66% Brookdale Hotel, Tregolls Rd,
TRURO ☎ 01872 73513 & 79305 22 ⇄

Wadebridge   Map 02 SW97

St Kew St Kew Highway PL30 3EF ☎ 01208 814500
An interesting, well-laid out 9-hole parkland course with 6
holes with water and 15 bunkers. In a picturesque setting
there are 10 par 4s and 8 par 3s. No handicap certificate
required but some experience of the game is essential.
9 holes, 4543yds, Par 64, SSS 62.
Club membership 200.
Visitors no restrictions. Start time system in operation
allowing prebooking.
Societies apply in writing, telephone or fax (same as
phone number).
Green Fees £12 per 18 holes; £7.50 per 9 holes. Weekly
ticket £50. Two weeks £80.
Facilities ⊗ Ⅲ Ⓚ ⬛ ♀ ⚡ ⛿ ⚑ ⚑ Tony Pitts.
Leisure fishing, buggies for hire, trolley for hire, driving
range, putting, pony trekking.
Location 2m N, main A39
Hotel ★★ 69% Port Gaverne Hotel, PORT
GAVERNE
☎ 01208 880244 16 ⇄ ⚑Annexe3 ⇄ ⚑

CUMBRIA

Alston   Map 12 NY74

Alston Moor The Hermitage, Middleton in Teesdale Rd
CA9 3DB ☎ 01434 381675 & 381354
Parkland course with lush fairways and naturally interesting
greens.
10 holes, 5518yds, Par 68, SSS 66, Course record 67.
Club membership 150.
Visitors usually turn up and play but some weekends
busy with competitions.
Societies telephone or write in advance.
Green Fees £8 per day (£10 weekends and bank holidays).
Facilities ⊗ by prior arrangement Ⅲ by prior arrangement
♀ ⚡
Leisure practice area.
Location 1 S of Alston on B6277

Hotel ★★ 68% Lowbyer Manor Country House
Hotel, ALSTON
☎ 01434 381230 8 ⇥ ☞Annexe4 ⇥

APPLEBY-IN-WESTMORLAND   Map 12 NY62

Appleby Brackenber Moor CA16 6LP
☎ 01768 351432
This remotely situated heather and moorland course
offers interesting golf with the rewarding bonus of
several long par-4 holes that will be remembered. There
are superb views.
18 holes, 5901yds, Par 68, SSS 68, Course record 63.
Club membership 800.
Visitors phone for details.
Societies must contact in advance by letter.
Green Fees £12 per day (£16 weekends & bank holidays).
Facilities ⊗ ⅲ ⅃ 里 ♀ ♨ 龠 ☏ Paul Jenkinson.
Leisure trolley for hire, putting green, practice area.
Location 1m E of Appleby 0.5m off A66
Hotel ★★★♨ 73% Appleby Manor Country
House Hotel, Roman Rd, APPLEBY-IN-
WESTMORLAND
☎ 017683 51571 23 ⇥ ☞Annexe7 ⇥ ☞

ASKAM-IN-FURNESS   Map 07 SD27

Dunnerholme Duddon Rd LA16 7AW ☎ 01229 462675
Unique 10-hole (18 tee) links course with view of Lakeland
hills, and a stream running through.
10 holes, 6154yds, Par 72, SSS 70.
Club membership 450.

Swim, Bubble and Golf!

**Enjoy your par 68 round on
Appleby's eighteen beautiful
moorland holes (5915 yds), then it's
five-minutes by car to return to your
favourite Country House Hotel for a
refreshing swim and a relaxing
jacuzzi in the indoor leisure club,
followed by a superb meal in the
award-winning restaurant.**

*Phone 017683 51571 now for a free
colour brochure with full details of
the hotel, leisure club and prices.*

Best Western
★★★
73% ⊛   APPLEBY•MANOR
COUNTRY HOUSE HOTEL
*Roman Road
Appleby-in-Westmorland
Cumbria CA16 6JB*
Telephone: 017683 51571

Visitors restricted times on Sun.
Societies apply in writing to the secretary.
Green Fees £12 per day (£15 weekends & bank holidays).
Facilities ⅃ 里 ♀ ♨
Leisure putting green, practice area.
Location 1m N on A595
Hotel ★★ 64% Lisdoonie Hotel, 307/309 Abbey Rd,
BARROW-IN-FURNESS
☎ 01229 827312 12 ⇥ ☞

BARROW-IN-FURNESS   Map 07 SD26

Barrow Rakesmoor Ln, Hawcoat LA14 4QB
☎ 01229 825444
Pleasant course laid out two levels on meadowland with
extensive views of the nearby Lakeland fells. Upper level is
affected by easterly winds.
18 holes, 6209yds, Par 71, SSS 70, Course record 66.
Club membership 620.
Visitors must be a member of a recognised golf club,
advisable to contact the professional regarding
tee time.
Societies small groups ring professional for details, groups
over 12 apply to the secretary in advance.
Green Fees £15 per day/round (£25 weekends & bank
holidays).
Facilities ⊗ ⅲ by prior arrangement ⅃ 里 ♀ ♨ 龠
☏ Neale Hyde.
Leisure putting green, practice area.
Location 2m N off A590
Hotel ★★ 64% Lisdoonie Hotel, 307/309 Abbey Rd,
BARROW-IN-FURNESS
☎ 01229 827312 12 ⇥ ☞

Furness Central Dr LA14 3LN ☎ 01229 471232
Links golf with a fairly flat first half but a much sterner
second nine played across subtle sloping ground. There are
good views of the Lakes, North Wales and the Isle of Man.
18 holes, 6363yds, Par 71, SSS 71, Course record 65.
Club membership 630.
Visitors must contact the secretary in advance.
Societies apply in writing, must be member of recognised
club with handicap certificate.
Green Fees £17 per day.
Facilities ⊗ ⅲ ⅃ 里 ♀ ♨ 龠
Leisure trolley for hire, putting green, practice area.
Location 1.75 W of town centre off A590
Hotel ★★ 64% Lisdoonie Hotel, 307/309 Abbey Rd,
BARROW-IN-FURNESS
☎ 01229 827312 12 ⇥ ☞

BOWNESS-ON-WINDERMERE   Map 07 SD49

Windermere Cleabarrow LA23 3NB ☎ 015394 43123
Enjoyable holiday golf on a short, slightly hilly but
sporting course in this delightful area of the Lake District
National Park, with superb views of the mountains as the
backcloth to the lake and the course.
18 holes, 5006yds, Par 67, SSS 65, Course record 58.
Club membership 1043.
Visitors contact pro shop 7 days before day of play,
9-12 & 2-4.30 by arrangement.
Societies by arrangement contact the secretary.
Green Fees £23 per day (£28 weekends & bank
holidays). ▶

TARN END HOUSE HOTEL AA ★★

Talkin Tarn, Brampton, Cumbria CA8 1LS   Tel: 016977 2340

Comfortable traditional family-run hotel set in own secluded grounds. All public rooms and bedrooms overlook the lovely tarn. All bedrooms are en-suite with tea/coffee & colour TV. Restaurant offers both à la carte and table d'hôte menus freshly prepared to order.

Special inclusive terms for golf parties, and a prize is given for the best round on the local course which runs alongside the hotel. Concessionary green fees available to our guests. We can also arrange visits etc. to the many other good golf courses in the area.

Please write or telephone for colour brochure & full details.

Facilities	⊗ 〴 ⓛ ♥ ♀ ♨ ⌂ ☂ ↾ W S M Rooke.
Leisure	motorised carts for hire, trolley for hire, putting green, practice area.
Location	B5284 1.5m from Bowness
Hotel	★★★ 71% Wild Boar Hotel, Crook, WINDERMERE ☎ 015394 45225 36 ⇆ ↾

See advertisement on page 43.

BRAMPTON   Map 12 NY56

Brampton Talkin Tarn CA8 1HN
☎ 016977 2255 & 2000
Challenging golf across glorious rolling fell country demanding solid driving and many long second shots. A number of particularly fine holes, the pick of which may arguably be, the 3rd and 11th. The course offers unrivalled panoramic views from its hilly position.
18 holes, 6407yds, Par 72, SSS 71, Course record 66.
Club membership 800.

Visitors	visitors intending to play at weekends are recommended to telephone in advance.
Societies	apply in writing to M Ogilvie (Hon Commercial Sec), 3 Warwick St, Carlisle, Cumbria CA3 8QW or telephone 01228 401996.
Green Fees	Apr-Oct '96; £20 per day (£23 weekends & bank holidays). Nov-Mar '96 £13 per day (£17 weekends & bank holidays).
Facilities	⊗ 〴 ⓛ ♥ ♀ ♨ ⌂ ☂ ↾ Stephen Harrison.
Leisure	trolley for hire, practice area.
Location	1.5m SE of Brampton on B6413
Hotel	★★ 63% The Tarn End House Hotel, Talkin Tarn, BRAMPTON ☎ 016977 2340 7 ⇆ ↾

CARLISLE   Map 11 NY35

Carlisle Aglionby CA4 8AG ☎ 01228 513303 & 513241
Majestic looking parkland course with great appeal. A complete but not too severe test of golf, with fine turf,
natural hazards, a stream and many beautiful trees.
18 holes, 6278yds, Par 71, SSS 70, Course record 63.
Club membership 800.

Visitors	may not play before 9am and between 12-1.30 and when tee is reserved. With member on Sat.
Societies	Mon, Wed & Fri, contact in advance for details.
Green Fees	£30 per day; £20 per round (Sun £35).
Facilities	⊗ 〴 ⓛ ♥ ♀ ♨ ⌂ ☂ ↾ John Smith More.
Leisure	trolley for hire, practice area.
Location	On A69 1m E of M6 junc 43
Hotel	★★★ 60% Central Plaza Hotel, Victoria Viaduct, CARLISLE ☎ 01228 20256 84 ⇆ ↾

Stony Holme Municipal St Aidans Rd CA1 1LS
☎ 01228 34856
Municipal parkland course, bounded on three sides by the River Eden.
18 holes, 5783yds, Par 69, SSS 68, Course record 68.
Club membership 350.

Visitors	must contact in advance.
Societies	must telephone in advance.
Green Fees	not confirmed.
Facilities	♀ ♨ ⌂ ☂ ↾ S Ling.
Location	3m E off A69
Hotel	B Forte Posthouse Carlisle, Parkhouse Rd, Kingstown, CARLISLE ☎ 01228 31201 93 ⇆ ↾

COCKERMOUTH   Map 11 NY13

Cockermouth Embleton CA13 9SG ☎ 017687 76223
Fell-land course, fenced, with exceptional views and a hard climb on the 3rd and 11th holes. Testing holes: 10th and 16th (rearranged by James Braid).
18 holes, 5496yds, Par 69, SSS 67, Course record 62.
Club membership 600.

Visitors	restricted Wed, Sat & Sun.
Societies	apply in writing to the secretary.

Green Fees £15 per day/round (£20 weekends & bank holidays).
Facilities ⊗ by prior arrangement 🍴 by prior arrangement 🍴 ▅ 💺 ♀ 🛆
Leisure putting green.
Location 3m E off A66
Hotel ★★★ 65% The Trout Hotel, Crown St, COCKERMOUTH ☎ 01900 823591 23 ⇔ ↑

CROSBY-ON-EDEN   Map 12 NY45

Eden CA6 4RA ☎ 01228 573003 & 573013
Open, championship-length parkland course following the River Eden. A large number of water hazards, including the river on certain holes, demands acuracy, as do the well designed raised greens. Flood-lit driving range and excellent clubhouse facilities.
18 holes, 6368yds, Par 72, SSS 72.
Club membership 500.
Visitors contact in advance.
Societies telephone to check availability.
Green Fees £15 per day (£20 weekends and bank holidays).
Facilities ⊗ 🍴 ▅ 💺 ♀ 🛆 🛍 ↑ 𝄐
Leisure trolley for hire, driving range, putting green, practice area.
Location 5m from M6 junc 44,on A689 towards Brampton
Hotel ★★★♨ 73% Crosby Lodge Country House Hotel, High Crosby, CROSBY-ON-EDEN ☎ 01228 573618 9 ⇔ ↑Annexe2 ⇔ ↑

GRANGE-OVER-SANDS   Map 07 SD47

Grange Fell Fell Rd LA11 6HB ☎ 015395 32536
Hillside course with magnificent views over Morecambe Bay and the surrounding Lakeland mountains.
9 holes, 5278yds, Par 70, SSS 66, Course record 67.
Club membership 400.
Visitors may normally play Mon-Sat.
Green Fees £15 per day (£20 weekends & bank holidays).
Facilities 💺 ♀ 🛆
Leisure putting green.
Location 1m W
Hotel ★★★ 65% Netherwood Hotel, Lindale Rd, GRANGE-OVER-SANDS ☎ 015395 32552 29 ⇔ ↑

Grange-over-Sands Meathop Rd LA11 6QX
☎ 015395 33180 or 33754
Interesting parkland course with well sited tree plantations, ditches and water features. The four par 3s are considered to be some of the best in the area.

18 holes, 5958yds, Par 70, SSS 69, Course record 68.
Club membership 570.
Visitors must contact in advance for play at weekends.
Societies apply in writing but may not play weekends and bank holidays.
Green Fees £20 per day; £15 per round (£25/£20 weekends & bank holidays).
Facilities ⊗ 🍴 ▅ 💺 ♀ 🛆 🛍 𝄐 Steve Sumner-Roberts.
Leisure trolley for hire, putting green, practice area.
Location NW of town centre off B5277
Hotel ★★★ 64% Grange Hotel, Station Square, GRANGE-OVER-SANDS ☎ 015395 33666 41 ⇔ ↑

KENDAL   Map 07 SD59

Kendal The Heights LA9 4PQ ☎ 01539 724079 & 733708
Elevated moorland course affording breathtaking views of Lakeland fells and surrounding district.
18 holes, 5515yds, Par 66, SSS 67, Course record 60.
Club membership 737.
Visitors must have a handicap certificate, weekends subject to availability.
Societies must contact in advance.
Green Fees £16 per day (£20 weekends).
Facilities ⊗ 🍴 ▅ 💺 ♀ 🛆 🛍 𝄐 D J Turner.
Leisure trolley for hire, putting green, practice area.
Location W side of town centre
Hotel ★★ 71% Garden House Hotel, Fowl-ing Ln, KENDAL ☎ 01539 731131 10 ⇔ ↑

KESWICK   Map 11 NY22

Keswick Threlkeld Hall CA12 4SX
☎ 017687 79324 & 79010
Varied fell and tree-lined course with commanding views of Lakeland scenery.
18 holes, 6225yds, Par 71, SSS 72, Course record 69.
Club membership 900.
Visitors must book tee 7 days in advance 017687 79010. Restricted on competition days.
Societies apply in writing to secretary.
Green Fees £15 per day (£20 weekends & bank holidays).
Facilities ⊗ 🍴 by prior arrangement ▅ 💺 ♀ 🛆 🛍 𝄐 Craig Hamilton.
Leisure fishing, trolley for hire, putting green, practice area.
Location 4m E of Keswick, off A66
Hotel ★★★★ 62% Keswick Country House Hotel, Station Rd, KESWICK ☎ 017687 72020 66 ⇔ ↑
Additional hotel ★★ 68% Chaucer House Hotel, Derwentwater Place, KESWICK ☎ 017687 72318 & 73223 35rm(28 ⇔ ↑)

KIRKBY LONSDALE   Map 07 SD67

Kirkby Lonsdale Scaleber Ln, Barbon LA6 2LE
☎ 015242 76365
Parkland course on the east bank of the River Lune and
crossed by Barbon Beck. Mainly following the lie of the land,
the gently undulating course uses the beck to provide water
hazards.
18 holes, 6472yds, Par 72, SSS 72, Course record 68.
Club membership 600.

Visitors	restricted on Sunday, must telephone in advance or call in at pro shop.
Societies	apply in writing for society package.
Green Fees	£16 per day (£20 weekends).
Facilities	⊗ ⅷ ⅊ ⚑ ♉ ♈ ⚐ Chris Barret.
Leisure	trolley for hire, putting green, practice area.
Location	6m S of Sedbergh
Hotel	★★ 67% Pheasant Inn, CASTERTON ☎ 015242 71230 10 ⇆ 🐾

MARYPORT   Map 11 NY03

Maryport Bank End CA15 6PA
☎ 01900 812605 & 815626
A tight seaside links course exposed to Solway breezes. Fine
views across Solway Firth.
18 holes, 6088yds, Par 70, SSS 69, Course record 70.
Club membership 400.

Visitors	no restrictions.
Societies	must apply in writing.
Green Fees	£15 per day/round (£20 weekends & bank holidays).
Facilities	⊗ ⅷ ⅊ ⚑ ♉ ⚐
Leisure	putting green, practice area.
Location	1m N on B5300
Hotel	★★ 64% Ellenbank Hotel, Birkby, MARYPORT ☎ 01900 815233 26 ⇆ 🐾

PENRITH   Map 12 NY53

Penrith Salkeld Rd CA11 8SG ☎ 01768 891919
A beautiful and well-balanced course, always changing
direction, and demanding good length from the tee. It is
set on rolling moorland with occasional pine trees and
some fine views.
18 holes, 6047yds, Par 69, SSS 69, Course record 63.
Club membership 850.

Visitors	contact in advance.
Societies	telephone in advance.
Green Fees	£25 for 2 rounds; £20 per round (£30/£25 weekends).
Facilities	⅊ ⚑ ♉ ⚐ ♈ ⚐ Garry Key.
Leisure	trolley for hire, driving range, putting green, practice area.
Location	0.75m N off A6
Hotel	★★ 68% George Hotel, Devonshire St, PENRITH ☎ 01768 862696 31 ⇆ 🐾

ST BEES   Map 11 NX91

St Bees CA27 0EJ ☎ 01946 824300
Links course, down hill and dale, with sea views.
9 holes, 5082yds, Par 64, SSS 65.
Club membership 275.

Visitors	no restrictions.
Green Fees	not confirmed.
Location	0.5m W of village off B5345
Hotel	★★★ 58% Blackbeck Bridge Inn, EGREMONT ☎ 01946 841661 22 ⇆ 🐾

SEASCALE   Map 06 NY00

Seascale The Banks CA20 1QL ☎ 019467 28202
A tough links requiring length and control. The natural
terrain is used to give a variety of holes and considerable
character. Undulating greens add to the challenge. Fine
views over the Western Fells, the Irish Sea and Isle of Man.
18 holes, 6416yds, Par 71, SSS 71, Course record 65.
Club membership 670.

Visitors	must contact in advance.
Societies	telephone to make provisional booking.
Green Fees	£25 per day; £20 per round (£30/£25 weekends & bank holidays).
Facilities	⊗ ⅷ ⅊ ⚑ ♉ ⚐
Leisure	motorised carts for hire, trolley for hire, driving range, putting green, practice area.
Location	NW side of village off B5344
Hotel	★★★ 58% Blackbeck Bridge Inn, EGREMONT ☎ 01946 841661 22 ⇆ 🐾

SEDBERGH   Map 07 SD69

Sedbergh Catholes, Abbot Holme LA10 5SS
☎ 015396 21551 & 20993
A tree-lined grassland course with superb scenery in the
Yorkshire Dales National Park. Feature hole is the par 3 2nd
(110yds) where the River Dee separates the tee from the
green.
9 holes, 5588yds, Par 70, SSS 68, Course record 66.
Club membership 300.

Visitors	must book to play on weekends & bank holidays.
Societies	must contact in advance.
Green Fees	£20 per day; £14 per 18 holes (£25/£18 weekends and bank holidays).
Facilities	⊗ ⅷ ⅊ ⚑ ♉ ⚐ ♈
Leisure	trolley for hire, practice area.
Location	1m S off A683
Hotel	★★ 71% Garden House Hotel, Fowl-ing Ln, KENDAL ☎ 01539 731131 10 ⇆ 🐾

SILECROFT   Map 06 SD18

Silecroft LA18 4NX ☎ 01229 774250
Seaside links course parallel to the coast of the Irish Sea.
Often windy. Easy walking. Spectacular views inland of
Lakeland hills.
9 holes, 5877yds, Par 68, SSS 68, Course record 67.
Club membership 300.

Visitors	may be restricted competition days & bank holidays,
Societies	must contact in writing.
Green Fees	£10 per day (£15 weekends).
Facilities	⅊ ⚑ ♉
Leisure	practice area.
Location	1m SW
Hotel	★ 59% Old King's Head Hotel, Station Rd, BROUGHTON IN FURNESS ☎ 01229 716293 5rm(1 🐾)

SILLOTH
Map 11 NY15

Silloth on Solway CA5 4BL
☎ 016973 31304 & 32440
Billowing dunes, narrow fairways, heather and gorse and
the constant subtle problems of tactics and judgement
make these superb links on the Solway an exhilarating
and searching test. The 13th is a good long hole. Superb
views.
18 holes, 6614yds, Par 72, SSS 72, Course record 65.
Club membership 700.
Visitors must contact in advance.
Societies telephone for times available.
Green Fees £25 per day (£30 per day weekends &
bank holidays). Weekday package incl meal
£35.
Facilities ⊗ ⅲ ⅃ 🏌 ♀ ⚲ 🖾 ꜛ Carl Weatherhead.
Leisure trolley for hire, putting green, practice area.
Location S side of village off B5300
Hotel ★★ 62% Golf Hotel, Criffel St, SILLOTH
☎ 016973 31438 22 ⇥ ⋔

ULVERSTON
Map 07 SD27

Ulverston Bardsea Park LA12 9QJ ☎ 01229 582824
Inland golf with many medium length holes on
undulating parkland. The 17th is a testing par 4.
Overlooking Morecambe Bay the course offers extensive
views to the Lakeland Fells.
18 holes, 6201yds, Par 71, SSS 70, Course record 67.
Club membership 750.

Birdie, Eagle, Albatross …
… or even if you're looking for the elusive 'hole in one', Windermere is the place.

Situated only a mile from this challenging
18 hole golf course, The Wild Boar Hotel
situated in the tranquil Gilpin Valley, with its
olde worlde charme offers you a friendly and
welcome atmosphere.

Reflect, whilst sampling the excellent cuisine
of our award winning restaurant on your 67 par
round. Enjoy free use of extensive leisure
facilities during your stay.

Discounted Green Fees for Residents

AA★★★
71%

Wild Boar Hotel
Crook, Nr. Windermere, Cumbria LA23 3NF.
Tel: Windermere (015 394) 45225
Fax: Windermere (015 394) 42498

Visitors must contact in advance, be a member of an
accredited golf club with a handicap
certificate. May not play on Sat competition
days or on Tue Ladies day.
Societies by arrangement in writing.
Green Fees Summer: £25 per day; £20 per round
(£30/£25 weekends & bank holidays).
Winter: £18 per day; £14 per round
(£20/£18 weekends & bank holidays), Nov-
Feb.
Facilities ⊗ ⅲ ⅃ 🏌 ♀ ⚲ 🖾 ꜛ ꜛ M R Smith.
Leisure trolley for hire, putting green, practice area.
Location 2m S off A5087
Hotel ★★★ 69% Whitewater Hotel, The
Lakeland Village, NEWBY BRIDGE
☎ 015395 31133 35 ⇥ ⋔

WINDERMERE
See **Bowness-on-Windermere**

WORKINGTON
Map 11 NX92

Workington Branthwaite Rd CA14 4SS ☎ 01900 67828
Meadowland course, undulating, with natural hazards created
by stream and trees. Good views of Solway Firth and
Lakeland Hills. 10th, 13th and 15th holes are particularly
testing.
18 holes, 6217yds, Par 72, SSS 70.
Club membership 735.
Visitors advisable to contact pro for weekday, weekends
are generally very busy.
Societies booking required for over 8 people.
Green Fees Summer: £19 per day; £15 per round (£25/£18
weekends & bank holidays).
Facilities ⊗ ⅲ ⅃ 🏌 ♀ ⚲ 🖾 ꜛ Aidrian Drabble.
Leisure buggies for hire, trolley for hire, putting green,
practice area.
Location 1.75m E off A596
Hotel ★★★ 68% Washington Central Hotel,
Washington St, WORKINGTON
☎ 01900 65772 40 ⇥ ⋔

DERBYSHIRE

ALFRETON
Map 08 SK45

Alfreton Wingfield Rd, Oakerthorpe DE66 7LH
☎ 01773 832070 & 831901
A small parkland course with tight fairways and many natural
hazards.
9 holes, 5074yds, Par 66, SSS 65, Course record 60.
Club membership 300.
Visitors must contact in advance, with member only
weekends.
Societies apply in writing or telephone in advance.
Green Fees £18 per day; £13 per round (18 holes).
Facilities ⊗ ⅲ by prior arrangement ⅃ 🏌 ♀ ⚲ 🖾
ꜛ Julian Mellors.
Leisure putting green, practice area.
Location 1m W on A615
▶

Hotel   ★★★★ 65% Swallow Hotel, Carter Ln East,
            SOUTH NORMANTON
            ☎ 01773 812000 161 ⇄ ↾

ASHBOURNE   Map 07 SK14

Ashbourne Clifton DE6 1BN ☎ 01335 342078
Undulating parkland course.
9 holes, 5359yds, Par 66, SSS 66.
Club membership 350.
Visitors   may not play on competition days. With member
            only at weekends.
Societies   telephone in advance.
Green Fees not confirmed.
Facilities ♀ ⅃
Location   1.5m SW on A515
Hotel   ★★★⚊ 75% Callow Hall, Mappleton Rd,
            ASHBOURNE
            ☎ 01335 343403 & 342412 16 ⇄ ↾

BAKEWELL   Map 08 SK26

Bakewell Station Rd DE45 1GB ☎ 01629 812307
Parkland course, hilly, with plenty of natural hazards to test
the golfer. Magnificent views across the Wye Valley.
9 holes, 5240yds, Par 68, SSS 66.
Club membership 360.
Visitors   with members only weekends.
Societies   apply in writing.
Green Fees not confirmed.
Facilities ⊗ ⅢⅡ ⅃ ⅊ ♀ (ex Mon) ⅃ 🏠
Leisure   putting green, practice area.
Location   E side of town off A6
Hotel   ★★ 67% Milford House Hotel, Mill St,
            BAKEWELL ☎ 01629 812130 12 ⇄ ↾

BAMFORD   Map 08 SK28

Sickleholme Saltergate Ln S30 2BH ☎ 01433 651306
Undulating downland course in the lovely Peak District, with
rivers and ravines and spectacular scenery.
18 holes, 6064yds, Par 69, SSS 69, Course record 62.
Club membership 700.
Visitors   must contact in advance, restricted weekends.
Societies   telephone in advance.
Green Fees £25 per day (£32 weekends & bank holidays).
Facilities ⊗ ⅢⅡ ⅃ ⅊ ♀ ⅃ 🏠 P H Taylor.
Location   0.75m S on A6013
Hotel   ★★ 69% Yorkshire Bridge Inn, Ashopton Rd,
            Yorkshire Bridge, BAMFORD
            ☎ 01433 651361 10 ⇄ ↾

BREADSALL   Map 08 SK33

Breadsall Priory Hotel, Golf & Country Club Moor Rd,
Morley DE7 6DL ☎ 01332 832235
Set in 200 acres of mature parkland, the Old Course is built
on the site of a 13th-century priory. Full use had been made
of natural features and fine old trees. In contrast the Moorland
Course, opened in Spring 1992, designed by Donald Steel and
built by Brian Piersen, features Derbyshire stone walls and
open moors heavily affected by winds.
*Priory Course: 18 holes, 6201yds, Par 72, SSS 70, Course
record 66.*

Moorland Course: 18 holes, 6028yds, Par 70, SSS 69.
Club membership 900.
Visitors   must contact in advance.
Societies   telephone in advance.
Green Fees Priory: £50 per day; £44 per round (£45 per
            round weekends & bank holidays). Moorland:
            £50 per day; £30 per round (£45 per round
            weekends & bank holidays).
Facilities ⊗ ⅢⅡ ⅃ ⅊ ♀ ⅃ 🏠 ⅂ ↾ ⅃ Andrew Smith.
Leisure   hard tennis courts, heated indoor swimming
            pool, buggies for hire, trolley for hire, putting
            green, practice area.
Location   0.75m W
Hotel   ★★★★ 64% Breadsall Priory Hotel, Country
            Club Resort, Moor Rd, MORLEY
            ☎ 01332 832235 14 ⇄ ↾Annexe77 ⇄ ↾

BUXTON   Map 07 SK07

Buxton & High Peak Townend, Waterswallows Rd
SK17 7EN ☎ 01298 23453 & 26263
Bracing, well-drained meadowland course; the highest in
Derbyshire. Challenging course where wind direction is a
major factor on some holes; others require blind shots to
sloping greens.
18 holes, 5966yds, Par 69, SSS 69, Course record 65.
Club membership 670.
Visitors   contact Mrs S Arnfield.
Societies   apply in writing to Mrs S Arnfield.
Green Fees £20 per day (£25 weekends & bank holidays).
Facilities ⊗ ⅢⅡ ⅃ ⅊ ♀ ⅃ 🏠 ⅂ ↾ Gary Brown.
Leisure   buggies for hire, trolley for hire, putting green,
            practice area, snooker.
Location   1m NE off A6
Hotel   ★★★ 66% Palace Hotel, Palace Rd, BUXTON
            ☎ 01298 22001 122 ⇄

Cavendish Gadley Ln SK17 6XD
☎ 01298 25052 & 79708
This parkland/moorland course with its comfortable
clubhouse nestles below the rising hills. Generally open
to the prevailing west wind, it is noted for its excellent
surfaced greens which contain many deceptive subtleties.
Designed by Dr Alastair McKenzie, good holes include
the 8th, 9th and 18th.
18 holes, 5833yds, Par 68, SSS 68, Course record 61.
Club membership 650.
Visitors   must contact in advance, weekends are
            restricted by competitions.
Societies   telephone professional on 01298 25052.
Green Fees £20 per round (£35 weekends & bank
            holidays).
Facilities ⊗ ⅢⅡ ⅃ ⅊ ♀ ⅃ 🏠 ⅂ ↾ ⅃ Paul Hunstone.
Leisure   trolley for hire, practice area.
Location   0.75m W of town centre off A53
Hotel   ★★★ 73% Lee Wood Hotel, 13
            Manchester Rd, BUXTON
            ☎ 01298 23002 36 ⇄ ↾Annexe2 ⇄ ↾

CHAPEL-EN-LE-FRITH   Map 07 SK08

Chapel-en-le-Frith The Cockyard, Manchester Rd
SK12 6UH ☎ 01298 812118
Scenic parkland course, with testing holes at the 15th (par 4)
and 17th (517 yds), par 5. Good views.

18 holes, 6054yds, Par 70, SSS 69.
Club membership 641.
Visitors must contact professional in advance.
Societies apply in advance to Secretary.
Green Fees £20 per day (£30 weekends & bank holidays).
Facilities ⊗ ⋈ ⫷ ⚑ ♀ ♨ 🖭 ⚷ David J Cullen.
Leisure trolley for hire, putting green, practice area,
    snooker.
Location On B5470
Hotel . ★★★ 73% Lee Wood Hotel, 13 Manchester
    Rd, BUXTON
    ☎ 01298 23002 36 ⇆ 🖝Annexe2 ⇆ 🖝

CHESTERFIELD   Map 08 SK37

Chesterfield Walton S42 7LA ☎ 01246 279256
A varied and interesting, undulating parkland course with
trees picturesquely adding to the holes and the outlook alike.
Stream hazard on back nine. Views over four counties.
18 holes, 6326yds, Par 71, SSS 70, Course record 65.
Club membership 500.
Visitors must contact in advance and must play with
    member at weekends and bank holidays. A
    handicap certificate is generally required.
Societies apply in writing.
Green Fees not confirmed.
Facilities ♀ ♨ 🖭 ⚷ M McLean.
Location 2m SW off A632
Hotel ★★★ 61% Chesterfield, Malkin St,
    CHESTERFIELD ☎ 01246 271141 73 ⇆ 🖝

Grassmoor Golf Centre North Wingfield Rd, Grassmoor
S41 5EA ☎ 01246 856044
An 18-hole heathland course with interesting and challenging
water features. 26-bay floodlit driving range, practice bunkers
and putting area.
18 holes, 5723yds, Par 69, SSS 69, Course record 67.
Club membership 420.
Visitors contact Manager in advance.
Societies telephone in Manager in advance.
Green Fees £7.50 (£9 weekends).
Facilities ⊗ ⋈ ⫷ ⚑ ♀ ♨ 🖭 ⚷ Peter Goldthorpe.
Leisure sauna, trolley for hire, floodlit driving range,
    putting green.
Location Between Chesterfield & Grassmoor, off B6038
Hotel ★★★ 61% Chesterfield, Malkin St,
    CHESTERFIELD
    ☎ 01246 271141 73 ⇆ 🖝

Stanedge Walton Hay Farm S45 0LW ☎ 01246 566156
Moorland course in hilly situation open to strong winds.
Some tricky short holes with narrow fairways, so accuracy is
paramount. Magnificent views over four counties.
9 holes, 4867yds, Par 64, SSS 64, Course record 64.
Club membership 310.
Visitors with member only Sat & Sun, and may not play
    after 2pm weekdays.
Societies apply in writing.
Green Fees £15 per round (18 holes).
Facilities ⫷ ♀ ♨
Leisure putting green, practice area.
Location 5m SW off B5057 nr Red Lion public house
Hotel ★★★ 61% Chesterfield, Malkin St,
    CHESTERFIELD
    ☎ 01246 271141 73 ⇆ 🖝

Tapton Park Municipal Tapton Park, Chesterfield S41 0EQ
☎ 01246 239500
Municipal parkland course with some fairly hard walking.
The 620 yd (par 5) 5th is a testing hole.
Tapton Main: 18 holes, 6013yds, Par 71, SSS 69.
Dobbin Clough: 9 holes, 2613yds, Par 34.
Club membership 750.
Visitors must contact in advance. No caddies allowed.
Societies apply in writing.
Green Fees not confirmed.
Facilities ♀ ♨ 🖭 🖝 ⚷ Fraser Scott.
Leisure putting, practice area, trolley hire.
Location 0.5m E of Chesterfield Station
Hotel ★★★ 61% Chesterfield, Malkin St,
    CHESTERFIELD ☎ 01246 271141 73 ⇆ 🖝

CODNOR   Map 08 SK44

Ormonde Fields Golf & Country Club Nottingham Rd
DE5 9RG ☎ 01773 570043 (Secretary) & 742987 (Pro)
Parkland course with undulating fairways and natural
hazards. The par 4 (4th) and the par 3 (11th) are notable.
There is a practice area.
18 holes, 6011yds, Par 69, SSS 69, Course record 68.
Club membership 500.
Visitors must contact in advance.
Societies telephone in advance.
Green Fees £15 per day (£20 per round weekends).
Facilities ⊗ ⋈ ⫷ ⚑ ♀ ♨ 🖭 ⚷ Peter Buttifant.
Leisure trolley for hire, putting green, practice area.
Location 1m SE on A610
Hotel ★★★ 75% Makeney Hall Country House
    Hotel, Makeney, Milford, BELPER
    ☎ 01332 842999 27 ⇆ 🖝Annexe18 ⇆ 🖝

DERBY   Map 08 SK33

Allestree Park Allestree Hall DE22 2EU
☎ 01332 550616
Municipal parkland course in rather hilly country.
18 holes, 5749yds, Par 68, SSS 68, Course record 66.
Club membership 275.
Visitors restricted weekends & bank holidays.
Societies restricted at weekends & bank holidays.
Green Fees not confirmed.
Facilities ♀ ♨ 🖭 🖝 ⚷ Colin Henderson.
Leisure fishing.
Location 3m N on A6
Hotel ★★ 69% Kedleston Country House Hotel,
    Kedleston Rd, DERBY
    ☎ 01332 559202 & 556507 14 ⇆ 🖝

Derby Shakespeare St, Sinfin DE24 9HD ☎ 01332 766323
Municipal parkland course. The front nine holes are rather
difficult.
18 holes, 6144yds, Par 70, SSS 69.
Club membership 450.
Visitors starting time must be booked at weekends.
Societies apply in writing in advance.
Green Fees not confirmed.
Facilities ♨ 🖭 🖝 ⚷
Location 3.5m S of city centre
Hotel ★★★ 63% International Hotel, Burton Rd
    (A5250), DERBY
    ☎ 01332 369321 41 ⇆ 🖝Annexe21 ⇆ 🖝

Mickleover Uttoxeter Rd, Mickleover DE3 5AD
☎ 01332 512092
Undulating parkland course in pleasant setting, affording
splendid country views. Some attractive par 3s and a number
of elevated greens..
18 holes, 5708yds, Par 68, SSS 68, Course record 64.
Club membership 800.
Visitors   must contact in advance.
Societies   apply in writing.
Green Fees £22 per day/round (£25 weekends & bank
    holidays).
Facilities   ⊗ ⅋ ᴸ ♨ ♀ ♁ ♠ ♦ ℓ Tim Coxon.
Leisure   trolley for hire, putting green, practice area,
    snooker.
Location   3m W off A516/B5020
Hotel   B Forte Posthouse Derby/Burton, Pastures Hill,
    Littleover, DERBY
    ☎ 01332 514933 62 ⇄ ╔

DRONFIELD   Map 08 SK37

Hallowes Hallowes Ln S18 6UA
☎ 01246 413734
Attractive moorland/meadowland course set in the
Derbyshire hills. Several testing par 4's and splendid views.
18 holes, 6342yds, Par 71, SSS 70, Course record 64.
Club membership 630.
Visitors   may only play with member at weekends. Must
    contact in advance.
Societies   must contact in advance.
Green Fees £27 per day; £20 per round.
Facilities   ⊗ ⅋ ᴸ ♨ ♀ ♁ ℓ Philip Dunn.
Leisure   trolley for hire, putting green, practice area.
Location   S side of town
Hotel   ★★ 64% Chantry Hotel, Church St,
    DRONFIELD ☎ 01246 413014 7 ⇄ ╔

DUFFIELD   Map 08 SK34

Chevin Golf Ln DE56 4EE
☎ 01332 841864
A mixture of parkland and moorland, this course is rather
hilly which makes for some hard walking. The 8th calls for a
very hard drive, possibly the hardest in the area.
18 holes, 6057yds, Par 69, SSS 69, Course record 65.
Club membership 750.
Visitors   not before 9.30am or off first tee between 12.30
    and 2pm. Proof of handicap required.
Societies   contact in advance.
Green Fees £27 per day.
Facilities   ⊗ ⅋ ᴸ ♨ ♀ ♁ ♠ ♦ ℓ Willie Bird.
Leisure   motorised carts for hire, trolley for hire, driving
    range, putting green, practice area, snooker.
Location   N side of town off A6
Hotel   ★★ 69% Kedleston Country House Hotel,
    Kedleston Rd, DERBY
    ☎ 01332 559202 & 556507 14 ⇄ ╔

GLOSSOP   Map 07 SK09

Glossop and District Hurst Ln, off Sheffield Rd SK13 9PU
☎ 01457 865247
Moorland course in good position, excellent natural hazards.
11 holes, 5800yds, Par 68, SSS 68.
Club membership 250.

Visitors   may not play on bank holidays.
Societies   must apply in writing to professional.
Green Fees not confirmed.
Facilities   ♀ (ex Mon) ♁ ♠ ℓ Gary S Brown.
Location   1m E off A57
Hotel   ★★ 69% York House Hotel, York Place,
    Richmond St, ASHTON-UNDER-LYNE
    ☎ 0161 330 5899 24 ⇄ ╔Annexe10 ⇄ ╔

HORSLEY   Map 08 SK34

Horsley Lodge Smalley Mill Rd DE21 5BL
☎ 01332 780838 & 781400
This course, opened in 1991 and set in 100 acres of
Derbyshire countryside, has some challenging holes. Also Par
3 course and floodlit driving range.
18 holes, 6400yds, Par 72, SSS 71, Course record 72.
Club membership 600.
Visitors   must contact professional in advance and have
    handicap. May not play weekends.
Societies   must telephone in advance.
Green Fees £18 per 18 holes.
Facilities   ⊗ ⅋ ᴸ ♨ ♀ ♁ ♠ ♦ ♣ ℓ
Leisure   fishing, sauna, solarium, motorised carts for hire,
    buggies for hire, trolley for hire, driving range,
    putting green, practice area.
Location   4m NE of Derby, off A38
Hotel   ★★★★ 64% Breadsall Priory Hotel, Country
    Club Resort, Moor Rd, MORLEY
    ☎ 01332 832235 14 ⇄ ╔Annexe77 ⇄ ╔

KEDLESTON   Map 08 SK34

Kedleston Park DE22 5JD ☎ 01332 840035
The course is laid out in flat mature parkland with fine
trees and background views of historic Kedleston Hall
(National Trust). Many testing holes are included in each
nine and there is an excellent modern clubhouse.
18 holes, 6583yds, Par 71, SSS 72, Course record 63.
Club membership 868.
Visitors   must contact in advance. With member only
    at weekends.
Societies   weekdays only, apply in writing.
Green Fees £35 per day; £27 per round weekdays only.
Facilities   ⊗ ⅋ ᴸ ♨ ♀ ♁ ♠ ♦ ℓ Jim Hetherington.
Leisure   sauna, trolley for hire, putting green,
    practice area.
Location   Signposted Kedleston Hall from A38
Hotel   ★★ 69% Kedleston Country House Hotel,
    Kedleston Rd, DERBY
    ☎ 01332 559202 & 556507 14 ⇄ ╔

MATLOCK   Map 08 SK36

Matlock Chesterfield Rd DE4 5LF
☎ 01629 582191 & 584934
Moorland course with fine views of the beautiful Peak District.
18 holes, 5991yds, Par 70, SSS 68, Course record 64.
Club membership 700.
Visitors   with member only weekends & bank holidays.
    Members only weekdays 12.30-1.30pm.
Societies   prior arrangement with Secretary.
Green Fees £25 per day/round.
Facilities   ⊗ by prior arrangement ⅋ by prior arrangement
    ᴸ ♨ ♀ ♁ ♠ ℓ M A Whithorn.

Leisure   trolley for hire, putting green, practice area.
Location   1.5m NE of Matlock on A632
Hotel   ★★★ 66% New Bath Hotel, New Bath Rd,
           MATLOCK ☎ 01629 583275 55 ⇄ ⁛

MICKLEOVER   Map 08 SK33

Pastures Pastures Hospital DE3 5DQ ☎ 01332 521074
Small course laid-out on undulating meadowland in the
grounds of a psychiatric hospital, with good views across the
Trent valley. Fishing and snooker.
9 holes, 5005yds, Par 64, SSS 64, Course record 62.
Club membership 320.
Visitors   must be accompanied by a member, may not
           play on Sun. Must contact in advance.
Societies must contact in advance.
Green Fees not confirmed.
Facilities ♀⚘
Leisure   fishing, bowls, table tennis.
Location   1m SW off A516
Hotel   ★★★ 63% International Hotel, Burton Rd
           (A5250), DERBY
           ☎ 01332 369321 41 ⇄ ⁛Annexe21 ⇄ ⁛

NEW MILLS   Map 07 SK08

New Mills Shaw Marsh SK12 4QE ☎ 01663 743485
Moorland course with panoramic views and first-class greens.
9 holes, 5633yds, Par 68, SSS 67.
Club membership 350.
Visitors   must play with member on Sunday & special
           days.
must contact in advance.
Green Fees not confirmed.
Facilities ♀⚘ 🕭⚞⁛
Leisure   putting green, practice area, trolley hire.
Location   0.5m N off B6101
Hotel   ★★ 70% Red Lion Inn, 112 Buxton Rd, High
           Ln, STOCKPORT
           ☎ 01663 765227 6 ⇄ ⁛

RENISHAW   Map 08 SK47

Renishaw Park Club House S31 9UZ ☎ 01246 432044
Part parkland and part meadowland with easy walking.
18 holes, 6253yds, Par 71, SSS 70, Course record 65.
Club membership 750.
Visitors   must contact in advance. Visitors not allowed
           Thu, weekends or competition days.
Societies must contact in advance.
Green Fees £28 per day; £20 per round (£33 per round/day
           weekends & bank holidays).
Facilities ⊗ ⅲ ᴸ ⬛ ♀⚘ 🕭⁛ John Oates.
Leisure   trolley for hire, putting green, practice area.
Location   0.5m NW on A616
Hotel   ★★★ 57% Sitwell Arms Hotel, Station Rd,
           RENISHAW ☎ 01246 435226 30 ⇄ ⁛

RISLEY   Map 08 SK43

Maywood Rushy Ln DE72 3ST ☎ 0115 030 2306
Wooded parkland course with numerous water hazards.
18 holes, 6424yds, Par 72, SSS 71, Course record 70.
Club membership 450.

Visitors   advisable to contact in advance during summer,
           may not play during competitions.
Societies by prior arrangement.
Green Fees £15 per round (£20 weekends).
Facilities ⊗ ⅲ ᴸ ⬛ ♀⚘ 🕭⁛ Colin Henderson.
Leisure   trolley for hire, putting green, practice area.
Hotel   ★★★ 70% Risley Hall Hotel, Derby Rd,
           RISLEY ☎ 01159 399000 16rm

SHIRLAND   Map 08 SK45

Shirlands Lower Delves DE55 6AU ☎ 01773 834935
Rolling parkland and tree-lined course with extensive views
of Derbyshire countryside.
18 holes, 6072yds, Par 71, SSS 70, Course record 71.
Club membership 600.
Visitors   contact professional in advance.
Societies contact Professional.
Green Fees £25 per day; £15 per round (£20 per round
           weekends).
Facilities ⊗ ⅲ ᴸ ⬛ ♀⚘ 🕭⁛⁛ Neville Hallam.
Leisure   trolley for hire, putting green, practice area.
Location   S side of village off A61
Hotel   ★★★★ 65% Swallow Hotel, Carter Ln East,
           SOUTH NORMANTON
           ☎ 01773 812000 161 ⇄ ⁛

STANTON-BY-DALE   Map 08 SK43

Erewash Valley DE7 4QR ☎ 0115 932 3258
Parkland/meadowland course overlooking valley and M1.
Unique 4th and 5th in Victorian quarry bottom: 5th-testing
par 3.
18 holes, 6487yds, Par 72, SSS 71, Course record 67.
Club membership 860.
Visitors   no restrictions
Societies contact in advance.
Green Fees not confirmed.
Facilities ♀⚘ 🕭⁛⁛ M J Ronan.
Leisure   bowling green.
Location   1m W
Hotel   ★★★ 70% Risley Hall Hotel, Derby Rd,
           RISLEY ☎ 01159 399000 16rm

DEVON

AXMOUTH   Map 03 SY29

Axe Cliff EX12 4AB ☎ 01297 24371
Undulating links course with coastal views.
18 holes, 5057yds, Par 67, SSS 65.
Club membership 400.
Visitors   may only play after 11am on Wed & Sun.
Societies must contact in advance.
Green Fees not confirmed.
Facilities ⚘🕭⁛ Mark Dack.
Location   0.75m S on B3172
Hotel   ★★ 64% Anchor Inn, BEER
           ☎ 01297 20386 8rm(5 ⇄ ⁛)

BIGBURY-ON-SEA   Map 03 SX64

Bigbury TQ7 4BB ☎ 01548 810557
Clifftop, heathland course with easy walking. Exposed to
winds, but with fine views over the sea and River Avon. 7th
hole particularly tricky.
18 holes, 6048yds, Par 70, SSS 69, Course record 65.
Club membership 850.
Visitors   must have handicap certificate.
Societies   must apply in writing.
Green Fees £20 per day (£24 weekends & bank holidays).
                 Half price after 4pm.
Facilities   ⊗ ⅢⅢ ♨ ➴ ♀ ♨ 🖬 ☞ ⌜ Simon Lloyd.
Leisure   motorised carts for hire, buggies for hire, trolley
                 for hire, putting green, practice area.
Location   1m S on B3392
Hotel   ★ 69% Henley Hotel, BIGBURY-ON-SEA ☎
                 01548 810240 8 ⇄ ♩

BLACKAWTON   Map 03 SX85

Dartmouth Golf & Country Club TQ9 7DQ
☎ 01803 712686 & 712650
The 9-hole Club course and the 18-hole Championship course
are both worth a visit and not just for the beautiful views. The
Championship is one of the most challenging courses in the
West Country with a 4th hole visitors will always remember.
Championship Course: 18 holes, 6663yds, Par 72, SSS 72.
Club Course: 9 holes, 5166yds, Par 66, SSS 65.
Club membership 800.
Visitors   must contact in advance, visitors welcome
                 subject to availability.
Societies   telephone in advance.
Green Fees Championship: £32 per day; £26 per round
                 (£35/£32 weekends). Club: £15 per 18 holes;
                 £10 per 10 holes.
Facilities   ⊗ ⅢⅢ ♨ ➴ ♀ ♨ 🖬 ☞ ⌜⌜ Peter Laugher.
Leisure   heated indoor swimming pool, sauna, solarium,
                 gymnasium, buggies for hire, trolley for hire,
                 driving range, putting green.
Location   On A3122 Totnes/Dartmouth road
Hotel   ★★★ 65% Stoke Lodge Hotel, Stoke Fleming,
                 DARTMOUTH ☎ 01803 770523 24 ⇄ ♩

BUDLEIGH SALTERTON   Map 03 SY08

East Devon North View Rd EX9 6DQ ☎ 01395 443370
An interesting course with downland turf, much heather
and gorse, and superb views over the bay. The early
holes climb to the cliff edge. The downhill 17th has a
heather section in the fairway, leaving a good second to
the green.
18 holes, 6239yds, Par 70, SSS 70, Course record 64.
Club membership 850.
Visitors   no visitors before 10am and between 12.30-
                 2pm. Visitors must be member of a
                 recognised club and must produce proof of
                 handicap.
Societies   must contact in advance. Large parties 16+
                 only on Thu.
Green Fees not confirmed.
Facilities   ♀ ♨ 🖬 ☞ ⌜ Trevor Underwood.
Leisure   putting green, practice area, trolley hire.
Location   W side of town centre

Hotel   ★★★ 63% The Imperial, The Esplanade,
                 EXMOUTH ☎ 01395 274761 57 ⇄ ♩

CHITTLEHAMHOLT   Map 03 SS62

Highbullen Hotel EX37 9HD ☎ 01769 540561
Mature parkland course with water hazards and outstanding
scenic views to Exmoor and Dartmoor. Excellent facilities
offered by the hotel.
18 holes, 5700yds, Par 67, SSS 66.
Club membership 100.
Visitors   to book tee time telephone 01769 540530
                 daytime, 01769 540561 evenings.
Green Fees £12-£14 (£14-£17 weekends and bank holidays).
Facilities   ⅢⅢ ♨ ➴ ♀ ♨ 🖬 ☞ ♨ ⌜ Paul Weston.
Leisure   hard tennis courts, outdoor and indoor heated
                 swimming pools, squash, fishing, sauna,
                 solarium, gymnasium, motorised carts for hire,
                 trolley for hire, putting green, indoor tennis,
                 beauty treatments.
Location   0.5m SE of village
Hotel   ★★★≜≜ 70% Highbullen Hotel,
                 CHITTLEHAMHOLT
                 ☎ 01769 540561 12 ⇄ Annexe25 ⇄ ♩

CHULMLEIGH   Map 03 SS61

Chulmleigh Leigh Rd EX18 7BL ☎ 01769 580519
Situated in a scenic area with views to distant Dartmoor, this
undulating meadowland course offers a good test for the most
experienced golfer and a challenge to newcomers to the
game. Short 18 hole summer course with a tricky 1st hole; in
winter the course is changed to 9 holes and made longer for
players to extend their game.
Summer Short Course: 18 holes, 1450yds, Par 54, Course
record 51.
Winter Course: 9 holes, 2372yds, Par 58.
Club membership 77.
Visitors   welcome anytime, closed on Mon from mid
                 Dec-1 Apr.
Societies   telephone in advance.
Green Fees £10 per day; £5.50 per 18 holes.
Facilities   ♨ ➴ ♀ ♨ 🖬 ☞
Location   SW side of village just off A377
Hotel   ★★★≜≜ 70% Northcote Manor,
                 BURRINGTON ☎ 01769 560501 12 ⇄ ♩

CHURSTON FERRERS   Map 03 SX95

Churston Dartmouth Rd TQ5 0LA
☎ 01803 842751 & 842218
A cliff-top downland course with splendid views over
Brixham harbour and Tor Bay. There is some gorse with a
wooded area inland. A variety of shot is called for, with
particularly testing holes at the 3rd, 9th and 15th, all par 4.
18 holes, 6219yds, Par 70, SSS 70, Course record 64.
Club membership 700.
Visitors   must telephone in advance and be a member
                 of recognised golf club with a handicap
                 certificate.
Societies   apply in writing or telephone.
Green Fees £22 per round (£27 weekends).
Facilities   ⊗ ⅢⅢ ♨ ➴ ♀ ♨ 🖬 ☞ ♨ ⌜ Neil Holman.
Location   NW side of village on A379

Hotel	★★ 63% Dainton Hotel, 95 Dartmouth Rd, Three Beaches, Goodrington, PAIGNTON ☎ 01803 550067 11 ⇌ ⌘

CREDITON
Map 03 SS80

Downes Crediton Hookway EX17 3PT
☎ 01363 773025 & 774464
Converted farmhouse course with lovely views. Parkland
with hilly back nine.
18 holes, 5859yds, Par 69, SSS 68.
Club membership 700.

Visitors	handicap certificate required, must contact in advance, restricted at weekends.
Societies	must contact in advance.
Green Fees	not confirmed.
Facilities	♀ ♨ ⌂ ♟ ℓ Howard Finch.
Leisure	putting,practice area,trolley for hire.
Location	1.5m SE off A377
Hotel	★★★ 72% Barton Cross Hotel & Restaurant, Huxham, STOKE CANON ☎ 01392 841245 7 ⇌ ⌘

CULLOMPTON
Map 03 ST00

Padbrook Park EX15 1RU
☎ 01884 38286
A 9-hole, 18 tee parkland course with many water and
woodland hazards and spectacular views. The dog-leg 2nd
and pulpit 2nd are of particular challenge to golfers of all
standards.
9 holes, 6108yds, Par 70, SSS 70.
Club membership 250.

Visitors	welcome at all times, tee may be reserved by telephoning in advance.
Societies	apply in writing or telephone.
Green Fees	£10 per 18 holes; £7 per 9 holes (£16/£8 weekends).
Facilities	⊗ �𝄢 ⚑ ♀ ♨ ⌂ ♟ ℓ Stewart Adwick.
Leisure	fishing, trolley for hire, putting green, practice area.
Location	Southern edge of Cullompton on B3181
Hotel	★★★ 62% The Tiverton Hotel, Blundells Rd, TIVERTON ☎ 01884 256120 75 ⇌ ⌘

DAWLISH WARREN
Map 03 SX97

Warren EX7 0NF ☎ 01626 862255 & 864002
Typical flat, genuine links course lying on spit between sea
and Exe estuary. Picturesque scenery, a few trees but much
gorse. Testing in windy conditions. The 7th hole provides the
opportunity to go for the green across a bay on the estuary.
18 holes, 5965yds, Par 69, SSS 69.
Club membership 600.

Visitors	must contact in advance & have handicap certificate.
Societies	prior arrangement essential.
Green Fees	£21 (£24 weekends & bank holidays).
Facilities	⊗ �𝄢 ⚑ ♀ ♨ ⌂ ℓ Andrew Naldrett.
Leisure	trolley for hire, practice area.
Location	E side of village
Hotel	★★★ 65% Langstone Cliff Hotel, Dawlish Warren, DAWLISH ☎ 01626 865155 64 ⇌ ⌘Annexe4 ⇌ ⌘

DOWN ST MARY
Map 03 SS70

Waterbridge EX17 5LG ☎ 01363 85111
A testing course of 9-holes set in a gently sloping valley. The
Par of 31 will not be easily gained with 4 par-4's and 5 par-
3's, although the course record holder has Par 29! The 3rd
hole which is a raised green is surrounded by water and the
4th (439 yards) is demanding for beginners.
9 holes, 3908yds, Par 62, SSS 62.

Visitors	no restrictions.
Societies	no restrictions.
Green Fees	not confirmed.
Facilities	⚑ ♟ ℓ David Ridyard.
Leisure	trolley for hire.
Location	From Exeter on A377 towards Barnstaple
Hotel	★★★♨ 70% Northcote Manor, BURRINGTON ☎ 01769 560501 12 ⇌ ⌘

EXETER
Map 03 SX99

Exeter Golf & Country Club Topsham Rd, Countess Wear
EX2 7AE ☎ 01392 874139
A sheltered parkland course with some very old trees and
known as the flattest course in Devon. 15th & 17th are testing
par 4 holes.
18 holes, 6000yds, Par 69, SSS 69.
Club membership 800.

Visitors	visitors welcome but may not play during match or competitions, very busy pre booking needed up to 1 week in advance.
Societies	welcome Thu only, booking available by telephone to starter tel 01392 876303.
Green Fees	£22 per day.
Facilities	⊗ �𝄢 ⚑ ⚑ ♀ ♨ ⌂ ℓ Mike Rowlett.
Leisure	hard tennis courts, heated indoor plus outdoor swimming pool, squash, sauna, solarium, gymnasium, trolley for hire, putting green, practice area.
Location	SE side of city centre off A379
Hotel	B Travel Inn, R98 Topsham Rd, Countess Wear Roundabout, Exeter Bypass, EXETER ☎ 01392 875441 44 ⇌ ⌘

Woodbury Park Woodbury Castle, Woodbury EX5 1JJ
☎ 01395 233382
Two courses set in the lovely wooded parkland of Woodbury
Castle.The 18-hole championship Oaks course is host to
professional Championships and the 9-hole is a
championship-standard training course.
Oaks: 18 holes, 6707yds, Par 72, SSS 72.
Acorn: 9 holes, 4582yds, Par 69, SSS 62.
Club membership 400.

Visitors	advisable to contact in advance.
Societies	contact in advance.
Green Fees	not confirmed.
Facilities	♀ (Mon-Sat) ♨ ⌂ ♟
Leisure	fishing.
Hotel	★★★ 67% Ebford House Hotel, Exmouth Rd, EBFORD ☎ 01392 877658 16 ⇌ ⌘

> Entries with a shaded background identify
> courses that are considered to be particularly
> interesting

HIGH BICKINGTON

Map 02 SS52

Libbaton EX37 9BS ☎ 01769 560269 & 560167
Parkland course on undulating land with no steep slopes.
Floodlit driving range.
18 holes, 6494yds, Par 73, SSS 72, Course record 72.
Club membership 500.
Visitors book in advance.
Societies telephone to book in advance.
Green Fees £22 per day; £18 per round (£26/£22 bank
holidays & weekends).
Facilities ⊗ ⅏ ﯞ ☕ ☂ ⚲ ♨ 🏠 ➹ 🍴 ⋈ 🏌 John Phillips.
Leisure fishing, gymnasium, motorised carts for hire,
buggies for hire, trolley for hire, driving range,
putting green, practice area.
Hotel ★★★▲▲ 70% Highbullen Hotel,
CHITTLEHAMHOLT
☎ 01769 540561 12 ⇆Annexe25 ⇆ 🐾

HOLSWORTHY

Map 02 SS30

Holsworthy Killatree EX22 6LP ☎ 01409 253177
Pleasant parkland course with gentle slopes and numerous
trees..
18 holes, 6062yds, Par 70, SSS 69, Course record 64.
Club membership 600.
Visitors may not play Sun am.
Societies by arrangement with secretary or professional.
Green Fees £15 per day/round (£20 weekends & bank
holidays).
Facilities ⊗ ⅏ ﯞ ☕ ☂ ⚲ ♨ 🏠 ➹ 🍴 Simon Chapman.
Leisure trolley for hire, putting green, practice area.
Location 1.5m W on A3072
Hotel ★★▲▲ 71% Court Barn Country House Hotel,
CLAWTON ☎ 01409 271219 8rm(7 ⇆ 🐾)

HONITON

Map 03 ST10

Honiton Middlehills EX14 8TR
☎ 01404 44422 & 42943
Level parkland course on a plateau 850ft above sea level.
Easy walking and good views. The 4th hole is a testing par 3.
The club was founded in 1896.
18 holes, 5902yds, Par 69, SSS 68.
Club membership 800.
Visitors must contact in advance.
Societies society bookings on Thursdays.
Green Fees £20 per day (£25 weekends).
Facilities ⊗ ⅏ ﯞ ☕ ☂ ⚲ ♨ 🏠 ➹ 🍴 Adrian Cave.
Leisure trolley for hire, putting green, practice area,
touring caravan site.
Location 1.25m SE of Honiton
Hotel ★★ 71% Home Farm Hotel, Wilmington,
HONITON
☎ 01404 831278 6 ⇆Annexe7 ⇆ 🐾

ILFRACOMBE

Map 02 SS54

Ilfracombe Hele Bay EX34 9RT ☎ 01271 862176
A sporting, clifftop, heathland course with views over the
Bristol Channel and moors from every tee and green.
18 holes, 5893yds, Par 69, SSS 69, Course record 66.
Club membership 642.

Visitors recommended to make tee reservation prior to
visit, member only 12-2 daily and before 10 am
on weekends.
Societies telephone in advance.
Green Fees £17 per day (£20 weekends & bank holidays).
Facilities ⊗ ⅏ ﯞ ☕ ☂ ⚲ ♨ 🏠 ➹ 🍴 David Hoare.
Leisure trolley for hire, driving range, putting, practice
area.
Location 1.5m E off A399
Hotel ★★ 69% Elmfield Hotel, Torrs Park,
ILFRACOMBE
☎ 01271 863377 11 ⇆ 🐾Annexe2 ⇆ 🐾

IPPLEPEN

Map 03 SX86

Dainton Park Totnes Rd, Ipplepen TQ12 5TN
☎ 01803 83812
The first full-length pay and play course serving the Torbay
area. A challenging parkland type course in typical Devon
countryside, with gentle contours, tree-lined fairways and
raised tees. Water hazards make the two opening holes
particularly testing. The 8th, a dramatic 180yard drop hole
totally surrounded by sand, is one of four tough Par 3's on the
course. It is advisable to book start times.
18 holes, 6207yds, Par 71, SSS 70, Course record 71.
Club membership 500.
Visitors prior booking by phone advisable to guarantee
start time.
Societies apply in writing.
Green Fees £20 per day; £12 per round (£24/£15 weekends
& bank holidays).
Facilities ⊗ ⅏ ﯞ ☕ ☂ ⚲ ♨ 🏠 ➹ 🍴 Martin Tyson.
Leisure motorised carts for hire, trolley for hire, driving
range, putting green, practice area.
Location 2m S of Newton Abbot on A381
Hotel ★★ 63% Old Church House Inn, Torbryan,
IPPLEPEN ☎ 01803 812372 6 ⇆ 🐾

IVYBRIDGE

Map 02 SX65

Dinnaton Sporting & Country Club Blachford Rd
PL21 9HU ☎ 01752 892512 & 892452
Challenging 9-hole moorland course overlooking the South
Hams. Mainly par 3 but with four recently added par 4 holes,
three lakes and tight fairways; excellent for improving the
short game Floodlit driving range.
9 holes, 4089yds, Par 64, SSS 60.
Club membership 275.
Visitors no restrictions.
Societies telephone in advance.
Green Fees weekdays £10 per day (£12.50 weekends & bank
holidays).
Facilities ⊗ ⅏ ﯞ ☕ ☂ ⚲ ♨ 🏠 ➹ 🍴 David Ridyard.
Leisure hard tennis courts, heated indoor swimming
pool, squash, sauna, solarium, gymnasium,
driving range, practice area.
Location Just off main A38
Hotel ★★▲▲ 74% Glazebrook House Hotel &
Restaurant, SOUTH BRENT
☎ 01364 73322 10 ⇆ 🐾

Entries with a shaded background identify
courses that are considered to be particularly
interesting

No Ordinary Golfing Hotel

Set on the edge of beautiful Dartmoor, the luxury and comfort of the Manor House Hotel complements a par 69 Championship course of stunning beauty, renowned as one of England's finest courses.

Enjoy a challenging game, modern facilities and the traditional comfort of our fine country house hotel. In addition, with 4 spacious meeting rooms and easy access to the M5, we are the ideal conference and team building venue. Ask about our self contained and luxurious North Lodge.

Book now on 01647 440355

MANOR HOUSE HOTEL & GOLF COURSE ★★★★
MORETONHAMPSTEAD, DEVON, TQ13 8RE.
A PRINCIPAL HOTEL

MORETONHAMPSTEAD
Map 03 SX78

Manor House Hotel TQ13 8RE ☎ 01647 440998
This enjoyable parkland course is a sporting circuit with just enough hazards (most of them natural) to make any golfer think. The Rivers Bowden and Bovey meander through the first eight holes. Driving range.
18 holes, 6016yds, Par 69, SSS 69, Course record 65.
Club membership 120.
Visitors must contact in advance and pre-arrange starting times.
Societies must telephone for reservation in advance.
Green Fees £28 per day; £22.50 per round (£35/£28 weekends).
Facilities ⊗ ⊪ ⓑ ♥ ♀ ♨ 🛋 ⵊ ⱺ (Richard Lewis.
Leisure hard tennis courts, fishing, motorised carts for hire, buggies for hire, trolley for hire, putting green, practice area.
Location 3m W of Moretonhampstead, off B3212
Hotel ★★★★ 63% Manor House Hotel, MORETONHAMPSTEAD ☎ 01647 440355 89 ⇆ ⏧

MORTEHOE
Map 02 SS44

Mortehoe & Woolacombe EX34 7EH
☎ 01271 870225 & 870745
Attached to a camping and caravan site, this 9-hole course has 2 par 3s and 7 par 4s. The gently sloping clifftop course has spectacular views across Morte Bay.
9 holes, 4690yds, Par 66, SSS 63, Course record 69.
Club membership 233.
Visitors no restrictions.
Societies must telephone or write in advance.
Green Fees £10 per 18 holes; £6 per 9 holes.
Facilities ⊗ ⊪ ⓑ ♥ ♀ ♨ 🛋 ⵊ
Leisure heated indoor swimming pool, trolley for hire, putting green, practice nets, camping & caravan site.
Location 0.25m before Mortehoe on station road
Hotel ★★★ 76% Watersmeet Hotel, Mortehoe, WOOLACOMBE ☎ 01271 870333 23 ⇆ ⏧

NEWTON ABBOT
Map 03 SX87

Newton Abbot (Stover) Bovey Rd TQ12 6QQ
☎ 01626 52460 (Secretary) & 62078 (Pro)
Wooded parkland course with a stream coming into play on eight holes. Fairly flat.
18 holes, 5862yds, Par 69, SSS 68, Course record 63.
Club membership 800.
Visitors must have proof of membership of recognised club or current handicap certificate.

Societies by arrangement on Thu only.
Green Fees £22 per day.
Facilities ⊗ ⊪ ⓑ ♥ ♀ ♨ 🛋 (Malcolm Craig.
Leisure trolley for hire, putting green, practice area.
Location 3m N on A382
Hotel ★★ 63% Queens Hotel, Queen St, NEWTON ABBOT ☎ 01626 63133 & 54106 22rm(19 ⇆ ⏧)

OKEHAMPTON
Map 02 SX59

Okehampton Tors Rd EX20 1EF ☎ 01837 52113
A good combination of moorland, woodland and river make this one of the prettiest, yet testing courses in Devon.
18 holes, 5243yds, Par 68, SSS 67, Course record 66.
Club membership 600.
Visitors advance booking recommended, limited times available at weekends.
Societies by prior arrangement.
Green Fees £16 per day (£22 Sat, £18 Sun).
Facilities ⊗ ⊪ ⓑ ♥ ♀ ♨ 🛋 ⵊ (Simon Jefferies.
Leisure trolley for hire, putting green, practice area.
Location 1m S off A30
Hotel ★★ 65% Oxenham Arms, SOUTH ZEAL ☎ 01837 840244 & 840577 8rm(7 ⇆ ⏧)

PLYMOUTH
Map 02 SX45

Elfordleigh Plympton PL7 5EB ☎ 01752 336428
Charming, saucer-shaped parkland course with alternate tees for 18 holes. Tree-lined fairways and three lakes. Fairly hard walking.
9 holes, 5664yds, Par 68, SSS 67.
Club membership 450.
Visitors must contact in advance & have handicap certificate.
Societies by arrangement.
Green Fees not confirmed.
Facilities ♀ ♨ 🛋 ⵊ ⱺ (Andrew Rickard.
Leisure hard tennis courts, outdoor and indoor heated swimming pools, squash, sauna, solarium, gymnasium, games room, jacuzzi, croquet.
Location 8m NE off B3416
Hotel ★★★ 68% Elfordleigh Hotel & Country Club, Colebrook, Plympton, PLYMOUTH ☎ 01752 336428 18 ⇆ ⏧

Staddon Heights Plymstock PL9 9SP
☎ 01752 402475 & 492630
Seaside course affording spectacular views across Plymouth Sound, Dartmoor and Bodmin Moor. Testing holes include the par 3 17th with its green cut into a hillside and the par 4 14th across a road. Easy walking. ▶

---

18 holes, 5869yds, Par 68, SSS 68, Course record 66.
Club membership 655.

Visitors must have handicap certificate and contact the pro or secretary.
Societies apply by telephone in advance.
Green Fees £20 per day (£25 weekends).
Facilities ⊗ ⅷ ℡ ♥ ♀ ♨ 🏠 ♍ ℄ Ian Marshall.
Leisure trolley for hire, putting green, practice area.
Location 5m SW of city centre
Hotel B Forte Posthouse Plymouth, Cliff Rd, The Hoe, PLYMOUTH ☎ 01752 662828 106 ⇔ ℟

SAUNTON   Map 02 SS43

Saunton EX33 1LG ☎ 01271 812436
Two traditional links courses (one championship). Windy, with natural hazards.
East Course: 18 holes, 6708yds, Par 73, SSS 73, Course record 65.
West Course: 18 holes, 6356yds, Par 71, SSS 71, Course record 68.
Club membership 1100.

Visitors prior booking recommended and must have handicap certificate.
Societies must apply in advance, handicap certificates required.
Green Fees £35 per day (£40 weekends & bank holidays).
Facilities ⊗ ⅷ ℡ ♥ ♀ ♨ 🏠 ♍ ℄ J A McGhee.
Leisure trolley for hire, putting green, practice area, snooker.
Location S side of village off B3231
Hotel ★★★★ 69% Saunton Sands Hotel, SAUNTON ☎ 01271 890212 92 ⇔ ℟

SIDMOUTH   Map 03 SY18

Sidmouth Cotmaton Rd, Peak Hill EX10 8SX
☎ 01395 513451 & 516407
Situated on the side of Peak Hill, offering beautiful coastal views. Club founded in 1889.
18 holes, 5100yds, Par 66, SSS 65, Course record 59.
Club membership 700.

Visitors by prior arrangement.
Societies by prior arrangement with the secretary.
Green Fees £20 per day.
Facilities ⊗ ⅷ ℡ ♥ ♀ ♨ 🏠 ♍ ℄ Haydn Barrell.
Leisure trolley for hire, putting green, limited practice area.
Location W side of town centre
Hotel ★★★★ 71% Victoria Hotel, Esplanade, SIDMOUTH ☎ 01395 512651 61 ⇔ ℟

SOUTH BRENT   Map 03 SX66

Wrangaton (S Devon) Golf Links Rd, Wrangaton TQ10 9HJ
☎ 01364 73229
Moorland/parkland course within Dartmoor National Park. Spectacular views towards sea and rugged terrain. Natural fairways and hazards include bracken, sheep and ponies.
18 holes, 6041yds, Par 69, SSS 69, Course record 63.
Club membership 700.

Visitors play any time.
Societies write or telephone.
Green Fees £17 per day (£23 weekends & bank holidays).

Facilities ⊗ ⅷ ℡ ♥ ♀ ♨ 🏠 ♍ ℄ Adrian Whitehead.
Leisure practice facilities.
Location 2.25 m SW off A38
Hotel ★★♨ 74% Glazebrook House Hotel & Restaurant, SOUTH BRENT ☎ 01364 73322 10 ⇔ ℟

SPARKWELL   Map 02 SX55

Welbeck Manor & Sparkwell Golf Course Blacklands PL7 5DF ☎ 01752 837219
A mature parkland course with several challenging holes, it features fairway and greenside bunkers, mature trees and streams. The house on the site, now the hotel, was built by Isambard Kingdom Brunel. Several of the holes have been named to commemorate some of his famous works - the 6th being The Great Western.This is a very challenging Par 5 tee which is out of bounds all the way up the left.
9 holes, 2886yds, Par 68, SSS 68, Course record 68.
Club membership 200.

Visitors no restrictions
Societies telephone in advance.
Green Fees £9 per 18 holes; £5 per 9 holes (£11/£6 weekends).
Facilities ⊗ ⅷ ℡ ♥ ♀ ♨ 🏠 ♍ ℄
Leisure trolley for hire, pitch & putt.
Location 1m N of A38 Plymouth/Ivybridge road
Hotel ★★★ 68% Boringdon Hall, Colebrook, Plympton, PLYMOUTH ☎ 01752 344455 41 ⇔ ℟

TAVISTOCK   Map 02 SX47

Hurdwick Tavistock Hamlets PL19 8PZ
☎ 01822 612746
This Executive parkland course with many bunkers and fine views opened in 1990. The idea of Executive golf originated in America and the concept is that a round should take no longer than 3 hours whilst offering solid challenge, thus suiting the busy business person.
18 holes, 4553yds, Par 67, SSS 64, Course record 69.
Club membership 180.

Visitors no restrictions.
Societies must contact in advance.
Green Fees £12 per day.
Facilities ℡ ♥ ♀ ♨ 🏠 ♍
Leisure buggies for hire, trolley for hire, putting green, practice area.
Location 1m N of Tavistock
Hotel ★★★ 62% Bedford Hotel, Plymouth Rd, TAVISTOCK ☎ 01822 613221 31rm(30 ⇔ ℟)

Tavistock Down Rd PL19 9AQ ☎ 01822 612344
Set on Whitchurch Down in south-west Dartmoor with easy walking and magnificent views over rolling countryside into Cornwall. Downland turf with some heather, and interesting holes on undulating ground.
18 holes, 6230yds, Par 70, SSS 70, Course record 64.
Club membership 700.

Visitors advisable to contact in advance.
Societies by arrangement with secretary.
Green Fees £18 per round/day (£23 weekends).
Facilities ⊗ ⅷ ℡ ♥ ♀ ♨ 🏠 ♍ ℄ D Rehaag.
Leisure trolley for hire, putting green, practice area.

Location	1m SE of town centre
Hotel	★★★ 62% Bedford Hotel, Plymouth Rd, TAVISTOCK
	☎ 01822 613221 31rm(30 ⇌ ↑)

TEDBURN ST MARY　　　　　　Map 03 SX89

Fingle Glen EX6 6AF ☎ 01647 61817
9-hole course containing six par 4's and three par 3's set in 52 acres of rolling countryside. Testing 4th, 5th and 9th holes. 12-bay floodlit driving range.
9 holes, 4818yds, Par 66, SSS 63, Course record 63.
Club membership 400.

Visitors	must contact in advance.
Societies	write or telephone in advance.
Green Fees	Summer: £13.50 per 18 holes; £9 per 9 holes (£16/£11.50 weekends). Winter: £6 per 9 holes (£8 weekends).
Facilities	⊗ ⅫⓂ ⅙ ⬛ ⅞ ⚲ 🏠 ⅞ ⋈ ♪ Stephen Gould.
Leisure	trolley for hire, driving range, practice area.
Location	5m W of Exeter, off A30
Hotel	B Travel Inn, R98 Topsham Rd, Countess Wear Roundabout, Exeter Bypass, EXETER
	☎ 01392 875441 44 ⇌ ↑

TEIGNMOUTH　　　　　　　　Map 03 SX97

Teignmouth Haldon Moor TQ14 9NY
☎ 01626 774194
This fairly flat heathland course is high up with a fine seascape from the clubhouse. Good springy turf with some heather and an interesting layout makes for very enjoyable holiday golf.
18 holes, 6200yds, Par 71, SSS 70, Course record 65.
Club membership 900.

Visitors	groups must contact in advance, restricted tee off times at weekends.
Societies	telephone in advance and confirm in writing.
Green Fees	£22 per day/round (£25 weekends).
Facilities	⊗ ⅫⓂ ⅙ ⬛ ⅞ ⚲ 🏠 ⅞ ♪ Peter Ward.
Leisure	trolley for hire, putting green, practice area.
Location	2m NW off B3192
Hotel	★★ 68% Ness House Hotel, Marine Dr, Shaldon, TEIGNMOUTH
	☎ 01626 873480 7 ⇌ ↑Annexe5 ⇌ ↑

THURLESTONE　　　　　　　Map 03 SX64

Thurlestone TQ7 3NZ ☎ 01548 560405
Situated on the edge of the cliffs with typical downland turf and good greens. The course, after an interesting opening hole, rises to higher land with fine seaviews, and finishes with an excellent 502-yard downhill hole to the clubhouse.
18 holes, 6340yds, Par 71, SSS 70, Course record 65.
Club membership 770.

Visitors	must contact in advance & have handicap certificate from a recognised club.
Green Fees	£24 per day/round. £90 7 consecutive days.
Facilities	⊗ Ⅻ by prior arrangement ⅙ ⬛ ⅞ ⚲ 🏠 ♪ Neville Whitley.
Leisure	hard and grass tennis courts, trolley for hire, putting green, practice area.
Location	S side of village

Hotel	★★★★ 70% Thurlestone Hotel, THURLESTONE
	☎ 01548 560382 68 ⇌ ↑

TIVERTON　　　　　　　　　Map 03 SS91

Tiverton Post Hill EX16 4NE ☎ 01884 252187
A parkland course where the many different species of tree are a feature and where the lush pastures ensure some of the finest fairways in the south-west. There are a number of interesting holes which visitors will find a real challenge.
18 holes, 6236yds, Par 71, SSS 71, Course record 65.
Club membership 725.

Visitors	must have a current handicap certificate.
Societies	apply in writing or telephone.
Green Fees	£21 (£27 weekends).
Facilities	⊗ ⅫⓂ ⅙ ⬛ ⅞ ⚲ 🏠 ♪ David Sheppard.
Leisure	trolley for hire, putting green, practice area.
Hotel	★★ 65% Hartnoll Hotel, Bolham, TIVERTON
	☎ 01884 252777 11 ⇌ ↑Annexe5 ↑

TORQUAY　　　　　　　　　Map 03 SX96

Torquay 30 Petitor Rd, St Marychurch TQ1 4QF
☎ 01803 329113
Unusual combination of cliff and parkland golf, with wonderful views over the sea and Dartmoor.
18 holes, 6175yds, Par 69, SSS 70, Course record 66.
Club membership 700.

Visitors	must contact in advance.
Societies	must apply in writing.
Green Fees	£20 per day/round (£25 weekends & bank holidays).
Facilities	⊗ ⅫⓂ ⅙ ⬛ ⅞ ⚲ 🏠 ⅞ ♪ Martin Ruth.
Leisure	motorised carts for hire, buggies for hire, trolley for hire, putting green.
Location	1.25m N
Hotel	★★ 60% Norcliffe Hotel, 7 Babbacombe Downs Rd, Babbacombe, TORQUAY
	☎ 01803 328456 27 ⇌ ↑

TORRINGTON　　　　　　　Map 02 SS41

Torrington Weare Trees, Great Torrington EX38 7EZ
☎ 01805 622229
Hard walking on hilly commonland 9 hole course. Challenging par 3 4th hole with a sloping green and difficult crosswinds. Small greens and outstanding views.
9 holes, 4419yds, Par 64, SSS 62, Course record 58.
Club membership 420.

Visitors	cannot play Sat & Sun before noon.
Societies	by arrangement.
Green Fees	£10 per day/round.
Facilities	⊗ Ⅻ by prior arrangement ⅙ ⬛ ⅞ ⚲ ⅞
Leisure	trolley for hire, putting green, practice area.
Location	1m W of Torringdon
Hotel	★★ 63% Beaconside Hotel, LANDCROSS
	☎ 01237 477205 8rm(6 ⇌ ↑)

CULLODEN HOUSE HOTEL
WESTWARD HO! (01237) 479421
Victorian elegance – modern comforts – most rooms en-suite – views across Bideford Bay and Atlantic – friendly and comfortable atmosphere.

SPECIAL GOLFING HOLIDAYS AVAILABLE – CHOICE OF 8 COURSES

AA ★★

UPOTTERY
Map 03 ST20

Otter Valley Golf Centre
☎ 01404 861266 (5m NW of Honiton off A30, on U pottery Rd) This Golf School set in beautiful Devon c ountryside was established in 1969. There are practice facilities with driving range, approach green, chipping green with bunkers and 5 practice holes. Weekend an d 5 day courses are available and there is self catering accommodation, telephone for details. All coaching is given personally by Andrew Thompson P.G.A.

WESTWARD HO!
Map 02 SS42

Royal North Devon EX39 1HD
☎ 01237 473817
Links course with sea views.
18 holes, 6644yds, Par 71, SSS 72.
Club membership 1100.

Visitors	advisable to telephone and book tee time, must have handicap certificate or letter of introduction from club.
Societies	apply in writing or telephone.
Green Fees	£28 per day; £24 per round.
Facilities	⊗ ⅷ by prior arrangement ⓛ ⓨ ♀ ⚲ ⌂ ⓣ ⓔ Graham Johnston.
Leisure	trolley for hire, driving range, putting green, practice area.
Location	N side of village off B3236
Hotel	★★ 62% Culloden House Hotel, Fosketh Hill, WESTWARD HO! ☎ 01237 479421 9rm(2 ⇄5 ⓝ)

WOOLFARDISWORTHY
Map 02 SS32

Hartland Forest Woolsery, Bideford EX39 5RA
☎ 01237 431442
This course is affected by winds and can be very windy at times.
18 holes, 6015yds, Par 71, SSS 69.
Club membership 240.

Visitors	no restrictions.
Societies	apply in writing.
Green Fees	not confirmed.
Facilities	♀ ⚲ ⓣ ⓔ
Leisure	hard tennis courts, heated indoor swimming pool, fishing, sauna, solarium, gymnasium.
Location	4m E of A39
Hotel	★★★★⚑⚑ 74% Penhaven Country House, PARKHAM ☎ 01237 451388 12 ⇄ ⓝ

YELVERTON
Map 02 SX56

Yelverton Golf Links Rd PL20 6BN
☎ 01822 852824
An excellent course on the moors with virtually no trees. It is exposed to high winds. The fairways are tight but there is plenty of room. The longest hole is the 8th, a 569-yard, par 5. Outstanding views.
18 holes, 6363yds, Par 71, SSS 70.
Club membership 650.

Visitors	subject to availability, advisable to contact in advance.
Societies	must be booked in advance, by telephone initially.
Green Fees	£22 per day/round (£25 weekends).
Facilities	⊗ ⅷ ⓛ ⓨ ♀ ⚲ ⌂ ⓣ ⓔ Tim McSherry.
Leisure	trolley for hire, putting green, practice area.
Location	1m S of Yelverton, off A386
Hotel	★★★ 69% Moorland Links Hotel, YELVERTON ☎ 01822 852245 45 ⇄ ⓝ

YELVERTON GOLF CLUB
Golf Links Road, Yelverton, Devon PL20 6BN.
Telephone: (01822) 852824
18 Hole moorland course within the Dartmoor National Park
8 miles north of Plymouth on the A386 road
Green Fee £22w/day £25 w/end; 6363 yards; S.S.S. 70; fully licensed with catering facilities

DORSET

BEAMINSTER
Map 03 ST40

Chedington Court South Perrott DT8 3HU
☎ 01935 891413
At present 9 holes, though due to be extended to 18, this course is laid out in parkland using the natural features of the rolling countryside. The Par 5 4th is 596yards and looks daunting but it is downhill from the tee to the green. The Par 4 9th is a tricky final hole with its hidden small lake waiting for the errant second shot. Preservation of wildlife and the natural flora are of prime concern in managing the course.
9 holes, 6754yds, Par 74, SSS 72, Course record 72.
Club membership 260.
Visitors   must book tee time.
Societies   apply in writing or telephone.
Green Fees £13 per 18 holes; £8 per 9 holes (£16/£10 weekends & bank holidays).
Facilities   ⊗ ⅃ ⬛ ♞ ♀ ☥ 🏠 ↰ ⋈
Leisure   trolley for hire, practice ground, pitch & putt.
Location   5m NE of Beaminster
Hotel   ★★★ 68% Bridge House Hotel, 3 Prout Bridge, BEAMINSTER
☎ 01308 862200 9 ⇥ ↜Annexe4 ⇥ ↜

BELCHALWELL
Map 03 ST70

Mid-Dorset DT11 0EG ☎ 01258 861386
Set in an area of outstanding natural beauty, rich in wildlife, which provides a picturesque backdrop to this stimulating, undulating course. Modern clubhouse with magnificent views.
18 holes, 6162yds, Par 70, SSS 70, Course record 69.
Club membership 270.
Visitors   no restrictions.
Societies   must telephone in advance.
Green Fees £20 per day; £12 per round (£28/£17 weekends & bank holidays).
Facilities   ⊗ ♏ ⅃ ⬛ ♀ ☥ 🏠 ↰ ⋈ Spencer Taylor.
Leisure   trolley for hire, driving range, putting green, practice area.
Hotel   ★★★ 68% Crown Hotel, 8 West St, BLANDFORD FORUM
☎ 01258 456626 32 ⇥

BLANDFORD FORUM
Map 03 ST80

Ashley Wood Wimborne Rd DT11 9HN ☎ 01258 452253
Undulating and well drained downland course with superb views over the Tarrant and Stour Valleys.
18 holes, 6335yds, Par 70, SSS 70, Course record 69.
Club membership 550.
Visitors   phone professional in advance (01258 480379).
Societies   apply to Secretary.
Green Fees £17 per day (£24 weekends).
Facilities   ⊗ ♏ ⅃ ⬛ ♀ ☥ 🏠 ↰ Spencer Taylor.
Leisure   motorised carts for hire, buggies for hire, trolley for hire, putting green, practice area.
Location   2m E on B3082
Hotel   ★★★ 68% Crown Hotel, 8 West St, BLANDFORD FORUM
☎ 01258 456626 32 ⇥

BOURNEMOUTH
Map 04 SZ09

Bournemouth & Meyrick Central Dr, Meyrick Park BH2 6LH ☎ 01202 292425
Picturesque muncipal parkland course founded in 1890.
18 holes, 5852yds, Par 70, SSS 69, Course record 64.
Club membership 500.
Visitors   advance booking is essential.
Societies   telephone in advance.
Green Fees £12.50 per round (£13.50 weekends & bank holidays).
Facilities   ♀ ☥ 🏠 ↰ ⋈ Lee Thompson.
Leisure   squash, trolley for hire, putting green, practice area.
Hotel   ★★★ 63% Burley Court Hotel, Bath Rd, BOURNEMOUTH
☎ 01202 552824 & 556704 38 ⇥ ↜

Knighton Heath Francis Av, West Howe BH11 8NX
☎ 01202 572633
Undulating heathland course on high ground inland from Bournemouth.
18 holes, 6064yds, Par 70, SSS 69.
Club membership 700.
Visitors   may not play weekend. Phone for availability.
Societies   must book in advance.
Green Fees £25 per day or round.
Facilities   ⊗ ♏ ⅃ ⬛ ♀ ☥ 🏠 ↰ Jane Miles.
Leisure   trolley for hire, putting green, practice area.
Location   N side of town centre off A348
Hotel   ★★★ 63% Bridge House Hotel, 2 Ringwood Rd, Longham, FERNDOWN
☎ 01202 578828 37 ⇥ ↜

Queen's Park Queens Park Dr West BH8 9BY
☎ 01202 396198
Undulating parkland course of pine and heather, with narrow, tree-lined fairways. Public course played over by 'Boscombe Golf Club' and 'Bournemouth Artisans Golf Club'.
18 holes, 6505yds, Par 72, SSS 72.
Visitors   must contact in advance.
Societies   must contact in advance.
Green Fees not confirmed.
Facilities   ♀ ☥ 🏠 ↰ Richard Hill.
Location   2m NE of town centre off A338
Hotel   ★★ 66% Hotel Riviera, West Cliff Gardens, BOURNEMOUTH
☎ 01202 552845 34 ⇥ ↜

BRIDPORT
Map 03 SY49

Bridport & West Dorset East Cliff, West Bay DT6 4EP
☎ 01308 421491 & 421095
Seaside links course on the top of the east cliff, with fine views over Lyme Bay and surrounding countryside. A popular feature is the pretty and deceptive 14th hole, its sunken green lying 90 feet below the tee and guarded by natural hazards and bunkers. New course layout from June 1996.
18 holes, 6500yds, Par 71, SSS 69.
Club membership 700.
Visitors   must contact in advance.
Societies   must contact in writing in advance.
Green Fees £25 per day (£18 after 2pm).
Facilities   ⊗ ⅃ ⬛ ♀ ☥ 🏠 ↰ David Parsons.   ▶

Bridport Arms Hotel

West Bay, Bridport, Dorset DT6 4EN

Tel: 01308 422994

A 16th century thatched hotel on the beach at West Bay. The Restaurant specialising in local sea foods is open to non residents. Bar meals are also available throughout the year. Very close to Bridport and West Dorset Golf Course.

Please contact for brochure.

Leisure	trolley for hire, putting green, pitch & putt (holiday season).
Location	2m S of Bridport
Hotel	★★ 67% Ullswater Hotel, West Cliff Gardens, BOURNEMOUTH ☎ 01202 555181 42 ⇥ ↸
Additional hotel	★★★ 59% Grosvenor Hotel, Bath Rd, East Cliff, BOURNEMOUTH ☎ 01202 558858 40 ⇥ ↸

BROADSTONE   Map 04 SZ09

Broadstone (Dorset) Wentworth Dr BH18 8DQ
☎ 01202 692595
Undulating and demanding heathland course with the 2nd, 7th, 13th and 16th being particularly challenging holes.
18 holes, 6315yds, Par 70, SSS 70, Course record 66.
Club membership 700.
Visitors restricted at weekends & bank holidays. Must contact in advance.
Societies contact in advance.
Green Fees £36 per day; £28 per round (£40 per round weekends & bank holidays).
Facilities ⊗ ⅲ ⅙ ⴹ ♀ ♨ 𐤟 ℓ Nigel Tokely.
Leisure motorised carts for hire, trolley for hire, driving range, putting green, practice area.
Location N side of village off B3074
Hotel ★★★ 60% King's Head Hotel, The Square, WIMBORNE ☎ 01202 880101 27 ⇥ ↸

CERNE ABBAS   Map 03 ST60

Lyons Gate Lyons Gate Farm, Lyons Gate DT2 7AZ
☎ 01300 345239
Since this course was opened in 1990, it has gained a reputation as 'the toughest 9-hole course in English golf' and the most spcetacular. Up to the time of publication no contender has reached par.
9 holes, 4000yds, Par 30, SSS 30, Course record 32.
Club membership 200.
Visitors no restrictions.
Societies telephone for details.
Green Fees not confirmed.
Facilities ⴹ 𐤠 𐤟
Location On A352, 11m N of Dorchester
Guesthouse QQQ Old Bakehouse Hotel, PIDDLETRENTHIDE ☎ 01300 348305 2 ⇥ Annexe7 ⇥ ↸

CHRISTCHURCH   Map 04 SZ19

Dudmoor Farm Dudmoor Farm Rd BH23 6AQ
☎ 01202 483980
A non-membership golf course with tree-lined par 3 and 4 fairways.
9 holes, 1428mtrs, Par 31.
Visitors no restrictions.
Societies telephone in advance.
Green Fees £4.50 per 18 holes.
Facilities ⴹ ⅄ 𐤟 𐤢
Leisure squash, fishing.
Hotel ★★★ 75% Waterford Lodge Hotel, 87 Bure Ln, Friars Cliff, Mudeford, CHRISTCHURCH ☎ 01425 272948 17 ⇥

Iford Bridge Barrack Rd BH23 2BA ☎ 01202 473817
Parkland course with the River Stour running through. Driving range.
9 holes, 2377yds, Par 34, SSS 32.
Club membership 350.
Visitors no restrictions.
Societies must contact in advance.
Green Fees not confirmed.
Facilities ♀ 𐤠 𐤟 ℓ Peter Troth.
Leisure hard and grass tennis courts, driving range,bowls,trolley hire.
Location W side of town centre on A35
Hotel ★★★ 75% Waterford Lodge Hotel, 87 Bure Ln, Friars Cliff, Mudeford, CHRISTCHURCH ☎ 01425 272948 17 ⇥

DORCHESTER   Map 03 SY69

Came Down Came Down DT2 8NR
☎ 01305 813494 & 812670
Scene of the West of England Championships on several occasions, this fine course lies on a high plateau commanding glorious views over Portland. Three par 5 holes add interest to a round. The turf is of the springy, downland type.
18 holes, 6244yds, Par 70, SSS 71.
Club membership 750.
Visitors advisable to phone in advance, must have handicap certificate. May play after 9am weekdays & after noon Sun.
Societies by arrangement on Wed only.
Green Fees £20 per day (£25 per day weekends & bank holidays).
Facilities ⊗ ⅲ ⅙ ⴹ ♀ ⅄ 𐤠 𐤟 ℓ Robert Preston.
Leisure buggies for hire, trolley for hire, driving range, putting green, practice area.

Location   2m S off A354
Guesthouse QQQQQ Yalbury Cottage Hotel &
            Restaurant, Lower Bockhampton,
            DORCHESTER ☎ 01305 262382 8 ⇋ ⏏

FERNDOWN   Map 04 SU00

Dudsbury Christchurch Rd BH22 8ST
☎ 01202 593499 & 594488 pro shop
Set in 150 acres of beautiful Dorset countryside rolling down
to the River Stour. Wide variety of interesting and
challenging hazards, notably water which comes into play on
14 holes.
*Main Course: 18 holes, 6508yds, Par 71, SSS 71, Course
record 64.*
Academy Course: 5 holes, 680yds, Par 16.
Club membership 650.
Visitors   welcome by arrangement with secretary or golf
            professional.
Societies   telephone in advance.
Green Fees Main: £40 per day; £30 per 18 holes.
Facilities ⊗ ⽊ ⅃ ⿆ ♀ ⅄ 🖻 ⏱ Kevin Spurgeon.
Leisure   fishing, motorised carts for hire, buggies for hire,
            trolley for hire, driving range, putting green,
            practice area.
Location   3m N of Bournemouth on B3073, between
            Parley and Longham
Hotel   ★★★★ 66% The Dormy, New Rd,
            FERNDOWN ☎ 01202 872121 128 ⇋ ⏏

Ferndown 119 Golf Links Rd BH22 8BU
☎ 01202 874602
Fairways are gently undulating amongst heather, gorse
and pine trees giving the course a most attractive
appearance. There are a number of dog-leg holes, and, on
a clear day, there are views across to the Isle of Wight.
*Championship Course: 18 holes, 6452yds, Par 71, SSS
71, Course record 64.*
*Presidents Course: 9 holes, 2797yds, Par 35, SSS 68,
Club membership 700.*
Visitors   must contact in advance & have handicap
            certificate, no visitors on Thursdays except on Presidents
            course, numbers restricted at weekends.
Societies   welcome Tue & Fri only, telephone in
            advance.
Green Fees Championship: £40 (£45 weekends).
            Presidents: £15 (£20 weekends and bank
            holidays).
Facilities ⊗ ⽊ ⅃ ⿆ ♀ ⅄ 🖻 ⏱ Iais Parker.
Leisure   buggies for hire, trolley for hire, putting
            green, practice area.
Location   S side of town centre off A347
Hotel   ★★★★ 66% The Dormy, New Rd,
            FERNDOWN ☎ 01202 872121 128 ⇋ ⏏

HALSTOCK   Map 03 ST50

Halstock Common Ln BA22 9SF ☎ 01935 891689
Halstock is a short tight course, but challenging. There are
plenty of trees and water hazards.
18 holes, 4351yds, Par 65, SSS 63, Course record 65.
Club membership 120.
Visitors   no restrictions.
Societies   telephone in advance.

Green Fees £9.50 per 18 holes; £5.50 per 9 holes (£11.50/£7
            weekends).
Facilities ⅃ ⅄ 🖻 ⏱
Leisure   trolley for hire, driving range, putting green,
            practice area.
Location   6m S of Yeovil
Hotel   ★★★(red)⚘ Summer Lodge, EVERSHOT
            ☎ 01935 83424 11 ⇋ ⏏Annexe6 ⇋ ⏏

HIGHCLIFFE   Map 04 SZ29

Highcliffe Castle 107 Lymington Rd BH23 4LA
☎ 01425 272210
Picturesque parkland course with easy walking.
18 holes, 4762yds, Par 64, SSS 63, Course record 58.
Club membership 500.
Visitors   must have handicap certificate or be a member
            of recognised club.
Societies   write or telephone in advance.
Green Fees not confirmed.
Facilities ♀ ⅄ 🖻 ⏱ ⏱ R E Crockford.
Leisure   putting green,practice area,trolley hire.
Location   SW side of town on A337
Hotel   ★★★ 75% Waterford Lodge Hotel, 87 Bure
            Ln, Friars Cliff, Mudeford, CHRISTCHURCH
            ☎ 01425 272948 17 ⇋

LYME REGIS   Map 03 SY39

Lyme Regis Timber Hill DT7 3HQ ☎ 01297 442963
Undulating cliff-top course with magnificent views of Golden
Cap and Lyme Bay.
18 holes, 6220yds, Par 71, SSS 70, Course record 65.
Club membership 575.
Visitors   must contact in advance & have handicap
            certificate or be a member of recognised golf
            club. No play on Thu & Sun mornings.
Societies   Tue, Wed & Fri; must contact in writing.
Green Fees not confirmed.
Facilities ♀ ⅄ 🖻 ⏱ Andrew Black.
Leisure   trolley hire, putting, practice area.
Location   1.5m N on A3052
Hotel   ★★★ 69% Alexandra Hotel, Pound St, LYME
            REGIS ☎ 01297 442010 27 ⇋ ⏏

LYTCHETT MATRAVERS   Map 03 SY99

Bulbury Woods Halls Rd BH16 6EP ☎ 01929 459574
Parkland course in 40 acres of woodland, with well guarded
greens, tight fairways and extensive views over the Purbecks,
Poole Bay and Wareham Forest. Not too hilly.
18 holes, 6065yds, Par 70, SSS 69, Course record 68.
Club membership 600.
Visitors   must contact in advance.
Societies   must contact in advance.
Green Fees £28 per day; £18 per round.
Facilities ⊗ ⅃ ⅃ ♀ ⅄ 🖻 ◵ ⏱ John Sharkey.
Leisure   buggies for hire, trolley for hire, putting green,
            practice area.
Location   A35 Poole to Dorchester, 1m from Bakers Arms
            roundabout
Hotel   ★★★(red)⚘ Priory Hotel, Church Green,
            WAREHAM
            ☎ 01929 551666 15 ⇋ ⏏Annexe4 ⇋ ⏏

AA 3 star & 80% rating –
2 AA Rosettes

Superb Waterside hotel with
outstanding food. 20 beautifully
furnished bedrooms overlooking Poole
Harbour and Brownsea Island. Many
top national awards presented for
exceptionally high of customer care and
outstanding service.
Only a pitch and a put away (¼ mile)
from Parkstone Golf Club!

**38 Salterns Way, Lilliput,
Poole, Dorset, BH14 8JR
Tel: 01202 707321**

Best
Western

POOLE   Map 04 SZ09

Parkstone Links Rd, Parkstone BH14 9QS
☎ 01202 707138
Very scenic heathland course with views of Poole Bay.
Club founded in 1910.
18 holes, 6250yds, Par 72, SSS 70, Course record 63.
Club membership 700.
Visitors   must contact in advance and have handicap
               certificate.
Societies   apply in writing.
Green Fees £36 per day; £27 per round (£42/£32
               weekends and bank holidays).
Facilities ⊗ ⅊ ≞ ♥ ♀ ♨ ☎ ⎛ Mark Thomas.
Leisure   trolley for hire, putting green, practice area.
Location   E side of town centre off A35
Hotel   ★★★ 80% Salterns Hotel, 38 Salterns
              Way, Lilliput, POOLE
              ☎ 01202 707321 20 ⇄ ⌂

SHERBORNE   Map 03 ST61

Sherborne Higher Clatcombe DT9 4RN
☎ 01935 814431
A sporting course of first-class fairways with far-
reaching views over the lovely Blackmore Vale and the
Vale of Sparkford. Parkland in character, the course has
many well-placed bunkers. The dog-leg 2nd calls for an
accurately placed tee shot, and another testing hole is the
7th, a 194-yard, par 3. There is a practice area.
18 holes, 5882yds, Par 70, SSS 68, Course record 63.
Club membership 900.

Visitors   must contact in advance & have handicap
              certificate.
Societies   prior booking only.
Green Fees £25 per day (£30 weekends and bank
              holidays).
Facilities ⊗ ⅊ ≞ ♥ ♀ ♨ ☎ ⎛ Stewart Wright.
Leisure   trolley for hire, putting green, practice area.
Location   2m N off B3145
Hotel   ★★★ 60% Sherborne Hotel, Horsecastles
              Ln, SHERBORNE
              ☎ 01935 813191 59 ⇄ ⌂

STURMINSTER MARSHALL   Map 03 ST90

Sturminster Marshall Moor Ln BH21 4BD
☎ 01258 858444
Opened in June 1992, this 9-hole is Pay-and-Play. A
membership scheme allows players to gain an official
handicap. Course was designed by John Sharkey.
9 holes, 4650yds, Par 68, SSS 63.
Club membership 350.
Visitors   no restrictions.
Societies   welcome.
Green Fees not confirmed.
Facilities ♨ ☎ ⎛ ⌂ John Sharkey.
Hotel   ★★★ 68% Crown Hotel, 8 West St,
              BLANDFORD FORUM
              ☎ 01258 456626 32 ⇄

SWANAGE   Map 04 SZ07

Isle of Purbeck BH19 3AB ☎ 01929 450361
A heathland course sited on the Purbeck Hills with grand
views across Swanage, the Channel and Poole Harbour.
Holes of note include the 5th, 8th, 14th, 15th, and 16th
where trees, gorse and heather assert themselves. The
very attractive clubhouse is built of the local stone.
Purbeck Course: 18 holes, 6295yds, Par 70, SSS 71.
Dene Course: 9 holes, 4014yds, Par 60.
Club membership 500.
Visitors   advisable to telephone.
Societies   must contact in advance.
Green Fees Purbeck: £32.50 per day; £25 per round
              (£37.50/£30 weekends). Dene: £10 (£12
              weekends).
Facilities ⊗ ⅊ by prior arrangement ≞ ♥ ♀ ♨ ☎
              ⎛ ⌂ Ian Brake.
Leisure   motorised carts for hire, buggies for hire,
              trolley for hire, putting green.
Location   2.5m N on B3351
Hotel   ★★★ 67% The Pines Hotel, Burlington Rd,
              SWANAGE ☎ 01929 425211 51rm(49 ⇄ ⌂)

VERWOOD   Map 04 SU00

Crane Valley BH31 7LE ☎ 01202 814088
Two secluded parkland courses set amid rolling Dorset
countryside and mature woodland - a 9-hole Pay and Play and
an 18-hole Valley course for golfers holding a handicap
certificate.The 6th nestles in the bend of the River Crane and
there are 4 long Par 5's ranging from 499 to 545 yards.
Valley: 18 holes, 6445yds, Par 72, SSS 72, Course record 69.
Woodland: 9 holes, 2090yds, Par 33.
Club membership 650.

EAST DORSET 🦌 GOLF CLUB

Calling Group Golf Organisers.
Recently opened The Dorchester Golf Lodge en-suite accommodation for 32 golfers.
An invitation to stage your Society or Corporate Golf Day at Dorsets golfing gem!
Attractive 18-hole Lakeland course with casual water features and 9-hole Woodland course set amongst trees
and rhododendrons. Floodlit 22-bay driving range. Visitors should contact in advance to book tee time.
For details call: Brian Lee, Telephone: 01929-472244
East Dorset Golf Club, Hyde, Wareham, Dorset BH20 7NT

Visitors	must have handicap certificate for Valley course.
Societies	telephone in advance.
Green Fees	Valley, £20 per round (£30 per round weekends). Woodland, £5.50 per 9 holes (£6.50 weekends).
Facilities	⊗ 🎽 🛍 💺 ♀ ⅋ 🏠 📮 🐎 ⃝ Paul Cannings.
Leisure	motorised carts for hire, buggies for hire, trolley for hire, driving range, putting green, practice area.
Location	6m N of Ferndown on B3081
Hotel	★★★★ 66% The Dormy, New Rd, FERNDOWN ☎ 01202 872121 128 ⇄ 📵

WAREHAM   Map 03 SY98

East Dorset Bere Regis BH20 7NT
☎ 01929 472244
Long 18-hole parkland course with natural water features. A second 9-hole, 18-tee course is set amongst trees and rhododendrons. Floodlit 22-bay driving range, club fitting centre, indoor putting area and extensive golf shop.
Lakeland Course: 18 holes, 6580yds, Par 72, SSS 73, Course record 68.
Woodland Course: 9 holes, 4887yards, Par 66, SSS 64.
Club membership 650.

Visitors	must contact in advance and handicap certificate required for Lakeland course.
Societies	apply in advance.
Green Fees	Lakeland: £28 per day; £23 per round (£33/£28 weekends). Woodland: £19 per day; £16 per round (£23/£20 weekends).
Facilities	⊗ 🎽 🛍 💺 ♀ ⅋ 🏠 📮 🐎 ⃝ Derwynne Honan.
Leisure	motorised carts for hire, buggies for hire, trolley for hire, covered and floodlit driving range, putting green, practice area.
Location	5m NW on unclass Puddletown Rd,off A352
Hotel	★★ 65% Kemps Country House Hotel, East Stoke, WAREHAM ☎ 01929 462563 5rm(4 ⇄ 📵)Annexe10 ⇄ 📵

Wareham Sandford Rd BH20 4DH
☎ 01929 554147 & 554156
Heathland/parkland course. The club was founded in 1926.
18 holes, 5603yds, Par 69, SSS 67, Course record 66.
Club membership 500.

Visitors	must contact the club in advance. Must be accompanied by a member at weekends & bank holidays.
Societies	must contact in advance.

Green Fees	£20 per day; £15 per round.
Facilities	⊗ 🛍 💺 ♀ ⅋
Leisure	trolley for hire, putting green, practice area.
Location	Adjacent to A351, nr Wareham railway station
Hotel	★★★ 71% Springfield Country Hotel & Leisure Club, Grange Rd, WAREHAM ☎ 01929 552177 32 ⇄ 📵

WEYMOUTH   Map 03 SY67

Weymouth Links Rd DT4 0PF
☎ 01305 773981 (Secretary) & 773997 (Pro)
Seaside parkland course. The 5th is played off an elevated green over copse.
18 holes, 5976yds, Par 70, SSS 69, Course record 63.
Club membership 750.

Visitors	must contact in advance.
Societies	Tue & Thu, apply in writing.
Green Fees	£25 per day; £20 per round (£30/£26 weekends).
Facilities	⊗ 🎽 🛍 💺 ♀ ⅋ 🏠 ⃝ Des Lochrie.
Leisure	putting green, practice area.
Location	N side of town centre off B3157
Hotel	★★ 66% Hotel Rex, 29 The Esplanade, WEYMOUTH ☎ 01305 760400 31 ⇄ 📵

CO DURHAM

BARNARD CASTLE   Map 12 NZ01

Barnard Castle Marwood DL12 8QN
☎ 01833 638355 & 631980
Perched high on the steep bank of the River Tees, the extensive remains of Barnard Castle with its splendid round tower dates back to the 12th and 13th centuries, when this was the main fortress of the Baliol family.
18 holes, 6406yds, Par 73, SSS 71.
Club membership 630.

Visitors	must contact in advance.
Societies	apply in writing.
Green Fees	£18 per day; £15 per round (£24 weekends).
Facilities	⊗ 🎽 🛍 💺 ♀ ⅋ 🏠 📮 ⃝ Darren Pearce.
Leisure	trolley for hire, putting green, practice area.
Location	1m N of town centre on B6278
Hotel	★★ 73% Rose & Crown Hotel, ROMALDKIRK ☎ 01833 650213 7 ⇄ 📵Annexe5 ⇄ 📵

BEAMISH

Map 12 NZ25

Beamish Park DH9 0RH ☎ 0191 370 1382
Parkland course. Designed by Henry Cotton and W Woodend.
18 holes, 6204yds, Par 71, SSS 70, Course record 64.
Club membership 630.
Visitors | must contact in advance and may not play weekends.
Societies | telephone in advance.
Green Fees | £20 per day; £16 per round.
Facilities | ⊗ ⦀ ⓑ ♥ ♀ ⚎ ⚑ ♈ ⟊ Chris Cole.
Leisure | trolley for hire, putting green, practice area.
Location | 1m NW off A693
Hotel | ★★★ 66% Beamish Park Hotel, Beamish Burn Rd, MARLEY HILL ☎ 01207 230666 47 ⇄ ℟

BILLINGHAM

Map 08 NZ42

Billingham Sandy Ln TS22 5NA
☎ 01642 533816 & 554494
Parkland course on edge of urban-rural district, with hard walking and water hazards; testing 15th hole.
18 holes, 6460yds, Par 73, SSS 71, Course record 63.
Club membership 1050.
Visitors | contact professional in advance.
Societies | apply in writing to Secretary/Manager.
Green Fees | £20 per day (£33 weekends).
Facilities | ⊗ ⦀ ⓑ ♥ ♀ ⚎ ⚑ ♈ ⟊ Michael Ure.
Leisure | trolley for hire, putting green, practice area.
Location | 1m W of town centre E of A19
Hotel | ★★★ 59% Billingham Arms Hotel, The Causeway, Billingham, STOCKTON-ON-TEES ☎ 01642 553661 & 360880 69 ⇄ ℟

BISHOP AUCKLAND

Map 08 NZ22

Bishop Auckland High Plains, Durham Rd DL14 8DL
☎ 01388 602198 & 663648
A rather hilly parkland course with many well-established trees offering a challenging round. A small ravine adds interest to several holes including the short 7th, from a raised tee to a green surrounded by a stream, gorse and bushes. Pleasant views down the Wear Valley.
18 holes, 6420yds, Par 72, SSS 71, Course record 64.
Club membership 950.
Visitors | must contact in advance. Handicap certificate advisable. Dress rules apply.
Societies | weekdays only; must contact in advance.
Green Fees | £24 per day; £20 per round (£26 per round weekends).
Facilities | ⊗ ⦀ ⓑ ♥ ♀ ⚎ ⚑ ⟊ David Skiffington.
Leisure | trolley for hire, driving range, putting green, practice area, snooker.
Location | 1m NE on A689
Hotel | ★★★ 64% Park Head Hotel, New Coundon, BISHOP AUCKLAND ☎ 01388 661727 8 ⇄ ℟Annexe7 ⇄

BURNOPFIELD

Map 12 NZ15

Hobson Municipal Hobson NE16 6BZ ☎ 01207 271605
Meadowland course opened in 1981.
18 holes, 6403yds, Par 69, SSS 68.
Club membership 700.
Visitors | no restrictions.
Societies | must contact in advance.
Green Fees | £9 per round (£12 weekends & bank holidays).
Facilities | ⊗ ⦀ ⓑ ♥ ♀ ⚎ ⚑ ♈ ⟊ Jack Ord.
Leisure | trolley for hire, putting green, practice area.
Location | 0.75m S on A692
Hotel | ★★★ 66% Swallow Hotel, High West St, GATESHEAD ☎ 0191 477 1105 103 ⇄ ℟

CHESTER-LE-STREET

Map 12 NZ25

Chester-le-Street Lumley Park DH3 4NS
☎ 0191 388 3218 (Secretary) & 389 0157 (Pro)
Parkland course in castle grounds, good views, easy walking.
18 holes, 6437yds, Par 71, SSS 71, Course record 71.
Club membership 650.
Visitors | must contact in advance and have an introduction from own club or handicap certificate.
Societies | must apply in writing.
Green Fees | £20 per day/round (£25 weekends & bank holidays).
Facilities | ⊗ ⦀ ⓑ ♥ ♀ ⚎ ⚑ ♈ ⟊ David Fletcher.
Leisure | motorised carts for hire, trolley for hire, putting green, practice area.
Location | 0.5m E off B1284
Hotel | ★★★ 72% Ramside Hall Hotel, Carrville, DURHAM ☎ 0191 386 5282 82 ⇄ ℟

Roseberry Grange Grange Villa DH2 3NF
☎ 0191 370 0670 & 370 0660
Testing holes on this parkland course include the uphill par 3 12th (147yds) and the par 4 8th (438yds) with a ditch crossing the fairway.
18 holes, 5628yds, Par 70, SSS 67.
Club membership 550.
Visitors | after 11.30am summer weekends, pay and play Mon-Fri.
Societies | booking form available on request.
Green Fees | £14 per day; £10 per round.
Facilities | ⊗ ⦀ ⓑ ♥ ♀ ⚎ ⚑ ♈ ⟊ Alan Hartley.
Leisure | trolley for hire, driving range, putting green.
Hotel | ★★★ 67% Washington Moat House, Stone Cellar Rd, District 12, High Usworth, WASHINGTON ☎ 0191 402 9988 105 ⇄ ℟

CONSETT

Map 12 NZ15

Consett & District Elmfield Rd DH8 5NN
☎ 01207 502186
Undulating parkland/moorland course with views across the Derwent Valley to the Cheviot Hills.
18 holes, 6013yds, Par 71, SSS 69.
Club membership 900.
Visitors | advised to contact in advance.
Societies | apply in writing.
Green Fees | £15 per day (£22 weekends & bank holidays).
Facilities | ⊗ ⦀ ⓑ ♥ ♀ ⚎ ⚑ ⟊ Craig Dilley.
Leisure | putting green, practice area.

Location	N side of town on A691
Hotel	★★★ 67% The Raven Hotel, Broomhill, EBCHESTER ☎ 01207 560367 28 ⇆ ༓

CROOK — Map 12 NZ13

Crook Low Jobs Hill DL15 9AA ☎ 01388 762429
Meadowland/parkland course in elevated position with natural hazards, varied holes and terrain. Panoramic views over Durham and Cleveland Hills.
18 holes, 6102yds, Par 70, SSS 69, Course record 64.
Club membership 660.

Visitors	must contact Secretary for weekend play, limited availability.
Societies	apply in writing to Secretary.
Green Fees	£12 per day (£20 weekends).
Facilities	⊗ ⅲ ⅃ ⚑ ♀ ⚘
Leisure	putting green, practice area.
Location	0.5m E off A690
Hotel	★★ 65% Kensington Hall Hotel, Kensington Ter, WILLINGTON ☎ 01388 745071 10 ⇆ ༓

DARLINGTON — Map 08 NZ21

Blackwell Grange Briar Close, Blackwell DL3 8QX
☎ 01325 464458
Pleasant parkland course with good views, easy walking.
18 holes, 5621yds, Par 68, SSS 67, Course record 63.
Club membership 700.

Visitors	restricted Wed & weekends.
Societies	welcome weekdays except Wed (Ladies Day).
Green Fees	£22 per day; £16 per round (£20 per round weekends & bank holidays).
Facilities	⊗ ⅲ ⅃ ⚑ ♀ ⚘ ⚒ ℓ Ralph Givens.
Leisure	trolley for hire, putting green.
Location	1m SW off A66, turn into Blackwell, signposted
Hotel	★★★ 68% Swallow King's Head Hotel, Priestgate, DARLINGTON ☎ 01325 380222 85 ⇆ ༓

Darlington Haughton Grange DL1 3JD ☎ 01325 355324
Fairly flat parkland course with tree-lined fairways, and large first-class greens. Championship standard.
18 holes, 6271yds, Par 71, SSS 70, Course record 64.
Club membership 850.

Visitors	may not play weekends unless accompanied by member.
Societies	by prior arrangement with the Secretary but not at weekends.
Green Fees	£22 per day weekdays.
Facilities	⊗ ⅲ ⅃ ⚑ ♀ ⚘ ⚒ ℓ Mark Rogers.
Leisure	motorised carts for hire, buggies for hire, trolley for hire, putting green, practice area.
Location	N side of town centre off A1150
Hotel	★★★★♨ 68% Headlam Hall Hotel, Headlam, Gainford, DARLINGTON ☎ 01325 730238 17 ⇆ ༓Annexe9 ⇆ ༓

Hall Garth Golf & Country Club Hotel Coatham Mundeville DL1 3LU ☎ 01325 300400
A 6900yard course with mature trees and Victorian deer folly. Three greens have been newly laid. The challenging 165 yard Par 3 3rd requires teeing over water, whilst the 500 yard Par 5 6th hole features the picturesque River Swale running alongside the fairway and the green.

9 holes, 6621yds, Par 72, SSS 72.

Visitors	advisable to book at least 1 week in advance.
Societies	prior booking by telephone.
Green Fees	£15 per day all week; £10 per 18 holes (£12.50 weekends).
Facilities	⊗ ⅲ ⅃ ⚑ ♀ ⚘ ⚒ ⚐ ⚙
Leisure	grass tennis courts, heated indoor swimming pool, sauna, solarium, gymnasium, putting green, practice area.
Location	0.5m from A1(M) off A167
Hotel	★★★ 70% Hall Garth Golf and Country Club Hotel, Coatham Mundeville, DARLINGTON ☎ 01325 300400 38 ⇆ ༓Annexe4 ⇆ ༓

Stressholme Snipe Ln DL2 2SA
☎ 01325 461002
Picturesque municipal parkland course, long but wide, with 98 bunkers and a par 3 hole played over a river.
18 holes, 6511yds, Par 71, SSS 71.
Club membership 650.

Visitors	must contact in advance.
Societies	apply to the steward or professional.
Green Fees	not confirmed.
Facilities	♀ ⚘ ⚒ ⚐ ℓ Tim Jenkins.
Location	SW side of town centre on A67
Hotel	★★★ 68% Swallow King's Head Hotel, Priestgate, DARLINGTON ☎ 01325 380222 85 ⇆ ༓

DURHAM — Map 12 NZ24

Brancepeth Castle Brancepeth Village DH7 8EA
☎ 0191 378 0075
Parkland course overlooked at the 9th hole by beautiful Brancepeth Castle.
18 holes, 6300yds, Par 70, SSS 70, Course record 64.
Club membership 780.

Visitors	may be restrictions at weekends for parties.
Societies	must contact in advance.
Green Fees	not confirmed.
Facilities	♀ ⚘ ⚒ ⚐ ℓ David Howdon.
Leisure	putting green,practice area,trolley hire.
Location	4.5m SW on A690
Hotel	★★★★ 70% Royal County Hotel, Old Elvet, DURHAM ☎ 0191 386 6821 150 ⇆ ༓

Durham City Littleburn, Langley Moor DH7 8HL
☎ 0191 378 0806 & 378 0029
Undulating parkland course bordered on several holes by the River Browney.
18 holes, 6321yds, Par 71, SSS 70.
Club membership 750.

Visitors	restricted on competition days.
Societies	apply in writing or telephone the club professional.
Green Fees	£20 per day (£30 weekends & bank holidays).
Facilities	⊗ ⅲ ⅃ ⚑ ♀ ⚘ ⚒ ℓ Steve Corbally.
Leisure	trolley for hire, putting green, practice area.
Location	2m W of Durham City, turn left off A690into Littleburn Ind Est
Hotel	★★★ 70% Three Tuns Hotel, New Elvet, DURHAM ☎ 0191 386 4326 47 ⇆ ༓

R·A·M·S·I·D·E
H·A·L·L H·O·T·E·L

THE NORTH EAST'S PREMIER PRIVATELY OWNED HOTEL
• WITH GOLF •

This marvellous 80-bedroomed hotel renowned for its popular bars and good food is now surrounded by 27 holes of golf with range and practice area.

For details of the North East's best kept secret, contact:

Ramside Hall Hotel,
Carrville Durham DH1 1TD

Phone: 0191-386 5282 Fax: 0191-386 0399

Mount Oswald South Rd DH1 3TQ ☎ 0191 386 7527
Flat, wooded parkland course with a Georgian clubhouse and good views of Durham cathedral on the back nine.
18 holes, 6101yds, Par 71, SSS 69.
Club membership 120.

Visitors	must contact in advance for weekends but may not play before 10am on Sun.
Societies	must contact in advance.
Green Fees	£10 per round (£12 weekends & bank holidays).
Facilities	⊗ ⴼ ⵌ ⵯ ⵯ ⵗ ⵗ ⵞ
Leisure	trolley for hire, putting green, practice area.
Location	On A181
Hotel	★★ 65% Bridge Toby Hotel, Croxdale, DURHAM ☎ 0191 378 0524 46 ⊶ ⵝ

Ramside Hall Carrville DH1 1TD ☎ 0191 386 9514
Three recently constructed 9-hole parkland courses - Princes, Bishops, Cathedral - with 14 lakes and panoramic views surrounding an impressive hotel. Excellent golf academy and driving range.
Princes: 9 holes, 3235yds, Par 36, SSS 36.
Bishops: 9 holes, 3285yds, Par 36, SSS 36.
Cathedral: 9 holes, 2874yds, Par 34, SSS 34.
Club membership 400.

Visitors	open at all times subject to tee availability.
Societies	telephone in advance.
Green Fees	£30 per day; £25 per 18 holes; £13.50 per 9 holes (£37.50/£30/£16 weekends & bank holidays).
Facilities	⊗ ⴼ ⵌ ⵯ ⵯ ⵗ ⵗ ⵯ ⵞ
Leisure	motorised carts for hire, buggies for hire, trolley for hire, driving range, putting green, practice area.

Location	500m from A1/A690 interchange
Hotel	★★★ 72% Ramside Hall Hotel, Carrville, DURHAM ☎ 0191 386 5282 82 ⊶ ⵝ

EAGLESCLIFFE   Map 08 NZ41

Eaglescliffe and District Yarm Rd TS16 0DQ
☎ 01642 780098 & 790122
This hilly course offers both pleasant and interesting golf to all classes of player. It lies in a delightful setting on a rolling plateau, shelving to the River Tees. There are fine views to the Cleveland Hills.
18 holes, 6275yds, Par 72, SSS 70, Course record 60.
Club membership 550.

Visitors	restricted Tue, Thu, Fri & weekends.
Societies	must contact in advance, apply to secretary on 01642 780238
Green Fees	£24 per day (£30 weekends & bank holidays).
Facilities	⊗ ⴼ ⵌ ⵯ ⵯ ⵗ ⵗ ⵞ Paul Bradley.
Leisure	trolley for hire, putting green, practice area.
Location	E side of village off A135
Hotel	★★★★ 63% Swallow Hotel, John Walker Square, STOCKTON-ON-TEES ☎ 01642 679721 125 ⊶ ⵝ

HARTLEPOOL   Map 08 NZ53

Castle Eden & Peterlee Castle Eden TS27 4SS
☎ 01429 836510
Beautiful parkland course alongside a nature reserve. Hard walking but trees provide wind shelter.

18 holes, 6262yds, Par 70, SSS 69.
Club membership 750.
Visitors with member only during 12-1.30pm & 4-6.30pm. Must contact in advance.
Societies must contact in advance tel: 01429 836689.
Green Fees not confirmed.
Facilities ♀ ᕕ 🏠 ⚐ (Graham J Laidlaw.
Leisure putting,practice,cart/buggy/trolley hire.
Location 2m S of Peterlee on B1281 off A19
Hotel ★★ 69% Hardwicke Hall Manor Hotel, HESLEDEN ☎ 01429 836326 11 ⇔ ⋒

Hartlepool Hart Warren TS24 9QF ☎ 01429 274398
A seaside course, half links, overlooking the North Sea. A good test and equally enjoyable to all handicap players. The 10th, par 4, demands a precise second shot over a ridge and between sand dunes to a green down near the edge of the beach, alongside which several holes are played.
18 holes, 6215yds, Par 70, SSS 70, Course record 64.
Club membership 700.
Visitors with member only on Sun.
Societies must apply in writing in advance.
Green Fees £20 per day (£30 weekends and bank holidays).
Facilities ⊗ ⫼ ᕒ ⚑ ♀ ᕕ 🏠 ⚐ (Malcolm E Cole.
Leisure trolley for hire, putting green, practice area.
Location N of Hartlepool, off A1086
Hotel ★★ 68% Ryedale Moor, 3 Beaconsfield St, Headland, HARTLEPOOL ☎ 01429 231436 14 ⇔ ⋒

MIDDLETON ST GEORGE Map 08 NZ31

Dinsdale Spa Neasham Rd DL2 1DW
☎ 01325 332297
A mainly flat, parkland course on high land above the River Tees with views of the Cleveland Hills. Water hazards front the 8th, 9th and 18th tees and the prevailing west wind affects the later holes. There is a practice area by the clubhouse.
18 holes, 6090yds, Par 71, SSS 69, Course record 65.
Club membership 850.
Visitors contact for further details.
Societies bookings through office, no weekends or Tue.
Green Fees not confirmed.
Facilities ⊗ ⫼ ᕒ ⚑ ♀ ᕕ 🏠 ⚐ (Craig Imlah.
Leisure motorised carts for hire, trolley for hire, putting green, practice area.
Location 1.5m SW
Hotel ★★★ 64% St George, Middleton St George, TEES-SIDE AIRPORT ☎ 01325 332631 59 ⇔ ⋒

NEWTON AYCLIFFE Map 08 NZ22

Aycliffe School Aycliffe Ln DL5 4EF
☎ 01325 312994
A parkland course in a country setting.
18 holes, 5430yds, Par 68, SSS 66, Course record 63.
Club membership 100.
Visitors must contact in advance (01325 310820).
Societies apply in writing.
Green Fees not confirmed.

Facilities ♀ ᕕ 🏠 ⚐ (Clive Burgess.
Leisure squash, cart/buggy/trolley hire,driving range.
Location 6m N of Darlington, off A6072
Hotel ★★★★ 72% Redworth Hall Hotel & Country Club, REDWORTH ☎ 01388 772442 100 ⇔ ⋒

SEAHAM Map 12 NZ44

Seaham Dawdon SR7 7RD
☎ 0191 581 2354 & 581 1268
Heathland links course with several holes affected by strong prevailing winds.
18 holes, 6017yds, Par 70, SSS 69, Course record 64.
Club membership 600.
Visitors with member only weekends until 3.30pm.
Societies must apply in advance.
Green Fees £11 (£15 weekends).
Facilities ⊗ by prior arrangement ⫼ by prior arrangement ᕒ by prior arrangement ⚑ ♀ ᕕ 🏠 ⚐ (Glyn Jones.
Leisure trolley for hire, putting green, practice area.
Location 3m E of A19, exit for Seaham
Hotel ★★★★ 60% Swallow Hotel, Queen's Pde, Seaburn, SUNDERLAND ☎ 0191 529 2041 65 ⇔ ⋒

SEATON CAREW Map 08 NZ52

Seaton Carew Tees Rd TS25 1DE
☎ 01429 261040 & 266249
A championship links course taking full advantage of its dunes, bents, whins and gorse. Renowned for its par 4 (17th); just enough fairway for an accurate drive followed by another precise shot to a pear-shaped, sloping green that is severely trapped.
The Old Course: 18 holes, 6604yds, Par 72, SSS 72.
Brabazon Course: 18 holes, 6849yds, Par 73, SSS 73.
Club membership 650.
Visitors restricted until after 10am at weekends & bank holidays.
Societies must apply in writing.
Green Fees not confirmed.
Facilities ♀ ᕕ 🏠 (W Hector.
Leisure putting green,cart/trolley hire.
Location SE side of village off A178
Hotel ★★ 68% Ryedale Moor, 3 Beaconsfield St, Headland, HARTLEPOOL ☎ 01429 231436 14 ⇔ ⋒

SEDGEFIELD Map 08 NZ32

Knotty Hill Golf Centre TS21 2BB ☎ 01740 620320
The 18-hole Princes course is rolling parkland with many holes routed through shallow valleys. Several holes are set wholly or partially within woodland. Water hazards abound. Bishops, a new 18-hole course was due to be completed in 1996.
Princes Course: 18 holes, 6517yds, Par 72, SSS 71.
Visitors no restrictions.
Societies package available on request.
Green Fees £12 per 18 holes; £7 per 9 holes.
Facilities ⊗ ⫼ ᕒ ⚑ ♀ ᕕ 🏠 ⚐ (Nick Todd.
Leisure motorised carts for hire, buggies for hire, trolley for hire, floodlit driving range, putting green, practice area. ▶

Location 1m N of Sedgefield on A177
Hotel ★★★ 64% Hardwick Hall Hotel,
SEDGEFIELD ☎ 01740 20253 17 ➡ ♠

ESSEX

STANLEY
Map 12 NZ15

South Moor The Middles, Craghead DH9 6AG
☎ 01207 232848
Moorland course with natural hazards designed by Dr Alistair McKenzie in 1926 and remains on of the most challenging of its type in north east England. Out of bounds features on 11 holes from the tee and the testing par 5 12th hole is uphill and usually against a strong headwind.
18 holes, 6445yds, Par 72, SSS 71, Course record 66.
Club membership 650.
Visitors must contact in advance but may only play Sun with member.
Societies apply in writing to Secretary.
Green Fees £21 per day; £14 per round (£25 per day/round weekends & bank holidays). Reduced winter fees end Oct-Mar.
Facilities ⊗ ⊞ ⓑ ♥ ♀ ♨ 🏌 Shaun Cowell.
Leisure buggies for hire, trolley for hire, putting green, practice area, snooker.
Location 1.5m SE on B6313
Hotel ★★★ 66% Beamish Park Hotel, Beamish Burn Rd, MARLEY HILL
☎ 01207 230666 47 ➡ ♠

STOCKTON-ON-TEES
Map 08 NZ41

Norton Norton TS20 1SU ☎ 01642 676385
An interesting parkland course with long drives from the 7th and 17th tees. Several water hazards.
18 holes, 5855yds, Par 70.
Visitors no restrictions.
Societies apply in advance.
Green Fees £13 per 27 holes; £8.50 per 18 holes (£15/£9 weekends).
Facilities ⊗ ⊞ ⓑ ♥ ♀ ♨ 🏌 Terry Myles.
Leisure trolley for hire, putting green, practice area.
Location At Norton 2m N off A19
Hotel ★★★ 59% Billingham Arms Hotel, The Causeway, Billingham, STOCKTON-ON-TEES
☎ 01642 553661 & 360880 69 ➡ ♠

Teesside Acklam Rd, Thornaby TS17 7JS
☎ 01642 676249
Flat parkland course, easy walking.
18 holes, 6472yds, Par 72, SSS 71.
Club membership 600.
Visitors with member only weekdays after 4.30pm, weekends after 11am.
Societies must contact in writing.
Green Fees not confirmed.
Facilities ♀ ♨ 🏌
Location 1.5m SE on A1130
Hotel B Forte Posthouse Teeside, Low Ln, Stainton Village, Thornaby, STOCKTON-ON-TEES
☎ 01642 591213 135 ➡ ♠

> Entries with a shaded background identify courses that are considered to be particularly interesting

ABRIDGE
Map 05 TQ49

Abridge Golf and Country Club Epping Ln, Stapleford Tawney RM4 1ST ☎ 01708 688396
A parkland course with easy walking. The quick drying course is by no means easy to play. This has been the venue of several professional tournaments. Abridge is a Golf and Country Club and has all the attendant facilities.
18 holes, 6692yds, Par 72, SSS 72, Course record 67.
Club membership 600.
Visitors must have current handicap certificate, contact in advance. Play with member only at weekends.
Societies telephone in advance.
Green Fees £30 per day/round.
Facilities ⊗ ⊞ ⓑ ♥ ♀ ♨ 🏌 Mike Herbert.
Leisure heated outdoor swimming pool, sauna, motorised carts for hire, buggies for hire, trolley for hire, driving range, putting green, practice area.
Location 1.75m NE
Hotel B Forte Posthouse Epping, High Rd, Bell Common, EPPING
☎ 01992 573137 Annexe79 ➡ ♠

BASILDON
Map 05 TQ78

Basildon Clay Hill Ln, Kingswood SS16 5JP
☎ 01268 533297
Undulating municipal parkland course. Testing 13th hole (par 4).
18 holes, 6153yds, Par 71, SSS 69, Course record 64.
Club membership 300.
Visitors contact professional in advance 01268 533532.
Societies may contact for details.
Green Fees £8.70 (£14.50 weekends).
Facilities ⊗ ⊞ ⓑ ♥ ♀ ♨ 🏌 W Paterson.
Location 1m S off A176
Hotel B Forte Posthouse Basildon, Cranes Farm Rd, BASILDON ☎ 01268 533955 110 ➡ ♠

Pipps Hill Country Club Cranes Farm Rd SS14 3DG
☎ 01268 523456
Flat course with ditches and pond.
9 holes, 2829yds, Par 34, SSS 34.
Club membership 400.
Visitors no restrictions.
Societies must contact in advance.
Green Fees not confirmed.
Facilities ♀ ♨
Location N side of town centre off A127
Hotel B Forte Posthouse Basildon, Cranes Farm Rd, BASILDON ☎ 01268 533955 110 ➡ ♠

BENFLEET
Map 05 TQ78

Boyce Hill Vicarage Hill, South Benfleet SS7 1PD
☎ 01268 793625 & 752565
Hilly parkland course with good views.
18 holes, 5956yds, Par 68, SSS 68, Course record 61.
Club membership 700.

Visitors	must have a handicap certificate, must contact 24hrs in advance, may not play at weekends.
Societies	Thu only, book well in advance by telephone.
Green Fees	£25 per day/round.
Facilities	⊗ ⅺ ╚ ■ ♀ ᕫ 🖆 (Graham Burroughs.
Leisure	motorised carts for hire, trolley for hire, putting green.
Location	0.75m NE of Benfleet Station
Hotel	B Forte Posthouse Basildon, Cranes Farm Rd, BASILDON ☎ 01268 533955 110 ⇌ ⋔

BILLERICAY   Map 05 TQ69

The Burstead Tythe Common Rd, Little Burstead
CM12 9SS ☎ 01277 631171
The Burstead is an attractive parkland course set amidst some
of the most attractive countryside in south Essex. It is an
excellent test of golf to players of all standards with the
greens showing maturity beyond their years. Challenging
holes include the Par 4 13th hole which at 342yds requires an
accurate tea shot to leave a second shot played over a lake
protecting an attractive contoured green. The 9th is the
longest hole on the course.
18 holes, 6177yds, Par 71, SSS 69, Course record 67.
Club membership 900.

Visitors	must have handicap certificate and may only play weekdays.
Societies	apply in writing or telephone for reservation.
Green Fees	£18 per 18 holes; £9 per 9 holes.
Facilities	⊗ ⅺ ╚ ■ ♀ ᕫ 🖆 ✝ (Keith Bridges.
Leisure	motorised carts for hire, buggies for hire, trolley for hire, putting green, practice area.
Hotel	★★★ 66% Chichester Hotel, Old London Rd, Wickford, BASILDON ☎ 01268 560555 2 ⇌ ⋔Annexe32 ⇌ ⋔

Stock Brook Manor Golf & Country Club Queens Park
Av, Stock CM12 0SP ☎ 01277 653616
Three gently undulating 9-hole parkland courses offering the
challenge of water on a large number of holes. Any
combination can be played, but the Stock and Brook courses
make the 18-hole championship course. Manor Course is the
easier 9 holes.
Stock & Brook Courses: 18 holes, 6728yds, Par 72, SSS 72,
Course record 66.
Manor Course: 9 holes, 2997yds, Par 35.
Club membership 750.

Visitors	must contact 24hrs in advance.
Societies	apply in writing or telephone.
Green Fees	£25 per day (£30 per round weekends).
Facilities	⊗ ⅺ ╚ ■ ♀ ᕫ 🖆 ✝ (Kevin Merry.
Leisure	sauna, trolley for hire, driving range, putting green, practice area.
Hotel	★★★ 64% The Heybridge Hotel, Roman Rd, INGATESTONE ☎ 01277 355355 22 ⇌ ⋔

BRAINTREE   Map 05 TL72

Braintree Kings Ln, Stisted CM7 8DA
☎ 01376 346079
Parkland course with many unique mature trees. Good par 3s
with the 14th -'Devils Lair'-regarded as one of the best in the
county.
18 holes, 6199yds, Par 70, SSS 69, Course record 65.
Club membership 850.

Visitors	weekdays only, contact the pro shop in advance 01376 343465.
Societies	society days Wed & Thu early booking advised.
Green Fees	£25 per day; £18 per round.
Facilities	⊗ ⅺ ╚ ■ ♀ ᕫ 🖆 (Tony Parcell.
Leisure	trolley for hire, putting green, practice area.
Location	1m E, off A120
Hotel	★★★ 61% White Hart Hotel, Bocking End, BRAINTREE ☎ 01376 321401 31 ⇌ ⋔

Towerlands Panfield Rd CM7 5BJ ☎ 01376 326802
Undulating, grassland course. Driving range and sports hall.
9 holes, 2703yds, Par 34, SSS 66.
Club membership 300.

Visitors	must not play before 12.30pm weekends. Correct dress at all times.
Societies	must contact in advance by telephone.
Green Fees	18 holes £12.50; 9 holes £9 (18 holes weekends & bank holidays £15).
Facilities	⊗ ⅺ ╚ ■ ♀ ᕫ 🖆 ✝
Leisure	trolley for hire, driving range, putting green, practice area, sportshall, indoor bowls.
Location	On B1053
Hotel	★★★ 61% White Hart Hotel, Bocking End, BRAINTREE ☎ 01376 321401 31 ⇌ ⋔

BRENTWOOD   Map 05 TQ59

Bentley Ongar Rd CM15 9SS ☎ 01277 373179
Parkland course with water hazards.
18 holes, 6709yds, Par 72, SSS 72.
Club membership 600.

Visitors	should contact in advance, may not play at weekends.
Societies	must write or telephone in advance.
Green Fees	£27 per 27-36 holes; £21 per round.
Facilities	⊗ ⅺ by prior arrangement ╚ ■ ♀ ᕫ 🖆 (Nick Garrett.
Leisure	trolley for hire, putting, practice area.
Location	3m NW on A128
Hotel	B Forte Posthouse Brentwood, Brook St, BRENTWOOD ☎ 01277 260260 111 ⇌

Hartswood King George's Playing Fields, Ingrave Rd CM14
5AE ☎ 01277 218850 & 214830
Municipal parkland course, easy walking.
18 holes, 6160yds, Par 70, SSS 69.
Club membership 500.

Visitors	pre-booking usually essential am.
Societies	must contact in advance.
Green Fees	not confirmed.
Facilities	♀ ᕫ 🖆 ✝ (
Leisure	putting green,trolley hire.
Location	0.75m SE on A128
Hotel	B Forte Posthouse Brentwood, Brook St, BRENTWOOD ☎ 01277 260260 111 ⇌

Warley Park Magpie Ln, Little Warley CM13 3DX
☎ 01277 224891
Parkland course with reasonable walking. Numerous water
hazards. There is also a golf-practice ground.
1st & 2nd: 18 holes, 5967yds, Par 69, SSS 68, Course record 68.
1st & 3rd: 18 holes, 6232yds, Par 71, SSS 69, Course record 67.
2nd & 3rd: 18 holes, 6223yds, Par 70, SSS 69, Course record 70.
Club membership 800. ▶

Visitors	must have handicap certificate and contact in advance. May not play at weekends.
Societies	telephone in advance for provisional booking.
Green Fees	£36 per day; £24 per 18 holes.
Facilities	⊗ ⋔ ℔ 🍺 ♀ ♣ 🖼 ℓ Jason Groat.
Leisure	motorised carts for hire, buggies for hire, trolley for hire, driving range, putting green, practice area.
Location	2.5m S off B186
Hotel	B Forte Posthouse Brentwood, Brook St, BRENTWOOD ☎ 01277 260260 111 ⊷

BULPHAN   Map 05 TQ68

Langdon Hills Hotel & Golf Complex Lower Dunton Rd RM14 3TY ☎ 01268 548444
The complex is the base of the European School of Golf. The 18-hole course is of championship standard and there is also a 9-hole public course. Practice facilities include a 22-bay covered floodlit driving range, short game practice area with greens and bunkers and three-hole practice course.
Langdon Course: 18 holes, 6485yds, Par 72.
Horndon Course: 9 holes, 2941yds, Par 36.
Club membership 620.

Visitors	may not play at weekends before 1pm in summer before noon in winter.
Societies	apply in writing or telephone.
Green Fees	Langdon £17.80 per day; £10.80 per round (£15.80 per round weekends). Horndon £5.90 per 18 holes (£7.50 weekends).
Facilities	⊗ ⋔ ℔ 🍺 ♀ ♣ 🖼 ⚑ 🛏 ℓ Andrew Lavers.
Leisure	motorised carts for hire, buggies for hire, trolley for hire, driving range, putting green, practice area.
Hotel	★★★★ 68% Marygreen Manor, London Rd, BRENTWOOD ☎ 01277 225252 3 ⊷ ⋔Annexe30 ⊷ ⋔

BURNHAM-ON-CROUCH   Map 05 TQ99

Burnham-on-Crouch Ferry Rd, Creeksea CM0 8PQ ☎ 01621 782282 & 785508
Undulating meadowland course, easy walking, windy.
18 holes, 6056yds, Par 70, SSS 69, Course record 66.
Club membership 534.

Visitors	must contact in advance, may not play weekends.
Societies	apply in writing.
Green Fees	£22 per day (weekdays only).
Facilities	⊗ ⋔ ℔ 🍺 ♀ ♣ 🖼
Leisure	motorised carts for hire, practice area.
Location	1.25m W off B1010
Hotel	★★ 64% Blue Boar Hotel, Silver St, MALDON ☎ 01621 852681 21 ⊷ ⋔Annexe8 ⊷ ⋔

CANEWDON   Map 05 TQ99

Ballards Gore Gore Rd SS4 2DA ☎ 01702 258917
A parkland course with several lakes.
18 holes, 7062yds, Par 73, SSS 74, Course record 69.
Club membership 500.

Visitors	may not play at weekends.
Societies	weekdays only, apply in advance.
Green Fees	£22 per day; £16 per round.

Facilities	⊗ ⋔ by prior arrangement ℔ 🍺 ♀ ♣ 🖼 ℓ Andrew Curry.
Leisure	buggies for hire, trolley for hire, putting green, practice area.
Location	2m NE of Rochford
Hotel	★★★ 66% Hotel Renouf, Bradley Way, ROCHFORD ☎ 01702 541334 24 ⊷ ⋔

CANVEY ISLAND   Map 05 TQ78

Castle Point Somnes Av SS8 9FG ☎ 01268 510830
A flat seaside links and part parkland course with water hazards on 13 holes and views of the estuary and Hadleigh Castle. Always a test for any golfer when the wind starts to blow.
18 holes, 6176yds, Par 71, SSS 69, Course record 69.
Club membership 275.

Visitors	must book for weekends.
Societies	phone or write for details.
Green Fees	£8.10 per round (£12.20 weekends).
Facilities	⊗ ⋔ ℔ 🍺 ♀ ♣ 🖼 ⚑ ℓ Paul Joiner.
Leisure	buggies for hire, trolley for hire, driving range, putting green.
Location	SE of Basildon, A130 to Canvey Island
Hotel	★★★ 66% Chichester Hotel, Old London Rd, Wickford, BASILDON ☎ 01268 560555 2 ⊷ ⋔Annexe32 ⊷ ⋔

CHELMSFORD   Map 05 TL70

Channels Belstead Farm Ln, Little Waltham CM3 3PT ☎ 01245 440005
Built on land from reclaimed gravel pits, 18 very exciting holes with plenty of lakes providing an excellent test of golf.
Channels Course: 18 holes, 6272yds, Par 71, SSS 71.
Belsteads: 18 holes, 4779yds, Par 67, SSS 63.
Club membership 650.

Visitors	Channels Course; must contact in advance and may only play with member at weekends. Belsteads Course; available anytime.
Societies	telephone starter on 01245 443311.
Green Fees	Channels £30 per day; £16 per rouund. Belsteads £15 per 18 holes; £9 per 9 holes.
Facilities	⊗ ⋔ ℔ 🍺 ♀ ♣ 🖼 ℓ Ian Sinclair.
Leisure	fishing, motorised carts for hire, buggies for hire, trolley for hire, driving range, putting green, practice area.
Location	2m NE on A130
Hotel	★★★ 58% South Lodge Hotel, 196 New London Rd, CHELMSFORD ☎ 01245 264564 25 ⊷ ⋔Annexe16 ⊷ ⋔

Chelmsford Widford Rd CM2 9AP ☎ 01245 256483
An undulating parkland course, hilly in parts, with 3 holes in woods and four difficult par 4's. From the reconstructed clubhouse there are fine views over the course and the wooded hills beyond.
18 holes, 5981yds, Par 68, SSS 69, Course record 66.
Club membership 650.

Visitors	must contact in advance. Society days Wed/Thu, Ladies Day Tue. With member only at weekends.
Societies	must contact in advance.
Green Fees	£35 per day; £25 per round.
Facilities	⊗ ⋔ ℔ 🍺 ♀ ♣ 🖼 ℓ Dennis Bailey.

Leisure	motorised carts for hire, buggies for hire, trolley for hire, putting green, practice area.
Location	1.5m S of town centre off A12
Hotel	★★★ 58% South Lodge Hotel, 196 New London Rd, CHELMSFORD ☎ 01245 264564 25 ⇌ ↟Annexe16 ⇌ ↟

CHIGWELL

Map 05 TQ49

Chigwell High Rd IG7 5BH ☎ 0181 500 2059
A course of high quality, mixing meadowland with parkland. For those who believe 'all Essex is flat' the undulating nature of Chigwell will be a refreshing surprise. The greens are excellent and the fairways tight with mature trees.
18 holes, 6279yds, Par 71, SSS 70, Course record 66.
Club membership 674.

Visitors	must contact in advance & have handicap certificate, but must be accompanied by member at weekends.
Societies	recognised societies welcome by prior arrangement.
Green Fees	£39 per day (£20 Dec-Feb). £28 per round (£20 Dec-Feb).
Facilities	⊗ ⅏ ⅃ ♨ ♀ ⚘ 🝙 ↟ Ray Beard.
Leisure	trolley for hire, putting green, practice area.
Location	0.5m S on A113
Hotel	★★ 62% Roebuck Hotel, North End, BUCKHURST HILL ☎ 0181 505 4636 29 ⇌ ↟

CHIGWELL ROW

Map 05 TQ49

Hainault Forest Romford Rd, Chigwell Row IG7 4QW
☎ 0181 500 2047
Club playing over Borough of Redbridge public courses; hilly parkland subject to wind. Two courses, driving range.
No 1 Course: 18 holes, 5744yds, Par 70, SSS 67, Course record 65.
No 2 Course: 18 holes, 6600yds, Par 71, SSS 71.
Club membership 600.

Visitors	no restrictions.
Societies	must contact in writing.
Green Fees	not confirmed.
Facilities	♀ ⚘ 🝙 ↟↟ ↟ T Dungate.
Location	0.5m S on A1112
Hotel	★★★ 65% Epping Forest Moat House, Oak Hill, WOODFORD GREEN ☎ 0181 787 9988 99 ⇌ ↟

CLACTON-ON-SEA

Map 05 TM11

Clacton West Rd CO15 1AJ ☎ 01255 421919
Windy, seaside course.
18 holes, 6494yds, Par 71, SSS 69.
Club membership 650.

Visitors	must contact in advance.
Societies	must contact in writing.
Green Fees	not confirmed.
Facilities	♀ ⚘ 🝙 ↟↟ ↟ S J Levermore.
Leisure	putting green,buggy/trolley hire.
Location	1.25m SW of town centre
Hotel	★★ 63% Maplin Hotel, Esplanade, FRINTON-ON-SEA ☎ 01255 673832 12rm(9 ⇌1 ↟)

COLCHESTER

Map 05 TL92

Birch Grove Layer Rd, Kingsford CO2 0HS
☎ 01206 734276
A pretty, undulating course surrounded by woodland - small but challenging with excellent greens. Challenging 6th hole cut through woodland with water hazards and out of bounds.
9 holes, 4038yds, Par 62, SSS 60, Course record 58.
Club membership 250.

Visitors	restricted Sun mornings.
Societies	apply in writing or telephone.
Green Fees	£10 per day; £7 per 9 holes.
Facilities	⊗ ⅏ ⅃ ♨ ♀ ⚘ 🝙
Leisure	trolley for hire, putting green, practice area.
Location	2.5m S on B1026
Hotel	★★ 70% Kingsford Park Hotel, Layer Rd, COLCHESTER ☎ 01206 734301 10 ⇌ ↟

Colchester Braiswick CO4 5AU
☎ 01206 853396 & 853920
A fairly flat, yet scenic, parkland course with tree-lined fairways and small copses. Mainly level walking.
18 holes, 6319yds, Par 70, SSS 69, Course record 64.
Club membership 700.

Visitors	weekends by prior arrangement.
Societies	apply in writing or by telephone, Mon, Thu & Fri only.
Green Fees	£25 per day; £20 per round (£30 per round weekends).
Facilities	⊗ ⅏ by prior arrangement ⅃ ♨ ♀ ⚘ 🝙 ↟ Mark Angel.
Leisure	trolley for hire, driving range, putting green, practice area.
Location	1.5m NW of town centre on B1508
Hotel	★★★ 66% George Hotel, 116 High St, COLCHESTER ☎ 01206 578494 47 ⇌ ↟

Stoke-by-Nayland Keepers Ln, Leavenheath CO6 4PZ
☎ 01206 262836
Two undulating courses (Gainsborough and Constable) situated in Dedham Vale. Some water hazards and hedges. On Gainsborough the 10th (par 4) takes 2 shots over a lake; very testing par 3 at 11th.
Gainsborough Course: 18 holes, 6581yds, Par 72, SSS 71, Course record 63.
Constable Course: 18 holes, 6544yds, Par 72, SSS 71, Course record 68.
Club membership 1400.

Visitors	write or telephone for details.
Societies	write or telephone for brochures and booking forms.
Green Fees	£29.50 per 36 holes (incl £1.50 meal voucher); £20 per 18 holes (£30/£24 weekends, 10-2pm).
Facilities	⊗ ⅏ ⅃ ♨ ♀ ⚘ 🝙 ↟ Kevin Lovelock.
Leisure	motorised carts for hire, buggies for hire, trolley for hire, driving range, putting green, practice area.
Location	1.5m NW of Stoke-by-Nayland on B1068
Hotel	★★★(red)⚑ Maison Talbooth, Stratford Rd, DEDHAM ☎ 01206 322367 10 ⇌ ↟

EARLS COLNE
Map 05 TL82

Colne Valley Station Rd CO6 2LT ☎ 01787 224233
An 18-hole course along the valley of the River Colne.
Opened in 1991.
18 holes, 6272yds, Par 71, SSS 70.
Club membership 600.
Visitors only after 10am at weekends, must dress
correctly,no sharing of clubs.
Societies apply in writing, minimum of 12 persons.
Green Fees not confirmed.
Facilities ♀⚑🏠 ⁆ Mrs Kimberley Martin.
Leisure sauna, range,putting,practice area,trolley hire.
Location Off A604
Hotel ★★★ 67% White Hart Hotel, Market End,
COGGESHALL
☎ 01376 561654 18 ⇌ ⁆

Earls Colne Golf & Leisure Centre CO6 2NS
☎ 01787 224466
Created on the site of a World War II airfield, this
challenging public course contains 14 lakes. Also 9-hole
course and 4-hole instruction course as well as a variety of
leisure facilities.
*County Course: 18 holes, 6800yds, Par 73, SSS 73, Course
record 69.*
Garden Course: 9 holes, 2190yds, Par 34, SSS 34.
Club membership 500.
Visitors contact the pro shop.
Societies apply in writting to the Society Secretary.
Green Fees £16 (£20 weekends).
Facilities ⊗ ⅷ ⅃ ⚑ ♀⚑🏠 ⁆ ⁆ Owen Mckenna.
Leisure hard tennis courts, heated indoor swimming
pool, fishing, sauna, solarium, gymnasium,
motorised carts for hire, buggies for hire, trolley
for hire, driving range, putting green, practice
area.
Location Off the A120 onto the B1024
Hotel ★★★ 67% White Hart Hotel, Market End,
COGGESHALL ☎ 01376 561654 18 ⇌ ⁆

EPPING
Map 05 TL40

Nazeing Middle St, Nazeing EN9 2LW
☎ 01992 893798 & 893915
Parkland course built with American sand based greens and
tees and five strategically placed lakes. One of the most
notable holes is the difficult par 3 13th with out of bounds
and a large lake coming into play.
18 holes, 6598yds, Par 72, SSS 71, Course record 65.
Club membership 500.
Visitors not compulsory to contact, weekends only
restricted times.
Societies prior arrangement required in writing.
Green Fees £35 per day; £20 Tue-Fri; £16 Mon (£28 after
midday weekends and bank holidays).
Facilities ⊗ ⅷ ⅃ ⚑ ♀⚑🏠 ⁆ ⁆ Robert Green.
Leisure motorised carts for hire, buggies for hire, trolley
for hire, driving range, practice area.
Location Just outside Waltham Abbey
Hotel ★★★ 63% Harlow Moat House, Southern Way,
HARLOW
☎ 01279 829988 118 ⇌ ⁆

FRINTON-ON-SEA
Map 05 TM22

Frinton 1 The Esplanade CO13 9EP
☎ 01255 674618 & 671618
Deceptive, flat seaside links course providing fast, firm and
undulating greens that will test the best putters and tidal
ditches that cross many of the fairways, requiring careful
placement of shots. Its open character means that every shot
has to be evaluated with both wind strength and direction in
mind. Easy walking.
*Long Course: 18 holes, 6265yds, Par 71, SSS 70, Course
record 64.*
Short Course: 9 holes, 1367yds, Par 29.
Club membership 850.
Visitors must contact in advance.
Societies by arrangement, apply in writing to the
secretary, Wed, Thu and some Fri.
Green Fees £22 per round, adjusted seasonally..
Facilities ⊗ ⅷ by prior arrangement ⅃ ⚑ ♀⚑🏠 ⁆ ⅙
⁆ Peter Taggart.
Leisure motorised carts for hire, buggies for hire, trolley
for hire, driving range, putting green, practice
area.
Location SW side of town centre
Hotel ★★ 63% Maplin Hotel, Esplanade, FRINTON-
ON-SEA ☎ 01255 673832 12rm(9 ⇌1 ⁆)

GOSFIELD
Map 05 TL72

Gosfield Lake The Manor House, Hall Dr CO9 1SE
☎ 01787 474747
Parkland course with bunkers, lake and water hazards.
Designed by Sir Henry Cotton/Mr Howard Swan and opened
in 1988. Also 9-hole course; ideal for beginners and
improvers.
*Lakes Course: 18 holes, 6707yds, Par 72, SSS 72, Course
record 68.*
Meadows Course: 9 holes, 4180yds, Par 64, SSS 61.
Club membership 650.
Visitors Lakes Course: must contact in advance,
handicap certificate required, Sat & Sun from
noon only. Meadows Course: restricted during
competitions, handicap certificate not required,
advisable to contact.
Societies welcome Mon-Fri by arrangement, telephone or
write.
Green Fees Lakes: £25 per day; £20 per round (£25 per
round weekends). Meadows: £10 per day; £8 per
round.
Facilities ⊗ ⅷ ⅃ ⚑ ♀⚑🏠 ⁆ Richard Wheeler.
Leisure sauna, trolley for hire, putting green, practice
area.
Location 1m W of Gosfield off B1017
Hotel ★★★ 61% White Hart Hotel, Bocking End,
BRAINTREE ☎ 01376 321401 31 ⇌ ⁆

HARLOW
Map 05 TL40

Canons Brook Elizabeth Way CM19 5BE
☎ 01279 421482 & 418357
Challenging parkland course designed by Henry Cotton in
1963. Accuracy is the key requiring straight driving from the
tees, especially on the par 5 11th to fly a gap with out of
bounds left and right before setting up the shot to the green.

18 holes, 6800yds, Par 73, SSS 72, Course record 65.
Club membership 850.

Visitors may not play at weekends.
Societies welcome Mon, Wed and Fri, must book in advance by telephone.
Green Fees £25 per day; £18 per round.
Facilities ⊗ ⅢⅢ ⅃⅃ ☰ ♀ ⚒ 🏠 ⛳ ℓ Alan McGinn.
Leisure buggies for hire, trolley for hire, putting green, practice area.
Location 3m S of M11
Hotel ★★★ 74% Churchgate Manor Hotel, Churchgate St, Old Harlow, HARLOW ☎ 01279 420246 85 ⇄

HARWICH Map 05 TM23

Harwich & Dovercourt Station Rd, Parkeston CO12 4NZ ☎ 01255 503616
Flat moorland course with easy walking.
9 holes, 5900yds, Par 70, SSS 69, Course record 58.
Club membership 420.

Visitors visitors with handicap certificate may play by prior arrangement, with member only at weekends.
Societies prior arrangement essential.
Green Fees on application.
Facilities ⊗ by prior arrangement ⅢⅢ by prior arrangement ⅃⅃ ♀ ⚒ 🏠 ☰
Leisure trolley for hire, putting green, practice area.
Location Off A120 near Ferry Terminal
Hotel ★★ 72% The Pier at Harwich, The Quay, HARWICH ☎ 01255 241212 6 ⇄

INGRAVE Map 05 TQ69

Thorndon Park Ingrave Rd CM13 3RH ☎ 01277 811666 & 810345
Among the best of the Essex courses with a fine new purpose-built clubhouse and a lake. The springy turf is easy on the feet. Many newly planted young trees now replace the famous old oaks that were such a feature of this course.
18 holes, 6492yds, Par 71, SSS 71.
Club membership 670.

Visitors must contact in advance, at weekends with member only.
Societies welcome n Tue and Fri but must apply in writing.
Green Fees £45 per day; £30 per round.
Facilities ⊗ ⅃⅃ ♀ ⚒ 🏠 ☰ ⛳ ℓ Brian White.
Leisure trolley for hire, putting green, practice area.
Location W side of village off A128
Hotel B Forte Posthouse Brentwood, Brook St, BRENTWOOD ☎ 01277 260260 111 ⇄

LOUGHTON Map 05 TQ49

High Beech Wellington Hill IG10 4AH ☎ 0181 508 7323
Short 9-hole course set in Epping Forest.
9 holes, Par 27, Course record 25 or 9 holes, Par 27, Course record 23.

Visitors welcome.
Green Fees Yellow; £3 per 9 holes. Red; £2.60 per 9 holes.
Facilities ♀ 🏠 ⛳ ℓ Clark Baker.
Leisure trolley for hire, putting green, practice nets.
Location Close to M25 Waltham Abbey junct

Loughton Clays Ln, Debden Green IG10 2RZ ☎ 0181 502 2923
Hilly 9-hole parkland course on the edge of Epping Forest.
9 holes, 4652yds, Par 64, SSS 63, Course record 65.
Club membership 180.

Visitors must contact in advance.
Societies telephone in advance.
Green Fees £8 per 18 holes; £5 per 9 holes (£10/£6 weekends & bank holidays).
Facilities ⅃⅃ ♀ ⚒ 🏠 ☰ ⛳ ℓ Stuart Layton.
Leisure trolley for hire, practice area.
Location 1.5m SE of Theydon Bois
Hotel B Forte Posthouse Epping, High Rd, Bell Common, EPPING ☎ 01992 573137 Annexe79 ⇄ ⚐

MALDON Map 05 TL80

Forrester Park Beckingham Rd, Great Totham CM9 8EA ☎ 01621 891406
Tight, undulating parkland course with tree-lined fairways and good views over the Blackwater estuary. Easy walking. Attractive 16th-century clubhouse.
18 holes, 6073yds, Par 71, SSS 69, Course record 69.
Club membership 1000.

Visitors must contact in advance but may not play before noon weekends & bank holidays.
Societies must apply in advance.
Green Fees £17 per round; £22 per day (£17 weekends).
Facilities ⊗ ⅃⅃ ♀ ⚒ 🏠 ☰ ℓ Gary Pike.
Leisure hard tennis courts, trolley for hire, putting green, practice area.
Location 3m NE of Maldon off B1022
Hotel ★★ 64% Blue Boar Hotel, Silver St, MALDON ☎ 01621 852681 21 ⇄ ⚐Annexe8 ⇄ ⚐

Maldon Beeleigh, Langford CM9 6LL ☎ 01621 853212
Flat, parkland course in a triangle of land by the River Chelmer, the Blackwater Canal and an old railway embankment. Alternate tees on 2nd nine holes. Testing par 3 14th (166yds) demanding particular accuracy to narrow green guarded by bunkers and large trees.
9 holes, 6197yds, Par 71, SSS 69.
Club membership 450.

Visitors telephone to check availability, may only play with member at weekends.
Societies intially telephone then confirm in writing.
Green Fees £20 per day; £15 per round (Mon-Fri).
Facilities ⊗ ⅢⅢ ⅃⅃ ♀ ⚒ 🏠 ☰
Leisure trolley for hire, practice area.
Location 1m NW off B1018
Hotel ★★ 64% Blue Boar Hotel, Silver St, MALDON ☎ 01621 852681 21 ⇄ ⚐Annexe8 ⇄ ⚐

ORSETT Map 05 TQ68

Orsett Brentwood Rd RM16 3DS ☎ 01375 891352 & 891226
A very good test of golf - this heathland course with its sandy soil is quick drying and provides easy walking. Close to the Thames estuary it is seldom calm and the main hazards are the prevailing wind and thick gorse. Any slight deviation can be exaggerated by the wind ▶

and a lost ball in the gorse results. The clubhouse has been modernised.

18 holes, 6614yds, Par 72, SSS 72, Course record 68.
Club membership 800.

Visitors	restricted weekends & bank holidays. Must contact in advance and have a handicap certificate.
Societies	must contact in advance.
Green Fees	£30 per day (£20 after 1pm).
Facilities	⊗ ⅷ ▙ ▟ ♀ ⚤ ☎ ℓ Robert Newberry.
Leisure	buggies for hire, trolley for hire, putting.
Location	1.5m SE off A128
Hotel	B Forte Posthouse Basildon, Cranes Farm Rd, BASILDON ☎ 01268 533955 110 ⇋ ☞

PURLEIGH   Map 05 TL80

Three Rivers Stow Rd CM3 6RR ☎ 01621 828631
Wooded parkland course with ponds, dog-legs and fine rural views.

Kings Course: 18 holes, 6536yds, Par 73, SSS 71.
Queens Course: 9 holes, 1071yds, Par 27.
Club membership 800.

Visitors	telephone before visit.
Societies	apply in writing or telephone.
Green Fees	Kings Course: £25 per day; £19 per round (£29/£24 weekends). Queens Course: £7.50 per day (£8.50 weekends).
Facilities	⊗ ⅷ ▙ ▟ ♀ ⚤ ☎ ⵏ ⛴ ℓ Graham Packer.
Leisure	hard tennis courts, squash, sauna, motorised carts for hire, buggies for hire, trolley for hire, putting green, practice area.
Location	1m from Purleigh on B1012
Hotel	★★ 64% Blue Boar Hotel, Silver St, MALDON ☎ 01621 852681 21 ⇋ ☞Annexe8 ⇋ ☞

ROCHFORD   Map 05 TQ89

Rochford Hundred Hall Rd SS4 1NW
☎ 01702 544302
Parkland course with ponds and ditches as natural hazards.

18 holes, 6292yds, Par 72, SSS 70, Course record 64.
Club membership 800.

Visitors	must have handicap certificate. Visitors may not play Tue morning (Ladies) or Sun without a member.
Societies	must contact in writing.
Green Fees	not confirmed.
Facilities	♀ ⚤ ☎ ℓ Graham Hill.
Leisure	putting green,cart/buggy/trolley hire.
Location	W on B1013
Hotel	★★★ 66% Hotel Renouf, Bradley Way, ROCHFORD ☎ 01702 541334 24 ⇋ ☞

SAFFRON WALDEN   Map 05 TL53

Saffron Walden Windmill Hill CB10 1BX
☎ 01799 522786
Undulating parkland course, beautiful views.

18 holes, 6585yds, Par 72, SSS 72.
Club membership 950.

Visitors	must contact in advance and have a handicap certificate. With member only at weekends.

Societies	must contact in advance.
Green Fees	not confirmed.
Facilities	♀ ⚤ ☎ ℓ Philip Davis.
Leisure	putting green,practice,cart/trolley hire.
Location	NW side of town centre off B184
Hotel	★★ 65% Saffron Hotel, 10-18 High St, SAFFRON WALDEN ☎ 01799 522676 20rm(17 ⇋ ☞)

SOUTHEND-ON-SEA   Map 05 TQ88

Belfairs Eastwood Rd North, Leigh on Sea SS9 4LR
☎ 01702 525345
Municipal parkland course run by the Borough Council. Tight second half through thick woods, easy walking.

18 holes, 5795yds, Par 70, SSS 68.
Club membership 300.

Visitors	restricted weekends & bank holidays.
Green Fees	not confirmed.
Facilities	☎ ⵏ ℓ
Leisure	hard tennis courts.
Location	3m W, N of A13
Hotel	★★★ 62% Balmoral Hotel, 34 Valkyrie Rd, Westcliffe-on-Sea, SOUTHEND-ON-SEA ☎ 01702 342947 22 ⇋ ☞

Thorpe Hall Thorpe Hall Av, Thorpe Bay SS1 3AT
☎ 01702 582205
Parkland course with narrow fairways where placement rather than length is essential.

18 holes, 6286yds, Par 71, SSS 71, Course record 64.
Club membership 995.

Visitors	must contact in advance, with member only weekends & bank holidays.
Societies	apply in writing, only a certain number a year.
Green Fees	£30 per day/round.
Facilities	⊗ ⅷ ▙ ▟ ♀ ⚤ ☎ ⵏ ℓ Bill McColl.
Leisure	squash, sauna, motorised carts for hire, buggies for hire, trolley for hire, putting green, practice area.
Location	2m E off A13
Hotel	★★★ 62% Balmoral Hotel, 34 Valkyrie Rd, Westcliffe-on-Sea, SOUTHEND-ON-SEA ☎ 01702 342947 22 ⇋ ☞

SOUTH OCKENDON   Map 05 TQ58

Belhus Park Municipal Belhus Park RM15 4PX
☎ 01708 854260
Municipal parkland type course with easy walking.

18 holes, 5450yds, Par 68, SSS 67.
Club membership 250.

Visitors	no restrictions. Must have proper golf shoes and shirts to be worn at all times.
Societies	must contact in writing.
Green Fees	not confirmed.
Facilities	♀ ⚤ ☎ ⵏ ℓ
Leisure	heated indoor swimming pool, squash, sauna, solarium, gymnasium, 11 bay floodlit driving range.
Location	2m SW off B1335
Hotel	★★★ 64% Stifford Moat House, High Rd, North Stifford, GRAYS ☎ 01708 719988 96 ⇋ ☞

Top Meadow Fen Ln, North Ockendon RM14 3PR
☎ 01708 852239
Set in the Essex countryside with a panoramic view of the area. Some holes are very difficult with the variable wind directions, especially 1st, 6th, 7th and 13th.
New Course: 18 holes, 5909yds, Par 69, SSS 68, Course record 67.
Old Course: 9 holes, 2010yds, Par 30, SSS 30, Course record 27.
Club membership 600.
Visitors New Course Mon-Fri, Old Course all week.
Societies telephone in advance.
Green Fees New Course: £12. Old Course: £5.
Facilities ⊗ ℋ ⅃ ⅃ ♀ ⅄ 🖰 ⑂ ⋈ ⅂ Paul King.
Leisure fishing, motorised carts for hire, buggies for hire, trolley for hire, driving range, putting green, practice area.
Hotel B Forte Travelodge, EAST HORNDEN
☎ 01277 810819 22 ⇥ ⋔

STAPLEFORD ABBOTTS   Map 05 TQ59

Stapleford Abbotts Horsemanside, Tysea Hill RM14 1JU
☎ 01708 381108 & 381278
Two championship courses and a 9-hole par 3. The main features of the Priors course are the numerous lakes and large sloping greeen. Abbots course has many hazards and will test players of all standards. It is rapidly maturing into one of the best in Essex.
Abbotts Course: 18 holes, 6501yds, Par 72, SSS 71.
Priors Course: 18 holes, 5720yds, Par 69, SSS 69.
Friars Course: 9 holes, 1140yds, Par 27, SSS 27.
Club membership 600.
Visitors may only play on Priors and par 3 Friars , advisable to telephone starter on 01277 373344.
Societies apply in writing, must be pre booked.
Green Fees Priors £10 (£15 weekends); Par 3 £5 (£8 weekends).
Facilities ⊗ ⅃ ⅃ ♀ ⅄ 🖰 ⑂ ⅂ Dominic Eagle.
Leisure fishing, sauna, gymnasium, buggies for hire, trolley for hire, putting green, practice area.
Location 1m E of Stapleford Abbotts, off B175
Hotel ★★★★ 68% Marygreen Manor, London Rd, BRENTWOOD ☎ 01277 225252 3 ⇥ ⋔Annexe30 ⇥ ⋔

THEYDON BOIS   Map 05 TQ49

Theydon Bois Theydon Rd CM16 4EH
☎ 01992 812460 & 83054
The course was originally a nine-hole built into Epping Forest. It was later extendend to 18-holes which were well-planned and well-bunkered but are situated out in the open on the hillside. The old nine in the Forest are short and have three bunkers among them, but even so a wayward shot can be among the trees. The autumn colours here are truly magnificent.
18 holes, 5480yds, Par 68, SSS 68, Course record 64.
Club membership 600.
Visitors may not play Wed, Thu, Sat & Sun mornings, ring 01992 812460 in advance to be sure tee is available.
Societies book through the secretary.
Green Fees £23 per round (£20 weekends after 2pm).
Facilities ⊗ ℋ ⅃ ⅃ ♀ ⅄ 🖰 ⑂ ⅂ R Hall.

Leisure trolley for hire, putting green, practice area.
Location 1m N
Hotel B Forte Posthouse Epping, High Rd, Bell Common, EPPING
☎ 01992 573137 Annexe79 ⇥ ⋔

TOLLESHUNT KNIGHTS   Map 05 TL91

Five Lakes Hotel Golf & Country Club Colchester Rd CM9 8HX ☎ 01621 868888 & 862307
Two 18-hole courses. The Links is a seaside course with a number of greenside ponds and strategically placed bunkers, while the Lakes is a championship course with large water features and mounding between fairways.
Links Course: 18 holes, 6250yds, Par 71, SSS 70, Course record 67.
Lakes Course: 18 holes, 6767yds, Par 72, SSS 72, Course record 63.
Club membership 600.
Visitors must contact in advance.
Societies must contact in advance.
Green Fees Links: £25 per day; £18 per round (£30/£22.50 weekends & bank holidays). Lakes: £37.50 per day; £25 per round (£45/£30 weekends and bank holidays) prices due to be reviewed.
Facilities ⊗ ℋ ⅃ ⅃ ♀ ⅄ 🖰 ⑂ ⋈ ⅂ Gary Carter.
Leisure hard tennis courts, heated indoor swimming pool, squash, sauna, solarium, gymnasium, motorised carts for hire, buggies for hire, trolley for hire, driving range, putting green.
Location 1.75m NE on B1026
Hotel ★★★★ 71% Five Lakes Hotel, Colchester Rd, Whitehouse Hill, TOLLESHUNT Knights
☎ 01621 868888 114 ⇥ ⋔

TOOT HILL   Map 05 TL50

Toot Hill School Rd CM5 9PU ☎ 01277 365523
Pleasant course with several water hazards and sand greens.
18 holes, 6053yds, Par 70, SSS 69, Course record 65.
Club membership 450.
Visitors welcome but may not play at weekends.
Societies Society days Tue & Thu contact in advance.
Green Fees £35 per day; £25 per round.
Facilities ⊗ ℋ ⅃ ⅃ ♀ ⅄ 🖰 ⑂ ⅂ Geoff Bacon.
Leisure motorised carts for hire, buggies for hire, trolley for hire, driving range, putting green, practice area.
Location 7m SE of Harlow, off A414
Hotel B Forte Posthouse Epping, High Rd, Bell Common, EPPING
☎ 01992 573137 Annexe79 ⇥ ⋔

WITHAM   Map 05 TL81

Braxted Park Braxted Park Estate CM8 3EN
☎ 01376 572372
A Pay and Play course in ancient parkland, surrounded by lakes and extremely pretty countryside. Suitable for beginners and average players.
9 holes, 2940yds, Par 35.
Club membership 71.
Visitors welcome weekdays from 7.30am onwards.
Societies telephone to arrange. ▶

Green Fees £12 per 18 holes; £9 per 9 holes.
Facilities ⊗ ь ♨ ♀ ⅄ 🛍 ⚑ ⌇ ʕ Michael Woollett.
Leisure fishing, trolley for hire, practice area.
Location 2m from A12 near Kelvedon
Hotel ★★★ 65% Jarvis Rivenhall Hotel, Rivenhall
End, WITHAM
☎ 01376 516969 7 ⇔ ʕ Annexe48 ⇔ ʕ

WOODHAM WALTER   Map 05 TL80

Bunsay Downs Little Baddow Rd CM9 6RU
☎ 01245 222648
Attractive 9-hole public course. Also Par 3 course.
9 holes, 2932yds, Par 70, SSS 68.
Badgers: 9 holes, 1319yds, Par 54.
Club membership 400.
Visitors no restrictions.
Societies Mon-Fri only. Must contact in advance.
Green Fees not confirmed.
Facilities ♀ ⅄ 🛍 ⌇ ʕ Mickey Walker.
Leisure putting, practice, cart/buggy/trolley hire.
Hotel ★★ 64% Blue Boar Hotel, Silver St,
MALDON
☎ 01621 852681 21 ⇔ ʕ Annexe8 ⇔ ʕ

Warren CM9 6RW ☎ 01245 223258 & 223198
Attractive parkland course with natural hazards and good
views.
18 holes, 6229yds, Par 70, SSS 70, Course record 65.
Club membership 765.
Visitors contact in advance, weekend pm only, Wed pm
only.
Societies arrange by telephone, confirm in writing,
weekdays ex Wed.
Green Fees £30 per day; £25 per round.
Facilities ⊗ ℳ by prior arrangement ь ♨ ♀ ⅄ 🛍 ⌇
ʕ Mickey Walker.
Leisure motorised carts for hire, buggies for hire, trolley
for hire, driving range, putting green, practice
area, teaching academy.
Location 0.5m SW
Hotel ★★ 64% Blue Boar Hotel, Silver St,
MALDON
☎ 01621 852681 21 ⇔ ʕ Annexe8 ⇔ ʕ

GLOUCESTERSHIRE

CHELTENHAM   Map 03 SO92

Cotswold Hills Ullenwood GL53 9QT ☎ 01242 515264
A gently undulating course with open aspects and views of
the Cotswolds.
18 holes, 6889yds, Par 71, SSS 74.
Club membership 750.
Visitors telephone in advance, handicap certificate
preferred.
Societies must apply in writing or telephone.
Green Fees £26 per day; £21 per round (£31/£26 weekends).
Facilities ⊗ ℳ ь ♨ ♀ ⅄ 🛍 ⌇ ʕ Noel Boland.
Leisure buggies for hire, trolley for hire, putting green,
practice area.

Location 3m SE on A435 and A436
Hotel B Forte Posthouse Gloucester, Crest Way,
Barnwood, GLOUCESTER
☎ 01452 613311 123 ⇔ ʕ

Lilley Brook Cirencester Rd, Charlton Kings GL53 8EG
☎ 01242 526785
Undulating parkland course. Magnificent views over
Cheltenham and surrounding coutryside.
18 holes, 6212yds, Par 69, SSS 70, Course record 63.
Club membership 800.
Visitors advisable to enquire of availability.
Societies apply in writing.
Green Fees £25 per day; £20 round (£30/£25 weekends).
Facilities ⊗ ℳ ь ♨ ♀ ⅄ 🛍 ⌇ ʕ Forbes Hadden.
Leisure motorised carts for hire, buggies for hire, trolley
for hire, putting green, practice area.
Location 2m S of Cheltenham on A435
Hotel ★★★★ 64% Cheltenham Park Hotel,
Cirencester Rd, Charlton Kings,
CHELTENHAM ☎ 01242 222021 144 ⇔ ʕ

CHIPPING SODBURY   Map 03 ST78

Chipping Sodbury BS17 6PU ☎ 01454 319042
Parkland courses of Championship proportions. The old
course may be seen from the large opening tee by the
clubhouse at the top of the hill. Two huge drainage dykes
cut through the course and form a distinctive hazard on
eleven holes.
*New Course: 18 holes, 6912yds, Par 73, SSS 73, Course
record 65.*
Old Course: 9 holes, 6184yds, Par 70, SSS 69.
Club membership 800.
Visitors no restriction on Old Course, must have a
handicap certificate and may only play until
after noon at weekends on New Course.
Societies must contact in writing.
Green Fees £30 per day; £25 per 27 holes (£35/£30
weekends and bank holidays).
Facilities ⊗ ℳ ь ♨ ♀ ⅄ 🛍 ⌇ ʕ Mike Watts.
Leisure motorised carts for hire, buggies for hire,
trolley for hire, putting green, practice area.
Location 0.5m N
Hotel ★★ 61% Cross Hands Hotel, OLD
SODBURY
☎ 01454 313000 24rm(3 ⇔17 ʕ)

CIRENCESTER   Map 04 SP00

Cirencester Cheltenham Rd, Bagendon GL7 7BH
☎ 01285 652465 & 656124 pro shop
Undulating Cotswold course.
18 holes, 6020yds, Par 70, SSS 69.
Visitors restricted play at weekends, contact professional
shop in advance.
Societies telephone Secretary/Manager.
Green Fees £20 per day (£25 weekends & bank holidays).
Facilities ⊗ ℳ ь ♨ ♀ ⅄ 🛍 ⌇ ʕ Geoff Robbins.
Leisure buggies for hire, trolley for hire, putting green,
practice area.
Location 2 N on A435
Hotel ★★★ 68% Stratton House Hotel, Gloucester
Rd, CIRENCESTER
☎ 01285 651761 41 ⇔ ʕ

CLEEVE HILL   Map 03 SO92

Cleeve Hill GL52 3PW ☎ 01242 672025
Undulating and open heathland course affected by crosswinds.
18 holes, 6411yds, Par 72, SSS 71, Course record 69.
Club membership 450.
Visitors   bookings taken 7 days in advance. Limited play weekends.
Societies   telephone in advance.
Green Fees £8 (£10 weekends & bank holidays).
Facilities   ⊗ ⅢⅢ ﾑ 👤 ➿ ➤ ➔ Ⅰ Richard Jenkins.
Leisure   trolley for hire, putting green, practice area.
Location   1m NE on B4632
Hotel   ★★★ 57% Hotel De La Bere, Southam, CHELTENHAM
               ☎ 01242 237771 32 ⇥ ⋔Annexe25 ⇥

COLEFORD   Map 03 SO51

Forest Hills Mile End Rd GL16 7BY ☎ 01594 810620
A parkland course on a plateau with panoramic views of Coleford and Forest of Dean. Some testing holes with the par-5 13th hole sitting tight on a water hazard, and the challenging 18th with 2nd shot over large pond to a green protected by another pond and bunker - all in front of the clubhouse.
18 holes, 6740yds, Par 68, SSS 68, Course record 66.
Visitors   no restrictions.
Societies   contact in advance.
Green Fees £20 per day; £13 per round (£25/£15 weekends).
Facilities   ⊗ ⅢⅢ ﾑ 👤 👤 ➿ ➤ ➔ Ⅰ J Nicholl.
Leisure   motorised carts for hire, buggies for hire, trolley for hire, driving range, putting green, practice area.
Hotel   ★★★ 65% The Speech House, Forest of Dean, COLEFORD ☎ 01594 822607 14 ⇥ ⋔

Forest of Dean Lords Hill GL16 8BD ☎ 01594 832583
Established in 1973 and now matured into an extremely pleasant parkland course. Well bunkered with light rough, a few blind tee shots and water in play on several holes.
18 holes, 5813yds, Par 69, SSS 68.
Club membership 500.
Visitors   are required to book tee-off times.
Societies   must telephone in advance.
Green Fees £13 per round (£15 weekends & bank holidays).
Facilities   ⊗ ⅢⅢ ﾑ 👤 👤 ➿ ➤ ➔ ⇥ Ⅰ Philip Worthing.
Leisure   hard tennis courts, outdoor swimming pool, motorised carts for hire, buggies for hire, trolley for hire, putting green, practice area, bowling green.
Hotel   ★★★ 65% The Speech House, Forest of Dean, COLEFORD ☎ 01594 822607 14 ⇥ ⋔

DURSLEY   Map 03 ST79

Stinchcombe Hill Stinchcombe Hill GL11 6AQ
☎ 01453 542015
High on the hill with splendid views of the Cotswolds, the River Severn and the Welsh hills. A downland course with good turf, some trees and an interesting variety of greens. Protected greens make this a challenging course in windy conditions.

18 holes, 5734yds, Par 68, SSS 68, Course record 63.
Club membership 550.
Visitors   restricted at weekends. Must contact professional in advance 01453 543878.
Societies   must apply in advance.
Green Fees £20 per day; £12.50 per round (£25 per round/day weekends & bank holidays, winter weekends £15 per round).
Facilities   ⊗ ⅢⅢ ﾑ 👤 👤 ➿ ➤ ➔ Ⅰ Paul Bushell.
Leisure   trolley for hire, putting green, practice area.
Location   1m W off A4135
Hotel   ★★ 65% Prince Of Wales Hotel, BERKELEY ROAD
               ☎ 01453 810474 41 ⇥ ⋔

GLOUCESTER   Map 03 SO81

Jarvis Gloucester Hotel & Country Club Matson Ln, Robinswood Hill GL4 6EA ☎ 01452 411331
Undulating, wooded course, built around a hill with superb views over Gloucester and the Cotswolds. The 12th is a drive straight up a hill, nicknamed 'Coronary Hill'.
18 holes, 6170yds, Par 70, SSS 69, Course record 65.
Club membership 600.
Visitors   can book up to 7 days in advance.
Societies   telephone in advance.
Green Fees £25 per day; £19 per round (£25 per round weekends).
Facilities   ⊗ ⅢⅢ ﾑ 👤 👤 ➿ ➤ ➔ ⇥ Ⅰ Peter Darnell.
Leisure   hard tennis courts, heated indoor swimming pool, squash, sauna, solarium, gymnasium, buggies for hire, trolley for hire, practice area, running track.
Location   2m SW off M5
Hotel   ★★★ 69% Jarvis Bowden Hall Hotel & Country Club, Bondend Ln, Upton St Leonards, GLOUCESTER
               ☎ 01452 614121 72 ⇥ ⋔

Rodway Hill Newent Rd, Highnam GL2 8DN
☎ 01452 384222
A challenging 18-hole course with superb panoramic views. Testing front 5 holes and the par 3 13th and par 5 16th being affected by strong croswinds off the River Severn.
18 holes, 5860yds, Par 70, SSS 68, Course record 72.
Club membership 400.
Visitors   no restrictions.
Societies   telephone in advance.
Green Fees £8 per 18 holes; £5 per 9 holes (£10/£6 weekends).
Facilities   ⊗ ﾑ 👤 👤 ➿ ➤ ➔ Ⅰ Tony Grubb.
Leisure   putting green, practice area.
Location   2m outside Gloucester on B4215
Hotel   ★★★ 62% Hatherley Manor Hotel, Down Hatherley Ln, GLOUCESTER
               ☎ 01452 730217 56 ⇥ ⋔

LYDNEY   Map 03 SO60

Lydney Lakeside Av GL15 5QA ☎ 01594 842614
Flat parkland/meadowland course with prevailing wind along fairways.
9 holes, 5298yds, Par 66, SSS 66, Course record 63.
Club membership 350.   ▶

Visitors	with member only at weekends & bank holidays.
Societies	apply in writing to the Secretary.
Green Fees	£12 per day.
Facilities	⬧ ♥ ♀⛳
Leisure	practice area.
Location	SE side of town centre
Hotel	★★★ 65% The Speech House, Forest of Dean, COLEFORD ☎ 01594 822607 14 ⇆ ⁿ

MINCHINHAMPTON

Map 03 SO80

Minchinhampton (New Course) New Course GL6 9BE
☎ 01453 833866 & 833840 bookings
The course is on an upland Costwold plateau. It is level and
open in design. Very good golf is needed to achieve par of 72.
Avening: 18 holes, 6244yds, Par 70, SSS 70, Course record 65.
*Cherington: 18 holes, 6320yds, Par 71, SSS 70, Course
record 66.*
Club membership 1100.

Visitors	must contact in advance.
Societies	must contact by telephone.
Green Fees	£25 per day; (£30 weekends & bank holidays).
Facilities	⊗ ⫪ ⬧ ♥ ♀⛳ ☎ ⚐ ⌁ Chris Steele.
Leisure	trolley for hire, driving range, putting green, practice area.
Location	2m E
Hotel	★★★ 65% Burleigh Court, Minchinhampton, STROUD ☎ 01453 883804 11 ⇆ ⁿAnnexe6 ⇆ ⁿ

Minchinhampton (Old Course) Old Course GL6 9AQ
☎ 01453 832642 & 836382
An open grassland course 600 feet above sea level. There is a
prevailing west wind that affects most holes. Panoramic
Cotswold views.
18 holes, 6205yds, Par 71, SSS 70, Course record 64.
Club membership 600.

Visitors	must contact in advance.
Societies	must contact by telephone.
Green Fees	£10 per day/round (£13 weekends & bank holidays).
Facilities	⊗ ⫪ ⬧ ♥ ♀⛳ ⚐
Leisure	trolley for hire, practice area.
Location	1m NW
Hotel	★★★ 65% Burleigh Court, Minchinhampton, STROUD ☎ 01453 883804 11 ⇆ ⁿAnnexe6 ⇆ ⁿ

NAUNTON

Map 04 SP12

Naunton Downs GL54 3AE ☎ 01451 850090
New in 1993, Naunton Downs course plays over beautiful
Cotswold countryside. A valley running through the course is
one of the main features, creating 3 holes that cross over it.
The prevailing wind adds extra challenge to the par 5's
(which play into the wind), combined with small undulating
greens.
18 holes, 6078yds, Par 71, SSS 69, Course record 73.
Club membership 1000.

Visitors	must contact in advance.
Societies	telephone for details.
Green Fees	£19.95 per day.
Facilities	⊗ ⫪ ⬧ ♥ ♀⛳ ⚐ ⌁ Martin Seddon.
Leisure	motorised carts for hire, buggies for hire, trolley for hire, putting green, practice area.

Location	B4068 Stow/Cheltenham
Hotel	★★★⬥⬥ 79% Lords of the Manor, UPPER SLAUGHTER ☎ 01451 820243 28 ⇆ ⁿ

PAINSWICK

Map 03 SO80

Painswick GL6 6TL ☎ 01452 812180
Downland course set on Cotswold Hills at Painswick Beacon,
with fine views. Short course more than compensated by
natural hazards and tight fairways.
18 holes, 4895yds, Par 67, SSS 64.
Club membership 420.

Visitors	with member only on Sun.
Societies	must apply in writing.
Green Fees	not confirmed.
Facilities	♀⛳ ⚐
Location	1m N on A46
Hotel	★★★ 76% Painswick Hotel, Kemps Ln, PAINSWICK ☎ 01452 812160 19 ⇆ ⁿ

TEWKESBURY

Map 03 SO83

Puckrup Hall Hotel Puckrup GL20 6EL
☎ 01684 296200
Set in 140 acres of undulating parkland with lakes, existing
trees and marvellous views of the Malvern hills. There are
water hazards at the 5th and a cluster of bunkers on the long
9th before the challnging tee shot across the water to the par-
3 18th.
18 holes, 6431yds, Par 71, SSS 71.
Club membership 250.

Visitors	must be a regular golfer familiar with rules and etiquette, must book a tee time, may book up to 6 days in advance.
Societies	telephone in advance.
Green Fees	£25 per day; £20 per round (£33/£25 weekends & bank holidays).
Facilities	⊗ ⫪ ⬧ ♥ ♀⛳ ⚐ ⌁ ⊠⌁ Kevin Pickett.
Leisure	heated indoor swimming pool, sauna, solarium, gymnasium, motorised carts for hire, buggies for hire, trolley for hire, driving range, putting green, practice area, aerobics hall.
Location	4m N, on main A38
Hotel	★★★ 74% Puckrup Hall Hotel and Golf Club, Puckrup, TEWKESBURY ☎ 01684 296200 84 ⇆ ⁿ

Tewkesbury Park Hotel Golf & Country Club Lincoln
Green Ln GL20 7DN ☎ 01684 295405
A parkland course in a sheltered situation beside the
River Severn. The par 3, 5th is an exacting hole calling
for accurate distance judgment. The hotel and country
club offer many sports facilities.
18 holes, 6533yds, Par 73, SSS 72.

Visitors	may play weekdays only.
Societies	telephone initially.
Green Fees	£25 weekdays.
Facilities	⊗ ⫪ ⬧ ♥ ♀⛳ ⚐ ⌁ ⊠⌁ Robert Taylor.
Leisure	hard tennis courts, heated indoor swimming pool, squash, sauna, solarium, gymnasium, motorised carts for hire, buggies for hire, trolley for hire, driving range, putting green, practice area.
Location	1m SW off A38

Hotel	★★★ 68% Tewkesbury Park Hotel, Country Club Resort, Lincoln Green Ln, TEWKESBURY ☎ 01684 295405 Annexe78 ⇆ ⋔

THORNBURY   Map 03 ST69

Thornbury Golf Centre Bristol Rd BS12 2XL
☎ 01454 281144
Two 18 hole pay & play courses designed by Hawtree and set in undulating terrain with estensive views towards the Severn estuary. The Low 18 is a Par 3 with holes ranging from 80 to 207 yards and is ideal for beginners. The High course puts to test the more experienced golfer. Excellent 25 bay floodlit driving range.
High Course: 18 holes, 6154yds, Par 71, SSS 69.
Low Course: 18 holes, 2195yds, Par 54.
Club membership 420.

Visitors	must contact in advance.
Societies	apply in writing for brochure.
Green Fees	£21 per day; £13 per round; £7.50 par 3 course.
Facilities	⊗ ⋔ ⅃ ⅂ ♀ ♨ 🏠 ⊀ ⋔ 🛈 Nicholas Lamb.
Leisure	trolley for hire, driving range, putting green, practice area.
Location	Off A38
Hotel	★★★(red)≜≜ Thornbury Castle Hotel, THORNBURY ☎ 01454 281182 18 ⇆ ⋔

PUCKRUP HALL HOTEL and GOLF CLUB

Puckrup, Tewkesbury, Gloucestershire GL20 6EL
Telephone: (01684) 296200
Fax: (01684) 850788

Puckrup Hall Hotel and Golf Club is set amidst 140 acres of rolling parkland between the Cotswolds and Malvern Hills, just a few minutes from junction 8 of the M5. The 18 hole par 71 championship golf course, with the addition of lakes to the natural water sources and astute use of specimen trees, will satisfy the most discerning golfer. The 84 luxury bedrooms, superb cuisine and extensive conference and private dining facilities are all complemented by "Generations" Leisure Club which hosts swimming pool, spa bath and crêche. Altogether the ideal location for a touring base, golfing break or management retreat.

WESTONBIRT   Map 03 ST88

Westonbirt Westonbirt School GL8 8QG
☎ 01666 880242
A parkland course with good views.
9 holes, 4504yds, Par 64, SSS 64.
Club membership 150.

Visitors	no restrictions.
Societies	no reserved tees.
Green Fees	not confirmed.
Facilities	⅃
Leisure	practice area.
Location	E side of village off A433
Hotel	★★★ 65% Hare & Hounds Hotel, Westonbirt, TETBURY ☎ 01666 880233 22 ⇆ ⋔Annexe8 ⇆ ⋔

WICK   Map 03 ST77

Tracy Park Tracy Park, Bath Rd BS15 5RN
☎ 0117 937 2251
Three undulating 9-hole parkland courses situated on the south-western escarpment of the Cotswolds, affording fine views. Whichever 18-hole combination is played, the variety of holes will ensure an enjoyable and interesting challenge to all levels of handicap. Natural water hazards affect a number of holes. The clubhouse dates back to 1600 and is a building of great beauty and elegance, set in the 220 acre estate of this golf and country club.
Avon Course: 9 holes, 3091yds, Par 35, SSS 35.
Bristol Course: 9 holes, 3332yds, Par 35, SSS 35.
Cotswold Course: 9 holes, 3098yds, Par 35, SSS 35.
Club membership 900.

Visitors	no restrictions.
Societies	must telephone or write to P A Murphy.
Green Fees	£30 per day; £20 per round (£30 weekends).
Facilities	⊗ ⋔ ⅃ ⅂ ♀ ♨ 🏠 ⊀ 🛈 Richard Berry.
Leisure	hard tennis courts, squash, motorised carts for hire, buggies for hire, trolley for hire, driving range, putting green, practice area.
Location	S side of village off A420
Hotel	★★★ 79% The Queensberry Hotel, Russel St, BATH ☎ 01225 447928 22 ⇆ ⋔

WOTTON-UNDER-EDGE   Map 03 ST79

Cotswold Edge Upper Rushmire GL12 7PT
☎ 01453 844167
Meadowland course situated in a quiet Cotswold valley with magnificent views. First half flat and open, second half more varied.
18 holes, 6170yds, Par 71, SSS 70.
Club membership 800.

Visitors	preferable to contact in advance, at weekends may only play with member.
Societies	must contact in writing or telephone in advance.
Green Fees	£15.50.
Facilities	⊗ ⅃ ⅂ ♀ ♨ 🏠 ⊀ 🛈 David Gosling.
Leisure	buggies for hire, trolley for hire, putting green, practice area.
Location	N of town on B4058 Wotton-Tetbury road
Hotel	★★ 66% Egypt Mill Hotel, NAILSWORTH ☎ 01453 833449 & 835449 6 ⇆ ⋔Annexe8 ⇆ ⋔

GREATER LONDON

Those courses which fall within the confines of the London Postal District area (ie have London postcodes - W1, SW1 etc) are listed under the county heading of **London** in the gazetteer (see page 147).

ADDINGTON   Map 05 TQ36

The Addington 205 Shirley Church Rd, Addington CR0 5AB ☎ 0181 777 1055
A world of heather, bracken, silver birch and pine referred to by Henry Longhurst as his favourite inland course. It is one where thought is required at every hole.
18 holes, 6242yds, Par 71, SSS 71, Course record 66.

Visitors	may not play weekends. Must be recognised of recognised club.
Societies	weekdays only, telephone for prior arrangement.
Green Fees	£30 per round or day weekdays only.
Facilities	⊗ ♥ ♀ ♣ 🏠 ⚑ ⚑ E Campbell.
Leisure	trolley for hire.
Hotel	★★★★ 68% Croydon Park Hotel, 7 Altyre Rd, CROYDON ☎ 0181 680 9200 212 ⇄ ⬚

Addington Court Featherbed Ln CR0 9AA ☎ 0181 657 0281
Challenging, well-drained courses designed by F. Hawtree. Two 18-hole courses, 9-hole course and a pitch-and-putt course.
Old Course: 18 holes, 5577yds, Par 67, SSS 67, Course record 60.
New Falconwood Course: 18 holes, 5360yds, Par 66, SSS 66.
Club membership 350.

Visitors	no restrictions.
Societies	must telephone in advance.
Green Fees	not confirmed.
Facilities	♀ ♣ 🏠 ⚑ ⚑ Geoffrey A Cotton.
Leisure	putting green, practice area, trolley hire.
Location	1m S off A2022
Hotel	★★★★ 65% Selsdon Park Hotel, Addington Rd, Sanderstead, CROYDON ☎ 0181 657 8811 170 ⇄ ⬚

Addington Palace Addington Park, Gravel Hill CR0 5BB ☎ 0181 654 3061
Hard-walking parkland course, with two (par 4) testing holes (2nd and 10th).
18 holes, 6286yds, Par 71, SSS 71, Course record 63.
Club membership 700.

Visitors	telephone in advance, must play with member at weekends & bank holidays.
Societies	Tue, Wed & Fri only, telephone in advance.
Green Fees	£30 per day/round.
Facilities	⊗ ⅷ by prior arrangement ⅼ ♥ ♀ ♣ 🏠 ⚑ Roger Williams.
Leisure	trolley for hire, putting green, practice area.
Location	0.5m SW on A212
Hotel	★★★★ 65% Selsdon Park Hotel, Addington Rd, Sanderstead, CROYDON ☎ 0181 657 8811 170 ⇄ ⬚

BARNEHURST   Map 05 TQ57

Barnehurst Mayplace Rd East DA7 6JU ☎ 01322 523746
Parkland course, easy walking.
9 holes, 5320yds, Par 66, SSS 66.
Club membership 300.

Visitors	restricted Tue, Thu, Sat (pm) & Sun.
Societies	by arrangement.
Green Fees	not confirmed.
Facilities	♀ ♣ 🏠 ⚑ ⚑ Tudor Morgan.
Leisure	practice area, trolley hire.
Location	0.75m NW of Crayford off A2000
Hotel	B Forte Posthouse Bexley, Black Prince Interchange, Southwold Rd, BEXLEY ☎ 01322 526900 103 ⇄ ⬚

BARNET   Map 04 TQ29

Arkley Rowley Green Rd EN5 3HL ☎ 0181 449 0394
Wooded parkland course situated on highest spot in Hertfordshire with fine views.
9 holes, 6045yds, Par 69, SSS 69.
Club membership 450.

Visitors	may play weekdays only (ex Tue).
Societies	must contact in advance.
Green Fees	£20 per day.
Facilities	⊗ ⅼ ♥ ♀ ♣ 🏠 ⚑ Mark Squire.
Leisure	trolley for hire, putting green, practice area.
Location	2m W off A411
Hotel	★★★ 74% Edgwarebury Hotel, Barnet Ln, ELSTREE ☎ 0181 953 8227 47 ⇄ ⬚

Dyrham Park Country Club Galley Ln EN5 4RA ☎ 0181 440 3361
Parkland course.
18 holes, 6369yds, Par 71, SSS 70, Course record 65.
Club membership 1200.

Visitors	must be guest of member.
Societies	Wed only, must book in advance.
Green Fees	not confirmed.
Facilities	♀ (all day) ♣ 🏠 ⚑ ⚑ Bill Large.
Leisure	hard tennis courts, heated outdoor swimming pool, fishing.
Location	3m NW off A1081
Hotel	B Forte Posthouse South Mimms, SOUTH MIMMS ☎ 01707 643311 120 ⇄ ⬚

Old Fold Manor Old Fold Ln, Hadley Green EN5 4QN ☎ 0181 440 9185
Heathland course, good test of golf.
18 holes, 6481yds, Par 71, SSS 71, Course record 66.
Club membership 520.

Visitors	with member only weekends & bank holidays.
Societies	must apply in writing.
Green Fees	£20 per round; Mon & Wed public days £11 per round.
Facilities	⊗ ⅷ ⅼ ♥ ♀ (ex Mon & Wed) ♣ 🏠 ⚑ Daniel Fitzsimmons.
Leisure	trolley for hire, putting green, practice area.
Location	Off A1000 between Barnet/Potters Bar
Hotel	★★★★⚘ 69% West Lodge Park Hotel, Cockfosters Rd, HADLEY WOOD ☎ 0181 440 8311 43 ⇄ ⬚ Annexe2 ⇄ ⬚

BECKENHAM   Map 05 TQ36

Beckenham Place The Mansion BR3 2BP
☎ 0181 650 2292
Picturesque course in the grounds of a public park. The course is played over by the Braeside Golf Club.
18 holes, 5722yds, Par 68, SSS 68.
Club membership 200.
Visitors   no restrictions.
Societies   must contact in advance.
Green Fees not confirmed.
Facilities   ♀ 🛆 🏠 ⚐ ℓ
Location   0.5m N on B2015
Hotel   ★★★ 69% Bromley Court Hotel, Bromley Hill, BROMLEY ☎ 0181 464 5011 118 ⇥ 🅿

Langley Park Barnfield Wood Rd BR6 2SZ
☎ 0181 658 6849
This is a pleasant, but difficult, well-wooded, parkland course with natural hazards including a lake at the 18th hole.
18 holes, 6488yds, Par 69, SSS 71, Course record 65.
Club membership 700.
Visitors   must contact in advance and may not play weekends.
Societies   Wed & Thu only, telephone to book.
Green Fees £35 per day/round (concessionary rate winter).
Facilities   ⊗ ⅃ 🝆 🝆 ♀ 🛆 🏠 ⚐ ℓ Colin Staff.
Leisure   trolley for hire, putting green, practice area.
Location   0.5 N on B2015
Hotel   ★★★ 69% Bromley Court Hotel, Bromley Hill, BROMLEY
☎ 0181 464 5011 118 ⇥ 🅿

BEXLEYHEATH   Map 05 TQ47

Bexleyheath Mount Rd DA6 8JS ☎ 0181 303 6951
Undulating course.
9 holes, 5162yds, Par 66, SSS 66, Course record 65.
Club membership 330.
Visitors   must contact Secretary in advance, may not play weekends.
Societies   telephone in advance.
Green Fees £20 per day.
Facilities   ⊗ ⅃ 🝆 🝆 ♀ 🛆
Leisure   putting green.
Location   1m SW
Hotel   B Forte Posthouse Bexley, Black Prince Interchange, Southwold Rd, BEXLEY
☎ 01322 526900 103 ⇥ 🅿

BIGGIN HILL   Map 05 TQ45

Cherry Lodge Jail Ln TN16 3AX ☎ 01959 572250
Undulating parkland course with good views, 600feet above sea level and affected by wind. 14th is 434 yards across a valley and uphill. Requires two good shots to reach the green.
18 holes, 6652yds, Par 72, SSS 73.
Club membership 700.
Visitors   must contact in advance but may not play at weekends.
Societies   must telephone in advance.
Green Fees not confirmed.

Facilities   ♀ 🛆 🏠 ℓ Nigel Child.
Leisure   sauna, putting, practice area, buggy/trolley hire.
Location   1m E
Hotel   ★★★ 68% Kings Arms Hotel, Market Square, WESTERHAM ☎ 01959 562990 16 ⇥ 🅿

BROMLEY   Map 05 TQ46

Bromley Magpie Hall Ln BR2 8JF ☎ 0181 462 7014
Flat course, ideal for beginners.
9 holes, 2745yds, Par 70, SSS 67.
Visitors   no restrictions.
Societies   apply in writing.
Green Fees £4.85 per 9 holes (£6.15 weekends and bank holidays).
Facilities   ⊗ 🝆 🝆 ♀ 🛆 ⚐ ℓ Peter Remy.
Leisure   trolley for hire, putting green, practice area.
Location   2m SE off A21
Hotel   ★★★ 69% Bromley Court Hotel, Bromley Hill, BROMLEY ☎ 0181 464 5011 118 ⇥ 🅿

Shortlands Meadow Rd, Shortlands BR2 0PB
☎ 0181 460 2471
Easy walking parkland course with a brook as a natural hazard.
9 holes, 5261yds, Par 65, SSS 66, Course record 59.
Club membership 410.
Visitors   must be guest of member.
Green Fees not confirmed.
Facilities   🛆 🏠 ℓ Jamie Bates.
Location   0.75m W off A222
Hotel   ★★★ 69% Bromley Court Hotel, Bromley Hill, BROMLEY ☎ 0181 464 5011 118 ⇥ 🅿

Sundridge Park Garden Rd BR1 3NE
☎ 0181 460 0278
The East course is longer than the West but many think the shorter of the two courses is the more difficult. The East is surrounded by trees while the West is more hilly, with good views. Both are certainly a good test of golf.
East Course: 18 holes, 6516yds, Par 70, SSS 71, Course record 63.
West Course: 18 holes, 6016yds, Par 68, SSS 69, Course record 65.
Club membership 1200.
Visitors   may only play on weekdays. Must contact in advance and must have a handicap certificate.
Societies   must contact well in advance.
Green Fees £36 per day.
Facilities   ⊗ ⅃ 🝆 🝆 ♀ 🛆 🏠 ℓ Bob Cameron.
Leisure   trolley for hire, putting green.
Location   N side of town centre off A2212
Hotel   ★★★ 69% Bromley Court Hotel, Bromley Hill, BROMLEY
☎ 0181 464 5011 118 ⇥ 🅿

CARSHALTON   Map 04 TQ26

Oaks Sports Centre Woodmansterne Rd SM5 4AN
☎ 0181 643 8363
Public parkland course with floodlit, covered driving range.
18 holes, 6025yds, Par 70, SSS 69, Course record 65 or 9 holes, 1443yds, Par 28, SSS 28.
Club membership 864.
Visitors   no restrictions.   ▶

Societies must apply in writing.
Green Fees £11 per round (£13 weekends). 9 hole: £5.20 per round (£6 weekends).
Facilities ⊗ ⊼ ⅃ ⅃ ♀ ♨ ☎ ♈ ⅃ G Horley/P Russell/M Pilkinton.
Leisure squash, trolley for hire, driving range, putting green.
Location 0.5m S on B278
Hotel B Forte Posthouse Croydon, Purley Way, CROYDON ☎ 0181 688 5185 83 ⇥ ♟

CHESSINGTON
Map 04 TQ16

Chessington Garrison Ln KT9 2LW ☎ 0181 391 0948
Tree-lined parkland course designed by Patrick Tallack.
9 holes, 1400yds, Par 27, SSS 28.
Club membership 250.
Visitors must book 7.30am-noon weekends only.
Societies must telephone 1 month in advance.
Green Fees not confirmed.
Facilities ♀ ♨ ☎ ♈ ⅃
Location Opp Chessington South Station nr Zoo
Hotel ★★ 65% Haven Hotel, Portsmouth Rd, ESHER ☎ 0181 398 0023 16 ⇥ ♟Annexe4 ⇥ ♟

CHISLEHURST
Map 05 TQ47

Chislehurst Camden Park Rd BR7 5HJ ☎ 0181 467 2782
Pleasantly wooded undulating parkland/heathland course.
Magnificent clubhouse with historical associations.
18 holes, 5106yds, Par 66, SSS 65, Course record 61.
Club membership 800.
Visitors with member only weekends.
Societies weekdays only.
Green Fees £25 per round/day.
Facilities ⊗ ⊼ by prior arrangement ⅃ ⅃ ♀ ♨ ☎ ♈ ⅃ Mark Lawrence.
Leisure trolley for hire, putting green.
Hotel ★★★ 69% Bromley Court Hotel, Bromley Hill, BROMLEY ☎ 0181 464 5011 118 ⇥ ♟

COULSDON
Map 04 TQ25

Coulsdon Manor Hotel Coulsdon Court Rd CR5 2LL
☎ 0181 660 6083
A public parkland course with good views. Clubhouse formerly owned by the Byron family.
18 holes, 6037yds, Par 70, SSS 68.
Visitors must telephone up to 5 days in advance.
Societies by arrangement.
Green Fees £13 per round (£16 weekends & bank holidays).
Facilities ⊗ ⊼ ⅃ ⅃ ♀ ♨ ☎ ♈ ⊨⅃ David Copsey.
Leisure hard tennis courts, squash, sauna, solarium, gymnasium, trolley for hire, putting green, practice area.
Location 0.75m E off A23 on B2030
Hotel ★★★★ 73% Coulsdon Manor Hotel, Coulsdon Court Rd, Coulsdon, CROYDON ☎ 0181 668 0414 35 ⇥ ♟

Woodcote Park Meadow Hill, Bridle Way CR5 2QQ
☎ 0181 668 2788
Slightly undulating parkland course.
18 holes, 6669yds, Par 71, SSS 72, Course record 66.
Club membership 650.

Visitors contact professional for details. Visitors may not play weekends.
Societies must contact Secretary in advance.
Green Fees £25 per round (Mon-Fri only).
Facilities ⊗ ⊼ ⅃ ⅃ ♀ ♨ ☎ ⅃ D Hudspith.
Leisure trolley for hire, putting green, practice area.
Location 1m N of town centre off A237
Hotel B Forte Posthouse Croydon, Purley Way, CROYDON ☎ 0181 688 5185 83 ⇥ ♟

CROYDON
Map 04 TQ36

Croham Hurst Croham Rd CR2 7HJ ☎ 0181 657 5581
Parkland course with tree-lined fairways and bounded by wooded hills. Easy walking.
18 holes, 6274yds, Par 70, SSS 70.
Club membership 800.
Visitors must contact in advance & have handicap certificate. With member only weekends & bank holidays.
Societies must book 1 year in advance.
Green Fees £32 per day/round (£42 weekends & bank holidays).
Facilities ⊗ ⊼ by prior arrangement ⅃ ⅃ ♀ ♨ ☎ ♈ ⅃ Eric Stillwell.
Leisure trolley for hire, putting green, practice area.
Location (1.5m SE)
Hotel ★★★★ 65% Selsdon Park Hotel, Addington Rd, Sanderstead, CROYDON ☎ 0181 657 8811 170 ⇥ ♟

Selsdon Park Addington Rd, Sanderstead CR2 8YA
☎ 0181 657 8811
Parkland course. Full use of hotel's sporting facilities by residents.
18 holes, 6473yds, Par 73, SSS 71.
Visitors booking advisable.
Societies telephone in advance.
Green Fees £25 per round; £15 early birdie/twilight (£30/£20 weekends & bank holidays).
Facilities ⊗ ⊼ ⅃ ⅃ ♀ ♨ ☎ ♈ ⊨⅃ Tom O'Keefe.
Leisure hard and grass tennis courts, outdoor and indoor heated swimming pools, squash, sauna, solarium, gymnasium, motorised carts for hire, buggies for hire, trolley for hire, driving range, putting green, practice area, other leisure facilities for residents of hotel only.
Location 3m S on A2022
Hotel ★★★★ 65% Selsdon Park Hotel, Addington Rd, Sanderstead, CROYDON ☎ 0181 657 8811 170 ⇥ ♟

Shirley Park 194 Addiscombe Rd CR0 7LB
☎ 0181 654 1143
This parkland course lies amid fine woodland with good views of Shirley Hills. The more testing holes come in the middle section of the course. The remarkable 7th hole calls for a 187-yard iron or wood shot diagonally across a narrow valley to a shelved green set right-handed into a ridge.
18 holes, 6210yds, Par 71, SSS 70, Course record 66.
Club membership 600.
Visitors should contact in advance. With member only at weekends.
Societies by arrangement.

Addington Road, Sanderstead,
S. Croydon, Surrey CR2 8YA
Tel: 0181 657 8811   Fax: 0181 651 6171

In a magnificent parkland settting, designed by J. H. Taylor and opened in 1929, this
challenging 18 hole, 6,473 yards course has now been brought up to championship
standard.
The Selsdon Park Golf Academy is located here and provides excellent tuition along
with master classes and special privileges. An annual season ticket is available.
The course is open to green fee players. Golf societies welcome.

Green Fees £29 weekdays only.
Facilities   ⊗ ⵗ ⵎ ⵗ ♀ ⵥ 🕿 ⵗ ℓ Nick Allen.
Leisure   trolley for hire, putting green, practice area.
Location   E side of town centre on A232
Hotel   ★★★★ 68% Croydon Park Hotel, 7 Altyre
Rd, CROYDON
🕿 0181 680 9200 212 ⇥ 📶

DOWNE   Map 05 TQ46

High Elms High Elms Rd BR6 7JL
🕿 01689 853232 & 858175 bookings
Municipal parkland course. Very tight 13th, 230 yds (par 3).
18 holes, 6210yds, Par 71, SSS 70, Course record 68.
Club membership 450.
Visitors   no restrictions.
Societies   telephone to book. Tel 01689 861813.
Green Fees   £9.75 per 18 holes (£12.80 weekends and bank
holidays).
Facilities   ⊗ ⵗ ⵎ ⵗ ♀ ⵥ 🕿 ⵗ ℓ Peter Remy.
Leisure   motorised carts for hire, buggies for hire, trolley
for hire, putting green, practice area.
Location   1.5m NE
Hotel   ★★★ 69% Bromley Court Hotel, Bromley Hill,
BROMLEY
🕿 0181 464 5011 118 ⇥ 📶

West Kent West Hill BR6 7JJ   🕿 01689 851323
Partly hilly downland course.
18 holes, 6399yds, Par 70, SSS 70.
Club membership 700.
Visitors   with member only at weekends. Must contact in
advance.
Societies   must apply in writing.
Green Fees   £40 per 36 holes; £26 per round.
Facilities   ⊗ ⵗ ⵎ ⵗ ♀ ⵥ 🕿 ℓ Roger Fidler.
Leisure   trolley for hire, practice area.
Location   0.75m SW
Hotel   ★★★ 69% Bromley Court Hotel, Bromley Hill,
BROMLEY   🕿 0181 464 5011 118 ⇥ 📶

ENFIELD   Map 04 TQ39

Crews Hill Cattlegate Rd, Crews Hill EN2 8AZ
🕿 0181 363 6674
Parkland course in country surroundings.
18 holes, 6250yds, Par 70, SSS 70, Course record 65.
Club membership 603.
Visitors   must play with member at weekends. Handicap
certificate required.
Societies   Wed-Fri; must apply in writing.
Green Fees   on application.

Facilities   ⊗ ⵗ ⵎ ⵗ ♀ ⵥ 🕿 ℓ John Reynolds.
Leisure   motorised carts for hire, buggies for hire, trolley
for hire, putting green.
Location   3m NW off A1005
Hotel   ★★★ 57% Enfield Hotel, 52 Rowantree Rd,
ENFIELD 🕿 0181 366 3511 34 ⇥ 📶

Enfield Old Park Rd South EN2 7DA
🕿 0181 363 3970
Parkland course. Salmons Brook crosses 7 holes.
18 holes, 6154yds, Par 72, SSS 70, Course record 61.
Club membership 700.
Visitors   must contact in advance & have handicap
certificate.
Societies   must contact the secretary in advance.
Green Fees   £30 per day; £22 per round.
Facilities   ⊗ ⵗ ⵎ ⵗ ♀ ⵥ 🕿 ℓ Lee Fickling.
Leisure   trolley for hire, putting green.
Location   W side of town centre off A110
Hotel   ★★★ 57% Enfield Hotel, 52 Rowantree Rd,
ENFIELD 🕿 0181 366 3511 34 ⇥ 📶

Whitewebbs Municipal Beggars Hollow, Clay Hill EN2 9JW
🕿 0181 363 4454
Flat wooded parkland course. 9th hole is a left-hand dog-leg
with second shot over a brook.
18 holes, 5755yds, Par 68, SSS 68.
Club membership 350.
Visitors   must play with member.
Societies   must apply in writing to the secretary.
Green Fees   not confirmed.
Facilities   🕿 ⵗ ℓ David Lewis.
Location   N side of town centre
Hotel   ★★★ 57% Enfield Hotel, 52 Rowantree Rd,
ENFIELD 🕿 0181 366 3511 34 ⇥ 📶

GREENFORD   Map 04 TQ18

C & L Golf & Country Club Westend Rd, Northolt
UB5 6RD   🕿 0181 845 5662
Parkland course.
18 holes, 4438yds, Par 64, SSS 63.
Club membership 150.
Visitors   welcome, but may not play Sun mornings.
Societies   contact for details.
Green Fees   £8 per 18 holes; £5 per 9 holes (£10/£6
weekends).
Facilities   ⊗ ⵗ ⵎ ⵗ ♀ ⵥ ℓ Richard Kelly.
Leisure   hard tennis courts, outdoor swimming pool,
squash, sauna, solarium, gymnasium.
Location   Junct Westend Road/A40
Hotel   ★★★ 70% The Bridge Hotel, Western Av,
GREENFORD 🕿 0181 566 6246 68 ⇥ 📶

Ealing Perivale Ln UB6 8SS ☎ 0181 997 0937
Flat, parkland course relying on natural hazards; trees, tight
fairways, and the River Brent which affects 9 holes.
18 holes, 6216yds, Par 70, SSS 70, Course record 64.
Club membership 700.
Visitors Mon-Fri only on application to pro shop.
Societies Mon, Wed & Thu only by arrangement.
Green Fees not confirmed.
Facilities ♀⚐🏌 Arnold Stickley.
Leisure putting, practice, buggy/trolley hire.
Hotel ★★★ 70% The Bridge Hotel, Western Av,
GREENFORD ☎ 0181 566 6246 68 ⇄ ↻

Horsenden Hill Whitten Av, Woodland Rise UB6 0RD
☎ 0181 902 4555
A well-kept, tree-lined short course.
9 holes, 1618yds, Par 28, SSS 28.
Club membership 135.
Visitors no restrictions.
Societies telephone for details.
Green Fees not confirmed.
Facilities ♀⚐🏌🏌 Anthony Ferrier.
Location 3m NE on A4090
Hotel ★★★ 70% The Bridge Hotel, Western Av,
GREENFORD ☎ 0181 566 6246 68 ⇄ ↻

Lime Trees Park Ruislip Rd, Northolt UB5 6QZ
☎ 0181 842 0442
Parkland course.
9 holes, 5836yds, Par 71, SSS 69.
Club membership 300.
Visitors no restrictions, but advisable to book for
weekends.
Societies contact for details.
Green Fees £10.50 per 18 holes; £5.50 per 9 holes.
Facilities ⊗🏌♀⚐🏌 Ian Godleman.
Leisure trolley for hire, driving range, putting green.
Location 300yds off A40 at Polish War Memorial/A4180
towards Hayes
Hotel ★★★ 70% The Bridge Hotel, Western Av,
GREENFORD ☎ 0181 566 6246 68 ⇄ ↻

Perivale Park Stockdove Way UB6 8TJ
☎ 0181 575 7116
Parkland course.
9 holes, 2600yds, Par 68, SSS 65.
Club membership 250.
Visitors no restrictions.
Green Fees not confirmed.
Facilities ⚐🏌🏌 Peter Bryant.
Leisure trolleys.
Location E side of town centre, off A40
Hotel ★★★ 69% Carnarvon Hotel, Ealing Common,
LONDON ☎ 0181 992 5399 145 ⇄ ↻

HADLEY WOOD
Map 04 TQ29

Hadley Wood Beech Hill EN4 0JJ
☎ 0181 449 4328 & 4486
A parkland course on the northwest edge of London. The
gently undulating fairways have a friendly width inviting
the player to open his shoulders, though the thick rough
can be very punishing to the unwary. The course is
pleasantly wooded and there are some admirable views.
18 holes, 6457yds, Par 72, SSS 71, Course record 66.
Club membership 600.

Visitors may not play Tue mornings & Sat. Must
book in advance Sun.
Societies must contact in advance.
Green Fees £40 per day; £30 per round (£35 Sun).
Facilities ⊗🏌🏌♀⚐🏌🏌 Peter Jones.
Leisure trolley for hire, driving range, putting green,
practice area.
Location E side of village
Hotel ★★★★♨ 69% West Lodge Park Hotel,
Cockfosters Rd, HADLEY WOOD
☎ 0181 440 8311 43 ⇄ ↻Annexe2 ⇄ ↻

HAMPTON
Map 04 TQ17

Fulwell Wellington Rd, Hampton Hill TW12 1JY
☎ 0181 977 3844 & 081-977 2733
Championship-length parkland course with easy walking. The
575-yd, 17th, is notable.
18 holes, 6544yds, Par 71, SSS 71.
Club membership 750.
Visitors may not play Tue & weekends. Must contact in
advance and have a handicap certificate.
Societies must apply in writing.
Green Fees not confirmed.
Facilities ♀⚐🏌🏌 David Haslam.
Location 1.5m N on A311
Hotel ★★★ 70% Richmond Hill, Richmond Hill,
RICHMOND UPON THAMES
☎ 0181 940 2247 & 0181 940 5466 124 ⇄ ↻

HAMPTON WICK
Map 04 TQ16

Home Park KT1 4AD ☎ 0181 977 2423
Flat, parkland course with easy walking.
18 holes, 6611yds, Par 71, SSS 71.
Club membership 550.
Visitors welcome all week subject to club competitions.
Societies apply in writing.
Green Fees £30 per 36 holes; £20 per 18 holes (£25 per 18
holes weekends & bank holidays).
Facilities ⊗🏌🏌♀⚐🏌 Len Roberts.
Leisure putting green, practice area.
Location Off A308 on W side of Kingston Bridge
Hotel ★★★ 70% Richmond Hill, Richmond Hill,
RICHMOND UPON THAMES
☎ 0181 940 2247 & 0181 940 5466 124 ⇄ ↻

HILLINGDON
Map 04 TQ08

Hillingdon Dorset Way, Vine Ln UB10 0JR
☎ 01895 233956
Parkland course west of London.
9 holes, 5490yds, Par 68, SSS 67.
Club membership 400.
Visitors may not play Thu, weekends, or bank holidays.
Must have an introduction from own club.
Societies must apply in writing.
Green Fees not confirmed.
Facilities ♀⚐🏌
Location W side of town off A4020
Hotel ★★★ 63% Master Brewer Hotel, Western Av,
HILLINGDON
☎ 01895 251199 106 ⇄ ↻

HOUNSLOW
Map 04 TQ17

Airlinks Southall Ln TW5 9PE
☎ 0181 561 1418
Meadowland/parkland course designed by P. Allis and D. Thomas.
18 holes, 6000yds, Par 72, SSS 68, Course record 63.
Club membership 500.
Visitors may not play before noon at weekends.
Societies must apply in writing.
Green Fees not confirmed.
Facilities ♀ ♨ 🏠 🏌 ⓕ Chris Woodcocks.
Leisure flood lit driving range,cart/buggy hire.
Location W of Hounslow off M4 junc 3
Hotel ★★★ 63% Master Robert Hotel, Great West Rd, HOUNSLOW
☎ 0181 570 6261 94 ⇌ ℾ

Hounslow Heath Municipal Staines Rd TW4 5DS
☎ 0181 570 5271
Parkland course in a conservation area, planted with an attractive variety of trees. The 15th hole lies between the fork of two rivers.
18 holes, 5901yds, Par 69, SSS 68, Course record 62.
Club membership 300.
Visitors pay & play, bookings taken for weekends & bank holidays seven days in advance.
Societies must telephone and confirm at least 14 days in advance.
Green Fees £7.50 per day (£10.50 weekends & bank holidays).
Facilities ⊗ ♨ ⟟ ♨ 🏠 🏌
Leisure trolley for hire, putting green, practice area.
Hotel B The Heathrow Crest, Sipson Rd, WEST DRAYTON
☎ 0181 759 2323 569 ⇌ ℾ

ILFORD
Map 05 TQ48

Ilford Wanstead Park Rd IG1 3TR
☎ 0181 554 2930
Fairly flat parkland course intersected five times by a river.
18 holes, 5308yds, Par 67, SSS 66, Course record 61.
Club membership 700.
Visitors must contact in advance, book with pro on 0181 554 0094.
Societies telephone for provisional date and booking form.
Green Fees £13.50 per round (£16 weekends).
Facilities ⊗ ⟟ ♨ ♨ ♀ ♨ 🏠 ⓕ S Dowsett.
Location NW side of town centre off A12
Hotel ★★★ 65% Epping Forest Moat House, Oak Hill, WOODFORD GREEN
☎ 0181 787 9988 99 ⇌ ℾ

ISLEWORTH
Map 04 TQ17

Wyke Green Syon Ln TW7 5PT
☎ 0181 560 8777 & 847 0685
Fairly flat parkland course.
18 holes, 6211yds, Par 69, SSS 70, Course record 64.
Club membership 650.
Visitors may not play before 3pm weekends and bank holidays, must have a handicap certificate required.

Societies must apply in writing or telephone in advance, Tue & Thu only.
Green Fees £25 per day (£42 weekends, after 3pm).
Facilities ⊗ ⟟ ♨ ♨ ♀ ♨ 🏠 ⓕ David Holmes.
Leisure motorised carts for hire, buggies for hire, trolley for hire, putting green, practice area.
Location 1.5m N on B454 off A4
Hotel ★★★ 63% Master Robert Hotel, Great West Rd, HOUNSLOW
☎ 0181 570 6261 94 ⇌ ℾ

KINGSTON UPON THAMES
Map 04 TQ16

Coombe Hill Golf Club Dr, Coombe Ln West KT2 7DG
☎ 0181 942 2284
A splendid course in wooded terrain. The undulations and trees make it an especially interesting course of great charm. And there is a lovely display of rhododendrons in May and June.
18 holes, 6293yds, Par 71, SSS 71, Course record 67.
Club membership 600.
Visitors must contact in advance. With member only at weekends.
Societies must book in advance.
Green Fees £50 per day/round; £30 after 3pm (weekdays).
Facilities ⊗ ⟟ ♨ ♨ ♀ ♨ 🏠 🏌 ⓕ Craig Defoy.
Leisure sauna, buggies for hire, trolley for hire, putting green, practice area, snooker.
Location 1.75m E on A238
Hotel ★★★ 68% Kingston Lodge Hotel, Kingston Hill, KINGSTON UPON THAMES ☎ 0181 541 4481 62 ⇌ ℾ

Coombe Wood George Rd, Kingston Hill KT2 7NS
☎ 0181 942 0388
Parkland course.
18 holes, 5210yds, Par 66, SSS 66.
Club membership 630.
Visitors must contact in advance & play with member at weekends.
Societies Wed, Thu & Fri; must contact in advance.
Green Fees £32 per day; £21 per 18 holes; £13 after 6pm.
Facilities ⊗ ⟟ by prior arrangement ♨ ♨ ♀ ♨ 🏠 ⓕ David Butler.
Leisure trolley for hire, putting green, practice area.
Location 1.25m NE on A308
Hotel ★★★ 68% Kingston Lodge Hotel, Kingston Hill, KINGSTON UPON THAMES
☎ 0181 541 4481 62 ⇌ ℾ

MITCHAM
Map 04 TQ26

Mitcham Carshalton Rd CR4 4HN ☎ 0181 648 4280
A wooded heathland course on a gravel base.
18 holes, 5935yds, Par 69, SSS 68, Course record 65.
Club membership 500.
Visitors must telephone & book in advance.
Societies must phone in advance.
Green Fees not confirmed.
Facilities ♀ ♨ 🏠 ⓕ Jeff Godfrey.
Leisure putting green,trolley hire.
Location 1m S
Hotel B Forte Posthouse Croydon, Purley Way, CROYDON ☎ 0181 688 5185 83 ⇌ ℾ

NEW MALDEN   Map 04 TQ26

Malden Traps Ln KT3 4RS ☎ 0181 942 0654
Parkland course with the hazard of the Beverley Brook which
affects 4 holes (3rd, 7th, 8th and 12th).
18 holes, 6295yds, Par 71, SSS 70.
Club membership 800.

Visitors	restricted weekends and bank holidays. Advisable to telephone.
Societies	must apply in writing.
Green Fees	on application.
Facilities	⊗ ℳ ⓛ 🞂 ♀ ♨ 🏠 ⓕ Robert Hunter.
Leisure	buggies for hire, trolley for hire, putting green.
Location	N side of town centre off B283
Hotel	★★★ 68% Kingston Lodge Hotel, Kingston Hill, KINGSTON UPON THAMES ☎ 0181 541 4481 62 ⇄ ⋔

NORTHWOOD   Map 04 TQ09

Haste Hill The Drive HA6 1HN
☎ 01923 822877 & 825224
Parkland course with stream running through. Excellent
views.
18 holes, 5787yds, Par 68, SSS 68.
Club membership 350.

Visitors	no restrictions.
Societies	must apply in advance.
Green Fees	not confirmed.
Facilities	♀ ♨ 🏠 ⓕ
Leisure	putting, cart/buggy/trolley hire.
Location	0.5m S off A404
Hotel	★★ 69% Harrow Hotel, Roxborough Bridge, 12-22 Pinner Rd, HARROW ☎ 0181 427 3435 57 ⇄ ⋔Annexe23 ⇄ ⋔

Northwood Rickmansworth Rd HA6 2QW
☎ 01923 821384
A very old club to which, it is said, golfers used to drive
from London by horse-carriage. They would find their
golf interesting as present-day players do. The course is
relatively flat although there are some undulations, and
trees and whins add not only to the beauty of the course
but also to the test of golf.
18 holes, 6553yds, Par 71, SSS 71, Course record 67.
Club membership 650.

Visitors	must contact in advance. May not play weekends.
Societies	must apply in writing.
Green Fees	£24 per round.
Facilities	⊗ ℳ ⓛ 🞂 ♀ ♨ 🏠 ⓕ ⓕ C J Holdsworth.
Leisure	trolley for hire, putting green, practice area.
Location	SW side of village off A404
Hotel	★★ 69% Harrow Hotel, Roxborough Bridge, 12-22 Pinner Rd, HARROW ☎ 0181 427 3435 57 ⇄ ⋔Annexe23 ⇄ ⋔

Sandy Lodge Sandy Lodge Ln HA6 2JD
☎ 01923 825429
A links-type, very sandy, heathland course.
18 holes, 6080yds, Par 71, SSS 70, Course record 64.
Club membership 780.

Visitors	must contact in advance.
Societies	must telephone in advance.

Green Fees	on application.
Facilities	⊗ ℳ ⓛ 🞂 ♀ ♨ 🏠 ⓕ Jeff Pinsent.
Leisure	trolley for hire, putting green, practice area.
Location	N side of town centre off A4125
Hotel	★★★ 62% The White House, Upton Rd, WATFORD ☎ 01923 237316 60 ⇄ ⋔Annexe26 ⇄ ⋔

ORPINGTON   Map 05 TQ46

Chelsfield Lakes Golf Centre Court Rd BR6 9BX
☎ 01689 896266
A downland course but some holes are played through the
orchards which used to occupy the site. The 9th and 18th
holes are separated by a hazardous lake.
18 holes, 6077yds, Par 71, SSS 69, Course record 64.
Club membership 438.

Visitors	must book in advance.
Societies	telephone in advance.
Green Fees	£14 per round (£17 weekends & bank holidays). 9 hole par 3 £5.50 (£6 weekends).
Facilities	⊗ ℳ ⓛ 🞂 ♀ ♨ 🏠 ⓕ ⓕ N Lee/B Hodkin/D Clark.
Leisure	trolley for hire, floodlit driving range, putting green, par 3 course.
Location	Exit M25 junct 4, on A224 Court Rd
Hotel	★★★ 69% Bromley Court Hotel, Bromley Hill, BROMLEY ☎ 0181 464 5011 118 ⇄ ⋔

Cray Valley Sandy Ln BR5 3HY
☎ 01689 39677 & 31927
An open parkland course with two man-made lakes and open
ditches.
18 holes, 5400yds, Par 70, SSS 67.
Club membership 640.

Visitors	no restrictions.
Societies	by arrangement.
Green Fees	not confirmed.
Facilities	♀ ♨ 🏠 ⓕ ⓕ John Gregory.
Location	1m off A20
Hotel	★★★ 69% Bromley Court Hotel, Bromley Hill, BROMLEY ☎ 0181 464 5011 118 ⇄ ⋔

Lullingstone Park Parkgate, Chelsfield BR6 7PX
☎ 01959 533793
Popular 27-hole public course set in 690 acres of undulating
parkland. Championship length 18-holes, plus 9-hole course
and a further 9-hole pitch and putt.
*Main Lullingstone Park Golf Course: 18 holes, 6759yds, Par
72, SSS 72, Course record 71 or 9 holes, 2432yds, Par 33,
SSS 33.*

Visitors	telephone for details.
Societies	must telephone in advance.
Green Fees	£9.30 per 18 holes; £5.80 per 9 holes (£11.70-£14.30/£7.80 weekends).
Facilities	⊗ ℳ ⓛ 🞂 ♀ ♨ 🏠 ⓕ ⓕ Alan Hodgson.
Leisure	motorised carts for hire, buggies for hire, trolley for hire, driving range, putting green, practice area, pitch & putt.
Location	Leave M25 junct 4 and take Well Hill turn
Hotel	★★★ 69% Bromley Court Hotel, Bromley Hill, BROMLEY ☎ 0181 464 5011 118 ⇄ ⋔

Ruxley Park Golf Centre Sandy Ln, St Paul's Cray
BR5 3HY ☎ 01689 871490
Parkland course with public, floodlit driving range. Difficult
6th hole, par 4. Easy walking and good views.
18 holes, 5703yds, Par 70, SSS 68.
Club membership 450.
Visitors book in advance.
Societies telephone for details 01689 839677.
Green Fees telephone for details.
Facilities ⊗ ⊞ ⅃ ♨ ♀ ⅄ 🖼 ⅂ ⅃ Richard Pilbury.
Leisure motorised carts for hire, buggies for hire, trolley
for hire, covered and floodlit driving range,
putting green, practice area, 9 hole par 3 course.
Location 2m NE on A223
Hotel ★★★ 69% Bromley Court Hotel, Bromley Hill,
BROMLEY
☎ 0181 464 5011 118 ⇥ ⅌

PINNER   Map 04 TQ18

Grims Dyke Oxhey Ln, Hatch End HA5 4AL
☎ 0181 428 4539
Pleasant, undulating parkland course.
18 holes, 5600yds, Par 69, SSS 67, Course record 62.
Club membership 580.
Visitors must contact in advance, may not play
weekends.
Societies by arrangement, booked in advance.
Green Fees £25 per day; £20 per round.
Facilities ⊗ ⊞ by prior arrangement ♨ ♀ ⅄ 🖼 ⅂
⅃ John Rule.
Leisure trolley for hire, putting green, practice area.
Location 3m N of Harrow on A4008
Hotel ★★ 69% Harrow Hotel, Roxborough Bridge,
12-22 Pinner Rd, HARROW
☎ 0181 427 3435 57 ⇥ ⅌Annexe23 ⇥ ⅌

Pinner Hill Southview Rd, Pinner Hill HA5 3YA
☎ 0181 866 0963 & 081-866 2109
A hilly, wooded parkland course.
18 holes, 6266yds, Par 72, SSS 70, Course record 63.
Club membership 770.
Visitors are required to have handicap certificate on Mon,
Tue & Fri. Public days Wed & Thu. Contact in
advance.
Societies Mon, Tue & Fri only, by arrangement.
Green Fees not confirmed.
Facilities ♀ ⅄ 🖼 ⅂ ⅃ Mark Grieve.
Location 2m NW off A404
Hotel ★★ 69% Harrow Hotel, Roxborough Bridge,
12-22 Pinner Rd, HARROW
☎ 0181 427 3435 57 ⇥ ⅌Annexe23 ⇥ ⅌

PURLEY   Map 05 TQ36

Purley Downs 106 Purley Downs Rd CR2 0RB
☎ 0181 657 8347
Hilly downland course. Notable holes are 6th and 12th.
18 holes, 6020yds, Par 70, SSS 69, Course record 64.
Club membership 700.
Visitors must have a handicap certificate, & play on
weekdays only with member.
Societies must contact in advance.
Green Fees not confirmed.
Facilities ♀ ⅄ 🖼 ⅃ Graham Wilson.

Leisure putting,trolley hire,practice area.
Location E side of town centre off A235
Hotel B Forte Posthouse Croydon, Purley Way,
CROYDON ☎ 0181 688 5185 83 ⇥ ⅌

RICHMOND UPON THAMES   Map 04 TQ17

Richmond Sudbrook Park, Petersham TW10 7AS
☎ 0181 940 4351
A beautiful and historic wooded, parkland course on the
edge of Richmond Park, with six par-3 holes. The 4th is
often described as the best short hole in the south of
England. Low scores are uncommon because cunningly
sited trees call for great accuracy. The clubhouse is one
of the most distinguished small Georgian mansions in
England.
18 holes, 6007yds, Par 70, SSS 69.
Club membership 700.
Visitors may not play weekends.
Societies must apply in writing.
Green Fees not confirmed.
Facilities ♀ ⅄ 🖼 ⅂ ⅃ Nick Job.
Location 1.5m S off A307
Hotel ★★★ 70% Richmond Hill, Richmond Hill,
RICHMOND UPON THAMES
☎ 0181 940 2247 & 0181 940 5466 124 ⇥ ⅌

Royal Mid-Surrey Old Deer Park TW9 2SB
☎ 0181 940 1894
A long playing parkland course. The flat fairways are
cleverly bunkered. The 18th provides an exceptionally
good par 4 finish with a huge bunker before the green to
catch the not quite perfect long second.
Outer Course: 18 holes, 6343yds, Par 69, SSS 70.
Inner Course: 18 holes, 5544yds, Par 67.
Club membership 1250.
Visitors may not play at weekends. Must contact in
advance and bring a handicap certificate.
Societies must apply in writing.
Green Fees not confirmed.
Facilities ⊗ ♨ ♀ ⅄ 🖼 ⅂ ⅃ David Talbot.
Leisure motorised carts for hire, trolley for hire.
Location 0.5m N of Richmond upon Thames off
A316
Hotel ★★★ 70% Richmond Hill, Richmond Hill,
RICHMOND UPON THAMES
☎ 0181 940 2247 & 0181 940 5466 124 ⇥ ⅌

ROMFORD   Map 05 TQ58

Maylands Golf Club & Country Park Colchester Rd, Harold
Park RM3 0AZ ☎ 01708 346466
Picturesque undulating parkland course.
18 holes, 6351yds, Par 71, SSS 70, Course record 67.
Club membership 700.
Visitors proof of membership or handicap certificate
required, with member only at weekends.
Societies Mon, Wed & Fri only, by arrangement.
Green Fees not confirmed.
Facilities ♀ ⅄ 🖼 ⅂ ⅃ John Hopkin.
Leisure putting, practice, cart/buggy/trolley hire.
Hotel B Forte Posthouse Brentwood, Brook St,
BRENTWOOD ☎ 01277 260260 111 ⇥

Risebridge Golf Centre Risebridge Chase, Lower Bedfords Rd RM1 4DG ☎ 01708 741429
A well matured parkland golf course, with many challenging holes especially the long 12th, the Par 4 13th and Par 5 14th with water and a two tiered green.
18 holes: 18 holes, 6000yds, Par 71, SSS 70, Course record 66.
9 holes: 9 holes, 459yds, Par 27, SSS 27.
Club membership 300.
Visitors   no restrictions.
Societies   must telephone in advance.
Green Fees £10 per round (£12 weekends & bank holidays) reduced rate twilight rounds on request.
Facilities ⊗ ⅋ ⬛ 🅿 ♀ 🛆 🏠 🎯 ✆ Paul Jennings.
Leisure   trolley for hire, driving range, putting green, practice area.
Location   Between Colier Row and Harold Hill
Hotel   ★★★ 61% Palms Hotel, Southend Arterial Rd, HORNCHURCH ☎ 01708 346789 137 ⇔ 🐾

Romford Heath Dr, Gidea Park RM2 5QB
☎ 01708 740986
A many-bunkered parkland course with easy walking. It is said there are as many bunkers as there are days in the year. The ground is quick drying making a good course for winter play when other courses might be too wet.
18 holes, 6374yds, Par 72, SSS 70.
Club membership 693.
Visitors   with member only weekends & bank holidays. Must contact in advance & have handicap certificate.
Societies   must telephone in advance.
Green Fees not confirmed.
Facilities ♀ 🛆 🏠 ✆ Harry Flatman.
Location   1m NE on A118
Hotel   B Forte Posthouse Brentwood, Brook St, BRENTWOOD ☎ 01277 260260 111 ⇔

RUISLIP   Map 04 TQ08

Ruislip Ickenham Rd HA4 7DQ ☎ 01895 638081
Municipal parkland course. Many trees.
18 holes, 5700yds, Par 69, SSS 68, Course record 65.
Club membership 500.
Visitors   advised to telephone in advance.
Societies   must contact in advance.
Green Fees £10 per day (£15 weekends & bank holidays).
Facilities ⊗ ⅋ ⬛ 🅿 ♀ 🛆 🏠 🎯 ✆ Paul Glozier.
Leisure   motorised carts for hire, buggies for hire, trolley for hire, driving range, putting green, pool tables, snooker.
Location   0.5m SW on B466
Hotel   ★★★ 63% Master Brewer Hotel, Western Av, HILLINGDON ☎ 01895 251199 106 ⇔ 🐾

SIDCUP   Map 05 TQ47

Sidcup 7 Hurst Rd DA15 9AE ☎ 0181 300 2150
Easy walking parkland course with natural water hazards.
9 holes, 5722yds, Par 68, SSS 68.
Club membership 380.
Visitors   contact in advance and may not play weekends.
Societies   must apply in writing.
Green Fees £18 per day/round.
Facilities ⊗ ⅋ ⬛ 🅿 ♀ 🛆 🏠 ✆ John Murray.
Leisure   putting green, practice area.

Location   N side of town centre off A222
Hotel   ★★★★ 71% Swallow Hotel, 1 Broadway, BEXLEYHEATH ☎ 0181 298 1000 142 ⇔ 🐾

SOUTHALL   Map 04 TQ17

West Middlesex Greenford Rd UB1 3EE ☎ 0181 574 3450
Gently undulating parkland course.
18 holes, 6242yds, Par 69, SSS 70, Course record 64.
Club membership 700.
Visitors   must contact in advance and may not play at weekends.
Societies   must apply in advance.
Green Fees £15.50 per round; £10 Mon & Wed.
Facilities ⊗ ⬛ 🅿 ♀ 🛆 🏠 ✆ I P Harris.
Leisure   trolley for hire, putting green, practice area.
Location   W side of town centre on A4127 off A4020
Hotel   ★★★ 63% Master Robert Hotel, Great West Rd, HOUNSLOW ☎ 0181 570 6261 94 ⇔ 🐾

STANMORE   Map 04 TQ19

Stanmore 29 Gordon Av HA7 2RL ☎ 0181 954 2599
North London parkland course.
18 holes, 5860yds, Par 68, SSS 68, Course record 61.
Club membership 560.
Visitors   may not play weekends. Contact professional (0181 954 2646).
Societies   phone in advance for booking sheet.
Green Fees Mon & Fri £13 per day; £10 per round. Tue-Thu £32 per day; £25 per round.
Facilities ⊗ ⅋ ⬛ 🅿 ♀ 🛆 🏠 ✆ V Law.
Leisure   trolley for hire, practice area.
Location   S side of town centre, between Stanmore & Belmont
Hotel   ★★ 69% Harrow Hotel, Roxborough Bridge, 12-22 Pinner Rd, HARROW ☎ 0181 427 3435 57 ⇔ 🐾Annexe23 ⇔ 🐾

SURBITON   Map 04 TQ16

Surbiton Woodstock Ln KT9 1UG
☎ 0181 398 3101 (Secretary) & 398 6619 (Pro)
Parkland course with easy walking.
18 holes, 6055yds, Par 70, SSS 69, Course record 63.
Club membership 700.
Visitors   with member only at weekends & bank holidays. No visitors Tue am (Ladies Day).
Societies   Mon & Fri only. Apply year in advance.
Green Fees £40.50 per day; £27 per round.
Facilities ⊗ ⅋ ⬛ 🅿 ♀ 🛆 🏠 ✆ Paul Milton.
Leisure   trolley for hire, putting green, practice area.
Location   2m S off A3
Hotel   ★★ 65% Haven Hotel, Portsmouth Rd, ESHER ☎ 0181 398 0023 16 ⇔ 🐾Annexe4 ⇔ 🐾

TWICKENHAM   Map 04 TQ17

Strawberry Hill Wellesley Rd, Strawberry Hill TW2 5SD
☎ 0181 894 0165
Parkland course with easy walking.
9 holes, 4762yds, Par 64, SSS 62, Course record 59.
Club membership 300.

Visitors	must contact in advance.
Societies	must apply in writing.
Green Fees	£26 per day; £20 per round.
Facilities	ⓑ ☕ ♀ ♣ 🏠 ⒧ Peter Buchan.
Leisure	trolley for hire, putting green, practice area.
Location	S side of town centre off A311
Hotel	★★★ 70% Richmond Hill, Richmond Hill, RICHMOND UPON THAMES ☎ 0181 940 2247 & 0181 940 5466 124 ⇆ ⓡ

Twickenham Staines Rd TW2 5JD
☎ 0181 783 1748 & 1698
Municipal commonland course.
9 holes, 3180yds, Par 36, SSS 69.

Visitors	must book in advance for weekends & bank holidays.
Societies	apply in advance
Green Fees	£12 per 18 holes; £6 per 9 holes (£14/£7 weekends & bank holidays).
Facilities	⊗ ⅏ ⓑ ☕ ♀ ♣ 🏠 ⒧ Steve LLoyd.
Leisure	trolley for hire, floodlit driving range, putting green.
Location	2m W on A305
Hotel	★★★ 70% Richmond Hill, Richmond Hill, RICHMOND UPON THAMES ☎ 0181 940 2247 & 0181 940 5466 124 ⇆ ⓡ

UPMINSTER   Map 05 TQ58

Upminster 114 Hall Ln RM14 1AU
☎ 01708 222788 (Secretary) 220000 (Pro)
Situated adjacent to a river, which features on several holes, this wooded parkland course provides a range of challenges for golfers of all abilities. Clubhouse is a beautiful Grade II listed building.
18 holes, 6076yds, Par 69, SSS 69, Course record 66.
Club membership 1000.

Visitors	contact in advance. Must have an introduction from own club.
Societies	telephone initially.
Green Fees	£30 per day; £25 per round weekdays.
Facilities	⊗ ⅏ ⓑ ☕ ♀ ♣ 🏠 ⒧ Neil Carr.
Leisure	trolley for hire, putting green.
Location	2m W from A127 junct with M25
Hotel	★★★ 61% Palms Hotel, Southend Arterial Rd, HORNCHURCH ☎ 01708 346789 137 ⇆ ⓡ

UXBRIDGE   Map 04 TQ08

Stockley Park Stockley Park UB11 1AQ
☎ 0181 813 5700
Hilly and challenging parkland championship course designed by Trent Jones in 1993 and situated within two miles of Heathrow Airport.
18 holes, 6548yds, Par 72, SSS 71.

Visitors	6 day in advance reservation facility.
Societies	please contact corporate Sales Manager.
Green Fees	£27 (£35 weekends).
Facilities	⊗ ⅏ ⓑ ☕ ♀ ♣ 🏠 ⒧ Alex Knox.
Leisure	trolley for hire, putting green.
Hotel	★★★ 63% Master Brewer Hotel, Western Av, HILLINGDON ☎ 01895 251199 106 ⇆ ⓡ

Uxbridge The Drive, Harefield Place UB10 8PA
☎ 01895 237287
Municipal parkland course, undulating and tricky.
18 holes, 5750yds, Par 68, SSS 68, Course record 66.
Club membership 700.

Visitors	no restrictions.
Societies	Thu by arrangment.
Green Fees	not confirmed.
Facilities	♀ ♣ 🏠 ⒧ ⒧ Phil Howard.
Leisure	buggies.
Location	2m N off B467
Hotel	★★★ 63% Master Brewer Hotel, Western Av, HILLINGDON ☎ 01895 251199 106 ⇆ ⓡ

WEMBLEY   Map 04 TQ18

Sudbury Bridgewater Rd HA0 1AL ☎ 0181 902 3713
Undulating parkland course very near centre of London.
18 holes, 6282yds, Par 69, SSS 70.
Club membership 650.

Visitors	must have handicap certificate. With member only at weekends.
Societies	must apply in writing.
Green Fees	not confirmed.
Facilities	♀ ♣ 🏠 ⒧ Neil Jordan.
Location	SW side of town centre on A4090
Hotel	★★★ 70% The Bridge Hotel, Western Av, GREENFORD ☎ 0181 566 6246 68 ⇆ ⓡ

WEST DRAYTON   Map 04 TQ07

Holiday Stockley Rd UB7 9BW ☎ 01895 444232
Fairly large, testing, hilly par 3 course suitable both for beginners and scratch players.
9 holes, 1618yds, Par 28, Course record 50.
Club membership 120.

Visitors	restricted Sun morning.
Societies	by arrangement.
Green Fees	not confirmed.
Facilities	♀ ♣ 🏠 ⒧ ⋈
Leisure	heated indoor swimming pool, sauna, solarium, gymnasium.
Location	1m SE off A408
Hotel	★★★★ 72% Holiday Inn Crowne Plaza, Stockley Rd, WEST DRAYTON ☎ 01895 445555 374 ⇆ ⓡ

WOODFORD GREEN   Map 05 TQ49

Woodford Sunset Av IG8 0ST
☎ 0181 504 3330 & 504 0553
Forest land course on the edge of Epping Forest. Views over the Lea Valley to the London skyline.
9 holes, 5806yds, Par 70, SSS 68, Course record 66.
Club membership 420.

Visitors	advisable to contact in advance. May not play Sat or Sun afternoon.
Societies	telephone for details.
Green Fees	£15 per day (£10 after 1pm in winter).
Facilities	⊗ ⓑ ☕ ♀ ♣ 🏠 ⒧ Ashley Johns.
Location	NW side of town centre off A104
Hotel	★★★ 65% Epping Forest Moat House, Oak Hill, WOODFORD GREEN ☎ 0181 787 9988 99 ⇆ ⓡ

GREATER MANCHESTER

ALTRINCHAM   Map 07 SJ78

Altrincham Stockport Rd WA15 7LP ☎ 0161 928 0761
Municipal parkland course with easy walking, water on many
holes, rolling contours and many trees. Driving range in
grounds.
18 holes, 6162yds, Par 71, SSS 69.
Club membership 350.
Visitors must book in advance.
Societies by prior arrangement.
Green Fees not confirmed.
Facilities ⚒ 🏌 ⛳ ℓ John Jackson.
Leisure driving range.
Location 0.75 E of Altrincham on A560
Hotel ★★★ 66% Cresta Court Hotel, Church St,
ALTRINCHAM ☎ 0161 927 7272 138 ⇄ 🏌

Dunham Forest Oldfield Ln WA14 4TY
☎ 0161 928 2605 & 928 2727
Attractive parkland course cut through magnificent beech
woods.
18 holes, 6636yds, Par 72, SSS 72.
Club membership 680.
Visitors may not play weekends & bank holidays.
Societies apply in writing or telephone in advance.
Green Fees £32 per day; £27 per round (£32 per round
weekends and bank holidays).
Facilities ⊗ ⍫ by prior arrangement ⏣ ⬛ ⚑ ⚒ 🏌 ⛳ 🏌
ℓ Ian Wrigley.
Leisure hard tennis courts, squash, motorised carts for
hire, buggies for hire, trolley for hire, putting
green, practice area.
Location 1.5m W off A56
Hotel ★★★ 60% Bowdon Hotel, Langham Rd,
Bowdon, ALTRINCHAM
☎ 0161 928 7121 82 ⇄ 🏌

Ringway Hale Mount, Hale Barns WA15 8SW
☎ 0161 904 9609
Parkland course, with interesting natural hazards. Easy
walking, good views.
18 holes, 6494yds, Par 71, SSS 71, Course record 67.
Club membership 700.
Visitors may not play before 9.30am or between 1-2pm,
play restricted Tue, Fri & Sat.
Societies Thu only May-Sep.
Green Fees £28 Mon-Thu (£34 weekends & bank holidays).
Facilities ⊗ ⍫ ⏣ ⬛ ⚑ ⚒ 🏌 ⛳ 🏌 ℓ Nick Ryan.
Leisure trolley for hire, putting green.
Location 2.5m SE on A538
Hotel ★★★ 66% Cresta Court Hotel, Church St,
ALTRINCHAM ☎ 0161 927 7272 138 ⇄ 🏌

ASHTON-IN-MAKERFIELD   Map 07 SJ59

Ashton-in-Makerfield Garswood Park, Liverpool Rd
WN4 0YT ☎ 01942 727267 & 719330
Well-wooded parkland course. Easy walking.
18 holes, 6250yds, Par 70, SSS 70.
Club membership 800.

Visitors with member only weekends & bank holidays.
No visitors Wed.
Societies apply in writing.
Green Fees not confirmed.
Facilities ⚑ ⚒ ⛳ 🏌 ℓ Peter Allan.
Leisure putting green, practice area, trolley hire.
Location 0.5m W of M6 (Junc 24) on A58
Hotel B Forte Posthouse Haydock, Lodge Ln, Newton-
Le-Willows, HAYDOCK
☎ 01942 717878 136 ⇄ 🏌

ASHTON-UNDER-LYNE   Map 07 SJ99

Ashton-under-Lyne Gorsey Way, Higher Hurst OL6 9HT
☎ 0161 330 1537
A testing, varied moorland course, with large greens. Easy
walking. Three new holes have improved the course.
18 holes, 6209yds, Par 70, SSS 70, Course record 68.
Club membership 550.
Visitors must contact in advance, with member only
weekends & bank holidays.
Societies apply in advance.
Green Fees £24 per day.
Facilities ⊗ ⍫ ⏣ ⬛ ⚑ ⚒ ⛳ ℓ Colin Boyle.
Leisure trolley for hire, putting green, practice area.
Location N off B6194
Hotel ★★ 69% York House Hotel, York Place,
Richmond St, ASHTON-UNDER-LYNE
☎ 0161 330 5899 24 ⇄ 🏌Annexe10 ⇄ 🏌

Dukinfield Lyne Edge, Yew Tree Ln SK16 5DF
☎ 0161 338 2340
Recently extended, tricky hillside course with several
difficult Par 3s and a very long par 5.
18 holes, 5303yds, Par 67, SSS 66.
Club membership 250.
Visitors may not play on Wed afternoons & must play
with member at weekends, advisable to contact
in advance.
Societies apply in writing or telephone.
Green Fees £16.50 per day.
Facilities ⊗ ⍫ ⏣ ⬛ ⚑ ⚒ ⛳ ℓ Jason Peel.
Leisure trolley for hire, practice area.
Location S off B6175
Hotel ★★ 69% York House Hotel, York Place,
Richmond St, ASHTON-UNDER-LYNE
☎ 0161 330 5899 24 ⇄ 🏌Annexe10 ⇄ 🏌

BOLTON   Map 07 SD70

Bolton Lostock Park, Chorley New Rd BL6 4AJ
☎ 01204 843067 & 843278
This well maintained heathland course is always a
pleasure to visit. The 12th hole should be treated with
respect and so too should the final four holes which have
ruined many a card.
18 holes, 6233yds, Par 70, SSS 70, Course record 66.
Club membership 612.
Visitors not able to play Tue before 2.30pm or on
competition days.
Societies write or telephone in advance, not accepted
Tue, Sat or Sun.
Green Fees £34 per day; £28 per round (£38/£32 Wed,
bank holidays and weekends).
Facilities ⊗ ⍫ ⏣ ⬛ ⚑ ⚒ ⛳ 🏌 ℓ R Longworth.

Leisure	trolley for hire, putting green, practice area.
Location	3m W of Bolton, on A673
Hotel	★★★★ 64% Georgian House Hotel, Manchester Rd, Blackrod, BOLTON ☎ 01942 814598 100 ⊭ ℾ

Breightmet Red Bridge, Ainsworth BL2 5PA
☎ 01204 527381
Long parkland course.
9 holes, 6416yds, Par 72, SSS 71, Course record 68.
Club membership 350.
Visitors may not play Wed or weekends.
Societies welcome Tue & Thu only, apply in advance in writing.
Green Fees not confirmed.
Facilities ♀🛆
Leisure putting green, practice area.
Location E side of town centre off A58
Hotel ★★★ 65% Egerton House Hotel, Blackburn Rd, Egerton, BOLTON ☎ 01204 307171 32 ⊭ ℾ

Deane Broadford Rd, Deane BL3 4NS
☎ 01204 61944 & 651808
Undulating parkland course with small ravines on approaches to some holes.
18 holes, 5583yds, Par 68, SSS 67, Course record 64.
Club membership 470.
Visitors must be a member of a golf club or member's guest. Restricted weekends.
Societies must telephone in advance and confirm in writing.
Green Fees £20 per day (£25 weekends).
Facilities ⊗ 〗🛆 🖢 ♀🛆 🖮 ℾ David Martindale.
Leisure trolley for hire, putting green, practice area.
Location 1m from exit 5 on M61 towards Bolton
Hotel ★★★ 64% Beaumont Hotel, Beaumont Rd, BOLTON ☎ 01204 651511 96 ⊭ ℾ

Dunscar Longworth Ln, Bromley Cross BL7 9QY
☎ 01204 303321
A scenic moorland course with panoramic views. A warm friendly club.
18 holes, 6085yds, Par 71, SSS 69, Course record 65.
Club membership 600.
Visitors must telephone 01204 592992 in advance.
Societies must apply in writing.
Green Fees £20 (£30 weekends & bank holidays).
Facilities ⊗ 〗🛆 🖢 ♀🛆 🖮 ℾ Gary Treadgold.
Leisure trolley for hire, putting green, practice area.
Location 2m N off A666
Hotel ★★★ 65% Egerton House Hotel, Blackburn Rd, Egerton, BOLTON ☎ 01204 307171 32 ⊭ ℾ

Great Lever & Farnworth Plodder Ln, Farnworth BL4 0LQ
☎ 01204 656137
Downland course with easy walking.
18 holes, 5986yds, Par 70, SSS 69, Course record 67.
Club membership 600.
Visitors must contact in advance.
Societies must contact in advance.
Green Fees £15 per day (£25 weekends & bank holidays).
Facilities ⊗ 〗🛆 🖢 ♀🛆 🖮 ℾ David Clarke.
Leisure trolley for hire, putting green, practice area.
Location SW side of town centre off A575

Hotel ★★★ 64% Beaumont Hotel, Beaumont Rd, BOLTON ☎ 01204 651511 96 ⊭ ℾ

Harwood Springfield, Roading Brook Rd, Harwood BL2 4JD ☎ 01204 522878
Mainly flat parkland course.
9 holes, 5993yds, Par 71, SSS 69, Course record 62.
Club membership 430.
Visitors must be members of a golf club and hold a current handicap cartificate. May not play at weekends.
Societies contact in writing.
Green Fees £15.
Facilities 🛆 🖢 ♀🛆 ℾ M Dance.
Leisure putting green, practice area.
Location 2.5m NE off B6196
Hotel ★★★ 65% Egerton House Hotel, Blackburn Rd, Egerton, BOLTON ☎ 01204 307171 32 ⊭ ℾ

Old Links Chorley Old Rd, Montserrat BL1 5SU
☎ 01204 842307
Championship moorland course.
18 holes, 6406yds, Par 72, SSS 72.
Club membership 600.
Visitors must contact in advance.
Societies apply by letter or telephone.
Green Fees £25 per day (£35 weekends and bank holidays).
Facilities ⊗ 〗🛆 🖢 ♀🛆 🖮 ℾ Paul Horridge.
Leisure trolley for hire, putting green, practice area.
Location NW of town centre on B6226
Hotel ★★★★ 64% Georgian House Hotel, Manchester Rd, Blackrod, BOLTON ☎ 01942 814598 100 ⊭ ℾ

Regent Park Links Rd, Chorley New Rd BL2 9XX
☎ 01204 844170
Parkland course.
18 holes, 6130yds, Par 70, SSS 69, Course record 67.
Club membership 200.
Visitors must book 6 days in advance.
Societies must telephone 01204 495421 in advance.
Green Fees £8 per round (£10 weekends).
Facilities ⊗ 〗🛆 🖢 ♀🛆 🖮 ℾℾ ℾ Bob Longworth.
Leisure trolley for hire, putting green, practice area.
Location 3.5m W off A673
Hotel ★★★ 64% Beaumont Hotel, Beaumont Rd, BOLTON ☎ 01204 651511 96 ⊭ ℾ

BRAMHALL Map 07 SJ88

Bramall Park 20 Manor Rd SK7 3LY ☎ 0161 485 3119
Well-wooded parkland course with splendid views of the Pennines.
18 holes, 6043yds, Par 70, SSS 69.
Club membership 600.
Visitors must contact in advance.
Societies apply in writing.
Green Fees not confirmed.
Facilities ♀🛆 🖮 ℾ
Location NW side of town centre off B5149
Hotel ★★★ 67% Bramhall Moat House, Bramhall Ln South, BRAMHALL ☎ 0161 439 8116 65 ⊭ ℾ

Bramhall Ladythorn Rd SK7 2EY ☎ 0161 439 6092
Undulating parkland course, easy walking.
18 holes, 6340yds, Par 70, SSS 70.
Club membership 700.
Visitors must contact in advance.
Societies apply in writing.
Green Fees £27 per day; £23 per round (£37/30 weekends).
Facilities ⊗ ℳ ﹫ ☷ ♀ ♨ ☎ ⏋ Richard Green.
Leisure motorised carts for hire, trolley for hire, driving
  range, putting green, practice area.
Location E side of town centre off A5102
Hotel ★★★ 67% Bramhall Moat House, Bramhall Ln
  South, BRAMHALL
  ☎ 0161 439 8116 65 ⇆ ⏏

BROMLEY CROSS   Map 07 SD71

Turton Wood End Farm, Chapeltown Rd BL7 9QH
☎ 01204 852235
Moorland course.
18 holes, 5690yds, Par 68, SSS 68.
Club membership 450.
Visitors avoid 11.30-2pm Wed Ladies day. Sat tee
  available after last competition.
Societies must contact in writing.
Green Fees £16 per day (£20 per day weekends).
Facilities ⊗ ℳ ﹫ ☷ ♀ ♨
Leisure putting green, practice area.
Location 3m N on A676
Hotel ★★★ 65% Egerton House Hotel, Blackburn
  Rd, Egerton, BOLTON
  ☎ 01204 307171 32 ⇆ ⏏

BURY   Map 07 SD81

Bury Unsworth Hall, Blackford Bridge BL9 9TJ
☎ 0161 766 2213 & 766 4897
Hard walking on hilly moorland course.
18 holes, 5961yds, Par 69, SSS 69, Course record 64.
Club membership 450.
Visitors must contact in advance.
Societies telephone 0161 766 4897.
Green Fees £22 per day (£28.50 weekends).
Facilities ⊗ ℳ ﹫ ☷ ♀ ♨ ☎ ⏋ S Crake.
Leisure trolley for hire, putting green, practice area.
Location 2m S on A56
Hotel ★★★ 63% Bolholt Country Park Hotel,
  Walshaw Rd, BURY
  ☎ 0161 764 5239 38 ⇆ ⏏Annexe9rm(8 ⇆ ⏏)

Lowes Park Hilltop, Lowes Rd BL9 6SU ☎ 0161 764 1231
Moorland course, with easy walking. Usually windy.
9 holes, 6009yds, Par 70, SSS 69, Course record 65.
Club membership 400.
Visitors may not play Wed & Sat, by appointment Sun.
  Must contact in advance.
Societies apply in writing.
Green Fees £15 per round (£20 Sun and bank holidays).
Facilities ⊗ ℳ ﹫ ☷ ♀ ♨ ☎
Leisure practice area.
Location N side of town centre off A56
Hotel ★★★ 63% Bolholt Country Park Hotel,
  Walshaw Rd, BURY
  ☎ 0161 764 5239 38 ⇆ ⏏Annexe9rm(8 ⇆ ⏏)

Walmersley Garretts Close, Walmersley BL9 6TE
☎ 0161 764 1429
Moorland hillside course, with wide fairways, large greens
and extensive views. Testing holes: 2nd (484 yds) par 5; 4th
(444 yds) par 4.
18 holes, 5341yds, Par 69, SSS 67.
Club membership 475.
Visitors welcome Mon & Tue after 5.30pm. With
  member only wed-Sun.
Societies must apply in writing.
Green Fees £20 per day.
Facilities ⊗ ℳ ﹫ ☷ ♀ ♨ ☎ ⏋ S Craike.
Leisure putting green, small practice area.
Location 2m N off A56
Hotel ★★★ 63% Old Mill Hotel, Springwood,
  RAMSBOTTOM
  ☎ 01706 822991 36 ⇆

CHEADLE   Map 07 SJ88

Cheadle Cheadle Rd SK8 1HW ☎ 0161 491 4452
Parkland course with hazards on every hole, from sand
bunkers and copses to a stream across six of the fairways.
9 holes, 5006yds, Par 64, SSS 65.
Club membership 425.
Visitors may not play Tue & Sat, & restricted Sun. Must
  contact in advance and have a handicap
  certificate and be member of a bona-fide golf
  club.
Societies apply in writing to secretary
Green Fees £15 per round 18 holes (£23 Sun & bank
  holidays).
Facilities ⊗ ℳ ﹫ ☷ ♀ ♨ ☎ ⏋ G J Norcott.
Leisure trolley for hire, putting green, practice area.
Location S side of village off A5149
Hotel ★★ 67% Wycliffe, 74 Edgeley Rd, Edgeley,
  STOCKPORT
  ☎ 0161 477 5395 20 ⇆ ⏏

DENTON   Map 07 SJ99

Denton Manchester Rd M34 2NU
☎ 0161 336 3218
Easy, flat parkland course with brook running through.
Notable hole is one called 'Death and Glory'.
18 holes, 6541yds, Par 72, SSS 71, Course record 66.
Club membership 585.
Visitors must contact in advance & may not play summer
  weekends.
Societies apply in advance.
Green Fees £22 (£27 weekends & bank holidays).
Facilities ⊗ ℳ ﹫ ☷ ♀ ♨ ☎ ⏋ M Hollingworth.
Leisure trolley for hire, putting green, practice area.
Location 1.5m W on A57
Hotel ★★ 69% York House Hotel, York Place,
  Richmond St, ASHTON-UNDER-LYNE
  ☎ 0161 330 5899 24 ⇆ ⏏Annexe10 ⇆ ⏏

FAILSWORTH   Map 07 SD80

Brookdale Medlock Rd M35 9WQ ☎ 0161 681 4534
Undulating parkland course, with river crossed 5 times in
play. Hard walking.
18 holes, 5841yds, Par 68, SSS 68, Course record 64.
Club membership 600.

Visitors advisable to contact in advance. May only play as guest of member at weekends.
Societies must contact in advance.
Green Fees £25 per day; £20 per round.
Facilities ⊗ by prior arrangement ⅷ by prior arrangement ⅃ ⬤ ♀ ⅄ 🏠 (Jason Spibey.
Leisure trolley for hire, putting green, practice area.
Location N side of Manchester
Hotel ★★ 69% York House Hotel, York Place, Richmond St, ASHTON-UNDER-LYNE ☎ 0161 330 5899 24 ⇋ (Annexe10 ⇋ (

FLIXTON   Map 07 SJ79

William Wroe Municipal Pennybridge Ln, Flixton Rd M41 5DX ☎ 0161 748 8680
Parkland course, with easy walking.
18 holes, 4395yds, Par 68, SSS 65.
Visitors must book in advance.
Societies contact for details.
Green Fees £6.50 (£8.70 weekends & bank holidays).
Facilities ⅄ 🏠 ✠ (Scott Partington.
Leisure putting green, practice area.
Location E side of village off B5158
Hotel ★ 64% Beaucliffe Hotel, 254 Eccles Old Rd, Pendleton, SALFORD ☎ 0161 789 5092 21rm(2 ⇋15 ()

GATLEY   Map 07 SJ88

Gatley Waterfall Farm, Styal Rd, Heald Green SK8 3TW ☎ 0161 437 2091
Parkland course. Moderately testing.
9 holes, 5934yds, Par 68, SSS 68.
Club membership 400.
Visitors may not play Tue & Sat. With member only weekends. Handicap certificate required.
Societies apply in writing.
Green Fees not confirmed.
Facilities ♀ ⅄ 🏠 (
Leisure squash.
Location S side of village off B5166
Hotel ★★★★ 62% Belfry Hotel, Stanley Rd, HANDFORTH ☎ 0161 437 0511 80 ⇋ (

HALE   Map 07 SJ78

Hale Rappax Rd WA15 0NU ☎ 0161 980 4225 & 904 0835
Beautiful, undulating parkland course, with the River Bollin winding round fairways.
9 holes, 5780yds, Par 70, SSS 68, Course record 65.
Club membership 300.
Visitors may not play before 4.30pm Thu; with member only weekends.
Societies apply in writing or telephone in advance.
Green Fees £20 per day/round.
Facilities ⊗ ⅷ by prior arrangement ⅃ ⬤ ♀ ⅄ 🏠 (Joy Jackson.
Leisure putting green, practice area.
Location 1.25m SE
Hotel ★★★ 60% Bowdon Hotel, Langham Rd, Bowdon, ALTRINCHAM ☎ 0161 928 7121 82 ⇋ (

HAZEL GROVE   Map 07 SJ98

Hazel Grove Buxton Rd SK7 6LU ☎ 0161 483 3978
Testing parkland course with tricky greens and water hazards coming into play on several holes.
18 holes, 6310yds, Par 71, SSS 71.
Club membership 600.
Visitors must contact in advance (0161 483 7272).
Societies must apply in writing, Thu & Fri only.
Green Fees £25 per day (£30 Fri/Sun & bank holidays).
Facilities ⊗ ⅷ ⅃ ⬤ ♀ ⅄ 🏠 ✠ (M E Hill.
Leisure trolley for hire, putting green, practice area, snooker room.
Location 1m E off A6
Hotel ★★★ 67% Bramhall Moat House, Bramhall Ln South, BRAMHALL ☎ 0161 439 8116 65 ⇋ (

HINDLEY   Map 07 SD60

Hindley Hall Hall Ln WN2 2SQ ☎ 01942 255131
Parkland course with mostly easy walking.
18 holes, 5913yds, Par 69, SSS 68, Course record 64.
Club membership 430.
Visitors must contact in advance and may not play weekends.
Societies apply in advance to Secretary
Green Fees £20 per day.
Facilities ⊗ ⅷ ⅃ ⬤ ♀ ⅄ 🏠 (Neil Brazell.
Leisure trolley for hire, putting green, practice area.
Location 1m N off A58
Hotel ★★★ 65% Oak Hotel, Riverway, WIGAN ☎ 01942 826888 88 ⇋ (

HYDE   Map 07 SJ99

Werneth Low Werneth Low Rd, Gee Cross SK14 3AF ☎ 0161 368 2503
Hard walking but good views from this moorland course. Exposed to wind.
11 holes, 6113yds, Par 70, SSS 70, Course record 69.
Club membership 375.
Visitors may not play Tue mornings or Sun and by prior arrangement on Sat.
Societies must contact in at least 14 days in advance.
Green Fees £18 per round (weekdays).
Facilities ⊗ ⅷ ⅃ ⬤ ♀ ⅄ 🏠 (Tony Bacchus.
Leisure putting green, practice area.
Location 2m S of town centre
Hotel ★★ 70% Red Lion Inn, 112 Buxton Rd, High Ln, STOCKPORT ☎ 01663 765227 6 ⇋ (

LEIGH   Map 07 SD60

Pennington St Helen's Rd WN7 4HW ☎ 01942 682852
Municipal parkland course, with natural hazards of brooks, ponds and trees, and easy walking.
9 holes, 2919yds, Par 35, SSS 34.
Club membership 200.
Visitors no restrictions.
Societies must contact in advance.
Green Fees not confirmed.   ▶

Facilities 🏠⛳🏌 Tim Kershaw.
Leisure trolleys for hire.
Location SW side of town centre off A572
Hotel ★★ 65% Kirkfield Hotel, 2/4 Church St,
NEWTON LE WILLOWS
☎ 01925 228196 14 ⇔🐦

LITTLEBOROUGH   Map 07 SD91

Whittaker Whittaker Ln OL15 0LH ☎ 01706 378310
Moorland 9-hole course.
9 holes, 5632yds, Par 68, SSS 67, Course record 61.
Club membership 150.
Visitors welcome except for Tue pm and Sun.
Societies apply to Secretary.
Green Fees not confirmed.
Facilities ♀🏔
Leisure putting green,practice area.
Location 3m NE of Rochdale, along A58
Hotel ★★★ 66% Norton Grange Hotel, Manchester
Rd, Castleton, ROCHDALE
☎ 01706 30788 50 ⇔🐦

MANCHESTER   Map 07 SJ89

Blackley Victoria Ave East, Blackley M9 6HW
☎ 0161 643 2980 & 654 7770
Parkland course. Course crossed by footpath.
18 holes, 6237yds, Par 70, SSS 70.
Club membership 730.
Visitors with member only Thu, weekends and bank
holidays.
Societies apply in advance.
Green Fees not confirmed.
Facilities ⊗⍨🍴🌬♀🏔🏠🏌 Martin Barton.
Leisure trolley for hire, putting green, practice area.
Location 4m N of city centre, on Rochdale Rd
Hotel ★★★ 61% Bower Hotel, Hollinwood Av,
Chadderton, OLDHAM
☎ 0161 682 7254 66 ⇔🐦

Chorlton-cum-Hardy Barlow Hall, Barlow Hall Rd,
Chorlton-cum-Hardy M21 7JJ
☎ 0161 881 5830 & 061-881 3139
Meadowland course with trees, stream and several ditches.
18 holes, 5980yds, Par 70, SSS 69, Course record 63.
Club membership 780.
Visitors handicap certificate required.
Societies on Thu only by prior booking.
Green Fees not confirmed.
Facilities ♀🏔🏠🏌 David Screeton.
Leisure putting,trolley hire,practice area.
Location 4m S of Manchester A5103/A5145
Hotel ★★★ 61% Willow Bank Hotel, 340-342
Wilmslow Rd, Fallowfield, MANCHESTER
☎ 0161 224 0461 116 ⇔🐦

Davyhulme Park Gleneagles Rd, Davyhulme M41 8SA
☎ 0161 748 2260
Parkland course.
18 holes, 6237yds, Par 72, SSS 70, Course record 65.
Visitors must contact in advance, may not play Wed,
weekends by prior notice. Must have an
introduction from own club.
Societies telephone in advance.

Green Fees £25 per day; £21 per round.
Facilities ⊗⍨🍴🌬♀🏠🏌 Dean Butler.
Leisure trolley for hire, putting green, practice area.
Location 8m S adj to Park Hospital
Hotel ★ 64% Beaucliffe Hotel, 254 Eccles Old Rd,
Pendleton, SALFORD
☎ 0161 789 5092 21rm(2 ⇔15 🐦)

Didsbury Ford Ln, Northenden M22 4NQ
☎ 0161 998 9278 (Secretary) & 998 2811 (Pro)
Parkland course.
18 holes, 6273yds, Par 70, SSS 70, Course record 63.
Club membership 750.
Visitors advised to check dates/times with professional.
Societies Thu & Fri, must contact in advance.
Green Fees £24 per day (£28 weekends & bank holidays).
Facilities ⊗⍨🍴🌬♀🏔🏠🏌 Peter Barber.
Leisure trolley for hire, putting green, practice area.
Location 6m S of city centre off A5145
Hotel B Forte Posthouse Manchester, Palatine Rd,
Northenden, MANCHESTER
☎ 0161 998 7090 190 ⇔🐦

Fairfield "Boothdale", Booth Rd, Audenshaw M34 5GA
☎ 0161 370 1641
Parkland course set around a reservoir. Course demands
particularly accurate placing of shots.
18 holes, 5654yds, Par 70, SSS 68.
Club membership 450.
Visitors may not play mornings at weekends & may be
restricted on Wed & Thu.
Societies prior booking through Secretary.
Green Fees £17 per round (£23 weekends & bank holidays).
Facilities ⊗⍨🍴🌬♀🏔🏠🏌 Nick Harding.
Leisure trolley for hire, sailing.
Location 1.5m W of Audenshaw off A635
Hotel ★★ 69% York House Hotel, York Place,
Richmond St, ASHTON-UNDER-LYNE
☎ 0161 330 5899 24 ⇔🐦Annexe10 ⇔🐦

Northenden Palatine Rd, Northenden M22 4FR
☎ 0161 998 4738
Parkland course surrounded by the River Mersey.
18 holes, 6503yds, Par 72, SSS 71, Course record 64.
Club membership 700.
Visitors Must contact in advance.
Societies Tue & Fri only, apply in advance to Secretary.
Green Fees £25 per day (£27.50 weekends & bank holidays).
Facilities ⊗⍨🍴🌬♀🏔🏠🏌 P A Scott.
Leisure trolley for hire, putting green, practice area.
Location 6.5m S of city centre on B1567 off A5103
Hotel B Forte Posthouse Manchester, Palatine Rd,
Northenden, MANCHESTER
☎ 0161 998 7090 190 ⇔🐦

Pike Fold Cooper Ln, Victoria Av, Blackley M9 6QQ
☎ 0161 740 1136
Picturesque, hilly course. Good test of golf.
9 holes, 5785yds, Par 70, SSS 68, Course record 66.
Club membership 200.
Visitors may not play Sun. Must be with member Sat &
bank holidays.
Societies apply in writing.
Green Fees not confirmed.
Facilities ♀🏔
Location 4m N of city centre off Rochdale Rd

Hotel ★★★ 61% Bower Hotel, Hollinwood Av,
Chadderton, OLDHAM
☎ 0161 682 7254 66 ⇋ ๖

Withington 243 Palatine Rd, West Didsbury M20 8UD
☎ 0161 445 9544
Flat parkland course.
18 holes, 6410yds, Par 71, SSS 71.
Club membership 600.
Visitors welcome except Thu, must contact in advance,
restricted at weekends.
Societies telephone in advance, welcome except Thu, Sat
& Sun.
Green Fees not confirmed.
Facilities ♀ 🛆 🖪 ໂ R J Ling.
Location 4m SW of city centre off B5167
Hotel B Forte Posthouse Manchester, Palatine Rd,
Northenden, MANCHESTER
☎ 0161 998 7090 190 ⇋ ๖

Worsley Stableford Av, Worsley M30 8AP
☎ 0161 789 4202
Well-wooded parkland course.
18 holes, 6252yds, Par 72, SSS 70, Course record 65.
Club membership 600.
Visitors no restrictions except during club competitions.
Societies apply in advance.
Green Fees £25 per day (£30 weekends & bank holidays).
Facilities ⊗ 🎞 ⅃ ⚑ ♀ 🛆 🖪 ໂ Ceri Cousins.
Leisure trolley for hire, putting green, practice area.
Location 6.5m NW of city centre off A572
Hotel ★★★ 61% Novotel, Worsley Brow,
WORSLEY
☎ 0161 799 3535 119 ⇋ ๖

MELLOR   Map 07 SJ98

Mellor & Townscliffe Gibb Ln, Tarden SK6 5NA
☎ 0161 427 2208
Scenic parkland and moorland course, undulating with some
hard walking. Good views. Testing 200 yd, 9th hole, par 3.
18 holes, 5925yds, Par 70, SSS 69.
Club membership 650.
Visitors with member only Sun.
Societies apply by letter.
Green Fees not confirmed.
Facilities ♀ 🛆 🖪 ໂ Gary R Broadley.
Location 0.5m S
Hotel ★ 74% Springfield Hotel, Station Rd,
MARPLE ☎ 0161 449 0721 6 ⇋ ๖

MIDDLETON   Map 07 SD80

Manchester Hopwood Cottage, Rochdale Rd M24 2QP
☎ 0161 643 3202
Moorland golf of unique character over a spaciously laid
out course with generous fairways sweeping along to
large greens. A wide variety of holes will challenge the
golfer's technique, particularly the testing last three
holes.
18 holes, 6519yds, Par 72, SSS 70, Course record 65.
Club membership 650.
Visitors must contact in advance, may not play Wed
and limited play weekends.
Societies telephone in advance.

Green Fees £40 per day; £30 per round (£45 weekends
& bank holidays).
Facilities ⊗ by prior arrangement 🎞 by prior
arrangement ⅃ ⚑ ♀ 🛆 🖪 ໂ Brian Connor.
Leisure motorised carts for hire, buggies for hire,
trolley for hire, driving range, putting green,
practice area.
Location 2.5m N off A664
Hotel ★★ 57% Midway Hotel, Manchester Rd,
Castleton, ROCHDALE
☎ 01706 32881 24 ⇋ ๖

North Manchester Rhodes House, Manchester Old Rd
M24 4PE ☎ 0161 643 9033
A long, tight heathland course with natural water hazards.
Excellent views of the Yorkshire Wolds.
18 holes, 6527yds, Par 72, SSS 72, Course record 66.
Club membership 800.
Visitors no restrictions.
Societies telephone in advance.
Green Fees not confirmed.
Facilities ♀ 🛆 🖪 ⚑ ໂ Peter Lunt.
Leisure putting green,trolley hire,practice area.
Location W side of town centre off A576
Hotel ★★★ 61% Bower Hotel, Hollinwood Av,
Chadderton, OLDHAM
☎ 0161 682 7254 66 ⇋ ๖

MILNROW   Map 07 SD91

Tunshill Kiln Ln OL16 3TS
☎ 01706 342095
Testing moorland course, particularly 6th and 15th (par 5's).
9 holes, 5804yds, Par 70, SSS 68.
Club membership 275.
Visitors must contact in advance, restricted weekends &
evenings.
Societies apply in writing.
Green Fees not confirmed.
Facilities ♀ 🛆
Leisure pool table.
Location 1m NE M62 exit junc 21 off B6225
Hotel ★★★ 66% Norton Grange Hotel, Manchester
Rd, Castleton, ROCHDALE
☎ 01706 30788 50 ⇋ ๖

OLDHAM   Map 07 SD90

Crompton & Royton Highbarn OL2 6RW
☎ 0161 624 0986
Undulating moorland course.
18 holes, 6214yds, Par 70, SSS 70, Course record 65.
Club membership 500.
Visitors must contact in advance and may not play Tue or
Sat, limited play Sun pm and Wed.
Societies apply in advance
Green Fees £24 (£30 weekends & bank holidays).
Facilities ⊗ 🎞 ⅃ ⚑ ♀ 🛆 🖪 ໂ David Melling.
Leisure trolley for hire, putting green, practice area.
Location 0.5m NE of Royton
Hotel ★★★ 61% Bower Hotel, Hollinwood Av,
Chadderton, OLDHAM
☎ 0161 682 7254 66 ⇋ ๖

Oldham Lees New Rd OL4 5PN
☎ 0161 624 4986
Moorland course, with hard walking.
18 holes, 5122yds, Par 66, SSS 65, Course record 62.
Club membership 370.
Visitors   no restrictions.
Societies   must contact in advance.
Green Fees   £16 (£22 weekends & bank holidays).
Facilities   ⊗ ⅏ ⅃ ⍷ ♀ ⌿ 🏠 ℓ Gavin Peter Mutch.
Leisure   trolley for hire, putting green.
Location   2.5m E off A669
Hotel   ★★ 69% York House Hotel, York Place,
                Richmond St, ASHTON-UNDER-LYNE
                ☎ 0161 330 5899 24 ⇄ ₨Annexe10 ⇄ ₨

Werneth Green Ln, Garden Suburb OL8 3AZ
☎ 0161 624 1190
Semi-moorland course, with a deep gulley and stream
crossing eight fairways. Testing hole: 3rd (par 3).
18 holes, 5363yds, Par 68, SSS 66.
Club membership 460.
Visitors   may not play on Tue or Thu and weekends. Must
                contact in advance.
Societies   must contact in advance.
Green Fees   not confirmed.
Facilities   ♀ ⌿ 🏠 ℓ
Location   S side of town centre off A627
Hotel   ★★ 69% York House Hotel, York Place,
                Richmond St, ASHTON-UNDER-LYNE
                ☎ 0161 330 5899 24 ⇄ ₨Annexe10 ⇄ ₨

PRESTWICH   Map 07 SD80

Heaton Park Municipal M25 2SW
☎ 0161 798 0295
A hilly parkland municipal course with lakes to cross,
including the 12th which requires an 183yd carry across the
water.
18 holes, 5766yds, Par 70, SSS 68.
Club membership 190.
Visitors   restricted to club members only between 8-10am
                Sat & Sun.
Societies   apply in writing to John Andrew.
Green Fees   not confirmed.
Facilities   ⌿ 🏠 ℓ Terry Morley.
Hotel   ★★★★ 63% Bolton Moat House, 1 Higher
                Bridge St, BOLTON
                ☎ 01204 879988 128 ⇄ ₨

Prestwich Hilton Ln M25 9XB ☎ 0161 773 2544
Parkland course, near to Manchester city centre.
18 holes, 4806yds, Par 64, SSS 63, Course record 60.
Club membership 507.
Visitors   weekdays by arrangement.
Societies   apply in writing or telephone.
Green Fees   not confirmed.
Facilities   ⊗ ⅏ ⅃ ⍷ ♀ ⌿ 🏠 ℓ Anthony Sposton.
Leisure   trolley for hire, putting green practice area.
Location   N side of town centre on A6044
Hotel   ★ 64% Beaucliffe Hotel, 254 Eccles Old Rd,
                Pendleton, SALFORD
                ☎ 0161 789 5092 21rm(2 ⇄15 ₨)

ROCHDALE   Map 07 SD81

Castle Hawk Chadwick Ln, Castleton OL11 3BY
☎ 01706 40841
Two parkland courses, with challenging par 3s, and a driving
range.
*New Course: 9 holes, 2699yds, Par 34, SSS 34, Course
record 30.*
*Old Course: 18 holes, 3460yds, Par 55, SSS 55, Course
record 54.*
Club membership 350.
Visitors   no restrictions.
Societies   must contact in advance.
Green Fees   £6 per day (£8 weekends & bank holidays).
Facilities   ⊗ ⅏ ⅃ ⍷ ♀ ⌿ 🏠 ℓ Mike Vipond.
Leisure   fishing, trolley for hire, driving range, putting
                green, practice area.
Location   S of Rochdale, nr junc 20 (M62)
Hotel   ★★★ 66% Norton Grange Hotel, Manchester
                Rd, Castleton, ROCHDALE
                ☎ 01706 30788 50 ⇄ ₨

Rochdale Edenfield Rd OL11 5YR ☎ 01706 43818
Parkland course with enjoyable golf and easy walking.
18 holes, 6050yds, Par 71, SSS 69, Course record 65.
Club membership 750.
Visitors   must telephone in advance.
Societies   apply in writing.
Green Fees   £23 per day (£27 weekends & bank holidays).
Facilities   ⊗ ⅏ by prior arrangement ⅃ ⍷ ♀ ⌿ 🏠 ℓ
                ℓ Andrew Laverty.
Leisure   trolley for hire, putting green, practice area.
Location   1.75m W on A680
Hotel   ★★ 57% Midway Hotel, Manchester Rd,
                Castleton, ROCHDALE
                ☎ 01706 32881 24 ⇄ ₨

Springfield Park Springfield Park, Bolton Rd OL11 4RE
☎ 01706 56401 (weekend only)
Parkland-moorland course situated in a valley. The River
Roch adds an extra hazard to the course.
18 holes, 5237yds, Par 67, SSS 66, Course record 64.
Club membership 300.
Visitors   must contact professional in advance.
Societies   telephone in advance.
Green Fees   under review.
Facilities   🏠 ℓ David Wills.
Location   1.5m SW off A58
Hotel   ★★ 57% Midway Hotel, Manchester Rd,
                Castleton, ROCHDALE
                ☎ 01706 32881 24 ⇄ ₨

ROMILEY   Map 07 SJ99

Romiley Goose House Green SK6 4LJ ☎ 0161 430 2392
Semi-parkland course on the edge of the Derbyshire Hills,
providing a good test of golf with a number of outstanding
holes, notably the 6th, 9th, 14th and 16th. The latter enjoys
magnificent views from the tee.
18 holes, 6454yds, Par 70, SSS 71, Course record 66.
Club membership 700.
Visitors   are advised to contact in advance, may not play
                Thu or Sat before 4pm.
Societies   Tue & Wed, must book in advance.

Green Fees £30 per day; £24 per round (£44/£33 weekends & bank holidays).
Facilities ⊗ ⅢⅢ ⓛ 💺 ♀ ⚘ 🛍 ⓕ Garry Butler.
Leisure trolley for hire, putting green.
Location E side of town centre off B6104
Hotel ★★ 70% Red Lion Inn, 112 Buxton Rd, High Ln, STOCKPORT ☎ 01663 765227 6 ⇄ ⓡ

SALE   Map 07 SJ79

Ashton on Mersey Church Ln M33 5QQ ☎ 0161 973 3220
Parkland course with easy walking.
9 holes, 6146yds, Par 72, SSS 69.
Club membership 450.
Visitors with member only Sun & bank holidays, not Sat.
Societies Thu only. Apply in writing.
Green Fees not confirmed.
Facilities ♀ ⚘ 🛍 ⓕ Mike Williams.
Leisure sauna, putting green, trolley hire.
Location 1m W of M63 junc 7
Hotel ★★★ 66% Cresta Court Hotel, Church St, ALTRINCHAM ☎ 0161 927 7272 138 ⇄ ⓡ

Sale Golf Rd M33 2XU
☎ 0161 973 1638 (Gen Man) & 973 1730 (Pro)
Tree-lined parkland course. Feature holes are the 13th - Watery Gap - and the par 3 (117yd) 17th.
18 holes, 6352yds, Par 71, SSS 70.
Club membership 700.
Visitors contact professional in advance.
Societies apply by letter.
Green Fees £25 per round weekdays.
Facilities ⊗ ⅢⅢ ⓛ 💺 ♀ ⚘ 🛍 ⓕ Mike Stewart.
Leisure trolley for hire, putting green, practice area.
Location NW side of town centre off A6144
Hotel ★★★ 66% Cresta Court Hotel, Church St, ALTRINCHAM ☎ 0161 927 7272 138 ⇄ ⓡ

SHEVINGTON   Map 07 SD50

Gathurst 62 Miles Ln WN6 8EW
☎ 01257 255235 (Secretary) & 254909 (Pro)
Testing parkland course, slightly hilly.
18 holes, 6016yds, Par 70, SSS 69, Course record 65.
Club membership 550.
Visitors may play anytime except competition days.
Societies welcome Mon, Tue, Thu & Fri. Apply in writing to Secretary.
Green Fees £20 weekdays.
Facilities ⊗ ⅢⅢ ⓛ 💺 ♀ ⚘ 🛍 ⓕ David Clarke.
Leisure trolley for hire, putting green, practice area.
Location W side of village B5375 off junc 27 of M6
Hotel ★★★ 65% Wigan/Standish Moat House, Almond Brook Rd, STANDISH ☎ 01257 499988 113 ⇄ ⓡ

STALYBRIDGE   Map 07 SJ99

Stamford Oakfield House, Huddersfield Rd SK15 3PY
☎ 01457 832126 & 834829
Undulating moorland course.
18 holes, 5701yds, Par 70, SSS 68, Course record 62.
Club membership 600.
Visitors limited play at weekends.
Societies apply in writing.

Green Fees £20 per day (£25 weekends).
Facilities ⊗ ⅢⅢ ⓛ 💺 ♀ ⚘ 🛍
Leisure trolley for hire, putting green.
Location 2m NE off A635
Hotel ★★ 69% York House Hotel, York Place, Richmond St, ASHTON-UNDER-LYNE ☎ 0161 330 5899 24 ⇄ ⓡ Annexe10 ⇄ ⓡ

STOCKPORT   Map 07 SJ89

Heaton Moor Heaton Mersey SK4 3NX ☎ 0161 432 2134
Parkland course, easy walking.
18 holes, 5907yds, Par 70, SSS 69, Course record 66.
Club membership 400.
Visitors restricted Tue & bank holidays.
Societies apply in writing.
Green Fees not confirmed.
Facilities ♀ ⚘ 🛍 ⚐ ⓕ C Loydall.
Location N of town centre off B5169
Hotel ★★ 67% Saxon Holme Hotel, 230 Wellington Rd, STOCKPORT ☎ 0161 432 2335 33 ⇄ ⓡ

Houldsworth Houldsworth Park, Reddish SK5 6BN
☎ 0161 442 9611 & 0161 442 1712
Flat parkland course, tree-lined and with water hazards. Testing holes 9th (par 5) and 13th (par 5).
18 holes, 6209yds, Par 71, SSS 70.
Club membership 680.
Visitors may not play weekends & bank holidays unless by prior arrangement with professional.
Societies by prior arrangement.
Green Fees not confirmed.
Facilities ♀ ⚘ 🛍 ⓕ David Naylor.
Leisure putting, trolley hire, practice area.
Location 4m SE of city centre off A6
Hotel ★★★ 61% Willow Bank Hotel, 340-342 Wilmslow Rd, Fallowfield, MANCHESTER ☎ 0161 224 0461 116 ⇄ ⓡ

Marple Barnsfold Rd, Hawk Green, Marple SK6 7EL
☎ 0161 427 2311
Parkland course.
18 holes, 5552yds, Par 68, SSS 67, Course record 66.
Club membership 640.
Visitors restricted Thu afternoon & weekend competition days.
Societies apply in writing to professional.
Green Fees £20 per day (£30 weekends & bank holidays).
Facilities ⊗ ⅢⅢ ⓛ 💺 ♀ ⚘ 🛍 ⓕ Nick Hamilton.
Leisure putting green.
Location S side of town centre
Hotel ★★ 70% Red Lion Inn, 112 Buxton Rd, High Ln, STOCKPORT ☎ 01663 765227 6 ⇄ ⓡ

Reddish Vale Southcliffe Rd, Reddish SK5 7EE
☎ 0161 480 2359
Undulating heathland course designed by Dr. A Mackenzie and situated in the River Thame valley.
18 holes, 6100yds, Par 69, SSS 69, Course record 64.
Club membership 550.
Visitors must play with member at weekends.
Societies must contact in writing.
Green Fees not confirmed.
Facilities ♀ ⚘ 🛍 ⓕ Richard Brown.
Location 1.5m N off Reddish road   ▶

Hotel ★★ 67% Wycliffe, 74 Edgeley Rd, Edgeley, STOCKPORT ☎ 0161 477 5395 20 ⇄ ♠

Stockport Offerton Rd, Offerton SK2 5HL
☎ 0161 427 8369 (Secretary) & 427 2421 (Pro)
A beautifully situated course in wide open countryside with views of the Cheshire and Derbyshire hills. It is not too long but requires that the player plays all the shots, to excellent greens. Demanding holes include the dog-leg 3rd and 12th, and the 460 yard opening hole is among the toughest on the course.
18 holes, 6326yds, Par 71, SSS 71, Course record 66.
Club membership 500.
Visitors must contact professional in advance, limited play weekends.
Societies Wed & Thu only, apply in writing to Secretary.
Green Fees £35 per day (£45 per round weekends & bank holidays).
Facilities ⊗ ℳ ╚ ☑ ♀ ♨ ⌂ ♠ ♈ ℓ Mike Peel.
Leisure trolley for hire.
Location 4m SE on A627
Hotel ★★ 70% Red Lion Inn, 112 Buxton Rd, High Ln, STOCKPORT ☎ 01663 765227 6 ⇄ ♠

SWINTON
Map 07 SD70

Swinton Park East Lancashire Rd M27 5LX
☎ 0161 794 0861
One of Lancashire's longest inland courses. Clubhouse extensions have greatly improved the facilities.
18 holes, 6726yds, Par 73, SSS 72, Course record 66.
Club membership 600.
Visitors may not play weekends or Thu. Must contact in advance and have handicap certificate.
Societies by letter.
Green Fees £25 per day.
Facilities ⊗ ℳ ╚ ☑ ♀ ♨ ⌂ ℓ James Wilson.
Leisure trolley for hire, putting green, practice area.
Location 1m W off A580
Hotel ★★★ 61% Novotel, Worsley Brow, WORSLEY ☎ 0161 799 3535 119 ⇄ ♠

UPPERMILL
Map 07 SD90

Saddleworth Mountain Ash OL3 6LT ☎ 01457 873653
Moorland course, with superb views of Pennines.
18 holes, 5976yds, Par 71, SSS 69, Course record 65.
Club membership 800.
Visitors must contact in advance, restricted at weekends.
Societies contact in advance.
Green Fees £23 per day (£26 weekends & bank holidays).
Facilities ⊗ ℳ ╚ ☑ ♀ ♨ ⌂ ♠ ℓ Tom Shard.
Leisure motorised carts for hire, buggies for hire, trolley for hire, putting green, practice area.
Location E side of town centre off A670
Hotel ★★★ 70% Hotel Smokies Park, Ashton Rd, Bardsley, OLDHAM ☎ 0161 624 3405 47 ⇄ ♠

URMSTON
Map 07 SJ79

Flixton Church Rd, Flixton M41 6EP ☎ 0161 748 2116
Meadowland course bounded by River Mersey.
9 holes, 6410yds, Par 71, SSS 71.
Club membership 400.

Visitors contact professional in advance, with member only weekends & bank holidays.
Societies apply in writing.
Green Fees £15 per day.
Facilities ⊗ ℳ by prior arrangement ╚ ☑ ♀ ♨ ⌂ ℓ John Watson.
Leisure trolley for hire, putting green, practice area, snooker.
Location S side of town centre on B5213
Hotel ★ 64% Beaucliffe Hotel, 254 Eccles Old Rd, Pendleton, SALFORD ☎ 0161 789 5092 21rm(2 ⇄ 15 ♠)

WALKDEN
Map 07 SD70

Brackley Municipal M38 9TR ☎ 0161 790 6076
Mostly flat course.
9 holes, 3003yds, Par 35, SSS 69.
Visitors no restrictions.
Green Fees not confirmed.
Facilities ⌂ ℓ
Location 2m NW on A6
Hotel ★★★ 61% Novotel, Worsley Brow, WORSLEY ☎ 0161 799 3535 119 ⇄ ♠

WESTHOUGHTON
Map 07 SD60

Westhoughton Long Island, School St BL5 2BR
☎ 01942 811085 & 840545
Compact downland course.
9 holes, 2886yds, Par 70, SSS 68, Course record 64.
Club membership 280.
Visitors with member only at weekends.
Societies telephone in advance or apply in writing.
Green Fees not confirmed.
Facilities ⊗ ℳ by prior arrangement ╚ ☑ ♀ ♨ ⌂ ℓ Jason Seed.
Leisure putting green, practice area, pool & snooker table.
Location 0.5m NW off A58
Hotel ★★★ 64% Beaumont Hotel, Beaumont Rd, BOLTON ☎ 01204 651511 96 ⇄ ♠

WHITEFIELD
Map 07 SD80

Stand The Dales, Ashbourne Grove M45 7NL
☎ 0161 766 3197
A semi-parkland course with five moorland holes. A fine test of golf with a very demanding finish.
18 holes, 6411yds, Par 72, SSS 71, Course record 67.
Club membership 500.
Visitors must contact professional in advance.
Societies Wed & Fri, apply by telephone.
Green Fees £25 per day (£30 weekends).
Facilities ⊗ ℳ ╚ ☑ ♀ ♨ ⌂ ♠ ℓ Mark Dance.
Leisure trolley for hire, putting green, practice area.
Location 1m W off A667
Hotel ★★★ 63% Bolholt Country Park Hotel, Walshaw Rd, BURY ☎ 0161 764 5239 38 ⇄ ♠ Annexe9rm(8 ⇄ ♠)

Whitefield Higher Ln M45 7EZ ☎ 0161 766 2904 & 2728
Fine sporting parkland course with well-watered greens.
18 holes, 6045yds, Par 69, SSS 69, Course record 64.

Visitors must contact in advance, play restricted weekends.
Societies must contact in advance.
Green Fees £25 (£35 weekends & bank holidays).
Facilities ⊗ ⅷ ⅊ ⅊ ⅊ ⅊ ⅊ ⅊ Paul Reeves.
Leisure hard tennis courts, motorised carts for hire, buggies for hire, trolley for hire, putting green, practice area.
Location N side of town centre on A665
Hotel ★★★★ 57% Portland Thistle, 3/5 Portland St, Piccadilly Gdns, MANCHESTER
☎ 0161 228 3400 205 ⇆ ℟

WIGAN
Map 07 SD50

Haigh Hall Haigh Country Park, Aspull WN2 1PE
☎ 01942 831107
Municipal parkland course, with hard walking, and a canal forms the west boundary. Adjacent to 'Haigh Country Park' with many facilities.
18 holes, 6423yds, Par 70, SSS 71, Course record 65.
Club membership 250.
Visitors must contact professional in advance.
Societies apply in writing to professional.
Green Fees £5.90 (£8.50 weekends).
Facilities ⅊ ⅊ ⅊ ⅊ ⅊ Ian Lee.
Leisure trolley for hire, putting green, practice area.
Location 2m NE off B5238
Hotel ★★ 64% Bel-Air Hotel, 236 Wigan Ln, WIGAN ☎ 01942 241410 12 ⇆ ℟

Wigan Arley Hall, Haigh WN1 2UH ☎ 01257 421360
Among the best of Lancashire's 9-hole courses. The fine old clubhouse is the original Arley Hall, and is surrounded by a moat.
9 holes, 6036yds, Par 70, SSS 69.
Club membership 200.
Visitors must contact in advance.
Societies apply by telephone.
Green Fees £25 per day (£30 weekends & bank holidays).
Facilities ⊗ ⅷ ⅊ ⅊ ⅊ ⅊
Leisure putting green.
Location 3m NE off B5238
Hotel ★★★ 65% Wigan/Standish Moat House, Almond Brook Rd, STANDISH
☎ 01257 499988 113 ⇆ ℟

WOODFORD
Map 07 SJ88

Avro Old Hall Ln SK7 1QR ☎ 0161 439 2709
An attractive, tight and challenging 9-hole course.
9 holes, 5735yds, Par 69, SSS 68.
Club membership 400.
Visitors restricted weekends and competition days.
Societies must contact The Hon Secretary, c/o 23 Meadowbank Avenue, Atherton, Manchester M49 9LB.
Green Fees not confirmed.
Facilities ⅊
Location W side of village on A5102
Hotel ★★★ 67% Bramhall Moat House, Bramhall Ln South, BRAMHALL
☎ 0161 439 8116 65 ⇆ ℟

WORSLEY
Map 07 SD70

Ellesmere Old Clough Ln M28 7HZ ☎ 0161 799 0554
Parkland course with natural hazards. Testing holes: 3rd (par 5), 9th (par 3), 13th (par 4). Hard walking.
18 holes, 6248yds, Par 70, SSS 70, Course record 67.
Club membership 600.
Visitors welcome except club competition days & bank holidays.
Societies apply in advance.
Green Fees £24 per day; £18 per round (£25 per day/round weekends).
Facilities ⊗ ⅷ ⅊ ⅊ ⅊ ⅊ ⅊ Terry Morley.
Leisure trolley for hire, putting green.
Location N side of village off A580
Hotel ★★★ 61% Novotel, Worsley Brow, WORSLEY
☎ 0161 799 3535 119 ⇆ ℟

HAMPSHIRE

ALDERSHOT
Map 04 SU85

Army Laffans Rd GU11 2HF ☎ 01252 540638
Picturesque heathland course with three par 3's, over 200 yds.
18 holes, 6550yds, Par 71, SSS 71, Course record 67.
Club membership 750.
Visitors may not play weekends.
Societies apply in writing.
Green Fees £22 per round; £30 per day.
Facilities ⊗ ⅷ ⅊ ⅊ ⅊ ⅊ ⅊ Graham Cowley.
Leisure putting green, practice area.
Location 1.5m N of town centre off A323/A325
Hotel ★★★ 69% Potters International Hotel, 1 Fleet Rd, ALDERSHOT
☎ 01252 344000 101 ⇆ ℟

ALRESFORD
Map 04 SU53

Alresford Cheriton Rd, Tichborne Down SO24 0PN
☎ 01962 733746
A testing downland course on well drained chalk. Now expanded to 18 holes, incorporating the original 12, but changing direction of play to give two starting points and two closing greens near clubhouse.
18 holes, 5905yds, Par 69, SSS 68, Course record 65.
Club membership 720.
Visitors must contact in advance but must play with member weekends & bank holidays.
Societies must telephone in advance.
Green Fees £30 per day; £18 per round (£37 per round weekends & bank holidays).
Facilities ⊗ ⅷ ⅊ ⅊ ⅊ ⅊ ⅊ Malcolm Scott.
Leisure trolley for hire, putting green, practice area.
Location 1m S on B3046
Hotel ★★ 61% Swan Hotel, 11 West St, ALRESFORD
☎ 01962 732302 & 734427 23rm(10 ⇆)

ALTON

Map 04 SU73

Alton Old Odiham Rd GU34 4BU ☎ 01420 82042
Undulating meadowland course.
9 holes, 5744yds, Par 68, SSS 68, Course record 64.
Club membership 350.
Visitors must contact in advance and must have a
handicap certificate to play at weekends.
Societies must contact in advance.
Green Fees not confirmed.
Facilities ⊗ ⊪ ⅄ ☘ ♀ ♨ 🖮 ℂ Paul Brown.
Leisure trolley for hire, putting green, practice area.
Location 2m N off A32
Hotel ★★★ 66% Alton House Hotel, Normandy St,
ALTON ☎ 01420 80033 39 ⇆ ℍ

Worldham Park Cakers Ln, Worldham GU34 3AG
☎ 01420 543151
The course is in a picturesque woodland setting with an
abundance of challenging holes (doglegs, water and sand).
Increased to 18-holes in the summer of 1995.
18 holes, 5800yds, Par 71, SSS 68.
Club membership 450.
Visitors normally may play Mon-Fri.
Societies Mon-Fri only. Must contact in advance.
Green Fees £10 per round (£12 weekends).
Facilities ⊗ ⊪ ⅄ ☘ ♀ 🖮 ♈
Leisure driving range, putting green.
Location B3004, 2mins from Alton
Hotel ★★★ 66% Grange Hotel, London Rd, ALTON
☎ 01420 86565 26 ⇆ ℍAnnexe4 ⇆ ℍ

AMPFIELD

Map 04 SU42

Ampfield Par Three Winchester Rd SO51 9BQ
☎ 01794 368480
Pretty parkland course designed by Henry Cotton in 1963.
Well-bunkered greens.
18 holes, 2478yds, Par 54, SSS 53, Course record 49.
Club membership 470.
Visitors must contact in advance & have a handicap
certificate to play at weekends & bank holidays.
Societies must contact in advance.
Green Fees £15 per day; £9 per round (£15.50 per round
weekends & bank holidays).
Facilities ⊗ ⊪ by prior arrangement ⅄ ☘ ♀ ♨ 🖮 ♈
ℂ Richard Benfield.
Leisure trolley for hire, putting green.
Location 4m NE of Romsey on A31
Hotel ★★★ 70% Potters Heron Hotel, Winchester
Rd, AMPFIELD
☎ 01703 266611 54 ⇆ ℍ

ANDOVER

Map 04 SU34

Andover 51 Winchester Rd SP10 2EF
☎ 01264 358040
Undulating downland course combining a good test of golf
for all abilities with breathtaking views across Hampshire
countryside. Well guarded greens and a notable par 3 9th
(225yds) with the tee perched on top of a hill, 100ft above the
green.
9 holes, 6096yds, Par 70, SSS 69, Course record 66.
Club membership 450.

South Lawn Hotel & Restaurant ★★★ ⍟

Milford-on-Sea, Lymington, Hampshire SO41 0RF
Tel: Lymington (01590) 643911 Fax: (01590) 644820

*Delightful Country House Hotel in peaceful
surroundings where comfort and good food
predominate. Owner/Chef Ernst Barten
supervises excellent cuisine. Specially
imported wines from Germany.*

*All rooms en-suite, colour TV, phone and
trouser press. Facilities nearby include
windsurfing and sailing from Keyhaven,
Golf at Brockenhurst and Barton-on-Sea,
the Beach at Milford and walking or riding
in the beautiful New Forest.*

Visitors must contact in advance.
Societies Mon-Wed only. Must contact in advance.
Green Fees £15 per day; £10 per round; (£22 Sun & bank
holidays).
Facilities ⊗ ⊪ ⅄ ☘ ♀ ♨ 🖮 ♈ ℂ D Lawrence.
Leisure trolley for hire, putting green, practice area.
Location 0.5m S on A3057
Hotel ★★ 61% Danebury Hotel, High St,
ANDOVER ☎ 01264 323332 23 ⇆ ℍ

ASHLEY HEATH

Map 04 SU10

Moors Valley Moors Valley Country Park, Horton Rd
BH24 2ET ☎ 01425 479776
This municipal course is set in the beautiful surroundings of a
country park. It offers a test for all standards. It is gently
undulating, with water hazards on six holes.
18 holes, 6200yds, Par 72, SSS 70.
Club membership 250.
Visitors must contact in advance.
Societies telephone for availability.
Green Fees £8.50 per 18 holes; £5 per 11 holes (£11/£6
weekends).
Facilities ⊗ ⊪ ⅄ ☘ ♀ ♨ 🖮 ♈ ℂ Michael Torrens.
Leisure driving range.
Location Signposted from A31 Ashley Heath roundabout
Hotel ★★★ 66% St Leonards Hotel, ST
LEONARDS ☎ 01425 471220 33 ⇆ ℍ

BARTON-ON-SEA
Map 04 SZ29

Barton-on-Sea Milford Rd BH25 5PP
☎ 01425 615308
Though not strictly a links course, it is right on a cliff edge with views over the Isle of Wight and Christchurch Bay. On a still day there is nothing much to it - but when it blows the course undergoes a complete change in character. Recently reconstructed to create 27 holes.
Becton-Needles: 18 holes, 6505yds, Par 72, SSS 71.
Needles-Stroller: 18 holes, 6444yds, Par 72, SSS 71.
Stroller-Becton: 18 holes, 6289yds, Par 72, SSS 70.
Club membership 920.
Visitors	must contact in advance and have a handicap certificate.
Societies	must telephone oin advance.
Green Fees	£25 per day (£30 weekends & bank holidays).
Facilities	⊗ ⅷ ⅬⅬ ☕ ♀ △ 🏠 🍴 ℓ Pat Coombs.
Leisure	motorised carts for hire, buggies for hire, trolley for hire, putting green, practice area, snooker.
Location	B3058 E side of town
Hotel	★★★★★(red)🛥 Chewton Glen Hotel, Christchurch Rd, NEW MILTON ☎ 01425 275341 55 ⇌ ℟Annexe2 ⇌ ℟
Additional hotel	★★★ 74% South Lawn Hotel, Lymington Rd, MILFORD ON SEA ☎ 01590 643911 24 ⇌ ℟

BASINGSTOKE
Map 04 SU65

Basingstoke Kempshott Park RG23 7LL
☎ 01256 465990
A well-maintained parkland course with wide and inviting fairways. You are inclined to expect longer drives than are actually achieved - partly on account of the trees. There are many two-hundred-year-old beech trees, since the course was built on an old deer park.
18 holes, 6350yds, Par 70, SSS 70, Course record 67.
Club membership 700.
Visitors	must contact in advance and play Mon-Fri only (ex bank holidays).
Societies	must contact in advance.
Green Fees	£32 per day; £21 per round.
Facilities	⊗ ⅷ ⅬⅬ ☕ ♀ △ 🏠 🍴 ℓ Ian Hayes.
Leisure	motorised carts for hire, buggies for hire, trolley for hire, putting green, practice area.
Location	3.5m SW on A30 M3 exit 7
Hotel	B Forte Posthouse Basingstoke, Grove Rd, BASINGSTOKE ☎ 01256 468181 84 ⇌ ℟

Dummer Nr Basingstoke RG25 2AR
☎ 01256 397888
Opened in July 1993 and designed by Peter Alliss/Clive Clark to consist of two 9-hole loops with water hazards. Gentle terrain makes the course suitable for players of all ages.
18 holes, 6556yds, Par 72.
Club membership 830.
Visitors	must contact in advance, handicap card required, limited at weekends.
Societies	contact in advance.
Green Fees	not confirmed.
Facilities	△ 🏠 🍴 ℓ

Leisure	sauna.
Location	Off junc 7 of M3 towards Dummer village
Hotel	★★★ 56% Wheatsheaf Hotel, NORTH WALTHAM ☎ 01256 398282 28 ⇌ ℟

Weybrook Park Aldermaston Rd, Sherborne St John RG24 9ND ☎ 01256 20347
A course designed to be enjoyable for all standards of player.
18 holes, 5988yds, Par 70, SSS 69.
Club membership 530.
Visitors	telephone for availability.
Societies	telephone in advance for availability and confirm in writing.
Green Fees	£15 per 18 holes (£25 weekends & bank holidays; £20 Nov-Mar).
Facilities	⊗ ⅷ ☕ ♀ △
Leisure	putting green, practice area.
Location	2m W of town centre, entrance via A339
Hotel	★★★ 61% Ringway Hotel, Popley Way, Aldermaston Roundabout, Ringway North (A339), BASINGSTOKE ☎ 01256 20212 134 ⇌ ℟

BORDON
Map 04 SU73

Blackmoor Firgrove Rd, Whitehill GU35 9EH
☎ 01420 472775
A first-class moorland course with a great variety of holes. Fine greens and wide pine tree-lined fairways are a distinguishing feature. The ground is mainly flat and walking easy.
18 holes, 6300yds, Par 69, SSS 70, Course record 65.
Club membership 750.
Visitors	must contact in advance and may not play at weekends.
Societies	must telephone in advance.
Green Fees	£30 per round.
Facilities	⊗ ⅷ ⅬⅬ ☕ ♀ △ 🏠 ℓ Stephen Clay.
Leisure	trolley for hire, putting green, practice area.
Hotel	★★★ 62% Swan Hotel, High St, ALTON ☎ 01420 83777 36 ⇌ ℟

BOTLEY
Map 04 SU51

Botley Park Hotel & Country Club Winchester Rd, Boorley Green SO32 2UA ☎ 01489 780888
Pleasantly undulating course with water hazards. Driving range and country club facilities.
18 holes, 6026yds, Par 70, SSS 70.
Club membership 750.
Visitors	must play with member. Must contact in advance & have handicap certificate.
Societies	contact in advance.
Green Fees	not confirmed.
Facilities	♀ △ 🏠 🍴 🛏 ℓ Tim Barter.
Leisure	hard tennis courts, heated indoor swimming pool, squash, sauna, solarium, gymnasium, croquet lawn & petanque.
Location	1m NW of Botley on B3354
Hotel	★★★★ 68% Botley Park Hotel & Country Club, Winchester Rd, Boorley Green, BOTLEY ☎ 01489 780888 100 ⇌ ℟

★★
The Watersplash Hotel
Brockenhurst in the New Forest

The Watersplash Hotel is recommended for its excellent food, friendly service and accommodation. Brokenhurst Manor Golf Club, situated just half a mile away, is one of ten courses within easy reach of the hotel. Personally supervised by resident proprietors Robin and Judy Foster who specialise in catering for the individual and small golf parties. Well-stocked bar and extensive wine list. All 23 bedrooms have private bathroom, colour TV, tea and coffee making facilities, direct dial telephone and radio. Heated outdoor pool in season. For further details ask for our colour brochure.

The Watersplash Hotel, The Rise, Brockenhurst, Hampshire SO42 7ZP.
Tel: (01590) 622344 Fax: (01590) 624047

BROCKENHURST   Map 04 SU20

Brokenhurst Manor Sway Rd SO41 7SG
☎ 01590 623332 (Secretary) & 623092 (Pro Shop)
An attractive woodland/heathland course set at the edge of the New Forest, with the unusual feature of three loops of six holes each to complete the round. Fascinating holes include the short 5th and 12th, and the 4th and 17th, both dog-legged. A stream also features on seven of the holes.
18 holes, 6222yds, Par 70, SSS 70, Course record 63.
Club membership 700.
Visitors   must contact in advance, numbers limited.
Societies   Thu only, apply in writing.
Green Fees £35 per day; £28 per round (£40 weekends & bank holidays).
Facilities   ⊗ ⫪ by prior arrangement ⛳ 🍺 ♀ ⛳ 🏠 ℓ John Lovell.
Leisure   trolley for hire, driving range, putting green, practice area.
Location   1m S on B3055
Hotel   ★★★ 66% Balmer Lawn Hotel, Lyndhurst Rd, BROCKENHURST
☎ 01590 623116 55 ⇄ 🐾
Additional hotel   ★★ 67% Watersplash Hotel, The Rise, BROCKENHURST
☎ 01590 622344 23 ⇄ 🐾

BURLEY   Map 04 SU20

Burley Cott Ln BH24 4BB
☎ 01425 402431
Undulating heather and gorseland. The 7th requires an accurately placed tee shot to obtain par 4. Played off different tees on second nine.
9 holes, 6149yds, Par 71, SSS 69, Course record 68.
Club membership 520.
Visitors   must contact in advance & have a handicap certificate. May not play before 4pm Sat.
Green Fees £14 per round/day (£16 weekends).
Facilities   ⊗ ⛳ 🍺 ♀ ⛳
Leisure   trolley for hire, putting green, practice area.
Location   E side of village
Hotel   ★★★ 60% Moorhill House, BURLEY
☎ 01425 403285 24 ⇄ 🐾

CORHAMPTON   Map 04 SU62

Corhampton Sheep's Pond Ln SO32 3LP
☎ 01489 877279 & 877638
Free draining downland course situated in the heart of the picturesque Meon Valley.
18 holes, 6444yds, Par 71, SSS 71.
Club membership 800.
Visitors   weekdays only and must contact in advance.
Societies   Mon & Thu only, contact in writing or telephone.
Green Fees £30 per day; £20 per round.
Facilities   ⊗ ⫪ ⛳ 🍺 ♀ ⛳ 🏠 ℓ Ian Roper.
Leisure   motorised carts for hire, buggies for hire, trolley for hire, driving range, putting green, practice area.
Location   1m W of Corhampton, off B3035
Hotel   ★★ 74% Old House Hotel, The Square, WICKHAM
☎ 01329 833049 9 ⇄ 🐾Annexe3 ⇄ 🐾

CRONDALL   Map 04 SU74

Oak Park Heath Ln GU10 5PB
☎ 01252 850880
Gently undulating course overlooking pretty village. 16-bay floodlit driving range, practice green and practice bunker. An additional 9-holes are due to be opened in Spring 1996.
Woodland: 18 holes, 6240yds, Par 70, SSS 70.
Village: 9 holes, 3279yds, Par 36.
Club membership 600.
Visitors   no restrictions for Village Course. Must book in advance and have a handicap certificate for Woodland Course.
Societies   must telephone in advance.
Green Fees Woodland: £25 per day; £16 per round (£40/£22.50 weekends & public holidays). Village: £8.50 per round.
Facilities   ⊗ ⫪ ⛳ 🍺 ♀ ⛳ 🏠 ℓ 🕴 Simon Coaker.
Leisure   motorised carts for hire, trolley for hire, driving range, putting green, practice area.
Location   0.5m E of village off A287
Hotel   ★★★♨ 60% Farnham House Hotel, Alton Rd, FARNHAM
☎ 01252 716908 20 ⇄ 🐾

DIBDEN
Map 04 SU40

Dibden Main Rd SO45 5TB
☎ 01703 207508 & 845596
Municipal parkland course with views over Southampton
Water. A pond guards the green at the par 5, 3rd hole.
Twenty-bay driving range.
*Course 1: 18 holes, 5900yds, Par 70, SSS 69, Course record
63.*
Course 2: 9 holes, 1400yds, Par 29.
Club membership 600.
Visitors must book in advance.
Societies must contact in writing.
Green Fees 18 holes: £7.25 (£10.50 weekends); 9 holes:
£3.40 (£4.75 weekends).
Facilities ⊗ ⦀ ♫ ▮ ♟ ♣ ☎ ⋔ ℓ Alan Bridge.
Leisure trolley for hire, driving range, putting green,
practice area.
Location 2m NW of Dibden Purlieu
Hotel ★★★ 65% Forest Lodge Hotel, Pikes Hill,
Romsey Rd, LYNDHURST
☎ 01703 283677 23 ⇆ ℕ

EASTLEIGH
Map 04 SU41

Fleming Park Magpie Ln SO50 9LS
☎ 01703 612797
Parkland course with stream-'Monks Brook'-running
through.
18 holes, 4436yds, Par 65, SSS 62.
Club membership 300.
Visitors no restrictions.
Societies must contact in advance.
Green Fees not confirmed.
Facilities ♟ ♣ ☎ ⋔ ℓ Chris Strickett.
Leisure putting green,trolley for hire.
Location E side of town centre
Hotel ★★★ 63% Southampton Park Hotel,
Cumberland Place, SOUTHAMPTON
☎ 01703 343343 72 ⇆ ℕ

EAST WELLOW
Map 04 SU32

Wellow Ryedown Ln SO51 6BD
☎ 01794 323833 & 322872
Three 9-hole courses set in 217 acres of parkland surrounding
Embley Park, former home of Florence Nightingale.
Ryedown: 9 holes, 2745yds, Par 34.
Embley: 9 holes, 3221yds, Par 36.
Blackwater: 9 holes, 3099, Par 36.
Club membership 500.
Visitors advisable to contact in advance weekdays and
weekends.
Societies apply in writing or telephone, Mon-Fri not bank
holidays.
Green Fees £17 per day; £15 per 18 holes; £9 per 9 holes
(£20/£18/£11 weekends & bank holidays).
Facilities ⊗ ⦀ ♫ ▮ ♟ ♣ ☎ ℓ Neil Bratley.
Leisure motorised carts for hire, buggies for hire, trolley
for hire, putting green, practice area.
Location 1m N from A36 to Salisbury then 1m right
Hotel ★★★ 62% White Horse Hotel, Market Place,
ROMSEY
☎ 01794 512431 33 ⇆ ℕ

FAREHAM
Map 04 SU50

Cams Hall Porchester Rd PO16 8UP
☎ 01329 827222 & 827732
Two Peter Alliss/Clive Clark designed golf courses opened in
1993.The Historic is in parkland and the Coastal has lakes
and undulating hills.
*Creek Course: 18 holes, 6244yds, Par 71, SSS 71, Course
record 69.*
Park Course: 9 holes, 3059yds, Par 36, SSS 71.
Club membership 940.
Visitors must contact in advance, tee times available any
time.
Societies telephone for details and society golf day pack.
Green Fees £23.50 per 27 holes; £15 per 18 holes; £9.50 per
9 holes (£30/£25/£12 weekends and bank
holidays).
Facilities ⊗ ⦀ ♫ ▮ ♟ ♣ ☎ ⋔ ℓ Jason Neve.
Leisure sauna, motorised carts for hire, buggies for hire,
trolley for hire, driving range, putting green.
Location M27 exit 11 to A27
Hotel ★★★ 67% Lysses House Hotel & Conference
Centre, 51 High St, FAREHAM
☎ 01329 822622 21 ⇆ ℕ

FARNBOROUGH
Map 04 SU85

Southwood Ively Rd, Cove GU14 0LJ ☎ 01252 548700
Municipal parkland course with stream running through.
18 holes, 5738yds, Par 69, SSS 68, Course record 61.
Club membership 650.
Visitors must book in advance.
Societies must contact in advance.
Green Fees Summer: £11.50 (£14 weekends). Winter £7.50
(£10.50 weekends).
Facilities ⊗ ⦀ ♫ ▮ ♟ ♣ ☎ ⋔ ℓ Bob Hammond.
Leisure motorised carts for hire, buggies for hire, trolley
for hire, putting green, practice area.
Location 0.5m W
Hotel B Forte Posthouse Farnborough, Lynchford Rd,
FARNBOROUGH
☎ 01252 545051 110 ⇆ ℕ

FLEET
Map 04 SU85

North Hants Minley Rd GU13 8RE ☎ 01252 616443
Picturesque tree-lined course with much heather and
gorse close to the fairways. A comparatively easy par-4
first hole may lull the golfer into a false sense of security,
only to be rudely awakened at the testing holes which
follow. The ground is rather undulating and, though not
tiring, does offer some excellent 'blind' shots, and more
than a few surprises in judging distance.
18 holes, 6257yds, Par 69, SSS 70, Course record 65.
Club membership 600.
Visitors must contact at least 48 hours in advance.
Must play with member at weekends.
Societies Tue & Wed only. Must telephone in
advance.
Green Fees £26 per round; £33 two rounds. With
member only at weekends.
Facilities ⊗ ⦀ ♫ ▮ ♟ ♣ ☎ ℓ Steve Porter.
Leisure trolley for hire, driving range, putting green,
practice area. ▶

Location	0.25m N of Fleet station on B3013
Hotel	★★★ 59% Lismoyne Hotel, Church Rd, FLEET ☎ 01252 628555 42 ⇄ ↾

GOSPORT   Map 04 SZ69

Gosport & Stokes Bay Off Fort Rd, Haslar PO12 2AT
☎ 01705 527941
A testing links course overlooking the Solent, with plenty of gorse and short rough. Changing winds.
9 holes, 5999yds, Par 70, SSS 69, Course record 65.
Club membership 460.
Visitors may not play at weekends & Thu.
Societies must contact in writing.
Green Fees £15 per round (£20 weekends).
Facilities ⊗ ⅏ ㄴ ♨ ♀ ⚐ ⛳ ↾
Leisure trolley for hire, putting green, practice area.
Location A32 S from Fareham,E on Fort rd to Haslar
Hotel ★★★ 60% Belle Vue Hotel, 39 Marine Pde East, LEE-ON-THE-SOLENT ☎ 01705 550258 24 ⇄ ↾Annexe3 ⇄ ↾

HARTLEY WINTNEY   Map 04 SU75

Hartley Wintney London Rd RG27 8PT ☎ 01252 844211
Easy walking, parkland course in pleasant countryside.
Played off different tees on back nine, with testing par 4s at 4th and 13th.
9 holes, 6096yds, Par 70, SSS 69.
Visitors must contact in advance.
Societies Tue & Thu only by prior arrangement.
Green Fees £17 per round; £25 per day (£20.25/£31.25 weekends).
Facilities ⊗ ⅏ by prior arrangement ㄴ ♨ ♀
Location NE side of village on A30
Hotel ★★★ 59% Lismoyne Hotel, Church Rd, FLEET ☎ 01252 628555 42 ⇄ ↾

HAYLING ISLAND   Map 04 SU70

Hayling Links Ln PO11 0BX
☎ 01705 464446 & 464491
A delightful links course among the dunes offering fine sea-scapes and views across to the Isle of Wight. Varying sea breezes and sometimes strong winds ensure that the course seldom plays the same two days running. Testing holes at the 12th and 13th, both par 4. Club selection is important.
18 holes, 5521yds, Par 71, SSS 71, Course record 65.
Club membership 800.
Visitors must contact in advance and have a handicap certificate, no jeans or denims allowed.
Societies welcome Tue & Wed, or half days Mon & Thu, apply in writing or telephone.
Green Fees £30 per day (£40 weekends).
Facilities ⊗ ⅏ ㄴ ♨ ㅅ ⚐ ⛳ ↾ ↾ Raymond Gadd.
Leisure trolley for hire, putting green, practice area.
Location SW side of island at West Town
Hotel B Forte Posthouse Havant, Northney Rd, HAYLING ISLAND ☎ 01705 465011 92 ⇄ ↾

KINGSCLERE   Map 04 SU55

Sandford Springs Wolverton RG26 5RT
☎ 01635 297881
The course has unique variety in beautiful surroundings and offers three distinctive loops of 9 holes. There are water hazards, woodlands and gradients to negotiate, providing a challenge for all playing categories. From its highest point there are extensive views.
The Park: 9 holes, 2963yds, Par 34.
The Lakes: 9 holes, 3180yds, Par 36.
The Wood: 9 holes, 3042yds, Par 35.
Club membership 650.
Visitors must contact in advance. Restricted at weekends.
Societies must contact in advance.
Green Fees £23 per 18 holes, £15 per 9 holes.
Facilities ⊗ ⅏ ㄴ ♨ ♀ ㅅ ⚐ ⛳
     ↾ Gary Edmunds/Kim Brake.
Leisure buggies for hire, trolley for hire, putting green, practice ground.
Location On A339
Hotel ★★★ 61% Millwaters Hotel & Restaurant, London Rd, NEWBURY ☎ 01635 528838 30 ⇄ ↾

KINGSLEY   Map 04 SU73

Dean Farm GU35 9NG ☎ 01420 489478 & 472313
Undulating downland course.
9 holes, 1500yds, Par 29.
Visitors no restrictions.
Societies must contact in writing.
Green Fees £6.50 per 18 holes; £4 per 9 holes.
Facilities ㄴ ♨ ⚐ ⛳
Leisure hard tennis courts, putting green.
Location W side of village off B3004
Hotel ★★★ 66% Grange Hotel, London Rd, ALTON ☎ 01420 86565 26 ⇄ ↾Annexe4 ⇄ ↾

LECKFORD   Map 04 SU33

Leckford SO20 6JG ☎ 01264 810320
A testing downland course with good views.
9 holes, 6444yds, Par 70, SSS 71.
Club membership 200.
Visitors must be accompanied by member and contact in advance.
Green Fees not confirmed.
Facilities ㅅ
Location 1m SW off A3057
Hotel ★★★ 62% Grosvenor Hotel, High St, STOCKBRIDGE ☎ 01264 810606 25 ⇄ ↾

LEE-ON-THE-SOLENT   Map 04 SU50

Lee-on-Solent Brune Ln PO13 9PB ☎ 01705 551170
A modest parkland/heathland course, yet a testing one. The five short holes always demand a high standard of play and the 13th is rated one of the best in the country.
18 holes, 5755yds, Par 69, SSS 69, Course record 64.
Club membership 750.
Visitors may not play before 9am. Handicap certificate required.

Societies must contact in advance.
Green Fees £25 per day/round (£35 weekends).
Facilities ⊗ ⋔ ᕒ ⬤ ♀ ⅄ 🛆 ℓ John Richardson.
Leisure trolley for hire, driving range, putting green, practice area.
Location 1m N off B3385
Hotel ★★★ 60% Belle Vue Hotel, 39 Marine Pde East, LEE-ON-THE-SOLENT
☎ 01705 550258 24 ⇥ ☏Annexe3 ⇥ ☏

LIPHOOK   Map 04 SU83

Liphook Wheatsheaf Enclosure GU30 7EH
☎ 01428 723271
Heathland course with easy walking and fine views.
18 holes, 6247yds, Par 70, SSS 70, Course record 67.
Club membership 800.
Visitors must contact in advance; may not play Tue, competition days etc.
Societies Wed-Fri only. Must contact in advance.
Green Fees £37 per day; £29 per round (£47/£37 Sat, £47 per round Sun).
Facilities ⊗ ᕒ ⬤ ♀ ⅄ 🛆 ⋔ ℓ Ian Large.
Leisure trolley for hire, putting green, practice area.
Location 1m S on B2030 (old A3)
Hotel ★★★★ 72% Lythe Hill Hotel, Petworth Rd, HASLEMERE
☎ 01428 651251 40 ⇥ ☏

Old Thorns Griggs Green GU30 7PE ☎ 01428 724555
A challenging 18-hole championship-standard course designed around magnificent oaks, beeches and Scots pine.
18 holes, 6041yds, Par 72, SSS 70.
Visitors no restrictions.
Societies must telephone in advance.
Green Fees not confirmed.
Facilities 🛆 ⬤ ⋔ ☏ ℓ
Leisure hard tennis courts, heated indoor swimming pool, sauna, solarium, caddy cars.
Location 1m W on B2131
Hotel ★★★ 76% Old Thorns Golf Course Hotel & Restaurant, Longmoor Rd, Griggs Green, LIPHOOK
☎ 01428 724555 28 ⇥ ☏Annexe5 ☏
See advertisement on page 198

LYNDHURST   Map 04 SU20

Bramshaw Brook SO43 7HE ☎ 01703 813433
Two 18-hole courses. The Manor Course is landscaped parkland with excellent greens, and features mature trees and streams. The Forest course is set amidst beautiful open forest. Easy walking. The Bell Inn Hotel, attached to the club, provides fine accommodation just a wedge shot from the first tee, and reserved tee times for its guests.
Manor Course: 18 holes, 6517yds, Par 71, SSS 71.
Forest Course: 18 holes, 5925yds, Par 69, SSS 68.
Club membership 950.
Visitors must be accompanied by member at weekends and bank holidays.
Societies apply in writing or telephone in advance.
Green Fees £30 per day; £20 per round.
Facilities ⊗ ⋔ ᕒ ⬤ ♀ ⅄ 🛆 ⋔ ℓ Clive Bonner.
Leisure motorised carts for hire, buggies for hire, trolley for hire, putting, golfing rates at Bell Inn.
Location On B3079 1m W of M27 junc 1
Hotel ★★★ 67% Bell Inn, BROOK
☎ 01703 812214 22 ⇥

New Forest Southampton Rd SO43 7BU
☎ 01703 282450
This picturesque heathland course is laid out in a typical stretch of the New Forest on high ground a little above the village of Lyndhurst. Natural hazards include the inevitable forest ponies. The first two holes are somewhat teasing, as is the 485-yard (par 5) 9th. Walking is easy.
18 holes, 5742yds, Par 69, SSS 68.
Club membership 900.
Visitors must contact in advance.
Societies must contact in advance.
Green Fees not confirmed.
Facilities ♀ ⅄ 🛆 ⬤ ℓ A Sackley.
Leisure putting green,trolley hire.
Location 0.5m NE off A35
Hotel ★★★ 71% Crown Hotel, High St, LYNDHURST ☎ 01703 282922 39 ⇥ ☏
Additional QQQ The Penny Farthing Hotel, Romsey
hotel Rd, LYNDHURST
☎ 01703 284422 11rm(10 ⇥ ☏)

NEW MILTON   Map 04 SZ29

Chewton Glen Hotel Christchurch Rd BH25 6QS
☎ 01425 275341
A 9-hole, Par 3 course with the hotel grounds plus a practice area. ONLY open to residents of the hotel or as a guest of a member of the club. ▶

9 holes, 854yds, Par 27.
Club membership 150.
Visitors non residents must play with member.
Societies must contact in advance.
Green Fees £10 (non residents).
Facilities ⊗ ⅏ ⅃ ♨ ♀ 🛍 ⚐ 🏌
Leisure hard tennis courts, outdoor and indoor heated
swimming pools, sauna, solarium, gymnasium,
driving range, putting, practice area.
Hotel ★★★★★(red)⚜ Chewton Glen Hotel,
Christchurch Rd, NEW MILTON
☎ 01425 275341 55 ⇥ ⚑Annexe 2 ⇥ ⚑

OVERTON   Map 04 SU54

Test Valley Micheldever Rd RG25 3DS ☎ 01256 771737
A new inland links course with fine turf fairways and greens
laid out in traditonal links style with pot bunkers as a feature.
There is strategic bunkering and ponds on this easy walking
course on a well drained chalk subsoil. The 2nd, 4th, 12th,
14th and 17th holes are particularly challenging but every
hole has its own appealing individual character.
18 holes, 6811yds, Par 72, SSS 73, Course record 66.
Club membership 500.
Visitors advisable to ring in advance.
Societies apply in writing or telephone in advance.
Green Fees £22 per day; £14 per 18 holes (£32/£20 weekends).
Facilities ⊗ ⅏ ⅃ ♨ ♀ ⚒ 🛍 ⚐ ⚐ ⚐ 🏌 ⚐ Terry Notley.
Leisure motorised carts for hire, buggies for hire, trolley
for hire, putting green, practice area.
Location 1.5m N of A303
Hotel ★★★ 56% Wheatsheaf Hotel, NORTH
WALTHAM ☎ 01256 398282 28 ⇥ ⚑

OWER   Map 04 SU31

Paultons Golf Centre Old Salisbury Rd SO51 6AN
☎ 01703 813992 & 813345
A Pay and Play 18-hole course built within the original
Paultons parkland which was laid out by 'Capability' Brown.
There is also a 9-hole academy course, ideal for beginners or
players wishing to improve their short games as well as a 20-
bay floodlit driving range.
18 holes, 6238yds, Par 71, SSS 70, Course record 72.
Academy: 9 holes, 1324yds, Par 27, SSS 27, Course record 24.
Visitors pay & play.
Societies telephone for details.
Green Fees £17.50 per 18 holes; £6.50 per 9 holes (£18.50
per 18 holes weekends).
Facilities ⊗ ⅏ ⅃ ♨ ♀ ⚒ 🛍 ⚐
⚐ John Cave & Heath Teschner.
Leisure motorised carts for hire, buggies for hire, trolley
for hire, floodlit driving range, putting green,
practice area.
Hotel ★★★ 60% Bartley Lodge, Lyndhurst Rd,
CADNAM ☎ 01703 812248 20 ⇥ ⚑

PETERSFIELD   Map 04 SU72

Petersfield Heath Rd GU31 4EJ
☎ 01730 262386 & 267732
Level part-heath and part-parkland course with a lake, two
par 5s, 5 par 3s and good views.
18 holes, 5603yds, Par 69, SSS 67, Course record 65.
Club membership 750.

Visitors advisable to contact in advance for weekdays,
must contact for weekends.
Societies booking form must be completed & deposit paid.
Green Fees £15 per round (£21 weekends & bank holidays),
£21 Mon-Fri 36 holes.
Facilities ⊗ ⅃ ♨ ♀ ⚒ 🛍 ⚐ Greg Hughes.
Leisure trolley for hire, practice area.
Location E side of town centre off A3
Hotel ★★★ 73% Spread Eagle Hotel, South St,
MIDHURST
☎ 01730 816911 37 ⇥ ⚑Annexe 4 ⚑

PORTSMOUTH & SOUTHSEA   Map 04 SU60

Great Salterns Public Course Eastern Rd PO3 5HH
☎ 01705 664549 & 699519
Easy walking, seaside course with open fairways and testing
shots onto well-guarded, small greens. Testing 13th hole, par
4, requiring 130yd shot across a lake.
18 holes, 5610yds, Par 69, SSS 66, Course record 64.
Club membership 700.
Visitors no restrictions.
Societies must contact in advance.
Green Fees not confirmed.
Facilities ♀ 🛍 ⚐ 🏌 ⚐ Terry Healy.
Location NE of town centre on A2030
Hotel ★★★ 65% Hospitality Inn, St Helens Pde,
SOUTHSEA
☎ 01705 731281 115 ⇥ ⚑

Southsea The Mansion, Great Salterns, Eastern Rd PO3 6QB
☎ 01705 664549
Municipal, meadowland course.
18 holes, 5800yds, Par 71, SSS 68, Course record 64.
Club membership 400.
Visitors no restrictions.
Societies must contact in advance, tel: 01705 664549.
Green Fees £10 per round.
Facilities ⊗ ⅏ ⅃ ♨ ♀ 🛍 ⚐ 🏌 ⚐ Terry Healy.
Leisure trolley for hire, driving range, practice area.
Location 0.5m off M27
Hotel ★★★ 65% Hospitality Inn, St Helens Pde,
SOUTHSEA ☎ 01705 731281 115 ⇥ ⚑

ROMSEY   Map 04 SU32

Dunwood Manor Shootash Hill SO51 0GF
☎ 01794 340549
Undulating parkland course with fine views. Testing 1st hole:
Reynolds Leap (par 4).
18 holes, 5925yds, Par 69, SSS 68.
Club membership 720.
Visitors always welcome advisable to contact in advance
but not essential.
Societies must contact in advance.
Green Fees £28 per day; £20 per round (weekends subject to
availability).
Facilities ⊗ ⅏ ⅃ ♨ ♀ ⚒ 🛍 ⚐ 🏌 ⚐
⚐ Johnathan Simpson.
Leisure motorised carts for hire, buggies for hire, trolley
for hire, putting green, practice area.
Location 4m W off A27
Hotel ★★★ 67% Bell Inn, BROOK
☎ 01703 812214 22 ⇥

Romsey Romsey Rd, Nursling SO16 0XW
☎ 01703 734637
Parkland/woodland course with narrow tree-lined fairways.
Six holes are undulating, rest are sloping. There are superb
views over the Test valley.
18 holes, 5851yds, Par 69, SSS 68.
Club membership 900.

Visitors	must play with member weekends and bank holidays.
Societies	Mon, Tue & Thu, must contact in advance.
Green Fees	£25 per day; £20 per round.
Facilities	⊗ ⅧⅢ ⓛ ☕ ♀ ♨ ⓐ ℓ Mark Desmond.
Leisure	trolley for hire, putting green, practice area.
Location	3m S on A3057
Hotel	★★★ 62% New Forest Heathlands, Romsey Rd, Ower, ROMSEY ☎ 01703 814333 52 ⇋ ♜

ROTHERWICK

Map 04 SU75

Tylney Park RG27 9AY ☎ 01256 762079
Parkland course. Practice area.
18 holes, 6109yds, Par 70, SSS 69, Course record 67.
Club membership 730.

Visitors	must be with member at weekends or have a handicap certificate.
Societies	must apply by phone in advance.
Green Fees	£23 per day; £18 per round (£28 per round weekends).
Facilities	⊗ ⅧⅢ ⓛ ☕ ♀ ♨ ⓐ ℓ Chris De Bruin.
Leisure	motorised carts for hire, buggies for hire, trolley for hire, putting green, practice area.
Location	0.5m SW
Hotel	★★★★(red)🏨 Tylney Hall Hotel, ROTHERWICK ☎ 01256 764881 35 ⇋Annexe56 ⇋

ROWLANDS CASTLE

Map 04 SU71

Rowlands Castle 31 Links Ln PO9 6AE
☎ 01705 412784
Exceptionally dry in winter, the flat parkland course is a
testing one with a number of tricky dog-legs and bunkers
much in evidence. The 7th, at 522yds, is the longest hole
on the course and leads to a well-guarded armchair green.
18 holes, 6618yds, Par 72, SSS 72, Course record 69.
Club membership 800.

Visitors	may not play Sat; must contact in advance.
Societies	Tue & Thu only; must contact in writing.
Green Fees	£25 per round (£30 weekends and bank holidays).
Facilities	⊗ ⅧⅢ ⓛ ☕ ♀ ♨ ⓐ ℓ Peter Klepacz.
Leisure	motorised carts for hire, buggies for hire, trolley for hire, driving range, putting green, practice area.
Location	W side of village off B2149
Hotel	★★★ 69% Brookfield Hotel, Havant Rd, EMSWORTH ☎ 01243 373363 & 376383 40 ⇋ ♜

SHEDFIELD

Map 04 SU51

Meon Valley Hotel Sandy Ln SO32 2HQ
☎ 01329 833455
It has been said that a golf course architect is as good as
the ground on which he has to work. Here Hamilton Stutt
had magnificent terrain at his disposal and a very good
and lovely parkland course is the result. There are three
holes over water. The hotel provides many sports
facilities.
*Meon Course: 18 holes, 6519yds, Par 71, SSS 71, Course
record 67.*
Valley Course: 9 holes, 5770yds, Par 70, SSS 68.
Club membership 910.

Visitors	may book up to seven days in advance, no available am weekends and bank holidays.
Societies	telephone in advance, written confirmation.
Green Fees	Meon Course: £30 per round (£40 weekends & bank holidays). Valley Course: £10 per round (£12 weekends & bank holidays).
Facilities	⊗ ⅧⅢ ⓛ ☕ ♀ ♨ ⓐ ℓ 🏌 ℓ Peter Green.
Leisure	hard tennis courts, heated indoor swimming pool, squash, sauna, solarium, gymnasium, motorised carts for hire, buggies for hire, trolley for hire, driving range, putting green, practice area.
Location	Off A334 between Botley and Wickham
Hotel	★★★ 64% Meon Valley Hotel, Country Club Resort, Sandy Ln, SHEDFIELD ☎ 01329 833455 83 ⇋ ♜

SOUTHAMPTON

Map 04 SU41

Chilworth Main Rd, Chilworth SO16 7JP
☎ 01703 733166
A course with two loops of nine holes, with a restricted
booking system to allow undisturbed play.
*Manor Golf Course: 18 holes, 5740yds, Par 69, SSS 69,
Course record 68.*
Club membership 700.

Visitors	must book in advance.
Societies	telephone in advance and complete booking form, various packages available.
Green Fees	£12 per 18 holes; £6 per 9 holes (£18/£9 weekends and bank holidays).
Facilities	⊗ ⅧⅢ ⓛ ☕ ♀ ♨ ℓ Martin Butcher/Jon Barnes.
Leisure	trolley for hire, driving range, floodlit driving range with 31 bays.
Location	A27 towards Romsey
Hotel	★★★ 61% County Hotel, Highfield Ln, Portswood, SOUTHAMPTON ☎ 01703 359955 66 ⇋ ♜

Southampton Golf Course Rd, Bassett SO16 7LE
☎ 01703 760478
This beautiful municipal parkland course always ensures a
good game, fast in summer, slow in winter. Three par 4's
over 450 yds.
18 holes, 6213yds, Par 69, SSS 70.
Club membership 500.

Visitors	no restrictions.
Societies	welcome.
Green Fees	not confirmed.
Facilities	♀ ♨ ⓐ 🏌 ℓ
Location	4m N of city centre off A33 ▶

Hotel ★★ 61% Star Hotel, High St,
SOUTHAMPTON
☎ 01703 339939 45rm(38 ⇌ ʀ̃)

Stoneham Monks Wood Close, Bassett SO16 3TT
☎ 01703 769272
A hilly, heather course with sand or peat sub-soil; the
fairways are separated by belts of woodland and gorse to
present a varied terrain. The interesting 4th is a difficult
par 4 and the fine 11th has cross-bunkers about 150 yards
from the tee.
18 holes, 6310yds, Par 72, SSS 69, Course record 63.
Club membership 800.
Visitors   advisable to contact in advance.
Societies   Mon, Thu & Fri only. Must telephone in
advance.
Green Fees £27 per day/round (£30 weekends & bank
holidays).
Facilities   ⊗ ⅺ ⅈ ♨ ♀ ⅄ 🏠 ⍾ ⅋ Ian Young.
Location   4m N of city centre off A27
Hotel   ★★★ 61% County Hotel, Highfield Ln,
Portswood, SOUTHAMPTON
☎ 01703 359955 66 ⇌ ʀ̃

SOUTHWICK   Map 04 SU60

Southwick Park Naval Recreation Centre Pinsley Dr
PO17 6EL ☎ 01705 380131
Set in 100 acres of parkland.
18 holes, 5972yds, Par 69, SSS 69.
Club membership 700.
Visitors   must contact in advance and may play weekday
mornings only.
Societies   Tue only, telephone in advance.
Green Fees not confirmed.
Facilities   ♀ ⅄ 🏠 ⍾ ⅋ John Green.
Leisure   pitch & putt, skittle alley.
Location   0.5m SE off B2177
Hotel   ★★ 74% Old House Hotel, The Square,
WICKHAM
☎ 01329 833049 9 ⇌ ʀ̃Annexe3 ⇌ ʀ̃

TADLEY   Map 04 SU66

Bishopswood Bishopswood Ln RG26 4AT ☎ 01734 812200
Wooded course, fairly tight, with stream and natural water
hazards.
9 holes, 6474yds, Par 72, SSS 71, Course record 66.
Club membership 485.
Visitors   must contact in advance. No play weekends or
bank holidays.
Societies   must contact by telephone.
Green Fees £8 per 9 holes, £13 per 18 holes.
Facilities   ⊗ ⅺ ⅈ ♨ ♀ ⅄ 🏠 ⅋ Steve Ward.
Leisure   floodlit driving range, putting green.
Location   1m W off A340
Hotel   ★★★ 73% Romans Hotel, Little London Rd,
SILCHESTER
☎ 01734 700421 11 ⇌ ʀ̃Annexe14 ⇌ ʀ̃

Entries with a shaded background identify
courses that are considered to be particularly
interesting

WATERLOOVILLE   Map 04 SU60

Portsmouth Crookhorn Ln, Purbrook PO7 5QL
☎ 01705 372210
Hilly, challenging course with good views of Portsmouth
Harbour. Rarely free from the wind and the picturesque 6th,
17th and 18th holes can test the best.
18 holes, 6139yds, Par 69, SSS 70, Course record 64.
Club membership 700.
Visitors   must book in advance.
Societies   must book in advance, in writing or by
telephone.
Green Fees Apr-Oct: £16 per day; £9.90 per 18 holes; £6 per
9 holes. Nov-Dec: £7.60 per 18 holes; £4.40 per
9 holes.
Facilities   ⊗ ⅺ ⅈ ♨ ♀ ⅄ 🏠 ⅋
⅋ Jason Banting/Mike Holman.
Leisure   putting green, practice area, lessons available.
Location   2m S, off A3
Hotel   ★★★ 61% The Bear Hotel, East St, HAVANT
☎ 01705 486501 42 ⇌ ʀ̃

Waterlooville Cherry Tree Av, Cowplain PO8 8AP
☎ 01705 263388
Parkland course, easy walking.
18 holes, 6647yds, Par 72, SSS 72.
Club membership 800.
Visitors   must contact in advance & may only play on
weekdays.
Societies   Thu only; apply by letter.
Green Fees not confirmed.
Facilities   ♀ ⅄ 🏠 ⅋ John Hay.
Leisure   putting green, practice area, trolley hire.
Location   NE side of town centre off A3
Hotel   B Forte Posthouse Havant, Northney Rd,
HAYLING ISLAND
☎ 01705 465011 92 ⇌ ʀ̃

WINCHESTER   Map 04 SU42

Hockley Twyford SO21 1PL ☎ 01962 713165
High downland course with good views.
18 holes, 6296yds, Par 71, SSS 70, Course record 69.
Club membership 650.
Visitors   are advised to phone in advance.
Societies   must telephone in advance and confirm in
writing with deposit.
Green Fees £28.
Facilities   ⊗ ⅺ ⅈ ♨ ♀ ⅄ 🏠 ⅋ Terry Lane.
Leisure   trolley for hire, driving range, putting green,
practice area.
Location   2m S via junct 12 on M27
Hotel   B Forte Posthouse Winchester, Paternoster Row,
WINCHESTER ☎ 01962 861611 94 ⇌ ʀ̃

Royal Winchester Sarum Rd SO22 5QE
☎ 01962 852462
The Royal Winchester course is a sporting downland
course centred on a rolling valley, so the course is hilly in
places. After a disastrous fire in 1994, a new clubhouse
was built (opened August 1995). Royal Winchester must
be included in any list of notable clubs, because of its age
(it dates from 1888) and also because the club was
involved in one of the very first professional matches.

18 holes, 6212yds, Par 71, SSS 70, Course record 7.
Club membership 772.

Visitors	must play with member at weekends. Must contact in advance and have a handicap certificate.
Societies	must contact in writing.
Green Fees	not confirmed.
Facilities	♀♣🏠🍴♟ Steven Hunter.
Leisure	practice area, trolley hire.
Location	1.5m W off A3090
Hotel	★★★★♨♨ 78% Lainston House Hotel, Sparsholt, WINCHESTER ☎ 01962 863588 38 ⇔ ♞

South Winchester Pitt SO22 5QW
☎ 01962 877800 & 840469
Opened in September 1993, this Peter Alliss/Clive Clark course incorporates downland, meadows and seven lakes. Visitors are only welcome if playing with a memember.
18 holes, 7086yds, Par 72, SSS 74.
Club membership 750.

Visitors	members guests only.
Societies	must contact in advance.
Green Fees	with member only £15 (£24 weekends).
Facilities	⊗🍴🍺♀♣🏠🍴♟ Richard Adams.
Leisure	motorised carts for hire, driving range, putting green, practice area.
Location	toff A3090)
Hotel	★★★ 70% Royal Hotel, Saint Peter St, WINCHESTER ☎ 01962 840840 75 ⇔ ♞

HEREFORD & WORCESTER

ALVECHURCH Map 07 SP07

Kings Norton Brockhill Ln, Weatheroak B48 7ED
☎ 01564 826706 & 826789
An old club with three, 9-hole courses; the Blue, Red and Yellow. Parkland with some exacting water hazards, it has housed important events. There is also a 12-hole, par 3 course.
Red Course: 9 holes, 3372yds, Par 36, SSS 36.
Blue Course: 9 holes, 3382yds, Par 36, SSS 36.
Yellow Course: 9 holes, 3290yds, Par 36, SSS 36.
Club membership 1000.

Visitors	must contact in advance. No visitors at weekends
Societies	must telephone in advance.
Green Fees	£29.50 per 27 holes; £27 per 18 holes.
Facilities	⊗🍴🍺♀♣🏠♟ Kevan Hayward.
Leisure	trolley for hire, putting green, practice area.
Location	M42 junct3, off A435
Hotel	★★★ 73% Pine Lodge Hotel, Kidderminster Rd, BROMSGROVE ☎ 01527 576600 114 ⇔ ♞

BEWDLEY
Map 07 SO77

Little Lakes Golf and Country Club Lye Head DY12 2UZ
☎ 01299 266385
A pleasant undulating parkland course extended to 18 holes
in April 1995. The course offers some pleasing views and
several demanding holes.
18 holes, 5812yds, Par 69.
Club membership 500.
Visitors must contact in advance.
Societies must telephone in advance.
Green Fees not confirmed.
Facilities ♀ ⚘ 🏠 ♪ Mark A Laing.
Leisure hard tennis courts, outdoor swimming pool,
fishing, putting green, cart/buggy/trolley hire.
Location 2.25m W off A456
Hotel ★★ 64% The George Hotel, Load St,
BEWDLEY
☎ 01299 402117 13rm(2 ⇔8 ♠)

Wharton Park Longbank DY12 2QW
☎ 01299 405222 & 405163
18-hole championship-standard course in 140 acres of
countryside. Some long Par 5s on the 6th (577yds) and the
9th (525yds)as well as superb par 3 holes at 3rd, 7th, 12th
make this a very challenging course.
18 holes, 6603yds, Par 73, SSS 72, Course record 66.
Club membership 330.
Visitors must contact in advance.
Societies prior booking required.
Green Fees £25 per day; £15 per round (£32/£22 weekends
and bank holidays).
Facilities ⊗ ⅢⅢ ⚘ 📷 ♀ ⚘ 🏠 ♪ Angus Hoare.
Leisure fishing, motorised carts for hire, buggies for hire,
trolley for hire, driving range, putting green.
Location Off A456 Bewdley bypass
Hotel ★★ 64% The George Hotel, Load St,
BEWDLEY
☎ 01299 402117 13rm(2 ⇔8 ♠)

BISHAMPTON
Map 03 SO95

Vale Golf & Country Club Hill Furze Rd WR10 2LZ
☎ 01386 462781
Opened in 1991 this course offers an American-style layout,
with large greens, trees and bunkers and several water
hazards. Its rolling fairways provide a testing round, as well
as superb views of the Malvern Hills. Picturesque and
peaceful. Also 9-hole course and 20-bay driving range.
International Course: 18 holes, 7114yds, Par 74, SSS 74.
Lenches Course: 9 holes, 2759yds, Par 35, SSS 34.
Club membership 650.
Visitors may play International course after 10.30am
weekends. Booking in advance.
Societies must apply in advance.
Green Fees International: £18 (£24 weekends). Lenches: 18
holes £12; 9 holes £7.50 (£16/£9.50 weekends).
Facilities ⊗ ⅢⅢ ⚘ 📷 ♀ ⚘ 🏠 ♪ ♪ Caroline Griffiths.
Leisure fishing, motorised carts for hire, buggies for hire,
trolley for hire, driving range, putting green,
practice area, archery, clay pigeon shooting.
Location Signposted off A4538
Hotel ★★ 65% The Chequers Inn, Chequers Ln,
FLADBURY
☎ 01386 860276 & 860527 8 ⇔ ♠

BLAKEDOWN
Map 07 SO87

Churchill and Blakedown Churchill Ln DY10 3NB
☎ 01562 700018
Pleasant course on hilltop with extensive views.
9 holes, 6472yds, Par 72, SSS 71, Course record 63.
Club membership 380.
Visitors with member only weekends & bank holidays.
Handicap certificate required.
Societies by arrangement through secretary.
Green Fees £17.50 per day/round.
Facilities ⊗ ⅢⅢ ⚘ 📷 ♀ ⚘ 🏠 ♪ K Wheeler.
Leisure trolley for hire, putting green, practice area.
Location W side of village off A456
Hotel ★★★★ 59% Stone Manor Hotel, Stone,
KIDDERMINSTER
☎ 01562 777555 52 ⇔ ♠

BRANSFORD
Map 03 SO75

Bank House Hotel Golf & Country Club WR6 5JD
☎ 01886 833551
Designed by Bob Sandow, the Pine Lakes course is in the
'Florida' style with fairways weaving between water courses,
13 lakes and sculptured mounds with colouful plant displays.
The 6,210yd course has doglegs, island greens and tight
fairways to challenge all standards of player. The 10th, 16th
and 18th (TheDevil's Elbow) are particularly tricky.
18 holes, 6101yds, Par 72, SSS 70.
Club membership 350.
Visitors all tee times must be booked, no play before
9.30am.
Societies contact the secretary, all tee times must be
booked in advance.
Green Fees not confirmed.
Facilities ♀ ⚘ 🏠 ♪ 🏐 ♪ Craig George.
Leisure outdoor swimming pool, fishing, sauna,
solarium, gymnasium, caddy cars, elec trolleys,
practice area.
Location 3m S of Worcester, A4103
Hotel ★★★ 68% Fownes Hotel, City Walls Rd,
WORCESTER
☎ 01905 613151 61 ⇔ ♠

BROADWAY
Map 04 SP03

Broadway Willersey Hill WR12 7LG
☎ 01386 853683
At the edge of the Cotswolds this downland course lies at an
altitude of 900 ft above sea level, with extensive views.
18 holes, 6216yds, Par 72, SSS 70, Course record 65.
Club membership 850.
Visitors may not play Sat between Apr-Sep before 3pm.
Restricted play Sun. Must contact in advance.
Societies Wed-Fri, must contact in advance.
Green Fees £33 per day; £27 per round (£33 per round/day
weekends & bank holidays).
Facilities ⊗ ⅢⅢ ⚘ 📷 ♀ ⚘ 🏠 ♪ ♪ Martyn Freeman.
Leisure trolley for hire, putting green, practice area.
Location 1.5m E on A44
Hotel ★★★ 68% Dormy House Hotel, Willersey Hill,
BROADWAY
☎ 01386 852711 26 ⇔ ♠Annexe23 ⇔

BROMSGROVE   Map 07 SO97

Blackwell Blackwell B60 1PY ☎ 0121 445 1994
Pleasantly undulating parkland with a variety of trees. Laid out in two 9-hole loops.
18 holes, 6202yds, Par 70, SSS 71, Course record 63.
Visitors   must contact in advance, must have handicap certificate.
Societies   must contact in advance.
Green Fees not confirmed.
Facilities   ♀♈☎ℓ Nigel Blake.
Leisure   putting green,cart/trolley hire.
Location   2m W of Alvechurch
Hotel   ★★★ 73% Pine Lodge Hotel, Kidderminster Rd, BROMSGROVE
              ☎ 01527 576600 114 ⇥ ℟

Bromsgrove Golf Centre Stratford Rd B60 1LD
☎ 01527 575886
Gently undulating parkland course with large contoured greens, generous tee surfaces and superb views over Worcestershire. Tricky par 3 16th across a lake. Also 41 bay floodlit driving range, floodlit practice bunker and new clubhouse with conference facilities.
18 holes, 5366mtrs, Par 68, SSS 68.
Club membership 900.
Visitors   dress restriction, no T-shirts, jeans, tracksuits etc. 7 day booking facilities available.
Societies   weekdays only, apply in writing or telephone.
Green Fees £11 per 18 holes; £6.50 per 9 holes (£13.50/£8 weekends & bank holidays).
Facilities   ⊗ ℳ ♞ ▆ ♀♈☎ℓ Graeme Long.
Leisure   trolley for hire, floodlit driving range, putting green, practice area.
Location   E side of Bromsgrove, 6m W of Alvechurch
Hotel   ★★★ 73% Pine Lodge Hotel, Kidderminster Rd, BROMSGROVE
              ☎ 01527 576600 114 ⇥ ℟

DROITWICH   Map 03 SO86

Droitwich Ford Ln WR9 0BQ
☎ 01905 774344 (Secretary) & 770207 (Pro)
Undulating parkland course.
18 holes, 6058yds, Par 70, SSS 69, Course record 62.
Club membership 732.
Visitors   with member only weekends & bank holidays.
Societies   must apply by telephone or letter.
Green Fees £24 per day.
Facilities   ⊗ ℳ ♞ ▆ ♀♈☎ℓ C Thompson.
Leisure   trolley for hire, putting green, practice area.
Location   1.5m N off A38
Hotel   ★★★★ 66% Chateau Impney Hotel, DROITWICH ☎ 01905 774411 67 ⇥ ℟

Ombersley Bishops Wood Rd, Lineholt, Ombersley WR9 0LE ☎ 01905 620747
Undulating course in beautiful countryside high above the edge of the Severn Valley. Covered driving range and putting green.
18 holes, 6139yds, Par 72, SSS 69.
Club membership 750.
Visitors   suitable dress expected, no jeans.
Societies   telephone in advance.
Green Fees £13.30 per 18 holes (£10 off peak).

Facilities   ⊗ ℳ ♞ ▆ ♀♈☎ℓ Graham Glenister.
Leisure   motorised carts for hire, buggies for hire, trolley for hire, driving range, putting green, practice area.
Location   3m W of Droitwich, off A449
Hotel   ★★★★ 61% Raven Hotel, St Andrews St, DROITWICH ☎ 01905 772224 72 ⇥ ℟

FLADBURY   Map 03 SO94

Evesham Craycombe Links, Old Worcester Rd WR10 2QS
☎ 01386 860395
Parkland, heavily wooded, with the River Avon running alongside 5th and 14th holes. Good views. Nine greens played from eighteen different tees.
9 holes, 6415yds, Par 72, SSS 71, Course record 68.
Club membership 383.
Visitors   must contact in advance. With members only at weekends.
Societies   must apply by letter.
Green Fees £15 per day/round.
Facilities   ⊗ by prior arrangement ℳ by prior arrangement ♞ ▆ ♀♈☎ℓ Charles Haynes.
Leisure   motorised carts for hire, trolley for hire, driving range, putting green, practice area.
Location   0.75m N on A4538
Hotel   ★★★ 69% The Evesham Hotel, Coopers Ln, off Waterside, EVESHAM
              ☎ 01386 765566 & 0800 716969 (Res) 40 ⇥ ℟
Additional ★★ 65% The Chequers Inn, Chequers Ln,
hotel   FLADBURY
              ☎ 01386 860276 & 860527 8 ⇥ ℟

HEREFORD

Map 03 SO53

Belmont Lodge Belmont HR2 9SA ☎ 01432 352666
Partly wooded course, the second half of which is on the
banks of the River Wye.
18 holes, 6490yds, Par 71.
Club membership 550.
Visitors advised to contact in advance at weekends.
Societies must telephone in advance.
Green Fees summer: £22 per day; £15 per round (£30/£25
weekends). winter: £18 per day; £10 per round
(£20/£16 weekends.
Facilities ⊗ ⅦⅠⅬ ♥ ♀ ⅄ ⿸ ⓣ ⿸ ⓕ Mike Welsh.
Leisure hard tennis courts, fishing, buggies for hire,
trolley for hire, putting green, practice area,
bowling green.
Location 2m S off A465
Hotel ★★★ 62% Belmont Lodge & Golf Course,
Belmont, HEREFORD
☎ 01432 352666 30 ⇄ ♠

Burghill Valley Tillington Rd, Burghill HR4 7RW
☎ 01432 760456
The course is situated in typically beautiful Herefordshire
countryside. The walking is easy on gently rolling fairways
with a background of hills and woods and in the distance, the
Welsh mountains. Some holes have been constructed through
mature cider orchards and there are two lakes to negotiate. A
fair but interesting test for players of all abilities.
18 holes, 6239yds, Par 71, SSS 70.
Club membership 600.
Visitors contact in advance.
Societies apply in writing or telephone in advance.
Green Fees £15 per round (£18 weekends & bank holidays).
Facilities ⊗ ⅦⅠⅬ ♥ ♀ ⅄ ⿸ ⓕ Nigel Clarke.
Leisure buggies for hire, trolley for hire, putting green,
practice area.
Location 4m NW of Hereford
Hotel ★★★ 62% The Green Dragon, Broad St,
HEREFORD ☎ 01432 272506 87 ⇄ ♠

Hereford Municipal Hereford Leisure Centre, Holmer Rd
HR4 9UD ☎ 01432 344376
This municipal parkland course is more challenging than first
appearance. The well-drained greens are open all year round
with good drainage for excellent winter golf.
9 holes, 3060yds, Par 35, SSS 69.
Club membership 85.
Visitors restrictions on race days.
Societies telephone in advance.
Green Fees £5.35 per 18 holes; £3.30 per 9 holes
(£7.20/£4.50 weekends).
Facilities ⊗ ⅦⅠⅬ ♥ ♀ ⅄ ⿸ ⓕ Philip Brookes.
Leisure squash, sauna, gymnasium, trolley for hire,
putting green, practice area.
Location Adjacent to race course & leisure centre
Hotel ★★ 64% The Merton Hotel & Governors
Restaurant, 28 Commercial Rd, HEREFORD
☎ 01432 265925 19 ⇄ ♠

HOLLYWOOD

Map 07 SP07

Gay Hill Hollywood Ln B47 5PP
☎ 0121 430 8544 & 6523
A meadowland course, some 7m from Birmingham.

18 holes, 6532yds, Par 72, SSS 71, Course record 64.
Club membership 740.
Visitors must contact in advance.
Societies telephone in advance.
Green Fees £28.50 per day (weekdays).
Facilities ⊗ ⅦⅠⅬ ♥ ♀ ⅄ ⿸ ⓣ ⓕ Andrew Hill.
Leisure trolley for hire, putting green, practice area.
Location N side of village
Hotel ★★★★ 61% Regency Hotel, Stratford Rd,
Shirley, SOLIHULL
☎ 0121 745 6119 112 ⇄ ♠

KIDDERMINSTER

Map 07 SO87

Habberley Low Trimpley DY11 5RG
☎ 01562 745756
Very hilly, wooded parkland course.
9 holes, 5481yds, Par 69, Course record 62.
Club membership 300.
Visitors may only play weekends with a member,
Societies telephone initially.
Green Fees on application.
Facilities ⊗ ⅦⅠⅬ ♥ ♀ ⅄
Location 2m NW
Hotel ★★★★ 59% Stone Manor Hotel, Stone,
KIDDERMINSTER
☎ 01562 777555 52 ⇄ ♠

Kidderminster Russell Rd DY10 3HT ☎ 01562 822303
Parkland course with natural hazards and some easy walking.
18 holes, 6405yds, Par 72, SSS 71, Course record 66.
Club membership 800.
Visitors with member only weekends & bank holidays.
Societies Thu only, apply in advance.
Green Fees £30 per day; £22 per round.
Facilities ⊗ ⅦⅠⅬ ♥ ♀ ⅄ ⿸ ⓣ ⓕ Nick Underwood.
Leisure trolley for hire, putting green, practice area.
Location 0.5m SE of town centre, signposted off A449
Hotel ★★★★ 59% Stone Manor Hotel, Stone,
KIDDERMINSTER
☎ 01562 777555 52 ⇄ ♠

KINGTON

Map 03 SO25

Kington Bradnor Hill HR5 3RE
☎ 01544 230340 & 231320
The highest 18-hole course in England, with magnificent
views over seven counties. A natural heathland course
with easy walking on mountain turf cropped by sheep.
There is bracken to catch any really bad shots but no sand
traps.
18 holes, 5980yds, Par 70, SSS 68, Course record 65.
Club membership 640.
Visitors contact the professional.
Societies must book in advance through the Hon
Secretary.
Green Fees £18 per day; £13 per round (£22/£16
weekends & bank holidays).
Facilities ⊗ ⅦⅠⅬ ♥ ♀ ⅄ ⿸ ⓣ ⓕ Dean Oliver.
Leisure trolley for hire, driving range, putting green,
practice area.
Location 0.5m N of Kington, off B4355
Hotel ★★ 67% Talbot Hotel, West St,
LEOMINSTER
☎ 01568 616347 20 ⇄ ♠

★★

TALBOT HOTEL

West Street - Leominster - Herefordshire - HR6 8EP

A coaching inn originating from the 15th century, oak beams, log fire and traditional hospitality. Leominster lies in an 'undiscovered' corner of England – memorable for its beautiful countryside, black and white villages and wealth of antique shops – an easy drive to Wye Valley, Malvern Hills, Welsh Marches and Ironbridge, home of the industrial revolution.

****

The Talbot Hotel Offers A Two Day Golfing Break

Dinner, Bed and Breakfast PLUS two days golf at Leominster 18 hole course – £127 per person

OR

Kington Golf Course £133 per person

Enquiries, Hotel Brochure and Further Information

Telephone 01568 616347

LEOMINSTER — Map 03 SO45

Leominster Ford Bridge HR6 0LE
☎ 01568 611402 & 610055
Sheltered parkland course alongside River Lugg with undulating land for nine holes.
18 holes, 6029yds, Par 70, SSS 69.
Club membership 550.

Visitors must contact in advance.
Societies must telephone in advance.
Green Fees £18 per day; £14.50 per round (£21 per day weekends & bank holidays).
Facilities Andrew Ferriday.
Leisure fishing, trolley for hire, driving range, putting green.
Location 3m S on A49
Hotel ★★ 57% Royal Oak Hotel, South St, LEOMINSTER
☎ 01568 612610 17 Annexe1
Additional hotel ★★ 67% Talbot Hotel, West St, LEOMINSTER ☎ 01568 616347 20

MALVERN WELLS — Map 03 SO74

Worcestershire Wood Farm, Hanley Rd WR14 4PP
☎ 01684 575992 & 573905
Fairly easy walking on windy downland course with trees, ditches and other natural hazards. Outstanding views of Malvern Hills and Severn Valley. 17th hole (par 5) is approached over small lake.
18 holes, 6449yds, Par 71, SSS 71, Course record 65.
Club membership 770.

Visitors only after 10am at weekends or with a member. Must contact in advance.
Societies Thu & Fri only, apply in writing.
Green Fees £25 per day (£30 weekends & bank holidays).
Facilities Grahame Harris.
Leisure trolley for hire, putting green, practice area.
Location 2m S of Gt Malvern on B4209
Hotel ★★★ 70% The Cottage in the Wood Hotel, Holywell Rd, Malvern Wells, MALVERN
☎ 01684 575859 8 Annexe12

REDDITCH — Map 07 SP06

Abbey Park Golf & Country Club Dagnell End Rd B98 9BE
☎ 01527 68006
Young parkland course opened in 1985, with rolling fairways. A 'Site of Special Scientific Interest', the course includes two fly-fishing lakes and is pleasant to play.
18 holes, 6411yds, Par 71, SSS 71, Course record 69.
Club membership 1000.

Visitors no restrictions.
Societies must apply in writing.
Green Fees not confirmed.
Facilities R K Cameron.
Leisure heated indoor swimming pool, fishing, sauna, solarium, gymnasium, driving range, trolley hire, practice area.
Location 1.25m N off A441 on B4101
Hotel ★★★ 62% Southcrest Hotel, Pool Bank, Southcrest, REDDITCH
☎ 01527 541511 58

Pitcheroak Plymouth Rd B97 4PB
☎ 01527 541054 & 541043
Woodland course, hilly in places.There is also a putting green and a practice ground.
9 holes, 4561yds, Par 65, SSS 62.
Club membership 200.

Visitors no restrictions.
Societies telephone to book.
Green Fees £6 per 18 holes; £4.50 per 9 holes (£7/£5 weekends).
Facilities David Stewart.
Leisure trolley for hire, putting green, practice area.
Location SW side of town centre off A448
Hotel ★★★ 62% Southcrest Hotel, Pool Bank, Southcrest, REDDITCH
☎ 01527 541511 58

Redditch Lower Grinsty, Green Ln, Callow Hill B97 5PJ
☎ 01527 543079
Parkland course, the hazards including woods, ditches and large ponds. The par 4, 14th is a testing hole.
18 holes, 6671yds, Par 72, SSS 72, Course record 68.
Club membership 650.

Visitors with member only weekends & bank holidays.
Societies telephone Secretary.
Green Fees £27.50 per day; £20 per 18 holes.
Facilities Frank Powell.
Leisure motorised carts for hire, buggies for hire, trolley for hire, putting green, practice area.
Location 2m SW
Hotel ★★★ 62% Southcrest Hotel, Pool Bank, Southcrest, REDDITCH
☎ 01527 541511 58

Pengethley Manor

GEORGIAN COUNTRY HOTEL & RESTAURANT

Nr. Ross-on-Wye, Herefordshire HR9 6LL
Tel: (01989) 730211 Fax: (01989) 730238

This delightful hotel and restaurant is quietly situated in 15 acres of gardens and grounds, has its own vineyard, with lovely views of the Herefordshire countryside. The attractive, elegant restaurant features fresh local produce and fresh herbs. A la Carte and Table d'hôte menus are available.
A separate Conference Centre provides everything you need for meetings 'away from it all'.
To help you relax, we have a heated outdoor swimming pool, 9 hole golf improvement course, designer walks, trout pond, croquet and snooker.

AA ★★★ 72% ☜☜ Egon Ronay
BTA Commended Country House Hotel
Derek Johansen Recommended Hotels

Cadmore Lodge

COUNTRY HOTEL ★★

Berrington Green, Tenbury Wells, WR15 8TQ
Tel/Fax: 01584 810044

Located 2½ miles west of Tenbury Wells, just off A4112 to Leominster. Brook Valley with lake and streams in constant play. **Green fees weekdays £7.00, weekends &10.00.** Hotel bar and restaurant – all meals catered for. 10 ensuite bedrooms. Visitors welcome. Society meetings welcome.
Secretary: Mr R. Farr,
Telephone: 01584 810306

ROSS-ON-WYE
Map 03 SO62

Ross-on-Wye Two Park, Gorsley HR9 7UT
☎ 01989 720267
The undulating, parkland course has been cut out of a silver birch forest; the fairways being well-screened from each other. The fairways are tight, the greens good.
18 holes, 6451yds, Par 72, SSS 73, Course record 68.
Club membership 760.

Visitors	must contact professional in advance 01989 720439.
Societies	must telephone in advance.
Green Fees	£35 day; £30 per 18 holes.
Facilities	⊗ 🍽 🛄 🍺 ♀ ⚒ 🏌
Leisure	trolley for hire, driving range, putting green, practice area.
Location	On B4221 N side of M50 junc 3
Hotel	★★★⚓ 72% Pengethley Manor, ROSS-ON-WYE ☎ 01989 730211 11 ⇌ 🐾Annexe14 ⇌ 🐾

TENBURY WELLS
Map 07 SO56

Cadmore Lodge Hotel & Country Club Berrington Green WR15 8TQ ☎ 01584 810044
A picturesque 9-hole course in a brook valley. Challenging holes include the 1st and 6th over the lake, 8th over the valley and 9th over hedges.

9 holes, 5129yds, Par 68, SSS 65.
Club membership 120.

Visitors	no restrictions but check availability.
Societies	telephone in advance.
Green Fees	not confirmed.
Facilities	♀ ⚒ 🏌
Leisure	hard tennis courts, fishing, practice net, bowling green.
Hotel	★★ 65% Cadmore Lodge Hotel & Country Club, Berrington Green, Tenbury Wells ☎ 01584 810044 8 ⇌ 🐾

UPPER SAPEY
Map 03 SO66

Sapey WR6 6XT ☎ 01886 853288
Parkland course with views of the Malvern Hills. Trees, lakes and water hazards. Not too strenuous a walk.
18 holes, 5935yds, Par 69, SSS 68, Course record 63.
Club membership 520.

Visitors	must contact in advance.
Societies	must contact in advance.
Green Fees	£22 per day; £15 per round (£25/£20 weekends & bank holidays).
Facilities	⊗ 🍽 🛄 🍺 ♀ ⚒ 🏠 🏌 🍴 Chris Knowles.
Leisure	motorised carts for hire, buggies for hire, trolley for hire, driving range, putting green, practice area, bowling green.
Location	B4203 Bromyard/Whitley Rd
Hotel	★★★ 70% The Elms, ABBERLEY ☎ 01299 896666 16 ⇌ 🐾Annexe9 ⇌ 🐾

WORCESTER   Map 03 SO85

Tolladine Tolladine Rd WR4 9BA ☎ 01905 21074
Parkland course, hilly and very tight, but with excellent views
of the surrounding hills and Worcester city.
9 holes, 2813yds, Par 68, SSS 67.
Club membership 350.
Visitors   with member only weekend & bank holidays.
Societies   must apply in writing.
Green Fees not confirmed.
Facilities   ⚲⚲⚲⚲ Clare George.
Location   1.5m E
Hotel   ★★★ 61% The Giffard, High St,
              WORCESTER ☎ 01905 726262 103 ⇆ ℝ

Worcester Golf & Country Club Boughton Park WR2 4EZ
☎ 01905 422555 & 422044 (Pro)
Fine parkland course with many trees, a lake, and views of
the Malvern Hills.
18 holes, 6251yds, Par 70, SSS 70, Course record 67.
Club membership 1000.
Visitors   with member only weekends. Must contact
              professional in advance.
Societies   telephone in advance.
Green Fees £25 per day.
Facilities   ⊗ ⅢⅢ ⬛ ⬛ ⚲⚲ ⬛ ℓ Colin Colenso.
Leisure   hard and grass tennis courts, squash, putting
              green, practice area.
Location   1½m from city centre on A4103
Hotel   ★★★ 61% The Giffard, High St,
              WORCESTER ☎ 01905 726262 103 ⇆ ℝ

WORMSLEY   Map 03 SO44

Herefordshire Ravens Causeway HR4 8LY
☎ 01432 830219
Undulating parkland course with expansive views.
18 holes, 6036yds, Par 70, SSS 69, Course record 61.
Club membership 800.
Visitors   must contact in advance.
Societies   must apply in advance.
Green Fees £20 per day; £15 per round (£18 per round
              weekends; £26 per day bank holidays).
Facilities   ⊗ ⅢⅢ ⬛ ⬛ ⚲⚲ ⬛ ℓ David Hemming.
Leisure   motorised carts for hire, buggies for hire, trolley
              for hire, putting green, practice area.
Location   E side of village
Hotel   ★★★ 62% The Green Dragon, Broad St,
              HEREFORD ☎ 01432 272506 87 ⇆ ℝ

WYTHALL   Map 07 SP07

Fulford Heath Tanners Green Ln B47 6BH
☎ 01564 824758
A mature parkland course encompassing two classic par
threes. The 11th, a mere 149 yards, shoots from an elevated
tee through a channel of trees to a well protected green. The
16th, a 166 yard par 3, elevated green, demands a 140 yard
carry over an imposing lake.
18 holes, 5971yds, Par 70, SSS 69.
Club membership 700.
Visitors   with member only weekend & bank holidays.
Societies   must apply in advance.
Green Fees £30 day/round weekdays.

Facilities   ⊗ ⅢⅢ ⬛ ⬛ ⚲⚲ ⬛ ℓ David Down.
Leisure   trolley for hire, putting green, practice area.
Location   1m SE off A435
Hotel   ★★★ 65% St John's Swallow Hotel, 651
              Warwick Rd, SOLIHULL
              ☎ 0121 711 3000 177 ⇆ ℝ

HERTFORDSHIRE

ALDBURY   Map 04 SP91

Stocks Hotel Golf & Country Club Stocks Rd HP23 5RX
☎ 01442 851341 & 851586
An 18-hole parkland course is one of the many facilities at
this country club. The course plays off blue, white (6,804
yards), yellow and red tees. There is also a driving range.
18 holes, 6804yds, Par 72, SSS 73, Course record 68.
Visitors   must contact in advance and have a handicap
              certificate. May not play before 2pm at
              weekends.
Societies   must contact well in advance.
Green Fees £30 per round (£40 weekends by arrangement).
Facilities   ⊗ ⅢⅢ ⬛ ⬛ ⚲⚲ ⬛ ⅛ ⅛ ℓ Peter Lane.
Leisure   hard tennis courts, heated outdoor swimming
              pool, sauna, solarium, gymnasium, motorised
              carts for hire, buggies for hire, trolley for hire,
              driving range, putting green, practice area,
              snooker, croquet, table tennis, steam room.
Location   2m from A41 at Tring
Hotel   ★★★★ 61% Pendley Manor, Cow Ln, TRING
              ☎ 01442 891891 71 ⇆ ℝ

ALDENHAM   Map 04 TQ19

Aldenham Golf and Country Club Church Ln WD2 8AL
☎ 01923 853929
Undulating parkland course.
Old Course: 18 holes, 6480yds, Par 70, SSS 71.
New Course: 9 holes, 2350yds, Par 33.
Club membership 550.
Visitors   Old Course restricted weekends before noon.
              New Course no restrictions.
Societies   must contact in advance.
Green Fees not confirmed.
Facilities   ⚲⚲ ⬛ ⅛ ⅛ ℓ Murray White.
Leisure   putting green,buggy/trolley hire.
Location   W side of village
Hotel   ★★★ 58% Dean Park Hotel, 30-40 St Albans
              Rd, WATFORD ☎ 01923 229212 90 ⇆ ℝ

BERKHAMSTED   Map 04 SP90

Berkhamsted The Common HP4 2QB
☎ 01442 865832
There are no sand bunkers on this Championship
heathland course but this does not make it any easier to
play. The natural hazards will test the skill of the most
able players, with a particularly testing hole at the 11th,
568 yards, par 5. Fine Greens, long carries and heather
and gorse. The clubhouse is very comfortable.   ▶

18 holes, 6605yds, Par 71, SSS 72, Course record 65.
Club membership 700.
Visitors must contact in advance.
Societies must contact in advance.
Green Fees £35 per day; £22.50 per round (£35
weekends after 11.30am). Winter: £30 per
day; £22.50 per round (£30 weekends after
11.30am).
Facilities ⊗ ⅏ ⅃ ☰ ♀ ⚘ 🏠 ⌢ Basil Proudfoot.
Leisure trolley for hire, putting green, practice area.
Location 1.5m E
Hotel ★★★★ 61% Pendley Manor, Cow Ln,
TRING ☎ 01442 891891 71 ⇄ ↾

BISHOP'S STORTFORD   Map 05 TL42

Bishop's Stortford Dunmow Rd CM23 5HP
☎ 01279 654715
Parkland course, fairly flat.
18 holes, 6404yds, Par 71, SSS 71.
Club membership 850.
Visitors must play with member at weekends.
Societies must contact in writing.
Green Fees £22 per day.
Facilities ⊗ ⅏ ⅃ ☰ ♀ ⚘ 🏠 ⌢ Vince Duncan.
Leisure motorised carts for hire, buggies for hire, trolley
for hire, putting green, practice area.
Location 0.5m W of M11 junc 8 on A1250
Hotel ★★★★ 69% Down Hall Country House Hotel,
Hatfield Heath, BISHOP'S STORTFORD
☎ 01279 731441 103 ⇄ ↾

Great Hadham Great Hadham Rd, Much Hadham SE10 6JE
☎ 01279 843558
An undulating open parkland course offering excellent
country views and a challenge with its ever present breeze.
18 holes, 6854yds, Par 72, SSS 73.
Club membership 700.
Visitors welcome all times except am Mon, Wed, Sat &
Sun.
Societies by advance booking in writing.
Green Fees £16 per 18 holes (£23 weekends & bank
holidays).
Facilities ⊗ ⅏ ⅃ ☰ ♀ ⚘ 🏠 ⌁ ⌢ Kevin Lunt.
Leisure motorised carts for hire, buggies for hire, trolley
for hire, driving range, putting green, practice
area.
Location On the B1004, 3m SW of Bishop's Stortford
Hotel ★★★★ 69% Down Hall Country House Hotel,
Hatfield Heath, BISHOP'S STORTFORD
☎ 01279 731441 103 ⇄ ↾

BRICKENDON   Map 05 TL30

Brickendon Grange SG13 8PD
☎ 01992 511258
Parkland course.
18 holes, 6349yds, Par 71, SSS 70, Course record 66.
Club membership 680.
Visitors must have handicap certificate. With member
only at weekends & bank holidays.
Societies by arrangement.
Green Fees not confirmed.
Facilities ♀ ⚘ 🏠 ⌢ John Hamilton.

Leisure putting,practice area,buggy/trolley hire.
Location W side of village
Hotel ★★★ 63% White Horse, Hertingfordbury,
HERTFORD ☎ 01992 586791 42 ⇄ ↾

BROOKMANS PARK   Map 04 TL20

Brookmans Park Golf Club Rd AL9 7AT
☎ 01707 652487
Brookman's Park is an undulating parkland course, with
several cleverly constructed holes. But it is a fair course,
although it can play long. The 11th, par 3, is a testing
hole which plays across a lake.
18 holes, 6460yds, Par 71, SSS 71, Course record 66.
Club membership 750.
Visitors must contact professional in advance 01707
652468 and have a handicap certificate;
must play with member at weekends & bank
holidays.
Societies must telephone in advance.
Green Fees £35 per day; £27 per round.
Facilities ⊗ ⅃ ☰ ♀ ⚘ 🏠 ⌢ Ian Jelley.
Leisure putting green, practice area.
Location N side of village off A1000
Hotel B Forte Posthouse South Mimms, SOUTH
MIMMS ☎ 01707 643311 120 ⇄ ↾

BUNTINGFORD   Map 05 TL32

East Herts Hamels Park SG9 9NA ☎ 01920 821922 (Pro)
An attractive undulating parkland course with magnificent
specimen trees.
18 holes, 6485yds, Par 71, SSS 71.
Club membership 750.
Visitors must contact in advance & have handicap
certificate, but may not play on Wed &
weekends.
Societies apply in writing.
Green Fees £24 per round.
Facilities ⊗ ⅏ ⅃ ☰ ♀ ⚘ 🏠 ⌁ ⌢ S Bryan.
Location 1m N of Puckeridge off A10
Hotel ★★★ 61% Vintage Court Hotel, Vintage
Corner, PUCKERIDGE
☎ 01920 822722 25 ⇄ ↾

BUSHEY   Map 04 TQ19

Bushey Golf & Country Club High St WD2 1BJ
☎ 0181 950 2283
Undulating parkland with challenging 2nd and 9th holes. The
latter has a sweeping dogleg left, playing to a green in front
of the club house. For the rather too enthusiatic golfer,
Bushey offers its own physiotherapist!
9 holes, 6000yds, Par 70, SSS 69, Course record 67.
Club membership 411.
Visitors must contact in advance.
Societies apply in writing or by telephone.
Green Fees £10 per round (£14 weekends & bank holidays).
Facilities ⊗ ⅏ ⅃ ☰ ♀ ⚘ 🏠 ⌁ ⌢ Michael Lovegrove.
Leisure squash, motorised carts for hire, buggies for hire,
trolley for hire, driving range, putting green,
physiotherapy.
Hotel ★★★ 74% Edgwarebury Hotel, Barnet Ln,
ELSTREE ☎ 0181 953 8227 47 ⇄ ↾

Bushey Hall Bushey Hall Dr WD2 2EP
☎ 01923 225802 & 222253
Parkland course.
18 holes, 6099yds, Par 70, SSS 69.
Club membership 500.
Visitors may book 7 days in advance.
Societies must contact in writing.
Green Fees not confirmed.
Facilities ♀ ♨ 🖥 🍴 ⎰ Ken Wickham.
Leisure practice area.
Location 1.5m NW on A4008
Hotel ★★★ 58% Dean Park Hotel, 30-40 St Albans
Rd, WATFORD
☎ 01923 229212 90 ⇄ 🐾

Hartsbourne Golf & Country Club Hartsbourne Ave
WD2 1JW ☎ 0181 950 1133
Parkland course with good views.
18 holes, 6305yds, Par 71, SSS 70, Course record 62.
Club membership 750.
Visitors must be guest of a member.
Societies phone for details.
Green Fees not confirmed.
Facilities ⊗ ⫴ ⓛ ⬛ ♀ ♨ 🖥 🍴 ⎰ Geoff Hunt.
Leisure motorised carts for hire, buggies for hire, trolley
for hire, driving range, putting.
Location 5m SE of Watford
Hotel ★★★ 58% Dean Park Hotel, 30-40 St Albans
Rd, WATFORD
☎ 01923 229212 90 ⇄ 🐾

CHESHUNT Map 05 TL30

Cheshunt Cheshunt Park, Park Ln EN7 6QD
☎ 01992 629777 & 624009
Municipal parkland course, well-bunkered with ponds, easy
walking.
18 holes, 6613yds, Par 71, SSS 71.
Club membership 350.
Visitors must book Tee-times through Pro shop.
Societies must apply in writing.
Green Fees not confirmed.
Facilities ♀ ♨ 🖥 🍴 ⎰ Chris Newton.
Leisure cart/trolley hire, practice area.
Location 1.5m NW off B156
Hotel B Marriott Hotel, Halfhide Ln, Turnford,
BROXBOURNE
☎ 01992 451245 150 ⇄ 🐾

CHORLEYWOOD Map 04 TQ09

Chorleywood Common Rd WD3 5LN
☎ 01923 282009
Heathland course with natural hazards and good views.
9 holes, 5676yds, Par 68, SSS 67.
Club membership 300.
Visitors must contact in advance, restricted weekends.
Societies must apply in writing.
Green Fees £14 per round; £17.50 weekends & bank
holidays.
Facilities ⊗ ⫴ ⓛ ⬛ ♨ 🖥
Location E side of village off A404
Hotel ★★★ 72% Bedford Arms, CHENIES
☎ 01923 283301 10 ⇄ 🐾

ELSTREE Map 04 TQ19

Elstree Watling St WD6 3AA ☎ 0181 953 6115
Parkland course.
18 holes, 6603yds, Par 73, SSS 72.
Club membership 650.
Visitors advisable to contact in advance, no restrictions
weekdays, may not play until after 2pm
weekends unless tee time available day prior.
Societies telephone in advance.
Green Fees not confirmed.
Facilities ♀ ♨ ⎰ Marc Warwick.
Leisure driving range, putting, trolley hire.
Location E of Bushey, on A5
Hotel ★★★ 74% Edgwarebury Hotel, Barnet Ln,
ELSTREE ☎ 0181 953 8227 47 ⇄ 🐾

ESSENDON Map 04 TL20

Hatfield London Country Club Bedwell Park AL9 6JA
☎ 01707 642624
Parkland course with many varied hazards, including ponds, a
stream and a ditch. 19th-century manor clubhouse. 9-hole
pitch and putt.
18 holes, 6880yds, Par 72, SSS 72.
Club membership 250.
Visitors must contact in advance.
Societies must contact in advance.
Green Fees Tue-Fri: £23 per day ticket; Mon £20 per day,
£11 per round (£19-£27 per round weekends &
bank holidays).
Facilities ⊗ ⫴ ⓛ ⬛ ♀ ♨ 🖥 🍴 ⎰ Norman Greer.
Leisure hard tennis courts, buggies for hire, trolley for
hire, driving range, putting green, practice area.
Location On B158 1m S
Hotel ★★★ 57% The Homestead Court, Homestead
Ln, WELWYN GARDEN CITY
☎ 01707 324336 58 ⇄ 🐾

GRAVELEY Map 04 TL22

Chesfield Downs Family Golf Centre Jack's Hill SG4 7EQ
☎ 01462 482929
A revolutionary new golf course with the emphasis on
facilities for the entire family. Its undulating, open downland
course has an inland links feel. There is a 25-bay floodlit,
covered driving range, a 9-hole Par 3 and many other
facilities.
Chesfield Downs: 18 holes, 6648yds, Par 71, SSS 72.
Lannock Links: 9 holes, 975yds, Par 27, SSS 27.
Club membership 500.
Visitors no restrictions.
Societies must telephone in advance.
Green Fees not confirmed.
Facilities ♀ ♨ 🖥 🍴 ⎰ Ross Whitehead.
Leisure putting, driving range, cart/trolley hire.
Hotel ★★★ 60% Hertfordpark Hotel, Danestrete,
STEVENAGE ☎ 01438 779955 98 ⇄ 🐾

HARPENDEN Map 04 TL11

Harpenden Hammonds End, Redbourn Ln AL5 2AX
☎ 01582 712580
Gently undulating parkland course, easy walking. ▶

18 holes, 6381yds, Par 70, SSS 70, Course record 67.
Club membership 800.

Visitors	must contact in advance. May not play Thu & weekends.
Societies	must apply in writing.
Green Fees	£34 per day; £24 per round (weekdays).
Facilities	⊗ ⅧL ᴸ ♥ ♀⚐ ᴖ ᵀ ℂ Peter Cherry.
Leisure	trolley for hire, driving range, putting green, practice area.
Location	1m S on B487
Hotel	★★★ 63% Harpenden House Hotel, 18 Southdown Rd, HARPENDEN ☎ 01582 764111 18 ⇋ ℝ Annexe35 ⇋ ℝ

Harpenden Common Cravells Rd, East Common AL5 1BL
☎ 01582 715959
Flat, easy walking, good greens, typical common course.
18 holes, 6214yds, Par 70, SSS 70.
Club membership 710.

Visitors	must contact in advance.
Societies	Thu & Fri only. Must apply in writing.
Green Fees	£27 per day; £22 per round (£27 per round weekends).
Facilities	⊗ L ♥ ♀⚐ ᴖ ᵀ ℂ Barney Puttick.
Leisure	trolley for hire, driving range, putting green, practice area.
Location	1m S on A1081
Hotel	★★★ 68% Glen Eagle Hotel, 1 Luton Rd, HARPENDEN ☎ 01582 760271 50 ⇋ ℝ

HEMEL HEMPSTEAD
Map 04 TL00

Boxmoor 18 Box Ln, Boxmoor HP3 0DJ
☎ 01442 242434
Challenging, very hilly, moorland course with sloping
fairways divided by trees. Fine views. Testing holes: 3rd (par
3), 4th (par 4).
9 holes, 4812yds, Par 64, SSS 63, Course record 62.
Club membership 280.

Visitors	may not play on Sun & bank holidays. Restricted some Sat.
Societies	must contact in advance.
Green Fees	£10 per day/round (£15 Sat).
Facilities	⊗ Ⅷ by prior arrangement L ♥ ♀⚐
Location	2m SW on B4505
Hotel	★★★ 64% The Two Brewers Inn, The Common, CHIPPERFIELD ☎ 01923 265266 20 ⇋ ℝ

Little Hay Box Ln, Bovingdon HP3 0DQ
☎ 01442 833798
Semi-parkland, inland links.
18 holes, 6678yds, Par 72, SSS 72.

Visitors	advisable to contact in advance.
Societies	telephone for details.
Green Fees	£9.50 per round (£13.50 weekends).
Facilities	⊗ Ⅷ by prior arrangement L ♥ ♀⚐ ⚐ ᴖ ℂ D Johnson/S Proudfoot.
Leisure	trolley for hire, floodlit driving range, putting green.
Location	1.5m SW on B4505 off A41
Hotel	B Forte Posthouse Hemel Hempstead, Breakspear Way, HEMEL HEMPSTEAD ☎ 01442 251122 146 ⇋ ℝ

Shendish Manor London Rd, Apsley HP3 0AA
☎ 01442 251806
A hilly course with plenty of trees and good greens. A tough
course for any golfer.
9 holes, 6076yds, Par 70, SSS 69.

Visitors	no restrictions.
Societies	must contact in advance.
Green Fees	not confirmed.
Facilities	♀⚐ ⚐ ᴖ ᵀ ℂ Kevin Hughes.
Leisure	practice area, trolley hire.
Hotel	★★★★ 61% Pendley Manor, Cow Ln, TRING ☎ 01442 891891 71 ⇋ ℝ

KNEBWORTH
Map 04 TL22

Knebworth Deards End Ln SG3 6NL ☎ 01438 812752
Parkland course, easy walking.
18 holes, 6492yds, Par 71, SSS 71, Course record 68.
Club membership 900.

Visitors	must have handicap certificate, but must play with member at weekends.
Societies	must contact in advance.
Green Fees	£29 per day/round.
Facilities	⊗ Ⅷ L ♥ ♀⚐ ⚐ ℂ Garry Parker.
Leisure	motorised carts for hire, buggies for hire, trolley for hire, putting green, practice area.
Location	N side of village off B197
Hotel	B Forte Posthouse Stevenage, Old London Rd, Broadwater, STEVENAGE ☎ 01438 365444 54 ⇋ ℝ

LETCHWORTH
Map 04 TL23

Letchworth Letchworth Ln SG6 3NQ ☎ 01462 683203
Planned more than 50 years ago by Harry Vardon, this
adventurous, parkland course is set in a peaceful corner
of 'Norman' England. To its variety of natural and
artificial hazards is added an unpredictable wind.
18 holes, 6181yds, Par 70, SSS 69.
Club membership 1000.

Visitors	with member only at weekends. Must contact in advance and have a handicap certificate.
Societies	Wed, Thu & Fri only, must telephone in advance.
Green Fees	not confirmed.
Facilities	♀⚐ ⚐ ℂ J Mutimer.
Leisure	putting green, practice area, trolley hire.
Location	S side of town centre off A505
Hotel	★★★ 63% Blakemore Thistle, Blakemore End Rd, Little Wymondley, HITCHIN ☎ 01438 355821 82 ⇋ ℝ

LITTLE GADDESDEN
Map 04 SP91

Ashridge HP4 1LY ☎ 01442 842244
Good parkland course, challenging but fair. Good clubhouse
facilities.
18 holes, 6547yds, Par 72, SSS 71, Course record 64.
Club membership 720.

Visitors	must contact in advance, be a member of a recognised club & have handicap certificate, may not play weekends & bank holidays.
Societies	must apply in writing and complete booking form.

Green Fees £50 per day; £35 per round.
Facilities ⊗ ⊪ ⅃ ⅃ ♀ ⅄ 🖻 ⅂ ⅃ Andrew Ainsworth.
Leisure trolley for hire, putting green, practice area.
Location 5m N of Berkhamsted on the B4506
Hotel ★★★ 75% The Bell Inn, ASTON CLINTON
🕾 01296 630252 6 ⇄ ⅃ Annexe15 ⇄ ⅃

POTTERS BAR
Map 04 TL20

Potters Bar Darkes Ln EN6 1DE 🕾 01707 652020
Undulating parkland course with water in play on many holes.
18 holes, 6279yds, Par 71, SSS 70.
Club membership 500.
Visitors with member only at weekends, Ladies Day
Wed morning.
Societies Mon Tue & Fri only, by arrangement with
Secretary.
Green Fees £30 per day; £20 per round.
Facilities ⊗ ⅃ ⅃ ♀ ⅄ 🖻 ⅂ ⅃ Gary Carver.
Leisure motorised carts for hire, buggies for hire, trolley
for hire, putting green, practice area.
Location 1m N of M25 junct 24
Hotel B Forte Posthouse South Mimms, SOUTH
MIMMS 🕾 01707 643311 120 ⇄ ⅃

RADLETT
Map 04 TL10

Porters Park Shenley Hill WD7 7AZ 🕾 01923 854127
A splendid, undulating parkland course with fine trees
and lush grass. The holes are all different and interesting
- on many accuracy of shot to the green is of paramount
importance.
18 holes, 6313yds, Par 70, SSS 70, Course record 64.
Club membership 820.
Visitors must book 24hrs in advance. With member
only weekends.
Societies Wed & Thu only, must apply in writing.
Green Fees £44 per day; £29 per round.
Facilities ⊗ ⅃ ⅃ ♀ ⅄ 🖻 ⅂ ⅃ David Gleeson.
Leisure trolley for hire, driving range, putting green,
practice area.
Location NE side of village off A5183
Hotel ★★★★ 65% The Noke Thistle, Watford
Rd, ST ALBANS
🕾 01727 854252 111 ⇄ ⅃

REDBOURN
Map 04 TL11

Redbourn Kinsbourne Green Ln AL3 7QA
🕾 01582 793493
Testing parkland course (five par 4's over 400 yds). Also 9-
hole par 3 course.
*Ver Course: 18 holes, 6506yds, Par 70, SSS 71, Course
record 67.*
Kingsbourne Course: 9 holes, 1361yds, Par 27.
Club membership 850.
Visitors must contact up to 3 days in advance for Ver
course. No restrictions for Par 3.
Societies must telephone in advance.
Green Fees 18 hole: £16 per round (£20 weekends & bank
holidays). 9 hole: £4.50 per round.
Facilities ⊗ ⅃ ⅃ ♀ ⅄ 🖻 ⅂ ⅃ Martin Wright.
Leisure motorised carts for hire, buggies for hire, trolley
for hire, driving range, putting green, practice
area,.

Location 1m N off A5183
Hotel ★★★ 63% Harpenden House Hotel, 18
Southdown Rd, HARPENDEN
🕾 01582 764111 18 ⇄ ⅃ Annexe35 ⇄ ⅃

RICKMANSWORTH
Map 04 TQ09

Moor Park WD3 1QN 🕾 01923 773146
Two parkland courses.
*High Golf Course: 18 holes, 6713yds, Par 72, SSS 72,
Course record 63.*
*West Golf Course: 18 holes, 5815yds, Par 69, SSS 68,
Course record 62.*
Club membership 1700.
Visitors must contact in advance but may not play at
weekends, bank holidays or before 1pm on
Tue & Thu.
Societies must contact in advance.
Green Fees High: £40 per round. West: £25 per round.
Facilities ⊗ ⅃ ⅃ ♀ ⅄ 🖻 ⅂ ⅃ Lawrence Farmer.
Leisure hard and grass tennis courts, motorised carts
for hire, buggies for hire, trolley for hire,
putting green, practice area.
Location 1.5m SE off A4145
Hotel ★★★ 58% Dean Park Hotel, 30-40 St
Albans Rd, WATFORD
🕾 01923 229212 90 ⇄ ⅃

Rickmansworth Public Course Moor Ln WD3 1QL
🕾 01923 775278
Undulating, municipal parkland course.
18 holes, 4469yds, Par 63, SSS 62.
Club membership 240.
Visitors must contact the club in advance.
Societies must contact in advance.
Green Fees £9 (£12.50 weekends).
Facilities ⊗ ⅃ ⅃ ♀ ⅄ 🖻 ⅂ ⅃ Alan Dobbins.
Leisure motorised carts for hire, buggies for hire, trolley
for hire, pool table.
Location 2m S of town off A4145
Hotel ★★★ 58% Dean Park Hotel, 30-40 St Albans
Rd, WATFORD
🕾 01923 229212 90 ⇄ ⅃

ROYSTON
Map 05 TL34

Barkway Park Nuthampstead Rd, Barkway SG8 8EN
🕾 01763 849070 & 848215
An undulating course criss-crossed by ditches which come
into play on several holes. The challenging par 3 7th features
a long, narrow green with out of bounds close to the right
edge of the green.
18 holes, 6997yds, Par 74, SSS 74.
Club membership 360.
Visitors telephone for tee times, weekends after 11.30am
only.
Societies apply for booking form.
Green Fees £18 per 36 holes; £12 per 18 holes; £6 per 9
holes (£17 per 18 holes/£8.50 per 9 holes
weekends).
Facilities ⊗ ⅃ ⅃ ♀ ⅄ 🖻 ⅃ Steve Fox.
Leisure buggies for hire, trolley for hire, putting green,
practice area.
Location Off B1368 from A10 ▶

Hotel ★★★ 66% Duxford Lodge Hotel, Ickleton Rd, DUXFORD
☎ 01223 836444 11 ⇨ ⋔Annexe4 ⇨ ⋔

Kingsway Cambridge Rd, Melbourn SG8 6EY
☎ 01763 262727 & 262943
Short and deceptively tricky 9-hole course providing a good test for both beginners and experienced golfers. Out of bounds and strategically placed bunkers come into play on several holes, in particular the tough par 3 7th.
9 holes, 2455yds, Par 33, SSS 32.
Club membership 150.
Visitors welcome.
Societies telephone for details.
Green Fees £9.50 per 18 holes; £5.50 per 9 holes. Pitch & Putt £4.25 per 18 holes; £3 per 9 holes..
Facilities ⊗ ⮞ ⚑ ♀ ⚒ 🛆 ⌁ ⋔ ⋌ Denise Hastings.
Leisure trolley for hire, driving range, putting green, practice area.
Location Off the A10
Hotel ★★★ 66% Duxford Lodge Hotel, Ickleton Rd, DUXFORD
☎ 01223 836444 11 ⇨ ⋔Annexe4 ⇨ ⋔

Royston Baldock Rd SG8 5BG ☎ 01763 242696
Heathland course on undulating terrain and fine fairways.The 8th, 9th and 18th are the most notable holes.
18 holes, 6052yds, Par 70, SSS 69, Course record 65.
Club membership 550.
Visitors with member only at weekends. Must contact in advance.
Societies by arrangement Mon-Fri.
Green Fees £20 per day/round.
Facilities ⊗ ⊪ ⮞ ⚑ ♀ 🛆 ⚒ ⌁ ⋌ Mark Hatcher.
Leisure trolley for hire, putting green, practice area, snooker table.
Location 0.5m W of town centre
Hotel ★★★ 66% Duxford Lodge Hotel, Ickleton Rd, DUXFORD
☎ 01223 836444 11 ⇨ ⋔Annexe4 ⇨ ⋔

St Albans Map 04 TL10

Abbey View Westminster Lodge Leisure Ctr, Hollywell Hill AL1 2DL ☎ 01727 841973
Abbey View is a public golf course designed for beginners, but is sufficiently challenging for experienced golfers who only have time for a short game. There is a resident professional for assistance and lessons.
9 holes, 2162yds.
Visitors welcome but no sharing clubs, suitable footwear & wide wheel trolleys.
Green Fees not confirmed.
Facilities 🛆 ⌁ ⋌ Mark Sibley.
Leisure swimming pool, leisure centre adjacent to course.
Hotel ★★★ 64% Hertfordshire Moat House, London Rd, Markyate, ST ALBANS
☎ 01582 449988 89 ⇨ ⋔

Batchwood Hall Batchwood Dr AL3 5XA
☎ 01727 844250 .
Municipal parkland course designed by J H Taylor and opened in 1935.
18 holes, 6487yds, Par 71, SSS 71.
Club membership 200.

Visitors must contact in advance, in person.
Societies must contact in advance.
Green Fees £8.50 per round (£11.50 weekends).
Facilities ⊗ ⅷ ⮞ ⚑ ♀ 🛆 ⌁ ⋌ Jimmy Thompson.
Leisure hard tennis courts, squash, solarium, gymnasium, trolley for hire, putting green, practice area, indoor tennis.
Location 1m NW off A5183
Hotel ★★★ 66% St Michael's Manor Hotel, Fishpool St, ST ALBANS ☎ 01727 864444 24 ⇨ ⋔

Verulam London Rd AL1 1JG ☎ 01727 853327
Parkland course with fourteen holes having out-of-bounds. Water affects the 5th, 6th and 7th holes. Samuel Ryder was Captain here in 1927 when he began the now celebrated Ryder Cup Competition.
18 holes, 6448yds, Par 72, SSS 71.
Club membership 630.
Visitors must contact in advance. With member only at weekends.
Societies must contact advance.
Green Fees Mon: £20 per 36 holes, £12 per 18 holes. Tue-Fri: £30 per 36 holes, £25 per 18 holes.
Facilities ⊗ ⅷ by prior arrangement ⮞ ⚑ ♀ 🛆 ⚒ ⌁ ⋌ Nick Burch.
Leisure motorised carts for hire, trolley for hire, practice area.
Location 1m from junc 22 of M25 off A1081
Hotel ★★★★ 74% Sopwell House Hotel & Country Club, Cottonmill Ln, Sopwell, ST ALBANS
☎ 01727 864477 92 ⇨ ⋔

Sawbridgeworth Map 05 TL41

Manor of Groves Golf & Country Club High Wych CM21 0LA ☎ 01279 722333 & 721486
The 6,280yd, Par 71 course is set over 150 acres of established parkland and rolling countryside and is a true test of golf for the club golfer.
18 holes, 6280yds, Par 71, SSS 70, Course record 65.
Club membership 450.
Visitors telephone bookings preferred, may not play until after 12 noon at weekends.
Societies Mon-Fri by prior arrangement, telephone in advance.
Green Fees £20 per round (£25 weekends). Twilight after 6pm £15. Price review Mar'96.
Facilities ⊗ ⅷ ⮞ ⚑ ♀ 🛆 ⚒ ⌁ ⋔ ⊨ ⋌ Craig Laurence.
Leisure hard tennis courts, outdoor swimming pool, gymnasium, motorised carts for hire, buggies for hire, trolley for hire, putting green, practice area.
Location 1.5m on west side of town
Hotel ★★★ 74% Churchgate Manor Hotel, Churchgate St, Old Harlow, HARLOW
☎ 01279 420246 85 ⇨

Stanstead Abbots Map 05 TL31

Briggens House Hotel Briggens Park, Stanstead Rd SG12 8LD ☎ 01279 793742
An attractive 9-hole course set in the grounds of a hotel and 80 acres of countryside.
9 holes, 2793yds, Par 36, SSS 69, Course record 31.
Club membership 180.

Visitors	may not play Thu 5-6pm and Sun am. No jeans. Must have own clubs.
Societies	must contact in advance.
Green Fees	£10.50 per 18 holes (£15 weekends).
Facilities	⊗ �𝄞 ⯊ ▆ ♀ ⯂ 🏠 ⛳ ⫉ Sean Carter.
Leisure	hard tennis courts, heated outdoor swimming pool, fishing, motorised carts for hire, buggies for hire, trolley for hire, practice area, pitch & putt (summer only).
Location	Off Stanstead road A414
Hotel	★★★ 64% County Hotel, Baldock St, WARE ☎ 01920 465011 50 ⇥ ♞

STEVENAGE   Map 04 TL22

Stevenage Golf Centre Aston Ln SG2 7EL
☎ 01438 880424
Municipal course designed by John Jacobs, with natural water hazards and some wooded areas.
18 holes, 6451yds, Par 72, SSS 71.
Club membership 600.

Visitors	no restrictions.
Societies	must contact 1 week in advance. Deposit required.
Green Fees	not confirmed.
Facilities	♀ (all day) ⯂ 🏠 ⛳ ⫉ Keith Bond.
Leisure	floodlit driving range.
Location	4m SE off B5169
Hotel	B Forte Posthouse Stevenage, Old London Rd, Broadwater, STEVENAGE ☎ 01438 365444 54 ⇥ ♞

WARE   Map 05 TL31

Chadwell Springs Hertford Rd SG12 9LE
☎ 01920 461447
Quick drying moorland course on high plateau subject to wind. The first two holes are par 5 and notable.
9 holes, 6418yds, Par 72, SSS 71, Course record 68.
Club membership 650.

Visitors	with member only at weekends.
Societies	bookings accepted, Mon, Wed & Fri only.
Green Fees	£15 per 18 holes.
Facilities	⊗ ⯊ ⯊ ▆ ♀ ⯂ 🏠 ⫉ Mark Wall.
Leisure	trolley for hire.
Location	0.75m W on A119
Hotel	★★★ 64% County Hotel, Baldock St, WARE ☎ 01920 465011 50 ⇥ ♞

Hanbury Manor Golf & Country Club SG12 0SD
☎ 01920 487722
Superb parkland course designed by Jack Nicklaus II. Large oval tees, watered fairways and undulating greens make up the first 9 holes. Attractive lakes and deep-faced bunkers are strategically sited. Second 9 holes offer open panoramas and challenging holes.
18 holes, 7016yds, Par 72, SSS 74, Course record 70.
Club membership 600.

Visitors	with handicap certificate, members guest and hotel residents welcome.
Societies	strictly limited to Mon-Thu and restricted tee times, must be booked in advance.
Green Fees	Hotel guests £50.
Facilities	⊗ ⯊ ⯊ ▆ ♀ ⯂ 🏠 ⛳ ⯌ ⫉ Peter Blaze.
Leisure	hard tennis courts, heated indoor swimming pool, squash, sauna, solarium, gymnasium,

motorised carts for hire, buggies for hire, trolley for hire, putting green, practice area.

Location	Adjacent to A10
Hotel	★★★★★ 75% Hanbury Manor, WARE ☎ 01920 487722 69 ⇥ ♞Annexe27 ⇥ ♞

Whitehill Dane End SG12 0JS ☎ 01920 438495
Undulating course providing a good test for both the average golfer and the low handicapper. Several lakes in challenging positions.
18 holes, 6681yds, Par 72, SSS 72.
Club membership 600.

Visitors	handicap certificate must be produced or competence test taken (free), appropriate clothing must be worn.
Societies	telephone or write for booking form.
Green Fees	£15 per round (£18 weekends).
Facilities	⊗ ⯊ ⯊ ▆ ♀ ⯂ 🏠 ⛳ ⫉ David Ling.
Leisure	motorised carts for hire, buggies for hire, trolley for hire, driving range, putting green, practice area.
Hotel	★★★ 64% County Hotel, Baldock St, WARE ☎ 01920 465011 50 ⇥ ♞

WATFORD   Map 04 TQ19

West Herts Cassiobury Park WD1 7SL
☎ 01923 236484
Another of the many clubs that were inaugurated in the 1890's when the game of golf was being given a tremendous boost by the the performances of the first star professionals, Baird, Vardon and Taylor. The West Herts course is close to Watford but its tree-lined setting is beautiful and tranquil. Set out on a plateau the course is exceedingly dry. It also has a very severe finish with the 17th, a hole of 378 yards, the toughest on the course. The last hole measures over 480 yards.
18 holes, 6400yds, Par 72, SSS 71, Course record 66.
Club membership 700.

Visitors	must contact in advance. No play at weekends.
Societies	must telephone in advance and confirm in writing.
Green Fees	£30 per day; £20 per round weekdays.
Facilities	⊗ ⯊ ⯊ ▆ ♀ ⯂ 🏠 ⛳ ⫉ Charles Gough.
Leisure	motorised carts for hire, buggies for hire, trolley for hire, putting green, practice area.
Location	W side of town centre off A412
Hotel	★★★ 58% Dean Park Hotel, 30-40 St Albans Rd, WATFORD ☎ 01923 229212 90 ⇥ ♞

WELWYN GARDEN CITY   Map 04 TL21

Mill Green Gypsy Ln AL6 4TY
☎ 01707 276900 & 270542 (Pro)
Opened in autumn 1993, the 18-hole, Peter Alliss/Clive Clark designed, Mill Green course makes use of woodland and meadows. The par 3 9-hole gives a good test for improving the short game.
18 holes, 6615yds, Par 72, SSS 72, Course record 68.
Club membership 700.

Visitors	must contact in advance.
Societies	apply in writing for details.
Green Fees	£27.50 per round (£32.50 weekends & bank holidays); Mon £12.

▶

Facilities	⊗ 〉Ⅲ ⅬⅬ ☕ ♀☖ 🏠 ⌀ Alan Hall.
Leisure	motorised carts for hire, buggies for hire, trolley for hire, driving range, putting green.
Location	Exit 4 of A1(M), A414 to Mill Green
Hotel	★★★ 57% The Homestead Court, Homestead Ln, WELWYN GARDEN CITY ☎ 01707 324336 58 ⇆ ☏

Panshanger Golf & Squash Complex Old Herns Ln AL7 2ED ☎ 01707 333350
Municipal parkland course overlooking Mimram Valley. Squash.
18 holes, 6347yds, Par 72, SSS 70, Course record 65.
Club membership 600.

Visitors	no restrictions.
Societies	telephone for details.
Green Fees	£20 per day; £11 per round (£15 per round weekends).
Facilities	⊗ ⅬⅬ ☕ ♀☖ 🏠 ⌀ ⌀ Bryan Lewis/Mick Corlass.
Leisure	squash, motorised carts for hire, buggies for hire, trolley for hire, putting green, practice area, pitch & putt.
Location	N side of town centre off B1000
Hotel	★★★ 57% The Homestead Court, Homestead Ln, WELWYN GARDEN CITY ☎ 01707 324336 58 ⇆ ☏

Welwyn Garden City Mannicotts, High Oaks Rd AL8 7BP ☎ 01707 325243
Undulating parkland course with a ravine. Course record holder is Nick Faldo.
18 holes, 6074yds, Par 70, SSS 69.
Club membership 975.

Visitors	must contact in advance but may not play Sun am.
Societies	must contact in advance.
Green Fees	£25 (£35 weekends).
Facilities	⊗ 〉Ⅲ ⅬⅬ ☕ ♀☖ 🏠 ⌀ Richard May.
Leisure	motorised carts for hire, buggies for hire, trolley for hire, putting green, practice area.
Location	W side of city, exit 6 off A1
Hotel	★★★ 57% The Homestead Court, Homestead Ln, WELWYN GARDEN CITY ☎ 01707 324336 58 ⇆ ☏

WHEATHAMPSTEAD   Map 04 TL11

Mid Herts Lamer Ln, Gustard Wood AL4 8RS
☎ 01582 832242
Commonland, wooded with heather and gorse-lined fairways.
18 holes, 6060yds, Par 69, SSS 69.
Club membership 760.

Visitors	may not play Tue, Wed afternoons & weekends.
Societies	must contact in writing.
Green Fees	on application.
Facilities	⊗ 〉Ⅲ ⅬⅬ ☕ ♀☖ 🏠 ⌀ Nick Brown.
Leisure	trolley for hire, putting green, practice area.
Location	1m N on B651
Hotel	★★★ 63% Harpenden House Hotel, 18 Southdown Rd, HARPENDEN ☎ 01582 764111 18 ⇆ ☏Annexe35 ⇆ ☏

ADDINGTON   Map 05 TQ65

West Malling London Rd ME19 5AR ☎ 01732 844785
Two 18-hole parkland courses.
Spitfire Course: 18 holes, 6142yds, Par 70, SSS 70, Course record 67.
Hurricane Course: 18 holes, 6268yds, Par 70, SSS 70, Course record 69.

Visitors	must contact in advance, may not play weekends until 2pm.
Societies	prior booking required.
Green Fees	£30 per day; £20 per round (£30 per round after 2pm weekends).
Facilities	⊗ 〉Ⅲ ⅬⅬ ☕ ♀☖ 🏠 ⌀ Jonathan Foss.
Leisure	squash, motorised carts for hire, buggies for hire, trolley for hire, putting green, practice area, snooker, table tennis.
Location	1m S off A20
Hotel	★★★ 64% Larkfield Priory Hotel, London Rd, LARKFIELD ☎ 01732 846858 52rm(51 ⇆ ☏)

ASH   Map 05 TQ66

The London South Ash Manor Estate TN15 7EN
☎ 01474 879899
Visitors may only play the courses at LGC as guests of members or prospective members by invitation.The courses, the Heritage and the International were designed by Jack Nicklaus: both include a number of lakes, generous fairways framed with native grasses and many challenging holes. A state-of-the-art drainage system ensures continuous play.
Heritage Course: 18 holes, 6771yds, Par 72, Course record 68.
International Course: 18 holes, 6574yds, Par 72.
Club membership 350.

Visitors	guest of member & prospective members invited by the membership office only.
Societies	companies only by application.
Green Fees	Guest of member. Heritage: £50 per round (£60 weekend & bank holidays). International: £40 per round (£45 weekend & bank holiday).
Facilities	⊗ 〉Ⅲ ⅬⅬ ☕ ♀☖ 🏠 ⌀ ⌀ Keith Morgan.
Leisure	sauna, motorised carts for hire, buggies for hire, trolley for hire, driving range, putting green, practice area.
Location	A20, 2m from Brands Hatch
Hotel	★★★ 64% Larkfield Priory Hotel, London Rd, LARKFIELD ☎ 01732 846858 52rm(51 ⇆ ☏)

ASHFORD   Map 05 TR04

Ashford Sandyhurst Ln TN25 4NT
☎ 01233 622655
Parkland course with good views and easy walking. Narrow fairways and tightly bunkered greens ensure a challenging game.
18 holes, 6263yds, Par 71, SSS 70, Course record 65.
Club membership 650.

Visitors	must contact in advance & have handicap certificate.

Societies   Tue & Thu only, by arrangement.
Green Fees £30 per day; £20 per round weekdays.
Facilities ⊗ ⅏ ⅃ ⅃ ♀ ♨ ☎ (Hugh Sherman.
Leisure   putting green.
Location   1.5m NW off A20
Hotel   ★★★★ 66% Ashford Moat House, Simone
            Weil Av, ASHFORD
            ☎ 01233 219988 200 ⇄ ♙
Additional QQQQ Elvey Farm Country Hotel, PLUCKLEY
hotel   ☎ 01233 840442 10 ⇄ ♙

Homelands Bettergolf Centre Ashford Rd, Kingsnorth
TN26 1NJ ☎ 01233 661620
Challenging 9-hole course designed by Donald Steel to
provide a stern test for experienced golfers and for others to
develop their game. With 4 par 3s and 5 par 4s it demands
accuracy rather than length. Floodlit driving range.
9 holes, 2205yds, Par 32, SSS 31.
Visitors   no restrictions, but booking recommended for
            weekend and summer evenings.
Societies   prior arrangements are essential.
Green Fees £10.50 per 18 holes; £7 per 9 holes (£14/£8
            weekends and bank holidays).
Facilities ⊗ ⅃ ⅃ ♀ ♨ ☎ ⚐ (Johnathan Callister.
Leisure   trolley for hire, driving range, putting green,
            practice area, 4 hole academy teaching course.
Hotel   ★★★ 62% Master Spearpoint Hotel,
            Canterbury Rd, Kennington, ASHFORD
            ☎ 01233 636863 35 ⇄ ♙

BARHAM   Map 05 TR25

Broome Park CT4 6QX ☎ 01227 831701
Championship standard parkland course in a valley, with a
350-year-old mansion clubhouse.
18 holes, 6610yds, Par 72, SSS 72, Course record 66.
Club membership 500.
Visitors   advisable to contact in advance, must have
            handicap certificate, but may not play Sat/Sun
            mornings.
Societies   Mon-Fri only, apply in writing or by telephone.
Green Fees £26 per round (£32 weekends & bank holidays).
            Dusk ticket £15 after 6pm.
Facilities ⊗ ⅏ ⅃ ⅃ ♀ ♨ ☎ ⚐ ⚑ (Tienne Britz.
Leisure   heated outdoor swimming pool, squash, sauna,
            solarium, gymnasium, motorised carts for hire,
            buggies for hire, trolley for hire, driving range,
            putting green, practice area.
Location   1.5m SE on A260
Hotel   ★★★ 64% Chaucer Hotel, Ivy Ln,
            CANTERBURY
            ☎ 01227 464427 42 ⇄ ♙

BEARSTED   Map 05 TQ85

Bearsted Ware St ME14 4PQ ☎ 01622 738198
Parkland course with fine views of the North Downs.
18 holes, 6437yds, Par 72, SSS 71.
Club membership 720.
Visitors   must have handicap certificate and may not play
            weekends unless with member. Must contact in
            advance.
Societies   write for reservation forms.
Green Fees £32 per day; £24 per round (£30 per round
            weekends).
Facilities ⊗ ⅏ ⅃ ⅃ ♀ ♨ ☎ (Tim Simpson.
Leisure   trolley for hire, putting green, practice area.
Location   2.5m E of Maidstone off A20
Hotel   ★★★★ 61% Tudor Park Hotel, Country Club
            Resort, Ashford Rd, Bearstead, MAIDSTONE
            ☎ 01622 734334 117 ⇄ ♙

BIDDENDEN   Map 05 TQ83

Chart Hills Weeks Ln TN27 8JX ☎ 01580 292222
Created by Nick Faldo and completed in 1993, this huge
course of grand design measures 7,000 yards from the back
tees. Facilities include a David Leadbetter Golf Academy.
18 holes, 7086yds, Par 72, SSS 74.
Club membership 280.
Visitors   contact for details.
Societies   telephone for details.
Green Fees not confirmed.
Facilities ⊗ ⅏ ⅃ ⅃ ♀ ♨ ☎ ⚐ (William Easdale.
Leisure   sauna, solarium, gymnasium, motorised carts for
            hire, buggies for hire, driving range, putting
            green, practice area.
Location   1m N of Biddenden off A274
Hotel   ★★ 67% Jarvis White Lion Hotel, High St,
            TENTERDEN
            ☎ 01580 765077 15 ⇄ ♙

BOROUGH GREEN   Map 05 TQ65

Wrotham Heath Seven Mile Ln TN15 8QZ
☎ 01732 884800
Parkland course, hilly, good views.
18 holes, 5954yds, Par 70, SSS 69.
Club membership 550.
Visitors   must contact in advance, may not play
            weekends.
Societies   Thu & Fri only, by arrangement.
Green Fees £32 per day; £22 per round.
Facilities ⊗ ⅏ ⅃ ⅃ ♀ ♨ ☎ (Harry Dearden.   ▶

Elvey Farm Country Hotel
Pluckley, Nr. Ashford, Kent TN27 0SU
Tel: Pluckley (01233) 840442   Fax/Guest Tel: (01233) 840726

Situated right in the heart of 'Darling Buds of May' country, we offer delux accommodation in our
Oast House, converted stables and 15thC. Kent Barn. Traditional English breakfast is served in
our unique dining room, dinner available when booked in advance, fully licensed. Ten double and
family rooms all with private bath/shower and colour T.V. Special rates for groups and societies,
many local courses including Faldo's designed Chart Hills.

*Junction 9, M20 only 12 minutes
away. Channel Tunnel 20 minutes*

KENT

Leisure — trolley for hire, putting green, practice area.
Location — 2.25m E on B2016
Hotel — B Forte Posthouse Maidstone/Sevenoaks, London Rd, Wrotham Heath, WROTHAM ☎ 01732 883311 106 ⇆ 🎇

BRENCHLEY   Map 05 TQ64

Moatlands Watermans Ln TN12 6ND
☎ 01892 724400
A rolling parkland course with dramatic views over the Weald of Kent. The challenging holes are the Par 4 8th with its tough dogleg, the 10th where there is a wooded copse with a Victorian bath-house to be avoided and the 14th where the approach to the green is guarded by oak trees.
18 holes, 6693yds, Par 72, SSS 72, Course record 71.
Club membership 453.
Visitors — must book in advance.
Societies — apply in writing or telephone.
Green Fees — £45 per day; £29 per round (£55/£39 weekends). Day prices summer only.
Facilities — ⊗ ⅏ ⓑ ♨ ♀ ♨ 🕋 🍴 Simon Wood.
Leisure — hard tennis courts, heated indoor swimming pool, sauna, gymnasium, motorised carts for hire, buggies for hire, trolley for hire, driving range, putting green, practice area.
Location — 3m N of Brenchley off B2160
Hotel — ★★★ 67% Jarvis Pembury Hotel, 8 Tonbridge Rd, Pembury, TUNBRIDGE WELLS (ROYAL) ☎ 01892 823567 80 ⇆ 🎇

BROADSTAIRS   Map 05 TR36

North Foreland Convent Rd, Kingsgate CT10 3PU
☎ 01843 862140
A picturesque course situated where the Thames Estuary widens towards the sea. North Foreland always seems to have a breath of tradition of golf's earlier days about it. Perhaps the ghost of one of its earlier professionals, the famous Abe Mitchell, still haunts the lovely turf of the fairways. Walking is easy and the wind is deceptive. The 8th and 17th, both par 4, are testing holes. There is also an approach and putting course.
18 holes, 6430yds, Par 71, SSS 71, Course record 65.
Short Course: 18 holes, 1752yds, Par 54, Course record 47.
Club membership 1200.
Visitors — for Main course are required to book in advance & have handicap certificate. May play afternoons only Mon and Tue, weekends restricted and no visitors Sun morning. Short course has no restrictions.
Societies — Wed & Fri only, by arrangement.
Green Fees — Main course £35 per day; £25 per round (£35 per round weekends). Short course £5.50/£6.50 per day.
Facilities — ⊗ ⅏ by prior arrangement ⓑ ♨ ♀ ♨ 🕋 🍴 Neil Hansen.
Leisure — hard tennis courts, motorised carts for hire, buggies for hire, trolley for hire, putting green, practice area.
Location — 1.5m N off B2052
Hotel — ★★★ 60% Royal Albion Hotel, Albion St, BROADSTAIRS ☎ 01843 868071 19 ⇆ 🎇

CANTERBURY   Map 05 TR15

Canterbury Scotland Hills, Littlebourne Rd CT1 1TW
☎ 01227 453532
Undulating parkland course, densely wooded in places, with elevated trees and difficult drives on several holes.
18 holes, 6249yds, Par 70, SSS 70, Course record 64.
Club membership 650.
Visitors — may only play after 3pm weekends & bank holidays. Must have a handicap certificate.
Societies — by arrangement.
Green Fees — £36 per day; £27 per round (£36 per round weekends and bank holidays).
Facilities — ⊗ ⅏ ⓑ ♨ ♀ ♨ 🕋 🍴 Paul Everard.
Leisure — trolley for hire, putting green, practice area.
Location — 1.5m E on A257
Hotel — ★★★ 64% Chaucer Hotel, Ivy Ln, CANTERBURY ☎ 01227 464427 42 ⇆ 🎇

CHART SUTTON   Map 05 TQ84

The Ridge Chartway St, East Sutton ME17 3DL
☎ 01622 844382
Opened in 1993, the course was designed by Patrick Dawson around mature orchards to challenge all levels of player. The par 5, 18th has two lakes to negotiate.
18 holes, 6254yds, Par 71, SSS 70, Course record 68.
Club membership 650.
Visitors — weekdays only, must have handicap certificate.
Societies — Tue & Thu, by arrangement.
Green Fees — £25 per day; £18 per round.
Facilities — ⊗ ⅏ ⓑ ♨ ♀ ♨ 🕋 🍴 Matthew Rackham.
Leisure — solarium, gymnasium, trolley for hire, driving range, putting green, practice area.
Location — 5m S of Bearsted, off A274
Hotel — ★★★★ 61% Tudor Park Hotel, Country Club Resort, Ashford Rd, Bearstead, MAIDSTONE ☎ 01622 734334 117 ⇆ 🎇

CRANBROOK   Map 05 TQ73

Cranbrook Benenden Rd TN17 4AL
☎ 01580 712833
Scenic, parkland course with easy terrain, backed by Hemstead Forest and close to Sissinghurst Castle (1m) and Bodiam Castle (6m). The most testing hole is the 12th (530 yds par 5). Venue for the County Championships.
18 holes, 6351yds, Par 70, SSS 70.
Club membership 480.
Visitors — may not play at weekends before 11am. Phone to book tee time up to one week in advance.
Societies — minimum of 12 write or telephone to book.
Green Fees — £30 per 36 holes; £20 per 18 holes (£27.50 per 18 holes weekends).
Facilities — ⊗ ⅏ ⓑ ♨ ♀ ♨ 🕋 🍴 Alan Gillard.
Leisure — trolley for hire, driving range, extensive practice area.
Location — 2m E
Hotel — ★★ 69% Hartley Mount Country House, Hartley Rd, CRANBROOK ☎ 01580 712230 6 ⇆ 🎇

DARTFORD
Map 05 TQ57

Birchwood Park Birchwood Rd, Wilmington DA2 7HJ
☎ 01322 662038 & 660554
18-hole course of two separate nines, reasonably demanding for good golfers. Last four holes very interesting. Additional 9-hole simple beginners/practice course and 38-bay floodlit driving range.
18 holes, 6364yds, Par 71, SSS 70, Course record 64 or 9 holes, 1259yds, Par 28.
Club membership 630.
Visitors   must contact in advance.
Societies   telephone for details.
Green Fees £14 (£23 weekends). 9 hole course £4 (£5 weekends).
Facilities ⊗ ⅲ ㅑ ♥ ♀ ㅅ 🏠 ☞ ☏ Martyn Hirst.
Leisure   floodlit driving range, putting green.
Location   B258 between Dartford & Swanley
Hotel   ★★★★ 71% Swallow Hotel, 1 Broadway, BEXLEYHEATH
☎ 0181 298 1000 142 ⇄ ☞

Dartford Upper Heath Ln, Dartford Heath DA1 2TN
☎ 01322 226455
Heathland course.
18 holes, 5914yds, Par 69, SSS 69, Course record 65.
Club membership 700.
Visitors   may not play at weekends. Must have a handicap certificate.
Societies   Mon & Fri only by prior arrangement with Secretary.
Green Fees £28 per day; £20 per round.
Facilities ⊗ ⅲ by prior arrangement ㅑ ♥ ♀ ㅅ 🏠 ☏ Gary Cooke.
Leisure   trolley for hire, putting green, practice area.
Hotel   B Forte Posthouse Bexley, Black Prince Interchange, Southwold Rd, BEXLEY
☎ 01322 526900 103 ⇄ ☞

DEAL
Map 05 TR35

Royal Cinque Ports Golf Rd CT14 6RF
☎ 01304 374007
Famous championship seaside links, windy but with easy walking. Outward nine is generally considered the easier, inward nine is longer and includes the renowned 16th, perhaps the most difficult hole. On a fine day there are wonderful views across the Channel.
18 holes, 6785yds, Par 72, SSS 72.
Club membership 850.
Visitors   restricted Wed mornings, weekends & bank holidays. Must contact in advance and have a handicap certificate.
Societies   must contact in advance.
Green Fees not confirmed.
Facilities ♀ ㅅ 🏠 ☞ ☏ Andrew Reynolds.
Leisure   putting,motor cart/buggy/trolley hire.
Location   Along seafront at N end of Deal
Hotel   B Forte Posthouse Dover, Singledge Ln, Whitfield, DOVER
☎ 01304 821222 67 ⇄ ☞

EDENBRIDGE
Map 05 TQ44

Edenbridge Golf & Country Club Crouch House Rd
TN8 5LQ ☎ 01732 865097 & 867381
Gently undulating course with a driving range.
Old Course: 18 holes, 6646yds, Par 73.
Skeynes Course: 18 holes, 5698yds, Par 67.
Club membership 1300.
Visitors   must contact in advance for Old Course.
Societies   contact in advance.
Green Fees Old Course: £15 (£20 weekends). Skeynes Course: £10 (£14 weekends, £12 after noon).
Facilities ⊗ ⅲ ㅑ ♥ ♀ ㅅ 🏠 ☞ ☏ Keith Burkin.
Leisure   hard tennis courts, gymnasium, motorised carts for hire, buggies for hire, trolley for hire, driving range, putting green, practice area, pitch & putt.
Location   1m W of town centre, signposted 'Golf Course'
Hotel   ★★★(red)♨ Gravetye Manor Hotel, EAST GRINSTEAD ☎ 01342 810567 18 ⇄ ☞

EYNSFORD
Map 05 TQ56

Austin Lodge Eynsford Station DA4 0HU
☎ 01322 868944
A well drained course designed to lie naturally in three secluded valleys in rolling countryside. Over 7000 yds from the medal tees. Practice ground, nets and a putting green add to the features.
18 holes, 6600yds, Par 73, SSS 71.
Club membership 600.
Visitors   must contact in advance, may not play until after 1pm on weekends and bank holidays.
Societies   telephone for bookings.
Green Fees not confirmed.
Facilities ♀ ㅅ 🏠 ☏ Nigel Willis.
Leisure   putting,cart/buggy/trolley hire.
Location   6m S of Dartford
Hotel   ★★★★ 61% Brands Hatch Thistle, BRANDS HATCH ☎ 01474 854900 137 ⇄ ☞

FAVERSHAM
Map 05 TR06

Faversham Belmont Park ME13 0HB
☎ 01795 890561
A beautiful inland course laid out over part of a large estate with pheasants walking the fairways quite tamely. Play follows two heavily wooded valleys but the trees affect only the loose shots going out of bounds. Fine views.
18 holes, 6030yds, Par 70, SSS 69.
Club membership 800.
Visitors   must have handicap certificate. With member only at weekends. Contacting the club in advance is advisable.
Societies   must contact in advance.
Green Fees not confirmed.
Facilities ♀ ㅅ 🏠 ☏ Stuart Rokes.
Location   3.5m S
Hotel   ★★★★♨ 75% Eastwell Manor, Eastwell Park, Boughton Lees, ASHFORD
☎ 01233 219955 23 ⇄ ☞

FOLKESTONE   Map 05 TR23

Etchinghill Canterbury Rd, Etchinghill CT18 8FA
☎ 01303 863863
A varied course incorporating parkland on the outward 9 holes and an interesting downland landscape with many challenging holes on the back 9.
18 holes, 6174yds, Par 70, SSS 69, Course record 67.
Club membership 600.
Visitors advisable to reserve tee time in advance.
Societies telephone or write, packages available.
Green Fees £15 (£20 weekends & bank holidays).
Facilities ⊗ ⅢIL ⬛ ♀ ⤴ 🖻 ⚑ ⌟ Trevor Dungate.
Leisure buggies for hire, trolley for hire, floodlit driving range, putting green, practice area, par 3 course.
Location N of M20, access from junct 11 or 12
Hotel ★★ 67% Wards Restaurant & Hotel, 39 Earls Ave, FOLKESTONE ☎ 01303 245166 10 ⇄ 🐾

GILLINGHAM   Map 05 TQ76

Gillingham Woodlands Rd ME7 2AP
☎ 01634 853017
Parkland course.
18 holes, 5347yds, Par 67, SSS 65.
Club membership 800.
Visitors contact in advance, weekends only with member.
Societies must apply in writing.
Green Fees £25 per day; £18 per round (£15/£10 weekends).
Facilities ⊗ ⅢIL ⬛ ♀ ⤴ 🖻 ⚑ ⌟ Brian Impett.
Leisure trolley for hire, driving range, putting green, practice area.
Location 1.5m SE on A2
Hotel B Forte Posthouse Rochester, Maidstone Rd, ROCHESTER ☎ 01634 687111 105 ⇄ 🐾

GRAVESEND   Map 05 TQ67

Mid Kent Singlewell Rd DA11 7RB ☎ 01474 568035
A well-maintained downland course with some easy walking and some excellent greens. The first hole is short, but nonetheless a real challenge. The slightest hook and the ball is out of bounds on the right.
18 holes, 6199yds, Par 69, SSS 69, Course record 60.
Club membership 900.
Visitors must contact in advance & have handicap certificate. May not play weekends.
Societies Tue only, apply in writing.
Green Fees £30 per day; £20 per round.
Facilities ⊗ ⅢIL ⬛ ♀ ⤴ 🖻 ⚑ ⌟ Mark Foreman.
Leisure trolley for hire, putting green, practice area.
Location S side of town centre off A227
Hotel ★★★ 61% Overcliffe Hotel, 15-16 The Overcliffe, GRAVESEND ☎ 01474 322131

HAWKHURST   Map 05 TQ73

Hawkhurst High St TN18 4JS ☎ 01580 752396
Undulating parkland course.
9 holes, 5751yds, Par 70, SSS 68, Course record 69.
Club membership 508.

Visitors may play weekdays and after 4pm weekends except with member.
Societies must apply in advance.
Green Fees £12 per round; £9 per 9 holes (£12 per round weekends after 4pm).
Facilities ⊗ ⅢI by prior arrangement IL ⬛ ♀ ⤴ 🖻 ⚑ ⌟ Tony Collins.
Leisure squash, buggies for hire, trolley for hire, driving range, putting green, practice area.
Location W side of village off A268
Hotel ★★★ 68% Tudor Court Hotel, Rye Rd, HAWKHURST ☎ 01580 752312 18 ⇄ 🐾

HERNE BAY   Map 05 TR16

Herne Bay Eddington CT6 7PG ☎ 01227 373964
Parkland course with bracing air.
18 holes, 4966yds, Par 65, SSS 64.
Club membership 500.
Visitors may not play mornings at weekends. Temporary course pending road works.
Societies apply in advance.
Green Fees £18 (£25 weekends and bank holidays).
Facilities ⊗ ⅢI by prior arrangement IL ⬛ ♀ ⤴ 🖻 ⚑ ⌟ D Lambert.
Leisure trolley for hire, practice area.
Location 1m S on A291
Hotel ★★★ 66% Falstaff Hotel, St Dunstans St, Westgate, CANTERBURY ☎ 01227 462138 24 ⇄ 🐾

HEVER   Map 05 TQ44

Hever TN8 7NG ☎ 01732 700771
The newly established Hever course has recently been voted one of the top ten developments in the British Isles. The 18-hole parkland course is set in 210 acres with water hazards and outstanding holes like the Par 3 12th which is similar to the 12th at Augusta.
18 holes, 7002yds, Par 72, SSS 75, Course record 69.
Club membership 620.
Visitors must book tee times Mon-Fri.
Societies telephone for details.
Green Fees not confirmed.
Facilities ♀ ⤴ 🖻 ⚑ ⌟ John Powell.
Hotel ★★★ 76% Spa Hotel, Mount Ephraim, TUNBRIDGE WELLS ☎ 01892 520331 76 ⇄ 🐾

HILDENBOROUGH   Map 05 TQ54

Nizels Nizels Ln TN11 8NX ☎ 01732 833138
Woodland course with many mature trees, wildlife and lakes that come into play on several holes. The 2nd hole is a 553yd Par 5, the green being guarded by bunkers hidden by a range of hillocks. The Par 4 7th has water on both sides of the fairway and a pitch over water to the green. The 10th is 539yd Par 5 with a sharp dogleg to the right, followed by a very narrow entry between trees for the 2nd shot.
18 holes, 6408yds, Par 72, SSS 71, Course record 68.
Club membership 650.
Visitors telephone professional shop for tee reservation 01732 838926.
Societies weekdays only, telephone initially.
Green Fees £35 all day, £25 per 18 holes (after 2pm).

Facilities ⊗ ⽊ 🝙 💼 ♀ 🝙 🝙 ʅ ➹ ʅ Richard Tinworth.
Leisure motorised carts for hire, buggies for hire, trolley for hire, putting green, practice area.
Location Off B245
Hotel ★★★ 58% Rose & Crown Hotel, 125 High St, TONBRIDGE
☎ 01732 357966 48 ⇆ ☔

HOO
Map 05 TQ77

Deangate Ridge ME3 8RZ ☎ 01634 251180
Parkland, municipal course designed by Fred Hawtree. 18-hole pitch and putt.
18 holes, 6300yds, Par 71, SSS 70.
Club membership 700.
Visitors no restrictions.
Societies must apply in writing.
Green Fees not confirmed.
Facilities ♀ 🝙 🝙 ➹ ʅ Richard Fox.
Leisure hard tennis courts, buggy/trolley hire, practice area.
Location 4m NE of Rochester off A228
Hotel B Forte Posthouse Rochester, Maidstone Rd, ROCHESTER ☎ 01634 687111 105 ⇆ ☔

HYTHE
Map 05 TR13

Hythe Imperial Princes Pde CT21 6AE
☎ 01303 267441
A 9-hole links course played off alternative tees on the second nine. Flat but interesting and testing. Hotel provides many leisure and sports facilities.
9 holes, 5560yds, Par 68, SSS 66, Course record 61.
Club membership 300.
Visitors course closed some Sun until 11am.
Societies must apply in writing.
Green Fees not confirmed.
Facilities ♀ 🝙 🝙 ➹ ʅ Gordon Ritchie.
Leisure hard and grass tennis courts, heated indoor swimming pool, squash, sauna, solarium, gymnasium, boule, bowling, croquet, health & beauty spa.
Location SE side of town
Hotel ★★★★ 73% The Hythe Imperial Hotel, Princes Pde, HYTHE ☎ 01303 267441 100 ⇆ ☔
Additional ★★★ 69% Stade Court Hotel, West Pde,
hotel HYTHE ☎ 01303 268263 42 ⇆ ☔

Sene Valley Sene CT18 8BL
☎ 01303 268513 (Manager) & 268514 (Pro)
A two-level downland course which provides interesting golf over an undulating landscape with sea views.
18 holes, 6196yds, Par 71, SSS 69, Course record 61.
Club membership 650.
Visitors must contact professional in advance.
Societies telephone in advance.
Green Fees £30 per day; £20 per round (£32/£25 weekends).
Facilities ⊗ ⽊ 🝙 💼 ♀ 🝙 ʅ Paul Moger.
Leisure trolley for hire, driving range, putting green, practice hire.
Location 1m NE off B2065
Hotel ★★★★ 73% The Hythe Imperial Hotel, Princes Pde, HYTHE
☎ 01303 267441 100 ⇆ ☔

KINGSDOWN
Map 05 TR34

Walmer & Kingsdown The Leas CT14 8EP
☎ 01304 373256
This course near Deal has through the years been overshadowed by its neighbours at Deal and Sandwich, yet it is a testing circuit with many undulations. The course is famous as being the one on which, in 1964, Assistant Professional, Roger Game became the first golfer in Britain to hole out in one at two successive holes; the 7th and 8th. The course is situated on top of the cliffs, with fine views.
18 holes, 6437yds, Par 72, SSS 71, Course record 66.
Club membership 600.
Visitors must contact in advance. Not before 9.30am weekdays and noon weekends & bank holidays.
Societies apply in writing.
Green Fees £28 per day; £22 per round (£30/£24 weekends & bank holidays).
Facilities ⊗ ⽊ 🝙 💼 ♀ 🝙 ʅ Matthew Paget.
Leisure trolley for hire, putting green, practice area.
Location 0.5m S off B2057
Hotel B Forte Posthouse Dover, Singledge Ln, Whitfield, DOVER
☎ 01304 821222 67 ⇆ ☔

LAMBERHURST
Map 05 TQ63

Lamberhurst Church Rd TN3 8DT ☎ 01892 890591
Parkland course crossing river twice. Fine views.
18 holes, 6345yds, Par 72, SSS 70, Course record 65.
Club membership 700.
Visitors may only play after noon weekends unless with member, handicap certificate required.
Societies Tue, Wed & Thu only from Apr-Oct, by arrangement.
Green Fees £30 per day; £20 per round (£36 weekends after noon, £20 Oct-Mar).
Facilities ⊗ ⽊ by prior arrangement 🝙 💼 ♀ 🝙 ʅ Mike Travers.
Leisure motorised carts for hire, buggies for hire, trolley for hire, putting green, practice area.
Location N side of village on B2162
Hotel ★★★ 67% Jarvis Pembury Hotel, 8 Tonbridge Rd, Pembury, TUNBRIDGE WELLS (ROYAL) ☎ 01892 823567 80 ⇆ ☔

LITTLESTONE
Map 05 TR02

Littlestone St Andrew's Rd TN28 8RB
☎ 01797 363355
Located in the Romney Marshes, this flattish seaside links course calls for every variety of shot. The 8th, 15th, 16th and 17th are regarded as classics by international golfers. Allowance for wind must always be made. Extensive practice area.
18 holes, 6460yds, Par 71, SSS 72, Course record 67.
Club membership 550.
Visitors must contact in advance, no visitors before 3pm weekends and bank holidays.
Societies must apply in advance.
Green Fees £36 per day; £26 per round (£45/£40 weekends). ▶

Facilities	⊗ ⌸ ⌸ ⌸ ♀ ⚲ 🛍 ⌿ Stephen Watkins.
Leisure	trolley for hire, putting green, practice area.
Location	N side of village
Hotel	★★★★ 73% The Hythe Imperial Hotel, Princes Pde, HYTHE ☎ 01303 267441 100 ⇄ 🏴

Romney Warren St Andrews Rd TN28 8RB
☎ 01797 362231
A traditional links course, newly developed alongside the 9-hole course at Littlestone.
18 holes, 5126yds, Par 67, SSS 65.
Club membership 340.
Visitors contact professional in advance.
Societies contact in advance.
Green Fees £18 per day; £10 per round (£25/£15 weekends & bank holidays).
Facilities ⊗ ⌸ ⌸ ⌸ ♀ ⚲ 🛍 ⌿ ⌿ Stephen Watkins.
Leisure trolley for hire, putting green, practice area.
Location N side of Littlestone
Hotel ★★★★ 73% The Hythe Imperial Hotel, Princes Pde, HYTHE ☎ 01303 267441 100 ⇄ 🏴

MAIDSTONE   Map 05 TQ75

Cobtree Manor Park Chatham Rd, Sandling ME14 3AZ
☎ 01622 681560
An undulating parkland course with some water hazards.
18 holes, 5716yds, Par 69, SSS 68, Course record 67.
Club membership 550.
Visitors no restrictions.
Societies Mon-Fri only, by arrangement.
Green Fees not confirmed.
Facilities ♀ ⚲ 🛍 ⌿ Martin Drew.
Location On A229 0.25m N of M20 junc 6
Hotel ★★ 61% Boxley House Hotel, The Street, Boxley, MAIDSTONE ☎ 01622 692269 11 ⇄ 🏴Annexe7 ⇄ 🏴

Leeds Castle Ashford Rd ME17 1PL ☎ 01622 880467
Situated around Leeds Castle, this is one of the most picturesque courses in Britain. Re-designed in the 1980s by Neil Coles, it is a challenging 9-hole course with the added hazard of the Castle moat. 18-holes may be played on weekdays.
9 holes, 2880yds, Par 34, SSS 34, Course record 32.
Visitors booking must be made. Bookings taken from 6 days in advance.
Societies apply in advance.
Green Fees £15 per 18 holes; £9 per 9 holes (£10 per 9 holes weekends).
Facilities ⊗ ⌸ ⌸ ⌸ ♀ ⚲ 🛍 ⌿
Leisure trolley for hire, putting green, practice area.
Location On A20, 4m E of Maidstone
Hotel ★★★★ 61% Tudor Park Hotel, Country Club Resort, Ashford Rd, Bearstead, MAIDSTONE ☎ 01622 734334 117 ⇄ 🏴

Tudor Park Country Club Ashford Rd, Bearsted ME14 4NQ ☎ 01622 734334
The course is set in a 220 acre former deerpark with the pleasant undulating Kent countyside as a backdrop. The natural features of the land have been incorporated into this picturesque course to form a challenge for those of both high and intermediate standard. The Par 5 14th is particularly

interesting. It can alter your score dramatically should you gamble with a drive to a narrow fairway. This hole has to be carefully thoughtout from tee to green depending on the wind direction.
18 holes, 6041yds, Par 70, SSS 69, Course record 63.
Club membership 750.
Visitors may not play Sat & Sun before noon. Contact pro shop 01622 739412 for bookings.
Societies please call the Golf Manager.
Green Fees £18 per round (£24 weekends & bank holidays).
Facilities ⊗ ⌸ ⌸ ⌸ ♀ ⚲ 🛍 ⌿ ⌿ John Slinger.
Leisure hard tennis courts, heated indoor swimming pool, sauna, solarium, gymnasium, motorised carts for hire, buggies for hire, trolley for hire, driving range, putting green, practice area.
Location On A20, 1.25m W of M20 junct 8
Hotel ★★★★ 61% Tudor Park Hotel, Country Club Resort, Ashford Rd, Bearstead, MAIDSTONE ☎ 01622 734334 117 ⇄ 🏴

RAMSGATE   Map 05 TR36

St Augustine's Cottington Rd, Cliffsend CT12 5JN
☎ 01843 590333
A comfortably flat course in this famous bracing Championship area of Kent. Neither as long nor as difficult as its lordly neighbours, St Augustine's will nonetheless extend most golfers. Dykes run across the course.
18 holes, 5197yds, Par 69, SSS 65, Course record 61.
Club membership 670.
Visitors must contact in advance.
Societies must contact in advance.
Green Fees £20.50 per day/round (£22.50 weekends and bank holidays). Afternoons £12.50 (£15 weekends).
Facilities ⊗ ⌸ ⌸ ⌸ ♀ ⚲ 🛍 ⌿ Derek Scott.
Leisure buggies for hire, trolley for hire, putting green, practice area.
Hotel ★★ 66% Jarvis Marina Hotel, Harbour Pde, RAMSGATE ☎ 01843 588276 59 ⇄ 🏴

ROCHESTER   Map 05 TQ76

Rochester & Cobham Park Park Pale ME2 3UL
☎ 01474 823411
A first-rate course of challenging dimensions in undulating parkland. All holes differ and each requires accurate drive placing to derive the best advantage. The clubhouse and course are situated a quarter of a mile from the western end of the M2. The club was formed in 1891.
18 holes, 6440yds, Par 72, SSS 71, Course record 66.
Club membership 720.
Visitors must contact in advance & have handicap certificate. No visitors weekends.
Societies apply in advance.
Green Fees £36 per day; £26 per round.
Facilities ⊗ ⌸ ⌸ ⌸ ♀ ⚲ 🛍 ⌿ Joe Blair.
Leisure trolley for hire, putting green, practice area.
Location 2.5m W on A2
Hotel ★★★★ 75% Bridgewood Manor Hotel, Bridgewood Roundabout, Maidstone Rd, ROCHESTER ☎ 01634 201333 100 ⇄ 🏴

ROYAL ST. GEORGE'S

SANDWICH *Kent* ☎ 01304 613090   Map 05 TR35

John Ingham writes: Sandwich is one of the most beautiful and unspoiled towns in southern England. Driving to this part of Kent is much like stepping back into history. The big golf course here, Royal St George's, is where Sandy Lyle won the Open Championship in 1985 by one shot from that colourful American, Payne Stewart.

Like the region, the clubhouse is old-fashioned and the seats near the window in the bar seem to have been there forever. The bar staff may know as much about fishing or lifeboats as they know about beer, and make a visit there a delight, providing you are not looking for modern sophistication.

The course itself is the truest links you will find in all England and the Royal & Ancient, in its wisdom, choose Royal St George's for major championships knowing it will find the pedigree player at the end of a week. Close to the sea, overlooking Pegwell Bay, any kind of wind can make this man-size test even tougher. The sweeping rough at the 1st can be daunting, so can the bunkers and the huge sandhills. But there are classic shots here.

Off-sea breezes can turn to incredible gales, and it is possible to find the course virtually unplayable. A smooth swing can be blown inside out and stories of three good woods to reach certain greens, into wind, are commonplace. Often the problem in high winds is simply to stand up and address the ball. Putting, too, can be almost impossible, with the ball blown off the surface and maybe into the sand. Christy O'Connor Jnr put together a 64 here, and no wonder it's the record!

Visitors	must contact in advance and have a handicap certificate. May not play at weekends or BHs
Societies	must apply in writing
Green fees	Midweek only £55 (18 holes); day £75
Facilities	⊗ ┗ �P ♀ ♨ ➡ ✈ ☏ (Andrew Brooks) motor carts, tolleys, caddy cars, putting green, practice area
Location	Sandwich CT13 9PB 1.5m E of town

18 holes, 6565yds, Par 70, SSS 72. Course record 64 (N. Faldo/P Stewart/Christy O'Connor)

WHERE TO STAY AND EAT NEARBY

HOTELS:

CANTERBURY
★★★ 66% Falstaff, St Dunstans St. ☎ 01227 462138. 24 (2 ╒ 22 ➡ ╒)
★★★ 64% Chaucer, Ivy Lane ☎ 01227 464427. 42 (1 ╒ 41 ➡ ╒)

DOVER
Forte Posthouse Dover, Singledge Ln, Whitfield (3m NW jct A2/A256) ☎ 01304 821222. 67 ➡ ╒

RAMSGATE
★★ 66% Jarvis Marina Hotel, Harbour Pde. ☎ 01843 588276. 59 ➡ ╒

RESTAURANTS:

CANTERBURY
❀ Ristorante Tuo e Mio, 16 The Borough. ☎ 01227 761471

ST MARGARET'S AT CLIFFE
❀❀❀ Wallets Court, West Cliffe ☎ 01304 852424

SANDWICH
Map 05 TR35

Prince's Prince's Dr, Sandwich Bay CT13 9QB
☎ 01304 611118
A 27 hole championship links of the highest calibre built
in three loops of nine holes from a modern clubhouse.
The course represents all that is best in traditional links
golf in the use of depression ridges and broken ground on
a predominantly flat surface with as little protection from
the wind as possible. The three 18 hole combinations all
demand the highest standard of distance judgement.
Dunes: 9 holes, 3343yds, Par 36, SSS 36.
Himalayas: 9 holes, 3163yds, Par 35, SSS 35.
Shore: 9 holes, 3347yds, Par 36, SSS 36.
Club membership 350.
Visitors must contact in advance.
Societies must contact in advance.
Green Fees £42 per day; £36 per round (£47/£39 Sat,
£52/£40 Sun).
Facilities ⊗ ⅏ ⅃ ▉ ♀ ⅄ 🏠 ⅂ ⅄ Chris Evans.
Leisure motorised carts for hire, buggies for hire,
trolley for hire, driving range, putting green,
practice area, snooker.
Location 2m E via toll road
Hotel ★★ 66% Jarvis Marina Hotel, Harbour Pde,
RAMSGATE ☎ 01843 588276 59 ⇔ ↕

ROYAL ST GEORGES See page 125

SEVENOAKS
Map 05 TQ55

Knole Park Seal Hollow Rd TN15 0HJ
☎ 01732 452150
The course is set in a majestic park with many fine trees
and deer running loose. It has a wiry turf seemingly
impervious to rain. Certainly a pleasure to play on.
Excellent views of Knole House and the North Downs.
Outstanding greens.
18 holes, 6259yds, Par 70, SSS 70, Course record 64.
Club membership 800.
Visitors may not play at weekends or bank holidays.
Must contact Secretary in advance.
Societies telephone initially.
Green Fees £42 per 36 holes; £32 per 18 holes.
Facilities ⊗ ▉ ▉ ♀ ⅄ 🏠 ⅂ P E Gill.
Leisure squash, trolley for hire, putting green,
practice area, snooker.
Location SE side of town centre off B2019
Hotel ★★★ 65% Royal Oak Hotel, Upper High
St, SEVENOAKS
☎ 01732 451109 21 ⇔ ↕Annexe16 ⇔ ↕

SHEERNESS
Map 05 TQ97

Sheerness Power Station Rd ME12 3AE
☎ 01795 662585
Marshland/meadowland course, few bunkers, but many
ditches and water hazards. Often windy.
18 holes, 6460yds, Par 72, SSS 71, Course record 66.
Club membership 750.
Visitors with member only at weekends.
Societies Tue-Thu only, telephone in advance.
Green Fees £20 per day; £15 per round.

Facilities ⊗ ⅏ by prior arrangement ▉ ▉ ♀ ⅄ 🏠
⅂ W Evans.
Leisure trolley for hire, putting green, practice area.
Location 1.5m E off A249
Hotel ★★★★ 75% Bridgewood Manor Hotel,
Bridgewood Roundabout, Maidstone Rd,
ROCHESTER
☎ 01634 201333 100 ⇔ ↕

SHOREHAM
Map 05 TQ56

Darenth Valley Station Rd TN14 7SA
☎ 01959 522944
Easy walking parkland course in beautiful valley. Testing
12th hole, par 4.
18 holes, 6327yds, Par 72, SSS 71, Course record 64.
Visitors must contact in advance.
Societies contact in advance.
Green Fees £12 per round (£17 weekends).
Facilities ⊗ ⅏ ▉ ▉ ♀ ⅄ 🏠 ⅂ ⅄ Scott Fotheringham.
Leisure fishing, trolley for hire, putting green, practice
area.
Location 1m E on A225
Hotel ★★★ 65% Royal Oak Hotel, Upper High St,
SEVENOAKS
☎ 01732 451109 21 ⇔ ↕Annexe16 ⇔ ↕

SITTINGBOURNE
Map 05 TQ96

The Oast Golf Centre Church Rd, Tonge ME9 9AR
☎ 01795 473527
A Par 3 Approach course of 9 holes with 18 tees augmented
by a 17-bay floodlit driving range and a putting green.
9 holes, 1664yds, Par 54, SSS 54.
Visitors no restrictions.
Societies telephone in advance.
Green Fees £5.50 per 18 holes; £4 per 9 holes.
Facilities ⊗ ⅏ ▉ ▉ ♀ ⅄
Leisure driving range, putting green, practice area,
bowls.
Location 2m NE
Hotel ★★★★ 75% Bridgewood Manor Hotel,
Bridgewood Roundabout, Maidstone Rd,
ROCHESTER
☎ 01634 201333 100 ⇔ ↕

Sittingbourne & Milton Regis Wormdale, Newington
ME9 7PX ☎ 01795 842261
A downland course with pleasant vistas. There are a few
uphill climbs, but the course is far from difficult. The 166-
yard, 2nd hole is a testing par 3.
18 holes, 6279yds, Par 71, SSS 70, Course record 64.
Club membership 670.
Visitors must contact in advance & may not play at
weekends.
Societies Tue & Thu, apply in advance.
Green Fees £32 per 36 holes; £20 per 18 holes.
Facilities ⊗ ⅏ ▉ ▉ ♀ ⅄ 🏠 ⅂ John Hearn.
Leisure motorised carts for hire, buggies for hire, trolley
for hire, putting green, practice area.
Location Turn off A249 at Dalaway
Hotel ★★★★ 75% Bridgewood Manor Hotel,
Bridgewood Roundabout, Maidstone Rd,
ROCHESTER
☎ 01634 201333 100 ⇔ ↕

SNODLAND
Map 05 TQ76

Oastpark Malling Rd ME6 5LG
☎ 01634 242661
A challenging parkland course for golfers of all abilities. The course has water hazards, orchards and views across the Valley of Dean.
18 holes, 6173yds, Par 69, SSS 69, Course record 71.
Club membership 620.
Visitors may book 3 days in advance.
Societies early booking with deposits required.
Green Fees £8.50 per 18 holes; £6 per 9 holes (£12/£7 weekends).
Facilities ⊗ ℡ ዄ ♥ ♀ ♈ 🏠 ℓ John Gregory.
Leisure trolley for hire, buggy for handicapped golfers.
Hotel ★★★ 64% Larkfield Priory Hotel, London Rd, LARKFIELD
☎ 01732 846858 52rm(51 ⇔ ℟)

TENTERDEN
Map 05 TQ83

Tenterden Woodchurch Rd TN30 7DR
☎ 01580 763987
Attractive parkland course, last 3 holes are hilly.
18 holes, 6050yds, Par 70, SSS 69, Course record 65.
Club membership 600.
Visitors contact professional shop. May only play with member weekends and bank holidays.
Societies must apply in writing.
Green Fees £20 per day.
Facilities ⊗ ℡ ዄ ♥ ♀ ♈ 🏠 ℓ Andrew Scullion.
Leisure motorised carts for hire, buggies for hire, trolley for hire, driving range, putting green, practice area.
Location 0.75m E on B2067
Hotel ★★ 67% Jarvis White Lion Hotel, High St, TENTERDEN
☎ 01580 765077 15 ⇔ ℟

TONBRIDGE
Map 05 TQ54

Poultwood Higham Ln TN11 9QR
☎ 01732 364039
With the opening of a 9-hole course in the summer of 1994 there are now two public 'pay and play' parkland courses in an idyllic woodland setting. The courses are ecologically designed, offering varied walking, water hazards, natural and interesting playing opportunities for all standards of golfer.
18 holes, 5569yds, Par 68, SSS 67 or 9 holes, 1281yds, Par 28.
Visitors non registered golfers may book up to 2 days in advance for 18 hole course, or take available tee times, pay and play system on 9 hole.
Societies apply in advance to the clubhouse manager.
Green Fees £10.50 (£15.50 weekends). 9 hole course £6.90 per 18 holes; £4.60 per 9 holes (£8.60/£5.70 weekends).
Facilities ⊗ ℡ ዄ ♥ ♀ ♈ 🏠 ✝ ℓ Chris Miller.
Leisure squash, trolley for hire, putting green, practice area.
Location Off A227, 3m N of Tonbridge
Hotel ★★★ 58% Rose & Crown Hotel, 125 High St, TONBRIDGE
☎ 01732 357966 48 ⇔ ℟

TUNBRIDGE WELLS (ROYAL)
Map 05 TQ53

Nevill Benhall Mill Rd TN2 5JW
☎ 01892 525818
Just within Sussex, the county boundary with Kent runs along the northern perimeter of the course. Open undulating ground, well-wooded with much heather and gorse for the first half. The second nine holes slope away from the clubhouse to a valley where a narrow stream hazards two holes.
18 holes, 6349yds, Par 71, SSS 70, Course record 63.
Club membership 900.
Visitors must contact 48 hours in advance, handicap certificate required, permission from secretary for weekends play.
Societies must apply in writing one month in advance.
Green Fees £33 per day; £25 per round (£46 per day/round weekends and bank holidays).
Facilities ⊗ ℡ ዄ ♥ ♀ ♈ 🏠 ✝ ℓ Paul Huggett.
Leisure buggies for hire, trolley for hire, putting green, practice area.
Location S of Tunbridge Wells, off forest road
Hotel ★★★ 76% Spa Hotel, Mount Ephraim, TUNBRIDGE WELLS
☎ 01892 520331 76 ⇔ ℟

Tunbridge Wells Langton Rd TN4 8XH ☎ 01892 523034
Somewhat hilly, well-bunkered parkland course with lake; trees form natural hazards.
9 holes, 4560yds, Par 65, SSS 62, Course record 59.
Club membership 450.
Visitors must contact in advance, limited availability weekends.
Societies weekdays, apply in advance.
Green Fees £15 per 18 holes; £10 per 9 holes (£25 per 19 holes weekend).
Facilities ⊗ ዄ ♥ ♀ ♈ 🏠 ✝ ℓ Keith Smithson.
Leisure trolley for hire, putting green.
Location 1m W on A264
Hotel ★★★ 76% Spa Hotel, Mount Ephraim, TUNBRIDGE WELLS
☎ 01892 520331 76 ⇔ ℟

WESTGATE ON SEA
Map 05 TR37

Westgate and Birchington 176 Canterbury Rd CT8 8LT
☎ 01843 831115
Seaside course.
18 holes, 4926yds, Par 64, SSS 64.
Club membership 310.
Visitors must contact in advance & have handicap certificate, restricted at weekends.
Societies must contact three months in advance.
Green Fees not confirmed.
Facilities ♀ ♈ 🏠 ℓ Roger Game.
Location E side of town centre off A28
Hotel ★★ 60% Ivyside Hotel, 25 Sea Rd, WESTGATE ON SEA
☎ 01843 831082 75rm(73 ⇔ ℟)

> Entries with a shaded background identify courses that are considered to be particularly interesting

WEST KINGSDOWN Map 05 TQ56

Woodlands Manor Woodlands TN15 6AB
☎ 01959 523806
Interesting, undulating parkland course with testing 1st, 9th and 15th holes.
18 holes, 6100yds, Par 69, SSS 68.
Club membership 650.
Visitors with member only weekend afternoons.
Societies apply in writing.
Green Fees not confirmed.
Facilities ⚐🏌️ Andrew Brooks.
Leisure hard tennis courts, driving range, putting green, trolley hire.
Location 2m S off A20
Hotel ★★★★ 61% Brands Hatch Thistle, BRANDS HATCH
☎ 01474 854900 137 ➤

WHITSTABLE Map 05 TR16

Chestfield (Whitstable) 103 Chestfield Rd CT5 3LU
☎ 01227 794411
Gently undulating parkland course with sea views. The Par 3 3rd is generally played into the wind and the Par 4th has a difficult lefthand dogleg.
18 holes.
Club membership 650.
Visitors with member weekends. Due to road works passing through the course the details on yardage cannot be given as the course is also undergoing changes to its structure.
Societies must apply in writing.
Green Fees £28 per day; £18 per round.
Facilities ⊗ 🍴 ⚐ Ⓣ John Brotherton.
Leisure motorised carts for hire, buggies for hire, trolley for hire, putting green, practice area.
Location 2m SE off A299
Hotel ★★★ 64% Chaucer Hotel, Ivy Ln, CANTERBURY
☎ 01227 464427 42 ➤

Whitstable & Seasalter Collingwood Rd CT5 1EB
☎ 01227 272020
Links course.
9 holes, 5314yds, Par 66, SSS 63, Course record 62.
Club membership 300.
Visitors must contact in advance. Must play with member at weekends.
Green Fees £12 per round.
Facilities 🍴 ⚐
Leisure putting green.
Location W side of town centre off B2205
Hotel ★★★ 64% Chaucer Hotel, Ivy Ln, CANTERBURY
☎ 01227 464427 42 ➤

A golf course name printed in **bold italics** means we have been unable to verify information with the club's management for the current year

LANCASHIRE

ACCRINGTON Map 07 SD72

Accrington & District Devon Av, Oswaldtwistle BB5 4LS
☎ 01254 381614 & 232734
Moorland course with pleasant views of the Pennines and surrounding areas.
18 holes, 6044yds, Par 70, SSS 69, Course record 64.
Club membership 600.
Visitors must contact in advance.
Societies contact in advance.
Green Fees £15 Mon-Thu (£20 Fri-Sun & bank holidays).
Facilities ⊗ 🍴 ⚐ 🏌️ Bill Harling.
Leisure motorised carts for hire, buggies for hire, trolley for hire, driving range, putting green, practise area.
Location Mid way between Accrington & Blackburn
Hotel ★★★ 66% Dunkenhalgh Hotel, Blackburn Rd, Clayton le Moors, ACCRINGTON
☎ 01254 398021 37 ➤ Annexe42 ➤

Baxenden & District Top o' th' Meadow, Baxenden BB5 2EA ☎ 01254 234555
Moorland course.
9 holes, 5740yds, SSS 68.
Visitors may not play Sat, Sun and bank holidays except with member.
Societies must contact in advance.
Green Fees not confirmed.
Facilities ⚐
Location 1.5m SE off A680
Hotel ★★★ 66% Dunkenhalgh Hotel, Blackburn Rd, Clayton le Moors, ACCRINGTON
☎ 01254 398021 37 ➤ Annexe42 ➤

Green Haworth Green Haworth BB5 3SL
☎ 01254 237580
Moorland course dominated by quarries and difficult in windy conditions.
9 holes, 5556yds, Par 68, SSS 67, Course record 65.
Club membership 360.
Visitors may not play Sun, Mar-Oct.
Societies apply in writing. Weekdays only before 5pm. Or contact secretary on above telephone number.
Green Fees not confirmed.
Facilities ⚐
Leisure putting green, practice area.
Location 2m S off A680
Hotel ★★★ 59% Blackburn Moat House, Preston New Rd, BLACKBURN
☎ 01254 899988 98 ➤

BACUP Map 07 SD82

Bacup Maden Rd OL13 8HY ☎ 01706 873170
Moorland course, predominantly flat except climbs to 1st and 10th holes.
9 holes, 6008yds, Par 70, SSS 69.
Club membership 350.
Visitors no restrictions.
Societies must contact in writing.
Green Fees not confirmed.

Facilities	⊗ ⋔ ╚ ▆ ♀ ⏝
Location	W side of town off A671
Hotel	★★ 65% Comfort Friendly Inn, Keirby Walk, BURNLEY ☎ 01282 427611 48 ⇆ ⎸

BARNOLDSWICK   Map 07 SD84

Ghyll Skipton Rd BB8 6JQ ☎ 01282 842466
Excellent, parkland course with outstanding views, especially from the 8th tee where you can see the Three Peaks. Testing 3rd hole is an uphill par 4.
9 holes, 5790yds, Par 68, SSS 66, Course record 62.
Club membership 345.

Visitors	may not play Tue, Fri after 4.30pm & Sun.
Societies	must contact in writing.
Green Fees	£14 per day (£18 weekends & bank holidays).
Facilities	⊗ by prior arrangement ⋔ by prior arrangement ╚ by prior arrangement ♀ evenings only ⏝
Leisure	putting green.
Location	1m NE on B6252
Hotel	★★★ 64% Stirk House Hotel, GISBURN ☎ 01200 445581 36 ⇆ ⎸Annexe12 ⇆ ⎸

BLACKBURN   Map 07 SD62

Blackburn Beardwood Brow BB2 7AX
☎ 01254 51122
Parkland course on a high plateau with stream and hills. Superb views of Lancashire coast and the Pennines.
18 holes, 6144yds, Par 71, SSS 70.
Club membership 550.

Visitors	must contact professional in advance.
Societies	must contact in advance.
Green Fees	£19.50 per day (£22.50 weekends).
Facilities	⊗ ⋔ ╚ ▆ ♀ ⏝ ⌂ ⏌ ⎸ Alan Rodwell.
Leisure	motorised carts for hire, buggies for hire, trolley for hire, putting green, practice area.
Location	1.25m NW of town centre off A677
Hotel	★★★ 59% Blackburn Moat House, Preston New Rd, BLACKBURN ☎ 01254 899988 98 ⇆ ⎸

BLACKPOOL   Map 07 SD33

Blackpool North Shore Devonshire Rd FY2 0RD
☎ 01253 352054
Undulating parkland course.
18 holes, 6400yds, Par 71, SSS 71.
Club membership 900.

Visitors	may not play Thu & Sat. Advisable to contact in advance.
Societies	must contact in advance.
Green Fees	not confirmed.
Facilities	⏝ ⌂ ⏌ ⎸ Brendan Ward.
Location	On A587 N of town centre
Hotel	★★ 70% Brabyns Hotel, Shaftesbury Av, North Shore, BLACKPOOL ☎ 01253 354263 22 ⇆ ⎸Annexe3 ⇆ ⎸

Herons Reach De Vere Hotel East Park Dr FY3 8LL
☎ 01253 766156 & 838866
The course was designed by Peter Alliss and Clive Clarke. There are 10 man-made lakes and several existing ponds. Built to a links design, well mounded but fairly easy walking. Water comes into play on 9 holes, better players can go for

the carry or shorter hitters can take the safe route. The course provides an excellent and interesting challenge for golfers of all standards.
18 holes, 6431yds, Par 72, SSS 71, Course record 67.
Club membership 500.

Visitors	can book up to 4 days in advance by tel 01253 766156, or if staying in hotel or a visiting society, there is no limit to how far in advance bookings can be made.
Societies	telephone or write to golf sales office 01253 838866 ext 573.
Green Fees	£20 per 18 holes (£30 weekends & bank holidays).
Facilities	♀ ⏝ ⌂ ⏌ ⎕ ⎸ Richard Hudson.
Leisure	hard tennis courts, heated indoor swimming pool, squash, sauna, solarium, gymnasium, driving range,buggies.
Location	Off A587 adjacent to Stanley Park & Zoo
Hotel	★★★★ 59% De Vere Hotel, East Park Dr, BLACKPOOL ☎ 01253 838866 166 ⇆ ⎸

Stanley Park Municipal North Park Dr FY3 8LS
☎ 01253 397916
The golf course, situated in Stanley Park is municipal. The golf club (Blackpool Park) is private but golfers may use the clubhouse facilities if playing the course.
18 holes, 6060yds, Par 70, SSS 69, Course record 64.
Club membership 600.

Visitors	must apply to Mrs A Hirst, Town Hall, Talbot Square, Blackpool.
Societies	must apply in writing to Mrs A Hirst, Blackpool Borough Council, Town Hall, Talbot Square, Blackpool.
Green Fees	£9 per 18 holes (£10.50 weekends & bank holidays).
Facilities	⊗ ⋔ ▆ ♀ ⏝ ⌂ ⏌ ⎸ Brian Purdie.
Leisure	trolley for hire, driving range, putting green, practice area.
Location	1m E of Blackpool Tower
Hotel	★★★ 58% Clifton Hotel, Talbot Square, BLACKPOOL ☎ 01253 21481 77 ⇆ ⎸

BURNLEY   Map 07 SD83

Burnley Glen View BB11 3RW
☎ 01282 421045 & 451281
Moorland course with hilly surrounds.
18 holes, 5899yds, Par 69, SSS 69, Course record 65.
Club membership 750.

Visitors	must contact in advance. May not play on Saturdays.
Societies	must apply in writing.
Green Fees	£20 per day (£25 weekends & bank holidays).
Facilities	⊗ ⋔ ╚ ▆ ♀ ⏝ ⌂ ⎸ William Tye.
Leisure	trolley for hire, putting green, practice area, snooker.
Location	1.5m S off A646
Hotel	★★ 65% Comfort Friendly Inn, Keirby Walk, BURNLEY ☎ 01282 427611 48 ⇆ ⎸

Towneley Towneley Park, Todmorden Rd BB11 3ED
☎ 01282 38473
Parkland course, with other sporting facilities.
18 holes, 5811yds, Par 70, SSS 68, Course record 67.
Club membership 290.

Visitors	must contact in advance. ▶

Societies must contact in advance in writing.
Green Fees £7.50 (£8.50 weekends & bank holidays).
Facilities ⊗ ⅷ ⅙ ⬛ ♀ ⚲ ☐ ⚑
Leisure trolley for hire, practice area.
Location 1m SE of town centre on A671
Hotel ★★★ 72% Oaks Hotel, Colne Rd, Reedley, BURNLEY ☎ 01282 414141 54 ⇆ ⚑

CHORLEY   Map 07 SD51

Chorley Hall o' th' Hill, Heath Charnock PR6 9HX
☎ 01257 480263
A splendid moorland course with plenty of fresh air. The well-sited clubhouse affords some good views of the Lancashire coast and of Angelzarke, a local beauty spot. Beware of the short 3rd hole with its menacing out-of-bounds.
18 holes, 6307yds, Par 71, SSS 70, Course record 63.
Club membership 550.
Visitors must contact in advance and may not play weekends or bank holidays.
Societies must contact in advance. Tue-Fri only.
Green Fees £25 day/round Mon-Fri.
Facilities ⊗ ⅷ ⅙ ⬛ ♀ ⚲ ☐ ⚑ Mark Tomlinson.
Leisure buggies for hire, trolley for hire, putting green, practice area.
Location 2.5m SE on A673
Hotel ★★★ 65% Pines Hotel, CLAYTON-LE-WOODS ☎ 01772 38551 39 ⇆ ⚑

Duxbury Jubilee Park Duxbury Hall Rd PR7 4AS
☎ 01257 265380 & 241634
Municipal parkland course.
18 holes, 6390yds, Par 71, SSS 70.
Club membership 250.
Visitors must contact in advance.
Societies must contact in advance.
Green Fees £6.40 per round (£8.50 weekends & bank holidays).
Facilities ⊗ ⅙ ⬛ ⚲ ☐ ⚑ S Middelman.
Leisure trolley for hire, putting green, practice area.
Location 2.5m S off A6
Hotel B Forte Travelodge, Mill Ln, CHARNOCK RICHARD ☎ 01257 791746 100 ⇆

Shaw Hill Hotel Golf & Country Club Preston Rd, Whittle-Le-Woods PR6 7PP ☎ 01257 269221
A fine course designed by one of Europe's most prominent golf architects and offering a considerable challenge as well as tranquillity and scenic charm. Seven lakes guard par 5 and long par 4 holes.
18 holes, 6405yds, Par 72, SSS 71, Course record 65.
Club membership 500.
Visitors denims and trainers not allowed on course or in clubhouse. Jacket and tie required in restaurant.
Societies must telephone in advance.
Green Fees not confirmed.
Facilities ♀ ⚲ ☐ ⚑ ⬗ ⚑ David Clark.
Leisure putting,cart/buggy/trolley hire.
Location On A6 1.5m N
Hotel ★★★ 68% Shaw Hill Hotel Golf & Country Club, Preston Rd, Whittle-le-Woods, CHORLEY ☎ 01257 269221 18 ⇆ ⚑Annexe4 ⇆ ⚑

CLITHEROE   Map 07 SD74

Clitheroe Whalley Rd, Pendleton BB7 1PP
☎ 01200 22292
One of the best inland courses in the country. Clitheroe is a parkland-type course with water hazards and good scenic views, particularly on towards Longridge, and Pendle Hill. The Club has been the venue for the Lancashire Amateur Championships.
18 holes, 6326yds, Par 71, SSS 71, Course record 67.
Club membership 725.
Visitors must contact in advance.
Societies must telephone in advance.
Green Fees £27 per day (£32 weekends & bank holidays).
Facilities ⊗ ⅷ ⅙ ⬛ ♀ ⚲ ☐ ⚑ ⚑ John Twissell.
Leisure trolley for hire, driving range, putting green, practice area.
Location 2m S on A671
Hotel ★★ 68% Shireburn Arms Hotel, HURST GREEN ☎ 01254 826518 16 ⇆ ⚑

COLNE   Map 07 SD84

Colne Law Farm, Skipton Old Rd BB8 7EB
☎ 01282 863391
Moorland course.
9 holes, 5961yds, Par 70, SSS 69, Course record 63.
Club membership 356.
Visitors restricted Thu. Must contact in advance.
Societies must contact in advance.

Green Fees £15 per round (£20 weekends).
Facilities ⊗ ⋔ 🏌 ▐ ♀ 🏌
Leisure putting green, practice area, snooker.
Location 1m E off A56
Hotel ★★★ 64% Stirk House Hotel, GISBURN
☎ 01200 445581 36 ⇔ 🏌Annexe12 ⇔ 🏌

DARWEN
Map 07 SD62

Darwen Winter Hill BB3 0LB ☎ 01254 701287
Moorland course.
18 holes, 5752yds, Par 68, SSS 68.
Club membership 600.
Visitors may not play on Sat.
Societies must telephone in advance.
Green Fees not confirmed.
Facilities ♀ 🏌 🏠 🏌 Wayne Lennon.
Leisure driving range,putting green,practice.
Location 1m NW
Hotel ★★★ 64% Whitehall Hotel, Springbank,
Whitehall, DARWEN
☎ 01254 701595 15 ⇔ 🏌

FLEETWOOD
Map 07 SD34

Fleetwood Princes Way FY7 8AF
☎ 01253 873661 & 773573
Championship length, flat seaside links where the player
must always be alert to changes of direction or strength
of the wind.
18 holes, 6723yds, Par 72, SSS 72.
Club membership 600.
Visitors may not play on competition days.
Societies must contact in advance. A deposit of £5 per
player is required.
Green Fees not confirmed.
Facilities ♀ 🏌 🏠 🏌 S McLaughlin.
Leisure putting green,trolley hire.
Location W side of town centre
Guesthouse QQQQQ The Victorian House, Trunnah Rd,
THORNTON-CLEVELEYS
☎ 01253 860619 3 ⇔ 🏌

GREAT HARWOOD
Map 07 SD73

Great Harwood Harwood Bar, Whallwy Rd BB6 7TE
☎ 01254 884391
Flat parkland course with fine views of the Pendle region.
9 holes, 6415yds, Par 73, SSS 71, Course record 68.
Club membership 320.
Visitors must contact in advance.
Societies welcome mid-week only, apply in writing.
Green Fees £16 per round (£22 weekends & bank holidays).
Facilities ⊗ ⋔ 🏌 ▐ ♀ 🏌
Leisure putting green, practice area.
Location E side of town centre on A680
Hotel ★★★ 66% Dunkenhalgh Hotel, Blackburn Rd,
Clayton le Moors, ACCRINGTON
☎ 01254 398021 37 ⇔ 🏌Annexe42 ⇔ 🏌

HASLINGDEN
Map 07 SD72

Rossendale Ewood Ln Head BB4 6LH ☎ 01706 831339
Testing, and usually windy meadowland course.

---

18 holes, 6293yds, Par 72, SSS 70, Course record 64.
Club membership 700.
Visitors must contact in advance. Must play with
member on Sat.
Societies must telephone in advance & confirm in writing.
Green Fees £22.50 per day (£27.50 weekends & bank
holidays).
Facilities ⊗ ⋔ 🏌 ▐ ♀ (ex Mon) 🏌 🏠
🏌 Stephen Nicholls.
Leisure trolley for hire, putting green, practice area.
Location 1.5m S off A56
Hotel ★★★ 63% Old Mill Hotel, Springwood,
RAMSBOTTOM ☎ 01706 822991 36 ⇔

HEYSHAM
Map 07 SD46

Heysham Trumacar Park, Middleton Rd LA3 3JH
☎ 01524 851011
Seaside parkland course, partly wooded. The 15th is a 459
yard Par 4 hole nearly always played into the prevailing south
west wind.
18 holes, 6258yds, Par 69, SSS 70, Course record 64.
Club membership 1100.
Visitors restricted at weekends.
Societies must contact in advance.
Green Fees £20 per day; £15 per round (£25 weekends).
Facilities ⊗ ⋔ 🏌 ▐ ♀ 🏌 🏠 🏌 Ryan Done.
Leisure motorised carts for hire, trolley for hire, putting
green, practice area, snooker.
Location 0.75m S off A589
Hotel ★★ 59% Clarendon Hotel, Marine Rd West,
West End Promenade, MORECAMBE
☎ 01524 410180 31rm(28 ⇔ 🏌)

KNOTT END-ON-SEA
Map 07 SD34

Knott End Wyreside FY6 0AA ☎ 01253 810576
Pleasant, undulating parkland course on banks of River Wyre.
Open to sea breezes.
18 holes, 5789yds, Par 69, SSS 68, Course record 63.
Club membership 500.
Visitors must contact in advance. May not play
weekends.
Societies must contact in advance.
Green Fees £21 per day; £18 per round (£24 per day
weekends).
Facilities ⊗ ⋔ 🏌 ▐ ♀ 🏌 🏠 🏌 Paul Walker.
Leisure trolley for hire, putting green, practice area.
Location W side of village off B5377
Guesthouse QQQQQ The Victorian House, Trunnah Rd,
THORNTON-CLEVELEYS
☎ 01253 860619 3 ⇔ 🏌

LANCASTER
Map 07 SD46

Lancaster Golf & Country Club Ashton Hall, Ashton-
with-Stodday LA2 0AJ ☎ 01524 751247
This course is unusual for parkland golf as it is exposed
to the winds coming off the Irish Sea. It is situated on the
Lune estuary and has some natural hazards and easy
walking. There are however several fine holes among
woods near the old clubhouse.
18 holes, 6282yds, Par 71, SSS 71.
Club membership 925. ▶

<table>
<tr><td>Visitors</td><td>residential visitors only at weekends. Must contact in advance and have a handicap certificate.</td></tr>
<tr><td>Societies</td><td>Mon-Fri only. Must contact in advance. Handicap certificate required.</td></tr>
<tr><td>Green Fees</td><td>not confirmed.</td></tr>
<tr><td>Facilities</td><td>♀☺☎♨ David Sutcliffe.</td></tr>
<tr><td>Leisure</td><td>putting,trolley hire,practice area.</td></tr>
<tr><td>Location</td><td>3m S on A588</td></tr>
<tr><td>Hotel</td><td>★★★★ 68% Lancaster House Hotel, Green Ln, Ellel, LANCASTER ☎ 01524 844822 80 ⊨ ☞</td></tr>
</table>

Lansil Caton Rd LA1 3PE ☎ 01524 61233
Parkland course.
9 holes, 5608yds, Par 70, SSS 67.
Club membership 375.

Visitors   may not play before 1pm at weekends.
Societies   weekdays only; must contact in writing.
Green Fees   not confirmed.
Facilities   ♀ (eves & weekends) ☺
Location   N side of town centre on A683
Hotel   B Forte Posthouse Lancaster, Waterside Park, Caton Rd, LANCASTER ☎ 01524 65999 115 ⊨ ☞

LANGHO   Map 07 SD73

Mytton Fold Farm Hotel Whalley Rd BB6 8AB
☎ 01254 240662
The course has panoramic views across the Ribble Valley and Pendle Hill. Tight fairways and water hazards are designed to make this a challenging course for any golfer.
18 holes, 6217yds, Par 72, SSS 70.
Club membership 200.

Visitors   must contact in advance.
Societies   telephone in advance.
Green Fees   £12 per day (£12 weekends & bank holidays).
Facilities   ⊗♏╟♥♀☺☎♈♨☎ Gary P Coope.
Leisure   motorised carts for hire, trolley for hire, putting green, practice area, pool table.·
Location   On A59 between Langho and Whalley
Hotel   ★★★ 65% Mytton Fold Farm Hotel, Whalley Rd, LANGHO ☎ 01254 240662 27 ⊨ ☞

LEYLAND   Map 07 SD52

Leyland Wigan Rd PR5 2UD
☎ 01772 436457 & 423425
Parkland course, fairly flat and usually breezy.
18 holes, 6123yds, Par 69, SSS 60, Course record 64.
Club membership 650.

Visitors   must contact in advance. With member only at weekends.
Societies   must contact in advance.
Green Fees   £25.
Facilities   ⊗♏╟♥♀☺☎ Colin Burgess.
Leisure   trolley for hire, putting green, practice area.
Location   E side of town centre on A49
Hotel   ★★★ 65% Pines Hotel, CLAYTON-LE-WOODS ☎ 01772 38551 39 ⊨ ☞

LONGRIDGE   Map 07 SD63

Longridge Fell Barn, Jeffrey Hill PR3 3TU
☎ 01772 783291
Moorland course 850 ft high with views of the Ribble Valley, Trough of Bowland, The Fylde and Welsh Mountains.
18 holes, 5975yds, Par 70, SSS 69, Course record 65.
Club membership 700.

Visitors   welcome.
Societies   welcome by prior arrangement.
Green Fees   £18 per day (£21 weekends and bank holidays).
Facilities   ⊗♏╟♥♀☺☎ Neil James.
Leisure   trolley for hire, putting green, practice area.
Location   8m NE of Preston off B6243
Hotel   ★★ 68% Shireburn Arms Hotel, HURST GREEN ☎ 01254 826518 16 ⊨ ☞

LYTHAM ST ANNES   Map 07 SD32

Fairhaven Lytham Hall Park, Ansdell FY8 4JU
☎ 01253 736741 (Secretary) 736976 (Pro)
A flat, but interesting parkland links course of good standard. There are natural hazards as well as numerous bunkers and players need to produce particularly accurate second shots.
18 holes, 6883yds, Par 74, SSS 73, Course record 66.
Club membership 750.

Visitors   telephone professional in advance.
Societies   must contact in advance.
Green Fees   £35 per day; £30 per round (£35 per round weekends).
Facilities   ⊗♏╟♥♀☺☎ Brian Plucknett.
Leisure   trolley for hire, putting green, practice area.
Location   E side of town centre off B5261
Hotel   ★★★ 65% Bedford Hotel, 307-311 Clifton Dr South, LYTHAM ST ANNES ☎ 01253 724636 36 ⊨ ☞

Lytham Green Drive Ballam Rd FY8 4LE
☎ 01253 737390
Pleasant parkland course, ideal for holidaymakers.
18 holes, 6157yds, Par 70, SSS 69, Course record 64.
Club membership 740.

Visitors   must contact in advance. May not play at weekends.
Societies   must apply in writing.
Green Fees   £30 per day; £24 per round.
Facilities   ⊗♏╟♥♀☺☎ Andrew Lancaster.
Leisure   trolley for hire, putting green, practice area.
Location   E side of town centre off B5259
Hotel   ★★★★ 61% Clifton Arms, West Beach, Lytham, LYTHAM ST ANNES ☎ 01253 739898 44 ⊨ ☞

ROYAL LYTHAM ST ANNES   See page 133

St Annes Old Links Highbury Rd FY8 2LD
☎ 01253 723597
Seaside links, qualifying course for Open Championship; compact and of very high standard, particularly greens. Windy, very long 5th, 17th and 18th holes. Famous hole: 9th (171 yds), par 3. Excellent club facilities.
18 holes, 6616yds, Par 72, SSS 72.
Club membership 950.   ▶

ROYAL LYTHAM AND ST ANNES

LYTHAM ST ANNES *Lancs*

☎ **01253 724206**

Map 07 SD32

John Ingham writes: Venue for many Open Championships, the most famous winner here was amateur Bobby Jones who, in 1926, put together a four-round total of 291 using wooden clubs and the old-fashioned ball. In the last round, when level with Al Watrous with two to play, Jones bunkered his teeshot at the 17th while Watrous hit a perfect drive and then a fine second on to the green. Jones climbed into the bunker, decided a 175-yard shot was needed if he had any chance, and hit a club similar to today's 4-iron. The shot was brilliant and finished, not only on the green, but nearer than his rival. Shaken, Watrous 3-putted, Jones got his four and finished with a perfect par while Watrous, rattled, had taken six. The club placed a plaque by the famous bunker and it's there to this day.

Since that time the course, which runs close to the railway but slightly inland from the sea, has staged other historic Opens. Bob Charles of New Zealand became the only left-hander to win the title while Tony Jacklin, in 1969, signalled the re-awakening of British golf by winning.

This huge links, founded in 1886 not far from Blackpool, is not easy. When the wind gets up it can be a nightmare. And not everyone approves a championship course that starts with a par 3 hole and it is, in fact, a rare thing in Britain. Some object to the close proximity of red-bricked houses, and aren't keen on trains that rattle past. Now there is an additional nine-hole course and a driving range.

But it's a test full of history and deserves to be played.

Visitors	weekdays only (unless guest at Dormy House). Must contact in advance, and have a handicap certificate
Societies	must apply to Secretary (large groups Mon & Thur only
Green fees	£75 per round (includes lunch)
Facilities	⊗ ⅲ ᒻ ▐ ♡ ⋈ 丛 ⌂ ℓ (E.Birchenough) driving range, putting, practice area, trollies
Leisure	snooker
Location	Links Gate, Lytham FY8 3LQ (0.5m E of St Annes town)

18 holes, 6334 yds, Par 71, SSS 74,

WHERE TO STAY AND EAT NEARBY

HOTELS:
LYTHAM ST ANNES
★★★ 65% Bedford, 307-311 Clifton Drive South. ☎ 01253 724636. 36 (15 ℝ 21 ⇄ ℝ)

★★★ 67% Chadwick, South Promenade. ☎ 01253 720061. 72 (7 ℝ 65 ⇄ ℝ)

★★ 66% Glendower, North Promenade. ☎ 01253 723241. 60 ⇄

★★ 65% St Ives, 7-9 South Promenade. ☎ 01253 720011. 70 (3 ℝ 60 ⇄)

RESTAURANT:
THORNTON
❀❀ The Victorian House, ☎ 01253 860619

Visitors	may not play on Sat or before 9.15am & between noon-2pm. Sundays by prior arrangement only. Handicap certificate requested.
Societies	must contact in advance.
Green Fees	not confirmed.
Facilities	♀⅃☎ℓ G Hardiman.
Leisure	putting,trolley hire,practice area.
Location	N side of town centre
Hotel	★★★ 65% Bedford Hotel, 307-311 Clifton Dr South, LYTHAM ST ANNES ☎ 01253 724636 36 ⇆ ℟

MORECAMBE
Map 07 SD46

Morecambe Bare LA4 6AJ
☎ 01524 412841 & 415596
Holiday golf at its most enjoyable. The well-maintained, wind-affected seaside parkland course is not long but full of character. Even so the panoramic views across Morecambe Bay and to the Lake District and Pennines make concentration difficult. The 4th is a testing hole.
18 holes, 5770yds, Par 67, SSS 68, Course record 63.
Club membership 850.

Visitors	must contact in advance.
Societies	must contact in advance.
Green Fees	on application.
Facilities	⊗ ⅷ ㏒ ♟ ♀⅃☎ℓ Simon Fletcher.
Leisure	trolley for hire, practice area, putting green.
Location	N side of town centre on A5105
Hotel	★★★ 66% Elms Hotel, Bare Village, MORECAMBE ☎ 01524 411501 40 ⇆ ℟

NELSON
Map 07 SD83

Marsden Park Nelson Municipal Golf Course, Townhouse Rd BB9 8DG ☎ 01282 67525
Hilly, parkland course open to the wind.
18 holes, 5806yds, Par 70, SSS 68, Course record 66.
Club membership 320.

Visitors	must telephone in advance at weekends.
Societies	may not play on Sat. Must contact in writing.
Green Fees	not confirmed.
Facilities	♀ (weekends or by prior arrangement) ⅃ ☎ ⚐ ℓ Nick Brown.
Location	E side of town centre off A56
Hotel	★★★ 72% Oaks Hotel, Colne Rd, Reedley, BURNLEY ☎ 01282 414141 54 ⇆ ℟

Nelson King's Causeway, Brierfield BB9 0EU
☎ 01282 611834
Hilly moorland course, usually windy, with good views. Testing 8th hole, par 4.
18 holes, 5967yds, Par 70, SSS 69, Course record 63.
Club membership 500.

Visitors	must telephone 01282 617000 in advance.
Societies	must contact in writing.
Green Fees	£25 per day (£30 weekends & bank holidays).
Facilities	⊗ ⅷ ㏒ ♟ ♀⅃☎ ⚐ ℓ Nigel Sumner.
Leisure	trolley for hire, putting green, practice area.
Location	1.5m SE
Hotel	★★★ 72% Oaks Hotel, Colne Rd, Reedley, BURNLEY ☎ 01282 414141 54 ⇆ ℟

ORMSKIRK
Map 07 SD40

Ormskirk Cranes Ln, Lathom L40 5UJ
☎ 01695 572112
A pleasantly secluded, fairly flat, parkland course with much heath and silver birch. Accuracy from the tees will provide an interesting variety of second shots.
18 holes, 6358yds, Par 70, SSS 70, Course record 63.
Club membership 300.

Visitors	restricted Sat.
Societies	must contact in writing.
Green Fees	not confirmed.
Facilities	♀⅃☎ℓ Jack Hammond.
Leisure	putting,practice,cart/buggy/trolley hire.
Location	1.5m NE
Hotel	★★★ 64% Holland Hall Hotel, 6 Lafford Ln, UPHOLLAND ☎ 01695 624426 28 ⇆ ℟Annexe6 ⇆ ℟

PLEASINGTON
Map 07 SD62

Pleasington BB2 5JF ☎ 01254 202177
Plunging and rising across lovely moorland turf this course tests judgement of distance through the air to greens of widely differing levels. The 11th and 17th are testing holes.
18 holes, 6417yds, Par 71, SSS 71.
Club membership 700.

Visitors	may play Mon & Wed-Fri only.
Societies	must contact in advance.
Green Fees	not confirmed.
Facilities	⊗ ⅷ ㏒ ♟ ♀⅃☎ℓ Ged Furey.
Leisure	trolley for hire, putting green, snooker.
Location	W side of village
Hotel	★★★ 59% Blackburn Moat House, Preston New Rd, BLACKBURN ☎ 01254 899988 98 ⇆ ℟

POULTON-LE-FYLDE
Map 07 SD33

Poulton-le-Fylde Breck Rd FY6 7HJ
☎ 01253 892444 & 893150
Municipal parkland course, with easy walking.
9 holes, 3028yds, Par 70, SSS 68.
Club membership 300.

Visitors	no restrictions.
Societies	contact in advance.
Green Fees	£5.50 (£7.50 weekends & bank holidays).
Facilities	⊗ ㏒ ♟ ♀⅃☎ ⚐ ℓ Lewis Ware.
Leisure	heated indoor swimming pool, trolley for hire, driving range, putting green, practice area.
Location	N side of town
Guesthouse	QQQQQ The Victorian House, Trunnah Rd, THORNTON-CLEVELEYS ☎ 01253 860619 3 ⇆ ℟

PRESTON
Map 07 SD52

Ashton & Lea Tudor Av, Lea PR4 0XA
☎ 01772 726480 & 735282
Heathland/parkland course with pond and streams, offering pleasant walks and some testing holes.
18 holes, 6346yds, Par 71, SSS 70, Course record 65.
Club membership 825.

Visitors must contact professional on 01772 724370.
Societies must contact in writing or by telephone.
Green Fees £20 per day (£23 weekends & bank holidays).
Facilities ⊗ ⅢⅡ ᗷ 📦 ♀ 🏌 📾 ⚑ ᚖ M Greenough.
Leisure trolley for hire, putting green, practice area.
Location 3m W on A5085
Hotel B Forte Posthouse Preston, Ringway,
PRESTON ☎ 01772 259411 121 ⇆ 🅟

Fishwick Hall Glenluce Dr, Farringdon Park PR1 5TD
☎ 01772 798300 & 795870
Meadowland course overlooking River Ribble. Natural hazards.
18 holes, 6092yds, Par 70, SSS 69, Course record 66.
Club membership 750.
Visitors advisable to contact in advance.
Societies must contact in advance.
Green Fees £20 per day (£25 weekends & bank holidays).
Facilities ⊗ ⅢⅡ ᗷ 📦 ♀ 🏌 📾 ᚖ Stuart Bence.
Leisure trolley for hire, putting green, practice area.
Hotel B Forte Posthouse Preston, Ringway,
PRESTON ☎ 01772 259411 121 ⇆ 🅟

Ingol Tanterton Hall Rd, Ingol PR2 7BY ☎ 01772 734556
Long, high course with natural water hazards.
18 holes, 6296yds, Par 72, SSS 70, Course record 67.
Club membership 800.
Visitors must contact in advance but may not play on competition days.
Societies must contact in writing.
Green Fees not confirmed.
Facilities ♀ 🏌 📾 ᚖ
Leisure squash.
Location 2m NW junc 32 of M55 off B5411
Hotel B Forte Posthouse Preston, Ringway,
PRESTON ☎ 01772 259411 121 ⇆ 🅟

Penwortham Blundell Ln, Penwortham PR1 0AX
☎ 01772 744630
A progressive golf club set close to the banks of the River Ribble. The course has tree-lined fairways, excellent greens, and provides easy walking. Testing holes include the 178-yd, par 3 third, the 480-yd, par 5 sixth, and the 398-yd par 4 sixteenth.
18 holes, 6056yds, Par 69, SSS 69.
Club membership 975.
Visitors must contact in advance; restricted Sun.
Societies must apply in writing.
Green Fees £25 per day; £22 per round (£28 weekends).
Facilities ⊗ ⅢⅡ ᗷ 📦 ♀ 🏌 📾 ᚖ John Wright.
Leisure trolley for hire, putting green, practice area.
Location 1.5m W of town centre off A59
Hotel ★★★ 66% Tickled Trout, Preston New Rd, Samlesbury, PRESTON
☎ 01772 877671 72 ⇆ 🅟

Preston Fulwood Hall Ln, Fulwood PR2 8DD
☎ 01772 700011
Pleasant inland golf at this course set in very agreeable parkland. There is a well-balanced selection of holes, undulating amongst groups of trees, and not requiring great length.
18 holes, 6233yds, Par 71, SSS 70.
Club membership 800.
Visitors may play midweek only. Must contact in advance and have a handicap certificate.

Societies must contact in writing/telephone.
Green Fees £27 per day; £22 per round.
Facilities ⊗ ⅢⅡ ᗷ 📦 ♀ 🏌 📾 ᚖ Pat Wells.
Leisure trolley for hire, putting green, practice area.
Location N side of town centre
Hotel ★★★★ 66% Broughton Park Hotel, Garstang Rd, Broughton, PRESTON
☎ 01772 864087 98 ⇆ 🅟

RISHTON
Map 07 SD73

Rishton Eachill Links, Hawthorn Dr BB1 4HG
☎ 01254 884442
Undulating moorland course.
9 holes, 6097yds, Par 70, SSS 69, Course record 68.
Club membership 270.
Visitors must play with member on weekends and bank holidays.
Societies must contact in writing.
Green Fees £13 per day.
Facilities ⊗ ⅢⅡ ᗷ 📦 ♀ by arrangement ᗷ
Leisure putting green, practice area.
Location S side of town off A678
Hotel ★★★ 66% Dunkenhalgh Hotel, Blackburn Rd, Clayton le Moors, ACCRINGTON
☎ 01254 398021 37 ⇆ 🅟 Annexe42 ⇆ 🅟

SILVERDALE
Map 07 SD47

Silverdale Redbridge Ln LA5 0SP ☎ 01524 701300
Difficult heathland course with rock outcrops. Excellent views.
12 holes, 5463yds, Par 69, SSS 67.
Club membership 500.
Visitors may only play on Sun in summer if accompanied by a member.
Societies must contact in writing.
Green Fees £12 per day (£17 weekends & bank holidays).
Facilities ⊗ ⅢⅡ ᗷ 📦 ♀ 🏌 📾 ᚖ S Sumner Roberts.
Leisure putting green.
Location Opposite Silverdale Station
Hotel ★ 62% Wheatsheaf Hotel, BEETHAM
☎ 015395 62123 6 ⇆ 🅟

UPHOLLAND
Map 07 SD50

Beacon Park Beacon Ln WN8 7RU
☎ 01695 622700
Undulating/hilly parkland course, designed by Donald Steel, with magnificent view of the Welsh hills and Blackpool Tower. Twenty-four-bay floodlit driving range.
18 holes, 6000yds, Par 72, SSS 69, Course record 68.
Club membership 200.
Visitors may book 6 days in advance.
Societies must contact in advance.
Green Fees £6 (£8 weekends & bank holidays).
Facilities ⊗ ⅢⅡ by prior arrangement ᗷ by prior arrangement 📦 ♀ 🏌 📾 ⚑ ᚖ Ray Peters.
Leisure trolley for hire, driving range, putting green, practice area.
Location S of Ashurst Beacon Hill
Hotel ★★★ 64% Holland Hall Hotel, 6 Lafford Ln, UPHOLLAND
☎ 01695 624426 28 ⇆ 🅟 Annexe6 ⇆ 🅟

Dean Wood Lafford Ln WN8 0QZ ☎ 01695 622219
This parkland course has a varied terrain - flat front nine,
undulating back nine. Beware the par 4, 11th and 17th
holes, which has ruined many a card. If there were a prize
for the best maintained course in Lancashire, Dean Wood
would be a strong contender.
18 holes, 6179yds, Par 71, SSS 71, Course record 66.
Club membership 800.

Visitors   must play with member Tue, Wed &
weekends. Must contact in advance.
Societies   must contact in advance.
Green Fees £24 per day.
Facilities ⊗ ⅫⅬ ▦ ♀♨ 🖻 ♈ ⎛ Tony Coop.
Leisure   trolley for hire, putting green, practice area.
Location   0.5m NE off A577
Hotel   ★★★ 64% Holland Hall Hotel, 6 Lafford
Ln, UPHOLLAND
☎ 01695 624426 28 ⇥ ⎛Annexe6 ⇥ ⎛

WHALLEY   Map 07 SD73

Whalley Long Leese Barn, Portfield Ln BB7 9DR
☎ 01254 822236
Parkland course on Pendle Hill, overlooking the Ribble
Valley. Superb views. Ninth hole over pond.
9 holes, 6258yds, Par 72, SSS 70.
Club membership 400.

Visitors   must telephone 01254 824766 in advance.
Societies   must apply in writing.
Green Fees £15 per day (£20 weekends & bank holidays).
Facilities ⊗ ⅫⅬ ▦ ♀♨ 🖻 ⎛ H Smith.
Leisure   trolley for hire, putting green, practice area.
Location   1m SE off A671
Hotel   ★★★★ 67% Foxfields Country Hotel &
Restaurant, Whalley Rd, BILLINGTON
☎ 01254 822556 28 ⇥ ⎛Annexe16 ⇥ ⎛

WHITWORTH   Map 07 SD81

Lobden Lobden Moor OL12 8XJ ☎ 01706 343228
Moorland course, with hard walking. Windy.
9 holes, 5697yds, Par 70, SSS 68, Course record 67.
Club membership 250.

Visitors   must contact in advance. May not play Sat.
Societies   must apply in writing to Secretary.
Green Fees £10 per day (£15 weekends & bank holidays).
Facilities ⊗ ⅫⅬ ▦ ♀♨
Leisure   putting, snooker.
Location   E side of town centre off A671
Hotel   ★★ 57% Midway Hotel, Manchester Rd,
Castleton, ROCHDALE
☎ 01706 32881 24 ⇥ ⎛

WILPSHIRE   Map 07 SD63

Wilpshire Whalley Rd BB1 9LF ☎ 01254 248260
Semi-moorland course. Testing 17th hole (229 yds) par 3.
Extensive views of Ribble Valley, the coast and the
Yorkshire Dales.
18 holes, 5921yds, Par 69, SSS 66, Course record 61.
Club membership 500.

Visitors   must contact in advance.
Societies   must contact by telephone and confirm in
writing.

Green Fees £25 per day/round (£30 weekends & bank
holidays).
Facilities ⊗ ⅫⅬ ▦ ♀♨ 🖻 ♈ ⎛ Walter Slaven.
Leisure   trolley for hire, putting green, practice area.
Hotel   ★★★ 59% Blackburn Moat House, Preston
New Rd, BLACKBURN
☎ 01254 899988 98 ⇥ ⎛

LEICESTERSHIRE

ASHBY-DE-LA-ZOUCH   Map 08 SK31

Willesley Park Measham Rd LE65 2PF
☎ 01530 414596
Undulating heathland and parkland course with quick
draining sandy sub-soil.
18 holes, 6304yds, Par 70, SSS 70, Course record 64.
Club membership 600.

Visitors   Must contact in advance. Restricted weekends.
Societies   Wed-Fri only. Must apply in writing.
Green Fees £28 per day (£33 weekends & bank holidays).
Facilities ⊗ Ⅺ by prior arrangement Ⅼ ▦ ♀♨ 🖻
⎛ C J Hancock.
Leisure   buggies for hire, trolley for hire, snooker.
Location   SW side of town centre on A453
Hotel   ★★★ 63% The Fallen Knight, Kilwardby St,
Ashby-de-la-Zouch
☎ 01530 412230 24 ⇥ ⎛

BIRSTALL   Map 04 SK50

Birstall Station Rd LE4 3BB ☎ 0116 267 4322
Parkland course with trees, shrubs, ponds and ditches.
18 holes, 6222yds, Par 70, SSS 70.
Club membership 650.

Visitors   with member only weekends; may not play Tue.
Societies   apply in writing.
Green Fees £25 per day; £20 per round.
Facilities ⊗ ⅫⅬ ▦ ♀♨ ⎛ David Clarke.
Leisure   trolley for hire, putting green, practice area.
Location   2m N of Leicester on A6
Hotel   ★★★ 58% Hotel Saint James, Abbey St,
LEICESTER
☎ 0116 251 0666 73 ⇥ ⎛

BOTCHESTON   Map 04 SK40

Forest Hill Markfield Ln LE9 9FJ ☎ 01455 824800
Parkland course with many trees, four Par 4s, but no steep
gradients.
18 holes, 6111yds, Par 72, SSS 69, Course record 72.
Club membership 450.

Visitors   must contact in advance for weekends.
Societies   must telephone in advance.
Green Fees not confirmed.
Facilities ♀♨ 🖻 ♈ ⎛ Martin Wing.
Leisure   driving range.
Hotel   ★★★ 63% Field Head Hotel, Markfield Ln,
MARKFIELD
☎ 01530 245454 28 ⇥ ⎛

COSBY   Map 04 SP59

Cosby Chapel Ln, Broughton Rd LE9 1RG
☎ 0116 286 4759
Undulating parkland course with a number of tricky, tight
driving holes.
18 holes, 6417yds, Par 71, SSS 71, Course record 68.
Club membership 750.
Visitors   restricted weekdays before 4pm. May not play at
                   weekends. Recommended to telephone in
                   advance.
Societies   book with secretary.
Green Fees   £26 per day; £22 per round.
Facilities   ⊗ ⅏ ╚ ■ ♀ ♨ 🏠 ⛳ ℓ Martin Wing.
Leisure   trolley for hire, putting green, practice area.
Location   S side of village
Hotel   B Forte Posthouse Leicester, Braunstone Ln
                   East, LEICESTER
                   ☎ 0116 263 0500 164 ⇄ ℝ

ENDERBY   Map 04 SP59

Enderby Mill Ln LE9 5HL ☎ 0116 2849 388
A gently undulating 9-hole course at which beginners are
especially welcome. The longest hole is the 2nd at 407 yards
and there are 5 Par 3's.
9 holes, 2133yds, Par 31, SSS 31, Course record 27.
Club membership 150.
Visitors   no restrictions.
Societies   must telephone in advance.
Green Fees   £5.25 per 18 holes; £4.25 per 9 holes
                   (£7.25/£5.25 weekends).
Facilities   ⊗ ⅏ ╚ ■ ♀ ♨ 🏠 ⛳ ℓ Chris D'Araujo.
Leisure   heated indoor swimming pool, squash, sauna,
                   solarium, gymnasium, trolley for hire.
Hotel   ★★ 63% Charnwood Hotel, 48 Leicester Rd,
                   NARBOROUGH ☎ 0116 286 2218 20 ⇄ ℝ

HINCKLEY   Map 04 SP49

Hinckley Leicester Rd LE10 3DR ☎ 01455 615124
Rolling parkland with lake features, and lined fairways.
18 holes, 6517yds, Par 71, SSS 71.
Club membership 1000.
Visitors   with member only weekends and bank holidays.
                   Must contact in advance and have a handicap
                   certificate.
Societies   apply by letter.
Green Fees   not confirmed.
Facilities   ♀ ♨ 🏠 ℓ Richard Jones.
Leisure   putting,practice area,buggy/trolley hire.
Location   1.5m NE on A47
Hotel   ★★ 67% Longshoot Toby Hotel, Watling St,
                   NUNEATON
                   ☎ 01203 329711 Annexe47 ⇄ ℝ

KETTON   Map 04 SK90

Luffenham Heath PE9 3UU
☎ 01780 720205 & 720298
This undulating heathland course with low bushes, much
gorse and many trees, lies in a conservation area for flora
and fauna. From the higher part of the course there is a
magnificent view across the Chater Valley.

18 holes, 6273yds, Par 70, SSS 70, Course record 64.
Club membership 550.
Visitors   must contact in advance.
Societies   write or telephone in advance.
Green Fees   £30 per day/round (£35 weekends & bank
                   holidays).
Facilities   ⊗ by prior arrangement ⅏ by prior
                   arrangement ╚ ■ ♀ ♨ 🏠 ⛳
                   ℓ Ian Burnett.
Leisure   trolley for hire, putting green, practice area.
Location   1.5m SW on A6121
Hotel   ★★★ 75% George of Stamford Hotel, St
                   Martins, STAMFORD
                   ☎ 01780 55171 47 ⇄ ℝ

KIBWORTH   Map 04 SP69

Kibworth Weir Rd, Beauchamp LE8 0LP
☎ 0116 279 2301
Parkland course with easy walking. A brook affects a number
of fairways
18 holes, 6333yds, Par 71, SSS 70, Course record 65.
Club membership 700.
Visitors   must contact in advance. With member only
                   weekends.
Societies   must contact in advance.
Green Fees   £28 per day; £22 per round.
Facilities   ⊗ ⅏ ╚ ■ ♀ ♨ 🏠 ⛳ ℓ Bob Larratt.
Leisure   trolley for hire, driving range, putting green,
                   practice area, snooker.
Location   S side of village
Hotel   ★★★ 68% Three Swans Hotel, 21 High St,
                   MARKET HARBOROUGH
                   ☎ 01858 466644 20 ⇄ ℝAnnexe16 ⇄ ℝ

KIRBY MUXLOE   Map 04 SK50

Kirby Muxloe Station Rd LE9 2EP ☎ 0116 239 3457
Pleasant parkland course with a lake in front of the 17th green
and a short 18th.
18 holes, 6351yds, Par 70, SSS 70, Course record 65.
Club membership 750.
Visitors   must contact in advance and a handicap certificate
                   is required. No visitors on Tue or at weekends.
Societies   must contact in advance.
Green Fees   £25 per day; £20 per round.
Facilities   ⊗ ⅏ ╚ ■ ♀ ♨ 🏠 ℓ Robert Stephenson.
Leisure   trolley for hire, driving range, putting green,
                   practice area, snooker.
Location   S side of village off B5380
Hotel   ★★★★ 60% Holiday Inn, St Nicholas Circle,
                   LEICESTER ☎ 0116 253 1161 188 ⇄ ℝ

LEICESTER   Map 04 SK50

Humberstone Heights Gypsy Ln LE5 0TB
☎ 0116 276 4674 & 276 3680
Municipal parkland course with 9 hole pitch and putt.
18 holes, 6343yds, Par 70, SSS 70, Course record 66.
Club membership 400.
Visitors   must contact in advance.
Societies   must telephone in advance.
Green Fees   £6 per round (£9 weekends).
Facilities   ⊗ ⅏ ╚ ■ ♀ ♨ 🏠 ⛳ ℓ Philip Highfield. ▶

Leisure trolley for hire, driving range, putting green, practice area.
Location 2.5m NE of city centre
Hotel ★★★ 72% Belmont House Hotel, De Montfort St, LEICESTER
☎ 0116 254 4773 44 ⇆ ʀ Annexe21 ⇆ ʀ

Leicestershire Evington Ln LE5 6DJ
☎ 0116 273 8825
Pleasantly undulating parkland course.
18 holes, 6312yds, Par 68, SSS 70, Course record 63.
Club membership 800.
Visitors must contact in advance.
Societies must contact in advance.
Green Fees £28 per day; £23 per round (£34/£29 weekends & bank holidays).
Facilities ⊗ Ⅲ ⅃ ⬤ ♀ ⚲ 🖾 ℓ John R Turnbull.
Leisure trolley for hire, putting green, practice area.
Location 2m E of city off A6030
Hotel ★★★ 64% Hermitage Hotel, Wigston Rd, Oadby, LEICESTER
☎ 0116 271 9441 57 ⇆ ʀ

Western Scudamore Rd, Braunstone Frith LE3 1UQ
☎ 0116 287 2339 & 287 6158
Pleasant, undulating parkland course with open aspect fairways in two loops of nine holes.Not too difficult but a good test of golf off the back tees.
18 holes, 6518yds, Par 72, SSS 71.
Club membership 400.
Visitors must contact in advance.
Societies must contact the secretary in advance.
Green Fees on application.
Facilities ⊗ Ⅲ⅃ ⬤ ♀ ⚲ 🖾 🗝ℓ Bruce Whipham.
Leisure trolley for hire, driving range, putting green, practice area.
Location 1.5m W of city centre off A47
Hotel B Forte Posthouse Leicester, Braunstone Ln East, LEICESTER
☎ 0116 263 0500 164 ⇆ ʀ

LOUGHBOROUGH
Map 08 SK51

Longcliffe Snell's Nook Ln, Nanpantan LE11 3YA
☎ 01509 239129
A re-designed course of natural heathland with outcrops of granite forming natural hazards especially on the 1st and 15th. The course is heavily wooded and has much bracken and gorse. There are a number of tight fairways and one blind hole.
18 holes, 6611yds, Par 72, SSS 72.
Club membership 660.
Visitors must contact in advance. With member only at weekends.
Societies telephone for availability, handicap certificate required.
Green Fees £30 per day; £22 per round.
Facilities ⊗ Ⅲ⅃ ⬤ ♀ ⚲ 🖾 ℓ Ian D Bailey.
Leisure trolley for hire, putting green, practice area.
Location 3m SW off B5350
Hotel ★★★ 65% Quality Friendly Hotel, New Ashby Rd, LOUGHBOROUGH
☎ 01509 211800 94 ⇆ ʀ

LUTTERWORTH
Map 04 SP58

Kilworth Springs South Kilworth Rd, North Kilworth LE17 6HJ ☎ 01858 575082 & 575974
An 18-hole course of two loops of 9: the front 9 are links style while the back 9 are in parkland with 4 lakes. On a windy day it is a very challenging course and the 6th hole is well deserving of its nickname 'the Devil's Toenail'.
18 holes, 6543yds, Par 72, SSS 71, Course record 66.
Club membership 800.
Visitors welcome subject to availability.
Societies contact in advance.
Green Fees not confirmed.
Facilities ♀ ⚲ 🖾 ℓ N Melvin.
Leisure driving range, buggies, caddys, trollies.
Location 4m E of M1 junc 20, A427 to Mkt Harborough
Hotel ★★★ 64% Denbigh Arms Hotel, High St, LUTTERWORTH
☎ 01455 553537 31 ⇆ ʀ

Lutterworth Rugby Rd LE17 4HN ☎ 01455 552532
Hilly course with River Swift running through.
18 holes, 6431yds, Par 71, SSS 71.
Club membership 700.
Visitors must play with member at weekends.
Societies must contact in advance.
Green Fees £24 per day; £18 per round.
Facilities ⊗ Ⅲ⅃ ⬤ ♀ ⚲ 🖾 🗝ℓ Roland Tisdall.
Leisure motorised carts for hire, buggies for hire, trolley for hire, putting green, practice area.
Location 0.5m S on A426
Hotel ★★★ 64% Denbigh Arms Hotel, High St, LUTTERWORTH
☎ 01455 553537 31 ⇆ ʀ

MARKET HARBOROUGH
Map 04 SP78

Langton Park Golf & Country Club Langton Hall, West Langton LE16 7TY ☎ 01858 545374
Set in the grounds of a former stately home, this attractive 9-hole course offers sufficient challenge to make it worthwhile playing them a second time.
9 holes, 3362yds, Par 72, SSS 72.
Club membership 135.
Visitors preferred on weekdays, preceedence given to members competitions at weekends.
Societies telephone enquiries welcome.
Green Fees £13.50 per 18 hole; £9 per 9 holes (£24/£12 weekends).
Facilities ⊗ Ⅲ⅃ ⬤ ♀ ⚲ ℓ Michael Balderstone.
Leisure trolley for hire, putting green, practice area.
Location Just off B6047, approx 5m N of Market Harborough
Hotel ★★★ 60% The Angel Hotel, 37 High St, MARKET HARBOROUGH
☎ 01858 462702 30 ⇆ ʀ

Market Harborough Oxendon Rd LE16 8NF
☎ 01858 463684
A parkland course situated close to the town. There are wide-ranging views over the surrounding countryside.
18 holes, 6022yds, Par 70, SSS 69, Course record 63.
Club membership 600.
Visitors must contact in advance and must play with member at weekends.

Societies must apply in writing.
Green Fees £22 per day; £16 per round.
Facilities ⊗ ⅲ ⅆ ⅌ ♀ ⅄ 🕮 ⅌ Frazer Baxter.
Leisure trolley for hire, putting green, practice area.
Location 1m S on A508
Hotel ★★★ 68% Three Swans Hotel, 21 High St,
MARKET HARBOROUGH
☎ 01858 466644 20 ⇔ ⅌Annexe16 ⇔ ⅌

MELTON MOWBRAY   Map 08 SK71

Melton Mowbray Waltham Rd, Thorpe Arnold LE14 4SD
☎ 01664 62118
Downland but flat course providing easy walking. Open to
the wind.
18 holes, 6222yds, Par 70, SSS 70.
Club membership 600.
Visitors must contact professional on 01664 69629.
Societies must contact in advance.
Green Fees £25 per day; £20 per round.
Facilities ⊗ ⅲ ⅆ ⅌ ♀ ⅄ 🕮 ⅌ Tony Westwood.
Leisure trolley for hire, putting green, practice area.
Location 2m NE on A607
Hotel ★★ 68% Sysonby Knoll Hotel, Asfordby Rd,
MELTON MOWBRAY
☎ 01664 63563 23 ⇔ ⅌Annexe1 ⇔ ⅌

OADBY   Map 04 SK60

Glen Gorse Glen Rd LE2 4RF ☎ 0116 271 4159
Fairly flat 18-hole parkland course with some strategically
placed mature trees, new saplings and ponds affecting play on
6 holes. Ridge and furrow is a feature of 5 holes.
18 holes, 6603yds, Par 72, SSS 72, Course record 65.
Club membership 600.
Visitors must contact in advance. Must play with
member at weekends.
Societies must telephone secretary in advance.
Green Fees £27 per day; £23 per round.
Facilities ⊗ ⅲ ⅆ ⅌ ♀ ⅄ 🕮 ⅌ Simon Ward.
Leisure trolley for hire, putting green, practice area,
snooker.
Location On A6 trunk road between Oadby/Great Glen
Hotel ★★★ 64% Hermitage Hotel, Wigston Rd,
Oadby, LEICESTER
☎ 0116 271 9441 57 ⇔ ⅌

Oadby Leicester Rd LE2 4AJ ☎ 0116 270 9052
Municipal parkland course.
18 holes, 6376yds, Par 72, SSS 70, Course record 60.
Club membership 500.
Visitors no restrictions.
Societies by arrangement contact pro shop.
Green Fees £6 per round (£9 weekends and bank holidays).
Facilities ⊗ ⅲ ⅆ ⅌ ♀ ⅄ 🕮 ⅌ Alan Kershaw.
Leisure trolley for hire, putting green, practice area.
Location West of Oadby, off A6
Hotel ★★★ 64% Hermitage Hotel, Wigston Rd,
Oadby, LEICESTER
☎ 0116 271 9441 57 ⇔ ⅌

ROTHLEY   Map 08 SK51

Rothley Park Westfield Ln LE7 7LH ☎ 0116 230 2809
Parkland course in picturesque situation.

18 holes, 6477yds, Par 71, SSS 71, Course record 67.
Club membership 600.
Visitors must contact professional on 0116 230 3023.
Societies apply in writing to secretary.
Green Fees £30 per day; £25 per round.
Facilities ⊗ ⅲ ⅆ ⅌ ♀ ⅄ 🕮 ⅌ Andrew Collins.
Location 0.75m W on B5328
Hotel ★★★ 61% Rothley Court Hotel, Westfield Ln,
ROTHLEY
☎ 0116 237 4141 14 ⇔ ⅌Annexe21 ⇔ ⅌

SCRAPTOFT   Map 04 SK60

Scraptoft Beeby Rd LE7 9SJ ☎ 0116 241 8863
Pleasant, inland country course.
18 holes, 6166yds, Par 69, SSS 69.
Club membership 550.
Visitors with member only weekends. Handicap
certificate required.
Societies apply in writing.
Green Fees not confirmed.
Facilities ♀ ⅄ 🕮 ⅌
Location 1m NE
Hotel ★★★ 64% Hermitage Hotel, Wigston Rd,
Oadby, LEICESTER
☎ 0116 271 9441 57 ⇔ ⅌

SEAGRAVE   Map 08 SK61

Park Hill Park Hill LE12 7NG ☎ 01509 815454
A new rolling parkland course with views over Charnwood
Forest. The opening hole is 420yards with a forced water
carry 100yards short of the green. The 10th is a 610yard Par 5
against the prevailing wind and there are 2 Par 5's to finish.
18 holes, 7219yds, Par 73, SSS 74.
Club membership 340.
Visitors must contact in advance.
Societies apply in writing.
Green Fees £24 per 36 holes; £20 per 27 holes; £16 per 18
holes (£32/£26/£20 weekends and bank
holidays).
Facilities ⊗ ⅲ ⅆ ⅌ ♀ ⅄ 🕮 ⅌ David C Mee.
Leisure trolley for hire, practice area.
Location 6m N of Leicester on A46
Hotel ★★★ 65% Quality Friendly Hotel, New Ashby
Rd, LOUGHBOROUGH
☎ 01509 211800 94 ⇔ ⅌

ULLESTHORPE   Map 04 SP58

Ullesthorpe Frolesworth Rd LE17 5BZ ☎ 01455 209023
Parkland course. Many leisure facilities.
18 holes, 6650yds, Par 72, SSS 72, Course record 67.
Club membership 650.
Visitors must contact in advance.
Societies contact well in advance.
Green Fees £21.50 per day, £13.50 per round.
Facilities ⊗ ⅲ ⅆ ⅌ ♀ ⅄ 🕮 Ⅿ ⅌ David Bowring.
Leisure hard tennis courts, heated indoor swimming
pool, sauna, solarium, gymnasium, motorised
carts for hire, buggies for hire, trolley for hire,
putting.
Location 0.5m N off B577
Hotel ★★★ 64% Denbigh Arms Hotel, High St,
LUTTERWORTH ☎ 01455 553537 31 ⇔ ⅌

WHETSTONE

Map 04 SP59

Whetstone Cambridge Rd, Cosby LE9 1SJ
☎ 0116 286 1424
Small and very flat parkland course adjacent to motorway.
18 holes, 5795yds, Par 68, SSS 68.
Club membership 500.
Visitors limited times at weekends
Societies must contact in advance.
Green Fees not confirmed.
Facilities ♀ ⚑ 🏠 𝒇 David Raitt.
Leisure driving range.
Location 1m S of village
Hotel ★★★ 65% Time Out Hotel & Leisure, Enderby Rd, Blaby, LEICESTER
☎ 0116 278 7898 25 ⇄ �“

WILSON

Map 08 SK42

Breedon Priory Green Ln DE73 1AT
☎ 01332 863081
A relatively short and forgiving course set in undulating countryside with magnificent views from several holes.
18 holes, 5530yds, Par 70, SSS 67, Course record 66.
Club membership 760.
Visitors may play any time if tee available, must book for weekends.
Societies apply in writing or telephone for booking form.
Green Fees £16 per day; £14 per round (£16 per round weekends).
Facilities ⚑ ♥ ♀ ⚒ 🏠
Leisure motorised carts for hire, buggies for hire, trolley for hire, driving range, putting green, practice area, teaching bays.
Location 4m W of A42/M1 junct 24
Hotel ★★★ 66% The Priest House, Kings Mills, CASTLE DONINGTON
☎ 01332 810649 27 ⇄ �“Annexe18 ⇄ �“

WOODHOUSE EAVES

Map 08 SK51

Charnwood Forest Breakback Ln LE12 8TA
☎ 01509 890259
Hilly heathland course with hard walking, but no bunkers.
9 holes, 5960yds, Par 69, SSS 69, Course record 64.
Club membership 210.
Visitors must contact in advance.
Societies Wed & Thu only. Must contact in advance.
Green Fees £25 per day; £15 per 18 holes (£25 weekends & bank holidays); £10 per 9 holes.
Facilities ⊗ ⌇ ⚑ ♥ ♀ ⚒
Leisure putting green.
Location 0.75m NW off B591
Hotel ★★★★ 71% Quorn Country Hotel, Charnwood House, Leicester Rd, QUORN
☎ 01509 415050 19 ⇄ �“

Lingdale Joe Moore's Ln LE12 8TF
☎ 01509 890703
Parkland course located in Charnwood Forest with some hard walking at some holes. The par 3, (3rd) and par 5, (8th) are testing holes. The 4th and 5th have water hazards.
18 holes, 6545yds, Par 71, SSS 71, Course record 68.
Club membership 610.

Visitors must telephone professional in advance.
Societies must contact in advance.
Green Fees £21 per day; £18 per round (£24 weekends).
Facilities ⊗ ⌇ ⚑ ♥ ♀ ⚒ 🏠 𝒇 Peter Sellears.
Leisure putting green, practice ground.
Location 1.5m S off B5330
Hotel ★★★★ 71% Quorn Country Hotel, Charnwood House, Leicester Rd, QUORN
☎ 01509 415050 19 ⇄ �“

● LINCOLNSHIRE

BELTON

Map 08 SK93

Belton Woods Hotel NG32 2LN
☎ 01476 593200
Two challenging 18-hole courses, a 9-hole Par 3 and a driving range. The Lakes Course has 13 lakes, while The Woodside boasts the third longest hole in Europe at 613 yards. Many leisure facilities.
The Lakes Course: 18 holes, 6808yds, Par 72, SSS 73, Course record 66.
The Woodside Course: 18 holes, 6834yds, Par 73, SSS 73.
Spitfire Course: 9 holes, 1164yds, Par 27.
Club membership 500.
Visitors available at all times, for further informatiom or reservation telephone the sales office.
Societies welcome all week, reservations to be made by telephone or letter.
Green Fees Lakes or Woodside: Apr-Oct, £35 per day; £25 per round. Nov-Mar, £18 per round. Spitfire £5 per round all year.
Facilities ⊗ ⌇ ⚑ ♥ ♀ ⚒ 🏠 𝒇 ⊨ 𝒇 Tony Roberts.
Leisure hard tennis courts, heated indoor swimming pool, squash, sauna, solarium, gymnasium, motorised carts for hire, buggies for hire, trolley for hire, driving range, putting green, practice area.
Location On A607, 2m N of Grantham
Hotel ★★★★ 75% Belton Woods Hotel, BELTON
☎ 01476 593200 136 ⇄ �“

BLANKNEY

Map 08 TF06

Blankney LN4 3AZ ☎ 01526 320263
Open parkland course with mature trees; fairly flat.
18 holes, 6479yds, Par 72, SSS 71, Course record 66.
Club membership 640.
Visitors must contact in advance, may not play Wed mornings, restricted at weekends.
Societies not Wed mornings, booking required.
Green Fees £25 per day; £17 per round (£30/£25 weekends & bank holidays).
Facilities ⊗ ⌇ ⚑ ♥ ♀ ⚒ 🏠 𝒇 ⊨ 𝒇 Graham Bradley.
Leisure squash, motorised carts for hire, trolley for hire, putting green, practice area.
Location 1m SW on B1188
Hotel ★★★ 60% Moor Lodge Hotel, Sleaford Rd, BRANSTON
☎ 01522 791366 26 ⇄ �“

BOSTON   Map 08 TF34

Boston Cowbridge, Horncastle Rd PE22 7EL
☎ 01205 350589
Parkland course many water hazards in play on ten holes.
18 holes, 6490yds, Par 72, SSS 71, Course record 69.
Club membership 650.
Visitors   contact in advance for tee time.
Societies   apply in writing.
Green Fees £22 per day; £17 per round (£30/£20 weekends
     & bank holidays).
Facilities   ⊗ ⅷ ﾑ ♥ ♀ ♨ 🏠 ⛳ ⛳ Terry Squires.
Leisure   trolley for hire, driving range, putting green,
     practice area.
Location   2m N of Boston on B1183
Hotel   ★★★ 59% New England, 49 Wide Bargate,
     BOSTON ☎ 01205 365255 25 ⇔ ↾

Kirton Holme Holme Rd, Kirton Holme PE20 1SY
☎ 01205 290669
A young parkland course designed for mid to high
handicappers. It is flat but has 2500 young trees, two natural
water course plus water hazards. The 2nd is a challenging,
386yard Par 4 dogleg.
9 holes, 5768yds, Par 70, SSS 68, Course record 71.
Club membership 350.
Visitors   no restrictions but booking advisable for
     weekends & summer evenings.
Societies   weekdays only, by prior arrangement.
Green Fees £7.70 per day; £4.40 per round (£8.80/£5.50
     weekends & bank holidays).
Facilities   ⊗ ⅷ ﾑ ♥ ♀ ♨ ⛳
Leisure   trolley for hire, practice area.
Location   4m W of Boston off A52
Hotel   ★★ 66% Comfort Friendly Inn, Bonnington Rd,
     Bicker Bar, BOSTON
     ☎ 01205 820118 55 ⇔ ↾

BOURNE   Map 08 TF02

Toft Hotel Toft PE10 0JT
☎ 01778 590614 & 590615
Parkland course on the verge of the Lincoln Edge. Includes
lake and uses contours of the hills to full effect.
18 holes, 6486yds, Par 72, SSS 71, Course record 63.
Club membership 550.
Visitors   advisable to book for weekends.
Societies   apply in advance by telephone.
Green Fees £18 per day; £10 per round (£25/£15 weekends
     & bank holidays).
Facilities   ⊗ ⅷ ﾑ ♥ ♀ ♨ 🏠 ⛳ ⇔ ⛳ Mark Jackson.
Leisure   motorised carts for hire, buggies for hire, trolley
     for hire, driving range, putting green, practice
     area.
Location   On A6121 Bourne/Stamford road
Hotel   ★★ 60% Angel Hotel, Market Place,
     BOURNE ☎ 01778 422346 14 ⇔ ↾

CLEETHORPES   Map 08 TA30

Cleethorpes Kings Rd DN35 0PN ☎ 01472 814060
Flat meadowland seaside course intersected by large dykes.
18 holes, 6018yds, Par 70, SSS 69, Course record 64.
Club membership 760.

Visitors   restricted Wed afternoons.
Societies   Tue,Thu or Fri only. Must contact in advance.
Green Fees not confirmed.
Facilities   ♀ ﾑ 🏠 ⛳ Eric Sharp.
Location   1.5m S off A1031
Hotel   ★★★ 69% Kingsway Hotel, Kingsway,
     CLEETHORPES
     ☎ 01472 601122 50 ⇔ ↾

ELSHAM   Map 08 TA01

Elsham Barton Rd DN20 0LS
☎ 01652 680291
Parkland course in country surroundings. Easy walking.
18 holes, 6411yds, Par 71, SSS 71, Course record 67.
Club membership 650.
Visitors   with member only weekends & bank holidays.
     Must contact in advance.
Societies   must apply in writing.
Green Fees £24 per day/round.
Facilities   ⊗ ⅷ ﾑ ♥ ♀ ♨ 🏠 ⛳ Stuart Brewer.
Leisure   motorised carts for hire, buggies for hire, trolley
     for hire, putting green, practice area.
Location   2m SW on B1206
Hotel   ★★★ 65% Wortley House Hotel, Rowland Rd,
     SCUNTHORPE
     ☎ 01724 842223 38 ⇔ ↾

GAINSBOROUGH   Map 08 SK88

Gainsborough Thonock DN21 1PZ
☎ 01427 613088
Scenic parkland course. Floodlit driving range.
18 holes, 6620yds, Par 73, SSS 72, Course record 66.
Club membership 600.
Visitors   welcome weekdays. Must contact in advance.
     Ladies Day Thu morning.
Societies   must telephone in advance.
Green Fees not confirmed.
Facilities   ♀ ﾑ 🏠 ⛳ Stephen Cooper.
Leisure   driving range,putting,trolley hire.
Location   1m N off A159
Hotel   ★★ 65% Hickman-Hill Hotel, Cox's Hill,
     GAINSBOROUGH
     ☎ 01427 613639 8rm(3 ⇔3 ↾)

GEDNEY HILL   Map 08 TF31

Gedney Hill West Drove PE12 0NT
☎ 01406 330922 & 330183
Flat parkland course similar to a links course. Made testing
by Fen winds and small greens. Also a 10-bay driving range.
18 holes, 5493yds, Par 70, SSS 66, Course record 67.
Club membership 300.
Visitors   no restrictions.
Societies   telephone in advance.
Green Fees not confirmed.
Facilities   ♀ ﾑ 🏠 ⛳ ⛳ David Creek.
Leisure   10 bay driving range.
Location   5m SE of Spalding
Hotel   ★★ 63% Queens Hotel, South Brink,
     WISBECH
     ☎ 01945 583933 11 ⇔ ↾Annexe6 ⇔ ↾

GRANTHAM
Map 08 SK93

Belton Park Belton Ln, Londonthorpe Rd NG31 9SH
☎ 01476 67399
Three 9-hole courses set in classic mature parkland of Lord
Brownlow's country seat, Belton House. Gently undulating
with streams, ponds, plenty of trees and beautiful scenery,
including a deer park. Famous holes: 5th, 12th, 16th and 18th.
Combine any of the three courses for a testing 18-hole round.
*Bronnlow: 18 holes, 6412yds, Par 71, SSS 71, Course record
66.*
Ancaster: 18 holes, 6109yds, Par 70, SSS 69.
Belmont: 18 holes, 5857yds, Par 69, SSS 68.
Club membership 900.
Visitors	contact for tee booking.
Societies	apply in writing.
Green Fees	£27.50 per 36 holes; £22 per round (£33/£27 weekends & bank holidays).
Facilities	⊗ ⅶ ⓑ ☂ ♀ ♨ ▾ ℓ Brian McKee.
Leisure	buggies for hire, trolley for hire, practice area.
Location	1.5m NE of Grantham
Hotel	★★★ 64% Kings Hotel, North Pde, GRANTHAM ☎ 01476 590800 22rm(21 ⇆ ♠)

Sudbrook Moor Charity St, Carlton Scroop NG32 3AT
☎ 01400 250796
A testing 9-hole parkland course in open countryside.
9 holes, 4566yds, Par 66, SSS 61, Course record 69.
Visitors	welcome by arrangement.
Green Fees	£5 per day (£7 weekends and bank holidays).
Facilities	⊗ ⓑ ☂ ♀ ♨ ▾ ℓ Tim Hutton.
Leisure	trolley for hire, putting green, practice area.
Location	6m NE of Grantham on A607
Hotel	★★★ 64% Kings Hotel, North Pde, GRANTHAM ☎ 01476 590800 22rm(21 ⇆ ♠)

GRIMSBY
Map 08 TA21

Grimsby Littlecoates Rd DN34 4LU ☎ 01472 342630
Parkland course with easy walking.
18 holes, 6098yds, Par 70, SSS 69, Course record 66.
Club membership 730.
Visitors	contact in advance.
Societies	by prior arrangement with secretary.
Green Fees	£25 per day; £18 per 18 holes (£25 per round weekends).
Facilities	⊗ ⅶ ⓑ ☂ ♀ ♨ ℓ Richard Smith.
Leisure	trolley for hire, putting green, practice area.
Location	W side of town centre off A1136
Hotel	B Forte Posthouse Grimsby, Littlecoates Rd, GRIMSBY ☎ 01472 350295 52 ⇆ ♠

HORNCASTLE
Map 08 TF26

Horncastle West Ashby LN9 5PP ☎ 01507 526800
Heathland course with many water hazards and bunkers; very
challenging. There is a 25-bay floodlit driving range.
18 holes, 5717yds, Par 70, SSS 70, Course record 71.
Par 3: 9 holes, 4025yds, Par 27, SSS 27.
Club membership 250.
Visitors	dress code must be adhered to, welcome anytime, may contact in advance.
Societies	apply in writing or telephone in advance.
Green Fees	£18 per day; £12 per round (£20/£15 weekends and bank holidays).
Facilities	⊗ ⅶ ⓑ ☂ ♀ ♨ ▾ ℓ E C Wright.
Leisure	fishing, trolley for hire, driving range, putting green, practice area.
Location	Off A158 Lincoln/Skegness road at Edlington
Hotel	★★ 65% Admiral Rodney Hotel, North St, HORNCASTLE ☎ 01507 523131 32 ⇆ ♠

IMMINGHAM
Map 08 TA11

Immingham St Andrews Ln, off Church Ln DN40 2EU
☎ 01469 575298
Parkland course with some water hazards and a public
footpath across holes 1, 2 & 8.
18 holes, 6191yds, Par 71, SSS 69.
Club membership 700.
Visitors	telephone in advance.
Societies	telephone (am) to arrange date.
Green Fees	£20 per day; £15 per round (£20 weekend and bank holidays).
Facilities	⊗ ⅶ by prior arrangement ⓑ ☂ ♀ ♨ ☎ ▾ ℓ Geoffrey Norton.
Leisure	trolley for hire, putting green, practice area.
Location	7m NW off Grimsby
Hotel	★★ 63% Old Chapel Hotel & Restaurant, 50 Station Rd, IMMINGHAM ☎ 01469 572377 14 ⇆ ♠

LACEBY
Map 08 TA20

Manor Barton St, Laceby Manor DN37 7EA
☎ 01472 873468
Upgraded to 18 holes in the summer of 1995. The first nine
holes as a parkland course, all the fairways lined with young
trees. The newly created second nine are mainly open
fairways. The 18th hole green is surrounded by water.
18 holes, 6354yds, Par 71, SSS 70.
Club membership 470.
Visitors	welcome but requested to book tee times.
Societies	telephone in advance.
Green Fees	£18 per day; £12 per round; Twilight £8.

Facilities ♖ ♙ ♗ 🖾
Leisure fishing, solarium, trolley for hire, driving range, putting green, practice area.
Location A18 Barton St - Laceby/Louth
Hotel ★★★ 63% Oaklands Hotel, Barton St, LACEBY ☎ 01472 872248 46 ⇥ ♞

LINCOLN   Map 08 SK97

Canwick Park Canwick Park, Washingborough Rd LN4 1EF ☎ 01522 522166 & 542912
Parkland course. Testing 14th hole (par 3).
18 holes, 6257yds, Par 70, SSS 70, Course record 66.
Club membership 700.
Visitors with member only Sat also Sun before 3pm.
Societies weekdays only by prior arrangement in writing.
Green Fees £19 per day; £13.50 per round Tue-Fri, £9.50 per round Mon.
Facilities ⊗ ⚏ ⅃ ♖ ♙ ♗ 🖾 ⚑ ⅋ S Williamson.
Leisure trolley for hire, putting green, practice area.
Location 1m E of Lincoln
Hotel B Forte Posthouse Lincoln, Eastgate, LINCOLN ☎ 01522 520341 70 ⇥ ♞

Carholme Carholme Rd LN1 1SE ☎ 01522 523725
Parkland course where prevailing west winds can add interest. Good views.
18 holes, 6243yds, Par 71, SSS 70, Course record 69.
Club membership 825.
Visitors must contact in advance. Weekends may no play before 2.30pm.
Societies apply in writing.
Green Fees £18 per day; £14 per round (£17 per round weekends and bank holidays,when available).
Facilities ⊗ ⚏ ⅃ ♖ ♙ ♗ 🖾 ⚑ ⅋ Gary Leslie.
Leisure trolley for hire, practice area.
Location 1m W of city centre on A57
Hotel ★★★★ 63% The White Hart, Bailgate, LINCOLN ☎ 01522 526222 48 ⇥

LOUTH   Map 08 TF38

Louth Crowtree Ln LN11 9LJ ☎ 01507 603681
Undulating parkland course, fine views.
18 holes, 6424yds, Par 72, SSS 71.
Club membership 700.
Visitors must contact in advance to make sure tee is not reserved for competition.
Societies a booking form will be sent on request.
Green Fees £20 day; £16 per round (£30/£25 weekends and bank holidays).
Facilities ⊗ ⚏ ⅃ ♖ ♙ ♗ 🖾 ⚑ ⅋ A Blundell.
Leisure squash, motorised carts for hire, buggies for hire, trolley for hire, putting green, practice area.
Location W side of Louth between A157/A153
Hotel ★★★ 62% Beaumont Hotel, 66 Victoria Rd, LOUTH ☎ 01507 605005 17 ⇥ ♞

MARKET RASEN   Map 08 TF18

Market Rasen & District Legsby Rd LN8 3DZ ☎ 01673 842319
Picturesque, well-wooded heathland course, easy walking, breezy with becks forming natural hazards. Good views of Lincolnshire Wolds.

18 holes, 6045yds, Par 70, SSS 69, Course record 65.
Club membership 565.
Visitors must play with member at weekends and must contact in advance.
Societies Tue & Fri only; must contact in advance.
Green Fees £24 per day; £16 per round.
Facilities ⊗ ⚏ ⅃ ♖ ♙ ♗ 🖾 ⚑ ⅋ A M Chester.
Leisure trolley for hire, putting, practice area.
Location 1m E, off A46
Hotel ★★★ 62% Beaumont Hotel, 66 Victoria Rd, LOUTH ☎ 01507 605005 17 ⇥ ♞

Market Rasen Race Course (Golf Course) Legsby Rd LN8 3EA ☎ 01673 843434 & 842307
This is a public course set within the bounds of Market Rasen race course - the entire racing area is out of bounds. The longest hole is the 4th at 454yards with the race course providing a hazard over the whole length of the drive.
9 holes, 2532yds, Par 32.
Visitors closed racedays apart from evening meetings when open until noon.
Societies telephone in advance to arrange.
Green Fees £6 per 18 holes; £4 per 9 holes (£8/£5 weekends).
Facilities ⅋
Location 2m E of Market Rasen
Hotel ★★★ 62% Beaumont Hotel, 66 Victoria Rd, LOUTH ☎ 01507 605005 17 ⇥ ♞

NORMANBY   Map 08 SE81

Normanby Hall Normanby Park DN15 9HU ☎ 01724 720226
Parkland course.
18 holes, 6548yds, Par 72, SSS 71.
Club membership 770.
Visitors book in advance by contacting professional.
Societies must contact in advance: Manager, Scunthorpe Leisure Centre, Carlton St, Scunthorpe, DN15 6TA.
Green Fees £16 per day; £10 per round (£12 per round weekends & bank holidays). Twilight ticket £5 (£6 weekends).
Facilities ⊗ ⚏ ♖ ♙ ♗ 🖾 ⚑ ⅋ Christopher Mann.
Leisure motorised carts for hire, buggies for hire, trolley for hire, putting green, practice area.
Location 3m N of Scunthorpe adj to Normanby Hall
Hotel ★★★ 62% Royal Hotel, Doncaster Rd, SCUNTHORPE ☎ 01724 282233 33 ⇥ ♞

SCUNTHORPE   Map 08 SE81

Ashby Decoy Burringham Rd DN17 2AB ☎ 01724 866561 (Office) & 868972 (Pro)
Very tight parkland course.
18 holes, 6281yds, Par 71, SSS 71, Course record 65.
Club membership 650.
Visitors may not play Sun or Tue. Sat with member only.
Societies apply in advance.
Green Fees £21 per day; £16 per round.
Facilities ⊗ ⚏ ⅃ ♖ ♙ ♗ 🖾 ⚑ ⅋ A Miller.
Leisure putting, practice area.
Location 2.5m SW on B1450 nr Asda Superstore
Hotel ★★★ 62% Royal Hotel, Doncaster Rd, SCUNTHORPE ☎ 01724 282233 33 ⇥ ♞

Forest Pines - Briggate Lodge Inn Hotel Ermine St, Broughton DN20 0AQ ☎ 01652 650770 & 650756
Set in 185 acres of mature parkland and open heathland and constructed in a similar design to that of Wentworth or Sunningdale, Forest Pines offers three challenging 9-hole courses - Forest, Pines and Beeches. Any combination can be played. Facilities include a 17-bay driving range and a spacious clubhouse.
Forest Course: 9 holes, 3291yds, Par 35.
Pines Course: 9 holes, 3591yds, Par 37.
Beeches: 9 holes, 3102yds, Par 35.
Visitors must contact in advance.
Societies telephone in advance.
Green Fees £35 per day; £25 per round (£40/£30 weekends and bank holidays). 9 holes £15.
Facilities ⊗ ⊪ ⓑ ♕ ♀ ⚲ 凾 ☜ ☝ ⓕ David Edwards.
Leisure motorised carts for hire, buggies for hire, trolley for hire, floodlit driving range, putting green, practice area.
Location 200yds from junct 4 M180
Hotel ★★★ 68% Briggate Lodge Inn, Ermine St, Broughton, SCUNTHORPE
☎ 01652 650770 50 ⇔ ⓡ

Holme Hall Holme Ln, Bottesford DN16 3RF
☎ 01724 862078
Heathland course with sandy subsoil. Easy walking.
18 holes, 6475yds, Par 71, SSS 71.
Club membership 724.
Visitors must play with member at weekends & bank holidays. Must contact in advance.
Societies must contact in advance.
Green Fees not confirmed.
Facilities ♀ ⚲ 凾 ☝ ⓕ Richard McKiernan.
Leisure putting, trolley hire, practice area.
Location 3m SE
Hotel ★★★ 62% Royal Hotel, Doncaster Rd, SCUNTHORPE
☎ 01724 282233 33 ⇔ ⓡ

Kingsway Kingsway DN15 7ER ☎ 01724 840945
Parkland course with many par 3's.
9 holes, 1915yds, Par 29, Course record 28.
Visitors no restrictions.
Green Fees £2.95 per 9 holes (£3.45 weekends).
Facilities ⚲ 凾 ☝ ⓕ Chris Mann.
Leisure trolley for hire, putting green, practice area, facilities for handicapped.
Location W side of town centre off A18
Hotel ★★★ 62% Royal Hotel, Doncaster Rd, SCUNTHORPE
☎ 01724 282233 33 ⇔ ⓡ

SKEGNESS　　　　　　　　　Map 09 TF56

North Shore Hotel & Golf Club North Shore Rd PE25 1DN
☎ 01754 763298
A half-links, half-parkland course designed by James Braid in 1910. Easy walking and good sea views.
18 holes, 6200yds, Par 71, SSS 71, Course record 67.
Club membership 450.
Visitors tee times must be booked.
Societies write or telephone in advance.
Green Fees £24 per day; £17 per round (£35/£25 weekdays).
Facilities ⊗ ⊪ ⓑ ♕ ♀ ⚲ 凾 ⇔ ⓕ J Cornelius.
Leisure trolley for hire, practice area.

Location 1m N of town centre off A52
Hotel ★★ 62% North Shore Hotel, North Shore Rd, SKEGNESS
☎ 01754 763298 30 ⇔ ⓡAnnexe3 ⇔ ⓡ

Seacroft Drummond Rd, Seacroft PE25 3AU
☎ 01754 763020
A typical seaside links with flattish fairways separated by low ridges and good greens. Easy to walk round. To the east are sandhills leading to the shore. Southward lies 'Gibraltar Point Nature Reserve'.
18 holes, 6479yds, Par 71, SSS 71, Course record 67.
Club membership 590.
Visitors must be a member of an affiliated golf club.
Societies contact in advance.
Green Fees £35 per day; £25 per round (£40/£30 weekends & bank holidays).
Facilities ⊗ ⊪ ⓑ ♕ ♀ ⚲ 凾 ⓕ Robin Lawie.
Leisure trolley for hire, putting green, practice area.
Location S side of town centre
Hotel ★★★ 62% Crown Hotel, Drummond Rd, Seacroft, SKEGNESS
☎ 01754 610760 27 ⇔ ⓡ

SLEAFORD　　　　　　　　　Map 08 TF04

Sleaford Willoughby Rd NG34 8PL ☎ 01529 488273
Inland links-type course, moderately wooded and fairly flat.
18 holes, 6443yds, Par 72, SSS 71, Course record 66.
Club membership 650.
Visitors may not play Sun in winter.
Societies telephone enquiry to fixture secretary.
Green Fees £21 per round/day (£28 weekends & bank holidays).
Facilities ⊗ ⊪ ⓑ ♕ ♀ ⚲ 凾 ⓕ James Wilson.
Leisure trolley for hire, putting green, practice area.
Location 2m W of Sleaford, off A153
Hotel ★★★ 62% Angel & Royal Hotel, High St, GRANTHAM ☎ 01476 65816 30 ⇔ ⓡ

SOUTH KYME　　　　　　　Map 08 TF14

South Kyme Skinners Ln LN4 4AT
☎ 01526 861113
A challenging fenland course described as an 'Inland links'. More water hazards, trees and fairway hazards added during 1995 so the course is improving all the time.
18 holes, 6597yds, Par 71, SSS 71, Course record 67 or 6 holes, 895yds.
Club membership 250.
Visitors telephone for advise on tee times.
Societies telephone for booking form.
Green Fees £15 per day; £10 per round (£18/£12 weekends). Fees due to be revised.
Facilities ⊗ ⊪ ⓑ ♕ ♀ ⚲ 凾 ☝ ⓕ Peter Chamberlain.
Leisure trolley for hire, putting green, practice area.
Location Off B1395 in South Kyme village
Hotel B Forte Travelodge, Holdingham, SLEAFORD
☎ 01529 414752 40 ⇔ ⓡ

Entries with a shaded background identify courses that are considered to be particularly interesting

WOODHALL SPA

WOODHALL SPA *Lincs* ☎ 01526 352511   Map 08 TF16

John Ingham writes: Opened in 1905 and regarded as the finest inland course in the British Isles, it has been purchased for £8 million by the English Golf Union to use as a headquarters. Many miles from the nearest towns, the heathland course is covered with silver birch and the fairways are made up of dry, springy turf and several big competitions have been played here.

In the 1960s I played in the Central England Mixed Foursomes and enjoyed the hospitality of the then owner, Neil Hotchkin, who had somehow helped create a wonderful clubhouse atmosphere, with country people behind the bar, giving the place a friendly glow. It remains the same today.

Although 18 miles south-east of Lincoln, I now understand it is wise to telephone to see whether the course can receive visitors for the day. If the answer is 'yes' then be prepared for a treat. Tony Jacklin brought his friend Tom Weiskopf to play and the American was thrilled with the shot-making that is required.

Designed by the great Harry Vardon, the course is a pleasant and fairly flat walk but because of the clever shaping of the holes, and the delightful isolation of almost each hole, hidden like a corridor through a stately home, the course becomes a most private place for a friendly four-ball. Measuring 6942 yards, it doesn't appear that long because of the fast-running fairways. The club don't like men visitors to have a handicap above 20 or the women above 30 and since the course is renowned for its huge bunkers, it is to the advantage of players to know how to escape from sand traps. In many ways, Woodhall Spa is like Sunningdale and as those who know that course would readily admit, there is no greater compliment.

Visitors	must be a member of a golf club affilliated to the appropriate Golf Union, max handicap-gentlemen 20, ladies 30. Handicap certificate must be produced
Societies	must book in advance
Green fees	£35 per round, £55 per day.
Facilities	⊗ ⊤┤ ┡ ⬛ ♀ ⚒ 🖻 ⌇ (C C Elliot) driving range putting green, practice area, trollies
Leisure	pitch & putt course
Location	The Broadway LN10 6PU (NE side of village B1191)

18 holes, 6947yards, Par 73 SSS 73
Course record 67

WHERE TO STAY NEARBY

HOTELS:

WOODHALL SPA
★★★ 65% Petwood House Hotel, Stixwould Rd ☎ 01526 352411. 46 ⇆ ℞

★★★ 63% Golf Hotel, The Broadway ☎ 01526 353535. 50 (14 ℞ 36 ⇆ ℞)

SPALDING

Map 08 TF22

Spalding Surfleet PE11 4EA ☎ 01775 680386 & 680234
A pretty, well laid-out course in a fenland area. The River
Glen runs beside the 1st and 2nd holes, and streams, ponds
and new tree plantings add to the variety of this well-
maintained course.
18 holes, 6478yds, Par 72, SSS 71.
Club membership 750.

Visitors	must contact in advance.
Societies	write to the secretary, Societies on Thu all day and Tue pm.
Green Fees	£24 per day (£30 weekends & bank holidays).
Facilities	⊗ ℳ ┗ ♥ ♀ ♨ ☎ ℓ John Spencer.
Leisure	putting green, practice area.
Location	4m N of Spaldingadjacent to A16
Hotel	★★ 60% Cley Hall Hotel, 22 High St, SPALDING ☎ 01775 725157 4 ⇌ ℝAnnexe7 ℝ

STAMFORD

Map 08 TF00

Burghley Park St Martins PE9 3JX
☎ 01780 62100 due to change to 762100
Open parkland course with superb greens, many new trees,
ponds and bunkers. Situated in the grounds of Burghley
House.
18 holes, 6238yds, Par 70, SSS 70, Course record 64.
Club membership 805.

Visitors	with member only weekends. Must contact in advance & have handicap certificate.
Societies	prior arrangement in writing, preferably by 1st Dec previous year.
Green Fees	£20 per day weekdays only.
Facilities	⊗ ℳ ┗ ♥ ♀ ♨ ☎ ℓ Glenn Davies.
Leisure	motorised carts for hire, buggies for hire, trolley for hire, putting green, practice area.
Location	1m S of town on B1081
Hotel	★★★ 75% George of Stamford Hotel, St Martins, STAMFORD ☎ 01780 55171 47 ⇌ ℝ

STOKE ROCHFORD

Map 08 SK92

Stoke Rochford NG33 5EW ☎ 01476 530275
Parkland course designed by C. Turner.
18 holes, 6251yds, Par 70, SSS 70, Course record 65.
Club membership 525.

Visitors	must contact in advance, restricted to 9am weekdays, 10.30am weekends & bank holidays.
Societies	contact one year in advance, in writing.
Green Fees	not confirmed.
Facilities	♀ ♨ ☎ ℓ Angus Dow.
Leisure	putting,cart/buggy/trolley hire.
Location	Off A1 5m S of Grantham
Hotel	★★★ 64% Kings Hotel, North Pde, GRANTHAM ☎ 01476 590800 22rm(21 ⇌ ℝ)

> A golf course name printed in ***bold italics***
> means we have been unable to verify
> information with the club's management for
> the current year

SUTTON BRIDGE

Map 09 TF42

Sutton Bridge New Rd PE12 9RQ ☎ 01406 350323
Parkland course.
9 holes, 5724yds, Par 70, SSS 68.
Club membership 350.

Visitors	may not play competition days, weekends & bank holidays, must contact in advance.
Societies	write or telephone in advance.
Green Fees	£15 per day.
Facilities	⊗ ℳ ┗ ♥ ♀ ♨ ☎ ℓ ℓ L Rawlings.
Leisure	trolley for hire, putting green, practice area.
Location	E side of village off A17
Hotel	★★★ 65% The Duke's Head, Tuesday Market Pl, KING'S LYNN ☎ 01553 774996 71 ⇌ ℝ

SUTTON ON SEA

Map 09 TF58

Sandilands Roman Bank LN12 2RJ ☎ 01507 441432
Flat links course on the sea shore.
18 holes, 5995yds, Par 70, SSS 69.
Club membership 230.

Visitors	no restrictions.
Societies	telephone in advance.
Green Fees	£20 per day; £15 per round (£20 per round weekends & bank holidays).
Facilities	⊗ ℳ ♥ ♀ ♨ ☎ ☞ ⋈
Leisure	grass tennis courts, trolley for hire, putting green, practice area.
Location	1.5m S off A52
Hotel	★★★ 68% Grange & Links Hotel, Sea Ln, Sandilands, MABLETHORPE ☎ 01507 441334 24 ⇌ ℝ

TORKSEY

Map 08 SK87

Lincoln LN1 2EG ☎ 01427 718210
A testing inland course with quick-drying sandy subsoil and
easy walking.
18 holes, 6438yds, Par 71, SSS 71, Course record 66.
Club membership 650.

Visitors	accepted on non event days.
Societies	apply in writing or telephone.
Green Fees	£28 per day; £22 per round.
Facilities	⊗ ℳ ┗ ♥ ♀ ♨ ☎ ℓ Ashley Carter.
Leisure	trolley for hire, putting green, practice field.
Location	SW side of village
Hotel	★★★★ 63% The White Hart, Bailgate, LINCOLN ☎ 01522 526222 48 ⇌

Millfield Sandfield Farm, Laughterton LN1 2LB
☎ 01427 718255
There is an unusual set-up at Millfield with a 15 hole 4,201
yard Family course on which anyone can play, as well as a 9-
hole Par 3 and an 18-hole course of nearly 6,000 yards. Due
to its location in flat Lincolnshire the courses are affected by
winds, which change every day.
18 holes, 5974yds, Par 69, SSS 69.
Family 15: 15 holes, 4201yds, Par 56.

Visitors	18 hole; shoes must be worn, no jeans etc. Family 15 hole no restrictions.
Societies	welcome on weekdays.
Green Fees	not confirmed.

Facilities ⛏ 🖻 🖾
Location On A1133 1m N of A57
Hotel ★★★★ 63% The White Hart, Bailgate,
LINCOLN
☎ 01522 526222 48 ⇌

WOODHALL SPA See page 145

WOODTHORPE   Map 09 TF48

Woodthorpe Hall LN13 0DD
☎ 01507 463664
Parkland course.
18 holes, 5010yds, Par 66, SSS 65.
Club membership 400.
Visitors contact in advance for weekends.
Societies Mon-Fri, telephone in first instance at least one
month prior to visit.
Green Fees £10 per day.
Facilities ⊗ ♨ ⅃ ⚑ ♀ 🖻 ✨ 🖾
Leisure fishing, trolley for hire.
Location 3m NNW of Alford on B1373
Hotel ★★★ 68% Grange & Links Hotel, Sea Ln,
Sandilands, MABLETHORPE
☎ 01507 441334 24 ⇌ ℝ

LONDON

Courses within the London Postal District area (ie those that have London Postcodes - W1, SW1 etc) are listed here in postal district order commencing East then North, South and West. Courses outside the London Postal area, but within Greater London are to be found listed under the county of **Greater London** in the gazetteer (see page 76).

E4 CHINGFORD

Royal Epping Forest Forest Approach, Chingford E4 7AZ
☎ 0181 529 2195
Woodland course. 'Red' garments must be worn.
18 holes, 6342yds, Par 71, SSS 70.
Club membership 400.
Visitors booking system in operation.
Societies must contact secretary in advance.
Green Fees £9.50 per round (£13 weekends).
Facilities 🖤 ♀ (members only) 🖻 ✨
ℓ R Gowers/J Francis.
Leisure trolley for hire.
Location 300 yds S of Chingford Station
Hotel ★★★ 65% Epping Forest Moat House, Oak
Hill, WOODFORD GREEN
☎ 0181 787 9988 99 ⇌ ℝ

West Essex Bury Rd, Sewardstonebury E4 7QL
☎ 0181 529 7558
Testing parkland course within Epping Forest. Notable holes
are 8th (par 4), 16th (par 4), 18th (par 5).
18 holes, 6289yds, Par 71, SSS 70.
Club membership 645.
Visitors must contact in advance & have handicap
certificate but may not play on Tue morning,
Thu afternoon & weekends.
Societies must contact in advance.
Green Fees not confirmed.
Facilities ♀ ⛏ 🖻 ℓ Robert Joyce.
Leisure buggies for hire.
Location Off N Circular Rd at Chingford on M25
Hotel ★★ 62% Roebuck Hotel, North End,
BUCKHURST HILL
☎ 0181 505 4636 29 ⇌ ℝ

E11 LEYTONSTONE

Wanstead Overton Dr, Wanstead E11 2LW
☎ 0181 989 3938
A flat, picturesque parkland course with many trees and
shrubs and providing easy walking. The par 3, 16th, involves
driving across a lake.
18 holes, 6004yds, Par 69, SSS 69, Course record 62.
Club membership 600.
Visitors must contact in advance and may only play Mon,
Tue & Fri.
Societies by prior arrangement.
Green Fees £25 per day.
Facilities ⊗ ♨ ⅃ ⚑ ♀ ⛏ 🖻 ℓ David Hawkins.
Leisure fishing, trolley for hire, putting green, practice
area.
Location From central London A11 NE to Wanstead
Hotel ★★★ 65% Epping Forest Moat House, Oak
Hill, WOODFORD GREEN
☎ 0181 787 9988 99 ⇌ ℝ

N2 EAST FINCHLEY

Hampstead Winnington Rd N2 0TU ☎ 0181 455 0203
Undulating parkland course.
18 holes, 5822yds, Par 68, SSS 68.
Club membership 526.
Visitors restricted Tue and weekends.
Societies small societies by prior arrangements.
Green Fees £30 all day; £25 per 18 holes (£32 per 18 holes
weekends and bank holidays).
Facilities ⊗ ⅃ ⚑ ♀ ⛏ 🖻 ℓ Peter Brown.
Leisure trolley for hire, putting green, practice area.
Location Off Hampstead Lane
Hotel B Forte Posthouse Hampstead, 215 Haverstock
Hill, LONDON ☎ 0171 794 8121 140 ⇌ ℝ

N6 HIGHGATE

Highgate Denewood Rd N6 4AH ☎ 0181 340 1906
Parkland course.
18 holes, 5985yds, Par 69, SSS 69, Course record 66.
Club membership 800.
Visitors may not play Wed & weekends.
Societies by arrangement.
Green Fees not confirmed.
Facilities ♀ ⛏ 🖻 ✨ ℓ Robin Turner.   ▶

Hotel ★★★★ 69% Marriott Hotel, 128 King Henry's Rd, LONDON ☎ 0171 722 7711 303 ⇥ ♞

N9 LOWER EDMONTON

Lee Valley Leisure Picketts Lock Sports Centre, Meridian Way, Edmonton N9 0AS ☎ 0181 803 3611
Tricky municipal parkland course with some narrow fairways and the River Lea providing a natural hazard.
18 holes, 4902yds, Par 66, SSS 64, Course record 66.
Club membership 200.
Visitors may telephone for advance bookings.
Societies must telephone in advance.
Green Fees £10 per round (£13 weekends).
Facilities ⊗ ⏃ ▙ ♥ ♀ ⚲ 🏠 ⚐ ⛳ R Gerken.
Leisure heated indoor swimming pool, squash, sauna, solarium, gymnasium, trolley for hire, floodlit driving range, putting green, practice area.
Hotel ★★★ 57% Enfield Hotel, 52 Rowantree Rd, ENFIELD ☎ 0181 366 3511 34 ⇥ ♞

N14 SOUTHGATE

Trent Park Bramley Rd, Oakwood N14 4UW ☎ 0181 366 7432
Parkland course set in 150 acres of green belt area. Seven holes played across Merryhills brook. Testing holes are 2nd (423 yds) over brook, 190 yds from the tee, and up to plateau green; 7th (463 yds) dog-leg, over brook, par 4.
18 holes, 6085yds, Par 70, SSS 69, Course record 68.
Club membership 1200.
Visitors must contact 7 days in advance.
Societies must telephone in advance.
Green Fees £10.60 (£13.50 weekends).
Facilities ⊗ ⏃ ▙ ♥ ♀ ⚲ 🏠 ⚐ ⛳ Mike Plumbridge.
Leisure trolley for hire, floodlit driving range, putting green.
Location Opposite Oakwood underground station
Hotel ★★★★♨ 69% West Lodge Park Hotel, Cockfosters Rd, HADLEY WOOD ☎ 0181 440 8311 43 ⇥ ♞Annexe2 ⇥ ♞

N20 WHETSTONE

North Middlesex The Manor House, Friern Barnet Ln, Whetstone N20 0NL ☎ 0181 445 1604 & 0181 445 3060
Short parkland course renowned for its tricky greens.
18 holes, 5625yds, Par 69, SSS 67, Course record 64.
Club membership 580.
Visitors advisable to contact in advance, contact professional shop.
Societies bookings in advance, winter offers & summer packages by prior arrangement.
Green Fees £27.50 per day; £22 per round (£30 per round, £25 after 3pm, weekends).
Facilities ⊗ ⏃ ▙ ♥ ♀ ⚲ 🏠 ⚐ ⛳ Steve Roberts.
Leisure trolley for hire, putting green.
Hotel ★★★ 74% Edgwarebury Hotel, Barnet Ln, ELSTREE ☎ 0181 953 8227 47 ⇥ ♞

South Herts Links Dr, Totteridge N20 8QU ☎ 0181 445 2035
An open undulating parkland course officially in Hertfordshire, but now in a London postal area. It is,

perhaps, most famous for the fact that two of the greatest of all British professionals, Harry Vardon and Dai Rees, CBE were professionals at the club. The course is testing, over rolling fairways, especially in the prevailing south-west wind.
18 holes, 6432yds, Par 72, SSS 71, Course record 65.
Club membership 850.
Visitors must be members of recognised golf club & have handicap certificate of 24 or less.
Societies Wed-Fri only, must apply in writing.
Green Fees £30 per round/day.
Facilities ⊗ ⏃ ▙ ♥ ♀ ⚲ 🏠 ⚐ ⛳ Bobby Mitchell.
Leisure motorised carts for hire, buggies for hire, trolley for hire, putting green, practice area.
Hotel B Forte Posthouse South Mimms, SOUTH MIMMS ☎ 01707 643311 120 ⇥ ♞

N21 WINCHMORE HILL

Bush Hill Park Bush Hill, Winchmore Hill N21 2BU ☎ 0181 360 5738
Pleasant parkland course surrounded by trees.
18 holes, 5809yds, Par 70, SSS 68.
Club membership 700.
Visitors may not play Wed mornings or weekends & bank holidays.
Societies by arrangement.
Green Fees not confirmed.
Facilities ♀ ⚲ 🏠 ⛳
Hotel ★★★ 57% Enfield Hotel, 52 Rowantree Rd, ENFIELD ☎ 0181 366 3511 34 ⇥ ♞

N22 WOOD GREEN

Muswell Hill Rhodes Av, Wood Green N22 4UT ☎ 0181 888 1764
Narrow parkland course featuring numerous water hazards.
18 holes, 6438yds, Par 71, SSS 71, Course record 65.
Club membership 560.
Visitors must contact in advance, restricted weekends.
Societies apply in writing or telephone.
Green Fees telephone for current rates.
Facilities ⊗ ⏃ ▙ ♥ ♀ ⚲ 🏠 ⚐ ⛳ David Wilton.
Leisure motorised carts for hire, buggies for hire, trolley for hire, putting green, practice area.
Location Off N Circular Rd at Bounds Green
Hotel ★★★ 67% Raglan Hall Hotel, 8-12 Queens Ave, Muswell Hill, LONDON ☎ 0181 883 9836 46 ⇥ ♞

NW7 MILL HILL

Finchley Nether Court, Frith Ln, Mill Hill NW7 1PU ☎ 0181 346 2436 & 346 5086
Easy walking on wooded parkland course.
18 holes, 6411yds, Par 72, SSS 71.
Club membership 500.
Visitors must contact in advance.
Societies must apply in writing.
Green Fees £30 per day; £24 per round (£36/£30 weekends and bank holidays).
Facilities ⊗ ▙ ♥ ♀ ⚲ 🏠 ⚐ ⛳ David Brown.
Leisure motorised carts for hire, buggies for hire, trolley for hire, putting green.

Location Near Mill Hill East Tube Station
Hotel ★★★ 74% Edgwarebury Hotel, Barnet Ln,
ELSTREE ☎ 0181 953 8227 47 ⇔ ♠

Hendon Sanders Ln, Devonshire Rd, Mill Hill NW7 1DG
☎ 0181 346 6023
Easy walking, parkland course with a good variety of trees,
and providing testing golf.
18 holes, 6266yds, Par 70, SSS 70.
Club membership 540.
Visitors must contact in advance. Restricted weekends &
bank holidays.
Societies Tue-Fri. Must contact in advance.
Green Fees £30 per day; £25 per round (£35 per round
weekends & bank holidays).
Facilities ⊗ ℳ by prior arrangement ♨ ☕ ♀ ♣ ♠ ♈
♦ Stuart Murray.
Leisure trolley for hire, putting green, practice area.
Location 10 mins from junc 2 of M1 southbound
Hotel ★★★ 74% Edgwarebury Hotel, Barnet Ln,
ELSTREE ☎ 0181 953 8227 47 ⇔ ♠

Mill Hill 100 Barnet Way, Mill Hill NW7 3AL
☎ 0181 959 2339
Undulating parkland course with all holes separated by good
tree and shrub cover.
18 holes, 6247yds, Par 69, SSS 70, Course record 65.
Club membership 550.
Visitors restricted weekends & bank holidays. Must
contact in advance.
Societies must contact in advance.
Green Fees not confirmed.
Facilities ♀ ♣ ♠ ♈ ♦ Alex Daniel.
Location On A1 S bound carriageway
Hotel ★★★ 74% Edgwarebury Hotel, Barnet Ln,
ELSTREE ☎ 0181 953 8227 47 ⇔ ♠

SE9 ELTHAM

Eltham Warren Bexley Rd, Eltham SE9 2PE
☎ 0181 850 4477 & 0181 850 1166
Parkland course with narrow fairways and small greens. The
course is bounded by the A210 on one side and Eltham Park
on the other.
9 holes, 5840yds, Par 69, SSS 68, Course record 66.
Club membership 440.
Visitors may not play at weekends. Must contact in
advance and have a handicap certificate.
Societies must book in advance. Deposit required.
Green Fees £25 per day.
Facilities ⊗ ℳ ♨ ☕ ♀ ♣ ♠ ♦ Ross Taylor.
Leisure trolley for hire, putting green, practice area,
snooker.
Hotel ★★★ 69% Bromley Court Hotel, Bromley Hill,
BROMLEY ☎ 0181 464 5011 118 ⇔ ♠

Royal Blackheath Court Rd SE9 5AF
☎ 0181 850 1795
A pleasant, parkland course of great character as befits
the antiquity of the Club; the clubhouse dates from the
17th century. Many great trees survive and there are two
ponds. The 18th requires a pitch to the green over a thick
clipped hedge, which also crosses the front of the 1st tee.
18 holes, 6219yds, Par 70, SSS 70.
Club membership 720.

Visitors must contact in advance but may play mid-
week only, handicap certificate is required.
Societies must apply in writing.
Green Fees £40 per day; £30 per round.
Facilities ⊗ ♨ ☕ ♀ ♣ ♠ ♈ ♦ Ian McGregor.
Leisure motorised carts for hire, buggies for hire,
trolley for hire, putting green, golf museum.
Hotel ★★★ 69% Bromley Court Hotel, Bromley
Hill, BROMLEY
☎ 0181 464 5011 118 ⇔ ♠

SE18 WOOLWICH
Map 05 TQ47

Shooters Hill Eaglesfield Rd, Shooters Hill SE18 3DA
☎ 0181 854 6368
Hilly and wooded parkland course with good view and
natural hazards.
18 holes, 5721 yds, Par 69, SSS 68, Course record 63.
Club membership 900.
Visitors must have handicap certificate and be a member
of a recognised golf club but may not play at
weekends.
Societies Tue & Thu only, by arrangement.
Green Fees £25 per day; £20 per round.
Facilities ⊗ ℳ ♨ ☕ ♀ ♣ ♠ ♦ Michael Ridge.
Leisure motorised carts for hire, buggies for hire, trolley
for hire, putting green.
Location Shooters Hill Rd from Blackheath
Hotel B Forte Posthouse Bexley, Black Prince
Interchange, Southwold Rd, BEXLEY
☎ 01322 526900 103 ⇔ ♠

SE21 DULWICH

Dulwich & Sydenham Hill Grange Ln, College Rd
SE21 7LH ☎ 0181 693 3961 & 693 8491
Parkland course overlooking London. Hilly with narrow
fairways.
18 holes, 6008yds, Par 69, SSS 69, Course record 63.
Club membership 850.
Visitors must contact in advance and have a handicap
certificate. May not play weekends or bank
holidays.
Societies must telephone in advance & confirm in writing.
Green Fees £30 per day; £25 per round.
Facilities ⊗ ℳ ♨ ☕ ♀ ♣ ♠ ♈ ♦ David Baillie.
Leisure motorised carts for hire, buggies for hire, trolley
for hire, putting green, practice area.
Hotel ★★★ 69% Bromley Court Hotel, Bromley Hill,
BROMLEY ☎ 0181 464 5011 118 ⇔ ♠

SE22 EAST DULWICH

Aquarius Marmora Rd, Honor Oak, Off Forest Hill Rd
SE22 0RY ☎ 0181 693 1626
Course laid-out on two levels around and over covered
reservoir; hazards include vents and bollards.
9 holes, 5246yds, Par 66, SSS 66, Course record 66.
Club membership 350.
Visitors must be accompanied by member and have a
handicap certificate.
Green Fees £10 per day/round.
Facilities ⊗ ℳ by prior arrangement ♨ ☕ ♀ ♣ ♠
♦ Frederick Private. ▶

Hotel   ★★★ 69% Bromley Court Hotel, Bromley Hill,
BROMLEY ☎ 0181 464 5011 118 ⇌ 🐾

SE28 WOOLWICH

Riverside Summerton Way, Thamesmead SE28 8PP
☎ 0181 310 7975
A delightful undulating course with a mix of mature trees,
new trees and water hazards. The 4th hole is a challenging
515yards down a narrow fairway.
9 holes, 5462yds, Par 70, SSS 66.
Club membership 150.
Visitors   no restrictions.
Societies   book by telephone or in writing.
Green Fees £8.50 per 18 holes; £5 per 9 holes (£10.50/£6.50
weekends).
Facilities   ⊗ 🍴 🛒 ⛳ ⚐ 🏌 Paul Jolner.
Leisure   driving range, putting green.
Hotel   ★★ 67% Bardon Lodge Hotel, Stratheden Rd,
LONDON ☎ 0181 853 4051 32rm(27 ⇌ 🐾)

SW15 PUTNEY

Richmond Park Roehampton Gate, Priory Ln
SW15 5JR ☎ 0181 876 1795
Two public parkland courses.
Princes Course: 18 holes, 5868yds, Par 69, SSS 68.
Dukes Course: 18 holes, 6036yds, Par 68, SSS 68.
Visitors   must contact in advance or pay and play.
Societies   must contact in advance.
Green Fees £4-£13 (£4-£16 weekends).
Facilities   ⊗ �🍴 🍴 🛒 ⛳ ⚐ 🏌
                 🏌 Stuart Hill & David Brown.
Leisure   motorised carts for hire, buggies for hire,
                 trolley for hire, driving range, putting green,
                 practice area.
Hotel   ★★★ 70% Richmond Hill, Richmond Hill,
                 RICHMOND UPON THAMES
                 ☎ 0181 940 2247 & 0181 940 5466 124 ⇌ 🐾

SW18 WANDSORTH

Springfield Park Burntwood Ln, Wandsworth SW18 0AT
☎ 0181 871 2468
Attractive flat parkland course in the middle of London. The
longest drive is the 430 yard 3rd to one of the course's superb
greens. Well placed bunkers trap the careless shot and the
course rewards the accurate player.
9 holes, 2250yds, Par 62, SSS 62.
Club membership 100.
Visitors   must contact in advance.
Societies   telephone or write to the secretary.
Green Fees £11 per 18 holes; £6 per 9 holes (£13/£8
weekends & bank holidays).
Facilities   ⊗ �🍴 🍴 🛒 ⛳ ⚐ 🏌 Jeremy Robson.
Leisure   trolley for hire, putting green, practice area.
Hotel   ★★★★ 76% Cannizaro House, West Side,
                 Wimbledon Common, LONDON
                 ☎ 0181 879 1464 46 ⇌ 🐾

Entries with a shaded background identify
courses that are considered to be particularly
interesting

SW19 WIMBLEDON

Royal Wimbledon 29 Camp Rd SW19 4UW
☎ 0181 946 2125
A club steeped in the history of the game, it is also of
great age, dating back to 1865. Of sand and heather like
so many of the Surrey courses its 12th hole (par 4) is
rated as the best on the course.
18 holes, 6300yds, Par 70, SSS 70.
Club membership 1050.
Visitors   must be guests of current club member.
Societies   welcome Wed-Thu. Must apply in writing.
Green Fees not confirmed.
Facilities   ⚐ 🏌 🏌
Hotel   ★★★★ 76% Cannizaro House, West Side,
                 Wimbledon Common, LONDON
                 ☎ 0181 879 1464 46 ⇌ 🐾

Wimbledon Common Camp Rd SW19 4UW
☎ 0181 946 0294
Quick-drying course on Wimbledon Common. Well wooded,
with tight fairways, challenging short holes but no bunkers. The
course is also played over by London Scottish Golf Club (0181
788 0135). All players must wear plain red upper garments.
18 holes, 5438yds, Par 68, SSS 66.
Club membership 250.
Visitors   with member only at weekends.
Societies   must telephone in advance.
Green Fees not confirmed.
Facilities   ⚐ ⛳ ⚐ 🏌 J S Jukes.
Hotel   ★★★★ 76% Cannizaro House, West Side,
                 Wimbledon Common, LONDON
                 ☎ 0181 879 1464 46 ⇌ 🐾

Wimbledon Park Home Park Rd, Wimbledon SW19 7HR
☎ 0181 946 1250
Easy walking on parkland course. Sheltered lake provides
hazard on 3 holes.
18 holes, 5465yds, Par 66, SSS 66.
Club membership 700.
Visitors   restricted weekends & bank holidays. Must
                 contact in advance and have handicap certificate
                 or letter of introduction.
Societies   must apply in writing.
Green Fees not confirmed.
Facilities   ⚐ ⛳ ⚐ 🏌 Dean Wingrove.
Leisure   putting green, trolley hire.
Location   400 yds from Wimbledon Park Station
Hotel   ★★★ 70% Richmond Hill, Richmond Hill,
                 RICHMOND UPON THAMES
                 ☎ 0181 940 2247 & 0181 940 5466 124 ⇌ 🐾

W7 HANWELL

Brent Valley 138 Church Rd, Hanwell W7 3BE
☎ 0181 567 1287
Municipal parkland course with easy walking. The River
Brent winds through the course.
18 holes, 5426yds, Par 67, SSS 66.
Club membership 350.
Visitors   no restrictions.
Societies   one month's notice required.
Green Fees not confirmed.
Facilities   ⚐ ⛳ ⚐ 🏌 Peter Byrne.
Hotel   ★★★ 63% Master Robert Hotel, Great West
                 Rd, HOUNSLOW ☎ 0181 570 6261 94 ⇌ 🐾

MERSEYSIDE

BEBINGTON
Map 07 SJ38

Brackenwood Brackenwood Park L63 2LY
☎ 0151 608 3093
Municipal parkland course with easy walking.
18 holes, 6285yds, Par 70, SSS 70.
Club membership 320.
Societies must apply in advance.
Green Fees not confirmed.
Facilities 🍴🏌♣
Location 0.75m N of M53 junc 4 on B5151
Hotel ★★★ 68% Thornton Hall Hotel, Neston Rd,
THORNTON HOUGH
☎ 0151 336 3938 5 ⇆ ♣Annexe58 ⇆ ♣

BIRKENHEAD
Map 07 SJ38

Arrowe Park Woodchurch L49 5LW ☎ 0151 677 1527
Pleasant municipal parkland course.
18 holes, 6435yds, Par 72, SSS 71, Course record 68.
Club membership 220.
Visitors no restrictions.
Societies must telephone in advance.
Green Fees not confirmed.
Facilities ♀🍴🏌♣ Clive Scanlon.
Leisure putting green, trolley hire.
Location 1m from M53 junc 3 on A551
Hotel ★★★ 68% Bowler Hat Hotel, 2 Talbot Rd,
Oxton, BIRKENHEAD
☎ 0151 652 4931 32 ⇆ ♣

Prenton Golf Links Rd, Prenton L42 8LW
☎ 0151 608 1053
Parkland course with easy walking and views of the Welsh
Hills.
18 holes, 6411yds, Par 71, SSS 71.
Club membership 610.
Visitors must contact in advance.
Societies must telephone in advance and confirm in
writing.
Green Fees £25 per day (£30 weekends & bank holidays).
Facilities ⊗ �🍴 by prior arrangement 🎯 ♣♀🍴🏌
♣ Robin Thompson.
Leisure trolley for hire, putting green, practice area,
snooker.
Location S side of town centre off B5151
Hotel ★★ 64% Riverhill Hotel, Talbot Rd, Oxton,
BIRKENHEAD ☎ 0151 653 3773 16 ⇆ ♣

Wirral Ladies 93 Bidston Rd, Oxton L43 6TS
☎ 0151 652 1255
Heathland course with heather and birch.
18 holes, 4966yds, SSS 70.
Club membership 450.
Visitors may not play over Christmas and Easter
holidays.
Societies must telephone in advance.
Green Fees not confirmed.
Facilities ♀🎯🍴♣ Philip Chandler.
Location W side of town centre on B5151

Hotel ★★★ 68% Bowler Hat Hotel, 2 Talbot Rd,
Oxton, BIRKENHEAD
☎ 0151 652 4931 32 ⇆ ♣

BLUNDELLSANDS
Map 07 SJ39

West Lancashire Hall Rd West L23 8SZ
☎ 0151 924 1076
Challenging, traditional links with sandy subsoil
overlooking the Mersey Estuary. The course provides
excellent golf throughout the year. The four short holes
are very fine.
18 holes, 6763yds, Par 72, SSS 73.
Club membership 650.
Visitors may not play on competition days; must
have a handicap certificate.
Societies must contact in advance.
Green Fees not confirmed.
Facilities ♀🎯🍴♣ David Lloyd.
Location N side of village
Hotel ★★★ 64% Blundellsands Hotel, The
Serpentine, BLUNDELLSANDS
☎ 0151 924 6515 41 ⇆ ♣

BOOTLE
Map 07 SJ39

Bootle 2 Dunnings Bridge Rd L30 2PP ☎ 0151 928 6196
Municipal seaside course, with prevailing north-westerly
wind. Testing holes: 5th (200 yds) par 3; 7th (415 yds) par 4.
18 holes, 6362yds, Par 70, SSS 70, Course record 64.
Club membership 380.
Visitors must contact in advance.
Societies must apply in writing.
Green Fees on application.
Facilities ⊗ ⍟ 🎯 ♣ ♀🍴🏌♣ Alan Bradshaw.
Leisure hard tennis courts, trolley for hire, putting green.
Location 2m NE on A5036
Hotel ★★★ 64% Blundellsands Hotel, The
Serpentine, BLUNDELLSANDS
☎ 0151 924 6515 41 ⇆ ♣

BROMBOROUGH
Map 07 SJ38

Bromborough Raby Hall Rd L63 0NW ☎ 0151 334 2155
Parkland course.
18 holes, 6650yds, Par 72, SSS 73, Course record 67.
Club membership 800.
Visitors are advised to contact professional on 0151 334
4499 in advance.
Societies normal society day Wed ; must apply in
advance.
Green Fees £26 per day (£30 weekends).
Facilities ⊗ ⍟ 🎯 ♣ ♀🍴♣ Geoff Berry.
Leisure motorised carts for hire, trolley for hire, putting
green.
Location 0.5m W of Station
Hotel B Travel Inn, High St, BROMBOROUGH
☎ 0151 334 2917 31 ⇆ ♣

> Entries with a shaded background identify
> courses that are considered to be particularly
> interesting

CALDY   Map 07 SJ28

Caldy Links Hey Rd L48 1NB
☎ 0151 625 5660
A parkland course situated on the estuary of the River Dee with many of the fairways running parallel to the river. Of Championship length, the course offers excellent golf all year, but is subject to variable winds that noticeably alter the day to day playing of each hole. There are excellent views of North Wales and Snowdonia.
18 holes, 6675yds, Par 72, SSS 73, Course record 68.
Club membership 800.
Visitors   may play on weekdays only. Must contact in advance and have an introduction from own club.
Societies   must telephone in advance.
Green Fees not confirmed.
Facilities   ♀ ♨ 🏠 ♪ K Jones.
Location   SE side of village
Hotel   ★★★ 68% Thornton Hall Hotel, Neston Rd, THORNTON HOUGH
    ☎ 0151 336 3938 5 ⇔ ♪Annexe58 ⇔ ♪

EASTHAM   Map 07 SJ38

Eastham Lodge 117 Ferry Rd L62 0AP
☎ 0151 327 3003 & 327 3008
A 15-hole parkland course with many trees. Three holes played twice to make 18, but restricted to 15 holes in winter.
18 holes, 5953yds, Par 69, SSS 69, Course record 67.
Club membership 800.
Visitors   with member only at weekends.
Societies   welcome Tue. Must apply in writing.
Green Fees £22 per day/round.
Facilities   ⊗ ⅢM by prior arrangement ⓑ ♥ ♀ ♨ 🏠 ♪ R Boobyer.
Leisure   trolley for hire, putting green, small practice area.
Location   1.5m N
Hotel   B Travel Inn, High St, BROMBOROUGH
    ☎ 0151 334 2917 31 ⇔ ♪

FORMBY   Map 07 SD30

Formby Golf Rd L37 1LQ
☎ 01704 872164
Championship seaside links through sandhills and partly through pine trees.It plays well throughout the year.
18 holes, 6496yds, Par 72, SSS 72, Course record 66.
Club membership 680.
Visitors   must contact in advance.
Societies   must contact well in advance.
Green Fees £50 per day/round.
Facilities   ⊗ ⅢM ⓑ ♥ ♀ ♨ 🏠 ♪ ⋈
    ♪ Clive Harrison.
Leisure   trolley for hire, putting green, practice area.
Location   N side of town
Hotel   ★★★ 64% Blundellsands Hotel, The Serpentine, BLUNDELLSANDS
    ☎ 0151 924 6515 41 ⇔ ♪

Formby Ladies Golf Rd L37 1YH ☎ 01704 873493
Seaside links - one of the few independent ladies clubs in the country. The course has contrasting hard-hitting holes in flat country and tricky holes in sandhills and woods.
18 holes, 5374yds, Par 71, SSS 71.
Club membership 423.
Visitors   must contact in advance and may not play Thu or before noon Sat & Sun.
Societies   must apply in advance.
Green Fees not confirmed.
Facilities   ♀ ♨ 🏠 ♪
Leisure   driving range,putting,trolley hire.
Location   N side of town
Hotel   ★★★ 64% Blundellsands Hotel, The Serpentine, BLUNDELLSANDS
    ☎ 0151 924 6515 41 ⇔ ♪

HESWALL   Map 07 SJ28

Heswall Cottage Ln L60 8PB ☎ 0151 342 1237
A pleasant parkland course in soft undulating country over-looking the estuary of the River Dee. There are excellent views of the Welsh hills and coastline, and a good test of golf. The clubhouse is modern and well-appointed with good facilities.
18 holes, 6492yds, Par 72, SSS 72, Course record 62.
Club membership 940.
Visitors   must contact in advance.
Societies   must apply in advance.
Green Fees £40 per day; £30 per round (£45/35 weekends).
Facilities   ⊗ ⅢM ⓑ ♥ ♀ ♨ 🏠 ♪ Alan Thompson.
Leisure   trolley for hire, putting green, practice area.
Location   1m S off A540
Hotel   ★★★ 68% Thornton Hall Hotel, Neston Rd, THORNTON HOUGH
    ☎ 0151 336 3938 5 ⇔ ♪Annexe58 ⇔ ♪

HOYLAKE   Map 07 SJ28

Hoylake Carr Ln, Municipal Links L47 4BG
☎ 0151 632 2956
Flat, generally windy semi-links course. Tricky fairways.
18 holes, 6313yds, Par 70, SSS 70, Course record 67.
Club membership 303.
Societies   must telephone 0151 632 4883 M E Down club steward or 0151 632 2956 club professional.
Green Fees not confirmed.
Facilities   ♀ (ex Fri) ♨ 🏠 ♪ ♪ Simon Hooton.
Leisure   practice ground no charge.
Location   SW side of town off A540
Hotel   ★★★ 66% Leasowe Castle Hotel, Leasowe Rd, MORETON ☎ 0151 606 9191 47 ⇔ ♪

Royal Liverpool Meols Dr L47 4AL ☎ 0151 632 3101
A world famous, windswept seaside links course.
18 holes, 6162yds, Par 71, SSS 71.
Club membership 650.
Visitors   must contact in advance & have a handicap certificate. Restricted before 9.30am & between 1-2pm. No play Thu am (ladies day). Limited play weekends.
Societies   must contact in advance.
Green Fees £65 per day; £47.50 per round (£95/£60 weekends).

Facilities	⊗ ⓘ ⚑ ♀ ⚐ 🕿 ⚐ (John Heggarty.
Leisure	trolley for hire, putting green, practice area.
Location	SW side of town on A540
Hotel	★★★ 66% Leasowe Castle Hotel, Leasowe Rd, MORETON
	☎ 0151 606 9191 47 ⇦ ⬧

HUYTON
Map 07 SJ49

Bowring Bowring Park, Roby Rd L36 4HD
☎ 0151 489 1901
Flat parkland course.
9 holes, 2796yds, Par 34.
Club membership 80.
Visitors no restrictions.
Green Fees not confirmed.
Facilities ⚐ 🕿 (
Location On A5080 adjacent M62 junc 5
Hotel ★ 59% Rockland Hotel, View Rd, RAINHILL
☎ 0151 426 4603 10rm(9 ⇦)

Huyton & Prescot Hurst Park, Huyton Ln L36 1UA
☎ 0151 489 3948
An easy walking, parkland course providing excellent golf.
18 holes, 5779yds, Par 68, SSS 68.
Club membership 700.
Visitors must contact in advance. Must play with member at weekends.
Societies must apply in writing.
Green Fees £22.
Facilities ⊗ ⫶ ⓘ ⚑ ♀ ⚐ (Malcolm Harrison.
Leisure trolley for hire, putting green, practice area.
Location 1.5m NE off B5199
Hotel ★ 59% Rockland Hotel, View Rd, RAINHILL
☎ 0151 426 4603 10rm(9 ⇦)

LIVERPOOL
Map 07 SJ39

Allerton Park Allerton Manor Golf Estate, Allerton Rd L18 3JT ☎ 0151 428 1046
Parkland course.
18 holes, 5459yds, Par 67, SSS 67.
Club membership 300.
Visitors must book with professional in advance.
Green Fees not confirmed.
Facilities ♀ 🕿 ⚐ (Barry Large.
Leisure putting green, trolley hire.
Location 5.5m SE of city centre off A562 and B5180
Hotel ★★★★ 55% Atlantic Tower, Chapel St, LIVERPOOL ☎ 0151 227 4444 226 ⇦ ⬧

The Childwall Naylors Rd, Gateacre L27 2YB ☎ 0151 487 0654
Parkland golf is played here over a testing course, where accuracy from the tee is well-rewarded. The course is very popular with visiting societies for the clubhouse has many amenities. Course designed by James Braid.
18 holes, 6425yds, Par 72, SSS 71, Course record 66.
Club membership 650.
Visitors must contact in advance.
Societies must apply in writing.
Green Fees £23 per day (£33 weekends).
Facilities ⊗ ⫶ ⓘ ⚑ ♀ ⚐ 🕿 ⚐ (Nigel M Parr.

Leisure trolley for hire, driving range, putting green, practice area.
Location 7m E of city centre off B5178
Hotel ★ 59% Rockland Hotel, View Rd, RAINHILL ☎ 0151 426 4603 10rm(9 ⇦)

Kirkby-Liverpool Municipal Ingoe Ln, Kirkby L32 4SS
☎ 0151 546 5435
Flat, easy course.
18 holes, 6588yds, Par 72, SSS 71, Course record 70.
Club membership 150.
Visitors must contact in advance.
Societies must contact 1 week in advance.
Green Fees not confirmed.
Facilities ♀ ⚐ 🕿 ⚐ (Dave Weston.
Location 7.5m NE of city centre on A506
Hotel ★★★★ 57% Liverpool Moat House Hotel, Paradise St, LIVERPOOL
☎ 0151 709 0181 251 ⇦ ⬧

Lee Park Childwall Valley Rd L27 3YA ☎ 0151 487 3882
Flat course with ponds in places.
18 holes, 5508mtrs, Par 71, SSS 69.
Club membership 600.
Visitors must dress acceptably.
Societies must contact in advance.
Green Fees not confirmed.
Facilities ♀ ⚐
Leisure putting green, practice area.
Location 7m E of city centre off B5178
Hotel ★★★★ 57% Liverpool Moat House Hotel, Paradise St, LIVERPOOL
☎ 0151 709 0181 251 ⇦ ⬧

West Derby Yew Tree Ln, West Derby L12 9HQ ☎ 0151 228 1540 & 0151 254 1034
A parkland course always in first-class condition, and so giving easy walking. The fairways are well-wooded. Care must be taken on the first nine holes to avoid the brook which guards many of the greens. A modern well-designed clubhouse with many amenities, overlooks the course.
18 holes, 6333yds, Par 72, SSS 70.
Club membership 550.
Visitors may not play before 9.30am.
Societies may not play on Sat, Sun & bank holidays; must contact in advance.
Green Fees not confirmed.
Facilities ♀ ⚐ 🕿 (Nick Brace.
Location 4.5m E of city centre off A57
Hotel ★★★★ 55% Atlantic Tower, Chapel St, LIVERPOOL ☎ 0151 227 4444 226 ⇦ ⬧

Woolton Speke Rd, Woolton L25 7TZ ☎ 0151 486 2298
Parkland course providing a good round of golf for all standards.
18 holes, 5717yds, Par 69, SSS 68.
Club membership 700.
Visitors must contact in advance. Restricted at weekends.
Societies must contact in advance.
Green Fees £20 per day (£30 weekends).
Facilities ⊗ ⫶ ⓘ ⚑ ♀ ⚐ 🕿 (Alan Gibson.
Leisure motorised carts for hire, putting green.
Location 7m SE of city centre off A562 ▶

Hotel   ★★★★ 55% Atlantic Tower, Chapel St,
LIVERPOOL
☎ 0151 227 4444 226 ⇄ ♚

NEWTON-LE-WILLOWS   Map 07 SJ59

Haydock Park Newton Ln WA12 0HX
☎ 01925 228525
A well-wooded parkland course, close to the well-known
racecourse, and always in excellent condition. The
pleasant undulating fairways offer some very interesting
golf and the 6th, 9th, 11th and 13th holes are particularly
testing. The clubhouse is very comfortable.
18 holes, 6043yds, Par 70, SSS 69, Course record 65.
Club membership 560.
Visitors   with member only weekends & bank
holidays. Must contact in advance.
Societies   must contact in advance.
Green Fees £25 per day/round.
Facilities ⊗ ⅷ ⅬⅬ ♚ ♀ ♤ ☎ ♪ Peter Kenwright.
Leisure   trolley for hire, putting green, practice area.
Location   0.75m NE off A49
Hotel   B Forte Posthouse Haydock, Lodge Ln,
Newton-Le-Willows, HAYDOCK
☎ 01942 717878 136 ⇄ ♚

ST HELENS   Map 07 SJ59

Grange Park Prescot Rd WA10 3AD
☎ 01744 26318
A course of Championship length set in plesant country
surroundings - playing the course it is hard to believe that
industrial St Helens lies so close at hand. The course is a
fine test of golf and there are many attractive holes liable
to challenge all grades.
18 holes, 6422yds, Par 72, SSS 71, Course record 65.
Club membership 730.
Visitors   play allowed any day except public
holidays. Advisable to contact professional
in advance (01744 28785)
Societies   phone initially.
Green Fees £29 per 36 holes; £23 per 27 holes (£35 per
27 holes weekends).
Facilities ⊗ ⅷ ⅬⅬ ♚ ♀ ♤ ☎ ♪ Paul Roberts.
Leisure   motorised carts for hire, trolley for hire,
putting, snooker.
Location   1.5m SW on A58
Hotel   ★★★★ 65% Chalon Court, Chalon Way,
Linkway West, ST HELENS
☎ 01744 453444 84 ⇄ ♚

Sherdley Park Sherdley Rd WA9 5DE
☎ 01744 813149
Fairly hilly course with ponds in places.
18 holes, 5941yds, Par 70, SSS 69.
Club membership 160.
Visitors   no restrictions.
Green Fees not confirmed.
Facilities ♤ ☎ ♪
Location   2m S off A570
Hotel   ★★★★ 65% Chalon Court, Chalon Way,
Linkway West, ST HELENS
☎ 01744 453444 84 ⇄ ♚

SOUTHPORT   Map 07 SD31

The Hesketh Cockle Dick's Ln, off Cambridge Rd
PR9 9QQ ☎ 01704 536897
Hesketh is the senior club in Southport, founded in 1885.
The Championship course comprises much of the
original territory plus a large area of reclaimed land on
the seaward side - essentially 'Links' in character.
18 holes, 6407yds, Par 71, SSS 72, Course record 66.
Club membership 600.
Visitors   must have a handicap certificate. May not
play Tue mornings (Ladies) or 12.30-2pm
daily.
Green Fees not confirmed.
Facilities ♀ ♤ ☎ ♪ John Donoghue.
Location   1m NE of town centre off A565
Hotel   ★★ 65% Bold Hotel, 585 Lord St,
SOUTHPORT
☎ 01704 532578 23 ⇄ ♚

Hillside Hastings Rd, Hillside PR8 2LU
☎ 01704 567169 & 568360
Championship links course with natural hazards open to
strong wind.
18 holes, 6850yds, Par 72, SSS 74.
Club membership 700.
Visitors   must contact in advance.
Societies   must apply to secretary in advance.
Green Fees £45 per day; £35 per round (£45 per round
Sun).
Facilities ⊗ ⅷ ⅬⅬ ♚ ♀ ♤ ☎ ♪ Brian Seddon.
Leisure   motorised carts for hire, buggies for hire,
trolley for hire, driving range, putting green,
practice area.
Location   3m S of town centre on A565
Hotel   ★★★ 68% Royal Clifton Hotel,
Promenade, SOUTHPORT
☎ 01704 533771 107 ⇄ ♚

ROYAL BIRKDALE   See page 155

Southport & Ainsdale Bradshaws Ln, Ainsdale PR8 3LG
☎ 01704 578000
'S and A', as it is known in the North is another of the
fine Championship courses for which this part of the
country is famed. This Club has staged many important
events and offers golf of the highest order.
18 holes, 6603yds, Par 72, SSS 73.
Club membership 815.
Visitors   welcome except Thu am, weekends & bank
holidays. Must contact club in advance &
have handicap certificate.
Societies   must apply in advance.
Green Fees not confirmed.
Facilities ♀ ♤ ☎ ♪ M Houghton.
Leisure   putting green,practice area,trolley hire.
Location   3m S off A565
Hotel   ★★★ 68% Royal Clifton Hotel,
Promenade, SOUTHPORT
☎ 01704 533771 107 ⇄ ♚

THE ROYAL BIRKDALE

SOUTHPORT *Lancs* ☎ 01704 567920   Map 07 SD31

John Ingham writes: There are few seaside links in the world that can be described as 'great', but Royal Birkdale, with its expanse of towering sandhills and willow scrub, is one of them. There have been some changes since the club was founded in 1889 and they have hosted everything that matters here, including the Open (which returns in 1998) and the Ryder Cup. Some changes have been made even since Arnold Palmer hit that wondrous recovery shot that helped him win an Open in the early sixties, and led to a plaque being erected at the spot from which the divot was taken.

Well bunkered, the sandhills run along the edges of the fairways and make ideal platforms from which to view the Open Championship - played frequently here because the examination is supreme in the United Kingdom.

The links, in a wind, may be too difficult for the weekender. Certainly it found out Dai Rees in 1961 when he was chasing Palmer for the title. In the last round the course struck at the very first hole. Rees had hit his teeshot a might to the left, and then had to wait for the players to hole out on the green ahead, before attempting a powerful shot with a lofted wood from the fairway. The ball smacked into the back of a bunker, and fell back into sand. Rees took an awful seven and Palmer beat him for the trophy - by one shot. The Welshman had stormed back in 31 but his chance to win an Open had gone forever. But Rees still touched his hat to the links, and held it in great respect as, indeed, does Arnold Palmer.

But for the amateur, another problem is simply hitting the ball far enough. If you play this terrific course from the Open Championship back tees, it measures 6690 yards and par 72 takes some getting, even with your handicap allowance!

Visitors must contact in advance, and have a handicap certificate. Normally not Fri & Sat; only Sun am. Play off yellow tees

Societies must apply in advance. Principle days: Wed, Thur

Green fees Weekdays £75 per day, £55 per round. Sun am only £75

Facilities ⊗ ⅺ Ⅼ ♖ ☕ ♀ ⅄ 🏠 ➶ ℓ (Richard Bradbeer) putting green, practice area

Location Waterloo Road, Birkdale, Southport PR8 2LX (2m S of town on A565)

18 holes, 6690yds, Par 72, SSS 73, Course record 63 (1991 Open, Jodie Mudd, USA)

WHERE TO STAY AND EAT NEARBY

HOTELS:

SOUTHPORT

★★★⊕ 68% Royal Clifton, Promenade. ☎ 01704 533771. 107 (6 ♠ 101 ⇋ ♠)

★★★ 67% Scarisbrick, Lord St. ☎ 01704 543000. 77 (2 ♠ 75 ⇋ ♠)

★★ 70% Balmoral Lodge, 41 Queens Rd. ☎ 01704 544298. 15⇋ ♠

★★★ 65% Stutelea Hotel & Leisure Club, Alexandra Rd. ☎ 01704 544220. 22(3 ♠ 19 ⇋ ♠)

RESTAURANT:

WRIGHTINGTON

⊕ High Moor Inn, Highmoor Ln (jct 27 off M6, take B5239). ☎ 01257 252364

155

Southport Municipal Park Rd West PR9 0JR
☎ 01704 535286
Municipal seaside links course. Played over by Southport
Municipal, Alt and Park golf clubs.
18 holes, 6400yds, Par 70, SSS 69, Course record 66.
Club membership 750.
Visitors   no restrictions.
Societies   must telephone 6 days in advance.
Green Fees   not confirmed.
Facilities   ♀⅄🏠🛈⚑ Bill Fletcher.
Location   N side of town centre off A565
Hotel   ★★★ 68% Royal Clifton Hotel, Promenade,
                  SOUTHPORT ☎ 01704 533771 107 ⇔ ℝ

Southport Old Links Moss Ln, Churchtown PR9 7QS
☎ 01704 28207
Seaside course with tree-lined fairways and easy walking.
One of the oldest courses in Southport, Henry Vardon won
the 'Leeds Cup' here in 1922.
9 holes, 6244yds, Par 72, SSS 71, Course record 68.
Club membership 450.
Visitors   advisable to contact in advance.
Societies   apply in writing.
Green Fees   £25.50 per day; £18.50 per round (£25.50 per
                  round weekends).
Facilities   ⊗ 🍴 🛂 🍺 ♀⅄
Leisure   putting green.
Location   NW side of town centre off A5267
Hotel   ★★ 65% Bold Hotel, 585 Lord St,
                  SOUTHPORT ☎ 01704 532578 23 ⇔ ℝ

Wallasey   Map 07 SJ29

Bidston Bidston Link Rd L44 2HR ☎ 0151 638 3412
Parkland course, with westerly winds.
18 holes, 5827yds, Par 70, SSS 71, Course record 66.
Club membership 650.
Visitors   must contact in advance, restricted weekends.
Societies   must apply in writing.
Green Fees   not confirmed.
Facilities   ♀⅄🏠⚑ J Law.
Leisure   putting green, practice area.
Location   0.5m W of M53 junc 1 entrance off A551
Hotel   ★★★ 66% Leasowe Castle Hotel, Leasowe Rd,
                  MORETON ☎ 0151 606 9191 47 ⇔ ℝ

Leasowe Moreton L46 3RD ☎ 0151 677 5852
Rather flat, semi-links, seaside course.
18 holes, 6227yds, Par 71, SSS 71.
Club membership 602.
Visitors   telephone professional (0151 678 5460).
                  Handicap certificate required.
Societies   contact in advance.
Green Fees   £20 per day (£25 weekends & bank holidays).
Facilities   ⊗ 🍴 🛂 🍺 ♀⅄🏠⚑ Neil Sweeney.
Leisure   trolley for hire, putting green, practice area.
Location   2m W on A551
Hotel   ★★★ 66% Leasowe Castle Hotel, Leasowe Rd,
                  MORETON ☎ 0151 606 9191 47 ⇔ ℝ

Wallasey Bayswater Rd L45 8LA ☎ 0151 691 1024
A well-established sporting links, adjacent to the Irish
Sea, with huge sandhills and many classic holes where
the player's skills are often combined with good fortune.
Large, firm greens and fine views but not for the faint-
hearted.

18 holes, 6607yds, Par 72.
Club membership 605.
Visitors   must contact one month in advance.
Societies   must apply in writing or telephone.
Green Fees   £32 per day; £27 per round (£37/£32
                  weekends & bank holidays).
Facilities   ⊗ 🛂 🍺 ♀⅄🏠⚑ Mike Adams.
Leisure   trolley for hire, putting green, practice area.
Location   N side of town centre off A554
Hotel   ★★★ 66% Leasowe Castle Hotel, Leasowe
                  Rd. MORETON ☎ 0151 606 9191 47 ⇔ ℝ

Warren Grove Rd L45 0JA ☎ 0151 639 8323
Short, undulating links course with first-class greens and
prevailing winds off the sea.
9 holes, 5854yds, Par 72, SSS 68.
Club membership 150.
Visitors   except Sun until 10.30.am.
Green Fees   not confirmed.
Facilities   🏠⚑ Ken Lamb.
Location   N side of town centre off A554
Hotel   ★★★ 66% Leasowe Castle Hotel, Leasowe Rd,
                  MORETON ☎ 0151 606 9191 47 ⇔ ℝ

NORFOLK

Barnham Broom   Map 05 TG00

Barnham Broom Hotel Golf and Country Club
Honingham Rd NR9 4DD
☎ 01603 759393
Attractive river valley courses with modern hotel and
leisure complex.
Hill Course: 18 holes, 6470yds, Par 71, SSS 71.
Valley Course: 18 holes, 6628yds, Par 72, SSS 72.
Club membership 500.
Visitors   must contact in advance. With member only
                  at weekends.
Societies   must contact in advance.
Green Fees   £33 per day; £27 per round.
Facilities   ⊗ 🍴 🛂 🍺 ♀⅄🏠⚑ 🖂
                  ⚑ Stephen Beckham.
Leisure   hard tennis courts, heated indoor swimming
                  pool, squash, sauna, solarium, gymnasium,
                  motorised carts for hire, buggies for hire,
                  trolley for hire, putting green, practice area,
                  snooker.
Location   1m N, S of A47
Hotel   ★★★ 69% Barnham Broom Hotel
                  Conference & Leisure, Centre, BARNHAM
                  BROOM ☎ 01603 759393 52 ⇔ ℝ
                  See advetisement on page 159.

Bawburgh   Map 05 TG10

Bawburgh Glen Lodge, Marlingford Rd NR9 3LU
☎ 01603 740404
An open-links. Driving range available.
18 holes, 6224yds, Par 70, SSS 70.
Club membership 700.

Visitors must contact in advance.
Societies must contact in advance.
Green Fees £20 per 36 holes; £15 per 18 holes (£20 per 18 holes weekends).
Facilities ⊗ ⅷ ┗ ⬤ ♀ ♨ 🖻 𝄢 Chris Potter.
Leisure motorised carts for hire, buggies for hire, trolley for hire, driving range, putting green, practice area.
Location S of Royal Norfolk Showground, on A47
Hotel ★★★ 68% Hotel Norwich, 121-131 Boundary Rd, NORWICH
☎ 01603 787260 107 ⇋ �

BRANCASTER   Map 09 TF74

Royal West Norfolk PE31 8AX
☎ 01485 210223 & 210616
If you want to see what golf courses were like years ago, then go to the Royal West Norfolk where tradition exudes from both clubhouse and course. Close by the sea, the links are laid out in the grand manner and is characterised by sleepered greens, superb cross-bunkering and salt marshes.
18 holes, 6428yds, Par 71, SSS 71, Course record 66.
Club membership 700.
Visitors must contact in advance.
Societies must contact Secretary in advance.
Green Fees £37.50 (£46.50 weekends).
Facilities ⊗ ⅷ ┗ ⬤ ♀ ♨ 🖻 ↷ 𝄢 R E Kimber.
Leisure trolley for hire, putting green, practice area.
Hotel ★★ 72% Titchwell Manor Hotel, TITCHWELL
☎ 01485 210221 11rm(7 ⇋ 🌙)Annexe4 ⇋ 🌙

CROMER   Map 09 TG24

Royal Cromer 145 Overstrand Rd NR27 0JH
☎ 01263 512884
Seaside course set out on cliff edge, hilly and subject to wind.
18 holes, 6447yds, Par 71, SSS 71, Course record 67.
Club membership 650.
Visitors must contact in advance & have handicap certificate. Restricted at weekends.
Societies must contact in advance.
Green Fees £27 per day (£32 weekends & bank holidays).
Facilities ⊗ ⅷ ┗ ⬤ ♀ ♨ 🖻 𝄢 Robin Page.
Leisure trolley for hire, putting green, practice area.
Location 1m E on B1159
Hotel ★★ 69% Red Lion, Brook St, CROMER
☎ 01263 514964 12 ⇋ 🌙

DENVER   Map 05 TF60

Ryston Park PE38 0HH ☎ 01366 382133
Parkland course.
9 holes, 6310yds, Par 70, SSS 70, Course record 66.
Club membership 330.
Visitors must contact in advance. May not play weekends or bank holidays.
Societies must apply in writing.
Green Fees £20 per day.
Facilities ⊗ ⅷ ┗ ⬤ ♀ ♨ 🖻

Leisure putting green, practice area.
Location 0.5m S on A10
Hotel ★★ 65% Castle Hotel, High St, DOWNHAM MARKET ☎ 01366 384311 12rm(9 ⇋ 🌙)

DEREHAM   Map 09 TF91

Dereham Quebec Rd NR19 2DS
☎ 01362 695900 & 685631
Parkland course.
9 holes, 6225yds, Par 71, SSS 70, Course record 64.
Club membership 400.
Visitors must contact in advance and have a handicap certificate; must play with member at weekends.
Societies must apply in writing.
Green Fees £20 per day.
Facilities ⊗ ⅷ ┗ ⬤ ♀ ♨ 🖻 𝄢 Robert Curtis.
Leisure trolley for hire, putting green, practice area.
Location N side of town centre off B1110
Hotel ★★ 63% King's Head Hotel, Norwich St, DEREHAM
☎ 01362 693842 & 693283 10rm(4 ⇋2 🌙)Annexe5 ⇋ 🌙

Reymerston Hingham Rd, Reymerston NR9 4QQ
☎ 01362 850297
The course was opened in June 1993 with large tees and greens which drain very well. Created from open farmland, it has many ditches and hedges and room for the 18th green to be over 1000sq.yds. The 17th green is protected by two large trees in front.
18 holes, 6609yds, Par 72, SSS 72, Course record 74.
Club membership 400.
Visitors must book tee times.
Societies telephone or write to arrange tee times.
Green Fees £30 per day; £20 per round (£35/£25 weekends).
Facilities ⊗ ⅷ ┗ ⬤ ♀ ♨ 🖻 𝄢 Alison Sheard.
Leisure motorised carts for hire, buggies for hire, trolley for hire, 9 hole pitch & putt, putting green, practice area.
Location 12m W of Norwich, off B1135
Hotel ★★ 63% King's Head Hotel, Norwich St, DEREHAM
☎ 01362 693842 & 693283 10rm(4 ⇋2 🌙)Annexe5 ⇋ 🌙

DISS   Map 05 TM18

Diss Stuston IP22 3JB ☎ 01379 642847
Commonland course with natural hazards.
18 holes, 6238yds, Par 73, SSS 70.
Club membership 650.
Visitors must contact in advance but may not play weekends & bank holidays.
Societies by arrangement.
Green Fees not confirmed.
Facilities ♀ ♨ 🖻 𝄢
Location 1.5m SE on B1118
Hotel ★★★ 64% Cornwallis Arms, BROME
☎ 01379 870326 11 ⇋ 🌙

Entries with a shaded background identify courses that are considered to be particularly interesting

FAKENHAM
Map 09 TF92

Fakenham Gallow Sports Centre, The Race Course
N21 7NY ☎ 01328 820316 & 862867
A well-wooded 9-hole course.
9 holes, 6000yds, Par 71, SSS 69, Course record 67.
Club membership 520.
Visitors   any time with member, restricted until after noon
              weekends and bank holidays.
Societies   apply in writing.
Green Fees   not confirmed.
Facilities   ♀⚘🏠ℓ J Westwood.
Leisure   hard tennis courts, squash.
Hotel   ★★ 63% Crown Hotel, Market Place,
              FAKENHAM ☎ 01328 851418 11 ⇔ ☏

GORLESTON-ON-SEA
Map 05 TG50

Gorleston Warren Rd NR31 6JT
☎ 01493 661911 & 662103
Seaside course.
18 holes, 6391yds, Par 71, SSS 71, Course record 68.
Club membership 860.
Visitors   advisable to contact in advance.
Societies   must apply in writing.
Green Fees   £21 per day/round (£25 weekends & bank
              holidays).
Facilities   ⊗ℳ⯑🍺♀⚘🏠☏ℓ Nick Brown.
Leisure   trolley for hire, putting green, practice area.
Location   S side of town centre
Hotel   ★★★ 72% Cliff Hotel, Gorleston, GREAT
              YARMOUTH ☎ 01493 662179 39 ⇔ ☏

GREAT YARMOUTH
Map 05 TG50

Great Yarmouth & Caister Beach House, Caister-on-
Sea NR30 5TD ☎ 01493 728699
This great old club, which celebrated its centenary in
1982, has played its part in the development of the game.
It is a fine old-fashioned links where not many golfers
have bettered the SSS in competitions. The 468-yard 8th
(par 4), is a testing hole.
18 holes, 6330yds, Par 70, SSS 70, Course record 67.
Club membership 770.
Visitors   must contact in advance. Restricted
              weekends.
Societies   must apply in writing or telephone.
Green Fees   £23.50 per day (£28 weekends).
Facilities   ⊗ℳ⯑🍺♀⚘🏠ℓ Robert Foster.
Leisure   motorised carts for hire, trolley for hire,
              putting green, practice area, snooker.
Location   0.5m N off A149
Hotel   ★★★ 66% Imperial Hotel, North Dr,
              GREAT YARMOUTH
              ☎ 01493 851113 39 ⇔ ☏

HUNSTANTON
Map 09 TF64

Hunstanton Golf Course Rd PE36 6JQ
☎ 01485 532811
A championship links course set among some of the most
natural golfing country in East Anglia. Known for its fast
and true greens. The wind is usually a factor in play and
it is a real test to play to handicap.

18 holes, 6735yds, Par 72, SSS 73, Course record 65.
Club membership 675.
Visitors   must contact in advance and be a club
              member with current handicap certificate.
              Restricted at weekends & may not play bank
              holiday weekends. Play in two ball format ie
              singles or foursomes.
Societies   apply in advance.
Green Fees   £40 per day (£50 weekends).
Facilities   ⊗ℳ⯑🍺♀⚘🏠☏ℓ John Carter.
Leisure   caddies available, motorised carts for hire,
              buggies for hire, trolley for hire, putting
              green, practice area.
Location   Off A149 in Old Hunstanton Village
              signposted
Hotel   ★★ 69% Caley Hall Motel, Old
              Hunstanton Rd, HUNSTANTON
              ☎ 01485 533486 Annexe33 ⇔

KING'S LYNN
Map 09 TF62

Eagles 39 School Rd, Tilney All Saints PE34 4RS
☎ 01553 827147
Parkland course with plenty of water hazards and bunkers.
Also Par-3 course and floodlit, covered driving range.
9 holes, 4284yds, Par 64, SSS 61, Course record 64.
Club membership 300.
Visitors   no restrictions.
Societies   must contact in advance.
Green Fees   £11.50 per 18 holes, £5.75 per 9 holes
              (£13.50/£6.75 weekends and bank holidays).
Facilities   ⊗ℳ⯑🍺♀⚘🏠☏ℓ Nigel Pickerell.
Leisure   trolley for hire, driving range, par 3, putting
              green, practice area.
Hotel   ★★★ 65% The Duke's Head, Tuesday Market
              Pl, KING'S LYNN
              ☎ 01553 774996 71 ⇔ ☏

King's Lynn Castle Rising PE31 6BD ☎ 01553 631654
Challenging, wooded parkland course.
18 holes, 6609yds, Par 72, SSS 72.
Club membership 1000.
Visitors   must contact in advance.
Societies   must contact in advance.
Green Fees   £32 per day/round (£40 weekends).
Facilities   ⊗ℳ⯑🍺♀⚘🏠ℓ Chris Hanlon.
Leisure   motorised carts for hire, trolley for hire, putting
              green, practice area, snooker.
Location   4m NE off A149
Hotel   ★★★ 65% The Duke's Head, Tuesday Market
              Pl, KING'S LYNN ☎ 01553 774996 71 ⇔ ☏

MATTISHALL
Map 09 TG01

Mattishall South Green NR20 3JZ ☎ 01362 850111
Mattishall has the distinction of having the longest hole in
Norfolk at a very demanding 615yds.
9 holes, 3109yds, Par 35, SSS 69.
Club membership 120.
Visitors   no restrictions.
Societies   welcome.
Green Fees   £5 per 9 holes.
Facilities   🍺♀⚘☏
Leisure   trolley for hire, putting green.

Hotel   ★★ 63% King's Head Hotel, Norwich St,
DEREHAM
☎ 01362 693842 & 693283 10rm(4 ⇄2
🐾)Annexe5 ⇄ 🐾

MIDDLETON   Map 09 TF61

Middleton Hall PE32 1RH ☎ 01553 841800
The 9-hole King's course (played off 18 tees) is a pleasant
parkland course constructed with conservation in mind
around numerous mature trees, pond and reservoir.
Additional Par 3 pitch and putt course.
9 holes, 5570yds, Par 68, SSS 67, Course record 69.
Club membership 300.
Visitors   no restrictions.
Societies   must contact in advance.
Green Fees not confirmed.
Facilities   ♀ ⚷ 🛍 ⚑ ♪ Brian McKee.
Leisure   driveing range,putting,trolley hire.
Location   4m from King's Lynn off A47
Hotel   ★★★ 66% Butterfly Hotel, Beveridge Way,
Hardwick Narrows, KING'S LYNN
☎ 01553 771707 50 ⇄ 🐾

MUNDESLEY   Map 09 TG33

Mundesley Links Rd NR11 8ES ☎ 01263 720279
Seaside course, good views, windy.
9 holes, 5410yds, Par 68, SSS 66.
Club membership 400.
Visitors   restricted Wed & weekends. Must contact in
advance.

AA
★ ★ ★

BARNHAM BROOM HOTEL

GOLF • CONFERENCE • LEISURE

Barnham Broom, Norwich NR9 4DD
Tel: (01603) 759393
Fax: (01603) 758224

In a beautiful valley, this modern hotel and leisure
complex has 52 bedrooms all with private bathrooms; a
spacious lounge with open log fire; two bars; and a host
of leisure facilities including two 18 hole championship
golf courses (one par 71, one par 72), practice holes
and putting green areas.
Inside the leisure centre are a heated indoor swimming
pool; sauna; solarium; steam room; a beauty and
hairdressing salon and a fully equipped gymnasium.
Other sports facilities include four squash courts, 3 all-
weather tennis courts and a full size snooker table.
The complex also contains a spacious and
comprehensively equipped conference centre.

Prices include full English breakfast.
Children charged for meals as taken.
Host: Richard Bond.

Access: From London and the South via A11; from Midlands and the
North via A47. 10 miles west of Norwich. Norwich Airport 10 miles.

Societies   must contact one month in advance.
Green Fees not confirmed.
Facilities   ♀ ⚷ 🛍 ♪ T G Symmons.
Leisure   putting green,practice area,trolley hire.
Location   W side of village off B1159
Hotel   ★★ 69% Red Lion, Brook St, CROMER
☎ 01263 514964 12 ⇄ 🐾

NORWICH   Map 05 TG20

Costessy Park Old Costessy NR8 5AL
☎ 01603 746333 & 747085
18 holes, 6104yds, Par 72, SSS 69.
Club membership 600.
Visitors   may not play competition days, prior booking
required for weekends.
Societies   welcome by prior arrangement.
Green Fees £15 (£18 weekends).
Facilities   ⊗ ⅢⅠ 🛍 ♪ ♀ ⚷ 🛍 ⚑ ♪ Simon Cook.
Leisure   trolley for hire, putting green, practice area.
Hotel   ★★★ 64% Norwich Sport Village & Hotel in
Broadland, Drayton High Rd, Hellesdon,
NORWICH ☎ 01603 789469 55 ⇄ 🐾

Eaton Newmarket Rd NR4 6SF
☎ 01603 451686 & 452881
An undulating, tree-lined parkland course with excellent
trees.
18 holes, 6135yds, Par 70, SSS 69, Course record 64.
Club membership 800.
Visitors   restricted before 11.30am weekends. Advised to
contact in advance.
Societies   must contact in advance.
Green Fees £28 per day; £15 per round (£35/£20 weekends).
Facilities   ⊗ ⅢⅠ 🛍 ♫ ♀ ⚷ 🛍 ♪ Nigel Bundy.
Leisure   trolley for hire, putting green, practice area.
Location   2.5m SW of city centre off A11
Hotel   ★★★ 64% Norwich Sport Village & Hotel in
Broadland, Drayton High Rd, Hellesdon,
NORWICH ☎ 01603 789469 55 ⇄ 🐾

Royal Norwich Drayton High Rd, Hellesdon NR6 5AH
☎ 01603 429928
Undulating heathland course.
18 holes, 6603yds, Par 72, SSS 72, Course record 67.
Club membership 700.
Visitors   must contact in advance. Restricted weekends &
bank holidays.
Societies   must contact in advance.
Green Fees £26 per day (£30 weekends & bank holidays).
Facilities   ⊗ ⅢⅠ 🛍 ♫ ♀ ⚷ 🛍 ♪ Gary Potter.
Leisure   trolley for hire, putting green, practice area.
Location   2.5m NW of city centre on A1067
Hotel   ★★★ 68% Hotel Norwich, 121-131 Boundary
Rd, NORWICH ☎ 01603 787260 107 ⇄ 🐾

Sprowston Park Wroxham Rd NR7 8RP ☎ 01603 410657
A Pay & Play course set in 100 acres of parkland. A very
tight course, so accuracy is required for good golf. The
facilities include a 27-bay driving range, a practice area and
tuition from a team of professionals.
18 holes, 5921yds, Par 70, SSS 69, Course record 64.
Club membership 550.
Visitors   no restrictions.
Societies   must contact in advance.
Green Fees £14 per round (£17 weekends).   ▶

Facilities ⊗ ⍢ 🐚 💺 ♀ 🎒 🏠 🏌 ⌜ Philip J Grice.
Leisure motorised carts for hire, buggies for hire, trolley for hire, driving range, putting green, practice area.
Location 4m NE from city centre on A1151
Hotel ★★★★ 74% Sprowston Manor, Sprowston Park, Wroxham Road, Sprowston, NORWICH ☎ 01603 410871 87 ⇆ ↾

Wensum Valley Beech Av, Taverham NR8 6HP
☎ 01603 261012
An undulating, picturesque golf course situated on the side of a valley. The greens in particular are very undulating and always give the average golfer a testing time. The 12th hole from a raised tee provides a blind and windy tee shot and a very slopey green.
Valley Course: 18 holes, 6059yds, Par 71, SSS 69, Course record 67.
Wensum Course: 9 holes, 2824yds, Par 35.
Club membership 900.
Visitors no restrictions but advisable to book tee times at weekends.
Societies apply in writing or by telephone.
Green Fees £12 day ticket (£15 weekends).
Facilities ⊗ ⍢ 🐚 💺 ♀ 🎒 🏠 🏌 ⌜ Tony Varney.
Leisure fishing, trolley for hire, driving range, putting green, practice area, bowling green, snooker.
Location 5m NE of Norwich
Hotel ★★★ 68% Hotel Norwich, 121-131 Boundary Rd, NORWICH ☎ 01603 787260 107 ⇆ ↾

SHERINGHAM Map 09 TG14

Sheringham Weybourne Rd NR26 8HG
☎ 01263 823488 & 822038
Splendid cliff-top links with gorse, good 'seaside turf' and plenty of space. Straight driving is essential for a low score. The course is close to the shore and can be very windswept, but offers magnificent views.
18 holes, 6464yds, Par 70, SSS 71, Course record 65.
Club membership 680.
Visitors must contact in advance & have handicap certificate. Restricted weekends.
Societies must apply in writing.
Green Fees £32.50 per day/round (£37.50 weekends & bank holidays).
Facilities ⊗ ⍢ 🐚 💺 ♀ 🎒 🏠 ⌜ R H Emery.
Leisure trolley for hire, practice area.
Location W side of town centre on A149
Hotel ★★ 66% Beaumaris Hotel, South St, SHERINGHAM ☎ 01263 822370 23 ⇆ ↾

SWAFFHAM Map 05 TF80

Swaffham Cley Rd PE37 8AE ☎ 01760 721611
Heathland course.
9 holes, 6252yds, Par 72, SSS 70.
Club membership 475.
Visitors must contact in advance. With member only at weekends.
Societies must contact in advance.
Green Fees £18 per day/round.
Facilities ⊗ ⍢ 🐚 💺 ♀ 🎒 🏠 🏌 ⌜ Peter Field.
Leisure trolley for hire, putting green, practice area.
Location 1.5m SW

Hotel ★★★ 62% George Hotel, Station Rd, SWAFFHAM ☎ 01760 721238 27rm(24 ⇆1 ↾)

THETFORD Map 05 TL88

Feltwell Thor Ave, Feltwell IP26 4AY
☎ 01842 827762 & 827644
In spite of being an inland links, this 9-hole course is still open and windy.
9 holes, 6175yds, Par 70, SSS 69.
Club membership 400.
Visitors dress restriction, no jeans,tracksuits or collarless shirts, golf shoes to be worn.
Societies apply in writing or telephone in advance.
Green Fees not confirmed.
Facilities ♀ (closed Mon) 🎒 🏠
Leisure trolleys for hire.
Hotel ★★★ 59% Bell Hotel, King St, THETFORD ☎ 01842 754455 47 ⇆ ↾

Thetford Brandon Rd IP24 3NE ☎ 01842 752169
This is a course with a good pedigree. It was laid-out by a fine golfer, C.H. Mayo, later altered by James Braid and then again altered by another famous course designer, Mackenzie Ross. It is a testing heathland course with a particularly stiff finish.
18 holes, 6879yds, Par 72, SSS 73, Course record 66.
Club membership 850.
Visitors pre booking advisable, may not play weekends or bank holidays except with member.
Societies must contact in advance, Wed-Fri only.
Green Fees £30 per day/round (weekdays).
Facilities ⊗ ⍢ 🐚 💺 ♀ 🎒 🏠 🏌 ⌜ Gary Kitley.
Leisure trolley for hire, putting green, practice area.
Location 2m W of Thetford on B1107
Hotel ★★★ 59% Bell Hotel, King St, THETFORD ☎ 01842 754455 47 ⇆ ↾

WATTON Map 05 TF90

Richmond Park Saham Rd IP25 6EA ☎ 01953 881803
Meadowland course dotted with newly planted trees and set on either side of the Little Wissey River.
18 holes, 6289yds, Par 71, SSS 70, Course record 69.
Club membership 600.
Visitors must contact in advance.
Societies must contact in advance.
Green Fees £20 per day; £15 per round (£20 per day/round weekends).
Facilities ⊗ ⍢ 🐚 💺 ♀ 🎒 🏠 ⌜ Alan Hemsley.
Leisure gymnasium, trolley for hire, driving range, putting green, practice area.
Location 500yds NW of town centre
Hotel ★★★ 62% George Hotel, Station Rd, SWAFFHAM ☎ 01760 721238 27rm(24 ⇆1 ↾)

WESTON LONGVILLE Map 09 TG11

Weston Park NR9 5JW ☎ 01603 872363
Testing course set in 200 acres of mature parkland with specimen trees.
18 holes, 6603yds, Par 72, SSS 72.
Club membership 250.

Visitors must telephone for tee times.
Societies must telephone for prices and tee times.
Green Fees £30 per day; £20 per 18 holes (£35/£25 weekends).
Facilities ⊗ ⅏ ⅃ ♨ ♀ ⅄ 🗄 ƒ Michael Few.
Leisure motorised carts for hire, buggies for hire, trolley for hire, putting green, practice area.
Location Off the A1067 Norwich/Fakenham road
Hotel ★★★ 65% Quality Friendly Hotel, 2 Barnard Rd, Bowthorpe, NORWICH
☎ 01603 741161 80 ⇔ ʀ

WEST RUNTON   Map 09 TG14

Links Country Park Hotel & Golf Club NR27 9QH
☎ 01263 837691
Parkland course 500 yds from the sea, with superb views overlooking West Runton. The hotel offers extensive leisure facilities.
9 holes, 4814yds, Par 66, SSS 64.
Club membership 250.
Visitors must have a handicap certificate.
Societies must telephone in advance.
Green Fees not confirmed.
Facilities ♀ ⅄ 🗄 ƒ ⇔ ƒ Mike Jubb.
Leisure hard tennis courts, heated indoor swimming pool, sauna, solarium.
Location S side of village off A149
Hotel ★★ 71% Dormy House Hotel, Cromer Rd, WEST RUNTON
☎ 01263 837537 16 ⇔ ʀ

• NORTHAMPTONSHIRE •

CHACOMBE   Map 04 SP44

Cherwell Edge OX17 2EN ☎ 01295 711591
Parkland course open since 1980.
18 holes, 5800yds, Par 70, SSS 68.
Club membership 650.
Visitors no restrictions but golf shoes to be worn (can be hired) and tidy appearance expected.
Societies must apply in writing.
Green Fees not confirmed.
Facilities ♀ ⅄ 🗄 ƒ ƒ Richard Jefferies.
Leisure putting green,cart/buggy/trolley hire,driving range,practice area.
Location 0.5m S off B4525
Hotel ★★★ 67% Whately Hall Hotel, Banbury Cross, BANBURY ☎ 01295 263451 74 ⇔ ʀ

COLD ASHBY   Map 04 SP67

Cold Ashby Stanford Rd NN6 6EP
☎ 01604 740548 & 740099
Undulating parkland course, nicely matured, with superb views. The 27 holes consist of three loops of nine which can be interlinked with each other. All three loops have their own challenge - the Ashby and the Winwick are Par 3's of 200 yards and the start of the Elkington offfers five holes of scenic beauty and testing golf.

Ashby-Elkington: 18 holes, 6250yds, Par 70, SSS 70, Course record 66.
Winwick-Ashby: 18 holes, 6004yds, Par 70, SSS 69.
Elkington-Winwick: 18 holes, 6308yds, Par 72, SSS 70.
Club membership 650.
Visitors restricted weekends.
Societies must contact in advance.
Green Fees £14 per round (£16 weekends).
Facilities ⊗ ⅏ ⅃ ♨ ♀ ⅄ 🗄 ƒ ƒ Shane Rose.
Leisure motorised carts for hire, trolley for hire, putting green, practice area.
Location 1m W
Hotel B Forte Posthouse Northampton/Rugby, CRICK
☎ 01788 822101 88 ⇔ ʀ

COLLINGTREE   Map 04 SP75

Collingtree Park Windingbrook Ln NN4 0XN
☎ 01604 700000
Superb 18-hole resort course designed by former U.S. and British Open champion Johnny Miller. Stunning island green at the 18th hole. Green fee includes buggy cart and range balls. The Golf Academy includes a driving range, practice holes, indoor video teaching room, golf custom-fit centre.
18 holes, 6695yds, Par 72, SSS 72, Course record 66.
Visitors must contact in advance & have handicap certificate.
Societies contact in advance.
Green Fees £30 per round (£40 weekends and bank holidays).
Facilities ⅃ ♨ ♀ ⅄ 🗄 ƒ ƒ Geoff Pook.
Leisure fishing, motorised carts for hire, buggies for hire, trolley for hire, driving range, putting green, practice area.
Location M1-junc 15 on A508 to Northampton
Hotel ★★★★ 67% Swallow Hotel, Eagle Dr, NORTHAMPTON
☎ 01604 768700 120 ⇔ ʀ

CORBY   Map 04 SP88

Corby Public Stamford Rd, Weldon NN17 3JH
☎ 01536 260756
Municipal course laid out on made-up quarry ground and open to prevailing wind. Wet in winter. Played over by Priors Hall Club.
18 holes, 6677yds, Par 72, SSS 72.
Club membership 600.
Visitors are advised to book in advance.
Societies must contact in advance.
Green Fees £7 per round (£9 weekends).
Facilities ⊗ by prior arrangement ⅃ ♨ ♀ ⅄ ƒ
Leisure putting green, practice area.
Location 4m NE on A43
Hotel ★★★ 66% The Talbot, New St, OUNDLE
☎ 01832 273621 39 ⇔ ʀ

DAVENTRY   Map 04 SP56

Daventry & District Norton Rd NN11 5LS
☎ 01327 702829
A hilly course with hard walking.
9 holes, 5555yds, Par 69, SSS 67, Course record 68.
Club membership 360.   ▶

Visitors restricted Sun mornings & weekends (Oct-Mar).
Societies contact the club professional.
Green Fees not confirmed.
Facilities ♀ ⚄ 🏠 ⚐ ☏ Michael Higgins.
Leisure putting,trolley hire,practice area.
Location 1m NE
Hotel ★★★ 69% The Daventry Hotel, Ashby Rd
(A361), DAVENTRY ☎ 01327 301777 138 ➪ ↾

FARTHINGSTONE
Map 04 SP65

Farthingstone Hotel & Golf Course NN12 8AH
☎ 01327 361533
Pleasant rambling course with open aspect and widespread
views.
18 holes, 6248yds, Par 71, SSS 71, Course record 67.
Club membership 500.
Visitors must contact in advance.
Societies must contact in advance.
Green Fees £10 per round (£15 weekends).
Facilities ⊗ 🏮 ⚄ 🍺 ♀ ⚄ 🏠 ⚐ ⚎ ☏ Tom Jones.
Leisure squash, motorised carts for hire, buggies for hire,
trolley for hire, putting green, indoor practice area.
Location 1m W
Hotel ★★ 64% Globe Hotel, High St, WEEDON
☎ 01327 340336 17 ➪ ↾

HELLIDON
Map 04 SP55

Hellidon Lakes Hotel & Country Club NN11 6LN
☎ 01327 262550
Spectacular parkland course designed by David Snell.
*18 holes, 6691yds, Par 72, SSS 72 or 9 holes, 2791yds,
Par 35.*
Club membership 500.
Visitors 18 hole course; must contact in advance & have
handicap certificate at weekends. 9 hole; open to
beginners.
Societies must telephone in advance.
Green Fees not confirmed.
Facilities ♀ ⚄ 🏠 ⚐ ⚎ ☏ Gary Wills.
Leisure hard tennis courts, heated indoor swimming
pool, fishing, sauna, solarium, gymnasium,
buggies, driving range, health studio.
Hotel ★★★★ 67% Hellidon Lakes Hotel & Country
Club, HELLIDON ☎ 01327 262550 45 ➪ ↾
See advertisement on page 221.

KETTERING
Map 04 SP87

Kettering Headlands NN15 6XA ☎ 01536 511104
A very pleasant, mainly flat meadowland course with easy
walking.
18 holes, 6081yds, Par 69, SSS 69, Course record 65.
Club membership 700.
Visitors welcome but with member only weekends &
bank holidays.
Societies Wed & Fri only, apply in writing.
Green Fees £22.
Facilities ⊗ 🏮 ⚄ 🍺 ♀ ⚄ 🏠 ⚐ ☏ Kevin Theobald.
Leisure trolley for hire, putting green, practice area.
Location S side of town centre
Hotel ★★★★ 73% Kettering Park Hotel, Kettering
Parkway, KETTERING
☎ 01536 416666 88 ➪ ↾

NORTHAMPTON
Map 04 SP76

Delapre Golf Complex Eagle Dr, Nene Valley Way
NN4 7DU ☎ 01604 764036
Rolling parkland course, part of municipal golf complex,
which includes two 9-hole, par 3 courses, pitch-and-putt and
33 bay driving-range.
*Main Course: 18 holes, 6269yds, Par 70, SSS 70, Course
record 66.*
Hardingstone Course: 9 holes, 2109yds, Par 32, SSS 32.
Club membership 900.
Visitors no restrictions.
Societies must book and pay full green fees 2 weeks in
advance.
Green Fees not confirmed.
Facilities ⊗ 🏮 ⚄ 🍺 ♀ ⚄ 🏠 ⚐ ☏ John Corby.
Leisure trolley for hire, driving range, putting green, par
3, pitch & putt.
Location 2m SE
Hotel ★★★ 61% Westone Hotel, Ashley Way,
Weston Favell, NORTHAMPTON
☎ 01604 739955 31 ➪ ↾Annexe35 ➪ ↾

Kingsthorpe Kingsley Rd NN2 7BU
☎ 01604 710610 & 711173
A compact, undulating parkland course set within the town
boundary. Not a long course but testing enough to attract a
competitive membership that boasts several County players.
18 holes, 5918yds, Par 69, SSS 69, Course record 63.
Club membership 630.
Visitors must contact in advance and have handicap
certificate. With member only weekends & bank
holidays.
Societies must contact in advance.
Green Fees £25 per day/round.
Facilities ⊗ 🏮 ⚄ 🍺 ♀ ⚄ 🏠 ☏ Paul Armstrong.
Leisure trolley for hire, putting green.
Location N side of town centre on A5095
Hotel ★★★ 61% Westone Hotel, Ashley Way,
Weston Favell, NORTHAMPTON
☎ 01604 739955 31 ➪ ↾Annexe35 ➪ ↾

Northampton Harlestone NN7 4EF
☎ 01604 845155
New parkland course with water in play on three holes.
18 holes, 6615yds, Par 72, SSS 71.
Club membership 750.
Visitors must contact in advance and have handicap
certificate. With member only at weekends.
Societies must contact in advance.
Green Fees £25 per day/round.
Facilities ⊗ 🏮 ⚄ 🍺 ♀ ⚄ 🏠 ☏ Kevin Dickens.
Leisure trolley for hire, putting green, practice area.
Location NW of town centre on A428
Hotel ★★★ 63% Northampton Moat House, Silver
St, NORTHAMPTON
☎ 01604 739988 140 ➪ ↾

Northamptonshire County Sandy Ln, Church Brampton
NN6 8AZ ☎ 01604 843025
Undulating heathland/woodland course with gorse, heather
and fine pine woods.
18 holes, 6503yds, Par 70, SSS 71, Course record 65.
Club membership 650.

Visitors	restricted weekends. Must contact in advance and have a handicap certificate.
Societies	Wed only, must contact in advance.
Green Fees	£37.50 per day summer; £27.50 winter.
Facilities	⊗ ⅲ ⅙ ⦿ ♀ ⅄ 🖾 ☂ ℓ Tim Rouse.
Leisure	trolley for hire, driving range, putting green, practice area.
Location	5m NW of Northampton, off A50
Hotel	★★★ 61% Westone Hotel, Ashley Way, Weston Favell, NORTHAMPTON ☎ 01604 739955 31 ⇆ ↾Annexe35 ⇆ ↾

OUNDLE   Map 04 TL08

Oundle Benefield Rd PE8 4EZ
☎ 01832 273267 (Gen Manager) & 272273 (Pro)
Undulating parkland course, shortish but difficult. A small brook affects some of the approaches to the greens.
18 holes, 6235yds, Par 71, SSS 70, Course record 68.

Visitors	may not play Tue (Ladies Day) or before 10am weekends unless with member.
Societies	must apply in advance.
Green Fees	£20 per day (£30 weekends); weekdays £12 after 3pm.
Facilities	⊗ ⅲ ⅙ ⦿ ♀ ⅄ 🖾 ☂ ℓ Richard Keys.
Leisure	trolley for hire, putting green, practice area.
Location	1m W on A427
Hotel	★★★ 66% The Talbot, New St, OUNDLE ☎ 01832 273621 39 ⇆ ↾

STAVERTON   Map 04 SP56

Staverton Park NN11 6JT ☎ 01327 302000
Open course, fairly testing with good views.
18 holes, 6661yds, Par 71, SSS 72, Course record 65.
Club membership 300.

Visitors	restricted weekends. Must contact in advance. Handicap certificates preferred.
Societies	must contact in advance.
Green Fees	Apr-Oct: £29 per day; £19 per round (£35/£22.50 weekends). Other times: £22 per day; £15 per round (£30/£19.50 weekends).
Facilities	⊗ by prior arrangement ⅲ by prior arrangement ⅙ ⦿ ♀ ⅄ 🖾 ☂ ⊨ ℓ Richard Mudge.
Leisure	sauna, gymnasium, motorised carts for hire, buggies for hire, trolley for hire, floodlit driving range, putting green, practice area, pool table.
Location	0.75m NE of Staverton on A425
Hotel	★★★ 69% The Daventry Hotel, Ashby Rd (A361), DAVENTRY ☎ 01327 301777 138 ⇆ ↾

WELLINGBOROUGH   Map 04 SP86

Rushden Kimbolton Rd, Chelveston NN9 6AN
☎ 01933 312581
Parkland course with brook running through the middle.
10 holes, 6335yds, Par 71, SSS 70.
Club membership 400.

Visitors	may not play Wed afternoon. With member only weekends.
Societies	must apply in writing.
Green Fees	not confirmed.
Facilities	♀ (ex Mon) ⅄
Leisure	putting green, practice area.

Location	2m E of Higham Ferrers on A45
Hotel	★★★ 63% Hind Hotel, Sheep St, WELLINGBOROUGH ☎ 01933 222827 34 ⇆ ↾

Wellingborough Great Harrowden Hall NN9 5AD
☎ 01933 677234 & 678752
An undulating parkland course with many trees. The 514-yd, 14th is a testing hole. The clubhouse is a stately home.
18 holes, 6617yds, Par 72, SSS 72, Course record 68.
Club membership 820.

Visitors	may not play at weekends & bank holidays or Tue between 10.30am and 2.30pm.
Societies	must apply in writing.
Green Fees	£30 per day; £25 per round.
Facilities	⊗ ⅲ ⅙ ⦿ ♀ ⅄ 🖾 ℓ David Clifford.
Leisure	outdoor swimming pool, motorised carts for hire, buggies for hire, trolley for hire, putting green, practice area, snooker.
Location	2m N on A509
Hotel	★★★ 63% Hind Hotel, Sheep St, WELLINGBOROUGH ☎ 01933 222827 34 ⇆ ↾

WHITTLEBURY   Map 04 SP64

West Park Golf & Country Club NN12 8XW
☎ 01327 858092
The 36 holes incorporate three loops of tournament-standard nines plus a short course. The 1905 Course is a reconstruction of the original parkland course built at the turn of the century, the Royal Whittlewood is a lakeland course playing around copses and the Grand Prix, next to Silverstone Motor Racing circuit has a strong links feel playing over gently undulating grassland with challenging lake features.
Grand Prix: 9 holes, 3339yds, Par 36, SSS 72.
1905: 9 holes, 3256yds, Par 36, SSS 71.
Royal Whittlewood: 9 holes, 3323yds, Par 36, SSS 71.
Wedgewood: 9 holes, 1664yds, Par 36, SSS 72.
Club membership 650.

Visitors	must contact in advance.
Societies	telephone 01327 857509 in advance.
Green Fees	£25 per 18 holes (£30 weekends & bank holidays). £5 per extra 9 holes.
Facilities	⊗ ⅲ ⅙ ⦿ ♀ ⅄ 🖾 ℓ Simon Murdoch.
Leisure	buggies for hire, trolley for hire, driving range, putting green, practice area.
Hotel	★★★ 64% The Saracens Head, 219 Watling St, TOWCESTER ☎ 01327 350414 21 ⇆ ↾

NORTHUMBERLAND

ALLENDALE   Map 12 NY85

Allendale High Studdon, Allenheads Rd NE47 9DQ
☎ 01434 683234 & 683237
Challenging and hilly parkland course set 1000 feet above sea level with superb views of Allendale. Holes with interesting features include the 3rd, 7th and 8th.
9 holes, 5044yds, Par 66, SSS 65, Course record 70.
Club membership 170.   ▶

Visitors may not play Aug bank holiday.
Societies must apply in writing to Secretary.
Green Fees £10 per day. Reductions after 5pm.
Facilities ♥ ♿
Leisure putting green.
Location 1.5m S on B6295
Hotel ★★ 62% County Hotel, Priestpopple,
HEXHAM ☎ 01434 602030 9 ⇌ ↾

ALNMOUTH   Map 12 NU21

Alnmouth Foxton Hall, Lesbury NE66 3BE
☎ 01665 830231
Coastal course with pleasant views.
18 holes, 6500yds, Par 69, SSS 69, Course record 65.
Visitors may not play Wed, Fri, weekends & bank
holidays.
Societies Mon, Tue or Thu only.
Green Fees £27 per day/round.
Facilities ⊗ ℳ ⓑ ♥ ♀ ♿ 🏠 🏪
Leisure trolley for hire, putting green, practice area.
Location 1m NE
Hotel ★★★ 61% White Swan Hotel, Bondgate
Within, ALNWICK
☎ 01665 602109 58 ⇌ ↾

Alnmouth Village Marine Rd NE66 2RZ ☎ 01665 830370
Seaside course with part coastal view.
9 holes, 6078yds, Par 70, SSS 70.
Club membership 480.
Visitors no restrictions.
Societies must contact in advance.
Facilities ♀ ♿
Location E side of village
Hotel ★★★ 61% White Swan Hotel, Bondgate
Within, ALNWICK
☎ 01665 602109 58 ⇌ ↾

ALNWICK   Map 12 NU11

Alnwick Swansfield Park NE66 2AT ☎ 01665 602632
Parkland course offering a fair test of golfing skills.
18 holes, 6284yds, Par 70, SSS 70.
Club membership 550.
Visitors must contact in advance.
Societies must contact in advance.
Green Fees £15 per day; £12 per round (£20 weekends &
bank holidays).
Facilities ⊗ ℳ ⓑ ♥ ♀ ♿
Leisure trolley for hire, putting green, practice area.
Location S side of town
Hotel ★★★ 61% White Swan Hotel, Bondgate
Within, ALNWICK
☎ 01665 602109 58 ⇌ ↾

BAMBURGH   Map 12 NU13

Bamburgh Castle NE69 7DE
☎ 01668 214378 & 214321
This is not a long, links course, but there are those who
have played golf all over the world who say that for sheer
breathtaking beauty this northern seaside gem cannot be
bettered. And the course itself is the greatest fun to play.
Magnificent views of Farne Island, Lindisfarne and Holy
Island.

18 holes, 5621yds, Par 68, SSS 67, Course record 64.
Club membership 650.
Visitors must contact in advance. Restricted weekends,
bank holidays and competition days.
Societies apply in writing. Weekdays only.
Green Fees £24 per day/round (£35 per day;£30 per
round weekends and bank holidays).
Facilities ⊗ ℳ ⓑ ♥ ♀ ♿
Leisure buggies for hire, trolley for hire, putting
green, practice area.
Location 6m E of A1 via B1341 or B1342
Hotel ★★ 69% Lord Crewe Arms, Front St,
BAMBURGH
☎ 01668 214243 25rm(20 ⇌ ↾)

BEDLINGTON   Map 12 NZ28

Bedlingtonshire Acorn Bank NE22 6AA
☎ 01670 822087 & 822457
Meadowland/parkland course with easy walking. Under
certain conditions the wind can be a distinct hazard.
18 holes, 6813mtrs, Par 73, SSS 73, Course record 68.
Club membership 960.
Visitors must contact in advance.
Societies must apply in writing.
Green Fees £18 per round.
Facilities ⊗ ℳ ⓑ ♥ ♀ ♿ 🏠 ⛳ ↾ Marcus Webb.
Leisure trolley for hire, putting green, practice area.
Location 1m SW on A1068
Hotel ★★★★ 58% Holiday Inn, Great North Rd,
SEATON BURN ☎ 0191 201 9988 150 ⇌ ↾

BELFORD   Map 12 NU13

Belford South Rd NE70 7HY ☎ 01668 213433
On the east coast, this course is often affected by crosswinds
especially the 4th - the compensation is spectacular views of
Holy Island. A number of other holes are affected by mature
trees.
9 holes, 3152yds, Par 72, SSS 70, Course record 72.
Club membership 200.
Visitors no restrictions.
Societies must contact in advance.
Green Fees £16 per day; £13 per 18 holes; £9 per 9 holes
(£21/£16/£10 weekends and bank holidays).
Facilities ⊗ ℳ ⓑ ♥ ♀ ♿ 🏠 ⛳
Leisure motorised carts for hire, trolley for hire, driving
range, practice area.
Location Off A1 between Alnwick & Berwick on Tweed
Hotel ★★★ 64% Blue Bell Hotel, Market Place,
BELFORD ☎ 01668 213543 17 ⇌ ↾

BELLINGHAM   Map 12 NY88

Bellingham Boggle Hole NE48 2DT
☎ 01434 220530 (Secretary) & 220152 (Clubhouse)
9-hole downland course with natural hazards and 18 tees.
9 holes, 5226yds, Par 67, SSS 66, Course record 63.
Club membership 450.
Visitors must contact in advance.
Societies must contact in advance.
Green Fees £10 per day/round (£15 weekends).
Facilities ⊗ ℳ ⓑ ♥ ♀ ♿
Leisure driving range, putting green, practice area.

Visitors are welcomed at

Berwick-upon-Tweed (Goswick) Golf Club

Signposted off the A1, south of Berwick, only 10 minutes from the centre.
The club is open all year to non-members
Anytime weekdays. Bookings weekends. Bar. Service/Catering. Residents Pro
Secretary Mr A. E. French **(01289) 387256**
Membership available
Paul Terras, Goswick Golf Club Pro Shop
Golf Club Repairs ★ Tuition ★ Sales ★ Tel: 01289 387380

Location N side of village on B6320
Hotel ★★ 68% Riverdale Hall Hotel,
BELLINGHAM ☎ 01434 220254 20 ⇔ ℉

BERWICK-UPON-TWEED   Map 12 NT95

Berwick-upon-Tweed (Goswick) Goswick TD15 2RW
☎ 01289 387256
Natural seaside links course, with undulating fairways,
elevated tees and good greens.
18 holes, 6425yds, Par 72, SSS 71, Course record 69.
Club membership 575.
Visitors must contact in advance for weekends,
advisable at other times.
Societies must telephone in advance (apply in writing
Apr-Sep).
Green Fees £24 per day; £18 per round (£32/£24
weekends).
Facilities ⊗ ℳ ㄴ ☕ ♀ ☖ ㅜ ㅜ ㇏ Paul Terras.
Leisure motorised carts for hire, buggies for hire,
trolley for hire, driving range, putting green,
practice area.
Location 6m S off A1
Hotel ★★★★ 69% Tillmouth Park Hotel,
CORNHILL-ON-TWEED
☎ 01890 882255 12 ⇔ ℉Annexe2 ⇔ ℉

Magdalene Fields Magdalene Fields TD15 1NE
☎ 01289 306384
Seaside course with natural hazards formed by sea bays. Last
9 holes open to winds. Testing 18th hole over bay (par 3).
18 holes, 6407yds, Par 72, SSS 71, Course record 66.
Club membership 400.
Visitors must contact in advance for weekend play.
Societies must contact in advance.
Green Fees £20 per day; £15.50 per round (£22/£17.50
weekends).
Facilities ⊗ ℳ ㄴ ☕ ♀ ☖
Leisure putting green.
Location E side of town centre
Hotel ★★★★ 69% Tillmouth Park Hotel,
CORNHILL-ON-TWEED
☎ 01890 882255 12 ⇔ ℉Annexe2 ⇔ ℉

BLYTH   Map 12 NZ38

Blyth New Delaval, Newsham NE24 4DB
☎ 01670 367728
Course built over old colliery. Parkland with water hazards.
18 holes, 6430yds, Par 72, SSS 71, Course record 66.
Club membership 820.
Visitors with member only after 3pm & at weekends.
Must contact in advance.

Societies apply in writing.
Green Fees £20 per day; £18 per round.
Facilities ⊗ ℳ ㄴ ☕ ♀ ☖ ☖ ㇏ Brian Rumney.
Leisure trolley for hire, putting green, practice area.
Location 6m N of Whitley Bay
Hotel ★★★ 64% Windsor Hotel, South Pde,
WHITLEY BAY ☎ 0191 251 8888 64 ⇔ ℉

CRAMLINGTON   Map 12 NZ27

Arcot Hall NE23 7QP ☎ 0191 236 2794 & 236 2147
A wooded parkland course, reasonably flat.
18 holes, 6380yds, Par 70, SSS 70, Course record 65.
Club membership 660.
Visitors must contact in advance. May not play
weekends.
Societies must contact in advance.
Green Fees £25 per day; £20 per round (£28 weekends).
Facilities ⊗ ℳ ㄴ ☕ ♀ ☖ ㅜ ㇏ Graham Cant.
Leisure trolley for hire, putting green, practice area.
Location 2m SW off A1
Hotel ★★★★ 58% Holiday Inn, Great North Rd,
SEATON BURN ☎ 0191 201 9988 150 ⇔ ℉

EMBLETON   Map 12 NU22

Dunstanburgh Castle NE66 3XQ ☎ 01665 576562
Rolling links designed by James Braid, with castle and bird
sanctuary either side. Superb views.
18 holes, 6298yds, Par 70, SSS 69, Course record 69.
Club membership 390.
Visitors advisable to contact in advance at weekends and
holiday periods.
Societies must contact in advance.
Green Fees £15 per day (£22 per day; £18 per round
weekends & bank holidays).
Facilities ⊗ ℳ ㄴ ☕ ♀ ☖ ㅜ
Location 0.5m E
Hotel ★★ 72% Beach House Hotel, Sea Front,
SEAHOUSES ☎ 01665 720337 14 ⇔ ℉

GREENHEAD   Map 12 NY66

Haltwhistle Banktop CA6 7HL
☎ 016977 47367 & 01434 320337 sec
Interesting course with panoramic views of Northumberland
National Park. The 515yard Par 5 8th hole is a real test of
golf skill, played from the highest point of the course through
an undulating fairway to a viciously sloping green. The
188yard Par 3 10th hole, played uphill, is particularly difficult
playing into the prevailing west wind.
12 holes, 5986yds, Par 71, SSS 69, Course record 78.
Club membership 287. ▶

Visitors course played over 18 holes, no visitors Sun mornings.
Societies apply in writing to: Hon Secretary, W E Barnes, Croftlynn, Haltwhistle, Northumberland NE49 9JR.
Green Fees not confirmed.
Facilities
Hotel ★★ 66% Kirby Moor Country House Hotel, Longtown Rd, BRAMPTON ☎ 016977 3893 6rm(5)

HEXHAM — Map 12 NY96

Hexham Spital Park NE46 3RZ ☎ 01434 603072
A very pretty undulating parkland course with interesting natural contours. From parts of the course, particularly the elevated 6th tee, there are the most exquisite views of the valley below. As good a parkland course as any in the North of England.
18 holes, 6000yds, Par 70, SSS 68, Course record 64.
Club membership 700.
Visitors advance booking advisable.
Societies welcome weekdays, contact in advance.
Green Fees not confirmed.
Facilities Martin Forster.
Leisure squash, putting,trolley hire,practice area.
Location 1m NW on B6531
Hotel ★★★ 65% Beaumont Hotel, Beaumont St, HEXHAM ☎ 01434 602331 23

Slaley Hall Slaley NE47 OBY ☎ 01434 673350 & 673154
Measuring 7021yds from the championship tees, this Dave Thomas designed course incorporates forest, parkland and moorland with an abundance of lakes and streams. The challenging par 4 9th (452yds) is played over water through a narrow avenue of towering trees and dense rhododendrons.
18 holes, 6759yds, Par 72, SSS 73, Course record 65.
Club membership 350.
Visitors must contact in advance, times subject to availability, restricted weekends, must provide proof of official handicap Gentlemen max28, Ladies max36.
Societies apply in writing to bookings co-ordinator, small groups 8 or less may book through pro shop.
Green Fees £55 per 36 holes; £45 per 27 holes; £35 per 18 holes (Standby rate £40/£35/£25). Twilight rate £25 per 18 holes (£22.50 winter).
Facilities To be appointed.
Leisure heated indoor swimming pool, fishing, sauna, solarium, gymnasium, motorised carts for hire, buggies for hire, trolley for hire, putting green, practice area.
Location 8m S of Hexham off A68

Tynedale Tyne Green NE46 3HQ ☎ 01434 608154
Flat, easy moorland course. Bounded by river and railway.
9 holes, 5643yds, Par 69, SSS 67, Course record 67.
Club membership 421.
Visitors may not play Sun mornings.
Societies must contact in advance.
Green Fees not confirmed.
Facilities Claire Brown.
Leisure practice net,pool table,darts.
Location N side of town
Hotel ★★★ 65% Beaumont Hotel, Beaumont St, HEXHAM ☎ 01434 602331 23

English Tourist Board HIGHLY COMMENDED

AA ★★★

The Beaumont Hotel,
Hexham, Northumberland
NE46 3LT
(01434) 602331
The perfect base for 3 of the North East's finest Golf Courses: Slaley, Hexham & Matfen Hall.
23 Bedrooms, with full facilities, excellent food and choice of bars make a wonderful 'Golfing Hotel'.
Special Golf Rates on Request

Best Western

MORPETH — Map 12 NZ28

Morpeth The Common NE61 2BT ☎ 01670 504942
Parkland course with views of the Cheviots.
18 holes, 6206yds, Par 71, SSS 69.
Club membership 700.
Visitors restricted weekends & bank holidays. Must contact in advance and have a handicap certificate.
Societies apply in writing.
Green Fees not confirmed.
Facilities
Leisure snooker.
Location S side of town centre on A197
Hotel ★★★★ 66% Longhirst Hall, Longhirst, MORPETH ☎ 01670 791348 75

NEWBIGGIN-BY-THE-SEA — Map 12 NZ38

Newbiggin-by-the-Sea Prospect Close NE64 6DW
☎ 01670 817344
Seaside-links course.
18 holes, 6452yds, Par 72, SSS 71, Course record 65.
Club membership 570.
Visitors must contact professional on arrival and may not play before 10am.
Societies must apply in writing.
Green Fees £14 per day/round (£19 weekends).
Facilities Marcus Webb.
Leisure trolley for hire, putting green, practice area, snooker.

Location N side of town
Hotel ★★★★ 66% Longhirst Hall, Longhirst, MORPETH ☎ 01670 791348 75 ⇔ ୮∿

PONTELAND
Map 12 NZ17

Ponteland 53 Bell Villas NE20 9BD ☎ 01661 822689
Open parkland course offering testing golf and good views.
18 holes, 6524yds, Par 72, SSS 71, Course record 66.
Club membership 720.
Visitors with member only Fri, weekends & bank holidays.
Societies welcome Tue & Thu only. Must contact in advance.
Green Fees £22.50 per day/round.
Facilities ⊗ ∭ ⬧ ⬛ ♀ ♨ ♨ ⌂ ୮ Alan Crosby.
Leisure trolley for hire, putting, practice area.
Location 0.5m E on A696
Hotel ★★★ 64% Newcastle Airport Moat House, Woolsington, NEWCASTLE UPON TYNE AIRPORT ☎ 0191 401 9988 100 ⇔ ୮∿

PRUDHOE
Map 12 NZ06

Prudhoe Eastwood Park NE42 5DX
☎ 01661 832466
Parkland course with natural hazards and easy walking along undulating fairways.
18 holes, 5812yds, Par 69, SSS 68, Course record 63.
Club membership 700.
Visitors must contact in advance. Weekends after 4.30pm
Societies must contact in writing.
Green Fees not confirmed.
Facilities ♀ ♨ ⌂ ୮ John Crawford.
Location E side of town centre off A695
Hotel ★★ 62% County Hotel, Priestpopple, HEXHAM ☎ 01434 602030 9 ⇔ ୮∿

ROTHBURY
Map 12 NU00

Rothbury Old Race Course NE65 7TR
☎ 01669 620718 & 621271
Very flat parkland course alongside the River Coquet.
9 holes, 5681yds, Par 68, SSS 68, Course record 65.
Club membership 400.
Visitors may play at weekends by arrangement only.
Societies may not play at weekends. Must contact in advance.
Green Fees not confirmed.
Facilities ♀ ♨
Location S side of town off B6342
Hotel ★★★ 61% White Swan Hotel, Bondgate Within, ALNWICK ☎ 01665 602109 58 ⇔ ୮∿

SEAHOUSES
Map 12 NU23

Seahouses Beadnell Rd NE68 7XT ☎ 01665 720794
Typical links course with many hazards, including the famous 10th, 'Logans Loch', water hole.
18 holes, 5462yds, Par 67, SSS 67, Course record 63.
Club membership 750.
Visitors must contact in advance.
Societies must contact in advance. May not play Sun.

Green Fees £16 per day (£20 weekends & bank holidays).
Facilities ⊗ ∭ ⬧ ⬛ ♀ ♨
Leisure trolley for hire, putting green, practice area.
Location S side of village on B1340
Hotel ★★ 72% Olde Ship Hotel, SEAHOUSES ☎ 01665 720200 12 ⇔ ୮∿Annexe4 ⇔ ୮∿

STOCKSFIELD
Map 12 NZ06

Stocksfield New Ridley Rd NE43 7RE
☎ 01661 843041 & 843101
Challenging course: parkland (9 holes), woodland (9 holes).
18 holes, 5978yds, Par 68, SSS 68.
Club membership 900.
Visitors welcome except Wed & weekends until 4pm. Must contact in advance.
Societies must contact in advance.
Green Fees £16-£19 (£24 weekends).
Facilities ⊗ by prior arrangement ∭ by prior arrangement ⬧ ⬛ ♀ ♨ ⌂ ┬ ୮ Steven McKenna.
Leisure motorised carts for hire, trolley for hire, putting green, practice area.
Location 2.5m SE off A695
Hotel ★★★ 65% Beaumont Hotel, Beaumont St, HEXHAM ☎ 01434 602331 23 ⇔ ୮∿

SWARLAND
Map 12 NU10

Swarland Hall Coast View NE65 9JG
☎ 01670 787010 & 787940
Parkland course set in mature woodland. There are seven Par 4 holes in excess of 400 yards.
18 holes, 6628yds, Par 72, SSS 72.
Club membership 400.
Visitors restricted on competition days.
Societies apply in writing.
Green Fees £17.50 per day; £12.50 per round (£15 per round weekends & bank holidays).
Facilities ⊗ ∭ ⬧ ⬛ ♀ ♨ ⌂ ┬ ୮ David Fletcher/Linzi Hardy.
Leisure motorised carts for hire, buggies for hire, trolley for hire, putting green, practice area, snooker.
Location Approx 1m W of A1
Hotel ★★★★⬥ 71% Linden Hall Hotel and Health Spa, LONGHORSLEY ☎ 01670 516611 50 ⇔ ୮∿

WARKWORTH
Map 12 NU20

Warkworth The Links NE65 0SW ☎ 01665 711596
Seaside links course, with good views and alternative tees for the back nine.
9 holes, 5856yds, Par 70, SSS 68, Course record 66.
Club membership 470.
Visitors welcome except Tue & Sat.
Societies must contact in advance.
Green Fees £12 per day (£20 weekends & bank holidays).
Facilities ⊗ ⬧ ⬛ ♀ ♨
Leisure practice area.
Location 0.5m E of village off A1068
Hotel ★★★ 61% White Swan Hotel, Bondgate Within, ALNWICK ☎ 01665 602109 58 ⇔ ୮∿

WOOLER   Map 12 NT92

Wooler Dod Law, Doddington NE71 6EA
☎ 01668 281137
Hilltop, moorland course with spectacular views over the
Glendale valley. Nine greens played from 18 tees. A very
challenging course when windy with one Par 5 of 580 yards.
The course is much under used during the week so is always
available.
9 holes, 6358yds, Par 72, SSS 70.
Club membership 300.
Visitors   normally no restrictions.
Societies   by prior arrangement with secretary.
Green Fees   £10 (£15 weekends & bank holidays).
Facilities   ⊗ ⅏ ⅃ ⬤ ♀ ⚒
Leisure   motorised carts for hire, buggies for hire, trolley
                  for hire, putting green, practice area.
Location   At Doddington on B6525 Wooler/Berwick Rd
Hotel   ★★ 62% Tankerville Arms Hotel, Cottage Rd,
                  WOOLER
                  ☎ 01668 281581 16 ⇔ ♙

NOTTINGHAMSHIRE

CALVERTON   Map 08 SK64

Ramsdale Park Golf Centre Oxton Rd, Calverton
NG14 6NU ☎ 0115 965 5600
The High course is a challenging and comprehensive test for
any standard of golfer. A relatively flat front nine is followed
by an undulating back nine that is renowned as one of the
best 9 holes of golf in the county. The Low course comprises
contoured and bunkered greens that is ideal for both beginner
and established golfer who wants to improve his iron and shot
play.
*High Course: 18 holes, 6546yds, Par 71, SSS 71, Course
record 70.*
Low Course: 18 holes, 2844yds, Par 54.
Club membership 400.
Visitors   may book up to 6 days in advance with credit
                  card.
Societies   welcome midweek, apply in writing or
                  telephone.
Green Fees   High: £13; Low: £7.20.
Facilities   ⊗ ⅏ ⅃ ⬤ ♀ ⚒ 🖼 ♙ ⚒ Robert Macey.
Leisure   driving range, video teaching bay.
Location   8m NE of Nottingham, off B6386
Hotel   ★★★ 65% Saracen's Head Hotel, Market
                  Place, SOUTHWELL
                  ☎ 01636 812701 27 ⇔ ♙

EAST LEAKE   Map 08 SK52

Rushcliffe Stocking Ln LE12 5RL
☎ 01509 852959
Hilly, tree-lined and picturesque parkland course.
18 holes, 6013yds, Par 70, SSS 69, Course record 63.
Club membership 700.
Visitors   restricted weekends & bank holidays 9.30-11am
                  & 3-4.30pm.

Societies   must apply in advance.
Green Fees   £22 per day (£25 weekends).
Facilities   ⊗ ⅏ ⅃ ⬤ ♀ 🖼 ⚒ Chris Hall.
Leisure   trolley for hire, putting green, practice area.
Location   1m N
Hotel   ★★★ 63% Yew Lodge, 33 Packington Hill,
                  KEGWORTH
                  ☎ 01509 672518 54 ⇔ ♙

KEYWORTH   Map 08 SK63

Stanton on the Wolds NG12 5BH
☎ 0115 937 2044
Parkland course, fairly flat with stream running through four
holes.
18 holes, 6437yds, Par 73, SSS 71, Course record 67.
Club membership 705.
Visitors   must play with member at weekends.
Societies   must apply in writing.
Green Fees   £25/£20 per day/round.
Facilities   ⊗ ⅏ ⅃ ⬤ ♀ ⚒ 🖼 ♙ ⚒ Nick Hernon.
Leisure   trolley for hire, putting green, practice area.
Location   E side of village
Hotel   ★★ 65% Rufford Hotel, 53 Melton Road, West
                  Bridgford, NOTTINGHAM
                  ☎ 0115 981 4202 35 ♙

KIRKBY IN ASHFIELD   Map 08 SK55

Notts Derby Rd NG17 7QR
☎ 01623 753225
Undulating heathland Championship course.
18 holes, 7030yds, Par 72, SSS 74, Course record 64.
Club membership 500.
Visitors   must contact in advance & have handicap
                  certificate. With member only weekends &
                  bank holidays.
Societies   must apply in advance.
Green Fees   £45 per day; £35 per round.
Facilities   ⊗ ⅏ ⅃ ⬤ ♀ ⚒ 🖼 ♙ ⚒ Brian Waites.
Leisure   trolley for hire, driving range, putting green,
                  practice area.
Location   1.5m SE off A611
Hotel   ★★★★ 65% Swallow Hotel, Carter Ln
                  East, SOUTH NORMANTON
                  ☎ 01773 812000 161 ⇔ ♙

LONG EATON   Map 08 SK43

Trent Lock Golf Centre Lock Ln, Sawley NG10 2FY
☎ 0115 9464398 & 9461184
Parkland course.
18 holes, 6211yds, Par 73, SSS 70, Course record 73.
Club membership 400.
Visitors   no restriction Mon-Fri am but booking system
                  12pm Fri-closing Sun.
Societies   apply in writing or telephone in advance.
Green Fees   £13 per day (£10 per 18 holes).
Facilities   ⊗ ⅏ ⅃ ⬤ ♀ ⚒ 🖼 ⚒ M Taylor/E McCausland.
Leisure   fishing, trolley for hire, driving range, putting
                  green.
Hotel   ★★★ 61% Novotel, Bostock Ln, LONG
                  EATON
                  ☎ 0115 946 5111 105 ⇔ ♙

MANSFIELD — Map 08 SK56

Sherwood Forest Eakring Rd NG18 3EW
☎ 01623 26689
As the name suggests, the Forest is the main feature of
this natural heathland course with its heather, silver birch
and pine trees. The homeward nine holes are particularly
testing. The 11th and 14th are notable par 4 holes on this
well-bunkered course designed by the great James Braid.
18 holes, 6698yds, Par 71, SSS 73, Course record 68.
Club membership 750.

Visitors	weekdays only by prior arrangement with the Secretary.
Societies	by arrangement with the Secretary.
Green Fees	on application.
Facilities	⊗ Ⅲ☰ ☰ ♀♣ ☎ ⟨ Ken Hall.
Leisure	trolley for hire, putting green, practice area, snooker table.
Location	E of Mansfield
Hotel	★★ 65% Pine Lodge Hotel, 281-283 Nottingham Rd, MANSFIELD ☎ 01623 22308 20rm(19 ⇄ ✿)

MANSFIELD WOODHOUSE — Map 08 SK56

Mansfield Woodhouse Leeming Ln North NG19 9EU
☎ 01623 23521
Easy walking on heathland.
9 holes, 2446yds, Par 68, SSS 64.
Club membership 130.

Visitors	no restrictions.
Societies	must contact by telephone.
Green Fees	not confirmed.
Facilities	♀ ☎ ⟨ Leslie Highfield.
Location	N side of town centre off A60
Hotel	★★ 65% Pine Lodge Hotel, 281-283 Nottingham Rd, MANSFIELD ☎ 01623 22308 20rm(19 ⇄ ✿)

NEWARK-ON-TRENT — Map 08 SK75

Newark Coddington NG24 2QX ☎ 01636 626282
Wooded, parkland course in secluded situation with easy
walking.
18 holes, 6421yds, Par 71, SSS 71, Course record 66.
Club membership 600.

Visitors	must contact in advance and have handicap certificate. May not play Tue (Ladies Day).
Societies	must contact in advance.
Green Fees	£27 per day; £22 per round.
Facilities	⊗ Ⅲ☰ ☰ ♀♣ ☎ ⟨ H A Bennett.
Leisure	trolley for hire, putting green, practice area.
Location	4m E on A17
Hotel	★★ 71% Grange Hotel, 73 London Rd, NEWARK ☎ 01636 703399 10 ⇄ ✿Annexe5 ⇄ ✿

NOTTINGHAM — Map 08 SK53

Beeston Fields Old Dr, Wollaton Rd, Beeston NG9 3DD
☎ 0115 925 7062
Parkland course with sandy subsoil and wide, tree-lined
fairways. The par 3, 14th has elevated tee and small bunker-
guarded green.

18 holes, 6402yds, Par 71, SSS 71, Course record 65.
Club membership 750.

Visitors	must contact in advance.
Societies	must apply in advance.
Green Fees	£30 per day; £20 per round (£25 per round weekends).
Facilities	⊗ Ⅲ☰ ☰ ♀♣ ☎ ⟨ Alun Wardle.
Leisure	trolley for hire, putting green, practice area.
Location	4m SW off A52
Hotel	B Forte Posthouse Nottingham/Derby, Bostocks Ln, SANDIACRE ☎ 0115 9397800 91 ⇄ ✿

Bramcote Hills Thoresby Rd, off Derby Rd, Bramcote
NG9 3EP ☎ 0115 928 1880
A Pay and Play, 18-hole Par 3 course with challenging
greens.
18 holes, 1500yds, Par 54.

Visitors	no restrictions.
Societies	telephone in advance.
Green Fees	£5.40 per 18 holes (£5.90 weekends).
Facilities	☰ ☎ ⟨
Location	Off A52 Derby rd
Hotel	★★ 70% Priory Hotel, Derby Rd, Wollaton Vale, NOTTINGHAM ☎ 0115 922 1691 31 ⇄ ✿

Bulwell Forest Hucknall Rd, Bulwell NG6 9LQ
☎ 0115 977 0576
Municipal heathland course with many natural hazards. Very
tight fairways and subject to wind.
18 holes, 5606yds, Par 68, SSS 67.
Club membership 450.

Visitors	restricted weekends. Must contact in advance.
Societies	must apply in writing.
Green Fees	not confirmed.
Facilities	♀♣ ☎ ⟨
Leisure	putting green.
Location	4m NW of city centre on A611
Hotel	★★★ 67% Nottingham Moat House, Mansfield Rd, NOTTINGHAM ☎ 0115 935 9988 172 ⇄ ✿

Chilwell Manor Meadow Ln, Chilwell NG9 5AE
☎ 0115 925 8958
Flat parkland course.
18 holes, 6379yds, Par 70, SSS 70.
Club membership 750.

Visitors	with member only weekends. Must contact in advance and have a handicap certificate.
Societies	welcome Mon, must apply in advance.
Green Fees	not confirmed.
Facilities	♣ ☎ ⟨
Location	4m SW on A6005
Hotel	★★ 62% Europa Hotel, 20 Derby Rd, LONG EATON ☎ 0115 972 8481 15 ⇄ ✿

Edwalton Municipal Wellin Ln, Edwalton NG12 4AS
☎ 0115 923 4775 & 923 1987
Gently sloping, 9-hole parkland course. Also 9-hole Par 3 and
large practice ground.
9 holes, 3372yds, Par 72, SSS 72, Course record 71.
Club membership 900.

Visitors	booking system in operation.
Societies	prior booking necessary.
Green Fees	not confirmed.
Facilities	♀♣ ☎ ⟨ John Staples.

▶

Leisure par 3 course.
Location S of Nottingham, off A606
Hotel ★★ 65% Rufford Hotel, 53 Melton Road,West Bridgford, NOTTINGHAM
☎ 0115 981 4202 35 ↑

Mapperley Central Av, Plains Rd, Mapperley NG3 5RH
☎ 0115 926 5611
Hilly meadowland course but with easy walking.
18 holes, 6283yds, Par 71, SSS 70, Course record 68.
Club membership 650.
Visitors must contact in advance. May not play Sat.
Societies must telephone in advance.
Green Fees £15 per day; £12 per 18 holes (£21/£18 weekends and bank holidays).
Facilities ⊗ �𝄂 ⓛ ⚑ ♀ ♧ 🖾 ↑ ↺
Leisure trolley for hire, putting green, practice area, pool table.
Location 3m NE of city centre off B684
Hotel B Forte Posthouse Nottingham, Saint James's St, NOTTINGHAM ☎ 0115 947 0131 130 ⇆ ↑

Nottingham City Bulwell Hall Park NG6 8BL
☎ 0115 927 6916 & 927 2767
A pleasant municipal parkland course on the city outskirts.
18 holes, 6218yds, Par 69, SSS 70, Course record 65.
Club membership 425.
Visitors restricted Sat 7am-3pm.
Societies welcome except weekends.
Green Fees not confirmed.
Facilities ♀ ♧ 🖾 ↑ ↺ Cyril Jepson.
Leisure putting green,practice area,trolley hire.
Location 4m NW of city centre off A6002
Hotel ★★★ 67% Nottingham Moat House, Mansfield Rd, NOTTINGHAM
☎ 0115 935 9988 172 ⇆ ↑

Wollaton Park Limetree Av, Wollaton Park NG8 1BT
☎ 0115 978 7574
A pleasant, fairly level course set in a park close to the centre of Nottingham, with red and fallow deer herds. The fairways are tree-lined. The 502-yd dog-leg 15th is a notable hole. The stately home - Wollaton Hall - is situated in the park.
18 holes, 6445yds, Par 71, SSS 71, Course record 64.
Club membership 650.
Visitors may not play Wed or competition days.
Societies must apply in advance.
Green Fees £35 per day; £21.50 per round (£35/£25 weekends).
Facilities ⊗ �𝄂 ⓛ ⚑ ♀ ♧ 🖾 ↺ John Lower.
Leisure trolley for hire, putting green, pitch & putt, practice area.
Location 2.5m W of city centre off A52
Hotel ★★★ 63% Swans Hotel & Restaurant, 84-90 Radcliffe Rd, West Bridgford, NOTTINGHAM ☎ 0115 981 4042 31 ⇆ ↑

OLLERTON   Map 08 SK66

Rufford Park Golf Centre Rufford Ln, Rufford NG22 9DG
☎ 01623 825253
Rufford Park is noted for its pictuesque 18 holes with its especially challenging Par 3's. From the unique 100yard Par 3 17th to the riverside 585yard 13th, the course offers everything the golfer needs from beginner to professional.

18 holes, 5953yds, Par 70, SSS 69.
Club membership 650.
Visitors are advised to book in advance.
Societies society packages on request, need to be booked in advance.
Green Fees £20 per day; £18 per round.
Facilities ⊗ ⟋ ⓛ ⚑ ♀ ♧ 🖾 ↺
↺ John Vaughan/James Thompson.
Leisure motorised carts for hire, buggies for hire, trolley for hire, driving range, putting green, practice area, 9 hole short course.
Location S Of Ollerton off A614
Hotel ★★ 65% Hop Pole Hotel, Main St, OLLERTON
☎ 01623 822573 11rm(10 ⇆ ↑)

OXTON   Map 08 SK65

Oakmere Park Oaks Ln NG25 0RH ☎ 0115 965 3545
Set in rolling parkland in the heart of picturesque Robin Hood country. The par 4 (16th) and par 5 (1st) are notable. Thirty-bay floodlit driving range.
North Course: 18 holes, 6617mtrs, Par 72, SSS 72.
South Course: 9 holes, 3216mtrs, Par 37, SSS 37.
Club membership 450.
Visitors correct golf attire required, please book for weekends.
Societies please apply in writing or telephone.
Green Fees not confirmed.
Facilities ♀ ♧ 🖾 ↺ ↺ Stephen Meade.
Leisure 30 bay floodlit driving range,caddy cars.
Location 1m NW off A6097
Hotel ★★★ 65% Saracen's Head Hotel, Market Place, SOUTHWELL
☎ 01636 812701 27 ⇆ ↑

RADCLIFFE-ON-TRENT   Map 08 SK63

Cotgrave Place Golf & Country Club Main Rd, Stragglethorpe NG12 3HB ☎ 01159 333344 & 334686
The course has been designed in three nines to play in three separate and self-contained styles. The first nine holes are dotted around a beautiful lake, man-made ponds and a canal. Water comes into play at every hole, but many are hidden from the tee waiting to catch the wayward drive. The second nine are in magnificent parkland with wide, lush fairways and with huge bunkers. The 13th is protected by enourmous tiers.The final nine are set amidst hedgerows and coppices requiring well-placed tee shots.
Lakeside: 9 holes, 3186yds, Par 36.
Parkland: 9 holes, 3117yds, Par 35.
Fox Coverts: 9 holes, 2755yds, Par 33.
Club membership 700.
Visitors must contact in advance.
Societies telephone in advance.
Green Fees £22 per day; £15 per 18 holes; £7.50 per 9 holes (£35/£25/£12.50 weekends).
Facilities ⊗ ⟋ ⓛ ⚑ ♀ ♧ 🖾 ↺ ↺ Greg Towne.
Leisure motorised carts for hire, buggies for hire, trolley for hire, driving range, putting green, practice area.
Location Off A52, 6miles from Nottingham
Hotel ★★⚘ 71% Langar Hall, LANGAR
☎ 01949 60559 12 ⇆ ↑

Radcliffe-on-Trent Drewberry Ln, Cropwell Rd NG12 2JH
☎ 0115 933 3000
Fairly flat, parkland course with three good finishing holes:
16th (427 yds) par 4; 17th (180 yds) through spinney, par 3;
18th (331 yds) dog-leg par 4. Excellent views.
18 holes, 6381yds, Par 70, SSS 71, Course record 64.
Club membership 620.
Visitors   must contact in advance.
Societies   welcome Wed. Must contact in advance.
Green Fees   £23 (£28 weekends).
Facilities   ⊗ � ♨ ♣ ♟ ♨ ☺ ⚑ ☂ 〔 Robert Ellis.
Leisure   trolley for hire, putting green, practice area.
Location   1m SE off A52
Hotel   ★★★ 63% Swans Hotel & Restaurant, 84-90
             Radcliffe Rd, West Bridgford, NOTTINGHAM
             ☎ 0115 981 4042 31 ⇥ 〔

RETFORD   Map 08 SK78

Retford Brecks Rd, Ordsall DN22 7UA
☎ 01777 860682 (Secretary) & 703733 (Pro)
A wooded, parkland course.
18 holes, 6301yds, Par 71, SSS 70, Course record 67.
Club membership 700.
Visitors   advisable to contact in advance, with member
             only at weekends and holidays.
Societies   apply in writing or telephone. Not welcome Tue
             morning or bank holidays, limited availability
             weekends.
Green Fees   £23 per day; £19 per round.
Facilities   ⊗ 〔 ♣ ♟ ♨ ☺ ⚑ ☂ 〔 Stuart Betteridge.
Leisure   motorised carts for hire, buggies for hire, trolley
             for hire, putting green, practice area.
Location   1.5m S A620, between Worksop &
             Gainsborough
Hotel   ★★★ 67% West Retford Hotel, 24 North Rd,
             RETFORD
             ☎ 01777 706333 Annexe60 ⇥ 〔

RUDDINGTON   Map 08 SK53

Ruddington Grange Wilford Rd NG11 6NB
☎ 0115 984 6141
Undulating parkland course with water hazards on 12 holes.
18 holes, 6543yds, Par 72, SSS 72.
Club membership 650.
Visitors   a handicap certificate is required, contact in
             advance if possible. Play may be restricted Sat &
             Wed mornings.
Societies   must contact in advance.
Green Fees   not confirmed.
Facilities   ♨ ☺ ⚑ 〔 Richard Daibell.
Leisure   putting green, practice area, trolley hire.
Location   5m S of Nottingham, A60 to Ruddington
Hotel   ★★★ 63% Swans Hotel & Restaurant, 84-90
             Radcliffe Rd, West Bridgford, NOTTINGHAM
             ☎ 0115 981 4042 31 ⇥ 〔

SERLBY   Map 08 SK68

Serlby Park DN10 6BA ☎ 01777 818268
Parkland course.
11 holes, 5325yds, Par 66, SSS 66, Course record 63.
Club membership 250.
Visitors   must be introduced by and play with member.

Societies   apply in writing before 31 Dec for following
             year.
Green Fees   not confirmed.
Facilities   ♨ ☺
Leisure   putting green & practice area.
Location   E side of village off A638
Hotel   ★★★ 63% Charnwood Hotel, Sheffield Rd,
             BLYTH ☎ 01909 591610 20 ⇥ 〔

SUTTON IN ASHFIELD   Map 08 SK45

Coxmoor Coxmoor Rd NG17 5LF ☎ 01623 557359
Undulating moorland/heathland course with easy walking
and excellent views. The clubhouse is modern with a
well-equipped games room. The course lies adjacent to
Forestry Commission land over which there are several
footpaths and extensive views.
18 holes, 6571yds, Par 73, SSS 72, Course record 64.
Club membership 700.
Visitors   must play with member weekends & bank
             holidays. Must contact in advance.
Societies   must apply in advance.
Green Fees   £25 per round.
Facilities   ⊗ 〔 ♣ ♟ ♨ ☺ ⚑ 〔 David Ridley.
Leisure   trolley for hire, putting green, practice area.
Location   2m SE off A611
Hotel   ★★★★ 65% Swallow Hotel, Carter Ln
             East, SOUTH NORMANTON
             ☎ 01773 812000 161 ⇥ 〔

WORKSOP   Map 08 SK57

Bondhay Golf & Country Club Bondhay Ln, Whitewell
S80 3EH ☎ 01909 724709 & 723608
The wind usually plays quite an active role in making this
pleasantly undulating course testing. Signatures holes are the
10th which requires a 2nd shot over water into a basin of
trees; the 11th comes back over the same expanse of water
and requires a mid to short iron to a long, narrow green; the
18th is a Par 5 with a lake right in lay up distance - the
dilemma is whether to lay up short or go for the carry.
Devonshire Course: 18 holes, 6720yds, Par 72, SSS 71,
Course record 67.
Family Course: 9 holes, 1118yds, Par 27, Course record 23.
Club membership 600.
Visitors   must contact in advance.
Societies   must telephone in advance.
Green Fees   Devonshire: £19.95 per day; £14.95 per round
             (£24.95 per day weekends). Family: £3.95 per 9
             holes.
Facilities   ⊗ 〔 ♣ ♟ ♨ ☺ ⚑ ☂ 〔 Martin Bell.
Leisure   fishing, motorised carts for hire, buggies for hire,
             trolley for hire, driving range, putting green.
Location   5m W of Worksop, off A616
Hotel   ★★ 62% Regancy Hotel, Carlton Rd,
             WORKSOP ☎ 01909 474108 13rm(7 〔)

Kilton Forest Blyth Rd S81 0TL
☎ 01909 485994 & 486563
Slightly undulating, parkland course on the north edge of
Sherwood Forest. Includes three ponds.
18 holes, 6424yds, Par 72, SSS 71, Course record 69.
Club membership 350.
Visitors   must contact in advance.
Societies   must contact in advance.   ▶

Green Fees £6.40 £(8.40 weekends).
Facilities ⊗ ⽭ by prior arrangement ⽬ ⽤ ♀ ⽻ ⽦ ⽨
        ⽧ Peter W Foster.
Leisure trolley for hire, putting green, practice area,
        bowling green.
Location 1m NE of town centre on B6045
Hotel ★★ 72% Lion Hotel, 112 Bridge St,
        WORKSOP ☎ 01909 477925 32 ⇌ ⽩

Lindrick Lindrick Common S81 8BH
☎ 01909 475282
Heathland course with some trees and masses of gorse.
18 holes, 6486yds, Par 71, SSS 72, Course record 65.
Club membership 500.
Visitors must contact in advance. Restricted Tue &
        weekends. Handicap certificate required.
Societies welcome except Tue (am) & weekends by
        prior arrangement with the Secretary.
Green Fees £40 per day (£45 weekends); £25 per
        day/round winter.
Facilities ⊗ ⽭ ⽬ ⽤ ♀ ⽻ ⽦ ⽧ Peter Cowen.
Leisure trolley for hire, putting green, practice area.
Location 4m NW on A57
Hotel ★★ 72% Lion Hotel, 112 Bridge St,
        WORKSOP
        ☎ 01909 477925 32 ⇌ ⽩

Worksop Windmill Ln S80 2SQ ☎ 01909 472696
Adjacent to Clumber Park this course has a heathland-type
terrain, with gorse, broom, oak and birch trees. Fast, true
greens, dry all year round.
18 holes, 6651yds, Par 72, SSS 73.
Club membership 500.
Visitors by arrangement with professional tel: 01909
        477732. No visitors Nov-Mar without member.
Societies must apply in advance.
Green Fees not confirmed.
Facilities ♀ ⽻ ⽦ ⽧ J R King.
Leisure putting green, trolley hire, practice area.
Location 1.75m S off A620
Hotel ★★★ 70% Clumber Park Hotel, Clumber Park,
        WORKSOP
        ☎ 01623 835333 48 ⇌ ⽩

OXFORDSHIRE

ABINGDON   Map 04 SU49

Drayton Park Steventon Rd, Drayton Village OX14 2RR
☎ 01235 550607
Set in the heart of the Oxfordshire countryside, an 18-hole
parkland course designed by Hawtree. Five lakes and sand
based greens.
18 holes, 6500yds, Par 67, SSS 67, Course record 63.
Club membership 500.
Visitors may phone to book, must have golf shoes, no
        jeans or tracksuits.
Societies contact in advance.
Green Fees not confirmed.
Facilities ♀ ⽻ ⽦ ⽧ Dinah Masey,Tony Williams.
Leisure putting green,trolley hire,driving range,9 hole
        par 3 course.

Location Between Oxford & Newbury,off A34 at Didcot
Hotel ★★★ 64% The Upper Reaches, Thames St,
        ABINGDON ☎ 01235 522311 25rm(19 ⇌ ⽩)

BURFORD   Map 04 SP21

Burford Swindon Rd OX18 4JG ☎ 01993 822583
Created out of open-farmland, this parkland course has high
quality fairways and greens.
18 holes, 6414yds, Par 71, SSS 71, Course record 64.
Club membership 830.
Visitors must contact in advance. May not play
        weekends.
Societies apply in writing.
Green Fees £28 per day.
Facilities ⊗ ⽭ ⽬ ⽤ ♀ ⽻ ⽦ ⽨ ⽧ Norman Allen.
Leisure practice area.
Location 0.5m S off A361
Hotel ★★ 66% Golden Pheasant Hotel, 91 High St,
        BURFORD
        ☎ 01993 823223 & 823417 12rm(11 ⇌ ⽩)

CHESTERTON   Map 04 SP52

Chesterton Golf & Country Club OX6 8TE
☎ 01869 242023 & 241204
Laid out over one-time farmland. Well-bunkered, and water
hazards increase the difficulty of the course.
18 holes, 6229yds, Par 71, SSS 70, Course record 68.
Club membership 500.
Visitors must pre-book up to 4 days ahead.
Societies must contact in advance.
Green Fees £15 per day; £10 per round (£20/£15 weekends
        & bank holidays).
Facilities ⊗ ⽬ ⽤ ♀ ⽻ ⽦ ⽧ J Wilkshire.
Leisure trolley for hire, driving range, putting green,
        practice area.
Location 0.5m W on A4095
Hotel ★★ 68% Jersey Arms Hotel, MIDDLETON
        STONEY
        ☎ 01869 343234 & 343505 6 ⇌ Annexe10 ⇌

CHIPPING NORTON   Map 04 SP32

Chipping Norton Southcombe OX7 5QH ☎ 01608 642383
Pleasant downland course open to winds.
18 holes, 6241yds, Par 71, SSS 70, Course record 65.
Club membership 900.
Visitors with member only at weekends & bank holidays.
Societies telephone in advance.
Green Fees £17 per round/day.
Facilities ⊗ ⽭ ⽬ ⽤ ♀ ⽻ ⽦ ⽧ Bob Gould.
Leisure trolley for hire, putting green, practice area.
Location 1.5m E on A44
Hotel ★★ 63% The White Hart Hotel, 16 High St,
        CHIPPING NORTON
        ☎ 01608 642572 16 ⇌ ⽩Annexe5 ⇌

Lyneham Lyneham OX7 6QQ ☎ 01993 831841
Lyneham was designed to use the natural features. It is set in
170 acres on the fringe of the Costwolds and bleds superbly
with its surroundings. Lakes and streams enhance the
challenge of the course with water coming into play on 8 of
the 18 holes. All greens are sand based, built ot USGA
specification.

18 holes, 6669yds, Par 72, SSS 72.
Club membership 600.

Visitors	must contact in advance.
Societies	apply in advance.
Green Fees	£13 (£16 weekends).
Facilities	⊗ ⅲ ⅼ ⅅ ♀ ☖ ⌂ ⛳ ℓ Mark Stancer.
Leisure	motorised carts for hire, buggies for hire, trolley for hire, driving range, putting green, practice area.
Location	Off A361, between Burford/Chipping Norton
Hotel	★★ 63% Shaven Crown Hotel, SHIPTON-UNDER-WYCHWOOD ☎ 01993 830330 9rm(8 ⇆ ⟨)

DIDCOT   Map 04 SU59

Hadden Hill Wallingford Rd OX11 9BJ ☎ 01235 510410
A challenging course on undulating terrain with excellent drainage so visitors can be sure of playing no matter what the weather conditions have been. Two loops of nine holes.

18 holes, 6563yds, Par 71, SSS 71, Course record 65.
Club membership 400.

Visitors	telephone to book tee times.
Societies	telephone to arrange times & dates & receive booking form.
Green Fees	£12 per 18 holes; £7 per 9 holes (£16/£9.50 weekends).
Facilities	⊗ ⅲ ⅼ ⅅ ♀ ☖ ⌂ ⛳ ℓ Dean Halford/Adrian Waters.
Leisure	motorised carts for hire, buggies for hire, trolley for hire, floodlit driving range, putting green, practice area.
Location	On A4130 1m E of Didcot
Hotel	★★★ 64% Abingdon Four Pillars Hotel, Marcham Rd, ABINGDON ☎ 01235 553456 63 ⇆ ⟨

FRILFORD   Map 04 SU49

Frilford Heath Abingdon OX13 5NW
☎ 01865 390864
54 holes of heathland courses. Both the Red and the Green courses are of outstanding interest and beauty. Heather, pine, birch and, in particular, a mass of flowering gorse enhance the terrain. The new Blue course is extremely testing in design, especially the four opening holes.
Red Course: 18 holes, 6843yds, Par 73, SSS 71, Course record 70.
Green Course: 18 holes, 6006yds, Par 69, SSS 68, Course record 64.
Blue Course: 18 holes, 6726yds, Par 72, SSS 71, Course record 69.
Club membership 1300.

Visitors	contact in advance.
Societies	apply in advance.
Green Fees	£45 per day (£55 weekends & bank holidays).
Facilities	⊗ ⅼ ⅅ ♀ ☖ ⌂ ⛳ ℓ Derek Craik.
Leisure	motorised carts for hire, buggies for hire, trolley for hire, putting green, practice area.
Location	1m N off A338
Hotel	★★★ 64% Abingdon Four Pillars Hotel, Marcham Rd, ABINGDON ☎ 01235 553456 63 ⇆ ⟨

HENLEY-ON-THAMES   Map 04 SU78

Aspect Park Remenham Hill RG9 3EH
☎ 01491 577562 & 578306
Parkland course.
18 holes, 6643yds, Par 72, SSS 72.
Club membership 500.

Visitors	must contact in advance.
Societies	must contact in advance.
Green Fees	not confirmed.
Facilities	ⅅ ♀ ☖ ⌂ ⛳ ℓ Roger Frost.
Leisure	motorised carts for hire, buggies for hire, trolley for hire, driving range, putting green, practice area, pitch & putt.
Hotel	★★★ 66% Red Lion Hotel, Hart St, HENLEY-ON-THAMES ☎ 01491 572161 26rm(23 ⇆ ⟨)

Badgemore Park RG9 4NR ☎ 01491 573667 & 572206
Parkland course with many trees and easy walking. The 13th is a very difficult par 3 hole played over a valley to a narrow green.
18 holes, 6112yds, Par 69, SSS 69, Course record 65.
Club membership 600.

Visitors	contact professional shop on 01491 574175.
Societies	contact General Manager to book.
Green Fees	£27 per day; £21 per round (£30 per round weekends).
Facilities	⊗ ⅼ ⅅ ♀ ☖ ⌂ ⛳ ℓ Jonathon Dunn.
Leisure	motorised carts for hire, buggies for hire, trolley for hire, putting green.
Location	1m W
Hotel	★★★ 66% Red Lion Hotel, Hart St, HENLEY-ON-THAMES ☎ 01491 572161 26rm(23 ⇆ ⟨)

Henley Harpsden RG9 4HG ☎ 01491 575742
Undulating parkland course. 6th hole, blind (par 4), with steep hill.
18 holes, 6329yds, Par 70, SSS 70, Course record 65.
Club membership 800.

Visitors	must contact in advance. Weekend only with a member.
Societies	Wed & Thu, apply in writing.
Green Fees	£30 per day/round.
Facilities	⊗ ⅲ ⅼ ⅅ ♀ ☖ ⌂ ℓ Mark Howell.
Leisure	trolley for hire, putting green, practice area.
Location	1.25m S off A4155
Hotel	★★★ 66% Red Lion Hotel, Hart St, HENLEY-ON-THAMES ☎ 01491 572161 26rm(23 ⇆ ⟨)

MILTON COMMON   Map 04 SP60

The Oxfordshire Rycote Ln OX9 2PU
☎ 01844 278300
Designed by Rees Jones, The Oxfordshire is considered to be one of the most exciting courses in the country. With four man-made lakes and 135 bunkers, it is a magnificent test of shot-making where almost every hole deserves special mention. Unfortunately it is only open to members and their guests.
18 holes, 6856mtrs, Par 72, SSS 73, Course record 68.
Club membership 900.

Visitors	Members guests only. ▶

Facilities ⊗ 🍴 ☕ ♀ ⚐ 🏠 ♟ ♟ Ian Mosey.
Leisure motorised carts for hire, buggies for hire, trolley for hire, driving range, putting green.
Location 1.5m from junct 7, M40
Hotel ★★★ 74% Spread Eagle Hotel, Cornmarket, THAME
☎ 01844 213661 33 ⇥ 🐾

NUFFIELD
Map 04 SU68

Huntercombe RG9 5SL ☎ 01491 641207
This heathland/woodland course overlooks the Oxfordshire plain and has many attractive and interesting fairways and greens. Walking is easy after the 3rd which is a notable hole. The course is subject to wind and grass pot bunkers are interesting hazards.
18 holes, 6301yds, Par 70, SSS 70, Course record 63.
Club membership 900.
Visitors must contact in advance and have a handicap certificate.
Societies must contact in advance.
Green Fees not confirmed.
Facilities ♀ ⚐ 🏠 ♟ John B Draycott.
Location N off A423
Hotel ★★★ 63% Shillingford Bridge Hotel, Shillingford, WALLINGFORD
☎ 01865 858567 34 ⇥ 🐾Annexe8 ⇥ 🐾

OXFORD
Map 04 SP50

North Oxford Banbury Rd OX2 8EZ
☎ 01865 54924 & 54415
Gently undulating parkland course.
18 holes, 5736yds, Par 67, SSS 67, Course record 62.
Club membership 700.
Visitors at weekends & bank holidays may only play after 4pm.
Societies must contact in advance.
Green Fees £25 per day/round.
Facilities ⊗ 🍴 🍴 ☕ ♀ ⚐ 🏠 ♟ Robert Harris.
Leisure trolley for hire, putting green.
Location 3m N of city centre on A423
Hotel ★★★ 63% Oxford Moat House, Godstow Rd, Wolvercote Roundabout, OXFORD
☎ 01865 59933 155 ⇥

Southfield Hill Top Rd OX4 1PF
☎ 01865 242158
Home of the City, University and Ladies Clubs, and well-known to graduates throughout the world. A challenging course, in varied parkland setting, providing a real test for players.
18 holes, 5973yds, Par 69, SSS 69.
Club membership 850.
Visitors with member only at weekends.
Societies must apply in writing.
Green Fees not confirmed.
Facilities ♀ ⚐ 🏠 ♟ Tony Rees.
Leisure putting,buggy/trolley hire.
Location 1.5m SE of city centre off B480
Hotel ★★★ 64% Eastgate Hotel, The High, Merton St, OXFORD
☎ 01865 248244 43 ⇥ 🐾

SHRIVENHAM
Map 04 SU28

Shrivenham Park Penny Hooks SN6 8EX
☎ 01793 783853 & 783854
Parkland course with easy walking. The par 4, 17th is a difficult dog-leg.
18 holes, 5713yds, Par 69, SSS 69.
Club membership 450.
Visitors phone in advance.
Societies phone for details.
Green Fees £14.50 per day; £10.50 per round; £6.50 per 10 holes (£16.50/£12.50/£8.50 weekends & bank holidays).
Facilities ⊗ 🍴 🍴 ☕ ♀ ⚐ 🏠 ♟ J McArthur.
Leisure motorised carts for hire, buggies for hire, trolley for hire, putting, practice area.
Location 0.5m NE of town centre
Hotel ★★★ 63% The Crest Hotel, Oxford Rd, Stratton St Margaret, SWINDON
☎ 01793 831333 91 ⇥ 🐾

TADMARTON
Map 04 SP33

Tadmarton Heath OX15 5HL ☎ 01608 737278
A mixture of heath and sandy land, the course, which is open to strong winds, incorporates the site of an old Roman encampment. The clubhouse is an old farm building with a 'holy well' from which the greens are watered. The 7th is a testing hole over water.
18 holes, 5917yds, Par 69, SSS 69, Course record 63.
Club membership 600.
Visitors weekday by appointment, with member only at weekends.
Societies by arrangement with club office.
Green Fees £26 per day; £18 after 2.30pm (Winter £15 per day).
Facilities ⊗ 🍴 🍴 ☕ ♀ ⚐ 🏠 ♟ ♟ Les Bond.
Leisure fishing, buggies for hire, trolley for hire, driving range, putting green, practice area.
Location 1m SW of Lower Tadmarton off B4035
Hotel ★★★ 65% Banbury House, Oxford Rd, BANBURY
☎ 01295 259361 49 ⇥ 🐾

WATERSTOCK
Map 04 SP60

Waterstock Thame Rd OX33 1HT
☎ 01844 338093
A 6,500yard course designed by Donald Steel with USGA greens and tees fully computer irrigated. Four Par 3's facing North, South, East and West. A brook and hidden lake affect six holes, with doglegs being 4th and 10th holes. Five Par 5's on the course, making it a challenge for players of all standards.
18 holes, 6535yds, Par 73, SSS 71, Course record 70.
Club membership 600.
Visitors no restrictions.
Societies apply in writing or telephone.
Green Fees not confirmed.
Facilities ♀ ⚐ 🏠 ♟ ♟ Andy Wyatt.
Leisure fishing, 22 bay floodlit range, caddy cars.
Location On junc 8 of M40
Hotel ★★★ 74% Spread Eagle Hotel, Cornmarket, THAME ☎ 01844 213661 33 ⇥ 🐾

RUTLAND

GREETHAM
Map 08 SK91

Greetham Valley Wood Ln LE15 7RG ☎ 01780 460444
Set in 200 acres, including mature woodland and water
hazards, Greetham Valley was opened in spring 1992. The
complex comprises an 18-hole course and clubhouse, a
floodlit 9-hole Par 3 and a 21-bay floodlit driving range.
18 holes, 6362yds, Par 71, SSS 71.
Club membership 850.
Visitors must contact in advance.
Societies must contact in advance.
Green Fees £16 per round (£25 weekends).
Facilities ⊗ �🝐 ⮭ ⛳ ♀ ⚂ 🏠 🍴 ⓕ Mark Cunningham.
Leisure fishing, motorised carts for hire, buggies for hire,
trolley for hire, driving range, putting green,
practice area, pool table, snooker, bowls,
archery, Par 3 course.
Location Off B668 in Greetham
Hotel ★★ 69% Ram Jam Inn, Great North Rd,
STRETTON ☎ 01780 410776 Annexe7 ⇆ 🐾

SHROPSHIRE

BRIDGNORTH
Map 07 SO79

Bridgnorth Stanley Ln WV16 4SF ☎ 01746 763315
A pleasant course laid-out on parkland on the bank of the
River Severn.
18 holes, 6673yds, Par 73, SSS 72, Course record 65.
Club membership 725.
Visitors must contact in advance but may not play on
Wed. Restricted weekends.
Societies must contact in writing.
Green Fees not confirmed.
Facilities ♀ ⚂ 🏠 ⓕ
Leisure fishing, putting green,practice area,trolley hire.
Location 1m N off B4373
Hotel ★★ 62% Falcon Hotel, Saint John St,
Lowtown, BRIDGNORTH
☎ 01746 763134 15rm(5 ⇆7 🐾)

CHURCH STRETTON
Map 07 SO49

Church Stretton Trevor Hill SY6 6JH ☎ 01694 722281
Hillside course constructed by James Braid on the lower
slopes of the Long Mynd.
18 holes, 5020yds, Par 66, SSS 65, Course record 63.
Club membership 400.
Visitors Tee reserved for members Sat 9-10.30 & 1-2.30,
Sun prior to 10.30 & 1-2.30.
Societies must contact in advance.
Green Fees £12 per day (£18 weekends & bank holidays).
Facilities ⊗ �🝐 ⮭ ⛳ ♀ ⚂ 🏠 ⇆ ⓕ P Seal (wknds only).
Leisure putting green.
Location W of the town
Hotel ★★ 71% Mynd House Hotel, Little Stretton,
CHURCH STRETTON
☎ 01694 722212 8 ⇆ 🐾

HIGHLEY
Map 07 SO78

Severn Meadows WV16 6HZ ☎ 01746 862212
Picturesque course set alongside the River Severn and
providing a tight test of golf with much of the course
bordered by mature trees.
9 holes, 5258yds, Par 68, SSS 67.
Club membership 170.
Visitors booking advisable for weekends.
Societies advance booking necessary.
Green Fees £10 per 18 holes; £6 per 9 holes (£12/£7
weekends and bank holidays).
Facilities ⊗ by prior arrangement 🝐 by prior arrangement
⮭ by prior arrangement ♀ ⚂ 🏠
Leisure putting green.
Hotel ★★★★ 65% Mill Hotel & Restaurant,
ALVELEY ☎ 01746 780437 21 ⇆ 🐾

LILLESHALL
Map 07 SJ71

Lilleshall Hall TF10 9AS ☎ 01952 603840
Heavily-wooded parkland course. Easy walking.
18 holes, 5906yds, Par 68, SSS 68.
Club membership 650.
Visitors must contact in advance and play with member
at weekends.
Societies must apply in writing by Dec for the following
year.
Green Fees not confirmed.
Facilities ♀ ⚂ 🏠 ⓕ Nigel Bramall.
Location 3m SE
Hotel ★★ 68% White House Hotel, Wellington Rd,
Muxton, TELFORD
☎ 01952 604276 & 603603 30 ⇆ 🐾

LUDLOW
Map 07 SO57

Ludlow Bromfield SY8 2BT ☎ 01584 856285
A long-established parkland course in the middle of the
racecourse. Very flat, quick drying, with broom and gorse-
lined fairways.
18 holes, 6277yds, Par 70, SSS 70, Course record 65.
Club membership 700.
Visitors advisable to contact in advance.
Societies apply in advance.
Green Fees £18 per day (£24 weekends).
Facilities ⊗ 🝐 ⮭ ⛳ ♀ ⚂ 🏠 ⓕ Russell Price.
Leisure motorised carts for hire, trolley for hire, putting
green, practice area.
Location 1m N of Ludlow, off A49
Hotel ★★★ 70% The Feathers at Ludlow, Bull Ring,
LUDLOW ☎ 01584 875261 39 ⇆ 🐾

MARKET DRAYTON
Map 07 SJ63

Market Drayton Sutton TF9 2HX ☎ 01630 652266
Parkland course in quiet, picturesque surroundings providing
a good test of golf. Bungalow on course is made available for
golfing holidays.
18 holes, 6400yds, Par 71, SSS 70, Course record 69.
Club membership 550.
Visitors may not play on Sun; must play with member on
Sat. Must contact in advance.
Societies must contact in advance. ▶

Green Fees not confirmed.
Facilities   ♀ ⚖ 📠 ℓ Russel Clewes.
Location   1m SW
Hotel   ★★★▲▲ 70% Goldstone Hall, Goldstone,
                  MARKET DRAYTON
                  ☎ 01630 661202 & 661487 8 ⇆ ⟨

MEOLE BRACE   Map 07 SJ41

Meole Brace SY2 6QQ ☎ 01743 364050
Pleasant municipal course.
9 holes, 5830yds, Par 68, SSS 68, Course record 66.
Club membership 300.
Visitors   may not play Wed and must book in advance for
                  weekends & bank holidays.
Societies   must contact Mr R Wootton, Shrewsbury &
                  Atcham Borough Council on 01743 231456.
Green Fees   £5.10 per 18 holes; £4 per 9 holes (£6.90/£5.10
                  weekends and bank holidays).
Facilities   📠 ⚑ ℓ Ian Doran.
Leisure   trolley for hire, pitch & putt, practice area.
Location   NE side of village off A49
Hotel   ★★★ 62% Lion Hotel, Wyle Cop,
                  SHREWSBURY ☎ 01743 353107 59 ⇆ ⟨

OSWESTRY   Map 07 SJ22

Mile End Mile End, Old Shrewsbury Rd SY11 4JE
☎ 01691 670580 & 671246
A gently undulating parkland-type course now featuring 18
holes, the new 9-holes offering a number of challenging holes
for all standards of golfing ability. Well-spaced holes in 70
acres.
9 holes, 6130yds, Par 70, SSS 69, Course record 71.
Visitors   welcome at all times please telephone in
                  advance.
Societies   must contact in advance.
Green Fees   £14 per day; £10 per 18 holes (£18/£14
                  weekends & bank holidays).
Facilities   ⊗ ⚖ ♥ ♀ ⚖ 📠 ℓ Scott Carpenter.
Leisure   trolley for hire, putting green, practice area.
Location   1m SE of Oswestry, just off A5
Hotel   ★★★ 70% Wynnstay Hotel, Church St,
                  OSWESTRY ☎ 01691 655261 27 ⇆ ⟨

Oswestry Aston Park SY11 4JJ ☎ 01691 610535
Parkland course laid-out on undulating ground.
18 holes, 6024yds, Par 70, SSS 69, Course record 62.
Club membership 960.
Visitors   must contact in advance.
Societies   must contact in advance.
Green Fees   £18 per day (£25 weekends and bank holidays).
Facilities   ⊗ ⚖ ♥ ♀ ⚖ 📠 ℓ David Skelton.
Leisure   motorised carts for hire, trolley for hire, putting
                  green, practice area.
Location   2m SE on A5
Hotel   ★★★ 70% Wynnstay Hotel, Church St,
                  OSWESTRY ☎ 01691 655261 27 ⇆ ⟨

PANT   Map 07 SJ22

Llanymynech SY10 8LB ☎ 01691 830983 & 830542
Upland course on the site of an early Iron Age/Roman hillfort
with far-reaching views. The 4th fairway crosses the Welsh
border.

18 holes, 6114yds, Par 70, SSS 69, Course record 65.
Club membership 600.
Visitors   must contact in advance, some weekends
                  restricted.
Societies   must contact Secretary.
Green Fees   £22 per day; £15 per round (£25/£20 weekends
                  & bank holidays).
Facilities   ⊗ ⚖ ⚖ ♥ ♀ ⚖ 📠 ℓ Andrew P Griffiths.
Leisure   trolley for hire, putting green, practice area.
Location   0.5m SW off A483
Hotel   ★★★ 70% Wynnstay Hotel, Church St,
                  OSWESTRY ☎ 01691 655261 27 ⇆ ⟨

SHIFNAL   Map 07 SJ70

Shifnal Decker Hill TF11 8QL ☎ 01952 460330
Well-wooded parkland course. Walking is easy and an
attractive country mansion serves as the clubhouse.
18 holes, 6468yds, Par 71, SSS 71, Course record 65.
Club membership 600.
Visitors   must contact in advance, may not play at
                  weekends.
Societies   must contact in advance.
Green Fees   £30 per day; £22 per round.
Facilities   ⊗ ⚖ ⚖ ♥ ♀ ⚖ 📠 ℓ Justin Flanagan.
Leisure   trolley for hire, putting green, practice area.
Location   1m N of Shifnal, off B4379
Hotel   ★★★★ 59% Park House Hotel, Park St,
                  SHIFNAL
                  ☎ 01952 460128 38 ⇆ ⟨Annexe16 ⇆ ⟨

SHREWSBURY   Map 07 SJ41

Arscott Arscot, Pontesbury SY5 0XP
☎ 01743 860114 & 860881
At 365feet above sea level, the views from Arscott Golf Club
of the hills of south Shropshire and Wales are superb. Arscott
is a new course, set in parkland with water features and holes
demanding all sorts of club choice. A challenge to all golfers
both high and low handicap.
18 holes, 6112yds, Par 70, SSS 69, Course record 65.
Club membership 550.
Visitors   most times available by prior arrangement.
Societies   apply in writing for tee reservation.
Green Fees   £12.50 per day (£20.50 weekends).
Facilities   ⊗ ⚖ ⚖ ♥ ♀ ⚖ 📠 ℓ Gary Sawyer.
Leisure   fishing, trolley for hire, putting green, practice
                  area.
Location   Off A488, S of Shrewsbury 3m from A5
Hotel   ★★★▲▲ 64% Rowton Castle Hotel, Halfway
                  House, SHREWSBURY
                  ☎ 01743 884044 19 ⇆

Shrewsbury Condover SY5 7BL ☎ 01743 872976
Parkland course. First nine flat, second undulating with good
views.
18 holes, 6300yds, Par 70, SSS 70.
Club membership 872.
Visitors   may only play between 10am-noon and after
                  2.15pm at weekends. Must contact in advance
                  and have a handicap certificate.
Societies   must contact in writing.
Green Fees not confirmed.
Facilities   ♀ ⚖ 📠 ℓ Peter Seal.
Location   4m S off A49

Hotel ★★★ 68% Prince Rupert Hotel, Butcher Row, SHREWSBURY ☎ 01743 499955 65 ⇌

TELFORD   Map 07 SJ60

The Shropshire Muxton Grange, Muxton TF2 8PQ
☎ 01952 677866
Pay and Play, 3 loops of 9-holes. Also tuition hole, practice green, 12 hole pitch and putt and 18-hole contoured putting green.
Blue Course: 9 holes, 3286yds, Par 35, SSS 35.
Silver Course: 9 holes, 3303yds, Par 36, SSS 36.
Gold Course: 9 holes, 3334yds, Par 36, SSS 36.
Club membership 250.
Visitors must book 7 days in advance.
Societies must book in advance.
Green Fees not confirmed.
Facilities ♀ ♨ 🖅 ⛳ 🏌 Kevin Craggs.
Leisure fishing, caddy car/trolley hire, pitch & putt.
Hotel ★★★ 69% Holiday Inn, St Quentin Gate, TELFORD ☎ 01952 292500 100 ⇌ 🐾

Telford Golf & Country Moat House Great Hay Dr, Sutton Hill TF7 4DT ☎ 01952 429977
Rolling parkland course with easy walking. Three lakes and large sand traps are hazards to the fine greens.
18 holes, 6754yds, Par 71, SSS 71, Course record 66.
Club membership 400.
Visitors must contact in advance.
Societies must book in advance 01952 429977 ext 297
Green Fees £25 weekdays (£31 per weekends).
Facilities ⊗ 🎪 ⓛ ♬ ♀ ♨ 🖅 ⛳ 🏌 Graham Farr.
Leisure heated indoor swimming pool, squash, sauna, solarium, gymnasium, motorised carts for hire, buggies for hire, trolley for hire, driving range, putting, clay pigeon, quad bikes.
Location 4m S of town centre off A442
Hotel ★★★ 68% Telford Golf & Country Moat House, Great Hay Dr, Sutton Hill, TELFORD ☎ 01952 429977 86 ⇌ 🐾

WELLINGTON   Map 07 SJ61

Wrekin Ercall Woods TF6 5BX ☎ 01952 244032
Downland course with some hard walking but rewarding views.
18 holes, 5699yds, Par 67, SSS 66, Course record 44.
Club membership 681.
Visitors must contact in advance.
Societies must apply in writing.
Green Fees £18 (£25 weekends & bank holidays).
Facilities ⊗ 🎪 ⓛ ♬ ♀ ♨ 🖅 🏌 K Housden.
Leisure trolley for hire, putting green, practice area.
Location 1.25m S off B5061
Hotel ★★★ 67% Buckatree Hall Hotel, The Wrekin, Wellington, TELFORD ☎ 01952 641821 64 ⇌ 🐾

WESTON-UNDER-REDCASTLE   Map 07 SJ52

Hawkstone Park Hotel SY4 5UY ☎ 01939 200611
In a beautiful setting, with natural hazards and good views, Hawkstone Course has been established for over 50 years and enjoys a superb setting. A new course, the Windmill, is being developed.

Hawkstone Course: 18 holes, 6465yds, Par 72, SSS 70.
Windmill Course: 18 holes, 6655yds, Par 72, SSS 72.
Academy Course: 6 holes, 741yds, Par 18.
Club membership 750.
Visitors must book 7 days in advance.
Societies must contact in advance by telephone.
Green Fees not confirmed.
Facilities ♀ ♨ 🖅 ⛳ 🏌
            🏌 Paul Brown & Damian Tudor.
Leisure grass tennis courts, fishing, putting, cart/buggy/trolley hire.
Location N side of village 0.75m E of A49

WHITCHURCH   Map 07 SJ54

Hill Valley Terrick Rd SY13 4JZ
☎ 01948 663584
Two testing parkland courses ideally suited to the club and scratch golfer alike. The West Course, cleverly designed by Peter Alliss and Dave Thomas, has fairways that thread their way through 160 acres of trees, lakes and streams to American-style greens trapped by sand and water. Shorter East Course with smaller greens requiring accurate approach shots.
West Course: 18 holes, 6240yds, Par 73, SSS 70, Course record 64.
East Course: 18 holes, 4862yds, Par 66, SSS 64.
Club membership 600.
Visitors must contact in advance. Restricted weekends.
Societies must contact in advance; a deposit will be required.
Green Fees West: £19 (£25 weekends); East £9 (£12 weekends). Reductions Jul-Aug.
Facilities ⊗ 🎪 ⓛ ♬ ♀ ♨ 🖅 ⛳ 🏌 A R Minshall.
Leisure hard tennis courts, sauna, gymnasium, motorised carts for hire, buggies for hire, trolley for hire, putting green, practice area, snooker.
Location 1m N
Hotel ★★★ 59% Dodington Lodge Hotel, Dodington, WHITCHURCH ☎ 01948 662539 10 ⇌ 🐾

WORFIELD   Map 07 SO79

Worfield Roughton WV15 5HE
☎ 01746 716372 & 716357
Opened in 1991, this undulating course with good-sized greens, well placed bunkers and 2 lakes, rated highly in a golf magazine survey.
18 holes, 6801yds, Par 73, SSS 73, Course record 68.
Visitors must contact in advance, weekends only after 10am.
Societies contact in advance.
Green Fees £20 per day; £15 per round (£25/£22 weekends).
Facilities ⊗ 🎪 ⓛ ♬ ♀ ♨ 🖅 🏌 Steve Russell.
Leisure buggies for hire, trolley for hire, driving range, putting green, practice area.
Location 3m W of Bridgenorth, off A454
Hotel ★★★🏅 77% Old Vicarage Hotel, WORFIELD ☎ 01746 716497 10 ⇌ 🐾Annexe4 ⇌ 🐾

SOMERSET

BACKWELL   Map 03 ST46

Tall Pines Cooks Bridle Path, Downside BS19 3DJ
☎ 01275 472076
Parkland course with views over the Bristol Channel.
18 holes, 5827yds, Par 70, SSS 68.
Club membership 500.
Visitors   must contact in advance.
Societies   prior arrangement by telephone for details.
Green Fees £12 per round; £6 second round (£14 per round;
             £7 second round weekends & bank holidays).
             Twilight £8.
Facilities   ⊗ �🏌 🛒 ⬤ ♀ 👥 🏠 ⬤ Terry Murray.
Leisure   motorised carts for hire, buggies for hire, trolley
             for hire, putting green, practice field.
Location   Adjacent to Bristol Airport, 1m off A38
Hotel   ★★★ 60% Walton Park Hotel, Wellington Ter,
             CLEVEDON ☎ 01275 874253 41 ⇄ 🐾

BATH   Map 03 ST76

Bath Sham Castle, North Rd BA2 6JG
☎ 01225 463834 & 425182
Considered to be one of the finest courses in the west,
this is the site of Bath's oldest golf club. An interesting
course situated on high ground overlooking the city and
with splendid views over the surrounding countryside.
The rocky ground supports good quality turf and there
are many good holes. The 17th is a dog-leg right past, or
over the corner of an out-of-bounds wall, and thence on
to an undulating green.
18 holes, 6429yds, Par 71, SSS 71, Course record 67.
Club membership 750.
Visitors   advisable to contact in advance.
Societies   Wed & Fri by prior arrangement.
Green Fees £30 per day; £25 per round (£35/£30
             weekends & bank holidays).
Facilities   ⊗ �🏌 🛒 ⬤ ♀ 👥 🏠 ⬤ ⬤ Peter J Hancox.
Leisure   trolley for hire, putting green, practice area.
Location   1.5m SE city centre off A36
Hotel   ★★★ 65% Francis Hotel, Queen Square,
             BATH ☎ 01225 424257 94 ⇄ 🐾

Entry Hill BA2 5NA ☎ 01225 834248
9 holes, 1922yds, Par 33, SSS 30.
Club membership 650.
Visitors   no restrictions.
Societies   bookings required in advance.
Green Fees not confirmed.
Facilities   👥 🏠 ⬤ ⬤ Tim Tapley.
Location   Off A367

Lansdown Lansdown BA1 9BT ☎ 01225 422138
A flat parkland course situated 800 feet above sea level,
providing a challenge to both low and high handicap golfers
due to the strong prevailing wind that comes into play at
every hole.
18 holes, 6316yds, Par 71, SSS 70, Course record 65.
Club membership 790.
Visitors   must contact in advance to ascertain availability.
Societies   apply in writing or telephone in advance.

Green Fees £24 per day; £18 per round (£30 per round/day
             weekends; £24 bank holidays).
Facilities   ⊗ �🏌 🛒 ⬤ ♀ 👥 🏠 ⬤ Terry Mercer.
Leisure   trolley for hire, putting green, practice area.
Location   6m SW of exit 18 of M4
Hotel   ★★★ 79% The Queensberry Hotel, Russel St,
             BATH ☎ 01225 447928 22 ⇄ 🐾

BRIDGWATER   Map 03 ST23

Cannington Cannington College, Cannington TA5 2LS
☎ 01278 652394
Nine hole golf course of 'links-like' appearance, designed by
Martin Hawtree of Oxford. The 4th hole is a challenging
464yard Par 4, slightly up hill and into the prevailing wind.
9 holes, 2929yds, Par 34, SSS 34.
Club membership 200.
Visitors   pay & play anytime ex Wed evening.
Societies   apply in writing.
Green Fees £10 per 18 holes (£12 weekends). Economy 9
             holes £6.50 after 2.30pm winter, 6.30pm
             summer.
Facilities   ⊗ ⬤ 👥 🏠 ⬤ ⬤ Ron Macrow.
Leisure   hard tennis courts, trolley for hire, practice area,
             pitch & putt.
Location   4m NW of Bridgwater of A39
Hotel   ★★ 67% Friarn Court Hotel, 37 St Mary St,
             BRIDGWATER
             ☎ 01278 452859 16 ⇄ 🐾

BURNHAM-ON-SEA   Map 03 ST34

Brean Coast Rd, Brean Sands TA8 2RF
☎ 01278 751595 office & 751570 pro
Level and open moorland course with water hazards.
Facilities of 'Brean Leisure Park' adjoining.
18 holes, 5715yds, Par 69, SSS 68, Course record 66.
Club membership 350.
Visitors   may not play on Sat & Sun before 1pm. Book in
             advance through professional.
Societies   contact office or professional in advance.
Green Fees £18 per day; £12 per round (£15 per round
             weekends).
Facilities   ⊗ �🏌 🛒 ⬤ ♀ 👥 🏠 ⬤ ⬤ G Coombe.
Leisure   heated indoor swimming pool, fishing, sauna,
             motorised carts for hire, buggies for hire, trolley
             for hire.
Location   6m N on coast rd
Hotel   ★★ 63% Royal Clarence Hotel, 31 The
             Esplanade, BURNHAM-ON-SEA
             ☎ 01278 783138 19rm(18 ⇄ 🐾)

Burnham & Berrow St Christopher's Way TA8 2PE
☎ 01278 785760
Links championship course with large sandhills.
Championship Course: 18 holes, 6447yds, Par 71, SSS 72.
9 Hole Course: 9 holes, 6332yds, Par 72, SSS 70.
Club membership 900.
Visitors   must contact in advance & have handicap
             certificate (22 or under gentlemen, 30 or
             under ladies) to play on the Championship
             course.
Societies   telephone in advance.
Green Fees £32 per day/round (£44 weekends & bank
             holidays); 9 hole £8 per day/round.

BURNHAM and BERROW GOLF CLUB

Championship links course with panoramic views of the Somerset hills and the Devon coast line sweeping across the reed beds and the Bristol Channel with the islands of Steepholm and Flatholm standing out against the background of the Welsh coast line.

18 holes. 6447 yards. Par 71, SSS 72, course record 66
9 hole course. 6332 yards. Par 72, SSS 70.

St Christophers Way, Burnham-on-Sea, Somerset TA8 2PE
Telephone: 01278 785760
Secretary: Mrs E L Sloman

Facilities	⊗ ⅢⅢ ⅬⅬ ⅬⅬ ♀ ⅄ 🏠 ⅎ 🎏
	ⅎ Mark Crowther-Smith.
Leisure	motorised carts for hire, trolley for hire, putting green, practice area.
Location	1m N of town on B3140
Hotel	★★ 63% Royal Clarence Hotel, 31 The Esplanade, BURNHAM-ON-SEA ☎ 01278 783138 19rm(18 ⇄ 🦰)
Additional hotel	★★🦽 65% Batch Farm Country Hotel, LYMPSHAM ☎ 01934 750371 8 ⇄

CHARD
Map 03 ST30

Windwhistle Golf, Squash & Country Club Cricket St Thomas TA20 4DG ☎ 01460 30231
Parkland course at 735 ft above sea level with outstanding views over the Somerset Levels to the Bristol Channel and South Wales.
East/West Course: 18 holes, 6500yds, Par 73, SSS 71.
Club membership 600.
Visitors must contact in advance.

Societies	by prior arrangement.
Green Fees	not confirmed.
Facilities	♀ ⅄ 🏠
Leisure	squash.
Location	3m E on A30
Hotel	★★ 66% Shrubbery Hotel, ILMINSTER ☎ 01460 52108 14 ⇄ 🦰

CLEVEDON
Map 03 ST47

Clevedon Castle Rd, Walton St Mary BS21 7AA
☎ 01275 874057
Situated on the cliff-top overlooking the Severn estuary and with distant views of the Welsh coast. Excellent parkland course in first-class condition overlooking the Severn estuary. Magnificent scenery and some tremendous 'drop' holes. Strong winds.
18 holes, 6117yds, Par 70, SSS 69, Course record 68.
Club membership 640.

Visitors	must contact in advance. No play Wed morning.
Societies	Mon & Tue only (not bank holidays), telephone or apply in writing.
Green Fees	£22 per 18/36 holes (£35 weekends & bank holidays).
Facilities	⊗ ⅢⅢ ⅬⅬ ♀ ⅄ 🏠 ⅎ ⅎ Martin Heggie.
Leisure	trolley for hire, putting green, practice area.
Location	1m NE of town centre
Hotel	★★★ 60% Walton Park Hotel, Wellington Ter, CLEVEDON ☎ 01275 874253 41 ⇄ 🦰

CONGRESBURY
Map 03 ST46

Mendip Spring Honeyhall Ln BS19 5JT
☎ 01934 852322 & 853337
Set in peaceful countryside with the Mendip Hills as a backdrop, this 18-hole course includes lakes and numerous water hazards covering some 12 acres of the course. The 12th is an island green surrounded by water and there are long drives on the 7th and 13th. The 9-hole Lakeside course is an easy walking course, mainly par 4. Floodlit driving range.
Brinsea Course: 18 holes, 6328yds, Par 71, SSS 70, Course record 70.
Lakeside: 9 holes, 4520yds, Par 68, SSS 68.
Club membership 370.

Visitors	must contact in advance for Brinsea course, Lakeside is play & pay anytime.
Societies	booking in advance by arrangement.
Green Fees	Brinsea: £22 per day; £17 per round (£25/£19 weekends). Lakeside: £6 per round.
Facilities	⊗ ⅢⅢ ⅬⅬ ♀ ⅄ 🏠 ⅎ ⅎ John Blackburn.
Leisure	buggies for hire, trolley for hire, driving range, putting green, practice area. ▶

Location	8m E of Weston-Super-Mare
Hotel	★★★⭑⭑ 69% Daneswood House Hotel, Cuck Hill, SHIPHAM
	☎ 01934 843145 & 843945 9
	⇔ 🐾Annexe3 ⇔ 🐾

ENMORE   Map 03 ST23

Enmore Park TA5 2AN
☎ 01278 671481 & 671519 (Pro)
Hilly, parkland course with water features on foothills of Quantocks. Wooded countryside and views of Quantocks and Mendips. 1st and 10th are testing holes.
18 holes, 6406yds, Par 71, SSS 71, Course record 64.
Club membership 750.

Visitors	phone professional for details.
Societies	must apply in writing.
Green Fees	£25 per day; £18 per round (£25 weekends).
Facilities	⊗ ⅢⅢ ⅃ᵇ ⚑ ♀ ⚐ 📅 🛈 ⁣ Nigel Wixon.
Leisure	motorised carts for hire, buggies for hire, trolley for hire, putting green, practice area.
Location	A39 to Minehead, at first set of lights trn left to Spaxton, then 1.5m to reservoir and turn left
Hotel	★★★ 72% Walnut Tree Hotel, North Petherton, BRIDGWATER
	☎ 01278 662255 32 ⇔

FARRINGTON GURNEY   Map 03 ST65

Farrington Marsh Ln BS18 5TS
☎ 01761 241274 & 241787
USGA spec greens on both challenging 9 and 18 hole courses. Newly completed 18 hole course with computerised irrigation, six lakes, four tees per hole and excellent views. Testing holes include the 12th (282yds) with the green set behind a lake at the base of a 100ft drop, and the 17th which is played between two lakes.
Executive Course: 9 holes, 3022yds, Par 54, SSS 53, Course record 57.
Main Course: 18 holes, 6693yds, Par 72, SSS 72.
Club membership 500.

Visitors	starting times at weekends.
Societies	welcome except for weekends & bank holidays, telephone or write in advance.
Green Fees	Executive: £10 per day; £6 per round (£12/£8 weekends). Main: £18 per day; £12 per round (£20/£15 weekends).
Facilities	⊗ ⅢⅢ ⅃ᵇ ⚑ ♀ ⚐ 📅 🛈 ⁣ Peter Thompson.
Leisure	sauna, buggies for hire, trolley for hire, floodlit driving range, putting green, practice area.
Hotel	★★ 69% Country Ways Hotel, Marsh Ln, FARRINGTON GURNEY
	☎ 01761 452449 6 ⇔ 🐾

FROME   Map 03 ST74

Orchardleigh BA11 2PH ☎ 01373 454200
This course is due to open April 1996 so please check any information before visiting. Originally designed by Ryder Cup golfer, Brian Huggett, as two returning nines through mature parkland. Five new lakes bring water into play on seven holes.
18 holes, 6810yds, Par 72, SSS 73.

Visitors	no visitors before 10.30am at weekends and bank holidays.

Societies	apply in writing or telephone in advance.
Green Fees	not confirmed.
Facilities	🛈
Leisure	fishing, driving range,putting green,practice area,cart/buggy/trolley hire.
Location	1m W of Frome on the A362
Hotel	★★ 67% The George at Nunney, 11 Church St, NUNNEY
	☎ 01373 836458 9 ⇔ 🐾

GURNEY SLADE   Map 03 ST64

Mendip BA3 4UT ☎ 01749 840570
Undulating downland course offering an interesting test of golf on superb fairways.
18 holes, 6330yds, Par 71, SSS 70, Course record 65.
Club membership 900.

Visitors	must contact in advance.
Societies	by arrangement with secretary.
Green Fees	not confirmed.
Facilities	⊗ ⅢⅢ ⅃ᵇ ⚑ ♀ ⚐ 📅 🛈 ⁣ Ron Lee.
Leisure	motorised carts for hire, buggies for hire, trolley for hire, putting green, practice area.
Location	1.5m S off A37
Hotel	★★★ 66% Centurion Hotel, Charlton Ln, MIDSOMER NORTON
	☎ 01761 417711 44 ⇔ 🐾

KEYNSHAM   Map 03 ST66

Stockwood Vale Stockwood Ln BS18 2ER
☎ 0117 986 6505
Undulating and challenging public course in a beautiful setting with interesting well bunkered holes, in particular the superb par 5 556 yrd 7th hole. Good views.
9 holes, 2760yds, Par 35, SSS 67.
Club membership 300.

Visitors	no restrictions, but must reserve a start time.
Societies	telephone in advance.
Green Fees	£10 per 18 holes; £5.50 per 9 holes (£12/£6 weekends).
Facilities	⊗ ⅢⅢ ⅃ᵇ ⚑ ♀ ⚐ 📅 🛈 ⁣ Kelvin Aitken.
Leisure	driving range, putting green.
Hotel	★★ 73% Chelwood House Hotel, CHELWOOD
	☎ 01761 490730 11 ⇔ 🐾

LANGPORT   Map 03 ST42

Long Sutton Long Sutton TA10 9JU
☎ 01458 241017
Gentle, undulating, Pay and Play course.
18 holes, 6367yds, Par 71, SSS 70, Course record 71.
Club membership 500.

Visitors	advisable to book in advance.
Societies	telephone in advance.
Green Fees	£12 per round (£16 weekends).
Facilities	⊗ ⅢⅢ ⅃ᵇ ⚑ ♀ ⚐ 📅 🛈 ⁣ Michael Blackwell.
Leisure	trolley for hire, floodlit driving range, putting green, practice area, snooker.
Location	5m NW of Yeovil off A372
Hotel	★★★ 70% The Hollies, Bower Hinton, MARTOCK
	☎ 01935 822232 Annexe30 ⇔ 🐾

LONG ASHTON Map 03 ST57

Long Ashton The Clubhouse BS18 9DW
☎ 01275 392316 & 392265
Wooded parkland course with nice turf, wonderful views of Bristol and surrounding areas and a spacious practice area. Good testing holes, especially the back nine, in prevailing south-west winds. The short second hole (126yds) cut from an old quarry and played over a road can ruin many a card! Good drainage ensures pleasant winter golf.
18 holes, 6077yds, Par 70, SSS 70, Course record 66.
Club membership 700.

Visitors recommended to telephone the professional.
Societies must contact the secretary in advance.
Green Fees £26 per round (£35 weekends & bank holidays).
Facilities Denis Scanlan.
Leisure trolley for hire, putting green, practice area.
Location 0.5m N on B3128
Hotel ★★★ 66% Redwood Lodge Hotel, Country Club Resort, Beggar Bush Ln, Failand, BRISTOL ☎ 01275 393901 108

Woodspring Golf & Country Club Yanley Ln BS18 9LR
☎ 01275 394378
Set in 180 acres of undulating heathland featuring superb natural water hazards, protected greens and a rising landscape. Designed by Peter Alliss and Clive Clark and laid out by Donald Steel, the course has three individual 9-hole courses, the Avon, Severn & Brunel. The 9th hole on the Brunel course is a feature hole here, with an elevated tee shot over a natural gorge. In undulating hills south of Bristol, long carries to tight fairways, elevated island tees and difficult approaches to greens make the most of the 27 holes.
Avon Course: 9 holes, 2960yds, Par 35.
Brunel Course: 9 holes, 3261yds, Par 37.
Severn Course: 9 holes, 3340yds, Par 36.
Club membership 800.

Visitors must contact in advance, weekends may be limited.
Societies must contact Head Professional in advance.
Green Fees £20 per 18 holes (£30 weekends & bank holidays).
Facilities Mark Pierce.
Leisure sauna, motorised carts for hire, buggies for hire, trolley for hire, driving range, putting green.
Location Off A38 Bridgewater Road
Hotel ★★★ 66% Redwood Lodge Hotel, Country Club Resort, Beggar Bush Ln, Failand, BRISTOL ☎ 01275 393901 108

MIDSOMER NORTON Map 03 ST65

Fosseway Country Club Charlton Ln BA3 4BD
☎ 01761 412214
Very attractive tree-lined parkland course, not demanding but with lovely views towards the Mendip Hills.
9 holes, 4278yds, Par 68, SSS 65.
Club membership 400.

Visitors may not play on Wed evenings, Sat & Sun mornings & competitions days.
Societies apply in writing or telephone.
Green Fees £8 (£10 weekends & bank holidays).
Facilities
Leisure heated indoor swimming pool, squash, putting green, practice area.

THE IDEAL VENUE
CENTURION HOTELS
20 MINUTES FROM BATH CITY CENTRE
44 LUXURY EN SUITE BEDROOMS
RESTAURANT • CONFERENCE FACILITIES
FULL SIZE 9 HOLE COURSE
BOWLING GREEN • SQUASH COURTS
SWIMMING POOL • INDOOR BOWL GREEN

Please see entry under MIDSOMER NORTON
★★★ AA
English Tourist Board
(01761) 417711
FAX (01761) 418357
CHARLTON LANE, MIDSOMER NORTON, BATH BA3 4BD
MAJOR CREDIT CARDS ACCEPTED

Location SE of town centre off A367
Hotel ★★★ 66% Centurion Hotel, Charlton Ln, MIDSOMER NORTON
☎ 01761 417711 44

MINEHEAD Map 03 SS94

Minehead & West Somerset The Warren TA24 5SJ
☎ 01643 702057
Flat seaside links, very exposed to wind, with good turf set on a shingle bank. The last five holes adjacent to the beach are testing. The 215-yard 18th is wedged between the beach and the club buildings and provides a good finish.
18 holes, 6228yds, Par 71, SSS 71, Course record 65.
Club membership 620.

Visitors must contact secretary in advance.
Societies telephone in advance.
Green Fees £22 (£25 weekends & bank holidays).
Facilities Ian Read.
Leisure trolley for hire, putting green, practice area.
Location E end of esplanade
Hotel ★★★ 68% Northfield Hotel, Northfield Rd, MINEHEAD
☎ 01643 705155 24

SALTFORD Map 03 ST66

Saltford Golf Club Ln BS18 3AA
☎ 01225 873220 & 872043
Parkland course with easy walking and panoramic views over the Avon Valley. The par 4, 2nd and 13th are notable. ▶

18 holes, 6081yds, Par 69, SSS 69.
Club membership 800.
Visitors   must contact in advance & have handicap
              certificate.
Societies   must telephone in advance.
Green Fees   not confirmed.
Facilities   ♀ ᚼ 🏠 🛈 ℂ Dudley Millinstead.
Leisure   caddy cars.
Location   S side of village
Hotel   ★★★(red)⚘ Hunstrete House Hotel,
              CHELWOOD
              ☎ 01761 490490 13 ⇔ ℝAnnexe11 ⇔ ℝ

SOMERTON   Map 03 ST42

Wheathill Wheathill TA11 7HG
☎ 01963 240667
A Par 68 parkland course with nice views in quiet
countryside. It is flat lying with the 13th hole along the river.
18 holes, 5362yds, Par 68, SSS 66.
Club membership 300.
Visitors   no restrictions.
Societies   telephone to arrange.
Green Fees   £12 per day; £10 per round (£15/£13 weekends).
Facilities   ⊗ ⅏ ᚼ 🍺 ♀ ᚼ 🏠 🛈 ℂ A England.
Leisure   motorised carts for hire, buggies for hire, trolley
              for hire, practice area.
Location   5m E of Somerton off B3153
Hotel   ★★★ 63% Wessex Hotel, High St, STREET
              ☎ 01458 443383 50 ⇔ ℝ

TAUNTON   Map 03 ST22

Oake Manor Oake TA4 1BA
☎ 01823 461993
A parkland/lakeland course situated in breathtaking Somerset
countryside with views of the Quantock, Blackdown and
Brendon Hills. Ten holes feature water hazards such as lakes,
cascades and a trout stream. The 15th hole (Par 5, 476yds) is
bounded by water all down the left with a carry over another
lake on to an island green. The course is great fun for all
standards of golfer.
18 holes, 6109yds, Par 70, SSS 69.
Club membership 600.
Visitors   no restrictions but visitors must book in advance.
Societies   contact Russell Gardner by telephone.
Green Fees   £22 per day; £14.50 per round; £8 3´ hours
              before dark. (£26/£16/£8 weekends).
Facilities   ⊗ ⅏ ᚼ 🍺 ♀ ᚼ 🏠 🛈 ℂ Russell Gardner.
Leisure   motorised carts for hire, trolley for hire, driving
              range, putting green, practice area, teaching
              academy.
Location   Exit M5 junct 26, take A38 towards Taunton and
              follow signs to Oake
Hotel   ★★★ 69% Rumwell Manor Hotel, Rumwell,
              TAUNTON
              ☎ 01823 461902 10 ⇔ ℝAnnexe10 ⇔ ℝ

Taunton & Pickeridge Corfe TA3 7BY
☎ 01823 421537
Downland course with extensive views.
18 holes, 5927yds, Par 69, SSS 68, Course record 61.
Club membership 600.
Visitors   must have a handicap certificate

Societies   must telephone in advance.
Green Fees   not confirmed.
Facilities   ♀ ᚼ 🏠 ℂ Gary Milne.
Leisure   putting green/practice area,trolley hire.
Location   4m S off B3170
Hotel   ★★★ 78% The Mount Somerset Hotel,
              Henlade, TAUNTON
              ☎ 01823 442500 11 ⇔ ℝ

Taunton Vale Creech Heathfield TA3 5EY
☎ 01823 412220 & 412880
An 18 hole and a 9 hole golf course in a parkland complex
occupying 156 acres in the Vale of Taunton. Complex
includes a floodlit driving range.
Charlton Course: 18 holes, 6142yds, Par 70, SSS 69, Course
record 66.
Durston Course: 9 holes, 2004yds, Par 64, SSS 60.
Club membership 640.
Visitors   telephone booking essential.
Societies   must book in advance.
Green Fees   18 holes: £20 per day; £14 per round
              (£25/£17.50 weekends). 9 holes: £10 per day; £7
              per round (£13/£8.75 weekends).
Facilities   ⊗ ᚼ 🍺 ♀ ᚼ 🏠 🛈 ℂ Martin Keitch.
Leisure   trolley for hire, driving range, putting green.
Location   Off A361 at junct with A38
Hotel   ★★★ 69% Rumwell Manor Hotel, Rumwell,
              TAUNTON
              ☎ 01823 461902 10 ⇔ ℝAnnexe10 ⇔ ℝ

Vivary Park Municipal Fons George TA1 3JU
☎ 01823 333875
A parkland course, tight and narrow with ponds.
18 holes, 4620yds, Par 63, SSS 63, Course record 60.
Club membership 700.
Visitors   may play anytime except weekends before
              10.30, bookings can be made 8 days in advance.
Societies   apply in writing.
Green Fees   £7.50 per day.
Facilities   ⊗ ⅏ ᚼ 🍺 ♀ ᚼ 🏠 🛈 ℂ Mike Steadman.
Leisure   hard tennis courts, trolley for hire, putting green,
              practice area.
Location   S side of town centre off A38
Hotel   ★★ 64% Falcon Hotel, Henlade, TAUNTON
              ☎ 01823 442502 11 ⇔ ℝ

WEDMORE   Map 03 ST44

Isle of Wedmore Lineage BS28 4QT
☎ 01934 713649 (Office) & 712452 (Pro)
Gentle undulating course designed to maintain natural
environment. Existing woodland and hedgerow enhanced by
new planting. Magnificent panoramic views of Cheddar
Valley and Glastonbury Tor.
18 holes, 5854yds, Par 70, SSS 68, Course record 70.
Club membership 560.
Visitors   phone professional in advance.
Societies   weekdays only, telephone in advance.
Green Fees   £20 per day; £15 per round (£25/£20 weekends).
Facilities   ⊗ ⅏ ᚼ 🍺 ♀ ᚼ 🏠 🛈 ℂ Graham Coombe.
Leisure   trolley for hire, putting green, practice area.
Location   Off B3139 between Wells & Burnham-on-Sea
Hotel   ★★★ 68% Swan Hotel, Sadler St, WELLS
              ☎ 01749 678877 38 ⇔ ℝ

Beachlands Hotel

AA
★★ 64%

Commended

Only a Wedge Shot from the 1st tee!!

Perhaps it's the Tom Dunne designed Championship course or the fact that the links are practically playable all year. On the othe hand it may be the excellent Hotel & Restaurant and its reputation for quality & service. complete with the 55 malts available in the bar, or the high level of comfort in the 18 ensuite bedrooms. Whatever it is, one thing is for sure – guests of the Beachlands Hotel & Weston-uper-Mare Links Golf Course come back time and time again!! Contact Charles Porter for details on Breaks for individuals, groups & societies from as little as £52.50 per person per day – Dinner, Bed & Breakfast and Green Fees.
Uphill Road North, Weston-super-Mare BS23 4NG. Tel: (01934) 621401 Fax: (01934) 621966

WELLS   Map 03 ST54

Wells (Somerset) East Horrington Rd BA5 3DS
☎ 01749 675005
Beautiful wooded course with wonderful views. The prevailing SW wind complicates the 448-yd, 3rd.
18 holes, 6015yds, Par 70, SSS 69, Course record 66.
Club membership 775.
Visitors   must contact in advance & have handicap certificate weekends. Tee times restricted at weekends to after 9.30pm
Societies   must apply in advance.
Green Fees   £20 per day; £18 per round (£25/£22 weekends & public holidays).
Facilities   ⊗ ⅲ ⯘ ☛ ♀ ⅄ 🖻 ⛳ ⛵ Adrian Bishop.
Leisure   motorised carts for hire, trolley for hire, putting green, practice area.
Location   1.5m E off B3139
Hotel   ★★★ 68% Swan Hotel, Sadler St, WELLS
                 ☎ 01749 678877 38 ➩ ☞

WESTON-SUPER-MARE   Map 03 ST36

Puxton Park Puxton Ln, Hewish BS24 6TA
☎ 01934 876942
A Pay and Play course built on flat moorland dissected by a network of waterways.
18 holes, 6636yds, Par 72, SSS 71.
Club membership 250.
Visitors   must contact in advance.
Societies   apply in advance.
Green Fees   not confirmed.
Facilities   ♀ ⅄ 🖻 ⛵ ⛳ Mike Smedley.
Leisure   practice area,trolley for hire.
Location   2m junc 21 of M5 on A370
Hotel   ★★★ 68% Commodore Hotel, Beach Rd, Sand Bay, Kewstoke, WESTON-SUPER-MARE
                 ☎ 01934 415778 12 ➩ ☞Annexe6 ➩ ☞

Weston-super-Mare Uphill Rd North BS23 4NQ
☎ 01934 626968 & 633360
A compact and interesting layout with the opening hole adjacent to the beach. The sandy, links-type course is slightly undulating and has beautifully maintained turf and greens. The 15th is a testing 455-yard, par 4.
18 holes, 6300yds, Par 70, SSS 70, Course record 65.
Club membership 840.
Visitors   must have handicap certificate to play at weekends.
Societies   apply in writing or telephone.
Green Fees   £24 per day, £15 after 5pm (£35 per day weekends).
Facilities   ⊗ ⅲ ⯘ ☛ ♀ ⅄ 🖻 ⛵ Paul Barrington.
Leisure   trolley for hire, putting green, practice area.
Location   S side of town centre off A370
Hotel   ★★ 64% Beachlands Hotel, 17 Uphill Rd North, WESTON-SUPER-MARE
                 ☎ 01934 621401 17 ➩ ☞
Additional   ★★ 64% Rozel Hotel, Madeira Cove,
hotel   WESTON-SUPER-MARE
                 ☎ 01934 415268 46 ➩ ☞

Worlebury Monks Hill BS22 9SX
☎ 01934 623789 & 623214
Situated on the ridge of Worlebury Hill, this seaside course offers fairly easy walking and extensive views of the Severn estuary and Wales.
18 holes, 5963yds, Par 70, SSS 69, Course record 66.
Club membership 590.
Visitors   must be recognised golfers, handicap certificate or proof of club membership may be required
Societies   apply in writing or telephone in advance.
Green Fees   £20 per day (£30 weekends, £12 Sun after 2pm).
Facilities   ⊗ ⅲ ⯘ ☛ ♀ ⅄ 🖻 ⛵ Gary Marks.
Leisure   trolley for hire, putting green, practice area.
Location   5m NE off A370
Hotel   ★★★ 59% Royal Pier Hotel, Birnbeck Rd, WESTON-SUPER-MARE
                 ☎ 01934 626644 40 ➩ ☞

and Worlebury & Weston Golf Clubs

Just minutes away from these most enjoyable and quite differing courses, the Commodore caters for the every need of those seeking rest, relaxation and recreation. Stylishly appointed modern bedrooms, traditional bar and a choice of buffet/carvery or modern English cuisine in "Alices" restaurant dedicated to fine food and excellent service. Please telephone our Sales Office for details of year round short breaks and weekly terms plus preferential green fees.

  Ashley Courtney
AA ★★★   English Tourist Board   Highly
Highly Commended   Recommended

The Commodore Hotel
Beach Road, Sand Bay, Kewstoke,
Weston-super-Mare, Avon BS22 9UZ
Telephone Weston-super-Mare
(01934) 415778

Additional ★★★ 68% Commodore Hotel, Beach Rd, Sand
hotel Bay, Kewstoke, WESTON-SUPER-MARE
☎ 01934 415778 12 ⇨ ♏Annexe6 ⇨ ♏

YEOVIL   Map 03 ST51

Yeovil Sherborne Rd BA21 5BW
☎ 01935 75949
The opener lies by the River Yeo before the gentle climb to high downs with good views. The outstanding 14th and 15th holes present a challenge, being below the player with a deep railway cutting on the left of the green.
Old Course: 18 holes, 6144yds, Par 72, SSS 69, Course record 64.
Newton Course: 9 holes, 4891yds, Par 68, SSS 65.
Club membership 1000.
Visitors must contact in advance. Members only before 9.30am and 12.30-2.
Societies telephone in advance.
Green Fees Old Course: £20 per day/round (£25 weekends). Newton Course: £12 per day/round (£15 weekends).
Facilities ⊗ ♏ ♒ ♋ ♀ ♏ 🏌 (Geoff Kite.
Leisure trolley for hire, putting green, practice area.
Location 1m E on A30
Hotel ★★★ 59% The Manor Hotel, Hendford,
YEOVIL
☎ 01935 23116 due to change to 423116 20
⇨ ♏Annexe21 ⇨ ♏

STAFFORDSHIRE

BARLASTON   Map 07 SJ83

Barlaston Meaford Rd ST15 8UX
☎ 01782 372795 & 372867
Picturesque meadowland course designed by Peter Alliss.
18 holes, 5800yds, Par 69, SSS 68.
Club membership 600.
Visitors may not play before 10am weekends and bank holidays.
Societies telephone or apply in writing.
Green Fees not confirmed.
Facilities ♀ ♋ ♏ (Ian Rogers.
Leisure putting green.
Hotel ★★★ 70% Stone House Hotel, Stafford Rd,
STONE ☎ 01785 815531 47 ⇨ ♏

BROCTON   Map 07 SJ91

Brocton Hall ST17 0TH
☎ 01785 661901
Parkland course with gentle slopes in places, easy walking.
18 holes, 6095yds, Par 69, SSS 69, Course record 67.
Club membership 665.
Visitors not competition days. Must contact in advance.
Societies must apply in advance.
Green Fees £25 per day (£30 weekends & bank holidays).
Facilities ⊗ ♏ ♒ ♔ ♀ ♋ ♏ 🏌 (R G Johnson.
Leisure trolley for hire, putting green, practice area.
Location NW side of village off A34
Hotel ★★★ 65% Garth Hotel, Wolverhampton Rd,
Moss Pit, STAFFORD
☎ 01785 56124 60 ⇨ ♏

BURTON-UPON-TRENT   Map 07 SK22

Branston Burton Rd, Branston DE14 3DP
☎ 01283 543207 & 512211
Parkland course, adjacent to River Trent, on undulating ground with natural water hazards.
18 holes, 6632yds, Par 71, SSS 72, Course record 70.
Club membership 800.
Visitors must contact in advance.
Societies must telephone in advance.
Green Fees £30 per day; £20 per round.
Facilities ⊗ ♏ ♒ ♔ ♀ ♋ ♏ 🏌 ♏ (Gary Prince.
Leisure heated indoor swimming pool, fishing, sauna, solarium, gymnasium, motorised carts for hire, buggies for hire, trolley for hire, driving range, putting green, practice area.
Location 1.5m SW on A5121
Hotel ★★★ 68% Riverside Hotel, Riverside Dr,
Branston, BURTON UPON TRENT
☎ 01283 511234 22 ⇨ ♏

Burton-upon-Trent 43 Ashby Rd East DE15 0PS
☎ 01283 544551 & 562240
Undulating parkland course with trees a major feature. There are testing par 3s at 10th and 12th. The 18th has a lake around its green.
18 holes, 6579yds, Par 71, SSS 71, Course record 63.
Club membership 600.

Visitors	must contact in advance and have a handicap certificate.
Societies	must contact in advance.
Green Fees	£27 per day; £23 per round (£33 per day; £28 per round weekends & bank holidays).
Facilities	⊗ 〗II by prior arrangement 🝙 ⚑ ♀ 🛆 🖻 ⛳ ╔ Gary Stafford.
Leisure	trolley for hire, putting green, practice area, snooker.
Location	3m E on A50
Hotel	★★★ 68% Riverside Hotel, Riverside Dr, Branston, BURTON UPON TRENT ☎ 01283 511234 22 ⇋ ╠

Craythorne Craythorne Rd, Stretton DE13 0AZ
☎ 01283 564329
A relatively short and challenging parkland course with tight fairways and views of the Trent Valley. Excellent greens. Suits all standards but particularly good for society players.
18 holes, 5255yds, Par 68, SSS 67, Course record 66.
Club membership 480.

Visitors	must contact in advance.
Societies	apply in writing or telephone for details.
Green Fees	£17 per round (£20 weekends).
Facilities	⊗ 〗II 🝙 ⚑ ♀ 🛆 🖻 ⛳ ╔ Steve Hadfield.
Leisure	trolley for hire, driving range, putting green, practice area.
Location	Off A38 through Stretton village
Hotel	★★★ 68% Riverside Hotel, Riverside Dr, Branston, BURTON UPON TRENT ☎ 01283 511234 22 ⇋ ╠

Hoar Cross Hall Health Spa Golf Course Hoar Cross DE13 8QS ☎ 01283 575671
Newly constructed academy course located in the grounds of a stately home, now a well appointed health spa resort and hotel. Driving range, bunker and practice areas.
Club membership 300.

Visitors	day guests & residents.
Societies	golfing societies that are resident only.
Green Fees	on application.
Facilities	⊗ 〗II 🝙 ⚑ ♀ after 6pm 🛆 🖻 ⛳ ╠╣ ╔ Neil Allsebrook.
Leisure	hard tennis courts, heated indoor swimming pool, sauna, solarium, driving range, putting green, practice area, health & beauty treatments.
Hotel	★★★★ 67% Hoar Cross Hall Health Spa, Hoar Cross, BURTON UPON TRENT ☎ 01283 575671 86 ⇋ ╠

CANNOCK Map 07 SJ91

Cannock Park Stafford Rd WS11 2AL
☎ 01543 578850
Part of a large leisure centre, this parkland-type course plays alongside Cannock Chase. Good drainage, open most of year.
18 holes, 5149yds, Par 67, SSS 65.
Club membership 250.

Visitors	must book in advance.
Societies	must contact in advance.
Green Fees	£6.50 per round (£7.50 weekends).
Facilities	⊗ 〗II 🝙 ⚑ ♀ 🛆 🖻 ⛳ ╔ David Dunk.

Leisure	hard tennis courts, heated indoor swimming pool, sauna, solarium, gymnasium, trolley for hire, putting green, indoor bowls, badminton.
Location	4m S of Brocton
Hotel	★★★ 66% Roman Way Hotel, Watling St, Hatherton, CANNOCK ☎ 01543 572121 56 ⇋ ╠

ENVILLE Map 07 SO88

Enville Highgate Common DY7 5BN
☎ 01384 872047 (Office) & 872585 (Pro shop)
Easy walking on two fairly flat parkland/moorland courses - the 'Highgate' and the 'Lodge'.
Highgate Course: 18 holes, 6556yds, Par 72, SSS 72, Course record 65.
Lodge Course: 18 holes, 6217yds, Par 70, SSS 70, Course record 65.
Club membership 900.

Visitors	must play with member at weekends.
Societies	phone initially for details.
Green Fees	£36 per 36 holes; £30 per 27 holes; £25 per 18 holes.
Facilities	⊗ 〗II 🝙 ⚑ ♀ 🛆 🖻 ╔ Sean Power.
Leisure	motorised carts for hire, buggies for hire, trolley for hire.
Location	Take A458 towards Bridgnorth, after 4.5m turn right. Golf club signposted
Hotel	★★ 65% Talbot Hotel, High St, STOURBRIDGE ☎ 01384 394350 25 ⇋ ╠

GOLDENHILL Map 07 SJ85

Goldenhill Mobberley Rd ST6 5SS
☎ 01782 784715
Rolling parkland course with water features on six of the back nine holes.
18 holes, 5957yds, Par 71, SSS 68.
Club membership 400.

Visitors	contact in advance for weekend play.
Societies	must apply in writing.
Green Fees	not confirmed.
Facilities	♀ 🛆 🖻 ⛳ ╔ Tony Clingan.
Location	On A50, 4m N of Stoke
Hotel	★★★ 66% Manor House Hotel, Audley Rd, ALSAGER ☎ 01270 884000 57 ⇋ ╠

HAZELSLADE Map 07 SK01

Beau Desert Ringeley Rd WS12 5PJ
☎ 01543 422626
Woodland course.
18 holes, 6310yds, Par 70, SSS 71, Course record 64.
Club membership 500.

Visitors	are advised to contact in advance.
Societies	must contact in advance.
Green Fees	£35 per day (£45 weekends).
Facilities	⊗ 〗II 🝙 ⚑ ♀ 🛆 🖻 ⛳ ╔ Barry Stevens.
Leisure	trolley for hire, putting green, practice area.
Location	0.5m NE of village
Hotel	★★★ 66% Roman Way Hotel, Watling St, Hatherton, CANNOCK ☎ 01543 572121 56 ⇋ ╠

HIMLEY
Map 07 SO89

Himley Hall Golf Centre Log Cabin, Himley Hall Park DY3
4DF ☎ 01902 895207
Parkland course set in grounds of Himley Hall Park, with
lovely views. Large practice area including a pitch-and-putt.
9 holes, 6215yds, Par 72, SSS 70, Course record 69.
Club membership 200.
Visitors restricted weekends.
Green Fees £7 per 18 holes; £4.80 per 9 holes (£7.50/£5
weekends).
Facilities ⚑🏠
Leisure trolley for hire, driving range, putting green,
practice area.
Location 0.5m E on B4176
Hotel ★★★ 59% Himley Country Hotel, School Rd,
HIMLEY ☎ 01902 896716 73 ⇆ ⌂

LEEK
Map 07 SJ95

Leek Birchall, Cheddleton Rd ST13 5RE ☎ 01538 384779
Undulating, challenging moorland course.
18 holes, 6240yds, Par 70, SSS 70, Course record 63.
Club membership 750.
Visitors must contact in advance.
Societies must apply in advance.
Green Fees £24 per day (£30 weekends & bank holidays).
Facilities ⊗ ⫼ ℔ ⬛ ♀ ⚐ 🏠 ℓ Peter A Stubbs.
Leisure trolley for hire, putting green, practice area.
Location 0.75m S on A520
Hotel ★★ 64% Bank End Farm Motel, Leek Old Rd,
Longsdon ☎ 01538 383638 10rm(9 ⇆ ⌂)

Westwood (Leek) Newcastle Rd ST13 1AA
☎ 01538 398385
A challenging moorland/parkland course.
18 holes, 6207yds, Par 70, SSS 69.
Club membership 700.
Visitors no visitors on Sun and Sat before 1pm.
Societies apply by phone or in writing.
Green Fees not confirmed.
Facilities ⊗ ⫼ ℔ ⬛ ♀ ⚑ 🏠 ℓ Darren Lewis.
Leisure trolley for hire, putting green, practice area.
Location On A53, S of Leek
Hotel ★★ 64% Bank End Farm Motel, Leek Old Rd,
Longsdon ☎ 01538 383638 10rm(9 ⇆ ⌂)

LICHFIELD
Map 07 SK10

Seedy Mill Elmhurst WS13 8HE ☎ 01543 417333
New, gently-rolling parkland course in picturesque rural
setting. Lakes and streams are abundant, and there are four
challenging Par 3s. Well contoured green, good bunkering.
Also a superb 9-hole Par 3 course.
18 holes, 6308yds, Par 72, SSS 70.
Club membership 800.
Visitors must contact in advance. May play weekends
after 1pm.
Societies phone for details,
Green Fees £17 (£22 weekends).
Facilities ⊗ ⫼ ℔ ⬛ ♀ ⚑ 🏠 ℓ Richard O'Hanlon.
Leisure motorised carts for hire, buggies for hire, trolley
for hire, driving range, 9 hole par 3 course,
putting, practice area.

Location At Elmhurst, 1.5m N of Lichfield, off A515
Hotel ★★★ 65% Little Barrow Hotel, Beacon St,
LICHFIELD ☎ 01543 414500 24 ⇆ ⌂

Whittington Heath Tamworth Rd WS14 9PW
☎ 01543 432317
18 magnificent holes winding their way through
heathland and trees, presenting a good test for the serious
golfer. Leaving the fairway can be severely punished.
The dog-legs are most tempting, inviting the golfer to
chance his arm. Local knowledge is a definite advantage.
Clear views of the famous three spires of Lichfield
Cathedral.
18 holes, 6448yds, Par 70, SSS 70, Course record 65.
Club membership 660.
Visitors must contact in advance. May not play at
weekends.
Societies welcome Wed & Thu, must apply in writing.
Green Fees £32 per day/round.
Facilities ⊗ ⫼ ℔ ⬛ ♀ ⚑ 🏠 ✈ ℓ Adrian Sadler.
Leisure trolley for hire, putting green, practice area.
Location 2.5m SE on A51
Hotel ★★★ 65% Little Barrow Hotel, Beacon St,
LICHFIELD
☎ 01543 414500 24 ⇆ ⌂

NEWCASTLE-UNDER-LYME
Map 07 SJ84

Newcastle Municipal Newcastle Rd, Keele ST5 5AB
☎ 01782 627596
Open course on the side of a hill without mature trees.
18 holes, 6396yds, Par 71, SSS 70, Course record 64.
Club membership 297.
Visitors must contact in advance.
Societies by prior arrangement to Newcastle-Under-Lyme
Borough Council, Civic Offices, Merrial St,
Newcastle-under-Lyme, Staffs.
Green Fees £6.40 per round (£8.60 weekends).
Facilities ⊗ ℔ ⬛ ♀ 🏠 ✈ ℓ Colin Smith.
Leisure trolley for hire, driving range, putting green.
Location 2m W on A525
Hotel B Forte Posthouse Newcastle under Lyme,
Clayton Rd, NEWCASTLE-UNDER-LYME
☎ 01782 717171 119 ⇆ ⌂

Newcastle-Under-
Lyme Whitmore Rd ST5 2QB ☎ 01782 617006
Parkland course.
18 holes, 6404yds, Par 72, SSS 71.
Club membership 600.
Visitors must contact in advance. With member only
weekends.
Societies must contact in advance.
Green Fees £25 per day/round.
Facilities ⊗ ⫼ ℔ ⬛ ♀ ⚑ 🏠 ✈ ℓ Paul Symonds.
Leisure trolley for hire, putting green.
Location 1m SW on A53
Hotel ★★ 63% Comfort Friendly Inn, Liverpool Rd,
Cross Heath, NEWCASTLE-UNDER-LYME
☎ 01782 717000 47 ⇆ ⌂Annexe21 ⇆ ⌂

Wolstanton Dimsdale Old Hall, Hassam Pde, Wolstanton
ST5 9DR ☎ 01782 622413
Meadowland/parkland course in an urban area.
18 holes, 5807yds, Par 68, SSS 68, Course record 63.
Club membership 700.

Visitors must contact in advance. With member only at weekends & bank holidays.
Societies must contact in advance.
Green Fees £18 per day/round.
Facilities ⊗ ⅷ by prior arrangement ᛚ 🏌 ♀ 👥 📷 ꞙ Colin Smith.
Leisure trolley for hire, putting green, snooker.
Location Turn off A34 at The Sportsman Inn
Hotel B Forte Posthouse Newcastle under Lyme, Clayton Rd, NEWCASTLE-UNDER-LYME ☎ 01782 717171 119 ⇌ ꞙ

ONNELEY   Map 07 SJ74

Onneley CW3 9QF ☎ 01782 750577
A tight, picturesque, hillside parkland course. An ideal test for the short game
9 holes, 5584yds, Par 70, SSS 67, Course record 67.
Club membership 480.
Visitors welcome except during competitions, but may not play on Sun and with member only Sat and bank holidays.
Societies packages available apply in writing to secretary.
Green Fees £15 per 18 holes.
Facilities ᛚ 🏌 ♀ 👥
Leisure putting green.
Location 2m from Woore on A525
Hotel ★★ 69% Wheatsheaf Inn at Onneley, Barhill Rd, ONNELEY ☎ 01782 751581 5 ꞙ

PATTINGHAM   Map 07 SO89

Patshull Park Hotel Golf & Country Club WV6 7HR
☎ 01902 700100
Picturesque course set in 280 acres of glorious Capability Brown landscaped parkland. Designed by John Jacobs, the course meanders alongside trout fishing lakes. Many leisure facilities.
18 holes, 6700yds, Par 72, SSS 71, Course record 63.
Club membership 400.
Visitors must contact in advance.
Societies must contact in advance.
Green Fees £22.50 per round (£27.50 weekends).
Facilities ⊗ ⅷ ᛚ 🏌 ♀ 👥 📷 ꞙ 🚣
ꞙ Joe Higgins/Richard Bissell.
Leisure heated indoor swimming pool, fishing, sauna, solarium, gymnasium, motorised carts for hire, buggies for hire, trolley for hire, putting green, practice area.
Location Off A464
Hotel ★★★ 66% Patshull Park Hotel Golf & Country Club, Patshull Park, PATTINGHAM ☎ 01902 700100 49 ⇌ ꞙ

PERTON   Map 07 SO89

Perton Park Wrottesley Park Rd WV6 7HL
☎ 01902 380103 & 380073
Flat meadowland course set in open countryside.
18 holes, 6620yds, Par 72, SSS 72.
Club membership 250.
Visitors must book in advance.
Societies must telephone in advance.
Green Fees £10 per day; £8 per round (£20/£15 weekends & bank holidays).

Facilities ⊗ ⅷ ᛚ 🏌 ♀ 👥 📷 ꞙ ꞙ Jeremy Harrold.
Leisure motorised carts for hire, buggies for hire, trolley for hire, driving range, putting green, bowling green, snooker.
Location 6m W of Wolverhampton, on A454
Hotel ★★ 68% Ely House Hotel, 53 Tettenhall Rd, WOLVERHAMPTON ☎ 01902 311311 18 ⇌ ꞙ

STAFFORD   Map 07 SJ92

Stafford Castle Newport Rd ST16 1BP ☎ 01785 223821
Parkland type course.
9 holes, 6382yds, Par 71, SSS 70, Course record 68.
Club membership 400.
Visitors must contact in advance. May not play at weekends.
Societies must apply in writing.
Green Fees £14 per day (£18 weekends & bank holidays).
Facilities ⊗ ⅷ ᛚ 🏌 ♀ 👥 📷
Leisure trolley for hire, putting green, practice area.
Location SW side of town centre off A518
Hotel ★★★ 65% Tillington Hall Hotel, Eccleshall Rd, STAFFORD ☎ 01785 53531 due to change to 253531 90 ⇌ ꞙ

STOKE-ON-TRENT   Map 07 SJ84

Burslem Wood Farm, High Ln, Tunstall ST6 7JT
☎ 01782 837006
On the outskirts of Tunstall, a moorland course with hard walking.
9 holes, 5354yds, Par 66, SSS 66.
Club membership 250.
Visitors except Sun & with member only Sat & bank holidays.
Societies must telephone in advance.
Green Fees not confirmed.
Facilities 👥
Location 4m N of city centre on B5049
Hotel ★★★ 65% George Hotel, Swan Square, Burslem, STOKE-ON-TRENT ☎ 01782 577544 30 ⇌ ꞙ

Greenway Hall Stanley Rd, Stockton Brook ST9 9LJ
☎ 01782 503158
Moorland course with fine views of the Pennines.
18 holes, 5678yds, Par 68, SSS 67.
Club membership 560.
Visitors may play weekdays only.
Societies must apply in writing.
Green Fees £14 per round.
Facilities ⊗ ᛚ 🏌 ♀ 👥
Leisure practice area, snooker.
Location 5m NE off A53
Hotel ★★★ 65% George Hotel, Swan Square, Burslem, STOKE-ON-TRENT ☎ 01782 577544 30 ⇌ ꞙ

Trentham 14 Barlaston Old Rd, Trentham ST4 8HB
☎ 01782 658109
Parkland course. The par 3, 4th is a testing hole reached over a copse of trees.
18 holes, 6644yds, Par 72, SSS 72, Course record 63.
Club membership 600.   ▶

Visitors must play with member at weekends.
Societies must contact in advance.
Green Fees £25 per day.
Facilities ⊗ ⅶ ⅊ ⅌ ♀ ⅄ ⋒ ᵀ ℓ Sandy Wilson.
Leisure squash, buggies for hire, trolley for hire, driving range, putting green, practice area.
Location 3m S off A5035
Hotel ★★★ 62% Haydon House Hotel, 1-13 Haydon St, Basford, STOKE-ON-TRENT
☎ 01782 711311 16 ⇄ ℝAnnexe14 ⇄ ℝ

Trentham Park Trentham Park ST4 8AE
☎ 01782 658800
Fine woodland course.
18 holes, 6425yds, Par 71, SSS 71, Course record 67.
Club membership 850.
Visitors must contact in advance.
Societies Wed & Fri, must apply in advance.
Green Fees £25 per day (£30 weekends).
Facilities ⊗ ⅶ ⅊ ⅌ ♀ ⅄ ⋒ ℓ Jim McLeod.
Leisure trolley for hire, practice area.
Location 3m SW off A34
Hotel B Forte Posthouse Newcastle under Lyme, Clayton Rd, NEWCASTLE-UNDER-LYME
☎ 01782 717171 119 ⇄ ℝ

STONE   Map 07 SJ93

Izaak Walton Eccleshall Rd, Cold Norton ST15 0NS
☎ 01785 760900
Opened in 1992, a gently undulating meadowland course with streams and ponds as features.
18 holes, 6281yds, Par 72, SSS 72, Course record 66.
Club membership 250.
Visitors must contact in advance for weekends play.
Societies must telephone in advance.
Green Fees £12 per round (£17 weekends).
Facilities ⊗ ⅶ ⅊ ⅌ ♀ ⅄ ⋒ ℓ Julie Brown.
Leisure driving range, putting green, practice area.
Hotel ★★★ 70% Stone House Hotel, Stafford Rd, STONE ☎ 01785 815531 47 ⇄ ℝ

Stone Filleybrooks ST15 0NB ☎ 01785 813103
9-hole parkland course with easy walking and 18 different tees.
9 holes, 6299yds, Par 71, SSS 70, Course record 68.
Club membership 310.
Visitors with member only weekends & bank holidays.
Societies must apply in writing.
Green Fees £15 per day or round.
Facilities ⊗ ⅶ ⅊ ⅌ ♀ ⅄
Leisure practice area.
Location 0.5m W on A34
Hotel ★★★ 70% Stone House Hotel, Stafford Rd, STONE ☎ 01785 815531 47 ⇄ ℝ

TAMWORTH   Map 07 SK20

Drayton Park Drayton Park B78 3TN ☎ 01827 251139
Parkland course designed by James Braid. Club established since 1897.
18 holes, 6214yds, Par 71, SSS 71, Course record 62.
Club membership 450.
Visitors with member only weekends. Must contact in advance.

Societies must apply in writing.
Green Fees £28 per day/round.
Facilities ⊗ ⅶ ⅊ ⅌ ♀ ⅄ ⋒ ℓ M W Passmore.
Leisure trolley for hire, putting green, practice area.
Location 2m S on A4091, next to Drayton Manor Leisure Park
Hotel ★★★★ 72% The Belfry, WISHAW
☎ 01675 470301 219 ⇄ ℝ

Tamworth Municipal Eagle Dr, Amington B77 4EG
☎ 01827 53850
First-class municipal, parkland course and a good test of golf.
18 holes, 6605ydss, Par 73, SSS 72, Course record 63.
Club membership 600.
Visitors must book in advance at weekends.
Societies must contact in advance.
Green Fees £8.50 per 18 holes; £5.60 for 9 holes.
Facilities ⊗ ⅶ ⅊ ⅌ ♀ ⅄ ⋒ ᵀ ℓ Barry Jones.
Leisure motorised carts for hire, buggies for hire, trolley for hire, putting greens, practice area.
Location 2.5m E off B5000
Hotel ★★ 62% Angel Croft Hotel, Beacon St, LICHFIELD
☎ 01543 258737 10rm(3 ⇄5 ℝ)Annexe8 ⇄ ℝ

UTTOXETER   Map 07 SK03

Uttoxeter Wood Ln ST14 8JR ☎ 01889 565108
Downland course with open aspect.
18 holes, 5468yds, Par 68, SSS 68, Course record 66.
Club membership 750.
Visitors restricted weekends and competition days.
Societies must apply in writing.
Green Fees £22 per day; £15 per round (£17 per round weekends & bank holidays).
Facilities ⊗ ⅶ ⅊ ⅌ ♀ ⅄ ⋒ ℓ John Pearsall.
Leisure trolley for hire, putting green, practice area, pool table.
Location 1m SE off B5017
Hotel ★★ 64% Bank House Hotel, Church St, UTTOXETER
☎ 01889 566922 16 ⇄ ℝ

WESTON   Map 07 SJ92

Ingestre Park ST18 0RE ☎ 01889 270845
Parkland course set in the grounds of Ingestre Hall, former home of the Earl of Shrewsbury, with mature trees and pleasant views.
18 holes, 6334yds, Par 70, SSS 70, Course record 67.
Club membership 850.
Visitors with member only weekends & bank holidays. Must play before 3.30pm weekdays . Advance booking preferred.
Societies must apply in advance.
Green Fees £21 per round.
Facilities ⊗ ⅶ ⅊ ⅌ ♀ ⅄ ⋒ ℓ Danny Scullion.
Leisure motorised carts for hire, buggies for hire, trolley for hire, driving range, putting green, practice area, snooker.
Location 2m SE off A51
Hotel ★★★ 65% Tillington Hall Hotel, Eccleshall Rd, STAFFORD
☎ 01785 53531 due to change to 253531 90 ⇄ ℝ

WHISTON

Map 07 SK04

Whiston Hall Whiston Hall ST10 2HZ
☎ 01538 266260 & 0850 903815
A challenging 18-hole course in scenic countryside and
incorporating many natural obstacles.
18 holes, 5742yds, Par 71, SSS 69.
Club membership 400.
Visitors   reasonable dress on the course. Must telephone
     in advance at weekends.
Societies   contact in advance.
Green Fees   £15 per day; £10 per round (£21/£14 weekends
     & bank holidays).
Facilities   ⊗ ⅢⅡ ⅃ ⅃ ⅃ ⅃
Leisure   fishing, trolley for hire, putting green, practice
     area, snooker.
Location   Off A52, 3m NE of Cheadle
Hotel   ★★(red) Old Beams Restaurant with Rooms,
     Leek Rd, WATERHOUSES
     ☎ 01538 308254 5rm

SUFFOLK

ALDEBURGH

Map 05 TM45

Aldeburgh Saxmundham Rd IP15 5PE
☎ 01728 452890
A most enjoyable and not unduly difficult seaside course;
ideal for golfing holidaymakers. A bracing and fairly
open terrain with some trees and heathland.
18 holes, 6330yds, Par 68, SSS 71, Course record 65.
River Course: 9 holes, 2114yds, Par 32, SSS 32.
Visitors   must contact in advance.
Societies   must contact in advance.
Green Fees   £33 per day; £22 after noon (£40/£28
     weekends & bank holidays). River Course:
     £12 per day; £10 after noon; £6 after 5pm.
Facilities   ⊗ ⅃ ⅃ ⅃ ⅃ ⅃ ⅃
Leisure   trolley for hire, putting green, practice area.
Location   1m W on A1094
Hotel   ★★★ 70% Wentworth Hotel, Wentworth
     Rd, ALDEBURGH
     ☎ 01728 452312 31rm(24 ➩4 ⓡ)Annexe7
     ➩ ⓡ

BECCLES

Map 05 TM49

Wood Valley The Common NR34 9YN ☎ 01502 712244
Heathland course with natural hazards and particularly
exposed to wind.
9 holes, 2779yds, Par 68, SSS 67.
Club membership 160.
Visitors   must play with member on Sun.
Societies   must contact in advance.
Green Fees   £10 per round (£12 weekends).
Facilities   ⊗ ⅃ ⅃ ⅃ ⅃ ⅃
Leisure   trolley for hire.
Location   NE side of town
Hotel   ★★★ 64% Hotel Hatfield, The Esplanade,
     LOWESTOFT ☎ 01502 565337 33 ➩ ⓡ

BUNGAY

Map 05 TM38

Bungay & Waveney Valley Outney Common NR35 1DS
☎ 01986 892337
Heathland course partly comprising Neolithic stone workings,
easy walking.
18 holes, 6026yds, Par 69, SSS 69.
Club membership 730.
Visitors   should contact in advance. With member only
     weekends & bank holidays.
Societies   must contact in advance.
Green Fees   £18 per day/round.
Facilities   ⊗ ⅢⅡ ⅃ ⅃ ⅃ ⅃ ⅃ ⅃ Nigel Whyte.
Leisure   motorised carts for hire, buggies for hire, trolley
     for hire, putting green, practice area.
Location   0.5m NW on A143
Hotel   ★★★ 64% Hotel Hatfield, The Esplanade,
     LOWESTOFT ☎ 01502 565337 33 ➩ ⓡ

BURY ST EDMUNDS

Map 05 TL86

Bury St Edmunds Tut Hill IP28 6LG ☎ 01284 755979
Undulating parkland course with easy walking and attractive
short holes.
18 holes, 6678yds, Par 72, SSS 72, Course record 69 or 9
holes, 2217yds, Par 62, SSS 62.
Club membership 850.
Visitors   with member only at weekends for 18 hole
     course.
Societies   must apply in writing.
Green Fees   18 hole course: £26 per day ; £24 per round. 9 hole
     course: £11 per 2 rounds (£12 weekends).   ▶

WENTWORTH
HOTEL   ★★★
Aldeburgh, Suffolk
Tel: (01728) 452312   Fax: (01728) 454343

*The Hotel has the comfort and style of a Country House.
Two comfortable lounges, with open fires and antique
furniture, provide ample space to relax. Each
individually decorated bedroom, many with sea views, is
equipped with a colour television, radio, hairdryer and
tea making facilities. The Restaurant serves a variety of
fresh produce whilst a light lunch can be chosen from the
Bar menu, eaten outside in the sunken terrace garden.
Aldeburgh is timeless and unhurried. There are quality
shops, two excellent golf courses within a short distance
from the hotel, long walks and some of the best
birdwatching at Minsmere Bird reserve. Music and the
Arts can be heard at the Internationally famous Snape
Malting Concert hall. Lastly, there are miles of beach to
sit upon and watch the sea!*

Facilities ⊗ ⅢⅢ by prior arrangement 🏌 ⚑ ♀ ⚲ 🏠
ℂ Mark Jillings.
Leisure trolley for hire.
Location 2m NW on B1106 off A45
Hotel ★★★ 68% Angel Hotel, Angel Hill, BURY ST EDMUNDS ☎ 01284 753926 42 ⇄ ℝ

Fornham Park St John's Hill Plantation, The Street, Fornham All Saints IP28 6JQ ☎ 01284 706777
Flat parkland course with many water hazards. Also country club facilities.
18 holes, 6209yds, Par 71, SSS 70, Course record 67.
Club membership 300.
Visitors no restrictions, but must book a tee time.
Societies by arrangement.
Green Fees not confirmed.
Facilities ♀ ⚲ 🏠 ⚡ ℂ Sean Clark.
Location 2m N off A134
Hotel ★★★⚑ 70% Ravenwood Hall Hotel, Rougham, BURY ST EDMUNDS ☎ 01359 270345 7 ⇄Annexe7 ⇄

CRETINGHAM   Map 05 TM26

Cretingham IP13 7BA ☎ 01728 685275
Parkland course.
9 holes, 4552yds, Par 66, SSS 64, Course record 61.
Club membership 350.
Visitors booking required for weekends.
Societies must contain in advance.
Green Fees £12 per day; £9 per 18 holes; £7 per 9 holes (£14/£11/£9 weekends & bank holidays).
Facilities ⊗ 🏌 ⚑ ♀ ⚲ 🏠 ⚡ ℂ Colin Jenkins.
Leisure hard tennis courts, outdoor swimming pool, trolley for hire, driving range, putting green, practice area, pitch & putt, snooker.
Location 2m from A1120 at Earl Soham
Hotel ★★ 67% Crown Hotel, Market Hill, FRAMLINGHAM ☎ 01728 723521 14 ⇄

FELIXSTOWE   Map 05 TM33

Felixstowe Ferry Ferry Rd IP11 9RY ☎ 01394 283060
Seaside links course, pleasant views, easy walking. Testing 491-yd, 7th hole.
18 holes, 6272yds, Par 72, SSS 70.
Club membership 800.
Visitors may not play weekends.
Societies Tue, Wed & Fri.
Green Fees £24 per day.
Facilities ⊗ ⅢⅢ 🏌 ⚑ ♀ ⚲ 🏠 ⚲⚡ ℂ Ian MacPherson.
Leisure trolley for hire, putting green, practice area.
Location NE side of town centre
Hotel ★★ 69% Waverley Hotel, 2 Wolsey Gardens, FELIXSTOWE ☎ 01394 282811 19 ⇄ ℝ

FLEMPTON   Map 05 TL86

Flempton IP28 6EQ ☎ 01284 728291
Breckland course.
9 holes, 6080yds, Par 70, SSS 70.
Club membership 300.
Visitors must have handicap certificate. With member only weekends & bank holidays.
Societies must apply in writing.

Green Fees not confirmed.
Facilities ♀ ⚲ 🏠 ℂ
Location 0.5m W on A1101
Hotel ★★ 65% Suffolk Hotel, 38 The Buttermarket, BURY ST EDMUNDS ☎ 01284 753995 33 ⇄ ℝ

HALESWORTH   Map 05 TM37

St Helena Bramfield Rd IP19 9XA ☎ 01986 875567
A 27-hole professionally designed parkland complex of three 9-hole courses, giving 6 playing options of 3 x 18-hole Par 72 and 3 x Par 36 9-hole.
Saint Helena: 18 holes, 6580yds, Par 72, SSS 72, Course record 71.
Halesworth: 9 holes, 3059yds, Par 36, SSS 36.
Club membership 500.
Visitors visitors welcome at all times except for Sunday before noon on the St Helena course.
Societies telephone for booking form.
Green Fees £19 per day; £15 per 18 holes; £7.50 per 9 holes (£21/£18/£7.50 weekends & bank holidays).
Facilities ⊗ ⅢⅢ 🏌 ⚑ ♀ ⚲ 🏠 ⚡ ℂ Philip Heil.
Leisure motorised carts for hire, buggies for hire, trolley for hire, driving range, putting green, practice area, equestrian centre.
Location 0.75m S of town, signposted on left of A144 road to Bramfield
Hotel ★★★ 69% Swan Hotel, Market Place, SOUTHWOLD ☎ 01502 722186 27 ⇄ ℝAnnexe18 ⇄

HAVERHILL   Map 05 TL64

Haverhill Coupals Rd CB9 7UW ☎ 01440 61951
Parkland course with good greens, plenty of trees and a small river running through three fairways and affecting 6 holes. A further 9-holes are under constrution and should be playable Spring 1997..
9 holes, 5717yds, Par 68, SSS 68, Course record 65.
Club membership 500.
Visitors telephone to check for club competitions.
Societies must contact in advance. Tue & Thu only.
Green Fees £15 per day; £12 per 18 holes (£20/£16 weekends & bank holidays).
Facilities ⊗ ⅢⅢ 🏌 ⚑ ♀ ⚲ 🏠 ⚡ ℂ Simon Mayfield.
Leisure buggies for hire, trolley for hire, putting green, practice area.
Location 1m SE off A604
Hotel ★★ 67% Bell Hotel, Market Hill, CLARE ☎ 01787 277741 9rm(3 ⇄4 ℝ)Annexe11 ⇄

HINTLESHAM   Map 05 TM04

Hintlesham Hall IP8 3NS ☎ 01473 652761
Magnificent new championship length course blending harmoniously with the ancient parkland surrounding this exclusive hotel. The 6630yd parkland course was designed by Hawtree and Son, one of the oldest established firms of golf course architects in the world. The course is fair but challenging for low and high handicappers alike. Hotel offers beautiful accommodation, excellent cuisine and many facilities.
18 holes, 6638yds, Par 72, SSS 72, Course record 67.
Club membership 350.

Visitors	must contact in advance.
Societies	must telephone in advance.
Green Fees	£45 per day; £26 per round (£75/£45 weekends & bank holidays).
Facilities	⊗ ⅲ ⅙ �& ♀ ⅄ 🏠 ⏋ 🏌 ⅛ Alastair Spink.
Leisure	hard tennis courts, heated outdoor swimming pool, sauna, solarium, gymnasium, motorised carts for hire, buggies for hire, trolley for hire.
Location	In village on A1071
Hotel	★★★★(red)♨ Hintlesham Hall Hotel, HINTLESHAM ☎ 01473 652334 & 652268 33 ⇄ ⟰

IPSWICH Map 05 TM14

Alnesbourne Priory Priory Park IP10 0JT
☎ 01473 727393 & 726373
A fabulous outlook facing due south across the River Orwell is one of the many good features of this course set in woodland. All holes run among trees with some fairways requiring straight shots. The 8th green is on saltings by the river.
9 holes, 1700yds, Par 29.
Club membership 50.

Visitors	closed on Tuesday.
Societies	Tue only, telephone in advance.
Green Fees	£10 weekdays, £11 Saturday, £12 Sunday.
Facilities	⊗ ⅲ ⅙ �& ♀ ⅄ ⏋ ⅛
Leisure	hard tennis courts, heated outdoor swimming pool, practice area.
Location	3m SE, off A14
Hotel	★★★ 69% Suffolk Grange Hotel, The Havens, Ransomes Europark, IPSWICH ☎ 01473 272244 60 ⇄ ⟰

Ipswich Purdis Heath IP3 8UQ
☎ 01473 728941
Many golfers are suprised when they hear that Ipswich has, at Purdis Heath, a first-class golf course. In some ways it resembles some of Surrey's better courses; a beautiful heathland/parkland course with two lakes and easy walking.
18 holes, 6405yds, Par 71, SSS 71 or 9 holes, 1930yds, Par 31, SSS 59.
Club membership 850.

Visitors	must contact in advance & have a handicap certificate for 18 hole courses.
Societies	must contact in advance.
Green Fees	not confirmed.
Facilities	♀ ⅄ 🏠 ⅛
Location	E side of town centre off A1156
Hotel	★★★ 69% Marlborough Hotel, Henley Rd, IPSWICH ☎ 01473 257677 22 ⇄ ⟰

Rushmere Rushmere Heath IP4 5QQ ☎ 01473 725648
Heathland course with gorse and prevailing winds. Testing 5th hole - dog leg, 419 yards (par 4).
18 holes, 6262yds, Par 70, SSS 68, Course record 66.
Club membership 792.

Visitors	not before 2.30pm weekends & bank holidays. Must have a handicap certificate.
Societies	weekdays ex Wed by arrangement.
Green Fees	£20 per day/round.

Facilities	⊗ ⅙ �& ♀ ⅄ 🏠 ⏋ ⅛ N T J McNeill.
Leisure	trolley for hire, putting green, practice area.
Location	3m E off A12
Hotel	★★★ 69% Marlborough Hotel, Henley Rd, IPSWICH ☎ 01473 257677 22 ⇄ ⟰

LOWESTOFT Map 05 TM59

Rookery Park Carlton Colville NR33 8HJ ☎ 01502 560380
Parkland course with a 9-hole, Par 3 adjacent.
18 holes, 6385yds, Par 72, SSS 72.
Club membership 1000.

Visitors	must have handicap certificate.
Societies	by arrangement.
Green Fees	not confirmed.
Facilities	♀ ⅄ 🏠 ⏋ ⅛
Location	3.5m SW on A146
Hotel	★★★ 64% Hotel Hatfield, The Esplanade, LOWESTOFT ☎ 01502 565337 33 ⇄ ⟰

NEWMARKET Map 05 TL66

Links Cambridge Rd CB8 0TG ☎ 01638 663000
Gently undulating parkland.
18 holes, 6574yds, Par 72, SSS 71, Course record 70.
Club membership 780.

Visitors	must have handicap certificate, may not play Sun before 11.30am.
Societies	telephone secretary in advance.
Green Fees	£26 (£30 weekends & bank holidays).
Facilities	⊗ ⅲ ⅙ �& ♀ ⅄ 🏠 ⏋ ⅛ John Sharkey.
Leisure	trolley for hire, putting green, practice area.
Location	1m SW on A1304
Hotel	★★★ 67% Heath Court Hotel, Moulton Rd, NEWMARKET ☎ 01638 667171 44 ⇄ ⟰

NEWTON Map 05 TL94

Newton Green Newton Green CO10 0QN
☎ 01787 377217 & 377501
Flat, 18-hole commonland course.
18 holes, 5960yds, Par 69, SSS 68.
Club membership 575.

Visitors	must contact in advance but may not play on Tue or Sat & Sun before 12.30.
Societies	apply in advance.
Green Fees	£20 per day; £14 per 18 holes.
Facilities	⊗ ⅲ ⅙ �& ♀ ⅄ 🏠 ⏋ ⅛ Tim Cooper.
Leisure	trolley for hire, putting green, practice area.
Location	W side of village on A134
Hotel	★★★ 64% Bull Hotel, Hall St, LONG MELFORD ☎ 01787 378494 25 ⇄ ⟰

RAYDON Map 05 TM03

Brett Vale Noakes Rd IP7 5LR ☎ 01473 310718
Brett Vale course takes you through a nature reserve and on lakeside walks. The excellent fairways demand an accurate tee and good approach shots. 1, 2, 3, 8, 10 and 15 are all affected by crosswinds, but once in the valley it is much more sheltered. Although only 5,808yards the course is testing and interesting at all levels of golf.
18 holes, 5808yds, Par 70, SSS 68, Course record 65.
Club membership 300. ▶

Visitors must book tee times and wear appropriate clothing.
Societies apply in writing or telephone.
Green Fees not confirmed.
Facilities ♀ ⚐ 🏌 ⌂ 🏌 🏌 Andrew Boulter.
Leisure indoor driving range.
Location B1070 at Raydon, 2m from A12
Hotel ★★★(red)🏌 Maison Talbooth, Stratford Rd, DEDHAM ☎ 01206 322367 10 ⇆ 🐾

SOUTHWOLD Map 05 TM57

Southwold The Common IP18 6TB
☎ 01502 723234 & 723248
Commonland course with 4-acre practice ground and panoramic views of the sea.
9 holes, 6052yds, Par 70, SSS 69, Course record 67.
Club membership 450.
Visitors restricted on competition days (Ladies-Wed, Gents-Sun.
Societies must contact in advance.
Green Fees £18 per day; £15 per 18 holes (£20 per round or day).
Facilities ⊗ 🍴 by prior arrangement 🏌 🏌 ♀ ⚐ ⌂ 🏌 🏌 Brian Allen.
Leisure motorised carts for hire, trolley for hire, putting green, practice area.
Location From A12 - B1140 to Southwold
Hotel ★★★ 69% Swan Hotel, Market Place, SOUTHWOLD
☎ 01502 722186 27 ⇆ 🐾 Annexe18 ⇆

STOWMARKET Map 05 TM05

Stowmarket Lower Rd, Onehouse IP14 3DA
☎ 01449 736473
Parkland course.
18 holes, 6107yds, Par 69, SSS 69, Course record 66.
Club membership 630.
Visitors must contact in advance.
Societies Thu or Fri, by arrangement.
Green Fees £27 per day; £22 per round (£38/£28 weekends and bank holidays).
Facilities ⊗ 🍴 by prior arrangement 🏌 🏌 ♀ ⚐ ⌂ 🏌
Leisure motorised carts for hire, trolley for hire, driving range, putting green, practice area.
Location 2.5m SW off B115
Hotel ★★ 63% Cedars Hotel, Needham Rd, STOWMARKET
☎ 01449 612668 24 ⇆ 🐾

THORPENESS Map 05 TM45

Thorpeness IP16 4NH ☎ 01728 452176 & 454926
The holes of this moorland course are pleasantly varied with several quite difficult par 4's. Natural hazards abound. The 15th, with its sharp left dog-leg, is one of the best holes. Designed by James Braid.
18 holes, 6271yds, Par 69, SSS 71, Course record 66.
Club membership 300.
Visitors contact in advance.
Societies telephone in advance, deposite required.
Green Fees £25 per day (£30 weekends & bank holidays).

Facilities ⊗ 🍴 🏌 🏌 ♀ ⚐ ⌂ 🏌 Mike Grantham.
Leisure motorised carts for hire, buggies for hire, trolley for hire, driving range, putting.
Location W side of village off B1353
Hotel ★ 65% White Horse Hotel, Station Rd, LEISTON
☎ 01728 830694 10rm(1 ⇆ 7 🐾)Annexe3 🐾

WALDRINGFIELD Map 05 TM24

Waldringfield Heath Newbourne Rd IP12 4PT
☎ 01473 736768 & 736426
Easy walking heathland course with long drives on 1st, 5th (586yds) and 10th tees.
18 holes, 6141yds, Par 71, SSS 69, Course record 68.
Club membership 600.
Visitors welcome Mon-Fri, weekends & bank holidays after noon.
Societies weekdays by arrangement.
Green Fees £18 per day; £12 per 18 holes (£15 per 18 holes weekends and bank holidays).
Facilities ⊗ 🏌 🏌 ♀ ⚐ ⌂ 🏌 Tony Dobson.
Leisure trolley for hire, putting green.
Location 3m NE of Ipswich off old A12
Hotel ★★★🏌 73% Seckford Hall Hotel, WOODBRIDGE
☎ 01394 385678 22 ⇆ 🐾 Annexe10 ⇆ 🐾

WITNESHAM Map 05 TM15

Fynn Valley IP6 9JA ☎ 01473 785267 & 785463
Undulating parkland course plus Par-3 nine-hole and driving range.
18 holes, 5807yds, Par 69, SSS 68, Course record 64.
Club membership 680.
Visitors members only Sun until noon.
Societies must apply in advance.
Green Fees £18 per day; £14 per 18 holes (£25/£18 weekends and bank holidays).
Facilities ⊗ 🍴 🏌 🏌 ♀ ⚐ ⌂ 🏌 Robin Mann/Glenn Crane.
Leisure buggies for hire, trolley for hire, covered and floodlit driving range, putting green, par 3 course.
Location 2m N of Ipswich on B1077
Hotel ★★★ 69% Marlborough Hotel, Henley Rd, IPSWICH
☎ 01473 257677 22 ⇆ 🐾

WOODBRIDGE Map 05 TM24

Seckford Seckford Hall Rd, Great Bealings IP13 6NT
☎ 01394 388000
An undulating course interspersed with young tree plantations and undulating greens. The 18th is almost completely surrounded by water.
18 holes, 5088yds, Par 69, SSS 66, Course record 63.
Club membership 300.
Visitors telephone in advance.
Societies telephone in advance.
Green Fees £14 per day; £12 per 18 holes; £8.50 per 9 holes (£18/£15/£10 weekends).
Facilities ⊗ 🍴 🏌 🏌 ♀ ⚐ ⌂ 🏌 🏌 Tony Pennock/J Skinner/S Jay.

Leisure   heated indoor swimming pool, fishing, sauna, solarium, gymnasium, trolley for hire, driving range, putting green, practice area.
Location   (3m W of Woodbridge, 0ff A12)
Hotel   ★★★▲▲ 73% Seckford Hall Hotel, WOODBRIDGE
☎ 01394 385678 22 ⇋ ♟Annexe10 ⇋ ♟

Ufford Park Hotel Golf & Leisure Yarmouth Rd, Ufford IP12 1QW ☎ 01394 383555
A challenging new course opened in autumn 1991. The 18-hole Par 70 course is set in ancient parkland has many natural features including 11 water hazards retaind from the original parkland. There is also an extensive hotel and leisure complex beside the course.
18 holes, 6300yds, Par 70, SSS 70, Course record 67.
Club membership 200.
Visitors   must book tee time from golf shop 01394 382836
Societies   contact in advance.
Green Fees   £20 per day; £14 per 18 holes (£27/£18 weekends & bank holidays).
Facilities   ⊗ Ⅷ ﹗ 💺 ♀ ♨ 🏠 ⚑ 🎏 ℓ Stuart Robertson.
Leisure   heated indoor swimming pool, sauna, solarium, gymnasium, motorised carts for hire, buggies for hire, trolley for hire, practice area.
Hotel   ★★★ 67% Ufford Park Hotel Golf & Leisure, Yarmouth Rd, Ufford, WOODBRIDGE
☎ 01394 383555 27rm(25 ⇋ ♟)

> **Woodbridge** Bromeswell Heath IP12 2PF
> ☎ 01394 382038
> A beautiful course, one of the best in East Anglia. It is situated on high ground and in different seasons present golfers with a great variety of colour. Some say that of the many good holes the 14th is the best.
> *18 holes, 6299yds, Par 70, SSS 70, Course record 64.*
> *also: 9 holes, 2243yds, Par 62, SSS 62.*
> *Club membership 900.*
> **Visitors**   must play with member at weekends & bank holidays. Must contact in advance and handicap certificate required for 18 hole course.
> **Societies**   by prior telephone call or in writing.
> **Green Fees**   £30 per day/round (18 hole); £14 (9 hole).
> **Facilities**   ⊗ Ⅷ ﹗ 💺 ♀ ♨ 🏠 ℓ Leslie Jones.
> **Leisure**   trolley for hire, putting green, practice area.
> **Location**   2.5m NE off A1152
> **Hotel**   ★★★▲▲ 73% Seckford Hall Hotel, WOODBRIDGE
> ☎ 01394 385678 22 ⇋ ♟Annexe10 ⇋ ♟

WORLINGTON   Map 05 TL67

> ***Royal Worlington & Newmarket*** IP28 8SD
> ☎ 01638 712216 & 717787
> Inland 'links' course. Favourite 9-hole course of many golf writers.
> *9 holes, 3105yds, Par 35, SSS 70, Course record 67.*
> *Club membership 325.*
> **Visitors**   with member only at weekends. Must contact in advance and have a handicap certificate.
> **Societies**   must apply in writing.
> **Green Fees**   not confirmed.
> **Facilities**   ♀ ♨ 🏠 ⚑ ℓ Malcolm Hawkins.
> **Leisure**   putting green,practice area,trolley hire.

Location   0.5m SE
Hotel   ★★★ 65% Riverside Hotel, Mill St, MILDENHALL ☎ 01638 717274 20 ⇋ ♟

SURREY

ADDLESTONE   Map 04 TQ06

Abbey Moor Green Ln KT15 2XV ☎ 01932 570741
A 9-hole course ideal for low or high handicap players, there are enough hazards to trouble the best without being too punishing to the not so good. The 4th is a drive over water to an angled approach to a green well protected by sand and water, usually with a left to right crosswind.
9 holes, 5150yds, Par 68, SSS 65.
Club membership 300.
Visitors   welcome providing they observe smart dress code & course etiquette, tee times should be booked in advance.
Societies   apply in writing or by telephone in advance.
Green Fees   not confirmed.
Facilities   ♀ 🏠 ⚑ ℓ Stephen Carter.
Leisure   practice putting green, trolley hire.
Location   Off junc 11 of the M25
Hotel   ★★★ 71% Ship Thistle, Monument Green, WEYBRIDGE ☎ 01932 848364 39 ⇋ ♟

> **New Zealand** Woodham Ln KT15 3QD
> ☎ 01932 345049
> Heathland course set in trees and heather.
> *18 holes, 6012yds, Par 68, SSS 69, Course record 66.*
> *Club membership 320.*
> **Visitors**   must contact in advance.
> **Societies**   telephone initially.
> **Green Fees**   £50 per day; £40 per round (£60 per round/day weekends and bank holidays).
> **Facilities**   ⊗ 💺 ♀ ♨ 🏠 ⚑ ℓ Vic Elvidge.
> **Leisure**   motorised carts for hire, buggies for hire, trolley for hire, putting green.
> **Location**   1.5m W of Weybridge
> **Hotel**   ★★★ 71% Ship Thistle, Monument Green, WEYBRIDGE ☎ 01932 848364 39 ⇋ ♟

ASHFORD   Map 04 TQ07

Ashford Manor Fordbridge Rd TW15 3RT
☎ 01784 252049
Parkland course, looks easy but is difficult.
18 holes, 6343yds, Par 70, SSS 70, Course record 66.
Club membership 700.
Visitors   advisable to telephone in advance, handicap certificate required, with member only at weekends.
Societies   welcome weekdays, must contact in advance.
Green Fees   £25 per day/round.
Facilities   ⊗ Ⅷ ﹗ 💺 ♀ ♨ 🏠 ℓ Mike Finney.
Leisure   trolley for hire, putting green, practice area.
Location   2m E of Staines via A308 Staines by-pass
Hotel   ★★★ 66% Thames Lodge Hotel, Thames St, STAINES ☎ 01784 464433 44 ⇋ ♟

BAGSHOT

Map 04 SU96

Pennyhill Park Hotel & Country Club London Rd
GU19 5ET ☎ 01276 471774
A nine-hole course set in 11.4 acres of beautiful parkland. It
is challenging to even the most experienced golfer.
9 holes, 2095yds, Par 32, SSS 32.
Club membership 100.
Visitors   prior booking must be made.
Societies   telephone in advance.
Green Fees not confirmed.
Facilities   ♀ ♨ ♈ ⬚
Leisure   hard tennis courts, heated outdoor swimming
                  pool, fishing, sauna.
Hotel   ★★★★(red)⚘ Pennyhill Park Hotel, London
                  Rd, BAGSHOT
                  ☎ 01276 471774 22 ⇌ ☞Annexe54 ⇌ ☞

Windlesham Grove End GU19 5HY
☎ 01276 452220
A parkland course with many tough Par 4 holes over 400
yards.
18 holes, 6600yds, Par 71, SSS 71, Course record 69.
Club membership 800.
Visitors   handicap certificate required.
Societies   apply in advance.
Green Fees £30 per round (£40 weekends).
Facilities   ⊗ �🝙 🍴 💺 ♀ ♨ 🏠 ♈ ℂ Alan Barber.
Leisure   buggies for hire, trolley for hire, driving range,
                  putting green.
Location   Junct of A30/A322
Hotel   ★★★★(red)⚘ Pennyhill Park Hotel, London
                  Rd, BAGSHOT
                  ☎ 01276 471774 22 ⇌ ☞Annexe54 ⇌ ☞

BANSTEAD

Map 04 TQ25

Banstead Downs Burdon Ln, Belmont, Sutton SM2 7DD
☎ 0181 642 2284
Downland course with narrow fairways and hawthorns.
18 holes, 6194yds, Par 69, SSS 69, Course record 64.
Club membership 835.
Visitors   must book in advance and have handicap
                  certificateor letter of introduction. With member
                  only weekends.
Societies   Thu, by prior arrangement
Green Fees £30 before noon; £20 afternoon.
Facilities   ⊗ 🍴 ♀ ♨ 🏠 ℂ Robert Dickman.
Leisure   trolley for hire, putting green, practice area,
                  covered driving nets.
Location   1.5m N on A217
Hotel   ★★ 63% Heathside Hotel, Brighton Rd,
                  BURGH HEATH ☎ 01737 353355 73 ⇌ ☞

Cuddington Banstead Rd SM7 1RD
☎ 0181 393 0952
Parkland course with easy walking and good views.
18 holes, 6394yds, Par 70, SSS 70, Course record 61.
Club membership 694.
Visitors   must contact in advance and have a handicap
                  certificate or letter of introduction.
Societies   welcome Thu, must apply in advance.
Green Fees £30 per day/round (£35 weekends).
Facilities   ⊗ 🍴 🍴 💺 ♀ ♨ 🏠 ♈ ℂ Mark Warner.
Leisure   trolley for hire, putting green, practice area.

Location   N of Banstead station on A2022
Hotel   ★★ 63% Heathside Hotel, Brighton Rd,
                  BURGH HEATH ☎ 01737 353355 73 ⇌ ☞

BRAMLEY

Map 04 TQ04

Bramley GU5 0AL ☎ 01483 892696
Downland course, fine views from top.
18 holes, 5990yds, Par 69, SSS 69, Course record 65.
Club membership 850.
Visitors   may not play Tue am (Ladies Morning) and
                  must play with member at weekends & bank
                  holidays. Must contact in advance.
Societies   must telephone the secretary in advance.
Green Fees £30 per day; £25 per round.
Facilities   ⊗ 🍴 💺 ♀ ♨ 🏠 ♈ ℂ Gary Peddie.
Leisure   motorised carts for hire, buggies for hire, trolley
                  for hire, driving range, putting green, practice
                  area.
Location   0.5m N on A281
Hotel   B Forte Posthouse Guildford, Egerton Rd,
                  GUILDFORD ☎ 01483 574444 111 ⇌ ☞

BROOKWOOD

Map 04 SU95

West Hill Bagshot Rd GU24 0BH ☎ 01483 474365
Worplesdon's next-door neighbour and a comparably
great heath-and-heather course. Slightly tighter than
Worplesdon with more opportunities for getting into
trouble - but a most interesting and challenging course
with wonderful greens. Water also provides natural
hazards. The 15th is a testing par 3.
18 holes, 6368yds, Par 69, SSS 70, Course record 62.
Club membership 500.
Visitors   must contact in advance & have handicap
                  certificate, may not play weekends & bank
                  holidays.
Societies   weekdays only (ex Wed). Telephone in
                  advance.
Green Fees £45 per day; £35 per round.
Facilities   ⊗ 🍴 🍴 💺 ♀ ♨ 🏠 ♈ ℂ John A Clements.
Leisure   trolley for hire, putting green, practice area.
Location   E side of village on A322
Hotel   ★★★★(red)⚘ Pennyhill Park Hotel,
                  London Rd, BAGSHOT
                  ☎ 01276 471774 22 ⇌ ☞Annexe54 ⇌ ☞

CAMBERLEY

Map 04 SU86

Camberley Heath Golf Dr GU15 1JG
☎ 01276 23258
One of the great 'heath and heather' courses so
frequently associated with Surrey. Several very good
short holes - especially the 8th. The 10th is a difficult and
interesting par 4, as also is the 17th, where the drive must
be held well to the left as perdition lurks on the right.
Course architect Harry Colt.
18 holes, 6128yds, Par 72, SSS 70, Course record 65.
Club membership 600.
Visitors   may not play at weekends. Must contact in
                  advance.
Societies   must apply in advance.
Green Fees £56 per day; £35 per round.
Facilities   ⊗ 🍴 💺 ♀ ♨ 🏠 ♈ ℂ Gary Smith.

Leisure	motorised carts for hire, buggies for hire, trolley for hire, driving range, putting green, practice area.
Location	1.25m SE of town centre off A325
Hotel	★★★★(red)▲▲ Pennyhill Park Hotel, London Rd, BAGSHOT ☎ 01276 471774 22 ⇄ ♔Annexe54 ⇄ ♔

CHERTSEY
Map 04 TQ06

Barrow Hills Longcross KT16 0DS ☎ 01344 635770
This parkland course with natural hazards is only open to guests of members.
18 holes, 3090yds, Par 56, SSS 53, Course record 58.
Club membership 235.
Visitors must play with member at all times.
Green Fees not confirmed.
Leisure putting green.
Location 3m W on B386
Hotel ★★★ 66% Thames Lodge Hotel, Thames St, STAINES ☎ 01784 464433 44 ⇄ ♔

Laleham Laleham Reach KT16 8RP ☎ 01932 564211
Well-bunkered parkland/meadowland course.
18 holes, 6211yds, Par 70, SSS 70.
Club membership 600.
Visitors members guests only at weekends.
Societies must contact in writing.
Green Fees £25 per day; £18 per round.
Facilities ⊗ ℳ by prior arrangement ㄴ ♥ ♀ ㅗ 🖻 ♔ Hogan Stott.
Leisure trolley for hire, putting green, practice area.
Location 1.5m N
Hotel ★★★ 66% Thames Lodge Hotel, Thames St, STAINES ☎ 01784 464433 44 ⇄ ♔

CHIPSTEAD
Map 04 TQ25

Chipstead How Ln CR5 3LN ☎ 01737 555781
Hilly parkland course, hard walking, good views. Testing 18th hole.
18 holes, 5491yds, Par 68, SSS 67, Course record 63.
Club membership 650.
Visitors must contact in advance. May not play weekends.
Societies must apply in writing.
Green Fees £25 per day (£20 after 2pm).
Facilities ⊗ ℳ by prior arrangement ㄴ ♥ ♀ ㅗ 🖻 ♔ Gary Torbett.
Leisure trolley for hire, putting green, practice area.
Location 0.5m N of village
Hotel ★★★★ 65% Selsdon Park Hotel, Addington Rd, Sanderstead, CROYDON ☎ 0181 657 8811 170 ⇄ ♔

CHOBHAM
Map 04 SU96

Chobham Chobham Rd, Knaphill GU21 2TZ ☎ 01276 855584 & 855748 pro
Designed by Peter Allis and CLive Clark, Chobham course sits among mature oaks and tree nurseries offering tree-lined fairways, together with six man-made lakes.
18 holes, 5821yds, Par 69, SSS 67, Course record 67.
Club membership 750.

Visitors booking in advance essential.
Societies by prior arrangement.
Green Fees £22 (£30 weekends & bank holidays).
Facilities ⊗ ㄴ ♥ ♀ ㅗ 🖻 ♔ Richard Thomas.
Leisure trolley for hire, putting green, practice area.
Hotel ★★★ 64% Falcon Hotel, 68 Farnborough Rd, FARNBOROUGH ☎ 01252 545378 30 ⇄ ♔

COBHAM
Map 04 TQ16

Silvermere Redhill Rd KT11 1EF ☎ 01932 866007
Parkland course with many very tight holes through woodland, 17th has 170-yd carry over the lake. Driving range.
18 holes, 6700yds, Par 73.
Club membership 740.
Visitors may not play at weekends until 1pm. Must contact in advance.
Societies must contact by telephone.
Green Fees £18.50 per round (£25 weekends & bank holidays).
Facilities ⊗ ℳ ㄴ ♥ ♀ ㅗ 🖻 ♔ Doug McClelland.
Leisure fishing, trolley for hire, driving range, putting green, practice area.
Location 2.25m NW off A245
Hotel ★★★★ 60% Woodlands Park Hotel, Woodlands Ln, STOKE D'ABERNON ☎ 01372 843933 58 ⇄ ♔

CRANLEIGH
Map 04 TQ03

Fernfell Golf & Country Club Barhatch Ln GU6 7NG ☎ 01483 268855
Scenic woodland/parkland course at the base of the Surrey hills, easy walking. Clubhouse in 400-year-old barn.
18 holes, 5636yds, Par 68, SSS 67, Course record 64.
Club membership 1000.
Visitors may only play at weekends after noon. Contact professional in advance 01483 277188
Societies telephone in advance.
Green Fees £25 per day (weekday only); £20 per round.
Facilities ⊗ ℳ by prior arrangement ㄴ ♥ ♀ ㅗ 🖻 ♔ Trevor Longmuir.
Leisure hard tennis courts, outdoor swimming pool, sauna, trolley for hire, driving range, putting green, practice area.
Location 0ff A281 Guildford to Horsham road, signposted Cranleigh
Hotel ★★★ 61% Gatton Manor Hotel Golf & Country Club, Standon Ln, OCKLEY ☎ 01306 627555 14 ⇄ ♔

Wildwood Horsham Rd, Alfold, Cranleigh GU6 8JE ☎ 01403 753255
Parkland with stands of old oaks dominating several holes, a stream fed by a natural spring winds through a series of lakes and ponds. The greens are smooth, undulating and large. The 5th and 16th are the most challenging holes.
18 holes, 655yds, Par 72, SSS 73, Course record 65.
Club membership 500.
Visitors welcome subject to availability & booking.
Societies apply in writing.
Green Fees not confirmed.
Facilities ♀ ㅗ 🖻 ♔ ♔ Nicholas Parfrement.
Leisure fishing, caddy cars can be booked. ▶

| Location | Off A281, approx 9m S of Guildford |
| Hotel | ★★★ 61% Gatton Manor Hotel Golf & Country Club, Standon Ln, OCKLEY ☎ 01306 627555 14 ⇔ ͡ |

DORKING

Map 04 TQ14

Betchworth Park Reigate Rd RH4 1NZ
☎ 01306 882052
Parkland course, with hard walking on southern ridge of Boxhill.
18 holes, 6266yds, Par 69, SSS 70, Course record 64.
Club membership 725.

Visitors	weekend play Sun pm only. Must contact in advance.
Societies	apply in writing.
Green Fees	weekday £31 per day/round am; £25 per round pm (Sun pm £43 per round).
Facilities	⊗ ͡ ♬ ♥ ♀ ♨ ☎ ⚓ ͡ Tocher.
Leisure	trolley for hire, putting green, practice area.
Location	1m E on A25
Hotel	★★★ 62% The White Horse, High St, DORKING ☎ 01306 881138 36 ⇔ ͡ Annexe32 ⇔ ͡

Dorking Chart Park, Deepdene Av RH5 4BX
☎ 01306 886917
Undulating parkland course, easy slopes, wind-sheltered.
Testing holes: 5th 'Tom's Puddle' (par 4); 7th 'Rest and Be Thankful' (par 4); 9th 'Double Decker' (par 4).
9 holes, 5120yds, Par 66, SSS 65, Course record 62.
Club membership 408.

Visitors	may not play Wed am and with member only weekends & bank holidays. Contact in advance.
Societies	Tue & Thu, telephone in advance.
Green Fees	£16 per day; £12 for 18 holes.
Facilities	⊗ by prior arrangement ♬ ♥ ♀ ♨ ☎ ⚓ ͡ Paul Napier.
Leisure	motorised carts for hire, trolley for hire, putting green.
Location	1m S on A24
Hotel	★★★★ 68% The Burford Bridge, Burford Bridge, Box Hill, DORKING ☎ 01306 884561 48 ⇔ ͡

EAST HORSLEY

Map 04 TQ05

Drift KT24 5HD ☎ 01483 284641
Woodland course with sheltered fairways and many ponds.
18 holes, 6424yds, Par 73, SSS 72, Course record 71.
Club membership 650.

Visitors	must contact in advance. With member only weekends & bank holidays.
Societies	telephone in advance.
Green Fees	£30 per day; £20 per round.
Facilities	⊗ ͡ ♬ ♥ ♀ ♨ ☎ ͡ Dominic Tunn.
Leisure	motorised carts for hire, buggies for hire, trolley for hire, putting green, practice area.
Location	1.5m N off B2039
Hotel	★★★ 63% Jarvis Thatchers Hotel, Epsom Rd, EAST HORSLEY ☎ 01483 284291 34 ⇔ ͡ Annexe20 ⇔ ͡

EFFINGHAM

Map 04 TQ15

Effingham Guildford Rd KT24 5PZ ☎ 01372 452203
Easy-walking downland course laid out on 27-acres with tree-lined fairways. It is one of the longest of the Surrey courses with wide subtle greens that provide a provocative but by no means exhausting challenge. Fine views.
18 holes, 6524yds, Par 71, SSS 71, Course record 64.
Club membership 800.

Visitors	contact in advance. With member only weekends & bank holidays.
Societies	Wed, Thu & Fri only and must book in advance.
Green Fees	£35 per day, £27.50 after 2pm. With member only weekends and bank holidays.
Facilities	⊗ ͡ ♬ ♥ ♀ ♨ ☎ ⚓ ͡ Steve Hoatson.
Leisure	motorised carts for hire, buggies for hire, trolley for hire, driving range, putting green, practice area.
Location	W side of village on A246
Hotel	★★★ 63% Jarvis Thatchers Hotel, Epsom Rd, EAST HORSLEY ☎ 01483 284291 34 ⇔ ͡ Annexe20 ⇔ ͡

ENTON GREEN

Map 04 SU94

West Surrey GU8 5AF ☎ 01483 421275
A good parkland-type course in rolling, well-wooded setting. Some fairways are tight with straight driving at a premium. The 17th is a testing hole with a long hill walk.
18 holes, 6259yds, Par 71, SSS 70, Course record 65.
Club membership 600.

Visitors	must contact in advance.
Societies	must apply in writing. All players to have a handicap.
Green Fees	£38.50 per day; £27 per round (£47.50 all day weekends & bank holidays).
Facilities	⊗ ͡ ♬ ♥ ♀ ♨ ☎ ͡ Alister Tawse.
Leisure	trolley for hire, putting green, practice area.
Location	S side of village
Hotel	★★★ 61% Bush Hotel, The Borough, FARNHAM ☎ 01252 715237 66 ⇔ ͡

EPSOM

Map 04 TQ26

Epsom Longdown Ln South KT17 4JR
☎ 01372 721666
Traditional downland course with many mature trees and well watered greens..
18 holes, 5701yds, Par 69, SSS 68, Course record 65.
Club membership 8900.

Visitors	restricted to after midday weekends & bank holidays.
Societies	must contact in advance.
Green Fees	£25 per day; £16.50 per round (£27/£18.50 weekends & bank holidays).
Facilities	⊗ ͡ ♬ ♥ ♀ ♨ ☎ ͡ Ron Goudie.
Leisure	trolley for hire, putting green, practice area.
Location	SE side of town centre on B288
Hotel	★★ 63% Heathside Hotel, Brighton Rd, BURGH HEATH ☎ 01737 353355 73 ⇔ ͡

Horton Park Country Club Hook Rd KT19 8QG
☎ 0181 394 2626
Parkland course.
18 holes, 5208yds, Par 69, SSS 65.
Club membership 534.
Visitors must book for weekends.
Societies must telephone in advance.
Green Fees not confirmed.
Facilities ⚑ ⛴ 🏌 ⛳ Gary Clements.
Leisure golf cart, driving range, putting green.
Hotel ★★ 63% Heathside Hotel, Brighton Rd, BURGH HEATH ☎ 01737 353355 73 ⇔ 🌊

ESHER   Map 04 TQ16

Moore Place Portsmouth Rd KT10 9LN
☎ 01372 463533
Public course on attractive, undulating parkland laid out some 60 years ago by Harry Vardon. Examples of most of the trees that will survive in the UK are to be found on the course. Testing short holes at 4th, 5th and 7th.
9 holes, 2128yds, Par 32, SSS 30, Course record 25.
Club membership 300.
Visitors no restrictions.
Societies must contact in advance.
Green Fees £5.50 (£7.40 weekends & bank holidays).
Facilities ⊗ ⋙ ⛴ 🍺 ⚑ ⛴ 🏌 ⛳ David Allen.
Leisure trolley for hire, putting green, practice area.
Location SW side of town centre on A244
Hotel ★★★ 71% Ship Thistle, Monument Green, WEYBRIDGE ☎ 01932 848364 39 ⇔ 🌊

Sandown Golf Centre Sandown Park, More Ln KT10 8AN
☎ 01372 463340
Flat parkland course in middle of racecourse. Additional facilities include a driving range, and a pitch-and-putt course.
New Course: 9 holes, 2828yds, Par 35, SSS 34.
Par 3: 9 holes, 1193yds, Par 27.
Club membership 650.
Visitors no restrictions.
Societies must apply in writing.
Green Fees not confirmed.
Facilities ⚑ ⛴ ⛳ 🏌
Leisure driving range,putting,trolley hire.
Location 1m NW off A307
Hotel ★★ 65% Haven Hotel, Portsmouth Rd, ESHER ☎ 0181 398 0023 16 ⇔ 🌊 Annexe4 ⇔ 🌊

Thames Ditton & Esher Portsmouth Rd KT10 9AL
☎ 0181 398 1551
Commonland course. There is a public right of way across the course.
18 holes, 5149yds, Par 66, SSS 65, Course record 63.
Club membership 250.
Visitors may not play on Sun mornings. Advisable to telephone for availability.
Societies must contact in advance.
Green Fees £10 per round (£12 weekends).
Facilities ⊗ ⋙ ⛴ by prior arrangement 🍺 ⚑ ⛴ 🏌 Mark Rodbard.
Leisure trolley for hire, putting green, practice area.
Location 1m NE on A307
Hotel ★★ 65% Haven Hotel, Portsmouth Rd, ESHER ☎ 0181 398 0023 16 ⇔ 🌊 Annexe4 ⇔ 🌊

FARNHAM   Map 04 SU84

Blacknest Binsted GU34 4QL ☎ 01420 22888 & 22999
Privately owned pay and play golf centre catering for all ages and levels of abilities. Facilities include a 20-bay driving range, gymnasium and a long and testing par 3 9-hole course with water hazards on 8 of the holes. Extension to 18 holes during 1997.
9 holes, 6726yds, Par 72, SSS 72.
Club membership 350.
Visitors welcome at all times but should telephone for tee times especially weekends.
Societies prior arrangements necessary telephone or write.
Green Fees £13 per 18 holes; £8 per 9 holes (£15/£10 weekends). Par 3 £7.50 per day; £6 per 18 holes; £3.50 per 9 holes.
Facilities ⊗ ⋙ by prior arrangement 🍺 ⛴ ⚑ ⛴ 🏌 Ian Benson.
Leisure gymnasium, driving range, par 3 course.
Location 0.5m S of A31 at Bentley
Hotel ★★★ 🏌 60% Farnham House Hotel, Alton Rd, FARNHAM ☎ 01252 716908 20 ⇔ 🌊

Farnham The Sands GU10 1PX ☎ 01252 782109
A mixture of meadowland and heath with quick drying sandy subsoil. Several of the earlier holes have interesting features, the finishing holes rather less.
18 holes, 6325yds, Par 72, SSS 70, Course record 66.
Club membership 500.
Visitors must be member of recognised club & have handicap certificate. With member only weekends.
Societies must apply in writing.
Green Fees £32 per day; £27 per round.
Facilities ⊗ ⋙ ⛴ 🍺 ⛴ ⚑ ⛴ 🏌 Grahame Cowlishaw.
Leisure trolley for hire, putting green, practice area.
Location 3m E off A31
Hotel ★★★ 61% Bush Hotel, The Borough, FARNHAM ☎ 01252 715237 66 ⇔ 🌊

Farnham Park Folly Hill, Farnham Park GU9 0AU
☎ 01252 715216
Municipal parkland course in Farnham Park.
9 holes, 1163yds, Par 27.
Visitors pay and play everyday.
Societies telephone in advance.
Green Fees 18 holes: £6.50 (£7.75 weekends). 9 holes: £3.75 (£4.25 weekends).
Facilities ⊗ ⋙ by prior arrangement 🍺 ⛴ ⚑ 🏌 ⛳ Peter Chapman.
Location N side of town centre on A287
Hotel ★★★ 61% Bush Hotel, The Borough, FARNHAM ☎ 01252 715237 66 ⇔ 🌊

GODALMING   Map 04 SU94

Broadwater Park Guildford Rd, Farncombe GU7 3BU
☎ 01483 429955
A Par-3 public course with floodlit driving range.
9 holes, 1287yds, Par 54, SSS 50.
Club membership 160.
Visitors must book for weekends & bank holidays.
Societies telephone in advance
Green Fees 18 holes £6.25; 9 holes £3.75 (£7.75/£4.25 weekends & bank holidays). ▶

Facilities ⊗)洲 ᕼ ➡ ♀亖 ⌁⌐ ᛏ ᚠ Kevin D Milton.
Leisure trolley for hire, driving range, putting green.
Location 4m SW of Guildford
Hotel ★★★ 65% Inn on the Lake, Ockford Rd, GODALMING ☎ 01483 415575 19 ⇋ 🐾

Hurtmore Hurtmore Rd, Hurtmore GU7 2RN
☎ 01483 426492 & 424440
A Peter Alliss/Clive Clark Pay and Play course with seven lakes and 100 bunkers. The 15th hole is the longest at 540yards. Played mainly into the wind there are 10 bunkers to negotiate. The 3rd hole at 440yds stroke Index 1 is a real test. A dogleg right around a lake and 9 bunkers makes this hole worthy of its stroke index.
18 holes, 5514yds, Par 70, SSS 67.
Club membership 200.
Visitors book by telephone up to 6 days in advance.
Societies telephone in advance.
Green Fees £14 per 18 holes (£10 weekends).
Facilities ⊗ ᕼ ➡ ♀亖 ⌁⌐ ᛏ ᚠ Maxine Burton.
Leisure trolley for hire.
Location 2m NW of Godalming between A3/A3100, access via unclass road
Hotel ★★★ 65% Inn on the Lake, Ockford Rd, GODALMING ☎ 01483 415575 19 ⇋ 🐾

Shillinglee Park Chiddingfold GU8 4TA
☎ 01428 653237 & 708158
Manicured parkland course with many natural features including seven ponds. The 4th and 7th are the signature holes requiring tee shots and second shots over ponds, to well-guarded greens.
9 holes, 5032yds, Par 64, SSS 64, Course record 65.

Club membership 400.
Visitors no restrictions but advisable to book starting times.
Societies apply for details.
Green Fees £13.50 per day; £11 per 18 holes; £7.50 per 9 holes (£16/£13/£8.50 weekends).
Facilities ⊗)洲 ᕼ ➡ ♀⅄ 🝙 ᛏ ᚠ Roger Mace.
Leisure motorised carts for hire, buggies for hire, trolley for hire, putting green, practice area.
Location 5m S of Godalming, off A283
Hotel ★★★ 65% Inn on the Lake, Ockford Rd, GODALMING ☎ 01483 415575 19 ⇋ 🐾

GUILDFORD   Map 04 SU94

Guildford High Path Rd, Merrow GU1 2HL
☎ 01483 63941
A downland course but with some trees and much scrub. The holes provide an interesting variety of play, an invigorating experience.
18 holes, 6090yds, Par 69, SSS 70, Course record 64.
Club membership 700.
Visitors must contact in advance. With member only weekends & bank holidays.
Societies welcome Mon-Fri. Must apply in advance.
Green Fees £35 per day; £25 per round.
Facilities ⊗)洲 by prior arrangement ᕼ ➡ ♀⅄ 🝙 ᛏ ᚠ P G Hollington.
Leisure motorised carts for hire, trolley for hire, putting green, practice area.
Location E side of town centre off A246
Hotel ★★★ 70% The Manor, Newlands Corner, GUILDFORD ☎ 01483 222624 19 ⇋ 🐾

Milford Station Ln, Milford GU8 5HS
☎ 01483 419200
A Peter Alliss/Clive Clark designed course opened summer 1993. The design has cleverly incorporated a demanding course within an existing woodland and meadow area.
18 holes, 5916yds, Par 69, SSS 68, Course record 67.
Club membership 750.

Visitors	telephone 01483 416291 up to 1 week in advance.
Societies	telephone in advance.
Green Fees	£25 per day; £19.50 per round; £10 per 9 holes (£35/£25/£12.50 weekends).
Facilities	⊗ ⅲ ⅃ ⬛ ♀ ♁ 🏠 ⛳ ↾ ✆ Grant Clough.
Leisure	motorised carts for hire, buggies for hire, trolley for hire, driving range, putting green, practice area.
Location	6m SW, leave A3 Milford then A3100 to Enton
Hotel	★★★ 65% Inn on the Lake, Ockford Rd, GODALMING ☎ 01483 415575 19 ⇔ ↾

Roker Park Rokers Farm, Aldershot Rd GU3 3PB
☎ 01483 236677
A Pay and Play 9-hole parkland course. A challenging course with two Par 5 holes.
9 holes, 3037yds, Par 36, SSS 72.
Club membership 200.

Visitors	no restrictions, pay & play, phone for reservations.
Societies	prior arrangement with deposit at least 14 days before, minimum 12 persons.
Green Fees	£11 per 18 holes; £6.50 per 9 holes (£14/£8 weekends).
Facilities	⊗ ⅲ ⅃ ⬛ ♀ ♁ 🏠 ⛳ ↾ ✆ Kevin Warn.
Leisure	motorised carts for hire, buggies for hire, trolley for hire, driving range, putting green.
Location	A323, 3m from Guildford
Hotel	★★★ 75% The Angel Posting House and Livery, 91 High St, GUILDFORD ☎ 01483 64555 11 ⇔ ↾

HINDHEAD
Map 04 SU83

Hindhead Churt Rd GU26 6HX
☎ 01428 604614
A good example of a Surrey heath-and-heather course, and most picturesque. Players must be prepared for some hard walking. The first nine fairways follow narrow valleys requiring straight hitting; the second nine are much less restricted.
18 holes, 6373yds, Par 70, SSS 70, Course record 63.
Club membership 850.

Visitors	must contact in advance and have a handicap certificate.
Societies	Wed & Thu only, contact in advance
Green Fees	£35 (£42 weekends & bank holidays), 9 holes £27 (£32 weekends & bank holdays).
Facilities	⊗ ⅲ ⅃ ⬛ ♀ ♁ 🏠 ↾ ✆ Neil Ogilvy.
Leisure	trolley for hire.
Location	1.5m NW on A287
Hotel	★★★★ 72% Lythe Hill Hotel, Petworth Rd, HASLEMERE ☎ 01428 651251 40 ⇔ ↾

KINGSWOOD
Map 04 TQ25

Kingswood Sandy Ln KT20 6NE ☎ 01737 832188
Flat parkland course, easy walking.
18 holes, 6880yds, Par 72, SSS 73.
Club membership 700.

Visitors	must contact professional at least 24 hrs in advance. May not play weekends.
Societies	must apply in advance.
Green Fees	£45 per day; £32 per round.
Facilities	⊗ ⅃ ⬛ ♀ ♁ 🏠 ⛳ ↾ ✆ James Dodds.
Leisure	squash, motorised carts for hire, buggies for hire, trolley for hire, driving range, putting green, practice area.
Location	5m S of village off A217
Hotel	★★ 63% Heathside Hotel, Brighton Rd, BURGH HEATH ☎ 01737 353355 73 ⇔ ↾

LEATHERHEAD
Map 04 TQ15

Leatherhead Kingston Rd KT22 0EE
☎ 01372 843966 & 843958
Parkland course with numerous ditches and only two hills, so walking is easy.
18 holes, 6203yds, Par 71, SSS 69, Course record 67.

Visitors	telephone pro shop 01372 843956 up to 10 days in advance.
Societies	telephone for booking form.
Green Fees	£40 per 36 holes; £27.50 per 18 holes (£40 per 18 holes weekends, pm only).
Facilities	⊗ ⅲ ⅃ ⬛ ♀ ♁ 🏠 ⛳ ↾ ✆ Richard Hurst.
Leisure	sauna, buggies for hire, trolley for hire, putting green, practice area.
Location	0.25m from junct 9 of M25, on A243
Hotel	★★★★ 60% Woodlands Park Hotel, Woodlands Ln, STOKE D'ABERNON ☎ 01372 843933 58 ⇔ ↾

Pachesham Park Golf Complex Oaklawn Rd KT22 0BT
☎ 01372 843453
A 9-hole undulating parkland course playing out over 18 holes at 5,400yards.
9 holes, 2805yds, Par 70, SSS 67.
Club membership 385.

Visitors	book 2 days in advance by phone. May play weekends after 12.30pm.
Societies	apply in advance.
Green Fees	£12.50 per 18 holes; £7.50 per 9 holes (£15/£9 weekends & bank holidays.
Facilities	⊗ ⅲ by prior arrangement ⅃ ⬛ ♀ ♁ 🏠 ⛳ ↾ ✆ Philip Taylor.
Leisure	trolley for hire, floodlit driving range, putting green, practice area.
Location	On A244, 0.5m from M25 junct 9
Hotel	★★★★ 60% Woodlands Park Hotel, Woodlands Ln, STOKE D'ABERNON ☎ 01372 843933 58 ⇔ ↾

Tyrrells Wood The Drive KT22 8QP ☎ 01372 376025
Parkland course with easy walking. Snooker.
18 holes, 6234yds, Par 71, SSS 70, Course record 65.
Club membership 700.

Visitors	must contact in advance. Restricted weekends.
Societies	must apply in advance.
Green Fees	£48 per day; £32 per round. ▶

Facilities ⊗ 〤 ㅂ ☕ ♀ ⅄ 🖻 🕈 Max Taylor.
Leisure trolley for hire, putting green & practice area.
Location 2m SE of town, off A24
Hotel ★★★★ 68% The Burford Bridge, Burford Bridge, Box Hill, DORKING
☎ 01306 884561 48 ⇄ 🌂

LIMPSFIELD Map 05 TQ45

Limpsfield Chart Westerham Rd RH8 0SL
☎ 01883 723405
Tight heathland course set in National Trust land.
9 holes, 5718yds, Par 70, SSS 68, Course record 64.
Club membership 300.
Visitors with member only or by appointment weekends & not before 3.30pm Thu (Ladies Day).
Societies must apply in advance.
Green Fees £18 per day/round. £10 four hours before sunset.
Facilities ⊗ by prior arrangement 〤 by prior arrangement ㅂ ☕ ♀ ⅄
Leisure putting green, practice area.
Location 1m E on A25
Hotel ★★★ 68% Kings Arms Hotel, Market Square, WESTERHAM
☎ 01959 562990 16 ⇄ 🌂

LINGFIELD Map 05 TQ34

Lingfield Park Lingfield Rd, Racecourse Rd RH7 6PQ
☎ 01342 834602
Difficult and challenging, tree-lined parkland course set in 210 acres of beautiful Surrey countryside. Driving range.
18 holes, 6473yds, Par 71, SSS 72, Course record 70.
Club membership 750.
Visitors must be accompanied by member on Sat & Sun. Advisable to telephone first.
Societies must telephone in advance.
Green Fees £25 per round.
Facilities ⊗ 〤 ㅂ ☕ ♀ ⅄ 🖻 🕈 Christopher Morley.
Leisure motorised carts for hire, buggies for hire, trolley for hire, driving range, putting green, practice area.
Location Entrance next to Lingfield race course
Hotel ★★★ 70% Woodbury House Hotel, Lewes Rd, EAST GRINSTEAD
☎ 01342 313657 13 ⇄ 🌂 Annexe1 🌂

NEWDIGATE Map 04 TQ14

Rusper Rusper Rd RH5 5BX
☎ 01293 871871 & 871456
New course set in mature woodland. The opening two holes give the golfer an encouraging start with the following holes demanding accurate playing through the trees. The 5th hole is a challenging Par 5 from the back tee with a gentle dogleg tempting the golfer to take a shortcut.
9 holes, 6069yds, Par 71, SSS 69, Course record 67.
Club membership 250.
Visitors welcome but telephone to reserve time, some restrictions if competitions being played.
Societies telephone for details.
Green Fees £11.50 per 18 holes; £7 per 9 holes (£15.50/£8.50 weekends).
Facilities ⊗ 〤 by prior arrangement ㅂ ☕ ♀ ⅄ 🖻 🕈
🕈 Karl Spurrier.

Leisure trolley for hire, driving range, putting green.
Location Between Newdigate/Rusper, off A24
Hotel ★★★★ 68% The Burford Bridge, Burford Bridge, Box Hill, DORKING
☎ 01306 884561 48 ⇄ 🌂

OCKLEY Map 04 TQ14

Gatton Manor Hotel Golf & Country Club Standon Ln RH5 5PQ ☎ 01306 627555
Undulating course through woods and over many challenging water holes.
18 holes, 6653yds, Par 72, SSS 72, Course record 68.
Club membership 300.
Visitors must give 2 weeks prior notice. Restricted Sun (am). Tee times to be booked through professional 01306 627557
Societies must apply in advance.
Green Fees £30 per day; £18 per round;(£50/£25 weekends). Twilight £12 (£15 weekends).
Facilities ⊗ 〤 ㅂ ☕ ♀ ⅄ 🖻 🕈 🖰 🕈 Rae Sargent.
Leisure grass tennis courts, fishing, sauna, solarium, gymnasium, motorised carts for hire, buggies for hire, trolley for hire, driving range, putting green, practice area.
Location 1.5m SW off A29
Hotel ★★★ 61% Gatton Manor Hotel Golf & Country Club, Standon Ln, OCKLEY
☎ 01306 627555 14 ⇄ 🌂

Gatton Manor Hotel
Golf and Country Club ★★
Ockley, Nr. Dorking RH5 5PQ
Tel: Oakwood Hill (01306) 627555/6
Fax: (01306) 627713

Gatton Manor Hotel, Golf & Country Club is an 18th Century manor house set within its own 18-hole championship length golf course and offering 14 well appointed en-suite bedrooms, with an à la carte restaurant serving both English and Continental cuisine. Adjacent to the restaurant is a large bar with a superb selection of wines and spirits.
The hotel also offers three tastefully decorated conference suites available with all the latest equipment. Other facilities include tennis, fishing, bowls and purpose built Gym & Health Suite.

OTTERSHAW
Map 04 TQ06

Foxhills Stonehill Rd KT16 0EL ☎ 01932 872050
A pair of parkland courses designed in the grand manner
and with American course-design in mind. One course is
tree-lined, the other, as well as trees, has massive bunkers
and artificial lakes which contribute to the interest. Both
courses offer testing golf and they finish on the same
long 'double green'. Par 3 'Manor' course also available.
Chertsey Course: 18 holes, 6734yds, Par 73, SSS 72.
Longcross Course: 18 holes, 6417yds, Par 72, SSS 71.
Manor Course: 9 holes, 1275yds, Par 27.
Visitors restricted before noon weekends.
Societies welcome Mon-Fri, must apply in advance.
Green Fees £65 per day; £45 per 36 holes (£55 per 18
holes weekends).
Facilities ⊗ ⅷ ▐▙ ⬛ ♀ ⚘ ⬟ ⚐ ⋈
ℂ A Goode/B Hunt/R Summerscales.
Leisure hard tennis courts, outdoor and indoor
heated swimming pools, squash, sauna,
solarium, gymnasium, motorised carts for
hire, buggies for hire, trolley for hire,
driving range, putting green, practice area,
health club.
Location 1m NW
Hotel ★★★ 66% The Crown Hotel, 7 London St,
CHERTSEY
☎ 01932 564657 Annexe30 ⇌ ℾ

PIRBRIGHT
Map 04 SU95

Goal Farm Gole Rd GU24 0PZ
☎ 01483 473183 & 473205
Beautiful lanscaped parkland 'Pay and Play' course with
excellent greens.
9 holes, 1273yds, Par 54, SSS 48.
Club membership 300.
Visitors may not play on Sat before 4pm or Thu
mornings.
Societies telephone in advance.
Green Fees £3.50 per round (£3.75 weekends & bank
holidays).
Facilities ▐▙ ⬛ ♀ ⚘ ⬟
Leisure putting green, practice area.
Location 1.5m NW on B3012
Hotel B Forte Posthouse Farnborough, Lynchford Rd,
FARNBOROUGH ☎ 01252 545051 110 ⇌ ℾ

PUTTENHAM
Map 04 SU94

Puttenham Heath Rd GU3 1AL ☎ 01483 810498
Picturesque tree-lined heathland course offering testing golf,
easy walking.
18 holes, 6214yds, Par 71, SSS 70.
Club membership 650.
Visitors with member only weekends & public holidays.
Must contact in advance.
Societies apply in advance to secretary.
Green Fees £30 per day; £23 per round.
Facilities ⊗ ⅷ ▐▙ ⬛ ♀ ⚘ ⬟ ℂ Gary Simmons.
Leisure trolley for hire, putting green, practice area.
Location 1m SE on B3000
Hotel ★★★ 61% Bush Hotel, The Borough,
FARNHAM ☎ 01252 715237 66 ⇌ ℾ

REDHILL
Map 04 TQ25

Redhill & Reigate Clarence Rd, Pendelton Rd RH1 6LB
☎ 01737 240777
Parkland course.
18 holes, 5238yds, Par 67, SSS 66.
Club membership 600.
Visitors may not play before 11am weekends or after
2pm Sun (Jun-Sep). Must contact in advance.
Societies must apply in writing.
Green Fees not confirmed.
Facilities ♀ ⚘ ⬟ ⚐ ℂ
Leisure putting, trolley hire.
Location 1m S on A23
Hotel ★★★ 65% Reigate Manor Hotel, Reigate Hill,
REIGATE ☎ 01737 240125 51 ⇌ ℾ

REIGATE
Map 04 TQ25

Reigate Heath Flanchford Rd RH2 8QR ☎ 01737 242610
Heathland course.
9 holes, 5658yds, Par 67, SSS 67, Course record 65.
Club membership 550.
Visitors with member only weekends & bank holidays.
Must contact in advance.
Societies must apply in writing.
Green Fees £20 per day; £16 morning; £12 afternoon.
Facilities ⊗ ⅷ by prior arrangement ▐▙ ⬛ ♀ ⚘ ⬟
ℂ Barry Davies.
Leisure trolley for hire, putting green, practice area.
Location 1.5m W off A25
Hotel ★★★ 65% Reigate Manor Hotel, Reigate Hill,
REIGATE ☎ 01737 240125 51 ⇌ ℾ

Reigate Hill Gatton Bottom RH2 0TU ☎ 01737 645577
Championship standard course opened in 1995 with fully
irrigated tees and greens. Feature holes include the 5th which
is divided by four bunkers and the par 5 14th involving a
tricky drive across a lake.
18 holes, 6175yds, Par 72, SSS 70.
Club membership 650.
Visitors must contact in advance to book tee time, may
not play weekends.
Societies welcome Mon-Fri but must book in advance.
Green Fees £25 per round.
Facilities ▐▙ ⬛ ♀ ⚘ ⬟ ⚐ ℂ Martin Platts.
Leisure trolley for hire, driving range, putting green,
practice area.
Location 2m from junct 8 of M25
Hotel ★★★ 63% Bridge House Hotel, Reigate Hill,
REIGATE
☎ 01737 246801 & 244821 40 ⇌ ℾ

RIPLEY
Map 04 TQ05

Wisley GU23 6QU ☎ 01483 211022
A 27-hole course designed by Robert Trent Jones Jnr,
and the first that this well-known American golf architect
has designed in the UK. Penncross Bent grasses have
been used to provide a superb playing surface.
The Church Course: 9 holes, 3355yds, Par 36, SSS 73.
The Mill Course: 9 holes, 3473yds, Par 36, SSS 73.
The Garden Course: 9 holes, 3385yds, Par 36, SSS 73.
Club membership 510. ▶

Visitors	may only play with member.
Green Fees	not confirmed.
Facilities	♀ ♨ 🍴 🏌 ⛳ Bill Reid.
Leisure	fishing, sauna.
Hotel	★★★ 63% Jarvis Thatchers Hotel, Epsom Rd, EAST HORSLEY ☎ 01483 284291 34 ⇌ 🐾 Annexe20 ⇌ 🐾

SHEPPERTON   Map 04 TQ06

Sunbury Charlton Ln TW17 8QA ☎ 01932 771414
There is a 9-hole course already in use at Sunbury which at 6210 yards, with two Par 5's and two Par 3's, is one of the longest in the south of England. There is also a new 18-hole course due to open in September 1996.
9 holes, 6210yds, Par 72, SSS 72, Course record 70.
Club membership 300.

Visitors	no restrictions.
Societies	advance booking necessary.
Green Fees	18 holes: £10 (£12 weekends & bank holidays). 9 holes: £6 (£7.50 weekends & bank holidays). Weekends after 4.30pm £5.
Facilities	⊗ 🍴 ♨ 🍴 ♀ ⛳ Alistair Hardaway.
Leisure	floodlit driving range, putting green, practice area.
Hotel	★★★ 65% Shepperton Moat House Hotel, Felix Ln, SHEPPERTON ☎ 01932 241404 156 ⇌ 🐾

TANDRIDGE   Map 05 TQ35

Tandridge RH8 9NQ ☎ 01883 712274
Rolling parkland, Colt designed course; good views.
18 holes, 6250yds, Par 70, SSS 70.
Club membership 750.

Visitors	must contact in advance. May play Mon, Wed, Thu.
Societies	Mon, Wed & Thu, apply in advance.
Green Fees	£40 per day; £31 per round (Winter £31/£21).
Facilities	⊗ 🍴 ♨ ♀ ♨ 🍴 ⛳ Allan Farquhar.
Leisure	motorised carts for hire, trolley for hire, driving range, putting green, practice area.
Location	2m SE junc 6 M25, 1.5m E of Godstone on A25
Hotel	★★★ 74% Nutfield Priory, NUTFIELD ☎ 01737 822066 52 ⇌ 🐾

TILFORD   Map 04 SU84

Hankley Common GU10 2DD ☎ 01252 792493
A natural heathland course subject to wind. Greens are first rate. The 18th, a long par 4, is most challenging, the green being beyond a deep chasm which traps any but the perfect second shot. The 7th is a spectacular one-shotter.
18 holes, 6418yds, Par 71, SSS 71.
Club membership 700.

Visitors	handicap certificate required, restricted to afternoons at weekends.
Societies	apply in writing.
Green Fees	not confirmed.
Facilities	♀ ♨ 🍴 ⛳ Peter Stow.
Location	0.75m SE
Hotel	★★★ 61% Bush Hotel, The Borough, FARNHAM ☎ 01252 715237 66 ⇌ 🐾

VIRGINIA WATER   Map 04 TQ06

WENTWORTH See page 203

WALTON-ON-THAMES   Map 04 TQ16

Burhill Burwood Rd KT12 4BL ☎ 01932 227345
A relatively short and easy parkland course with some truly magnificent trees. The 18th is a splendid par 4 requiring a well-placed drive and a long firm second. This course is always in immaculate condition.
18 holes, 6224yds, Par 69, SSS 70, Course record 64.
Club membership 1200.

Visitors	may not play Fri-Sun unless introduced by member. Must contact in advance.
Societies	apply in writing.
Green Fees	£44 per day; £30 per round.
Facilities	⊗ 🍴 ♨ ♀ ♨ 🍴 ⛳ Lee Johnson.
Leisure	squash, trolley for hire, driving range, putting green, practice area.
Location	2m S
Hotel	★★★ 71% Ship Thistle, Monument Green, WEYBRIDGE ☎ 01932 848364 39 ⇌ 🐾

WALTON-ON-THE-HILL   Map 04 TQ25

WALTON HEATH See page 205

WEST BYFLEET   Map 04 TQ06

West Byfleet Sheerwater Rd KT14 6AA
☎ 01932 343433
An attractive course set against a background of woodland and gorse. The 13th is the famous 'pond' shot with a water hazard and two bunkers fronting the green. No less than six holes of 420 yards or more.
18 holes, 6211yds, Par 70, SSS 70.
Club membership 650.

Visitors	with member only weekends. Restricted Thu (Ladies Day).
Societies	must apply in writing.
Green Fees	not confirmed.
Facilities	♀ ♨ 🍴 ⛳ David Regan.
Location	W side of village on A245
Hotel	★★★ 63% Jarvis Thatchers Hotel, Epsom Rd, EAST HORSLEY ☎ 01483 284291 34 ⇌ 🐾 Annexe20 ⇌ 🐾

WEST CLANDON   Map 04 TQ05

Clandon Regis Epsom Rd GU4 7TT ☎ 01483 224888
High quality parkland course with challenging lake holes on the back nine. European Tour specification tees and greens.
18 holes, 6412yds, Par 72, SSS 71.

Visitors	a visitor is allowed to play 10 times a year mid-week only.
Societies	telephone in advance.
Green Fees	not confirmed.
Facilities	♀ ♨ 🍴 ⛳ Sean Brady.
Leisure	sauna, indoor practice area.

▶

WENTWORTH CLUB

VIRGINIA WATER *Surrey*
☎ 01344 842201   Map O4 TQO6

John Ingham writes: Among the really famous inland courses in England you have to name Wentworth. The challenge, in terms of sheer yards, is enormous. But the qualities go beyond this, and include the atmosphere, the heathland, the silver birch and fairway-side homes.

The West Course is the one every visitor wishes to play. You can't possibly name the best hole. Bernard Gallacher, the course professional, has his view, but you may select the 7th where the drive rolls downhill and the second shot has to be played high up to a stepped green. The closing holes really sort out the best of them too.

The clubhouse offers Country Club facilities not typical of many British golf courses. The pro shop resembles a plush city store; evening hospitality events are frequent and society meetings here are catered for as at few other centres for sport, and it's all done in five-star style. Probably it is during the World Match-Play championship when Wentworth can be seen at its best. The tents are up, the superstars pile in and out of huge cars and the air is one of luxury and opulence.

One of the attractions of Wentworth is that the great players, including Ben Hogan and Sam Snead, have played here. Gary Player has won marvellously at Wentworth, beating Tony Lema after being seven down in the 36-hole match! Great competitors from the past have stamped their mark here. Arnold Palmer, back in the 1960s, beat Neil Coles in the Match-Play final but then, a generation later, faced young Seve Ballesteros. The Spaniard saved his bacon by pitching in for an eagle three at the last against Palmer, to take the clash into extra holes, where he won.

Visitors	weekdays only. Must contact in advance with letter from own club or a current handicap certificate
Societies	apply in advance (handicap restrictions)
Green fees	(per round) West Course £120; East Course £85; Edinburgh Course £75 (winter rates cheaper).
Facilities	⊗ ⋔ ⌱ ⚑ ♀ (all day) Breakfast from 7a.m. (private rooms) ⚒ 🖎 ⚑ ᚛ (Bernard Gallacher) driving range, putting green, practice area, motor carts caddy/ buggy/ trolley hire,
Leisure	tennis (hardcourt & grass), outdoor swimming pool, gym, snooker, private fishing
Location	Wentworth Drive, GU25 4LS (Wside of Virginia Water, at jnctn of A30 and A329)

54 holes. West Course: 18 holes, 6957yds, Par 73, SSS 74, Course record 63 (Wayne Riley) East Course: 18 holes, 6176yds, Par 68, SSS 70, Course record 62 (Doug Sewell) Edinburgh: 18 holes, 6979yds, Par 72, SSS 73, Course record 67 (Gary Orr)

WHERE TO STAY AND EAT NEARBY

HOTELS:
ASCOT
★★★★ ❀❀ 68% The Berystede, Bagshot Rd, Sunninghill. ☎ 01344 23311
91 (1 ☛ 90 ⇌ ☛)

★★71% Highclere, 19 Kings Road, Sunninghill. ☎ 01344 25220. 11 ⇌ ☛

BAGSHOT
★★★★(Red) ❀❀❀ ♨ Pennyhill Park, London Rd. ☎ 01276 471774 22 ⇌ ☛ Annexe 54 ⇌ ☛.

RESTAURANTS:
BRAY
❀❀❀❀❀ Waterside Inn, River Cottage, Ferry Rd. ☎ 01628 20691.

Location From A246 Guildford/Leatherhead direction
Hotel ★★★ 63% Jarvis Thatchers Hotel, Epsom Rd, EAST HORSLEY
☎ 01483 284291 34 ⊨ ♖Annexe20 ⊨ ♖

WEST END   Map 04 SU96

Windlemere Windlesham Rd GU24 5LS
☎ 01276 858727
A parkland course, undulating in parts with natural water hazards. There is also a floodlit driving range.
9 holes, 2673yds, Par 34, SSS 33, Course record 30.
Visitors no restrictions.
Societies advisable to contact in advance.
Green Fees 18 holes £14 (£17 weekends); 9 holes £8 (£9.50 weekends).
Facilities ⊗ ⓑ ♖ ♀ ⌷ ♖ ♖ David Thomas.
Leisure trolley for hire, driving range.
Location N side of village at junct of A319/A322
Hotel ★★★★(red)♖♖ Pennyhill Park Hotel, London Rd, BAGSHOT
☎ 01276 471774 22 ⊨ ♖Annexe54 ⊨ ♖

WEYBRIDGE   Map 04 TQ06

St George's Hill KT13 0NL ☎ 01932 847758
Comparable and similar to Wentworth, a feature of this course is the number of long and difficult par 4s. To score well it is necessary to place the drive - and long driving pays handsomely. Walking is hard on this undulating, heavily wooded course with plentiful heather and rhododendrons.
A+B Course: 18 holes, 6569yds, Par 70, SSS 71.
A+C Course: 18 holes, 6097yds, Par 70, SSS 69.
B+C Course: 18 holes, 6210yds, Par 70, SSS 70.
Club membership 600.
Visitors must contact in advance and have a handicap certificate.
Societies must contact in advance.
Green Fees not confirmed.
Facilities ♀ ♖ ⌷ ♖ A C Rattue.
Location 2m S off B374
Hotel ★★★ 71% Ship Thistle, Monument Green, WEYBRIDGE ☎ 01932 848364 39 ⊨ ♖

WOKING   Map 04 TQ05

Hoebridge Golf Centre Old Woking Rd GU22 8JH
☎ 01483 722611
Three public courses set in parkland on Surrey sand belt. 24-bay floodlit driving range.
Main Course: 18 holes, 6536yds, Par 72, SSS 71, Course record 68.
Shey Course: 9 holes, 2294yds, Par 33, SSS 31.
Maybury Course: 18 holes, 2230yds, Par 54.
Club membership 600.
Visitors welcome every day, course and reservation desk open dawn to dusk. Credit card reservations 6 days in advance.
Societies Mon-Fri only, telephone in advance
Green Fees Main: £22.50 per day; £14 per 18 holes; £7.50 per 9 holes. Shey: £7.50 per 9 holes. Maybury: £7 per 18 holes; £4.25 per 9 holes. Prices under review.
Facilities ⊗ ⅷ ⓑ ♖ ♀ ♖ ⌷ ♖ ♖ Tim Powell.

Leisure motorised carts for hire, buggies for hire, trolley for hire, floodlit driving range, putting green.
Location On B382 Old Woking to West Byfleet road
Hotel ★★★★(red)♖♖ Pennyhill Park Hotel, London Rd, BAGSHOT
☎ 01276 471774 22 ⊨ ♖Annexe54 ⊨ ♖

Pyrford Warren Ln, Pyrford GU22 8XR ☎ 01483 723555
Opened in September 1993 this inland links style course was designed by Peter Alliss and Clive Clark. Set between Surrey woodlands, the fairways weave between 23 acres of water courses while the greens and tees are connected by rustic bridges. The signature hole is the Par 5 9th at 595 yards, with a dogleg and final approach over water and a sand shelf.
18 holes, 6230yds, Par 72, SSS 70, Course record 69.
Club membership 600.
Visitors must book in advance.
Societies must contact in advance.
Green Fees £45 per day; £35 per 18 holes (£50 bank holidays and weekends). £10 per 9 holes.
Facilities ⊗ ⅷ ⓑ ♖ ♀ ♖ ⌷ ♖ ♖ Jeremy Bennett.
Leisure trolley for hire, driving range, putting green, practice area.
Location Off A3 Ripley to Pyrford
Hotel ★★★★(red)♖♖ Pennyhill Park Hotel, London Rd, BAGSHOT
☎ 01276 471774 22 ⊨ ♖Annexe54 ⊨ ♖

Woking Pond Rd, Hook Heath GU22 0JZ
☎ 01483 760053
An 18-hole course on Surrey heathland with few changes from the original course designed in 1892 by Tom Dunn. Bernard Darwin a past Captain and President has written ' the beauty of Woking is that there is something distinctive about every hole...'.
18 holes, 6340yds, Par 70, SSS 70, Course record 65.
Club membership 550.
Visitors must contact secretary at least 7 days prior to playing. No visitors weekends & bank holidays.
Societies telephone intially then confrim in writing, normally 12 months notice.
Green Fees not confirmed.
Facilities ♀ ♖ ⌷ ♖ John Thorne.
Leisure caddy cars available.
Hotel ★★★★(red)♖♖ Pennyhill Park Hotel, London Rd, BAGSHOT
☎ 01276 471774 22 ⊨ ♖Annexe54 ⊨ ♖

Worplesdon Heath House Rd GU22 0RA
☎ 01483 472277
The scene of the celebrated mixed-foursomes competition. Accurate driving is essential on this heathland course. The short 10th across a lake from tee to green is a notable hole, and the 18th provides a wonderfully challenging par-4 finish.
18 holes, 6440yds, Par 71, SSS 71, Course record 64.
Club membership 590.
Visitors must play with member at weekends & bank holidays. Must contact in advance and have a handicap certificate.
Societies must contact in writing.
Green Fees not confirmed.
Facilities ♖ ⌷ ♖ ♖ J Christine.
Leisure trolley hire.
Location 3.5m SW off B380   ▶

WALTON HEATH

WALTON-ON-THE-HILL *Surrey*
☎ 01737 812380/812060   Map O4 TQ25

John Ingham writes: Several historic names are etched on the Honours Board at Walton Heath, almost 700 feet above sea level. The rare atmosphere here is justified because these Surrey courses can claim to be the toughest inland examination in Britain. Walton Heath is famous for staging the Ryder Cup and the European Open Championship but older players will remember it best for the Match-Play Championship battles that involved Sir Henry Cotton and Dai Rees as well as huge money matches that brought names such as Bobby Locke and Fred Daly to public prominence.

Once owned by the News of the World newspaper, MP's, Lords and significant members of the press would be invited down to Walton Heath by Sir Emsley Carr, who was one of the first to employ a lady as Secretary and manager of a well-known championship venue.

The courses were designed in 1903 by Herbert Fowler, who used natural hollows and channels for drainage, so the fairways equal the best on any seaside links and quickly dry out, even after a severe storm.

Erratic shots, wide of the prepared surface, are wickedly punished and weekend players are tormented in awful fashion. Nobody escapes undamaged from the gorse and bracken but it is the heather, with those tough stems, that really snarl up any attempt at an over-ambitious recovery shot. So be advised - if you're caught off the fairway, don't attempt anything fancy. Play back on the shortest route to comparative security.

While the Old Course is most frequently played by visitors, the New Course is very challenging and requires all the subtle shots required if you are to get the ball near the hole. And, in the clubhouse, they serve a spectacular lunch.

Visitors	limited play weekends. Must contact in advance and have a handicap certificate or letter of introduction
Societies	telephone in advance or apply in writing
Green fees	per day: £65 before 11.30, £50 after 11.30; weekends £65
Facilities	⊗ (3.30-7pm) 🍴 🍷 ♀ ⛳ 🏌 🛒 🏌 (Ken Macpherson) practice area, putting green, trolleys
Location	Tadworth KT20 7TP Deans Lane (SE side of village, off B2032)

36 holes. Old Course: 18 holes, 6801yds, Par 72, SSS 73, Course record 65 (Peter Townsend) New Course: 18 holes, 6609 yds, Par 72, SSS 72, Course record 64 (Clive Clark)

WHERE TO STAY AND EAT NEARBY

HOTELS:
BURGH HEATH
★★ 63% Heathside, Brighton Rd. ☎ 01737 353355. 73 ⇆ 🟤

DORKING
★★★★ 66% The Burford Bridge, Burford Bridge, Box Hill (2m NE A24) ☎ 01306 884561. 48 ⇆ 🟤

REIGATE
★★★ 64% Reigate Manor, Reigate Hill. ☎ 01737 240125. 51 (11 🟤 40 ⇆ 🟤)

STOKE D'ABERNON
★★★★ ❀❀ 60% Woodlands Park, Woodlands Ln. ☎ 01372 843933. 58 ⇆ 🟤

RESTAURANTS:
DORKING
❀❀Partners West Street, 2-4 West St. ☎ 01306 882826.

SUTTON
❀❀Partners Brasserie, 23 Stonecot Hill. ☎ 0181-644 7743.

| Hotel | ★★★★(red)▲▲ Pennyhill Park Hotel, London Rd, BAGSHOT ☎ 01276 471774 22 ⇆ ⚑Annexe54 ⇆ ⚑ |

WOLDINGHAM

Map 05 TQ35

North Downs Northdown Rd CR3 7AA ☎ 01883 652057
Downland course, 850 ft above sea-level, with several testing holes.
18 holes, 5843yds, Par 69, SSS 68.
Club membership 700.

Visitors	must play with member at weekends and bank holidays. Must contact in advance and have a handicap certificate.
Societies	must contact in writing.
Green Fees	not confirmed.
Facilities	♀ ♣ ⌂ ⚑
Location	0.75m S
Hotel	★★★ 68% Kings Arms Hotel, Market Square, WESTERHAM ☎ 01959 562990 16 ⇆ ⚑

SUSSEX, EAST

BEXHILL

Map 05 TQ70

Cooden Beach Cooden Sea Rd TN39 4TR
☎ 01424 842040
The course is close by the sea, but is not real links in character. Despite that, it is dry and plays well throughout the year. There are some excellent holes such as the 4th, played to a built-up green, the short 12th, and three good holes to finish.
18 holes, 6470yds, Par 72, SSS 71, Course record 65.
Club membership 730.

Visitors	must have a handicap certificate. Restricted at weekends. Book in advance with professional 01424 843938
Societies	must contact in advance by telephoning secretary.
Green Fees	£29 per day/round, Nov-Mar £26 (£35/£33 weekends & bank holidays).
Facilities	⊗ ⅷ ⅃ ♥ ♀ ♣ ⌂ 🏌 ⇆ ⚑ Jeffrey Sim.
Leisure	motorised carts for hire, buggies for hire, trolley for hire, putting green, practice area, snooker.
Location	2m W on A259
Hotel	★★★ 67% Jarvis Cooden Beach Hotel, COODEN BEACH ☎ 01424 842281 33 ⇆ ⚑Annexe8 ⇆ ⚑

Highwoods Ellerslie Ln TN39 4LJ ☎ 01424 212625
Undulating course.
18 holes, 6218yds, Par 70, SSS 70, Course record 66.
Club membership 820.

Visitors	must play with member on Sun. Must contact in advance and have an introduction from own club. Handicap required.
Societies	must contact 6 months in advance.
Green Fees	not confirmed.
Facilities	♀ ♣ ⌂ ⚑ M Andrews.

| Location | 1.5m NW |
| Hotel | ★★★ 60% Grand Hotel, Sea Rd, BEXHILL-ON-SEA ☎ 01424 215437 50 ⇆ ⚑ |

BRIGHTON & HOVE

Map 04 TQ30

Brighton & Hove Devils Dyke Rd BN1 8YJ
☎ 01273 556482
Downland course with sea views.
9 holes, 5710yds, Par 68, SSS 68, Course record 65.
Club membership 400.

Visitors	must contact in advance, restricted play Wed, Fri & weekends.
Societies	must contact secretary in advance.
Green Fees	Apr-Oct £15 per round (£25 weekends); Nov-Mar £13.50 per round (£23 weekends).
Facilities	⊗ ⅷ by prior arrangement ⅃ ♥ ♀ ♣ ⌂ ⚑ Clive Burgess.
Leisure	trolley for hire, putting green, practice area, snooker.
Location	4m NW
Hotel	★★ 65% St Catherines Lodge Hotel, Seafront, Kingsway, Hove ☎ 01273 778181 50rm(40 ⇆ ⚑)

Dyke Dyke Rd, Devils Dyke BN1 8YJ
☎ 01273 857296
This downland course has some glorious views both towards the sea and inland. The best hole on the course is probably the 17th; it is one of those teasing short holes of just over 200 yards, and is played across a gully to a high green.
18 holes, 6611yds, Par 72, SSS 72, Course record 66.
Club membership 750.

Visitors	must contact in advance.
Societies	apply by telephone or in writing.
Green Fees	Winter £31 per day: £21 per round (£31 weekends). Summer £35 per day: £25 per round (£35 weekends).
Facilities	⊗ ⅷ ⅃ ♥ ♀ ♣ ⌂ 🏌 ⚑ Martin Ross.
Leisure	motorised carts for hire, buggies for hire, trolley for hire, putting green, practice area.
Location	4m N of Brighton, between A23 & A27
Hotel	★★ 65% St Catherines Lodge Hotel, Seafront, Kingsway, Hove ☎ 01273 778181 50rm(40 ⇆ ⚑)

East Brighton Roedean Rd BN2 5RA
☎ 01273 604838
Undulating downland course, overlooking the sea. Windy.
18 holes, 6346yds, Par 72, SSS 70, Course record 67.
Club membership 650.

Visitors	contact in advance & may only play weekends after 11am.
Societies	must contact in advance, handicap certificate required.
Green Fees	£22 per day; £17 per round (£30 per day weekends, £20 after 1pm winter 3pm summer).
Facilities	⊗ ⅷ by prior arrangement ⅃ ♥ ♀ ♣ ⌂ 🏌 ⚑ Robin S Goodway.
Leisure	trolley for hire, putting green, practice area.
Location	2m E of Palace Pier, overlooking marina
Hotel	★★★ 54% Jarvis Norfolk Hotel, 149 Kings Rd, BRIGHTON ☎ 01273 738201 121 ⇆ ⚑

Hollingbury Park Ditchling Rd BN1 7HS
☎ 01273 552010
Municipal course in hilly situation on the Downs,
overlooking the sea.
18 holes, 6500yds, Par 72, SSS 71, Course record 66.
Club membership 300.
Visitors	no restrictions
Societies	telephone the secretary for details.
Green Fees	£11 weekday (£15 weekends & bank holidays).
Facilities	⊗ 🍴 ♟ ♀ ♨ 🏠 🏌 🥃 Peter Brown.
Leisure	motorised carts for hire, buggies for hire, trolley for hire, putting green, practice area.
Location	2m N of town centre
Hotel	★★★ 54% Jarvis Norfolk Hotel, 149 Kings Rd, BRIGHTON ☎ 01273 738201 121 ⇄ ⋒

Waterhall Seddlescombe Rd, (Off Devils Dyke Road) BN1
8YN ☎ 01273 508658
Hilly downland course with hard walking and open to the
wind. Private club playing over municipal course.
18 holes, 5773yds, Par 69, SSS 68, Course record 66.
Club membership 300.
Visitors	must contact in advance, may not play at start of day.
Societies	must contact the secretary in writing.
Green Fees	£17 per day; £11 per round (£15 per round weekends).
Facilities	⊗ 🍴 ♟ ♀ ♨ 🏠 🏌 🥃 Paul Charmon.
Leisure	trolley for hire, putting green, practice area.
Location	3m N off A27
Hotel	★★ 65% St Catherines Lodge Hotel, Seafront, Kingsway, Hove ☎ 01273 778181 50rm(40 ⇄ ⋒)

West Hove Church Farm, Hangleton BN3 8AN
☎ 01273 419738
A downland course designed by Hawtree & Sons.
18 holes, 6237yds, Par 70, SSS 70.
Club membership 700.
Visitors	tee times by arrangement.
Societies	by arrangement.
Green Fees	not confirmed.
Facilities	♀ ♨ 🏠 🥃 David Mills.
Leisure	putting,cart/buggy/trolley hire.
Hotel	★★ 65% St Catherines Lodge Hotel, Seafront, Kingsway, Hove ☎ 01273 778181 50rm(40 ⇄ ⋒)

CROWBOROUGH
Map 05 TQ53

Crowborough Beacon Beacon Rd TN6 1UJ
☎ 01892 661511
A picturesque course in pleasant heathland. Though most
fairways are wide and open, one or two are distinctly

tight where a wayward shot results in a lost ball. By no
means an easy course, with testing holes at the 2nd, 6th
and 16th.
18 holes, 6279yds, Par 71, SSS 70, Course record 66.
Club membership 700.
Visitors	must contact in advance & have handicap certificate but may not play at weekends & bank holidays.
Societies	apply in writing to secretary.
Green Fees	£40 per day; £25 per round.
Facilities	⊗ 🍴 ♟ ♀ ♨ 🏠 🏌 🥃 D C Newnham.
Leisure	trolley for hire, putting green, practice area.
Location	1m SW on A26
Hotel	★★★ 76% Spa Hotel, Mount Ephraim, TUNBRIDGE WELLS ☎ 01892 520331 76 ⇄ ⋒

Dewlands Manor Cottage Hill, Rotherfield TN6 3JN
☎ 01892 852266
A pretty, moderately hilly, Pay and Play parkland course with
water features.
9 holes, 3186yds, Par 36, SSS 70.
Visitors	must telephone in advance.
Societies	telephone for availability.
Green Fees	not confirmed.
Facilities	⊗ by prior arrangement 🍴 by prior arrangement ♀ ♨ 🏠 🏌 🥃 Nick Godin.
Leisure	motorised carts for hire, buggies for hire, trolley for hire, putting green, practice area, indoor teaching facility.
Location	0.5m S of Rotherfield
Inn	QQQQ The Rose & Crown Inn, Fletching St, MAYFIELD ☎ 01435 872200 4 ⇄ ⋒

DITCHLING
Map 05 TQ31

Mid Sussex Spatham Ln BN6 8XJ ☎ 01273 846567
Mature parkland course with many trees, water hazards,
strategically placed bunkers and superbly contoured greens.
The 14th hole, a spectacular par 5, demands accurate
shotmaking to avoid the various hazards along its length.
18 holes, 6431yds, Par 71, SSS 71, Course record 69.
Visitors	telephone in advance to book tee times, members only at weekends.
Societies	advance booking required.
Green Fees	Weekdays only, £30 per day £20 per round.
Facilities	⊗ 🍴 ♟ ♀ ♨ 🏠 🏌 🥃 Chris Connell.
Leisure	motorised carts for hire, buggies for hire, trolley for hire, driving range, putting green, practice area.
Location	1m E of Ditchling village
Hotel	★★★ 76% Shelleys, High St, LEWES ☎ 01273 472361 19 ⇄ ⋒

EASTBOURNE   Map 05 TV69

Eastbourne Downs East Dean Rd BN20 8ES
☎ 01323 720827
Downland/seaside course.
18 holes, 6645yds, Par 72, SSS 72, Course record 67.
Club membership 650.
Visitors   must contact in advance. A handicap certificate
             is required for weekend play and may not play
             weekends before 11am.
Societies   must contact secretary in advance.
Green Fees   £18 per day, £14 per round (£20/£18 weekends).
Facilities   ⊗ ⅏ ⅃ 里 ♀ ⚘ 🝐 ⬤ ⟮ T Marshall.
Leisure   trolley for hire, putting green, practice area.
Location   1m W of town centre on A259
Hotel   ★★★★ 56% Cavendish Hotel, Grand Pde,
             EASTBOURNE ☎ 01323 410222 112 ⇄ ⋔

Royal Eastbourne Paradise Dr BN20 8BP
☎ 01323 729738 & 736986
A famous club which celebrated its centenary in 1987.
The course plays longer than it measures. Testing holes
are the 8th, a par 3 played to a high green and the 16th, a
par 5 righthand dogleg.
Devonshire Course: 18 holes, 6109yds, Par 71, SSS 69,
Course record 62.
Hartington Course: 9 holes, 2147yds, Par 64, SSS 61.
Club membership 800.
Visitors   must contact in advance, may not play
             weekends except by arrangement.
Societies   must apply in advance.
Green Fees   Devonshire £20/25; Hartington £8/12.

7 Courses to choose from!
Any 2 days - 12 January - 31 December 1997
Your break includes 2 days' free golf (up to 36 holes
each day), accommodation, newspaper (except Sunday),
full English breakfast, light lunch at the golf club, with
a 4 course Dinner and coffee at the hotel. Guaranteed
tee-off times. Handicap certificates required.

All our 122 rooms are en suite with every modern
facility inc. Satellite TV.

The cost of your golf break from 12 Jan-28 Feb £124:
1-31 Mar £130: 1 Apr-31 May £140: 1 Jun-30 Sep £150:
1 Oct-31 Dec £135. Extra days pro rata.

You may, subject to availability, play at a selection of
7 golf clubs (all 18-hole) in this lovely area.
Please write or telephone for our Golfing Break folder.

Lansdowne Hotel ⊛   AA
                                           ★★★
King Edward's Parade · Eastbourne BN21 4EE   75%
Tel: (01323) 725174   Fax: (01323) 739721

Facilities   ⊗ ⅏ by prior arrangement ⅃ 里 ♀ ⚘ 🝐
             🝐 ⬤ ⟮ Richard Wooller.
Leisure   motorised carts for hire, buggies for hire,
             trolley for hire, putting green, practice area.
Location   0.5m W of town centre
Hotel   ★★★ 75% Lansdowne Hotel, King
             Edward's Pde, EASTBOURNE
             ☎ 01323 725174 122 ⇄ ⋔

Willingdon Southdown Rd, Willingdon BN20 9AA
☎ 01323 410981
Unique, hilly downland course set in oyster-shaped
amphitheatre.
18 holes, 6118yds, Par 69, SSS 69.
Club membership 570.
Visitors   by application, may not play at weekends.
Societies   apply in writing.
Green Fees   £24 per day/round (£14 winter).
Facilities   ⊗ ⅃ 里 ♀ ⚘ 🝐 ⬤ ⟮ James Debenham.
Leisure   motorised carts for hire, buggies for hire, trolley
             for hire, putting green, practice area.
Location   0.5m N of town centre off A22
Hotel   ★★★ 60% Wish Tower Hotel, King Edward's
             Pde, EASTBOURNE
             ☎ 01323 722676 65 ⇄ ⋔

FOREST ROW   Map 05 TQ43

Ashdown Forest Hotel Chapel Ln RH18 5BB
☎ 01342 824866
Two natural undulating heathland and woodland courses cut
out of the Ashdown Forest. No sand bunkers, just equally
testing heather dunes with the 14th hole on the Hotel course
being regarded as the best of the 36 holes. The hotel
specialises in catering for golf breaks and societies.
Hotel Course: 18 holes, 5586yds, Par 68, SSS 67.
Old Course: 18 holes, 6477yds, Par 72, SSS 71.
Club membership 180.
Visitors   must contact in advance.
Societies   must telephone in advance.
Green Fees   on request.
Facilities   ⊗ ⅏ ⅃ 里 ♀ ⚘ 🝐 ⬤
             ⟮ Martyn Landsborough.
Leisure   trolley for hire, driving range, putting green,
             practice area.
Location   4m S of East Grinstead off A22 & B2110

Royal Ashdown Forest Chapel Ln RH18 5LR
☎ 01342 822018
Undulating heathland course. Long carries off the tees
and magnificent views over the Forest. Not a course for
the high handicapper.
Old Course: 18 holes, 6477yds, Par 72, SSS 71, Course
record 67.
New Course: 18 holes, 5586yds, Par 68, SSS 67.
Club membership 450.
Visitors   restricted weekends & Tue. Must have a
             handicap certificate on Old Course. No
             restrictions on New Course.
Societies   must contact in advance.
Green Fees   £36 per day; £30 per round (£42/£36
             weekends & bank holidays).
Facilities   ⊗ ⅃ 里 ♀ ⚘ 🝐 ⬤
             ⟮ Martyn Landsborough.

Leisure	trolley for hire, putting green, practice area.
Location	SE side of village, off B2110
Hotel	★★★ 70% Woodbury House Hotel, Lewes Rd, EAST GRINSTEAD ☎ 01342 313657 13 ⇌ ♠Annexe1 ♠

HAILSHAM   Map 05 TQ50

Wellshurst Golf & Country Club North St, Hellingly
BN27 4EE ☎ 01435 813456 & 813636
There are outstanding views of the South Downs and the
Weald Valley from this 18-hole, well-manicured, undulating
course. There are varied features and some water hazards. A
practice sand bunker, putting green and driving range are
available to improve your golf.
18 holes, 5717yds, Par 70, SSS 68.
Club membership 260.

Visitors	no restrictions but advisable to book.
Societies	telephone in advance to book tee times.
Green Fees	£20 per day; £12 per 18 holes (£26/£16/ weekends & bank holidays).
Facilities	⊗ Ⅲ ⓛ 🐴 ♟ ⚒ 🏠 ⛳ 🛏 ⬚ ℓ Matthew Round.
Leisure	motorised carts for hire, buggies for hire, trolley for hire, driving range, putting green, practice area.
Location	2.5m N of Hailsham, on A267
Hotel	★★ 65% The Olde Forge, Magham Down, HAILSHAM ☎ 01323 842893 8rm(6 ⇌ ♠)

The Beauport Park Hotel

Hastings, Sussex TN38 8EA ★★★

Telephone: 01424 851222

Fax: 01424 852465

A Georgian country house hotel set in 33 acres of
parkland with its own swimming pool, tennis courts,
putting green, croquet lawn, French boules, outdoor
chess and country walks. Candle-lit restaurant and
open log fires. Adjacent to an 18 hole and 9 hole golf
course, floodlight driving range, riding stables and
squash courts. Convenient for East Sussex National
Golf Course – and many other interesting courses.

**Full inclusive golfing breaks
available all year. Please send for
our colour brochure and tariff.**

HASTINGS & ST LEONARDS   Map 05 TQ80

Beauport Park St Leonards-on-Sea TN38 0TA
☎ 01424 852977
Played over Hastings Public Course. Undulating parkland
with stream and fine views.
18 holes, 6033yds, Par 70, SSS 70.
Club membership 290.

Visitors	no restrictions.
Societies	must contact in writing.
Green Fees	not confirmed.
Facilities	♟ ⚒ 🏠 ⛳ ℓ
Location	3m N of Hastings on A2100
Hotel	★★★⚑ 72% Beauport Park Hotel, Battle Rd, HASTINGS ☎ 01424 851222 23 ⇌ ♠

HEATHFIELD   Map 05 TQ52

Horam Park Chiddingly Rd, Horam TN21 0JJ
☎ 01435 813477
A woodland course with lakes.
9 holes, 5965yds, Par 70, SSS 68, Course record 64.
Club membership 450.

Visitors	contact for tee times.
Societies	prior booking required.
Green Fees	£15 per day; £12.50 per 18 holes; £8 per 9 holes (£17/£14/£8.50 weekends and bank holidays).
Facilities	⊗ Ⅲ ⓛ 🐴 ♟ ⚒ 🏠 ⛳ ℓ Mark Jarvis.
Leisure	motorised carts for hire, buggies for hire, trolley for hire, driving range, putting green, practice area.
Location	Off A267
Hotel	★★ 62% Horse Shoe Inn, Windmill Hill, HERSTMONCEUX ☎ 01323 833265 13 ⇌ ♠

HOLTYE   Map 05 TQ43

Holtye TN8 7ED ☎ 01342 850635
Undulating forest/heathland course with tree-lined fairways
providing testing golf. Difficult tees on back nine.
9 holes, 5289yds, Par 66, SSS 66, Course record 65.
Club membership 500.

Visitors	may not play weekend or Thu mornings.
Societies	Tue & Fri only, by arrangement.
Green Fees	not confirmed.
Facilities	♟ ⚒ 🏠 ℓ Kevin Hinton.
Location	N side of village on A264
Hotel	★★★(red)⚑ Gravetye Manor Hotel, EAST GRINSTEAD ☎ 01342 810567 18 ⇌ ♠

LEWES   Map 05 TQ41

Lewes Chapel Hill BN7 2BB ☎ 01273 483474 & 473245
Downland course. Fine views.
18 holes, 6213yds, Par 71, SSS 70, Course record 65.
Club membership 638.

Visitors	may not play at weekends before 2pm. Bookings taken up to 7 days in advance.
Societies	must contact in advance.
Green Fees	£18 (£30 weekends & bank holidays).
Facilities	⊗ Ⅲ ⓛ 🐴 ♟ ⚒ 🏠 ℓ Paul Dobson.
Leisure	motorised carts for hire, buggies for hire, trolley for hire, putting green, practice area. ▶

Location	E side of town centre
Hotel	★★ 68% White Hart Hotel, 55 High St, LEWES

☎ 01273 476694 23rm(19 ⇄ ↑)Annexe29 ⇄ ↑

NEWHAVEN
Map 05 TQ40

Peacehaven Brighton Rd BN9 9UH
☎ 01273 512571
Downland course, sometimes windy. Testing holes: 1st (par 3), 4th (par 4), 9th (par 3), 10th (par 3), 18th (par 3).
9 holes, 5305yds, Par 69, SSS 66.
Club membership 270.

Visitors	may not play before 11am weekends.
Societies	telephone in advance.
Green Fees	£11 per 18 holes; £8 per 9 holes (£17/£11 weekends).
Facilities	⊗ ⅷ ⅃ ⬛ ♀ ⚎ 🏠 ⚏ ℓ Gerry Williams.
Leisure	trolley for hire, putting green.
Location	0.75m W on A259
Hotel	★★★ 66% The Star Inn, ALFRISTON ☎ 01323 870495 34 ⇄ ↑

RYE
Map 05 TQ92

Rye New Lydd Rd, Camber TN31 7QS
☎ 01797 225241
Typical links course with superb greens and views.
Old Course: 18 holes, 6317yds, Par 68, SSS 71.
Jubilee Course: 9 holes, 6141yds, Par 71, SSS 70.
Club membership 1100.

Visitors	must be invited/introduced by a member.
Green Fees	contact secretary.
Facilities	⚎ 🏠 ⚏ ℓ Michael Lee.
Leisure	trolley for hire, putting green, practice area.
Location	2.75m SE off A259
Hotel	★★★ 62% George Hotel, High St, RYE ☎ 01797 222114 22 ⇄ ↑

SEAFORD
Map 05 TV49

Seaford Firle Rd, East Blatchington BN25 2JD
☎ 01323 892442
The great H. Taylor did not perhaps design as many courses as his friend and rival, James Braid, but Seaford's original design was Taylor's. It is a splendid downland course with magnificent views and some fine holes.
18 holes, 6551yds, Par 69, SSS 71.
Club membership 600.

Visitors	must contact in advance, may not play weekends.
Societies	must contact in advance.
Green Fees	Apr-Oct: £35 per day; £25 per round. Nov-Mar: £25 per day; £20 per round. Twilight after 3.30 £20.
Facilities	⊗ ⅷ ⅃ ⬛ ♀ ⚎ 🏠 ⟠ ℓ Mark Smith.
Leisure	motorised carts for hire, buggies for hire, trolley for hire, driving range, putting green, practice area.
Location	Turn inland at war memorial off A259
Hotel	★★★ 66% The Star Inn, ALFRISTON ☎ 01323 870495 34 ⇄ ↑

Seaford Head Southdown Rd BN25 4JS
☎ 01323 890139 & 894843
A links type course situated on the cliff edge giving exception views over the Seven Sisters and coastline. The upper level is reached via a short hole with elevated green - known as the 'Hell Hole' and the 18th Par 5 tee is on the 'Head' being 300 feet above sea level.
18 holes, 5848yds, Par 71, SSS 68.
Club membership 450.

Visitors	no restrictions.
Societies	write or telephone the Pro's shop.
Green Fees	not confirmed.
Facilities	♀ ⚎ 🏠 ⚏ ℓ Tony Lowles.
Hotel	★★★ 63% Deans Place, ALFRISTON ☎ 01323 870248 36 ⇄ ↑

SEDLESCOMBE
Map 05 TQ71

Sedlescombe Kent St TN33 0SD ☎ 01424 870898
This course was established in 1989 and is windswept and challenging. The Par 5 9th holes has a green surrounded by lakes.
18 holes, 6359yds, Par 71, SSS 68.
Club membership 300.

Visitors	please telephone and reserve tee times.
Societies	please telephone to reserve tee times.
Green Fees	£15 per day; £12.50 per 18 holes; £8 per 9 holes (£17/£14/£8.50). Golf & Food all day £29.50.
Facilities	⊗ ⅷ ⅃ ⬛ ♀ ⚎ 🏠 ⚏ ℓ
Leisure	motorised carts for hire, buggies for hire, trolley for hire, driving range, putting green, practice area.
Location	A21, 4m N of Hastings
Hotel	★★★ 62% Brickwall Hotel, The Green, SEDLESCOMBE ☎ 01424 870253 23 ⇄ ↑

TICEHURST
Map 05 TQ63

Dale Hill TN5 7DQ ☎ 01580 200112
Picturesque course with woodland, water and gently undulating fairways. Hotel and leisure centre within grounds.
18 holes, 6106yds, Par 70, SSS 69.
Club membership 650.

Visitors	must play after noon weekends.
Societies	must contact in advance.
Green Fees	£35 per day; £20 per round (£30 per round weekends and bank holidays). Twilight reductions.
Facilities	⊗ ⅷ ⅃ ⬛ ♀ ⚎ 🏠 ⚏ ⟠ ℓ Liam Greasley.
Leisure	heated indoor swimming pool, sauna, solarium, gymnasium, buggies for hire, trolley for hire, driving range, putting green, practice area.
Location	N side of village off B2087
Hotel	★★★ 72% Dale Hill Hotel & Golf Club, TICEHURST ☎ 01580 200112 32 ⇄ ↑

UCKFIELD
Map 05 TQ42

EAST SUSSEX NATIONAL See page 211

Piltdown Piltdown TN22 3XB ☎ 01825 722033
Natural heathland course with much heather and gorse. No bunkers, easy walking, fine views.
▶

EAST SUSSEX NATIONAL

Uckfield *East Sussex* ☎ 01825 880088   Map 05 TQ42

John Ingham writes: Designed by Bob Cupp on a grand championship scale and opened in 1989, East Sussex National presents two massive courses, more than 7000 yards long. Both are ideal for big-hitting professionals and already they have staged the European Open here. Boasting a driving range and a Golf Academy, Bob Cupp, once a designer for Jack Nicklaus, decided to use what they call 'bent' grass from tee to green - and the result is an American-type course to test everyone, depending upon which tee you drive from.

Could either course, brand spanking new, compare with the other Sussex classics of Pulborough (West Sussex) and Royal Ashdown Forest, a gem of a place near Forest Row and a course without a single bunker? When first I drove into the vastness of the car park and eyed the huge redbrick clubhouse, I admit it all looked daunting. The experience is not unlike entering an hotel-country club complex in the United States, signing in as one does at the reception area before walking across a suspended corridor towards the huge and well-stocked professional's shop.

The East Sussex National offers the most modern day's golf in the United Kingdom. The greens on both the East and West courses are immaculate and groomed to perfection. Strike the putt solidly and on-line, and it must go in! While it's true that 50,000 spectators can watch you hole out on the last green, it's just as true that on a quiet day out, you can enjoy letting out plenty of shaft without fear of hitting valuable balls into thick woods.

The West course is reserved for members and their guests, but visitors are welcomed on the other course.

Visitors	must contact in advance. No handicap certificate required. Must accompany a member on West Course
Societies	Societies must contact Corporate Hospitality (01825 880230)
Green fees	£49.50 all day winter inc. lunch or brunch £65 all day summer inc. lunch or brunch, £49.50 18 holes, £29.50 twilight (5 hours)
Facilities	⊗ ⊪ ⅃ ➤ ♀ ⋈ ⚲ 🏌 ♟ driving range, putting green, ℓ Philip Lewin motor cart, practice area, buggies, trolleys. 3-hole academy course
Leisure	hard court tennis, indoor swimming, riding, sauna, croquet
Location	Little Horsted TN22 5ES (S on A22)

36 holes. East Course 18 holes, 7081yds, Par72 SSS 74
Course record 65 (Gordon Brand Jr)
West Course 18 holes, 7154yds, Par 72, SSS74

WHERE TO STAY AND EAT NEARBY

HOTELS:

UCKFIELD
★★★(Red) ✿✿✿ ♨ 78% Horsted Place, Little Horsted ☎ 01825 750581. 17 ⇆ ➧)

HALLAND
★★★ 63% Halland Forge ☎ 01825 840456. Annexe 20 (3 ➧ 17 ⇆ ➧)

AA ★★★
Open 7 days a week

The ideal 19th hole

Play golf to your heart's content in Sussex.
Then dine in style and stay a while at the
Halland Forge Hotel and Restaurant.
The Forge Restaurant – à la Carte and Table d'Hôte
Luncheon and Dinner. Coffee Shop/Carvery –
Open for Breakfast, Lunch and Tea from 8.00am to 6.00pm
Anvil Lounge Bar – *Fully Licensed.*
20 Bedrooms with private facilities.
▲ We are the ideal golfing centre for South East England ▲

Hotel Restaurant and Coffee
Shop/Carvery
Halland, nr. Lewes, East Sussex
On A22/B2192 roundabout,
4 miles south of Uckfield just
beyond East Sussex National
Tel: Halland (01825) 840456 Fax: (01825) 840773

18 holes, 6070yds, Par 68, SSS 69, Course record 67.
Club membership 400.

Visitors	must telephone pro shop in advance 01825 722389 and have a handicap certificate. Play on Tue, Thu and weekends is restricted.
Societies	must contact in writing.
Green Fees	£32 per day; £27.50 per round. Reductions after 4pm..
Facilities	⊗ ⫢ by prior arrangement ⬚ ⬚ ⬚ ⬚ ⬚ ⬚ ⬚ John Amos.
Leisure	motorised carts for hire, buggies for hire, trolley for hire, driving range, putting green, practice area.
Location	3m NW off A272
Hotel	★★★ 63% Halland Forge Hotel & Restaurant, HALLAND ☎ 01825 840456 Annexe20 ⇄ ♞

SUSSEX, WEST

ANGMERING　　　　　　　　　　　　Map 04 TQ00

Ham Manor BN16 4JE ☎ 01903 783288
Two miles from the sea, this parkland course has fine
springy turf and provides an interesting test in two loops
of nine holes each.
18 holes, 6267yds, Par 70, SSS 70, Course record 64.
Club membership 780.

Visitors	must have a handicap certificate. Telephone pro shop in advance 01903 783732.
Societies	telephone for details
Green Fees	£28 (£35 weekends).
Facilities	⊗ ⫢ ⬚ ⬚ ⬚ ⬚ ⬚ ⬚ Simon Buckley.
Leisure	trolley for hire, putting green, practice area, bowling green, table tennis.
Location	Off A259
Hotel	★★★ 59% Chatsworth Hotel, Steyne, WORTHING ☎ 01903 236103 107 ⇄ ♞

ARUNDEL　　　　　　　　　　　　　　Map 04 TQ00

Avisford Park Yapton Ln, Walberton BN18 0LS
☎ 01243 554611
Newly extended course - now 18-holes - enjoying a country
hotel complex setting. The course opens with a real challenge
as there is out of bounds water and tree hazards the whole
length of this 414yard drive.
18 holes, 5703yds, Par 70, SSS 68.
Club membership 100.

Visitors	must contact in advance for weekend play.
Societies	apply in writing or telephone.
Green Fees	Summer rates - Mon-Fri £14 per 18 holes (£16 weekends).
Facilities	⊗ ⫢ ⬚ ⬚ ⬚ ⬚ ⬚ ⬚ ⬚ Richard Beach.
Leisure	buggies for hire, trolley for hire.
Location	Off A27
Hotel	★★★ 66% Norfolk Arms Hotel, High St, ARUNDEL ☎ 01903 882101 21 ⇄ Annexe13 ⇄

BOGNOR REGIS　　　　　　　　　　　Map 04 SZ99

Bognor Regis Downview Rd, Felpham PO22 8JD
☎ 01243 821929 (Secretary) & 865867
This flattish, parkland course has more variety than is to be
found on some of the South Coast courses. The club is also
known far and wide for its enterprise in creating a social
atmosphere. The course is open to the prevailing wind.
18 holes, 6238yds, Par 70, SSS 70, Course record 64.
Club membership 700.

Visitors	must play with member at weekends Apr-Sep. Must contact in advance (pro shop 01243 865209).
Societies	phone initially.
Green Fees	£25 per day or round (£30 weekends & bank holidays).
Facilities	⊗ ⬚ ⬚ ⬚ ⬚ ⬚ ⬚
Leisure	motorised carts for hire, buggies for hire, trolley for hire, putting green,practice area.
Location	1.5m NE off A259
Hotel	★★ 67% Black Mill House Hotel, Princess Av, Aldwick, BOGNOR REGIS ☎ 01243 821945 & 865596 22rm(18 ⇄ ♞)Annexe4rm

BURGESS HILL　　　　　　　　　　　Map 04 TQ31

Burgess Hill Cuckfield Rd RH15 8RE ☎ 01444 258585
Presently under construction and due to open in February
1997 is an academy course bordered by a tributary of the

River Adur. Facilities currently available for public use include a floodlit driving range and a large sweeping putting green.
9 holes.
Visitors details not yet available.
Societies contact in advance.
Green Fees to be advised.
Facilities ♨ ⚐ ⚑ ♟ ♥ 𝄐 Steven Dunkley.
Leisure floodlit driving range, putting green, practice area.
Location N of town on B2036
Hotel ★★★♨♨ 76% Ockenden Manor, Ockenden Ln, CUCKFIELD ☎ 01444 416111 22 ⇆ ℝ

CHICHESTER Map 04 SU80

Chichester Golf Centre Hoe Farm, Hunston PO20 6AX
☎ 01243 533833
Set amongst lush farmland, the Tower course has four lakes which bring water into play on seven holes. The Florida-style Cathedral course was opened in spring 1994. There is also a 9-hole par 3 and a floodlit driving range.
Tower Course: 18 holes, 6174yds, Par 71, SSS 69, Course record 67.
Cathedral Course: 18 holes, 6461yds, Par 72, SSS 69, Course record 70.
Club membership 300.
Visitors a strict dress code is in operation. It is advisable to contact in advance.
Societies must contact in advance.
Green Fees not confirmed.
Facilities ⚐ ⚑ ♟ ♥ 𝄐 Carl Rota.
Leisure driving range,putting,buggy/trolley hire.
Location 3m S of Chichester, on B2145 at Hunston
Hotel ★★★ 65% The Dolphin & Anchor, West St, CHICHESTER ☎ 01243 785121 49 ⇆ ℝ

COPTHORNE Map 05 TQ33

Copthorne Borers Arms Rd RH10 3LL
☎ 01342 712033 & 712508
Despite it having been in existence since 1892, this club remains one of the lesser known Sussex courses. It is hard to know why because it is most attractive with plenty of trees and much variety
18 holes, 6505yds, Par 71, SSS 71, Course record 67.
Club membership 550.
Visitors must contact in advance, may not play weekends before 1pm.
Societies must contact in advance.
Green Fees £35 per day; £27 per round (£30 per round weekends after 1pm).
Facilities ⊗ ⊮ ᕮ ♨ ⚐ ⚑ ♥ 𝄐 Joe Burrell.
Leisure trolley for hire, putting green, practice area.
Location E side of village junc 10 of M23 off A264
Hotel ★★★★ 64% The Copthorne, Copthorne Way, COPTHORNE ☎ 01342 714971 227 ⇆ ℝ

Effingham Park RH10 3EU ☎ 01342 716528 & 712138
Parkland course.
9 holes, 1769yds, Par 30, SSS 57, Course record 28.
Club membership 390.
Visitors restricted at weekends after 11am and not after 4pm Apr-Oct.

Societies Mon-Fri, and Sat/Sun after 1pm, must write/telephone in advance.
Green Fees not confirmed.
Facilities ⚐ ⚑ ♟ ♥ 𝄐 Duncan Arnold.
Leisure heated indoor swimming pool, sauna, solarium, gymnasium, practice area, putting green, trolley hire.
Location 2m E on B2028
Hotel ★★★★ 64% The Copthorne Effingham Park, West Park Rd, COPTHORNE
☎ 01342 714994 122 ⇆ ℝ

CRAWLEY Map 04 TQ23

Cottesmore Buchan Hill, Pease Pottage RH11 9AT
☎ 01293 528256
The course was originally founded in 1974.The Griffin course is undulating with four holes are over water. The newer Phoenix course is shorter and less testing. But both are lined by silver birch, pine and oak, with rhododendrons ablaze in June.
Griffin Course: 18 holes, 6280yds, Par 72, SSS 70.
Phoenix Course: 18 holes, 5489yds, Par 69, SSS 68.
Club membership 1500.
Visitors may only play after 11am at weekends and bank holidays. Must contact in advance.
Societies weekdays, must telephone in advance.
Green Fees Griffin: £30 per day (£40 weekends); £24 per round (£30 weekends). Phoenix: £20 per day (£26 weekends); £15 per round (£20 weekends).
Facilities ⊗ ⊮ ᕮ ♨ ⚐ ⚑ ♥ 𝄐 Andrew Prior.
Leisure hard tennis courts, heated indoor swimming pool, squash, sauna, solarium, gymnasium, motorised carts for hire, buggies for hire, trolley for hire, putting green, practice area.
Location 3m SW 1m W of M23 junc 11
Hotel ★★★ 58% George Hotel, High St, CRAWLEY ☎ 01293 524215 86 ⇆ ℝ

Gatwick Manor Lowfield Heath RH10 2ST
☎ 01293 538587
Interesting, pay and play short course.
9 holes, 2492yds, Par 56, SSS 50.
Club membership 63.
Visitors no restrictions.
Societies must telephone in advance.
Green Fees not confirmed.
Facilities ⚐ ⚑ ♥ 𝄐 C Jenkins.
Location 2m N on A23
Hotel B Forte Travelodge, Church Rd, Lowfield Heath, Crawley, CRAWLEY
☎ 01293 533441 121 ⇆ ℝ

Ifield Golf & Country Club Rusper Rd, Ifield RH11 0LN
☎ 01293 520222 (Manager) & 523088 (Pro)
Parkland course.
18 holes, 6330yds, Par 70, SSS 70, Course record 65.
Club membership 850.
Visitors must contact professional in advance. Must be guest of member at weekends.
Societies apply in advance.
Green Fees £30 per day; £20 per round.
Facilities ⊗ ⊮ by prior arrangement ᕮ ♨ ⚐ ⚑ 𝄐 Jonathan Earl.
Leisure squash, motorised carts for hire, buggies for hire, trolley for hire, putting green, practice area. ▶

Location 1m W side of town centre off A23
Hotel ★★★ 58% George Hotel, High St,
CRAWLEY ☎ 01293 524215 86 ⇥ ⋔

Tilgate Forest Golf Centre Titmus Dr RH10 5EU
☎ 01293 530103
Designed by former Ryder Cup players Neil Coles and Brian Huggett, the course has been carefully cut through a silver birch and pine forest. It is possibly one of th most beautiful public courses in the country. The 17th is a treacherous Par 5 demanding an uphill third shot to a green surrounded by rhododendrons.
18 holes, 6359yds, Par 72, SSS 69 or 9 holes, 1136yds, Par 27.
Visitors may book up to 7 days in advance.
Societies telephone in advance for details.
Green Fees £11.85 per 18 holes, £4.40 per 9 holes (£16.25/£5.80 weekends).
Facilities ⊗ ⫾ ⶫ ⓛ ⬙ ♀ ⚥ ⛫ ⛿ Ⲓ Sean Trussell.
Leisure trolley for hire, floodlit driving range, putting green.
Hotel ★★★ 58% George Hotel, High St,
CRAWLEY ☎ 01293 524215 86 ⇥ ⋔

GOODWOOD   Map 04 SU80

Goodwood PO18 0PN ☎ 01243 774968
Downland course designed by the master architect, James Braid. Many notable holes, particularly the finishing ones: 17 down an avenue of beech trees and 18 along in front of the terrace. Superb views of the downs and the coast.
18 holes, 6434yds, Par 72, SSS 71.
Club membership 930.
Visitors telephone for details,
Societies Wed & Thu, telephone secretary in advance.
Green Fees £28 per day/round (£38 weekends).
Facilities ⊗ ⫾ ⶫ ⓛ ⬙ ♀ ⚥ ⛫ ⛿ Ⲓ Keith MacDonald.
Leisure trolley for hire, putting green, practice area.
Location 3m NE of Chichester off A27
Hotel ★★★ 70% Goodwood Park Hotel, Country Club Resort, GOODWOOD
☎ 01243 775537 88 ⇥ ⋔

HAYWARDS HEATH   Map 05 TQ32

Haywards Heath High Beech Ln RH16 1SL
☎ 01444 414457
Pleasant parkland course with several challenging par 4s and 3s.
18 holes, 6204yds, Par 71, SSS 70, Course record 68.
Club membership 770.
Visitors must have a handicap certificate. Must contact in advance.

Societies Wed & Thu only by prior arrangement with the secretary.
Green Fees £36 per 36 holes; £26 per 18 holes (£40/£35 weekends).
Facilities ⊗ ⫾ ⶫ ⓛ ⬙ ♀ ⚥ ⛫ Ⲓ Michael Henning.
Leisure trolley for hire, driving range, putting green, practice area.
Location 1.25m N off B2028
Hotel ★★★⚜ 76% Ockenden Manor, Ockenden Ln, CUCKFIELD ☎ 01444 416111 22 ⇥ ⋔

Paxhill Park East Mascalls Ln, Lindfield RH16 2QN
☎ 01444 484467
A relatively flat parkland course designed by Patrick Tallack.
18 holes, 6117yds, Par 70, SSS 69.
Club membership 375.
Visitors welcome but may not play weekend mornings.
Societies must contact in advance.
Green Fees £20 per day; £15 per round (£20 per round weekend & bank holidays).
Facilities ⊗ ⶫ ⓛ ⬙ ♀ ⚥ ⛫ ⛿ Ⲓ Steve Dunkerley.
Leisure trolley for hire, putting green, practice area.
Hotel ★★★ 60% The Birch Hotel, Lewes Rd, HAYWARDS HEATH
☎ 01444 451565 53 ⇥ ⋔

HORSHAM   Map 04 TQ13

See also Slinfold

Horsham Golf Park Worthing Rd RH13 7AX
☎ 01403 271525
A short but challenging course with six Par 4s and three Par 3s''s, two of which are played across water. Designed for beginners and intermediates but also challenges better players with a standard scratch of six below par.
9 holes, 4122yds, Par 33, SSS 30, Course record 55.
Club membership 250.
Visitors no restrictions but may not play until after 11am on Sat.
Societies apply in advance.
Green Fees £7 per 18 holes; £6 per 9 holes (£12/£10 weekends & bank holidays).
Facilities ⊗ ⶫ ⓛ ⬙ ♀ ⚥ ⛫ ⛿ Ⲓ Neil Burke.
Leisure gymnasium, trolley for hire, driving range, putting green.
Location Off A24 rdbt, between Horsham/Southwater, by garage on B2237
Hotel ★★ 67% Ye Olde King's Head Hotel, HORSHAM
☎ 01403 253126 42rm(41 ⇥ ⋔)

HURSTPIERPOINT

Map 04 TQ21

Singing Hills Albourne BN6 9EB
☎ 01273 835353
Three distinct nines (Lake, River & Valley) can be combined to make a truly varied game. Gently undulating fairways and spectacular waterholes make Singing Hills a test of accurate shotmaking. The opening 2 holes of the Rive Nine have long drives, while the second hole on the Lake course is an Island green where the tee is also protected by two bunkers.
Lake: 9 holes, 3253yds, Par 35.
River: 9 holes, 2826yds, Par 34.
Valley: 9 holes, 3348yds, Par 36.
Club membership 390.
Visitors no restrictions.
Societies apply in advance.
Green Fees £18 per 18 holes (£26 weekends & bank holidays).
Facilities ⊗ ␛ ⛳ ♨ ♀ ♨ ☗ ⚑ ⚐ Wallace Street.
Leisure trolley for hire, driving range, putting green.
Location On B2117
Hotel ★★★ 64% The Hickstead Hotel, Jobs Ln, Bolney, ☎ 01444 248023 50 ⇄ ⏪

LITTLEHAMPTON

Map 04 TQ00

Littlehampton Rope Walk, West Beach BN17 5DL
☎ 01903 717170
A delightful seaside links in an equally delightful setting - and the only links course in the area.
18 holes, 6244yds, Par 70, SSS 70, Course record 66.
Club membership 650.
Visitors must have handicap certificate.
Societies welcome weekdays.
Green Fees not confirmed.
Facilities ♀ ♨ ☗ ⚐ Guy McQuitty.
Leisure putting,cart/buggy/trolley hire.
Location 1m W off A259
Hotel ★★★ 77% Bailiffscourt Hotel, CLIMPING
☎ 01903 723511 10 ⇄ ⏪Annexe17 ⇄ ⏪

LOWER BEEDING

Map 04 TQ22

Brookfield Brookfield Farm Hotel, Plummers Plain RH13 6LU ☎ 01403 891568
This is an unusual golf course in that it has only 7 holes par 3 and 4. However, it has been especially designed as an executive course for beginners and those who find it difficult to play a full 18 holes. It is very popular.
6 holes, 3015yds, Par 57, SSS 53, Course record 53.
Club membership 200.
Visitors no restrictions.
Societies apply in writing or telephone.
Green Fees not confirmed.
Facilities ♀ ♨ ⚑ ⚐ Mike Denny.
Leisure fishing, sauna.
Farmhouse QQQ Brookfield Farm Hotel, Winterpit Ln, Plummers Plain, LOWER BEEDING
☎ 01403 891568 20 ⇄ ⏪
Additional hotel ★★★★♨♨ 76% South Lodge Hotel, Brighton Rd, LOWER BEEDING
☎ 01403 891711 39 ⇄

MANNINGS HEATH

Map 04 TQ22

Mannings Heath Fullers, Hammerpond Rd RH13 6PG
☎ 01403 210228
The course meanders up hill and down dale over heathland with streams affecting 11 of the holes. Wooded valleys protect the course from strong winds. Famous holes at 12th (the 'Waterfall', par 3), 13th (the 'Valley', par 4).
Waterfall: 18 holes, 6378yds, Par 71, SSS 70, Course record 66.
Kingfisher: 18 holes, 6305yds, Par 70, SSS 70.
Club membership 760.
Visitors may book up to 14 days in advance.
Societies must contact in advance.
Green Fees £40 per 36 holes; £30 per 18 holes (£55/£40 weekends and bank holidays).
Facilities ⊗ ␛ ⛳ ♨ ♀ ♨ ☗ ⚑ ⚐ Clive Tucker.
Leisure hard tennis courts, fishing, sauna, trolley for hire, covered driving range, putting green, practice area, indoor teaching facility.
Location N side of village
Hotel ★★★★♨♨ 76% South Lodge Hotel, Brighton Rd, LOWER BEEDING
☎ 01403 891711 39 ⇄

MIDHURST

Map 04 SU82

Cowdray Park Petworth Rd GU29 0BB ☎ 01730 813599
Parkland course, hard walking up to 4th green.
18 holes, 6212yds, Par 70, SSS 70, Course record 66.
Club membership 720.
▶

SOUTH LODGE HOTEL

South Lodge Hotel is a fine Victorian Country House set in 93 acres of secluded wooded parkland with views over the South Downs.
Delicious cuisine by Chef Timothy Neal, using local game and fish, with soft fruits and herbs from the hotel's own walled garden.
Superbly appointed bedrooms and suites each individually decorated in true country house style.
Enjoy tennis, croquet, petanque, putting, snooker or golf at our spectacular 18 hole Championship Course at Mannings Heath.
South Lodge is the perfect location for London and the South Coast and for many famous Gardens and National Trust Properties in the area.
For full information please contact:
SOUTH LODGE HOTEL,
Brighton Road, Lower Beeding,
near Horsham, West Sussex RH13 6PS.
Telephone: (01403) 891711 Fax: (01403) 891766

Visitors may play after 9.30am or 2pm. Must contact in advance.
Societies telephone in advance, mainly Wed & Thu available.
Green Fees £20 per day/round (£25 weekends & bank holidays).
Facilities ⊗ ⍶ ▮ ☕ ♀ ♨ 🖼 ⛴ ⛾ Simon Blanshard.
Leisure trolley for hire, putting green, practice area.
Location 1m E on A272
Hotel ★★★ 73% Spread Eagle Hotel, South St, MIDHURST
☎ 01730 816911 37 ⇆ ⛾Annexe4 ⛾

PULBOROUGH   Map 04 TQ01

West Sussex Golf Club Ln, Wiggonholt RH20 2EN
☎ 01798 872563
Heathland course.
18 holes, 6221yds, Par 68, SSS 70, Course record 61.
Club membership 850.
Visitors must contact in advance, may not play weekends.
Societies Wed & Thu only, apply in writing.
Green Fees £42 per 2 rounds; £31.50 per round weekdays.
Facilities ⊗ ▮ ☕ ♀ ♨ 🖼 ⛴ ⛾ Tim Packham.
Leisure trolley for hire, putting green, practice area.
Location 1.5m E off A283
Hotel ★★★ 71% Roundabout Hotel, Monkmead Ln, WEST CHILTINGTON
☎ 01798 813838 23 ⇆ ⛾

PYECOMBE   Map 04 TQ21

Pyecombe Clayton Hill BN45 7FF ☎ 01273 845372
Typical downland course on the inland side of the South Downs. Hilly, but magnificent views.
18 holes, 6278yds, Par 71, SSS 70, Course record 67.
Club membership 700.
Visitors must contact in advance and may only play after 9.15am weekdays and after 2.15pm weekends
Societies telephone secretary in advance.
Green Fees £25 per day; £20 per round (£30/£25 weekends).
Facilities ⊗ ⍶ ▮ ☕ ♀ ♨ 🖼 ⛾ C R White.
Leisure trolley for hire, driving range, putting.
Location E side of village on A273
Hotel ★★★ 64% Courtlands Hotel, 21-27 The Drive, HOVE
☎ 01273 731055 43 ⇆ ⛾Annexe12 ⇆ ⛾

SELSEY   Map 04 SZ89

Selsey Golf Links Ln PO20 9DR ☎ 01243 602203
Fairly difficult seaside course, exposed to wind and has natural ditches.
9 holes, 5834yds, Par 68, SSS 68, Course record 64.
Club membership 360.
Visitors must contact in advance.
Societies must contact in advance.
Green Fees £17 per day; £12 per 18 holes; £9 per 9 holes (£20/£15/£10 weekends & bank holidays). Weekly rate £50.
Facilities ⊗ ⍶ ▮ ☕ ♀ ♨ 🖼 ⛾ Peter Grindley.
Leisure hard tennis courts, trolley for hire, putting green, practice area.

Location 1m N off B2145
Hotel ★★★ 65% The Dolphin & Anchor, West St, CHICHESTER
☎ 01243 785121 49 ⇆ ⛾

SLINFOLD   Map 04 TQ13

Slinfold Park Golf & Country Club Stane St RH13 7RE
☎ 01403 791555
Opened for play in spring 1993, Slinfold course enjoys splendid views among mature trees. The 10th tee is spectacularly located on the centre of one of the two large landscaped lakes. The 166-yard 16th has water running in front of of the tee and everything sloping towards it!
Championship Course: 18 holes, 6407yds, Par 72, SSS 71, Course record 64.
Short Course: 9 holes, 1315yds, Par 28.
Club membership 611.
Visitors subject to booking.
Societies advance booking required, weekends and bank holidays not available.
Green Fees Championship: £30 per day; £20 per round (£35/25 weekends). Short Course £6.50 per 18 holes; £4 per round.
Facilities ⊗ by prior arrangement ⍶ by prior arrangement ▮ ☕ ♀ ♨ 🖼 ⛴ ⛾ G McKay.
Leisure trolley for hire, driving range, putting green.
Location 4m W on the A29
Hotel ★★★ 72% Random Hall Hotel, Stane St, Slinfold, HORSHAM
☎ 01403 790558 15 ⇆ ⛾

WEST CHILTINGTON   Map 04 TQ01

West Chiltington Broadford Bridge Rd RH20 2YA
☎ 01798 813574
The Main Course is situated on gently undulating, well-drained greensand and offers panoramic views of the Sussex Downs. Three large double greens provide an interesting feature to this new course. Also 9-hole short course and 13-bay driving range.
Windmill: 18 holes, 5888yds, Par 70, SSS 69, Course record 66 or 9 holes, 1360yds, Par 28.
Visitors book tee times in advance.
Societies by prior arrangement.
Green Fees £13 per round (£17.50 weekends, £20 before 11am Sun).
Facilities ⊗ ⍶ ▮ ☕ ♀ ♨ 🖼 ⛴ ⛾ Giles Downer.
Leisure motorised carts for hire, trolley for hire, driving range, putting green.
Location On N side of village
Hotel ★★★ 71% Roundabout Hotel, Monkmead Ln, WEST CHILTINGTON
☎ 01798 813838 23 ⇆ ⛾

WORTHING   Map 04 TQ10

Hill Barn Municipal Hill Barn Ln BN14 9QE
☎ 01903 237301
Downland course with views of both Isle of Wight and Brighton.
18 holes, 6224yds, Par 70, SSS 70.
Club membership 1000.
Visitors no restrictions.
Societies must telephone in advance.

Green Fees not confirmed.
Facilities 🏌⛳🏠⚑ A Higgins.
Leisure putting,practice,cart/buggy/trolley hire.
Location N side of town at junction of A24/A27
Hotel ★★★ 59% Chatsworth Hotel, Steyne,
WORTHING ☎ 01903 236103 107 ⇆ 🐾

Worthing Links Rd BN14 9QZ ☎ 01903 260801
The High Course, short and tricky with entrancing views,
will provide good entertainment. 'Lower Course' is
considered to be one of the best downland courses in the
country.
Lower Course: 18 holes, 6530yds, Par 71, SSS 72,
Course record 62.
Upper Course: 18 holes, 5243yds, Par 66, SSS 66.
Club membership 1200.
Visitors advisable to contact in advance. Only as
guest of member at weekends.
Societies contact in advance.
Green Fees £30 per day both courses; £25 per round
Lower Course, £20 per round Upper Course.
Facilities ⊗🏌🍺⛳🏠⚑ Stephen Rolley.
Leisure trolley for hire, driving range, putting green,
practice area.
Location N side of town centre off A27
Hotel ★★★ 66% Ardington Hotel, Steyne
Gardens, WORTHING
☎ 01903 230451 47rm(45 ⇆ 🐾)

TYNE & WEAR

BACKWORTH
Map 12 NZ37

Backworth The Hall NE27 0AH ☎ 0191 268 1048
Parkland course with easy walking, natural hazards and good
scenery.
9 holes, 5930yds, Par 71, SSS 69, Course record 64.
Club membership 480.
Visitors visitors may not play Tue (Ladies Day) &
weekend mornings.
Societies apply in writing to secretary.
Green Fees £16 per day; £12 per round (£16 per round
weekends & bank holidays).
Facilities ⊗🍺🍺
Leisure putting green, bowls.
Location W side of town on B1322
Hotel ★★★★ 58% Holiday Inn, Great North Rd,
SEATON BURN ☎ 0191 201 9988 150 ⇆ 🐾

BIRTLEY
Map 12 NZ25

Birtley Birtley Ln DH3 2LR ☎ 0191 410 2207
Parkland course.
9 holes, 5660yds, Par 66, SSS 67.
Club membership 270.
Visitors must play with member at weekends.
Societies apply in writing, must contact 1 month in
advance in summer.
Green Fees not confirmed.
Facilities 🏌⛳
Leisure putting green,practice area.

Hotel B Forte Posthouse Washington, Emerson
District 5, WASHINGTON
☎ 0191 416 2264 138 ⇆ 🐾

BOLDON
Map 12 NZ36

Boldon Dipe Ln, East Boldon NE36 0PQ
☎ 0191 536 5360 & 0191 536 4182
Parkland links course, easy walking, distant sea views, windy.
18 holes, 6362yds, Par 72, SSS 70, Course record 67.
Club membership 700.
Visitors may not play after 3.30pm at weekends & bank
holidays. Must contact in advance.
Societies must contact in advance.
Green Fees not confirmed.
Facilities 🏌⛳🏠⚑
Location S side of village off A184
Hotel ★★★ 67% Quality Friendly Hotel, Witney
Way, Boldon Business Park, BOLDON
☎ 0191 519 1999 82 ⇆ 🐾

CHOPWELL
Map 12 NZ15

Garesfield NE17 7AP ☎ 01207 561309
Undulating parkland course with good views and picturesque
woodland surroundings.
18 holes, 6603yds, Par 72, SSS 72, Course record 68.
Club membership 770.
Visitors weekends after 4.30pm only, unless with
member. Must contact in advance.
Societies must contact secretary in advance.
Green Fees not confirmed.
Facilities ⊗🏌🍺⛳🏠⚑ David Race.
Leisure trolley for hire, putting green, practice area.
Location 0.5m N
Hotel ★★★ 64% Swallow Hotel, Newgate St,
NEWCASTLE UPON TYNE
☎ 0191 232 5025 93 ⇆ 🐾

FELLING
Map 12 NZ26

Heworth Gingling Gate, Heworth NE10 8XY
☎ 01632 692137
Fairly flat, parkland course.
18 holes, 6437yds, Par 71, SSS 71.
Club membership 500.
Visitors may not play Sat & before 10am Sun, Apr-Sep.
Societies must apply in writing.
Green Fees not confirmed.
Facilities 🏌⛳
Leisure practice area.
Location On A195, 0.5m NW of junc with A1(M)
Hotel B Forte Posthouse Washington, Emerson
District 5, WASHINGTON
☎ 0191 416 2264 138 ⇆ 🐾

GATESHEAD
Map 12 NZ26

Ravensworth Moss Heaps, Wrekenton NE9 7UU
☎ 0191 487 2843
Moorland/parkland course 600 ft above sea-level with fine
views. Testing 13th hole (par 3).
18 holes, 5872yds, Par 68, SSS 68.
Club membership 600.
▶

Visitors apply in advance.
Societies apply in writing to secretary.
Green Fees not confirmed.
Facilities ⊗ by prior arrangement Ⅺ by prior arrangement ⅃ 🍴 🏌 🏠 ⌷ Shaun Cowell.
Leisure trolley for hire, putting green, practice area.
Location 3m SE off A6127
Hotel ★★★ 66% Swallow Hotel, High West St, GATESHEAD ☎ 0191 477 1105 103 ⇆ 🏴

GOSFORTH   Map 12 NZ26

Gosforth Broadway East NE3 5ER ☎ 0191 285 3495
Parkland course with natural water hazards, easy walking.
18 holes, 6024yds, Par 69, SSS 68.
Club membership 500.
Visitors must contact in advance. Restricted play on competition days.
Societies telephone in advance.
Green Fees £20 per day.
Facilities ⊗ Ⅺ ⅃ 🍴 🏌 🏠 ⌷ G Garland.
Leisure trolley for hire.
Location N side of town centre off A6125
Hotel ★★★★ 69% Swallow Gosforth Park Hotel, High Gosforth Park, Gosforth, NEWCASTLE UPON TYNE ☎ 0191 236 4111 178 ⇆ 🏴

Parklands Gosforth Park Golfing Complex, High Gosforth Park NE3 5HQ ☎ 0191 236 4867 & 0191 236 4480
Parklands course is set in pleasant parkland with challenging shots around and sometimes over attractive water hazards. The first 9 holes are easier but the second 9 test even the most experienced golfer.
18 holes, 6060yds, Par 71, SSS 69, Course record 66.
Club membership 750.
Visitors a daily start sheet operates with bookings taken from 4.30pm the previous day during weekdays, and from 8am Fri & Sat for weekends.
Societies by prior arrangement with club secretary.
Green Fees not confirmed.
Facilities 🏌 🏠 ⌷ Brian Rumney.
Leisure 45bay driving range,putting,trolley hire.
Location 3m N, at the end A1 Western by Pass
Hotel ★★★★ 69% Swallow Gosforth Park Hotel, High Gosforth Park, Gosforth, NEWCASTLE UPON TYNE ☎ 0191 236 4111 178 ⇆ 🏴

HOUGHTON-LE-SPRING   Map 12 NZ35

Elemore Elemore Ln, Hetton-le-hole DH5 0QB ☎ 0191 526 9020
A new course.
18 holes, 6000yds, Par 72.
Club membership 600.
Visitors no restrictions.
Societies apply in writing, telephone enquiries welcome.
Green Fees not confirmed.
Facilities 🏌 🏠 ⌷
Leisure practice area,putting green,trolley hire.
Location 3m S
Hotel ★★ 58% Chilton Lodge Country Pub & Motel, Black Boy Rd, Chilton Moor, Fencehouses, HOUGHTON-LE-SPRING ☎ 0191 385 2694 18 ⇆ 🏴

Houghton-le-Spring Copt Hill DH5 8LU ☎ 0191 584 1198 & 584 0048
Hilly, downland course with natural slope hazards.
18 holes, 6443yds, Par 72, SSS 71, Course record 64.
Club membership 600.
Visitors may not play on Sun until 4pm.
Societies must contact secretary in advance.
Green Fees £25 per day; £18 per round (£30/£25 weekends).
Facilities ⊗ Ⅺ ⅃ 🍴 🏌 🏠 ⌷ Kevin Gow.
Leisure putting green, practice area.
Location 0.5m E on B1404
Hotel ★★ 58% Chilton Lodge Country Pub & Motel, Black Boy Rd, Chilton Moor, Fencehouses, HOUGHTON-LE-SPRING ☎ 0191 385 2694 18 ⇆ 🏴

NEWCASTLE UPON TYNE   Map 12 NZ26

City of Newcastle Three Mile Bridge NE3 2DR ☎ 0191 285 1775
A well-manicured parkland course in the Newcastle suburbs, subject to wind.
18 holes, 6508yds, Par 72, SSS 71, Course record 64.
Club membership 460.
Visitors no restrictions but advisable to telephone first.
Societies telephone in advance
Green Fees £20 per day (£25 weekends & bank holidays).
Facilities ⊗ Ⅺ ⅃ 🍴 🏌 🏠 ⌷ Anthony Matthew.
Leisure trolley for hire, putting green, practice area.
Location 3m N on A1
Hotel ★★★ 64% Newcastle Airport Moat House, Woolsington, NEWCASTLE UPON TYNE AIRPORT ☎ 0191 401 9988 100 ⇆ 🏴

Newcastle United Ponteland Rd, Cowgate NE5 3JW ☎ 0191 286 4693
Moorland course with natural hazards.
18 holes, 6484yds, Par 72, SSS 71, Course record 68.
Club membership 500.
Visitors must play with member at weekends.
Societies must contact in writing.
Green Fees not confirmed.
Facilities 🏌 🏠 🏠
Location 1.25m NW of city centre off A6127
Hotel ★★★ 68% Imperial Swallow Hotel, Jesmond Rd, NEWCASTLE UPON TYNE ☎ 0191 281 5511 122 ⇆ 🏴

Northumberland High Gosforth Park NE3 5HT ☎ 0191 236 2498
Many golf courses have been sited inside racecourses, although not so many survive today. One which does is the Northumberland Club's course at High Gosforth Park. Naturally the course is flat but there are plenty of mounds and other hazards to make it a fine test of golf. It should be said that not all the holes are within the confines of the racecourse, but both inside and out there are some good holes. This is a Championship course.
18 holes, 6629yds, Par 72, SSS 72, Course record 65.
Club membership 580.
Visitors may not play at weekends or competition days. Must contact in advance.
Societies must apply in writing.
Green Fees £35 per day; £30 per round.
Facilities ⊗ Ⅺ ⅃ 🍴 🏌 🏠

Leisure	trolley for hire, putting green, practice area.
Location	4m N of city centre off A1
Hotel	★★★★ 69% Swallow Gosforth Park Hotel, High Gosforth Park, Gosforth, NEWCASTLE UPON TYNE ☎ 0191 236 4111 178 ⇄ ঙ

Westerhope Whorlton Grange, Westerhope NE5 1PP
☎ 0191 286 7636
Attractive parkland course with tree-lined fairways, and easy walking. Good open views towards the airport.
18 holes, 6444yds, Par 72, SSS 71, Course record 64.
Club membership 778.

Visitors   with member only at weekends. Must contact in advance.
Societies   must contact Secretary in advance.
Green Fees £22 per day; £16 per round.
Facilities   ⊗ ⅏ ┗ ☰ ♀ ♨ 🖢 ╏ Nigel Brown.
Leisure   motorised carts for hire, buggies for hire, trolley for hire, putting green, practice area, pool table.
Location   4.5m NW of city centre off B6324
Hotel   ★★★★ 69% Swallow Gosforth Park Hotel, High Gosforth Park, Gosforth, NEWCASTLE UPON TYNE ☎ 0191 236 4111 178 ⇄ ঙ

RYTON   Map 12 NZ16

Ryton Clara Vale NE40 3TD ☎ 0191 413 3737
Parkland course.
18 holes, 6042yds, Par 70, SSS 69, Course record 68.
Club membership 600.
Visitors   with member only at weekends.
Societies   apply in advance.
Green Fees £20 per day; £15 per round.
Facilities   ⊗ ⅏ ┗ ☰ ♀ ♨
Leisure   putting green, practice area.
Location   NW side of town off A695
Hotel   ★★★ 70% Gibside Arms Hotel, Front St, WHICKHAM ☎ 0191 488 9292 45 ⇄ ঙ

Tyneside Westfield Ln NE40 3QE ☎ 0191 413 2742
Open parkland course, not heavily bunkered. Water hazard, hilly, practice area.
18 holes, 6042yds, Par 70, SSS 69, Course record 65.
Club membership 900.
Visitors   must contact in advance to play at weekends.
Societies   must apply in advance.
Green Fees £25 per day; £20 per round (£30 per round weekends).
Facilities   ⊗ ⅏ ┗ ☰ ♀ ♨ 🖢 ╏ Malcolm Gunn.
Leisure   trolley for hire, putting green, practice area.
Location   NW side of town off A695
Hotel   ★★★ 70% Gibside Arms Hotel, Front St, WHICKHAM ☎ 0191 488 9292 45 ⇄ ঙ

SOUTH SHIELDS   Map 12 NZ36

South Shields Cleadon Hills NE34 8EG ☎ 0191 456 8942
A slightly undulating downland course on a limestone base ensuring good conditions underfoot. Open to strong winds, the course is testing but fair. There are fine views of the coastline.
18 holes, 6264yds, Par 71, SSS 70, Course record 64.
Club membership 800.

Visitors   must contact in advance.
Societies   by arrangement.
Green Fees £20 per day (£25 weekends & bank holidays).
Facilities   ⊗ ⅏ ┗ ☰ ♀ ♨ 🖢 ╏ Gary Parsons.
Leisure   trolley for hire, putting green, practice area.
Location   SE side of town centre off A1300
Hotel   ★★★ 61% Sea Hotel, Sea Rd, SOUTH SHIELDS ☎ 0191 427 0999 33 ⇄ ঙ

Whitburn Lizard Ln NE34 7AF
☎ 0191 529 4944 & 0191 529 2144
Parkland course.
18 holes, 5780yds, Par 69, SSS 68, Course record 66.
Club membership 650.
Visitors   restricted weekends. Contact professional in advance.
Societies   must apply in writing to secretary
Green Fees £17.50 per day (£22.50 weekends & bank holidays).
Facilities   ⊗ ⅏ ┗ ☰ ♀ ♨ 🖢 ╏ David Stephenson.
Leisure   trolley for hire, putting green, practice area, snooker table.
Location   2.5m SE off A183
Hotel   ★★★★ 60% Swallow Hotel, Queen's Pde, Seaburn, SUNDERLAND ☎ 0191 529 2041 65 ⇄ ঙ

SUNDERLAND   Map 12 NZ35

Ryhope Leechmore Way, Ryhope SR2 ODH
☎ 0191 523 7333
A municipal course recently extended to 18 holes.
18 holes, 4601yds, Par 65, SSS 63.
Club membership 350.
Visitors   no restrictions.
Societies   apply in writing, telephone enquiries welcome.
Green Fees not confirmed.
Facilities   ♀ ♨ 🖢 ⍟
Leisure   trolley hire.
Location   3.5m S of city centre
Hotel   ★★★★ 60% Swallow Hotel, Queen's Pde, Seaburn, SUNDERLAND ☎ 0191 529 2041 65 ⇄ ঙ

Wearside Coxgreen SR4 9JT ☎ 0191 534 2518
Open, undulating parkland course rolling down to the River Wear and beneath the shadow of the famous Penshaw Monument. Built on the lines of an Athenian temple it is a well-known landmark. Two ravines cross the course presenting a variety of challenging holes.
18 holes, 6373yds, Par 71, SSS 74.
Club membership 729.
Visitors   may not play before 9.30am & after 4pm.
Societies   must apply in writing.
Green Fees not confirmed.
Facilities   ♀ ♨ 🖢 ╏ Doug Brolls.
Leisure   putting,trolley hire,practice area.
Location   3.5m W off A183
Hotel   ★★★★ 60% Swallow Hotel, Queen's Pde, Seaburn, SUNDERLAND ☎ 0191 529 2041 65 ⇄ ঙ

TYNEMOUTH

Map 12 NZ36

Tynemouth Spital Dene NE30 2ER ☎ 0191 257 4578
Well-drained parkland/downland course, easy walking.
18 holes, 6082yds, Par 70, SSS 69.
Club membership 824.

Visitors	must play with member weekends & bank holidays.
Societies	must contact in writing.
Green Fees	not confirmed.
Facilities	♀⚐⚑ J P McKenna.
Leisure	putting,buggy/trolley hire,practice area.
Location	0.5m W
Hotel	★★★ 61% Park Hotel, Grand Pde, TYNEMOUTH ☎ 0191 257 1406 49rm(43 ⇔ ♞)

WALLSEND

Map 12 NZ26

Wallsend Rheydt Av, Bigges Main NE28 8SU
☎ 0191 262 1973
Parkland course.
18 holes, 6608yds, Par 72, SSS 72, Course record 68.
Club membership 750.

Visitors	may not play before 12.30pm weekends.
Societies	must apply in writing.
Green Fees	not confirmed.
Facilities	♀⚐⚑ Ken Phillips.
Leisure	putting green,trolley hire,driving range.
Location	NW side of town centre off A193
Hotel	★★★ 61% Europa Hotel, Coast Rd, WALLSEND ☎ 0191 202 9955 147 ⇔ ♞

WASHINGTON

Map 12 NZ25

Washington Moat House Stone Cellar Rd, High Usworth
NE37 1PH ☎ 0191 402 9988
Championship-standard course. Also a 9-hole (par 3) course,
putting green and 21-bay floodlit driving range. 'Bunkers
Bar' at the 10th tee is one of the few 'spike' bars in the
country.
18 holes, 6267yds, Par 73, SSS 71.
Club membership 700.

Visitors	must contact in advance. May not play before 10am or between noon & 2pm at weekends.
Societies	book in advance.
Green Fees	£17 per round (£25 weekends).
Facilities	⊗ �🁢 ⚐ 🛒 ♀⚑ 🏌 Warren Marshall.
Leisure	heated indoor swimming pool, squash, sauna, solarium, gymnasium, trolley for hire, floodlit driving range, putting green, practice area.
Hotel	★★★ 67% Washington Moat House, Stone Cellar Rd, District 12, High Usworth, WASHINGTON ☎ 0191 402 9988 105 ⇔ ♞

WHICKHAM

Map 12 NZ26

Whickham Hollinside Park, Fellside Rd NE16 5BA
☎ 0191 488 1576
Parkland course, some uphill walking, fine views.
18 holes, 5878yds, Par 68, SSS 68, Course record 61.
Club membership 630.

Visitors	must contact in advance. Must have an introduction from own club.
Societies	by arrangement.
Green Fees	£20 per day/round (£25 weekends & bank holidays).
Facilities	⊗ �🁢 ⚐ 🛒 ♀⚑ 🏌 Brian Ridley.
Leisure	trolley for hire, putting green, practice area.
Location	1.5m S
Hotel	★★★ 66% Swallow Hotel, High West St, GATESHEAD ☎ 0191 477 1105 103 ⇔ ♞

WHITLEY BAY

Map 12 NZ37

Whitley Bay Claremont Rd NE26 3UF
☎ 0191 252 0180 & 252 5568
Downland course close to the sea. A stream runs through the
undulating terrain.
18 holes, 6600yds, Par 72, SSS 71, Course record 66.
Club membership 800.

Visitors	apply in advance for occasional Sun play.
Societies	telephone initially.
Green Fees	£25 per day; £20 per round (£30 Sun).
Facilities	⊗ �🁢 ⚐ 🛒 ♀⚑ Gary Shipley.
Leisure	trolley for hire, putting green, practice area.
Location	NW side of town centre off A1148
Hotel	★★ 61% Holmedale Hotel, 106 Park Av, WHITLEY BAY ☎ 0191 251 3903 & 0191 253 1162 18 ⇔ ♞

WARWICKSHIRE

ATHERSTONE

Map 04 SP39

Atherstone The Outwoods, Coleshill Rd CV9 2RL
☎ 01827 713110
Parkland course, established in 1894 and laid out on hilly
ground.
18 holes, 6006yds, Par 72, SSS 69.
Club membership 480.

Visitors	handicap certificate required. With member only weekends and bank holidays. Also with holder of handicap certificate by permission of Club Secretary.
Societies	contact in advance.
Green Fees	£17 per day/round.
Facilities	⊗ �🁢 ⚐ 🛒 ♀⚑
Leisure	putting green.
Location	0.5m S on B4116
Hotel	★★ 73% Chapel House Hotel, Friar's Gate, ATHERSTONE ☎ 01827 718949 12 ⇔ ♞

BIDFORD-ON-AVON

Map 04 SP15

Bidford Grange Stratford Rd B50 4LY ☎ 01789 490319
Designed by Howard Swan & Paul Tillman, this very long,
championship standard course is built to represent a links
course and is fully irrigated. There are water hazards on the
first 7 holes, and particularly challenging holes on the 16th
(223yds,par 3), 8th (600yds, par 5) and an uphill par 4 at the
13th.
18 holes, 7233yds, Par 72, SSS 74.
Club membership 500.

Visitors	no restrictions.

Societies	apply in writing or phone, minimum 12, maximum 36.
Green Fees	not confirmed.
Facilities	♀ ⚲ 🖿
Leisure	fishing.
Location	4m W of Stratford upon Avon, B439
Hotel	★★★ 76% Salford Hall Hotel, ABBOT'S SALFORD
	☎ 01386 871300 14 ⇆ 🐾Annexe19 ⇆ 🐾

BRANDON   Map 04 SP47

City of Coventry-Brandon Wood Brandon Ln, Wolston CV8 3GQ ☎ 01203 543141
Municipal parkland course surrounded by fields and bounded by River Avon on east side. Floodlit driving range.
18 holes, 6610yds, Par 72, SSS 72, Course record 68.
Club membership 580.

Visitors	telephone for details.
Societies	telephone secretary for details
Green Fees	£8.70 per round (£11.60 weekends).
Facilities	⊗ ∭ ⓛ ⚑ ♀ ⚲ 🖿 ⚷ 𝄢 Chris Gledhill.
Leisure	buggies for hire, trolley for hire, driving range, putting green, practice area.
Location	Off A45 southbound
Hotel	★★★ 64% The Brandon Hall, Main St, BRANDON ☎ 01203 542571 60 ⇆ 🐾

COLESHILL   Map 04 SP28

Maxstoke Park Castle Ln B46 2RD ☎ 01675 466743
Parkland course with easy walking. Numerous trees and a lake form natural hazards.
18 holes, 6442yds, Par 71, SSS 71.
Club membership 720.

Visitors	with member only at weekends & bank holidays.
Societies	contact in advance.
Green Fees	£25 per round.
Facilities	⊗ ∭ ⓛ ⚑ ♀ ⚲ 🖿 ⚷ 𝄢 Neil McEwan.
Leisure	trolley for hire, putting green, practice area.
Location	2m E
Hotel	★★ 66% Coleshill Hotel, 152 High St, COLESHILL
	☎ 01675 465527 15 ⇆ 🐾Annexe8 ⇆ 🐾

KENILWORTH   Map 04 SP27

Kenilworth Crewe Ln CV8 2EA ☎ 01926 858517
Parkland course in open hilly situation. Club founded in 1887.
18 holes, 6413yds, Par 73, SSS 71, Course record 62.
Club membership 725.

Visitors	must contact in advance.
Societies	apply in writing.

Green Fees	£26 per day/round (£37 weekends).
Facilities	⊗ ∭ by prior arrangement ⓛ ⚑ ♀ ⚲ 🖿 ⚷ 𝄢 Steven Yates.
Leisure	motorised carts for hire, trolley for hire, putting green, practice area, par 3 course.
Location	0.5m NE
Hotel	★★ 64% Clarendon House Hotel, Old High St, KENILWORTH
	☎ 01926 57668 Cen. Res. 0800 616883 30 ⇆ 🐾

LEA MARSTON   Map 04 SP29

Lea Marston Hotel & Leisure Complex Haunch Ln B76 0BY ☎ 01675 470468
Par 3, 'pay-and-play' course, with water hazards, out of bounds, and large bunkers. The venue for the past two years of the Midlands Professional Par 3 Competition. Golf driving range.
9 holes, 783yds, Par 27, SSS 27, Course record 46.

Visitors	no restrictions.
Societies	must telephone in advance.
Green Fees	not confirmed.
Facilities	♀ 🖿 ⚷ 𝄢 Andrew Stokes.
Leisure	hard tennis courts, heated indoor swimming pool, sauna, solarium, gymnasium, driving range,putting green.
Hotel	★★★ 69% Lea Marston Hotel & Leisure Complex, Haunch Ln, LEA MARSTON
	☎ 01675 470468 49 ⇆ 🐾

LEAMINGTON SPA   Map 04 SP36

Leamington & County Golf Ln, Whitnash CV31 2QA ☎ 01926 425961
Undulating parkland course with extensive views.
18 holes, 6488yds, Par 71, SSS 71, Course record 65.
Club membership 802.

Visitors	must contact in advance.
Societies	telephone in advance.
Green Fees	£30 per day; £25 per round (£40 per round weekends & bank holidays).
Facilities	⊗ ∭ ⓛ ⚑ ♀ ⚲ 🖿 𝄢 Iain Grant.
Leisure	buggies for hire, trolley for hire, putting green, practice area, snooker.
Location	S side of town centre
Hotel	★★★ 61% Manor House Hotel, Avenue Rd, LEAMINGTON SPA ☎ 01926 423251 53 ⇆ 🐾

Newbold Comyn Newbold Ter East CV32 4EW ☎ 01926 421157
Municipal parkland course with hilly front nine. The par 4, 9th is a 467-yd testing hole.
18 holes, 6315yds, Par 70, SSS 70, Course record 69.
Club membership 420. ▶

Visitors   no restrictions.
Societies   apply to professional.
Green Fees not confirmed.
Facilities   ⛿ 🏠 ⛴ 𝄢 Don Knight.
Leisure   heated indoor swimming pool, gymnasium.
Location   0.75m E of town centre off B4099
Hotel   ★★★ 61% Manor House Hotel, Avenue Rd,
              LEAMINGTON SPA
              ☎ 01926 423251 53 ⇆ ↸

LEEK WOOTTON   Map 04 SP26

The Warwickshire CV35 7QT ☎ 01926 409409
Opened in 1993, this is an unusual championship standard
course. Designed by Karl Litten, the 36 holes are laid out as
four interchangeable loops of 9 holes to create six contrasting
yet superb courses in a parkland and woodland setting.
South East Course: 18 holes, 7000yds, Par 72, SSS 72,
Course record 68.
North West Course: 18 holes, 7000yds, Par 72, SSS 72.
Par 3: 9 holes, 1133yds, Par 27, SSS 27.
Club membership 1100.
Visitors   can book up to 7 days in advance.
Societies   apply to sales office for details.
Green Fees £40 per round.
Facilities   ⊗ �🍺 🍴 🗡 ♀ ⛿ 🏠 ⛴ 𝄢 John Cook.
Leisure   motorised carts for hire, buggies for hire, trolley
              for hire, floodlit driving range, putting, practice
              area.
Location   On B4115
Hotel   ★★ 56% Warwick Arms Hotel, 17 High St,
              WARWICK ☎ 01926 492759 35 ⇆ ↸

NUNEATON   Map 04 SP39

Nuneaton Golf Dr, Whitestone CV11 6QF
☎ 01203 347810
Undulating moorland and woodland course.
18 holes, 6429yds, Par 71, SSS 71.
Club membership 675.
Visitors   with member only at weekends.
Societies   apply in writing.
Green Fees not confirmed.
Facilities   ⛿ 🏠 𝄢 Graham Davison.
Location   2m SE off B4114
Hotel   ★★ 67% Longshoot Toby Hotel, Watling St,
              NUNEATON
              ☎ 01203 329711 Annexe47 ⇆ ↸

Oakridge Arley Ln, Ansley Village CV10 9PH
☎ 01676 541389 & 540542
There are a number of water hazards on the back nine which
add to the natural beauty of the countryside. The undulating
course is affected by winter cross winds on several holes.
Overall it will certainly test golfing skills.
18 holes, 6242yds, Par 71, SSS 70.
Club membership 450.
Visitors   contact in advance, with members only at
              weekends.
Societies   apply in writing or telephone in advance.
Green Fees £25 per 36 holes: £15 per round.
Facilities   ⊗ ⍗ 🍺 🍴 ♀ ⛿ 🏠 ⛴ 𝄢 Ian Sadler.
Leisure   buggies for hire, trolley for hire, putting green,
              practice area, snooker, games room.
Location   4m W

Hotel   ★★★ 64% Weston Hall, Weston Ln, Weston in
              Arden, Bulkington, NUNEATON
              ☎ 01203 312989 36 ⇆ ↸

Purley Chase Pipers Ln, Ridge Ln CV10 0RB
☎ 01203 393118
Meadowland course with tricky water hazards on eight holes
and undulating greens. 13-bay driving range.
18 holes, 6772yds, Par 72, SSS 72, Course record 67.
Club membership 650.
Visitors   welcome except before noon weekends.
Societies   Telephone for provisional booking.
Green Fees £13 per round (£20 weekends & bank holidays).
Facilities   ⊗ ⍗ 🍺 🍴 ♀ ⛿ 🏠 ⛴ 𝄢 Roy Young.
Leisure   fishing, motorised carts for hire, trolley for hire,
              driving range, putting green.
Location   2m NW off B4114
Hotel   ★★ 67% Longshoot Toby Hotel, Watling St,
              NUNEATON
              ☎ 01203 329711 Annexe47 ⇆ ↸

RUGBY   Map 04 SP57

Rugby Clifton Rd CV21 3RD ☎ 01788 542306
Parkland course with brook running through the middle and
crossed by a viaduct.
18 holes, 5457yds, Par 68, SSS 67, Course record 62.
Club membership 550.
Visitors   weekends & bank holidays with member only.
Societies   apply in writing.
Green Fees not confirmed.
Facilities   ♀ ⛿ 🏠 ⛴ 𝄢 Andy Peach.
Leisure   caddy carts for hire.
Location   1m NE on B5414
Hotel   ★★★ 60% Grosvenor Hotel, Clifton Rd,
              RUGBY ☎ 01788 535686 21 ⇆ ↸

Whitefields Hotel & Golf Complex Coventry Rd,
Thurlaston CV23 9JR ☎ 01788 522393 & 521800
Whitefields has superb drainage and has never had to close.
There are four water features and the 12th has a stunning
dogleg 442yard Par 4 with a superb view across Draycote
Water. The 16th is completely surrounded by water and is
particularly difficult.
18 holes, 6433yds, Par 71, SSS 71, Course record 69.
Club membership 550.
Visitors   advisable to book unless hotel guest.
Societies   contact secretary in advance.
Green Fees £18 (£22 weekends & bank holidays).
Facilities   ⊗ ⍗ 🍺 🍴 ♀ ⛿ 🏠 ⛴ 𝄢
Leisure   motorised carts for hire, buggies for hire, trolley
              for hire, putting green, planned driving range.
Location   A45 Coventry road

STONELEIGH   Map 04 SP37

Stoneleigh The Old Deer Park, Coventry Rd CV8 3DR
☎ 01203 639991
Parkland course in old deer park with many mature trees. The
River Avon meanders through the course and comes into play
on 4 holes. Also 9-hole course.
Tantara Course: 18 holes, 6083yds, Par 71, SSS 69.
Avon Course: 9 holes, 1251yds, Par 27.
Club membership 750.

Visitors must contact in advance, no visitors at weekends except by prior arrangement.
Societies by prior arrangement.
Green Fees not confirmed.
Facilities ♀ ⛳ 🏠 ⓕ Sid Mouland.
Leisure practice area,cart/buggy/trolley hire.
Location 3m NE of Kenilworth
Hotel ★★★ 64% De Montfort Hotel, The Square, KENILWORTH ☎ 01926 55944 96 ⇄ ⓡ

STRATFORD-UPON-AVON Map 04 SP25

Stratford Oaks Bearley Rd, Snitterfield CV37 0EZ
☎ 01789 731571
American styled, parkland course designed by Howard Swan.
18 holes, 6100yds, Par 71, SSS 69, Course record 66.
Club membership 600.
Visitors no restrictions.
Societies telephone in advance.
Green Fees not confirmed.
Facilities ♀ ⛳ 🏠 ⓕ ⓕ Fraser Leek.
Location 4m N of Stratford-upon-Avon
Hotel ★★★ 74% Stratford Manor, Warwick Rd, STRATFORD-UPON-AVON ☎ 01789 731173 104 ⇄ ⓡ

Stratford-upon-Avon Tiddington Rd CV37 7BA
☎ 01789 205749
Beautiful parkland course. The par 3, 16th is tricky and the par 5, 17th and 18th, provide a tough end.

18 holes, 6309yds, Par 72, SSS 70, Course record 64.
Club membership 750.
Visitors restricted on Wed. Must contact in advance.
Societies must telephone in advance.
Green Fees not confirmed.
Facilities ♀ ⛳ 🏠 ⓕ ⓕ N D Powell.
Location 0.75m E on B4086
Hotel ★★★★ 65% Alveston Manor Hotel, Clopton Bridge, STRATFORD-UPON-AVON ☎ 01789 204581 106 ⇄ ⓡ

Welcombe Hotel Warwick Rd CV37 0NR
☎ 01789 295252
Wooded parkland course of great character and boasting superb views of the River Avon, Stratford and the Cotswolds. Set within the hotel's 157-acre estate, it has two lakes and water features.
18 holes, 6217yds, Par 70, SSS 68, Course record 65.
Club membership 400.
Visitors must contact in advance.
Societies booking via Hotel.
Green Fees £35 per day; £30 per round (£45/£40 weekends & bank holidays).
Facilities ⊗ 🥋 🍴 ♀ ⛳ 🏠 ⓕ 🏌
Leisure hard tennis courts, fishing, motorised carts for hire, buggies for hire, trolley for hire, driving range, putting green, practice area.
Location 1.5m NE off A46
Hotel ★★★★ 72% Welcombe Hotel and Golf Course, Warwick Rd, STRATFORD-UPON-AVON ☎ 01789 295252 76 ⇄ ⓡ

TANWORTH-IN-ARDEN   Map 04 SP17

Ladbrook Park Poolhead Ln B94 5ED
☎ 01564 742264
Parkland course lined with trees.
18 holes, 6427yds, Par 71, SSS 71, Course record 65.
Club membership 700.
Visitors   with member only weekends. Must contact in
              advance & have handicap certificate.
Societies   apply in advance.
Green Fees   Winter: £20 per day/round. Summer: £35 per
              days, £30 per 27 holes, £25 per round.
Facilities   ⊗ ⅊ ⅃ ⅃ ⅃ ⅃ 𝒓 Richard Mountford.
Leisure   trolley for hire, putting green, practice area.
Location   2.5m SE of M42 junct 3
Hotel   ★★★(red)⇞ Nuthurst Grange Country House
              Hotel, Nuthurst Grange Ln, HOCKLEY
              HEATH
              ☎ 01564 783972 15 ⇨ 𝒓

UPPER BRAILES   Map 04 SP32

Brailes Sutton Ln, Lower Brailes OX15 5BB
☎ 01608 685336 & 685633
Undulating meadowland on 130 acres of Cotswold
countryside. Sutton brook passes through the course and is
crossed 5 times.The Par 5 17th offers the most spectacular
view of three counties from the tee. There is a prevailing
cross wind.
18 holes, 6270yds, Par 71, SSS 70, Course record 73.
Club membership 420.
Visitors   advance telephone advisable.
Societies   telephone or write for information to the
              secretary.
Green Fees   £24 per 27/36 holes; £16 per 18 holes (£33/£22
              weekends & bank holidays) Twilight £10 (£13).
Facilities   ⊗ ⅊ ⅃ ⅃ ⅃ ⅃ 𝒓 Mike Bendall.
Leisure   trolley for hire, putting green, practice area.
Location   4m E of Shipston-on-Stour, on B4035
Hotel   ★★ 63% The Red Lion Hotel, Main St, Long
              Compton, SHIPSTON ON STOUR
              ☎ 01608 684221 5 ⇨ 𝒓

WARWICK   Map 04 SP26

Warwick The Racecourse CV34 6HW
☎ 01926 494316
Parkland course with easy walking. Driving range with
floodlit bays.
9 holes, 2682yds, Par 34, SSS 66, Course record 67.
Club membership 150.
Visitors   must contact in advance. May not play Sun
              before 12.30pm
Societies   contact in advance.
Green Fees   £4 per 9 holes (£5 weekends).
Facilities   ⅃ ⅃ ⅃ ⅃ 𝒓 Phil Sharp.
Leisure   trolley for hire, driving range.
Location   W side of town centre
Hotel   ★★ 56% Warwick Arms Hotel, 17 High St,
              WARWICK
              ☎ 01926 492759 35 ⇨ 𝒓

WEST MIDLANDS

ALDRIDGE   Map 07 SK00

Druids Heath Stonnall Rd WS9 8JZ
☎ 01922 55595 (Office) & 59523 (Pro)
Testing, undulating heathland course.
18 holes, 6659yds, Par 72, SSS 73.
Club membership 590.
Visitors   contact in advance recommended. Weekend play
              permitted after 2pm.
Societies   phone initially.
Green Fees   £25 per day (£32 weekends).
Facilities   ⊗ ⅊ ⅃ ⅃ ⅃ ⅃ 𝒓 Simon Elliott.
Leisure   trolley for hire, putting, practice area.
Location   NE side of town centre off A454
Hotel   ★★★ 70% The Fairlawns at Aldridge, 178
              Little Aston Rd, Aldridge, WALSALL
              ☎ 01922 55122 35 ⇨ 𝒓

BIRMINGHAM   Map 07 SP08

Brandhall Heron Rd, Oldbury, Warley B68 8AQ
☎ 0121 552 2195
Private golf club on municipal parkland course, easy walking,
good hazards. Testing holes: 1st-502 yds (par 5); 10th-455
yds dog-leg (par 5).
18 holes, 5734yds, Par 70, Course record 66.
Club membership 250.
Visitors   restricted weekends.
Societies   by arrangement.
Green Fees   not confirmed.
Facilities   ⅃ ⅃ 𝒓
Leisure   practice area.
Location   5.5m W of city centre off A4123
Hotel   B Forte Posthouse Birmingham Great Barr,
              Chapel Ln, GREAT BARR
              ☎ 0121 357 7444 192 ⇨ 𝒓

Cocks Moors Woods Municipal Alcester Rd South, Kings
Heath B14 4ER ☎ 0121 444 3584
Tree-lined, parkland course.
18 holes, 5888yds, Par 69, SSS 68.
Club membership 250.
Visitors   no restrictions.
Societies   must contact in advance.
Green Fees   not confirmed.
Facilities   ⅃ ⅃ ⅃ 𝒓
Leisure   heated indoor swimming pool, solarium,
              gymnasium, putting green,trolley hire.
Location   5m S of city centre on A435
Hotel   B Forte Posthouse Birmingham City,
              Smallbrook Queensway, BIRMINGHAM
              ☎ 0121 643 8171 251 ⇨ 𝒓

Edgbaston Church Rd, Edgbaston B15 3TB
☎ 0121 454 1736
Parkland course in lovely country.
18 holes, 6106yds, Par 69, SSS 69.
Club membership 850.
Visitors   recommended to contact in advance, must
              have handicap certificate.
Societies   must apply in writing.

Green Fees £42.50 (£50 weekends & bank holidays); Winter £35.50/£42.50.
Facilities ⊗ ⅢⅢ ▙ ▆ ♀ ▵ 📠 ▜ ⌇ Andrew H Bownes.
Leisure motorised carts for hire, buggies for hire, trolley for hire, putting green, practice area.
Location 1m S of city centre on B4217 off A38
Hotel ★★★ 66% Plough & Harrow, 135 Hagley Rd, Edgbaston, BIRMINGHAM
☎ 0121 454 4111 44 ⇌ ⋒

Great Barr Chapel Ln, Great Barr B43 7BA
☎ 0121 357 5270
Parkland course with easy walking. Pleasant views of Barr Beacon National Park.
18 holes, 6523yds, Par 72, SSS 71.
Club membership 600.
Visitors restricted at weekends.
Societies must contact in writing.
Green Fees not confirmed.
Facilities ♀ ▵ 📠 ▜ ⌇ Richard Spragg.
Location 6m N of city centre off A 34
Hotel B Forte Posthouse Birmingham Great Barr, Chapel Ln, GREAT BARR
☎ 0121 357 7444 192 ⇌ ⋒

Handsworth 11 Sunningdale Close, Handsworth Wood B20 1NP ☎ 0121 554 0599 & 554 3387
Undulating parkland course with some tight fairways but subject to wind.
18 holes, 6267yds, Par 70, SSS 70, Course record 65.
Club membership 800.
Visitors restricted weekends, bank holidays & Xmas. Must contact in advance and have a handicap certificate.
Societies must contact in advance.
Green Fees £30 per day Mon-Fri.
Facilities ⊗ ⅢⅢ ▙ ▆ ♀ ▵ 📠 ⌇ Lee Bashford.
Leisure squash, trolley for hire, putting green, practice area.
Location 3.5m NW of city centre off A4040
Hotel ★★★ 67% Birmingham/West Bromwich Moat House, Birmingham Rd, WEST BROMWICH
☎ 0121 609 9988 171 ⇌ ⋒

Harborne 40 Tennal Rd, Harborne B32 2JE
☎ 0121 427 3058 & 427 3512
Parkland course in hilly situation, with brook running through.
18 holes, 6230yds, Par 70, SSS 70, Course record 65.
Club membership 636.
Visitors must contact in advance, may not play weekends except with member, Ladies have priority Tue.
Societies Mon, Wed-Fri apply to secretary.
Green Fees £35 per day; £30 per round.
Facilities ⊗ ⅢⅢ ▙ ▆ ♀ ▵ 📠 ▜ ⌇ Alan Quarterman.
Leisure trolley for hire, putting green.
Location 3.5 m SW of city centre off A4040
Hotel ★★★ 66% Plough & Harrow, 135 Hagley Rd, Edgbaston, BIRMINGHAM
☎ 0121 454 4111 44 ⇌ ⋒

Harborne Church Farm Vicarage Rd, Harborne B17 0SN
☎ 0121 427 1204
Parkland course with water hazards and easy walking. Some holes might prove difficult.

9 holes, 2457yds, Par 66, SSS 64, Course record 62.
Club membership 200.
Visitors must contact in advance.
Societies must telephone in advance.
Green Fees £7 per 18 holes; £4.50 per 9 holes (£8/£5 weekends).
Facilities ⊗ ⅢⅢ ▆ ▵ 📠 ▜ ⌇ Mark Hampton.
Leisure trolley for hire, putting green.
Location 3.5m SW of city centre off A4040
Hotel ★★★ 66% Plough & Harrow, 135 Hagley Rd, Edgbaston, BIRMINGHAM
☎ 0121 454 4111 44 ⇌ ⋒

Hatchford Brook Coventry Rd, Sheldon B26 3PY
☎ 0121 743 9821
Fairly flat, municipal parkland course.
18 holes, 6202yds, Par 69, SSS 70, Course record 69.
Club membership 500.
Visitors are restricted early Sat & Sun.
Societies must contact in advance.
Green Fees £8.50 per round (£9 weekends).
Facilities ⊗ ▆ ▵ 📠 ▜ ⌇ Paul Smith.
Leisure trolley for hire, putting green, practice area.
Location 6m E of city centre on A45
Hotel B Forte Posthouse Birmingham Airport, Coventry Rd, BIRMINGHAM
☎ 0121 782 8141 136 ⇌ ⋒

Hilltop Park Ln, Handsworth B21 8LJ ☎ 0121 554 4463
Testing and hilly municipal parkland course.
18 holes, 6254yds, Par 71, SSS 70.
Club membership 400.
Visitors no restrictions but booking recommended.
Societies telephone in advance.
Green Fees not confirmed.
Facilities ▵ 📠 ▜ ⌇ Kevin Highfield.
Leisure putting green, practice area, trolley hire.
Location 3.5m N of city centre off A4040
Hotel ★★★ 67% Birmingham/West Bromwich Moat House, Birmingham Rd, WEST BROMWICH
☎ 0121 609 9988 171 ⇌ ⋒

Moseley Springfield Rd, Kings Heath B14 7DX
☎ 0121 444 2115
Parkland course with a lake, pond and stream to provide natural hazards. The par-3, 5th goes through a cutting in woodland to a tree and garden-lined amphitheatre, and the par-4, 6th entails a drive over a lake to a dog-leg fairway.
18 holes, 6300yds, Par 70, SSS 70, Course record 64.
Club membership 600.
Visitors may only play at weekends by prior arrangement.
Societies by prior arrangement.
Green Fees not confirmed.
Facilities ♀ ▵ 📠 ⌇ Gary Edge.
Leisure putting, trolley hire, practice area.
Location 4m S of city centre on B4146 off A435
Hotel ★★ 67% Norwood Hotel, 87-89 Bunbury Rd, Northfield, BIRMINGHAM
☎ 0121 411 2202 18 ⇌ ⋒

North Worcestershire Frankley Beeches Rd, Northfield B31 5LP ☎ 0121 475 1047
Designed by James Braid and established in 1907, this is a mature parkland course. Tree plantations rather than heavy rough are the main hazards. ▶

18 holes, 5959yds, Par 69, SSS 68, Course record 64.
Club membership 600.

Visitors	by prior arrangement with professional, no visitors before 10.30 or at weekends. All visitors must have an official CONGU handicap.
Societies	apply in advance in writing or by telephone to the professional tel: 0121 475 5721.
Green Fees	Tue-Fri £25.50 per day; £18.50 per round. Mon £15 per round No visitors weekends.
Facilities	⊗ 〠 ⓛ 🖵 ♀ ⚲ 🖻 ☂ ℓ Keith Jones.
Leisure	trolley for hire, putting green, practice area.
Location	7m SW of Birmingham city centre, off A38
Hotel	★★ 67% Norwood Hotel, 87-89 Bunbury Rd, Northfield, BIRMINGHAM ☎ 0121 411 2202 18 ⇄ ⋔

Rose Hill Rosehill, Rednal B45 8RR ☎ 0121 453 3159
Hilly municipal course overlooking the city.
18 holes, 6010yds, Par 69, SSS 69, Course record 64.
Club membership 300.

Visitors	may not play between 9 & 10.30am weekends.
Societies	must contact in advance.
Green Fees	not confirmed.
Facilities	⚲ 🖻 ☂ ℓ Mike March.
Leisure	tennis courts, putting green.trolley hire,bowls.
Location	10m SW of city centre on B4096
Hotel	★★ 67% Norwood Hotel, 87-89 Bunbury Rd, Northfield, BIRMINGHAM ☎ 0121 411 2202 18 ⇄ ⋔

Warley Lightswood Hill, Warley B67 5ED
☎ 0121 429 2440
Municipal parkland course in Warley Woods.
9 holes, 5370yds, Par 68, SSS 66, Course record 66.
Club membership 200.

Visitors	no restrictions. Advance booking available at reduced cost.
Green Fees	£8 per round (£8.50 weekends).
Facilities	⊗ ⓛ 🖵 ⚲ 🖻 ☂ ℓ David Owen.
Leisure	trolley for hire, putting green.
Location	4m W of city centre off A456
Hotel	★★★ 66% Plough & Harrow, 135 Hagley Rd, Edgbaston, BIRMINGHAM ☎ 0121 454 4111 44 ⇄ ⋔

COVENTRY
Map 04 SP37

Ansty Golf Centre Brinklow Rd, Ansty CV7 9JH
☎ 01203 621341 & 621305
18-hole Pay and Play course of two 9-hole loops.Membership competitions for handicaps. Driving range and putting green.
18 holes, 5793yds, Par 70, SSS 68, Course record 66.
Club membership 300.

Visitors	no restrictions.
Societies	welcome.
Green Fees	not confirmed.
Facilities	♀ ⚲ 🖻 ☂ ℓ John Reay.
Leisure	putting/range/practice,cart/trolley hire.
Location	3m from city centre via A4600
Hotel	★★★ 64% Ansty Hall, ANSTY ☎ 01203 612222 25 ⇄ ⋔Annexe6 ⇄ ⋔

Coventry St Martins Rd, Finham Park CV3 6PJ
☎ 01203 414152 & 411298
The scene of several major professional events, this undulating parkland course has a great deal of quality.

More than that, it usually plays its length, and thus scoring is never easy, as many professionals have found to their cost.
18 holes, 6613yds, Par 73, SSS 72, Course record 64.
Club membership 500.

Visitors	must contact in advance. May not play at weekends and bank holidays.
Societies	must apply in writing.
Green Fees	£30 per day.
Facilities	⊗ 〠 ⓛ 🖵 ♀ ⚲ 🖻 ℓ Philip Weaver.
Leisure	trolley for hire, putting green, practice area.
Location	3m S of city centre on A444
Hotel	★★★ 66% Hylands Hotel, Warwick Rd, COVENTRY ☎ 01203 501600 54 ⇄ ⋔

Coventry Hearsall Beechwood Av CV5 6DF
☎ 01203 713470
Parkland course with fairly easy walking. A brook provides an interesting hazard.
18 holes, 5983yds, Par 70, SSS 69.
Club membership 650.

Visitors	with member only at weekends.
Societies	apply in writing to secretary.
Green Fees	£25 per day.
Facilities	⊗ 〠 ⓛ 🖵 ♀ ⚲ 🖻 ℓ Mike Tarn.
Leisure	motorised carts for hire, trolley for hire, putting green, practice area.
Location	1.5m SW of city centre off A429
Hotel	★★★ 66% Hylands Hotel, Warwick Rd, COVENTRY ☎ 01203 501600 54 ⇄ ⋔

GPT The Grange, Copsewood, Binley Rd CV3 1HS
☎ 01203 563127
Flat parkland course with very tight out of bounds on a number of holes, and a river which affects play on five of them. Well-bunkered, with plenty of trees.
9 holes, 6002yds, Par 72, SSS 69.
Club membership 300.

Visitors	may not play after 2pm weekdays or before noon on Sun. No visitors Sat.
Societies	must contact in advance.
Green Fees	not confirmed.
Facilities	♀ ⚲
Leisure	putting green,practice area.
Location	2m E of city centre on A428
Hotel	★★★ 60% The Chace Hotel, London Rd, Toll Bar End, COVENTRY ☎ 01203 303398 67 ⇄ ⋔

Windmill Village Birmingham Rd, Allesley CV5 9AL
☎ 01203 407241
An 18-hole course over rolling parkland with lakes and ponds. Other leisure facilities available.
18 holes, 5129yds, Par 70, SSS 67.
Club membership 500.

Visitors	welcome except before noon at weekends. Must contact in advance.
Societies	telephone and confirm in writing.
Green Fees	£10.95 per round (£15 weekends).
Facilities	⊗ 〠 ⓛ 🖵 ♀ ⚲ 🖻 ☂ 🖼 ℓ Robert Hunter.
Leisure	hard tennis courts, heated indoor swimming pool, fishing, sauna, solarium, gymnasium, motorised carts for hire, buggies for hire, trolley for hire, putting green, bowling, beauty salon.
Location	On A45 W of Coventry

Hotel   ★★★ 72% Brooklands Grange Hotel &
Restaurant, Holyhead Rd, COVENTRY
☎ 01203 601601 30 ➪ ↿

DUDLEY   Map 07 SO99

Dudley Turner's Hill, Rowley Regis, Warley B65 9DP
☎ 01384 233877
Exposed and very hilly parkland course.
18 holes, 6000yds, Par 69, SSS 68.
Club membership 550.
Visitors   contact in advance, may not play at weekends.
Societies   must contact in advance.
Green Fees £18 per day.
Facilities ⊗ ⅷ ↳ ▆ ♀ ⅍ 🖻 ↿ Paul Taylor.
Leisure   trolley for hire, putting green, practice area,.
Location   2m S of town centre off B4171
Hotel   ★★★ 59% Himley Country Hotel, School Rd,
HIMLEY ☎ 01902 896716 73 ➪ ↿

Swindon Bridgnorth Rd, Swindon DY3 4PU
☎ 01902 897031 & 895226
Attractive undulating woodland/parkland course, with
spectacular views.
Old Course: 18 holes, 6091yds, Par 71, SSS 69.
New Course: 9 holes, 1135yds, Par 27.
Club membership 700.
Visitors   must contact in advance.
Societies   must apply in writing.
Green Fees £28 per day; £18 per round (£40/£27 weekends
& bank holidays).
Facilities ⊗ ⅷ ↳ ▆ ♀ ⅍ 🖻 ↿ Phil Lester.
Leisure   fishing, buggies for hire, trolley for hire, driving
range, putting green, snooker.
Location   On B4176, 3m from A449 at Himley
Hotel   ★★★ 59% Himley Country Hotel, School Rd,
HIMLEY ☎ 01902 896716 73 ➪ ↿

HALESOWEN   Map 07 SO98

Corngreaves Hall Corngreaves Rd B64
☎ 01384 567880
Mature course offering a good challenge to the best golfers
with American specification greens and most holes holding a
testing start. Magnificent views of the Clent Hills.
Congreaves Hall Golf Course: 9 holes, 2800.
Visitors   at anytime by prior arrangement.
Societies   apply in writing in advance.
Green Fees £6.90 per 18 holes; £4.90 per 9 holes
(£7.80/£5.50 weekends).
Facilities ⊗ ▆ ⅋ ↿ S Joyce/C Yates.
Leisure   trolley for hire, putting green.
Hotel   ★★ 65% Talbot Hotel, High St,
STOURBRIDGE
☎ 01384 394350 25 ➪ ↿

Halesowen The Leasowes, Leasowes Ln B62 8QF
☎ 0121 501 3606
Parkland course in convenient position.
18 holes, 5754yds, Par 69, SSS 68.
Visitors   may only play weekends or bank holidays with
member
Societies   must apply in writing.
Green Fees £25 per day; £18 per round.
Facilities ⊗ ⅷ ↳ ▆ ♀ ⅍ 🖻 ⅋ ↿ Jon Nicholas.

Leisure   trolley for hire, putting green, practice area.
Location   1m E
Hotel   ★★ 65% Talbot Hotel, High St,
STOURBRIDGE ☎ 01384 394350 25 ➪ ↿

KNOWLE   Map 07 SP17

Copt Heath 1220 Warwick Rd B93 9LN
☎ 01564 772650
Parkland course designed by H. Vardon.
18 holes, 6508yds, Par 71, SSS 71.
Club membership 700.
Visitors   must contact in advance. May not play weekends
& bank holidays.
Societies   must contact in advance.
Green Fees £40 per day; £35 per round.
Facilities ⊗ ⅷ ↳ ▆ ♀ ⅍ 🖻 ↿ Brian J Barton.
Leisure   motorised carts for hire, buggies for hire, trolley
for hire, driving range, putting green, practice
area.
Location   On A4141, 0.50m S of junc 5 of M42
Hotel   ★★★ 65% St John's Swallow Hotel, 651
Warwick Rd, SOLIHULL
☎ 0121 711 3000 177 ➪ ↿

MERIDEN   Map 04 SP28

Forest of Arden Hotel Golf and Country Club
Shepherd's Ln CV7 7HR
☎ 01676 22335
Two parkland courses, set within the grounds of Packington
Park, with extensive water hazards and offering a fine test of
golf. On-site hotel with many leisure facilities.
*Arden Course: 18 holes, 6472yds, Par 72, SSS 71, Course
record 64.*
Aylesford Course: 18 holes, 6258yds, Par 72, SSS 69.
Club membership 800.
Visitors   must have handicap certificate, but may not play
weekends (unless hotel resident). Must contact
in advance.
Societies   by arrangement.
Green Fees not confirmed.
Facilities ♀ ⅍ 🖻 ⅋ ⅷ ↿ Mike Tarn.
Leisure   hard tennis courts, heated indoor swimming
pool, squash, fishing, sauna, solarium,
gymnasium, steam room, beauty salon.
Location   1m SW on B4102
Hotel   ★★★★ 68% Forest of Arden Hotel, Maxstoke
Ln, MERIDEN
☎ 01676 522335 154 ➪ ↿

North Warwickshire Hampton Ln CV7 7LL
☎ 01676 22259
Parkland course with easy walking.
9 holes, 6390yds, Par 72, SSS 70, Course record 65.
Club membership 425.
Visitors   must contact in advance.
Societies   must apply in writing to secretary.
Green Fees £18 per round.
Facilities ↳ ▆ ♀ ⅍ 🖻 ↿ David Ingram.
Leisure   trolley for hire, putting green, practice area.
Location   1m SW on B4102
Hotel   ★★★ 68% Manor Hotel, Main Rd, MERIDEN
☎ 01676 522735 74 ➪ ↿

SEDGLEY   Map 07 SO99

Sedgley Golf Centre Sandyfields Rd DY3 3DL
☎ 01902 880503
Public Pay and Play course. Undulating contours and mature
trees with extensive views over surrounding countryside.
9 holes, 3147yds, Par 72, SSS 70.
Club membership 150.
Visitors   booking advisable for weekends.
Societies   must contact in advance.
Green Fees   £7 per 18 holes (£7.50 weekends & bank
                 holidays); £5 per 9 holes (£5.50 weekends &
                 bank holidays).
Facilities   🦌 🏠 ℓ Garry Mercer.
Leisure   trolley for hire, driving range, putting green,
                 practice area, golf lessons.
Location   0.5m from town centre off A463
Hotel   ★★★ 59% Himley Country Hotel, School Rd,
                 HIMLEY ☎ 01902 896716 73 ⇆ 🐾

SOLIHULL   Map 07 SP17

Olton Mirfield Rd B91 1JH ☎ 0121 705 1083
Parkland course with prevailing southwest wind.
18 holes, 6265yds, Par 69, SSS 71, Course record 63.
Club membership 600.
Visitors   must contact in advance. No visitors at weekend.
Societies   apply in writing.
Green Fees   £35 per day.
Facilities   ⊗ ⅊ 🦌 🦌 ♀ ⅄ 🏠 🍸 ℓ Mark Daubney.
Leisure   trolley for hire, putting green, practice area.
Location   Exit M42 junct 5 and take A41 for 1.5m
Hotel   ★★★ 65% St John's Swallow Hotel, 651
                 Warwick Rd, SOLIHULL
                 ☎ 0121 711 3000 177 ⇆ 🐾

Robin Hood St Bernards Rd B92 7DJ ☎ 0121 706 0061
Pleasant parkland course with easy walking and open to good
views.Tree lined fairways and varied holes, culminating in
two excellent finishing holes. Modern clubhouse.
18 holes, 6635yds, Par 72, SSS 72, Course record 68.
Club membership 650.
Visitors   must contact in advance. With member only at
                 weekends.
Societies   must contact in advance.
Green Fees   £35 per day; £29 per round.
Facilities   ⊗ ⅊ 🦌 🦌 ♀ ⅄ 🏠 🍸 ℓ Alan Harvey.
Leisure   trolley for hire, driving range, putting green,
                 practice area.
Location   2m W off B4025
Hotel   ★★★ 65% St John's Swallow Hotel, 651
                 Warwick Rd, SOLIHULL
                 ☎ 0121 711 3000 177 ⇆ 🐾

Shirley Stratford Rd, Monkpath B90 4EW
☎ 0121 744 6001
Fairly flat parkland course.
18 holes, 6510yds, Par 72, SSS 71.
Club membership 500.
Visitors   may not play bank holidays & with member only
                 at weekends. Handicap certificate is required.
Societies   must contact in advance.
Green Fees   not confirmed.
Facilities   ♀ ⅄ 🏠 ℓ C J Wicketts.
Leisure   putting,practice area,trolley hire.

Location   3m SW off A34
Hotel   ★★★★ 61% Regency Hotel, Stratford Rd,
                 Shirley, SOLIHULL
                 ☎ 0121 745 6119 112 ⇆ 🐾

STOURBRIDGE   Map 07 SO98

Hagley Golf & Country Club Wassell Grove, Hagley
DY9 9JW ☎ 01562 883701
Undulating parkland course set beneath the Clent Hills; there
are superb views. Testing 15th, par 5, 557 yards.
18 holes, 6353yds, Par 72, SSS 72, Course record 66.
Club membership 700.
Visitors   restricted Wed (Ladies Day) & with member
                 only at weekends.
Societies   Mon-Fri only, must apply in writing.
Green Fees   £25 per day; £20 per round.
Facilities   ⊗ ⅊ 🦌 🦌 ♀ ⅄ 🏠 ℓ Iain Clark.
Leisure   squash, motorised carts for hire, buggies for hire,
                 trolley for hire, putting green, practice area.
Location   1m E of Hagley off A456
Hotel   ★★ 65% Talbot Hotel, High St,
                 STOURBRIDGE ☎ 01384 394350 25 ⇆ 🐾

Stourbridge Worcester Ln, Pedmore DY8 2RB
☎ 01384 395566
Parkland course.
18 holes, 6231yds, Par 70, SSS 69, Course record 67.
Club membership 857.
Visitors   contact secretary, no casual visitors weekends.
Societies   must apply in writing.
Green Fees   £25 per day.
Facilities   ⊗ ⅊ by prior arrangement 🦌 🦌 ♀ ⅄ 🏠
                 ℓ W H Firkins.
Leisure   trolley for hire, putting green, practice area.
Location   2m from town centre
Hotel   ★★ 65% Talbot Hotel, High St,
                 STOURBRIDGE ☎ 01384 394350 25 ⇆ 🐾

SUTTON COLDFIELD   Map 07 SP19

THE BELFRY See page 229

Boldmere Monmouth Dr B73 6Jl
☎ 0121 354 3379
Established municipal course with 10 par 3s and a lake
coming into play on the 16th and 18th holes.
18 holes, 4482yds, Par 63, SSS 62, Course record 57.
Club membership 300.
Visitors   must contact in advance.
Societies   midweek only, apply in writing.
Green Fees   £8 per 18 holes; £5 per 9 holes (£8.50/£5.50
                 weekends).
Facilities   ⊗ 🦌 🦌 ♀ ⅄ 🏠 🍸 ℓ Trevor Short.
Leisure   trolley for hire, putting green.
Location   Adjacent to Sutton Park
Hotel   ★★★ 69% Moor Hall Hotel, Moor Hall Dr,
                 Four Oaks, SUTTON COLDFIELD
                 ☎ 0121 308 3751 75 ⇆ 🐾

Little Aston Streetly B74 3AN ☎ 0121 353 2942
Parkland course.
18 holes, 6670yds, Par 72, SSS 73, Course record 64.
Club membership 350.   ▶

THE BELFRY

SUTTON COLDFIELD *West Midlands*

☎ 01675 470301   **Map 07 SP19**

John Ingham writes: When professional people are commissioned to turn a piece of farmland into a golf course and hotel complex, they are flattered - and delighted. This happened to Peter Alliss and Dave Thomas, two celebrated tournament competitors. The challenge they were offered: turn an unsympathetic piece of land into a good golf course. The resulting Belfry Golf Club was opened in 1977.

Since that date the two architects have every reason to be proud. The course, set in 370 acres of parkland, has staged more than one of the popular Ryder Cup matches, and the two courses - the Brabazon and the Derby - named after two Lords, have received thousands of visitors. These visitors have been entertained with a kindly reception, enhanced by a really excellent hotel. A third course - the PGA National Course - is due to be completed in Spring 1997. The Belfry is also home to the PGA Training Academy.

In the nineteen years since its establishment, the saplings and newly-created greens have settled down very well and presented a worthwhile face to the world. One of the big challenges of The Belfry are the lakes and many water hazards that gobble up wild shots. Many a famous player, such as Seve Ballesteros, has had balls sinking without trace at the Brabazon's famously testing 18th hole. This monster requires the player to clear the lake twice in its 455-yard drive to reach an uphill, three-tiered, 60-yard long green.

As a public course, The Belfry is open to all-comers every day. This obviously means a great deal of traffic, although there are many other worthwhile courses in the West Midlands such as Hansworth and Little Aston. However, The Belfry is excellently managed and kept in top condition by a team now fully experienced in catering for every golfer. Recently, bunkering and new tees have improved several of the holes and spectator mounding has improved viewing of the golf tournaments.

In its fine parkland setting the club has become well known for its accommodation and fine business facilities and, being so well placed for the NEC, Birmingham and the international airport, it attracts a variety of golfers.

Visitors	must contact 24 hours in advance. A handicap certificate is required for the Brabazon course
Societies	must contact in advance
Green fees	Brabazon £55 per round; Derby £27.50 per round. Reduced fees in winter
Facilities	⊗ ⅷ ⅃ ⅊ ♣ ♀ ⋈ ⚓ 🏠 ⚐ ⚑ (P McGovern) putting green, driving range
Leisure	hard tennis courts, heated indoor swimming pool, squash, snooker, sauna, solarium, gym. Nightclub in grounds
Location	Sutton Coalfield B76 9PR Lichfield Rd, Wishaw (exit junc 9 M42 4m E)

36 holes. **Brabazon: 18 holes, 7220yds, Par 72, SSS 72. Course record 63**
Derby: 18 holes, 6103yds Par70, SSS 70

WHERE TO STAY AND EAT NEARBY

HOTELS:

WISHAW
★★★★👑👑 72%The Belfry, Lichfield Rd.☎ 01675 470301
219 (3 🛏 216 ⇥ 🛏)

★★★58% Moxhull Hall, Holly Lane.
☎ 0121-329 2056. 11(3 🛏 8 ⇥ 🛏)
Annex 9

LEA MARSTON
★★★69% Lea Marston Hotel and Leisure Complex. ☎ 01675 470468
49 (2 🛏 47 ⇥ 🛏)

SUTTON COLDFIELD
★★★ 60% Sutton Court, 60-66 Lichfield Rd. ☎ 0121-355 6071, 56 (9 🛏 47 ⇥ 🛏)
Annexe 8 ⇥ 🛏

★★★★(Red)👑👑 ♨ New Hall,
Walmley Rd. ☎ 0121-378 2442. 62 ⇥ 🛏

MOXHULL HALL HOTEL

Holly Lane, Wishaw, Sutton Coldfield, Warwickshire B76 9PD
Tel: 0121 329 2056 Fax: 0121 311 1980

Privately owned ★★★ Country House Hotel set in eight acres of gardens and woodlands. All rooms en-suite, colour television, telephone, etc. Only one mile from international golf at the Belfry.

Visitors must contact in advance & may not play at weekends.
Societies must apply in writing.
Green Fees £45 per day.
Facilities ⊗ ℳ 💺 ♀ ⅄ 🛍 ℓ John Anderson.
Leisure trolley for hire, putting green, practice area.
Location 3.5m NW off A454
Hotel ★★★ 69% Moor Hall Hotel, Moor Hall Dr, Four Oaks, SUTTON COLDFIELD
☎ 0121 308 3751 75 ⇌ ๒

Moor Hall Moor Hall Dr B75 6LN ☎ 0121 308 6130
Parkland course. The 14th is a notable hole.
18 holes, 6249yds, Par 70, SSS 70.
Club membership 600.
Visitors must contact in advance. With member only weekends & bank holidays.
Societies must apply in writing.
Green Fees not confirmed.
Facilities ♀ ⅄ 🛍 ๙ ℓ
Location 2.5m N of town centre off A453
Hotel ★★★ 69% Moor Hall Hotel, Moor Hall Dr, Four Oaks, SUTTON COLDFIELD
☎ 0121 308 3751 75 ⇌ ๒

Pype Hayes Eachel Hurst Rd, Walmley B76 1EP
☎ 0121 351 1014
Attractive, fairly flat course with excellent greens.
18 holes, 5996yds, Par 71, SSS 68, Course record 66.
Club membership 400.
Visitors phone professional in advance.
Societies contact professional in advance.
Green Fees £8.50 per round; £5 per 9 holes (£9/£5.50 weekends).
Facilities ⊗ ℳ 💺 💺 🛍 ๙ ℓ James Bayliss.
Leisure trolley for hire, putting green, practice area.
Location 2.5m S off B4148
Hotel ★★★ 67% Marston Farm Hotel, Bodymoor Heath, SUTTON COLDFIELD
☎ 01827 872133 37 ⇌ ๒

Sutton Coldfield 110 Thornhill Rd, Streetly B74 3ER
☎ 0121 353 9633
A fine natural, heathland course, with tight fairways, gorse, heather and trees; which is surprising as the high-rise buildings of Birmingham are not far away.
18 holes, 6541yds, Par 72, SSS 71, Course record 65.
Club membership 550.
Visitors must contact in advance. Restricted at weekends.
Societies must apply in writing.
Green Fees £35 per day.
Facilities ⊗ 💺 💺 ♀ ⅄ 🛍 ℓ Jerry Hayes.
Leisure trolley for hire, putting green, practice area.
Location 3m NW on B4138

Hotel ★★★ 69% Moor Hall Hotel, Moor Hall Dr, Four Oaks, SUTTON COLDFIELD
☎ 0121 308 3751 75 ⇌ ๒

Walmley Brooks Rd, Wylde Green B72 1HR
☎ 0121 373 0029 & 377 7272
Pleasant parkland course with many trees. The hazards are not difficult.
18 holes, 6559yds, Par 72, SSS 72, Course record 67.
Club membership 650.
Visitors must contact in advance. May only play weekdays unless guest of member.
Societies must contact in advance.
Green Fees £30 per day; £25 per round.
Facilities ⊗ ℳ 💺 💺 ♀ ⅄ ๙ ℓ M J Skerritt.
Leisure trolley for hire.
Location 2m S off A5127
Hotel ★★★ 67% Marston Farm Hotel, Bodymoor Heath, SUTTON COLDFIELD
☎ 01827 872133 37 ⇌ ๒

WALSALL   Map 07 SP09

Bloxwich Stafford Rd, Bloxwich WS3 3PQ
☎ 01922 405724 & 476593
Undulating parkland course with natural hazards and subject to strong north wind.
18 holes, 6260yds, Par 71, SSS 70, Course record 68.
Club membership 532.
Visitors may not play at weekends.
Societies must contact in advance.
Green Fees £25 per day; £20 per round.
Facilities ⊗ ℳ 💺 💺 ♀ ⅄ 🛍 ℓ Daryl Scott.
Leisure trolley for hire, putting green, practice area.
Location 3m N of town centre on A34
Hotel ★★★ 70% The Fairlawns at Aldridge, 178 Little Aston Rd, Aldridge, WALSALL
☎ 01922 55122 35 ⇌ ๒

Calderfields Aldridge Rd WS4 2JS
☎ 01922 640540
Parkland course with lake.
18 holes, 6590yds, Par 73, SSS 72.
Club membership 700.
Visitors no restrictions.
Societies telephone in advance.
Green Fees not confirmed.
Facilities ♀ ⅄ 🛍 ๙ ℓ Roger Griffin.
Leisure fishing.
Location On A454
Hotel ★★★ 70% The Fairlawns at Aldridge, 178 Little Aston Rd, Aldridge, WALSALL
☎ 01922 55122 35 ⇌ ๒

Walsall The Broadway WS1 3EY ☎ 01922 613512
Well-wooded parkland course with easy walking.
18 holes, 6300yds, Par 70, SSS 70, Course record 67.
Club membership 600.
Visitors must contact in advance. May not play weekends
& bank holidays.
Societies must apply in writing.
Green Fees £40 per day; £33 per round.
Facilities ⊗ ℿ ⅃ ☧ ♀ ⚐ 🗑 ℂ Richard Lambert.
Leisure trolley for hire, putting green, practice area.
Location 1m S of town centre off A34
Hotel ★★★ 66% Boundary Hotel, Birmingham Rd,
WALSALL ☎ 01922 33555 94 ⇔ 🌑

WEST BROMWICH   Map 07 SP09

Dartmouth Vale St B71 4DW ☎ 0121 588 2131
Meadowland course with undulating but easy walking. The
617 yd (par 5) first hole is something of a challenge.
9 holes, 6060yds, Par 71, SSS 70, Course record 66.
Club membership 350.
Visitors with member only at weekends. May not play
bank holidays or medal weekends.
Societies must apply in writing.
Green Fees not confirmed.
Facilities ♀ ⚐ 🗑 ℂ Carl Yates.
Leisure practice area, putting green.
Location E side of town centre off A4041
Hotel ★★★ 67% Birmingham/West Bromwich Moat
House, Birmingham Rd, WEST BROMWICH
☎ 0121 609 9988 171 ⇔ 🌑

Sandwell Park Birmingham Rd B71 4JJ
☎ 0121 553 4637 & 553 4384
Undulating parkland course situated in the Sandwell Valley.
18 holes, 6470yds, Par 71, SSS 72, Course record 68.
Club membership 550.
Visitors must contact in advance. May not play at
weekends.
Societies must contact in advance.
Green Fees £25 per round.
Facilities ⊗ ℿ ℄ ☧ ♀ ⚐ 🗑 ℂ Nigel Wylie.
Leisure trolley for hire, putting green, practice area.
Location SE side of town centre off A4040
Hotel ★★★ 67% Birmingham/West Bromwich
Moat House, Birmingham Rd, WEST
BROMWICH ☎ 0121 609 9988 171 ⇔ 🌑

WOLVERHAMPTON   Map 07 SO99

Oxley Park Stafford Rd, Bushbury WV10 6DE
☎ 01902 25892 & 25445
Parklands course with easy walking on the flat.
18 holes, 6222yds, Par 71, SSS 70, Course record 68.
Club membership 550.
Visitors must contact in advance.
Societies must contact in advance.
Green Fees £24 per day; £20 per round.
Facilities ⊗ ℿ ℄ ☧ ♀ ⚐ 🗑 ℂ Les Burlison.
Leisure buggies for hire, trolley for hire, putting green,
snooker.
Location N of town centre off A449
Hotel ★★ 68% Ely House Hotel, 53 Tettenhall Rd,
WOLVERHAMPTON
☎ 01902 311311 18 ⇔ 🌑

Penn Penn Common, Penn WV4 5JN
☎ 01902 341142
Heathland course just outside the town.
18 holes, 6462yds, Par 70, SSS 71, Course record 68.
Club membership 650.
Visitors must play with member at weekends.
Societies must contact in advance.
Green Fees £25 per day.
Facilities ⊗ ℿ ℄ ☧ ♀ ⚐ 🗑 ℾ ℂ A Briscoe.
Leisure motorised carts for hire, trolley for hire, putting
green.
Location SW side of town centre off A449
Hotel ★★★ 60% Jarvis Park Hall, Ednam Rd,
Goldthorn Park, WOLVERHAMPTON
☎ 01902 331121 57 ⇔ 🌑

South Staffordshire Danescourt Rd, Tettenhall WV6 9BQ
☎ 01902 751065 & 754816
A parkland course.
18 holes, 6513yds, Par 71, SSS 71.
Club membership 500.
Visitors must contact in advance but may not play
weekends & before 2pm Tue.
Societies must apply in writing.
Green Fees £37 per day; £32 per round.
Facilities ⊗ ℿ ℄ ☧ ♀ ⚐ 🗑 ℂ Jim Rhodes.
Leisure buggies for hire, trolley for hire, putting green,
practice area.
Location 3m NW off A41
Hotel ★★ 68% Ely House Hotel, 53 Tettenhall Rd,
WOLVERHAMPTON ☎ 01902 311311 18 ⇔ 🌑

Three Hammers Short Course Old Stafford Rd, Coven
WV10 7PP ☎ 01902 790940
Well maintained short course designed by Henry Cotton and
providing a unique challenge to golfers of all standards.
18 holes, 1438yds, Par 54, SSS 54, Course record 43.
Visitors no restrictions.
Societies contact for details.
Green Fees £5 per day (£6 weekends).
Facilities ⊗ ℿ ℄ ☧ ♀ ⚐ 🗑 ℾ ℂ
Leisure driving range.
Location On A449 N of junct 2 M54
Hotel ★★★ 66% Roman Way Hotel, Watling St,
Hatherton, CANNOCK
☎ 01543 572121 56 ⇔ 🌑

Wergs Keepers Ln, Tettenhall WV6 8UA
☎ 01902 742225
Open parkland course.
18 holes, 6949yds, Par 72, SSS 73.
Club membership 250.
Visitors are advised to contact in advance.
Societies must contact in advance.
Green Fees £12.50 per day (£15 weekends & bank holidays).
Facilities ⊗ ℿ ℄ ☧ ♀ ⚐ 🗑 ℂ Martin Payne.
Leisure motorised carts for hire, buggies for hire, trolley
for hire, putting green, practice area.
Hotel ★★ 68% Ely House Hotel, 53 Tettenhall Rd,
WOLVERHAMPTON ☎ 01902 311311 18 ⇔ 🌑

Entries with a shaded background identify
courses that are considered to be particularly
interesting

WIGHT, ISLE OF

COWES
Map 04 SZ49

Cowes Crossfield Av PO31 8HN
☎ 01983 292303
Fairly level, tight parkland course with difficult par 3s and
Solent views.
9 holes, 5934yds, Par 70, SSS 68, Course record 66.
Club membership 300.
Visitors   restricted Thu & Sun mornings.
Societies   Mon-Wed, must contact in advance.
Green Fees   £15 per day/round (£18 weekends).
Facilities   ⓑ ♥ ♀ ⚘ ⚑
Leisure   trolley for hire, putting green, practice area.
Location   NW side of town
Hotel   ★★ 62% The Fountain Hotel, High St,
                  COWES ☎ 01983 292397 20 ⇄ ⋔

EAST COWES
Map 04 SZ59

Osborne Osborne House Estate PO32 6JX
☎ 01983 295421
Undulating parkland course in the grounds of Osborne House.
Quiet and peaceful situation.
9 holes, 6372yds, Par 70, SSS 70.
Club membership 400.
Visitors   may not play Tue before 1pm, weekends before
                  noon & bank holidays before 11am.
Societies   telephone initially.
Green Fees   £16 (£19 weekends & bank holidays).
Facilities   ⊗ ⋔ ⓑ ♥ ♀ ⚘ 🖼
Leisure   trolley for hire, putting green, practice area.
Location   E side of town centre off A3021
Hotel   ★★ 62% The Fountain Hotel, High St,
                  COWES ☎ 01983 292397 20 ⇄ ⋔

FRESHWATER
Map 04 SZ38

Freshwater Bay Afton Down PO40 9TZ
☎ 01983 752955
A downland/seaside links with wide fairways and spectacular
coastal views of the Solent and Channel.
18 holes, 5725yds, Par 69, SSS 68.
Club membership 450.
Visitors   may play daily after 9.30 ex Thu & Sun (10.30).
Societies   apply to secretary.
Green Fees   £20 per day (£24 weekends & bank holidays).
Facilities   ⊗ ⋔ ⓑ ♥ ♀ ⚘ ⚑
Leisure   trolley for hire, putting green, practice area.
Location   0.5m E of village off A3055
Hotel   ★★★ 64% Albion Hotel, FRESHWATER
                  ☎ 01983 753631 42 ⇄ ⋔

NEWPORT
Map 04 SZ58

Newport St George's Down, Shide PO30 2JB
☎ 01983 525076
Downland course, fine views.
9 holes, 5710yds, Par 68, SSS 68.
Club membership 350.

Visitors   may not play Wed noon-3.30pm or before 3pm
                  Sat & noon Sun.
Societies   contact Secretary in advance.
Green Fees   £15 per day (£17.50 weekends & bank holidays).
Facilities   ⊗ ⋔ by prior arrangement ⓑ ♥ ♀ ⚘ ⚑
Leisure   trolley for hire, putting green, practice area.
Location   1.5m S off A3020
Hotel   ★★ 62% The Fountain Hotel, High St,
                  COWES ☎ 01983 292397 20 ⇄ ⋔

RYDE
Map 04 SZ59

Ryde Binstead Rd PO33 3NF ☎ 01983 614809
Downland course with wide views over the Solent.
9 holes, 5287yds, Par 66, SSS 66.
Club membership 500.
Visitors   may not play Wed afternoons, Sun mornings or
                  before 10.30 Sat.
Societies   must contact in writing.
Green Fees   £15 (£20 weekends).
Facilities   ⊗ ⋔ by prior arrangement ⓑ ♥ ♀ ⚘ 🖼 ⚑
Leisure   trolley for hire, practice area.
Location   1m W on A3054
Hotel   ★★ 65% Biskra House Beach Hotel, 17 Saint
                  Thomas's St, RYDE
                  ☎ 01983 567913 9 ⇄ ⋔

SANDOWN
Map 04 SZ58

Shanklin & Sandown The Fairway, Lake PO36 9PR
☎ 01983 403217
Heathland course.
18 holes, 6063yds, Par 70, SSS 69, Course record 64.
Club membership 600.
Visitors   must contact in advance & have handicap
                  certificate,
Societies   apply in writing.
Green Fees   £22 (£24 weekends).
Facilities   ⊗ ⋔ by prior arrangement ⓑ ♥ ♀ ⚘ 🖼
                  ⚑ Peter Hammond.
Leisure   trolley for hire, putting green, practice area.
Location   1m NW
Hotel   ★★ 58% Birdham Hotel, 1 Steyne Rd,
                  BEMBRIDGE
                  ☎ 01983 872875 14rm(12 ⇄)

VENTNOR
Map 04 SZ57

Ventnor Steephill Down Rd PO38 1BP
☎ 01983 853326
Downland course subject to wind. Fine seascapes.
12 holes, 5767yds, Par 70, SSS 68.
Club membership 297.
Visitors   may not play Fri noon-3pm or Sun mornings.
Societies   telephone initially.
Green Fees   £10-£12 per day (£12-£14 weekends & bank
                  holidays).
Facilities   ⊗ by prior arrangement ⋔ by prior arrangement
                  ⓑ ♥ ♀ ⚘ ⚑
Leisure   trolley for hire.
Location   1m NW off B3327
Hotel   ★★★ 63% Ventnor Towers Hotel, Madeira Rd,
                  VENTNOR
                  ☎ 01983 852277 27 ⇄ ⋔

WILTSHIRE

BISHOPS CANNINGS

Map 04 SU06

North Wilts SN10 2LP ☎ 01380 860627
High, downland course with fine views.
18 holes, 6322yds, Par 70, SSS 70, Course record 69.
Club membership 800.
Visitors welcome, a handicap certificate is required at weekends.
Societies must book in advance.
Green Fees not confirmed.
Facilities ♀ ♨ 🏠 ⚑ ⌕ Graham Laing.
Leisure putting green,practice,cart/trolley hire.
Location 2m NW
Hotel ★★★ 61% Bear Hotel, Market Place, DEVIZES ☎ 01380 722444 24 ⇥ ⋔

CALNE

Map 03 ST97

Bowood Golf & Country Club Derry Hill SN11 9PQ
☎ 01249 822228
A long, undulating course designed by Dave Thomas. Set in a Grade I listed Capability Brown park full of mature trees and acres of wildflowers, the course is a real test of golf. A 10-bay driving range and grass teeing area are enhanced by a 3-hole Academy course and putting greens
18 holes, 6890yds, Par 72, SSS 73, Course record 67.
Club membership 350.
Visitors welcome except before noon on Sat and Sun. Advisable to book.
Societies booking by telephone.
Green Fees £40 per 36 holes; £35 per 27 holes; £30 per 18 holes.
Facilities ⊗ ⋔ ♨ ♨ ♀ ♨ 🏠 ⚑ ⍾ ⌕ N Blenkarne.
Leisure motorised carts for hire, buggies for hire, trolley for hire, driving range, putting green, practice area, croquet.
Location Off A6 between Chippenham & Calne
Hotel ★★ 62% Lansdowne Strand Hotel & Restaurant, The Strand, CALNE
☎ 01249 812488 21 ⇥ ⋔Annexe5 ⇥ ⋔

CASTLE COMBE

Map 03 ST87

Manor House SN14 7PL
☎ 01249 782982
Opened in 1992 and set in one of the finest locations in England, this 18-hole Peter Alliss/Clive Clark course was designed to marry neatly with the surrounding conservation area. Many mature trees have been used to great effect giving individuality and challenge to every shot. There are spectacular holes at the 17th & 18th with lakes and waterfalls making them memorable.
18 holes, 6340yds, Par 73, SSS 71.
Club membership 500.
Visitors must have a handicap certificate.
Societies contact in advance.
Green Fees not confirmed.
Facilities ♀ ♨ 🏠 ⚑ ⍾ ⌕ Chris Smith.
Leisure hard tennis courts, heated outdoor swimming pool, fishing, sauna, putting, buggy/trolley hire.

Location 5m NW of Chippenham
Hotel ★★★★(red)♨ Manor House Hotel, CASTLE COMBE
☎ 01249 782206 16 ⇥ ⋔Annexe24 ⇥ ⋔

CHAPMANSLADE

Map 03 ST84

Thoulstone Park BA13 4AQ
☎ 01373 832825
A rolling parkland course with natural lakes and mature tees. Hole 7, stroke index 1 has a second shot over a large lake to the green so a straight drive is essential.
18 holes, 6312yds, Par 71, SSS 70.
Club membership 500.
Visitors restricted Sat & Sun mornings.
Societies telephone in advance.
Green Fees not confirmed.
Facilities ♀ ♨ 🏠 ⚑ ⌕ Derek Thomson.
Leisure sauna, 20 bay floodlit driving range.
Location On A36 between Bath/Warminster
Hotel ★★★ 62% Mendip Lodge Hotel, Bath Rd, FROME
☎ 01373 463223 40 ⇥

CHIPPENHAM

Map 03 ST97

Chippenham Malmesbury Rd SN15 5LT
☎ 01249 652040
Easy walking on downland course. Testing holes at 1st and 15th.
18 holes, 5559yds, Par 69, SSS 67, Course record 64.
Club membership 650.
Visitors must contact in advance and have a handicap certificate.
Societies must contact in writing; handicap certificates required.
Green Fees not confirmed.
Facilities ♀ ♨ 🏠 ⚑ ⌕ Bill Creamer.
Location 1.5m N on A429
Hotel ★★★★(red)♨ Manor House Hotel, CASTLE COMBE
☎ 01249 782206 16 ⇥ ⋔Annexe24 ⇥ ⋔

CRICKLADE

Map 04 SU09

Cricklade Hotel & Country Club Common Hill SN6 6HA
☎ 01793 750751
A challenging 9-hole course with undulating greens and beautiful views. Par 3 6th (128yds) signature hole from an elevated tee to a green protected by a deep pot bunker.
9 holes, 1830yds, Par 62, SSS 57.
Club membership 140.
Visitors welcome.
Societies apply in writing.
Green Fees not confirmed.
Facilities ⊗ ⋔ ♨ ♨ ♀ ♨ ⚑ ⌕ Ian Bolt.
Leisure hard tennis courts, heated indoor swimming pool, solarium, gymnasium, trolley for hire, snooker & pool table, croquet.
Location On the B4040 out of Cricklade, towards Malmesbury
Hotel ★★★ 70% Stanton House Hotel, The Avenue, Stanton Fitzwarren, SWINDON
☎ 01793 861777 86 ⇥ ⋔

ERLESTOKE   Map 03 ST95

Erlestoke Sands SN10 5UA ☎ 01380 831069
The course is set on the lower slopes of Salisbury Plain with distant views to the Cotswolds and Marlborough Downs. The 7th plunges from an elevated three-tiered tee, high in the woods, to a large green with a spectacular backdrop of a meandering river and hills. The course was built to suit every standard of golfer from the novice to the very low handicapper and its two tiers offer lakes and rolling downland.
18 holes, 6406yds, Par 73, SSS 71, Course record 69.
Club membership 706.
Visitors   phone for tee booking in advance 01380 831027.
Societies   must book in advance.
Green Fees £14 per 18 holes (£18 weekends & bank holidays).
Facilities   ⊗ ⅷ ┗ ♥ ♀ ♨ 🏌 ⌞ Tony Valentine.
Leisure   motorised carts for hire, buggies for hire, trolley for hire, driving range, putting green, practice area.
Location   On B3098 Devizes/Westbury road
Hotel   ★★ 67% The Cedar Hotel, Warminster Rd, WESTBURY
                 ☎ 01373 822753 8 ⇔ ⬧Annexe8 ⇔ ⬧

GREAT DURNFORD   Map 04 SU13

High Post SP4 6AT ☎ 01722 782356
An interesting downland course on Wiltshire chalk with good turf and splendid views over the southern area of Salisbury Plain. The par 3, 17th and the two-shot 18th require good judgement.
18 holes, 6297yds, Par 70, SSS 70, Course record 64.
Club membership 580.
Visitors   a handicap certificate is required at weekends & bank holidays. Telephone professional in advance 01722 782219.,
Societies   apply by telephone to manager.
Green Fees £30 per day; £23 per round (£35/£28 weekends).
Facilities   ⊗ ⅷ ┗ ♥ ♀ ♨ 🏌 ⌞ Ian Welding.
Leisure   trolley for hire, driving range, putting green, practice area.
Location   1.75m SE on A345
Hotel   ★★★ 68% Rose & Crown Hotel, Harnham Rd, Harnham, SALISBURY
                 ☎ 01722 327908 28 ⇔ ⬧

HIGHWORTH   Map 04 SU29

Highworth Community Golf Centre Swindon Rd SN6 7SJ ☎ 01793 766014
Public downland course, situated in a high position affording good views.
9 holes, 3120yds, Par 35, SSS 35.
Club membership 150.
Visitors   no restrictions.
Societies   advisable to contact in advance.
Green Fees £5 per 9 holes (£6 weekends).
Facilities   ♥ ♨ 🏌 ⌞ Mark Toombs.
Leisure   trolley for hire, putting green, practice area, pitch & putt.
Location   Off A361 Swindon to Letchlade road

Hotel   ★★★ 63% The Crest Hotel, Oxford Rd, Stratton St Margaret, SWINDON
                 ☎ 01793 831333 91 ⇔ ⬧

Wrag Barn Golf & Country Club Shrivenham Rd SN6 7QQ ☎ 01793 861327
This course, designed by Hawtree, is some 6,500yards long. The Par of 72 can be demanding as it maximises the natural features of gentle contours, tess and water. The Par 3 5th is particularly tricky. A long approach shot has to carry over a stream 5 yards in front of the tree-protected green. The large greenside bunker to the right attracts an alarming number of balls!
18 holes, 6500yds, Par 72.
Club membership 600.
Visitors   no restrictions but may not play before noon at weekends.
Societies   contact in advance.
Green Fees £30 per day; £18 per round (£25 per round weekends & bank holidays).
Facilities   ⊗ ⅷ ┗ ♥ ♀ ♨ 🏌 ⌞ Barry Loughrey.
Leisure   motorised carts for hire, buggies for hire, trolley for hire, driving range, putting green, practice area.
Location   On B4000 Shrivenham Road
Hotel   ★★★ 70% Stanton House Hotel, The Avenue, Stanton Fitzwarren, SWINDON
                 ☎ 01793 861777 86 ⇔ ⬧

KINGSDOWN   Map 03 ST86

Kingsdown SN13 8BS ☎ 01225 742530
Fairly flat, open downland course with very sparse tree cover but surrounding wood.
18 holes, 6445yds, Par 72, SSS 71, Course record 64.
Club membership 650.
Visitors   welcome except at weekends. Must contact in advance & handicap certificate required.
Societies   apply by letter.
Green Fees £22 per day.
Facilities   ⊗ ⅷ ┗ ♥ ♀ ♨ 🏌 ⌞ Andrew Butler.
Leisure   trolley for hire, putting green, practice area.
Location   W side of village
Hotel   ★★ 68% Box House Hotel, London Rd, BOX
                 ☎ 01225 744447 9 ⇔ ⬧

LANDFORD   Map 04 SU21

Hamptworth Golf & Country Club Hamptworth Rd, Hamptworth SP5 2DU ☎ 01794 390155
Hamptworth enjoys ancient woodland and an abundance of wildlife in a beautiful setting on the edge of the New Forest. The 14th is one of its most challenging holes having a narrow fairway guarded by established forest oaks. The 2nd is a dogleg of 543yds and plays differently all year.
18 holes, 6516yds, Par 72, SSS 71, Course record 68.
Club membership 450.
Visitors   telephone to check availability.
Societies   weekdays only, write or telephone in advance.
Green Fees £28 per day; £17.50 per 18 holes (£33/22.50 weekends).
Facilities   ⊗ ┗ ♥ ♀ ♨ 🏌
Leisure   buggies for hire, trolley for hire, practice area.
Location   1m NW
Hotel   ★★★ 60% Bartley Lodge, Lyndhurst Rd, CADNAM ☎ 01703 812248 20 ⇔ ⬧

MARLBOROUGH

Map 04 SU16

Marlborough The Common SN8 1DU ☎ 01672 512147
Downland course open to prevailing wind. Extensive views.
18 holes, 6526yds, Par 72, SSS 71.
Club membership 920.
Visitors restricted at certain times; must have a handicap
certificate at weekends. Must contact in advance.
Societies must telephone in advance.
Green Fees not confirmed.
Facilities ♀ ♨ 🏠 🥃 L Ross.
Location N side of town centre on A345
Hotel ★★★ 59% Castle & Ball Hotel, High St,
MARLBOROUGH
☎ 01672 515201 34 ⊨ 🐾Annexe2 ⊨ 🐾

OAKSEY

Map 03 ST99

Oaksey Park Golf & Leisure SN16 9SB
☎ 01666 577995
A testing nine-hole parkland course set on the west side of the
Cotswold Water Parks.
9 holes, 3100yds, Par 70, SSS 69, Course record 66.
Club membership 250.
Visitors no restrictions.
Societies telephone for details.
Green Fees £8 per 18 holes; £5 per 9 holes (£13/£8
weekends & bank holidays).
Facilities ⊗ ♨ 🥃 ♀ ♨ 🛏 🥃 David Carroll.
Leisure fishing, driving range, putting green, practice
area, shooting, water sports, horse riding.
Location Between A419 & A429
Hotel ★★★ 68% Stratton House Hotel, Gloucester
Rd, CIRENCESTER
☎ 01285 651761 41 ⊨ 🐾

OGBOURNE ST GEORGE

Map 04 SU27

Ogbourne Downs SN8 1TB ☎ 01672 841327 & 841287
Downland turf and magnificent greens.
18 holes, 6226yds, Par 71, SSS 70, Course record 65.
Club membership 890.
Visitors welcome weekdays only, handicap certificate
required. Must contact in advance.
Societies must apply for booking form in advance.
Green Fees £20 per day/round (£30 weekends by prior
arrangement only).
Facilities ⊗ ♨ 🥃 ♀ ♨ 🏠 🥃 Colin Harraway.
Leisure motorised carts for hire, buggies for hire, trolley
for hire, driving range, putting green, practice area.
Location N side of village on A436
Hotel ★★★ 73% Ivy House Hotel & Garden
Restaurant, High St, MARLBOROUGH
☎ 01672 515333 12 ⊨ 🐾Annexe16 ⊨ 🐾

SALISBURY

Map 04 SU12

Salisbury & South Wilts Netherhampton SP2 8PR
☎ 01722 742645
Gently undulating and well drained parkland course in
country setting with panoramic views of the cathedral and
surrounding country. Any of the three 9-hole courses - Main,
Old and Drummony can be combined for a challenging 18-
hole round

*Main Course: 18 holes, 6528yds, Par 71, SSS 71, Course
record 61.*
Old Course: 18 holes, 6177yds, Par 70, SSS 70.
*Drummond: 18 holes, 6121yds, Par 69, SSS 69, Course
record 63.*
Club membership 1000.
Visitors must telephone in advance.
Societies telephone initially.
Green Fees £25 per day (£40 weekends & bank holidays).
£12 per day on 9 hole course of the day.
Facilities ⊗ ♨ 🥃 ♀ ♨ 🏠 🥃 Gary Emerson.
Leisure trolley for hire, driving range, putting green,
practice area.
Location 2m W on A3094
Hotel ★★★ 66% Rose & Crown Hotel, Harnham Rd,
Harnham, SALISBURY
☎ 01722 327908 28 ⊨ 🐾

SWINDON

Map 04 SU18

Broome Manor Golf Complex Pipers Way SN3 1RG
☎ 01793 532403
Two courses and a 20-bay floodlit driving range. Parkland
with water hazards, open fairways and short cut rough.
Walking is easy on gentle slopes.
*18 holes, 6283yds, Par 71, SSS 70, Course record 62 or 9
holes, 2690yds, Par 66, SSS 66.*
Club membership 800.
Visitors casual times available but advisable to contact in
advance.
Societies must be prebooked.
Green Fees £8.50 per 18 holes; £5 per 9 holes (£10/£6
weekends).
Facilities ⊗ ♨ 🥃 🥃 ♀ ♨ 🏠 🥃 Barry Sandry.
Leisure trolley for hire, driving range, putting green,
practice area.
Location 1.75m SE of town centre off B4006
Hotel ★★★ 63% The Crest Hotel, Oxford Rd,
Stratton St Margaret, SWINDON
☎ 01793 831333 91 ⊨ 🐾

TIDWORTH

Map 04 SU24

Tidworth Garrison Bulford Rd SP9 7AF
☎ 01980 842301
A breezy, dry downland course with lovely turf, fine
trees and views over Salisbury Plain and the surrounding
area. The 3rd and 12th holes are notable. The 564-yard
13th, going down towards the clubhouse, gives the big
hitter a chance to let fly.
18 holes, 6101yds, Par 69, SSS 69, Course record 62.
Club membership 700.
Visitors must contact in advance, weekend & bank
holiday bookings may not be made until
Thursday prior.
Societies Tue & Thu, bookings required 12-18 months
in advance.
Green Fees £18 per day.
Facilities ⊗ ♨ 🥃 🥃 ♀ ♨ 🏠 🥃 Terry Gosden.
Leisure trolley for hire, driving range, putting green,
practice area.
Location W side of village off A338
Hotel ★★ 61% Danebury Hotel, High St,
ANDOVER
☎ 01264 323332 23 ⊨ 🐾

UPAVON   Map 04 SU15

Upavon Douglas Av SN9 6BQ
☎ 01980 630787 & 630281
Downland course set on sides of infamous valley, with some
wind affecting play. The 2nd, 9th, 11th and 18th are all par 3
to small greens. A well-drained course.
9 holes, 5601yds, Par 69, SSS 67, Course record 66.
Club membership 450.

Visitors	must contact in advance and may not play before noon at weekends.
Societies	telephone in advance.
Green Fees	£18 per day; £12 per round (£24 weekends; £12 after 4pm).
Facilities	⊗ by prior arrangement ⅶ by prior arrangement ♣ ☕ ♀ ⚲ 🏌 ✆ ₵ Richard Blake.
Leisure	hard tennis courts, trolley for hire, putting green, practice area.
Location	2m E on A342
Hotel	★★★ 61% Bear Hotel, Market Place, DEVIZES ☎ 01380 722444 24 ⇌ ⋒

WARMINSTER   Map 03 ST84

West Wilts Elm Hill BA12 0AU
☎ 01985 212702 & 213133
A hilltop course among the Wiltshire downs without
trees and somewhat windswept. First-class springy turf
with many interesting holes.
18 holes, 5709yds, Par 70, SSS 68, Course record 62.
Club membership 650.

Visitors	must contact in advance.
Societies	apply by letter.
Green Fees	£24 per day/round in summer; £24 per day, £16 per round in winter (£35 weekends).
Facilities	⊗ ⅶ ♣ ☕ ♀ ⚲ 🏌 ✆ ₵ Andrew Lamb.
Leisure	trolley for hire, putting, practice area.
Location	N side of town centre off A350
Hotel	★★★★ 70% Bishopstrow House, WARMINSTER ☎ 01985 212312 30 ⇌ ⋒

WOOTTON BASSETT   Map 04 SU08

Brinkworth Longmans Farm, Brinkworth SN15 5DG
☎ 01666 510277
Fairly long and open course with ditches and water hazards
on the 2nd and 18th holes. Several testing par 3s with
crosswinds and three long and tricky par 5s, notably the 4th,
8th and 14th holes.
18 holes, 5884yds, Par 70, SSS 70.
Club membership 70.

Visitors	welcome any time no contact needed.
Societies	telephone in advance or apply in writing.
Green Fees	£6.50 per 18 holes (£8.50 weekends & bank holidays).
Facilities	☕ ♀ ⚲ 🏌
Leisure	trolley for hire, putting green, practice area.
Location	Just off B4042 between Malmesbury/Wootton Bassett
Hotel	★★★ 69% Marsh Farm Hotel, Coped Hall, WOOTTON BASSETT ☎ 01793 848044 4 ⇌ ⋒Annexe24 ⇌ ⋒

Wiltshire Vastern SN4 7PB ☎ 01793 849999
A Peter Alliss/Clive Clark design set in rolling Wiltshire
countryside. A number of lakes add a challenge for both low
and high handicappers.
18 holes, 6496yds, Par 72, SSS 71.
Club membership 800.

Visitors	must contact in advance.
Societies	contact in advance.
Green Fees	£25 per day; £20 per round (£30/£25 weekends).
Facilities	⊗ ⅶ ♣ ☕ ♀ ⚲ 🏌 ✆ ₵ Andy Gray.
Leisure	motorised carts for hire, buggies for hire, trolley for hire, putting green, practice area.
Location	Leave M4 at junc 16, on A3102
Hotel	★★★ 69% Marsh Farm Hotel, Coped Hall, WOOTTON BASSETT ☎ 01793 848044 4 ⇌ ⋒Annexe24 ⇌ ⋒

YORKSHIRE, EAST RIDING OF

BEVERLEY   Map 08 TA03

Beverley & East Riding The Westwood HU17 8RG
☎ 01482 869519
Picturesque parkland course with some hard walking and
natural hazards - trees and gorse bushes. Also cattle and
sheep (spring to autumn); horse-riders are an occasional
hazard in the early morning.
18 holes, 6127yds, Par 69, SSS 69, Course record 65.
Club membership 500.

Visitors	advised to contact pro shop 01482 869519.
Societies	telephone then written confirmation.
Green Fees	£16 per day; £12 per round (£21/£16 weekends & bank holidays).
Facilities	⊗ ⅶ ♣ ☕ ♀ ⚲ 🏌 ✆ ₵ Ian Mackie.
Leisure	trolley for hire, putting green, practice area.
Location	1m SW on B1230
Hotel	★★★ 65% Beverley Arms Hotel, North Bar Within, BEVERLEY ☎ 01482 869241 57 ⇌ ⋒

BRANDESBURTON   Map 08 TA14

Hainsworth Park Burton Holme YO25 8RT
☎ 01964 542362
A parkland course with easy walking.
18 holes, 6003yds, Par 71, SSS 69, Course record 62.
Club membership 500.

Visitors	contact in advance.
Societies	telephone initially.
Green Fees	£12 per round (£15 weekends & bank holidays).
Facilities	⊗ ⅶ ♣ ☕ ♀ ⚲ 🏌 ✆ ⇌
Leisure	grass tennis courts, fishing, trolley for hire, putting green, practice area.
Location	SW side of village on A165
Hotel	★★ 68% Burton Lodge Hotel, BRANDESBURTON ☎ 01964 542847 8rm(7 ⇌ ⋒)Annexe2 ⇌ ⋒

BRIDLINGTON
Map 08 TA16

Bridlington Belvedere Rd YO15 3NA
☎ 01262 606367 & 672092
Clifftop, seaside course, windy at times, with hazards of
bunkers, ponds, ditches and trees.
18 holes, 6294yds, Par 71, SSS 71, Course record 65.
Club membership 600.

Visitors	preferably book in advance, limited at weekends.
Societies	telephone bookings in advance.
Green Fees	£18 per day; £12 per round (£25/£20 weekends & bank holidays).
Facilities	⊗ ⑪ ⓑ 🛍 ♥ ♀ ♨ 🏠 👕 ⌊ Anthony Howarth.
Leisure	motorised carts for hire, trolley for hire, putting green, practice area.
Location	1m S off A165
Hotel	★★★ 65% Expanse Hotel, North Marine Dr, BRIDLINGTON ☎ 01262 675347 48 ⇌ 🐾

BROUGH
Map 08 SE92

Brough Cave Rd HU15 1HB ☎ 01482 667291 & 667374
Parkland course.
18 holes, 6159yds, Par 68, SSS 69.
Club membership 800.

Visitors	with member only at weekends. Must have handicap certificate and contact in advance.
Societies	apply by letter.
Green Fees	not confirmed.
Facilities	♀ ♨ 🏠 👕 ⌊ Gordon Townhill.
Location	0.5m N
Hotel	B Forte Posthouse Hull, Ferriby High Rd, NORTH FERRIBY ☎ 01482 645212 96 ⇌ 🐾

DRIFFIELD (GREAT)
Map 08 TA05

Driffield Sunderlandwick YO25 9AD ☎ 01377 253116
An easy walking, parkland course.
18 holes, 6199yds, Par 70, SSS 69, Course record 67.
Club membership 398.

Visitors	must adhere to club dress rule.
Societies	apply in writing or telephone.
Green Fees	£18 per day/round (£25 weekends).
Facilities	⊗ ⑪ ⓑ 🛍 ♥ ♀ ♨ 🏠 ⌊ Ian Mackie.
Leisure	fishing, trolley for hire, putting green, practice area.
Location	2m S off A164
Hotel	★★★ 69% Bell Hotel, 46 Market Place, DRIFFIELD ☎ 01377 256661 14 ⇌ 🐾

FLAMBOROUGH
Map 08 TA27

Flamborough Head Lighthouse Rd YO15 1AR
☎ 01262 850333 & 850417
Undulating seaside course.
18 holes, 5483yds, Par 66, SSS 66, Course record 63.
Club membership 500.

Visitors	may not play before noon on Sun or Wed between 10.30 and 1.30.
Societies	must contact in advance.
Green Fees	£15 per day; £12 per round (£18 weekends & bank holidays).
Facilities	⊗ ⑪ ⓑ 🛍 ♥ ♀ ♨ 🏠
	⌊ G Hutchinson (summer only).

Leisure	trolley for hire, putting green, practice area.
Location	2m E off B1259
Hotel	★ 64% Flaneburg Hotel, North Marine Rd, FLAMBOROUGH ☎ 01262 850284 13rm(8 🐾)

HESSLE
Map 08 TA02

Hessle Westfield Rd, Raywell HU16 5YL
☎ 01482 650171 & 650190
Well-wooded downland course, easy walking, windy.
18 holes, 6638yds, Par 72, SSS 72, Course record 63.

Visitors	not Tue between 9-1 and may not play before 11am on Sat & Sun.
Societies	by prior arrangement.
Green Fees	£23 per day; £18 per round (£25 per round weekends & bank holidays).
Facilities	⊗ ⑪ ⓑ 🛍 ♥ ♀ ♨ 🏠 ⌊ Grahame Fieldsend.
Leisure	trolley for hire, putting green, practice area.
Location	3m SW of Cottingham
Hotel	B Forte Posthouse Hull, Ferriby High Rd, NORTH FERRIBY ☎ 01482 645212 96 ⇌ 🐾

HORNSEA
Map 08 TA14

Hornsea Rolston Rd HU18 1XG
☎ 01964 532020 & 534989
Flat, parkland course with good greens.
18 holes, 6685yds, Par 72, SSS 72, Course record 66.
Club membership 600.

Visitors	with member only at weekends & after 3pm. Must contact in advance.
Societies	contact Secretary in advance.
Green Fees	£25 per day; £18 per round.
Facilities	⊗ ⑪ ⓑ 🛍 ♥ ♀ ♨ 🏠 👕 ⌊ Brian Thompson.
Leisure	trolley for hire, putting green, practice area, snooker.
Location	1m S on B1242, follow signs for Hornsea Pottery
Hotel	★★★ 65% Beverley Arms Hotel, North Bar Within, BEVERLEY ☎ 01482 869241 57 ⇌ 🐾

HULL
Map 08 TA02

Ganstead Park Longdales Ln, Coniston HU11 4LB
☎ 01482 874754 & 811121
Parkland course, easy walking.
18 holes, 6801yds, Par 72, SSS 73, Course record 67.

Visitors	contact in advance.
Societies	telephone in advance.
Green Fees	£15 (£24 weekends).
Facilities	⊗ ⑪ ⓑ 🛍 ♥ ♀ ♨ 🏠 ⌊ Michael J Smee.
Leisure	trolley for hire, putting green, practice area.
Location	6m NE off A165
Hotel	★★ 63% Waterfront Hotel, Dagger Ln, HULL ☎ 01482 227222 30 ⇌ 🐾

Hull The Hall, 27 Packman Ln HU10 7TJ ☎ 01482 658919
Parkland course.
18 holes, 6242yds, Par 70, SSS 70.
Club membership 840.

Visitors	only weekdays. Contact professional 01482 653074.
Societies	only on Tue and Thu by prior arrangement.
Green Fees	£30 per day; £25 per round. ▶

Facilities ⊗ ⅶ ⮾ ⬤ ♀ ♨ 🕭 ℓ David Jagger.
Leisure trolley for hire, putting green, practice area.
Location 5m W of city centre off A164
Hotel ★★★ 69% Willerby Manor Hotel, Well Ln,
WILLERBY ☎ 01482 652616 34 ⇄ ⏃

Springhead Park Willerby Rd HU5 5JE ☎ 01482 656309
Municipal parkland course with tight, tree-lined, undulating
fairways.
18 holes, 6402yds, Par 71, SSS 71.
Club membership 667.
Visitors welcome ex Sun (tee reserved).
Green Fees not confirmed.
Facilities 🕭 ⯈ ℓ Barry Herrington.
Location 5m W off A164
Hotel ★★★ 69% Willerby Manor Hotel, Well Ln,
WILLERBY ☎ 01482 652616 34 ⇄ ⏃

Sutton Park Salthouse Rd HU8 9HF ☎ 01482 374242
Municipal parkland course.
18 holes, 6251yds, Par 70, SSS 69, Course record 67.
Club membership 300.
Visitors no restrictions.
Societies prior arrangement via club, telephone and
confirm in writing.
Green Fees £5.50 (£7.50 weekends).
Facilities ♀ ♨ 🕭 ⯈ ℓ Paul Rushworth.
Leisure trolley for hire, putting green, practice area.
Location 3m NE on B1237 off A165
Hotel ★★ 63% Waterfront Hotel, Dagger Ln, HULL
☎ 01482 227222 30 ⇄ ⏃

SOUTH CAVE   Map 08 SE93

Cave Castle Golf Hotel Church Hill, South Cave HU15 2EU
☎ 01430 421286
A young but challenging course at the foot of the Wolds with
superb views. There is a keen interest in ladies golf and
tuition and golf clinics are available.
18 holes, 6500yds, Par 73, SSS 71.
Club membership 400.
Visitors must contact in advance.
Societies by arrangement with Manager.
Green Fees £18 per day; £12.50 per round (£25/£18
weekends and bank holidays).
Facilities ⊗ ⅶ ⮾ ⬤ ♀ ♨ 🕭 ⯈ ℓ Karl Worby.
Leisure fishing, trolley for hire, putting green, practice
area.
Hotel ★★ 65% Fox & Coney Inn, Market Place,
South Cave ☎ 01430 422275 8 ⇄ ⏃

WITHERNSEA   Map 08 TA32

Withernsea Chesnut Av HU19 2PG ☎ 01964 612078
Exposed seaside links with narrow, undulating fairways,
bunkers and small greens.
9 holes, 5112yds, Par 66, SSS 64.
Club membership 550.
Visitors with member only at weekends.
Societies apply in writing.
Green Fees not confirmed.
Facilities ♨ 🕭 ℓ Graham Harrison.
Location S side of town centre off A1033
Hotel ★★ 64% Pearson Park Hotel, Pearson Park,
HULL ☎ 01482 343043 32 ⇄ ⏃

YORKSHIRE, NORTH

ALDWARK   Map 08 SE46

Aldwark Manor YO6 2NF ☎ 01347 838353
An easy walking, scenic 18-hole parkland course with holes
both sides of the River Ure. The course surrounds the
Victorian Aldwark Manor Golf Hotel.
18 holes, 6171yds, Par 71, SSS 70, Course record 69.
Club membership 430.
Visitors must contact in advance, restricted weekends.
Societies must telephone in advance.
Green Fees £20 per day; £16 per round (£24/£20 weekends
& bank holidays).
Facilities ⊗ ⅶ ⮾ ⬤ ♀ ♨ 🕭 ⯈ ⋈
Leisure fishing, trolley for hire, putting green, practice
area.
Location 5m SE of Boroughbridge off A1
Hotel ★★★⚘ 70% Aldwark Manor Hotel,
ALDWARK
☎ 01347 838146 17 ⇄ ⏃Annexe3 ⇄ ⏃

BEDALE   Map 08 SE28

Bedale Leyburn Rd DL8 1EZ ☎ 01677 422451
Secluded parkland course with many trees.
18 holes, 6565yds, Par 72, SSS 71, Course record 68.
Club membership 600.
Visitors welcome when course is free.
Societies must apply in advance.

ALDWARK
MANOR
GOLF HOTEL

Aldwark, Alne, York YO6 2NF
Telephone: (01347) 838146/7
Golf Shop: (01347) 838353
Fax: (01347) 838867

Extensively refurbished Victorian Country
House Hotel – set in 110 acres of rural
Yorkshire. 20 luxury bedrooms –
Conference and Banqueting up to 90 persons
– excellent cuisine. Special breaks available.

The hotel is surrounded by its own 18 hole
6171 yd par 71 golf course, spanning both
sides of the river Ure. Located 12 miles
north of the historic city of York and the
spa town of Harrogate.

Green Fees £18 per day/round (£28 weekends & bank holidays).
Facilities ⊗ ⅢⅢ ⅬⅬ ⯀ ♀ ♨ 🏠 (Tony Johnson.
Leisure trolley for hire, putting green, practice area.
Location 0.25 N of town on A684
Hotel ★★ 62% Motel Leeming, Great North Rd, Leeming Bar ☎ 01677 422122 40 ⇔ ㋫

BENTHAM   Map 07 SD66

Bentham Robin Ln LA2 7AG ☎ 01524 262455
Moorland course with glorious views.
9 holes, 5760yds, Par 70, SSS 69, Course record 69.
Club membership 480.
Visitors no restrictions.
Societies must apply in advance.
Green Fees not confirmed.
Facilities ♀ ♨
Leisure putting green, practice area.
Location N side of High Bentham
Hotel ★★ 67% The Traddock, AUSTWICK ☎ 015242 51224 11 ⇔ ㋫

CATTERICK GARRISON   Map 08 SE29

Catterick Garrison Leyburn Rd DL9 3QE
☎ 01748 833268
Scenic parkland/moorland course of Championship standard, with good views of the Pennines and Cleveland hills. Testing 1st and 3rd holes.
18 holes, 6313yds, Par 71, SSS 70, Course record 68.
Club membership 700.
Visitors telephone professional shop for tee availability.
Societies by arrangement.
Green Fees £20 per day/round (£25 weekends).
Facilities ⊗ ⅢⅢ ⅬⅬ ⯀ ♀ ♨ 🏠 ┳ (Andy Marshall.
Leisure motorised carts for hire, buggies for hire, trolley for hire, putting green, practice area.
Location 0.5m W of Catterick Garrison Centre
Hotel ★★ 59% Bridge House Hotel, CATTERICK BRIDGE ☎ 01748 818331 16rm(4 ⇔9 ㋫)

COPMANTHORPE   Map 08 SE54

Pike Hills Tadcaster Rd YO2 3UW
☎ 01904 706566 & 700797
Parkland course surrounding nature reserve. Level terrain.
18 holes, 6140yds, Par 71, SSS 69, Course record 67.
Club membership 800.
Visitors with member only weekends & bank holidays.
Societies must apply in advance.
Green Fees £20 per day; £15 per round.
Facilities ⊗ ⅢⅢ ⅬⅬ ⯀ ♀ ♨ 🏠 ┳ (Ian Gradwell.
Leisure motorised carts for hire, buggies for hire, trolley for hire, 2 putting greens, practice area.
Location 3m SW of York on A64
Hotel ★★★★ 64% Swallow Hotel, Tadcaster Rd, YORK ☎ 01904 701000 113 ⇔ ㋫

EASINGWOLD   Map 08 SE56

Easingwold Stillington Rd YO6 3ET ☎ 01347 821964
Parkland course with easy walking. Trees are a major feature and on six holes water hazards come into play.

18 holes, 6285yds, Par 72, SSS 70, Course record 65.
Club membership 600.
Visitors prior enquiry essential.
Societies prior application in writing essential.
Green Fees £25 per day (£30 weekends).
Facilities ⊗ ⅢⅢ ⅬⅬ ⯀ ♀ ♨ 🏠 (John Hughes.
Leisure trolley for hire, putting green, practice area.
Location 1m S
Hotel ★★ 65% George Hotel, Market Place, EASINGWOLD ☎ 01347 821698 14 ⇔ ㋫

FILEY   Map 08 TA18

Filey West Av YO14 9BQ ☎ 01723 513293 & 513134
Parkland course with good views, windy. Stream runs through course. Testing 9th and 13th holes.
18 holes, 6112yds, Par 70, SSS 69.
Club membership 900.
Visitors must telephone to reserve tee time.
Societies contact by telephone.
Green Fees Apr-Oct: £20 per day (£25 weekends). Nov-Mar £14 per day (£18 weekends).
Facilities ⊗ ⅢⅢ ⅬⅬ ⯀ ♀ ♨ 🏠 ┳ (
Leisure motorised carts for hire, buggies for hire, trolley for hire, putting green, practice area.
Location 0.5m S of Filey
Hotel ★★ 63% Sea Brink Hotel, The Beach, FILEY ☎ 01723 513257 11 ⇔ ㋫

GANTON   Map 08 SE97

Ganton YO12 4PA ☎ 01944 710329
Championship course, heathland, gorse-lined fairways and heavily bunkered; variable winds.
18 holes, 6720yds, Par 73, SSS 74, Course record 65.
Club membership 500.
Visitors by prior arrangement.
Societies prior arrangement in writing.
Green Fees not confirmed.
Facilities ⊗ ⅢⅢ ⅬⅬ ⯀ ♀ ♨ 🏠 ┳ (Gary Brown.
Leisure motorised carts for hire, buggies for hire, trolley for hire, putting green, practice area.
Location 0.25m NW off A64
Hotel ★★★ 63% East Ayton Lodge Country House, Moor Ln, Forge Valley, EAST AYTON ☎ 01723 864227 11 ⇔ ㋫Annexe20 ⇔ ㋫

HARROGATE   Map 08 SE35

Harrogate Forest Ln Head, Starbeck HG2 7TF
☎ 01423 862999 & 862547
One of Yorkshire's oldest and best courses was designed in 1897 by 'Sandy' Herd. A perfect example of golf architecture, its greens and fairways offer an interesting but fair challenge. The undulating parkland course once formed part of the ancient Forest of Knaresborough. Excellent clubhouse.
18 holes, 6241yds, Par 69, SSS 70, Course record 64.
Club membership 650.
Visitors advisable to contact professional in advance.
Societies must contact in writing or intially by telephone.
Green Fees £32 per day; £28 per round (£40 day/round weekends & bank holidays). ▶

Facilities ⊗ ⅷ ⓑ 🍽 ♀ ⚲ 🏠 ⓣ Paul Johnson.
Leisure trolley for hire, putting green, practice area.
Location 2.25m N on A59
Hotel ★★★ 73% Balmoral Hotel & Henry's Restaurant, Franklin Mount, HARROGATE ☎ 01423 508208 20 ⇆ ☏

Oakdale Oakdale HG1 2LN
☎ 01423 567162 & 567188
A pleasant, undulating parkland course which provides a good test of golf for the low handicap player without intimidating the less proficient. A special feature is an attractive stream which comes in to play on four holes. Excellent views from the clubhouse which has good facilities.
18 holes, 6456yds, Par 71, SSS 71.
Club membership 1034.
Visitors no party bookings weekends.
Societies telephone followed by letter.
Green Fees £30 per day; £25 per round (£30 per round weekends and bank holidays).
Facilities ⊗ ⅷ ⓑ 🍽 ♀ ⚲ 🏠 ⓣ ⓣ Clive Dell.
Leisure motorised carts for hire, buggies for hire, trolley for hire, putting green, practice area.
Location N side of town centre off A61
Hotel ★★★ 69% Grants Hotel, 3-13 Swan Rd, HARROGATE ☎ 01423 560666 42 ⇆ ☏

Rudding Park HG3 1DJ ☎ 01423 872100
Opened in Spring 1995, Rudding Park has been designed by Hawtree of Oxford as a parkland course with 5 water features to be operated on a Pay and Play basis.
18 holes, 6871yds, Par 72, SSS 73, Course record 73.
Visitors handicap certificate required, tee reservation available but not essential.
Societies apply by telephone in advance.
Green Fees £16 per round (£19 weekends and bank holidays).
Facilities ⊗ ⅷ ⓑ 🍽 ♀ ⚲ 🏠 ⇆ ⓣ Christopher Steele.
Leisure heated outdoor swimming pool, motorised carts for hire, buggies for hire, trolley for hire, driving range, putting green.
Location 2m SE of Harrogate town centre
Hotel ★★★ 64% Studley Hotel, Swan Rd, HARROGATE ☎ 01423 560425 36 ⇆ ☏

HOWDEN   Map 08 SE72

Boothferry Spaldington Ln DN14 7NG ☎ 01430 430364
A heavily bunkered meadowland course with several dykes.
18 holes, 6651yds, Par 73, SSS 72, Course record 64.
Club membership 650.
Visitors must contact in advance.
Societies must contact for booking form.
Green Fees £8.50 per 18 holes; £5.50 per 9 holes (£12/£7.50 weekends).
Facilities ⊗ ⅷ ⓑ 🍽 ♀ ⚲ 🏠 ⓣ ⓣ Stewart Wilkinson.
Leisure trolley for hire, driving range, putting green, practice area.
Location 2.5m N of Howden off B1228
Hotel ★★ 66% Clifton Hotel, 1 Clifton Gardens, Boothferry Rd, GOOLE ☎ 01405 761336 9rm(5 ⇆3 ☏)

KIRKBYMOORSIDE   Map 08 SE68

Kirkbymoorside Manor Vale YO6 6EG ☎ 01751 431525
Hilly parkland course with narrow fairways, gorse and hawthorn bushes. Beautiful views.
18 holes, 6000yds, Par 69, SSS 69, Course record 65.
Club membership 650.
Visitors are advised to contact in advance, may not play before 9.30 or between 12.30-1.30.
Societies must apply in advance.
Green Fees £17 per day (£25 weekends & bank holidays).
Facilities ⊗ ⅷ ⓑ 🍽 ♀ ⚲ ⓣ
Leisure trolley for hire, putting green, practice area.
Location N side of village
Hotel ★★⚤ 71% Appleton Hall Country House Hotel, APPLETON-LE-MOORS ☎ 01751 417227 & 417452 10 ⇆ ☏

KNARESBOROUGH   Map 08 SE35

Knaresborough Boroughbridge Rd HG5 0QQ
☎ 01423 862690 & 864865
Undulating parkland course with mature trees.
18 holes, 6496yds, Par 70, SSS 71.
Club membership 796.
Visitors restricted start times summer weekends.
Societies apply by telephone or letter, no bookings for Sat, Sun or Tue.
Green Fees £25 per day; £18.50 per round (£30/£25 weekends).
Facilities ⊗ ⅷ ⓑ 🍽 ♀ ⚲ 🏠 ⓣ Gary J Vickers.
Leisure buggies for hire, putting green, practice area.
Location 1.25 N on A6055
Hotel ★★★ 70% Dower House Hotel, Bond End, KNARESBOROUGH ☎ 01423 863302 28 ⇆ ☏Annexe4 ⇆ ☏

MALTON   Map 08 SE77

Malton & Norton Welham Park, Norton YO17 9QE
☎ 01653 693882 & 697912
Parkland course with panoramic views of the moors. Very testing 1st hole (564 yds dog-leg, left).
Welham Course: 18 holes, 6456yds, Par 72, SSS 71.
Park Course: 18 holes, 6242yds, Par 72, SSS 70.
Derwent Course: 18 holes, 6286yds, Par 72, SSS 70.
Club membership 825.
Visitors anytime except during competitions.
Societies telephone and confirm in writing.
Green Fees £22 per day/round (£28 weekends & bank holidays).
Facilities ⊗ ⅷ ⓑ 🍽 ♀ ⚲ ⓣ ⓣ S Robinson.
Leisure trolley for hire, putting green, practice area.
Location 1m S
Hotel ★★★⚤ 70% Burythorpe House Hotel, Burythorpe, MALTON ☎ 01653 658200 11 ⇆ ☏

MASHAM   Map 08 SE28

Masham Burnholme, Swinton Rd HG4 4HT
☎ 01765 689379
Flat parkland course crossed by River Burn, which comes into play on two holes.

9 holes, 6102yds, Par 70, SSS 69.
Club membership 327.

Visitors must play with member at weekends & bank holidays.
Societies write or telephone well in advance.
Green Fees £15 per day/round.
Facilities ⊗ ⅃ ☕ ♀ ♨
Leisure putting green.
Location 1m SW off A6108
Hotel ★ 67% Buck Inn, THORNTON WATLASS ☎ 01677 422461 7rm(5 ⇔ ♟)

MIDDLESBROUGH   Map 08 NZ41

Middlesbrough Brass Castle Ln, Marton TS8 9EE
☎ 01642 311515
Undulating parkland course, prevailing winds. Testing 9th, 16th and 17th holes.
18 holes, 6167yds, Par 70, SSS 70.
Club membership 960.

Visitors restricted Tue & Sat.
Societies Wed, Thu & Fri only. Must contact the club in advance.
Green Fees not confirmed.
Facilities ♀ ♨ ☕ ⨍ Don Jones.
Leisure putting green, practice area, trolley hire.
Location 4m S off A172
Hotel ★★ 62% Marton Way Toby Hotel, Marton Rd, MIDDLESBROUGH ☎ 01642 817651 53 ⇔ ♟

Middlesbrough Municipal Ladgate Ln TS5 7YZ
☎ 01642 315533
Parkland course with good views. The front nine holes have wide fairways and large, often well-guarded greens while the back nine demand shots over tree-lined water hazards and narrow entrances to subtly contoured greens. Driving range.
18 holes, 6333yds, Par 71, SSS 70, Course record 67.
Club membership 540.

Visitors book on the day weekdays, 7days in advance for weekends & bank holidays.
Societies apply in writing giving at least 2 weeks in advance.
Green Fees £8.50 per round (£11.50 weekends).
Facilities ⊗ ⅃ ☕ ♀ ♨ ☕ ⅋ ⨍ Alan Hope.
Leisure buggies for hire, trolley for hire, driving range, putting green, practice area.
Location 2m S of Middlesbrough on the A174
Hotel ★★ 62% Marton Way Toby Hotel, Marton Rd, MIDDLESBROUGH ☎ 01642 817651 53 ⇔ ♟

PANNAL   Map 08 SE35

Pannal Follifoot Rd HG3 1ES ☎ 01423 872628
Fine championship course. Moorland turf but well-wooded with trees closely involved with play.
18 holes, 6618yds, Par 72, SSS 72, Course record 62.
Club membership 780.

Visitors preferable to contact in advance, weekends limited.
Societies apply in advance.
Green Fees £38 per day; £30 per round (£38 per round weekends).
Facilities ⊗ ⅃ ⅃ ☕ ♀ ♨ ☕ ⅋ ⨍ Murray Burgess.
Leisure trolley for hire, putting green, practice area.

Location E side of village off A61
Hotel ★★★★ 59% The Majestic, Ripon Rd, HARROGATE ☎ 01423 568972 156 ⇔ ♟

RAVENSCAR   Map 08 NZ90

Raven Hall Hotel Golf Course YO13 0ET
☎ 01723 870353
Opened by the Earl of Cranbrook in 1898, this 9-hole clifftop course is sloping and with good quality small greens. Because of its clifftop position it is subject to strong winds which make it great fun to play, especially the 6th hole.
9 holes, 1894yds, Par 32, SSS 32.
Club membership 120.

Visitors spikes essential, no jeans/T shirts, busy at weekends.
Societies telephone in advance.
Green Fees not confirmed.
Facilities ♀ ⅋ ⊟
Leisure hard tennis courts, heated indoor plus outdoor swimming pool, sauna, putting green.
Location Situated on cliff top
Hotel ★★★ 60% Raven Hall Hotel, RAVENSCAR ☎ 01723 870353 53 ⇔ ♟

REDCAR   Map 08 NZ62

Cleveland Queen St TS10 1BT ☎ 01642 471798
Links championship course.
18 holes, 6707yds, Par 72, SSS 72, Course record 67.
Club membership 820.

Visitors must contact in advance, may not play Sat.
Societies must apply in writing.
Green Fees £20 per day/round (£30 weekends & bank holidays).
Facilities ⊗ ⅃ ⅃ ☕ ♀ ♨ ☕ ⨍ Stephen Wynn.
Leisure putting green, practice area.
Location 8m E of Middlesbrough
Hotel ★★ 62% Marton Way Toby Hotel, Marton Rd, MIDDLESBROUGH ☎ 01642 817651 53 ⇔ ♟

Wilton Wilton Castle TS10 4QY ☎ 01642 465265
Parkland course with some fine views.
18 holes, 6104yds, Par 70, SSS 69.
Club membership 750.

Visitors restricted Sat.
Societies must telephone in advance.
Green Fees not confirmed.
Facilities ♀ ♨ ☕ ⨍ R Smith.
Location 3m W on on A174
Hotel ★★ 62% Marton Way Toby Hotel, Marton Rd, MIDDLESBROUGH ☎ 01642 817651 53 ⇔ ♟

RICHMOND   Map 07 NZ10

Richmond Bend Hagg DL10 5EX
☎ 01748 823231(Secretary) & 825319
Parkland course.
18 holes, 5769yds, Par 70, SSS 68, Course record 64.
Club membership 600.

Visitors may not play before 11.30am on Sun.
Societies must contact in writing. ▶

Green Fees not confirmed.
Facilities   ♀ ♿ 🏋 ⛳ 🍴 ⛴ Paul Jackson.
Leisure   putting green,trolley hire.
Location   0.75m N
Hotel   ★★ 68% King's Head Hotel, Market Place,
              RICHMOND
              ☎ 01748 850220 24 ⇄ ⌽Annexe4 ⇄ ⌽

RIPON   Map 08 SE37

Ripon City Palace Rd HG4 3HH ☎ 01765 603640
Hard-walking on undulating parkland course; two testing par
3's at 5th and 7th.
18 holes, 6120yds, Par 71, SSS 69.
Club membership 675.
Visitors   book with professional. Limited play Sat
              especially Apr-Aug.
Societies   contact in writing or telephone.
Green Fees   £18 per day (£25 weekends & bank holidays).
Facilities   ⊗ ⅲ 🏋 ⛳ ♀ ♿ 🍴 ⛴ S T Davis.
Leisure   motorised carts for hire, buggies for hire, trolley
              for hire, putting green.
Location   1m NW on A6108
Hotel   ★★★ 67% Ripon Spa Hotel, Park St, RIPON
              ☎ 01765 602172 40 ⇄ ⌽

SALTBURN-BY-THE-SEA   Map 08 NZ62

Saltburn by the Sea Hob Hill, Guisborough Rd TS12 1NJ
☎ 01287 622812
Undulating meadowland course surrounded by woodland.
Particularly attractive in autumn. There are fine views of the
Cleveland Hills and of Tees Bay.
18 holes, 5846yds, Par 70, SSS 68, Course record 62.
Club membership 900.
Visitors   telephone in advance.
Societies   apply in writing.
Green Fees   £19 (£24 weekends).
Facilities   ⊗ ⅲ 🏋 ⛳ ♀ ♿ 🍴 ⛴ Alan Hope.
Leisure   trolley for hire, putting green.
Location   0.5m out of Saltburn on Guisborough road
Hotel   ★★ 62% Marton Way Toby Hotel, Marton Rd,
              MIDDLESBROUGH
              ☎ 01642 817651 53 ⇄ ⌽

SCARBOROUGH   Map 08 TA08

Scarborough North Cliff North Cliff Av YO12 6PP
☎ 01723 360786
Seaside parkland course begining on cliff top overlooking
bay and castle. Good views.
18 holes, 6425yds, Par 71, SSS 71, Course record 66.
Club membership 860.
Visitors   must be member of a club with handicap
              certificate. May not play before 10.30am Sun.
Societies   prior booking with secretary for parties of 8-40.
Green Fees   £25 per day; £18 per round (£28/ £22 weekends
              & bank holidays).
Facilities   ⊗ ⅲ 🏋 ⛳ ♀ ♿ 🍴 ⛴ Simon N Deller.
Leisure   motorised carts for hire, trolley for hire, putting
              green, practice area.
Location   2m N of town centre off A165
Hotel   ★★★ 63% Esplanade Hotel, Belmont Rd,
              SCARBOROUGH ☎ 01723 360382 73 ⇄ ⌽

Scarborough South Cliff Deepdale Av YO11 2UE
☎ 01723 374737
Parkland/seaside course designed by Dr Mackenzie.
18 holes, 6039yds, Par 70, SSS 69, Course record 66.
Club membership 700.
Visitors   contact in advance may not play before 9.30am
              Mon-Fri, 10am Sat and 10.30am Sun.
Societies   must contact Secretary in advance.
Green Fees   not confirmed.
Facilities   ♀ ♿ 🍴 ⛴ A R Skingle.
Leisure   putting green,practice area,trolley hire.
Location   1m S on A165
Hotel   ★★ 64% Bradley Court, 7-9 Filey Rd, South
              Cliff, SCARBOROUGH
              ☎ 01723 360476 40 ⇄ ⌽

SELBY   Map 08 SE63

Selby Brayton Barff YO8 9LD ☎ 01757 228622
Mainly flat, links-type course; prevailing SW wind. Testing
holes including the 3rd, 7th and 16th.
18 holes, 6246yds, Par 70, SSS 70.
Club membership 840.
Visitors   contact professional on 01757 228785, members
              and guests only at weekends.
Societies   welcome Wed-Fri, must apply in advance.
Green Fees   £25 per day; £22 per round.
Facilities   ⊗ ⅲ 🏋 ⛳ ♀ ♿ 🍴 ⛴ Andrew Smith.
Leisure   motorised carts for hire, buggies for hire, trolley
              for hire, putting green, practice area, snooker.
Location   Off A19 at Brayton
Hotel   ★★★★ 68% Monk Fryston Hall, MONK
              FRYSTON ☎ 01977 682369 28 ⇄ ⌽

SETTLE   Map 07 SD86

Settle Buckhaw Brow, Giggleswick BD24 0DH
☎ 01729 825288
Picturesque parkland course.
9 holes, 4400yds, Par 64, SSS 62, Course record 59.
Club membership 380.
Visitors   may not play before 4pm on Sun.
Societies   apply in writing or telephone 4 weeks in
              advance.
Green Fees   £10 per day.
Facilities   ♀ ♿
Location   1m N on A65
Hotel   ★★★ 64% Falcon Manor Hotel, Skipton Rd,
              SETTLE
              ☎ 01729 823814 15 ⇄ ⌽Annexe5 ⇄ ⌽

SKIPTON   Map 07 SD95

Skipton Off North West By-Pass BD23 1LL
☎ 01756 795657 & 793257
Undulating parkland course with some water hazards and
panoramic views.
18 holes, 6049yds, Par 70, SSS 69, Course record 69.
Club membership 750.
Visitors   welcome by prior arrangement.
Societies   must apply in writing.
Green Fees   £18 (£22 Sun & bank holidays).
Facilities   ⊗ ⅲ 🏋 ⛳ ♀ ♿ 🍴 ⛴ Peter Robinson.
Leisure   driving range, practice area.
Location   1m N on A65

Hotel ★★★(red) Devonshire Arms Country House Hotel, BOLTON ABBEY
☎ 01756 710441 41 ⇌ ⋔

STOCKTON-ON-THE-FOREST   Map 08 SE65

Forest Park YO3 9UW ☎ 01904 400425 & 400688
A parkland/meadowland course, opened in 1991, with natural features including a stream and mature and new trees.
Old Foss Course: 18 holes, 6600yds, Par 71, SSS 72.
The West Course: 9 holes, 6384yds, Par 70, SSS 70.
Club membership 650.
Visitors welcome, subject to tee availability. Advisable to contact club in advance.
Societies by prior arrangement.
Green Fees Old Foss: £14.50 per round (£20 weekends & bank holidays). West Course: £12 per 18 holes, £7 per 9 holes (£16/£9 weekends and bank holidays).
Facilities ⊗ ⮚ ♉ ♀ ⩗ 🖻 ⭐
Leisure trolley for hire, driving range, putting green, practice area.
Location 1.5m from end of A64, York bypass
Hotel ★★★ 69% York Pavilion Hotel, 45 Main St, Fulford, YORK
☎ 01904 622099 13 ⇌ ⋔Annexe22 ⇌ ⋔

TADCASTER   Map 08 SE44

Cocksford Cocksford, Stutton LS24 9NG ☎ 01937 834253
Three 9-hole courses; the old 18-hole combination set on undulating meadowland with the famous Cock Beck featuring on 8 of the original 18 holes. Whatever combination you choose the course is relatively short featuring a number of drivable par 4s, but beware danger surrounds many of the greens!
Old Course: 18 holes, 5570yds, Par 71, SSS 69.
Plews Course: 18 holes, 5559yds, Par 70, SSS 68.
Quarry Hills Course: 18 holes, 4951yds, Par 67, SSS 65.
Club membership 450.
Visitors welcome.
Societies telephone the secretary.
Green Fees £20 per day; £16 per round (£25/£22 weekends).
Facilities ⊗ ⯊ ⮚ ♉ ♀ ⩗ 🖻 ⭐ ⟿
⟆ Graham Thompson.
Leisure outdoor swimming pool, motorised carts for hire, trolley for hire, putting green, practice area.
Location Between York & Leeds, A162 from Tadcaster
Hotel ★★★⚘ 71% Wood Hall Hotel, Trip Ln, Linton, WETHERBY
☎ 01937 587271 37 ⇌ ⋔Annexe6 ⇌ ⋔

THIRSK   Map 08 SE48

Thirsk & Northallerton Thornton-le-Street YO7 4AB
☎ 01845 522170 & 526216
The course has good views of the nearby Hambleton Hills. Testing course, mainly flat land.
9 holes, 6342yds, Par 72, SSS 70, Course record 67.
Club membership 420.
Visitors no play on Sun, must have handicap certificate.
Societies must apply in writing.
Green Fees £15 per day; £10 per 18 holes (£20 Sat & bank holidays).
Facilities ⊗ ⯊ ⮚ ♉ ♀ ⩗ 🖻 ⭐ ⟆ Robert Garner.
Leisure trolley for hire, putting green, practice area.

Location 2m N on A168
Hotel ★★ 62% Three Tuns Hotel, Market Place, THIRSK ☎ 01845 523124 11 ⇌ ⋔

WHITBY   Map 08 NZ81

Whitby Low Straggleton, Sandsend Rd YO21 3SR
☎ 01947 600660
Seaside course on cliff top. Good views and fresh sea breeze.
18 holes, 6134yds, Par 71.
Club membership 800.
Visitors may not play on competition days.
Societies must contact in writing.
Green Fees £20 per day/round (£25 weekends and bank holidays).
Facilities ⊗ ⯊ ⮚ ♉ ♀ ⩗ 🖻 ⭐ ⟆ Richard Wood.
Leisure trolley for hire, putting green, practice area.
Location 1.5m NW on A174
Hotel ★★ 67% White House Hotel, Upgang Lane, West Cliff, WHITBY
☎ 01947 600469 12rm(7⇌4 ⋔)

YORK   Map 08 SE65

Forest of Galtres Moorlands Rd, Skelton YO3 3RF
☎ 01904 766198
Level parkland course situated in the heart of the ancient Forest of Galtres with mature oak trees and interesting water hazards coming into play on the 5th, 6th, 14th and 17th holes. Views towards York Minster.
18 holes, 6312yds, Par 72, SSS 70, Course record 66.
Club membership 400.
Visitors telephone to book, may play any time.
Societies booking system, telephone for forms.
Green Fees £20 per day; £15 per round (£22.50/£18.50 weekends and bank holidays).
Facilities ⊗ ⯊ ⮚ ♉ ♀ ⩗ 🖻 ⭐ ⟆ Neil Suckling.
Hotel ★★ 66% Jacobean Lodge Hotel, Plainville Ln, Wigginton, YORK
☎ 01904 762749 8 ⇌ ⋔Annexe6 ⇌ ⋔

Fulford Heslington Ln YO1 5DY ☎ 01904 413579
A flat, parkland/moorland course well-known for the superb quality of its turf, particularly the greens, and now famous as the venue for some of the best golf tournaments in the British Isles.
18 holes, 6775yds, Par 72, SSS 72, Course record 62.
Club membership 700.
Visitors must contact in advance.
Societies not Tue am, book with the manager.
Green Fees £35 per day; £25 per round (£40 per round weekends & bank holidays).
Facilities ⊗ ⯊ ⮚ ♉ ♀ ⩗ 🖻 ⭐ ⟆ Bryan Hessay.
Leisure trolley for hire, driving range, putting green, practice area.
Location 2m S of York off A19
Hotel ★★★★ 64% Swallow Hotel, Tadcaster Rd, YORK ☎ 01904 701000 113 ⇌ ⋔

Heworth Muncaster House, Muncastergate YO3 9JX
☎ 01904 422389
11-hole parkland course, easy walking. Holes 3 to 9 played twice from different tees.
11 holes, 6141yds, Par 70, SSS 69, Course record 67.
Club membership 550.

▶

Visitors   advisable to telephone the professional in advance.
Societies   apply in writing.
Green Fees £14 per day; £10 per round (£17/£14 weekends & bank holidays).
Facilities ⊗ ⊪ ⬛ ⬛ ♀ ♁ 🏠 🇹 (Gregg Roberts.
Location   1.5m NE of city centre on A1036
Hotel   ★★★ 72% Dean Court Hotel, Duncombe Place, YORK ☎ 01904 625082 41 ⇆ 🐾

Swallow Hall Crockey Hill YO1 4SG
☎ 01904 448889
A small 18-hole, Par 3 course with 2 par 4s. Attached to a caravan park.
18 holes, 3100yds, Par 56, SSS 56, Course record 61.
Club membership 100.
Visitors   no restrictions.
Societies   must telephone in advance.
Green Fees £7 per 18 holes; £3.50 per 9 holes (£8/£4 weekends & bank holidays).
Facilities ⬛ ♁ 🇹 🛒
Leisure   hard tennis courts, trolley for hire, driving range, putting green, practice area.
Location   Off A19, signposted to Wheldrake
Hotel   ★★★ 69% York Pavilion Hotel, 45 Main St, Fulford, YORK
☎ 01904 622099 13 ⇆ 🐾 Annexe22 ⇆ 🐾

York Lords Moor Ln, Strensall YO3 5XF
☎ 01904 491840 & 490304
A pleasant, well-designed, heathland course with easy walking. The course is of good length but being flat the going does not tire. There are two testing pond holes.
18 holes, 6323yds, Par 70, SSS 70, Course record 66.
Club membership 700.
Visitors   with member only weekends, must contact in advance.
Societies   more than 16 contact secretary, under 16 contact professional.
Green Fees £28 per day/£20 per round.
Facilities ⊗ ⊪ ⬛ ⬛ ♀ ♁ 🏠 (A B Mason.
Leisure   trolley for hire, driving range, putting green, practice area.
Location   6m NE, E of Strensall village
Hotel   ★★★ 72% Dean Court Hotel, Duncombe Place, YORK
☎ 01904 625082 41 ⇆ 🐾

YORKSHIRE, SOUTH

BARNSLEY   Map 08 SE30

Barnsley Wakefield Rd, Staincross S75 6JZ
☎ 01226 382856
Undulating municipal parkland course with easy walking apart from last 4 holes. Testing 8th and 18th holes.
18 holes, 6042yds, Par 69, SSS 69, Course record 64.
Club membership 450.
Visitors   no restrictions.
Societies   by arrangement.

Green Fees not confirmed.
Facilities ♀ ♁ 🏠 🇹 (Mike Melling.
Location   3m N on A61
Hotel   ★★★ 66% Ardsley House Hotel, Doncaster Rd, Ardsley, BARNSLEY
☎ 01226 309955 73 ⇆ 🐾

Sandhill Middlecliffe Ln, Little Houghton S72 0HW
☎ 01226 753444
Opened in 1993, the course is reasonably flat with generously wide fairways laid out between and amongst 25 acres of newly planted woodlands. Holes of note are the 4th which is a 311 yard Par 4 to a horseshoe green around a 9-foot deep bunker; the 7th Par 3 to blind reverse Mackenzie Green and the 11th 416 yard Par 4 dogleg where the brave can take on the out of bounds.
18 holes, 6214yds, Par 71, SSS 70, Course record 69.
Club membership 275.
Visitors   welcome by prior booking.
Societies   telephone for availability, write to confirm.
Green Fees not confirmed.
Facilities ♀ ♁ 🏠
Leisure   18 bay floodlit driving range.
Location   5m E of Barnsley, off A635
Hotel   ★★★ 66% Ardsley House Hotel, Doncaster Rd, Ardsley, BARNSLEY
☎ 01226 309955 73 ⇆ 🐾

BAWTRY   Map 08 SK69

Austerfield Park Cross Ln, Austerfield DN10 6RF
☎ 01302 710841 & 710850
Long moorland course with postage stamp 8th and testing 618-yd 7th. Driving range attached.
18 holes, 6854yds, Par 70, SSS 70, Course record 64.
Club membership 600.
Visitors   telephone in advance.
Societies   must contact in advance.
Green Fees £19 per day; £15 per round (£23/£19 weekends).
Facilities ⊗ ⊪ ⬛ ⬛ ♀ ♁ 🏠 (Peter Rothery.
Leisure   trolley for hire, driving range, putting green, practice area, par 3 course, bowling green.
Location   2m from Bawtry on A614
Hotel   ★★★ 65% The Crown Hotel, High St, BAWTRY
☎ 01302 710341 57 ⇆ 🐾

CONISBROUGH   Map 08 SK59

Crookhill Park Municipal Carr Ln DN12 2BE
☎ 01709 862979
A rolling parkland course.
18 holes, 5839yds, Par 70, SSS 68.
Club membership 500.
Visitors   restricted weekends before 9am. Must contact in advance.
Societies   by arrangement.
Green Fees not confirmed.
Facilities ♀ ♁ 🏠 🇹 (Richard Swaine.
Leisure   pool table.
Location   1.5m SE on B6094
Hotel   ★★★ 62% Danum Swallow Hotel, High St, DONCASTER ☎ 01302 342261 66 ⇆ 🐾

DONCASTER
Map 08 SE50

Doncaster 278 Bawtry Rd, Bessacarr DN4 7PD
☎ 01302 868316 & 865632
Pleasant undulating heathland course with wooded surroundings. Quick drying, ideal autumn, winter and spring.
18 holes, 6220yds, Par 69, SSS 70, Course record 66.
Club membership 600.

Visitors	must contact in advance. Times restricted on Wed & weekends.
Societies	must contact in advance.
Green Fees	£25 per day; £20 per round (£30/25 weekends & bank holidays).
Facilities	⊗ ⅫⅬ ⅃ 🛑 ♀ ⅄ 🛍 ℓ Graham Bailey.
Leisure	trolley for hire, putting green, practice area.
Location	4m SE on A638
Hotel	★★★ 64% Mount Pleasant Hotel, Great North Rd, ROSSINGTON
☎ 01302 868696 & 868219 29 ⇋ 🐾

Doncaster Town Moor Bawtry Rd, Belle Vue DN4 5HU
☎ 01302 535286 & 533167
Easy walking, but testing, heathland course with good true greens. Friendly club. Notable hole is 11th (par 4), 464 yds. Situated in centre of racecourse.
18 holes, 6072yds, Par 69, SSS 69, Course record 66.
Club membership 520.

Visitors	may not play on Sun morning.
Societies	must contact in advance.
Green Fees	not confirmed.
Facilities	♀ ⅄ 🛍 ℓ Steven C Poole.
Leisure	practice area, trolley hire.
Location	1.5m E, at racecourse, on A638
Hotel	★★★ 62% Danum Swallow Hotel, High St, DONCASTER ☎ 01302 342261 66 ⇋ 🐾

Owston Park Owston Hall, Ownston DN6 9JF
☎ 01302 330821
A flat course surrounded by woodland. A lot of mature trees and a few ditches in play. A practice putting green and chipping area.
9 holes, 3042yds, Par 36, SSS 71.

Visitors	no restrictions.
Societies	telephone in advance.
Green Fees	£3.90 per 9 holes.
Facilities	⅃ ⅄ 🛍 ⅂ℓ Mike Parker.
Leisure	trolley for hire, putting green.
Location	5m N of Doncaster off A19
Hotel	★★★ 62% Danum Swallow Hotel, High St, DONCASTER ☎ 01302 342261 66 ⇋ 🐾

Wheatley Armthorpe Rd DN2 5QB
☎ 01302 831655
Fairly flat well-bunkered, lake-holed, parkland course.
18 holes, 6169yds, Par 70, SSS 69.
Club membership 600.

Visitors	must contact in advance and have an introduction from own club.
Societies	must contact in advance.
Green Fees	not confirmed.
Facilities	♀ ⅄ 🛍 ℓ T C Parkinson.
Location	NE side of town centre off A18
Hotel	★★★ 62% Grand St Leger, Bennetthorpe, DONCASTER ☎ 01302 364111 20 ⇋ 🐾

HICKLETON
Map 08 SE40

Hickleton DN5 7BE ☎ 01709 896081
Undulating parkland course with stream running through; designed by Neil Coles and Brian Huggett.
18 holes, 6403yds, Par 71, SSS 71.
Club membership 600.

Visitors	restricted weekends after 2.30pm. Must contact in advance.
Societies	must contact in advance on 01709 888436.
Green Fees	not confirmed.
Facilities	♀ ⅄ 🛍 ⅂ℓ Paul Shepherd.
Location	0.5m W on B6411
Hotel	★★★ 62% Danum Swallow Hotel, High St, DONCASTER ☎ 01302 342261 66 ⇋ 🐾

HIGH GREEN
Map 08 SK39

Tankersley Park S30 4LG ☎ 0114 246 8247
Akin to an inland links, this parkland course is hilly, windy and has good views.
18 holes, 6212yds, Par 69, SSS 70, Course record 65.
Club membership 634.

Visitors	must contact in advance.
Societies	must apply in writing.
Green Fees	£24.50 per day/weekends; £19.50 per round.
Facilities	⊗ ⅫⅬ ⅃ 🛑 ♀ ⅄ 🛍 ⅂ℓ Ian Kirk.
Leisure	motorised carts for hire, trolley for hire, putting green, practice area.
Location	Off A61/M1 onto A616, Stocksbridge bypass
Hotel	★★★ 68% Tankersley Manor, Church Ln, TANKERSLEY ☎ 01226 744700 40 ⇋ 🐾

RAWMARSH
Map 08 SK49

Wath Abdy Ln S62 7SJ ☎ 01709 872149 & 878677
Parkland course, not easy in spite of its length; 17th hole (par 3) is a difficult 244yds with narrow driving area.
18 holes, 5857yds, Par 68, SSS 68.
Club membership 550.

Visitors	must play with member at weekends. Must contact in advance and have a handicap certificate.
Societies	must contact in writing, may not play at weekends.
Green Fees	not confirmed.
Facilities	♀ ⅄ 🛍 ℓ Chris Bassett.
Leisure	putting green, practice area, trolley hire.
Location	2.5m N off A633
Hotel	★★ 66% Brentwood Hotel, Moorgate Rd, ROTHERHAM ☎ 01709 382772 33 ⇋ 🐾 Annexe10 ⇋ 🐾

ROTHERHAM
Map 08 SK49

Grange Park Upper Wortley Rd S61 2SJ
☎ 01709 559497
Parkland/meadowland course, with panoramic views especially from the back nine. The golf is testing, particularly at the 1st, 4th and 18th holes (par 4), and 8th, 12th and 15th (par 5).
18 holes, 6461yds, Par 71, SSS 70.
Club membership 325.

▶

Visitors	no restrictions.
Societies	apply in writing.
Green Fees	not confirmed.
Facilities	♀ ⚐ ♙ ⛳ ♪ Eric Clark.
Location	3m NW off A629
Hotel	★★ 66% Brentwood Hotel, Moorgate Rd, ROTHERHAM ☎ 01709 382772 33 ⇄ ♪Annexe10 ⇄ ♪

Phoenix Pavilion Ln, Brinsworth S60 5PA
☎ 01709 363864 & 382624
Undulating meadowland course with variable wind.
18 holes, 6182yds, Par 71, SSS 69, Course record 65.
Club membership 1100.

Visitors	must contact in advance.
Societies	must apply in writing.
Green Fees	£21 per day (£28 weekends & bank holidays).
Facilities	⊗ ℼ ⛳ ♙ ♀ ⚐ ♙ ⛳ ♪
Leisure	hard tennis courts, squash, gymnasium, trolley for hire, driving range, putting green, practice green.
Location	SW side of town centre off A630
Hotel	★★ 66% Brentwood Hotel, Moorgate Rd, ROTHERHAM ☎ 01709 382772 33 ⇄ ♪Annexe10 ⇄ ♪

Rotherham Golf Club Ltd Thrybergh Park, Doncaster Rd, Thrybergh S65 4NU
☎ 01709 850812 (Secretary) & 850480 (Pro)
Parkland course with easy walking along tree-lined fairways.
18 holes, 6324yds, Par 70, SSS 70, Course record 65.
Club membership 500.

Visitors	must contact in advance.
Societies	must contact secretary in advance.
Green Fees	£26.50 per day/round (£31.50 weekends & bank holidays).
Facilities	⊗ ℼ ⛳ ♙ ♀ ⚐ ♙ ⛳ ♪ Simon Thornhill.
Leisure	motorised carts for hire, buggies for hire, trolley for hire, putting green, practice area.
Location	3.5m E on A630
Hotel	★★ 66% Brentwood Hotel, Moorgate Rd, ROTHERHAM ☎ 01709 382772 33 ⇄ ♪Annexe10 ⇄ ♪

Sitwell Park Shrogswood Rd S60 4BY ☎ 01709 541046
Parkland course with easy walking.
18 holes, 6209yds, Par 71, SSS 70, Course record 61.
Club membership 450.

Visitors	must contact in advance.
Societies	must contact in advance.
Green Fees	£27 per day; £23 per round (£31/£27 weekends & bank holidays).
Facilities	⊗ ℼ ⛳ ♙ ♀ ⚐ ♙ ⛳ ♪ Nic Taylor.
Leisure	motorised carts for hire, trolley for hire, putting green, practice area.
Hotel	★★ 66% Brentwood Hotel, Moorgate Rd, ROTHERHAM ☎ 01709 382772 33 ⇄ ♪Annexe10 ⇄ ♪

SHEFFIELD

Map 08 SK38

Abbeydale Twentywell Ln, Dore S17 4QA
☎ 0114 236 0763
Parkland course, well-kept and wooded. Testing hole: 12th, par 3.
18 holes, 6419yds, Par 72, SSS 71.
Club membership 750.

Visitors	restricted Wed 10am-1.30pm.
Societies	must apply in writing.
Green Fees	not confirmed.
Facilities	♀ ⚐ ⚑ ♪
Location	4m SW of city centre off A621
Hotel	B Forte Posthouse Sheffield, Manchester Rd, Broomhill, SHEFFIELD ☎ 0114 267 0067 135 ⇄ ♪

Beauchief Municipal Abbey Ln S8 0DB ☎ 0114 236 7274
Municipal course with natural water hazards. The rolling land looks west to the Pennines and a 12th-century abbey adorns the course.
18 holes, 5452yds, Par 67, SSS 66, Course record 65.
Club membership 450.

Visitors	are advised to book in advance in summer.
Societies	weekdays only, must apply in writing to: Recreation Department, Tower Lodge, Firth Park Road, Sheffield S5 6WS.
Green Fees	£8 per round (£8.70 weekends).
Facilities	⊗ ⛳ ♙ ♀ ⚐ ⚑ ♪ A Highfield.
Leisure	trolley for hire, putting green, practice area.
Location	4m SW of city centre off A621
Hotel	★★★ 72% Beauchief Hotel, 161 Abbeydale Rd South, SHEFFIELD ☎ 0114 262 0500 41 ⇄ ♪

Birley Wood Birley Ln S12 3BP ☎ 0114 264 7262
Undulating meadowland course with well-varied features, easy walking and good views. Practice range and area.
18 holes, 5100yds, Par 66, SSS 65, Course record 64.
Club membership 300.

Visitors	no restrictions.
Societies	apply in advance.
Green Fees	£4.20 (£8.10 weekends).
Facilities	⚐ ♙ ⛳ ♪ Peter Ball.
Leisure	putting green, practice area.
Location	4.5m SE of city centre off A621
Hotel	★★★ 65% Mosborough Hall Hotel, High St, Mosborough, SHEFFIELD ☎ 0114 248 4353 23 ⇄ ♪

Concord Park Shiregreen Ln S5 6AE ☎ 0114 234 9802
Hilly municipal parkland course with some fairways wood-flanked, good views, often windy. Eight par 3 holes.
18 holes, 4321yds, Par 65, SSS 62, Course record 57.
Club membership 150.

Visitors	no restrictions.
Green Fees	£9.75 per 36 holes; £6.50 per 18 holes. Prices under review..
Facilities	⛳ ♙ ♀ ⚐
Leisure	hard tennis courts, heated indoor swimming pool, squash, solarium, gymnasium, practice area.
Location	3.5m N of city centre on B6086 off A6135
Hotel	B Forte Posthouse Sheffield, Manchester Rd, Broomhill, SHEFFIELD ☎ 0114 267 0067 135 ⇄ ♪

Dore & Totley Bradway Rd, Bradway S17 4QR
☎ 0114 236 0492
Flat parkland course.
18 holes, 6265yds, Par 70, SSS 70, Course record 65.
Club membership 580.

| Visitors | must contact in advance a handicap certificate may be requested, may not play 9.30am-noon & after 2.30pm. |

Societies must apply in writing.
Green Fees not confirmed.
Facilities ♀ ♣ 🖭 ᶜ Neil Cheetham.
Leisure putting green,practice area,trolley hire.
Location 7m S of city centre on B6054 off A61
Hotel B Forte Posthouse Sheffield, Manchester Rd,
Broomhill, SHEFFIELD
☎ 0114 267 0067 135 ⇥ ᶜ

Hallamshire Golf Club Ltd Sandygate S10 4LA
☎ 0114 230 2153 (Secretary) & 230 5222 (Pro)
Situated on a shelf of land at a height of 850 ft.
Magnificent views to the west. Moorland turf, long
carries over ravine. Good natural drainage.
18 holes, 6359yds, Par 71, SSS 71, Course record 63.
Club membership 600.
Visitors contact professional in advance. Tees
reserved for members 8-9.30 and noon-1.30.
Societies parties of 12+ should book in advance with
secretary.
Green Fees £31 per day (£36 weekends & bank
holidays).
Facilities ⊗ by prior arrangement 🌙 by prior
arrangement ♭ ♟ ♀ ♣ 🖭 ᶠ
ᶜ G R Tickell.
Leisure trolley for hire, putting green, practice area.
Location Off A57 at Crosspool onto Sandygate Rd,
clubhouse 0.75m on right
Hotel B Forte Posthouse Sheffield, Manchester
Rd, Broomhill, SHEFFIELD
☎ 0114 267 0067 135 ⇥ ᶜ

Hillsborough Worrall Rd S6 4BE
☎ 0114 234 9151 (Secretary) & 233 2666 (Pro)
Beautiful moorland/woodland course 500 ft above sea-level,
reasonable walking. Challenging first four holes into a
prevailing wind and a tight, testing 14th hole.
18 holes, 6216yards, Par 71, SSS 70, Course record 64.
Club membership 650.
Visitors contact professional in advance. May not play
Tue (Ladies Day), Thu and weekends before
2pm
Societies must apply in writing to secretary.
Green Fees £28 per day (£35 weekends & bank holidays);
£20 per round Sun.
Facilities ⊗ 🌙 ♭ ♟ ♀ ♣ 🖭 ᶠ ᶜ Graham Walker.
Leisure trolley for hire, driving range, putting green,
practice area.
Location 3m NW of city centre off A616
Hotel ★★★ 59% Rutland Hotel, 452 Glossop Rd,
Broomhill, SHEFFIELD
☎ 0114 266 4411 70 ⇥ ᶜAnnexe17 ⇥ ᶜ

Lees Hall Hemsworth Rd, Norton S8 8LL
☎ 0114 255 4402
Parkland/meadowland course with panoramic view of city.
18 holes, 6137yds, Par 71, SSS 69, Course record 63.
Club membership 725.
Visitors restricted Wed.
Societies must apply in writing.
Green Fees not confirmed.
Facilities ♀ ♣ 🖭 ᶜ J R Wilkinson.
Location 3.5m S of city centre off A6102
Hotel B Forte Posthouse Sheffield, Manchester Rd,
Broomhill, SHEFFIELD
☎ 0114 267 0067 135 ⇥ ᶜ

Tinsley Park Municipal Golf High Hazels Park WN6 8EW
☎ 0114 256 0237
Undulating meadowland course with plenty of trees and
rough.
18 holes, 6064yds, Par 71, SSS 69.
Club membership 420.
Visitors no restrictions.
Societies apply in writing to Sheffield City Council,
Recreation Dept., Meersbrook Park, Sheffield.
Green Fees not confirmed.
Facilities ♀ ♣ 🖭 ᶠ ᶜ A P Highfield.
Leisure putting green,trolley hire.
Location 4m E of city centre off A630
Hotel ★★★ 65% Mosborough Hall Hotel, High St,
Mosborough, SHEFFIELD
☎ 0114 248 4353 23 ⇥ ᶜ

SILKSTONE   Map 08 SE20

Silkstone Field Head, Elmhurst Ln S75 4LD
☎ 01226 790328
Parkland/downland course, fine views over the Pennines.
Testing golf.
18 holes, 6069yds, Par 70, SSS 70, Course record 64.
Club membership 508.
Visitors with member only at weekends.
Societies contact in advance.
Green Fees £25 per day/round.
Facilities ⊗ 🌙 ♭ ♟ ♀ ♣ 🖭 ᶜ Kevin Guy.
Leisure trolley for hire, putting green, practice area,
snooker.
Location 1m E off A628
Hotel ★★★ 66% Ardsley House Hotel, Doncaster Rd,
Ardsley, BARNSLEY
☎ 01226 309955 73 ⇥ ᶜ

STOCKSBRIDGE   Map 08 SK29

Stocksbridge & District 30 Royd Ln, Townend, Deepcar
S30 5RZ ☎ 0114 288 2003
Hilly moorland course.
18 holes, 5200yds, Par 65, SSS 65, Course record 64.
Club membership 300.
Visitors contact the professional.
Societies apply to professional.
Green Fees £16 per day (£25 weekends & bank holidays).
Facilities ⊗ 🌙 ♭ ♟ ♀ ♣ 🖭 ᶜ Timothy Brookes.
Leisure putting green, practice area.
Location S side of town centre
Hotel B Forte Posthouse Sheffield, Manchester Rd,
Broomhill, SHEFFIELD
☎ 0114 267 0067 135 ⇥ ᶜ

THORNE   Map 08 SE61

Thorne Kirton Ln DN8 5RJ ☎ 01405 812084 & 815173
Picturesque parkland course with 6000 newly planted trees.
18 holes, 5366yds, Par 68, SSS 66, Course record 62.
Club membership 300.
Visitors no restrictions.
Societies telephone in advance.
Green Fees £8.50 per round (£10 weekends & bank
holidays).
Facilities ⊗ 🌙 ♭ ♟ ♀ ♣ 🖭 ᶠ ᶜ Richard Highfield.
Leisure trolley for hire, putting green, practice area. ▶

Location   14m SE of Pontefract off of M18
Hotel   ★★ 67% Belmont Hotel, Horsefair Green,
THORNE ☎ 01405 812320 23 ⇥ ⌐

WORTLEY   Map 08 SK39

Wortley Hermit Hill Ln S30 7DF
☎ 0114 288 8469 (Secretary) & 288 6490 (Pro)
Well-wooded, undulating parkland course sheltered from
prevailing wind.
18 holes, 6028yds, Par 69, SSS 68, Course record 62.
Club membership 510.
Visitors   may not play between 11.30am and 1pm. Must
contact professional in advance.
Societies   telephone in advance and confirm in writing
with deposit.
Green Fees £24 (£30 weekends & bank holidays).
Facilities   ⊗ ⫚ ⅃ ☴ ♀ ♨ 🏠 🏴 ⌐ Ian Kirk.
Leisure   trolley for hire, putting green, practice area.
Location   0.5m NE of village off A629
Hotel   B Forte Posthouse Sheffield, Manchester Rd,
Broomhill, SHEFFIELD
☎ 0114 267 0067 135 ⇥ ⌐

YORKSHIRE, WEST

ALWOODLEY   Map 08 SE24

Alwoodley Wigton Ln LS17 8SA ☎ 0113 268 1680
A fine heathland course with length, trees and abundant
heather. Many attractive situations - together a severe test
of golf.
18 holes, 6686yds, Par 72, SSS 72, Course record 67.
Club membership 455.
Visitors   must contact in advance,
Societies   must apply in advance.
Green Fees £50 per day/round (£60 weekends & bank
holidays).
Facilities   ⊗ ⫚ ⅃ ☴ ♀ ♨ 🏠 🏴 ⌐ John Green.
Leisure   motorised carts for hire, trolley for hire,
putting green, practice area.
Location   5m N off A61
Hotel   ★★★ 63% Harewood Arms Hotel,
Harrogate Rd, HAREWOOD
☎ 0113 288 6566 13 ⇥ ⌐Annexe11 ⇥ ⌐

BAILDON   Map 07 SE13

Baildon Moorgate BD17 5PP ☎ 01274 595162 & 584266
Moorland course with much bracken rough. The 5th is a hard
climb.
18 holes, 6225yds, Par 70, SSS 70, Course record 64.
Club membership 500.
Visitors   contact in advance, restricted Tue & weekends.
Societies   large numbers apply in writing, small numbers
check with the professional.
Green Fees £16 per day/round.
Facilities   ⊗ ⫚ ⅃ ☴ ♀ ♨ 🏠 🏴 ⌐ Richard Masters.
Leisure   trolley for hire, putting green, practice area.
Location   3m N of Bradford, off A6038

Hotel   ★★★ 70% Hollins Hall, Hollins Hill, Baildon,
SHIPLEY
☎ 01274 530053 59 ⇥ ⌐

BINGLEY   Map 07 SE13

Bingley St Ives Golf Club House, St Ives Estate, Harden
BD16 1AT ☎ 01274 562436 & 511788
Parkland/moorland course.
18 holes, 6485yds, Par 71, SSS 71, Course record 69.
Club membership 450.
Visitors   contact professional on 01274 562506, no green
fees Sat.
Societies   telephone in advance, the professional 01274
562506.
Green Fees £27 per day, £25 per round.
Facilities   ⊗ ⫚ ⅃ ☴ ♀ ♨ 🏠 ⌐ Ray Firth.
Leisure   motorised carts for hire, buggies for hire, trolley
for hire, putting green, practice area.
Location   0.75m W off B6429
Hotel   ★★★ 66% Oakwood Hall Hotel, Lady Ln,
BINGLEY
☎ 01274 564123 & 563569 20 ⇥ ⌐

BRADFORD   Map 07 SE13

Bradford Moor Scarr Hall, Pollard Ln BD2 4RW
☎ 01274 638313 & 626107
Parkland course, hard walking.
9 holes, 5900yds, Par 70, SSS 68, Course record 66.
Club membership 330.
Visitors   no visitors at weekends.
Societies   can book starting times by application in writing.
Green Fees £12 per day/round.
Facilities   ⊗ ⫚ ⅃ ☴ ♀ ♨ 🏠 🏴 ⌐ Ron Hughes.
Leisure   trolley for hire, putting green, practice area.
Location   2m NE of city centre off A658
Hotel   ★★ 66% Park Drive Hotel, 12 Park Dr,
BRADFORD ☎ 01274 480194 11 ⇥ ⌐

Clayton Thornton View Rd, Clayton BD14 6JX
☎ 01274 880047
Moorland course, difficult in windy conditions.
9 holes, 5407yds, Par 68, SSS 67.
Club membership 350.
Visitors   may not play after 4pm on Sun.
Societies   apply in writing to the Secretary or Captain.
Green Fees not confirmed.
Facilities   ♀ ☴
Leisure   putting green.
Location   2.5m SW of city centre on A647
Hotel   ★★★ 64% Novotel, Merrydale Rd,
BRADFORD
☎ 01274 683683 127 ⇥ ⌐

East Bierley South View Rd, East Bierley BD4 6PP
☎ 01274 681023
Hilly moorland course with narrow fairways. Two par 3 holes
over 200 yds.
9 holes, 4700yds, Par 64, SSS 63.
Club membership 200.
Visitors   restricted Sat (am), Sun & Mon evening. Must
contact in advance.
Societies   must apply in writing.
Green Fees not confirmed.

Facilities ♀☖
Location 4m SE of city centre off A650
Hotel ★★★ 64% Novotel, Merrydale Rd,
BRADFORD ☎ 01274 683683 127 ⇥ ◖

Headley Headley Ln, Thornton BD13 3LX
☎ 01274 833481
Hilly moorland course, short but very testing, windy, fine
views.
9 holes, 4996yds, Par 64, SSS 64, Course record 61.
Club membership 300.
Visitors must contact in advance, may not play
weekends/BHs.
Societies must contact in advance.
Green Fees £11 weekdays.
Facilities ⊗ ℍ ⅃ ♥ ♀☖
Leisure putting green, practice area.
Location 4m W of city centre off B6145 at Thornton
Hotel ★★ 66% Park Drive Hotel, 12 Park Dr,
BRADFORD ☎ 01274 480194 11 ⇥ ◖

Phoenix Park Phoenix Park, Thornbury BD3 7AT
☎ 01274 667573
Very short, tight, moorland course, rather testing.
9 holes, 2491yds, Par 66, SSS 64, Course record 66.
Club membership 260.
Visitors restricted weekends.
Societies must apply in advance.
Green Fees not confirmed.
Facilities ♀☖☖
Location E side of city centre on A647
Hotel ★★ 66% Park Drive Hotel, 12 Park Dr,
BRADFORD ☎ 01274 480194 11 ⇥ ◖

Queensbury Brighouse Rd, Queensbury BD13 1QF
☎ 01274 882155 & 816864
Undulating woodland/parkland course.
9 holes, 5024yds, Par 66, SSS 65, Course record 63.
Club membership 380.
Visitors preferable to telephone in advance, restricted at
weekends.
Societies apply in writing.
Green Fees £10 per day (£20 weekends & bank holidays).
Facilities ⊗ ℍ by prior arrangement ⅃ ♥ ♀☖☖ ⊶
◖ Geoff Howard.
Leisure putting green, practice area.
Location 4m from Bradford on A647
Hotel ★★ 66% Park Drive Hotel, 12 Park Dr,
BRADFORD ☎ 01274 480194 11 ⇥ ◖

South Bradford Pearson Rd, Odsal BD6 1BH
☎ 01274 679195
Hilly course with good greens, trees and ditches. Interesting
short 2nd hole (par 3) 200 yds, well-bunkered and played
from an elevated tee.
9 holes, 6068yds, Par 70, SSS 68, Course record 65.
Club membership 300.
Visitors must contact in advance.
Societies must apply in writing to the secretary.
Green Fees £10 (£22 weekends).
Facilities ⊗ ℍ ⅃ ♥ ♀☖☖ Ian Marshall.
Leisure trolley for hire, putting green, practice area.
Location 2m S of city centre off A638
Hotel ★★★ 64% Novotel, Merrydale Rd,
BRADFORD ☎ 01274 683683 127 ⇥ ◖

West Bowling Newall Hall, Rooley Ln BD5 8LB
☎ 01274 724449 & 728036
Undulating, tree-lined parkland course. Testing hole: 'the
coffin' short par 3, very narrow.
18 holes, 5763yds, Par 69, SSS 68, Course record 65.
Club membership 500.
Visitors must contact in advance, weekend very limited.
Societies must apply in writing.
Green Fees £26 per round (£34 weekends). Handicap
certificate £4 discount.
Facilities ⊗ ℍ ⅃ ♥ ♀☖☖ ◖ Allan Swaine.
Leisure trolley for hire, putting green, practice area,
snooker.
Location S side of city centre off A638
Hotel ★★★★ 63% Cedar Court Hotel Bradford,
Mayo Av, Off Pooley Ln, BRADFORD
☎ 01274 406606 & 406601 127 ⇥ ◖

West Bradford Chellow Grange Rd BD9 6NP
☎ 01274 542767
Parkland course, windy, especially 3rd, 4th, 5th and 6th
holes. Hilly but not hard.
18 holes, 5741yds, Par 69, SSS 68.
Club membership 440.
Visitors restricted Sat.
Societies must apply in writing.
Green Fees not confirmed.
Facilities ♀ (ex Mon) ☖☖ ◖ Nigel M Barber.
Leisure putting,trolley hire.
Location W side of city centre off B6269
Hotel ★★★ 70% Hollins Hall, Hollins Hill, Baildon,
SHIPLEY
☎ 01274 530053 59 ⇥ ◖

CLECKHEATON
Map 08 SE12

Cleckheaton & District Bradford Rd BD19 6BU
☎ 01274 851266
Parkland course with gentle hills.
18 holes, 5769yds, Par 71, SSS 68.
Club membership 550.
Visitors must contact in advance and have an
introduction from own club.
Societies weekdays only; must contact in advance.
Green Fees not confirmed.
Facilities ♀☖☖ ⊶ ◖ Mike Ingham.
Location 1.5m NW on A638 junc 26 M62
Hotel ★★★ 66% Gomersal Park Hotel, Moor Ln,
GOMERSAL
☎ 01274 869386 52 ⇥ ◖

DEWSBURY
Map 08 SE22

Hanging Heaton White Cross Rd WF12 7DT
☎ 01924 461606
Arable land course, easy walking, fine views. Testing 4th
hole (par 3).
9 holes, 5400mtrs, Par 69, SSS 67.
Club membership 550.
Visitors must play with member at weekends & bank
holidays. Must contact in advance.
Societies must telephone in advance.
Green Fees not confirmed.
Facilities ♀☖☖ ◖ S Hartley.
Location 0.75m NE off A653 ▶

Hotel   ★★ 70% Healds Hall Hotel, Leeds Rd,
              Liversedge, DEWSBURY
              ☎ 01924 409112 25 ⇌ ℝ

ELLAND   Map 07 SE12

Elland Hammerstones, Leach Ln HX5 0TA
☎ 01422 372505
Parkland course.
9 holes, 2815yds, Par 66, SSS 66, Course record 64.
Club membership 450.
Visitors   welcome.
Societies   must contact in writing.
Green Fees £14 per day/round (£25 weekends and bank
                holidays).
Facilities ⊗ �𝕄 ⓛ ⌿ ♀ ♨ 🏠 ℓ N Bell.
Location   1m SW
Hotel   ★★ 70% Rock Inn Hotel & Churchills,
                HOLYWELL GREEN
                ☎ 01422 379721 18 ⇌ ℝ

FENAY BRIDGE   Map 08 SE11

Woodsome Hall HD8 0LQ ☎ 01484 602739 & 602971
A parkland course with good views and an historic
clubhouse.
18 holes, 6081yds, Par 69, SSS 69, Course record 65.
Club membership 800.
Visitors   must contact in advance.
Societies   must apply in writing.
Green Fees £30 per day; £25 per round (£35/£30 weekends
                & bank holidays).
Facilities ⊗ �𝕄 ⓛ ⌿ ♀ ♨ 🏠 ℓ M Higginbotton.
Leisure   trolley for hire, putting green, practice area.
Location   1.5m SW off A629
Hotel   ★★★ 70% Springfield Park Hotel, Penistone
                Rd, KIRKBURTON
                ☎ 01484 607788 44 ⇌ ℝ

GARFORTH   Map 08 SE43

Garforth LS25 2DS ☎ 0113 286 2021
Parkland course with fine views, easy walking.
18 holes, 6005yds, Par 69, SSS 69.
Club membership 500.
Visitors   must contact in advance and have handicap
                certificate. With member only weekends & bank
                holidays.
Societies   must apply in advance.
Green Fees not confirmed.
Facilities ♨ 🏠 ℯ ℓ
Location   1m N
Hotel   B Hilton National Leeds/Garforth, Wakefield
                Rd, GARFORTH ☎ 0113 286 6556 144 ⇌ ℝ

GUISELEY   Map 08 SE14

Bradford Hawksworth Ln LS20 8NP ☎ 01943 875570
Moorland course with eight par 4 holes of 360 yds or more.
18 holes, 6259yds, Par 71, SSS 71.
Club membership 600.
Visitors   must have a handicap certificate. May not play
Sat.
Societies   make prior arrangements with secretary.

Green Fees £25 per day; £20 per round (£32/£25 weekends).
Facilities ⊗ �𝕄 ⓛ ⌿ ♀ ♨ 🏠 ℓ Sydney Weldon.
Leisure   trolley for hire, putting green, practice area.
Location   SW side of town centre off A6038
Hotel   ★★★ 56% Cow & Calf Hotel, Moor Top,
                ILKLEY ☎ 01943 607335 20 ⇌ ℝ

HALIFAX   Map 07 SE02

Halifax Bob Hall, Union Ln, Ogden HX2 8XR
☎ 01422 244171 & 240047
Hilly moorland course crossed by streams, natural hazards,
and offering fine views. Testing 172-yd 17th (par3).
18 holes, 6037yds, Par 70, SSS 70, Course record 63.
Club membership 700.
Visitors   contact professional for tee times.
Societies   contact manager for dates.
Green Fees £20 per day; £15 per round (£30 weekends).
Facilities ⊗ ⟨ ⓛ ⌿ ♀ ♨ 🏠 ⟨ ℓ Michael Allison.
Location   A629 Halifax/Keighley
Hotel   ★★★ 74% Holdsworth House Hotel,
                Holmfield, HALIFAX
                ☎ 01422 240024 40 ⇌ ℝ

Lightcliffe Knowle Top Rd, Lightcliffe HX3 8SW
☎ 01422 202459
Heathland course.
9 holes, 5388yds, Par 68, SSS 68.
Club membership 545.
Visitors   must be a member of a recognised Golf Club.
Societies   must contact 21 days in advance.
Green Fees not confirmed.
Facilities ♀ ♨ 🏠 ℓ Robert Kershaw.
Leisure   putting green.
Location   3.5m E on A58
Hotel   ★★★ 74% Holdsworth House Hotel,
                Holmfield, HALIFAX
                ☎ 01422 240024 40 ⇌ ℝ

West End Paddock Ln, Highroad Well HX2 0NT
☎ 01422 341878 & 363293
Semi-moorland course.
18 holes, 5951yds, Par 69, SSS 69, Course record 62.
Visitors   contact in advance.
Societies   must apply in writing to Secretary.
Green Fees £22 per day; £17 per round (£27/£20 weekends
                & bank holidays).
Facilities ⊗ ⟨ ⓛ ⌿ ♀ ♨ 🏠 ⟨ ℓ David Rishworth.
Leisure   trolley for hire, putting green, practice area.
Location   W side of town centre off A646
Hotel   ★★★ 74% Holdsworth House Hotel,
                Holmfield, HALIFAX
                ☎ 01422 240024 40 ⇌ ℝ

HEBDEN BRIDGE   Map 07 SD92

Hebden Bridge Mount Skip, Wadsworth HX7 8PH
☎ 01422 842896 & 842732
Moorland course with splendid views.
9 holes, 5064yds, Par 68, SSS 65, Course record 64.
Club membership 300.
Visitors   weekends after 4pm only.
Societies   apply in writing.
Green Fees £12 per day (£15 weekends).
Facilities ♀ (evenings only) ♨

Leisure putting green.
Location 1.5m E off A6033
Hotel ★★ 65% Hebden Lodge Hotel, New Rd,
HEBDEN BRIDGE ☎ 01422 845272 12 ⇔ ﾃ

HOLYWELL GREEN   Map 07 SE01

Halifax Bradley Hall HX4 9AN ☎ 01422 374108
Moorland/parkland course, tightened by recent tree planting,
easy walking.
18 holes, 6213yds, Par 70, SSS 70, Course record 65.
Club membership 500.
Visitors contact in advance.
Societies must apply in writing.
Green Fees £20 per day; £16 per round (£35/£28 weekends
& bank holidays).
Facilities ⊗ Ⅲ ﾑ ■ ♀ ♈ 合 ☂ ﾃ Peter Wood.
Leisure trolley for hire, putting green, practice area.
Location S on A6112
Hotel ★★ 70% Rock Inn Hotel & Churchills,
HOLYWELL GREEN ☎ 01422 379721 18 ⇔ ﾃ

HUDDERSFIELD   Map 07 SE11

Bagden Hall Wakefield Rd, Scissett HD8 9LE
☎ 01484 864839
Picturesque tree-lined course offering a challenging test of
golf for all levels of handicap. Lake guarded greens require
pin-point accuracy.
9 holes, 3002, Par 56, SSS 55, Course record 60.
Club membership 150.
Visitors anytime.
Societies company day packages available.
Green Fees £9 per 18 holes (£12 weekends).
Facilities ⊗ Ⅲ ﾑ ■ ♀ ♈ 合 ☂ ﾃ Ian Darren.
Leisure trolley for hire, putting green.
Hotel ★★★ 69% Bagden Hall, Wakefield Rd,
Scissett, HUDDERSFIELD
☎ 01484 865330 17 ⇔ ﾃ

Bradley Park Off Bradley Rd HD2 1PZ ☎ 01484 539988
Parkland course, challenging with good mix of long and short
holes. Also 14-bay floodlit driving range and 9-hole par 3
course, ideal for beginners. Superb views.
18 holes, 6284yds, Par 70, SSS 70, Course record 65.
Club membership 300.
Visitors may book by phone for weekends from the
preceeding Thu.
Societies welcome midweek only, apply in writing to
professional.
Green Fees £9.50 per round (£11.50 weekends).
Facilities ⊗ Ⅲ ﾑ ■ ♀ ♈ 合 ☂ ﾃ Parnell E Reilly.
Leisure motorised carts for hire, buggies for hire, trolley
for hire, driving range, putting green, practice
area, par 3 course.
Location 2.5m from junct 25 of M62
Hotel ★★★ 65% The George Hotel, St George's
Square, HUDDERSFIELD
☎ 01484 515444 60 ⇔ ﾃ

Crosland Heath Felk Stile Rd, Crosland Heath HD4 7AF
☎ 01484 653216
Moorland course with fine views over valley.
18 holes, 5972yds, Par 70, SSS 70.
Club membership 350.

Visitors welcome, but advisable to check with
professional. Must contact in advance and have
an introduction from own club.
Societies must telephone in advance.
Green Fees not confirmed.
Facilities ﾑ 合 ﾃ Chris Gaunt.
Location SW off A62
Hotel ★★★ 65% The George Hotel, St George's
Square, HUDDERSFIELD
☎ 01484 515444 60 ⇔ ﾃ

Huddersfield Fixby Hall, Lightridge Rd, Fixby HD2 2EP
☎ 01484 426203
A testing heathland course of championship standard laid out
in 1891.
18 holes, 6432yds, Par 71, SSS 71, Course record 64.
Club membership 759.
Visitors must book tee times with professional.
Societies welcome Mon & Wed-Fri, prior arrangement
required.
Green Fees Summer:£40 per day; £30 per round (£50/£40
weekends). Winter: £20 per day/round (£30
weekends).
Facilities ⊗ Ⅲ ﾑ ■ ♀ ♈ 合 ﾃ Paul Carman.
Leisure trolley for hire, putting green, practice area.
Location 2m N off A641
Hotel ★★★ 65% The George Hotel, St George's
Square, HUDDERSFIELD
☎ 01484 515444 60 ⇔ ﾃ

Longley Park Maple St, Off Somerset Rd HD5 9AX
☎ 01484 422304
Lowland course.
9 holes, 5269yds, Par 66, SSS 66.
Club membership 440.
Visitors must contact in advance & have handicap
certificate, restricted Thu & weekends.
Societies must apply in writing.
Green Fees not confirmed.
Facilities ♀ ♈ 合 ☂ ﾃ Paul Middleton.
Leisure putting green, trolley hire.
Location 0.5m SE of town centre off A629
Hotel ★★★ 65% The George Hotel, St George's
Square, HUDDERSFIELD
☎ 01484 515444 60 ⇔ ﾃ

ILKLEY   Map 07 SE14

Ben Rhydding High Wood, Ben Rhydding LS29 8SB
☎ 01943 608759
Moorland/parkland course with splendid views over the
Wharfe valley.
9 holes, 4711yds, Par 65, SSS 64, Course record 64.
Club membership 260.
Visitors contact in advance. May only play at weekend as
guest of member.
Societies advance notice in writing. In view of limited
resources requests considered by monthly
committee meeting.
Green Fees £10 per day (£15 bank holidays).
Facilities ♀ ♈
Leisure putting green.
Location SE side of town
Hotel ★★ 74% Rombalds Hotel & Restaurant, 11
West View, Wells Rd, ILKLEY
☎ 01943 603201 15 ⇔ ﾃ

Ilkley Nesfield Rd, Myddleton LS29 0BE
☎ 01943 600214
This beautiful parkland course is situated in Wharfedale and the Wharfe is a hazard on each of the first seven holes. In fact, the 3rd is laid out entirely on an island in the middle of the river.
18 holes, 5953yds, Par 69, SSS 70, Course record 66.
Club membership 450.
Visitors　advisable to contact in advance.
Societies　apply in writing.
Green Fees £35 per day/round (£40 weekends & bank holidays).
Facilities　⊗ ℳ ⓛ ⚐ ♀ ♨ 🏠 ⚑ 𝄆 John L Hammond.
Leisure　fishing, trolley for hire, putting green, practice area.
Location　W side of town centre off A65
Hotel　★★ 74% Rombalds Hotel & Restaurant, 11 West View, Wells Rd, ILKLEY
☎ 01943 603201 15 ⇔ ⦅

KEIGHLEY　　　　　　　　　　　Map 07 SE04

Branshaw Branshaw Moor, Oakworth BD22 7ES
☎ 01535 643235
Picturesque moorland course with fairly narrow fairways and good greens. Extensive views.
18 holes, 6000yds, Par 69, SSS 69.
Club membership 500.
Visitors　welcome most times, restrictions at weekends advisable to ring.
Societies　apply in writing to the secretary.
Green Fees £15 per day; £12 per round (£20/£18 weekends).
Facilities　⊗ ℳ ⓛ ⚐ ♀ ♨ 🏠 𝄆
Leisure　trolley for hire, practice area.
Location　2m SW on B6149
Hotel　★★ 66% Dalesgate Hotel, 406 Skipton Rd, Utley, KEIGHLEY ☎ 01535 664930 21 ⇔ ⦅

Keighley Howden Park, Utley BD20 6DH
☎ 01535 604778
Parkland course with good views down the Aire Valley.
18 holes, 6149yds, Par 69, SSS 70, Course record 65.
Club membership 600.
Visitors　restricted Sat & Sun. Must contact in advance.
Societies　must apply in advance.
Green Fees not confirmed.
Facilities　♀ ♨ 🏠 𝄆 Mike Bradley.
Leisure　putting green, practice area, trolley hire.
Location　1m NW of town centre off B6143
Hotel　★★ 66% Dalesgate Hotel, 406 Skipton Rd, Utley, KEIGHLEY
☎ 01535 664930 21 ⇔ ⦅

LEEDS　　　　　　　　　　　　　Map 08 SE33

Brandon Holywell Ln, Shadwell LS17 8EZ
☎ 0113 273 7471
An 18-hole links type course enjoying varying degrees of rough, water and sand hazards.
18 holes, 3650yds, Par 56.
Visitors　pay & play course booking not usually necessary.
Societies　telephone or write in advance.
Green Fees £5 per round (£6 weekend & bank holidays).

Facilities　💼 🏠 ⚑
Leisure　trolley for hire, putting, practice area.
Hotel　★★★ 79% Haley's Hotel & Restaurant, Shire Oak Rd, Headingley, LEEDS
☎ 0113 278 4446 22 ⇔ ⦅

Gotts Park Armley Ridge Rd LS12 2QX ☎ 0113 263 8232
Municipal parkland course; hilly and windy with narrow fairways. Some very steep hills to some greens. A challenging course requiring accuracy rather than length from the tees.
18 holes, 4960yds, Par 65, SSS 64, Course record 63.
Club membership 300.
Visitors　no restrictions.
Green Fees not confirmed.
Facilities　♀ (evenings) 🏠 ⚑ 𝄆 John F Simpson.
Location　3m W of city centre off A647
Hotel　★★★★ 68% The Queen's, City Square, LEEDS ☎ 0113 243 1323 190 ⇔ ⦅

Headingley Back Church Ln, Adel LS16 8DW
☎ 0113 267 9573 0113 267 5100
An undulating course with a wealth of natural features offering fine views from higher ground. Its most striking hazard is the famous ravine at the 18th. Leeds's oldest course, founded in 1892.
18 holes, 6298yds, Par 69, SSS 70, Course record 64.
Club membership 675.
Visitors　must contact in advance.
Societies　must telephone in advance and confirm in writing.
Green Fees £30 per day; £25 per round (£36 per day/round weekends & bank holidays).
Facilities　⊗ ℳ ⓛ 💼 ♀ ♨ 🏠 ⚑ 𝄆 Steven Foster.
Leisure　trolley for hire, putting green, practice area.
Location　5.5m N of city centre off A660
Hotel　B Forte Posthouse Leeds/Bradford, Leeds Rd, BRAMHOPE ☎ 0113 284 2911 124 ⇔ ⦅

Horsforth Layton Rise, Layton Rd, Horsforth LS18 5EX
☎ 0113 258 6819
Moorland course overlooking airport.
18 holes, 6243yds, Par 71, SSS 70.
Club membership 750.
Visitors　restricted Sat & with member only Sun.
Societies　must apply in writing.
Green Fees not confirmed.
Facilities　♀ ♨ 🏠 𝄆 Peter Scott.
Leisure　putting green, trolley hire, practice area.
Location　6.5m NW of city centre off A65
Hotel　B Forte Posthouse Leeds/Bradford, Leeds Rd, BRAMHOPE ☎ 0113 284 2911 124 ⇔ ⦅

Leeds Elmete Ln LS8 2LJ ☎ 0113 265 8775
Parkland course with pleasant views.
18 holes, 6097yds, Par 69, SSS 69.
Club membership 600.
Visitors　with member only weekends, yellow tees only. Must contact in advance.
Societies　must apply in writing.
Green Fees not confirmed.
Facilities　♀ ♨ 🏠 ⚑ 𝄆 Simon Longster.
Location　5m NE of city centre on A6120 off A58
Hotel　★★★ 79% Haley's Hotel & Restaurant, Shire Oak Rd, Headingley, LEEDS
☎ 0113 278 4446 22 ⇔ ⦅

Leeds Golf Centre Wike Ridge Ln, Shadwell LS17 9JW
☎ 0113 288 6000
Two courses - the 18-hole Wike Ridge, a traditional
heathland course designed by Donald Steele. The sand-based
greens are constructed to USGA specification and there are
an excellent variety of holes with some very challenging Par
5's. The 9-hole Oaks is complemented by a floodlit driving
range and other practice facilities. The course is the home of
the Leeds Golf Academy.
Wike Ridge Course: 18 holes, 6482yds, Par 72, SSS 71.
Oaks: 9 holes, 1355yds, Par 27.
Club membership 500.
Visitors no restrictions, telephone booking advisable.
Societies tee reservation available in advance.
Green Fees Wike Ridge: £20 per day; £12.50 per 18 holes,
£6.50 per 9 holes. Oaks: £6.50 per 18 holes; £5
per 9 holes.
Facilities ⊗ ℳ 🛅 🏌 ♀ 🏌 🏠 ⚑ 𝄢 John Clapham.
Leisure motorised carts for hire, buggies for hire, trolley
for hire, driving range, putting green.
Location 5m N,take A58 course on N side of Shadwell
Hotel ★★★ 79% Haley's Hotel & Restaurant, Shire
Oak Rd, Headingley, LEEDS
☎ 0113 278 4446 22 ⇆ 𝄢

Middleton Park Municipal Middleton Park, Middleton LS10
3TN ☎ 0113 270 0449
Parkland course.
18 holes, 5263yds, Par 68, SSS 66.
Club membership 300.
Visitors may only use the club 6 times in one year.
Green Fees not confirmed.
Facilities ♀ 🏠 ⚑ 𝄢
Leisure putting green,practice area.
Location 3m S off A653
Hotel ★★★★ 68% The Queen's, City Square,
LEEDS ☎ 0113 243 1323 190 ⇆ 𝄢

Moor Allerton Coal Rd, Wike LS17 7EA
☎ 0113 266 1154
The Moor Allerton Club has 27 holes set in 220 acres of
undulating parkland, with magnificent views extending
across the Vale of York. The Championship Course was
designed by Robert Trent Jones, the famous American
course architect, and is the only course of his design in
the British Isles.
Lakes Course: 18 holes, 6470yds, Par 71, SSS 72.
Blackmoor Course: 18 holes, 6673yds, Par 71, SSS 73.
High Course: 18 holes, 6841yds, Par 72, SSS 74.
Club membership 1200.
Visitors contact professional (0113 266 5209).
Societies must apply in advance.
Green Fees £36 (£60 Sat, no casual visitors Sun).
Facilities ⊗ ℳ 🛅 🏌 ♀ 🏠 ⚑ 𝄢 Richard Lane.
Leisure hard tennis courts, sauna, motorised carts for
hire, buggies for hire, trolley for hire,
covered driving range, putting green,
practice field.
Location 5.5m N of city centre on A61
Hotel ★★★ 63% Harewood Arms Hotel,
Harrogate Rd, HAREWOOD
☎ 0113 288 6566 13 ⇆ 𝄢Annexe11 ⇆ 𝄢

Moortown Harrogate Rd, Alwoodley LS17 7DB
☎ 0113 268 6521
Championship course, tough but fair. Springy moorland
turf, natural hazards of heather, gorse and streams,
cunningly placed bunkers and immaculate greens.
18 holes, 6782yds, Par 72, SSS 73, Course record 66.
Club membership 566.
Visitors must contact in advance.
Societies apply in writing in advance.
Green Fees £45 per day; £40 per round (£50/£45
weekends).
Facilities ⊗ ℳ 🛅 🏌 ♀ 🏠 ⚑ 𝄢
𝄢 Bryon Hutchinson.
Leisure motorised carts for hire, buggies for hire,
trolley for hire, putting green, practice area.
Location 6m N of city centre on A61
Hotel ★★★ 63% Harewood Arms Hotel,
Harrogate Rd, HAREWOOD
☎ 0113 288 6566 13 ⇆ 𝄢Annexe11 ⇆ 𝄢

Oulton Park Rothwell LS26 8EX ☎ 0113 282 3152
27-hole championship-length municipal course. Although
municipal, a dress rule is applied. 16-bay driving range.
*Main Course: 18 holes, 6450yds, Par 71, SSS 71, Course
record 65.*
Short Course: 9 holes, 3250yds, Par 35, SSS 35.
Club membership 450.
Visitors must apply 24hrs in advance.
Societies Mon-Fri. Must contact in advance.
Green Fees £20 per 18 holes; £7.50 per 9 holes.
Facilities ⊗ ℳ 🛅 🏌 ♀ 🏠 ⚑ 🏌 𝄢 Stephen Gromett.
Leisure heated indoor swimming pool, squash, sauna,
solarium, gymnasium, motorised carts for hire,
buggies for hire, trolley for hire, driving range.
Location Junc 30 on M62
Hotel ★★★★★ 70% Oulton Hall Hotel, Rothwell Ln,
Oulton, LEEDS ☎ 0113 282 1000 152 ⇆ 𝄢

Roundhay Park Ln LS8 2EJ ☎ 0113 266 2695 & 249 2523
Attractive municipal parkland course, natural hazards, easy
walking.
9 holes, 5223yds, Par 70, SSS 65, Course record 61.
Club membership 400.
Visitors must contact professional at all times.
Societies telephone or write to the professional.
Green Fees £7 per round (£8 weekends & bank holidays).
Facilities 🏠 ⚑ 𝄢 James Pape.
Leisure trolley for hire, putting green, practice area.
Location 4m NE of city centre off A58
Hotel ★★★ 79% Haley's Hotel & Restaurant, Shire
Oak Rd, Headingley, LEEDS
☎ 0113 278 4446 22 ⇆ 𝄢

Sand Moor Alwoodley Ln LS17 7DJ ☎ 0113 268 5180
A beautiful, undulating course overlooking Lord
Harewood's estate and the Eccup Reservoir. The course
is wooded with some holes adjacent to water. The 12th is
perhaps the most difficult where the fairway falls away
towards the reservoir.
18 holes, 6429yds, Par 71, SSS 71, Course record 63.
Club membership 553.
Visitors restricted weekends & bank holidays.
Societies must apply in advance.
Green Fees not confirmed.
Facilities ♀ 🏠 ⚑ 𝄢 Peter Tupling. ▶

> **Leisure** practice area.
> **Location** 5m N of city centre off A61
> **Hotel** B Forte Posthouse Leeds/Bradford, Leeds
> Rd, BRAMHOPE
> ☎ 0113 284 2911 124 ⇄ ⋔

South Leeds Gipsy Ln, Beeston LS11 5TU
☎ 0113 277 1676
Parkland course, windy, hard walking, good views.
18 holes, 5769yds, Par 69, SSS 68, Course record 64.
Club membership 500.
Visitors probably difficult for weekend play.
Societies must apply in advance.
Green Fees £18 per round/day (£26 weekends).
Facilities ⊗ ⅢⅢ ⅃ ⬛ ♀ ⅄ 🖻 ⅋ Mike Lewis.
Leisure trolley for hire, putting green, practice area.
Location 3m S of city centre off A653
Hotel ★★★★ 68% The Queen's, City Square,
LEEDS ☎ 0113 243 1323 190 ⇄ ⋔

Temple Newsam Temple-Newsam Rd LS15 0LN
☎ 0113 264 5624
Two parkland courses. Testing long 13th (563 yds) on second
course.
Lord Irwin: 18 holes, 6460yds, Par 69, SSS 71.
Lady Dorothy: 18 holes, 6276yds, Par 70, SSS 70.
Club membership 520.
Visitors no restrictions.
Societies must apply in advance.
Green Fees not confirmed.
Facilities ♀ ⅄ 🖻 ⅋ David Bulmer.
Location 3.5m E of city centre off A63
Hotel ★★★ 79% Haley's Hotel & Restaurant, Shire
Oak Rd, Headingley, LEEDS
☎ 0113 278 4446 22 ⇄ ⋔

MARSDEN   Map 07 SE01

Marsden Mount Rd, Hemplow HD7 6NN
☎ 01484 844253
Moorland course with good views, natural hazards, windy.
9 holes, 5702yds, Par 68, SSS 68.
Club membership 200.
Visitors must play with member at weekends.
Societies Mon-Fri; must contact in advance.
Green Fees not confirmed.
Facilities ♀ ⅄ 🖻 ⅋ A J Bickerdike.
Leisure hard tennis courts.
Location S side off A62
Hotel ★★★ 62% Briar Court Hotel, Halifax Rd,
Birchencliffe, HUDDERSFIELD
☎ 01484 519902 47 ⇄ ⋔

MELTHAM   Map 07 SE01

Meltham Thick Hollins Hall HD7 3DQ
☎ 01484 850227 & 851521
Parkland course with good views. Testing 548 yd, 13th hole
(par 5).
18 holes, 6305yds, Par 70, SSS 70, Course record 65.
Club membership 500.
Visitors may not play Sat & Wed (Ladies Day), desirable
to contact professional in advance.
Societies must apply in writing.

Green Fees £20 per day (£25 weekends & bank holidays).
Facilities ⊗ ⅢⅢ ⅃ ⬛ ♀ ⅄ 🖻 ⅋ Paul Davies.
Leisure trolley for hire, putting green, practice area.
Location SE side of village off B6107
Hotel ★★★ 65% The George Hotel, St George's
Square, HUDDERSFIELD
☎ 01484 515444 60 ⇄ ⋔

MIRFIELD   Map 08 SE21

Dewsbury District Sands Ln WF14 8HJ
☎ 01924 492399
Heathland/parkland course with panoramic view from top,
hard walking. Ponds in middle of 3rd fairway, left of 5th
green and 17th green.
18 holes, 6267yds, Par 71, SSS 71.
Club membership 650.
Visitors weekends after 1pm, on non competition days.
Telephone in advance.
Societies telephone bookings.
Green Fees £20 per day; £16 per round (£18 per round
weekends after 1pm).
Facilities ⊗ ⅢⅢ ⅃ ⬛ ♀ ⅄ 🖻 ⅋ Nigel P Hirst.
Leisure trolley for hire, putting green, practice area.
Location 1m S off A644
Hotel ★★★ 65% The George Hotel, St George's
Square, HUDDERSFIELD
☎ 01484 515444 60 ⇄ ⋔

MORLEY   Map 08 SE22

Howley Hall Scotchman Ln LS27 0NX
☎ 01924 478417 & 473852
Parkland course with easy walking and good views.
18 holes, 6058yds, Par 71, SSS 69.
Club membership 700.
Visitors standard course only, may not play Sat.
Societies contact for details.
Green Fees £25 per day; £21 per round (£30 day/round Sun
& bank holidays).
Facilities ⊗ ⅢⅢ ⅃ ⬛ ♀ ⅄ 🖻 ⅋ Stephen Spinks.
Leisure motorised carts for hire, trolley for hire, putting
green, practice area.
Location 1.5m S on B6123
Hotel ★★ 66% Alder House Hotel, Towngate Rd, off
Healey Ln, BATLEY
☎ 01924 444777 22rm(21 ⇄ ⋔)

NORMANTON   Map 08 SE32

Normanton Snydale Rd WF6 1PN ☎ 01924 892943
A pleasant, flat course with tight fairways in places and an
internal out-of-bounds requiring accuracy.
9 holes, 5288yds, Par 66, SSS 66.
Club membership 250.
Visitors may not play on Sun.
Societies mid-week only.
Green Fees not confirmed.
Facilities ♀ ⅄ 🖻 ⅋ Martin Evans.
Location 0.5m SE on B6133
Hotel ★★★ 68% Swallow Hotel, Queens St,
WAKEFIELD
☎ 01924 372111 64 ⇄ ⋔

OSSETT   Map 08 SE22

Low Laithes Parkmill Ln, Flushdyke WF5 9AP
☎ 01924 274667
Testing parkland course.
18 holes, 6463yds, Par 72, SSS 71, Course record 65.
Club membership 600.
Visitors   may not play weekends and bank holidays. Must
                   contact in advance.
Societies   by prior arrangement.
Green Fees   £22 per day; £18 per round.
Facilities   ⊗ ⴉⵏ ⴊ ⴋ ⵕ ⴻ ⵌ ⵍ Paul Browning.
Leisure   trolley for hire, putting green, practice area.
Location   1.5m SE off A128
Hotel   B Forte Posthouse Northampton/Rugby, CRICK
                   ☎ 01788 822101 88 ⇌ ⵟ

OTLEY   Map 08 SE24

Otley Off West Busk Ln LS21 3NG
☎ 01943 465329
An expansive course with magnificent views across
Wharfedale. It is well-wooded with streams crossing the
fairway. The 4th is a fine hole which generally needs two
woods to reach the plateau green. The 17th is a good
short hole.
18 holes, 6225yds, Par 70, SSS 70, Course record 66.
Club membership 700.
Visitors   telephone to check tee time.
Societies   telephone enquiries welcome, bookings in
                   writing.
Green Fees   £30 per 36 holes; £24 per 27 holes (£35/£30
                   weekends and bank holidays).
Facilities   ⊗ ⴉⵏ ⴊ ⴋ ⵕ ⴻ ⵌ ⵍ Simon Poot.
Leisure   trolley for hire, putting green, practice area.
Location   1.5m SW off A6038
Hotel   B Forte Posthouse Leeds/Bradford, Leeds
                   Rd, BRAMHOPE
                   ☎ 0113 284 2911 124 ⇌ ⵟ

OUTLANE   Map 07 SE01

Outlane Slack Ln HD3 3YL ☎ 01422 374762
Moorland course.
18 holes, 6015yds, Par 71, SSS 70, Course record 67.
Club membership 600.
Visitors   telephone in advance, must be correctly
                   equipped and attired.
Societies   apply in writing.
Green Fees   £18 per day (£27 weekends & bank holidays).
Facilities   ⊗ ⴉⵏ ⴊ ⴋ ⵕ ⴻ ⵌ ⵍ David Chapman.
Leisure   trolley for hire, putting green, practice area.
Location   S side of village off A640
Hotel   ★★★ 69% Old Golf House Hotel, New Hey
                   Rd, Outlane, HUDDERSFIELD
                   ☎ 01422 379311 50 ⇌ ⵟ

PONTEFRACT   Map 08 SE42

Mid Yorkshire Havercroft Ln, Darrington WF8 3BP
☎ 01977 704522
An 18-hole championship-standard course opened in 1992.
18 holes, 6500yds, Par 72, SSS 72, Course record 68.
Club membership 500.

Visitors   must contact in advance, with member only at
                   weekends.
Societies   apply in writing to the secretary.
Green Fees   not confirmed.
Facilities   ⵕ ⴻ ⵌ ⵍ Peter Scott.
Leisure   golf academy with 28 driving bays.
Location   2m SE
Hotel   ★★★ 68% Wentbridge House Hotel,
                   WENTBRIDGE ☎ 01977 620444 16 ⇌ ⵟ

Pontefract & District Park Ln WF8 4QS ☎ 01977 792241
Parkland course.
18 holes, 6227yds, Par 72, SSS 70.
Club membership 800.
Visitors   welcome except Wed & weekends. Must contact
                   in advance and have a handicap certificate.
Societies   welcome except Wed & weekends.
Green Fees   not confirmed.
Facilities   ⵕ ⴻ ⵌ ⵍ Nick Newman.
Leisure   putting green,trolley hire,practice area.
Location   1.5m W on B6134
Hotel   ★★★ 68% Wentbridge House Hotel,
                   WENTBRIDGE ☎ 01977 620444 16 ⇌ ⵟ

PUDSEY   Map 08 SE23

Calverley Woodhall Ln LS28 5QY ☎ 0113 256 9244
Two parkland courses on top of a hill.The course was
established 10 years ago and has a few water hazards and
some bunkers.
18 holes, 5567yds, Par 68, SSS 67, Course record 67.
Club membership 572.
Visitors   must contact pro shop in advance.
Societies   contact in writing or telephone.
Green Fees   £18 per day; £12 per round (£17 per round
                   weekends). 9 hole course £6 at all times.
Facilities   ⊗ ⴉⵏ ⴊ ⴋ ⵕ ⴻ ⵌ ⵍ Derek Johnson.
Leisure   trolley for hire, putting green, practice area.
Hotel   ★★ 66% Park Drive Hotel, 12 Park Dr,
                   BRADFORD ☎ 01274 480194 11 ⇌ ⵟ

Fulneck LS28 8NT ☎ 0113 256 5191
Picturesque, hilly parkland course. Compact but strenuous.
9 holes, 5456yds, Par 66, SSS 67, Course record 65.
Club membership 250.
Visitors   with member only weekends & bank holidays.
Societies   must apply in writing.
Green Fees   £14 per day.
Facilities   ⴊ ⴋ ⵕ ⴻ
Leisure   putting green.
Location   S side of town centre
Hotel   ★★★ 64% Novotel, Merrydale Rd,
                   BRADFORD ☎ 01274 683683 127 ⇌ ⵟ

Woodhall Hills Calverley LS28 5UN
☎ 0113 255 4594 & 256 2857
Meadowland course, prevailing SW winds, fairly hard
walking. Testing holes: 8th, 377 yd (par 4); 14th,
206 yd (par 3).
18 holes, 6102yds, Par 71, SSS 69, Course record 63.
Club membership 570.
Visitors   any day advise secretary/professional in
                   advance.
Societies   must apply in writing.
Green Fees   £20.50 per day/round (£25.50 weekends & bank
                   holidays).   ▶

Facilities ⊗ ⍦ ﹀ ♨ ♀ ⚘ ☎ ⎇ Warren Lockett.
Leisure trolley for hire, putting green, practice area.
Location 2.5m NW off A647
Hotel ★★ 66% Park Drive Hotel, 12 Park Dr, BRADFORD ☎ 01274 480194 11 ⇌ ⌗

RAWDON　　　　　　　　　　　　　Map 08 SE23

Rawdon Golf & Lawn Tennis Club Buckstone Dr LS19 6BD
☎ 0113 250 6040
Undulating parkland course.
9 holes, 5980yds, Par 72, SSS 69.
Club membership 700.
Visitors must contact in advance & have handicap certificate. With member only at weekends.
Societies must contact in advance.
Green Fees not confirmed.
Facilities ♀ ⚘ ☎ ⎇ Syd Wheldon.
Leisure hard and grass tennis courts.
Location S side of town off A65
Hotel ★★★ 65% Apperley Manor, Apperley Ln, Apperley Bridge, BRADFORD ☎ 0113 250 5626 13 ⇌ ⌗

RIDDLESDEN　　　　　　　　　　　Map 07 SE04

Riddlesden Howden Rough BD20 5QN ☎ 01535 602148
Undulating moorland course with prevailing west winds, some hard walking and beautiful views. Ten par 3 holes and spectacular 6th and 15th holes played over old quarry sites.
18 holes, 4295yds, Par 63, SSS 61.
Club membership 350.
Visitors restricted before 2pm weekends.
Societies apply by telephone or in writing.
Green Fees £10 per round (£15 weekends).
Facilities ⊗ ﹀ ♨ ♀ ⚘
Location 1m NW
Hotel ★★ 66% Dalesgate Hotel, 406 Skipton Rd, Utley, KEIGHLEY ☎ 01535 664930 21 ⇌ ⌗

SCARCROFT　　　　　　　　　　　Map 08 SE34

Scarcroft Syke Ln LS14 3BQ ☎ 0113 289 2311
Undulating parkland course with prevailing west wind and easy walking.
18 holes, 6031yds, Par 71, SSS 69.
Club membership 667.
Visitors must contact in advance.
Societies must contact in advance.
Green Fees not confirmed.
Facilities ♀ ⚘ ☎ ⎇ ⍦ ⎇ Darren Tear.
Leisure putting green, practice area, trolley hire.
Location 0.5m N of village off A58
Hotel ★★★ 63% Harewood Arms Hotel, Harrogate Rd, HAREWOOD ☎ 0113 288 6566 13 ⇌ ⌗Annexe11 ⇌ ⌗

SHIPLEY　　　　　　　　　　　　Map 07 SE13

Northcliffe High Bank Ln BD18 4LJ
☎ 01274 596731 & 587193
Parkland course with magnificent views of moors. Testing 1st hole (18th green 100 feet below tee).

18 holes, 6104yds, Par 71, SSS 69, Course record 65.
Club membership 700.
Visitors no restrictions.
Societies book via secretary in advance, weekdays only.
Green Fees on application.
Facilities ⊗ ﹀ ♨ ♀ ⚘ ☎ ⍦ ⎇ M Hillas.
Leisure motorised carts for hire, trolley for hire, putting green, practice area.
Location 1.25m SW of Shipley, off A650
Hotel ★★★ 70% Hollins Hall, Hollins Hill, Baildon, SHIPLEY ☎ 01274 530053 59 ⇌ ⌗

SILSDEN　　　　　　　　　　　　Map 07 SE04

Silsden High Brunthwaite BD20 0NH
☎ 01535 652998
Tight downland course which can be windy. Good views of the Aire Valley.
14 holes, 4870yds, Par 65, SSS 64, Course record 61.
Club membership 300.
Visitors may not play before 11am on Sun.
Societies must apply in advance.
Green Fees not confirmed.
Facilities ♀ ⚘
Location 1m E
Hotel ★★ 66% Dalesgate Hotel, 406 Skipton Rd, Utley, KEIGHLEY ☎ 01535 664930 21 ⇌ ⌗

SOWERBY　　　　　　　　　　　　Map 07 SE02

Ryburn The Shaw, Norland HX6 3QP
☎ 01422 831355
Moorland course, easy walking.
9 holes, 4984yds, Par 66, SSS 64, Course record 64.
Club membership 200.
Visitors must contact in advance.
Societies apply in writing.
Green Fees not confirmed.
Facilities ⊗ ﹀ ♨ ♀ ⚘
Location 1m S of Sowerby Bridge off A58
Hotel ★★ 69% The Hobbit Hotel, Hob Ln, Norland, SOWERBY BRIDGE ☎ 01422 832202 17 ⇌ ⌗Annexe5 ⇌ ⌗

TODMORDEN　　　　　　　　　　Map 07 SD92

Todmorden Rive Rocks, Cross Stone Rd OL14 8RD
☎ 01706 812986
Pleasant moorland course.
9 holes, 5382yds, Par 68, SSS 68, Course record 67.
Club membership 240.
Visitors restricted Thu & weekends. Advisable to contact in advance.
Societies must apply in writing.
Green Fees £15 per day (£20 weekends & bank holidays).
Facilities ⊗ by prior arrangement ⍦ by prior arrangement ♨ ♀ ⚘
Leisure putting green, practice area.
Location NE off A646
Hotel ★★★⚘ 64% Scaitcliffe Hall, Burnley Rd, TODMORDEN ☎ 01706 818888 13 ⇌ ⌗

WAKEFIELD — Map 08 SE32

City of Wakefield Lupset Park, Horbury Rd WF2 8QS
☎ 01924 367442 & 360282
Parkland course.
18 holes, 6319yds, Par 72, SSS 70, Course record 67.
Club membership 600.
Visitors restricted weekends.
Societies must apply in advance to stewardess 01924
367242.
Green Fees £7.90 per round (£9.90 weekends and bank
holidays).
Facilities ⊗ ⅶ ㄴ ☛ ♀ ♨ 合 ↑ ℓ Roger Holland.
Leisure trolley for hire, putting green, practice area.
Location 1.5m W of city centre on A642
Hotel B Forte Posthouse Wakefield, Queen's Dr,
Ossett, WAKEFIELD
☎ 01924 276388 99 ⇄ ⋔

Painthorpe House Painthorpe Ln, Painthorpe, Crigglestone
WF4 3HE ☎ 01924 274527 & 255083
Undulating meadowland course, easy walking.
9 holes, 4544yds, Par 62, SSS 62, Course record 64.
Club membership 150.
Visitors no visitors Sun.
Societies must telephone in advance.
Green Fees £5 per 18 holes (£8 Sat & bank holidays).
Facilities ⊗ ⅶ ㄴ ☛ ♀ ♨
Leisure putting green, practice area.
Location 2m S off A636
Hotel B Forte Posthouse Wakefield, Queen's Dr, Ossett,
WAKEFIELD ☎ 01924 276388 99 ⇄ ⋔

Wakefield Woodthorpe Ln, Sandal WF2 6JH
☎ 01924 258778
A well-sheltered meadowland/heath course with easy walking
and good views.
18 holes, 6613yds, Par 72, SSS 72, Course record 66.
Club membership 540.
Visitors contact must be made in advance.
Societies must apply in writing.
Green Fees £27.50 per day; £22 per round (£30 weekends &
bank holidays).
Facilities ⊗ ⅶ ㄴ ☛ ♀ ♨ 合 ℓ Ian M Wright.
Leisure trolley for hire, putting green, practice area.
Location 3m S off A61
Hotel B Forte Posthouse Wakefield, Queen's Dr, Ossett,
WAKEFIELD ☎ 01924 276388 99 ⇄ ⋔

WETHERBY — Map 08 SE44

Wetherby Linton Ln LS22 4JF
☎ 01937 580089
Parkland course with fine views.
18 holes, 6235yds, Par 71, SSS 70, Course record 66.
Club membership 650.
Visitors may not play Mon & Tues morning.
Societies apply in writing or telephone in advance.
Green Fees £28 per day; £23 per round (£34 per day/round
weekends).
Facilities ⊗ ⅶ ㄴ ☛ ♀ ♨ 合 ℓ D Padgett.
Leisure trolley for hire, putting green, practice area.
Location 1m W off A661
Hotel ★★★ 57% Jarvis Wetherby Hotel, Leeds Rd,
WETHERBY ☎ 01937 583881 72 ⇄ ⋔

CHANNEL ISLANDS

ALDERNEY

ALDERNEY — Map 16

Alderney Route des Carrieres GY9 3YD
☎ 01481 822835
Undulating seaside course with sea on all sides and offering
magnificent views from its high tees and greens. Course
designed by Frank Pennink.
9 holes, 5006yds, Par 64, SSS 65, Course record 65.
Club membership 400.
Visitors may not play before 10am at weekends.
Advisable to contact in advance.
Societies must contact in advance.
Green Fees £12.50 per day (£17.50 weekends and bank
holidays).
Facilities ㄴ ☛ ♀ ♨ ↑
Leisure trolley for hire, putting green, practice area,
bowling green.
Location 1m E of St Annes
Hotel ★★ 73% Inchalla Hotel, St Anne,
ALDERNEY
☎ 01481 823220 10 ⇄ ⋔

GUERNSEY

L'ANCRESSE VALE — Map 16

Royal Guernsey GY3 5BY
☎ 01481 46523
Not quite as old as its neighbour Royal Jersey, Royal
Guernsey is a sporting course which was re-designed
after World War II by Mackenzie Ross, who has many
fine courses to his credit. It is a pleasant links, well-
maintained, and administered by the States of Guernsey
in the form of the States Tourist Committee. The 8th
hole, a good par 4, requires an accurate second shot to the
green set amongst the gorse and thick rough. The 18th,
with lively views, needs a strong shot to reach the green
well down below. The course is windy, with hard
walking. There is a junior section.
18 holes, 6206yds, Par 70, SSS 70, Course record 64.
Club membership 934.
Visitors must have a handicap certificate; may not
play on Thu, Sat afternoons & Sun.
Green Fees £28 per day.
Facilities ⊗ ⅶ ㄴ ☛ ♀ ♨ 合 ↑ ℓ Norman Wood.
Leisure trolley for hire, driving range, putting green.
Location 3m N of St Peter Port
Hotel ★★★★ 71% St Pierre Park Hotel, Rohais,
ST PETER PORT
☎ 01481 728282 135 ⇄ ⋔

St Peter Port   Map 16

St Pierre Park Golf Club Rohais GY1 1FD
☎ 01481 728282
Par 3 parkland course with delightful setting, with lakes,
streams and many tricky holes.
9 holes, 2511yds, Par 54, SSS 50.
Club membership 200.

Visitors	contact in advance.
Societies	must contact in advance.
Green Fees	£14 per 18 holes (£16 weekends). Prices under review..
Facilities	⊗ ⑪ ⓛ ⬛ ♀ ♨ 🏠 ⚑ ⛳
Leisure	hard tennis courts, heated indoor swimming pool, sauna, solarium, gymnasium, trolley for hire, driving range, croquet, crazy golf, snooker.
Location	1m W off Rohais Rd
Hotel	★★★★ 71% St Pierre Park Hotel, Rohais, ST PETER PORT ☎ 01481 728282 135 ⇋ 🐾

JERSEY

Grouville   Map 16

Royal Jersey JE3 9BD ☎ 01534 854416
A seaside links, historic because of its age: its centenary
was celebrated in 1978. It is also famous for the fact that
Britain's greatest golfer, Harry Vardon, was born in a
little cottage on the edge of the course and learned his
golf here.
18 holes, 6059yds, Par 70, SSS 70, Course record 64.
Club membership 1364.

Visitors	restricted to 10am-noon & 2pm-4pm.
Societies	welcome Mon-Fri. Must apply in writing.
Green Fees	not confirmed.
Facilities	♀ ♨ 🏠 ⚑ ⛳ Tommy Horton.
Leisure	putting,trolley hire,practice area.
Location	4m E of St Helier off coast rd
Hotel	★★★ 65% Old Court House Hotel, GOREY ☎ 01534 854444 58 ⇋ 🐾

La Moye   Map 16

La Moye La Route Orange JE3 8GQ ☎ 01534 43401
Seaside championship links course (venue for the Jersey
Open) situated in an exposed position on the south
western corner of the island overlooking St Ouens Bay.
Offers spectacular views, two start points, full course all
year - no temporary greens.
18 holes, 6664yds, Par 72, SSS 72, Course record 69.
Club membership 1300.

Visitors	must contact in advance.
Societies	apply in writing.
Green Fees	£40 per round (£45 weekends).
Facilities	⊗ ⑪ ⓛ ⬛ ♨ 🏠 ⛳ Mike Deeley.
Leisure	practice ground.
Location	W side of village off A13
Hotel	★★★★ 75% The Atlantic Hotel, La Moye, ST BRELADE ☎ 01534 44101 50 ⇋ 🐾

St Clement   Map 16

St Clement Jersey Recreation Grounds JE2 6PN
☎ 01534 21938
Very tight moorland course. Holes cross over fairways,
impossible to play to scratch. Suitable for middle to high
handicaps.
9 holes, 2244yds, Par 30.
Club membership 500.

Visitors	must contact in advance.
Green Fees	not confirmed.
Facilities	♨
Leisure	hard tennis courts.
Location	E side of St Helier on A5
Hotel	★★★★(red)♨♨ Longueville Manor Hotel, ST SAVIOUR ☎ 01534 25501 32 ⇋ 🐾

St Ouen   Map 16

Les Mielles Golf & Country Club JE3 7PQ
☎ 01534 482787
Challenging American-style parkland course with bent grass
greens, dwarf rye fairways and picturesque ponds situated in
the Island's largest conservation area within St Ouen's Bay.
18 holes, 5633yds, Par 70, SSS 68, Course record 62.
Club membership 1500.

Visitors	welcome all times, prior booking recommended.
Societies	write in advance to avoid disappointment.
Green Fees	£25 per day; £17 per 18 holes; £11.50 per 9 holes (£27.50/£19/£12.50 weekends).
Facilities	⊗ ⑪ ⓛ ⬛ ♀ ♨ 🏠 ⚑ ⛳ Jeremy Philips.
Leisure	motorised carts for hire, buggies for hire, trolley for hire, driving range, putting green, practice area.
Hotel	★★★ 67% Mermaid Hotel, ST PETER ☎ 01534 41255 68 ⇋ 🐾

ISLE OF MAN

Castletown   Map 06 SC26

Castletown Golf Links Fort Island, Derbyhaven 1M9 1VA
☎ 01624 822201
Set on the Langness Peninsula, this superb Championship
course is surrounded on three sides by the sea, and holds
many surprises from its Championship tees. The hotel offers
many leisure facilities.
18 holes, 6750yds, Par 72, SSS 72, Course record 65.
Club membership 600.

Visitors	contact in advance. Sat reserved for hotel residents.
Societies	must telephone in advance.
Green Fees	£20 per day (£25 weekends & bank holidays).
Facilities	⊗ ⑪ ⓛ ⬛ ♀ ♨ 🏠 ⚑ ⛳ Murray Crowe.
Leisure	heated indoor swimming pool, fishing, sauna, solarium, motorised carts for hire, buggies for hire, trolley for hire, putting green, practice area.
Hotel	★★★ 67% Castletown Golf Links Hotel, Fort Island, CASTLETOWN ☎ 01624 822201 58 ⇋ 🐾

Douglas   Map 06 SC37

Douglas IM2 1AE ☎ 01624 675952
Hilly, parkland and moorland course under the control of
Douglas Corporation.
18 holes, 6080yds, Par 69, SSS 68.
Club membership 430.
Visitors   no restrictions.
Societies   must apply in writing.
Green Fees not confirmed.
Facilities   ♀ ⚘ 📠 ⛳ ℓ K Parry.
Leisure   trolley hire.
Location   1m W off A1
Hotel   ★★★ 72% The Empress Hotel, Central
               Promenade, DOUGLAS
               ☎ 01624 661155 102 ⇥ ☈

Mount Murray Hotel & Country Club Mount Murray,
Santon IM4 2HT ☎ 01624 661111
A moorland course with fantastic views of the island, the
course has some serious challenges. The 7th hole is a Par 5
but with 612yd drive, it is the longest on the island. The 18th
is 538yds ensuring there is no let up, especially as it has to
carry over a lake in front of the hotel.
18 holes, 6664yds, Par 72, SSS 72.
Club membership 220.
Visitors   no restrictions.
Societies   telephone in advance.
Green Fees £18 per day/round (£24 weekends).
Facilities   ⊗ ⍟ ⓛ ⚑ ♀ ⚘ 📠 ⛳ ℓ Andrew Dyson.
Leisure   hard tennis courts, heated indoor swimming
               pool, squash, sauna, gymnasium, motorised carts
               for hire, buggies for hire, trolley for hire, driving
               range, putting green, practice area, crown green
               bowling.
Location   4.5m W, on north side of A5
Hotel   ★★★★ 71% Mount Murray Hotel & Country
               Club, Santon, DOUGLAS
               ☎ 01624 661111 89 ⇥ ☈

Onchan   Map 06 SC47

King Edward Bay Golf & Country Club Howstrake,
Groudle Rd IM3 2JR ☎ 01624 620430
Club plays over King Edward Bay course. Hilly seaside links
course with natural hazards and good views.
18 holes, 5457yds, Par 67, SSS 66.
Club membership 470.
Visitors   must have a handicap certificate.
Societies   must contact in advance.
Green Fees not confirmed.
Facilities   ♀ ⚘ 📠 ⛳ ℓ Donald Jones.
Leisure   sauna, solarium, caddy cars for hire, also buggies.
Location   E side of town off A11
Hotel   ★★★ 67% Sefton Hotel, Harris Promenade,
               DOUGLAS ☎ 01624 626011 79 ⇥

Peel   Map 06 SC28

Peel Rheast Ln IM5 1BG ☎ 01624 842227
Moorland course, with natural hazards and easy walking.
Good views. 11th hole is a par 4, dog-leg.
18 holes, 5914yds, Par 69, SSS 68.
Club membership 856.

Visitors   limited availability weekends.
Societies   apply in writing.
Green Fees £15 per day (£18 weekends & bank holidays).
Facilities   ⊗ ⍟ ⓛ ⚑ ♀ ⚘ 📠 ℓ Murray Crowe.
Leisure   trolley for hire, putting green, practice area.
Location   SE side of town centre on A1
Hotel   ★★★ 72% The Empress Hotel, Central
               Promenade, DOUGLAS
               ☎ 01624 661155 102 ⇥ ☈

Port Erin   Map 06 SC16

Rowany Rowany Dr IM9 6LN
☎ 01624 834108 or 834072
Undulating seaside course with testing later holes.
18 holes, 5840yds, Par 70, SSS 69, Course record 66.
Club membership 550.
Visitors   must contact in advance.
Societies   telephone in advance.
Green Fees £15 per day; £10 per round.
Facilities   ⊗ ⍟ ⓛ ⚑ ♀ ⚘ 📠 ⛳
Leisure   motorised carts for hire, trolley for hire, putting
               green, practice area.
Location   N side of village off A32
Hotel   ★★★ 66% Cherry Orchard Hotel, Bridson St,
               PORT ERIN ☎ 01624 833811 31 ⇥ ☈

Port St Mary   Map 06 SC26

Port St Mary Kallow Point Rd
☎ 01624 834932
Slightly hilly course with beautiful scenic views over Port St
Mary and the Irish Sea.
9 holes, 5418yds, Par 68, SSS 66, Course record 62.
Club membership 432.
Visitors   anytime except between 8-10.30 weekends.
Societies   contact for details.
Green Fees £9 daily (£11 weekends).
Facilities   ⊗ ⍟ ⓛ ⚑ ♀ ⚘ 📠 ⛳
Leisure   hard tennis courts, trolley for hire, putting green,
               practice area.
Hotel   ★★★ 66% Cherry Orchard Hotel, Bridson St,
               PORT ERIN
               ☎ 01624 833811 31 ⇥ ☈

Ramsey   Map 06 SC49

Ramsey Brookfield IM8 2AH
☎ 01624 812244 & 813365
Parkland course, with easy walking. Windy. Good views.
Testing holes: 1st, par 5; 18th, par 3.
18 holes, 5960yds, Par 70, SSS 69, Course record 64.
Club membership 960.
Visitors   contact in advance, visitors may not play before
               10am weekdays.
Societies   must apply in advance.
Green Fees £16 (£20 weekends & bank holidays).
Facilities   ⊗ ⍟ ⓛ ⚑ ♀ ⚘ 📠 ℓ Calum Wilson.
Leisure   trolley for hire, putting green, practice area.
Location   SW side of town
Hotel   ★★★ 72% The Empress Hotel, Central
               Promenade, DOUGLAS
               ☎ 01624 661155 102 ⇥ ☈

SCOTLAND

*"Golf's big prize is an invitation to play
Royal Dornoch, or Muirfield!"*

Most true golfers, by the nature of things, must have had at least one drop of Scottish blood bestowed on them. How else can you account for the quickening of the pulse as the border is reached? Some of us feel that if we haven't been to Scotland at least once in the year, irritation sets in. The lure of the people, the tartan, heather and the history is compelling. No wonder Keith Prowse, the travel agents, now offer a special package to pilgrims wishing to tee off at St Andrews.

Although this northern city, made of grey stone and exposed to a harsh winter climate, is the acknowledged Home of Golf, the Old Course there is overplayed and deserves Sundays off, which it duly gets! Undoubtedly a monument to our royal and ancient game, newcomers depart with private views about the experience they enjoyed, and assess the value of the £60 green fee they paid to walk across those hallowed humps and hollows.

But Scotland, wall-to-wall with courses and seaside links of incredible calibre, is sadly taken for granted by locals who seem not to appreciate what they have. Again, we must nominate favourites or mention known jewels, such as the Royal Dornoch, the second oldest place where golf began, with a club that opened in 1880. Senior professional John Panton, once dubbed the laird of the Highlands, rates this course, and Muirfield (near Edinburgh) among Scotland's finest. Receiving an invitation to play either is something akin to winning golf's premier prize

SWEET-SMELLING PINE

If planning a golf invasion of Scotland my advice would be to seek out the established tests, even though some speak highly of newer creations, designed by others than ancient Britons. When I teed off at Gleneagles with the late Henry Longhurst for a pre-dinner friendly, there was nowhere else in the world to compare. Affectionately called 'The Glen', the pure air is filled with sweet-smelling pine, heather, bracken and wildlife abounds, and the scenery is breathtaking.

Good motor transport is essential to prise open the best of Scotland. In the old days the railways chose to buy several Scottish courses with Cruden Bay, 23 miles north of

Aberdeen being, like Gleneagles, a prime example of past railway ownership. Founded at the end of the 19th century, Cruden Bay was designed by Tom Simpson and is hailed as one of the nations finest links - and nearby there is an additional 9-holer, St Olaf, for the ladies who, some reckon, are not always treated too well by elite clubs, although times may be changing.

While motoring in the Aberdeen area, the A92 takes a wise player to Murcar which further adds glitter to this part of the north-east. Although I have not played there, friends say it has views of the sea, rolling duneland, streams and fine turf and, at only 6219 yards in length, must be on my list since I don't hit the ball vast lengths.

TURNBERRY; CROWN JEWEL

My favourite Scottish links is Turnberry (Ayrshire) and if the wind off the sea isn't too fierce, and the sun shines, the place sparkles out by that lighthouse and everone feels almost turbo-charged. It's true that to play Turnberry today as a visitor is expensive and to enjoy a meal at the deeply impressive hotel is a somewhat costly experience.

Although now owned by overseas investors, the injection of foreign money has improved every aspect of Turnberry, underlining its status as one of the world's finest links. Whatever happens to the world economy in the future this is now one upgraded, king-size jewel in the crown of

British sport, on par with Muirfield, the oldest course which defends its private status and old-world elegance against all predators, and, sometimes, against visitors, too! According to an American list of the world's 100 greatest courses, Muirfield is rated at number two, behind Pine Valley.

UNTAMED AND NATURAL

Scotland is home to the Loch Ness Monster and that golfing monster known as Carnoustie. Ben Hogan won on this whopping links - and never returned. I don't know why this legend chose to stay home, but can guess. While the last few holes, over the Barry Burn that winds across fairways like an angry serpent, are indeed memorable, the whole challenge is too much like hard work in the wind.

While Prestwick, founded in 1851, may have been left behind by modern wonders such as Loch Lomond or Peter de Savary's course at Skibo Castle, it stays in my mind as highly desirable. There are some 14 blind shots you must hit over the sandhills and wherever you walk, you feel the spirits of champions past.

Anywhere else? Oh yes. We flew in a small aircraft to the Isle of Islay. The island folk were very special, as was their hospitality! I failed to hit a decent, or sober, shot. But for pure, untamed natural golf, there is nothing better. If life is kind, I shall return, and use my own clubs before sipping a drop.

SCOTLAND

The directory which follows has been divided into three geographical regions. Counties have not been shown against individual locations as recent legislation has created a number of smaller counties which will be unfamiliar to the visitor. The postal authorities have confirmed that it is no longer necessary to include a county name in addresses, provided a post code is shown. All locations appear in the atlas section at the end of this guide in their appropriate counties.

HIGHLANDS & ISLANDS

This region includes the counties of Aberdeen City, Aberdeenshire, Highland, Moray, Orkney, Shetland and Western Isles which reflect the recent national changes.

ABERDEEN   Map 15 NJ90

Auchmill Bonnyview Rd, West Heatheryfold AB2 7FQ
☎ 01224 715214
This course is definitely not for beginners - the fairways are tree-lined and very tight on most holes. Three holes are quite hilly and although the remainder is flat there are nice views over Aberdeen. The course is not recommended for anyone over 22 handicap unless they have plenty of golf balls!
18 holes, 5123metres, Par 68, SSS 67, Course record 67.
Club membership 300.
Visitors   members have priority Sat & Wed for club competitions.
Societies   apply in writing to Leisure and Recreation Dept, Aberdeen District Council.
Green Fees £7 per round.
Facilities   ⊗ by prior arrangement ⅢⅢ by prior arrangement �󠁬 ♥ ♀ ⅄
Leisure   putting green, practice area.
Location   Outskirts Aberdeen, A96 Aberdeen/Inverness
Hotel   ★★★ 66% The Craighaar, Waterton Rd, Bucksburn, ABERDEEN
                 ☎ 01224 712275 55 ⇥ ⋔

Balnagask St Fitticks Rd AB1 3QT
☎ 01224 876407 & 01224 871286
Links course. Used by the Nigg Bay Club.
18 holes, 5986ydss, SSS 69.
Visitors   no restrictions.
Societies   apply to council.
Facilities   ⅄
Location   2m E of city centre
Hotel   ★★★ 69% Caledonian Thistle, 10 Union Ter, ABERDEEN ☎ 01224 640233 80 ⇥ ⋔

Deeside Golf Rd, Bieldside AB1 9DL
☎ 01224 869457
An interesting riverside course with several tree-lined fairways. A stream comes into play at 9 of the 18 holes on the main course. There is a subsidiary 9-hole course.
18 holes, 5971yds, Par 71, SSS 69, Course record 63.
Club membership 800.
Visitors   must contact in advance.
Societies   apply in writing.
Green Fees £25 per day (£30 weekends & bank holidays). 9 hole £8 per day..
Facilities   ⊗ ⅢⅢ ⅓ ♥ ♀ ⅄ 🛍 ⅂ Frank J Coutts.
Leisure   trolley for hire, putting green, practice area.
Location   3m W of city centre off A93
Hotel   ★★★★ 70% Ardoe House, Blairs, South Deeside Rd, ABERDEEN
                 ☎ 01224 867355 71 ⇥ ⋔

Hazelhead Public Hazelhead AB1 8BD
☎ No telephone
A tree-lined course.
18 holes, 6595yds, Par 70, SSS 70.
Visitors   no restrictions.
Societies   must contact in advance.
Green Fees not confirmed.
Facilities   ⅄ 🛍 ⅂
Location   4m W of city centre off A944
Hotel   ★★★★ 70% Ardoe House, Blairs, South Deeside Rd, ABERDEEN
                 ☎ 01224 867355 71 ⇥ ⋔

Kings Links AB2 1NR ☎ 01224 632269
A typical links course with no tree lines and plenty of bunkers.The 14th hole is tricky - a long par 4 with a raised green and not much fairway round the green. The course is playable all year. Nearby there is a 6-hole course. The Bon Accord Club, Caledonian Club and Northern Club play over this course.
18 holes, 6384yds, Par 72, SSS 71.
Visitors   contact starters box on 01224 632269 regarding booking of tee times.
Societies   write to the Arts & Recreation Dept, St Nicholas House, Broad Street, Aberdeen.
Green Fees municipal rates.
Facilities   ⅄
Location   0.75m NE of city centre
Hotel   ★★★ 69% Caledonian Thistle, 10 Union Ter, ABERDEEN ☎ 01224 640233 80 ⇥ ⋔

Murcar Bridge of Don AB23 8BD
☎ 01224 704345
Seaside links course, prevailing NE wind, hard-walking. Testing 4th and 14th holes.
18 holes, 6241yds, Par 71, SSS 71, Course record 65.
Club membership 800.
Visitors   must contact in advance.
Societies   advance booking required.
Green Fees £35 per day; £25 per round (£40 per day/round weekends & bank holidays).
Facilities   ⊗ ⅢⅢ ⅓ ♥ ♀ ⅄ 🛍 ⅂ Alan White.
Leisure   trolley for hire, putting green, practice area.
Location   5m NE of city centre off A92
Hotel   ★★★ 66% The Craighaar, Waterton Rd, Bucksburn, ABERDEEN
                 ☎ 01224 712275 55 ⇥ ⋔

Royal Aberdeen Balgownie, Bridge of Don AB23 8AT
☎ 01224 702571
Championship links course. Windy, easy walking.
*Balgownie Course: 18 holes, 6372yds, Par 71, SSS 71,
Course record 63.*
Silverburn Course: 18 holes, 4066yds, Par 64, SSS 60.
Club membership 500.
Visitors | times for visitors 10-11.30 and 2-3.30pm
weekdays, after 3.30pm weekends.
Societies | apply in writing.
Green Fees | £48 per day; £37 per round (£48 per round
weekends).
Facilities | ⊗ ⅏ ⅃ ☂ ♀ ⅄ ⛫ ⛛ ⅂ Ronnie MacAskill.
Leisure | trolley for hire, putting green, practice area.
Location | 2.5m N of city centre off A92
Hotel | ★★★ 69% Caledonian Thistle, 10 Union Ter,
ABERDEEN ☎ 01224 640233 80 ⊨ ⋔

Westhill Westhill Heights, Westhill, Skene AB32 6RY
☎ 01224 742567
A highland course.
18 holes, 5921yds, Par 69, SSS 69, Course record 65.
Club membership 800.
Visitors | must contact in advance.
Societies | telephone in advance.
Green Fees | £16 per day; £12 per round (£22/18 weekends
and bank holidays).
Facilities | ⊗ ⅏ ⅃ ☂ ♀ ⅄ ⛫ ⛛ ⅂ Ronnie McDonald.
Leisure | motorised carts for hire, buggies for hire, trolley
for hire, putting green, practice area.
Location | 6m NW of city centre off A944
Hotel | ★★★ 63% Westhill Hotel, WESTHILL
☎ 01224 740388 37 ⊨ ⋔Annexe13 ⊨ ⋔

COUNTRY HOTEL AND RESTAURANT

Return to the Quality of Life

Varied à la carte menu
including vegetarian
dishes.
Seafood our speciality.
Only 10 minutes from
Royal Aberdeen
Murcar and Cruden
Bay courses.
A warm welcome
awaits you from the
Craig Family.

NEWBURGH, ABERDEENSHIRE
Tel: (01358) 789444

ABOYNE
Map 15 NO59

Aboyne Formaston Park AB34 5HP ☎ 013398 86328
Beautiful parkland with outstanding views. Two lochs on
course.
18 holes, 5975yds, Par 69, SSS 68, Course record 62.
Club membership 906.
Visitors | no restrictions. Advisable to contact in advance.
Societies | prior booking essential.
Green Fees | £21 per day; £16 per round (£25/£20 weekends).
Facilities | ⊗ ⅏ ⅃ ☂ ♀ ⅄ ⛫ ⛛ ⅂ Innes Wright.
Leisure | trolley for hire, putting green, practice area.
Location | E side of village, N of A93
Hotel | ★★ 70% Birse Lodge Hotel, Charleston Rd,
ABOYNE ☎ 013398 86253 12 ⊨ ⋔

ALFORD
Map 15 NJ51

Alford Montgarrie Rd AB33 8AE ☎ 019755 62178
A flat parkland course in scenic countryside. Divided into
sections by a road, a railway and a burn.
18 holes, 5290yds, Par 69, SSS 65, Course record 64.
Club membership 600.
Visitors | advisable to contact in advance.
Societies | telephone in advance.
Green Fees | £15 per day; £11 per round (£22/£17 weekends).
Facilities | ⊗ ⅏ ⅃ ☂ ♀ ⅄ ⛛ ⅂
Leisure | trolley for hire, trolley hire.
Hotel | ★★★(red)⚘ Kildrummy Castle Hotel,
KILDRUMMY ☎ 019755 71288 16 ⊨ ⋔

ALNESS
Map 14 NH66

Alness Ardross Rd IV17 0PQ ☎ 01349 883877
A short, but testing, parkland course with beautiful views
over the Cromarty Firth and the Black Isle.
9 holes, 2606yds, Par 66, SSS 64.
Club membership 220.
Visitors | telephone in advance for weekend play.
Societies | must contact in advance.
Green Fees | £7 per day (£9 weekends).
Facilities | ⅃ ☂ ♀ ⅄ ⛛
Leisure | fishing, practice area.
Location | 0.5m N off A9
Hotel | ★★★ 68% Morangie House Hotel, Morangie
Rd, TAIN ☎ 01862 892281 26 ⊨ ⋔

ARISAIG
Map 13 NM68

Traigh PH39 4NT ☎ 01687 450645
According to at least one newspaper Traigh is 'probably the
most beautifully sited nine-hole golf course in the world'.
Whether that is true or not, Traigh lies by the sea alongside
sandy beaches with views to Skye and the Inner Hebrides.
The feature of the course is a line of grassy hills, originally
sand dunes, that rise to some 60 feet. The nine-hole course
was completely redesigned for the 1995 season.
9 holes, 2405yds, Par 68, SSS 65, Course record 67.
Club membership 125.
Visitors | no restrictions.
Societies | contact in advance.
Green Fees | £40 per week; £10 per day.
Facilities | ☂ ⛫ ⛛
Leisure | trolley for hire, putting green, practice area. ▶

Location	6m S of Malling on A830
Hotel	★★ 65% Arisaig Hotel, ARISAIG ☎ 01687 450210 15rm(6 ⇋)

AUCHENBLAE   Map 15 NO77

Auchenblae AB30 1BU ☎ 01561 378869
Picturesque, small, undulating parkland course offering good views.
9 holes, 2174yds, Par 32, SSS 30, Course record 60.
Club membership 78.
Visitors   restricted Wed & Fri evenings.
Societies   must telephone in advance.
Green Fees not confirmed.
Location   0.5m NE
Hotel   ★★ 61% County Hotel, Arduthie Rd, STONEHAVEN ☎ 01569 764386 14 ⇋ 🐾

BALLATER   Map 15 NO39

Ballater Victoria Rd AB35 5QX ☎ 013397 55567
Moorland course with testing long holes and beautiful scenery.
18 holes, 5638yds, Par 67, SSS 67, Course record 62.
Club membership 650.
Visitors   must contact in advance.
Societies   prior booking recommended.
Green Fees £26 per 2 rounds; £17 per round (£30/£20 weekends).
Facilities   ⊗ �🍽 🏌 🍺 ♀ ⅄ 🏠 ⛳ 𝄢 Frank Smith.
Leisure   hard tennis courts, fishing, motorised carts for hire, trolley for hire, putting green, practice area.
Location   W side of town
Hotel   ★★★ 72% Darroch Learg Hotel, Braemar Rd, BALLATER ☎ 013397 55443 14 ⇋ 🐾Annexe5 ⇋ 🐾

BANCHORY   Map 15 NO69

Banchory Kinneskie Rd AB31 3TA ☎ 01330 822365
Sheltered parkland course situated beside the River Dee, with easy walking and woodland scenery. 11th and 12th holes are testing.
18 holes, 5522yds, Par 67, SSS 65, Course record 60.
Club membership 975.
Visitors   telephone for details on 01330 822447
Societies   must book in advance, no parties Thu & weekends.
Green Fees £22 per day, £16 per round (£25/£20 weekends). Weekly £70..
Facilities   ⊗ ⍝ 🏌 🍺 ♀ ⅄ 🏠 ⛳ 𝄢 J Charles Dernie.
Location   A93, 300 yds from W end of High St
Hotel   ★★★(red)⚜ Banchory Lodge Hotel, BANCHORY ☎ 01330 822625 22 ⇋ 🐾

BANFF   Map 15 NJ66

Duff House Royal The Barnyards AB45 3SX ☎ 01261 812062
Well-manicured flat parkland, bounded by woodlands and River Deveron. Well bunkered and renowned for its large, two-tier greens.
18 holes, 6161yds, Par 68, SSS 69, Course record 63.
Club membership 1000.
Visitors   a handicap certificate is preferred. Some time restrictions.
Societies   must apply in writing.
Green Fees not confirmed.
Facilities   ♀ ⅄ 🏠 ⛳ 𝄢 Bob Strachan.
Location   0.5m S on A98
Hotel   ★★★ 61% Banff Springs Hotel, Golden Knowes Rd, BANFF ☎ 01261 812881 30 ⇋ 🐾

BOAT OF GARTEN — Map 14 NH91

Boat of Garten PH24 3BQ ☎ 01479 831282
This parkland course was cut out from a silver birch
forest though the fairways are adequately wide. There are
natural hazards of broom and heather, good views and
walking is easy. A round provides great variety.
18 holes, 5866yds, Par 69, SSS 69, Course record 64.
Club membership 600.
Visitors must contact in advance.
Societies must telephone in advance.
Green Fees £20 per day (£23 weekends).
Facilities ⊗ 𝍩 ᵇ ♥ ♀ ♨ 🏌
Leisure hard tennis courts, trolley for hire, putting
   green.
Location E side of village
Hotel ★★★ 65% Boat Hotel, BOAT OF
   GARTEN ☎ 01479 831258 32 ⇆ ⏀

BONAR BRIDGE — Map 14 NH69

Bonar Bridge-Ardgay Migdale Rd IV24 3EJ
☎ 01863 766375
Wooded moorland course with picturesque views of hills and
loch.
9 holes, 4640yds, Par 66, SSS 63, Course record 63.
Club membership 250.
Visitors restricted during competitions.
Societies apply in writing.
Green Fees £10 per day; £50 per week.
Facilities ᵇ ♥ ♨
Location 0.5m E
Hotel ★★ 66% Dornoch Castle Hotel, Castle St,
   DORNOCH
   ☎ 01862 810216 4 ⇆ ⏀Annexe13 ⇆ ⏀

BRAEMAR — Map 15 NO19

Braemar Cluniebank Rd AB35 5XX ☎ 013397 41618
Flat course, set amid beautiful countryside on Royal Deeside,
with River Clunie running through several holes. The 2nd
hole is one of the most testing in the area.
18 holes, 5000yds, Par 65, SSS 64, Course record 61.
Club membership 450.
Visitors are advised to book 24 hours in advance to play
   at weekends.
Societies must contact secretary in advance 01224
   704471.
Green Fees £16 per day; £12 per round (£20 per day; £15
   per round weekends).
Facilities ⊗ ᵇ ♀ ♨ 🖴 🏌
Leisure trolley for hire.
Location 0.5m S
Hotel ★★★ 68% Invercauld Arms, BRAEMAR
   ☎ 013397 41605 68 ⇆ ⏀

BRORA — Map 14 NC90

Brora Golf Rd KW9 6QS ☎ 01408 621417
Typical seaside links with little rough and fine views. Some
testing holes.
18 holes, 6110yds, Par 69, SSS 69, Course record 61.
Club membership 704.
Visitors advisable to book in advance May-Oct.

Societies advisable to book in advance.
Green Fees £16 per day.
Facilities ⊗ 𝍩 ᵇ ♥ ♀ ♨ 🖴 🏌
Leisure trolley for hire, putting green, practice area.
   limited fishing.
Location E side of village
Hotel ★★★ 64% The Links Hotel, Golf Rd, BRORA
   ☎ 01408 621225 23 ⇆ ⏀

BUCKIE — Map 15 NJ46

Buckpool Barhill Rd, Buckpool AB56 1DU
☎ 01542 832933
Windy, seaside course, with easy walking. Overlooking
Moray Firth, its fairways are lined by whin and broom.
18 holes, 6257yds, Par 70, SSS 70, Course record 64.
Club membership 430.
Visitors apply in advance.
Societies apply in advance.
Green Fees £12 per day; £8 per round (£18/£10 weekends).
Facilities ⊗ 𝍩 ♥ ♀ ♨
Leisure squash, trolley for hire, putting green.
Location Off A98
Hotel ★★ 68% Marine Hotel, Marine Place,
   BUCKIE ☎ 01542 832249 12 ⇆ ⏀

Strathlene Strathlene Rd AB56 1DJ ☎ 01542 831798
Windy seaside links course with magnificent view. A special
feature of the course is approach shots to raised greens (holes
4,5,6 & 13).
18 holes, 5980yds, Par 69, SSS 69, Course record 65.
Club membership 370.
Visitors booking essential at weekends.
Societies telephone for Mon-Fri & apply in writing for
   weekends.
Green Fees £14 per day; £10 per round (£18/£14 weekends).
Facilities ⊗ ᵇ ♥ ♨ 🖴
Leisure trolley for hire, putting green.
Location 3m E on A942
Hotel ★★ 64% Mill House Hotel, Tynet, BUCKIE
   ☎ 01542 850233 15 ⇆ ⏀

CAIRNBULG — Map 15 NK06

Inverallochy AB43 5YL ☎ 01346 582000
Windy seaside links course with natural hazards, tricky par 3s
and easy walking. Panoramic views of North Sea at every hole.
18 holes, 5137yds, Par 64, SSS 65, Course record 60.
Club membership 300.
Visitors restricted at weekends and competition days.
Societies apply in writing.
Green Fees not confirmed.
Facilities ♨
Leisure practice area.
Location ⸴ E side of village off B9107
Hotel ★★ 65% Tufted Duck Hotel, ST COMBS
   ☎ 01346 582481 & 582482/3 18 ⇆ ⏀

CARRBRIDGE — Map 14 NH92

Carrbridge Inverness Rd PH23 3AU ☎ 01479 841623
Short part-parkland, part-moorland course with magnificent
views of the Cairngorms.
9 holes, 5402yds, Par 71, SSS 68, Course record 64.
Club membership 650. ▶

AA ★★
Les Routiers
Highly Recommended
01542 840432

Cullen Bay Hotel

Banffshire AB56 2XA

STB ●●●●
Commended
Fax: 840900

Central on the Moray/Banff golf course coastal belt, next to Cullen links (early tee-off?), our
family run hotel offers a warm homely atmosphere. 18 courses within 20 miles, most on
inclusive ticket to uncrowded greens.
Panoramic hilltop views of rocky coastline provide backdrop to our award winning chefs
cuisine. Relax by lounge bars' log fire with Scotlands finest malts. 14 newly refurbished
ensuite bedrooms, most with sea views.
Parties of 8+ play for trophy and special incentive to win!

Visitors	during May-Sep, course open to visitors after 5pm Wed & 4pm Sun.
Societies	small parties welcome, apply in writing.
Green Fees	£10-£11 per day (£12 weekends). Evening (after 6.30pm) £5-£7.
Facilities	⬛ 💺 ♿ ⛳
Leisure	trolley for hire, putting green.
Location	N side of village
Hotel	★★♨ 71% Dalrachney Lodge, CARRBRIDGE ☎ 01479 841252 11 ⇄ 🐾

CRUDEN BAY   Map 15 NK03

Cruden Bay AB42 7NN ☎ 01779 812285
A seaside links which provides golf of a high order. It
was designed by a master architect, Tom Simpson, and
although changed somewhat from his original design it is
still a great golf course. Magnificent views.
*Main Course: 18 holes, 6395yds, Par 70, SSS 72, Course
record 63.*
St Olaf Course: 9 holes, 2553yds, Par 64, SSS 65.
Club membership 1100.

Visitors	welcome on weekdays, at weekends only when there are no competitions.
Societies	weekdays only telephone in advance.
Green Fees	Main Course £30 per day (£40 weekends); St Olaf £10 per day (£15 weekends).
Facilities	⊗ �🍽 ⬛ 💺 ♀ ⛳ ⛳ ⛳ Robert Stewart.
Leisure	trolley for hire, driving range, putting green, practice area.
Location	SW side of village on A975
Hotel	★★ 65% Red House Hotel, Aulton Rd, CRUDEN BAY ☎ 01779 812215 6rm(5 ⇄ 🐾)
Additional hotel	★★ 68% Udny Arms Hotel, Main St, NEWBURGH ☎ 01358 789444 26 ⇄ 🐾

CULLEN   Map 15 NJ56

Cullen The Links AB56 2UU ☎ 01542 840685
Interesting links on two levels with rocks and ravines offering
some challenging holes. Spectacular scenery.
18 holes, 4610yds, Par 63, SSS 62, Course record 58.
Club membership 600.

Visitors	no restrictions but during summer club medal matches given preference on Mon/Wed/Sat.
Societies	advance applications advisable.
Green Fees	£12 per day; £7 per round (£15/£9 weekends).
Facilities	⊗ ⍾ by prior arrangement ⬛ 💺 ♀♿
Leisure	trolley for hire, putting green, practice area.
Location	0.5m W off A98
Hotel	★★ 63% Cullen Bay Hotel, Cullen, BUCKIE ☎ 01542 840432 14 ⇄ 🐾

DORNOCH   Map 14 NH78

Royal Dornoch Golf Rd IV25 3LW
☎ 01862 810219 & 811220
Very challenging seaside championship links, designed
by Tom Morris and John Sutherland.
*Championship: 18 holes, 6514yds, Par 70, SSS 73,
Course record 65.*
Struie Course: 18 holes, 5438yds, Par 69, SSS 66.
Club membership 1150.

Visitors	must have a handicap of 24 for gentlemen (ladies 35) on Championship Course. Must contact in advance and have a handicap certificate.
Societies	must apply in advance.
Green Fees	Championship course: £40 per round summer; £27 winter (£45/30 weekends). Struie course £16 per day; £11 per round (£8/£5.50 winter).
Facilities	⊗ ⍾ ⬛ 💺 ♀♿ 🏠 ⛳ ⛳ W E Skinner.
Leisure	hard tennis courts, fishing, motorised carts for hire, trolley for hire, putting green, practice area.
Location	E side of town
Hotel	★★ 66% Dornoch Castle Hotel, Castle St, DORNOCH ☎ 01862 810216 4 ⇄ 🐾Annexe13 ⇄ 🐾

Skibo Castle The Carnegie Club, Skibo Castle
IV25 3RG ☎ 01862 894600
Set within the grounds of an enchanting castle, with the
sea on three sides and the hills of Sutherland and Ross-
shire all around, this splendid course enjoys a
magnificent position. Although not long by modern
standards, strong and fickle winds will test even the most
experienced golfer. Excellent leisure facilities.
18 holes, 6403yds, Par 71, SSS 71.
Club membership 350.

Visitors	weekdays only by written application to the secretary.
Green Fees	£50 per 18 holes.
Facilities	⊗ 💺 ♀♿ 🏠 ⛳ ⛳ ⛳ William Milne.
Leisure	hard tennis courts, heated indoor swimming pool, fishing, sauna, solarium, gymnasium, trolley for hire, driving range, putting green, practice area.
Location	Off A9 3m before Dornoch
Hotel	★★ 66% Dornoch Castle Hotel, Castle St, DORNOCH ☎ 01862 810216 4 ⇄ 🐾Annexe13 ⇄ 🐾

★★

Dornoch Castle

DORNOCH,
SUTHERLAND
IV25 3SD
Tel. (01862) 810216
Fax: (01862) 810981

Play GOLF on the famous Royal Dornoch Championship Course, and stay at the charming Dornoch Castle. All rooms have private facilities: those in the new wing have modern decor, while those in the Castle enjoy the highest level of traditional atmosphere and elegance. Beaches and golf courses are within walking distance. Superb food ("Taste of Scotland" recommended) in one of the finest Restaurants of the area with a cellar to match will make your visit an experience not to be forgotten.

STB ● ● ● ● COMMENDED

DUFFTOWN   Map 15 NJ33

Dufftown Methercluny, Tomintoul Rd AB55 4BX
☎ 01340 820325
A short and undulating inland course with good views. Highest hole over 1000 ft above sea level.
18 holes, 5308yds, Par 67, SSS 67, Course record 67.
Club membership 250.
Visitors   tee reserved Tue & Wed 4.30-6.30 & Sun 7.30-9
              & 12.30-2.
Societies   apply in writing.
Green Fees £15 per day; £10 per round.
Facilities   ♀ ♨ ♈
Leisure   trolley for hire, putting green.
Location   0.75m SW off B9009
Hotel   ★★★ 72% Craigellachie Hotel,
           CRAIGELLACHIE ☎ 01340 881204 30 ➪ ℞

DURNESS   Map 14 NC46

Durness Balnakeil IV27 4PG ☎ 01971 511364 & 511262
A 9-hole course set in tremendous scenery overlooking Balnakeil Bay. Part links and part inland with water hazards. Off alternative tees for second 9 holes giving surprising variety. Tremendous last hole played across the sea to the green over 100 yards away.
9 holes, 5555yds, Par 70, SSS 69, Course record 72.
Club membership 150.
Visitors   restricted 10am-12.30 on Sun during Jun-Sep.
Societies   must telephone in advance 01971 511364 (ex
            Sun).
Green Fees £11 per day.
Facilities   ⊗ ♥ ♨ ♈
Leisure   fishing, trolley for hire, putting green, practice
           area.
Location   1m W of village
Guesthouse QQQ Port-Na-Con House, Loch Eriboll, By
            Altnaharra ☎ 01971 511367 4rm(1 ℞)

ELGIN   Map 15 NJ26

Elgin Hardhillock, Birnie Rd, New Elgin IV30 3SX
☎ 01343 542338
Possibly the finest inland course in the north of Scotland, with undulating greens and compact holes that demand the highest accuracy. There are thirteen par 4's and one par 5 hole on its parkland layout.
18 holes, 6411yds, Par 69, SSS 71, Course record 64.
Club membership 1000.
Visitors   must contact in advance, weekend play only
            by prior arrangement.
Societies   telephone secretary for details.

Green Fees £25 per day; £19 per round (£32/£26
            weekends).
Facilities   ⊗ ⋔ ﬞ▙ ♥ ♀ ♨ 🕮 ℓ Ian P Rodger.
Leisure   trolley for hire, driving range, putting green,
           practice area.
Location   1m S on A941
Hotel   ★★★ 70% Mansefield House Hotel,
           Mayne Rd, ELGIN
           ☎ 01343 540883 17 ➪ ℞

ELLON   Map 15 NJ93

McDonald Hospital Rd AB41 9AW ☎ 01358 720576
Tight, parkland course with streams and a pond.
18 holes, 5986yds, Par 70, SSS 69.
Club membership 710.
Visitors   no restrictions.
Green Fees not confirmed.
Facilities   ♀ ♨
Location   0.25m N on A948
Hotel   ★ 66% Meldrum Arms Hotel, The Square,
           OLDMELDRUM ☎ 01651 872238 7 ℞

FORRES   Map 14 NJ05

Forres Muiryshade IV36 0RD ☎ 01309 672250
An all-year parkland course laid on light, well-drained soil in wooded countryside. Walking is easy despite some hilly holes. A test for the best golfers.
18 holes, 6240yds, Par 70, SSS 70, Course record 64.
Club membership 950.
Visitors   welcome although club competitions take
           priority. Weekends may be restricted in
           summer.
Societies   must telephone 2-3 weeks in advance.
Green Fees not confirmed.
Facilities   ♀ ♨ 🕮 ♈ ℓ Sandy Aird.
Leisure   putting green,cart/buggy/trolley hire.
Location   SE side of town centre off B9010
Hotel   ★★ 69% Ramnee Hotel, Victoria Rd,
           FORRES ☎ 01309 672410 20 ➪ ℞

FORT AUGUSTUS   Map 14 NH30

Fort Augustus Markethill PH32 4AU ☎ 01320 366660
Moorland course, with narrow fairways and good views. Bordered by the tree-lined Caledonian Canal.
9 holes, 5454yds, Par 67, SSS 67, Course record 67.
Club membership 170.
Visitors   may not play Sat 1.30-4 & occasional Sun.
Societies   telephone in advance.   ▶

Green Fees £10 per day.
Facilities ♀ 飞 ☂
Location 1m SW on A82
Hotel ★★ 67% Lovat Arms Hotel, FORT AUGUSTUS
☎ 01320 366206 & 366204 21 ⇌ ⋔

FORTROSE   Map 14 NH75

Fortrose & Rosemarkie Ness Rd East IV10 8SE
☎ 01381 620529
Seaside links course, set on a peninsula with sea on three sides. Easy walking, good views. Designed by James Braid; the club was formed in 1888.
18 holes, 5858yds, Par 71, SSS 69, Course record 64.
Club membership 770.
Visitors restricted 8.45-10.15am & 1-2.15 then 4.45-6.30pm.
Societies must telephone in advance.
Green Fees £21 per day; £15 per round (£30/£21 weekends & bank holidays).
Facilities ⊗ ⅃ ☕ ♀ ⟁ 🖻 ☂
Leisure trolley for hire, putting green, practice area.
Location E side of town centre
Hotel ★★ 67% Royal Hotel, Marine Ter, CROMARTY ☎ 01381 600217 10 ⇌ ⋔

FORT WILLIAM   Map 14 NN17

Fort William Torlundy PH33 7SN ☎ 01397 704464
Spectacular moorland location looking onto the cliffs of Ben Nevis. Tees and greens are in excellent condition and major drainage improvements to the fairways were implemented in 1995.
18 holes, 6500yds, Par 72, SSS 71, Course record 67.
Club membership 230.
Visitors no restrictions.
Societies must contact in writing.
Green Fees £14 per day; £12 per round.
Facilities ☕ ♀ ⟁ ☂
Leisure trolley for hire, putting green.
Location 3m NE on A82
Hotel ★★★ 75% Moorings Hotel, Banavie, FORT WILLIAM
☎ 01397 772797 21 ⇌ ⋔Annexe3 ⋔

FRASERBURGH   Map 15 NJ96

Fraserburgh Philorth AB43 5TL ☎ 01346 516616
Testing seaside course.
Corbie: 18 holes, 6278yds, Par 70, SSS 70, Course record 64.
Rosehill: 9 holes, 3380yds, Par 70, SSS 71.
Club membership 750.
Visitors no restrictions but advised to check availability.
Societies must contact in advance.
Green Fees £14 per day; £11 per round (£20/£15 weekends). 9 hole course £10 per day.
Facilities ⊗ ⅃ ☕ ⅃ ♀ ⟁ 🖻 ☂
Leisure trolley for hire, putting green, practice area.
Location 1m SE on B9033
Hotel ★★ 65% Tufted Duck Hotel, ST COMBS
☎ 01346 582481 & 582482/3 18 ⇌ ⋔

GAIRLOCH   Map 14 NG87

Gairloch IV21 2BE ☎ 01445 712407
Fine seaside links course running along Gairloch Sands with good views over the sea to Skye. In windy conditions each hole is affected.
9 holes, 4514yds, Par 62, SSS 64, Course record 61.
Club membership 250.
Visitors handicap certificate required.
Societies apply in writing to secretary.
Green Fees £12 per day; £45 per week.
Facilities ☕ ⟁ 🖻 ☂
Leisure trolley for hire, practice area.
Location 1m S on A832
Hotel ★★ 63% The Old Inn, Flowerdale, GAIRLOCH ☎ 01445 712006 14 ⇌ ⋔

GARMOUTH   Map 15 NJ36

Garmouth & Kingston Spey St IV32 7NJ
☎ 01343 870388
Seaside course with several parkland holes and tidal waters. Naturally flat.
18 holes, 5616yds, Par 67, SSS 67, Course record 62.
Club membership 450.
Visitors must contact in advance for weekend play.
Societies advisable to phone in advance.
Green Fees £17 per day; £11 per round (£22/£16 weekends).
Facilities ⊗ ⅃ ⅃ ☕ ♀ ⟁
Leisure fishing, trolley for hire, practice area.
Location In village on B9015
Hotel ★★★ 70% Mansefield House Hotel, Mayne Rd, ELGIN ☎ 01343 540883 17 ⇌ ⋔

GOLSPIE   Map 14 NH89

Golspie Ferry Rd KW10 6ST ☎ 01408 633266
Founded in 1889, Golspie's seaside course offers easy walking and natural hazards including beach heather and whins. Spectacular scenery.
18 holes, 5800yds, Par 68, SSS 68, Course record 64.
Club membership 300.
Visitors contact in advance.
Societies contact in advance.
Green Fees £15 per day/round (£20 weekends & bank holidays).
Facilities ⊗ by prior arrangement ⅃ by prior arrangement ⅃ by prior arrangement ☕ by prior arrangement ♀ ⟁
Leisure trolley for hire, putting green, practice area.
Location 0.5m S off A9
Hotel ★★ 61% Golf Links Hotel, GOLSPIE ☎ 01408 633408 9 ⇌ ⋔

GRANTOWN-ON-SPEY   Map 14 NJ02

Grantown-on-Spey Golf Course Rd PH26 3HY
☎ 01479 872079 (Apr-Oct)
Parkland and woodland course. Part easy walking, remainder hilly. The 7th to 13th really sorts out the golfers.
18 holes, 5517yds, Par 69, SSS 68.
Club membership 650.
Visitors advisable to contact in advance. No visitors before 10am weekends.

Societies clubhouse open Apr-Oct, apply in advance to secretary.
Green Fees £15 per day (£20 weekends). Evenings after 6pm £10.
Facilities ⊗ ⅷ by prior arrangement ⅑ ♨ ♀ ⚖ ⌂ ⚑ ℓ Bill Mitchell.
Leisure trolley for hire, putting green, practice area.
Location SE side of town centre
Hotel ★★★ 67% Garth Hotel, Castle Rd, GRANTOWN-ON-SPEY
☎ 01479 872836 & 872162 17 ⇆ ⋔

HELMSDALE   Map 14 ND01

Helmsdale Golf Rd KW8 6JA ☎ 01431 821339
Sheltered, undulating course following the line of the Helmsdale River.
9 holes, 1860yds, Par 62, SSS 61.
Club membership 90.
Visitors no restrictions.
Societies apply in writing.
Green Fees not confirmed.
Facilities ⚖
Location NW side of town on A896
Hotel ★★★ 64% The Links Hotel, Golf Rd, BRORA
☎ 01408 621225 23 ⇆ ⋔

HOPEMAN   Map 15 NJ16

Hopeman IV30 2YA ☎ 01343 830578
Links-type course with beautiful views over the Moray Firth. The 12th hole, called the Priescach, is a short hole with a drop of 100 feet from tee to green. It can require anything from a wedge to a wood depending on the wind.
18 holes, 5531yds, Par 67, SSS 67, Course record 64.
Club membership 600.
Visitors must contact in advance, restricted tee times at weekend.
Societies contact in advance.
Green Fees £12 per day (£17 weekends).
Facilities ⊗ ⅷ ⅑ ♨ ♀ ⚖ ⌂ ⚑
Leisure trolley for hire, practice area.
Location E side of village off B9040
Hotel ★★★ 62% Stotfield Hotel, Stotfield Rd, LOSSIEMOUTH ☎ 01343 812011 45 ⇆ ⋔

HUNTLY   Map 15 NJ53

Huntly Cooper Park AB54 4SH ☎ 01466 792643
A parkland course lying between the Rivers Deveron and Bogie.
18 holes, 5399yds, Par 67, SSS 66.
Club membership 800.

Visitors may not play before 8am.
Societies must contact the secretary.
Green Fees £13 per day (£20 weekends); weekly ticket £65.
Facilities ⊗ ⅷ ⅑ ♨ ♀ ⚖ ⌂
Leisure trolley for hire, driving range, putting green, practice area.
Location N side of Huntly, turn off A96 at bypass roundabout
Hotel ★★★♨ 64% Castle Hotel, HUNTLY
☎ 01466 792696 20 ⇆ ⋔

INSCH   Map 15 NJ62

Insch Golf Ter AB52 6XN ☎ 01464 820363
A challenging 9-hole course soon be extended to 18. With the prevailing westerly winds the Par 5 1st and Par 4 4th play into the wind and are particularly challenging.
9 holes, 5632yds, Par 70, SSS 67, Course record 66.
Club membership 400.
Visitors restricted during club conpetitions and Tee times.
Societies apply in writing or telephone, bookings accepted.
Green Fees not confirmed.
Facilities ♀ ⚖ ⌂
Hotel ★★ 63% Lodge Hotel, OLD RAYNE
☎ 01464 851205 3 ⋔Annexe4 ⇆ ⋔

INVERGORDON   Map 14 NH76

Invergordon King George St IV18 0BD ☎ 01349 852715
Fairly easy but windy 18-hole parkland course, with woodland, wide fairways and good views over Cromarty Firth. Very good greens and a fair challenge, especially if the wind is from the west..
18 holes, 6030yds, Par 69, SSS 69.
Club membership 240.
Visitors visitors advised to avoid Tue & Thu 4.30-6, Mon & Wed 5-6 and Sat 8.30-10 & 1-2pm.
Societies must contact in advance.
Green Fees £10 per day Mon-Fri/per round weekends.
Facilities ⅑ ♀ ⚖ ⚑
Leisure trolley for hire, putting green, practice area.
Location W side of town centre on B817
Hotel ★★★ 68% Morangie House Hotel, Morangie Rd, TAIN ☎ 01862 892281 26 ⇆ ⋔

INVERNESS   Map 14 NH64

Inverness Culcabock IV2 3XQ ☎ 01463 239882
Fairly flat parkland course with burn running through it. Windy in winter. The 14th is one of the most difficult Par 4's in the north of Scotland. ▶

18 holes, 6226yds, Par 69, SSS 70.
Club membership 1100.

Visitors	restricted at weekends.
Societies	must telephone in advance.
Green Fees	not confirmed.
Facilities	♀⅄🕿⚐ℓ Alistair P Thomson.
Leisure	putting green,practice area,trolley hire.
Hotel	★★★★ 67% Kingsmills Hotel, Culcabock Rd, INVERNESS ☎ 01463 237166 78 ⇄ ♠Annexe6 ⇄ ♠

Torvean Glenurquhart Rd IV3 6JN ☎ 01463 711434
Municipal parkland course, easy walking, good views.
18 holes, 5784yds, Par 69, SSS 68, Course record 64.
Club membership 415.

Visitors	must contact in advance.
Societies	advance bookings through Inverness District Council, Town House, Inverness.
Green Fees	£11.90 per day; £8.90 per round (£13.40/£10.30 weekends).
Facilities	⊗ by prior arrangement ⅃ ♥ ♀⅄🕿⚐
Leisure	trolley for hire, putting green.
Location	1.5m SW on A82
Hotel	★★(red)⚘ Dunain Park Hotel, INVERNESS ☎ 01463 230512 14rm(10 ⇄ ♠)

INVERURIE   Map 15 NJ72

Inverurie Blackhall Rd AB51 5JB ☎ 01467 624080
Parkland course, part of which is exposed and windy, and part through wooded area.
18 holes, 5711yds, Par 69, SSS 68, Course record 64.
Club membership 700.

Visitors	book tee time through shop up to 24 hrs in advance 01467 620207.
Societies	telephone administrator.
Green Fees	£18 per day (£24 weekends).
Facilities	⊗ ⅊ ⅃ ♥ ♀⅄🕿⚐ℓ Howard Ferguson.
Leisure	trolley for hire, putting green, practice area.
Location	W side of town off A96
Hotel	★★★ 68% Strathburn Hotel, Burghmuir Dr, INVERURIE ☎ 01467 624422 25 ⇄ ♠

KEITH   Map 15 NJ45

Keith Fife Park AB55 3DF ☎ 01542 882469
Parkland course, with natural hazards over first 9 holes.
Testing 7th hole, 232 yds, par 3.
18 holes, 5767yds, Par 69, SSS 68.
Club membership 500.

Visitors	no restrictions except competitions.
Societies	by arrangement with outings secretary.
Green Fees	£12 per day; £10 per round (£15/£12 weekends).
Facilities	⅃ ♥ ♀⅄
Leisure	trolley for hire, putting green, practice area.
Location	NW side of town centre off A96
Hotel	★★★ 72% Craigellachie Hotel, CRAIGELLACHIE ☎ 01340 881204 30 ⇄ ♠

KEMNAY   Map 15 NJ71

Kemnay Monymusk Rd AB51 5RA
☎ 01467 642225 shop & 643746 office
Undulating parkland course with superb views. A stream crosses four holes.

---

18 holes, 5903yds, Par 70, SSS 69, Course record 69.
Club membership 800.

Visitors	telephone shop for booking.
Societies	must telephone in advance.
Green Fees	£18 per day; £14 per round (£20/£16 weekends).
Facilities	⊗ ⅊ ⅃ ♥ ♀⅄🕿⚐
Leisure	trolley for hire, practice area.
Location	W side of village on B993
Hotel	★★★ 63% Westhill Hotel, WESTHILL ☎ 01224 740388 37 ⇄ ♠Annexe13 ⇄ ♠

KINGUSSIE   Map 14 NH70

Kingussie Gynack Rd PH21 1LR
☎ 01540 661600
Hilly upland course with natural hazards and magnificent views. Stands about 1000ft above sea level at its highest point, and the River Gynack comes into play on five holes.
18 holes, 5500yds, Par 66, SSS 68, Course record 63.
Club membership 800.

Visitors	must contact in advance.
Societies	must contact in advance.
Green Fees	£16 per day; £13 per round (£20/£15 weekends).
Facilities	⊗ ⅊ ⅃ ♥ ♀⅄🕿⚐
Leisure	motorised carts for hire, buggies for hire, trolley for hire, putting green.
Location	0.25m N off A86
Hotel	★★ 71% Columba House Hotel, Manse Rd, KINGUSSIE ☎ 01540 661402 7 ⇄ ♠

KINTORE
Map 15 NJ71

Kintore Balbithan Rd AB51 0UR ☎ 01467 632631
The course covers a large area of ground from the Don Basin, near the clubhouse, to mature woodland at the far perimeter. One of the main attractions is the excellent drainage which results in very few days of lost play.
18 holes, 5997yds, Par 70, SSS 69, Course record 64.
Club membership 700.
Visitors	during season booking system is in operation & slots for visitors are available. Other times can be booked 24 hours in advance.
Societies	apply in writing or telephone.
Green Fees	£13 per day; £10 per round (£18/£15 weekends).
Facilities	⊗ ⬛ ⬛ ♀ ⬛
Leisure	putting green, practice area.
Location	1m from village centre on B977
Hotel	★★ 60% Torryburn Hotel, School Rd, KINTORE ☎ 01467 632269 9rm(8 ♠)

LEWIS, ISLE OF
Map 13 NB43

STORNOWAY
Map 13 NB43

Stornoway Lady Lever Park HS2 0XP ☎ 01851 702240
Picturesque, tree-lined parkland course, fine views. The 11th hole, 'Dardanelles' - most difficult par 5.
18 holes, 5252yds, Par 68, SSS 67, Course record 62.
Club membership 400.
Visitors	no golf on Sun.
Societies	apply in writing.
Green Fees	£10 per day/round.
Facilities	⬛ ⬛ ♀ ⬛ ⬛
Leisure	trolley for hire, putting green, practice area.
Location	N side of town centre off A857
Hotel	★★★ 66% Caberfeidh Hotel, STORNOWAY ☎ 01851 702604 46 ⇔ ♠

LOCHCARRON
Map 14 NG83

Lochcarron East End ☎ 01520 2257
Seaside links course with some parkland with an interesting 2nd hole. A short course but great accuracy is required. There are plans to extend to 18-holes on an additional 500 acres.
9 holes, 1750yds, SSS 60.
Club membership 150.
Visitors	restricted Fri evening & Sat 2-5pm.
Societies	welcome but restricted Fri evening & Sat 2-5pm.
Green Fees	not confirmed.
Facilities	⬛
Location	1m E
Hotel	★★ 66% Lochcarron Hotel, Main St, LOCHCARRON ☎ 01520 722226 10rm(9 ⇔ ♠)

LOSSIEMOUTH
Map 15 NJ27

Moray IV31 6QS ☎ 01343 812018
Two fine Scottish Championship links courses, known as Old and New (Moray), and situated on the Moray Firth where the weather is unusually mild.
Old Course: 18 holes, 6643yds, Par 71, SSS 73.
New Course: 18 holes, 6005yds, Par 69, SSS 69.

Visitors	must contact in advance.
Societies	must contact in advance.
Green Fees	Old Moray course £32 per day; £22 per round (£43/33 weekends). New Moray course £22 per day; £17 per round (£27/£22 weekends).
Facilities	♭ Alistair Thomson.
Leisure	putting green, practice area.
Location	N side of town
Hotel	★★★ 62% Stotfield Hotel, Stotfield Rd, LOSSIEMOUTH ☎ 01343 812011 45 ⇔ ♠

LYBSTER
Map 15 ND23

Lybster Main St KW3 6AE
Picturesque, short heathland course, easy walking.
9 holes, 1896yds, Par 62, SSS 62.
Club membership 80.
Visitors	no restrictions.
Societies	must contact in advance.
Green Fees	not confirmed.
Facilities	⬛ ⬛
Location	E side of village
Hotel	★★ 65% Portland Arms, LYBSTER ☎ 01593 721208 19 ⇔ ♠

MACDUFF
Map 15 NJ76

Royal Tarlair Buchan St AB44 1TA
☎ 01261 832897
Seaside clifftop course, can be windy. Testing 13th, 'Clivet' (par 3).
18 holes, 5866yds, Par 71, SSS 68.
Club membership 576.
Visitors	no restrictions.
Societies	apply in writing.
Green Fees	not confirmed.
Facilities	♀ ⬛ ⬛
Leisure	trolley hire.
Location	0.75m E off A98
Hotel	★★ 58% The Highland Haven, Shore St, MACDUFF ☎ 01261 832408 20 ⇔ ♠

MUIR OF ORD
Map 14 NH55

Muir of Ord Great North Rd IV6 7SX
☎ 01463 870825
Old established (1875), heathland course with tight fairways and easy walking. Testing 11th, 'Castle Hill' (par 3).
18 holes, 5202yds, Par 67, SSS 66, Course record 61.
Club membership 750.
Visitors	may not play before 11am weekends without prior agreement and during club competitions.
Societies	telephone followed by letter of confirmation.
Green Fees	£14.50 per day; £12.50 per round (£18.50/£16.50 weekends).
Facilities	⊗ ⬛ by prior arrangement ⬛ ⬛ ♀ ⬛ ⬛ ⬛ ♭ Graham Vivers.
Leisure	trolley for hire, putting green, practice area.
Location	S side of village on A862
Hotel	★★★ 68% Priory Hotel, The Square, BEAULY ☎ 01463 782309 22 ⇔ ♠

NAIRN   Map 14 NH85

Nairn Seabank Rd IV12 4HB ☎ 01667 453208
Championship, seaside links founded in 1887 and created
from a wilderness of heather and whin. Designed by A.
Simpson, old Tom Morris and James Braid. Opening
holes stretch out along the shoreline with the turn for
home at the 10th. Regularly chosen for national
championships.
18 holes, 6452yds, Par 71, SSS 73, Course record 65.
Club membership 1150.
Visitors	book in advance through secretary, may not play between 8-10.30 & 12-2.30.
Societies	subject to availability bookings through secretary's office.
Green Fees	£35 per round (£42 weekends).
Facilities	⊗ ⅢⅢ ⅞ ⅌ ♀ ⅍ ⏸ ⅋ ⅌ Robin P Fyfe.
Leisure	trolley for hire, driving range, putting green, practice area, 9 hole juniors/beginners course.
Hotel	★★★★ 62% Golf View Hotel & Leisure Club, Seabank Rd, NAIRN ☎ 01667 452301 47 ⇔ ⋔

Nairn Dunbar Lochloy Rd IV12 5AE
☎ 01667 452741
Links course with sea views and testing gorse-and whin-lined
fairways. Breezy at holes 6, 7 and 8. Testing hole: 'Long
Peter' (527 yds).
18 holes, 6712yds, Par 72, SSS 73.
Club membership 700.
Visitors	must contact in advance.
Societies	must contact in advance.
Green Fees	£25 per day; £20 per round (£30/£25 weekends).
Facilities	⊗ ⅢⅢ ⅞ ⅌ ♀ ⅍ ⏸ ⅋ ⅌ Brian Mason.
Leisure	motorised carts for hire, trolley for hire, putting green, practice area.
Location	E side of town off A96
Hotel	★★ 62% Alton Burn Hotel, Alton Burn Rd, NAIRN ☎ 01667 452051 19rm(14 ⇔3 ⋔)Annexe7 ⇔ ⋔

NETHY BRIDGE   Map 14 NJ02

Abernethy PH25 3EB ☎ 01479 821305
Picturesque moorland course.
9 holes, 2551yds, Par 33, SSS 33.
Club membership 350.
Visitors	contact in advance.
Societies	must contact in advance.
Green Fees	£9 per day (£12 weekends).
Facilities	⊗ ⅞ ⅌ ⅍ ⅋
Leisure	trolley for hire, putting green.
Location	N side of village on B970
Hotel	★★★⅖ 68% Muckrach Lodge Hotel, DULNAIN BRIDGE ☎ 01479 851257 10 ⇔ ⋔Annexe4 ⇔ ⋔

NEWBURGH ON YTHAN   Map 15 NJ92

Newburgh on Ythan Newburgh Links AB41 0FD
☎ 01358 789058 & 789436
This seaside coursewas founded in 1888 and is adjacent to
bird sanctuary. Testing 550-yd dog leg (par 5).

18 holes, 6162yds, Par 72, SSS 69.
Club membership 400.
Visitors	must contact in advance.
Societies	apply in advance.
Green Fees	£13 per day (£15 weekends).
Facilities	⅞ ⅌ ⅍
Leisure	practice area.
Location	E side of village on A975
Hotel	★★ 68% Udny Arms Hotel, Main St, NEWBURGH ☎ 01358 789444 26 ⇔ ⋔

NEWMACHAR   Map 15 NJ81

Newmachar Swailend AB2 0UU
☎ 01651 863002
Championship-standard parkland course designed by Dave
Thomas and opened in 1991. Several lakes affect five of the
holes and there are well developed birch and Scots pine trees.
Hawkshill Course: 18 holes, 6623yds, Par 72, SSS 74,
Course record 68.
Club membership 750.
Visitors	must contact in advance & have handicap certificate, restricted at weekends.
Societies	apply in writing.
Green Fees	not confirmed.
Facilities	⅌ ⅍ ⏸ ⅌ Glenn Taylor.
Leisure	putting, cart/buggy/trolley hire.
Location	2m N of Dyce, off A947
Hotel	★★★ 68% Strathburn Hotel, Burghmuir Dr, INVERURIE ☎ 01467 624422 25 ⇔ ⋔

NEWTONMORE   Map 14 NN79

Newtonmore Golf Course Rd PH20 1AT
☎ 01540 673328 & 673878
Inland course beside the River Spey. Beautiful views and
easy walking. Testing 17th hole (par 3).
18 holes, 6029yds, Par 70, SSS 68, Course record 68.
Club membership 420.
Visitors	contact in advance.
Societies	apply in writing to secretary.
Green Fees	£15 per day; £10 per round (£20/£14 weekends).
Facilities	⊗ ⅢⅢ ⅞ ⅌ ♀ ⅍ ⏸ ⅋ ⅌ Robert Henderson.
Leisure	motorised carts for hire, buggies for hire, trolley for hire, putting green, practice area.
Location	E side of town off A9
Hotel	★★ 75% The Scot House Hotel, Newtonmore Rd, KINGUSSIE ☎ 01540 661351 9 ⇔ ⋔

OLDMELDRUM   Map 15 NJ82

Old Meldrum Kirkbrae AB51 0DJ
☎ 01651 872648
Parkland course with tree-lined fairways and superb views.
Challenging 196 yard, Par 3, 11th over two ponds to a green
surrounded by bunkers.
18 holes, 5988yds, Par 70, SSS 69, Course record 67.
Club membership 800.
Visitors	may not play during Club competitions. Must contact in advance. To book tee time tel: 01651 873555.
Societies	apply in writing to secretary
Green Fees	£12 per day (£18 weekends).
Facilities	⊗ ⅢⅢ ⅞ ⅌ ♀ ⅍ ⏸

Leisure trolley for hire, putting green, practice area.
Location E side of village off A947
Hotel ★ 66% Meldrum Arms Hotel, The Square, OLDMELDRUM ☎ 01651 872238 7 ╟

ORKNEY Map 16

KIRKWALL Map 16 HY41

Orkney Grainbank KW15 1RB ☎ 01856 872457
Open parkland course with few hazards and superb views over Kirkwall and Islands.
18 holes, 5411yds, Par 70, SSS 67, Course record 65.
Club membership 376.
Visitors may not play on competition days.
Societies write or telephone if possible.
Green Fees £10 per day; £35 per week; £50 per fortnight.
Facilities ╚ ╙ ╗ ╔ ╟
Leisure trolley for hire, putting green, practice area.
Location 0.5m W off A965
Hotel ★★★ 62% Ayre Hotel, Ayre Rd, KIRKWALL ☎ 01856 873001 33 ╘ ╟

STROMNESS Map 16 HY20

Stromness KW16 3DW ☎ 01856 850772
Testing parkland/seaside course with easy walking. Beautiful holiday course with magnificent views of Scapa Flow.
18 holes, 4762yds, Par 65, SSS 63, Course record 61.
Club membership 275.
Visitors no restrictions except during major competitions.
Societies no restrictions.
Green Fees £12 per day/round.
Facilities ╗ ╔
Leisure hard tennis courts, putting green, bowling green.
Location S side of town centre off A965
Hotel ★★★ 62% Ayre Hotel, Ayre Rd, KIRKWALL ☎ 01856 873001 33 ╘ ╟

WESTRAY Map 16 HY44

Westray Rosevale KW17 2DH ☎ 01857 677373
Interesting, picturesque seaside course, easy walking.
9 holes, 2405yds, Par 33.
Club membership 60.
Visitors No restrictions.
Green Fees not confirmed.
Facilities ╟
Location 1m NW of Pierowall off B9066
Hotel ★★★ 62% Ayre Hotel, Ayre Rd, KIRKWALL ☎ 01856 873001 33 ╘ ╟

PETERCULTER Map 15 NJ80

Peterculter Oldtown, Burnside Rd AB1 0LN
☎ 01224 734994
The course is a tight Par 68 (from Yellow tees) with a beautiful Par 2 2nd and two Par 5 holes in excess of 500 yards. Surrounded by wonderful scenery and bordered by the River Dee, there is a variety of birds, deer and foxes on the course, which also has superb views up the Dee Valley.
18 holes, 5947yds, Par 68, SSS 68, Course record 68.
Club membership 1035.

Visitors welcome after 2.30pm weekdays & 4pm weekends.
Societies contact up to 7 days in advance.
Green Fees £16 per day; £11 per round after 2pm (£21 per day; £15 per round after 4pm weekends).
Facilities ⊗ ╫ ╚ ╙ ╗ ╔ ╣ ╟ ╒ Dean Vannet.
Leisure motorised carts for hire, buggies for hire, trolley for hire, putting green, practice area.
Location On A93
Hotel ★★★ 63% Westhill Hotel, WESTHILL ☎ 01224 740388 37 ╘ ╟Annexe13 ╘ ╟

PETERHEAD Map 15 NK14

Peterhead Craigewan Links AB42 6LT
☎ 01779 472149
Natural links course bounded by the sea and the River Ugie.
Old Course: 18 holes, 6173yds, Par 70, SSS 71, Course record 64.
New Course: 9 holes, 2228yds.
Club membership 800.
Visitors telephone for details. Competition day Sat.
Societies apply in writing, not weekends.
Green Fees Old Course: £22 per day; £16 per round (£27/£20 weekends). New Course: £9 per day/round.
Facilities ╚ ╙ ╗ ╔
Leisure practice area.
Location N side of town centre off A952
Hotel ★★★ 67% Waterside Inn, Fraserburgh Rd, PETERHEAD ☎ 01779 471121 70 ╘ ╟Annexe40 ╘ ╟

PORTLETHEN Map 15 NO99

Portlethen Badentoy Rd AB1 4YA
☎ 01224 782575 & 781090
Set in pleasant parkland, this new course features mature trees and a stream which affects a number of holes.
18 holes, 6707yds, Par 72, SSS 72, Course record 63.
Club membership 1000.
Visitors may not play Sat. Contact in advance.
Societies apply in advance.
Green Fees £20 per day; £13 per round (£20 per round weekends).
Facilities ⊗ ╫ ╚ ╙ ╗ ╔ ╣ ╟ ╒ Muriel Thomson.
Leisure trolley for hire, putting green, practice area.
Location Off A90 S of Aberdeen
Hotel ★★ 61% County Hotel, Arduthie Rd, STONEHAVEN ☎ 01569 764386 14 ╘ ╟

PORTMAHOMACK Map 14 NH98

Tarbat IV20 1YQ ☎ 01862 871236
Picturesque links course with magnificent views.
9 holes, 5046yds, Par 66, SSS 65.
Club membership 180.
Visitors no restrictions.
Societies must telephone in advance.
Green Fees not confirmed.
Facilities ╔
Location E side of village
Hotel ★★★ 68% Morangie House Hotel, Morangie Rd, TAIN ☎ 01862 892281 26 ╘ ╟

REAY   Map 14 NC96

Reay KW14 7RE ☎ 01847 811288
Picturesque seaside links with natural hazards, following the
contours of Sandside Bay. Tight and testing.
18 holes, 5884yds, Par 69, SSS 68, Course record 64.
Club membership 450.
Visitors   restricted competition days
Societies   apply in writing.
Green Fees £12 per day/round.
Facilities   ♀ ⚒
Leisure   practice area.
Location   0.5m E off A836
Hotel   ★★ 64% Melvich Hotel, MELVICH
                   ☎ 01641 531206 14 ⏴

ROTHES   Map 15 NJ24

Rothes Blackhall AB38 7AN ☎ 01340 831443
A hilly course opened in 1990 on an elevated site overlooking
the remains of Rothes castle and the Spey valley. The 2nd
fairway and most of the 3rd are sheltered by woodland. The
ground alongside the 5th & 6th falls away steeply.
9 holes, 4972yds, Par 68, SSS 65.
Club membership 280.
Visitors   course reserved Mon 5-6.30 & Tue 5-7.30.
Societies   apply in writing to secretary.
Green Fees £8 per 18 holes (£10 weekends).
Facilities   ♀ ⚒
Location   9m S of Elgin on A941
Hotel   ★★★ 61% Rothes Glen Hotel, ROTHES
                   ☎ 01340 831254 16 ⏴ ⏴

SHETLAND   Map 16

LERWICK   Map 16 HU44

Shetland PO Box 18 ZE1 0YW ☎ 01595 84369
Challenging moorland course, hard walking. A burn runs the
full length of the course and provides a natural hazard.
Testing holes include the 3rd (par 4), 5th (par 4).
*Dale Course: 18 holes, 5800yds, Par 68, SSS 68, Course
record 68.*
Club membership 450.
Visitors   advisable to contact in advance.
Societies   telephone in advance.
Green Fees £10 per day.
Facilities   ⓑ ⛻ ♀ ⚒ ⏴
Leisure   putting green.
Location   4m N on A970
Hotel   ★★★ 62% Lerwick Hotel, 15 South Rd,
                   LERWICK ☎ 01595 692166 35 ⏴ ⏴

WHALSAY, ISLAND OF   Map 16 HU56

Whalsay Skaw Taing ZE2 9AA
☎ 01806 566450 & 566481
The most northerly golf course in Britain, with a large part of
it running round the coastline, offering spectacular holes in an
exposed but highly scenic setting. There are no cut fairways
as yet, these are defined by marker posts, with preferred lies
in operation all year round.

18 holes, 6009yds, Par 70, SSS 68, Course record 65.
Club membership 134.
Visitors   are advised to telephone, and on arrival on
                   Whalsay call at the shop by the harbour.
Societies   telephone in advance.
Green Fees £5 per day; £20 per week.
Facilities   ⛻ ♀ ⚒
Location   N end of Island
Hotel   ★★★⚌ 66% Busta House Hotel, BRAE
                   ☎ 01806 522506 20 ⏴ ⏴

SKEABOST BRIDGE   Map 13 NG44

Skeabost Skeabost House Hotel IV51 9NP
☎ 01470 532202
Short woodland and seaside course featuring some very tight
fairways and greens.
9 holes, 3056yds, Par 62, SSS 60, Course record 58.
Club membership 80.
Visitors   must contact in advance.
Societies   contact in advance.
Green Fees £6 per day.
Facilities   ⊗ ⛻ ⓑ ⛻ ♀ ⚒ ⛿ ⏴ ⏴
Leisure   fishing, trolley for hire, putting green, practice
                   area.
Hotel   ★★★⚌ 64% Skeabost House Hotel,
                   SKEABOST BRIDGE
                   ☎ 01470 532202 21 ⏴ ⏴Annexe5 ⏴ ⏴

SKYE, ISLE OF   Map 13 NG53

SCONSER   Map 13 NG53

Isle of Skye IV48 8TD ☎ 01478 650351
Seaside course, often windy, splendid views.
9 holes, 4798yds, Par 66, SSS 64, Course record 64.
Club membership 220.
Visitors   contact in advance to avoid competition times.
Societies   apply in advance.
Green Fees £10 per day; £40 per week.
Facilities   ⚒ ⏴
Location   0.5m E of village on A850
Hotel   ★★ 71% Rosedale Hotel, PORTREE
                   ☎ 01478 613131 20 ⏴ ⏴Annexe3 ⏴ ⏴

SOUTH UIST, ISLE OF   Map 13 NF72

ASKERNISH   Map 13 NF72

Askernish Lochboisdale PA81 5SY
☎ No telephone
Golfers play on machair (hard-wearing short grass), close to
the Atlantic shore.
9 holes, 5042yds, Par 68, SSS 67, Course record 64.
Club membership 15.
Visitors   no restrictions.
Societies   welcome.
Green Fees £5 per day; £3.50 per round.
Facilities   ⊗ ⛻ ⓑ ⛻ ♀ ⏴
Location   5m NW of Lochboisdale off A865 via ferry

SPEY BAY

Map 15 NJ36

Spey Bay IV32 7PJ ☎ 01343 820424
Seaside links course over gently undulating banks and well-drained ground. Good views along Moray coast. Driving range.
18 holes, 6092yds, Par 70, SSS 69, Course record 66.
Club membership 350.
Visitors telephone for details.
Societies book by telephone.
Green Fees £15 per day; £10 per round (£18/£13 weekends).
Facilities ⊗ ⽊ ⅃ ⬛ ♀ ⅄ ⌐ ⬢ ⅂ Hamish MacDonald.
Leisure hard tennis courts, trolley for hire, driving range, putting green, practice area.
Location 4.5m N of Fochabers on B9104
Hotel ★★ 64% Mill House Hotel, Tynet, BUCKIE ☎ 01542 850233 15 ⇥ ↾

STONEHAVEN

Map 15 NO88

Stonehaven Cowie AB3 2RH ☎ 01569 762124
Challenging meadowland course overlooking sea with three gullies and splendid views.
18 holes, 5103yds, Par 66, SSS 65, Course record 61.
Club membership 850.
Visitors prefer prior booking, may not play before 4pm Sat.
Societies must contact in advance for booking form.
Green Fees £15 per day (£20 weekends).
Facilities ⊗ ⽊ ⅃ ⬛ ♀ ⅄ ⬢
Leisure trolley for hire, putting green, practice area.
Location 1m N off A92
Hotel ★★ 61% County Hotel, Arduthie Rd, STONEHAVEN ☎ 01569 764386 14 ⇥ ↾

STRATHPEFFER

Map 14 NH45

Strathpeffer Spa IV14 9AS ☎ 01997 421219
Upland course with many natural hazards (no sand bunkers), hard walking and fine views. Testing 3rd hole (par 3) across loch.
18 holes, 4792yds, Par 65, SSS 64, Course record 60.
Club membership 550.
Visitors advisable to contact in advance.
Societies apply in writing.
Green Fees £16 per day; £12 per round. Weekly ticket (Mon-Fri) £50.
Facilities ⊗ ⅃ ⬛ ♀ ⅄ ⬢ ⅂
Leisure trolley for hire, practice area.
Location 0.25m N of village off A834
Hotel ★★ 69% Brunstane Lodge Hotel, Golf Rd, STRATHPEFFER ☎ 01997 421261 7rm(6 ⇥ ↾)

TAIN

Map 14 NH78

Tain Chapel Rd IV19 1PA ☎ 01862 892314
Heathland/links course with river affecting 3 holes; easy walking, fine views.
18 holes, 6246yds, Par 70, SSS 70, Course record 62.
Club membership 500.
Visitors no restrictions.
Societies must book in advance.

Green Fees £22 per 36 holes; £15 per round (£24/£18 weekends).
Facilities ⊗ ⽊ by prior arrangement ⅃ ⬛ ♀ ⅄ ⬢ ⅂
Leisure motorised carts for hire, buggies for hire, putting green, practice area.
Location E side of town centre off B9174
Hotel ★★★ 68% Morangie House Hotel, Morangie Rd, TAIN ☎ 01862 892281 26 ⇥ ↾

TARLAND

Map 15 NJ40

Tarland Aberdeen Rd AB3 4YN ☎ 013398 81413
Difficult upland course, but easy walking.
9 holes, 5888yds, Par 67, SSS 68, Course record 66.
Club membership 350.
Visitors must contact in advance.
Societies must telephone in advance.
Green Fees prices under review.
Facilities ⅃ ⬛ ♀ ⅄
Location 6E side of village off B9119)
Hotel ★★ 70% Birse Lodge Hotel, Charleston Rd, ABOYNE ☎ 013398 86253 12 ⇥ ↾

THURSO

Map 15 ND16

Thurso Newlands of Geise KW14 7XF ☎ 01847 63807
Parkland course, windy, but with fine views of Dunnet Head and the Orkney Islands.
18 holes, 5828yds, SSS 69, Course record 63.
Club membership 252.
Visitors no restrictions.
Societies contact in advance.
Green Fees £11 per day; £35 per week.
Facilities ♀ ⅄ ⬢ ⅂
Leisure trolley for hire, practice area.
Location 2m SW on B874
Hotel ★★ 63% Pentland Hotel, Princes St, THURSO ☎ 01847 893202 53rm(28 ⇥11 ↾)

TORPHINS

Map 15 NJ60

Torphins Bog Rd AB31 4JU ☎ 013398 82115
Heathland/parkland course built on a hill with views of the Cairngorms.
9 holes, 4800yds, Par 64, SSS 64, Course record 63.
Club membership 380.
Visitors must contact in advance. Restricted on competition days.
Societies apply in advance.
Green Fees £10 per day (£12 weekends).
Facilities ⅃ ⬛ ⅄
Leisure trolley for hire, putting green.
Location 0.25m W of village off A980
Hotel ★★★ 66% Tor-na-Coille Hotel, BANCHORY ☎ 01330 822242 24 ⇥ ↾

TURRIFF

Map 15 NJ74

Turriff Rosehall AB53 7HB ☎ 01888 562982
A well-maintained parkland course alongside the River Deveron in picturesque surroundings. 6th and 12th particularly challenging in a testing course.
18 holes, 6145yds, Par 69, SSS 68, Course record 63.
Club membership 860.

▶

Visitors	may not play before 10am weekends. Must contact in advance.
Societies	apply in writing to the secretary.
Green Fees	not confirmed.
Facilities	♀ ♨ 🏠 ❜ ❜ Robin Smith.
Leisure	putting green,practice area,trolley hire.
Location	1m W off B9024
Hotel	★★★ 61% Banff Springs Hotel, Golden Knowes Rd, BANFF ☎ 01261 812881 30 ⇆ 🐾

WICK
Map 15 ND35

Wick Reiss KW1 4RW ☎ 01955 602726
Typical seaside links course, windy, easy walking.
18 holes, 5976yds, Par 69, SSS 69, Course record 63.
Club membership 352.

Visitors	no restrictions.
Societies	apply in writing or telephone in advance.
Green Fees	not confirmed.
Facilities	♀
Location	3.5m N off A9
Hotel	★★ 60% Mackay's Hotel, Union St, WICK ☎ 01955 602323 26 ⇆ 🐾

CENTRAL SCOTLAND

This region includes the counties of Angus, Argyll & Bute, Clackmannanshire, City of Edinburgh, Dundee City, East Lothian, Falkirk, Fife, Inverclyde, Midlothian, Perthshire & Kinross, Stirling and West Lothian which reflect the recent national changes.

ABERDOUR
Map 11 NT18

Aberdour Seaside Place KY3 0TX ☎ 01383 860080
Parkland course with lovely views over Firth of Forth.
18 holes, 5460yds, Par 67, SSS 66, Course record 63.
Club membership 800.

Visitors	must contact in advance.
Societies	telephone secretary in advance.
Green Fees	£28 per day; £17 per round.
Facilities	⊗ ⍭ ♨ ♥ ♀ ♨ 🏠 ❜ ❜ Gordon McCallum.
Leisure	motorised carts for hire, trolley for hire, putting green, practice area.
Location	S side of village
Hotel	★★ 66% Woodside Hotel, High St, ABERDOUR ☎ 01383 860328 20 ⇆ 🐾

ABERFELDY
Map 14 NN84

Aberfeldy Taybridge Rd PH15 2BH ☎ 01887 820535
Founded in 1895, this flat, parkland course is situated by River Tay near the famous Wade Bridge and Black Watch Monument and enjoys some splendid scenery. The new layout will test the keen golfer.
18 holes, 4907yds, Par 68, SSS 66.
Club membership 333.

Visitors	are advised to book in advance especially at weekends.
Societies	must contact in advance.
Green Fees	£22 per day; £14 per round (Weekly £55).
Facilities	⊗ ⍭ ♨ ♥ ♀ ♨ 🏠 ❜
Leisure	fishing, trolley for hire.
Location	N side of town centre
Hotel	★★ 63% The Weem, Weem, ABERFELDY ☎ 01887 820381 12 ⇆ 🐾

ABERFOYLE
Map 11 NN50

Aberfoyle Braeval FK8 3UY ☎ 01877 382493
Scenic heathland course with mountain views.
18 holes, 5210yds, Par 66, SSS 66.
Club membership 665.

Visitors	may not tee off before 10.30am Sat & Sun.
Societies	must contact in advance.
Green Fees	not confirmed.
Facilities	♀ ♨
Leisure	putting green,trolley hire.
Location	1m E on A81
Hotel	★★ 75% Lake Hotel, PORT OF MENTEITH ☎ 01877 385258 15 ⇆ 🐾

ABERLADY
Map 12 NT47

Kilspindie EH32 0QD ☎ 01875 870358
Seaside course, short but tight and well-bunkered. Testing holes: 2nd, 3rd, 4th and 7th.
18 holes, 5471yds, Par 69, SSS 66, Course record 62.
Club membership 750.

Visitors	must contact in advance.
Societies	contact secretary in advance.
Green Fees	£30 per day; £20 per round (£35/£25 weekends).
Facilities	⊗ ⮴ 🕭 ⚑ ♀ ⚒ 🖂 🏴‍ 🍴 Ⓒ Graham J Sked.
Leisure	trolley for hire, putting green, practice area.
Location	W side of village off A198
Hotel	★★ 67% Kilspindie House Hotel, Main St, ABERLADY ☎ 01875 870682 26 ⇆ 🐾

Luffness New EH32 0QA ☎ 01620 843114 & 843336
Seaside course.
18 holes, 6122yds, Par 69, SSS 69, Course record 62.
Club membership 700.

Visitors	must contact in advance but may not play at weekends & bank holidays.
Societies	must contact in writing.
Green Fees	£40 per day; £27 per round.
Facilities	♀ ⚒ 🖂
Leisure	putting,practice area,trolleys,caddies.
Location	1m E on A198
Hotel	★★★(red)⚜ Greywalls Hotel, Muirfield, GULLANE ☎ 01620 842144 17 ⇆ 🐾Annexe5 ⇆ 🐾

ALLOA   Map 11 NS89

Alloa Schawpark, Sauchie FK10 3AX
☎ 01259 722745 & 724476
Undulating, wooded parkland course.
18 holes, 6229yds, Par 69, SSS 71, Course record 63.
Club membership 910.

Visitors	7 day booking system through professional.
Societies	apply in writing.
Green Fees	£25 per day; £16 per round (£30/£20 weekends).
Facilities	⊗ 𝍖 ⮴ 🕭 ♀ ⚒ 🖂 🏴‍ 🍴 Bill Bennett.
Leisure	trolley for hire, practice area.
Location	1.5m NE on A908
Hotel	★★★⚜ 73% Gean House, Gean Park, Tullibody Rd, ALLOA ☎ 01259 219275 7 ⇆ 🐾

Braehead Cambus FK10 2NT ☎ 01259 722078 & 725766
Attactive parkland course at the foot of the Ochil Hills, and offering spectacular views.
18 holes, 6041yds, Par 70, SSS 69, Course record 64.
Club membership 800.

Visitors	advisable to telephone in advance.
Societies	must contact the clubhouse manager in advance tel 01259 725766.
Green Fees	£22 per day; £14 per round (£30/£22 weekends).
Facilities	⊗ 𝍖 ⮴ 🕭 ♀ ⚒ 🖂 🏴‍ 🍴 Ⓒ Paul Brookes.
Leisure	motorised carts for hire, trolley for hire, putting green, practice area.
Location	1m W on A907
Hotel	★★★⚜ 73% Gean House, Gean Park, Tullibody Rd, ALLOA ☎ 01259 219275 7 ⇆ 🐾

ALVA   Map 11 NS89

Alva Beauclerc St FK12 5LH ☎ 01259 760431
A 9-hole course at the foot of the Ochil Hills which gives it its characteristic sloping fairways and fast greens.
9 holes, 2423yds, Par 66, SSS 64, Course record 62.
Club membership 314.

Visitors	may not play during medal competitions or Thu evening (Ladies night).
Societies	apply in writing or telephone in advance.
Green Fees	£15 per day; £9 per round (£12 per round weekends). Weekly ticket (weekdays) £30.
Facilities	♀ ⚒
Location	7m from Stirling,A91 Stirling/St Andrews rd
Hotel	★★ 64% Harviestoun Country Inn, Dollar Rd, TILLICOULTRY ☎ 01259 752522 10 ⇆ 🐾

ALYTH   Map 15 NO24

Alyth Pitcrocknie PH11 8HF
☎ 01828 632268 & 632241
Windy, heathland course with easy walking.
18 holes, 6205yds, Par 71, SSS 71, Course record 65.
Club membership 1000.

Visitors	advance booking advisable
Societies	must telephone in advance.
Green Fees	£30 per day; £18 per round (£35/£23 weekends).
Facilities	⊗ 𝍖 ⮴ 🕭 ♀ ⚒ 🖂 🏴‍ 🍴 Tom Melville.
Leisure	motorised carts for hire, trolley for hire, driving range, putting green, practice area.
Location	1m E on B954
Hotel	★★ 61% Alyth Hotel, ALYTH ☎ 01828 632447 8 ⇆ 🐾

Strathmore Golf Centre Leroch PH11 8NZ
☎ 01828 633322
The course is set on rolling parkland and heath with splendid views over Strathmore. The course is laid out in two loops of nine which both start and finish at the clubhouse. Among the challenging holes is the 480yard 5th with a 180yard carry over water from a high tee position (a cop out route available!).
Rannaleroch Course: 18 holes, 6490yds, Par 72, SSS 71.
Leitfie Course: 9 holes, 1719yds, Par 29.
Club membership 200.

Visitors	no restrictions.
Societies	phone enquiry recommended.
Green Fees	Rannaleroch: £20 per day; £12 per round (£25/£16 weekends). Leitfie: £8 per day; £5 per round (£10/£6 weekends).
Facilities	⊗ 𝍖 ⮴ 🕭 ♀ ⚒ 🖂 🏴‍
Leisure	motorised carts for hire, buggies for hire, trolley for hire, driving range, putting, practice area.
Location	5m SE of Alyth,off B954 at Meigle onto A926
Hotel	★★ 61% Alyth Hotel, ALYTH ☎ 01828 632447 8 ⇆ 🐾

ANSTRUTHER   Map 12 NO50

Anstruther Shore Rd, "Marsfield" KY10 3DZ
☎ 01333 310956 & 312283
Seaside links course with some excellent par 3 holes; always in good condition.
9 holes, 4144mtrs, Par 62, SSS 63.
Club membership 600.

Visitors	advised to phone in advance.
Societies	welcome except Jun-Aug. Must apply in writing.
Green Fees	not confirmed.
Facilities	♀ Jun-Aug ⚒
Location	SW off A917
Hotel	★★ 60% Smugglers Inn, High St, ANSTRUTHER ☎ 01333 310506 8 ⇆ 🐾

ARBROATH
Map 12 NO64

Arbroath Elliot DD11 2PE
☎ 01241 872069
Municipal seaside links course, with bunkers guarding greens. Played upon by Arbroath Artisan Club.
18 holes, 6185yds, Par 70, SSS 69.
Club membership 550.
Visitors contact professional 01241 875837.
Societies contact professional 01241 875837.
Green Fees £18 per day; £13 per round (£30/£18 weekends).
Facilities ⊗ ⦉ ╚ ⚑ ♀ ♨ ✆ ℓ Lindsay Ewart.
Leisure trolley for hire, driving range, putting green, practice area.
Location 2m SW on A92
Hotel ★★ 62% Hotel Seaforth, Dundee Rd, ARBROATH
☎ 01241 872232 20 ⇌ ℝ

Letham Grange Colliston DD11 4RL
☎ 01241 890373
Often referred to as the 'Augusta of Scotland', the Old Course provides championship standards in spectacular surroundings with attractive lochs and burns. The New Course is less arduous and shorter using many natural features of the estate.
Old Course: 18 holes, 6632yds, Par 73, SSS 73, Course record 69.
New Course: 18 holes, 5528yds, Par 68, SSS 68, Course record 63.
Club membership 750.
Visitors no visitors weekends before 9.30am, Old Course before 10am Tue & New Course before 10am Fri.
Societies telephone in advance.
Green Fees Old Course: £35 per day; £23 per round (£64/£32 weekends). New Course: £21 per day; £14.50 per round d (£27/£17 weekends).
Facilities ⊗ ⦉ ╚ ⚑ ♀ ♨ ✆ ⚒
Leisure motorised carts for hire, buggies for hire, trolley for hire, putting green, practice area, curling rink (winter).
Location 4m N on A933
Hotel ★★★ 69% Letham Grange Hotel & Golf Course, Colliston, ARBROATH
☎ 01241 890373 19 ⇌ ℝ

AUCHTERARDER
Map 11 NN91

Auchterarder Orchil Rd PH3 1LS
☎ 01764 662804 (Secretary) & 663711 (Pro)
Parkland course with easy walking.
18 holes, 5775yds, Par 69, SSS 68, Course record 64.
Club membership 715.
Visitors must contact professional in advance.
Societies must contact in advance.
Green Fees £25 per day; £16 per round (£35/£22 weekends).
Facilities ⊗ ⦉ ╚ ⚑ ♀ ♨ ✆ ⚒ ℓ Gavin Baxter.
Leisure trolley for hire, putting green, practice area.
Location 0.75m SW on A824
Hotel ★★★★★(red) The Gleneagles Hotel, AUCHTERARDER
☎ 01764 662231 234 ⇌ ℝ

THE GLENEAGLES HOTEL
See page 279

BARRY
Map 12 NO53

Panmure Burnside Rd DD7 7RT
☎ 01241 855120
A nerve-testing, adventurous course set amongst sandhills - its hazards belie the quiet nature of the opening holes. This tight links has been used as a qualifying course for the Open Championship, and features Ben Hogan's favourite hole, the dog-leg 6th, which heralds the toughest stretch, around the turn.
18 holes, 6317yds, Par 70, SSS 70, Course record 62.
Club membership 700.
Visitors may not play Sat. Parties of 6 or more must contact in advance.
Societies must contact secretary in advance.
Green Fees not confirmed.
Facilities ♀ ♨ ✆ ⚒ ℓ Andrew Cullen.
Leisure buggy, caddy cars, caddies.
Location S side of village off A930
Hotel ★★ 64% Glencoe Hotel, Links Pde, CARNOUSTIE
☎ 01241 853273 7 ⇌ ℝ

BATHGATE
Map 11 NS96

Bathgate Edinburgh Rd EH48 1BA
☎ 01506 630553 & 652232
Moorland course. Easy walking. Testing 11th hole, par 3.
18 holes, 6250yds, Par 71, SSS 70.
Club membership 750.
Visitors must contact in advance & may not play at weekends.
Societies apply in writing.
Green Fees £20 per day; £15 per round.
Facilities ⊗ ⦉ ╚ ⚑ ♀ ♨ ✆ ℓ Sandy Strachan.
Leisure motorised carts for hire, buggies for hire, trolley for hire, putting green, practice area.
Location E side of town off A89
Hotel ★★ 56% Dreadnought Hotel, 17/19 Whitburn Rd, BATHGATE
☎ 01506 630791 19rm(18 ⇌ ℝ)

BLAIR ATHOLL
Map 14 NN86

Blair Atholl PH18 5TG ☎ 01796 481407
Parkland course, river runs alongside 3 holes, easy walking.
9 holes, 5710metres, Par 69, SSS 70, Course record 64.
Club membership 400.
Visitors apply in advance to avoid competition times.
Societies apply in writing.
Green Fees £11 per day (£14 weekends). Weekly ticket £50.
Facilities ⊗ ╚ ⚑ ♀ ♨ ✆
Leisure trolley for hire, practice area.
Location 0.5m S off B8079
Hotel ★★ 64% Atholl Arms Hotel, BLAIR ATHOLL
☎ 01796 481205 30 ⇌ ℝ

Entries with a shaded background identify courses that are considered to be particularly interesting

THE GLENEAGLES HOTEL

AUCHTERARDER *Perthshire & Kinross*

☎ **01764 662231**　　　　　　　　　**Map 11 NN91**

John Ingham writes: Between Perth and Stirling you'll find those delightful courses, the King's and Queen's designed by James Braid and opened in 1919 to universal acclaim. There is nothing better – anywhere! They represent the best in beautiful, undulating moorland golf set alongside the massive and famous hotel – once the Caledonian Railway Hotel. The splendid Gleneagles Hotel courses are loved by its residents and for very good reasons – they are the stuff of dreams, of springy fairways, heather, bracken and pheasants that dart away when a shot misses the short grass and plunges into the wild life.

The motto there 'High Above the High' is apt as the 395 yard twelfth on the King's, named Tappit Hen (maybe it should be 'tap it in') is more than 600 feet above sea level with magnificent panoramas providing, of course, that mellow Scottish mists allow.

Only visitors to the hotel can play the courses. Years ago I stayed at the Glen with the late Henry Longhurst. 'We'll just have a quick 18 before dinner' he had said and delighted in showing me round the superb course. Since those days Jack Nicklaus has built his type of course there, the Monarch, in an American style. So now all tastes are catered for at this 5-star escape,

Without doubt the Gleneagles experience will impress any golfer and if the weather is fine, there is no better place to be. I used to go there every autumn for the Gleneagles Foursomes and at that time of the year, with the leaves golden, you feel that anything is possible.

Visitors	must be resident in the hotel. A handicap certificate is not required but advance booking is essential
Societies	must be resident in the hotel
Green fees	Kings, Queens, Monarchs: resident rate £65 per round. Wee: £15 per round
Facilities	⊗ ⅻ ⅊ ⅌ ♀ 🚗 ⚲ 🏠 ♟ driving range, putting greens, practice area, ⅃ (Greg Schofield) motor carts (Monarch only), buggies, trollies. Golf academy
Leisure	tennis, squash, swimming, gymnasuim, riding, fishing, shooting etc
Location	Perthshire PH3 1NF 2 miles SW of A823

63 holes. **Kings:** 18 holes, 6125yds, Par 68, SSS 71
Queens: 18 holes, 5660 yds, Par 68, SSS 68
Monarch: 18 holes, 6551yds, Par 72, SSS 73
Wee: 9 holes, 1481yds, Par 27

WHERE TO STAY AND EAT NEARBY

HOTELS:
AUCHTERARDER
★★★★★ (Red) ❀❀ The Gleneagles Hotel
☎ 01764 662231 234 ➳ ♞

KINLOCH HOUSE HOTEL
AA ★★★ (red)
By Blairgowrie, Perthshire, PH10 6SG
Telephone: Blairgowrie (01250) 884 237 Fax: (01250) 884 333
Kinloch House is an award winning, family run, Country house hotel in the heart of Sporting Perthshire. Located approximately 1½ hours from Glasgow, Edinburgh, Inverness and Aberdeen, the hotel has 30 golf courses within an hour's drive, including many Championship ones. Full drying facilities for clothes and equipment are available, we would be delighted to help plan your golf and book your tee times.
Please write or telephone for a brochure. *DAVID AND SARAH SHENTALL*

BLAIRGOWRIE Map 15 NO14

Blairgowrie Rosemount PH10 6LG ☎ 01250 872622
Two 18-hole heathland courses, also a 9-hole course.
Rosemount Course: 18 holes, 6588yds, Par 72, SSS 72.
Lansdowne Course: 18 holes, 6895yds, Par 72, SSS 73.
Wee Course: 9 holes, 4654yds, Par 64, SSS 63.
Club membership 1200.

Visitors must contact in advance & have handicap certificate, restricted Wed, Fri & weekends.
Societies must contact in writing.
Green Fees not confirmed.
Facilities Gordon Kinnoch.
Location 2m S off A93
Hotel ★★★(red) Kinloch House Hotel, BLAIRGOWRIE ☎ 01250 884237 21

BONNYBRIDGE Map 11 NS88

Bonnybridge Larbert Rd FK4 1NY ☎ 01324 812822
Testing heathland course, with tightly guarded greens. Easy walking.
9 holes, 6060yds, Par 72, SSS 69.
Club membership 325.

Visitors must contact in advance and be accompanied by member.
Societies must contact in advance.
Green Fees not confirmed.
Facilities
Location 1m NE off A883
Hotel ★★★ 68% Inchyra Grange Hotel, Grange Rd, POLMONT ☎ 01324 711911 43

BONNYRIGG Map 11 NT36

Broomieknowe 36 Golf Course Rd EH19 2HZ
☎ 0131 663 9317
Easy walking mature parkland course laid out by Ben Sayers and extended by James Braid. Elevated site with excellent views.
18 holes, 6150yds, Par 70, SSS 69, Course record 65.

Visitors must contact in advance.
Societies contact for details.
Green Fees £25 two rounds; £17 per round (£20 per round weekends).
Facilities Mark Patchett.
Leisure trolley for hire, putting green, practice area.
Location 0.5m NE off B704
Hotel ★★ 62% Eskbank Hotel, 29 Dalhousie Rd, DALKEITH ☎ 0131 663 3234 16

BRECHIN Map 15 NO56

Brechin Trinity DD9 7PD
☎ 01356 622383 & 01356 625270 (Pro)
Rolling parkland course, with easy walking and good views of Strathmore Valley and Grampian Mountains. The course was extended in 1993.
18 holes, 6092yds, Par 72, SSS 70, Course record 66.
Club membership 620.

Visitors contact in advance.
Societies must contact club steward in advance.
Green Fees £19 per day; £14 per round (£27/£18 weekends). 5 day ticket £45.
Facilities Stephen Rennie.
Leisure squash, motorised carts for hire, buggies for hire, trolley for hire, putting green, practice area.
Location 1m N on B966
Hotel ★★ 58% Northern Hotel, Clerk St, BRECHIN ☎ 01356 622156 & 625505 20rm(4 12)

BRIDGE OF ALLAN Map 11 NS79

Bridge of Allan Sunnylaw FK9 4LY ☎ 01786 832332
Parkland course, very hilly with good views of Stirling Castle and beyond to the Trossachs. Testing 1st hole, 221 yds (par 3) uphill 6 ft wall 25 yds before green.
9 holes, 4932yds, Par 66, SSS 65, Course record 62.
Club membership 400.

Visitors restricted Sat.
Societies must contact in advance.
Green Fees not confirmed.
Facilities
Leisure pool table.
Location 0.5m N off A9
Hotel ★★★ 65% Royal Hotel, Henderson St, BRIDGE OF ALLAN ☎ 01786 832284 32

BROXBURN Map 11 NT07

Niddry Castle Castle Rd, Winchburgh EH52 6RQ
☎ 01506 891097
A 9-hole parkland course. While not very long, it requires accurate golf to score well.
9 holes, 5514yds, Par 70, SSS 67.
Club membership 320.

Visitors advisable to contact at weekends, restricted during competition time.
Societies must contact in advance.
Green Fees not confirmed.
Facilities
Location 9m W of Edinburgh off junc 1

Hotel ★★★ 60% Forth Bridges Hotel, Forth Bridge, SOUTH QUEENSFERRY
☎ 0131 331 1199 108 ⇌ ⟨

BURNTISLAND   Map 11 NT28

Burntisland Golf House Club Dodhead, Kirkcaldy Rd KY3 9EW ☎ 01592 874093 (Manager) & 873247 (Pro)
This hill course has fine sea views.
18 holes, 5965yds, Par 70, SSS 69, Course record 62.
Club membership 800.
Visitors weekend play restricted. Book by telephoning professional.
Societies apply in writing to manager.
Green Fees £25 per day; £15 per round (£35/£23 weekends).
Facilities ⊗ ⏏ ⓑ ⓛ ⓠ ⓐ ⓣ ⓕ Jacky Montgomery.
Leisure trolley for hire, driving range, putting green, practice area.
Location 1m E on B923
Hotel ★★ 65% Inchview Hotel, 69 Kinghorn Rd, BURNTISLAND ☎ 01592 872239 12 ⇌ ⟨

BUTE, ISLE OF   Map 10 NS05

KINGARTH   Map 10 NS05

Bute Kingarth, Rothesay PA20 9HN
☎ 01700 831648
Flat seaside course with good fenced greens.
9 holes, 2497yds, Par 68, SSS 64, Course record 65.
Club membership 120.
Visitors restricted Sat until after 12.30pm.
Societies apply in advance.
Green Fees not confirmed.
Facilities ⓐ
Location 1m W off A844
Hotel ★★♨ 72% Ardmory House Hotel, Ardmory Rd, ARDBEG ☎ 01700 502346 5 ⇌ ⟨

PORT BANNATYNE   Map 10 NS06

Port Bannatyne Bannatyne Mains Rd PA20 0PH
☎ 01700 505223
Seaside hill course with panoramic views. Difficult hole: 4th (par 3).
13 holes, 5085yds, Par 68, SSS 65, Course record 66.
Club membership 200.
Visitors no restrictions.
Societies must telephone in advance.
Green Fees not confirmed.
Facilities ⓐ
Location W side of village off A844
Hotel ★★♨ 72% Ardmory House Hotel, Ardmory Rd, ARDBEG ☎ 01700 502346 5 ⇌ ⟨

ROTHESAY   Map 10 NS06

Rothesay Canada Hill PA20 9HN ☎ 01700 502244
A scenic island course designed by James Braid and Ben Sayers. The course is fairly hilly, with views of the Firth of Clyde, Rothesay Bay or the Kyles of Bute from every hole. Winds are a regular feature which makes the two par 5 holes extremely challenging.

---

18 holes, 5043yds, Par 69, SSS 65, Course record 62.
Club membership 350.
Visitors pre-booking essential for weekends, telephone professional.
Societies contact in advance, booking essential at weekends.
Green Fees not confirmed.
Facilities ⓠ ⓐ ⓑ ⓣ ⓕ James M Dougal.
Leisure caddy cars, putting green, trolley hire, practice area.
Location Off road to Kingarth
Hotel ★★♨ 72% Ardmory House Hotel, Ardmory Rd, ARDBEG ☎ 01700 502346 5 ⇌ ⟨

CALLANDER   Map 11 NN60

Callander Aveland Rd FK17 8EN
☎ 01877 330090 & 330975
Parkland course, with fairly tightly guarded greens. Designed by Tom Morris Snr and overlooked by the Trossachs.
18 holes, 5151yds, Par 66, SSS 66, Course record 61.
Club membership 750.
Visitors prior booking 24-48 hrs is advised in the playing season.
Societies write or telephone for booking form.
Green Fees £22.50 per day; £17 per round (£28/£22.50 weekends).
Facilities ⊗ ⏏ by prior arrangement ⓑ ⓛ ⓠ ⓐ ⓑ ⓣ ⓕ William Kelly.
Leisure trolley for hire.
Location E side of town off A84
Hotel ★★★♨ 69% Roman Camp Hotel, CALLANDER ☎ 01877 330003 14 ⇌ ⟨

CARDENDEN   Map 11 NT29

Auchterderran Woodend Rd KY5 0NH
☎ 01592 721579
This is a relatively flat course requiring a lot of thought. There are two or three holes to test the best.
9 holes, 5250yds, Par 66, SSS 66, Course record 63.
Club membership 120.
Visitors no visitors between 7-11am & 1-3pm Sat, also some Sun in season.
Societies apply in writing.
Green Fees not confirmed.
Facilities ⓠ ⓐ
Location N end Cardendon, Kirkcaldy/Glenrothes road
Hotel ★★★ 57% Dean Park Hotel, Chapel Level, KIRKCALDY
☎ 01592 261635 20 ⇌ ⟨Annexe12 ⟨

CARDROSS   Map 10 NS37

Cardross Main Rd G82 5LB ☎ 01389 841754
Undulating parkland course, testing with good views.
18 holes, 6469yds, Par 71, SSS 72, Course record 65.
Club membership 800.
Visitors may not play at weekends unless introduced by member. Contact professional in advance 01359 841350
Societies must contact in writing.
Green Fees £32 per day; £22 per round.
Facilities ⊗ ⏏ by prior arrangement ⓑ ⓛ ⓠ ⓐ ⓑ ⓣ ⓕ Robert Farrell.

▶

Leisure motorised carts for hire, buggies for hire, trolley for hire, putting green, practice area.
Location In centre of village on A814
Hotel ★★ 68% Commodore Toby Hotel, 112 West Clyde St, HELENSBURGH
☎ 01436 676924 45 ⇔ ℝ

CARNOUSTIE
Map 12 NO53

CARNOUSTIE GOLF LINKS See page 283

CARRADALE
Map 10 NR83

Carradale PA28 6SG ☎ 01583 431643
Pleasant seaside course built on a promontory overlooking the Isle of Arran. Natural terrain and small greens are the most difficult natural hazards. Described as the most sporting 9-hole course in Scotland. Testing 7th hole (240 yds), par 3.
9 holes, 2392yds, Par 62, SSS 64.
Club membership 320.
Visitors no restrictions
Societies contact in advance.
Green Fees £7 per day also weekly and monthly rates available.
Facilities ⌂
Leisure trolley for hire, putting green.
Location S side of village
Hotel ★★ 65% Seafield Hotel, Kilkerran Rd, CAMPBELTOWN
☎ 01586 554385 3 ℝAnnexe6 ℝ

COLONSAY, ISLE OF
Map 10 NR39

SCALASAIG
Map 10 NR39

Colonsay PA61 7YP ☎ 01951 200316
Traditional links course on natural machair (hard wearing short grass), challenging, primitive. Colonsay Hotel, 2 miles away, is the headquarters of the club, offering accommodation and facilities.
18 holes, 4775yds, Par 72, SSS 72.
Club membership 120.
Visitors no restrictions.
Societies apply in writing.
Green Fees not confirmed.
Facilities ⸙
Location 2m W on A870
Hotel ★ 75% Colonsay Hotel, SCALASAIG
☎ 01951 200316 10rm(1 ⇔7 ℝ)Annexe1rm

COMRIE
Map 11 NN72

Comrie PH6 2LR ☎ 01764 760055 & 760941
Scenic highland course.
9 holes, 6040yds, Par 70, SSS 69, Course record 62.
Club membership 315.
Visitors apply in advance.
Societies must contact in advance.
Green Fees £10 per day (£15 per day/£12 per round weekends).
Facilities ⊗ Ꮟ ⌂ ⸙
Leisure fishing, buggies for hire, trolley for hire, practice area.
Location E side of village off A85
Guesthouse QQQ Mossgiel Guest House, Burrell St, COMRIE ☎ 01764 670567 5rm

COWDENBEATH
Map 11 NT19

Cowdenbeath Seco Place KY4 8PD ☎ 01383 511918
A parkland-based 9-hole golf course.
Dora Course: 9 holes, 6552yds, Par 72, SSS 71, Course record 68.
Club membership 400.
Visitors no restrictions.
Societies must contact at least 2 weeks in advance.
Green Fees not confirmed.
Facilities ♀
Leisure putting green,practice area.
Location 6m E of Dunfermline
Hotel ★★ 66% Woodside Hotel, High St, ABERDOUR ☎ 01383 860328 20 ⇔ ℝ

CRAIL
Map 12 NO60

Crail Golfing Society Balcomie Clubhouse, Fifeness KY10 3XN ☎ 01333 450686 & 450416
Perched on the edge of the North Sea on the very point of the golfing county of Fife, the Crail Golfing Society's course at Balcomie is picturesque and sporting. And here again golf history has been made for Crail Golfing Society began its life in 1786. The course is highly thought of by students of the game both for its testing holes and the standard of its greens.
18 holes, 5922yds, Par 69, SSS 69.
Club membership 950.
Visitors must contact in advance, restricted 10am-noon & 2-4.30pm.
Societies must contact in advance, as much notice as possible for weekend play.
Green Fees £26 per day; £18 per round (£34/£23 weekends). ▶

CARNOUSTIE GOLF LINKS

CARNOUSTIE *Angus* ☎ **01241 853789**   **Map 12 NO53**

John Ingham writes: You love it, or hate it - but you respect it. Carnoustie can be a graveyard. Simply standing up to the buffeting is bad enough, but those closing holes, across the Barry Burn (or into it) are a prospect which can gnaw at the mind. The burn twists through the links like an angry serpent and has to be crossed no fewer than seven times.

Back in 1953 they came to see Ben Hogan play in the Open Championship. This little man from Texas had a magic about him, and the huge terrifying links, the dread of any short hitter, certainly promised to be a platform on which to examine the finest golfer of his day, and maybe of any day.

Not since 1860 had any golfer won the Open on his first attempt. Certainly Hogan hadn't come to this awesome place for the money which, in those days, was a pittance. He had come to prove he was the best player in the world. That was pressure!

When Mr Hogan saw the 'Stone Age' course, dating back to the birth of the game, he was shocked because it lacked trees and colour, and looked drab. But he beat the 7200-yard monster course for the 1953 Championship, which was, as they say, something else.

'Winning the British Open at Carnoustie gave me my greatest pleasure' he told the *Fort Worth Star-Telegram*. 'Certainly the other victories were pleasurable, but none gave me the feeling, the desire to perform, that gripped me in Scotland'.

Sadly, Hogan never returned and then the great links was taken from the Open Championship rota. Today there are hopes it may be re-instated.

Visitors	must contact golf links in advance. Restricted hours. Must have a handicap certificate for Championship course
Societies	prior arrangement required either in writing or by telephone
Green fees	Championship: £78 per day; £45 per round. Burnside: £26 per day; £17 per round; Buddon Links: £18 per day; £12 per round. Combination day tickets: Championship & Burnside £54; Championship & Buddon Links £50; Burnside & Buddon Links £22
Facilities	⌂
Location	Carnoustie DD7 7JE Links Parade (SW side of town, off A930)

54 holes. Championship Course: 18 holes, 6936 yds, Par 72, SSS 74, Course record 68 (Colin Montgomerie). Burnside Course: 18 holes, 6020 yds, Par 68, SSS 69. Buddon Links: 18 holes, 5420 yds, Par 66, SSS 66

WHERE TO STAY AND EAT NEARBY

HOTELS:

ARBROATH
★★ 62% Hotel Seaforth, Dundee Rd, ☎ 01241 872232. 20 (14 ⇆ 6 ⇆ ↸)

CARNOUSTIE
★★ 67% Carlogie House, Carlogie Rd ☎ 01241 853185. 12 (10 ↸ 1 ⇆ 1 ⇆ ↸) Annexe 1 ↸

★★64% Glencoe, Links Pde. ☎ 01241 853273. 7 (4 ↸ 3 ⇆ ↸)

RESTAURANT:

INVERKEILOR
🌑 Gordon's, Homewood House, Main St. ☎ 01241 830364

Facilities ⊗ ⵊ ⅃ ⅃ ⅃ ⅃ ⅃ ⅃ ⅃ Graheme Lennie.
Leisure trolley for hire, driving range, putting green, practice area.
Location 2m NE off A917
Hotel ★★ 63% Balcomie Links Hotel, Balcomie Rd, CRAIL ☎ 01333 450237 11 ⇔ ⋐
Additional hotel QQQQ The Spindrift, Pittenweem Rd, ANSTRUTHER ☎ 01333 310573 8 ⇔ ⋐

CRIEFF
Map 11 NN82

Crieff Ferntower, Perth Rd PH7 3LR
☎ 01764 652909 & 652397 bookings
This course is what you might call 'up and down' but the turf is beautiful and the highland air fresh and invigorating. There are views from the course over Strathearn. Of the two courses the Ferntower is the more challenging. Both parkland, the Dornock has one water hazard.
Ferntower Course: 18 holes, 6402yds, SSS 71, Course record 65.
Dornock Course: 9 holes, 4772yds, Par 64, SSS 63.
Club membership 720.
Visitors must contact professional in advance.
Societies must contact professional in advance.
Green Fees Ferntower: £30 per day, £18 per round (£40/£25 weekends). Dornock: £12/£15.
Facilities ⊗ ⵊ ⅃ ⅃ ⅃ ⅃ ⅃ ⅃ David Murchie.
Location 0.5m NE on A85
Hotel ★★ 69% Murraypark Hotel, Connaught Ter, CRIEFF ☎ 01764 653731 20 ⇔ ⋐

CUPAR
Map 11 NO31

Cupar Hilltarvit KY15 5NZ ☎ 01334 53549
Hilly parkland course with fine views over north east Fife.5th/14th hole is most difficult - uphill and into the prevailing wind.
9 holes, 5500yds, Par 68, SSS 65, Course record 62.
Club membership 450.
Visitors welcome except Sat.
Societies must contact in advance.
Green Fees not confirmed.
Facilities ⅃ ⅃
Leisure practice putting green.
Location 0.75m S off A92
Hotel ★★ 67% Eden House Hotel, 2 Pitscottie Rd, CUPAR ☎ 01334 652510 9 ⇔ ⋐Annexe2 ⇔ ⋐

DALKEITH
Map 11 NT36

Newbattle Abbey Rd EH22 3AD
☎ 0131 663 2123 & 0131 660 1631
Undulating parkland course on three levels, surrounded by woods.
18 holes, 6005yds, Par 69, SSS 70, Course record 61.
Club membership 700.
Visitors Mon-Fri ex public holidays, before 4pm.
Societies welcome weekdays ex public holidays, before 4pm.
Green Fees £24 per day; £16 per round.
Facilities ⊗ ⵊ ⅃ ⅃ ⅃ ⅃ ⅃ David Torrance.
Leisure trolley for hire, putting green, small practice area.

Location SW side of town off A68
Hotel ★★ 62% Eskbank Hotel, 29 Dalhousie Rd, DALKEITH ☎ 0131 663 3234 16 ⇔ ⋐

DALMALLY
Map 10 NN12

Dalmally Old Saw Mill PA33 1AE ☎ 01838 200370
A 9-hole flat parkland course alongside the River Orchy. The course is surrounded by mountains and there are plenty of water hazards.
9 holes, 2257yds, Par 64, SSS 63, Course record 64.
Club membership 100.
Visitors no visitors on Sun between 9-10 & 1-2.
Societies telephone in advance.
Green Fees £8 per day.
Facilities ⅃ by prior arrangement ⅃ by arrangement ⅃ ⅃
Leisure fishing, practice area.
Location On A85, 1.5m W of Dalmally
Hotel ★★ 57% Polfearn Hotel, TAYNUILT ☎ 01866 2251 16rm(3 ⇔ 11 ⋐)

DOLLAR
Map 11 NS99

Dollar Brewlands House FK14 7EA ☎ 01259 742400
Compact hillside course.
18 holes, 5242yds, Par 69, SSS 66, Course record 62.
Club membership 470.
Visitors weekdays course available but restricted Wed ladies day, weekends must contact in advance.
Societies write or telephone in advance.
Green Fees £14 per day; £10 per round (£18.50 per day/round).
Facilities ⊗ ⵊ ⅃ ⅃ ⅃ ⅃ ⅃
Leisure trolley for hire, practice area.
Location 0.5m N off A91
Hotel ★★★ 65% Royal Hotel, Henderson St, BRIDGE OF ALLAN ☎ 01786 832284 32 ⇔ ⋐

DRYMEN
Map 11 NS48

Buchanan Castle G63 0HY ☎ 01360 660307
Parkland course, with easy walking and good views.
18 holes, 6086yds, Par 70, SSS 69.
Club membership 830.
Societies must contact in advance.
Green Fees not confirmed.
Facilities ⅃ ⅃ ⅃ ⅃ ⅃ Keith Baxter.
Leisure putting, trolley hire, practice area.
Location 1m W
Hotel ★★★ 67% Buchanan Arms Hotel, DRYMEN ☎ 01360 660588 51 ⇔ ⋐

DUNBAR
Map 12 NT67

Dunbar East Links EH42 1LT ☎ 01368 862317
Another of Scotland's old links. It is said that it was some Dunbar members who first took the game of golf to the North of England. The club dates back to 1856. The wind, if blowing from the sea, is a problem.
18 holes, 6426yds, Par 71, SSS 71, Course record 64.
Club membership 1000. ▶

Visitors may not play Thu, between 12.30-2 weekdays, 12-2 weekends or before 9.30am any day.
Societies telephone in advance.
Green Fees £30 per day (£40 weekends).
Facilities ⊗ 🄱 ▆ ♀ ⚐ 🕇 ℯ Derek Small.
Leisure trolley for hire, putting green, practice area.
Location 0.5m E off A1087
Hotel ★★ 61% Bayswell Hotel, Bayswell Park, DUNBAR ☎ 01368 862225 13 ➡ 📷

Winterfield North Rd EH42 1AY ☎ 01368 863562
Seaside course with superb views.
18 holes, 5220yds, SSS 64.
Club membership 200.
Visitors must contact in advance.
Green Fees not confirmed.
Facilities ♀ ⚐ 📷 🕇
Location W side of town off A1087
Hotel ★★ 61% Bayswell Hotel, Bayswell Park, DUNBAR ☎ 01368 862225 13 ➡ 📷

DUNBLANE
Map 11 NN70

Dunblane New Golf Club Perth Rd FK15 0LJ
☎ 01786 823711
Well maintained parkland course, with reasonably hard walking. Testing 6th and 9th holes.
18 holes, 5876yds, Par 69, SSS 68.
Club membership 800.
Visitors may play 9.30am-noon & 2.30-4pm Mon-Fri. Must contact in advance.
Societies welcome Mon, Wed-Fri, contact in advance.
Green Fees not confirmed.
Facilities ♀ ⚐ 📷 🕇 ℯ
Leisure putting,trolley hire,practice area.
Location E side of town on A9
Hotel ★★★(red)🏨 Cromlix House Hotel, Kinbuck, DUNBLANE ☎ 01786 822125 14 ➡ 📷

DUNDEE
Map 11 NO43

Caird Park Mains Loan DD4 9BX ☎ 01382 453606
Municipal parkland course.
18 holes, 5494yds, Par 69, SSS 68.
Club membership 400.
Visitors no restrictions.
Societies must contact Dundee District Council on 01382 223141 in advance.
Green Fees not confirmed.
Facilities ♀ 📷 🕇 ℯ J Black.
Location 1.5m N of city centre off A972
Hotel ★★★ 62% The Queen's Hotel, 160 Nethergate, DUNDEE ☎ 01382 322515 47 ➡ 📷

Camperdown Camperdown House, Camperdown Park DD2 4TF ☎ 01382 621145
Parkland course. Testing 2nd hole.
18 holes, 5999yds, Par 71, SSS 69.
Club membership 600.
Visitors must contact in advance.
Societies must contact in advance.
Green Fees not confirmed.
Facilities ⚐ 📷 ℯ

Leisure hard tennis courts.
Location 3m NW of city centre off A923
Hotel ★★★ 63% The Angus Thistle, 101 Marketgait, DUNDEE ☎ 01382 226874 58 ➡ 📷

Downfield Turnberry Av DD2 3QP
☎ 01382 825595
A fine inland course of recent Championship rating set in undulating woodland to the north of Dundee. The Gelly burn provides a hazard for several holes.
18 holes, 6822yds, Par 73, SSS 73, Course record 65.
Club membership 750.
Visitors must contact in advance, no visitors at weekends.
Societies must contact in advance.
Green Fees £39 per day; £27 per round.
Facilities ⊗ 🍽 🄱 ▆ ♀ ⚐ 📷 🕇 ℯ Kenny Hutton.
Leisure trolley for hire, putting green, practice area.
Location N of city centre off A923
Hotel ★★★ 63% The Angus Thistle, 101 Marketgait, DUNDEE ☎ 01382 226874 58 ➡ 📷

DUNFERMLINE
Map 11 NT08

Canmore Venturefair Av KY12 0PF
☎ 01383 724969
Undulating parkland course affording excellent views.
18 holes, 5474yds, Par 67, SSS 66.
Club membership 620.
Visitors no restrictions. Sat not usually available.
Societies apply in writing to secretary.
Green Fees not confirmed.
Facilities ♀ ⚐ 📷 ℯ
Location 1m N on A823
Hotel ★★★ 62% King Malcolm Thistle, Queensferry Rd, Wester Pitcorthie, DUNFERMLINE ☎ 01383 722611 48 ➡ 📷

Dunfermline Pitfirrane, Crossford KY12 8QV
☎ 01383 723534
Gently undulating parkland course with interesting contours. Sixteenth-century clubhouse.
18 holes, 6237yds, Par 72, SSS 70, Course record 65.
Par 3 course: 9 holes, 1144yds, Par 27.
Club membership 690.
Visitors may not play Sat. Contact to check times.
Societies must contact in advance.
Green Fees not confirmed.
Facilities ♀ ⚐ 📷 ℯ Steve Craig.
Leisure putting,trolley hire,practice area.
Location 2m W on A994
Hotel ★★★ 62% King Malcolm Thistle, Queensferry Rd, Wester Pitcorthie, DUNFERMLINE ☎ 01383 722611 48 ➡ 📷

Pitreavie Queensferry Rd KY11 5PR
☎ 01383 722591
Picturesque woodland course with panoramic view of the River Forth Valley. Testing golf.
18 holes, 6086yds, Par 70, SSS 69, Course record 65.
Club membership 700.
Visitors welcome except for competition days.
Societies must write or telephone in advance.
Green Fees not confirmed.
Facilities ♀ ⚐ 📷 🕇 ℯ Jim Forrester. ▶

Leisure putting green,practice area,trolley hire.
Location SE side of town on A823
Hotel ★★★ 62% King Malcolm Thistle, Queensferry
Rd, Wester Pitcorthie, DUNFERMLINE
☎ 01383 722611 48 ⇌ ⋒

DUNKELD   Map 11 NO04

Dunkeld & Birnam Fungarth PH8 0HU
☎ 01350 727524
Interesting heathland course with spectacular views of
surrounding countryside.
9 holes, 5322yds, Par 68, SSS 66, Course record 64.
Club membership 430.
Visitors must contact in advance.
Societies apply in writing.
Green Fees on application.
Facilities ⊗ ⋔ ⋤ ⬛ ♀ ⚲ ⌂ ⋔
Leisure trolley for hire, driving range, putting green,
practice area.
Location 1m N of village on A923
Hotel ★★★(red)⛟ Kinnaird, Kinnaird Estate,
DUNKELD ☎ 01796 482440 9 ⇌ ⋒

DUNNING   Map 11 NO01

Dunning Rollo Park PH2 0RH
☎ 01764 684372 & 684747
Parkland course.
9 holes, 4836yds, Par 66, SSS 64.
Club membership 580.
Visitors may not play on Sat before 4pm or Sun before
1pm. With member only after 5pm Mon-Fri.
Societies must contact in advance in writing.
Green Fees not confirmed.
Facilities ⚲
Location Off A9 NW
Hotel ★★★⛟ 70% Duchally House Hotel,
AUCHTERARDER
☎ 01764 663071 13rm(12 ⇌ ⋒)

DUNOON   Map 10 NS17

Cowal Ardenslate Rd PA23 8LT ☎ 01369 705673
Moorland course. Panoramic views of Clyde Estuary and
surrounding hills.
18 holes, 6063yds, Par 70, SSS 70, Course record 63.
Club membership 700.
Visitors advisable to book in advance.
Societies must telephone in advance.
Green Fees £24 per day; £16 per round (£35/£24 weekends).
Facilities ⊗ ⋔ ⋤ ⬛ ♀ ⚲ ⌂ ⋔ ⋔ Russell Weir.
Leisure trolley for hire, putting green, practice area.
Location 1m N
Hotel ★★ 76% Enmore Hotel, Marine Pde, Kirn,
DUNOON ☎ 01369 702230 11 ⇌ ⋒

EDINBURGH   Map 11 NT27

Baberton 50 Baberton Av, Juniper Green EH14 5DU
☎ 0131 453 4911
Parkland course.
18 holes, 6123yds, Par 69, SSS 70, Course record 64.
Club membership 900.

Visitors may not play at weekends or after 3.30pm
weekdays. Contact in advance.
Societies must contact in advance.
Green Fees £28.50 per day; £18.50 per round.
Facilities ⊗ ⋔ ⋤ ⬛ ♀ ⚲ ⌂ ⋔ Ken Kelly.
Leisure trolley for hire, putting green, practice area.
Location 5m W of city centre off A70
Hotel ★★★ 67% Bruntsfield Hotel, 69/74 Bruntsfield
Place, EDINBURGH
☎ 0131 229 1393 50 ⇌ ⋒

Braid Hills Braid Hills Approach EH10 6JZ
☎ 0131 447 6666
Municipal heathland course with good views of Edinburgh
and the Firth of Forth.
*Course No 1: 18 holes, 6172yds, Par 70, SSS 68, Course
record 62.*
Course No 2: 18 holes, 4832yds, Par 65, SSS 63.
Visitors may not play on Sat mornings.
Societies apply in writing to Leisure Management Unit,
Edinburgh District Council, 141 London Road,
Edinburgh.
Green Fees not confirmed.
Facilities ⚲ ⌂ ⋔ ⋔
Leisure putting green,trolley hire,practice area.
Location 2.5m S of city centre off A702
Hotel ★★★ 67% Braid Hills Hotel, 134 Braid Rd,
Braid Hills, EDINBURGH
☎ 0131 447 8888 68 ⇌ ⋒

Bruntsfield Links Golfing Society 32 Barnton Av EH4 6JH
☎ 0131 336 1479
Parkland course with good views of Forth Estuary. 4th and
14th holes testing.
18 holes, 6407yds, Par 71, SSS 71, Course record 67.
Club membership 1100.
Visitors Must contact in advance.
Societies apply in writing.
Green Fees £45 per day; £35 per round (£50/£40 weekends).
Facilities ⊗ ⬛ ♀ ⚲ ⌂ ⋔ ⋔ Brian Mackenzie.
Leisure motorised carts for hire, buggies for hire, trolley
for hire, driving range, putting green. practice
area.
Location 4m NW of city centre off A90
Hotel ★★★ 64% The Barnton Thistle, Queensferry
Rd, Barnton, EDINBURGH
☎ 0131 339 1144 50 ⇌ ⋒

Carrick Knowe Carrick Knowe Municipal, Glendevon Park
EH12 5UZ ☎ 0131 337 1096
Flat parkland course. Played over by two clubs, Carrick
Knowe and Carrick Vale.
18 holes, 6299yds, Par 71, SSS 70.
Club membership 450.
Visitors may be restricted at weekends.
Societies apply in writing to: Leisure Management Unit,
Meadowbank Sports Centre, London Road,
Edinburgh.
Green Fees not confirmed.
Facilities ⋔
Leisure trolley hire,practice area.
Location 3m W of city centre, S of A8
Hotel B Forte Posthouse Edinburgh, Corstorphine Rd,
EDINBURGH
☎ 0131 334 0390 204 ⇌ ⋒

Craigentinny Fillyside Rd, Lochend
☎ 0131 554 7501
To the north east of Edinburgh, Craigentinny course is
between Leith and Portobello. It is generally flat although
there are some hillocks with gentle slopes. The famous
Arthur's Seat dominates the southern skyline.
18 holes, 5418yds, Par 67, SSS 65.
Societies   must apply in writing to: Leisure Management
Unit,Meadowbank Sports Centre, London Road,
Edinburgh.
Green Fees not confirmed.
Facilities   ☂
Leisure   trolley hire, practice area.
Location   NE side of city, between Leith & Portobello
Hotel   ★★★ 70% King James Thistle, 107 Leith St,
EDINBURGH
☎ 0131 556 0111 147 ⇌ ⋒

Craigmillar Park 1 Observatory Rd EH9 3HG
☎ 0131 667 0047
Parkland course, with good views.
18 holes, 5851yds, Par 70, SSS 69, Course record 63.
Club membership 750.
Visitors   must contact in advance, may not play weekends
and after 3.30pm weekdays.
Societies   must contact in writing.
Green Fees £25 per day; £17 per round.
Facilities   ⊗ ⍢ ⓛ ⬛ ♀ ⌙ 🖻 ☂ ⚑ B McGhee.
Leisure   trolley for hire, putting green, practice area.
Location   2m S of city centre off A7
Hotel   ★★★ 59% Donmaree Hotel, 21 Mayfield
Gardens, EDINBURGH
☎ 0131 667 3641 15 ⇌ ⋒Annexe2 ⇌ ⋒

> *Dalmahoy Hotel Golf & Country Club* Kirknewton
> EH27 8EB ☎ 0131 333 1845
> Two upland courses, one Championship.
> *East Course: 18 holes, 6677yds, Par 72, SSS 72, Course
> record 64.*
> *West Course: 18 holes, 5185yds, Par 68, SSS 66, Course
> record 62.*
> *Club membership 700.*
> **Visitors**   weekend by application.
> **Societies**   telephone or write for information.
> **Green Fees** not confirmed.
> **Facilities**   ♀ ⌙ 🖻 ☂ ⨝
>   ⚑ Brian Anderson/Stuart Callan.
> **Leisure**   hard tennis courts, heated indoor swimming
>   pool, squash, sauna, solarium, gymnasium,
>   range, putting, cart/buggy/trolley hire.
> **Location**   7m W of city centre on A71
> **Hotel**   ★★★★ 71% Dalmahoy Hotel, Country
>   Club Resort, Kirknewton, EDINBURGH
>   ☎ 0131 333 1845 43 ⇌ ⋒Annexe108 ⇌ ⋒

Duddingston Duddingston Rd West EH15 3QD
☎ 0131 661 7688
Parkland, semi-seaside course with burn as a natural hazard.
Testing 11th hole. Easy walking and windy.
18 holes, 6647yds, Par 72, SSS 72.
Club membership 700.
Visitors   may not play at weekends.
Societies   Tue & Thu only. Must contact in advance.
Green Fees not confirmed.
Facilities   ♀ ⌙ 🖻 ☂ ⚑ Alastair McLean.
Location   2.5m SE of city centre off A1

Hotel   ★★★ 59% Donmaree Hotel, 21 Mayfield
Gardens, EDINBURGH
☎ 0131 667 3641 15 ⇌ ⋒Annexe2 ⇌ ⋒

Kingsknowe 326 Lanark Rd EH14 2JD ☎ 0131 441 1145
Hilly parkland course with prevailing SW winds.
18 holes, 5979ydss, Par 69, SSS 69, Course record 69.
Club membership 800.
Visitors   contact in advance and subject to availability of
tee times.
Societies   apply in writing or telephone to secretary.
Green Fees £21 per day; £17 per round (£25 per round
weekends).
Facilities   ⊗ ⓛ ⬛ ♀ ⌙ 🖻 ⚑ Andrew Marshall.
Leisure   trolley for hire, putting green, practice area.
Location   4m SW of city centre on A70
Hotel   ★★★ 67% Bruntsfield Hotel, 69/74 Bruntsfield
Place, EDINBURGH
☎ 0131 229 1393 50 ⇌ ⋒

Liberton 297 Gilmerton Rd EH16 5UJ ☎ 0131 664 3009
Undulating, wooded parkland course.
18 holes, 5299yds, Par 67, SSS 67.
Club membership 650.
Visitors   may only play before 5pm on Tue & Thu Apr-
Sep. Must contact in advance.
Societies   must contact in writing.
Green Fees not confirmed.
Facilities   ⌙ 🖻 ⚑
Location   3m SE of city centre on A7
Hotel   ★★ 62% Eskbank Hotel, 29 Dalhousie Rd,
DALKEITH ☎ 0131 663 3234 16 ⇌ ⋒

Lothianburn 106A Biggar Rd, Fairmilehead EH10 7DU
☎ 0131 445 2206 & 0131 445 5067
Hillside course with a 'T' shaped wooded-area, situated in the
Pentland foothills. Sheep on course. Testing in windy
conditions.
18 holes, 5750yds, Par 71, SSS 68, Course record 66.
Club membership 850.
Visitors   weekends after 3.30pm contact professional,
weekdays up to 4pm.
Societies   apply to the secretary or telephone in the first
instance.
Green Fees £20 per day; £14 per round (£25/£20 weekends).
Facilities   ⊗ ⓛ ⬛ ♀ ⌙ 🖻 ☂ ⚑ Kurt Mungall.
Leisure   trolley for hire, putting green, practice area.
Location   4.5m S of city centre on A702
Hotel   ★★★ 67% Braid Hills Hotel, 134 Braid Rd,
Braid Hills, EDINBURGH
☎ 0131 447 8888 68 ⇌ ⋒

Merchants of Edinburgh 10 Craighill Gardens EH10 5PY
☎ 0131 447 1219
Testing hill course.
18 holes, 4889mtrs, Par 65, SSS 64, Course record 59.
Club membership 750.
Visitors   must play with member at weekends.
Societies   must contact in secretary in writing.
Green Fees £15 per day/round.
Facilities   ⊗ ⓛ ⬛ ♀ ⌙ 🖻 ☂ ⚑ Neil Colquhoun.
Leisure   trolley for hire, putting green.
Location   2m SW of city centre off A702
Hotel   ★★★ 67% Braid Hills Hotel, 134 Braid Rd,
Braid Hills, EDINBURGH
☎ 0131 447 8888 68 ⇌ ⋒

Mortonhall 231 Braid Rd EH10 6PB
☎ 0131 447 6974
Moorland course with views over Edinburgh.
18 holes, 6557yds, Par 72, SSS 72, Course record 66.
Club membership 500.
Visitors   advisable to contact by phone.
Societies   may not play at weekends. Must contact in
                 writing.
Green Fees £28 per day; £23 per round (£38/£28 weekends).
Facilities   ⊗ ⅷ by prior arrangement ⅖ ⬛ ♀ ⅄ 🖻 ⅌
                 ♦ Douglas Horn.
Leisure   trolley for hire, putting green, practice area.
Location   3m S of city centre off A702
Hotel   ★★★ 67% Braid Hills Hotel, 134 Braid Rd,
                 Braid Hills, EDINBURGH
                 ☎ 0131 447 8888 68 ⇆ ♠

Murrayfield 43 Murrayfield Rd EH12 6EU
☎ 0131 337 3478
Parkland course on the side of Corstorphine Hill, with
fine views.
18 holes, 5725yds, Par 70, SSS 69.
Club membership 750.
Visitors   contact in advance, may not play at weekends.
Green Fees £28 per day; £22 per round.
Facilities   ⊗ ⅖ ⬛ ♀ ⅄ 🖻 ⅌ ♦ J J Fisher.
Leisure   trolley for hire, putting green, practice area.
Location   2m W of city centre off A8
Hotel   B Forte Posthouse Edinburgh, Corstorphine Rd,
                 EDINBURGH
                 ☎ 0131 334 0390 204 ⇆ ♠

Portobello Stanley St EH15 1JJ
☎ 0131 669 4361
Public parkland course, easy walking.
9 holes, 2400yds, Par 32, SSS 32.
Club membership 70.
Visitors   may not play Sat 8.30-10am & 12.30-2pm and
                 on competition days.
Societies   must contact in advance.
Green Fees not confirmed.
Facilities   ⅌
Leisure   trolley hire.
Location   3m E of city centre off A1
Hotel   ★★★ 59% Donmaree Hotel, 21 Mayfield
                 Gardens, EDINBURGH
                 ☎ 0131 667 3641 15 ⇆ ♠Annexe2 ⇆ ♠

Prestonfield Priestfield Rd North EH16 5HS
☎ 0131 667 9665
Parkland course with beautiful views.
18 holes, 6212yds, Par 70, SSS 70, Course record 62.
Club membership 850.
Visitors   contact secretary in advance.
Societies   must contact secretary.
Green Fees £30 per day; £20 per round (£40 per day; £30
                 per round weekends & bank holidays).
Facilities   ⊗ ⅷ ⅖ ⬛ ♀ ⅄ 🖻 ⅌ ♦ Graham MacDonald.
Leisure   trolley for hire, putting green, practice area.
Location   1.5m S of city centre off A68
Hotel   ★★★ 59% Donmaree Hotel, 21 Mayfield
                 Gardens, EDINBURGH
                 ☎ 0131 667 3641 15 ⇆ ♠Annexe2 ⇆ ♠

Ravelston 24 Ravelston Dykes Rd EH4 5NZ
☎ 0131 315 2486
Parkland course.
9 holes, 5200yds, Par 66, SSS 65, Course record 64.
Club membership 610.
Visitors   must contact in advance but may not play at
                 weekends & bank holidays.
Green Fees £15 per round.
Facilities   ⬛ ⅄
Leisure   practice nets.
Location   3m W of city centre off A90
Hotel   B Forte Posthouse Edinburgh, Corstorphine Rd,
                 EDINBURGH
                 ☎ 0131 334 0390 204 ⇆ ♠

Royal Burgess 181 Whitehouse Rd, Barnton EH4 6BZ
☎ 0131 339 2075
No mention of golf clubs would be complete without
mention of the Royal Burgess, which was instituted in
1735, thus being the oldest golfing society in the world.
Its course is a pleasant parkland, and one with very much
variety. A club which all those interested in the history of
the game should visit.
18 holes, 6111yds, Par 71, SSS 71, Course record 66.
Club membership 620.
Visitors   must contact in advance. Gentlemen only.
Societies   must contact in advance.
Green Fees not confirmed.
Facilities   ♀ ⅄ 🖻 ⅌ ♦ George Yuille.
Location   5m W of city centre off A90
Hotel   ★★★ 64% The Barnton Thistle,
                 Queensferry Rd, Barnton, EDINBURGH
                 ☎ 0131 339 1144 50 ⇆ ♠

Silverknowes Silverknowes, Parkway EH4 5ET
☎ 0131 336 3843
Public links course on coast overlooking the Firth of Forth.
18 holes, 6216yds, Par 71, SSS 70.
Club membership 500.
Visitors   restricted Sat & Sun.
Societies   must apply in writing to: Leisure Management
                 Unit, Meadowbank Sports Centre, London Road,
                 Edinburgh.
Green Fees not confirmed.
Facilities   🖻 ⅌
Leisure   putting,trolley hire,practice area.
Location   4m NW of city centre N of A902
Hotel   ★★ 65% Murrayfield Hotel, 18 Corstorphine
                 Rd, EDINBURGH
                 ☎ 0131 337 1844 23 ⇆ ♠Annexe10 ♠

Swanston 111 Swanston Rd, Fairmilehead EH10 7DS
☎ 0131 445 2239
Hillside course with steep climb at 12th & 13th holes.
18 holes, 5024yds, Par 66, SSS 65.
Visitors   contact in advance. Must contact in advance.
Societies   telephone for details.
Green Fees £18 per day; £12 per round (£22/£17 weekends
                 & public holidays).
Facilities   ⊗ ⅷ ⅖ ⬛ ♀ ⅄ 🖻 ♦
Location   4m S of city centre off B701
Hotel   ★★★ 67% Braid Hills Hotel, 134 Braid Rd,
                 Braid Hills, EDINBURGH
                 ☎ 0131 447 8888 68 ⇆ ♠

Torphin Hill Torphin Rd, Colinton EH13 0PG
☎ 0131 441 1100
Beautiful hillside, heathland course, with fine views of
Edinburgh and the Forth Estuary.
18 holes, 4580mtrs, Par 67, SSS 66, Course record 64.
Club membership 550.
Visitors   must contact in advance.
Societies   must contact in advance.
Green Fees £15 per day (£25 weekends).
Facilities ⊗ Ⅻ ┗ ⬤ ♀ ♨ 🏠 ⌘ Jamie Browne.
Leisure   putting green, practice area.
Location   5m SW of city centre S of A720
Hotel   ★★★ 67% Braid Hills Hotel, 134 Braid Rd,
            Braid Hills, EDINBURGH
            ☎ 0131 447 8888 68 ⇋ ⌘

Turnhouse 154 Turnhouse Rd EH12 0AD
☎ 0131 339 1014
Hilly, parkland/heathland course, good views.
18 holes, 5622yds, Par 69, SSS 70, Course record 63.
Club membership 800.
Visitors   may not play at weekends or Wed.
Societies   must contact in writing.
Green Fees not £24 per day, £16 per round.
Facilities ⊗ Ⅻ ┗ ⬤ ♀ ♨ 🏠 ⌘ John Murray.
Leisure   buggies for hire, trolley for hire, putting green,
            practice area.
Location   6m W of city centre N of A8
Hotel   ★★★ 64% The Barnton Thistle, Queensferry
            Rd, Barnton, EDINBURGH
            ☎ 0131 339 1144 50 ⇋ ⌘

EDZELL   Map 15 NO66

Edzell High St DD9 7TF
☎ 01356 647283 (Secretary) & 648462 (Pro)
This delightful course is situated in the foothills of the
Scottish Highlands and provides good golf as well as
conveying to everyone who plays there a feeling of peace
and quiet. The village of Edzell is one of the most
picturesque in Scotland.
18 holes, 6348yds, Par 71, SSS 71, Course record 65.
Club membership 650.
Visitors   may not play 4.45-6.15 weekdays & 7.30-
            10, 12-2 weekends. Not before 2pm on 1st
            Sat each month.
Societies   must contact secretary at least 14 days in
            advance.
Green Fees £25.50 per day; £19 per round (£37.50 per
            day; £25 per round weekends & bank
            holidays). Weekday rates after 4pm
            weekends.
Facilities ⊗ Ⅻ ┗ ⬤ ♀ ♨ 🏠 ⌘ A J Webster.
Leisure   trolley for hire, putting green, practice area.
Location   S side of village on B966
Hotel   ★★★ 62% Glenesk Hotel, High St,
            EDZELL
            ☎ 01356 648319 25rm(23 ⇋ ⌘)

Entries with a shaded background identify
courses that are considered to be particularly
interesting

ELIE   Map 12 NO40

Golf House Club KY9 1AS ☎ 01333 330301
One of Scotland's most delightful holiday courses with
panoramic views over the Firth of Forth. Some of the
holes out towards the rocky coastline are splendid. This
is the course which has produced many good
professionals, including the immortal James Braid.
18 holes, 6273yds, Par 70, SSS 69, Course record 62.
Club membership 600.
Visitors   advisable to contact in advance, limited
            availability at weekends May-Sep.
Societies   must contact in advance.
Green Fees £40 per day; £28.50 per round (£50/£36
            weekends).
Facilities ⊗ Ⅻ ┗ ⬤ ♀ ♨ 🏠 ⌘ Robin Wilson.
Leisure   hard tennis courts, trolley for hire, driving
            range, putting green, practice area.
Location   W side of village off A917
Hotel   ★★★ 69% Old Manor Hotel, Leven Rd,
            LUNDIN LINKS
            ☎ 01333 320368 19 ⇋ ⌘

FALKIRK   Map 11 NS88

Falkirk 136 Stirling Rd, Camelon FK2 7YP
☎ 01324 611061
Parkland course with trees, gorse and streams.
18 holes, 6230yds, Par 71, SSS 70, Course record 66.
Club membership 800.
Visitors   telephone starter 01324 612219, visiting parties
            only on Sun.
Societies   telephone 01324 612219 in advance.
Green Fees £20 per day; £15 per round (weekdays). £30 per
            day on Sun..
Facilities ⊗ Ⅻ ┗ ⬤ ♀ ♨ 🏠 ⌘ Colin Gillies.
Leisure   trolley for hire, putting green, practice area.
Location   1.5m W on A9
Hotel   ★★★ 68% Inchyra Grange Hotel, Grange Rd,
            POLMONT ☎ 01324 711911 43 ⇋ ⌘

FALKLAND   Map 11 NO20

Falkland The Myre KY7 7AA ☎ 01337 857404
A flat, well kept course with excellent greens and views of
East Lomond Hill and Falkland Palace.
9 holes, 5216yds, Par 68, SSS 65, Course record 62.
Club membership 325.
Visitors   parties must make prior arrangements.
Societies   must contact in advance.
Green Fees not confirmed.
Facilities ♀ ♨
Location   N side of town on A912
Hotel   ★★ 65% Lomond Hills Hotel, Parliament
            Square, FREUCHIE
            ☎ 01337 857329 & 857498 25 ⇋ ⌘

FAULDHOUSE   Map 11 NS96

Greenburn 6 Greenburn Rd EH47 9HG ☎ 01501 770292
Exposed rolling course with sparse tree cover. Water hazards
from a pond and a burn.
18 holes, 6045yds, Par 71, SSS 70, Course record 65.
Club membership 800.   ▶

Visitors contact for details.
Societies by prior arrangement.
Green Fees £19 per day; £13 per round (£23/£16 weekends).
Facilities ⊗ ℿ ⓛ ♥ ♀ ⚘ 🏌 Malcolm Leighton.
Leisure trolley for hire, putting green, practice area.
Location 3m SW of Whitburn
Hotel ★★ 56% Dreadnought Hotel, 17/19 Whitburn Rd, BATHGATE
☎ 01506 630791 19rm(18 ⇄ ⋔)

FORFAR

Map 15 NO45

Forfar Cunninghill, Arbroath Rd DD8 2RL
☎ 01307 463773 & 462120
Moorland course with wooded, undulating fairways and fine views.
18 holes, 6053yds, Par 69, SSS 70, Course record 61.
Club membership 820.
Visitors no restrictions.
Societies must contact in advance.
Green Fees £24 per day; £16 per round (£32 weekends & bank holidays £20 after 3pm).
Facilities ⊗ ℿ ⓛ ♥ ♀ ⚘ 🏌 Peter McNiven.
Leisure trolley for hire, putting green, practice area.
Location 1.5m E of Forfar on A932
Hotel ★★★⚌ 64% Idvies House Hotel, Letham, FORFAR ☎ 01307 818787 10 ⇄ ⋔

GIFFORD

Map 12 NT56

Gifford Edinburgh Rd EH41 4QN ☎ 01620 810267
Parkland course, with easy walking.
9 holes, 6243yds, Par 71, SSS 70, Course record 64.
Club membership 470.
Visitors restricted weekends, not after 4pm Sat & noon Sun.
Societies telephone in advance.
Green Fees £10 per day (£10 per round weekends).
Facilities ⚘
Leisure trolley for hire, putting green, practice area.
Location 1m SW off B6355
Hotel ★★ 69% Tweeddale Arms Hotel, GIFFORD
☎ 01620 810240 16 ⇄ ⋔

GIGHA ISLAND

Map 10 NR64

Gigha PA41 7AA ☎ 01583 505287
A 9-hole course with scenic views of the Sound of Gigha to the east and to the north the Kilberry Hills. The 9th hole is a good par 3, especially with a strong blow of wind from the west.
9 holes, 5042 yds, Par 66, SSS 65.
Club membership 40.

Visitors no restrictions.
Societies telephone for details.
Green Fees £10 per day; £7 per 18 holes.
Facilities ⚘
Location 0.5m N of Druimeonbeg farm shop

GLENROTHES

Map 11 NO20

Glenrothes Golf Course Rd KY6 2LA
☎ 01592 754561 & 758686
Testing and hilly parkland course with burn crossed four times. Good views.
18 holes, 6444yds, Par 71, SSS 71, Course record 67.
Club membership 770.
Visitors no restrictions.
Societies write to secretary.
Green Fees £17 per day; £10 per round (£19/£12.50 weekends). Prices under review.
Facilities ⊗ ℿ ⓛ ♥ ♀ ⚘
Leisure putting green, practice area.
Location W side of town off B921
Hotel ★★★ 69% Balgeddie House Hotel, Balgeddie Way, GLENROTHES
☎ 01592 742511 18 ⇄ ⋔

GLENSHEE (SPITTAL OF)

Map 15 NO16

Dalmunzie Dalmunzie Estate PH10 7QG
☎ 01250 885226
Well maintained Highland course with difficult walking. Testing 5th hole. Small but good greens.
9 holes, 2035yds, Par 30, SSS 30.
Club membership 70.
Visitors restricted Sun 10.30-11.30am.
Societies advance contact preferred.
Green Fees £8.50 per day; £5 per round; £34 weekly.
Facilities ⊗ ℿ ♥ ♀ ⚘ 🏌 ⚘
Leisure hard tennis courts, fishing, stalking & clay pigeon shooting.
Location 2m NW of Spittal of Glenshee
Hotel ★★⚌ 65% Dalmunzie House Hotel, SPITTAL OF GLENSHEE
☎ 01250 885224 18rm(16 ⇄ ⋔)

GOREBRIDGE

Map 11 NT36

Vogrie Vogrie Estate Country Park EH23 4NU
☎ 01875 821716
A 9-hole municipal course located with a country park. The wide fairways are particularly suited to beginners.
9 holes, 2530yds, Par 33.
Visitors book by telephone 24 hrs in advance.
Green Fees not confirmed.

Dalmunzie House
the hotel in the hills

Spittal o' Glenshee, Blairgowrie, Perthshire PH10 7QG
Telephone: 01250 885224 Fax: 01250 885225
Family run country house with its own 9 hole golf course offers 16 bedrooms with private bathroom, log fire, personal service and 'Taste of Scotland' cooking. Many golf courses within 1 hours drive such as Blairgowrie, Alyth, Pitlochry, Kirriemuir, Aboyne and Ballater.

STB 3 CROWNS COMMENDED

Facilities ⛏
Location Off B6372
Hotel ★★★🏌 62% Johnstounburn House, HUMBIE
☎ 01875 833696 11rm(10 ⇄ ♞)Annexe9 ⇄ ♞

GOUROCK
Map 10 NS27

Gourock Cowal View PA19 6HD
☎ 01475 631001
Moorland course with hills and dells. Testing 8th hole, par 5.
Magnificent views over Firth of Clyde.
18 holes, 6492yds, Par 73, SSS 73, Course record 64.
Club membership 720.
Visitors by introduction or with member.
Societies welcome weekdays, must contact in advance.
Green Fees not confirmed.
Facilities ♀⛏🏠⚲ʈ A M Green.
Leisure putting,trolley hire,practice area.
Location SW side of town off A770
Hotel ★★★🏌 63% Manor Park Hotel, LARGS
☎ 01475 520832 10 ⇄ ♞Annexe13 ⇄ ♞

GREENOCK
Map 10 NS27

Greenock Forsyth St PA16 8RE
☎ 01475 720793
Testing moorland course with panoramic views of Clyde
Estuary.
18 holes, 5838yds, Par 69, SSS 69.
Club membership 730.
Visitors may not play Sat. Must contact in advance and
have a handicap certificate.
Societies must telephone in advance.
Green Fees not confirmed.
Facilities ♀⛏🏠ʈ Graham Ross.
Leisure Putting green,trolley hire.
Location SW side of town off A770
Hotel ★★★🏌 63% Manor Park Hotel, LARGS
☎ 01475 520832 10 ⇄ ♞Annexe13 ⇄ ♞

Whinhill Beith Rd PA16 9LN
☎ 01475 724694 evenings & weekends only
Picturesque heathland public course.
18 holes, 5454yds, Par 66, SSS 68, Course record 64.
Club membership 270.
Visitors may only use club facilities with member.
Green Fees not confirmed.
Facilities ♀⛏
Leisure putting green.
Location 1.5m SW off B7054
Hotel ★★★🏌 63% Manor Park Hotel, LARGS
☎ 01475 520832 10 ⇄ ♞Annexe13 ⇄ ♞

GULLANE
Map 12 NT48

Gullane EH31 2BB ☎ 01620 842255
Gullane is a delightful village and one of Scotland's great
golf centres. Gullane club was formed in 1882. There are
three Gullane courses and the No 1 is of championship
standard. It differs from most Scottish courses in as much
as it is of the downland type and really quite hilly. The
first tee is literally in the village. The views from the top
of the course are magnificent and stretch far and wide in
every direction - in fact, it is said that 14 counties can be
seen from the highest spot.

Course No 1: 18 holes, 6466yds, Par 71, SSS 72, Course
record 65.
Course No 2: 18 holes, 6244yds, Par 71, SSS 70.
Course No 3: 18 holes, 5251yds, Par 68, SSS 66.
Club membership 1200.
Visitors advance booking recommended.
Societies advance booking advised.
Green Fees Course No 1: £63 per day; £42 per round
(£53 per round weekends). Course No. 2:
£31.50 per day; £21 per round (£40/£26.50
weekends). Course No. 3: £19 per round;
£12.50 per round (£24/£16 weekends).
Facilities ⊗�𝄢🍴♀⛏🏠⚲ʈ Jimmy Hume.
Leisure motorised carts for hire, buggies for hire,
trolley for hire, putting green, practice area.
Location At west end of village on A198
Hotel ★★★(red)🏌 Greywalls Hotel, Muirfield,
GULLANE
☎ 01620 842144 17 ⇄ ♞Annexe5 ⇄ ♞

MUIRFIELD
(Honourable Company of Edinburgh Golfers) See page 293

HADDINGTON
Map 12 NT57

Haddington Amisfield Park EH41 4PT ☎ 01620 823627
Inland course, tree-lined and bunkered, but not hilly.
18 holes, 6280yds, Par 71, SSS 70.
Club membership 600.
Visitors may not play between 7am-10am & noon-2pm at
weekends. Must contact in advance.
Societies must contact in advance; deposits required.
Green Fees not confirmed.
Facilities ♀⛏🏠ʈ John Sandilands.
Leisure pool table.
Location E side off A613
Hotel ★★ 69% Tweeddale Arms Hotel, GIFFORD
☎ 01620 810240 16 ⇄ ♞

HELENSBURGH
Map 10 NS28

Helensburgh 25 East Abercromby St G84 9JD
☎ 01436 674173
Sporting moorland course with superb views of Loch
Lomond and River Clyde.
18 holes, 6104yds, Par 69, SSS 70, Course record 64.
Club membership 880.
Visitors may not play at weekends.
Societies must contact in writing.
Green Fees £23.50 per day; £15.50 per round.
Facilities ⊗𝄢🍴♀⛏🏠⚲ʈ David Fotheringham.
Leisure trolley for hire, driving range, putting green,
practice area.
Location NE side of town off B832
Hotel ★★ 68% Commodore Toby Hotel, 112 West
Clyde St, HELENSBURGH
☎ 01436 676924 45 ⇄ ♞

INNELLAN
Map 10 NS17

Innellan Knockamillie Rd PA23 7SG
☎ 01369 830242 & 703327
Situated above the village of Innellan, this undulating hilltop
course has extensive views of the Firth of Clyde. ▶

9 holes, 4683yds, Par 64, SSS 64, Course record 63.
Club membership 199.

Visitors	welcome but may not play after 5pm on Mondays.
Societies	telephone initially.
Green Fees	£8 (£10 weekends).
Facilities	ⓑ ☕ ♀
Location	4m S of Dunoon
Hotel	★★ 76% Enmore Hotel, Marine Pde, Kirn, DUNOON ☎ 01369 702230 11 ⇄ ♥

INVERARAY
Map 10 NN00

Inveraray Lochgilphead Rd ☎ 01499 302508
Testing parkland course with beautiful views overlooking Loch Fyne.
9 holes, 5790yds, Par 70, SSS 68.
Club membership 130.

Visitors	welcome.
Societies	write or telephone to the secretary.
Green Fees	£10 per 18 holes.
Facilities	⚒
Leisure	practice area.
Location	1m S of Inveraray
Hotel	★ 64% Fernpoint Hotel, INVERARAY ☎ 01499 302170 7 ⇄ ♥

ISLAY, ISLE OF
Map 10 NR34

PORT ELLEN
Map 10 NR34

Machrie Hotel Machrie PA42 7AN ☎ 01496 302310
Championship links course opened in 1891, where golf's first £100 Open Championship was played in 1901. Fine turf and many blind holes. Par 4.
18 holes, 6226yds, Par 71, SSS 71, Course record 65.
Club membership 250.

Visitors	no restrictions.
Societies	apply in writing.
Green Fees	£25 per day; £16.50 per round.
Facilities	⊗ ⋔ ⓑ ☕ ♀ ⚒ ☎ ♉ ☳
Leisure	fishing, buggies for hire, trolley for hire, putting green, practice area.
Location	4m N off A846
Hotel	★★ 57% Lochside Hotel, 19 Shore St, BOWMORE ☎ 01496 810244 8 ⇄ ♥

KENMORE
Map 14 NN74

Kenmore PH15 2HN ☎ 01887 830226
Testing course in mildly undulating natural terrain. Beautiful views in tranquil setting by Loch Tay.
9 holes, 6052yds, Par 70, SSS 69, Course record 71.
Club membership 100.

Visitors	advance booking advisable.
Societies	telephone in advance.
Green Fees	£16 per day; £10 per 18 holes; £7 per 9 holes (£18/£12/£8 weekends).
Facilities	⊗ ⋔ ⓑ ☕ ♀ ⚒ ☎ ♉ ☳
Leisure	fishing, motorised carts for hire, buggies for hire, trolley for hire, putting green, practice area.
Location	On A827

Hotel	★★ 59% Fortingall Hotel, FORTINGALL ☎ 01887 830367 & 830368 9 ⇄ ♥

Taymouth Castle PH15 2NT ☎ 01887 830228
Parkland course set amidst beautiful mountain and loch scenery. Easy walking. Fishing.
18 holes, 6066yds, Par 69, SSS 69, Course record 62.
Club membership 250.

Visitors	must book in advance.
Societies	must contact in advance.
Green Fees	£26 per day; £16 round (£36/£20 weekends).
Facilities	⊗ ⋔ ⓑ ☕ ♀ ⚒ ☎ ♉ ☳
Leisure	fishing, motorised carts for hire, buggies for hire, trolley for hire, putting green, practice area.
Location	1m E on A827
Hotel	★★ 59% Fortingall Hotel, FORTINGALL ☎ 01887 830367 & 830368 9 ⇄ ♥

KILLIN
Map 11 NN53

Killin FK21 8TX ☎ 01567 820312
Parkland course with good views. Glorious setting.
9 holes, 2600yds, Par 66, SSS 65, Course record 61.
Club membership 250.

Visitors	may not play competition days.
Societies	previous record of courses visited required.
Green Fees	£14 per day; £11 per round; £40 per week 5 days.
Facilities	⊗ ⋔ ⓑ ☕ ♀ ⚒ ☎ ♉
Leisure	motorised carts for hire, buggies for hire, trolley for hire, putting green, practice area.
Location	1m N on A827
Hotel	★★★ 59% Dall Lodge Country House Hotel, Main St, KILLIN ☎ 01567 820217 10 ⇄ ♥

KILMACOLM
Map 10 NS36

Kilmacolm Porterfield Rd PA13 4PD ☎ 01505 872139
Moorland course, easy walking, fine views. Testing 7th, 13th and 14th holes.
18 holes, 5961yds, Par 69, SSS 69, Course record 64.
Club membership 850.

Visitors	must contact in advance.
Societies	apply in writing.
Green Fees	£30 per day; £20 per round.
Facilities	⊗ ⓑ ☕ ♀ ⚒ ☎ ♉ David Stewart.
Leisure	trolley for hire, driving range, putting green, practice area.
Location	SE side of town off A761
Hotel	★★★★ 72% Gleddoch House Hotel, LANGBANK ☎ 01475 540711 39 ⇄ ♥

KINCARDINE
Map 11 NS98

Tulliallan Alloa Rd FK10 4BB ☎ 01259 730396
Partially hilly parkland course with testing 3rd hole (par 4).
18 holes, 5982yds, Par 69, SSS 69.
Club membership 525.

Visitors	restricted at weekends.
Societies	may not play on Sat; must contact in advance.
Green Fees	not confirmed.
Facilities	♀ ⚒ ☎ ♉ ♉ Steven Kelly.
Location	1m NW on A977
Hotel	★★★ 59% Dall Lodge Country House Hotel, Main St, KILLIN ☎ 01567 820217 10 ⇄ ♥

MUIRFIELD

(Honourable Company of Edinburgh Golfers)

GULLANE *East Lothian* ☎ **01620 842123   Map 12 NT 48**

John Ingham writes: Ask an American superstar to name the best golf course in Great Britain, or maybe even in the entire world, and the likely answer will be Muirfield. It certainly features in the top ten of any meaningful selection.

Purely on shape and balance, the course has everything. Ask competitors in the Open Championship what they think of the last nine holes, and they will tell you it can wreck the stoutest heart. But ask Isoa Aoki of Japan what he thinks, and he will smile and maybe tell of his course record 63 here.

Established in 1744, it is just ten years older than the Royal & Ancient itself but not as old as Royal Blackheath. However, these dates show that Muirfield certainly has seniority and tradition. Quite simply, it is exclusive and entirely excellent. Muirfield has staged some outstanding Open Championships with one, I suspect, standing out in people's minds more than any other.

Back in 1972, Tony Jacklin was Europe's best player and looked set to prove it again at Muirfield when he had appeared to wear down Lee Trevino, the defending champion. At the 71st hole, Trevino seemed to be frittering away strokes as he mis-hit a shot downwind through the dry, fast, green. The next few minutes were truly hair-raising 'I was mad' recalled Trevino. 'My next shot from the bank was strictly a give-up one. And the ball went straight in the hole.' Jacklin had chipped up, well short. Then he missed his putt, turned for the return putt, and missed again. We all did mental arithmetic. Jacklin had blown it and when he bogeyed the last, furious at himself, he suddenly wasn't the winner - Trevino was.

Those of us who were there recall Trevino had holed one bunker shot, and chipped in three times. Muirfield looked on his brilliance with favour and sad Jacklin never won an Open again.

Visitors	Tue & Thur only; contact in advance and have handicap certificate
Societies	telephone in advance. But restricted to Tue and Thur
Green fees	£77 per day; £57 per round
Facilities	⊗ ☕ ♀ ⅄ ⚐ practice area, putting green
Location	Duncur Rd, Muirfield, Gullane EH31 2EG (off A198 on NE side of village)

18 holes, 6601 yards, Par 70, SSS 73, Course record 63 (R Davies, Isoa Aoki).

WHERE TO STAY AND EAT NEARBY

HOTELS:

ABERLADY
★★ 67% Kilspindie House, Main St. ☎ 01875 870682.   26 (8 ⚑ 18 ⇌ ⚑)

GULLANE
★★★(Red)⊛⊛ ♨ Greywalls, Muirfield. ☎ 01620 842144. 17 ⇌ ⚑ Annexe 5 ⇌ ⚑

NORTH BERWICK
★★★ 65% The Marine, Cromwell Rd. ☎ 01620 892406.   83 (3 ⇌ 80 ⇌ ⚑)

★★ 62% Nether Abbey, 20 Dirleton Ave. ☎ 01620 892802.   16 (6 ⚑ 4 ⇌)

★★ 64% Point Garry, West Bay Rd. ☎ 01620 892380. 15(8 ⚑ 2 ⇌ 5 ⇌ ⚑)

RESTAURANT:

GULLANE
⊛⊛⊛ La Potinière, Main St. ☎ 01620 843214.

KINGHORN   Map 11 NT28

Kinghorn Macduff Cres KY3 9RE ☎ 01592 890345
Municipal course, 300 ft above sea level with views over
Firth of Forth and North Sea. Undulating and quite testing.
Facilities shared by Kinghorn Ladies.
18 holes, 5269yds, Par 65, SSS 67.
Club membership 190.
Visitors   no restrictions.
Societies   must contact in writing.
Green Fees not confirmed.
Facilities   ♀♣
Location   S side of town on A921
Hotel   ★★★ 57% Dean Park Hotel, Chapel Level,
              KIRKCALDY
              ☎ 01592 261635 20 ⇥ ⚑Annexe12 ⚑

KINROSS   Map 11 NO10

Green Hotel 2 The Muirs KY13 7AS ☎ 01577 863407
Two interesting and picturesque parkland courses, with easy
walking.
Red Course: 18 holes, 6257yds, Par 72, SSS 70.
Blue Course: 18 holes, 6456yds, Par 71, SSS 71.
Club membership 600.
Visitors   must contact in advance.
Societies   must contact in advance.
Green Fees £25 per day; £15 per round (£35/£25 weekends).
Facilities   ⊗ ⫪ ⭐ 🍺 ♀♣ 🏠 ⚑ 🚽 ⚑ Stuart Geraghty.
Leisure   hard tennis courts, heated indoor swimming
             pool, squash, fishing, sauna, solarium, trolley for
             hire, putting green, practice area.

Location   NE side of town on B996
Hotel   ★★★ 70% Green Hotel, 2 The Muirs,
              KINROSS ☎ 01577 863467 47 ⇥ ⚑

Kinross Beeches Park KY13 7EU ☎ 01577 862237
Parkland course on the banks of Loch Leven.
Blue Course: 18 holes, 6456yds, Par 71, SSS 71.
Red Course: 18 holes, 6257yds, Par 72, SSS 70.
Club membership 540.
Visitors   no restrictions.
Green Fees not confirmed.
Facilities   ♀♣ 🏠 ⚑ ⚑ Stuart Geraghty.
Leisure   caddy cars.
Location   NE side of town on B996
Hotel   ★★★ 70% Green Hotel, 2 The Muirs,
              KINROSS ☎ 01577 863467 47 ⇥ ⚑

KIRKCALDY   Map 11 NT29

Dunnikier Park Dunnikier Way KY1 3LP
☎ 01592 261599
Parkland, rolling fairways, not heavily bunkered, views of
Firth of Forth.
18 holes, 6036metres, Par 72, SSS 72, Course record 65.
Club membership 660.
Visitors   visitors must contact course starter in person.
Societies   apply in writing.
Green Fees £18 per day; £11 per round (£20/£15 weekends).
Facilities   ⊗ ⫪ ⭐ 🍺 ♀♣ 🏠 ⚑ Gregor Whyte.
Leisure   trolley for hire, practice area.
Location   2m N on B981
Hotel   ★★★ 57% Dean Park Hotel, Chapel Level,
              KIRKCALDY
              ☎ 01592 261635 20 ⇥ ⚑Annexe12 ⚑

Kirkcaldy Balwearie Rd KY2 5LT ☎ 01592 205240
Parkland course.
18 holes, 6004yds, Par 71, SSS 69, Course record 65.
Club membership 700.
Visitors   may not play Sat. Must contact in advance.
Societies   apply in writing.
Green Fees £20 per day; £15 per round (£30/£20 Sun).
Facilities   ⊗ ⫪ ⭐ 🍺 ♀♣ 🏠 ⚑ Scott McKay.
Leisure   trolley for hire, putting green, practice area.
Location   SW side of town off A910
Hotel   ★★★ 57% Dean Park Hotel, Chapel Level,
              KIRKCALDY
              ☎ 01592 261635 20 ⇥ ⚑Annexe12 ⚑

KIRRIEMUIR   Map 15 NO35

Kirriemuir Shielhill Rd, Northmuir DD8 4LN
☎ 01575 573317
Parkland and heathland course set at the foot of the Angus
glens, with good view.
18 holes, 5553yds, Par 68, SSS 67, Course record 62.
Club membership 750.
Visitors   must play with member at weekends.
Societies   must apply in advance, may not play weekends.
Green Fees £19 per day; £14 per round.
Facilities   ⊗ ⫪ ⭐ 🍺 ♀♣ 🏠 ⚑ A Caira.
Leisure   trolley for hire, putting green.
Location   1m N off B955
Hotel   ★★★🏆 73% Castleton House Hotel,
              GLAMIS ☎ 01307 840340 6 ⇥ ⚑

LADYBANK
Map 11 NO30

Ladybank Annsmuir KY15 7RA ☎ 01337 830814
Picturesque parkland/heathland course, popular with visitors.
Qualifying course for the British Open.
18 holes, 6641yds, Par 71, SSS 72, Course record 63.
Club membership 900.
Visitors advance booking essential.
Societies must telephone or write in advance.
Green Fees £35 per day; £26 per round.
Facilities ⊗ ⋔ ⓑ ⬛ ♀ ♨ ☎ ⚵ ⓒ Martin Gray.
Leisure motorised carts for hire, buggies for hire, trolley for hire, putting green, practice area.
Location N side of village off B9129
Hotel ★★ 65% Lomond Hills Hotel, Parliament Square, FREUCHIE
☎ 01337 857329 & 857498 25 ⇔ ⓒ

LARBERT
Map 11 NS88

Falkirk Tryst 86 Burnhead Rd FK5 4BD
☎ 01324 562054 & 562091
Moorland course, fairly level with trees and broom, well-bunkered. Winds can affect play.
18 holes, 6053yds, Par 70, SSS 69.
Club membership 850.
Visitors must contact in advance no play at weekends.
Societies visitors welcome Mon-Fri must book or phone depending on numbers.
Green Fees £25 per day; £15 per round.
Facilities ⊗ ⋔ ⓑ ⬛ ♀ ☎ ⚵ ⓒ Steven Dunsmore.
Leisure trolley for hire, putting green, practice area.
Location 1m NE off A88/B905
Hotel ★★★ 68% Inchyra Grange Hotel, Grange Rd, POLMONT ☎ 01324 711911 43 ⇔ ⓒ

Glenbervie Clubhouse Stirling Rd FK5 4SJ
☎ 01324 562605
Parkland course with good views.
18 holes, 6469yds, Par 70, SSS 70, Course record 65.
Club membership 600.
Visitors must contact in advance. May not play at weekends.
Societies Tue & Thu only. Apply in writing.
Green Fees not confirmed.
Facilities ♀ ♨ ☎ ⓒ John Chillas.
Location 2m NW on A9
Hotel ★★★ 68% Inchyra Grange Hotel, Grange Rd, POLMONT ☎ 01324 711911 43 ⇔ ⓒ

LESLIE
Map 11 NO20

Leslie Balsillie Laws KY6 3EZ ☎ 01592 620040
Challenging parkland course.
9 holes, 4686yds, Par 63, SSS 64, Course record 63.
Club membership 230.
Visitors contact secretary in writing.
Societies letter to the Secretary.
Green Fees £8 per day (£10 weekends).
Facilities ⊗ by prior arrangement ⋔ by prior arrangement ⓑ by prior arrangement ⬛ by prior arrangement ♨
Location N side of town off A911

Hotel ★★★ 69% Balgeddie House Hotel, Balgeddie Way, GLENROTHES
☎ 01592 742511 18 ⇔ ⓒ

LEUCHARS
Map 12 NO42

St Michael's KY16 0DX ☎ 01334 839365
Parkland course with open views over Fife and Tayside. The undulating course weaves its way through tree plantations. The short Par 4 7th, parallel to the railway and over a pond to a stepped green, poses an interesting challenge.
18 holes, 5802yds, Par 70.
Club membership 550.
Visitors may not play on Sun before noon.
Societies must apply in writing, limited weekends
Green Fees £22.50 per day; £15 per round.
Facilities ⊗ ⋔ ⓑ ⬛ ♀ ♨
Leisure trolley for hire, putting green.
Location NW side of village on A919
Hotel ★★ 65% St Michaels Inn, LEUCHARS
☎ 01334 839220 7 ⇔ ⓒ

LEVEN
Map 11 NO30

Leven Links The Promenade KY8 4HS
☎ 01333 428859
Leven Links has the classic ingredients which make up a golf links in Scotland; undulating fairways with hills and hallows, out of bounds and a 'burn' or stream. A top class championship links course used for British Open final qualifying stages, it has fine views over Largo Bay.
18 holes, 6436yds, Par 71, SSS 70, Course record 63.
Club membership 500.
Visitors contact in advance. Limited availability Fri pm & Sat, contact for these times no more than 5 days in advance.
Societies apply in advance.
Green Fees £30 per day; £20 per round (£36/£24 weekends).
Facilities ⊗ ⋔ ⓑ ⬛ ♀ ♨ ☎ ⚵
Leisure trolley for hire, putting green, practice area.
Hotel ★★★ 56% Caledonian Hotel, 81 High St, LEVEN ☎ 01333 424101 24 ⇔ ⓒ

Scoonie North Links KY8 4SP ☎ 01333 27057
A pleasant inland links course suitable for all ages.
18 holes, 4967mtrs, SSS 66.
Club membership 150.
Visitors no restrictions.
Societies apply in writing.
Green Fees not confirmed.
Facilities ♀ ♨ ⚵
Hotel ★★★ 56% Caledonian Hotel, 81 High St, LEVEN ☎ 01333 424101 24 ⇔ ⓒ

LINLITHGOW
Map 11 NS97

Linlithgow Braehead EH49 6QF ☎ 01506 842585
Slightly hilly parkland course in beautiful setting.
18 holes, 5800yds, Par 70, SSS 68.
Club membership 400.
Visitors may not play Sat. Must book in advance Sun.
Societies must contact in writing.
Green Fees not confirmed.
Facilities ♀ ♨ ☎ ⓒ Derek Smith. ▶

Location	1m S off Bathgate Road off A803
Hotel	★★★ 63% The Earl O'Moray Inn, Bonsyde, LINLITHGOW ☎ 01506 842229 8 ⇆ ⬥

West Lothian Airngath Hill EH49 7RH ☎ 01506 826030
Hilly parkland course with superb views of River Forth.
18 holes, 6406yds, Par 71, SSS 71, Course record 64.
Club membership 800.

Visitors	Weekends by arrangement. Advisable to contact in high season.
Societies	apply in writing.
Green Fees	£20 day ; £15 per round (£28/20 weekends).
Facilities	⊗ ⅃ 밤 ☕ ♀ ♨ 🏠 ♈ ℓ Neil Robertson.
Leisure	trolley for hire, putting green, practice area.
Location	1m S off A706
Hotel	★★★ 63% The Earl O'Moray Inn, Bonsyde, LINLITHGOW ☎ 01506 842229 8 ⇆ ⬥

LIVINGSTON
Map 11 NT06

Deer Park Golf & Country Club Golfcourse Rd EH54 9EG
☎ 01506 431037
Long testing course, fairly flat, championship standard.
18 holes, 6688yds, Par 72, SSS 72, Course record 65.
Club membership 650.

Visitors	must book in advance, Sun after 10am.
Societies	telephone or write
Green Fees	£22 per day; £16 per round (£36.50/£26 weekends).
Facilities	⊗ ⅃ 밤 ☕ ♀ ♨ 🏠 ♈ ℓ William Yule.
Leisure	heated indoor swimming pool, squash, sauna, solarium, gymnasium, motorised carts for hire, buggies for hire, trolley for hire, putting green, practice area.
Location	N side of town off A809
Hotel	★★ 56% Dreadnought Hotel, 17/19 Whitburn Rd, BATHGATE ☎ 01506 630791 19rm(18 ⇆ ⬥)

Pumpherston Drumshoreland Rd, Pumpherston EH53 0LF
☎ 01506 432122
Undulating parkland course with testing 6th hole (par 3), and
view of Pentland Hills.
9 holes, 5434yds, Par 66, SSS 67.
Club membership 430.

Visitors	must be accompanied by a member.
Societies	apply in writing to the secretary.
Green Fees	£10 per 18 holes with member.
Facilities	밤 ☕ ♀ ♨
Leisure	puttimg green, practice area.
Location	1m E between A71 & A89
Hotel	★★ 56% Dreadnought Hotel, 17/19 Whitburn Rd, BATHGATE ☎ 01506 630791 19rm(18 ⇆ ⬥)

LOCHGELLY
Map 11 NT19

Lochgelly Cartmore Rd KY5 9PB ☎ 01592 780174
Parkland course with easy walking and often windy.
18 holes, 5491yds, Par 68, SSS 67.
Club membership 650.

Visitors	no restrictions.
Societies	must apply in writing.
Green Fees	not confirmed.
Facilities	⊗ ⅃ 밤 ☕ ♀ ♨
Leisure	putting green.

Location	W side of town off A910
Hotel	★★★ 57% Dean Park Hotel, Chapel Level, KIRKCALDY ☎ 01592 261635 20 ⇆ ⬥Annexe12 ⬥

Lochore Meadows Lochore Meadows Country Park,
Crosshill KY5 8BA ☎ 01592 860086
Lochside course with natural stream running through, and
woodland nearby. Country park offers many leisure facilities.
9 holes, 5554yds, Par 72, SSS 71.
Club membership 200.

Visitors	no restrictions.
Societies	must contact in advance.
Green Fees	not confirmed.
Facilities	♨
Leisure	fishing, putting green,practice area.
Location	2m N off B920
Hotel	★★★ 70% Green Hotel, 2 The Muirs, KINROSS ☎ 01577 863467 47 ⇆ ⬥

LOCHGILPHEAD
Map 10 NR88

Lochgilphead Blarbuie Rd PA31 8LE ☎ 01546 602340
A varied course with short but interesting holes. Some
elevated greens and tees and some tight fairways.
9 holes, 2242yds, Par 64, SSS 63, Course record 58.
Club membership 250.

Visitors	restricted during weekend club competitions. apply in advance, restricted wekends.
Green Fees	£10 per day; £30 per week. Winter £5 per day.
Facilities	밤 by prior arrangement ☕ ♀ ♨ 🏠
Leisure	putting green, practice area.
Hotel	★★ 63% The Stag Hotel, Argyll St, LOCHGILPHEAD ☎ 01546 602496 17 ⇆ ⬥

LONGNIDDRY
Map 12 NT47

Longniddry Links Rd EH32 0NL ☎ 01875 852141
Undulating seaside links and partial parkland course. One
of the numerous courses which stretch east from
Edinburgh right to Dunbar. The inward half is more open
and less testing than the wooded outward half.
18 holes, 6219yds, Par 69, SSS 70, Course record 63.
Club membership 1000.

Visitors	may book tee times up to 7 days in advance, welcome most times except during competitions.
Societies	Mon-Thu, apply in writing, handicap certificate required.
Green Fees	£35 per day; £25 per round (£35 per round weekends).
Facilities	⊗ ⅃ 밤 ☕ ♀ ♨ 🏠 ♈ ℓ John Gray.
Leisure	trolley for hire, putting green, practice area.
Location	W side of village off A198
Hotel	★★ 67% Kilspindie House Hotel, Main St, ABERLADY ☎ 01875 870682 26 ⇆ ⬥

LUNDIN LINKS
Map 12 NO40

Lundin Golf Rd KY8 6BA ☎ 01333 320202
The Leven Links and the course of the Lundin Club
adjoin each other. The course is part seaside and part
inland. The holes are excellent but those which can be
described as seaside holes have a very different nature
from the inland style ones.

18 holes, 6387yds, Par 71, SSS 71, Course record 63.
Club membership 820.

Visitors	visitors welcome weekdays 9-3.30 (3pm Fridays) and Sat after 2.30pm, no vistors Sun. Book well in advance.
Societies	book well in advance by telephoning Secretary.
Green Fees	Mon-Fri £35 per day; £25 per round. Sat after 2.30pm £35 per round (Winter£15/£10/£15).
Facilities	⊗ Ⅻ ⓛ ♥ ♀ ♣ 🏠 ♛ David Webster.
Leisure	trolley for hire, putting green, practice area.
Location	W side of village off A915
Hotel	★★★ 69% Old Manor Hotel, Leven Rd, LUNDIN LINKS ☎ 01333 320368 19 ⇆ ♛ *See advertisement on page 302.*

Lundin Ladies Woodielea Rd KY8 6AR
☎ 01333 320832
Short, lowland course with Roman stones on the second
fairway, and coastal views.
9 holes, 2365yds, Par 68, SSS 67, Course record 67.
Club membership 350.

Visitors	contact in advance. Competition days Wed and some weekends.
Societies	telephone secretary.
Green Fees	£7.50 per day (£9.50 weekends).
Facilities	♣ ♛
Leisure	trolley for hire, putting green.
Location	W side of village off A915
Hotel	★★★ 69% Old Manor Hotel, Leven Rd, LUNDIN LINKS ☎ 01333 320368 19 ⇆ ♛

LUSS   Map 10 NS39

Loch Lomond Rossdhu House G83 8NT
☎ 01436 860223
This is a Members Only club. Visitors are not permitted to
play on this Tom Weiskopf/Jay Morrish designed course
except as guest of members.
18 holes, 6698yds, Par 72, SSS 72, Course record 69.
no visitors strictly private.

Facilities	♣ 🏠 ♛ Colin Campbell.

MACHRIHANISH   Map 10 NR62

Machrihanish PA28 6PT
☎ 01586 810213
Magnificent seaside links of championship status. The
1st holes is the famous drive across the Atlantic. Sandy
soil allows for play all year round. Large greens, easy
walking, windy. Fishing.
18 holes, 6228yds, Par 70, SSS 70.

Visitors	no restrictions.
Societies	apply in writing.
Green Fees	£28 per day; £20 per round (£35 per day Sat). Winter £20 per day.
Facilities	⊗ Ⅻ ⓛ ♥ ♀ ♣ 🏠 ♛
Location	5m W of Campbeltown on B843
Hotel	★★ 65% Seafield Hotel, Kilkerran Rd, CAMPBELTOWN ☎ 01586 554385 3 ♛Annexe6 ♛

MARKINCH   Map 11 NO20

Balbirnie Park Balbirnie Park KY7 6NR
☎ 01592 752006
Scenic parkland course with several interesting holes.
18 holes, 6214yds, Par 71, SSS 70, Course record 65.
Club membership 900.

Visitors	must contact in advance. Numbers restricted weekends and visitors must play from yellow tees.
Societies	booking forms sent out on request by asst secretary.
Green Fees	£28 per day; £20 per round (£36/£28 weekends).
Facilities	⊗ Ⅻ ⓛ ♥ ♀ ♣ 🏠 ♛
Leisure	trolley for hire, putting green.
Location	2m E of Glenrothes
Hotel	★★★★(red)♨ Balbirnie House, Balbirnie Park, MARKINCH ☎ 01592 610066 30 ⇆ ♛

MILNATHORT   Map 11 NO10

Milnathort South St KY13 7XA ☎ 01577 864069
Undulating parkland course.
9 holes, 5969yds, Par 71, SSS 69, Course record 65.
Club membership 600.

Visitors	must contact in advance.
Societies	advisable to book in advance.
Green Fees	£10 per day (£15 weekends).
Facilities	♥ ♀ ♣
Leisure	driving range, putting green, practice area.
Location	S side of town on A922
Hotel	★★★ 70% Green Hotel, 2 The Muirs, KINROSS ☎ 01577 863467 47 ⇆ ♛

MONIFIETH   Map 12 NO43

Monifieth The Links DD5 4AW ☎ 01382 532767
The chief of the two courses at Monifieth is the Medal
Course. It has been one of the qualifying venues for the
Open Championship on more than one occasion. A
seaside links, but divided from the sand dunes by a
railway which provides the principal hazard for the first
few holes. The 10th hole is outstanding, the 17th is
excellent and there is a delightful finishing hole. The
other course here is the Ashludie, and both are played
over by a number of clubs who share the links.
Medal Course: 18 holes, 6655yds, Par 71, SSS 72,
Course record 63.
Ashludie Course: 18 holes, 5123yds, Par 68, SSS 66.
Club membership 1750.

Visitors	must contact in advance. Restricted to after 2pm Sat & 10am Sun.
Societies	must contact in advance by telephone or writing to Medal Starter's Box, Princes St, Monifieth.
Green Fees	Medal Course: £32 per day, £22 per round (£38/£26 weekends). Ashludie Course: £20 per day, £14 per round (£22/£15 weekends).
Facilities	⊗ Ⅻ ⓛ ♥ ♀ ♣ 🏠 ♛ ♛ Ian McLeod.
Leisure	trolley for hire, putting green, practice area.
Location	NE side of town on A930
Hotel	★★ 67% Carlogie House Hotel, Carlogie Rd, CARNOUSTIE ☎ 01241 853185 12 ⇆ ♛Annexe1 ♛

MONTROSE GOLF COURSES

(Montrose Links Trust)

Medal Course, generally recognised as one of the oldest sites of golf in the world – ranked 5th.

INDIVIDUAL ROUND AND DAY TICKETS AVAILABLE ON BOTH COURSES . . . OR

GOLFERS – How's this for a great day out?

TWO LINKS COURSES: Medal Course Par 71, SSS 72
Broomfield Course Par 66, SSS 63

Available throughout the year for clubs, societies, parties and casual visitors.

Prices for 1997 range from £28.00 to £49.00 per day

This includes: 1 day's golf (36 holes), morning coffee and bacon roll, light lunch (soup and sandwiches), high tea.

Special packages available in conjunction with local hotels

Great Scottish Golf Tour ticket welcome here

Enquiries to: Mrs M Stewart, Secretary,
Montrose Links Trust, Traill Drive,
Montrose DD10 8SW.
Tel: 01674 672932
Fax: 01674 671800

MONTROSE Map 15 NO75

Montrose Links Trust Traill Dr DD10 8SW
☎ 01674 672932
The links at Montrose like many others in Scotland are on commonland and are shared by three clubs. The Medal course at Montrose - the fifth oldest in the world - is typical of Scottish seaside links, with narrow, undulating fairways and problems from the first hole to the last. The Broomfield course is flatter and easier.
Medal Course: 18 holes, 6470yds, Par 71, SSS 72, Course record 64.
Broomfield Course: 18 holes, 4765yds, Par 66, SSS 63.
Club membership 1300.
Visitors | may not play on the Medal Course on Sat & before 10am on Sun. Must have a handicap certificate for Medal Course. Contact in advance.
Societies | must contact secretary in advance.
Green Fees | not confirmed.
Facilities | ⊗ ⊞ ⅃ ♥ ♀ ♣ 🏠 ♈ ℓ Kevin Stables.
Leisure | trolley for hire, putting green, practice area.
Location | NE side of town off A92
Hotel | ★★★ 61% Park Hotel, 61 John St, MONTROSE
☎ 01674 673415 59rm(48 ⇆5 ℝ)

MUCKHART Map 11 NO00

Muckhart FK14 7JH ☎ 01259 781423
Scenic heathland/downland course.
18 holes, 6034yds, Par 71, SSS 70.

Club membership 750.
Visitors | telephone to book - steward 01259 781423 or professional 01259 781493.
Societies | booking by prior arrangement.
Green Fees | £20 per 36 holes; £14 per round (£28/£20 weekends).
Facilities | ⊗ ⊞ ⅃ ♥ ♀ ♣ 🏠 ♈ ℓ Keith Salmoni.
Leisure | trolley for hire, putting green, practice area.
Location | SW of village off A91
Hotel | ★★★ 66% Whinsmuir Country Inn, POWMILL
☎ 01577 840595 13 ⇆ ℝ

MULL, ISLE OF Map 10 NM73

CRAIGNURE Map 10 NM73

Craignure Scallastle PA65 6PB
A flat links course, overlooking the sea.
9 holes, 5072yds, Par 70, SSS 65, Course record 72.
Club membership 100.
Visitors | may not play on competition days.
Societies | write to the secretary in advance.
Green Fees | £9 per day; £40 per week.
Facilities | ♣ ♈
Location | 0.5m N of Craignure A849
Hotel | ★★★ 72% Western Isles Hotel, TOBERMORY ☎ 01688 302012 26 ⇆ ℝ

TOBERMORY Map 13 NM55

Tobermory PA75 6PE ☎ 01688 302020 & 302493
A physically demanding, hilly seaside cliff-top course. No sand-bunkers, superb views over the Sound of Mull. Testing 3rd hole (par 3) and interesting 7th much affected by the winds.
9 holes, 4890yds, Par 64, SSS 64, Course record 65.
Club membership 150.
Visitors | no restrictions except competition days.
Societies | prefrable to contact in advance.
Green Fees | £12 per day/round; £40 per week.
Facilities | ♈
Leisure | practice area.
Location | 0.5m N off A848
Hotel | ★★★ 72% Western Isles Hotel, TOBERMORY ☎ 01688 302012 26 ⇆ ℝ

MUSSELBURGH Map 11 NT37

Musselburgh Monktonhall EH21 6SA ☎ 0131 665 2005
Testing parkland course with natural hazards including trees and a burn, easy walking.
18 holes, 6614yds, Par 71, SSS 73, Course record 65.
Club membership 900.
Visitors | must contact in advance.
Societies | must contact in advance.
Green Fees | £25 per day; £17 per round (£30/£21 weekends).
Facilities | ⊗ ⊞ ⅃ ♥ ♀ ♣ 🏠 ♈ ℓ Fraser Mann.
Leisure | motorised carts for hire, buggies for hire, trolley for hire, putting green, practice area.
Location | 1m S on B6415
Hotel | ★★★ 59% Donmaree Hotel, 21 Mayfield Gardens, EDINBURGH
☎ 0131 667 3641 15 ⇆ ℝAnnexe2 ⇆ ℝ

Musselburgh Old Course Millhill EH21 7RP
☎ 0131 665 6981
A links type course.
9 holes, 2371yds, Par 33, SSS 33, Course record 67.
Club membership 70.
Visitors may not play at weekends.
Societies must contact in advance.
Green Fees not confirmed.
Facilities ♀ ᛤ
Location 1m E of town off A1
Hotel ★★★ 59% Donmaree Hotel, 21 Mayfield
Gardens, EDINBURGH
☎ 0131 667 3641 15 ⇥ ☞Annexe2 ⇥ ☞

MUTHILL
Map 11 NN81

Muthill Peat Rd PH5 2DA ☎ 01764 681523
Parkland course with fine views. Not too hilly, tight with
narrow fairways.
9 holes, 4700yds, Par 66, SSS 63.
Club membership 500.
Visitors no restrictions.
Societies book in advance.
Green Fees £12 per day (£15 weekends). 5 day ticket £40.
Facilities ⊗ ᛤ 🍷 ᛤ 🏠
Leisure trolley for hire, putting green.
Location W side of village off A822
Hotel ★★ 69% Murraypark Hotel, Connaught Ter,
CRIEFF ☎ 01764 653731 20 ⇥ ☞

NORTH BERWICK
Map 12 NT58

Glen East Links, Tantallon Ter EH39 4LE
☎ 01620 895288 & 892726
An interesting course with a good variety of holes. The views
of the town, the Firth of Forth and the Bass Rock are
breathtaking.
18 holes, 6089yds, Par 69, SSS 69, Course record 64.
Club membership 650.
Visitors booking advisable.
Societies advance booking recommended.
Green Fees £23 per day; £15.50 per round (£28/£20
weekends).
Facilities ⊗ ᛤ ᛤ 🍷 ♀ ᛤ 🏠 ᛏ
Leisure buggies for hire, trolley for hire, putting green,
practice area.
Location 1m E of B198
Hotel ★★ 62% Nether Abbey Hotel, 20 Dirleton Av,
NORTH BERWICK
☎ 01620 892802 16rm(4 ⇥6 ☞)

North Berwick Beach Rd EH39 4BB ☎ 01620 892135
Another of East Lothian's famous courses, the links at
North Berwick is still popular. A classic championship
links, it has many hazards including the beach, streams,
bunkers, light rough and low walls. The great hole on the
course is the 15th, the famous 'Redan', selected for
televisions best 18 in the UK. Used by both the Tantallon
and Bass Rock Golf Clubs.
18 holes, 6420yds, Par 71, SSS 71, Course record 64.
Club membership 730.
Visitors must contact in advance.
Societies must contact in advance.
Green Fees £40 per day; £22 per round (£55/£40
weekends).

Facilities ⊗ ᛤ ᛤ 🍷 ♀ ᛤ 🏠 ᛏ ᛤ D Huish.
Leisure trolley for hire, putting green, practice area.
Location W side of town on A198
Hotel ★★★ 63% The Marine Hotel, Cromwell
Rd, NORTH BERWICK
☎ 01620 892406 83 ⇥ ☞
Additional Q Castle Inn, DIRLETON
hotel ☎ 01620 850221 4 ⇥ ☞Annexe4rm

OBAN
Map 10 NM83

Glencruitten Glencruitten Rd PA34 4PU
☎ 01631 62868
There is plenty of space and considerable variety of hole
on this downland course - popular with holidaymakers. In
a beautiful, isolated situation, the course is hilly and
testing, particularly the 1st and 12th, par 4's, and 10th
and 15th, par 3's.
18 holes, 4452yds, Par 61, SSS 63, Course record 55.
Club membership 600.
Visitors restricted Thu & weekends
Societies must contact in writing.
Green Fees £15.50 per day; £12.50 per round
(£16.50/£14.50 weekends).
Facilities ⊗ ᛤ ᛤ 🍷 ♀ ᛤ 🏠
Leisure trolley for hire, practice area.
Location NE side of town centre off A816
Hotel ★★★ 55% Caledonian Hotel, Station
Square, OBAN
☎ 01631 563133 70 ⇥

The Castle Inn
Dirleton, North Berwick,
East Lothian EH39 5EP

Fully licensed hotel with 8 bedrooms,
4 en suite. Accommodates 14. Cask
conditioned ales. Bar lunches & suppers.

Warm, friendly atmosphere. Surrounded
by many well known golf courses –
North Berwick, Muirfield, Gullane
and Luffness

Open all year.
Telephone: (01620) 850221

PENICUIK   Map 11 NT25

Glencorse Milton Bridge EH26 0RD
☎ 01968 677189 & 676481
Picturesque parkland course with burn affecting ten holes.
Testing 5th hole (237 yds) par 3.
18 holes, 5217yds, Par 64, SSS 66, Course record 60.
Club membership 700.
Visitors	contact professional.
Societies	contact secretary for details.
Green Fees	£24 per day; £18 per round (£24 per round weekends and bank holidays).
Facilities	⊗ ℳ ⮮ ☂ ♀ ⚂ 🏠 ⌇ Cliffe Jones.
Leisure	trolley for hire, driving range, practice area.
Location	1.5m N of Penicuik on A701
Hotel	★★ 60% Roslin Glen Hotel, 2 Penicuik Rd, ROSLIN ☎ 0131 440 2029 7 ⇌ 🐾

PERTH   Map 11 NO12

Craigie Hill Cherrybank PH2 0NE
☎ 01738 620829 & 622644
Slightly hilly, parkland course. Good views over Perth.
18 holes, 5386yds, Par 66, SSS 67, Course record 60.
Club membership 560.
Visitors	restricted access Sat. Telephone up to 3 days in advance.
Societies	must contact in writing.
Green Fees	£20 per day; £15 per round (£25 Sun).
Facilities	⊗ ℳ ⮮ ☂ ♀ ⚂ 🏠 ⌇ Steven Harrier.
Leisure	trolley for hire, putting green, practice area.
Location	1m SW of city centre off A952
Hotel	★★★ 61% The Royal George, Tay St, PERTH ☎ 01738 624455 42 ⇌ 🐾

King James VI Moncreiffe Island PH2 8NR
☎ 01738 445132 (Secretary) & 632460 (Pro)
Parkland course, situated on island in the middle of River
Tay. Easy walking.
18 holes, 6038yds, Par 70, SSS 69, Course record 62.
Club membership 650.
Visitors	visitors restricted on competition days. Contact professional for bookings.
Societies	book by telephone.
Green Fees	£22 per day; £15 per round (£28/£18 weekends). Winter £9 per round..
Facilities	⊗ ℳ ⮮ ☂ ♀ ⚂ 🏠 ⌇ Tom Coles.
Leisure	buggies for hire, trolley for hire, putting green, practice area.
Location	SE side of city centre
Hotel	★★★ 61% Queens Hotel, Leonard St, PERTH ☎ 01738 442222 51 ⇌ 🐾

Murrayshall Country House Hotel Murrayshall, Scone
PH2 7PH ☎ 01738 552784
This course is laid out in 130 acres of parkland with tree-lined
fairways. Hotel and driving range.
18 holes, 6446yds, Par 73, SSS 71.
Club membership 350.
Visitors	no restrictions.
Societies	telephone in advance.
Green Fees	£30 per day; £20 per round (£40 per day; £25 per round weekends).
Facilities	⊗ ℳ ⮮ ☂ ♀ ⚂ 🏠 ⌇ 🛒 ⌇ George Finlayson.
Leisure	hard tennis courts, motorised carts for hire, buggies for hire, trolley for hire, driving range, putting green, practice area.
Location	E side of village off A94
Hotel	★★★ 74% Murrayshall Country House Hotel & Golf Course, New Scone, PERTH ☎ 01738 551171 19 ⇌ 🐾
Additional hotel	★★ 65% The Tayside Hotel, Mill St, Stanley ☎ 01738 828249 16rm(4 ⇌ 10 🐾)

North Inch North Inch, off Hay St PH1 5PH
☎ 01738 636481
An enjoyable short and often testing course incorporating
mature trees, open parkland with fine views and attractive
riverside.
18 holes, 5178yds, Par 65, Course record 60.
Club membership 476.
Visitors	advisable to telephone in advance.
Green Fees	£3.20-£7.40.
Facilities	⊗ ⮮ ☂ ♀
Leisure	squash, gymnasium, trolley for hire, putting green.
Hotel	★★★ 61% The Royal George, Tay St, PERTH ☎ 01738 624455 42 ⇌ 🐾

PITLOCHRY   Map 14 NN95

Pitlochry Pitlochry Estate Office PH16 5QY
☎ 01796 472792
A varied and interesting heathland course with fine views
and posing many problems. Its SSS permits few errors in
its achievement.
18 holes, 5811yds, Par 69, SSS 68.
Club membership 400.
Visitors	may not play before 9.30am.
Societies	must contact in writing.
Green Fees	not confirmed.
Facilities	♀ ⚂ 🏠 🛒 ⌇ George Hampton.
Location	N side of town off A924
Hotel	★★★ 72% Pine Trees Hotel, Strathview Ter, PITLOCHRY ☎ 01796 472121 20rm(19 ⇌ 🐾)

POLMONT

Map 11 NS97

Grangemouth Polmont Hill FK2 0YE
☎ 01324 711500
Windy parkland course. Testing holes: 3rd, 4th (par 4's); 5th
(par 5); 7th (par 3) 216 yds over reservoir (elevated green);
8th, 9th, 18th (par 4's).
18 holes, 6314yds, Par 71, SSS 71.
Club membership 700.
Visitors must contact in advance.
Societies must contact in writing.
Green Fees not confirmed.
Facilities ♀ △ 🏠 ℓ
Leisure pool tables.
Location On unclass rd 0.5m N of M9 junc 4
Hotel ★★★ 68% Inchyra Grange Hotel, Grange Rd,
POLMONT
☎ 01324 711911 43 ⇔ 🐾

Polmont Manuelrigg, Maddiston FK2 0LS
☎ 01324 711277
Parkland course, hilly with few bunkers. Views of the River
Forth and Ochil Hills.
9 holes, 3073yds, Par 72, SSS 69, Course record 71.
Club membership 300.
Visitors no visitors on Sat, Mon-Fri must tee of before 5pm.
Societies apply in writing to club secretary.
Green Fees £7 per 18 holes (£12 Sun).
Facilities ⊗ ⅷ ⅃ 🍺 ♀ △
Leisure putting green.
Location E side of village off A803
Hotel ★★★ 68% Inchyra Grange Hotel, Grange Rd,
POLMONT
☎ 01324 711911 43 ⇔ 🐾

PORT GLASGOW

Map 10 NS37

Port Glasgow Devol Rd PA14 5XE ☎ 01475 704181
A moorland course set on a hilltop overlooking the Clyde,
with magnificent views to the Cowal hills.
18 holes, 5712yds, Par 68, SSS 68.
Club membership 390.
Visitors may not play on Sat.
Societies apply in writing.
Green Fees not confirmed.
Facilities ♀ △ 🏠
Leisure putting green.
Location 1m S
Hotel ★★★⚕ 72% Gleddoch House Hotel,
LANGBANK
☎ 01475 540711 39 ⇔ 🐾

PRESTONPANS

Map 11 NT37

Royal Musselburgh Prestongrange House EH32 9RP
☎ 01875 810276
Tree-lined parkland course overlooking Firth of Forth.
18 holes, 6237yds, Par 70, SSS 70, Course record 64.
Club membership 970.
Visitors must contact professional in advance, restricted
Fri afternoons & weekends.
Societies must contact in advance,
Green Fees £35 per day; £20 per round (£35 round
weekends).

Facilities ⊗ ⅷ ⅃ 🍺 ♀ △ 🏠 🍴 ℓ John Henderson.
Leisure trolley for hire, putting green, practice area,
snooker.
Location W side of town centre off A59
Hotel ★★ 67% Kilspindie House Hotel, Main St,
ABERLADY
☎ 01875 870682 26 ⇔ 🐾

RATHO

Map 11 NT17

Ratho Park EH28 8NX
☎ 0131 333 2566 0131 333 1752
Flat parkland course.
18 holes, 5900yds, Par 69, SSS 68, Course record 62.
Club membership 850.
Visitors must contact in advance.
Societies must contact in writing.
Green Fees not confirmed.
Facilities ♀ △ 🏠 ℓ Alan Pate.
Leisure putting green,practice area,trolley hire.
Location 0.75m E, N of A71
Hotel B Forte Posthouse Edinburgh, Corstorphine Rd,
EDINBURGH
☎ 0131 334 0390 204 ⇔ 🐾

ST ANDREWS

Map 12 NO51

British Golf Museum
☎ 01334 478880 (Situated opposite Royal &
Ancient Golf Club). The museum which tells the
history of golf from its origins to the present day, is
of interest to golfers and non-golfers alike. Themed
galleries and interactive displays explore the history
of the major championships and the lives of the
famous players, and trace the development of golfing
equipment and costume. An audio-visual theatre
shows historic golfing moments. **Open**: mid April-
mid Oct 10-5.30pm. **Admission**: There is a charge.
☎ for details.

ST ANDREWS LINKS See page 303

ST FILLANS

Map 11 NN62

St Fillans South Loch Earn Rd PH6 2NJ
☎ 01764 685312
Fairly flat, beautiful parkland course. Wonderfully rich in
flora, animal and bird life.
9 holes, 5796yds, Par 68, SSS 67, Course record 73.
Club membership 400.
Visitors advisable to contact in advance.
Societies Apr-Oct, apply to starter.
Green Fees £10 per day (£15 per day weekends & bank
holidays).
Facilities 🍺 🍺 △ 🍴
Leisure fishing, trolley for hire.
Location E side of village off A85
Hotel ★★★ 67% The Four Seasons Hotel, Loch Earn,
ST FILLANS
☎ 01764 685333 12 ⇔ 🐾

SALINE   Map 11 NT09

Saline Kinneddar Hill KY12 9LT
☎ 01383 852591
Hillside course with panoramic view of the Forth Valley.
9 holes, 5302yds, SSS 66, Course record 68.
Club membership 420.

Visitors	advisable to contact in advance and may not play Sat, some restrictions Sun.
Societies	contact in advance.
Green Fees	£9 per day (£11 Sun).
Facilities	⊗ by prior arrangement ⋔ by prior arrangement 🅱 ⛳ ♀ ⚒
Leisure	driving range, putting green, practice area.
Location	0.5m E at junc B913/914
Hotel	★★★ 62% King Malcolm Thistle, Queensferry Rd, Wester Pitcorthie, DUNFERMLINE ☎ 01383 722611 48 ⇆ ℝ

SOUTHEND   Map 10 NR60

Dunaverty PA28 6RW
☎ 01586 830677
Undulating, seaside course.
18 holes, 4799yds, Par 66, SSS 63, Course record 59.
Club membership 400.

Visitors	limited Sat, contact in advance.
Societies	apply in advance.
Green Fees	£18 per day; £12 per round; £45 per week.
Facilities	⊗ by prior arrangement ⋔ by prior arrangement 🅱 ⚒ ⚒ 🖿

▶

ST ANDREWS LINKS

ST ANDREWS *Fife* ☎ 01334 475757   Map 12   N051

*J*ohn Ingham *writes:* If golf has a mother, then without doubt it is St Andrews, the most famous links in all the world. Sir Winston Churchill is said to have claimed golf was invented by the Devil, and if this is so then the famous Old Course must be the Devil's playground. How can one reconcile these two thoughts; the birthplace and mother of the game - and yet the very Devil of a test?

The great Bobby Jones started by hating St Andrews and shredded his card into a hundred pieces, letting it blow in the wind. But eventually he came to love the place, and earn the affection of all golf. However you view St Andrews, you cannot ignore it. That master shot-maker from America, Sam Snead, took one look and claimed they should plant cattle fodder on the bumpy acres. Gary Player once said it should be towed out to sea, and sunk. But Jack Nicklaus loved it so much that when he won an Open title here, he threw his putter into the air. And he went away, and copied several of the St Andrews features in other courses that now decorate this earth.

St Andrews is much more than an 18-hole test. It is a whole experience and a walk in history. Name the famous players of yesteryear, and they played here, taking divots from the very spot that you can also take divots - merely by paying for a ticket. You too can wander out with your clubs to conquer some holes, maybe, and to be brought to a humbling halt by others.

Jack Nicklaus won his most remarkable victory on this course, thanks to an historic missed putt of just 3 feet 6 inches by Doug Sanders, who had needed a final hole par 4 to win the 1970 Open Championship. The all-time course record is 62, shot by Curtis Strange in the 1987 Dunhill Cup. Surely nobody can ever beat that?

Visitors	must telephone in advance
Societies	must book at least a month in advance.
Green fees	Old course: £60; New Course £25; Jubilee £25, Eden £18; Strathtyrum £14, Balgove £6 (18 holes)
Facilities	⊗ ⅺ ⅃ ♨ ☂ ㅅ 🏠 🏌 driving range, putting green, practice area, trolleys.
Location	St. Andrews KY16 9SF NW of town off the A91

Old Course: 18 holes, 6566yds, Par 72, SSS 72
New (West Sands Rd): 18 holes, 6604yds, Par 71, SSS 72
Jubilee (West Sands Rd): 18 holes, 6805yds, Par 72, SSS 73
Eden (Dundee Rd): 18 holes, 6112yds, Par 70, SSS 69
Strathtyrum): 18 holes, 5195yds, Par 69
Balgove 9 holes 3060 yds

WHERE TO STAY AND EAT NEARBY

HOTELS:
ST ANDREWS
★★★★★ 🏵🏵 63% Old Course St Andrews, Old Station Rd.
☎ 01334 474371. 125 ⇄ ℕ

★★★🏵 73% St Andrews Golf, 40 The Scores. ☎ 01334 472611.
23 (3 ℕ 20 ⇄ ℕ)

★★★67% Scores, 76 The Scores
☎ 01334 472451. 30 (2 ℕ 28 ⇄ ℕ)

RESTAURANTS:
CUPAR
🏵🏵🏵 Ostlers Close, Bonnygate
☎ 01334 655574

Leisure fishing, putting green, practice area.
Location 10m S of Campbeltown on B842
Hotel ★★ 65% Seafield Hotel, Kilkerran Rd,
CAMPBELTOWN
☎ 01586 554385 3 ᏁAnnexe6 Ꮪ

SOUTH QUEENSFERRY
Map 11 NT17

Dundas Parks c/o Secretary, 3 Stewart Clark Av EH30 9QF
☎ 0131 331 2363 (evenings only)
Parkland course situated on the estate of Lady Jane Stewart-
Clark, with excellent views. For 18 holes, the 9 are played twice.
9 holes, 6024yds, Par 70, SSS 69, Course record 66.
Club membership 500.
Visitors must contact in advance.
Societies must contact in advance.
Green Fees not confirmed.
Facilities Ꮬ
Leisure putting green, practice ground, bunker &
driving bay.
Location 1m S on A8000
Hotel ★★★ 60% Forth Bridges Hotel, Forth Bridge,
SOUTH QUEENSFERRY
☎ 0131 331 1199 108 ⇋ Ꮪ

STIRLING
Map 11 NS79

Stirling Queens Rd FK8 3AA ☎ 01786 464098
Undulating parkland course with magnificent views. Testing
15th, 'Cotton's Fancy', 384 yds (par 4).
18 holes, 6438yds, Par 72, SSS 71, Course record 65.
Club membership 1100.
Visitors may reserve tee off times mid week 9-4.30pm.
At weekends tee off times may be reserved on
day of play subject to availability.
Societies must apply in writing or telephone.
Green Fees £26 per day; £18 per round (£10 per day/round
Nov-Mar).
Facilities ⊗ ℳ Ꮭ 🍺 ⴹ Ꮬ 🗠 ⴲ Ᏼ Ian Collins.
Leisure trolley for hire, driving range, putting green,
practice area.
Location W side of town on B8051
Hotel ★★ 64% Terraces Hotel, 4 Melville Ter,
STIRLING ☎ 01786 472268 18 ⇋ Ꮪ

STRATHTAY
Map 14 NN95

Strathtay PH15 ☎ 01350 727797
A wooded mainly hilly course with pleasing panoramic views.
5th hole 'Spion Kop' is especially difficult. It is steep, with
heavy rough on both sides of the hilly fairway and an unsighted
green of the back of the hill which is affected by winds.
9 holes, 4082yds, Par 63, SSS 63, Course record 61.
Club membership 158.
Visitors restricted May-Sep; Sun 12.30-5pm & Mon 6-
8pm. Also some Wed & Thu evenings.
Societies by letter or telephone to Secretary T D Lind,
Lorne Cottage, Dalguise, Dunkeld, Perthshire
PH8 0JX.
Green Fees not confirmed.
Facilities ᏜᏜ
Location Eastern end of minor rd to Weem, off A827
Hotel ★★ 63% The Weem, Weem, ABERFELDY
☎ 01887 820381 12 ⇋ Ꮪ

TARBERT
Map 10 NR86

Tarbert PA29 6XX ☎ 01880 820536
Beautiful moorland course. Four fairways crossed by streams.
9 holes, 4460yds, Par 66, SSS 63, Course record 62.
Visitors may not play Sat pm.
Societies apply in writing.
Green Fees £15 per day; £10 per 18 holes; £5 per 9 holes.
Location N1m W on B8024)
Hotel ★★★▲▲ 64% Stonefield Castle Hotel,
TARBERT ☎ 01880 820836 33 ⇋ Ꮪ

TAYPORT
Map 12 NO42

Scotscraig Golf Rd DD6 9DZ ☎ 01382 552515
A rather tight course on downland-type turf with an
abundance of gorse. The sheltered position of this Open
qualifying course ensures good weather throughout the year.
18 holes, 6550yds, Par 71, SSS 72, Course record 69.
Club membership 750.
Visitors restricted at weekends. Must contact in advance.
Societies advance booking.
Green Fees £36 per day; £25 per round (£42/£30
weekends).
Facilities ⊗ ℳ Ꮭ 🍺 ⴹ Ꮬ 🗠 ⴲ Ᏼ
Leisure trolley for hire, driving range, putting green,
practice area.
Location S side of village off B945
Hotel ★★★ 62% The Queen's Hotel, 160 Nethergate,
DUNDEE ☎ 01382 322515 47 ⇋ Ꮪ

THORNTON
Map 11 NT29

Thornton Station Rd KY1 4DW ☎ 01592 771111
Undulating and fairly difficult parkland course.
18 holes, 6177yds, Par 70, SSS 69, Course record 64.
Club membership 700.
Visitors restricted at weekends before 10am & between
12.30-2pm, also Tue 1-1.30 & Thu 9-10.
Booking in advance recommended.
Societies apply in advance.
Green Fees £20 per day; £14 per round (£30/£20 weekends).
Facilities ⊗ ℳ Ꮭ 🍺 ⴹ Ꮬ
Leisure trolley for hire, putting green, practice area.
Location 1m E of town off A92
Hotel ★★★ 69% Balgeddie House Hotel, Balgeddie
Way, GLENROTHES
☎ 01592 742511 18 ⇋ Ꮪ

TIGHNABRUAICH
Map 10 NR97

Kyles of Bute PA21 2EE ☎ 01700 811603
Moorland course which is hilly and exposed to wind. Good
views of the Kyles of Bute.
9 holes, 4778yds, Par 66, SSS 64, Course record 62.
Club membership 150.
Visitors may not play Wed pm or Sun am.
Societies telephone in advance.
Green Fees £6 per day/round.
Facilities 🍺 Ꮬ ⴲ
Leisure trolley for hire.
Location 1.25m S off B8000
Hotel ★★ 76% Kilfinan Hotel, KILFINAN
☎ 01700 821201 11 ⇋

TILLICOULTRY   Map 11 NS99

Tillicoultry Alva Rd FK13 6BL ☎ 01259 750124
Parkland course at foot of the Ochil Hills entailing some hard walking.
9 holes, 4904metres, Par 68, SSS 66, Course record 61.
Club membership 400.
Visitors   must contact in advance.
Societies   apply to the secretary.
Green Fees £10 per round before 4pm, £12 after 4pm (£15 weekends).
Facilities   ⊗ ⅷ ㏒ ☕ ♀ ⌂
Location   A91, 9m E of Stirling
Hotel   ★★ 64% Harviestoun Country Inn, Dollar Rd, TILLICOULTRY ☎ 01259 752522 10 ⇄ ⋒

UPHALL   Map 11 NT07

Uphall EH52 6JT ☎ 01506 856404 & 855553 (Pro)
Windy parkland course, easy walking.
18 holes, 5567yds, Par 69, SSS 67, Course record 62.
Club membership 500.
Visitors   restricted weekends.
Societies   must contact in advance.
Green Fees not confirmed.
Facilities   ♀ ⌂ 🖥 ⛴ ⋒ Gordon Law.
Location   W side of village on A899
Hotel   ★★ 56% Dreadnought Hotel, 17/19 Whitburn Rd, BATHGATE
☎ 01506 630791 19rm(18 ⇄ ⋒)

WEST CALDER   Map 11 NT06

Harburn EH55 8RS ☎ 01506 871131
Moorland, reasonably flat.
18 holes, 5921yds, Par 69, SSS 69, Course record 62.
Club membership 870.
Visitors   contact secretary, limited weekends.
Societies   must contact in writing.
Green Fees £21 two rounds; £16 per round (£26/£19 Fri, £32/£21 weekends & bank holidays).
Facilities   ⊗ ㏒ ☕ ♀ ⌂ ⋒ Tom Stangoe.
Leisure   motorised carts for hire, buggies for hire, trolley for hire, putting green, practice area.
Location   On B7008
Hotel   ★★★ 61% The Hilcroft Hotel, East Main St, WHITBURN ☎ 01501 740818 30 ⇄ ⋒

WHITBURN   Map 11 NS96

Polkemmet Country Park EH47 0AD ☎ 01501 743905
Public parkland course surrounded by mature woodland and rhododendron bushes. 15-bay floodlit driving range.
9 holes, 2969mtrs, Par 37.
Visitors   no restrictions.
Green Fees per 9 holes summer £2.85 (£3.60 Sun) prices due to be reviewed.
Facilities   ⊗ ⅷ ㏒ ☕ ♀
Leisure   trolley for hire, driving range, practice area.
Location   2m W off B7066
Hotel   ★★★ 61% The Hilcroft Hotel, East Main St, WHITBURN ☎ 01501 740818 30 ⇄ ⋒

SOUTHERN LOWLANDS & BORDERS

This region includes the counties of City of Glasgow, Dumbarton & Clydebank, Dumfries & Galloway, East Ayrshire, East Dunbartonshire, East Renfrewshire, North Ayrshire, North Lanarkshire, Renfrewshire, Scottish Borders, South Ayrshire and South Lanarkshire which reflect the recent national changes..

AIRDRIE   Map 11 NS76

Airdrie Rochsoles ML6 0PQ ☎ 01236 762195
Picturesque parkland course with good views.
18 holes, 6004yds, Par 69, SSS 69, Course record 64.
Club membership 450.
Visitors   must contact in advance. With member only weekends & bank holidays.
Societies   apply in writing.
Green Fees not confirmed.
Facilities   ♀ ⌂ 🖥 ⋒ A McCloskey.
Leisure   putting green, practice area, trolley hire.
Location   1m N on B802
Hotel   ★★★★ 64% Westerwood Hotel Golf & Country Club, 1 St Andrews Dr, Westerwood, CUMBERNAULD ☎ 01236 457171 47 ⇄ ⋒

Easter Moffat Mansion House, Plains ML6 8NP
☎ 01236 842878
Moorland/parkland course.
18 holes, 6221yds, Par 72, SSS 70.
Club membership 450.
Visitors   may only play on weekdays.
Societies   must contact in advance.
Green Fees not confirmed.
Facilities   ♀ ⌂ 🖥 ⋒ Brian Dunbar.
Location   2m E on old Edinburgh-Glasgow road
Hotel   ★★★★ 64% Westerwood Hotel Golf & Country Club, 1 St Andrews Dr, Westerwood, CUMBERNAULD ☎ 01236 457171 47 ⇄ ⋒

ARRAN, ISLE OF   Map 10 NR94

BLACKWATERFOOT   Map 10 NR82

Shiskine Shore Rd KA27 8AH ☎ 01770 860226
Unique 12-hole links course with gorgeous outlook to the Mull of Kintyre.
12 holes, 2990yds, Par 41, SSS 42.
Club membership 520.
Visitors   must contact in advance.
Societies   must contact in writing in advance. Jul and Aug no parties.
Green Fees £12 per 2 rounds; £8 per round.
Facilities   ⊗ ⅷ ㏒ ☕ ⌂ 🖥
Leisure   hard tennis courts, buggies for hire, trolley for hire, putting green, outdoor all weather bowling green.
Location   W side of village off A841   ▶

Hotel ★★ 64% The Lagg Hotel, Kilmory, BRODICK
☎ 01770 870255 15 ⇄ ↑

BRODICK   Map 10 NS03

Brodick KA27 8DL ☎ 01770 302349 & 302513
Short seaside course, very flat.
18 holes, 4405yds, Par 62, SSS 62, Course record 60.
Club membership 552.
Visitors	must contact in advance but may not play on competition days.
Societies	must contact in advance.
Green Fees	not confirmed.
Facilities	♀ ▲ 🏠 ↑ Peter McCalla.
Leisure	caddy cars, practice area.
Location	N side of village
Hotel	★★★ 76% Auchrannie Country House Hotel, BRODICK ☎ 01770 302234 28 ⇄ ↑

CORRIE   Map 10 NS04

Corrie Sannox KA27 8JD ☎ 01770 810223
A heathland course on the coast with beautiful mountain scenery. An upward climb to 6th hole, then a descent from the 7th. All these holes are subject to strong winds in bad weather.
9 holes, 1948yds.
Club membership 280.
Visitors	welcome except Sat pm and two first Thu afternoons of the month.
Societies	maximum size of party 16, apply in advance.
Green Fees	£7 per day.
Facilities	⊗ ⏍ ⓛ ♥ 🏠 ↑
Location	2m N on A841
Hotel	★★★ 76% Auchrannie Country House Hotel, BRODICK ☎ 01770 302234 28 ⇄ ↑

LAMLASH   Map 10 NS03

Lamlash KA27 8JU ☎ 01770 600296 & 600196 (Starter)
Undulating heathland course with magnificent views of the mountains and sea.
18 holes, 4640yds, Par 64, SSS 64, Course record 62.
Club membership 400.
Visitors	contact in advance.
Societies	must contact in writing.
Green Fees	£12 per day (£15 weekends).
Facilities	⊗ ⏍ ⓛ ♥ ♀ ▲ ◫
Leisure	trolley for hire, putting green, trolley hire.
Location	0.75m N of Lamlash on A841
Hotel	★★★ 76% Auchrannie Country House Hotel, BRODICK ☎ 01770 302234 28 ⇄ ↑

LOCHRANZA   Map 10 NR95

Lochranza KA27 8HL ☎ 01770 830273
This course opened in 1991 is mainly on the level, set amid spectacular scenery where the fairways are grazed by wild red deer, while overhead buzzards and golden eagles may be seen. There are water hazards including the river which is lined by mature trees. The final three holes are nicknamed the Bermuda Triangle provide an absorbing finish right to the 18th hole - a 530 yard dogleg through trees and over the river.The nine large greens are played off 18 tees. The course is closed during the winter from 1 November to mid April.

9 holes, 5033mtrs, Par 70, SSS 70, Course record 74.
Visitors	no restrictions; course closed Nov-mid Apr.
Societies	advance booking preferred.
Green Fees	£15 per day; £10 per 18 holes; £5 per 9 holes.
Facilities	♥ ▲ 🏠 ↑
Leisure	trolley for hire, putting green.
Hotel	★★ 64% The Lagg Hotel, Kilmory, BRODICK ☎ 01770 870255 15 ⇄ ↑

MACHRIE   Map 10 NR83

Machrie Bay KA27 8DZ ☎ 01770 850232
Fairly flat seaside course. Designed at turn of century by William Fernie.
9 holes, 4396yds, Par 66, SSS 66, Course record 56.
Club membership 315.
Visitors	no restrictions.
Societies	write in advance.
Green Fees	£5 per day.
Facilities	⊗ ♥ ▲
Leisure	hard tennis courts, fishing, putting green.
Location	9m W of Brodick via String Rd
Hotel	★★ 64% The Lagg Hotel, Kilmory, BRODICK ☎ 01770 870255 15 ⇄ ↑

WHITING BAY   Map 10 NS02

Whiting Bay KA27 8QT ☎ 01770 700347
Heathland course.
18 holes, 4405yds, Par 63, SSS 63, Course record 59.
Club membership 350.
Visitors	tee reserved 8.45-9.30am, also Sun 11.45-1pm.
Societies	apply by telephone and confirm in writing with deposit.
Green Fees	not confirmed.
Facilities	♀ ▲ 🏠
Leisure	putting green, motor cart, buggy/trolley hire.
Location	NW side of village off A841
Hotel	★★ 64% The Lagg Hotel, Kilmory, BRODICK ☎ 01770 870255 15 ⇄ ↑

AYR   Map 10 NS32

Belleisle Belleisle Park KA7 4DU ☎ 01292 441258
Parkland course with beautiful sea views. First-class conditions.
Belleisle Course: 18 holes, 6540yds, Par 70, SSS 72.
Seafield Course: 18 holes, 5498yds, Par 68, SSS 67.
Club membership 300.
Visitors	advised to contact in advance.
Societies	advised to contact in advance.
Green Fees	not confirmed.
Facilities	♀ ▲ 🏠 ↑ ◫ ↑ David Gemmell.
Leisure	putting,cart/trolley hire.
Location	2m S on A719
Hotel	★★★ 59% Quality Friendly Hotel, Burns Statue Square, AYR ☎ 01292 263268 75 ⇄ ↑
Additional hotel	★★★ 62% Jarvis Caledonian, Dalblair Rd, AYR ☎ 01292 269331 114 ⇄ ↑

> Entries with a shaded background identify courses that are considered to be particularly interesting

Golfing Breaks in Ayr

Visitors to Scotland's beautiful west coast are at the heart of golf when they stay in Ayrshire. The Jarvis Caledonian Hotel is situated in the heart of the town. Yet only a short stroll to Ayr's sandy beaches.

The hotel offers you comfortable bedrooms all with own private bathroom. You'll have complimentary use of the Leisure Club & Swimming Pool during your stay. Hudson's Bar & Grill is a "lively place to meet and eat" 22 Golf Courses within 1 hours drive from the Hotel.

To find out more call:

The Jarvis Caledonian Hotel
Dalblair Road
Ayr KA7 1UG
(01292) 269331

Dalmilling Westwood Av KA8 0QY ☎ 01292 263893
Meadowland course, with easy walking.
18 holes, 5724yds, Par 69, SSS 68.
Club membership 140.
Visitors   must contact in advance.
Societies   must contact in advance.
Green Fees not confirmed.
Facilities   ♀⚐🏠🏌♪ Philip Cheyney.
Leisure   caddy cars for hire.
Location   1.5m E of town centre off A719
Hotel   ★★ 65% Carlton Toby Hotel, 187 Ayr Rd,
PRESTWICK
☎ 01292 476811 39 ⇔ ↑

BALLOCH
Map 10 NS38

Cameron House Hotel & Country Estate Loch Lomond
G83 8QZ ☎ 01389 757211
Only available for residents of the hotel or a party booked in advance. A challenging 9-hole course with water hazards.
The Wee Demon Course: 9 holes, 2266yds, Par 32.
Club membership 200.
Visitors   must be residents or party booked in advance.
Societies   apply in writing.
Green Fees not confirmed.
Facilities   ♀⚐♪🏠
Leisure   hard tennis courts, heated indoor swimming pool, squash, fishing, sauna, solarium, gymnasium, practice nets, trolley hire.
Hotel   ★★★★ 75% Cameron House Hotel and Country Estate, BALLOCH
☎ 01389 755565 68 ⇔ ↑

BALMORE
Map 11 NS57

Balmore Golf Course Rd G64 4AW ☎ 01360 620240
Parkland course with fine views.
18 holes, 5530yds, Par 66, SSS 67, Course record 63.
Club membership 700.
Visitors   must contact in advance and be accompanied by member.
Societies   apply in writing.
Green Fees not confirmed.
Facilities   ⊗⚐🏠♣🏌
Leisure   putting green, practice area.
Location   N off A807
Hotel   ★★★ 65% Black Bull Thistle, Main St,
MILNGAVIE ☎ 0141 956 2291 27 ⇔ ↑

BARASSIE
Map 10 NS33

Kilmarnock (Barassie) 29 Hillhouse Rd KA10 6SY
☎ 01292 313920
A magnificent seaside course, relatively flat with much heather. The turf and greens are quite unequalled. The 15th is a testing par 3 at 220 yards.
18 holes, 6473yds, Par 71, SSS 72, Course record 63.
Club membership 600.
Visitors   with member only Wed & weekends. May not play Fri am. Contact secretary in advance.
Societies   must telephone in advance and confirm in writing.
Green Fees £40 per day; £30 per round (£28.50/£21.50 winter).
Facilities   ⊗⚐🏠♣🏌⚑🏌♪ W R Lockie.
Leisure   trolley for hire, putting green, practice area.
Location   E side of village on B746
Hotel   ★★★★ 65% Marine Highland Hotel,
TROON ☎ 01292 314444 72 ⇔ ↑

BARRHEAD
Map 11 NS45

Fereneze Fereneze Av G78 1HJ
☎ 0141 881 1519
Hilly moorland course, with a good view at the end of a hard climb to the 3rd, then levels out.
18 holes, 5821yds, Par 70, SSS 68.
Club membership 700.
Visitors   must contact in advance but may not play at weekends.
Societies   apply in writing.
Green Fees not confirmed.
Facilities   ♀⚐🏠🏌♪ Darren Robinson.
Leisure   putting green, practice area, pool table.
Location   NW side of town off B774
Hotel   ★★★ 60% Dalmeny Park Country House,
Lochlibo Rd, BARRHEAD
☎ 0141 881 9211 19 ⇔ ↑

BEARSDEN
Map 11 NS57

Bearsden Thorn Rd G61 4BP ☎ 0141 942 2381
Parkland course, with 16 greens and 11 teeing grounds. Easy walking and views over city.
9 holes, 6014yds, Par 68, SSS 69, Course record 67.
Club membership 450.

▶

Visitors must be accompanied by and play with member.
Societies apply by writing.
Green Fees no fees given as must be with member.
Facilities ⊗ ⅏ � ⅃ ♀ ⅄
Leisure putting green, practice area.
Location 1m W off A809
Hotel ★★★ 65% Black Bull Thistle, Main St,
MILNGAVIE ☎ 0141 956 2291 27 ⇋ ⋔

Douglas Park Hillfoot G61 2TJ ☎ 0141 942 2220
Parkland course with wide variety of holes.
18 holes, 5957yds, Par 69, SSS 69.
Club membership 900.
Visitors Must be accompanied by member and must
contact in advance.
Societies Wed & Thu. Must telephone in advance.
Green Fees not confirmed.
Facilities ♀ ⅄ ⓐ ⋔ David Scott.
Leisure caddy cars.
Location E side of town on A81
Hotel ★★★ 65% Black Bull Thistle, Main St,
MILNGAVIE ☎ 0141 956 2291 27 ⇋ ⋔

Glasgow Killermont G61 2TW ☎ 0141 942 2011
One of the finest parkland courses in Scotland.
18 holes, 5968yds, Par 70, SSS 69.
Club membership 800.
Visitors must contact in advance & have handicap
certificate.
Green Fees not confirmed.
Facilities ♀ (members guest only) ⅄ ⓐ ⋔ ⋔ J Steven.
Location SE side off A81
Hotel ★★★ 65% Black Bull Thistle, Main St,
MILNGAVIE ☎ 0141 956 2291 27 ⇋ ⋔

Windyhill Baljaffray Rd G61 4QQ
☎ 0141 942 2349 & 0141 942 7157 pro
Hard walking parkland/moorland course; testing 12th hole.
18 holes, 6254yds, Par 71, SSS 70, Course record 64.
Club membership 520.
Visitors may not play at weekends. Must contact
professional in advance.
Societies must apply in writing.
Green Fees £20 per day.
Facilities ⊗ ⅏ ▬ ⅃ ♀ ⅄ ⓐ ⋔ ⋔ G Collinson.
Leisure trolley for hire, putting green, practice area.
Location 2m NW off B8050
Hotel ★★★ 65% Black Bull Thistle, Main St,
MILNGAVIE ☎ 0141 956 2291 27 ⇋ ⋔

BEITH
Map 10 NS35

Beith Threepwood Rd KA15 2JR ☎ 01505 503166
Hilly course, with panoramic views over 7 counties.
18 holes, 5616yds, Par 68, SSS 68.
Club membership 420.
Visitors contact for details.
Societies apply in writing to secretary at least 1 month in
advance.
Green Fees contact for details.
Facilities ▬ ⅃ ⅄
Location 1.5m NE off A737
Hotel ★★★ 65% Bowfield Hotel & Country Club,
HOWWOOD ☎ 01505 705225 12 ⇋ ⋔

BELLSHILL
Map 11 NS76

Bellshill Community Rd, Orbiston ML4 2RZ
☎ 01698 745124
Parkland course.
18 holes, 5900yds, Par 69, SSS 69.
Club membership 500.
Visitors apply in writing in advance, may not play on
competition Sat & Sun.
Societies apply in writing in advance.
Green Fees £18 per day (£25 weekends).
Facilities ⊗ ⅏ ▬ ⅃ ♀ ⅄
Leisure putting green, practice area.
Location 1m SE off A721
Hotel ★★ 62% Silvertrees Hotel, Silverwells
Crescent, BOTHWELL
☎ 01698 852311 7 ⇋ ⋔Annexe19 ⇋ ⋔

BIGGAR
Map 11 NT03

Biggar The Park, Broughton Rd ML12 6AH
☎ 01899 220319
Flat parkland course, easy walking and fine views.
18 holes, 5600yds, Par 67, SSS 66, Course record 61.
Club membership 340.
Visitors Must contact in advance. Smart casual wear
required.
Societies must book in advance, observe dress code.
Green Fees £9 per day (£14 weekends & bank holidays).
Facilities ⊗ ⅏ ▬ ⅃ ♀ ⅄ ⓐ
Leisure hard tennis courts, motorised carts for hire,
buggies for hire, trolley for hire, putting green,
practice area.
Location S side of town
Hotel ★★★★ 70% Shieldhill Hotel, Quothquan,
BIGGAR ☎ 01899 220035 11 ⇋ ⋔

BISHOPBRIGGS
Map 11 NS67

Bishopbriggs Brackenbrae Rd G64 2DX
☎ 0141 772 1810
Parkland course with views to Campsie Hills.
18 holes, 6041yds, Par 69, SSS 69, Course record 63.
Club membership 600.
Visitors must be accompanied by member, contact in
advance and have an introduction from own
club.
Societies apply in writing to the Committee one month in
advance.
Green Fees not confirmed.
Facilities ♀ ⅄ ⓐ
Location 0.5m NW off A803
Hotel ★★★ 65% Black Bull Thistle, Main St,
MILNGAVIE ☎ 0141 956 2291 27 ⇋ ⋔

Cawder Cadder Rd G64 3QD
☎ 0141 772 5167
Two parkland courses; Cawder Course is hilly, with 5th, 9th,
10th, 11th-testing holes. Keir Course is flat.
Cawder Course: 18 holes, 6295yds, Par 70, SSS 71.
Keir Course: 18 holes, 5877yds, Par 68, SSS 68.
Club membership 1150.
Visitors must contact in advance & may play on
weekdays only.

Societies must contact in writing.
Green Fees not confirmed.
Facilities ♀♙☎🕻🕻
Location 1m NE off A803
Hotel ★★★ 65% Black Bull Thistle, Main St,
MILNGAVIE ☎ 0141 956 2291 27 ⇔ 🏌

BISHOPTON   Map 10 NS47

Erskine PA7 5PH ☎ 01505 862302
Parkland course.
18 holes, 6287yds, Par 71, SSS 70.
Club membership 700.
Visitors must be accompanied by member and must have
a handicap certificate.
Societies apply in writing.
Green Fees not confirmed.
Facilities ♀♙☎🕻 Peter Thomson.
Location 0.75 NE off B815
Hotel B Forte Posthouse Glasgow Erskine, North Barr,
ERSKINE ☎ 0141 812 0123 166 ⇔ 🏌

BONHILL   Map 10 NS37

Vale of Leven North Field Rd G83 9ET
☎ 01389 52351
Hilly moorland course, tricky with many natural hazards -
gorse, burns, trees. Overlooks Loch Lomond.
18 holes, 5162yds, Par 67, SSS 66, Course record 61.
Club membership 640.
Visitors may not play Sat Apr-Sep.
Societies apply to the secretary.
Green Fees not confirmed.
Facilities ♀♙☎🕻
Location E side of town off A813
Hotel ★★ 61% Dumbuck Hotel, Glasgow Rd,
DUMBARTON ☎ 01389 734336 22 ⇔ 🏌

BOTHWELL   Map 11 NS75

Bothwell Castle Blantyre Rd G71 8PJ ☎ 01698 853177
Flat parkland course in residential area.
18 holes, 6200yds, Par 71, SSS 70, Course record 63.
Club membership 1000.
Visitors may only play Mon-Fri 9.30-10.30am & 2-3pm.
Green Fees £28 per day; £20 per round.
Facilities ⊗🎜🝆🝅♀♙☎🕻🕻 Gordon Niven.
Leisure trolley for hire, putting green, practice area.
Location NW of village off B7071
Hotel ★★ 62% Silvertrees Hotel, Silverwells
Crescent, BOTHWELL
☎ 01698 852311 7 ⇔ 🏌Annexe19 ⇔ 🏌

BRIDGE OF WEIR   Map 10 NS36

Ranfurly Castle The Clubhouse, Golf Rd PA11 3HN
☎ 01505 612609
A highly challenging, 240 acre, picturesque moorland course.
18 holes, 6284yds, Par 70, SSS 71, Course record 65.
Club membership 825.
Visitors contact in advance.
Societies apply in writing.
Green Fees £35 per day; £25 per round.
Facilities 🎜🝆🝅♀♙☎🕻🕻 Tom Eckford.

Leisure buggies for hire, trolley for hire, putting green,
practice area.
Location 5m NW of Johnstone
Hotel ★★★ 65% Bowfield Hotel & Country Club,
HOWWOOD ☎ 01505 705225 12 ⇔ 🏌

BURNSIDE   Map 11 NS66

Blairbeth Fernbrae Av, Fernhill G73 4SF
☎ 0141 634 3355
Parkland course.
18 holes, 5518yds, Par 70, SSS 68, Course record 64.
Club membership 600.
Visitors must contact in advance & may not play
weekends.
Societies apply in advance.
Green Fees £16 per day Mon-Fri.
Facilities ⊗🎜🝆🝅♀♙
Leisure putting green.
Location S off A749
Hotel ★★★ 64% Macdonald Thistle, Eastwood Toll,
GIFFNOCK ☎ 0141 638 2225 56 ⇔ 🏌

Cathkin Braes Cathkin Rd G73 4SE
☎ 0141 634 6605
Moorland course, prevailing westerly wind, small loch hazard
at 5th hole.
18 holes, 6208yds, Par 69, SSS 69.
Club membership 890.
Visitors must contact in advance & have handicap
certificate but may not play at weekends.
Societies apply in writing.
Green Fees not confirmed.
Facilities ♀♙☎🕻 Stephen Bree.
Leisure putting green, practice area, trolley hire.
Location 1m S on B759
Hotel ★★★ 64% Macdonald Thistle, Eastwood Toll,
GIFFNOCK ☎ 0141 638 2225 56 ⇔ 🏌

CARLUKE   Map 11 NS85

Carluke Mauldslie Rd, Hallcraig ML8 5HG
☎ 01555 771070
Parkland course with views over the Clyde Valley. Testing
11th hole, par 3.
18 holes, 5853yds, Par 70, SSS 68, Course record 63.
Club membership 750.
Visitors must contact in advance & may not play
weekends.
Societies prior arrangement required.
Green Fees £25 per day; £18 per round.
Facilities ⊗🎜🝆🝅♀♙☎🕻 Richard Forrest.
Leisure putting green.
Location 1m W off A73
Hotel ★★★ 66% Popinjay Hotel, Lanark Rd,
ROSEBANK
☎ 01555 860441 36 ⇔ 🏌Annexe5 ⇔ 🏌

CARNWATH   Map 11 NS94

Carnwath 1 Main St ML11 8JX ☎ 01555 840251
Picturesque parkland course slightly hilly, with small greens
calling for accuracy. Panoramic views.
18 holes, 5953yds, Par 70, SSS 69.
Club membership 470.   ▶

Visitors restricted after 5pm, no visitors Sat.
Societies apply in writing or telephone.
Green Fees not confirmed.
Facilities ♀ ⚴ 📷
Location W side of village on A70
Hotel ★★★ 67% Cartland Bridge Hotel, Glasgow Rd, LANARK ☎ 01555 664426 18 ⇄ ♠

CASTLE DOUGLAS   Map 11 NX76

Castle Douglas Abercromby Rd DG7 1BB
☎ 01556 502180 or 502099
Parkland course, one severe hill.
9 holes, 2704yds, Par 68, SSS 66.
Club membership 500.
Visitors welcome except Tue & Thu after 4pm & during competitions. Must contact secretary in advance.
Societies apply by writing to secretary.
Green Fees £12 per day/round.
Facilities ⊗ ﮐ 🍺 ♀ ⚴ 🏌
Leisure trolley for hire, putting green, practice area.
Location W side of town
Hotel ★★ 66% Douglas Arms, King St, CASTLE DOUGLAS ☎ 01556 502231 20rm(15 ⇄ ♠)

CLARKSTON   Map 11 NS55

Cathcart Castle Mearns Rd G76 7YL
☎ 0141 638 0082
Tree-lined parkland course, with undulating terrain.
18 holes, 5832yds, Par 68, SSS 68.
Club membership 990.
Visitors must have a letter of introduction from own club.
Societies Tue & Thu only; must apply in writing.
Green Fees not confirmed.
Facilities ♀ ⚴ 📷 ♪ David Naylor.
Location 0.75m SW off A726
Hotel ★★★ 64% Macdonald Thistle, Eastwood Toll, GIFFNOCK ☎ 0141 638 2225 56 ⇄ ♠

CLYDEBANK   Map 11 NS56

Clydebank & District Glasgow Rd, Hardgate G81 5QY
☎ 01389 873289
An undulating parkland course established in 1905 overlooking Clydebank.
18 holes, 5823yds, Par 68, SSS 68, Course record 64.
Club membership 889.
Visitors Round only, weekdays only. Must tee off before 4pm. Apply to professional 01389 878686.
Societies must apply in writing.
Green Fees £13 per round.
Facilities ⊗ ﮐ 🍺 ♀ ⚴ 📷 ♪ David Pirie.
Leisure putting green, practice area.
Location 2m E of Erskine Bridge
Hotel ★★★ 65% Patio Hotel, 1 South Av, Clydebank Business Park, CLYDEBANK ☎ 0141 951 1133 80 ⇄ ♠

Clydebank Municipal Overtoun Rd, Dalmuir G81 3RE
☎ 0141 941 1331
Hilly, compact parkland course with tough finishing holes.
18 holes, 5349yds, Par 67, SSS 67.
Visitors no restrictions.

Societies contact in advance.
Green Fees not confirmed.
Facilities ⚴ 📷 ♪ ♪ Stewart Savage.
Leisure trolley hire.
Location 2m NW of town centre
Hotel ★★★ 65% Patio Hotel, 1 South Av, Clydebank Business Park, CLYDEBANK ☎ 0141 951 1133 80 ⇄ ♠

COATBRIDGE   Map 11 NS76

Drumpellier Drumpellier Av ML5 1RX
☎ 01236 424139 & 428723
Parkland course.
18 holes, 6227yds, Par 71, SSS 70, Course record 60.
Club membership 827.
Visitors must contact in advance.
Societies apply in advance.
Green Fees not confirmed.
Facilities ⊗ ﮡ ﮐ 🍺 ♀ ⚴ 📷 ♪ ♪ David Ross.
Leisure trolley for hire, putting green, practice area.
Location 0.75m W off A89
Hotel ★★★ 63% Bothwell Bridge Hotel, 89 Main St, BOTHWELL ☎ 01698 852246 74 ⇄ ♠

COLDSTREAM   Map 12 NT83

Hirsel Kelso Rd TD12 4NJ
☎ 01890 882678 & 883052
Parkland course, with hard walking and sheltered trees. Testing 3rd and 6th holes. A further 9 holes have been developed.
18 holes, 6092yds, Par 70, SSS 69.
Club membership 680.
Visitors contact for details.
Societies write or telephone the secretary in advance.
Green Fees £15 per day (£20 weekends & bank holidays).
Facilities ⊗ ﮡ ﮐ 🍺 ♀ ⚴ 📷 ♪
Leisure motorised carts for hire, trolley for hire, putting green, practice area.
Location At W end of Coldstream on A697
Hotel ★★★⚴ 69% Tillmouth Park Hotel, CORNHILL-ON-TWEED ☎ 01890 882255 12 ⇄ ♠Annexe2 ⇄ ♠

COLVEND   Map 11 NX85

Colvend Sandyhills DG5 4PY
☎ 01556 630398
Picturesque and challenging course on Solway coast. Superb views.
9 holes, 4480yds, Par 66, SSS 62, Course record 63.
Club membership 490.
Visitors restricted Apr-Sep on Tue at 2pm, Thu at 5.30pm and some weekends for members competitions.
Societies must telephone in advance.
Green Fees £12 per day.
Facilities ⊗ ﮡ ﮐ 🍺 ♀ ⚴ ♪
Leisure trolley for hire, putting green, practice area.
Location 6m from Dalbeattie on A710 Solway Coast Rd
Hotel ★★ 65% Clonyard House Hotel, COLVEND ☎ 01556 630372 15 ⇄ ♠

CUMBERNAULD
Map 11 NS77

Dullatur 1A Glen Douglas Dr G68 0DW ☎ 01236 723230
Parkland course, with natural hazards and wind. Testing 17th hole, par 5.
18 holes, 6219yds, Par 70, SSS 70, Course record 65.
Club membership 700.

Visitors telephone for availability. May not play weekends.
Societies must apply in writing to secretary.
Green Fees £25 per day; £15 per round.
Facilities ⊗ ⁄‖‖ �℔ ▪ ♀ ♨ ♿ Duncan Sinclair.
Leisure tennis courts, sauna, solarium, gymnasium, motorised carts for hire, buggies for hire, trolley for hire, putting green, practice area.
Location 1.5m N
Hotel ★★★★ 64% Westerwood Hotel Golf & Country Club, 1 St Andrews Dr, Westerwood, CUMBERNAULD ☎ 01236 457171 47 ⇌ ♠

Palacerigg Palacerigg Country Park G67 3HU
☎ 01236 734969
Parkland course.
18 holes, 6444yds, Par 72, SSS 71, Course record 66.
Club membership 400.

Visitors anytime except club competitions, advance booking advisable.
Societies apply in writing to the Secretary.
Green Fees £8 per round.
Facilities ⊗ ⁄‖‖ ⅃ ▪ ♀ ♨ ♿
Leisure driving range, putting green, practice area.
Location 2m S
Hotel ★★★★ 64% Westerwood Hotel Golf & Country Club, 1 St Andrews Dr, Westerwood, CUMBERNAULD ☎ 01236 457171 47 ⇌ ♠

Westerwood Hotel Golf & Country Club 1 St Andrews Dr, Westerwood G68 0EW ☎ 01236 457171
Undulating parkland/woodland course designed by Dave Thomas and Seve Ballesteros. Holes meander through silver birch, firs, heaths and heathers, and the spectacular 15th, 'The Waterfall', has its green set against a 40ft rockface. Buggie track. Hotel facilities.
18 holes, 6721yds, Par 73, SSS 73, Course record 65.
Club membership 1500.

Visitors advised to book in advance.
Societies all bookings through golf coordinator on 01256 457171 ext 215.
Green Fees £22.50 (£27.50 weekends).
Facilities ⊗ ⁄‖‖ ⅃ ▪ ♀ ♨ ♿ ⚐ ♠ Steven Killen.
Leisure hard tennis courts, heated indoor swimming pool, sauna, solarium, gymnasium, motorised carts for hire, buggies for hire, trolley for hire, driving range, putting green, practice area, golf school.
Location Adjacent to A80
Hotel ★★★★ 64% Westerwood Hotel Golf & Country Club, 1 St Andrews Dr, Westerwood, CUMBERNAULD ☎ 01236 457171 47 ⇌ ♠

CUMMERTREES
Map 11 NY16

Powfoot DG12 5QE ☎ 01461 700276
The hills of Cumbria, away beyond the Solway Firth, and from time to time a sight of the Isle of Man, make

playing at this delightfully compact semi-links seaside course a scenic treat. Lovely holes include the 2nd, the 8th and the 11th.
18 holes, 6283yds, Par 71, SSS 70.
Club membership 820.

Visitors contact in advance. May not play 8.45-10 & noon-1.30 weekdays and until after 2pm weekends.
Societies must book in advance.
Green Fees £27 per day; £20 per round (£20 Sun after 2pm).
Facilities ⊗ ⁄‖‖ ⅃ ▪ ♀ ♨ ♿ ♠ Gareth Dick.
Leisure trolley for hire, putting green, practice area.
Location 0.5m off B724
Hotel ★★ 64% Golf Hotel, Links Av, POWFOOT ☎ 01461 700254 19rm(14 ⇌ ♠)

DUMBARTON
Map 10 NS37

Dumbarton Broadmeadow G82 2BQ ☎ 01389 732830
Flat parkland course.
18 holes, 5992yds, Par 71, SSS 69, Course record 64.
Club membership 700.

Visitors may not play weekends & public holidays.
Societies advance booking with secretary.
Green Fees not confirmed.
Facilities ♀ ♨
Leisure putting green, practice area.
Location 0.25m N off A814
Hotel ★★ 61% Dumbuck Hotel, Glasgow Rd, DUMBARTON ☎ 01389 734336 22 ⇌ ♠

DUMFRIES
Map 11 NX97

Dumfries & County Nunfield, Edinburgh Rd DG1 1JX
☎ 01387 253585
Parkland course alongside River Nith, with views over the
Queensberry Hills.
18 holes, 5928yds, Par 69, SSS 68.
Club membership 800.
Visitors	must contact in advance but may not play most weekends between 9.30-11 & 2-3.30.
Societies	apply in writing.
Green Fees	£22 per day/round (£25 weekends).
Facilities	⊗ ⅢⅢ ঌ ⬛ ♀ ঌ ঌ ᵀ ℓ Gordon Gray.
Leisure	trolley for hire, putting green, practice area.
Location	1m NE off A701
Hotel	★★★ 63% Station Hotel, 49 Lovers Walk, DUMFRIES ☎ 01387 254316 32 ⇔ ⁿ
Additional hotel	★★★ 69% Hetland Hall Hotel, CARRUTHERSTOWN ☎ 01387 840201 27 ⇔ ⁿ

See advert on page 311

Dumfries & Galloway 2 Laurieston Av DG2 7NY
☎ 01387 263848
Parkland course.
18 holes, 5803yds, Par 68, SSS 68.
Club membership 800.
Visitors	may not play on competition days.
Societies	apply in writing.
Green Fees	not confirmed.
Facilities	♀ ঌ ঌ ᵀ ℓ Joe Fergusson.
Leisure	putting green,practice area,trolley hire.
Location	W side of town centre on A75
Hotel	★★★ 63% Station Hotel, 49 Lovers Walk, DUMFRIES ☎ 01387 254316 32 ⇔ ⁿ

DUNS
Map 12 NT75

Duns Longformacus Rd TD11 3NR
☎ 01361 882717 & 882194
Interesting upland course, with natural hazards of water and
hilly slopes. Views south to the Cheviot Hills.
9 holes, 5864yds, Par 68, SSS 68, Course record 65.
Club membership 340.
Visitors	welcome except competition days and Mon, Tue and Wed after 3pm.
Societies	write or telephone the secretary in advance for booking details.
Green Fees	£10 per day/round (50% reduction Nov-15 Mar).
Facilities	ঌ ⬛ ♀ (evenings) ঌ
Leisure	trolley for hire, putting green, practice area.
Location	1m W off A6105
Hotel	★★★ 69% Marshall Meadows Country House Hotel, BERWICK-UPON-TWEED ☎ 01289 331133 18 ⇔ ⁿ

EAGLESHAM
Map 11 NS55

Bonnyton Kirktonmoor Rd G76 0QA ☎ 01355 302781
Windy, moorland course.
18 holes, 6255yds, Par 72, SSS 71.
Club membership 960.
Visitors	welcome weekdays only (ex Tue), must contact in advance.
Societies	must telephone in advance.
Green Fees	£30 per 2 rounds; £20 per round.
Facilities	⊗ ⅢⅢ ঌ ⬛ ♀ ঌ ঌ ᵀ ℓ Kendal McWade.
Leisure	buggies for hire, trolley for hire, putting green, practice area.
Location	0.25m SW off B764
Hotel	★★★ 63% Bruce Swallow Hotel, Cornwall St, EAST KILBRIDE ☎ 013552 29771 78 ⇔ ⁿ

EAST KILBRIDE
Map 11 NS65

East Kilbride Chapelside Rd, Nerston G74 4PF
☎ 013552 20913
Parkland and hill course. Very windy. Testing 7th, 9th and
14th holes.
18 holes, 6419yds, Par 71, SSS 71.
Club membership 800.
Visitors	by appointment. Must be a member of recognised golfing society.
Societies	must telephone in advance & submit formal application.
Green Fees	not confirmed.
Facilities	♀ ঌ ঌ ᵀ ℓ A Taylor.
Location	0.5m N off A749
Hotel	★★★ 63% Bruce Swallow Hotel, Cornwall St, EAST KILBRIDE ☎ 013552 29771 78 ⇔ ⁿ

Torrance House Calderglen Country Park, Strathaven Rd
G75 0QZ ☎ 013552 48638
A parkland course.
18 holes, 6415yds, Par 72, SSS 69, Course record 71.
Club membership 1000.
Visitors	welcome, may book up to six days in advance.
Societies	Mon-Fri. Apply in writing to John Dunlop, East Kilbride District Council, Civic Centre, East Kilbride.
Green Fees	not confirmed.
Facilities	♀ ঌ ᵀ ℓ John Dunlop.
Leisure	practice area, caddy cars.
Location	1.5m SE of Kilbride on A726
Hotel	★★★ 63% Bruce Swallow Hotel, Cornwall St, EAST KILBRIDE ☎ 013552 29771 78 ⇔ ⁿ

EYEMOUTH
Map 12 NT96

Eyemouth Gunsgreen House TD14 5SF
☎ 01890 750551
With the exception of a steep climb to the 1st tee, this is a
compact, flat and popular seaside course. Fast smooth greens
and fine views are typified by the 15th, played from an
elevated tee to a green on a peninsula over a North Sea inlet.
9 holes, 4608mtrs, Par 66, SSS 65, Course record 60.
Club membership 250.
Visitors	may not play before 10.30am Sat or noon Sun.
Societies	apply in writing.
Green Fees	not confirmed.
Facilities	♀ (evenings) ঌ ঌ ℓ Craig Maltman.
Location	E side of town
Hotel	★★★ 69% Marshall Meadows Country House Hotel, BERWICK-UPON-TWEED ☎ 01289 331133 18 ⇔ ⁿ

GALASHIELS
Map 12 NT43

Galashiels Ladhope Recreation Ground TD1 2NJ
☎ 01896 753724
Hillside course, superb views from the top; 10th hole very steep.
18 holes, 5185yds, Par 67, SSS 66, Course record 61.
Club membership 343.
Visitors must contact the secretary in advance especially for weekends.
Societies arrangements with secretary especially for weekends.
Green Fees £16 per day; £12 per round (£20/£14 weekends).
Facilities ⊗ ℿ ⓛ ♣ ♬ ♀
Leisure trolley for hire, changing room being built, clubhouse.
Location N side of town centre off A7
Hotel ★★★ 64% Kingsknowes Hotel, Selkirk Rd, GALASHIELS
☎ 01896 758375 11rm(10 ➡ ⁅⁆)

Torwoodlee TD1 2NE ☎ 01896 752260
Parkland course with natural hazards designed by James Braid. Testing 3rd hole (par 3).
18 holes, 6200yds, Par 70, SSS 69, Course record 65.
Club membership 550.
Visitors restricted Thu - ladies day and Sat - mens competitions.
Societies letter to secretary.
Green Fees £20 per day; £12 5er round (£25/£20 weekends).
Facilities ⊗ ℿ ⓛ ♣ ♀ ♬ ☎
Leisure trolley for hire, putting green, practice area.
Location 1.75m NW off A7
Hotel ★★★ 65% Woodlands House Hotel & Restaurants, Windyknowe Rd, GALASHIELS
☎ 01896 754722 9 ➡ ⁅⁆

GALSTON
Map 11 NS53

Loudoun Edinburgh Rd KA4 8PA ☎ 01563 821993
Pleasant, testing parkland course.
18 holes, 5844yds, Par 67, SSS 68, Course record 61.
Club membership 750.
Visitors must contact in advance. No play at weekends.
Societies telephone in advance.
Green Fees £29 per day; £17 per round.
Facilities ⊗ ℿ ⓛ ♣ ♀ ♬ ☎
Leisure trolley for hire, putting green, practice area.
Location NE side of town on A71
Hotel ★★★ 66% Strathaven Hotel, Hamilton Rd, STRATHAVEN ☎ 01357 521778 10 ➡ ⁅⁆

GARTCOSH
Map 11 NS66

Mount Ellen G69 8EY ☎ 01236 872277 & 872421
Downland course with 73 bunkers. Testing hole: 10th ('Bedlay'), 156 yds, par 3.
18 holes, 5525yds, Par 68, SSS 68.
Club membership 500.
Visitors may play Mon-Fri 9am-4pm. Must contact in advance.
Societies must contact in advance.
Green Fees not confirmed.
Facilities ♀ ♬ ☎ ⁅ Gerry Rielly.

Leisure putting green, cart/buggy/trolley hire.
Location 0.75m N off A752
Hotel ★★★★ 60% The Copthorne, George Square, GLASGOW ☎ 0141 332 6711 141 ➡ ⁅⁆

GATEHOUSE-OF-FLEET
Map 11 NX55

Gatehouse Laurieston Rd DG7 2PW ☎ 01644 450263
Set against a background of rolling hills with scenic views of Fleet Bay and the Solway Firth.
9 holes, 2398yds, Par 66, SSS 64, Course record 60.
Club membership 315.
Visitors restricted Sun before 11.30am.
Societies telephone in advance.
Green Fees £10 per day/round.
Facilities ♬
Leisure putting green.
Location 0.25m N of town
Hotel ★★★★☆ 67% Cally Palace Hotel, GATEHOUSE OF FLEET
☎ 01557 814341 56 ➡

GIRVAN
Map 10 NX19

Brunston Castle Bargany, Dailly KA26 9RH
☎ 01465 811471
Sheltered inland parkland course. A championship design by Donald Steel, the course is bisected by the River Girvan and shaped to incorporate all the natural surroundings. It finishes with the 17th 185 yards over a man made lake. Driving range.
Burns: 18 holes, 6858yds, Par 72, SSS 73, Course record 69.
Club membership 400. ▶

Visitors reserved for members at weekends 8-10 & 12.30-1.30.
Societies telephone to book.
Green Fees £35 per day; £22.50 per round (£39/£27.50 weekends).
Facilities ⊗ ⅢⅠ ⊾ ☕ Y △ ⌂ ⛳ ⟨ Derek J McKenzie.
Leisure motorised carts for hire, buggies for hire, trolley for hire, driving range, putting green, practice area.
Location 6m SE of Turnberry
Hotel ★★★ 73% Malin Court, TURNBERRY ☎ 01655 331457 17 ⇌ ⛳

Girvan Golf Course Rd KA26 9HW
☎ 01465 714272
Municipal seaside and parkland course. Testing 17th hole (223-yds) uphill, par 3. Good views.
18 holes, 5098yds, Par 64, SSS 65.
Club membership 175.
Visitors no restrictions.
Societies may not play Jul & Aug.
Green Fees not confirmed.
Facilities Y △
Location N side of town off A77
Hotel ★★★ 73% Malin Court, TURNBERRY ☎ 01655 331457 17 ⇌ ⛳

GLASGOW Map 11 NS56

Alexandra Alexandra Park, Alexandra Pde G31 8SE
☎ 0141 552 1294
Parkland course, hilly with some woodland.
9 holes, 2800yds, Par 31, Course record 25.
Club membership 85.
Visitors no restrictions.
Societies telephone 24 hrs in advance or by writing one week in advance.
Green Fees prices under review.
Facilities △
Leisure practice area.
Location 2m E of city centre off M8/A8
Hotel ★★★ 68% The Town House Hotel, 54 West George St, GLASGOW ☎ 0141 332 3320 34 ⇌ ⛳

Cowglen Barrhead Rd G43 1AU
☎ 0141 632 0556
Parkland course with good views over Clyde valley to Campsie Hills.
18 holes, 5976yds, Par 69, SSS 69, Course record 63.
Club membership 775.
Visitors play on shorter course. Must contact in advance and have a handicap certificate. No visitors at weekends.
Societies must telephone in advance.
Green Fees not confirmed.
Facilities Y △ ⌂ ⟨ John McTear.
Leisure putting,practice area,driving range.
Location 4.5m SW of city centre on B762
Hotel ★★★ 64% Macdonald Thistle, Eastwood Toll, GIFFNOCK ☎ 0141 638 2225 56 ⇌ ⛳

Haggs Castle 70 Dumbreck Rd, Dumbreck G41 4SN
☎ 0141 427 1157
Wooded, parkland course where Scottish National Championships and the Glasgow and Scottish Open have been held. Quite difficult.
18 holes, 6464yds, Par 73, SSS 72.
Club membership 900.
Visitors may not play at weekends. Must contact in advance.
Societies apply in writing.
Green Fees £38 per day; £27 per round.
Facilities ⊗ ⅢⅠ ⊾ ☕ Y △ ⌂ ⛳ ⟨ Jim McAlister.
Leisure buggies for hire, trolley for hire, putting green, practice area.
Location 2.5m SW of city centre on B768
Hotel ★★★ 59% Sherbrooke Castle Hotel, 11 Sherbrooke Av, Pollokshields, GLASGOW ☎ 0141 427 4227 10 ⇌ ⛳ Annexe11 ⇌ ⛳

Kirkhill Greenless Rd, Cambuslang G72 8YN
☎ 0141 641 8499
Meadowland course designed by James Braid.
18 holes, 5889yds, Par 69, SSS 69, Course record 63.
Club membership 650.
Visitors must play with member at weekends. Must contact in advance.
Societies must contact in advance.
Green Fees not confirmed.
Facilities Y △
Location 5m SE of city centre off A749
Hotel ★★★ 59% Stuart Hotel, 2 Cornwall Way, EAST KILBRIDE ☎ 013552 21161 39 ⇌ ⛳

Knightswood Lincoln Av G71 5QZ
☎ 0141 959 2131
Parkland course within easy reach of city. Two dog-legs.
9 holes, 2700yds, Par 33, SSS 33.
Club membership 60.
Visitors no restrictions.
Societies welcome.
Green Fees not confirmed.
Location 4m W of city centre off A82
Hotel ★★★ 64% Jurys Glasgow Hotel, Great Western Rd, GLASGOW ☎ 0141 334 8161 133 ⇌ ⛳

Lethamhill 1240 Cumbernauld Rd, Millerston G33 1AH
☎ 0141 770 6220
Municipal parkland course.
18 holes, 5859yds, Par 70, SSS 68.
Visitors must have an introduction from own club.
Societies must contact in advance.
Facilities △
Location 3m NE of city centre on A80
Hotel ★★★★ 60% The Copthorne, George Square, GLASGOW ☎ 0141 332 6711 141 ⇌ ⛳

Linn Park Simshill Rd G44 5EP ☎ 0141 637 5871
Municipal parkland course with six par 3's in outward half.
18 holes, 4952yds, Par 65, SSS 65, Course record 61.
Club membership 80.
Visitors no restrictions.
Green Fees not confirmed.
Facilities △
Location 4m S of city centre off B766

Hotel ★★★ 63% Bruce Swallow Hotel, Cornwall St, EAST KILBRIDE ☎ 013552 29771 78 ⇥ ♠

Pollok 90 Barrhead Rd G43 1BG ☎ 0141 632 4351
Parkland course with woods and river.
18 holes, 6254yds, Par 71, SSS 70, Course record 62.
Club membership 620.
Visitors no ladies. Must play with member at weekends. Must contact in advance.
Societies must contact in writing.
Green Fees £33 per day; £26 per round.
Facilities ⊗ ∭ ᕮ 里 ♀ ᕟ 🖻 ✆
Leisure putting green, practice area.
Location 4m SW of city centre on A762
Hotel ★★★ 63% Tinto Firs Thistle, 470 Kilmarnock Rd, GLASGOW ☎ 0141 637 2353 28 ⇥ ♠

Williamwood Clarkston Rd G44 3YR ☎ 0141 637 4311
Inland course, fairly hilly with wooded areas, a small lake and pond.
18 holes, 5878yds, SSS 69, Course record 61.
Club membership 800.
Visitors apply in writing to secretary, no weekend play.
Societies midweek bookings only, apply in writing to secretary.
Green Fees not confirmed.
Facilities ⊗ ∭ ᕮ 里 ♀ ᕟ 🖻 ✆ Jack Gardner.
Leisure trolley for hire, practice area.
Location 5m S of city centre on B767
Hotel ★★★ 64% Macdonald Thistle, Eastwood Toll, GIFFNOCK ☎ 0141 638 2225 56 ⇥ ♠

GLENLUCE
Map 10 NX15

Wigtownshire County Mains of Park DG8 0NN
☎ 01581 300420
Seaside links course on the shores of Luce Bay, easy walking but affected by winds. The 12th hole, a dogleg with out of bounds to the right,is named after the course's designer, Gordon Cunnigham.
18 holes, 5847yds, Par 70, SSS 68, Course record 67.
Club membership 450.
Visitors may play any day by prior arrangement ex competition days.
Societies must contact in advance.
Green Fees £20 per day ; £16 per round (£22/£18 weekends).
Facilities ⊗ ∭ ᕮ 里 ♀ ᕟ 🖻 ✆
Leisure trolley for hire, putting green, practice area.
Location 1.5m W off A75
Hotel ★★★★ 68% North West Castle Hotel, STRANRAER ☎ 01776 704413 71 ⇥ ♠

GREAT CUMBRAE ISLAND
(MILLPORT)
Map 10 NS15

Millport Golf Rd KA28 0HB ☎ 01475 530305 & 530311
Pleasantly situated on the west side of Cumbrae looking over Bute to Arran and the Mull of Kintyre. Exposure means conditions may vary according to wind strength and direction. A typical seaside resort course welcoming visitors.
18 holes, 5828yds, Par 68, SSS 69, Course record 64.
Club membership 470.
Visitors advisable to phone and book tee times especially in summer months.
Societies telephone or write in advance.

Green Fees £15 per day; £11 per round (£20/£15 weekends and bank holidays) Due to be reviewed..
Facilities ⊗ ∭ ᕮ 里 ♀ ᕟ 🖻 ✆ Kenneth Docherty.
Leisure trolley for hire, putting green, practice area.
Location Approx 4m from ferry slip
Hotel ★★★ 66% Brisbane House, 14 Greenock Rd, Esplanade, LARGS ☎ 01475 687200 23 ⇥ ♠

GRETNA
Map 11 NY36

Gretna Kirtle View DG16 5HD ☎ 01461 338464
A nice parkland course on gentle hills. Opened in 1991, it offers a good test of skill.
9 holes, 3214yds, Par 72, SSS 71, Course record 71.
Club membership 250.
Visitors no restrictions.
Societies telephone in advance.
Green Fees £8 per day (£10 weekends & bank holidays).
Facilities ⊗ by prior arrangement ∭ by prior arrangement ᕮ by prior arrangement 里 ♀ ᕟ
Leisure trolley for hire, driving range.
Location 0.5m W of Gretna on B721,signposted
Hotel ★★ 66% Solway Lodge Hotel, Annan Rd, GRETNA
☎ 01461 338266 3 ⇥ ♠Annexe7 ⇥ ♠

HAMILTON
Map 11 NS75

Hamilton Carlisle Rd, Ferniegair ML3 7TU
☎ 01698 282872
Beautiful parkland course.
18 holes, 6243yds, Par 70, SSS 71, Course record 62.
Visitors must contact in advance, may not play weekends. Must be accompanied by member.
Societies apply in writing.
Green Fees not confirmed.
Facilities ⊗ ∭ ᕮ 里 ♀ ᕟ 🖻 ✆ Maurice Moir.
Location 1.5m SE on A72
Hotel ★★ 62% Silvertrees Hotel, Silverwells Crescent, BOTHWELL
☎ 01698 852311 7 ⇥ ♠Annexe19 ⇥ ♠

Strathclyde Park Mote Hill ML3 6BY
☎ 01698 266155
Municipal parkland course.
9 holes, 3128yds, Par 36, SSS 70, Course record 64.
Club membership 200.
Visitors same day booking system in operation, telephone above number (Regional Authority).
Societies must contact in advance on above telephone number.
Green Fees £2.50 per round.
Facilities 里 ♀ ᕟ 🖻 ✆ William Walker.
Leisure driving range, putting green, practice area.
Location N side of town off B7071
Hotel ★★ 62% Silvertrees Hotel, Silverwells Crescent, BOTHWELL
☎ 01698 852311 7 ⇥ ♠Annexe19 ⇥ ♠

HAWICK
Map 12 NT51

Hawick Vertish Hill TD9 0NY ☎ 01450 372293
Hill course with good views.
18 holes, 5929yds, Par 68, SSS 69, Course record 63.
Club membership 600.

▶

Tweed Valley Hotel

As a centre for golf the Tweed Valley is a natural choice. Quiet, friendly and well appointed, with a noteworthy reputation for good food. Including its own smokehouse, fine wines and huge selection of whiskies at the bar. Special rates throughout the year. Enjoy countryside golf on 17 scenic courses. All arranged for you.

Tweed Valley Hotel, Walkerburn, Peeblesshire EH43 6AA
Tel: 01896 870636   Fax: 01896 870639

Visitors must contact in advance.
Societies write or telephone for booking arrangement.
Green Fees £24 per day; £16 per round (£24 day/round).
Facilities ⊗ ⅏ ⅃ ♨ ♀ ♁ 🏠
Leisure trolley for hire, putting green, practice area.
Location SW side of town
Hotel ★★ 71% Kirklands Hotel, West Stewart Place, HAWICK ☎ 01450 372263 5 ⇄ 🐾Annexe7 ⇄ 🐾

INNERLEITHEN   Map 11 NT33

Innerleithen Leithen Water, Leithen Rd EH44 6NL
☎ 01896 830951
Moorland course, with easy walking. Burns and rivers are natural hazards. Testing 5th hole (100 yds) par 3.
9 holes, 6056yds, Par 70, SSS 69, Course record 65.
Club membership 240.
Visitors advisable to check for availability for weekends.
Societies by prior booking.
Green Fees £15 per day; £10 per round (£18/£12 weekends).
Facilities ⊗ by prior arrangement ⅏ by prior arrangement ♨ ♀ by prior arrangement ♀ ♁
Leisure putting green, practice area.
Location 1.5m N on B709
Hotel ★★★♨ 61% Tweed Valley Hotel & Restaurant, Galashiels Rd, WALKERBURN ☎ 01896 870636 16 ⇄ 🐾

IRVINE   Map 10 NS33

Glasgow Gailes KA11 5AE ☎ 0141 942 2011
A lovely seaside links. The turf of the fairways and all the greens is truly glorious and provides tireless play. Established in 1787, this is the ninth oldest course in the world and is a qualifying course for the Open Championship.
18 holes, 6510yds, Par 71, SSS 72, Course record 64.
Club membership 1100.
Visitors must contact in advance but may not play weekends & bank holidays before 2.30pm.
Societies initial contact by telephone.
Green Fees £37 per day; £30 per round (£33 afternoon round weekends).
Facilities ⊗ ⅏ by prior arrangement ♨ ♀ ♁ 🏠 🐾 ♙ J Steven.
Leisure trolley for hire, putting green, practice area.
Location 2m S off A737
Hotel ★★★★ 52% Hospitality Inn, 46 Annick Rd, IRVINE ☎ 01294 274272 128 ⇄ 🐾

Irvine Bogside KA12 8SN ☎ 01294 275626
Testing links course; only two short holes.
18 holes, 6400yds, Par 71, SSS 71, Course record 65.
Club membership 450.
Visitors may not play before 3pm Sat & Sun. Must contact in advance.
Societies are welcome weekdays, telephone 01294 275979 to book in advance.
Green Fees not confirmed.
Facilities ♀ ♁ 🏠 🐾 Keith Erskine.
Location N side of town off A737
Hotel ★★★★ 52% Hospitality Inn, 46 Annick Rd, IRVINE ☎ 01294 274272 128 ⇄ 🐾

Irvine Ravenspark 13 Kidsneuk Ln KA12 8SR
☎ 01294 271293
Parkland course.
18 holes, 6702yds, Par 71, SSS 71, Course record 65.
Club membership 600.
Visitors may not play Sat before 2pm.
Societies not allowed Sat, contact club steward in advance.
Green Fees £11 per day; £7 per round (£17/£11 weekends).
Facilities ⊗ ⅏ ♨ ♀ ♁ 🏠 🐾 Peter Bond.
Leisure putting green, practice ground.
Location N side of town on A737
Hotel ★★★♨ 71% Montgreenan Mansion House Hotel, Montgreenan Estate, KILWINNING ☎ 01294 557733 21 ⇄ 🐾

Western Gailes Gailes by Irvine KA11 5AE
☎ 01294 311649
A magnificent seaside links with glorious turf and wonderful greens. The view is open across the Firth of Clyde to the neighbouring islands. It is a well-balanced course crossed by 3 burns. There are 2 par 5's, the 6th and 14th, and the 11th is a testing 445-yd, par 4, dog-leg.
18 holes, 6664yds, Par 71, SSS 73, Course record 65.
Visitors welcome Mon, Tue, Wed & Fri. Must contact in advance and have a handicap certificate.
Societies must contact in advance.
Green Fees not confirmed.
Facilities ♀ ♁
Leisure caddies & caddy cars for hire.
Location 2m S off A737
Hotel ★★★♨ 71% Montgreenan Mansion House Hotel, Montgreenan Estate, KILWINNING ☎ 01294 557733 21 ⇄ 🐾

JEDBURGH   Map 12 NT62

Jedburgh Dunion Rd TD8 6DQ ☎ 01835 863587
Undulating parkland course, windy, with young trees.
9 holes, 5760yds, Par 68, SSS 67.
Club membership 265.

Visitors restricted at weekends during competitions.
Societies must contact at least one month in advance.
Green Fees not confirmed.
Facilities ♀ (Apr-Sep) ⚐ 🏠
Location 1m W on B6358
Hotel L Larkhall Burn, JEDBURGH
☎ 01835 862040 6 ⇉ ⌕

JOHNSTONE Map 10 NS46

Cochrane Castle Scott Av, Craigstone PA5 0HF
☎ 01505 320146
Fairly hilly parkland course,wooded with two small streams
running through it.
18 holes, 6223yds, Par 71, SSS 71, Course record 65.
Club membership 660.
Visitors may not play at weekends. Must contact in
writing.
Societies apply in writing.
Green Fees £25 per day; £17 per round.
Facilities ⊗ ⥸ ⓛ ⚐ ♀ ⚐ 🏠 ⌕ Stuart Campbell.
Leisure trolley for hire, putting green, practice area.
Location 0.5m W off A737
Hotel ★★★ 64% Lynnhurst Hotel, Park Rd,
JOHNSTONE ☎ 01505 324331 21 ⇉ ⌕

Elderslie 63 Main Rd, Elderslie PA5 9AZ ☎ 01505 322835
Parkland course, undulating, with good views.
18 holes, 6175yds, Par 70, SSS 70.
Club membership 940.
Visitors may not play at weekends & bank holidays.
Must contact club in advance and preferably
have a handicap certificate.
Societies must telephone in advance.
Green Fees not confirmed.
Facilities ♀ ⚐ 🏠 ⌕ Richard Bowman.
Leisure putting green,trolley hire,practica area.
Location E side of town on A737
Hotel ★★★ 64% Lynnhurst Hotel, Park Rd,
JOHNSTONE ☎ 01505 324331 21 ⇉ ⌕

KELSO Map 12 NT73

Kelso Racecourse Rd TD5 7SL ☎ 01573 223009
Parkland course. Easy walking.
18 holes, 6046yds, Par 70, SSS 69, Course record 64.
Club membership 500.
Visitors advisable to telephone in advance.
Societies apply in writing.
Green Fees £20 per day; £12 per round (£27/£18 weekends).
Facilities ⊗ ⥸ ⓛ ⚐ ♀ ⚐ 🏠 ⌕
Leisure trolley for hire, putting green, practice area.
Location N side of town centre off B6461
Hotel ★★★ 61% Cross Keys Hotel, 36-37 The
Square, KELSO ☎ 01573 223303 24 ⇉ ⌕

KILBIRNIE Map 10 NS35

Kilbirnie Place Largs Rd KA25 7AT ☎ 01505 683398
Easy walking parkland course.
18 holes, 5400yds, Par 69, SSS 67.
Club membership 450.
Visitors no restrictions.
Societies must apply in writing in advance.
Green Fees not confirmed.

Facilities ♀ ⚐
Leisure putting green,practice area.
Location 1m W on A760
Hotel ★★ 69% Elderslie Hotel, John St, Broomfields,
LARGS ☎ 01475 686460 26rm(9 ⇉ 5 ⌕)

KILMARNOCK Map 10 NS43

Annanhill Irvine Rd KA1 2RT ☎ 01563 521644
Municipal, tree-lined parkland course played over by private
clubs.
18 holes, 6269yds, Par 71, SSS 70, Course record 66.
Club membership 394.
Visitors book at starters office.
Societies apply in writing.
Green Fees £14.25 per day; £9 per round (£17.50/£14.25
weekends).
Facilities ⊗ by prior arrangement ⥸ by prior arrangement
ⓛ by prior arrangement ⚐ by prior arrangement
♀ ⚐
Leisure putting green, practice area.
Location 1m W on A71
Hotel ★★★⚑ 75% Chapeltoun House Hotel,
STEWARTON ☎ 01560 482696 8 ⇉ ⌕

Caprington Ayr Rd KA1 4UW ☎ 01563 23702
Municipal parkland course.
18 holes, 5718yds, Par 69, SSS 68.
Club membership 400.
Visitors may not play on Sat.
Societies must contact in advance.
Green Fees not confirmed.
Facilities ♀ ⚐ 🏠
Location 1.5m S on B7038
Hotel ★★★⚑ 75% Chapeltoun House Hotel,
STEWARTON ☎ 01560 482696 8 ⇉ ⌕

KILSYTH Map 11 NS77

Kilsyth Lennox Tak Ma Doon Rd G65 0RS
☎ 01236 824115 & 823089
Hilly moorland course, hard walking. Course and facilities
revamped with 18-holes after a serious fire early in 1993.
18 holes, 5912yds, Par 70, SSS 70, Course record 66.
Club membership 500.
Visitors advisable to contact in advance. No restrictions
weekdays up to 5pm, may play Sun on
application but not Sat.
Societies must contact in advance.
Green Fees £16 per day; £10 per round (£18/£12 weekends).
Facilities ⊗ ⥸ ⓛ ⚐ ♀ ⚐ 🏠 ⌕ R Abercrombie.
Leisure buggies for hire, putting green.
Location N side of town off A803
Hotel ★★★ 64% Kirkhouse Inn, STRATHBLANE
☎ 01360 770621 15 ⇉ ⌕

KIRKCUDBRIGHT Map 11 NX65

Kirkcudbright Stirling Crescent DG6 4EZ
☎ 01557 330314
Parkland course. Hilly, with hard walking. Good views.
18 holes, 5598yds, Par 68, SSS 68, Course record 63.
Club membership 500.
Visitors advisable to contact in advance.
Societies contact in advance. ▶

Green Fees £20 per day/round (£15 per round).
Facilities ⊗ ⅷ ﬤ ☂ ♀ ⚐
Leisure trolley for hire, driving range, putting green.
Location NE side of town off A711
Hotel ★★ 72% Selkirk Arms Hotel, Old High St, KIRKCUDBRIGHT
☎ 01557 330402 15 ⇆ ╒Annexe1 ⇆ ╒

KIRKINTILLOCH
Map 11 NS67

Hayston Campsie Rd G66 1RN
☎ 0141 776 1244
An undulating, tree-lined course with a sandy subsoil.
18 holes, 6042yds, Par 70, SSS 70, Course record 62.
Club membership 800.
Visitors must apply in advance, may not play weekends,
Societies Tue & Thu, apply in writing
Green Fees £25 per day; £18 per round.
Facilities ⊗ ⅷ ﬤ ☂ ♀ ⚐ ╒ ╒ Steven Barnett.
Leisure trolley for hire, putting green, practice area.
Location 1m NW off A803
Hotel ★★★ 64% Kirkhouse Inn, STRATHBLANE
☎ 01360 770621 15 ⇆ ╒

Kirkintilloch Campsie Rd G66 1RN
☎ 0141 776 1256
Parkland course in rural setting.
18 holes, 5269yds, Par 70, SSS 66.
Club membership 650.
Visitors must be introduced by member.
Societies apply in writing.
Green Fees not confirmed.
Facilities ⚐ ╒
Location 1m NW off A803
Hotel ★★★ 64% Kirkhouse Inn, STRATHBLANE
☎ 01360 770621 15 ⇆ ╒

LANARK
Map 11 NS84

Lanark The Moor, Whitelees Rd ML11 7RX
☎ 01555 663219
Chosen as one of the pre-qualifying tests for the Open Championship held at Lanark from 1977 to 1983. The address of the club, 'The Moor', gives some indication as to the kind of golf to be found there. Golf has been played at Lanark for well over a century and the Club dates from 1851.
Old Course: 18 holes, 6423yds, Par 70, SSS 71, Course record 62.
9 Hole: 9 holes, 2980yds, Par 56.
Club membership 880.
Visitors must contact in advance, no visitors weekends,
Societies apply in advance.
Green Fees £35 per day; £23 per round. 9 hole course £4 per day.
Facilities ⊗ ⅷ ﬤ ☂ ♀ ⚐ ╒ ╒ Ron Wallace.
Leisure motorised carts for hire, buggies for hire, trolley for hire, putting green, practice area.
Location E side of town centre off A73
Hotel ★★★ 67% Cartland Bridge Hotel, Glasgow Rd, LANARK
☎ 01555 664426 18 ⇆ ╒

LANGBANK
Map 10 NS37

Gleddoch Golf and Country Club PA14 6YE
☎ 01475 540304
Parkland and heathland course with other sporting facilities available to temporary members. Good views over Firth of Clyde.
18 holes, 5661yds, Par 68, SSS 67.
Club membership 600.
Visitors must contact in advance.
Societies must contact in advance.
Green Fees not confirmed.
Facilities ♀ ⚐ ╒ ╒ ⇆ ╒ Keith Campbell.
Leisure grass tennis courts, heated indoor swimming pool, squash, sauna, archery, clay pigeon shooting.
Location B789-Old Greenock Road
Hotel ★★★⚓ 72% Gleddoch House Hotel, LANGBANK ☎ 01475 540711 39 ⇆ ╒

LANGHOLM
Map 11 NY38

Langholm Whitaside DG13 0JR ☎ 013873 80673
Hillside course with fine views, hard walking.
9 holes, 5744yds, Par 70, SSS 68, Course record 63.
Club membership 200.
Visitors restricted Sat & Sun.
Societies apply in writing to secretary.
Green Fees £10 per day/round.
Facilities ⊗ by prior arrangement ⅷ by prior arrangement ﬤ by prior arrangement ☂ by prior arrangement ♀
Leisure putting green, practice area.
Location E side of village off A7
Hotel ★★ 57% Eskdale Hotel, Market Place, LANGHOLM
☎ 013873 80357 & 81178 15rm(11 ⇆ ╒)

LARGS
Map 10 NS25

Largs Irvine Rd KA30 8EU ☎ 01475 673594
A parkland, tree-lined course with views to the Clyde coast and Arran Isles.
18 holes, 6220yds, Par 70, SSS 71, Course record 64.
Club membership 850.
Visitors may not play weekends & competition days. Must contact in advance.
Societies apply in writing.
Green Fees not confirmed.
Facilities ♀ ⚐ ╒ ╒ ╒
Location 1m S of town centre on A78
Hotel ★★ 69% Elderslie Hotel, John St, Broomfields, LARGS ☎ 01475 686460 26rm(9 ⇆5 ╒)

Routenburn Routenburn Rd KA30 8QA
☎ 01475 673230
Heathland course with fine views over Firth of Clyde.
18 holes, 5675yds, Par 68, SSS 68.
Club membership 500.
Visitors no restrictions.
Societies apply in writing.
Green Fees not confirmed.
Facilities ♀ ⚐ ╒ ╒ J Grieg McQueen.
Leisure caddy car for hire.

Location 1m N off A78
Hotel ★★★♨♨ 63% Manor Park Hotel, LARGS
☎ 01475 520832 10 ⇆ ⚘Annexe13 ⇆ ⚘

LARKHALL
Map 11 NS75

Larkhall Burnhead Rd ML9 3AB ☎ 01698 881113
Small, inland parkland course.
9 holes, 6700yds, Par 72, SSS 71, Course record 69.
Club membership 250.
Visitors restricted Tue & Sat.
Green Fees not confirmed.
Facilities ♀
Location E side of town on B7019
Hotel ★★★ 66% Popinjay Hotel, Lanark Rd,
ROSEBANK
☎ 01555 860441 36 ⇆ ⚘Annexe5 ⇆ ⚘

LAUDER
Map 12 NT54

Lauder Galashiels Rd TD2 6RS ☎ 01578 722526
Inland course and practice area on gently sloping hill.
9 holes, 3001yds, Par 72, SSS 70, Course record 70.
Club membership 200.
Visitors restricted Wed 4.30-5.30pm and Sun before
noon.
Societies telephone in advance.
Green Fees not confirmed.
Facilities ⚐
Location On Galashiels Rd, off A68, 0.5m from Lauder
Hotel ★★ 63% Lauderdale Hotel, 1 Edinburgh Rd,
LAUDER ☎ 01578 722231 9 ⇆ ⚘

LEADHILLS
Map 11 NS81

Leadhills ML12 6XR ☎ no telephone
A testing, hilly course with high winds. At 1500ft above sea
level it is the highest golf course in Scotland.
9 holes, 4354yds, Par 66, SSS 64.
Club membership 80.
Visitors no restrictions.
Societies must contact in advance.
Green Fees not confirmed.
Location E side of village off B797
Hotel ★★ 61% Mennockfoot Lodge Hotel, Mennock,
SANQUHAR
☎ 01659 50382 & 50477 1 ⇆Annexe8 ⇆ ⚘

LENNOXTOWN
Map 11 NS67

Campsie Crow Rd G65 7HX ☎ 01360 310244
Scenic hillside course.
18 holes, 5507yds, Par 70, SSS 67, Course record 65.
Club membership 640.
Visitors contact professional 1360 310920.
Societies wrtten application.
Green Fees £20 per day; £12 per round (£15 per round
weekends).
Facilities ⊗ �🍴 ⚑ ⚐ ♀ ♨ 🏠 ℓ Mark Brennan.
Leisure putting green, practice area.
Location 0.5m N on B822
Hotel ★★★ 64% Kirkhouse Inn, STRATHBLANE
☎ 01360 770621 15 ⇆ ⚘

LENZIE
Map 11 NS67

Lenzie 19 Crosshill Rd G66 5DA
☎ 0141 776 1535 & 0141 776 6020
Pleasant moorland course.
18 holes, 5984yds, Par 69, SSS 69, Course record 64.
Club membership 890.
Visitors must contact in advance and may not play
weekends.
Societies apply in writing.
Green Fees £24 per day; £16 per round.
Facilities ⊗ �🍴 ⚑ ⚐ ♀ ♨ 🏠 ℓ Jim McCallum.
Leisure motorised carts for hire, trolley for hire, putting
green, practice area.
Location S side of town on B819
Hotel ★★★ 64% Kirkhouse Inn, STRATHBLANE
☎ 01360 770621 15 ⇆ ⚘

LESMAHAGOW
Map 11 NS83

Holland Bush Acretophead ML11 0JS
☎ 01555 893484 & 893646
Fairly difficult, tree-lined municipal parkland and moorland
course. 1st half is flat, while 2nd half is hilly. No bunkers.
18 holes, 6110yds, Par 71, SSS 69, Course record 63.
Club membership 500.
Visitors no restrictions.
Societies contact the professional in advance.
Green Fees £12 per day (£15 weekends) under review.
Facilities ⊗ ⍾ ⚑ ⚐ ♀ ♨ 🏠 ⚘ ℓ Ian Rae.
Leisure trolley for hire, practice area.
Hotel ★★★ 66% Strathaven Hotel, Hamilton Rd,
STRATHAVEN ☎ 01357 521778 10 ⇆ ⚘

LOCHMABEN
Map 11 NY08

Lochmaben Castlehillgate DG11 1NT
☎ 01387 810552
Comfortable-walking parkland course between two lochs
with fine old trees and fast greens all year round.
18 holes, 5357yds, Par 67, SSS 66, Course record 60.
Club membership 850.
Visitors advised to contact in advance.
Societies must contact in advance.
Green Fees £16 per day; £14 per round (£20/£16 weekends).
Facilities ⊗ ⍾ ⚑ ⚐ ♀ ♨
Leisure fishing, putting green, practice area.
Location S side of village off A709
Hotel ★★★ 69% Dryfesdale Hotel, LOCKERBIE
☎ 01576 202427 15 ⇆ ⚘

LOCHWINNOCH
Map 10 NS35

Lochwinnoch Burnfoot Rd PA12 4AN ☎ 01505 842153
Parkland course, slightly hilly in middle, with testing golf.
Overlooks bird sanctuary and boating loch.
18 holes, 6243yds, Par 71, SSS 70.
Club membership 650.
Visitors may not play at weekends and bank holidays
unless accompanied by member. Restricted
during competition days.
Societies apply in writing to club administrator.
Green Fees not confirmed.
Facilities ♀ ♨ 🏠 ℓ Gerry Reilly. ▶

Location W side of town off A760
Hotel ★★★ 65% Bowfield Hotel & Country Club, HOWWOOD ☎ 01505 705225 12 ⇋ ↾

LOCKERBIE   Map 11 NY18

Lockerbie Corrie Rd DG11 2ND
☎ 01576 202462 & 203363
Parkland course with fine views and featuring the only pond hole in Dumfriesshire.
18 holes, 5614yds, Par 68, SSS 67, Course record 64.
Club membership 620.
Visitors restricted Sun. Advisable to book in advance.
Societies must contact secretary in advance.
Green Fees £18 per day (£22 per day Sat; £18 per round Sun).
Facilities ⊗ ⅧⅢ ⅛ ⚏ ⚐ ⚒
Leisure trolley for hire, putting green, practice area.
Location E side of town centre off B7068
Hotel ★★★ 69% Dryfesdale Hotel, LOCKERBIE
☎ 01576 202427 15 ⇋ ↾

MAUCHLINE   Map 11 NS42

Ballochmyle Catrine Rd KA5 6LE ☎ 01290 550469
Wooded parkland course.
18 holes, 5952yds, Par 70, SSS 69, Course record 65.
Club membership 730.
Visitors no visitors on Mon from Oct-Mar except with member.
Societies apply in writing.
Green Fees £25 per day; £18 per round (£30 per day weekends).
Facilities ⊗ ⅧⅢ by prior arrangement ⅛ ⚏ ⚐ ⚒ ⛶
Leisure trolley for hire, putting green, practice area.
Location 1m SE on B705
Hotel ★★ 57% Royal Hotel, 1 Glaisnock St, CUMNOCK
☎ 01290 420822 11rm(6 ⇋ ↾)

MAYBOLE   Map 10 NS20

Maybole Municipal Memorial Park KA19 7DX
Hilly parkland course.
9 holes, 2635yds, Par 33, SSS 65, Course record 64.
Club membership 100.
Visitors no restrictions.
Societies must contact in advance.
Green Fees not confirmed.
Hotel ★★(red)⚕ Ladyburn, MAYBOLE
☎ 01655 740585 8rm(4 ⇋3 ↾)

MELROSE   Map 12 NT53

Melrose Dingleton TD6 9HS
☎ 01896 822855 & 822391
Undulating tree-lined fairways with spendid views.
9 holes, 5579yds, Par 70, SSS 68, Course record 61.
Club membership 380.
Visitors competitions all Sats and many Suns Apr-Oct, ladies priority Tue, junior priority Wed am in holidays.
Societies apply in writing.
Green Fees £15 per round/day.

Facilities ⊗ by prior arrangement ⅧⅢ by prior arrangement ⅛ by prior arrangement ⚐ ⚒
Leisure practice area.
Location S side of town centre on B6359
Hotel ★★★ 64% Burt's Hotel, The Square, MELROSE ☎ 01896 822285 21 ⇋ ↾

MILNGAVIE   Map 11 NS57

Clober Craigton Rd G62 7HP ☎ 0141 956 1685 & 6963
Parkland course. Testing 5th hole, par 3.
18 holes, 5042yds, Par 65, SSS 65, Course record 61.
Club membership 600.
Visitors may not play after 4.30pm Mon-Thu and after 4pm Fri & last Tue in month (Mar-Sep). Must play with member weekends and bank holidays.
Societies must contact in advance.
Green Fees not confirmed.
Facilities ⚐ ⚒ ⌂
Leisure putting green, trolley hire.
Location NW side of town
Hotel ★★★ 65% Black Bull Thistle, Main St, MILNGAVIE ☎ 0141 956 2291 27 ⇋ ↾

Dougalston Strathblane Rd G62 8HJ ☎ 0141 956 5750
Tree-lined with water features.
18 holes, 6683yds, Par 72, SSS 71.
Club membership 500.
Visitors are restricted at weekends.
Societies weekdays only.
Green Fees £15 per round; £20 per 36 holes.
Facilities ⊗ ⅧⅢ ⅛ ⚏ ⚐ ⚒ ⛶
Leisure trolley for hire, putting green, practice area.
Location NE side of town on A81
Hotel ★★★ 65% Black Bull Thistle, Main St, MILNGAVIE ☎ 0141 956 2291 27 ⇋ ↾

Hilton Park Auldmarroch Estate, Stockiemuir Rd G62 7HB
☎ 0141 956 4657
Moorland courses set amidst magnificent scenery.
Hilton Course: 18 holes, 6054yds, Par 70, SSS 70, Course record 65.
Allander Course: 18 holes, 5374yards, Par 69, SSS 66, Course record 66.
Club membership 1100.
Visitors must contact in advance but may not play at weekends.
Societies apply in advance to secretary.
Green Fees £26 per day; £20 per round.
Facilities ⊗ ⅧⅢ ⅛ ⚏ ⚐ ⚒ ⌂ ⛶ ✆ William Condichie.
Leisure buggies for hire, trolley for hire, putting green, practice area.
Location 3m NW on A809
Hotel ★★★ 65% Black Bull Thistle, Main St, MILNGAVIE ☎ 0141 956 2291 27 ⇋ ↾

Milngavie Laigh Park G62 8EP ☎ 0141 956 2073
Moorland course, hard walking, sometimes windy, good views. Testing 1st and 4th holes (par 4).
18 holes, 5818yds, Par 68, SSS 68, Course record 59.
Club membership 700.
Visitors must contact in advance, may not play weekends.
Societies apply in writing.
Green Fees £25 per day; £15 per round.
Facilities ⊗ ⅧⅢ ⅛ ⚏ ⚐ ⚒

Leisure	putting green, practice area.
Location	1.25m N
Hotel	★★★ 65% Black Bull Thistle, Main St, MILNGAVIE ☎ 0141 956 2291 27 ⇉ ↾

MINTO   Map 12 NT52

Minto Denholm TD9 8SH
☎ 01450 870220
Pleasant, undulating parkland course featuring mature trees and panoramic views of Scottish Border country. Short but quite testing.
18 holes, 5460yds, Par 68, SSS 67, Course record 65.
Club membership 670.

Visitors	advisable to telephone in advance, and essential for weekends.
Societies	telephone or write.
Green Fees	£20 per day; £15 per round (£30/£25 weekends & bank holidays).
Facilities	⊗ ⅢⅡ ⅊ ♀ ⅄
Leisure	motorised carts for hire, buggies for hire, trolley for hire, practice area.
Location	5m from Hawick, 1.25m off A698 at Denholm
Hotel	★★ 71% Kirklands Hotel, West Stewart Place, HAWICK ☎ 01450 372263 5 ⇉ ↾Annexe7 ⇉ ↾

MOFFAT   Map 11 NT00

Moffat Coatshill DG10 9SE ☎ 01683 220020
Scenic moorland course overlooking the town, with panoramic views.
18 holes, 5218yds, Par 69, SSS 67, Course record 60.
Club membership 350.

Visitors	advised to contact in advance.
Societies	apply in writing to the clubmistress.
Green Fees	£17.50 per day (£25.50 weekends & bank holidays). Weekdays (ex Wed) £12.50 per round after 3pm.
Facilities	⊗ ⅢⅡ ⅊ ♀ ⅄ ⋒ ⅌
Leisure	trolley for hire, putting green, games room.
Location	1m SW off A701
Hotel	★★★ 63% Moffat House Hotel, High St, MOFFAT ☎ 01683 220039 16 ⇉ ↾Annexe4 ⇉ ↾

MONREITH   Map 10 NX34

St Medan DG8 8NJ ☎ 01988 700358
Links course with panoramic views of the Solway and Isle of Man.
9 holes, 4608yds, Par 64, SSS 63, Course record 60.
Club membership 300.

Visitors	no restrictions.
Societies	apply in advance.
Green Fees	£15 per day; £12 per 18 holes; £7 per 9 holes.
Facilities	⊗ ⅢⅡ ⅊ ♀ ⅄ ⅌
Leisure	trolley for hire, putting green.
Location	1m SE off A747
Hotel	★★★♨ 65% Corsemalzie House Hotel, PORT WILLIAM ☎ 01988 860254 14 ⇉ ↾

MOTHERWELL   Map 11 NS75

Colville Park New Jerviston House, Jerviston Estate, Merry St ML1 4UG ☎ 01698 265779
Parkland course. First nine, tree-lined, second nine, more exposed. Testing 10th hole par 3, 16th hole par 4.
18 holes, 6250yds, Par 71, SSS 70, Course record 63.
Club membership 800.

Visitors	must contact in advance in writing.
Societies	apply in writing.
Green Fees	not confirmed.
Facilities	⊗ ⅢⅡ ⅊ ♀ ⅄ ⋒
Leisure	putting green, practice area.
Location	1.25m NE on A723
Hotel	★★ 62% Silvertrees Hotel, Silverwells Crescent, BOTHWELL ☎ 01698 852311 7 ⇉ ↾Annexe19 ⇉ ↾

MUIRHEAD   Map 11 NS66

Crow Wood Garnkirk House, Cumbernauld Rd G69 9JF
☎ 0141 779 4954 & 0141 779 2011
Parkland course.
18 holes, 6261yds, Par 71, SSS 71, Course record 62.
Club membership 800.

Visitors	must contact in advance but may not play weekends & bank holidays.
Societies	apply in advance.
Green Fees	£25 per day; £17 per round.
Facilities	⊗ ⅢⅡ ⅊ ♀ ⅄ ⋒ ⅋ Brian Moffat.
Leisure	trolley for hire, putting green, practice area.
Location	0.5m W on A80
Hotel	★★★ 68% Malmaison Hotel, 278 West George St, GLASGOW ☎ 0141 221 6400 21 ⇉ ↾

NEWCASTLETON   Map 12 NY48

Newcastleton Holm Hill TD9 0QD ☎ 01387 375257
Hill course.
9 holes, 5748yds, Par 70, SSS 68.
Club membership 100.

Visitors	contact in advance.
Societies	contact by telephone or in writing in advance.
Green Fees	£7 per day/round (£8 weekends).
Facilities	⅄ ⅌
Leisure	fishing, putting green.
Location	W side of village
Hotel	★★ 57% Eskdale Hotel, Market Place, LANGHOLM ☎ 013873 80357 & 81178 15rm(11 ⇉ ↾)

NEW CUMNOCK   Map 11 NS61

New Cumnock Lochhill, Cumnock Rd KA18 4PN
☎ 01290 338848
Parkland course.
9 holes, 5176yds, Par 68, SSS 68, Course record 68.
Club membership 280.

Visitors	restricted on Sun competition days.
Societies	apply in writing.
Green Fees	£7 per day.
Facilities	⅄ ⊠
Leisure	fishing, practice area.
Location	0.75m N on A76 ▶

Hotel ★★ 57% Royal Hotel, 1 Glaisnock St, CUMNOCK ☎ 01290 420822 11rm(6 ⇔ ℟)

NEW GALLOWAY   Map 11 NX67

New Galloway DG7 3RN
☎ 01644 420737 & 01644 430455
Set on the edge of the Galloway Hills and overlooking Loch Ken, the course has excellent tees and first class greens.
9 holes, 5006yds, Par 68, SSS 67, Course record 63.
Club membership 350.
Visitors restricted on Sun (competition days).
Societies contact secretary in advance.
Green Fees £10 per day.
Facilities ☜ ♀ ᐃ
Leisure putting green, practice area,.
Location S side of town on A762
Hotel ★★ 66% Douglas Arms, King St, CASTLE DOUGLAS ☎ 01556 502231 20rm(15 ⇔ ℟)

NEWTON MEARNS   Map 11 NS55

East Renfrewshire Pilmuir G77 8PS ☎ 01355 500258
Undulating moorland with loch; prevailing SW wind.
18 holes, 6097yds, Par 70, SSS 70, Course record 64.
Club membership 900.
Visitors telephone for details.
Societies must contact in advance.
Green Fees not confirmed.
Facilities ♀ ᐃ 🏠 ℓ Gordon Clarke.
Leisure driving range, putting green, practice area,trolley hire.
Location 3m SW on A77
Hotel ★★★ 64% Macdonald Thistle, Eastwood Toll, GIFFNOCK ☎ 0141 638 2225 56 ⇔ ℟

Eastwood Muirshield, Loganswell G77 6RX
☎ 01355 500280
Moorland course.
18 holes, 5864yds, Par 68, SSS 69, Course record 62.
Club membership 900.
Visitors contact in advance, may only play with member at weekends.
Societies must contact in advance.
Green Fees £30 per day; £20 per round.
Facilities ⊗ ⅏ ᒪ ☜ ♀ ᐃ 🏠 ℓ Alan McGinness.
Leisure trolley for hire, putting green, practice area.
Location 2.5m S on A77
Hotel ★★★ 64% Macdonald Thistle, Eastwood Toll, GIFFNOCK ☎ 0141 638 2225 56 ⇔ ℟

Whitecraigs 72 Ayr Rd G46 6SW
☎ 0141 639 4530 & 0141 639 2140 pro
Beautiful parkland course.
18 holes, 6230yds, Par 70, SSS 70, Course record 65.
Club membership 1078.
Visitors must contact professional in advance and have a handicap certificate. With member only weekends and bank holidays.
Green Fees £35 per day; £28 per round.
Facilities ⊗ ⅏ ᒪ ☜ ♀ ᐃ 🏠 ⍑ ℓ Alistair Forrow.
Leisure trolley for hire, putting green, practice area.
Location 1.5m NE on A77
Hotel ★★★ 64% Macdonald Thistle, Eastwood Toll, GIFFNOCK ☎ 0141 638 2225 56 ⇔ ℟

NEWTON STEWART   Map 10 NX46

Newton Stewart Kirroughtree Av, Minnigaff DG8 6PF
☎ 01671 402172
Parkland course in picturesque setting. Short but quite tight.
18 holes, 5970yds, Par 69, SSS 69.
Club membership 300.
Visitors must contact in advance.
Societies must contact in advance.
Green Fees £19 per day; £16 per round (£23/£19 weekends & bank holidays).
Facilities ⊗ ⅏ ᒪ ☜ ♀ ᐃ 🏠 ⍑
Leisure trolley for hire, practice area.
Location 0.5m N of town centre
Hotel ★★ 67% Creebridge House Hotel, NEWTON STEWART ☎ 01671 402121 20 ⇔ ℟

PAISLEY   Map 11 NS46

Barshaw Barshaw Park PA1 3TJ ☎ 0141 889 2908
Municipal parkland course.
18 holes, 5703yds, Par 68, SSS 67, Course record 63.
Club membership 100.
Visitors no restrictions.
Societies by prior arrangement with Parks Manager, Dept of Sports & Leisure, Renfrewshire Council, Mirren House, 6 Maxwell St, Paisley PA3 2AB.
Green Fees £6 per round.
Facilities ☜ ᐃ ⍑ ℓ John Scott.
Leisure putting green.
Location 1m E off A737
Hotel ★★★ 68% Glynhill Hotel & Leisure Club, Paisley Rd, RENFREW ☎ 0141 886 5555 125 ⇔ ℟

Paisley Braehead PA2 8TZ
☎ 0141 884 3903 & 884 4114
Moorland course, windy but with good views.
18 holes, 6466yds, Par 71, SSS 72, Course record 66.
Club membership 800.
Visitors must contact in advance. Visitors may not play weekends or public holidays.
Societies weekdays only, excluding bank holidays. Contact in advance.
Green Fees £28 per day; £20 per round.
Facilities ⊗ ⅏ ᒪ ☜ ♀ ᐃ 🏠 ℓ Grant Gilmour.
Leisure trolley for hire, putting green, practice area.
Location S side of town off B774
Hotel ★★★ 68% Glynhill Hotel & Leisure Club, Paisley Rd, RENFREW ☎ 0141 886 5555 125 ⇔ ℟

Ralston Strathmore Av, Ralston PA1 3DT
☎ 0141 882 1349
Parkland course.
18 holes, 6071yds, Par 71, SSS 69.
Club membership 750.
Visitors must be accompanied by member.
Green Fees not confirmed.
Facilities ♀ ᐃ 🏠
Location 2m E off A737
Hotel ★★★ 66% Swallow Hotel, 517 Paisley Rd West, GLASGOW ☎ 0141 427 3146 117 ⇔ ℟

PATNA　　　　　　　　Map 10 NS41

Doon Valley Hillside Park KA6 7JT
☎ 01292 531607 & 550411
Established parkland course located on an undulating hillside.
9 holes, 5654yds, Par 70, SSS 68.
Club membership 90.
Visitors　　mid week tee times available any time, advisable
　　　　　　　to contact for weekends.
Societies　　telephone to arrange.
Green Fees £13.80 per day; £9 per round.
Facilities　　⛳
Leisure　　fishing.
Location　　10m S of Ayr on the A713
Hotel　　★★(red)🏨 Ladyburn, MAYBOLE
　　　　　　　☎ 01655 740585 8rm(4 ⇌3 ↾)

PEEBLES　　　　　　　Map 11 NT24

Peebles Kirkland St EH45 8EU ☎ 01721 720197
Parkland course with fine views.
18 holes, 6160yds, Par 70, SSS 70, Course record 63.
Club membership 690.
Visitors　　must contact in advance, may not play Sat.
Societies　　apply by telephone or in writing in advance.
Green Fees £23 per day; £17 per round (£30/£23 weekends).
Facilities　　⊗ 🍴 ▙ 🍷 ♀ ⛳ 🏠 ↾
Leisure　　motorised carts for hire, buggies for hire, trolley
　　　　　　　for hire, putting green, practice area.
Location　　W side of town centre off A72
Hotel　　★★★ 71% Peebles Hydro Hotel, PEEBLES
　　　　　　　☎ 01721 720602 137 ⇌ ↾

PORTPATRICK　　　　　Map 10 NX05

Portpatrick Golf Course Rd DG9 8TB ☎ 01776 810273
Seaside links-type course, set on cliffs overlooking the Irish
Sea, with magnificent views.
*Dunskey Course: 18 holes, 5882yds, Par 70, SSS 68, Course
record 65.*
Dinvin Course: 9 holes, 1504yds, Par 27, SSS 27.
Club membership 720.
Visitors　　must contact in advance.
Societies　　must contact in advance.
Green Fees 18 holes: £25 per day; £17 per round (£30/£20
　　　　　　　weekends) 9 holes: £12 per day; £6 per round.
Facilities　　⊗ 🍴 ▙ 🍷 ♀ ⛳ 🏠 ↾
Leisure　　trolley for hire, putting green, practice area.
Location　　300 yds right from war memorial
Hotel　　★★★ 66% Fernhill Hotel, PORTPATRICK
　　　　　　　☎ 01776 810220 14 ⇌ ↾Annexe6 ⇌ ↾

PRESTWICK　　　　　　Map 10 NS32

Prestwick 2 Links Rd KA9 1QG ☎ 01292 477404
Seaside links with natural hazards and fine views.
18 holes, 6544yds, Par 71, SSS 72.
Club membership 575.
Visitors　　restricted Thu; may not play at weekends.
　　　　　　　Must contact in advance and have a
　　　　　　　handicap certificate.
Societies　　must contact in writing.
Green Fees not confirmed.
Facilities　　⛳ 🏠 ↾ ↾ F C Rennie.

Location　　In town centre off A79
Hotel　　★★ 62% Parkstone Hotel, Esplanade,
　　　　　　　PRESTWICK ☎ 01292 477286 15 ⇌ ↾

Prestwick St Cuthbert East Rd KA9 2SX
☎ 01292 477101
Parkland course with easy walking, natural hazards and
sometimes windy.
18 holes, 6470yds, Par 71, SSS 71, Course record 64.
Club membership 880.
Visitors　　must contact in advance but may not play at
　　　　　　　weekends & bank holidays.
Societies　　Mon-Fri, apply in writing.
Green Fees £27 per day; £20 per round.
Facilities　　⊗ 🍴 ▙ 🍷 ♀ ⛳
Leisure　　trolley for hire, putting green, practice area.
Location　　0.5m E of town centre off A77
Hotel　　★★ 61% St Nicholas Hotel, 41 Ayr Rd,
　　　　　　　PRESTWICK ☎ 01292 479568 17rm(12 ⇌ ↾)

Prestwick St Nicholas Grangemuir Rd KA9 1SN
☎ 01292 477608
Seaside links course with whins, heather and tight fairways. It
provides easy walking and has an unrestricted view of the
Firth of Clyde.
18 holes, 5952yds, Par 69, SSS 69, Course record 63.
Club membership 650.
Visitors　　except weekends & public holidays. Must
　　　　　　　contact in advance.
Societies　　must contact in advance.
Green Fees £35 per day; £22 per round.
Facilities　　⊗ 🍴 ▙ 🍷 ♀ ⛳ 🏠
Leisure　　putting green.
Location　　S side of town off A79
Hotel　　★★ 62% Parkstone Hotel, Esplanade,
　　　　　　　PRESTWICK ☎ 01292 477286 15 ⇌ ↾

RENFREW　　　　　　　Map 11 NS46

Renfrew Blythswood Estate, Inchinnan Rd PA4 9EG
☎ 0141 886 6692
Tree-lined parkland course.
18 holes, 6818yds, Par 72, SSS 73.
Club membership 800.
Visitors　　restricted to Mon, Tue & Thu, apply in advance.
Societies　　apply in writing in advance.
Green Fees not confirmed.
Facilities　　♀ ⛳ 🏠 ↾ Stuart Kerr.
Leisure　　putting green,trolley hire.
Location　　0.75m W off A8
Hotel　　★★★ 68% Glynhill Hotel & Leisure Club,
　　　　　　　Paisley Rd, RENFREW
　　　　　　　☎ 0141 886 5555 125 ⇌ ↾

RIGSIDE　　　　　　　Map 11 NS83

Douglas Water Old School, Ayr Rd ML11 9NP
☎ 01555 880361
A 9-hole course of 3,000 yards with good variety and some
hills and spectacular views. An interesting course with a
challenging longest hole of 564 yards but, overall, not too
testing for average golfers.
9 holes, 5890yds, Par 72, SSS 69.
Club membership 250.　　　　　　　　　　　　　　▶

Visitors no restrictions weekdays or Sun, competitions on Sat normal restrictions.
Societies apply in writing/telephone in advance.
Green Fees not confirmed.
Facilities ♀ (prior arrangement) ⚐
Location Ayr rd A70
Hotel ★★★ 67% Tinto Hotel, Symington, BIGGAR
☎ 01899 308454 29 ⇔ ↑

ST BOSWELLS

Map 12 NT53

St Boswells Braeheads TD6 0DE
☎ 01835 823527
Attractive parkland course by the banks of the River Tweed; easy walking.
9 holes, 5250yds, Par 66.
Club membership 320.
Visitors contact in advance.
Societies booking by writing to secretary.
Green Fees £15 per day; £10 per round (£15 per day/round weekends).
Facilities ♥ ♀ ⚐
Leisure fishing.
Location 500yds off A68 east end of village
Hotel ★★★⚑ 76% Dryburgh Abbey Hotel, ST BOSWELLS
☎ 01835 822261 25 ⇔ ↑Annexe1 ⇔ ↑

SANQUHAR

Map 11 NS70

Sanquhar Euchen Golf Course, Blackaddie Rd DG4 6JZ
☎ 01659 50577
Moorland course, fine views.
9 holes, 5594yds, Par 70, SSS 68 or 55 holes.
Club membership 200.
Visitors no restrictions.
Societies must pre-book.
Green Fees £10 per day (£12 weekends).
Facilities ⊗ by prior arrangement ⅏ by prior arrangement ♥ ♀ ⚐
Leisure putting green, practice area.
Location 0.5m SW off A76
Hotel ★★ 61% Mennockfoot Lodge Hotel, Mennock, SANQUHAR
☎ 01659 50382 & 50477 1 ⇔ ↑Annexe8 ⇔ ↑

SELKIRK

Map 12 NT42

Selkirk Selkirk Hill TD7 4NW
☎ 01750 22508
Pleasant moorland course set around Selkirk Hill. Unrivalled views.
9 holes, 5620yds, Par 68, SSS 67, Course record 61.
Club membership 364.
Visitors may not play Mon evening, competition/match days.
Societies must telephone in advance.
Green Fees not confirmed.
Facilities ⚐
Location 1m S on A7
Hotel ★★ 62% Heatherlie House Hotel, Heatherlie Park, SELKIRK
☎ 01750 21200 7rm(6 ↑)

SHOTTS

Map 11 NS86

Shotts Blairhead ML7 5BJ ☎ 01501 820431 & 826628
Moorland course.
18 holes, 6205yds, Par 70, SSS 70, Course record 63.
Club membership 500.
Visitors may not play weekends.
Societies apply in writing.
Green Fees £17 per day.
Facilities ⊗ ⅏ ⚑ ♥ ♀ ⚐ ⚞ ↑
Leisure buggies for hire, trolley for hire, putting green, practice area.
Location 2m from M8 off Benhar Road
Hotel ★★★ 61% The Hilcroft Hotel, East Main St, WHITBURN ☎ 01501 740818 30 ⇔ ↑

SKELMORLIE

Map 10 NS16

Skelmorlie Beithglass PA17 5ES ☎ 01475 520152
Parkland/moorland course with magnificent views over Firth of Clyde. Designed by James Braid, the club celebrated its centenary in 1991. The first five holes are played twice.
13 holes, 5056yds, Par 64, SSS 65.
Club membership 385.
Visitors no visitors before 4pm Sat.
Societies apply by telephone.
Green Fees £16 per day; £12 per 18 holes (£18/£13 weekends).
Facilities ♥ ♀ ⚐ ↑
Leisure fishing.
Location E side of village off A78
Hotel ★★★⚑ 63% Manor Park Hotel, LARGS
☎ 01475 520832 10 ⇔ ↑Annexe13 ⇔ ↑

SOUTHERNESS

Map 11 NX95

Southerness DG2 8AZ ☎ 01387 880677
Natural links, Championship course with panoramic views. Heather and bracken abound.
18 holes, 6566yds, Par 69, SSS 73, Course record 65.
Club membership 830.
Visitors must contact in advance.
Societies must contact in advance.
Green Fees £25 per day (£35 weekends & bank holidays).
Facilities ⊗ ⅏ ⚑ ♥ ♀ ⚐ ⚞
Leisure trolley for hire, putting green, practice area.
Location 3.5m S of Kirkbean off A710
Hotel ★★ 65% Clonyard House Hotel, COLVEND
☎ 01556 630372 15 ⇔ ↑

STEVENSTON

Map 10 NS24

Ardeer Greenhead KA20 4JX ☎ 01294 464542
Parkland course with natural hazards.
18 holes, 6500yds, Par 72, SSS 72, Course record 64.
Club membership 560.
Visitors may not play Sat.
Societies must contact in advance.
Green Fees not confirmed.
Facilities ♀ ⚐ ⚞
Location 0.5m N off A78
Hotel ★★★⚑ 71% Montgreenan Mansion House Hotel, Montgreenan Estate, KILWINNING
☎ 01294 557733 21 ⇔ ↑

ROYAL TROON

TROON *South Ayrshire* ☎ 01292 311555   **Map 10 NS33**

John Ingham writes: When Jack Nicklaus first played Royal Troon in the 1962 Open, he was 22 and hit the ball a long way. At that time Nicklaus told me 'There are only two holes that I might not reach with my second shot. My favourite shot is the drive, which I hit up to 350 yards. Just before I swing,' he said, 'all my concentration is directed on one thing and that is to give the ball as big a hit - and as square a hit - as I physically can.'

While sheer length from the back tees at Royal Troon is a great advantage, bearing in mind the full course measures 7097 yards, where you hit the ball is more important than how far. The reason is that this championship links-type course is peppered with bunkers not visible from the tee.

That particular Open was won by Arnold Palmer, in those days a longish hitter as well. However, Palmer also had a delightful putting touch, essential for Royal Troon greens, which can prove hard to read.

Royal Troon is one of the finest links in the world and in an American list appears at number 36. Created in 1878, it was then mercifully free of jumbo jets from nearby Prestwick and has provided entertaining and testing golf for players from all over the world. Greg Norman holds the record with a 10-under-par round of 64. A round which put him in a tie for the 1989 Open which he lost to Mark Calcavecchia.

In the 1960s I played a round at this grand links with the late Henry Longhurst, a good club single figure man who had once won the German Amateur championship. To my best drives, lashed in the breeze, he would just hiss 'Wrong line' and, sure enough, when we got up the fairway, the ball would be submerged in soft sand. In fact I'm told there are 365 bunkers, one for every day of the year!

The Marine Higland hotel is on the edge of the course and, as there are 22 other courses in the area, this makes a great place for a holiday.

So great is Royal Troon, in fact, that the Royal and Ancient has announced that the 1997 Open will again be staged there - for the seventh time since 1923!

Visitors	may not play Wed, Fri, weekends. Must write in advance and have a letter of introduction from own club and a handicap certificate of under 20. Ladies and under 18s may only play on the Portland
Societies	apply in writing
Green fees	£90 per day (Portland only £55) inc lunch.
Facilities	⊗ 川 ᪤ ᪣ ♀ ♨ 🛍 ☏ ⛳ 𝄃 (J D Montgomerie)
Location	Craigend Rd Troon KA10 6EP (S side of town on B749)

36 holes. Old Course: 18 holes, 7097yds, Par 73, SSS 74, course record 64 (Greg Norman)
Portland: 18 holes, 6274yds, Par 71, SSS 71

WHERE TO STAY AND EAT NEARBY

HOTELS:
TROON
★★★⊛⊛ ⚌ 81% Lochgreen House, Monktenhill Rd, Southwood ☎ 01292 313343. 7 ⇥ 📻

★★★★ 65% Marine Highland. ☎ 01292 314444, 72 ⇥ 📻

★★★⊛⊛ 74% Highgrove House ☎ 01292 312511. 9 (2 📻 7 ⇥ 📻)

★★★⊛ 66% Piersland House, Craigend Rd. ☎ 01292 314747. 15 (1 ⇥ 14 ⇥ 📻) Annexe 8 ⇥ 📻

Auchenharvie Moor Park Rd West KA20 3HU
☎ 01294 603103
Long and flat municipal course with narrow greens and a
pond affecting the 3rd and 12th holes. Easy walking.
9 holes, 5048yds, Par 65, SSS 65.
Visitors municipal course 6 day advance booking system.
Societies apply to professional.
Green Fees £3.30 per 9 holes (£5.50 weekends).
Facilities ⊗ ⅄ ☎ ♀ ♨ 🏠 ᵀ ⌁ Bob Rogers.
Leisure trolley for hire, driving range, putting green,
practice area.
Hotel ★★★⚌ 71% Montgreenan Mansion House
Hotel, Montgreenan Estate, KILWINNING
☎ 01294 557733 21 ⇆ ♞

STRANRAER   Map 10 NX06

Stranraer Creachmore by Stranraer DG9 0LF
☎ 01776 870245
Parkland course with beautiful view of Lochryan.
18 holes, 6308yds, Par 70, SSS 71, Course record 66.
Club membership 596.
Visitors must contact in advance. Members times
reserved throughout year.
Societies must telephone in advance.
Green Fees £24 per day; £17.50 per round (£30/£23
weekends).
Facilities ♀ ♨ 🏠
Leisure trolleys, practice area.
Location 2.5m NW on A718
Hotel ★★★★ 68% North West Castle Hotel,
STRANRAER ☎ 01776 704413 71 ⇆ ♞

STRATHAVEN   Map 11 NS64

Strathaven Glasgow Rd ML10 6NL ☎ 01357 520421
Gently undulating, tree-lined, Championship parkland course
with panoramic views over town and Avon valley.
18 holes, 6224yds, Par 71, SSS 71, Course record 63.
Club membership 950.
Visitors welcome weekdays up to 4pm only. Must
contact in advance.
Societies apply in writing to general manager.
Green Fees £30 per day; £20 per round.
Facilities ⊗ ⅏ ⅄ ☎ ♀ ♨ 🏠 ⌁ Matt McCrorie.
Leisure trolley for hire, putting green, practice area.
Location NE side of town on A726
Hotel ★★★ 66% Strathaven Hotel, Hamilton Rd,
STRATHAVEN ☎ 01357 521778 10 ⇆ ♞

THORNHILL   Map 11 NX89

Thornhill Blacknest DG3 5DW
☎ 01848 330546 & 331779
Moorland/parkland course with fine views.
18 holes, 6011yds, Par 71, SSS 70.
Club membership 700.
Visitors apply in advance, restricted competition days.
Societies apply in writing.
Green Fees £18 per day (£22 weekends & bank holidays).
Facilities ⊗ ⅏ ⅄ ☎ ♀ ♨
Leisure trolley for hire, putting green, practice area.
Location 1m E of town off A92
Hotel ★★ 72% Trigony House Hotel, Closeburn,
THORNHILL ☎ 01848 331211 8 ⇆ ♞

TROON   Map 10 NS33

ROYAL TROON See page 325

Troon Municipal Harling Dr KA10 6NE
☎ 01292 312464
Three links courses, two Championship.
Lochgreen Course: 18 holes, 6785yds, Par 74, SSS 73.
Darley Course: 18 holes, 6501yds, Par 71, SSS 71.
Fullarton Course: 18 holes, 4822yds, Par 64, SSS 63.
Club membership 3000.
Visitors no restrictions.
Societies apply in writing.
Green Fees not confirmed.
Facilities ♀ ♨ 🏠 ᵀ ⌁ Gordon McKinley.
Leisure putting, trolley hire, practice area.
Location 100yds from railway station
Hotel ★★ 62% Craiglea Hotel, South Beach,
TROON
☎ 01292 311366 20rm(10 ⇆ ♞)

TURNBERRY   Map 10 NS20

TURNBERRY HOTEL GOLF COURSES See page 327

UDDINGSTON   Map 11 NS66

Calderbraes 57 Roundknowe Rd G71 7TS
☎ 01698 813425
Parkland course with good view of Clyde Valley. Testing 4th
hole (par 4), hard uphill.
9 holes, 5046yds, Par 66, SSS 67, Course record 65.
Club membership 230.
Visitors weekdays before 5pm.
Societies welcome.
Green Fees not confirmed.
Facilities ♀ ♨
Leisure putting green, practice area.
Location 1.5m NW off A74
Hotel ★★ 67% Redstones Hotel, 8-10 Glasgow Rd,
UDDINGSTON
☎ 01698 813774 & 814843 18rm(16 ⇆ ♞)

UPLAWMOOR   Map 10 NS45

Caldwell G78 4AU
☎ 01505 850366 (Secretary) & 850616 (Pro)
Parkland course.
18 holes, 6294yds, Par 71, SSS 70, Course record 63.
Club membership 600.
Visitors must be with member at weekends & bank
holidays. Must contact professional in advance.
Societies writing to professional.
Green Fees £28 per day; £20 per round.
Facilities ⊗ ⅏ ⅄ ☎ ♀ ♨ 🏠 ⌁ Stephen Forbes.
Leisure trolley for hire, putting green, practice area.
Location 0.5m SW A736
Hotel ★★★ 60% Dalmeny Park Country House,
Lochlibo Rd, BARRHEAD
☎ 0141 881 9211 19 ⇆ ♞

TURNBERRY HOTEL GOLF COURSES

TURNBERRY *South Ayrshire*

☎ 01655 331000   Map 10 NS20

John Ingham writes: The hotel is sumptuous, the Ailsa and Arran courses beneath it are total magic. The air reaches down into your inner lung and of all places in Scotland, Turnberry has to be among the finest.

Tunberry is delightfully off the beaten track and, although the courses are principally for residents of the hotel, if you wish to fly in, then Prestwick Airport is only seventeen miles from the first tee. What makes the place so desirable is the warmness of the welcome and, course professional Brian Gunson will tell you, this is literally so on occasions, as the links is on the friendliest of gulf streams.

The Ailsa course has been the venue for the Open in 1977 and 1986 and hosted it again in 1994. It was here in the 1977 Open, that Jack Nicklaus put up such a brave fight against Tom Watson. Then, in 1986, we had a wondrous victory from Greg Norman. He has fond memories of Turnberry, where a few hours after the prize-giving he was able to sit with his wife on the edge of the great links, drinking champagne, and watching the moon roll round the pure white lighthouse out by the 9th green.

Without any doubt, Turnberry is the stuff of dreams and you must go there if you possibly can.

Visitors	The golf courses are principally for residents of the hotel, so must contact in advance
Societies	contact in advance as courses are for residents of the hotel
Green fees	Arran £30, Ailsa £60 fees include a round on Arran if played on same day
Facilities	⊗ ⍟ ⤋ ♨ ♀ ⇤ ⚲ 🏠 ⚑ ((Brian Gunson) practice area, putting green, trollies
Leisure	tennis (hardcourt), swimming pool, squash, snooker, health spa
Location	Turnberry KA26 9LT. On A719 N side of village

36 holes. Ailsa Course: 18 holes, 6440 yds, Par 69, SSS 72, Course record 63 (Greg Norman & Maric Hayes) Arran Course: 18 holes, 6014yds, Par 68, SSS 69. Course record 65 (E Macintosh/C Ronald/S McGregor)

WHERE TO STAY AND EAT NEARBY

HOTELS:

MAYBOLE
★★(Red)🏵 ⚘ Ladyburn
☎ 01655 740585. 8(7 ⇥ 🎝)

TURNBERRY
★★★★★(Red) 🏵🏵 Turnberry Hotel,
Golf Courses & Spa.
☎ 01655 331000. 132 ⇥ 🎝

★★★ 🏵 73%Malin Court.
☎ 01655 31457. 17 ⇥ 🎝

WEST KILBRIDE
Map 10 NS24

West Kilbride 33-35 Fullerton Dr, Seamill KA23 9NQ
☎ 01294 823911
Seaside links course on Firth of Clyde, with fine views of Isle
of Arran from every hole.
18 holes, 5974yds, Par 70, SSS 70, Course record 63.
Club membership 840.
Visitors may not play at weekends, must contact in
advance.
Societies Tue & Thu only; must contact in advance.
Green Fees £35 per day; £21 per round.
Facilities ⊗ ⅢⅡ ㅂ ♥ ♀ ♨ 📠 ℓ Gregor Howie.
Leisure trolley for hire, driving range, putting green,
practice area.
Location W side of town off A78
Hotel ★★ 69% Elderslie Hotel, John St, Broomfields,
LARGS
☎ 01475 686460 26rm(9 ⇌5 ℝ)

WEST LINTON
Map 11 NT15

West Linton EH46 7HN
☎ 01968 660256 & 660970
Moorland course with beautiful views of Pentland Hills.
18 holes, 6132yds, Par 69, SSS 70, Course record 63.
Club membership 725.
Visitors weekdays anytime, weekends not before 1pm.
Societies contact the secretary in writing.
Green Fees £24 per day; £16 per round (£25 per round
weekends). Five day ticket (Mon-Fri) £75.
Facilities ⊗ ⅢⅡ ㅂ ♥ ♀ ♨ 📠 ℓ Ian Wright.
Leisure motorised carts for hire, trolley for hire, putting
green, practice area.
Location NW side of village off A702
Hotel ★★★ 71% Peebles Hydro Hotel, PEEBLES
☎ 01721 720602 137 ⇌ ℝ

WIGTOWN
Map 10 NX45

Wigtown & Bladnoch Lightlands Ter DG8 9EF
☎ 01988 403354 & 403209
Slightly hilly parkland course with fine views over Wigtown
Bay to Galloway Hills.
9 holes, 5462yds, Par 68, SSS 67, Course record 62.
Club membership 150.
Visitors advisable to contact in advance for weekend
play.
Societies contact secretary in advance.
Green Fees £15 per day; £10 per round.
Facilities ⊗ ㅂ ♥ ♀ ♨
Leisure putting green, practice area.
Location SW on A714
Hotel ★★ 67% Creebridge House Hotel, NEWTON
STEWART
☎ 01671 402121 20 ⇌ ℝ

WISHAW
Map 11 NS75

Wishaw 55 Cleland Rd ML2 7PH ☎ 01698 372869
Parkland course with many tree-lined areas. Bunkers protect
17 of the 18 greens.
18 holes, 6073yds, Par 69, SSS 69, Course record 64.
Club membership 940.
Visitors may not play Sat.
Societies apply in writing.
Green Fees £20 per day; £12 per round (Sun £25 per
day/round).
Facilities ⊗ ⅢⅡ ㅂ ♥ ♀ ♨ 📠 ℉ ℓ John Campbell.
Leisure motorised carts for hire, buggies for hire, trolley
for hire, putting green, practice area.
Location NW side of town off A721
Hotel ★★★ 66% Popinjay Hotel, Lanark Rd,
ROSEBANK
☎ 01555 860441 36 ⇌ ℝAnnexe5 ⇌ ℝ

WALES

'Dai was a Welsh winner; so is every visitor'

Dai Rees once told me to hit down on the ball, and get the hands 'here' to drive shots low into the wind. For me this advice led to a powerful hook! But he knew the secrets for sure because Welshman Dai led the British Ryder Cup team to that 1957 victory, and collected titles all over the world. Ian Woosnam is, without doubt, the great modern-day 'Taffie' and could pocket our premier title soon to add to his US Masters. So Wales, you see, can produce stars other than rugby players.

Wales can be proud, too, about certain excellent courses. Sometimes wild and exposed, they provide a wholesome day out for us, and a friendly welcome to 'foreigners' from over the border. Some of the great tests started in a humble way. During the last century, for instance, a fellow called Tony Ruck collected flower pots from a lady in the village, sank them into fairly basic greens and created the Aberdovey course in Merioneth, at the mouth of the Dovey estuary.

To return to Dai Rees, he won the PGA Close Championship at Ashburnham (Burry Port) in 1959 and when I went there to see him win, I found the holes near the clubhouse not too impressive.Further out the course shows itself in great colours. Well worth a trip back, we decided.

PORTHCAWL RATED TOP

It's pointless to say which is the best course in Wales. We tend to judge this on how we played, and whether we won! But Royal Porthcawl (near Bridgend) is a top rated course by our American researchers. I love the place, and not just because you can have a view of the sea from every single hole. Go there, but with an introduction from someone significant.

In 1893, an Honourable Finch-Hatton, just back from Australia, was showing chums the boomerang on the Morfa, a low-lying piece of land beneath the famous castle at Harlech. Great place for golf, thought Finch-Hatton and thus the splendid St David's course was created. Edward VII became club patron and the Duke of Windsor was captain in 1935. St David's welcomes everyone, even into the clubhouse and no travel agents have set money-making traps. Try it.

The St Pierre clubhouse, just across the Severn Bridge, is as ancient as the country. It is a fine, lush parkland course with a large lake and magnificent trees. Why haven't we mentioned Southerndown (Bridgend). Downland, above the sea with views across the Bristol Channel, and if you look over there, that is the direction to Ireland...... where yet another golf feast awaits.

WALES

The directory which follows has been divided into three geographical regions. Counties have not been shown against individual locations as recent legislation has created a number of smaller counties which will be unfamiliar to the visitor. The postal authorities have confirmed that it is no longer necessary to include a county name in addresses, provided a post code is shown. All locations appear in the atlas at the end of this guide in their appropriate counties.

NORTH WALES

This region includes the counties of Aberconwy & Colwyn, Anglesey, Denbighshire, Flintshire, Gwynedd and Wrexham which reflect the recent national changes.

ABERDOVEY (ABERDYFI) Map 06 SN69

Aberdovey LL35 0RT ☎ 01654 767493
A beautiful championship course at the mouth of the Dovey estuary, Aberdovey has all the true characteristics of a seaside links. It has some fine holes among them the 3rd, the 12th, an especially good short hole, and the 15th. There are some striking views to be had from the course.
18 holes, 6445yds, Par 71, SSS 71, Course record 66.
Club membership 1000.
Visitors must contact in advance, restrictions at weekends.
Societies prior arrangement essential.
Green Fees £34 per day; £22 per round (£40/£27 weekends).
Facilities ⊗ ℳ ᒣ ⓛ ▼ ♀ ♣ 🏌 ☔ John Davies.
Leisure motorised carts for hire, buggies for hire, trolley for hire, putting green, practice area.
Location 0.5m W on A493
Hotel ★★★ 69% Trefeddian Hotel, ABERDOVEY ☎ 01654 767213 46 ⇔ ℟

ABERGELE Map 06 SH97

Abergele & Pensarn Tan-y-Gopa Rd LL22 8DS
☎ 01745 824034
A beautiful parkland course with views of the Irish Sea and Gwrych Castle. There are splendid finishing holes, a testing par 5, 16th; a 185 yd, 17th to an elevated green, and a superb par 5 18th with out of bounds just behind the green.
18 holes, 6520yds, Par 72, SSS 71, Course record 66.
Club membership 1250.
Visitors must contact in advance. Limited play weekends.

Societies must contact in advance.
Green Fees £22 per day (£28 weekends & bank holidays).
Facilities ⊗ ℳ ᒣ ⓛ ▼ ♀ ♣ 🏌 Iain R Runcie.
Leisure trolley for hire, putting green, practice area.
Location 0.5m W off A547/A55
Hotel ★★★ 63% Kinmel Manor Hotel, St Georges Rd, ABERGELE ☎ 01745 832014 42 ⇔ ℟
Additional hotel ★★★ 60% Colwyn Bay Hotel, Penmaenhead, COLWYN BAY ☎ 01492 516555 43 ⇔ ℟

ABERSOCH Map 06 SH32

Abersoch LL53 7EY ☎ 01758 712622
Seaside links, with five parkland holes.
18 holes, 5819yds, Par 69, SSS 68.
Club membership 650.
Visitors must contact in advance. Competition days Sun & Thu.
Societies must apply in advance.
Green Fees £18 per day (£20 weekends).
Facilities ⊗ ℳ ᒣ ⓛ ▼ ♀ ♣ 🏌 A D Jones.
Leisure trolley for hire, driving range.
Location S side of village
Hotel ★★★ 64% Abersoch Harbour Hotel, ABERSOCH ☎ 01758 712406 9 ⇔ ℟Annexe5 ⇔ ℟

ANGLESEY, ISLE OF Map 06

Golf Courses on the island of Anglesey are listed below.

AMLWCH Map 06 SH49

Bull Bay LL68 9RY ☎ 01407 830960
Wales's northernmost course,Bull Bay is a pleasant coastal, heathland course with natural meadow, rock, gorse and wind hazards. Views from all tees across Irish Sea to Isle of Man.
18 holes, 6217yds, Par 70, SSS 70, Course record 65.
Club membership 825.
Visitors advisable to contact in advance.
Societies advance booking essential.
Green Fees £20 per day; £15 per round (£25/£20 Fri & weekends). Winter £13/£10 (£16/£13 Fri & weekends).
Facilities ⊗ ℳ ᒣ ⓛ ▼ ♀ ♣ 🏌 ☔ 🏌
Leisure trolley for hire, putting green, practice area, snooker.
Location 1m W on A5025
Hotel ★★ 60% Trecastell Hotel, Bull Bay, AMLWCH ☎ 01407 830651 12rm(8 ⇔3 ℟)

BEAUMARIS Map 06 SH67

Baron Hill LL58 8YW ☎ 01248 810231
Undulating course with natural hazards of rock and gorse. Testing 3rd and 4th holes (par 4's). Nole 5/14 plays into the prevailing wind with an elevated tee across two streams. The hole is between two gorse covered mounds.
9 holes, 5062mtrs, Par 68, SSS 69, Course record 62.
Club membership 400.
Visitors ladies have priority on Tue & club competitions Sun.
Societies apply in writing to secretary.
Green Fees £14 per day, £40 weekly.

Facilities ⊗ 𝍢 ♨ ♥ ♀ ♨
Location 1m SW off A545
Hotel ★★ 70% Bishopsgate House Hotel, 54 Castle
St, BEAUMARIS
☎ 01248 810302 9 ⇌ ℝAnnexe2rm

HOLYHEAD
Map 06 SH28

Holyhead Lon Garreg Fawr, Trearddur Bay LL65 2YG
☎ 01407 763279
Treeless, undulating seaside course which provides a
varied and testing game, particularly in a south wind. The
fairways are bordered by gorse, heather and rugged
outcrops of rock. Accuracy from most tees is paramount
as there are 43 fairway and greenside bunkers and lakes.
Designed by James Braid. Indoor driving range.
18 holes, 6058yds, Par 70, SSS 70, Course record 64.
Club membership 1000.
Visitors must contact in advance.
Societies must contact in advance.
Green Fees £20 per day; £15 per round (£25/£20
weekends & bank holidays).
Facilities ⊗ 𝍢 ♨ ♥ ♀ ♨ ♔ ☐ ♔ ♔ ♔ Stephen Elliot.
Leisure trolley for hire, covered driving range,
putting green, practice area.
Location 1.25m S on B4545
Hotel ★★★ 71% Trearddur Bay Hotel,
TREARDDUR BAY
☎ 01407 860301 31 ⇌ ℝ

LLANGEFNI
Map 06 SH47

Llangefni (Public) LL77 7LJ
☎ 01248 722193
Picturesque parkland course designed by Hawtree & Son.
9 holes, 1342yds, Par 28, SSS 28.
Visitors no restrictions.
Societies must contact in advance.
Facilities ♨ ☐ ♔ ♔
Location 1.5m off A5
Hotel ★★★(red) Tre-Ysgawen Hall, Capel Coch,
LLANGEFNI
☎ 01248 750750 19 ⇌ ℝ

RHOSNEIGR
Map 06 SH37

Anglesey Station Rd LL64 5QX
☎ 01407 811202
Links course, low and fairly level with sand dunes and tidal
river.
18 holes, 6300yds, Par 68, SSS 68.
Club membership 400.
Visitors phone in advance, some times are reserved for
members.
Societies telephone & confirm in writing.
Green Fees not confirmed.
Facilities ♀ ♨ ☐ ♔ Mark Harrison.
Leisure putting green,trolley hire,practice area.
Location NE side of village on A4080
Hotel ★★★ 71% Trearddur Bay Hotel,
TREARDDUR BAY
☎ 01407 860301 31 ⇌ ℝ

BALA
Map 06 SH93

Bala Penlan LL23 7YD ☎ 01678 520359 & 521361
Mountainous course with natural hazards. All holes except
first and last affected by wind.
10 holes, 4962yds, Par 66, SSS 64, Course record 64.
Club membership 200.
Visitors book in advance.
Societies must contact in advance.
Green Fees £12 per day (£15 weekends & bank holidays).
Facilities ⊗ by prior arrangement 𝍢 by prior arrangement
♨ by prior arrangement ♥ by prior arrangement
♀ ♨ ♔
Leisure trolley for hire, putting green, practice area,
snooker, pool.
Location 0.5m SW off A494
Hotel ★★ 63% Plas Coch Hotel, High St, BALA
☎ 01678 520309 10 ⇌ ℝ

BANGOR
Map 06 SH57

St Deiniol Penybryn LL57 1PX ☎ 01492 353098
Elevated parkland course with panoramic views of
Snowdonia, Menai Straits, and Anglesey.
18 holes, 5068mtrs, Par 68, SSS 67, Course record 61.
Club membership 700.
Visitors must contact in advance.
Societies must contact in advance.
Green Fees £12 per week (£16 weekends).
Facilities ⊗ by prior arrangement 𝍢 by prior arrangement
♨ ♥ ♀ ♨ ☐ ♔
Leisure trolley for hire, putting green.
Location E side of town centre off A5122
Hotel ★★★ 68% Menai Court Hotel, Craig y Don Rd,
BANGOR ☎ 01248 354200 13 ⇌ ℝ

BETWS-Y-COED
Map 06 SH75

Betws-y-Coed LL24 0AL ☎ 01690 710556
Attractive flat meadowland course set between two rivers in
Snowdonia National Park.
9 holes, 4996yds, Par 64, SSS 64.
Club membership 350.
Visitors no restrictions.
Societies must telephone in advance.
Green Fees not confirmed.
Facilities ♀ ♨
Location NE side of village off A5
Hotel ★★★ 69% The Royal Oak Hotel, Holyhead Rd,
BETWS-Y-COED ☎ 01690 710219 27 ⇌ ℝ

BODELWYDDAN
Map 06 SJ07

Kimnel Park LL18 5SR ☎ 01745 833548
Flat parkland pay and play course that is suitable for
beginners.
9 holes, 3100, Par 58, SSS 58.
Visitors no restrictions.
Societies telephone for details.
Green Fees £3 for 18 holes.
Facilities ⊗ ♨ ♥ ♀ ♨ ♔ ♔ Peter Stebbings.
Leisure driving range.
Hotel ★★★ 64% Oriel House Hotel, Upper Denbigh
Rd, ST ASAPH ☎ 01745 582716 19 ⇌ ℝ

BRYNFORD
Map 07 SJ17

Holywell Brynford CH8 8LQ ☎ 01352 713937 & 710040
Exposed moorland course, with bracken and gorse flanking
undulating fairways. 720 ft above sea level.
18 holes, 6100yds, Par 70, SSS 70, Course record 69.
Club membership 505.
Visitors must contact in advance.
Societies by prior arrangement with the secretary.
Green Fees £15 per round (£20 weekends & bank holidays).
Facilities ⊗ ⅋ ᕾ ♥ ♀ ⚲ 🏠 ℓ Saen O'Conner.
Leisure trolley for hire, putting green, practice area.
Location 1.25m SW off B5121
Hotel ★★ 67% Stamford Gate Hotel, Halkyn Rd,
HOLYWELL ☎ 01352 712942 12 ⇄ ℟

CAERNARFON
Map 06 SH46

Caernarfon Llanfaglan LL54 5RP
☎ 01286 673783 & 678359
Parkland course with gentle gradients.
18 holes, 5891yds, Par 69, SSS 68.
Club membership 730.
Visitors must contact in advance.
Societies must apply in advance.
Green Fees £18 per day; £15 per round (£22/£20 weekends
& bank holidays).
Facilities ⊗ ⅋ ᕾ ♥ ♀ ⚲ 🏠 ℓ Aled Owen.
Leisure motorised carts for hire, buggies for hire, trolley
for hire, putting green, practice area.
Location 1.75m SW
Hotel ★★ 63% Stables Hotel, LLANWNDA
☎ 01286 830711 & 830935 Annexe14 ⇄ ℟

CAERWYS
Map 06 SJ17

Caerwys Nine Of Clubs CH7 5AQ ☎ 01352 720692
Following the natural contours of the land and with a south-
west aspect, this course could be considered a litle gem. Each
approach to every green is different and there are many
interesting and challenging holes.
9 holes, 3080yds, Par 60, Course record 61.
Club membership 150.
Visitors no restrictions.
Societies telephone then confirm in writing.
Green Fees £8.50 per day; £4.50 per 18 holes (£10.50/£5.50
weekends & bank holidays).
Facilities ⊗ ᕾ ⚲ 🏠 ♈
Leisure trolley for hire, putting green, practice area,
snooker.
Location 1.5m SW of A55, midway between St Asaph
and Holywell
Hotel ★★ 65% Bryn Awel Hotel, Denbigh Rd, MOLD
☎ 01352 758622 7 ⇄ ℟Annexe10 ⇄ ℟

CHIRK
Map 07 SJ23

Chirk Golf & Country Club LL14 5AD ☎ 01691 774407
Overlooked by the National Trust's Chirk Castle, is a
championship-standard 18-hole course with a 664 yard, par 5
at the 9th - one of the longest in Europe. Also a 9-hole course,
driving range and golf academy.
*Manor Course: 18 holes, 7045yds, Par 72, SSS 73, Course
record 72.*

Mine Rock: 9 holes, 1141yds, Par 27.
Club membership 750.
Visitors advisable to contact in advance. May not play in
members preferred tee times 7-11 daily.
Societies must telephone for provisonal booking.
Green Fees £22 per day; £15 per round (£28/£22 weekends).
9 holes: £4 per round (£5 weekends).
Facilities ⊗ ⅋ ᕾ ♥ ♀ ⚲ 🏠 ♈ ℓ James Waugh.
Leisure squash, fishing, buggies for hire, trolley for hire,
driving range, putting green, practice area, clay
pigeon shotingby arrangement.
Location 5m N of Oswestry
Hotel ★★★ 67% Hand Hotel, Church St, CHIRK
☎ 01691 772479 14 ⇄ ℟

COLWYN BAY
Map 06 SH87

Old Colwyn Woodland Av, Old Colwyn LL29 9NL
☎ 01492 515581
Hilly, meadowland course with sheep and cattle grazing on it
in parts.
9 holes, 5243yds, Par 68, SSS 66, Course record 63.
Club membership 267.
Visitors welcome ex Sat. Contact in advance.
Societies must contact in advance.
Green Fees £10 per day (£15 weekends and bank holidays).
May-Sep 9 holes after 7pm £5.
Facilities ♀ (weekends/evenings) ⚲
Leisure practice area.
Location E side of town centre on B5383
Hotel ★★★ 64% Hopeside Hotel, Princes Dr, West
End, COLWYN BAY
☎ 01492 533244 19 ⇄ ℟

★★★
Penmaenhead
THE
Old Colwyn
COLWYN
Colwyn Bay
BAY
Clwyd LL29 9LD
HOTEL
Tel: 01492 516555
Fax: 01492 515565
Previously called Hotel 70°

Occupying an enviable position commanding panoramic
views of the Irish Sea, Colwyn Bay and the dramatic
mountains of Snowdonia.
This splendid modern Hotel offers a very high standard of
comfort, service and luxury through-out. All bedrooms en
suite with full facilities and sea views.
Elegant restaurants serving excellent cuisine in superb
surroundings.
Ideally located for touring Snowdonia National Park and
Conwy. Numerous golf courses nearby for the discerning
golf enthusiast.
Excellent conference and banqueting facilities available
for up to 200 persons.

CONWY
Map 06 SH77

Conwy (Caernarvonshire) Beacons Way, Morfa
LL32 8ER ☎ 01492 592423
Founded in 1890, Conwy has hosted national and
international championships since 1898. Set among
sandhills, possessing true links greens and a profusion of
gorse on the latter holes, especially the 16th, 17th and
18th. This course provides the visitor with real golfing
enjoyment against a background of stunning beauty.
18 holes, 6647yds, Par 72, SSS 72, Course record 69.
Club membership 1050.
Visitors must contact secretary in advance.
Societies must contact in advance.
Green Fees £23 per day (£28 weekends & bank
holidays).
Facilities ⊗ ℍ ㄥ ☰ ♀ ㅿ 🏠 ⛳ ℓ Peter Lees.
Leisure motorised carts for hire, buggies for hire,
trolley for hire, putting green, practice area.
Location 1m W of town centre on A55
Hotel ★★★ 58% Sychnant Pass Hotel, Sychnant
Pass Rd, CONWY
☎ 01492 596868 10 ⇌ 🐾

CRICCIETH
Map 06 SH43

Criccieth Ednyfed Hill LL52 0PH ☎ 01766 522154
Hilly course on Lleyn Peninsula. Good views.
18 holes, 5787yds, Par 69, SSS 68.
Club membership 350.
Visitors must contact in advance.
Societies telephone in advance.
Green Fees £12 per day Mon-Sat (£15 Sun and bank
holidays).
Facilities ⊗ ℍ ㄥ ☰ ♀ ㅿ 🏠
Leisure trolley for hire, putting green.
Location 1m NE
Hotel ★★★🏌 70% Bron Eifion Country House
Hotel, CRICCIETH ☎ 01766 522385 19 ⇌ 🐾

DENBIGH
Map 06 SJ06

Bryn Morfydd Hotel Llanrhaedr LL16 4NP
☎ 01745 890280
In a beautiful setting in the Vale of Clwyd, the original 9-hole
Duchess course was designed by Peter Alliss in 1982. In
1992, the 18-hole Dukes course was completed: a parkland
course designed to encourage use of finesse in play.
Dukes Course: 18 holes, 5650yds, Par 70, SSS 67.
Duchess Course: 9 holes, 2098yds, Par 54.
Club membership 450.
Visitors advance reservation advisable.
Societies apply in writing.
Green Fees not confirmed.
Facilities ♀ ㅿ 🏠 ⛳ 🍴
Leisure heated outdoor swimming pool, putting green,
practice area, trolley hire.
Location On A525 between Denbigh and Ruthin

Denbigh Henllan Rd LL16 5AA ☎ 01745 814159
Parkland course, giving a testing and varied game. Good
views.
18 holes, 5712yds, Par 69, SSS 68, Course record 64.
Club membership 725.

Visitors must contact in advance.
Societies apply in writing.
Green Fees £19 per day (£25 Sun, round only Sat).
Facilities ⊗ ℍ ㄥ ☰ ♀ ㅿ 🏠 ℓ Mike Jones.
Leisure trolley for hire, putting green, practice area.
Location 1.5m NW on B5382
Hotel ★★★ 65% Talardy Park Hotel, The Roe,
ST ASAPH
☎ 01745 584957 18 ⇌ 🐾

DOLGELLAU
Map 06 SH71

Dolgellau Pencefn Rd LL40 2ES
☎ 01341 422603
Undulating parkland course. Good views of mountains and
Mawddach estuary.
9 holes, 4671yds, Par 66, SSS 63, Course record 62.
Club membership 280.
Visitors may not play on Sat.
Societies must contact in advance.
Green Fees £13 (£16 weekends & bank holidays).
Facilities ⊗ ℍ ㄥ ☰ ♀ ㅿ
Location 0.5m N
Hotel ★★ 64% Royal Ship Hotel, Queens Square,
DOLGELLAU
☎ 01341 422209 24rm(18 ⇌ 🐾)

EYTON
Map 07 SJ34

Plassey LL13 0SP
☎ 01978 780028
Plesant 9-hole course set in naturally contoured parkland with
water hazards. It is within Plassey Leisure Park and Craft
Centre and all park facilities are available to golfers.
9 holes, 2300yds.
Club membership 200.
Visitors must contact in advance,
Societies telephone then confirm in writing.
Green Fees £5 (£6 weekends & bank holidays).
Facilities ⊗ ℍ ㄥ ☰ ♀ ㅿ 🏠 ⛳ ℓ Richard Hughes.
Leisure heated indoor swimming pool, fishing, sauna,
solarium, trolley for hire, putting green, practice
area.
Location 2.5m off A483 Chester/Oswestry
Hotel ★★ 65% Cross Lanes Hotel & Restaurant,
Cross Lanes, Bangor Rd, MARCHWIEL
☎ 01978 780555 16 ⇌ 🐾

FFESTINIOG
Map 06 SH74

Ffestiniog Y Cefn LL41 4LS
☎ 01766 762637
Moorland course set in Snowdonia National Park.
9 holes, 4570yds, Par 68, SSS 66.
Club membership 150.
Visitors welcome except during competitions.
Societies must telephone in advance.
Green Fees not confirmed.
Facilities ㅿ
Location 1m E on B4391
Hotel ★★(red)🏌 Maes y Neuadd Hotel,
TALSARNAU
☎ 01766 780200 12 ⇌ 🐾Annexe4 ⇌ 🐾

FLINT
Map 07 SJ27

Flint Cornist Park CH6 5HJ ☎ 01352 732327 & 812974
Parkland course incorporating woods and streams. Excellent
views of Dee estuary.
9 holes, 6984yds, Par 69, SSS 69, Course record 65.
Club membership 260.
Visitors must contact in advance.
Societies not weekends.
Green Fees £10 per round.
Facilities ⊗ ⅢⅠ ╚ 🐴 ♀ 占
Leisure hard tennis courts, practice area.
Location 1m W
Hotel ★★ 67% Stamford Gate Hotel, Halkyn Rd,
HOLYWELL ☎ 01352 712942 12 ⇌ ↑

HARLECH
Map 06 SH53

Royal St Davids LL46 2UB ☎ 01766 780361
Championship links, with easy walking and natural
hazards.
18 holes, 6427yds, Par 69, SSS 72.
Club membership 700.
Visitors pre booking essential, must hold current
handicap certificate.
Societies telephone secretary in advance. Handicap
certificates required.
Green Fees £26 per day (£32 weekends & bank
holidays).
Facilities ⊗ ⅢⅠ ╚ 🐴 ♀ 占 ➡ ↑ John Barnett.
Leisure motorised carts for hire, buggies for hire,
trolley for hire, putting green, practice area.
Location W side of town on A496
Hotel ★★ 64% Ty Mawr Hotel, LLANBEDR
☎ 01341 241440 10 ⇌ ↑

HAWARDEN
Map 07 SJ36

Hawarden Groomsdale Ln CH5 3EH
☎ 01244 531447 & 520809
Parkland course with comfortable walking and good views.
18 holes, 5842yds, Par 69, SSS 69.
Club membership 550.
Visitors arrange visit with the professional.
Societies by prior arrangement.
Green Fees £12 (£15 weekends).
Facilities ⊗ ⅢⅠ ╚ 🐴 ♀ 占 ➡ ↑ Chris Hope.
Leisure putting green, practice area.
Location W side of town off B5125
Hotel ★★★ 72% The Gateway To Wales Hotel,
Welsh Rd, Sealand, Deeside, CHESTER
☎ 01244 830332 39 ⇌ ↑

LLANDUDNO
Map 06 SH78

Llandudno (Maesdu) Hospital Rd LL30 1HU
☎ 01492 876450
Part links, part parkland, this championship course starts
and finishes on one side of the main road, the remaining
holes, more seaside in nature, being played on the other
side. The holes are pleasantly undulating and present a
pretty picture when the gorse is in bloom. Often windy,
this varied and testing course is not for beginners.
18 holes, 6545yds, Par 72, SSS 72, Course record 66.
Club membership 1045.
Visitors must book in advance.
Societies must apply in advance to secretary.
Green Fees £22 per day (£30 weekends & bank
holidays). £16 per round after 3pm (£20
weekends & bank holidays).
Facilities ⊗ ⅢⅠ ╚ 🐴 ♀ 占 ➡ ↑ Simon Boulden.
Leisure motorised carts for hire, buggies for hire,
trolley for hire, putting green, practice area.
Location S side of town centre on A546
Hotel ★★★ 67% Imperial Hotel, The Promenade,
LLANDUDNO
☎ 01492 877466 100 ⇌ ↑
Additional ★★ 60% Esplanade Hotel, Glan-y-Mor
hotel Pde, Promenade, LLANDUDNO
☎ 01492 860300 59 ⇌ ↑

North Wales 72 Bryniau Rd, West Shore LL30 2DZ
☎ 01492 875325 & 876878
Challenging seaside links with superb views of Anglesey
and Snowdonia.
18 holes, 6247yds, Par 71, SSS 71, Course record 65.
Club membership 525.
Visitors must contact in advance.
Societies must contact in advance.
Green Fees £22 per day (£28 weekends & bank
holidays).
Facilities ⊗ ⅢⅠ ╚ 🐴 ♀ 占 ➡ ➤ ↑ Richard Bradbury.
Leisure motorised carts for hire, buggies for hire,
trolley for hire, practice ground, practice
area.
Location W side of town on A546
Hotel ★★(red) St Tudno Hotel, Promenade,
LLANDUDNO ☎ 01492 874411 21 ⇌ ↑

Rhos-on-Sea Penryhn Bay LL30 3PU
☎ 01492 549641 & 549100
Seaside course, with easy walking and panoramic views.
18 holes, 6064yds, Par 69, SSS 69.
Club membership 400.
Visitors advised to telephone beforehand to guarantee tee
times.

ESPLANADE HOTEL ★★
Glan-y-Mor Parade, Promenade, Llandudno LL30 2LL
Tel: (01492) 860300 Fax: (01492) 860418
SPECIAL ATTENTION GIVEN TO GOLFING PARTIES
MEMBERSHIP FOR NORTH WALES GOLF CLUB
Premier seafront position. Ideally situated for town and leisure facilities. 60 rooms all with
bathroom and toilet en-suite, tea/coffee making facilities, colour TV, intercom and baby listening
service, direct dial telephone. Central heating throughout. Car park. Fully licensed. Lift. Small
ballroom. Open all year. Christmas and New Year festivities. Spring and Autumn breaks.

Societies booking essential, telephone in advance.
Green Fees £10 per day (£20 weekends).
Facilities ⊗ ⅷ ⅃ ♥ ♀ ♨ 🖃 ♨ ⚓
Leisure trolley for hire, putting green.
Location 0.5m W off A546
Hotel ★★★ 62% Gogarth Abbey Hotel, West Shore, LLANDUDNO ☎ 01492 876211 40 ⇄ ♠

LLANFAIRFECHAN   Map 06 SH67

Llanfairfechan Llannerch Rd LL33 0ES ☎ 01248 680144
Hillside course with panoramic views of coast.
9 holes, 3119yds, Par 54, SSS 57, Course record 53.
Club membership 189.
Visitors booking necessay for Sun play.
Societies apply in writing.
Green Fees £10 per day (£15 weekends & bank holidays).
Facilities ⅃ ♀ ♨
Leisure putting green.
Location W side of town on A55
Hotel ★★★ 58% Sychnant Pass Hotel, Sychnant Pass Rd, CONWY ☎ 01492 596868 10 ⇄ ♠

LLANGOLLEN   Map 07 SJ24

Vale of Llangollen Holyhead Rd LL20 7PR
☎ 01978 860906
Parkland course, set in superb scenery by the River Dee.
18 holes, 6661yds, Par 72, SSS 72, Course record 67.
Club membership 760.
Visitors must contact in advance. Restricted club competition days.
Societies apply in writing to the secretary.
Green Fees £20 per day (£25 weekends & bank holidays).
Facilities ⊗ ⅷ ⅃ ♥ ♀ ♨ 🖃 ⚓ David Vaughan.
Leisure motorised carts for hire, buggies for hire, trolley for hire, putting green, practice area.
Location 1.5m E on A5
Hotel ★★★♨ 69% Bryn Howel Hotel & Restaurant, LLANGOLLEN ☎ 01978 860331 36 ⇄ ♠

MOLD   Map 07 SJ26

Old Padeswood Station Rd, Padeswood CH7 4JL
☎ 01244 547401 & 550414
Meadowland course, undulating in parts.
18 holes, 6685yds, Par 72, SSS 72, Course record 66.
Club membership 600.
Visitors welcome, subject to tee availability.
Societies telephone in advance.
Green Fees £16 (£20 weekends & bank holidays).
Facilities ⊗ ⅷ ⅃ ♥ ♀ ♨ 🖃 ⚓ Tony Davies.
Leisure buggies for hire, trolley for hire, putting green, practice area.
Location 3m SE off A5118
Hotel ★★ 65% Bryn Awel Hotel, Denbigh Rd, MOLD
☎ 01352 758622 7 ⇄ ♠Annexe10 ⇄ ♠

Padeswood & Buckley The Caia, Station Ln CH7 4JD
☎ 01244 550537
Gently undulating parkland course, with natural hazards and good views of the Welsh Hills.
18 holes, 5982yds, Par 70, SSS 69, Course record 66.
Club membership 700.

Visitors weekdays only, contact secretary in advance
Societies apply in writing.
Green Fees £25 per day, £20 per round (£25 bank holiday).
Facilities ⊗ ⅷ ⅃ ♥ ♀ ♨ 🖃 ⚓ David Ashton.
Leisure motorised carts for hire, buggies for hire, trolley for hire, driving range, putting green, practice area, snooker.
Location 3m SE off A5118
Hotel ★★ 65% Bryn Awel Hotel, Denbigh Rd, MOLD
☎ 01352 758622 7 ⇄ ♠Annexe10 ⇄ ♠

MORFA NEFYN   Map 06 SH24

Nefyn & District LL53 6DA
☎ 01758 720966
A 27-hole course played as two separate 18's, Neffyn is a cliff top links where you never lose sight of the sea. A well-maintained course which will be a very tough test for the serious golfer, is still user friendly for the casual visitor. Every hole has a different challenge and the old 13th fairway is approximately 30 yards arcross from sea-to-sea. The course has an added bonus of a pub on the beach roughly halfway round for those whose golf may need some bolstering!
Old Course: 18 holes, 6201yds, Par 71, SSS 71, Course record 67.
New Course: 18 holes, 6548yds, Par 71, SSS 71, Course record 67.
Club membership 800.
Visitors advisable to contact in advance.
Societies apply by telephone.
Green Fees £25 per day; £20 per round (£35/£25 weekends & bank holidays).
Facilities ⊗ ⅷ ⅃ ♥ ♀ ♨ 🖃 ⚓ John Froom.
Leisure motorised carts for hire, buggies for hire, trolley for hire, putting green, practice area.
Location 0.75m NW
Hotel ★★★ 64% Riverside Hotel, ABERSOCH ☎ 01758 712419 12 ⇄ ♠

NORTHOP   Map 07 SJ26

Northop Country Park CH7 6WA
☎ 01352 840440
Designed by former British Ryder Cup captain, John Jacobs, the parkland course gives the impression of having been established for many years. No two holes are the same and designed to allow all year play.
18 holes, 6750yds, Par 72, SSS 73, Course record 65.
Club membership 500.
Visitors advisable to prebook.
Societies apply in writing or by telephone in advance.
Green Fees £28 per round (£35 weekends & bank holidays).
Facilities ⊗ ⅷ ⅃ ♥ ♀ ♨ 🖃 ♨ ⚓ David Llewllyn.
Leisure hard tennis courts, heated indoor swimming pool, sauna, solarium, gymnasium, motorised carts for hire, buggies for hire, trolley for hire, driving range, putting green, practice area.
Location 150 yds from Connahs Quay turnoff on A55
Hotel ★★★★ 69% St Davids Park Hotel, St Davids Park, EWLOE
☎ 01244 520800 121 ⇄ ♠

PANTYMWYN

Map 07 SJ16

Mold Cilcain Rd CH7 5EH ☎ 01352 740318 & 741513
Meadowland course with some hard walking and natural
hazards. Fine views.
18 holes, 5528yds, Par 67, SSS 67, Course record 64.
Club membership 600.
Visitors contact in advance.
Societies provisional booking by telephone.
Green Fees £16 per day (£21 per day, £18 per round
weekends & bank holidays).
Facilities ⊗ ⅷ ⅃ ⅃ ♀ ♨ 🖿 🖈 ʲ Martin Carty.
Leisure motorised carts for hire, trolley for hire, putting
green, practice area.
Location E side of village
Hotel ★★ 65% Bryn Awel Hotel, Denbigh Rd,
MOLD
☎ 01352 758622 7 ⇆ 🐾Annexe10 ⇆ 🐾

PENMAENMAWR

Map 06 SH77

Penmaenmawr Conway Old Rd LL34 6RD
☎ 01492 623330
Hilly course with magnificent views across the bay to
Llandudno and Anglesey. Dry-stone wall natural hazards.
9 holes, 5350yds, Par 67, SSS 66, Course record 64.
Club membership 600.
Visitors advisable to contact in advance. May not play
Sat.
Societies must contact in advance.
Green Fees £12 per day (£18 Sun & bank holidays).
Facilities ⊗ ⅷ ⅃ ⅃ ♀ ♨
Leisure putting green, practice area.
Location 1.5m NE off A55
Hotel ★★★ 62% The Castle, High St, CONWY
☎ 01492 592324 29 ⇆ 🐾

PORTHMADOG

Map 06 SH53

Porthmadog Morfa Bychan LL49 9TP
☎ 01766 514124 & 513828
Seaside links,very interesting but with easy walking and good
views.
18 holes, 6350yds, Par 71, SSS 71.
Club membership 900.
Visitors must contact in advance.
Societies apply telephone initially.
Green Fees £18 per day (£25 weekends & bank holidays).
Facilities ⊗ ⅷ ⅃ ⅃ ♀ ♨ 🖿 ʲ Peter L Bright.
Leisure trolley for hire, putting green, practice area.
Location 1.5m SW
Hotel ★★ 62% Plas Isa Hotel, Porthmadog Rd,
CRICCIETH ☎ 01766 522443 14 ⇆ 🐾

PRESTATYN

Map 06 SJ08

Prestatyn Marine Rd East LL19 7HS ☎ 01745 854320
Very flat seaside links exposed to stiff breeze. Testing holes:
9th, par 4, bounded on 3 sides by water; 10th, par 4; 16th, par
4.
18 holes, 6564yds, Par 72, SSS 72, Course record 66.
Club membership 660.
Visitors welcome except Sat & Tue mornings. Must
contact in advance.

Societies prior booking required.
Green Fees £20 per day (£25 weekends & bank holidays).
Facilities ⊗ ⅷ ⅃ ⅃ ♀ ♨ 🖿 🖈 ʲ Malcolm Staton.
Leisure trolley for hire, putting green, practice area.
Location 0.5m N off A548
Hotel ★★ 61% Hotel Marina, Marine Dr, RHYL
☎ 01745 342371 26rm(20 ⇆2 🐾)

St Melyd The Paddock, Meliden Rd LL19 8NB
☎ 01745 854405
Parkland course with good views of mountains and Irish Sea.
Testing 1st hole (423 yds) par 4. 18 tees.
9 holes, 5829yds, Par 68, SSS 68, Course record 65.
Club membership 400.
Visitors must contact in advance.
Societies must telephone in advance.
Green Fees not confirmed.
Facilities ♀ ♨ 🖿 ʲ Richard Bladbury.
Location 0.5m S on A547
Hotel ★★ 61% Hotel Marina, Marine Dr, RHYL
☎ 01745 342371 26rm(20 ⇆2 🐾)

PWLLHELI

Map 06 SH33

Pwllheli Golf Rd LL53 5PS ☎ 01758 701644
Easy walking on flat seaside course with outstanding views of
Snowdon, Cader Idris and Cardigan Bay.
18 holes, 6091yds, Par 69, SSS 69.
Club membership 880.
Visitors restricted Tue,Thu & weekends.
Societies must telephone in advance.
Green Fees not confirmed.
Facilities ♀ ♨ 🖿 ʲ
Leisure putting green, practice area, trolley hire.
Location 0.5m SW off A497
Hotel ★★★ 64% Riverside Hotel, ABERSOCH
☎ 01758 712419 12 ⇆ 🐾

RHUDDLAN

Map 06 SJ07

Rhuddlan Meliden Rd LL18 6LB ☎ 01745 590217
Attractive, gently undulating parkland course with good
views. Well bunkered with trees and water hazards. The 476
yard 8th and 431 yard 11th require both length and accuracy.
The clubhouse has been refurbished.
18 holes, 6482yds, Par 71, SSS 71, Course record 67.
Club membership 1060.
Visitors must contact in advance. Sun with member only.
Societies telephone to book reservation.
Green Fees £24 per day (£30 per round Sat).
Facilities ⊗ ⅷ ⅃ ⅃ ♀ ♨ 🖿 🖈 ʲ Andrew Carr.
Leisure trolley for hire, putting green, practice area.
Location E side of town on A547
Hotel ★★★ 64% Oriel House Hotel, Upper Denbigh
Rd, ST ASAPH ☎ 01745 582716 19 ⇆ 🐾

RHYL

Map 06 SJ08

Rhyl Coast Rd LL18 3RE ☎ 01745 353171
Seaside course.
9 holes, 6165yds, Par 70, SSS 70, Course record 65.
Club membership 350.
Visitors must contact in advance. Limited availability at
weekends due to club competitions.
Societies must contact in advance.

Hotel Marina

AA★★ WTB ♛♛♛ Commended

MARINE DRIVE, RHYL, LL18 3AU

TELEPHONE: (01745) 342371

SET ON THE LOVELY EAST PARADE

Situated near Sun Centre on Rhyl's lovely East Parade, the hotel has 26 bedrooms all en suite. The hotel also has a late night Piano Bar and a recently refurbished night club called Quaffers Place and its own Steak Bar. We can cater for large or small parties either requiring accommodation or food only. Discounts available for organised groups. Large car park and lift.

Green Fees £10 per 18 holes (£15 weekends & bank holidays).
Facilities ⊗ ⫿ ℔ ▬ ♀ ⚘ 🏠 ⛳ ℓ Tim Leah.
Leisure trolley for hire, putting green, practice area.
Location 1m E on A548
Hotel ★★ 61% Hotel Marina, Marine Dr, RHYL
☎ 01745 342371 26rm(20 ⇌2 ₨)

RUABON
Map 07 SJ34

Penycae Ruabon Rd, Penycae LL14 1TP
☎ 01978 810108
An architecturally designed and built 9-hole course with an opening hole from an elevated tee wooded to one side and backed by trees and a river. The 2nd at 262 yards crosses water twice as the river meanders down the fairway. Th 5th is very narrow being wooded on either side and with a slight dogleg. The 6th also a par 3, needs a high shot to clear the mature birch in the path.
9 holes, 2140yds, Par 64, SSS 62, Course record 62.
Club membership 200.
Visitors advisable to book in advance.
Societies telephone or write in advance.
Green Fees £6 per 18 holes; £4 per 9 holes (£8/£5 weekends & bank holidays).
Facilities ⊗ ⫿ by prior arrangement ℔ ▬ ♀ ⚘ 🏠 ⛳ ℓ Nick Rothe.
Leisure trolley for hire, putting green.
Location 1m on A5
Hotel ★★★ 67% Hand Hotel, Church St, CHIRK
☎ 01691 772479 14 ⇌ ₨

RUTHIN
Map 06 SJ15

Ruthin-Pwllglas Pwllglas LL15 2PE ☎ 01824 703427
Hilly parkland course in elevated position with panoramic views. Stiff climb to 3rd and 9th holes.
10 holes, 5362yds, Par 66, SSS 66.
Club membership 380.
Visitors welcome except for competition days.
Societies apply in writing.
Green Fees not confirmed.
Facilities ♀ ⚘
Location 2.5m S off A494
Hotel ★★★ 63% Ruthin Castle, RUTHIN
☎ 01824 702664 58 ⇌ ₨

ST ASAPH
Map 06 SJ07

Llannerch Park North Wales Golf Range, Llannerch Park LL17 0BD ☎ 01745 730805
9 holes, 1587yds, Par 30.
Visitors pay & play.
Societies telephone in advance.
Green Fees £2 per 9 holes.
Facilities ▬ 🏠 ⛳
Leisure driving range.
Location 1.5m S off A525

WREXHAM
Map 07 SJ35

Clays Farm Golf Centre Bryn Estyn Rd, Llan-y-Pwll LL13 9UB ☎ 01978 661406 & 661416
Parkland course in a rural setting with views of the Welsh mountains and noted for the difficulty of its par 3s.
18 holes, 5624yds, Par 69, SSS 69, Course record 70.
Club membership 420.
Visitors must contact in advance.
Societies at busy times prior arrangement required by telephone.
Green Fees £11 per round (£14 weekends).
Facilities ⊗ ⫿ ℔ ▬ ♀ ⚘ 🏠 ⛳ ℓ Paul Williams.
Leisure motorised carts for hire, buggies for hire, trolley for hire, driving range, putting green, practice area.
Hotel ★★★⚘ 65% Llwyn Onn Hall Hotel, Cefn Rd, WREXHAM ☎ 01978 261225 13 ⇌ ₨

Wrexham Holt Rd LL13 9SB ☎ 01978 351476
Inland, sandy course with easy walking. Testing dog-legged 7th hole (par 4), and short 14th hole (par 3) with full carry to green.
18 holes, 6233yds, Par 70, SSS 70, Course record 64.
Club membership 600.
Visitors may not play competition days, and are advised to contact in advance. A handicap certificate is required.
Societies welcome except for Tue, Wed & weekends. Apply in writing
Green Fees £20 (£25 weekends).
Facilities ⊗ ⫿ ℔ ▬ ♀ ⚘ 🏠 ℓ David Larvin.
Leisure trolley for hire, putting green, practice area.
Location 2m NE on A534
Hotel ★★★⚘ 65% Llwyn Onn Hall Hotel, Cefn Rd, WREXHAM ☎ 01978 261225 13 ⇌ ₨

MID WALES

This region includes the counties of Cardiganshire, Carmarthenshire, Pembrokeshire and Powys which reflect the recent national changes.

ABERYSTWYTH
Map 06 SN58

Aberystwyth Brynymor Rd SY23 2HY
☎ 01970 615104
Undulating meadowland course. Testing holes: 16th (The Loop) par 3; 17th, par 4; 18th, par 3. Good views over Cardigan Bay.
18 holes, 6109yds, Par 71, SSS 71, Course record 67.
Club membership 450.
Visitors	must contact in advance.
Societies	write or telephone in advance.
Green Fees	£18 per day; £15 per round (£20/£18 weekends and bank holidays).
Facilities	⊗ ⏣ ⓛ ☂ ♀ ♨ 🏠 🏴 ℓ Kevin Bayliss.
Leisure	trolley for hire, driving range, putting green, practice area.
Location	N side of town
Hotel	★★★ 66% Belle Vue Royal Hotel, Marine Ter, ABERYSTWYTH ☎ 01970 617558 36 ⇔ 🐾

AMMANFORD
Map 03 SN61

Glynhir Glynhir Rd, Llandybie SA18 2TF
☎ 01269 850472 & 851365
Parkland course with good views, latter holes close to Upper Loughor River. The 14th is a 394-yd dog leg.
18 holes, 5986yds, Par 69, SSS 69, Course record 66.
Club membership 700.
Visitors	no visitors Sun. Contact professional in advance (01269 851010).
Societies	welcome weekdays only. Contact in advance.
Green Fees	£15 per day (£20 Sat & bank holidays).
Facilities	⊗ ⏣ ⓛ ☂ ♀ ♨ 🏠 🏴 ℓ Ian Roberts.
Leisure	trolley for hire, putting green.
Location	2m N of Ammanford
Hotel	★★ 67% Mill at Glynhir, Glyn-Hir, Llandybie, AMMANFORD ☎ 01269 850672 11 ⇔ 🐾

BORTH
Map 06 SN69

Borth & Ynyslas SY24 5JS ☎ 01970 871202
Seaside links, over 100 years old, with strong winds at times. Some narrow fairways.
18 holes, 6116yds, Par 70, SSS 70, Course record 65.
Club membership 625.
Visitors	must contact in advance, may play weekends ring to check no competitions in progress.
Societies	telephone in advance.
Green Fees	£18 per day (£22 weekends & bank holidays).
Facilities	⊗ ⏣ ⓛ ☂ ♀ ♨ 🏠 🏴 ℓ J G Lewis.
Leisure	trolley for hire, practice area.
Location	0.5m N on B4353
Hotel	★★ 65% Four Seasons Hotel, 50-54 Portland St, ABERYSTWYTH ☎ 01970 612120 14rm(13 ⇔ 🐾)

BRECON
Map 03 SO02

Brecon Newton Park LD3 8PA ☎ 01874 622004
Parkland course, with easy walking. Natural hazards include two rivers on its boundary. Good river and mountain scenery.
9 holes, 5256yds, Par 66, SSS 66, Course record 61.
Club membership 420.
Visitors	advisable to contact in advance, limited availability at weekends.
Societies	apply in writing.
Green Fees	£10 per day.
Facilities	ⓛ ♀ ♨
Leisure	practice area.
Location	0.75m W of town centre on A40
Hotel	★★ 62% Castle of Brecon Hotel, Castle Square, BRECON ☎ 01874 624611 33 ⇔ 🐾Annexe12 🐾

Cradoc Penoyre Park, Cradoc LD3 9LP ☎ 01874 623658
Parkland with wooded areas, lakes and spectacular views over the Brecon Beacons. Challenging golf.
18 holes, 6301yds, Par 71, SSS 71, Course record 65.
Club membership 700.
Visitors	must contact secretary in advance.
Societies	apply in writing or telephone in advance to secretary.
Green Fees	£18 per day (£22 weekends & bank holidays).
Facilities	⊗ ⏣ ⓛ ☂ ♀ ♨ 🏠 ℓ Richard Davies.

Leisure	trolley for hire, putting green, practice area.
Location	2m N on B4520
Hotel	★★ 62% Castle of Brecon Hotel, Castle Square, BRECON
	☎ 01874 624611 33 ⇔ ♠Annexe12 ♠

BUILTH WELLS Map 03 SO05

Builth Wells The Clubhouse, Golf Links Rd LD2 3NF
☎ 01982 553296
Well guarded greens and a stream running thorough the centre of the course add interest to this 18-hole undulating parkland course. The clubhouse is a converted 16th-century Welsh long house.
18 holes, 5386yds, Par 66, SSS 67, Course record 65.
Club membership 380.

Visitors	contact secretary.
Societies	by prior arrangement.
Green Fees	£16 per day; £12 per round (£22/ £18 weekends and bank holidays).
Facilities	⊗ ∭ ⓑ ♥ ♀ ☖ ☎ ☏ ♠ Roy Truman.
Location	N of A483
Hotel	★★★⚖ 64% Caer Beris Manor Hotel, BUILTH WELLS
	☎ 01982 552601 22 ⇔ ♠

BURRY PORT Map 02 SN40

Ashburnham Cliffe Ter SA16 0HN
☎ 01554 832269 & 833846
This course has a lot of variety. In the main it is of the seaside type although the holes in front of the clubhouse are of an inland character. They are, however, good holes which make a very interesting finish. Course record holder, Sam Torrance.
18 holes, 6916yds, Par 72, SSS 74, Course record 70.
Club membership 730.

Visitors	must be bona fide member of affiliated golf club and produce handicap certificate, very limited weekend times.
Societies	telephone for initial enquiry.
Green Fees	£30 per day; £25 per round (£40/£30 weekends).
Facilities	⊗ ∭ ⓑ ♥ ♀ ☖ ☎ ☏ ♠ Robert Ryder.
Leisure	trolley for hire, putting green, practice area.
Location	5m W of Llanelli, A484 road
Hotel	★★★ 64% Diplomat Hotel, Felinfoel, LLANELLI
	☎ 01554 756156 23 ⇔ ♠Annexe8 ⇔ ♠

CAERSWS Map 06 SO09

Mid-Wales Golf Centre SY17 5SB ☎ 01686 688303
A 9-hole, Par 3 course with sand bunkers and three ponds.
9 holes, 2554yds, Par 54, SSS 54.
Club membership 95.

Visitors	welcome, restricted during competitions on Sun am.
Societies	telephone in advance.
Green Fees	£6 per day (£8 weekends & bank holidays).
Facilities	⊗ by prior arrangement ∭ by prior arrangement ⓑ ♥ ♀ ☖ ☎ ☏
Leisure	trolley for hire, driving range, putting green, practice area.
Location	0.75m off A470 out of Caersws

Hotel	★★ 64% Elephant & Castle, Broad St, NEWTOWN
	☎ 01686 626271 25 ⇔ ♠Annexe11 ⇔ ♠

CARDIGAN Map 02 SN14

Cardigan Gwbert-on-Sea SA43 1PR ☎ 01239 612035
A links course, very dry in winter, with wide fairways, light rough and gorse. Every hole overlooks the sea.
18 holes, 6641yds, Par 72, SSS 72.
Club membership 500.

Visitors	may not play between 1-2pm. Must have a handicap certificate.
Societies	must telephone in advance.
Green Fees	not confirmed.
Facilities	♀ ☖ ☎ ☏ ♠ Colin Parsons.
Leisure	squash, putting,cart/buggy/trolley hire.
Location	3m N off B4548
Hotel	★★★ 65% Cliff Hotel, GWBERT
	☎ 01239 613241 70 ⇔ ♠

CARMARTHEN Map 02 SN42

Carmarthen Blaenycoed Rd SA33 6EH
☎ 01267 281588 & 281214
Hilltop course with good views.
18 holes, 6210yds, Par 71, SSS 70, Course record 68.
Club membership 700.

Visitors	must have a handicap certificate, telephone for times at weekends.
Societies	apply in writing minimum of ten days in advance.
Green Fees	£18 per round (£25 weekends & bank holidays).
Facilities	⊗ ∭ ⓑ ♥ ♀ ☖ ☎ ☏ ♠ Pat Gillis.
Leisure	trolley for hire, putting green, practice area.
Location	4m N of town
Hotel	★★★ 60% The Ivy Bush Royal, Spilman St, CARMARTHEN
	☎ 01267 235111 73 ⇔ ♠

Derllys Court Llysonnen Rd SA33 5DT ☎ 01267 211575
Gently undulating parkland course with challenging par 3s (5th and 8th) and a testing par 5 involving a shot across a lake.
9 holes, 2859yds, Par 35, SSS 66, Course record 33.
Club membership 60.

Visitors	welcome at all times.
Societies	telephone in advance.
Green Fees	£9 per 18 holes; £5 per 9 holes.
Facilities	⊗ ⓑ ♥ ☖ ☎ ☏ ⇔
Leisure	trolley for hire, practice area.
Location	Just off A40 between Carmarthen/St Clears
Hotel	★★★ 60% The Ivy Bush Royal, Spilman St, CARMARTHEN
	☎ 01267 235111 73 ⇔ ♠

GWBERT-ON-SEA Map 02 SN15

Cliff Hotel SA43 1PP ☎ 01239 613241
This is a short course with 2 Par 4's and the remainder are challenging Par 3's. Particularly interesting holes are played across the sea on to a small island.
9 holes, 1545yds, Par 29.

Visitors	telephone to book in advance.
Societies	telephone in advance. ▶

Cliff Hotel

GWBERT, CARDIGAN,
WEST WALES
TEL: CARDIGAN (01239) 613241

AA ★★★ Hotel in breathtaking
position on cliffs overlooking
Cardigan Bay. Outdoor pool, Squash,
Gym, Snooker, Sauna. FREE Golf on
hotel's own 9-hole course. Cardigan
Golf Course (18 holes) only ½ mile
away. Bargain breaks available.
Also self-catering in Gate House.

Green Fees £5.50 per 9 holes (£6.75 weekends and bank
holidays).
Facilities ⊗ ⅲ ⅃ ⅃ ⅃ ⅃ ⅃ ↯ ⋈
Leisure heated outdoor swimming pool, squash, fishing,
sauna, solarium, gymnasium, motorised carts for
hire, putting green, snooker table.
Hotel ★★★ 65% Cliff Hotel, GWBERT
☎ 01239 613241 70 ⇆ ⧆

HAVERFORDWEST   Map 02 SM91

Haverfordwest Arnolds Down SA61 2XQ
☎ 01437 764523
Parkland course in attractive surroundings.
18 holes, 6005yds, Par 70, SSS 69.
Club membership 770.
Visitors restricted at weekends.
Societies apply in writing or telephone for booking form.
Green Fees £16 per day (£20 weekends).
Facilities ⊗ ⅲ ⅃ ⅃ ⅃ ⅃ ⅃ ↯ ⧆ Alex Pile.
Leisure motorised carts for hire, buggies for hire, trolley
for hire, putting green, practice area.
Location 1m E on A40
Hotel ★★ 65% Hotel Mariners, Mariners Square,
HAVERFORDWEST
☎ 01437 763353 30 ⇆ ⧆

Entries with a shaded background identify
courses that are considered to be particularly
interesting

HAY-ON-WYE   Map 03 SO24

Rhosgoch Rhosgoch, Builth Wells LD2 3JY
☎ 01497 851251
The course is parkland, quite challenging, with beautiful
scenery.
9 holes, 4842yds, Par 68, SSS 64, Course record 68.
Club membership 165.
Visitors no restrictions.
Societies please telephone in advance.
Green Fees not confirmed.
Facilities ⅃ ⅃ ⧆
Location 5m N of Hay-on-Wye
Hotel ★★★ 67% The Swan-at-Hay Hotel, Church St,
HAY-ON-WYE
☎ 01497 821188 15 ⇆ ⧆Annexe3 ⇆ ⧆

Summerhill Hereford Rd, Clifford HR3 5EW
☎ 01497 820451
Undulating parkland course set deep in the Wye Valley on
the Welsh Border overlooking the Black Mountains.
9 holes, 2929yds, Par 70, SSS 67.
Visitors welcome anytime.
Societies contact for information.
Green Fees £8 per round (£10 weekends and bank holidays).
Facilities ⊗ ⅲ ⅃ ⅃ ⅃ ⅃ ⅃ ↯ ⧆
Location B4350 Whitney toll bridge road
Hotel ★★★ 67% The Swan-at-Hay Hotel, Church St,
HAY-ON-WYE
☎ 01497 821188 15 ⇆ ⧆Annexe3 ⇆ ⧆

KIDWELLY   Map 02 SN40

Pontnewydd Golf Centre Trimsaran SA17 4LB
☎ 01554 810278
In the Gwendraeth valley, a new 18-hole parkland course
with greens well protected by the planting of 35,000 trees.
There is a covered practice area and 9-hole course under
construction.
18 holes, 6173yds, Par 70, SSS 69, Course record 68.
Club membership 300.
Visitors advisable to book for weekends.
Societies must contact in advance.
Green Fees not confirmed.
Facilities ⅃ ⅃ ⧆ ↯
Leisure covered practice area.
Location 4.5m E, off B4317
Hotel ★★★ 60% The Ivy Bush Royal, Spilman St,
CARMARTHEN
☎ 01267 235111 73 ⇆ ⧆

KNIGHTON   Map 07 SO27

Knighton Frydd Wood LD7 1EF ☎ 01547 528646
Hill course with hard walking.
9 holes, 5320yds, Par 68, SSS 66, Course record 65.
Club membership 150.
Visitors may not play on Sun until after 4.30pm.
Societies must contact in advance.
Green Fees not confirmed.
Facilities ⅃ ⅃
Location 0.5m S off B4355
Hotel ★★★ 60% The Knighton Hotel, Broad St,
KNIGHTON ☎ 01547 520530 15 ⇆ ⧆

LETTERSTON Map 02 SM92

Priskilly Forest Castlemorris SA62 5EH
☎ 01348 840276
Testing parkland course surrounded by rhododendrons. Challenging dog-leg 4th with hazards both sides.
9 holes, 5712yds, Par 70, SSS 68, Course record 76.
Visitors advance booking advisable at weekends during summer.
Societies telephone in advance.
Green Fees £10 per day; £8per 18 holes; £5 per 9 holes.
Facilities ⊗ ☕ ♁ ⌂ ⚑ 🛏
Leisure fishing, motorised carts for hire, buggies for hire, trolley for hire.
Hotel ★★ 63% Abergwaun Hotel, The Market Square, FISHGUARD
☎ 01348 872077 11rm(7 ⇌ ↱)

LLANDRINDOD WELLS Map 03 SO06

Llandrindod Wells LD1 5NY
☎ 01597 822010 & 823873 (sec)
Moorland course, designed by Harry Vardon, with easy walking and panoramic views. One of the highest courses in Wales. (1,100 ft above sea level).
18 holes, 5759yds, Par 68, SSS 67, Course record 65.
Club membership 650.
Visitors no restrictions.
Societies must telephone in advance.
Green Fees not confirmed.
Facilities 🍷 ♁ ⌂ ⚑
Leisure putting green,practice area,trolley hire.
Location 1m SE off A483
Hotel ★★★ 65% Hotel Metropole, Temple St, LLANDRINDOD WELLS
☎ 01597 823700 121 ⇌ ↱

LLANDYSSUL

Saron Saron SA44 5EL ☎ 01559 370705
Set in 50 acres of mature parkland with large trees and magnificent Teifi Valley views. Numerous water hazards and bunkers.
9 holes, 2400yds, Par 32, Course record 34.
Visitors may play at all times no arrangements required.
Societies telephone for details.
Green Fees £6 per 18 holes; £4.50 per 9 holes.
Facilities ⚑
Leisure trolley for hire.
Location Off A484 at Saron
Hotel ★★ 72% Ty Mawr Country Hotel & Restaurant, BRECHFA
☎ 01267 202332 5rm(4 ⇌ ↱)

LLANGATTOCK Map 03 SO21

Old Rectory NP8 1PH ☎ 01873 810373
Sheltered course with easy walking.
9 holes, 2200yds, Par 54, SSS 59, Course record 53 or 53yds.
Club membership 180.
Visitors telephone for information.
Societies telephone for booking.
Green Fees £10 per day; £5 per 18 holes.
Facilities ⊗ Ⅲ ▙ ☕ 🍷 ♁ ⚑ 🛏
Leisure outdoor swimming pool.
Location SW of village
Hotel ★★♣♣ 71% Gliffaes Country House Hotel, CRICKHOWELL
☎ 01874 730371 19 ⇌ ↱Annexe3 ⇌ ↱

LLANGYBI Map 02 SN65

Cilgwyn SA48 8NN ☎ 01570 493286
Picturesque parkland course in secluded valley, with natural hazards of ponds, stream and woodland.
9 holes, 5309yds, Par 68, SSS 66.
Club membership 300.
Visitors no restrictions, apart from Sun when advisable to telephone.
Societies apply in advance by letter or telephone.
Green Fees £15 per day; £10 per round (£20/£15 weekends & bank holidays).
Facilities ⊗ Ⅲ ▙ ☕ 🍷 ♁ ⌂ ⚑ 🛏
Leisure trolley for hire, putting green, practice area.
Location 5m N of Lampeter on A485
Hotel ★★★♣♣ 69% Falcondale Country House Hotel, LAMPETER ☎ 01570 422910 19 ⇌ ↱

LLANIDLOES Map 06 SN98

St Idloes Penrallt SY18 6LG ☎ 01686 412559
Hill-course, slightly undulating but walking is easy. Good views.
9 holes, 2755yds, Par 66, SSS 66, Course record 61.
Club membership 300.
Visitors may not play on Sun mornings.
Societies apply in writing to the secretary at least one month in advance.
Green Fees £10 (£12 weekends).
Facilities ⊗ Ⅲ ▙ ☕ 🍷 ♁ ⌂ ⚑ (Phillip Parkin.
Leisure trolley for hire, putting green, practice area.
Location 1m N off B4569
Hotel ★★ 67% Glansevern Arms Hotel, Pant Mawr, LLANGURIG ☎ 0686 440240 7 ⇌ ↱

LLANRHYSTUD Map 06 SN56

Penrhos Golf & Country Club SY23 5AY
☎ 01974 202999
Beautifully scenic course incorporating five lakes and spectacular coastal and inland views. Many leisure facilities.
Penrhos: 18 holes, 6641yds, Par 72, SSS 73, Course record 71.
Academy: 9 holes, 1827yds, Par 31.
Club membership 300.
Visitors must telephone, no jeans allowed on main course.
Societies must telephone in advance.
Green Fees £15 per round plus £5 per extra round (£18 per round weekends & bank holidays).
Facilities ⊗ Ⅲ ▙ ☕ 🍷 ♁ ⌂ ⚑ 🛏 (Paul Diamond.
Leisure hard tennis courts, heated indoor swimming pool, sauna, solarium, gymnasium, motorised carts for hire, buggies for hire, trolley for hire, driving range, putting green, practice area.
Location Turn off A487 onto B4337 in Llanrhystud
Hotel ★★★♣♣ 67% Conrah Hotel, Ffosrhydygaled, Chancery, ABERYSTWYTH
☎ 01970 617941 11 ⇌ ↱Annexe9 ⇌ ↱

LLANSTEFFAN
Map 02 SN31

Llansteffan SA33 5LU ☎ 01267 241526
A Pay and Play downland course with superb views of the sea
and Gower Coast. Quite challenging in a sea breeze!
9 holes, 2165yds, Par 30.
Visitors   no restrictions, visitors welcome at all times.
Societies   contact in advance for bank holidays.
Green Fees not confirmed.
Facilities   🍴 ⛳
Leisure   putting green,practice area,trolley hire.
Location   S of Carmarthen off B4312
Hotel   ★★ 66% Forge Restaurant & Motel, ST
      CLEARS ☎ 01994 230300 Annexe18 ⇌ 🏮

MACHYNLLETH
Map 06 SH70

Machynlleth Ffordd Drenewydd SY20 8UH
☎ 01654 702000
Lowland course with mostly natural hazards.
9 holes, 5726yds, Par 68, SSS 67, Course record 65.
Club membership 250.
Visitors   Thur ladies day, Sun morning mens competition.
Societies   telephone in advance.
Green Fees £12 per day (£15 weekends & bank holidays).
Facilities   ⊗ 🏌 ♥ ♀ ⚒
Leisure   trolley for hire, putting green, practice area.
Location   0.5m E off A489
Hotel   ★★ 65% Wynnstay Arms Hotel, Maengwyn St,
      MACHYNLLETH ☎ 01654 702941 20 ⇌ 🏮

MILFORD HAVEN
Map 02 SM90

Milford Haven Woodbine House, Hubberstone SA73 3RX
☎ 01646 692368
Parkland course with excellent greens and views of the
Milford Haven waterway.
18 holes, 6030yds, Par 71, SSS 70.
Club membership 450.
Visitors   no restrictions, advisable to contact in advance.
Societies   telephone to book.
Green Fees not confirmed.
Facilities   ♀ ⚒ 🍴 ⛳
Leisure   putting green,practice area,trolley hire.
Location   1.5m W
Hotel   ★★ 63% Lord Nelson Hotel, Hamilton Ter,
      MILFORD HAVEN
      ☎ 01646 695341 32 ⇌ 🏮

NEWPORT
Map 02 SN03

Newport (Pemb) The Golf Club SA42 0NR
☎ 01239 820244
Seaside links course, with easy walking and good view of the
Preselli Hills and Newport Bay.
9 holes, 5815yds, Par 70, Course record 61.
Club membership 350.
Visitors   telephone in advance.
Societies   must telephone in advance.
Green Fees £15 per 18 holes; £10 per 9 holes.
Facilities   ⊗ 🏌 🏌 ♥ ♀ ⚒ 🍴 ⛳ 🏮 ⚓ 🏮 Colin Parsons.
Leisure   motorised carts for hire, buggies for hire, trolley
      for hire, driving range, putting green, practice
      area.

Location   1.25m N
Hotel   ★★ 65% Trewern Arms, NEVERN
      ☎ 01239 820395 9 ⇌ 🏮

NEWTOWN
Map 06 SO19

St Giles Pool Rd SY16 3AJ
☎ 01686 625844
Inland country course with easy walking. Testing 2nd hole,
per 3, and 4th hole, par 4. River Severn skirts four holes.
9 holes, 5936yds, Par 70, SSS 69, Course record 67.
Club membership 350.
Visitors   may not play at weekends.
Societies   must contact in advance.
Green Fees £12.50 per day (£15 weekends and bank
      holidays).
Facilities   ⊗ 🏌 🏌 ♥ ♀ ⚒ 🍴 ⛳ 🏮 D P Owen
Leisure   fishing, trolley for hire, putting green, practifce
      area.
Location   0.5m NE on A483
Hotel   ★★ 64% Elephant & Castle, Broad St,
      NEWTOWN
      ☎ 01686 626271 25 ⇌ 🏮Annexe11 ⇌ 🏮

PEMBROKE DOCK
Map 02 SM90

South Pembrokeshire Defensible Barracks SA72 6SE
☎ 01646 621453
Parkland course overlooking the Cleddau River.
9 holes, 5804yds, Par 70, SSS 69, Course record 65.
Club membership 350.
Visitors   must contact in advance, especially during
      season.
Societies   apply in advance.
Green Fees £10 per day to be reviewed when 18 hole course
      is open.
Facilities   ⊗ 🏌 🏌 ♥ ♀ ⚒
Leisure   practice area.
Location   SW side of town centre off B4322
Hotel   ★★ 60% Old Kings Arms, Main St,
      PEMBROKE
      ☎ 01646 683611 21 ⇌ 🏮

ST DAVID'S
Map 02 SM72

St David's City Whitesands Bay SA62 6PT
☎ 01437 720312 & 721751
Links course with alternative tees for 18 holes. Panoramic
views of St David's Head and Ramsey Island.
9 holes, 6117yds, Par 70, SSS 70, Course record 67.
Club membership 200.
Visitors   prior booking with secretary is encouraged but
      no always necessary, please check for weekends,
      Ladies Day Fri pm.
Societies   book with the secretary in advance.
Green Fees £14 per day.
Facilities   ♥ ⚒
Leisure   trolley for hire, putting green, practice net.
Location   2m W overlooking Whitesands Bay
Hotel   ★★★ 68% Warpool Court Hotel, ST
      DAVID'S
      ☎ 01437 720300 25 ⇌ 🏮

PENALLY ABBEY ★★ ◉◉ 81%
Penally, Tenby, Dyfed SA70 7PY
Telephone: (01834) 843033 Fax: (01834) 844714

Penally Abbey, one of Pembrokeshire's loveliest country houses, is a 12 bedroom, gothic style, stone built mansion. Situated in an elevated position overlooking the golf course, adjacent to the church, on the village green in the picturesque floral village of Penally, 2 miles from Tenby.

TENBY
Map 02 SN10

Tenby The Burrows SA70 7NP
☎ 01834 844447
The oldest club in Wales,this fine old seaside links, with sea views and natural hazards provides good golf.
18 holes, 6232yds, Par 69, SSS 71.
Club membership 750.
Visitors	subject to competition & tee reservation. Must produce handicap certificate.
Societies	must apply in advance.
Green Fees	not confirmed.
Facilities	♀ ⚠ 🏠 ⭐ T Mountford.
Leisure	putting,trolley hire,practice area.
Hotel	★★★ 70% Atlantic Hotel, Esplanade, TENBY ☎ 01834 842881 & 844176 40 ⇌ ♟
Additional hotel	★★ 80% Penally Abbey Country House, Penally, TENBY ☎ 01834 843033 8 ⇌ ♟Annexe4 ⇌

WELSHPOOL
Map 07 SJ20

Welshpool Golfa Hill SY21 9AQ
☎ 01938 83249
Undulating, hilly, heathland course with bracing air. Testing holes are 2nd (par 5), 14th (par 3), 17th (par 3) and a memorable 18th.
18 holes, 5708yds, Par 70, SSS 69, Course record 68.
Club membership 550.
Visitors	restricted at weekends.
Societies	must book in advance.
Green Fees	not confirmed.
Facilities	♀ ⚠ 🏠
Location	3m W off A458
Hotel	★★ 67% Royal Oak Hotel, WELSHPOOL ☎ 01938 552217 24 ⇌ ♟

Entries with a shaded background identify courses that are considered to be particularly interesting

---

A golf course name printed in ***bold italics*** means we have been unable to verify information with the club's management for the current year

---

SOUTH WALES

This region includes the counties of Blaenau Gwent, Bridgend, Caerphilly, Cardiff, Merthyr Tydfil, Monmouthshire, Neath Port Talbot, Newport, Rhondda Cynon Taff, Swansea, Torfaen and Vale of Glamorgan which reflect the recent national changes.

ABERDARE
Map 03 SO00

Aberdare Abernant CF44 0RY
☎ 01685 872797 & 878735
Mountain course with parkland features overlooking Cynon Valley.
18 holes, 5767yds, Par 69, SSS 69, Course record 65.
Club membership 550.
Visitors	must contact in advance, may only play on Sat with member, Sun by arrangement with secretary.
Societies	apply in writing in advance to the secretary.
Green Fees	£14 per day (£18 weekends & bank holidays).
Facilities	⊗ �𝍂 🐍 💼 ♀ ⚠ 🏠 ⭐ A Palmer.
Leisure	trolley for hire, putting green, practice area.
Location	0.75m E
Hotel	★★★ 59% The Baverstock Hotel, The Heads Of Valley Rd, MERTHYR TYDFIL ☎ 01685 386221 53 ⇌ ♟

ABERGAVENNY
Map 03 SO21

Monmouthshire Gypsy Ln, LLanfoist NP7 9HE
☎ 01873 853171
This parkland course is very picturesque, with the beautifully wooded River Usk running alongside. There are a number of par 3 holes and a testing par 4 at the 15th.
18 holes, 5961yds, Par 72, SSS 70.
Club membership 700.
Visitors	must play with member at weekends. Must contact in advance & have handicap certificate.
Societies	must contact in writing.
Green Fees	not confirmed.
Facilities	⚠ 🏠 ⭐ ⭐
Leisure	fishing.
Location	2m S off B4269
Hotel	★★ 70% Llanwenarth Arms Hotel, Brecon Rd, ABERGAVENNY ☎ 01873 810550 18 ⇌ ♟

Wernddu Golf Centre Old Ross Rd NP7 8NG
☎ 01873 856223
Two 9-hole parkland courses. The old course is an ideal starter course with wind hazards on the 4th; the new course in longer and more challenging with winds hazards on the 3rd and 9th holes and water affecting the 5th and 7th holes. There is also a 26-bay floodlit driving range and a practice putting green.
Old Course: 9 holes, 2001yds, Par 31, SSS 30.
New Course: 9 holes, 3564yds, Par 36, SSS 35.
Club membership 300.
Visitors   ring in advance for details.
Societies   telephone in advance.
Green Fees   £12 per 18 holes; £8 per 9 holes.
Facilities   ⊗ ⅶ ⅃ 里 ♀ ⚐ ⅲ ⅰ Alan Ashmead.
Leisure   trolley for hire, driving range, putting green, practice area.
Location   1.5m NE on B4521
Hotel   ★★ 70% Llanwenarth Arms Hotel, Brecon Rd, ABERGAVENNY
☎ 01873 810550 18 ⇋ ℝ

BARGOED   Map 03 ST19

Bargoed Heolddu CF8 9GF ☎ 01443 830143
Mountain parkland course, testing par 4, 13th hole.
18 holes, 5836yds, Par 70, SSS 70, Course record 65.
Club membership 500.
Visitors   must play with member at weekends.
Societies   must contact in advance.
Green Fees   not confirmed.
Facilities   ♀ ⚐
Leisure   putting green.
Location   NW side of town
Hotel   ★★★ 67% Maes Manor Hotel, BLACKWOOD
☎ 01495 224551 & 220011 8 ⇋Annexe14 ⇋

BARRY   Map 03 ST16

Brynhill Port Rd CF62 8PN
☎ 01446 720277 & 735061
Meadowland course with some hard walking. Prevailing west wind.
18 holes, 5947yds, Par 70, SSS 68.
Club membership 750.
Visitors   must contact in advance. May not play on Sun.
Societies   phone secretary for details.
Green Fees   £20 per round (£25 Sat).
Facilities   ⊗ ⅶ ⅃ 里 ♀ ⚐ ⅰ Peter Fountain.
Leisure   trolley for hire, putting green, practice area.
Location   1.25m N on B4050
Hotel   ★★★ 60% Mount Sorrel Hotel, Porthkerry Rd, BARRY ☎ 01446 740069 43 ⇋ ℝ

RAF St Athan St Athan CF62 4WA
☎ 01446 797186 & 751043
This is a very windy course with wind straight off the sea to make all holes interesting. Further interest is added by this being a very tight course with lots of trees.
9 holes, 6452yds, Par 71, SSS 71.
Club membership 450.
Visitors   contact in advance.
Societies   apply in advance.
Green Fees   £10 (£15 weekends & bank holidays).

Facilities   ⊗ ⅶ ⅃ 里 ♀ ⚐ ⅰ
Leisure   trolley for hire, putting green, practice area.
Location   Between Barry & Llantwit Major
Hotel   ★★ 67% West House Country Hotel & Restaurant, West St, LLANTWIT MAJOR
☎ 01446 792406 & 793726 21 ⇋ ℝ

St Andrews Major Coldbrook Rd, Argae Ln, Cadoxton CF6 3BB ☎ 01446 722227
A new 9-hole, Pay and Play course with 6 Par 4s and 1 Par 5.
9 holes, 3000yds, Par 70, SSS 68.
Club membership 520.
Visitors   must contact in advance.
Societies   contact in advance.
Green Fees   £8 per 9 holes; £13 per 18 holes.
Facilities   ⊗ ⅶ ⅃ 里 ♀ ⚐ ⅰ
Leisure   trolley for hire, putting green.
Location   Off Barry new link road
Hotel   ★★★⚑ 74% Egerton Grey Country House Hotel, Porthkerry, BARRY
☎ 01446 711666 10 ⇋ ℝ

BETTWS NEWYDD   Map 03 SO30

Alice Springs NP5 1JY
☎ 01873 880772 & 880708
Two 18-hole undulating parkland courses set back to back with magnificent views of the Usk Valley. The Queen's course has testing 7th and 15th holes. The King's Course which opened in summer 1992, is 6662yds long.
Queens Course: 18 holes, 6041yds, Par 67, SSS 69.
Kings Course: 18 holes, 6662yds, Par 72, SSS 71.
Club membership 350.
Visitors   should contact the club in advance for weekend play.
Societies   must telephone in advance.
Green Fees   not confirmed.
Facilities   ♀ ⚐ ⅰ Jim Howard.
Leisure   caddy cars.
Hotel   ★★★ 73% Glen-yr-Afon House Hotel, Pontypool Rd, USK
☎ 01291 672302 & 673202 27 ⇋ ℝ

BLACKWOOD   Map 03 ST19

Blackwood Cwmgelli NP2 1EL
☎ 01495 222121 & 223152
Heathland course with sand bunkers. Undulating, with hard walking. Testing 2nd hole par 4. Good views.
9 holes, 5332yds, Par 66.
Club membership 310.
Visitors   contact club or turn up and pay greens staff, may not play at weekends & bank holidays unless with member.
Societies   by prior arrangement for members of a recognised golf club.
Green Fees   £13 weekdays.
Facilities   ⊗ by prior arrangement ⅶ by prior arrangement ⅃ by prior arrangement 里 by prior arrangement ♀ ⚐
Leisure   putting green, practice area.
Location   0.25m N of Blackwood, off A4048
Hotel   ★★★ 67% Maes Manor Hotel, BLACKWOOD
☎ 01495 224551 & 220011 8 ⇋Annexe14 ⇋

BRIDGEND
Map 03 SS97

Coed-Y-Mwstwr The Clubhouse, Coychurch CF35 6AF
☎ 01656 862121
Challenging holes on this 9-hole course include the par 3 3rd (142yds) involving a drive across a lake and the par 4 5th (448yds) which is subject to strong prevailing winds.
9 holes, 5758yds, Par 70, SSS 68.
Club membership 260.
Visitors must have handicap certificate, advisable to contact in advance.
Societies by prior application.
Green Fees £15 per 18 holes; £10 per 9 holes.
Facilities ⊗ ℑ ╚ ☕ ♀ ♨ ♨ ☎ Peter Evans.
Leisure trolley for hire, putting green, practice area.
Location 1m out of Coychurch turn at village garage
Hotel ★★★ 74% Coed-y-Mwstwr Hotel, Coychurch, BRIDGEND ☎ 01656 860621 23 ⇔ ♣

Southerndown Ewenny CF32 0QP
☎ 01656 880476 & 880326
Downland championship course with rolling fairways and fast greens. The par-3 5th is played across a valley and the 18th, with its split level fairway, is a demanding finishing hole. Superb views.
18 holes, 6417yds, Par 70, SSS 72, Course record 64.
Club membership 710.
Visitors must contact in advance & have handicap certificate.
Societies on Tue & Thu by arrangement with secretary.
Green Fees £30 (£36 weekends and bank holidays).

Facilities ⊗ ℑ ╚ ☕ ♀ ♨ ♨ ☎ D G McMonagle.
Leisure trolley for hire, putting green, practice area.
Location 3m SW on B4524
Hotel ★★★ 74% Coed-y-Mwstwr Hotel, Coychurch, BRIDGEND ☎ 01656 860621 23 ⇔ ♣

CAERLEON
Map 03 ST39

Caerleon NP6 1AY ☎ 01633 420342
Parkland course.
9 holes, 2900yds, Par 34, SSS 34, Course record 29.
Club membership 120.
Visitors contact for details.
Societies telephone.
Green Fees £5.15 per 18 holes; £3.45 per 9 holes (£6.50/£4.30 weekends).
Facilities ╚ ☕ ♀ ♨ ☎ Alex Campbell.
Leisure trolley for hire, driving range, putting green.
Location 3m from M4 turn off for Caerleon
Hotel ★★★★ 65% Celtic Manor Hotel, Golf & Country Club, Coldra Woods, NEWPORT ☎ 01633 413000 72 ⇔ ♣

CAERPHILLY
Map 03 ST18

Caerphilly Penchapel, Mountain Rd CF8 1HJ
☎ 01222 883481 & 863441
Undulating mountain course with woodland affording good views especially from 10th hole, 700 ft above sea level. Recently upgraded to 18 holes. ▶

14 holes, 6032yds, Par 73, SSS 71.
Club membership 750.

Visitors	telephone in advance, must produce a current handicap certificate or letter from club secretary,may not play at weekends except with member, no visitors bank holidays.
Societies	apply in writing in advance to the secretary.
Green Fees	£20 (weekly tickets available).
Facilities	⊗ ⅺ by prior arrangement ᕊ ⬛ ♀ ᕒ 🖿 ⌀ Richard Barter.
Leisure	trolley for hire, putting green, practice area.
Location	0.5m S on A469
Hotel	★★★ 73% Manor Parc Country Hotel & Restaurant, Thornhill Rd, Thornhill, CARDIFF ☎ 01222 693723 12 ⇥ ♞

Mountain Lakes & Castell Heights Blaengwynlais
CF8 3lNG ☎ 01222 861128 & 886666
The 9-hole Castell Heights course within the Mountain Lakes complex was established in 1982 on a 45-acre site. In 1988 a further 18-hole course was designed by Bob Sandow to take advantage of 150-acres of mountain heathland, combining both mountain top golf and parkland. Most holes are tree lined and there are 16 'lakes' as hazards. Host of major PGA tournaments.
Mountain Lakes Course: 18 holes, 6046mtrs, Par 74, SSS 73, Course record 69.
Castell Heights Course: 9 holes, 2688mtrs, Par 34, SSS 32.
Club membership 500.

Visitors	advisable to check availability, Castell Heights is pay as you play.
Societies	written or telephone notice in advance.
Green Fees	Mountain Lakes: £20 per day; £15 per round. Castell Heights: £5 (£5.50 weekends).
Facilities	⊗ ᕊ ⬛ ♀ ᕒ 🖿 ⌀ Sion Bebb.
Leisure	motorised carts for hire, buggies for hire, trolley for hire, driving range, putting green, practice area.
Location	Near Black Lock Inn, Caerphilly Mountain
Hotel	★★★ 73% Manor Parc Country Hotel & Restaurant, Thornhill Rd, Thornhill, CARDIFF ☎ 01222 693723 12 ⇥ ♞

Virginia Park Golf Club Virginia Park CF38 3SW
☎ 01222 863919 & 585368
Beside Caerphilly leisure centre, the course is totally flat but with plenty of trees and bunkers and 2 lakes. It is a tight, challenging course with 6 par 4 and 3 par 3 holes. Also a 20-bay flodlit driving range.
9 holes, 2566yds, Par 33.
Club membership 250.

Visitors	telephone in advance.
Societies	telephone then write to confirm.
Green Fees	£11 per 18 holes; £6 per 9 holes.
Facilities	ᕊ ⬛ ♀ ᕒ 🖿 ⌀
Leisure	trolley for hire, driving range, leisure centre adjacent.
Location	Off Pontyewindy Rd
Hotel	★★★ 73% Manor Parc Country Hotel & Restaurant, Thornhill Rd, Thornhill, CARDIFF ☎ 01222 693723 12 ⇥ ♞

CAERWENT
Map 03 ST49

Dewstow NP6 4AH
☎ 01291 430444
A newly-established, picturesque parkland course with spectacular views over the Severn estuary towards Bristol. Testing holes include the Par three 7th, which is approached over water, some 50 feet lower than the tee. There is also a 26-bay floodlit driving range.
Valley Course: 18 holes, 6123yds, Par 72, SSS 70, Course record 69.
Park Course: 18 holes, 6147yds, Par 69, SSS 69, Course record 72.
Club membership 850.

Visitors	may book two days in advance (six days in advance in winter).
Societies	apply in writing or telephone for details.
Green Fees	£18 per day; £11 per 18 holes; £7 per 9 holes (£15 per round; £9 per 9 holes weekends & bank holidays).
Facilities	⊗ ⅺ ᕊ ⬛ ♀ ᕒ 🖿 ⌀ ⌀ Gareth Bebb.
Leisure	motorised carts for hire, buggies for hire, trolley for hire, driving range, putting green.
Location	0.5m S of A48 at Caerwent
Hotel	★★★★ 72% St Pierre Hotel, Country Club Resort, St Pierre Park, CHEPSTOW ☎ 01291 625261 143 ⇥ ♞

CARDIFF
Map 03 ST17

Cardiff Sherborne Av, Cyncoed CF2 6SJ
☎ 01222 753320
Parkland course, where trees form natural hazards. Interesting variety of holes, mostly bunkered.
18 holes, 6016yds, Par 70, SSS 70, Course record 66.
Club membership 900.

Visitors	contact in advance.
Societies	Thu only, pre-booking essential.
Green Fees	£30 per day summer (£20 winter).
Facilities	⊗ ⅺ ᕊ ⬛ ♀ ᕒ 🖿 ⌀ Terry Hanson.
Leisure	trolley for hire, putting green, practice area.
Location	3m N of city centre
Hotel	B Forte Posthouse Pentwyn, Pentwyn Rd, Pentwyn, CARDIFF ☎ 01222 731212 142 ⇥ ♞

Llanishen Cwm Lisvane CF4 5UD
☎ 01222 755078
Mountain course, with hard walking overlooking the Bristol Channel.
18 holes, 5296yds, Par 68, SSS 66, Course record 63.
Club membership 600.

Visitors	must play with member at weekends & bank holidays. Must contact in advance.
Societies	contact in advance.
Green Fees	£24 per weekday.
Facilities	⊗ ⅺ ᕊ ⬛ ♀ ᕒ 🖿 ⌀ Adrian Jones.
Leisure	trolley for hire, putting green, practice area.
Location	5m N of city centre off A469
Hotel	B Forte Posthouse Pentwyn, Pentwyn Rd, Pentwyn, CARDIFF ☎ 01222 731212 142 ⇥ ♞

Peterstone Peterstone, Wentloog CF3 8TN
☎ 01633 680009
Parkland course with abundant water features and several long drives (15th, 601yds).
18 holes, 6555yds, Par 72, SSS 71, Course record 67.
Club membership 709.
Visitors   contact in advance suggested.
Societies   telephone enquiries welcome.
Green Fees £20 per day; £15 per round (£27.50/£22.50 weekends).
Facilities ⊗ ⅷ ╚ ➤ ♀ ♨ 🏠 🍴 ⚑ Mike Pycroft.
Leisure   motorised carts for hire, buggies for hire, trolley for hire, putting green, practice area.
Location   3m from Castleton off A48
Hotel   B Forte Posthouse Pentwyn, Pentwyn Rd, Pentwyn, CARDIFF
            ☎ 01222 731212 142 ⇌ ♟

Radyr Drysgol Rd, Radyr CF4 8BS
☎ 01222 842408
Hillside, parkland course which can be windy. Good views.
18 holes, 6031yds, Par 69, SSS 70, Course record 63.
Club membership 870.
Visitors   must play with member at weekends. Must contact in advance and have an introduction from own club.
Societies   must contact in advance.
Green Fees not confirmed.
Facilities ♀ ♨ 🏠 ⚑ Steve Gough.
Location   4.5m NW of city centre off A4119
Hotel   ★★★★ 62% Park Thistle, Park Place, CARDIFF ☎ 01222 383471 119 ⇌ ♟

St Mellons St Mellons CF3 8XS
☎ 01633 680408
This parkland course comprises quite a few par-3 holes and provides some testing golf. It is indeed a challenge to the single handicap golfer. The 12th hole runs over a stream, making an accurate drive virtually essential.
18 holes, 6275yds, Par 70, SSS 70, Course record 63.
Club membership 700.
Visitors   must contact in advance. With member only at weekends.
Societies   must contact in advance.
Green Fees £25 per day.
Facilities ⊗ ⅷ ╚ ➤ ♀ ♨ 🏠 ⚑ Barry Thomas.
Leisure   buggies for hire, trolley for hire, putting green, practice area.
Location   5m NE off A48
Hotel   B Forte Posthouse Pentwyn, Pentwyn Rd, Pentwyn, CARDIFF
            ☎ 01222 731212 142 ⇌ ♟

Whitchurch Pantmawr Rd, Whitchurch CF4 6XD
☎ 01222 620985 sec & 614660 pro
Well manicured parkland course, with easy walking.
18 holes, 6321yds, Par 71, SSS 71, Course record 62.
Club membership 750.
Visitors   contact secretary/professional in advance.
Societies   Thu only. Must contact in advance.
Green Fees £30 per day (£35 weekends & bank holidays).
Facilities ⊗ ⅷ ╚ ➤ ♀ ♨ 🏠 ⚑ Eddie Clark.
Leisure   trolley for hire, putting green, practice area.
Location   4m N of city centre on A470
Hotel   ★★★★ 62% Park Thistle, Park Place, CARDIFF ☎ 01222 383471 119 ⇌ ♟

Marriott

ST. PIERRE
HOTEL & COUNTRY CLUB

St Pierre Park Chepstow Gwent NP6 6YA

Telephone: (01291) 625261

CHEPSTOW   Map 03 ST59

ST PIERRE HOTEL, COUNTRY CLUB RESORT
See page 349

CLYDACH   Map 03 SN60

Inco SA6 5PQ ☎ 01792 844216
Flat meadowland course.
12 holes, 6303yds, Par 71, SSS 70.
Club membership 300.
Visitors   no restrictions.
Societies   must contact in advance.
Green Fees not confirmed.
Facilities ♀ ♨
Location   0.75m SE on B4291
Hotel   ★★ 62% Oak Tree Parc Hotel, Birchgrove Rd, BIRCHGROVE ☎ 01792 817781 10 ⇌ ♟

CREIGIAU (CREIYIAU)   Map 03 ST08

Creigiau Llantwit Rd CF4 8NN ☎ 01222 890263
Downland course, with small greens.
18 holes, 6015yds, Par 71, SSS 69.
Club membership 1020.
Visitors   must contact in advance.
Societies   Wed only min number 20, must book in advance.
Green Fees £26 per day/round.
Facilities ⊗ ⅷ ╚ ➤ ♀ ♨ 🏠 ⚑ Iain Luntz.   ▶

Leisure trolley for hire, practice area.
Location 6m NW of Cardiff on A4119
Hotel ★★★★ 65% Miskin Manor Hotel, MISKIN
☎ 01443 224204 32 ⇄ ſ

CWMBRAN
Map 03 ST29

Green Meadow Golf & Country Club Treherbert Rd,
Croesyceiliog NP44 2BZ
☎ 01633 869321 & 860655
Undulating parkland course with panoramic views. The 7th
hole is played partly down hill with the front half of the green
enclosed with water; the 13th is exposed to winds with large
mature trees along righthand side of green.
18 holes, 6029yds, Par 71, SSS 72.
Club membership 400.
Visitors by prior arrangement advised especially at
weekends, tel 01633 862626. Correct standard of
dress compulsory.
Societies telephone for brochure, Golf Shop 01633
862626.
Green Fees £15 per day; £12 per 18 holes (£18/£15
weekends).
Facilities ⊗ ⅷ ⅃ ▇ ♀ ♨ ☎ ✈ ſ Dave Woodman.
Leisure hard tennis courts, motorised carts for hire,
buggies for hire, trolley for hire, driving range,
driving range, practice area.
Location 5m N of junct 26 M4, off A4042
Hotel ★★★★ 63% Parkway Hotel, Cwmbran Dr,
CWMBRAN
☎ 01633 871199 70 ⇄ ſ

Pontnewydd Maesgwyn Farm, West Pontnewydd NP44 1AB
☎ 01633 482170
Mountainside course, with hard walking. Good views across
the Severn Estuary.
10 holes, 5353yds, Par 68, SSS 67, Course record 63.
Club membership 250.
Visitors must play with member weekends & bank
holidays.
Green Fees not confirmed.
Facilities ♀ ♨
Location N side of town centre
Hotel ★★★★ 63% Parkway Hotel, Cwmbran Dr,
CWMBRAN
☎ 01633 871199 70 ⇄ ſ

DINAS POWIS
Map 03 ST17

Dinas Powis Old High Walls CF64 4AJ
☎ 01222 512727
Parkland/downland course with views over the Bristol
Channel and the seaside resort of Barry.
18 holes, 5486yds, Par 67, SSS 67, Course record 60.
Club membership 550.
Visitors must contact in advance. No visitors during
weekends.
Societies telephone in advance.
Green Fees £22.50 per day (with member only weekends).
Facilities ⊗ ⅷ ⅃ ▇ ♀ ♨ ☎ ſ Gareth Bennett.
Leisure trolley for hire, putting green, practice area.
Location NW side of village
Hotel ★★★ 60% Mount Sorrel Hotel, Porthkerry Rd,
BARRY
☎ 01446 740069 43 ⇄ ſ

GLYNNEATH
Map 03 SN80

Glynneath Pen-y-graig, Pontneathvaughan SA11 5UH
☎ 01639 720452
Attractive hillside golf overlooking the Vale of Neath in the
foothills of the Brecon Beacons National Park. Reasonably
level farmland/wooded course.
18 holes, 5533yds, Par 68, SSS 67, Course record 66.
Club membership 600.
Visitors restricted starting times at weekend.
Societies apply in writing in advance.
Green Fees £15 per day (£20 weekends and bank holidays).
Facilities ⊗ ⅃ ▇ ♀ ♨ ☎
Leisure buggies for hire, trolley for hire, snooker.
Location 2m NE on B4242
Hotel ★★ 62% Oak Tree Parc Hotel, Birchgrove Rd,
BIRCHGROVE
☎ 01792 817781 10 ⇄ ſ

LLANWERN
Map 03 ST38

Llanwern Tennyson Av NP6 2DY
☎ 01633 412029 & 412380
Parkland Course.
*New Course: 18 holes, 6115yds, Par 70, SSS 69, Course
record 63.*
Club membership 650.
Visitors welcome, but with member only at weekends.
Societies telephone and confirm in writing.
Green Fees £20 per day (£25 weekends).
Facilities ⊗ ⅷ ⅃ ▇ ♀ ♨ ☎ ſ Stephen Price.
Leisure putting green, practice area, snooker room.
Location 0.5m S off A455
Hotel ★★★★ 65% Celtic Manor Hotel, Golf &
Country Club, Coldra Woods, NEWPORT
☎ 01633 413000 72 ⇄ ſ

MAESTEG
Map 03 SS89

Maesteg Mount Pleasant, Neath Rd CF34 9PR
☎ 01656 734106 & 732037
Reasonably flat hill-top course with scenic views.
18 holes, 5929yds, Par 70, SSS 69, Course record 69.
Club membership 720.
Visitors must be a member of a recognised golf club &
have a handicap certificate.
Societies apply in writing.
Green Fees £17 per day (£20 weekends & bank holidays).
Facilities ⊗ ⅷ ⅃ ♀ ♨ ☎ ✈ ſ John Black.
Leisure trolley for hire, putting green, practice area.
Location 0.5m W off B4282
Hotel ★★★ 60% Aberavon Beach Hotel, PORT
TALBOT ☎ 01639 884949 52 ⇄

MAESYCWMMER
Map 03 ST19

Bryn Meadows Golf & Country Hotel The Bryn CF8 7SM
☎ 01495 225590 or 224103
A heavily wooded parkland course with panoramic views of
the Brecon Beacons.
18 holes, 6132yds, Par 72, SSS 69, Course record 68.
Club membership 540.
Visitors may not play Sun mornings. Must contact in
advance. ▶

St Pierre

ST PIERRE PARK, CHEPSTOW *Monmouthshire*
☎ **01291 625261**   **Map 03 ST59**

John Ingham writes: Just over the Severn Bridge, and a mile down the old Newport road, is St Pierre, the parkland course where huge trees stand in the way of any golf shot not hit on the perfect line!

Set in 400 yards of glorious deer park, with a lake preserved as a wild life sanctuary, a clubhouse which was once a great mansion and the 800-year-old church of St Pierre nearby, you cannot help but be impressed by the place, and the atmosphere.

There are two courses to sample. The Old was designed by C K Cotton in 1962 while the Mathern was created by Bill Graham, a Geordie businessman who snapped up the place after driving past in his car after World War II. He immediately saw the potential as the fast motorway link with London and the south was being created.

The courses have staged several successful tournaments including the old Dunlop Masters which I used to cover for a London newspaper. Competitors would get pretty cross when they found their towering drives achieved nothing because the ball, when they got up to it, was 'snookered' by huge trees, several hundred years old. Among other hazards there was none more fearsome than the lake that guards the short 18th hole - a 'mere' 245 yards across water. Television cameras here filmed Tony Jacklin and Peter Oosterhuis almost holing in one, But they missed Arwyn Griffiths who arrived on the last tee needing a par-3 for an amazing course record 63. Unhappily, Mr Griffiths found the ordeal too much and took a ghastly 11 shots, although he still won the amateur event and was thus able to celebrate at the very excellent 19th hole!

Accommodation is sumptuous within the historic buildings, making it a very special place for a few days away from it all.

While there are stories of spirits walking in the night I suspect they had something to do with the tough Old course which at 6785yards cannily sorts out even the best players while the shorter Mathern, at 5732 yards with a par 68 can also throw up a few nightmare situations if you become stymied behind a whopping oak tree!

Visitors	must contact in advance and on the Old Course play to a proficient standard so as not to restrict play apply in writing. Handicap certificate required
Societies	Monday to Friday only. Must make an advance reservation
Green fees	Midweek only Old Course £40, Mathern Course £30. Day ticket (both courses) £55
Facilities	⊗ ⏝ ┗ ▆ ♀ ⇔ ♨ 🖙 ↑ putting green, practice area, ƚ (Renton Doig) buggies, trolleys
Leisure	hard tennis courts, indoor swimming, squash, snooker, crown bowling, croquet, jacuzzi, health spa
Location	Chepstow NP6 6YA 3m SW off A48

36 holes. Old Course: 18 holes, 6785yds, Par71 SSS 73
Mathern Course: 18 holes, 5732yds, Par 68, SSS 67

WHERE TO STAY AND EAT NEARBY

HOTELS:
CHEPSTOW
★★★★⊛ 72% Marriott St Pierre Hotel & Country Club ☎ 01291 625261 143 ⇔ ♠

★★ 66% The George Hotel, Moor St ☎ 01291 625363. 14 ⇔ ♠

★★65% Castle View, 16 Bridge St ☎ 01291 620349. 9(8 ⇔ 1 ♠) Annexe 4 ⇔

RESTAURANTS:
TINTERN
⊛ Royal George Hotel (★★) ☎ 01291 689205

WHITEBROOK
⊛⊛⊛ The Crown at Whitebrook (★★) ☎ 01600 860254

Societies	Tue & Thu only.
Green Fees	not confirmed.
Facilities	♀ ♨ 🏠 ⛳ 🍴 🏌 Bruce Hunter.
Leisure	heated indoor swimming pool, sauna, gymnasium, buggy/trolley hire,practice area.
Location	On the A4048 Blackwood to Ystrad Mynach rd
Hotel	★★★ 67% Maes Manor Hotel, BLACKWOOD ☎ 01495 224551 & 220011 8 ⇥Annexe14 ⇥

MARGAM   Map 03 SS78

Lakeside Water St SA13 2PA
☎ 01639 899959
A nine hole course with four Par 4's and five Par 3's.
Old Course: 9 holes, 2500yds, Par 31, SSS 31, Course record 63.
New Course: 9 holes, 2500yds, Par 34.
Club membership 250.

Visitors	no restrictions. New course due to open June 96.
Societies	apply in advance by letter or telephone.
Green Fees	£8 per 18 holes; £5 per 9 holes.
Facilities	⊗ ⅲ ⚑ ♨ ♀ ♨ 🏠 ⛳ 🏌 Mathew Wootton.
Leisure	trolley for hire, driving range.
Location	Off junct 38 of M4
Hotel	★★★ 60% Aberavon Beach Hotel, PORT TALBOT ☎ 01639 884949 52 ⇥

MERTHYR TYDFIL   Map 03 SO00

Merthyr Tydfil (Cilanws) Cilsanws, Cefn Coed CF48 2NU
☎ 01685 723308
Mountain-top course with good views and water hazards.
Requires accuracy off the tee.
11 holes, 5956yds, Par 70, SSS 69, Course record 65.
Club membership 210.

Visitors	may not play on Sun.
Societies	by prior arrangement.
Green Fees	£12 per day (£16 weekends & bank holidays).
Facilities	♨
Location	Off A470 at Cefn Coed
Hotel	★★ 66% Nant Ddu Lodge Hotel, Cwm Taf, Merthyr Tydfil ☎ 01685 379111 12 ⇥ 🏌Annexe4 ⇥

Morlais Castle Pant, Dowlais CF48 2UY
☎ 01685 722822
Beautiful moorland course in National Park adjacent to
Brecon Beacons. Rocky terrain off the fairways makes for a
testing game.
18 holes, 6320yds, Par 71, SSS 71.
Club membership 450.

Visitors	must contact in advance for weekends.
Societies	apply in writing.
Green Fees	£14 per day (£16 weekends & bank holidays).
Facilities	⊗ by prior arrangement ⅲ by prior arrangement ⚑ ♨ ♀ ♨ 🏠 🏌 P Worthing.
Leisure	practice area.
Location	2.5m N off A465
Hotel	★★ 66% Nant Ddu Lodge Hotel, Cwm Taf, Merthyr Tydfil ☎ 01685 379111 12 ⇥ 🏌Annexe4 ⇥

MONMOUTH   Map 03 SO51

Monmouth Leasebrook Ln NP5 3SN
☎ 01600 712212
Parkland course in scenic setting. High, undulating land with
good views. Testing 1st and 4th holes.
18 holes, 5689yds, Par 69, SSS 69, Course record 68.
Club membership 600.

Visitors	advisable to contact in advance, bank holidays only with member.
Societies	advance notice advisable, write or telephone secretary.
Green Fees	£15 per day.
Facilities	⊗ ⅲ ⚑ ♨ ♀ ♨ 🏠
Leisure	motorised carts for hire, trolley for hire, putting green, practice area.
Location	1.5m NE off A40
Hotel	★★ 68% Riverside Hotel, Cinderhill St, MONMOUTH ☎ 01600 715577 & 713236 17 ⇥ 🏌

Rolls of Monmouth The Hendre NP5 4HG
☎ 01600 715353
A hilly and challenging parkland course encompassing
several lakes and ponds and surrounded by woodland. Set
within a beautiful private estate complete with listed
mansion.
18 holes, 6733yds, Par 72, SSS 73.
Club membership 200.

Visitors	telephone in advance.
Societies	must contact in advance.
Green Fees	£30 per day (£35 weekends & bank holidays). Monday special £25 per 18 holes,lunch & coffee.
Facilities	⊗ ⅲ ⚑ ♨ ♀ ♨ 🏠 ⛳
Leisure	motorised carts for hire, buggies for hire, trolley for hire, putting green, practice area.
Location	4m W on B4233
Hotel	★★ 68% Riverside Hotel, Cinderhill St, MONMOUTH ☎ 01600 715577 & 713236 17 ⇥ 🏌

MOUNTAIN ASH   Map 03 ST09

Mountain Ash Cefnpennar CF45 4DT ☎ 01443 479459
Mountain course.
18 holes, 5553yds, Par 69, SSS 67, Course record 63.
Club membership 600.

Visitors	contact in advance for details.
Societies	must contact in writing.
Green Fees	£15 per day (£18 weekends).
Facilities	⊗ ⅲ ⚑ ♨ ♀ ♨ 🏠 🏌 Ceri Hiscox.
Leisure	trolley for hire, putting green.
Location	1m NW off A4059
Hotel	★★★ 59% The Baverstock Hotel, The Heads Of Valley Rd, MERTHYR TYDFIL ☎ 01685 386221 53 ⇥ 🏌

A golf course name printed in ***bold italics***
means we have been unable to verify
information with the club's management for
the current year

NANTYGLO
Map 03 SO11

West Monmouthshire Golf Rd, Winchestown NP3 4QT
☎ 01495 310233
Established in 1906, this mountain and heathland course was
officially designated in 1994 by the Guiness Book of Record
as being the highest above sea level, with the 14th tee at a
height of 1513ft. The course has plenty of picturesque views,
hard walking and natural hazards. Testing 3rd hole, par 5, and
7th hole, par 4.
18 holes, 6013yds, Par 71, SSS 69, Course record 65.
Club membership 350.

Visitors	welcome, must be guest of member for play on Sun.
Societies	apply in writing or contact golf shop 01495 313052.
Green Fees	£18 per day (Mon-Sat).
Facilities	⊗ ⅏ 丨 ⅃ ♀ ⏚ 🏠
Leisure	trolley for hire, putting green, practice area,.
Location	0.25m W off A467
Hotel	★★★ 54% Angel Hotel, Cross St, ABERGAVENNY ☎ 01873 857121 29 ⇌ 🐾

NEATH
Map 03 SS79

Earlswood Jersey Marine SA10 6JP ☎ 01792 812198
Earlswood is a hillside course offering spectacular scenic
views over Swansea Bay. The terrain is gently undulating
parkland with natural hazards and is designed to appeal to
both the new and the experienced golfer.
18 holes, 5084yds, Par 68, SSS 68.

Visitors	no restrictions.
Societies	advisable to contact in advance.
Green Fees	£8 per 18 holes.
Facilities	丨 ⅃ 🏠 ⏚ 丨 ⅃ Mike Day.
Leisure	trolley for hire, catering can be arranged at Swansea Bay Golf Club.
Location	Approx 4m E of Swansea, off A483
Hotel	★★ 65% Castle Hotel, The Parade, NEATH ☎ 01639 641119 & 643581 28 ⇌ 🐾

Neath Cadoxton SA10 8AH
☎ 01639 643615 & 632759
Mountain course, with spectacular views. Testing holes: 10th
par 4; 12th par 5; 15th par 4.
18 holes, 6492yds, Par 72, SSS 72, Course record 66.
Club membership 700.

Visitors	with member only at weekends & bank holidays.
Societies	should either telephone or write in advance.
Green Fees	not confirmed.
Facilities	♀ ⅃ 🏠 丨 ⅃ E M Bennett.
Leisure	putting green,trolley hire.
Location	2m NE off A4230
Hotel	★★ 65% Castle Hotel, The Parade, NEATH ☎ 01639 641119 & 643581 28 ⇌ 🐾

Swansea Bay Jersey Marine SA10 6JP
☎ 01792 812198 & 814153
Fairly level seaside links with part-sand dunes.
18 holes, 6605yds, Par 72, SSS 72.
Club membership 500.

Visitors	welcome.
Societies	telephone enquiry or letter stating requirements.
Green Fees	£16 per day (£22 weekends & bank holidays).

Facilities	⊗ ⅏ by prior arrangement 丨 ⅃ ♀ ⅃ 🏠 丨 ⅃ Mike Day.
Leisure	trolley for hire, putting green, practice area.
Location	4m SW off A48
Hotel	★★ 65% Castle Hotel, The Parade, NEATH ☎ 01639 641119 & 643581 28 ⇌ 🐾

NELSON
Map 03 ST19

Whitehall The Pavilion CF46 6ST ☎ 01443 740245
Windy hilltop course. Testing 4th hole (225 yds) par 3, and
6th hole (402 yds) par 4. Pleasant views.
9 holes, 5666yds, Par 69, SSS 68, Course record 63.
Club membership 300.

Visitors	must be a member of a recognised golf club & have a handicap certificate. Must contact in advance to play at weekends.
Societies	must contact in writing 4 weeks in advance.
Green Fees	not confirmed.
Facilities	♀ ⅃
Location	Turn off A470 to Nelson and take A4054 S
Hotel	★★★ 63% Llechwen Hall Hotel, Llanfabon, PONTYPRIDD ☎ 01443 742050 & 740305 11 ⇌ 🐾

NEWPORT
Map 03 ST38

Newport Great Oak, Rogerstone NP1 9FX
☎ 01633 896794 & 892643
An undulating parkland course, part-wooded. The 2nd
hole is surrounded by bunkers - a difficult hole. The 11th
hole is a bogey 4 and the fairway runs through an avenue
of trees, making a straight drive preferable. Set 300ft
above sea level, it offers fine views.
18 holes, 6431yds, Par 72, SSS 71, Course record 64.
Club membership 800.

Visitors	must contact in advance & have handicap certificate. With member only on Sat.
Societies	must contact in writing.
Green Fees	not confirmed.
Facilities	♀ ⅃ 🏠 丨 ⅃ Roy Skuse.
Leisure	putting green,practice area,trolley hire.
Location	3m NW of city centre off B4591
Hotel	★★★★ 65% Celtic Manor Hotel, Golf & Country Club, Coldra Woods, NEWPORT ☎ 01633 413000 72 ⇌ 🐾

Parc Church Ln, Coedkernew NP1 9TU
☎ 01633 680933
A challenging but enjoyable 18-hole course with water
hazards and accompanying wildlife. The 38-bay driving
range is floodlit until 10pm.
18 holes, 5512yds, Par 70, SSS 70, Course record 71.
Club membership 400.

Visitors	book in advance 01633 680933.
Societies	telephone in advance.
Green Fees	£10 per round (£12 weekends and bank holidays).
Facilities	⊗ ⅏ 丨 ⅃ ♀ ⅃ 🏠 丨 ⅃ B Thomas/L Bond.
Leisure	trolley for hire, driving range, putting green, practice area.
Location	3m SW of Newport, off A48
Hotel	★★★ 60% Jarvis Wentloog Hotel, CASTLETON ☎ 01633 680591 55 ⇌ 🐾

THE CELTIC MANOR

- *Luxurious Bedrooms*
- *Award Winning Restaurant*
- *Health & Leisure Centre*
- *Beauty Therapy Suites*
- *Ian Woosnam Golf Academy*
- *Two 18 Hole Courses*

Designed by Robert Trent Jones

The Complete Resort

AA ★ ★ ★ ★

"*Both our courses are a golfer's dream; challenging, interesting and set in beautiful Welsh countryside.*"

IAN WOOSNAM MBE, TOURING PROFESSIONAL

THE CELTIC MANOR HOTEL,
GOLF & COUNTRY CLUB
Coldra Woods, Newport, Gwent NP6 2YA
Tel: 01633 413000 Fax: 01633 412910/410284

Tredegar Park Bassaleg Rd NP9 3PX
☎ 01633 894433 & 894517
A parkland course with River Ebbw and streams as natural hazards. The ground is very flat with narrow fairways and small greens. The 17th hole (par 3) is played on to a plateau where many players spoil their medal round.
18 holes, 6095yds, Par 71, SSS 70.
Club membership 750.
Visitors   must be a member of a golf club affiliated to a national golf union, please contact in advance.
Societies   apply to secretary.
Green Fees   £23 per day; £15 in winter (£30 weekends & bank holidays).
Facilities   ⊗ ⚞ ⚎ ⚍ ♀ ♨ ➊ ✦ ✆ M L Morgan.
Leisure   trolley for hire, putting green, practice area.
Location   2m SW off A467 exit 27 of M4
Hotel   ★★★ 62% Kings Hotel, High St, NEWPORT ☎ 01633 842020 47 ⇆ ♠

OAKDALE   Map 03 ST19

Oakdale Llwynon Ln NP2 0NF ☎ 01495 220044
9 holes, 1344yds, Par 28, Course record 27.
Visitors   no restrictions pay & play.
Societies   telephone for further information and arrangements.
Green Fees   £3.75 per 9 holes; £2.25 additional round.
Facilities   ⚎ ➊ ✦ ✆ Clive Coombs.
Leisure   trolley for hire, driving range.
Location   B4251 E of Blackwood

PENARTH   Map 03 ST17

Glamorganshire Lavernock Rd CF64 5UP
☎ 01222 701185
Parkland course, overlooking the Bristol Channel.
18 holes, 6181yds, Par 70, SSS 70, Course record 64.
Club membership 1000.
Visitors   contact professional in advance.
Societies   must contact in advance.
Green Fees   £24 per day (£30 weekends & bank holidays).
Facilities   ⊗ ⚞ ⚎ ⚍ ♀ ♨ ➊ ✦ ✆ Andrew Kerr-Smith.
Leisure   squash, motorised carts for hire, buggies for hire, trolley for hire, driving range, putting green, practice area.
Location   S side of town centre on B4267
Hotel   ★ 66% Walton House Hotel, 37 Victoria Rd, PENARTH ☎ 01222 707782 13rm(11 ⇆ ♠)

PENCOED   Map 03 SS98

St Mary's Hotel Golf & Country Club St Mary Hill CF35 5EA ☎ 01656 861100
A parkland course with many American style features. The Par 3 13th called 'Alcatraz' has a well deserved reputation.
St Mary's Course: 18 holes, 5120yds, Par 67, SSS 66, Course record 67.
Sevenoaks Course: 9 holes, 2426yds, Par 35, SSS 34.
Club membership 1100.
Visitors   must produce a handicap certificate.
Societies   telephone Kay Brazell.
Green Fees   not confirmed.
Facilities   ♀ ♨ ➊ ✦ ✦ ✆ Jason Harris.
Leisure   hard tennis courts, 15 bay driving range.
Hotel   ★★★ 70% St Mary's Hotel & Country Club, St Marys Golf Club, PENCOED
☎ 01656 861100 24 ⇆ ♠
See advertisement on page 345.

PENRHYS   Map 03 ST09

Rhondda Golf Club House CF43 3PW ☎ 01443 441384
Mountain course with good views.
18 holes, 6205yds, Par 70, SSS 70, Course record 67.
Club membership 600.
Visitors   contact secretary for weekend play.
Societies   contact for details.
Green Fees   £15 (£20 weekends & bank holidays).
Facilities   ⊗ ⚞ ⚎ ⚍ ♀ ♨ ➊ ✆ Rhys Davies.
Leisure   motorised carts for hire, buggies for hire, trolley for hire, putting green, practice area.
Location   0.5m W off B4512
Hotel   ★★ 64% Wyndham Hotel, Dunraven Place, BRIDGEND
☎ 01656 652080 & 657431 24 ⇆ ♠

PONTARDAWE   Map 03 SN70

Pontardawe Cefn Llan SA8 4SH
☎ 01792 830041 & 830977
Meadowland course situated on plateau 600 ft above sea-level with good views over Bristol Channel and Brecon Beacons.
18 holes, 6038yds, Par 70, SSS 70, Course record 64.
Club membership 500.

Visitors must contact in advance, but may not play on weekends.
Societies apply in writing.
Green Fees £19 per day.
Facilities ⊗ ⅶ ⅃ ♭ ♥ ♀ ♣ 🏠 ℭ Gary Hopkins.
Leisure trolley for hire, putting green, practice area.
Location N side of town centre M4 junc 45 off A4067
Hotel ★★ 62% Oak Tree Parc Hotel, Birchgrove Rd, BIRCHGROVE
☎ 01792 817781 10 ⇆ ℝ

PONTLLIW
Map 02 SS69

Allt-y-Graban Allt-y-Graban Rd SA4 1DT
☎ 01792 885757
A new course opened for 1994.It is a 9-hole course but with plans for 12 holes. There are 6 par-4 holes and 3 par-3 holes. The 4th is a challenging hole with a blind tee shoot into the valley and a dogleg to the left onto an elevated green.
9 holes, 2210yds, Par 66, SSS 66.
Club membership 158.
Visitors no restrictions,
Societies telephone in advance.
Green Fees £12 per day; £9 per 18 holes; £6 per 9 holes (£8 per 18 holes; £5 per 9 holes in winter).
Facilities ♭ ♥ ♀ ♣ 🏠 ⅌ ℭ Steven Rees.
Leisure trolley for hire, putting green, practice area.
Hotel ★★★ 61% Fforest Hotel, Pontardulais Rd, Fforestfach, SWANSEA
☎ 01792 588711 34 ⇆ ℝ

PONTYPOOL
Map 03 SO20

Pontypool Trevethin NP4 8TR
☎ 01495 763655
Undulating, mountain course with magnificent views.
18 holes, 6046yds, Par 69, SSS 69.
Club membership 638.
Visitors must have a handicap certificate.
Societies apply in writing or by phone, deposit payable.
Green Fees £18 per day; £24 weekends and bank holidays.
Facilities ⊗ ⅶ ⅃ ♭ ♥ ♀ ♣ 🏠 ⅌ ℭ James Howard.
Leisure motorised carts for hire, buggies for hire, trolley for hire, putting green, practice area.
Location 1.5m N off A4043
Hotel ★★★ 73% Glen-yr-Afon House Hotel, Pontypool Rd, USK
☎ 01291 672302 & 673202 27 ⇆ ℝ

Woodlake Park Golf & Country Club Glascoed NP4 0TE
☎ 01291 673933
Undulating parkland course with magnificent views over Llandegfedd Reservoir. Superb green constructed to USGA specification. Holes 4, 7 & 16 are Par 3's which are particularly challenging. Holes 6 & 17 are long Par 4's which can be wind affected. An indoor golf centre with chipping/pitching & 4 bunker positions, plus an indoor driving range ensure golf can be played whatever the weather!
18 holes, 6278yds, Par 71, SSS 72, Course record 68.
Club membership 350.
Visitors book in advance.
Societies telephone or write for society package.
Green Fees £27.50 per day; £20 per round.
Facilities ⊗ ⅶ ⅃ ♭ ♥ ♀ ♣ 🏠 ⅌ ℭ Adrian Pritchard.

Leisure fishing, motorised carts for hire, buggies for hire, trolley for hire, putting green, practice area.
Location Overlooking Llandegfedd Reservoir
Hotel ★★★ 73% Glen-yr-Afon House Hotel, Pontypool Rd, USK
☎ 01291 672302 & 673202 27 ⇆ ℝ

PONTYPRIDD
Map 03 ST09

Pontypridd Ty Gwyn Rd CF37 4DJ
☎ 01443 409904 & 402359
Well-wooded mountain course with springy turf. Good views of the Rhondda Valleys and coast.
18 holes, 5721yds, Par 69, SSS 68.
Club membership 850.
Visitors must play with member on weekends & bank holidays. Must have a handicap certificate.
Societies weekdays only. Must apply in writing.
Green Fees not confirmed.
Facilities ♀ ♣ 🏠 ℭ Wade Walters.
Location E side of town centre off A470
Hotel ★★★ 66% Heritage Park Hotel, Coed Cae Rd, Trehafod, PONTYPRIDD
☎ 01443 687057 50 ⇆ ℝ

PORT TALBOT
Map 03 SS78

British Steel Port Talbot Sports & Social Club, Margam SA13 2NF ☎ 01639 814182 & 871111
A 9 hole course with two lakes. All the holes are affected by crosswinds and the 7th, Par 3, is alongside a deep stream, so is very tight.
9 holes, 4726yds, Par 62, SSS 63, Course record 60.
Club membership 250.
Visitors contact in advance, may not play at weekends.
Societies by prior arrangement.
Green Fees £8 per 18 holes.
Facilities ⊗ ♭ ♥ ♀ ♣
Leisure hard tennis courts, practice area.
Hotel ★★★ 60% Aberavon Beach Hotel, PORT TALBOT
☎ 01639 884949 52 ⇆

PORTHCAWL
Map 03 SS87

Royal Porthcawl CF36 3UW
☎ 01656 782251
This championship-standard heathland/downland links course is always in sight of the sea, and has hosted many major tournaments.
18 holes, 6406yds, Par 72, SSS 73.
Club membership 800.
Visitors must contact in advanced & produce handicap certificate limit men 20, ladies 30. Restricted at weekends & bank holidays.
Societies apply in writing.
Green Fees £45 per day (£50 weekends if available).
Facilities ⊗ ⅶ ⅃ ♭ ♥ ♀ ♣ 🏠 ⅌ ⤙ ℭ Peter Evans.
Leisure trolley for hire, driving range, putting green, practice area.
Location 1.5m NW of town centre
Hotel ★★★ 61% Seabank Hotel, The Promenade, PORTHCAWL
☎ 01656 782261 61 ⇆ ℝ

PYLE

Map 03 SS88

Pyle & Kenfig Waun-Y-Mer CF33 4PU
☎ 01656 783093 & 771613
Links and downland course, with sand-dunes. Easy walking.
Often windy.
18 holes, 6081mtrs, Par 71, SSS 73, Course record 68.
Club membership 1010.

Visitors	by arrangement midweek, guests of members only at weekends.
Societies	for large numbers apply in writing, small numbers telephone booking accepted.
Green Fees	£30 per day/round.
Facilities	⊗ ⅏ ⓛ 𝕃 ♀ ♨ 🖻 ⚐ 𝕁 Robert Evans.
Leisure	motorised carts for hire, buggies for hire, trolley for hire, driving range, putting green, practice area.
Location	S side of Pyle off A4229
Hotel	★★★ 61% Seabank Hotel, The Promenade, PORTHCAWL ☎ 01656 782261 61 ⇌ 🅻

RAGLAN
.
Map 03 SO40

Raglan Park Park Lodge NP5 2ER ☎ 01291 690077
New parkland course with well laid greens and a mature back
9 that are already the source of local praise. Several testing
holes where a combination of wind and water make golf
challenging. Easy walking.
18 holes, 6391yds, Par 72, SSS 72.
Club membership 300.

Societies	advance arrangement required.
Green Fees	£15 per day.
Facilities	⊗ ⅏ ⓛ 𝕃 ♀ ♨ 🖻
Leisure	buggies for hire, putting green under construction, practice area.
Hotel	★★★ 66% Llansantffraed Court, Llanvihangel Gobion, ABERGAVENNY ☎ 01873 840678 21 ⇌ 🅻

SOUTHGATE

Map 02 SS58

Pennard 2 Southgate Rd SA3 2BT
☎ 01792 233131 & 233451
Undulating, cliff-top seaside links with good coastal views.
18 holes, 6265yds, Par 71, SSS 71, Course record 69.
Club membership 912.

Visitors	advisable to contact in advance.
Societies	by prior arrangement, telephone in advance.
Green Fees	£24 (£30 weekends & bank holidays).
Facilities	⊗ ⅏ ⓛ 𝕃 ♀ ♨ 🖻 ⚐ 𝕁 M V Bennett.
Leisure	squash, trolley for hire.
Location	8m W of Swansea by A4067 and B4436
Hotel	★★ 61% Nicholaston House Hotel, Nicholaston, PENMAEN ☎ 01792 371317 13 ⇌ 🅻

SWANSEA

Map 03 SS69

Clyne 120 Owls Lodge Ln, The Mayals, Blackpyl SA3 5DP
☎ 01792 401989
Moorland course, very open to the wind and with grazing
rights for local commoners.
18 holes, 6334yds, Par 70, SSS 71, Course record 64.
Club membership 800.

Visitors	must be member of a club with handicap certificate and contact in advance.
Societies	must telephone in advance.
Green Fees	not confirmed.
Facilities	♀ ♨ 🖻 𝕁 Mark Bevan.
Leisure	range, putting, practice area, trolley hire.
Location	3.5m SW on B4436 off A4067
Hotel	★★ 69% Langland Court, Langland Court Rd, LANGLAND ☎ 01792 361545 16 ⇌ 🅻 Annexe5 ⇌ 🅻

Langland Bay Langland Bay SA3 4QR
☎ 01792 366023
Parkland course overlooking Gower coast. The par 4, 6th is
an uphill dog-leg open to the wind, and the par 3, 16th (151
yds) is aptly named 'Death or Glory'.
18 holes, 5857yds, Par 70, SSS 69.
Club membership 850.

Visitors	no restrictions.
Societies	must telephone in advance.
Green Fees	not confirmed.
Facilities	♀ ♨ 🖻 𝕁
Location	6m W on A4067
Hotel	★★ 69% Langland Court, Langland Court Rd, LANGLAND ☎ 01792 361545 16 ⇌ 🅻 Annexe5 ⇌ 🅻

Morriston 160 Clasemont Rd SA6 6AJ
☎ 01792 796528 & 772335
Pleasant parkland course.
18 holes, 5891yds, Par 68, SSS 68, Course record 64.
Club membership 700.

Visitors	may not play at weekends.
Societies	apply in writing.
Green Fees	£21 per day.
Facilities	⊗ ⅏ ⓛ 𝕃 ♀ ♨ 🖻 ⚐ 𝕁 D A Rees.
Leisure	trolley for hire, putting green, practice area.
Location	5m N on A48
Hotel	★★ 62% Oak Tree Parc Hotel, Birchgrove Rd, BIRCHGROVE ☎ 01792 817781 10 ⇌ 🅻

TALBOT GREEN

Map 03 ST08

Llantrisant & Pontyclun Llanelry Rd CF7 8HZ
☎ 01443 222148
Parkland course.
12 holes, 5712yds, Par 68, SSS 68.
Club membership 600.

Visitors	must have a club membership card & handicap certificate and should be accompanied by a member.
Societies	apply in writing.
Green Fees	not confirmed.
Facilities	♨ 🖻 ⚐ 𝕁
Location	N side of village off A473
Hotel	★★★★ 65% Miskin Manor Hotel, MISKIN ☎ 01443 224204 32 ⇌ 🅻

TREDEGAR

Map 03 SO10

Tredegar and Rhymney Cwmtysswg, Rhymney NP2 3BQ
☎ 01685 840743 & 843400
Mountain course with lovely views.
9 holes, 5504yds, Par 68, SSS 68, Course record 69.
Club membership 194.

Visitors	no restrictions.
Societies	must contact in writing.
Green Fees	not confirmed.
Facilities	♀ (by arrangement) ⏣
Location	1.75m SW on B4256
Hotel	★★ 68% Tregenna Hotel, Park Ter, MERTHYR TYDFIL ☎ 01685 723627 & 382055 24 ⇌ ♚

UPPER KILLAY   Map 02 SS59

Fairwood Park Blackhills Ln SA2 7JN
☎ 01792 203648 & 297849
Championship parkland course on Gower coast with good
views and easy walking.
18 holes, 6741yds, Par 72, SSS 72.
Club membership 720.

Visitors	welcome except when championship or club matches are being held. Must contact in advance.
Societies	must contact in advance.
Green Fees	not confirmed.
Facilities	♀ ⏣ ▥ ♈ ℓ
Location	1.5m S off A4118
Hotel	★ 76% Windsor Lodge Hotel, Mount Pleasant, SWANSEA ☎ 01792 642158 & 652744 18 ⇌ ♚

WENVOE   Map 03 ST17

Wenvoe Castle CF5 6BE ☎ 01222 594371
Parkland course which is hilly for first 9 holes. Lake, situated
280 yds from tee at 10th hole, is a hazard.
18 holes, 6422yds, Par 72, SSS 71, Course record 64.
Club membership 600.

Visitors	must be a member of a recognised golf club & have a handicap certificate. Must play with member at weekends.
Societies	must contact in writing.
Green Fees	not confirmed.
Facilities	♀ ⏣ ▥ ℓ Robin Day.
Leisure	carts/buggy/trolley hire,practice area.
Location	1m S off A4050
Hotel	★★★⚉ 74% Egerton Grey Country House Hotel, Porthkerry, BARRY ☎ 01446 711666 10 ⇌ ♚

YSTALYFERA   Map 03 SN70

Palleg Lower Cwm-twrch SA9 1QT
☎ no telephone
Heathland course liable to become heavy going after winter
rain.
9 holes, 6400yds, Par 72, SSS 72.
Club membership 200.

Visitors	restricted Sat (Apr-Sep) & Sun mornings in winter.
Societies	must contact two months in advance.
Green Fees	not confirmed.
Facilities	♀ (ex Mon) ⏣
Location	1.5m N off A4068
Hotel	★★ 62% Oak Tree Parc Hotel, Birchgrove Rd, BIRCHGROVE ☎ 01792 817781 10 ⇌ ♚

IRELAND

The Irish welcome is overwhelming. Few clubs circle the waggons to keep visiors out...'

Picturesque public houses in Cork are irrisistible. This particular bar, no bigger than our kitchen, had a lino floor, former church pews against unpainted walls and a dozen customers, all telling farmer's yarns, and taking no notice of intruders, namely two American girls (one my wife) asking to sample a glass of the black stuff. We had been to Killarney Golf Club where the parkland grass is lush green, the scenery too dramatic to keep your head down and where the clubhouse is vast and modern. So, obviously, we had to recapture the non-tourist atmosphere at a Ballingeary watering-hole, and plan to take Christy O'Connor's advice and go to Dingle, another day. Nothing had changed since previous visits....

Previous visits. Odd, how one recalls every one so vividly. We flew into Dublin, checked in at Ryans for a hire car and were playing Royal Dublin (Dollymount), just four miles away, the same afternoon. The first nine holes go outwards, away from the clubhouse and, down a fierce breeze, I reached the turn in 34. On the inward nine, against the gale (well, that's the excuse) I took 43 back!

Royal Dublin is a grand course, but so is the mighty Portmarnock which we played the following day. It is giant-sized and I recall the old Canada Cup there with Arnold Palmer and Sam Snead winning. While it has none of the beauty of the Killarney course, it is a proper links, created in 1893 with a shack as its clubhouse. South African Bobby Locke, who used to play down the road at Woodbrook, near Bray, said Portmarnock was the finest links in Europe. Off the back tees in a wind, it's unplayable for such as me, although I did start with a birdie before blowing up and mentally quitting. Anyone who plays this test is qualified to talk about it for the rest of time - which we tend to do!

EUROPE'S FINEST

The West Coast of Ireland means Shannon Airport to some, and Ballybunion Golf Course to seasoned golfers. I know top Americans who love the place and rate it number one in Europe. The official list of the world's 100 Greatest Courses has it in there at number eight. Designed in 1906 by someone called Murphy, it overlooks the ocean. Point out to sea and the next stop is

America! When the wind howls and the white horses, dolphins and what have you are in full flight, you aim your teeshot wide of the fairway and watch it curve back - you hope.

Your next stop in County Clare (because that's where we are) must be the Lahinch Golf Club. Played over in 1891 by members of the Black Watch, it was designed by Tom Morris and later upgraded by Dr A Mackenzie. Why anyone is allowed to mess about with the classics of golf is beyond me, but there is usually someone on the committee who has a 'bright' idea. Happily, this one remains true and at 6,300 yards, you'll take the road via Ennis with a great deal to look forward to - and that Irish welcome.

Usually, I never admit that Newcastle's Royal County Down Golf Course is somewhere I have never played. Shame overpowers me, because I know for a fact, that it is a magnificent course. In 1889 Tom Morris was instructed to lay the place out 'at a cost not exceeding £4'. Today, someone like Jack Nicklaus instructs committees that he will require not less than £1 million! Played beneath the shadow of Slieve Donard, the highest of the Mourne Mountains, the views are said to be the finest from any course in the British Isles.

FAULKNER'S FAVOURITE

Since we are now in Northern Ireland, I can confirm that Royal Portrush Golf Course is etched in my mind. I reported an Amateur Championship win by Ireland's Joe Carr and as we all looked out towards the sea, wild and raging as it was, with bright sunshine illuminating the scene, folk talked of the day England's Max Faulkner had won the Open Championship in 1951 on this superb links. And they recall that Harry Colt, the man who designed it, claimed it was the best example of his work.

There are views of the Giant's Causeway, the Paps of Jura can be seen on a clear day and, if you don't hit your drives dead straight, you can end in 'Purgatory' at the hole that follows one called 'Calamity Corner'. And at the end of it all, you will hope they can bring the Open back here again, then you will enjoy sinking into a chair to recall that, although you went into the rough here and there, at least it was adorned with briar roses and wild flowers. And you will find it difficult to go home......

THE NEXT 50 YEARS

So that's our Round Britain trip. In my lifetime, golf in the United Kingdom has changed from a middle-class club game for those with disposable income, to a sport for the masses. Because of this, certain clubs have circled waggons, and limit visitors. In the next 50 years, we shall see popular golf emerge, and clubhouses may return to what they were - basic, plank pavilions with an ordinary course, unpretentious and available, like a seat in the cinema. A dream?

NORTHERN IRELAND

CO ANTRIM

ANTRIM
Map 01 D5

Masereene 51 Lough Rd BT41 4DQ ☎ 01849 428096
The first nine holes are parkland, while the second,
adjacent to the shore of Lough Neagh, have more of a
links character with sandy ground.
18 holes, 6559yds, Par 72, SSS 71, Course record 66.
Club membership 969.
Visitors must contact in advance.
Societies book in advance.
Green Fees £20 (£25 weekends & bank holidays).
Facilities ⊗ ⅢⓁ ♥ ♀ ♨ 🏠 ⚑ ℯ Jim Smyth.
Leisure trolley for hire, putting green.
Location 1m SW of town
Hotel ★★★★ 71% Galgorm Manor,
BALLYMENA ☎ 01266 881001 23 ⇆ ☏

BALLYCASTLE
Map 01 D6

Ballycastle Cushendall Rd BT54 6QP
☎ 01265 762536
An unusual mixture of terrain beside the sea, with
magnificent views from all parts. The first five holes are
inland type; the middle holes on the Warren are links type
and the rest, on high ground, are heath type.
18 holes, 5201mtrs, Par 71, SSS 68, Course record 64.
Club membership 950.
Visitors are welcome during the week.
Societies apply in writing.
Green Fees £17 per day (£22 per round weekends).
Facilities ⊗ Ⅲ Ⓛ ♥ ♀ ♨ 🏠 ℯ Ian McLaughlin.
Leisure trolley for hire.
Location Between Portrush & Cushendall (A2)
Hotel ★★ 57% Thornlea Hotel, 6 Coast Rd,
CUSHENDALL
☎ 012667 71223 13 ⇆ ☏

BALLYCLARE
Map 01 D5

Ballyclare 23 Springdale Rd BT39 9JW
☎ 01960 322696 & 342352
Parkland course with lots of trees and shrubs and water
hazards provided by the river, streams and lakes.
18 holes, 5745mtrs, Par 71, SSS 71, Course record 67.
Club membership 580.
Visitors no restrictions.
Societies must contact in advance.
Green Fees £15 (£20 weekends & bank holidays).
Facilities ⊗ Ⅲ Ⓛ ♥ ♀ ♨
Leisure buggies for hire, trolley for hire, driving range,
putting green, practice area.
Location 1.5m N
Hotel ★★★★ 63% Stormont Hotel, 587 Upper
Newtonards Rd, BELFAST
☎ 01232 658621 109 ⇆ ☏

BALLYGALLY
Map 01 D5

Cairndhu 192 Coast Rd BT40 2QG ☎ 01574 583324
Built on a hilly headland, this course is both testing and
scenic, with wonderful coastal views.
18 holes, 5611mtrs, Par 70, SSS 69, Course record 64.
Club membership 830.
Visitors may not play on Sat.
Societies must apply in writing.
Green Fees £25 per day; £17 per round (£30/£22 Sun &
bank holidays).
Facilities ⊗ Ⅲ Ⓛ ♥ ♀ ♨ 🏠 ⚑ ℯ Robert Walker.
Leisure trolley for hire, putting green, practice area.
Location 4m N of Larne on coast road
Hotel ★★★ 61% Ballygally Castle Hotel, 274 Coast
Rd, BALLYGALLY
☎ 01574 583212 30 ⇆ ☏

BALLYMENA
Map 01 D5

Ballymena 128 Raceview Rd BT42 4HY ☎ 01266 861487
Parkland course of level heathland with plenty of bunkers.
18 holes, 5654yds, Par 68, SSS 67.
Visitors may not play on Tue or Sat.
Societies must contact in advance.
Green Fees not confirmed.
Facilities ♀ ⚑ ℯ James Gallagher.
Leisure bowling green.
Location 2m E on A42
Hotel ★★★★ 71% Galgorm Manor, BALLYMENA
☎ 01266 881001 23 ⇆ ☏

Galgorm Castle Golf & Country Club Galgorm Rd
BT42 1HL ☎ 01266 46161
Challenging, American-style championship course scheduled
to open in the summer of 1997. Set in 240 acres of mature,
undulating parkland within the estate of one of Ireland's
unique 17th-century castles, it will feature two rivers and five
beautifully positioned lakes.
18 holes, 6800mtrs, Par 72.
Club membership 400.
Visitors scheduled to open summer 1997. Contact for
details
Societies apply in writing or telephone in advance.
Green Fees not confirmed.
Facilities ⊗ Ⅲ Ⓛ ♥ ♀ ♨ 🏠 ⚑ ℯ
Leisure fishing, trolley for hire, driving range, putting
green, practice area.
Location S from Ballymena

CARRICKFERGUS
Map 01 D5

Carrickfergus 25 North Rd BT38 8LP
☎ 019603 363713 & 351803
Parkland course, fairly level but nevetheless demanding, with
a notorious water hazard at the 1st. Well maintained with
nice views.
18 holes, 5759yds, Par 68, SSS 68.
Club membership 815.
Visitors restrictions at weekends.
Societies must contact in advance.
Green Fees not confirmed.
Facilities ♀ ♨ 🏠 ℯ Raymond Stevenson.
Leisure caddy cars.

Location   9m NE of Belfast on A2
Hotel   ★★★ 58% Chimney Corner Hotel, 630 Antrim Rd, NEWTOWNABBEY
    ☎ 01232 844925 & 844851 63 ⇔ ☝

Greenisland 156 Upper Rd, Greenisland
☎ 01232 862236
9 holes, 5536mtrs, Par 71, SSS 68.
Visitors   welcome, may be restricted on Sat.
Societies   by prior arrangement.
Green Fees   not confirmed.
Facilities
Hotel   ★★★ 58% Chimney Corner Hotel, 630 Antrim Rd, NEWTOWNABBEY
    ☎ 01232 844925 & 844851 63 ⇔ ☝

CUSHENDALL   Map 01 D6

Cushendall 21 Shore Rd ☎ 01266 771318
Scenic course with spectacular views over the Sea of Moyle and Red Bay to the Mull of Kintyre. The River Dall winds through the course, coming into play in seven of the nine holes.
9 holes, 4386mtrs, Par 66, SSS 63.
Club membership 714.
Visitors   restricted on Sun.
Societies   must contact in writing.
Green Fees   not confirmed.
Facilities   ♀ ⅄
Hotel   ★★ 57% Thornlea Hotel, 6 Coast Rd, CUSHENDALL
    ☎ 012667 71223 13 ⇔ ☝

LARNE   Map 01 D5

Larne 54 Ferris Bay Rd, Islandmagee BT40 3RT
☎ 01960 382228
An exposed part links, part heathland course offering a good test, particularly on the last three holes along the sea shore.
9 holes, 6686yds, Par 70, SSS 69, Course record 64.
Club membership 430.
Visitors   may not play on Sat.
Societies   apply in writing or telephone in advance.
Green Fees   £8 per round (£15 weekends & bank holidays).
Facilities   ⊗ by prior arrangement ⅢＴ by prior arrangement ☝ by prior arrangement ♀ ⅄
Leisure   putting green, practice area, snooker room.
Location   6m N of Whitehead on Browns Bay rd
Hotel   ★★★ 61% Ballygally Castle Hotel, 274 Coast Rd, BALLYGALLY
    ☎ 01574 583212 30 ⇔ ☝

LISBURN   Map 01 D5

Aberdelghy Bell's Ln, Lambeg BT27 4QH
☎ 01846 662738
This parkland course has no bunkers but the par-3 3rd high on the hill and the 5th hole over the dam provide a challenge. The par-4 6th hole is a long dog leg.
9 holes, 2192mtrs, Par 33, SSS 65.
Club membership 150.
Visitors   restricted Sat 8-11am.
Societies   telephone in advance.
Green Fees   not confirmed.
Facilities   ⅄ ☎ ☂ ☝ Ian Murdoch.

Leisure   practice area, lessons, trolley hire.
Location   1.5m N of Lisburn off A1
Hotel   B Forte Posthouse Belfast, Kingsway, Dunmurry, BELFAST
    ☎ 01232 612101 82 ⇔ ☝

Lisburn Blaris Lodge, 68 Eglantine Rd BT27 5RQ
☎ 01846 677216
Meadowland course, fairly level, with plenty of trees and shrubs. Challenging last three holes.
18 holes, 6647yds, Par 72, SSS 72, Course record 67.
Club membership 1421.
Visitors   must play with member at weekends. Must tee off before 3pm weekdays.
Societies   must contact in writing.
Green Fees   £25 per round (£30 weekends & bank holidays).
Facilities   ⊗ Ⅲ ♀ ⅄ ☎ ☂ ☝ Blake Campbell.
Leisure   trolley for hire, putting.
Location   2m from town on A1
Hotel   ★★★★ 63% Stormont Hotel, 587 Upper Newtonards Rd, BELFAST
    ☎ 01232 658621 109 ⇔ ☝

MAZE   Map 01 D5

Down Royal Park Dunygarton Rd BT27 5RT
☎ 01846 621339
The 9-hole Valley course and the 18-hole Down Royal Park are easy walking, undulating heathland courses. Down Royal's 2nd hole is 628yards and thought to be among the best par 5 holes in Ireland.
Down Royal Park Course: 18 holes, 6824yds, Par 72, Course record 73.
Valley Course: 9 holes, 2500yds, Par 33.
Visitors   no restrictions.
Societies   reservations in advance.
Green Fees   not confirmed.
Facilities   ♀ ⅄ ☎
Leisure   putting green.
Location   Inside Down Royal Race Course
Hotel   ★★★ 62% Dukes Hotel, 65 University St, BELFAST
    ☎ 01232 236666 21 ⇔ ☝

NEWTOWNABBEY   Map 01 D5

Ballyearl Golf & Leisure Centre 585 Doagh Rd, Mossley BT36 8RZ ☎ 01232 848287
9 holes, 2520yds, Par 27.
Visitors   no restrictions.
Societies   telephone in advance.
Green Fees   £4 (£5 weekends).
Facilities   ☂ ⅄ ☎ ☝ Jim Robinson.
Leisure   squash, gymnasium, driving range, practice area.

Mallusk Antrim Rd BT36 ☎ 01232 843799
Attractive 9-hole parkland course featuring 3 small par 4s and several water hazards, notably on the tricky, dog-leg 7th hole.
9 holes, 4444yds, Par 62, SSS 62, Course record 62.
Club membership 150.
Visitors   no restrictions.
Societies   contact for details.
Green Fees   £5.50 (£7.50 weekends).
Facilities   ☂ ♀ ⅄ ⋈
Leisure   hard tennis courts, sauna, putting green.

PORTBALLINTRAE　　　　　　　　　Map 01 C6

Bushfoot 50 Bushfoot Rd, Portballintrae BT57 8RR
☎ 01265 731317
A seaside links course with superb views in an area of
outstanding beauty. A challenging par-3 7th is ringed by
bunkers with out-of-bounds beyond, while the 3rd has a blind
approach. Also a putting green and pitch & putt course.
9 holes, 5876yds, Par 70, SSS 67, Course record 68.
Club membership 850.
Visitors　　must contact in advance.
Societies　　must contact in advance.
Green Fees £13 per round (£16 weekends & bank holidays).
Facilities　⊗ ⅷ ᴌ ☳ ♀ ♨ ⚑
Leisure　　trolley for hire, putting green, practice area.
Location　　Off Ballaghmore rd
Hotel　　★★ 60% Beach House Hotel, The Sea Front,
　　　　　　　PORTBALLINTRAE
　　　　　　　☎ 012657 31214 32 ⇄ ℾ

PORTRUSH　　　　　　　　　　　　Map 01 C6

ROYAL PORTRUSH　See page 361

WHITEHEAD　　　　　　　　　　　Map 01 D5

Bentra Municipal Slaughterford Rd BT38 9TG
☎ 01960 378996
A well matured course designed with the experienced golfer
and novice in mind with wide fairways and some particularly
long holes.
9 holes, 2885mtrs, Par 37, SSS 35.
Green Fees £6.75 per 18 holes (£10.50 weekends & bank
　　　　　　　holidays).
Facilities　⊗ ⅷ ᴌ ☳ ♀ ♨ ⚑
Leisure　　trolley for hire, driving range, putting green.
Hotel　　★★★ 58% Chimney Corner Hotel, 630 Antrim
　　　　　　　Rd, NEWTOWNABBEY
　　　　　　　☎ 01232 844925 & 844851 63 ⇄ ℾ

Whitehead McCrae's Brae
☎ 01960 353631
Undulating parkland course with magnificent sea views.
18 holes, 6426yds, Par 72, SSS 71, Course record 67.
Club membership 850.
Visitors　　may not play on Sat. Must play with member on
　　　　　　　Sun.
Societies　　must contact in advance.
Green Fees not confirmed.
Facilities　♀ ♨ ⚑ ℾ
Leisure　　putting green.
Location　　0.5m N
Hotel　　★★★ 58% Chimney Corner Hotel, 630 Antrim
　　　　　　　Rd, NEWTOWNABBEY
　　　　　　　☎ 01232 844925 & 844851 63 ⇄ ℾ

> Entries with a shaded background identify
> courses that are considered to be particularly
> interesting

CO ARMAGH

ARMAGH　　　　　　　　　　　　Map 01 C5

County Armagh The Demesne, Newry Rd BT60 1EN
☎ 01861 525861
Mature parkland course with excellent views of Armagh city
and its surroundings.
18 holes, 5649mtrs, Par 70, SSS 69, Course record 63.
Club membership 1000.
Visitors　　time sheet operates at weekends.
Societies　　must contact in writing.
Green Fees £12 per round (£18 weekends & bank holidays).
Facilities　⊗ ⅷ ᴌ ☳ ♀ ♨ ⚑ ℾ Alan Rankin.
Leisure　　trolley for hire, putting green, practice area.
Location　　On the Newry road
Hotel　　★★★★ 63% Stormont Hotel, 587 Upper
　　　　　　　Newtonards Rd, BELFAST
　　　　　　　☎ 01232 658621 109 ⇄ ℾ

LURGAN　　　　　　　　　　　　Map 01 D5

Craigavon Golf & Ski Centre Turmoyra Ln, Silverwood
BT66 6NG ☎ 01762 326606
Parkland course with a lake and stream providing water
hazards.
18 holes, 6496yds, Par 72, SSS 72.
Club membership 400.
Visitors　　restricted Sat am.
Societies　　telephone in advance.
Green Fees £10 per day (£13 weekends & bank holidays).
Facilities　⊗ ⅷ ☳ ♨ ⚑
Leisure　　trolley for hire, floodlit driving range, putting
　　　　　　　green, practice area.
Location　　2m N at Silverwood off the M1
Hotel　　★★★★ 63% Stormont Hotel, 587 Upper
　　　　　　　Newtonards Rd, BELFAST
　　　　　　　☎ 01232 658621 109 ⇄ ℾ

Lurgan The Demesne BT67 9BN ☎ 01762 322087
Testing parkland course bordering Lurgan Park Lake with a
need for accurate shots. Drains well in wet weather and suits
a long straight hitter.
18 holes, 6382yds, Par 70, SSS 70, Course record 66.
Club membership 800.
Visitors　　may not play Sat, contact in advance.
Societies　　must contact in advance, not Sat.
Green Fees £15 per round (£20 weekends & bank holidays).
Facilities　⊗ ⅷ ᴌ ☳ ♀ ♨ ⚑ ℾ Des Paul.
Leisure　　putting green, practice area.
Location　　0.5m from town centre near Lurgan Park
Hotel　　★★★★ 63% Stormont Hotel, 587 Upper
　　　　　　　Newtonards Rd, BELFAST
　　　　　　　☎ 01232 658621 109 ⇄ ℾ

PORTADOWN　　　　　　　　　　Map 01 D5

Portadown 192 Gilford Rd BT63 5LF
☎ 01762 355356
Well wooded parkland course on the banks of the River
Bann, which features among the water hazards.
18 holes, 5649mtrs, Par 70, SSS 70, Course record 65.
Club membership 1004.　　　　　　　　　　　　　▶

ROYAL PORTRUSH

PORTRUSH *Co Antrim* ☎ 01265 822311   Map 01 D4

John Ingham writes: It was more than thirty years ago that I first saw Royal Portrush, but the memory lingers on. That week in 1960, the great Joe Carr won the British Amateur Championship for his third, and last, time. But everyone there was a winner; the sun shone, and the course glistened as the foaming ocean was almost blown inland on to the briar roses that dotted the rough.

What a splendid seaside paradise this is, I wrote in a London evening newspaper, whose readers were keen to follow players such as Joe Carr and Michael Bonallack. There among the gallery was the late Fred Daly, winner of the 1947 Open and the only Irishman ever to win.

The man who designed this course was Harry S Colt, a name that appears as a creator of many fine courses. This one is considered among the six best in the United Kingdom. It is spectacular, breathtaking, but one of the tightest driving tests known to man because, if you get in the long stuff, you may stay there. On a clear day, you have a fine view of Islay and the Paps of Jura - seen from the 3rd tee. Then there's the Giant's Causeway, from the 5th, as good a downhill dogleg hole as you'll find anywhere.

While the greens have to be 'read' from the start, there are fairways up and down valleys, and holes called Calamity Corner and Purgatory for good reason. The second hole, called Giant's Grave, is 509 yards but there's an even longer one waiting for you at the 17th, while the last hole, a 479-yarder, nearly cost Max Faulkner his 1951 Open title. He hit a crooked drive, and had to bend his second shot with a wooden club. Dressed in primrose-coloured slacks, his colourful plumage and out-going attitude attracted most of the small crowd.

The Open did not return to Portrush and championship golf is the loser because the place is a gem. Founded in 1888, it was also the venue of the first professional golf event held in Ireland, when in 1895, Sandy Herd beat Harry Vardon in the final.

You'll love it.

Visitors must contact in advance, have a letter of introduction from their own club and a handicap certificate. Restricted Saturday and Sunday morning

Societies must apply in writing.

Green fees Dunluce Links £45 per day (£55 weekends) Valley Links £20 per day (£30 weekends)

Facilities ⊗ ⅏ ⅃ ⚑ ♀ (all day) ♨ 🏠 ☂ 2 practice grounds, caddies & caddy cars ☏ (Dai Stevenson)

Leisure snooker

Location Bushmills Rd Portrush BT56 8JQ (0.5m from Portrush on main road to Bushmills)

45 holes. Dunluce Links: 18 holes, 6794 yds, Par 72, SSS 73, course record 66

Valley Links: 18 holes, 6273 yds, Par 70, SSS 70, course record 65

Skerries Course: 9 holes, 1187 yds

WHERE TO STAY AND EAT NEARBY

HOTELS:
PORTRUSH
★★★ 61% Causeway Coast, 36 Ballyreagh Rd.
☎ 01265 822435. 21 ⇄ 🐾

RESTAURANT:
PORTRUSH
⊛⊛ Ramore, The Harbour.
☎ 01265 824313.

Visitors may not play on Tue & Sat.
Societies apply in writing.
Green Fees £16 per round (£20 weekends & bank holidays).
Facilities ⊗ ⅢⓁ ⓛ ⓦ ⅋ ⚒ ⚏ ⚐ ⚑ Paul Stevenson.
Leisure squash, motorised carts for hire, trolley for hire, putting green, practice area.
Location SE via A59
Hotel ★★★★ 63% Stormont Hotel, 587 Upper Newtonards Rd, BELFAST
☎ 01232 658621 109 ⇆ ⚐

TANDRAGEE
Map 01 D5

Tandragee Markethill Rd BT62 2ER
☎ 01762 841272
Pleasant hilly parkland with mature trees.
18 holes, 5446mtrs, Par 69, SSS 69, Course record 62.
Club membership 1175.
Visitors contact in advance.
Societies must contact in advance.
Green Fees £15 per round (£21 weekends & bank holidays).
Facilities ⊗ ⅢⓁ ⓛ ⓦ ⅋ ⚒ ⚏ ⚐ ⚑ Paul Stevenson.
Leisure sauna, gymnasium, trolley for hire, driving range, putting green, practice area.
Location On B3 out of Tandragee towards Markethill
Farmhouse QQQQ Brook Lodge Farmhouse, 79 Old Ballynahinch Rd, Cargacroy, LISBURN
☎ 01846 638454 6rm(4 ⚐)

● CO BELFAST ●

BELFAST
Map 01 D5

See also The Royal Belfast, Hollywood, Co Down.

Balmoral 518 Lisburn Rd BT9 6GX
☎ 01232 381514
Parkland course, mainly level, with tree-lined fairways and a stream providing a water hazard.
18 holes, 6238yds, Par 69, SSS 70.
Visitors preferred Mon & Thu.
Societies must contact in advance.
Green Fees not confirmed.
Facilities ⅋ ⚐ ⚑ Geoff Bleakley.
Location 3m SW
Hotel ★★★★ 63% Stormont Hotel, 587 Upper Newtonards Rd, BELFAST
☎ 01232 658621 109 ⇆ ⚐

Cliftonville 44 Westland Rd BT14 6NH
☎ 01232 744158 & 746595
Parkland course with rivers bisecting two fairways.
9 holes, 6242yds, Par 70, SSS 70, Course record 66.
Club membership 430.
Visitors may not play: after 5pm unless with member, on Sat or on Sun mornings.
Societies must contact in writing.
Green Fees £12 (£15 weekends & bank holidays).
Facilities ⊗ ⅢⓁ ⓛ ⓦ ⅋ ⚏ ⚒
Leisure trolley for hire, putting green, practice area.

Location Between Cavehill Rd & Cliftonville Circus
Hotel ★★★★ 63% Stormont Hotel, 587 Upper Newtonards Rd, BELFAST
☎ 01232 658621 109 ⇆ ⚐

Dunmurry 91 Dunmurry Ln, Dunmurray BT17 9JS
☎ 01232 610834
Maturing very nicely, this tricky parkland course has several memorable holes which call for skilful shots.
18 holes, 5832yds, Par 69, SSS 69, Course record 64.
Club membership 900.
Visitors telephone in advance. May only play Sat after 5pm, restricted Fri (Ladies Day).
Societies must contact in writing.
Green Fees £17 per round (£26.50 weekends & bank holidays).
Facilities ⊗ ⅢⓁ ⓛ ⓦ ⅋ ⚏ ⚒ ⚐ ⚑ Paul Leonard.
Leisure trolley for hire, putting green, practice area, snooker.
Hotel ★★★★ 63% Stormont Hotel, 587 Upper Newtonards Rd, BELFAST
☎ 01232 658621 109 ⇆ ⚐

Fortwilliam Downview Ave BT15 4EZ
☎ 01232 370770 (Office) & 770980 (Pro)
Parkland course in most attractive surroundings. The course is bisected by a lane.
18 holes, 5789yds, Par 70, SSS 68, Course record 65.
Club membership 1000.
Visitors contact professional in advance.
Societies must contact in advance.
Green Fees £19 per round (£25 weekends & bank holidays). Ladies £17 (£21 Sun & bank holidays, no play Sat).
Facilities ⊗ ⅢⓁ ⓛ ⓦ ⅋ ⚏ ⚒ ⚐ ⚑ Peter Hanna.
Leisure trolley for hire, putting green, practice area.
Location Off Antrim road
Hotel ★★★★ 63% Stormont Hotel, 587 Upper Newtonards Rd, BELFAST
☎ 01232 658621 109 ⇆ ⚐

Malone 240 Upper Malone Rd, Dunmurry BT17 9LB
☎ 01232 612758 (Office) & 614917 (Pro)
Two parkland courses, extremely attractive with a large lake, mature trees and flowering shrubs and bordered by the River Lagan. Very well maintained and offering a challenging round.
Main Course: 18 holes, 6654yds, Par 71, SSS 71, Course record 68.
Edenderry: 9 holes, 6402yds, Par 72, SSS 71.
Club membership 1300.
Visitors advisable to contact pro-shop in advance.
Societies apply in writing or fax to club manager. Large group normally Mon & Thu only.
Green Fees £30 (£35 weekends). Ladies £20/£28. 9 hole course: £15 (£20 weekends). Ladies £12/£15.
Facilities ⊗ ⅢⓁ ⓛ ⓦ ⅋ ⚏ ⚒ ⚐ ⚑ Michael McGee.
Leisure squash, trolley for hire, putting green, practice area.
Location 4.5m S
Hotel ★★★★ 63% Stormont Hotel, 587 Upper Newtonards Rd, BELFAST
☎ 01232 658621 109 ⇆ ⚐

Mount Ober Golf, Ski & Leisure 24 Ballymaconaghy Rd
BT8 4QZ ☎ 01232 401811
Inland parkland course which has recently been refurbished.
18 holes, 5391yds, Par 67, SSS 68, Course record 67.
Club membership 400.
Visitors	must contact in advance at weekends & bank holidays.
Societies	must contact in writing.
Green Fees	not confirmed.
Facilities	♀ ⚐ 🏌 ⛳ ⚑ Geoff Loughrey/Chris Spence.
Leisure	driving ranges,putting,buggy etc. hire.
Hotel	★★★★ 63% Stormont Hotel, 587 Upper Newtonards Rd, BELFAST ☎ 01232 658621 109 ⇔ ℝ

Ormeau Ravenshill Rd
☎ 01232 641069 & 640999
Parkland.
9 holes, 2653mtrs, Par 68, SSS 65.
Club membership 520.
Visitors	welcome weekdays except Tue after 2pm. May play Sat after 5.30pm & Sun by arrangement.
Societies	contact in advance.
Green Fees	not confirmed.
Facilities	♀ ⚐ 🏌 ⚑ Bertie Wilson.
Leisure	putting green,trolley hire,practice area.
Location	S of city centre
Hotel	★★★ 62% Dukes Hotel, 65 University St, BELFAST ☎ 01232 236666 21 ⇔ ℝ

Shandon Park 73 Shandon Park BT5 6NY
☎ 01232 401856
Fairly level parkland offering a pleasant challenge.
18 holes, 6261yds, Par 70, SSS 70.
Club membership 1100.
Visitors	may not play on competition days. Must contact in advance and have a handicap certificate.
Societies	may play Mon & Fri only, applications to club.
Green Fees	not confirmed.
Facilities	♀ ⚐ 🏌 ⚑ Barry Wilson.
Leisure	putting green,trolley hire,practice area.
Location	Off Knock road
Hotel	★★★★ 63% Stormont Hotel, 587 Upper Newtonards Rd, BELFAST ☎ 01232 658621 109 ⇔ ℝ

DUNDONALD   Map 01 D5

Knock Summerfield BT16 0QX
☎ 01232 483251 & 482249
Parkland course with huge trees, deep bunkers and a river cutting across several fairways. This is a hard but fair course and will test the best of golfers.
18 holes, 6435yds, Par 70, SSS 71, Course record 66.
Club membership 890.
Visitors	with member only on Sat.
Societies	must contact in advance.
Green Fees	£20 per day (£25 weekends & bank holidays).
Facilities	⊗ 🍴 🛏 ♟ ♀ ⚐ 🏌 ⚑ Gordon Fairweather.
Leisure	buggies for hire, trolley for hire, putting green, practice area.
Hotel	★★★★ 71% Culloden Hotel, Bangor Rd, Holywood, BELFAST ☎ 01232 425223 87 ⇔ ℝ

NEWTOWNBREDA   Map 01 D5

The Belvoir Park 73 Church Rd BT8 4AN
☎ 01232 491693
This undulating parkland course is not strenuous to walk, but is certainly a test of your golf, with tree-lined fairways and a particularly challenging finish at the final four holes.
18 holes, 6516yds, Par 71, SSS 71, Course record 65.
Club membership 1000.
Visitors	must contact in advance, may not play Sat.
Societies	must contact in writing.
Green Fees	£30 per day (£35 Wed, weekends & holidays).
Facilities	⊗ 🍴 🛏 ♟ ♀ ⚐ 🏌 ⚑ Maurice Kelly.
Leisure	motorised carts for hire, buggies for hire, trolley for hire, putting green, practice area.
Location	3m from centre off Saintfield/Newcastle rd
Hotel	★★★★ 63% Stormont Hotel, 587 Upper Newtonards Rd, BELFAST ☎ 01232 658621 109 ⇔ ℝ

CO DOWN

ARDGLASS   Map 01 D5

Ardglass Castle Pl BT30 7TP ☎ 01396 841219
A scenic cliff-top seaside course with spectacular views and some memorable holes.
18 holes, 5498mtrs, Par 70, SSS 69, Course record 65.
Club membership 800.
Visitors	must contact in advance.
Societies	must contact in advance, welcome weekdays & restricted times Sun.
Green Fees	£17 per day (£22 per round weekends & bank holidays).
Facilities	⊗ 🍴 🛏 ♟ ♀ ⚐ 🏌 ⚑ Philip Farrell.
Leisure	trolley for hire, putting green, practice area.
Hotel	★★★ 65% Slieve Donard Hotel, Downs Rd, NEWCASTLE ☎ 013967 23681 118 ⇔ ℝ

ARDMILLAN   Map 01 D5

Mahee Island 14 Mahee Island, Comber BT23 6EP
☎ 01238 541234
An undulating parkland course, almost surrounded by water, with magnificent views of Strangford Lough and its islands, with Scrabo Tower in the background.
9 holes, 5590yds, Par 68, SSS 67, Course record 63.
Club membership 450.
Visitors	may not play on Wed after 5pm or Sat before 5pm.
Societies	apply in writing.
Green Fees	£10 per round (£15 weekends & public holidays).
Facilities	⚐ 🏌
Leisure	trolley for hire, putting green, practice area.
Location	On Comber/Killyleagh road 0.5m from Comber
Hotel	★★★★ 63% Stormont Hotel, 587 Upper Newtonards Rd, BELFAST ☎ 01232 658621 109 ⇔ ℝ

BALLYNAHINCH   Map 01 D5

Spa 20 Grove Rd BT24 8PN
☎ 01238 562365
Parkland course with tree-lined fairways and scenic views of
the Mourne Mountains.
18 holes, 6003mtrs, Par 72, SSS 72, Course record 67.
Club membership 877.
Visitors   must contact in advance.
Societies   must contact in advance.
Green Fees £14 (£18 weekends & bank holidays).
Facilities   ⊗ ⅻ ⅃ ⬛ ⬤ ⬣ ⬕ ⬖ ⬗
Leisure   buggies for hire, trolley for hire, putting green,
                 practice area.
Location   1m S on the Grove Rd
Hotel   ★★★ 65% Slieve Donard Hotel, Downs Rd,
                 NEWCASTLE
                 ☎ 013967 23681 118 ⇥ ⬕

BANBRIDGE   Map 01 D5

Banbridge 116 Huntly Rd BT32 3UR
☎ 01820 662211
A picturesque course with excellent views of the Movene
mountains. The holes are not long, but are tricky, and six new
holes opened in 1992 completed the 18.
18 holes, 5003mtrs, Par 69, SSS 67, Course record 66.
Club membership 700.
Visitors   may not play Tue, Sat or before 11am on Sun.
Societies   must contact in writing.
Green Fees not confirmed.
Facilities   ⬤ ⬕
Leisure   putting green, driving range, trolley hire,
                 practice area.
Location   0.5m along Huntly road
Hotel   ★★★ 65% Slieve Donard Hotel, Downs Rd,
                 NEWCASTLE
                 ☎ 013967 23681 118 ⇥ ⬕

BANGOR   Map 01 D5

Bangor Broadway BT20 4RH
☎ 01247 270922
Undulating parkland course in the town. It is well maintained
and pleasant and offers a challenging round, particularly at
the 5th.
18 holes, 6424yds, Par 71, SSS 71, Course record 62.
Club membership 1147.
Visitors   may not play Sat & weekdays 1-2. Wed
                 unrestricted before 4.45pm.
Societies   Must contact in advance, Mon/Wed by
                 telephone, Fri by letter.
Green Fees £17.50 per round (£25 Sun). Winter: £15 (£20
                 Sun).
Facilities   ⊗ ⅻ ⅃ ⬛ ⬤ ⬣ ⬕ ⬖ ⬗ Norman V Drew.
Leisure   trolley for hire, putting green, practice area.
Location   1m from town on Donaghadee road
Hotel   ★★★ 63% Royal Hotel, Seafront, BANGOR
                 ☎ 01247 271866 34 ⇥ ⬕

---

*Entries with a shaded background identify
courses that are considered to be particularly
interesting*

Blackwood Golf Centre 150 Crawfordsburn Rd, Clandeboye
BT19 1GB ☎ 01247 852706
The golf centre is a pay and play development with a
computerised booking system for the 18-hole championship-
standard Hamilton course. The course is built on mature
woodland with man-made lakes that come into play on 3
holes. The Temple course is an 18-hole Par 3 course with
holes ranging from the 75yd 1st to the 'hit it out of your
boots' 185yd 10th, which has a lake on the right of the green.
Banked by gorse with streams crossing throughout, this Par 3
course is no pushover.
Hamilton Course: 18 holes, 6304yds, Par 71, SSS 70.
Temple Course: 18 holes, 2492yds, Par 54.
Visitors   pay as you play, computerized booking system
                 for the Hamilton Course.
Societies   telephone in advance.
Green Fees Hamilton: £12 per 18 holes (£16 weekends &
                 bank holidays). Temple: £7 per 18 holes (£9
                 weekends).
Facilities   ⊗ ⅻ ⅃ ⬛ ⬤ ⬣ ⬕ ⬖ ⬗ ⬘ ⬙ Tony White.
Leisure   trolley for hire, driving range, putting green,
                 practice area.
Location   2m from Bangor, off A2 to Belfast
Hotel   ★★★ 74% Clandeboye Lodge Hotel, 10 Estate
                 Rd, Clandeboye, BANGOR
                 ☎ 01247 852500 43 ⇥ ⬕

Carnalea Station Rd BT19 1EZ
☎ 01247 270368
A scenic course on the shores of Belfast Lough.
18 holes, 5574yds, Par 68, SSS 67, Course record 63.
Club membership 1200.
Visitors   restricted Sat.
Societies   must contact in advance.
Green Fees £11 (£15 weekends & bank holidays).
Facilities   ⊗ ⅻ ⅃ ⬛ ⬤ ⬣ ⬕ ⬖ ⬗
Leisure   trolley for hire, putting green, practice area.
Location   2m W adjacent to railway station
Hotel   ★★★ 66% Old Inn, 15 Main St,
                 CRAWFORDSBURN
                 ☎ 01247 853255 33 ⇥ ⬕

Clandeboye Tower Rd, Conlig, Newtownards BT23 3PN
☎ 01247 271767
Parkland/heathland courses. The Dufferin is the
championship course and offers a tough challenge.
Nevertheless, the Ava has much to recommend it, with a
notable 2nd hole.
Dufferin Course: 18 holes, 6469yds, Par 71, SSS 71.
Ava Course: 18 holes, 5656yds, Par 70, SSS 68.
Club membership 1200.
Visitors   must play with member at weekends.
Societies   Mon-Wed & Fri, Apr-Sep; Mon & Wed, Oct-
                 Mar. Must contact in advance.
Green Fees not confirmed.
Facilities   ⬤ ⬣ ⬕ ⬖ ⬗ ⬘ Peter Gregory.
Location   2m S on A21
Hotel   ★★★ 63% Royal Hotel, Seafront, BANGOR
                 ☎ 01247 271866 34 ⇥ ⬕

Helen's Bay Golf Rd, Helen's Bay
☎ 01247 852815
A parkland course on the shores of Belfast Lough. The 4th
hole Par 3 is particularly challenging as the green is screened
by high trees.
9 holes, 5168mtrs, Par 68, SSS 67.

Visitors welcome Sun, Mon, Wed, Thu (before 1.30pm), Fri (after 11.30am during Jul & Aug) & Sat after 6pm. Book in advance with secretary.
Societies welcome Mon, Wed, Thu (before 1.30pm) & Fri. Telephone secretary in advance.
Green Fees £13 per day (£15 Sun & bank holidays). Sat after 6pm £6.50.
Facilities ⊗ ⅢⓁ ➍ ♀ ⚘ ⚐
Leisure trolley for hire.
Location A2 from Belfast
Hotel ★★★ 66% Old Inn, 15 Main St, CRAWFORDSBURN
☎ 01247 853255 33 ⇄ ⌁

CLOUGHEY
Map 01 D5

Kirkistown Castle 142 Main Rd, Cloughey BT22 1JA
☎ 012477 71233
A seaside semi-links popular with visiting golfers because of its quiet location. The course is exceptionally dry and remains open when others in the area have to close. The Par 4 10th is particularly distinctive with a long drive and a slight dogleg to a raised green with a gorse covered motte waiting for the wayward approach shot.
18 holes, 6167yds, Par 69, SSS 70, Course record 65.
Club membership 920.
Visitors must contact in advance, restricted weekends.
Societies apply in writing.
Green Fees £13 (£25 weekends & bank holidays).
Facilities ⊗ Ⅲ Ⓛ ➍ ♀ ⚘ ➌ ⚐ ⚑ Jonathan Peden.
Leisure trolley for hire, driving range, putting green, practice area.
Hotel ★★★ 66% Old Inn, 15 Main St, CRAWFORDSBURN
☎ 01247 853255 33 ⇄ ⌁

DONAGHADEE
Map 01 D5

Donaghadee Warren Rd BT21 0PQ
☎ 01247 883624
Undulating seaside course requiring a certain amount of concentration. Splendid views.
18 holes, 5570mtrs, Par 71, SSS 69, Course record 65.
Club membership 1190.
Visitors contact in advance.
Societies telephone in advance.
Green Fees £14 per round (£18 Sat after 4pm, Sun & bank holidays).
Facilities ⊗ Ⅲ Ⓛ ➍ ♀ ⚘ ➌ ⚐ ⚑ Gordon Drew.
Leisure trolley for hire, putting green, practice area.
Hotel ★★★ 66% Old Inn, 15 Main St, CRAWFORDSBURN
☎ 01247 853255 33 ⇄ ⌁

DOWNPATRICK
Map 01 D5

Bright Castle 14 Coniamstown Rd, Bright BT30 8LU
☎ 01396 841319
Parkland course in elevated position with views of the Mountains of Mourne. A good challenge for the energetic golfer.
18 holes, 7300yds, Par 74, SSS 74.
Visitors no restrictions.
Societies must contact in advance.
Green Fees not confirmed.

Facilities
Location 5m S
Hotel ★★★ 65% Slieve Donard Hotel, Downs Rd, NEWCASTLE
☎ 013967 23681 118 ⇄ ⌁

Downpatrick 43 Saul Rd BT30 6PA
☎ 01396 615947 & 615167
This undulating parkland course has recently been extended, with Hawtree & Son as architects. It provides a good challenge.
18 holes, 6100yds, Par 70, SSS 69, Course record 66.
Club membership 800.
Visitors must contact in advance.
Societies must telephone in advance.
Green Fees £15 per day (£20 weekends & bank holidays).
Facilities ⊗ Ⅲ Ⓛ ➍ ♀ ⚘ ➌ ⚐
Leisure motorised carts for hire, buggies for hire, trolley for hire, putting green, practice area.
Location 1.5m from town centre
Hotel ★★ 64% Enniskeen House Hotel, 98 Bryansford Rd, NEWCASTLE
☎ 013967 22392 12 ⇄ ⌁

HOLYWOOD
Map 01 D5

Holywood Nuns Wall, Demesne Rd
☎ 01232 423135
Hilly parkland course with some fine views and providing an interesting game.
18 holes, 5480mtrs, Par 69, SSS 68, Course record 64.
Club membership 1100.
Visitors must contact in advance.
Societies must contact in writing.
Green Fees £15 per round (£21 weekends).
Facilities ⊗ Ⅲ Ⓛ ➍ ♀ ⚘ ➌ ⚐ ⚑ Michael Bannon.
Leisure trolley for hire, driving range, putting green, practice area.
Hotel ★★ 74% Rayanne Country House & Restaurant, 60 Desmesne Rd, HOLYWOOD
☎ 01232 425859 6 ⇄ ⌁

The Royal Belfast Station Rd, Craigavad BT18 0BP
☎ 01232 428165
On the shores of Belfast Lough, this attractive course consists of wooded parkland on undulating terrain which provides a pleasant, challenging game.
18 holes, 5963yds, Par 70, SSS 69.
Club membership 1200.
Visitors may not play on Wed or Sat before 4.30pm; must be accompanied by a member or present a letter of introduction from their own golf club.
Societies must contact in writing.
Green Fees not confirmed.
Facilities ♀ ⚘ ➌ ⚐ ⚑
Leisure hard tennis courts, squash, caddy cars.
Location 2m E on A2
Hotel ★★★★ 71% Culloden Hotel, Bangor Rd, Holywood, BELFAST
☎ 01232 425223 87 ⇄ ⌁

KILKEEL   Map 01 D5

Kilkeel Mourne Park BT34 4LB ☎ 016937 65095
Picturesquely situated at the foot of the Mourne Mountains,
Kilkeel was recently upgraded to an 18-hole course. Eleven
holes now have tree-lined fairways with the remainder in
open parkland. The 13th hole is testing and a well positioned
tee shot is essential.
18 holes, 6615yds, Par 72, SSS 72.
Club membership 650.
Visitors   May not play Sat. Must contact in advance.
Societies   must contact in writing.
Green Fees £16 (£18 weekends & bank holidays).
Facilities ⊗ ⍟ ⓛ ♥ ⅍ ⚲
Leisure   fishing, trolley for hire, driving range, putting
                green, practice area.
Location   On Newry road
Hotel   ★★(red) Glassdrumman Lodge, 85 Mill Rd,
                ANNALONG
                ☎ 013967 68451 8 ⇋ ⋔Annexe2 ⇋ ⋔

MAGHERALIN   Map 01 D5

Edenmore Edenmore House, 70 Drumnabreeze Rd BT67
0RH ☎ 01846 611310 & 619199
Set in mature parkland with gently rolling slopes. There are 9
well-established holes and an additional 9 holes opened in the
summer of 1994. The original Par 5 4th is played across a
lake and between two large oak trees. The Par 3 8th has an
elevated tee and a green nestled among lime trees.
18 holes, 6244yds, Par 71, SSS 70.
Club membership 300.
Visitors   telephone in advance, may not play until after
                2pm Sat or Sun.
Societies   telephone in advance.
Green Fees £8 per 18 holes; £5 per 9 holes (£10/£7
                weekends & bank holidays).
Facilities ⊗ ⍟ ♥ ⚲ ⓐ ⋔
Leisure   trolley for hire, putting green, practice area.
Hotel   B Forte Posthouse Belfast, Kingsway, Dunmurry,
                BELFAST ☎ 01232 612101 82 ⇋ ⋔

NEWCASTLE   Map 01 D5

ROYAL COUNTY DOWN   See page 367

NEWRY   Map 01 D5

Newry 11 Forkhill Rd BT35 8LZ ☎ 01693 63871
Short 18-hole course enjoying panoramic views of the
Mourne Mountains and across Newry.
18 holes, 3000mtrs, Par 53, SSS 52, Course record 51.
Club membership 150.
Visitors   welcome anytime.
Societies   apply in writing or telephone.
Green Fees £3.50 (£4.50 weekends & bank holidays).
Facilities ⊗ ⍟ ⓛ ♥ ⅍ ⚲ ⓐ
Leisure   motorised carts for hire, buggies for hire,
                practice area.
Hotel   ★★ 64% Enniskeen House Hotel, 98
                Bryansford Rd, NEWCASTLE
                ☎ 013967 22392 12 ⇋ ⋔

NEWTOWNARDS   Map 01 D5

Scrabo 233 Scrabo Rd BT23 4SL ☎ 01247 812355
Hilly and picturesque, this course offers a good test of golf.
18 holes, 5722mtrs, Par 71, SSS 71, Course record 65.
Club membership 956.
Visitors   may not play on Sat or Sun before 11.30am.
                Contact in advance.
Societies   must contact in advance.
Green Fees £15 per round (£20 Sun).
Facilities ⊗ ⍟ ⓛ ♥ ⅍ ⚲ ⓐ ⋔ Alistair Cardwell.
Leisure   trolley for hire, putting green, practice area.
Hotel   ★★★★ 63% Stormont Hotel, 587 Upper
                Newtonards Rd, BELFAST
                ☎ 01232 658621 109 ⇋ ⋔

WARRENPOINT   Map 01 D5

Warrenpoint Lower Dromore Rd BT34 3LN
☎ 016937 53695
Parkland course with marvellous views and a need for
accurate shots.
18 holes, 6108yds, Par 71, SSS 70.
Club membership 1100.
Visitors   must contact in advance.
Societies   must contact in advance.
Green Fees £17 (£23 weekends & bank holidays).
Facilities ⊗ ⍟ ⓛ ♥ ⅍ ⚲ ⓐ ⋔ ⋔ Nigel Shaw.
Leisure   squash, trolley for hire, putting green, practice
                area.
Location   1m W
Hotel   ★★★ 65% Slieve Donard Hotel, Downs Rd,
                NEWCASTLE ☎ 013967 23681 118 ⇋ ⋔

CO FERMANAGH

ENNISKILLEN   Map 01 C5

Ashwoods Golf Centre Sligo Rd BT74 7JY
☎ 01365 325321 & 322908
Only 1 mile from Lough Erne, this course is open
meadowland. It has been well planted with many young trees.
9 holes, 1290yds, Par 27.
Visitors   no restrictions.
Societies   must book in advance.
Green Fees not confirmed.
Facilities ⚲ ⓐ ⋔ ⋔ Pat Trainor.
Leisure   putting,trolley hire,practice area.
Hotel   ★★★ 54% Killyhevlin Hotel, ENNISKILLEN
                ☎ 01365 323481 44 ⇋ ⋔Annexe26rm

Castle Hume Castle Hume BT93 7ED ☎ 01365 327077
Castle Hulme is a particularly scenic and challenging course.
Set in undulating parkland with large rolling greens, rivers,
lakes and water hazards all in play on a championship
standard course.
18 holes, 6400yds, Par 72, SSS 70, Course record 69.
Club membership 150.
Visitors   advisable to telephone in advance.
Societies   telephone in advance.   ▶

ROYAL COUNTY DOWN

NEWCASTLE ***Co Down*** **☏ 013967 23314 Map 01 D5**

Charlie Mulqueen writes: Where the mountains of Mourne sweep down to the sea – that's the location for one of the game's most beautiful and challenging golf courses, Royal Co Down alongside the lovely seaside town of Newcastle. There can be few grander places when the sun shines on the Mournes and on the Irish Sea and on the furze bushes that dot the sides of almost every fairway, turning the whole scene into one of riotous colour in early summer.

The most prestigious Championships, including the British Amateur, men's and ladies', and the Curtis Cup have come to Newcastle where the game began in 1889. Legend has it that Old Tom Morris was commissioned to lay out a course at a cost not exceeding £4. Another of golf's early greats, Harry Vardon, reconstructed the links in 1908, the same year it was made 'Royal' by Edward VII. Slight changes here and there over the decades have served only to make Newcastle a finer and fairer challenge.

Most people's favourite hole at Newcastle is the 9th, a none too difficult par five of less than 500 yards, but it has been suggested that the chief hazards of the hole are the distracting views of the sea and Slieve Donard, the highest of the Mourne Mountains – a breathtaking sight perhaps unrivalled in all of golf. .

However, nobody should run away with the idea that this is anything other than an outstanding test of golf where length, accuracy and a sure touch on the many fiercely undulating greens are all essential attributes. The 13th is such a beautiful hole that it was copied at a course in Cincinatti, Ohio...Newcastle is that kind of place, a jewel among golf courses.

Visitors	may not play No 2 course on Saturdays. May not play on Championship Course on Sun am or Wed pm
Societies	must contact in advance
Green fees	Championship: wkdays Winter £35, Summer £50. W/e Winter £45, Summer £60. Add £12 for full day. No 2: summer£15 w/e £25. winter £10 w/e £18
Facilities	⊗ ♨ ☕ ♀ ⛺ 🏠 ✈ (Kevan Whitson) practice area, putting green, driving range trollies
Location	Newcastle BT33 0AN

36 holes.
Championship Course 18 holes, 6692yds, Par71 SSS 72
No 2 Course 18 holes, 4681yds, Par 66 SSS 65

WHERE TO STAY AND EAT NEARBY

HOTELS:

NEWCASTLE

★★★ 65% Slieve Donard Hotel ☏ 013967 23681. 118 ⇌ ↱

★★ 64% Enniskeen Hotel, 98 Bryansford Rd ☏ 013967 22392 12 (3 ↱ 8 ⇌ 1 ⇌ ↱)

Green Fees £12 per round (£18 weekends & bank holidays).
Facilities ⊗ ⫽ ┗ 💺 ♀ ☂ ➅ ⚐
Leisure fishing, motorised carts for hire, buggies for hire, trolley for hire, putting green, practice area.
Location 4m from Enniskillen on the Belleek Rd
Hotel ★★★ 54% Killyhevlin Hotel, ENNISKILLEN
☎ 01365 323481 44 ⇌ ☜Annexe26rm

Enniskillen Castlecoole BT74 6HZ
☎ 01365 325250
Meadowland course in Castle Coole estate.
18 holes, 5588mtrs, Par 71, SSS 69, Course record 67.
Club membership 500.
Visitors restricted Tue and weekends.
Societies must contact club steward in advance.
Green Fees not confirmed.
Facilities ♀ ☂ ⚐
Location 1m E
Hotel ★★★ 54% Killyhevlin Hotel, ENNISKILLEN
☎ 01365 323481 44 ⇌ ☜Annexe26rm

CO LONDONDERRY

AGHADOWEY   Map 01 C6

Brown Trout Golf & Country Inn 209 Agivey Rd
BT51 4AD ☎ 01265 868209
A challenging course with two par 5s. During the course of the 9 holes, players have to negotiate water 7 times and all the fairways are lined with densely packed fir trees.
9 holes, 5510yds, Par 70, SSS 68, Course record 70.
Club membership 150.
Visitors no restrictions.
Societies must contact by telephone, restricted tee-off times Sun.
Green Fees £8 per day (£12 weekends & bank holidays).
Facilities ⊗ ⫽ ┗ 💺 ♀ ☂ ⚐ ⊨ ⚐ Ken Revie.
Leisure fishing, gymnasium, practice area.
Location Junc of A54 & B66
Hotel ★★ 67% Brown Trout Golf & Country Inn, 209
Agivey Rd, AGHADOWEY
☎ 01265 868209 17 ⇌ ☜

CASTLEDAWSON   Map 01 C5

Moyola Park 15 Curran Rd BT45 8DG
☎ 01648 468468
Parkland course with some difficult shots, calling for length and accuracy. The Moyola River provides a water hazard at the 8th.
18 holes, 6522yds, Par 71, SSS 70, Course record 67.
Club membership 1000.
Visitors contact professional in advance. May not play weekends until late afternoon.
Societies must contact in advance, preferably in writing
Green Fees £12 per day (£17 weekends & bank holidays).
Facilities ⊗ ⫽ ┗ 💺 ♀ ☂ ➅ ⚐ Vivian Teague.
Leisure trolley for hire, putting green, practice area.
Location 3m NE of Magherafelt
Hotel ★★★★ 71% Galgorm Manor, BALLYMENA
☎ 01266 881001 23 ⇌ ☜

CASTLEROCK   Map 01 C6

Castlerock 65 Circular Rd BT51 4TJ ☎ 01265 848314
A most exhilarating course with three superb par 4s, four testing short holes and two par 5s. After an uphill start, the hazards are many, including the river and a railway, and both judgement and accuracy are called for. A challenge in calm weather, any trouble from the elements will test your golf to the limits.
Mussenden Course: 18 holes, 6499yds, Par 73, SSS 72, Course record 67.
Bann Course: 9 holes, 2457mtrs, Par 35, SSS 33.
Club membership 960.
Visitors contact in advance.
Societies Mon-Thu only, must contact in advance.
Green Fees Mussenden: £17 per round (£25 weekends & bank holidays). Bann: £7 per 18 holes (£10 weekends & bank holidays).
Facilities ⊗ ⫽ ┗ 💺 ♀ ☂ ➅ ⚐ ⚐ Robert Kelly.
Leisure trolley for hire, putting green, practice area.
Location 6m from Coleraine on A2
Hotel ★★★ 61% Causeway Coast Hotel, 36
Ballyreagh Rd, PORTRUSH
☎ 01265 822435 21 ⇌ ☜

KILREA   Map 01 C5

Kilrea Drumagarner Rd
A relatively short undulating inland course with tight fairways and small greens. The opening hole is a long par 3, particularly into the wind.
9 holes, 3956mtrs, Par 62, SSS 62, Course record 61.
Club membership 300.
Visitors welcome but restricted Tue am, Wed pm during summer and Sat all year.
Societies contact D P Clark (Sec), 37 Townhill Rd, Portglenope, Co Antrim BT44 8AD.
Green Fees £10 per round (£12.50 weekends & bank holidays).
Facilities ☂
Hotel ★★ 67% Brown Trout Golf & Country Inn, 209
Agivey Rd, AGHADOWEY
☎ 01265 868209 17 ⇌ ☜

LIMAVADY   Map 01 C6

Benone 53 Benone Ave BT49 0LQ ☎ 015047 50555
9 holes, 1458yds, Par 27.
Visitors no reservations.
Societies telephone in advance.
Green Fees £3.75 per day (£4.50 weekends & public holidays). Prices under review.
Facilities 💺 ☂ ⚐
Leisure hard tennis courts, heated outdoor swimming pool, driving range, putting green, bowling green.
Location Between Coleraine/Limavady on A2

Radisson Roe Park Hotel & Golf Resort Roe Park
BT49 9LB ☎ 015047 22222
A parkland course opened in 1992 on an historic Georgian estate. The course surrounds the original buildings and a driving range has been created in the old walled garden. Final holes 15-18 are particularly memorable with water, trees, out-of-bounds, etc to provide a testing finish.

18 holes, 6318yds, Par 70, SSS 71.
Club membership 300.
Visitors advance booking recommended.
Societies contact in advance.
Green Fees £16 per round (£20 weekends & bank holidays) reduced fees for hotel guests.
Facilities ⊗ ⅏ ⅃ ☞ ♀ ⅄ 🏠 ☞ ♘ ⅂ Seamus Duffy.
Leisure heated indoor swimming pool, fishing, sauna, solarium, gymnasium, motorised carts for hire, buggies for hire, trolley for hire, driving range, putting green, practice area.
Location On Ballykelly rd A2

LONDONDERRY   Map 01 C5

City of Derry 49 Victoria Rd BT47 2PU ☎ 01504 46369
Two parkland courses on undulating parkland with good views and lots of trees. The 9-hole course will particularly suit novices.
Prehen Course: 18 holes, 6406yds, Par 71, SSS 71, Course record 68.
Dunhugh Course: 9 holes, 4708yds, Par 63.
Club membership 732.
Visitors must make a booking to play on Prehen Course at weekends or before 4.30pm on weekdays.
Societies must contact in advance.
Green Fees not confirmed.
Facilities ♀ ⅄ 🏠 ⅂ Michael Doherty.
Location 2m S
Hotel ★★★ 65% Everglades Hotel, Prehen Rd, LONDONDERRY ☎ 01504 46722 52 ⇥ ⏚

PORTSTEWART   Map 01 C6

Portstewart 117 Strand Rd BT55 7PG ☎ 01265 832015
Three links courses with spectacular views, offering a testing round on the Strand course in particular.
Strand Course: 18 holes, 6784yds, Par 72, SSS 72.
Town Course: 18 holes, 4733yds, Par 64, SSS 62.
3: 9 holes, 2622yds, Par 32.
Visitors preferred on weekdays.
Societies must contact in advance.
Green Fees not confirmed.
Facilities ♀ ☞ ⅂ Alan Hunter.
Leisure indoor bowling.
Hotel ★★★ 61% Causeway Coast Hotel, 36 Ballyreagh Rd, PORTRUSH ☎ 01265 822435 21 ⇥ ⏚

CO TYRONE

COOKSTOWN   Map 01 C5

Killymoon 200 Killymoon Rd BT80 8TW
☎ 016487 63762 & 62254
Parkland course on elevated, well drained land.
18 holes, 5481mtrs, Par 70, SSS 69, Course record 64.
Club membership 950.
Visitors booking essential through proshop on 016487 63460.
Societies must contact in advance.

Green Fees £15 per round (£18 Sun & bank holidays).
Facilities ⊗ ⅏ ⅃ ☞ ♀ ⅄ 🏠 ⅂ Gary Chambers.
Leisure trolley for hire, putting green, practice area.
Hotel ★★ 63% Royal Arms Hotel, 51 High St, OMAGH ☎ 01662 243262 19 ⇥ ⏚

DUNGANNON   Map 01 C5

Dungannon 34 Springfield Ln BT70 1QX
☎ 01868 722098 or 727338
Parkland course with five par 3s and tree-lined fairways.
18 holes, 5950yds, Par 71, SSS 68, Course record 62.
Club membership 600.
Visitors contact in advance, may not play before 4pm Sat.
Societies apply in writing to secretary.
Green Fees £15 per day (£18 weekends & bank holidays).
Facilities ⊗ ⅃ ☞ ♀ ⅄ 🏠
Leisure trolley for hire, putting green.
Location 0.5m outside town on Donaghmore road
Hotel L The Cohannon Inn, 212 Ballynakilly Rd, DUNGANNON ☎ 01868 724488 Annexe22 ⇥ ⏚

FINTONA   Map 01 C5

Fintona Ecclesville Demesne BT78 2AF ☎ 01662 841480
Attractive 9-hole parkland course with a notable water hazard - a trout stream that meanders through the course causing many problems for badly executed shots.
9 holes, 5765mtrs, Par 72, SSS 70.
Club membership 365.
Societies apply in writing well in advance, weekends not advisable as competitions played.
Green Fees £10 per 18 holes.
Facilities ⅃ ☞ ♀ ⅄
Hotel ★★ 66% Mahons Hotel, IRVINESTOWN ☎ 013656 21656 18 ⇥ ⏚

NEWTOWNSTEWART   Map 01 C5

Newtownstewart 38 Golf Course Rd BT78 4HU
☎ 016626 61466
Parkland course bisected by a stream.
18 holes, 5468mtrs, Par 70, SSS 69, Course record 66.
Club membership 700.
Visitors contact in advance.
Societies must contact secretary in advance.
Green Fees £10 per round (£15 weekends & bank holidays).
Facilities ⊗ ⅏ by prior arrangement ⅃ ☞ ♀ ⅄ 🏠 ☞
Leisure hard tennis courts, motorised carts for hire, buggies for hire, trolley for hire, putting green, practice area.
Location 2m SW on B84
Hotel ★★ 63% Royal Arms Hotel, 51 High St, OMAGH ☎ 01662 243262 19 ⇥ ⏚

OMAGH   Map 01 C5

Omagh 83a Dublin Rd BT78 1HQ ☎ 01662 243160
Undulating parkland course beside the River Drummagh.
18 holes, 5636mtrs, Par 71, SSS 70.
Visitors play restricted Sat.
Societies must contact in advance.   ▶

· ·

Green Fees £10 (£15 weekends & bank holidays).
Facilities ⚠
Leisure putting green.
Location On S outskirts of town
Hotel ★★ 63% Royal Arms Hotel, 51 High St,
OMAGH ☎ 01662 243262 19 ⇌ ⬧

STRABANE
Map 01 C5

Strabane Ballycolman Rd ☎ 01504 382271 & 382007
Testing parkland course with the River Mourne running
alongside and creating a water hazard.
18 holes, 5552mtrs, Par 69, SSS 69.
Club membership 550.
Visitors may not play on Sat.
Societies must contact in writing.
Green Fees not confirmed.
Facilities ⚑⚠
Hotel ★★ 63% Royal Arms Hotel, 51 High St,
OMAGH ☎ 01662 243262 19 ⇌ ⬧

REPUBLIC OF IRELAND

CO CARLOW

BORRIS
Map 01 C3

Borris Deerpark ☎ 0503 73143 & 73310
Testing parkland course with tree-lined fairways situated within the McMorrough Kavanagh Estate at the foot of Mount Leinster.
9 holes, 6096yds, Par 70, SSS 69, Course record 66.
Club membership 350.
Visitors	advisable to contact in advance, weekends very restricted.
Societies	applications in writing.
Green Fees	IR£12 per 18 holes.
Facilities	🏌 💷 ♀ 🏌
Leisure	trolley for hire, putting green, practice area.
Hotel	★★★★(red)🏖 Mount Juliet Hotel, THOMASTOWN ☎ 056 24455 32 🏳 🏴Annexe21 🏳 🏴

CARLOW
Map 01 C3

Carlow Deerpark ☎ 0503 31695
Created in 1922 to a design by Tom Simpson, this testing and enjoyable course is set in a wild deer park, with beautiful dry terrain and a varied character. With sandy sub-soil, the course is playable all year round. There are water hazards at the 2nd, 10th and 11th and only two par 5s, both offering genuine birdie opportunities.
18 holes, 5599mtrs, Par 70, SSS 69, Course record 62.
Club membership 1100.
Visitors	are welcome, although play is limited on Tue and difficult on Sat & Sun. Must contact in advance.
Societies	must book in advance.
Green Fees	IR£20 per day (IR£25 per round weekends & bank holidays).
Facilities	⊗ 🏌 💷 ♀ 🏌 Andrew Gilbert.
Leisure	trolley for hire, putting green, practice area.
Location	2m N of Carlow
Guesthouse	QQQQ Barrowville Town House, Kilkenny Rd, CARLOW ☎ 0503 43324 7 🏳 🏴

CO CAVAN

BALLYCONNELL
Map 01 C4

Slieve Russell Hotel Golf & Country Club
☎ 049 26444 & 26474
An 18-hole course with a new 9-hole Par 3 to complement it. On the main course, the 2nd plays across water while the 16th has water surrounding the green. The course finishes with a 519 yard, Par 5 18th.

18 holes, 6650yds, Par 72, SSS 72, Course record 68.
Club membership 770.
Visitors	must book in advance.
Societies	write or telephone in advance, not allowed Sat.
Green Fees	IR£25 per day (IR£30 Sat). Reduced rate for hotel residents.
Facilities	⊗ 🏌 💷 ♀ 🏌 Liam McCool.
Leisure	hard tennis courts, heated indoor swimming pool, squash, sauna, solarium, gymnasium, buggies for hire, trolley for hire, practice area.
Location	1.5m E of Ballyconnell
Hotel	★★★★ 66% Slieve Russell Hotel & Country Club, BALLYCONNELL ☎ 049 26444 151 🏳 🏴

BELTURBET
Map 01 C4

Belturbet Erne Hill ☎ 049 22287
Beautifully maintained parkland course with predominantly family membership and popular with summer visitors.
9 holes, 5480yds, Par 68, SSS 65, Course record 64.
Club membership 150.
Visitors	restrictions the same as for members.
Societies	must contact secretary or captain in advance.
Green Fees	not confirmed.
Facilities	♀ 🏌
Hotel	★★★★ 66% Slieve Russell Hotel & Country Club, BALLYCONNELL ☎ 049 26444 151 🏳 🏴

BLACKLION
Map 01 C5

Blacklion Toam ☎ 072 53024
Parkland course established in 1962, with coppices of woodland and mature trees. The lake comes into play on two holes and there are some magnificent views of the lake, islands and surrounding hills. It has been described as one of the best maintained nine-hole courses in Ireland.
9 holes, 5614mtrs, Par 72, SSS 69.
Club membership 250.
Visitors	no restrictions.
Societies	must contact in advance.
Green Fees	IR£8 per day (IR£10 weekends & bank holidays).
Facilities	🏌 💷 ♀ 🏌
Leisure	fishing, trolley for hire, putting green, small practice area.
Hotel	★★★ 70% Sligo Park Hotel, Pearse Rd, SLIGO ☎ 071 60291 89 🏳 🏴

CAVAN
Map 01 C4

County Cavan Drumelis ☎ 049 31541 & 31283
Parkland course.
18 holes, 5519mtrs, Par 70, SSS 69, Course record 66.
Club membership 830.
Visitors	welcome but restricted at weekends.
Societies	contact for details.
Green Fees	not confirmed.
Facilities	♀ 🏌
Leisure	putting green, practice area.
Location	On Killeshandra rd

▶

Hotel ★★★ 64% Kilmore Hotel, Dublin Rd,
CAVAN
☎ 049 32288 39 ⇄ ⬥

VIRGINIA   Map 01 C4

Virginia ☎ 049 47235 & 40223
9 holes, 4139mtrs, Par 64, SSS 62.
Club membership 400.
Visitors may not play Thu & Sun.
Societies must apply in writing to secretary.
Green Fees IR£10.
Facilities ⬥ ⬥
Location By Lough Ramor
Hotel ★★ 60% Conyngham Arms Hotel, SLANE
☎ 041 24155 16rm(15 ⇄ ⬥)

CO CLARE

CLONLARA   Map 01 B3

Clonlara Golf & Leisure
☎ 061 354141
A 9-hole parkland course, Par 35, on the banks of the River
Shannon with views of Clare Hills. Set in grounds of 63 acres
surrounding the 17th century Landscape House, there is also
a leisure complex for self-catering holidays.
9 holes, 5328mtrs, Par 70, SSS 68.
Club membership 70.
Visitors players only no accompanying persons.
Societies welcome subject to availability prior notice
required.
Green Fees not confirmed.
Facilities ♀⬥⬥⬥
Leisure hard tennis courts, sauna, games room.
Location 7m NE of Limerick
Hotel ★★★★ 68% Castletroy Park Hotel, Dublin Rd,
LIMERICK
☎ 061 335566 107 ⇄ ⬥

ENNIS   Map 01 B3

Ennis Drumbiggle ☎ 065 24074
On rolling hills, this immaculately manicured course presents
an excellent challenge to both casual visitors and aspiring
scratch golfers, with tree-lined fairways and well protected
greens.
18 holes, 5275mtrs, Par 69, SSS 68, Course record 65.
Club membership 1000.
Visitors advisable to contact in advance, course available
Mon-Sat at most times.
Societies apply in writing.
Green Fees IR£16 per day.
Facilities ⊗ ⽒ ⬥ ⬥ ♀⬥ ⬥ ⬥ ⬥ Martin Ward.
Leisure trolley for hire, putting green, practice area.
Hotel ★★★ 68% Auburn Lodge Hotel, Galway Rd,
ENNIS
☎ 065 21247 100 ⇄ ⬥

KILKEE   Map 01 B3

Kilkee East End ☎ 065 56048
Well established course on the cliffs of Kilkee Bay, with
beautiful views.
18 holes, 6500yds, Par 72, SSS 71, Course record 68.
Club membership 390.
Visitors must book in advance.
Societies apply in writing.
Green Fees IR£15 per round.
Facilities ⊗ ⽒ ⬥ ⬥ ♀⬥ ⬥ ⬥
Leisure squash, sauna, buggies for hire, trolley for hire,
putting green, practice area.
Hotel ★★ 60% Halpin's Hotel, Erin St, KILKEE
☎ 065 56032 12 ⇄ ⬥

KILRUSH   Map 01 B3

Kilrush Parknamoney ☎ 065 51138
Parkland course that was extended to 18 holes in the summer
of 1994.
18 holes, 5986yds, Par 70, SSS 70, Course record 68.
Club membership 375.
Visitors welcome, contact for details.
Societies by prior arrangement.
Green Fees IR£15 per day.
Facilities ⊗ ⽒ ⬥ ⬥ ♀⬥ ⬥ ⬥
Leisure trolley for hire, putting green, small practice
area.
Hotel ★★ 60% Halpin's Hotel, Erin St, KILKEE
☎ 065 56032 12 ⇄ ⬥

LAHINCH   Map 01 B3

Lahinch ☎ 065 81003
Originally designed by Tom Morris and later modified by
Dr Alister MacKenzie, Lahinch has hosted every
important Irish amateur fixture and the Home
Internationals. The par five 5th - The Klondike - is
played along a deep valley and over a huge dune; the par
three 6th may be short, but calls for a blind shot over the
ridge of a hill to a green hemmed in by hills on three
sides.
Old Course: 18 holes, 6696yds, Par 72, SSS 73.
Castle Course: 18 holes, 5619yds, Par 70, SSS 70.
Club membership 1840.
Visitors must contact in advance.
Societies apply in writing
Green Fees Old Course IR£40; Castle Course IR£25.
Facilities ⊗ ⽒ ⬥ ⬥ ♀⬥ ⬥ ⬥ ⬥ R McCavery.
Location 2m W of Ennisstymon on N67
Hotel ★★ 70% Sheedy's Spa View Hotel &
Orchid Restaurant, LISDOONVARNA
☎ 065 74026 11 ⇄ ⬥

MILLTOWN MALBAY   Map 01 B3

Spanish Point ☎ 065 84198
A 9-hole links course with 3 elevated greens and 4 elevated
tees. The 8th hole is a 75-metre par 3, locally known as 'the
Terror'.
9 holes, 4600mtrs, Par 64, SSS 62, Course record 63.
Club membership 250.
Visitors contact in advance.

Societies apply in writing to the secretary 065 84219
Green Fees IR£10 per day.
Facilities ㅑ ☴ ♀ ᗱ ⚑
Hotel ★★★ 65% West County Inn Hotel, Clare Rd,
ENNIS ☎ 065 28421 110 ⇆ ⭑

NEWMARKET-ON-FERGUS   Map 01 B3

Dromoland Castle ☎ 061 368444 & 368144
Set in 200 acres of parkland, the course is enhanced by
numerous trees and a lake. Three holes are played around the
lake which is in front of the castle.
18 holes, 6098yds, Par 71, SSS 72, Course record 67.
Club membership 500.
Visitors must contact in advance.
Societies contact in writing.
Green Fees IR£22 per day (IR£27 weekends & bank
holidays).
Facilities ⊗ ⵏ ㅑ ☴ ♀ ᗱ 亩 ⚑ ⋈ ⚑ Philip Murphy.
Leisure hard tennis courts, fishing, motorised carts for
hire, buggies for hire, trolley for hire, driving
range, putting green, practice area.
Location 2m N, on main Limerick/Galway rd
Hotel ★★★ 64% Clare Inn Hotel, NEWMARKET-
ON-FERGUS
☎ 061 368161 121 ⇆ ⭑

SCARRIFF   Map 01 B3

East Clare Bodyke ☎ 061 921322
Beside Lough Derg, East Clare was opened in June 1992 as a
9-hole course in 148 acre site with natural trees and water on
well-drained land. An 18-hole championship course deigned
by Arthur Spring is in preparation.
9 holes, 52yds, Par 70, SSS 70 or 32 holes.
Club membership 130.
Visitors no restrictions unless there is a club competition
or a society playing.
Societies apply in writing, deposit required.
Green Fees not confirmed.
Facilities ᗱ ⚑
Hotel ★★★ 65% West County Inn Hotel, Clare Rd,
ENNIS
☎ 065 28421 110 ⇆ ⭑

SHANNON AIRPORT   Map 01 B3

Shannon ☎ 061 471849
Superb parkland course with tree-lined fairways, strategically
placed bunkers, water hazards and excellent greens, offering
a challenge to all levels of players - including the many
famous golfers who have played here.
18 holes, 6874yds, Par 72, SSS 74.
Club membership 800.
Visitors must contact in advance & have handicap
certificate. Restricted play at certain times.
Societies must contact in writing.
Green Fees not confirmed.
Facilities ♀ ᗱ 亩 ⚑ ⚑ Artie Pyke.
Leisure putting green, practice area, motorised carts,
buggy & trolley hire.
Location 2m from Shannon Airport
Hotel ★★★ 63% Fitzpatrick Bunratty Shamrock
Hotel, BUNRATTY
☎ 061 361177 115 ⇆ ⭑

CO CORK

BANDON   Map 01 B2

Bandon Castlebernard ☎ 023 41111
Lovely parkland course in pleasant rural surroundings.
18 holes, 5663mtrs, Par 70, SSS 69, Course record 66.
Club membership 800.
Visitors welcome but may not play during club
competitions. Must contact in advance.
Societies must apply in writing.
Green Fees not confirmed.
Facilities ♀ ᗱ 亩 ⚑ ⚑ Paddy O'Boyle.
Leisure hard tennis courts, caddy cars.
Hotel ★★ 70% Inishannon House Hotel,
INISHANNON
☎ 021 775121 13 ⇆ ⭑Annexe1 ⇆ ⭑

BANTRY   Map 01 B2

Bantry Park Donemark ☎ 027 50579
An undulating 9-hole course with some magnificent sea views.
9 holes, 5946mtrs, Par 72, SSS 72.
Club membership 300.
Visitors contact in advance.
Societies must apply in writing.
Green Fees IR£13 per day.
Facilities ⊗ ⵏ ㅑ ☴ ♀ ᗱ ⚑
Leisure trolley for hire, putting green.
Hotel ★★★⚑⚑ 70% Sea View Hotel,
BALLYLICKEY
☎ 027 50073 & 50462 17 ⇆ ⭑

BLARNEY   Map 01 B2

Muskerry Carrigrohane ☎ 021 385297
An adventurous game is guaranteed at this course, with
its wooded hillsides and the meandering Shournagh River
coming into play at a number of holes. The 15th is a
notable hole - not long, but very deep - and after that all
you need to do to get back to the clubhouse is stay out of
the water.
18 holes, 6327yds, Par 71, SSS 71.
Club membership 706.
Visitors may not play Wed afternoon & Thu
morning. Some limited opportunities at
weekends.
Societies must telephone in advance and then confirm
in writing.
Green Fees not confirmed.
Facilities ♀ ᗱ 亩 ⚑ ⚑
Leisure practice area,trolley hire.
Location 7.5m NW of Cork
Hotel ★★★ 68% Blarney Park Hotel,
BLARNEY
☎ 021 385281 76 ⇆ ⭑

CASTLETOWNBERE   Map 01 A2

Berehaven Millcove ☎ 027 70700
Seaside links founded in 1902.
9 holes, 2398mtrs, Par 68, SSS 66, Course record 63.   ▶

Visitors no restrictions ex first week June.
Societies apply to J J McLaughlin, Main St, Castletownbere.
Green Fees IR£8 per day (IR£10 weekends & bank holidays).
Facilities ⊗ ⓛ ▆ ♥ ♀ ⚐ ⚑
Leisure hard tennis courts, sauna, trolley for hire, practice area, camp site.
Location 2m E on Glen Garriff Rd
Hotel ★★★★ 70% Sea View Hotel, BALLYLICKEY
☎ 027 50073 & 50462 17 ⇥ ⚑

CHARLEVILLE   Map 01 B2

Charleville ☎ 063 81257
Wooded parkland course offering not too strenuous walking.
18 holes, 6212yds, Par 71, SSS 69, Course record 65.
Club membership 1000.
Visitors only prebooked at weekends.
Societies contact in advance.
Green Fees IR£12 (IR£15 weekends & bank holidays).
Facilities ⊗ ⅲ ⓛ ▆ ♥ ♀ ⚐ ⚑
Leisure trolley for hire, putting green, practice area.
Hotel ★★★(red)♨ Longueville House Hotel, MALLOW
☎ 022 47156 & 47306 16 ⇥ ⚑

CLONAKILTY   Map 01 B2

Dunmore Dunmore, Muckross ☎ 023 33352
A hilly, rocky 9-hole course overlooking the Atlantic.
9 holes, 4464yds, Par 64, SSS 61, Course record 57.
Club membership 250.
Visitors must contact in advance, may not play weekends.
Societies apply in writing.
Green Fees IR£10 per 18 holes.
Facilities ⊗ ⅲ ⓛ ▆ ♥ ♀ ⚑ ⋈
Leisure trolley for hire.
Location 3.5m S of Clonakilty
Hotel ★★ 64% Courtmacsherry, COURTMACSHERRY
☎ 023 46198 13rm(9 ⇥ 1 ⚑)

CORK   Map 01 B2

Cork Little Island ☎ 021 353451
This championship-standard course is always kept in superb condition and is playable all year round. It has many memorable and distinctive features including holes at the water's edge and holes in a disused quarry.
18 holes, 5910mtrs, Par 72, SSS 70.
Club membership 750.
Visitors may not play 12.30-2pm or on Thu (Ladies Day), and only after 2pm Sat & Sun.
Societies must contact in advance.
Green Fees IR£30 (IR£35 weekends).
Facilities ⊗ ⅲ ⓛ ▆ ♥ ♀ ⚐ ⚑ ⚑ ⚑ Peter Hickey.
Leisure trolley for hire, putting green, practice area.
Location 5m E, on N25
Hotel ★★★★ 70% Jurys Hotel, Western Rd, CORK ☎ 021 276622 185 ⇥ ⚑

Fitzpatrick Silver Springs Tivoli
☎ 021 507533 & 505128
Five Par 4s and 4 Par3s make up this short 9-hole course. The 4th has a 189 metre drive with out of bounds on the righthand side.
9 holes, 1786mtrs, Par 32, Course record 26.
Club membership 70.
Visitors no restrictions.
Societies apply by telephone.
Green Fees IR£5 (IR£7 weekends and bank holidays).
Facilities ⓛ ▆ ♥ ♀ ⚐ ⚑ ⋈ ⚑ Freddy Twomey.
Leisure hard tennis courts, heated indoor swimming pool, squash, sauna, solarium, gymnasium, buggies for hire, trolley for hire, putting green.
Location 1m E of city centre
Hotel ★★★★ 66% Fitzpatrick Silver Springs Hotel, Tivoli, CORK
☎ 021 507533 109 ⇥ ⚑

Fota Island Carrigtwohill ☎ 021 883700 & 883710
Fota Island Golf Club is in the heart of the 780 acre island in Cork Harbour which is recognised as one of Ireland's most outstanding landscapes. The course is gently undulating parkland routed among mature woodlands with occasional views of the harbour. The overall design is very traditional, featuring pot bunkers, a double green and undulating putting surfaces. The 10th and 18th holes are narrow Par 5's that require great accuracy and shotmaking skills.
18 holes, 6500yds, Par 72, SSS 72, Course record 67.
Club membership 300.
Visitors advisable to contact in advance.
Societies contact in advance.
Green Fees IR£27 per round (IR£30 weekends). Extra 18 Holes IR£10.
Facilities ⊗ ⅲ ⓛ ▆ ♥ ♀ ⚐ ⚑ ⚑ Kevin Morris.
Leisure motorised carts for hire, buggies for hire, trolley for hire, driving range, putting green, practice area.
Location Off N25 E of Cork City
Hotel ★★★ 66% Midleton Park, MIDLETON
☎ 021 631767 40 ⇥ ⚑

Mahon Municipal Blackrock ☎ 021 362480
Municipal course which stretches alongside the river estuary, with some holes across water.
18 holes, 4818mtrs, Par 67, SSS 66.
Club membership 380.
Visitors may not play mornings at weekends.
Green Fees not confirmed.
Facilities ♀ ⚐ ⚑ ⚑
Location 2m from city centre
Hotel ★★★★ 66% Fitzpatrick Silver Springs Hotel, Tivoli, CORK ☎ 021 507533 109 ⇥ ⚑

DONERAILE   Map 01 B2

Doneraile ☎ 022 24137
Parkland.
9 holes, 5528yds, SSS 66.
Visitors no restrictions
Societies welcome.
Green Fees not confirmed.
Location Off T11
Hotel ★★★(red)♨ Longueville House Hotel, MALLOW
☎ 022 47156 & 47306 16 ⇥ ⚑

DOUGLAS

Map 01 B2

Douglas ☎ 021 895297
Level inland course overlooking the city of Cork. Suitable for golfers of all ages and abilities.
18 holes, 5383mtrs, Par 70, SSS 68.
Club membership 810.
Visitors advisable to play Mon & Wed-Fri, contact in advance.
Societies must contact in writing, dates allocated early Feb.
Green Fees IR£20 (IR£22 weekends).
Facilities ⊗ ⅲ ⅂ ⤵ ♀ ⅄ 🏠 ✈ ⌇ Gary Nicholson.
Leisure trolley for hire, putting green, practice area.
Hotel ★★★★ 70% Jurys Hotel, Western Rd, CORK ☎ 021 276622 185 ⇥ ⌇

FERMOY

Map 01 B2

Fermoy Corrin Cross ☎ 025 31472
Rather exposed heathland course, bisected by a road.
18 holes, 5586mtrs, Par 70, SSS 69.
Club membership 1000.
Visitors contact in advance.
Societies advisable to write in advance.
Green Fees IR£13 (IR£16 weekends).
Facilities ⊗ ⅲ ⅂ ⤵ ♀ ⅄ 🏠 ✈ ⌇ John Savage.
Leisure buggies for hire, trolley for hire, putting green, practice area.
Location 2m SW
Hotel ★★★(red)🕮 Longueville House Hotel, MALLOW ☎ 022 47156 & 47306 16 ⇥ ⌇

GLENGARRIFF

Map 01 B2

Glengarriff ☎ 027 63150
Founded 1935.
9 holes, 2042mtrs, SSS 62.
Club membership 300.
Visitors welcome, details not supplied
Societies apply to club.
Green Fees not confirmed.
Facilities ♀ ⅄ ✈
Leisure practice area,trolley hire.
Location On N71
Hotel ★★★ 58% Westlodge Hotel, BANTRY ☎ 027 50360 90 ⇥ ⌇

KINSALE

Map 01 B2

Kinsale Farrangalway ☎ 021 772197
In addition to the existing 9-hole (Ringenane) course, a new 18-hole (Farrangalway) course was opened in 1994. Set in unspoilt farmland and surrounded by peacefull rolling countryside, it offers a stiff yet fair challenge to be enjoyed by all standards of golfers. New putting green.
Farrangalway: 18 holes, 6608yds, Par 71, SSS 71, Course record 70.
Ringenane: 9 holes, 2552yds, Par 70, SSS 66, Course record 63.
Club membership 740.
Visitors must contact in advance.
Societies apply in writing.

Green Fees Farrangalway: IR£15 per round (IR£20 weekends). Ringenane: IR£10 per 18 holes.
Facilities ⅄ ✈
Leisure trolley for hire, putting green, practice area.
Location On main Cork/Kinsale rd
Hotel ★★★ 68% Trident Hotel, Worlds End, KINSALE ☎ 021 772301 58 ⇥ ⌇

LITTLE ISLAND

Map 01 B2

Harbour Point Clash Rd ☎ 021 353094
A new championship-standard course in rolling countryside on the banks of the River Lee at Cork's scenic harbour. A distinctive and testing course for every standard of golfer.
18 holes, 5883metres, Par 72, SSS 71, Course record 71.
Visitors must contact in advance.
Societies telephone for bookings.
Green Fees IR£10 per round before 11am Mon, Wed, Thu & Fri; IR£20 other times.
Facilities ⊗ ⅲ ⅂ ⤵ ♀ ⅄ 🏠 ✈
Leisure motorised carts for hire, buggies for hire, trolley for hire, driving range, putting green, practice area.
Location 5m E of Cork
Hotel ★★★★ 66% Fitzpatrick Silver Springs Hotel, Tivoli, CORK ☎ 021 507533 109 ⇥ ⌇

MACROOM

Map 01 B2

Macroom Lackaduve ☎ 026 41072
A particularly scenic parkland course located on undulating ground along the banks of the River Sullane. Bunkers and mature trees make a variable and testing course and the 18th has a 50 yards carry over the river to the green.
18 holes, 5574mtrs, Par 72, SSS 70.
Club membership 550.
Visitors restricted some weekends, contact in advance.
Societies apply in writing.
Green Fees IR£12 (IR£15 weekends & bank holidays).
Facilities ⊗ ⅂ ⤵ ♀ ⅄ ✈
Leisure trolley for hire, putting green.
Location Through castle entrance in town square
Hotel ★★ 70% Castle Hotel, Main St, MACROOM ☎ 026 41074 26 ⇥ ⌇

MALLOW

Map 01 B2

Mallow Ballyellis ☎ 022 21145
A well wooded parkland course overlooking the Blackwater Valley, Mallow is straightforward, but no less of a challenge for it. The front nine is by far the longer, but the back nine is demanding in its call for accuracy and the par 3 18th provides a tough finish.
18 holes, 5769metres, Par 72, SSS 71, Course record 67.
Club membership 1400.
Visitors must contact in advance.
Societies apply in advance.
Green Fees IR£17 per round (IR£20 weekends & bank holidays).
Facilities ⊗ ⅲ ⅂ ⤵ ♀ ⅄ 🏠 ✈ ⌇ Sean Conway.
Leisure hard tennis courts, squash, sauna, trolley for hire, putting green, practice area.
Hotel ★★★(red)🕮 Longueville House Hotel, MALLOW ☎ 022 47156 & 47306 16 ⇥ ⌇

MIDLETON   Map 01 C2

East Cork Gortacrue ☎ 021 631687
A well wooded course calling for accuracy of shots.
18 holes, 5207mtrs, Par 69, SSS 67.
Club membership 511.
Visitors   may not play Sun mornings.
Societies   must apply in writing or telephone.
Green Fees   not confirmed.
Facilities   ♀⚲ ⚑
Leisure   squash, fishing, driving range, putting green,
                  practice area, trolley hire.
Location   On the A626
Hotel   ★★★ 66% Midleton Park, MIDLETON
                  ☎ 021 631767 40 ⇄ 🐾

MITCHELSTOWN   Map 01 B2

Mitchelstown Limerick Rd, Gurrane ☎ 025 24072
Attractive, gently undulating parkland course set in the
Golden Vale, noted for the quality of the greens, the
magnificent views of the Galtee Mountains and its friendly
atmosphere. Ideal for golfers seeking tranquility and a golfing
challenge.
18 holes, 5160mtrs, Par 67, SSS 68, Course record 65.
Club membership 400.
Visitors   advisable to book for weekend play.
Societies   apply in writing.
Green Fees   IR£10 per day.
Facilities   ⚲ ⚑ ♀⚲
Leisure   trolley for hire, putting green, practice area.
Location   0.75m on Limerick rd from Mitchelstown
Hotel   ★★★(red)⚕ Longueville House Hotel,
                  MALLOW ☎ 022 47156 & 47306 16 ⇄ 🐾

MONKSTOWN   Map 01 B2

Monkstown Parkgariffe, Monkstown ☎ 021 841376
Undulating parkland course with five tough finishing holes.
18 holes, 5441mtrs, Par 70, SSS 68, Course record 66.
Club membership 960.
Visitors   restricted weekends, must contact in advance.
Societies   apply in writing or telephone. Large groups
                  (24+) should book before Xmas.
Green Fees   IR£23 Mon-Thu; IR£26 Fri-Sun & bank
                  holidays.
Facilities   ⊗ ⅏ ⚲ ⚑ ♀⚲ ⚍ ⚑ ⚑ ⚑ Batt Murphy.
Leisure   motorised carts for hire, trolley for hire,
                  putting green, practice area.
Location   0.5m SE of Monkstown village
Hotel   ★★★★ 70% Jurys Hotel, Western Rd,
                  CORK ☎ 021 276622 185 ⇄ 🐾

OVENS   Map 01 B2

Lee Valley Golf & Country Club Clashanure
☎ 021 331721
An undulating test of all golfing abilities designed by Ryder
Cup star Christy O'Connor Junior. Seven of the 18 holes have
water and the unusual feature of two fairy forts which are
over 300 years old - can they be blamed for errors on the
testing Par 5 8th and 12th holes?! The 508yard, Par 5 8th is
already regarded as one of the best holes in Ireland with its
spectacular lake a feature from tee to green.

18 holes, 6434mtrs, Par 72, SSS 70, Course record 68.
Club membership 400.
Visitors   telephone in advance.
Societies   telephone in advance.
Green Fees   IR£30 per 36 holes, IR£20 per round
                  (IR£35/IR£25 weekends & bank holidays).
Facilities   ⊗ ⅏ ⚲ ⚑ ♀⚲ ⚑ ⚑ ⚍ ⚑ Brendan McDaid.
Leisure   motorised carts for hire, buggies for hire, trolley
                  for hire, driving range, putting green, practice area.
Location   8m from Cork on Cork/Killarney road N22
Hotel   ★★ 57% Vienna Woods Hotel, Glanmire,
                  CORK ☎ 021 821146 20 ⇄ 🐾

SKIBBEREEN   Map 01 B2

Skibbereen & West Carbery Licknavar ☎ 028 21227
Expanded to an 18-hole course in May 1993. Slightly hilly
course in scenic locatio.
18 holes, 6004yds, Par 71, SSS 69, Course record 68.
Club membership 640.
Visitors   advisable to contact in advance, may be
                  restricted Sun for competitions.
Societies   apply in writing.
Green Fees   IR£12 per day (IR£15 July/Aug).
Facilities   ⊗ ⅏ ⚲ ⚑ ♀⚲
Leisure   trolley for hire, putting green, practice area.
Location   20m S of Bantry, off N71
Hotel   ★★★ 68% Liss Ard Lake Lodge, SKIBBEREEN

YOUGHAL   Map 01 C2

Youghal Knockaverry ☎ 024 92787
For many years the host of various Golfing Union
championships, Youghal offers a good test of golf and is
well maintained for year-round play. There are panoramic
views of Youghal Bay and the Blackwater estuary.
18 holes, 5700mtrs, Par 70, SSS 70, Course record 67.
Club membership 600.
Visitors   may not play Wed (Ladies Day) and should
                  contact in advance for weekends.
Societies   must apply in writing a few months in
                  advance.
Green Fees   not confirmed.
Facilities   ♀⚲ ⚑ ⚑ ⚑ Liam Burns.
Leisure   putting green,trolley hire,practice area.
Hotel   ★★ 64% Devonshire Arms Hotel and
                  Restaurant, Pearse Square, YOUGHAL
                  ☎ 024 92827 & 92018 10 ⇄ 🐾

CO DONEGAL

BALLINTRA   Map 01 B5

Donegal Murvagh, Laghy ☎ 073 34054
This massive links course was opened in 1973 and
provides a world-class facility in peaceful surroundings.
It is a very long course with some memorable holes,
including five par 5s, calling for some big hitting.
Donegal is the home club of former Curtis Cup captain,
Maire O'Donnell.

18 holes, 6243mtrs, Par 73, SSS 73, Course record 68.
Club membership 750.

Visitors	must contact in advance, limited availability at weekends.
Societies	must contact in advance.
Green Fees	IR£17 per day (IR£22.50 per round weekends & bank holidays).
Facilities	⊗ ⅷ ⅼ ♥ ♀ ⅄
Leisure	buggies for hire, trolley for hire, putting green, practice area.
Location	6m S of Donegal on Ballyshannon road
Hotel	★★★ 73% Sand House Hotel, ROSSNOWLAGH ☎ 072 51777 46 ⇆ 🏌

BALLYBOFEY
Map 01 C5

Ballybofey & Stranorlar Stranorlar ☎ 074 31093
A most scenic course incorporating pleasant valleys backed
by mountains with three of its holes bordered by a lake. There
are three Par 3s on the first nine and two on the second. The
most difficult hole is the long uphill Par 4 16th. The only Par
5 is the 7th.
18 holes, 5366mtrs, Par 68, SSS 68, Course record 64.
Club membership 450.

Visitors	may play on weekdays. Advisable to book in advance
Green Fees	not confirmed.
Facilities	♀ ⅄
Leisure	squash.
Location	0.25m from Stranorlar
Hotel	★★★ 62% Kee's Hotel, Stranolar, BALLYBOFEY ☎ 074 31018 36 ⇆ 🏌

BALLYLIFFEN
Map 01 C6

Ballyliffin ☎ 077 76119
The Old course is a links course with rolling fairways,
surrounded by rolling hills and bounded on one side by the
ocean. Nick Faldo said 'This is the most natural golf links I
have ever played.' It has an old-fashioned charm with its
uniquely contoured fairways. The new 18-hole course, the
Glaslady (opened summer 1995), offers a modern (and
arguably 'fairer') championship test.
*Old Links: 18 holes, 6384yds, Par 72, SSS 70, Course record
68.*
Glashedy Links: 18 holes, 6982yds, Par 71, SSS 72.
Club membership 903.

Visitors	telephone in advance.
Societies	telephone in advance.
Green Fees	not confirmed.
Facilities	♀ ⅄ 🏠
Leisure	putting green,practice area,trolley hire.
Guesthouse	QQQQ Mount Royd Country Home, CARRIGANS ☎ 074 40163 4 🏌

BUNCRANA
Map 01 C6

Buncrana Municipal Ballmacarry ☎ 077 62279
A 9-hole course with a very challenging Par-3 3rd with all
carry out of bounds on either side.
9 holes, 2125yds, Par 62, SSS 60, Course record 59.
Club membership 100.

Visitors	during open competitions only visitors with club handicaps.
Societies	write in advance.
Green Fees	not confirmed.
Facilities	♀ ⅄ 🏠
Guesthouse	QQQQ Mount Royd Country Home, CARRIGANS ☎ 074 40163 4 🏌

North West Lisfannon, Fahan ☎ 077 61027
A traditional-style links course on gently rolling sandy
terrain with some long par 4s. Good judgement is
required on the approaches and the course offers a
satisfying test coupled with undemanding walking.
18 holes, 5968yds, Par 69, SSS 68, Course record 64.
Club membership 580.

Visitors	contact in advance for weekends. Wed - Ladies Day
Societies	telephone in advance.
Green Fees	IR£12 (IR£17 weekends).
Facilities	⊗ ⅷ ⅼ ♥ ♀ ⅄ 🏠 ℓ Seamus McBriarty.
Leisure	motorised carts for hire, buggies for hire, trolley for hire, practice area, putting green.
Guesthouse	QQQQ Mount Royd Country Home, CARRIGANS ☎ 074 40163 4 🏌

BUNDORAN
Map 01 B5

Bundoran ☎ 072 41302
This popular course, acknowledged as one of the best in
the country, runs along the high cliffs above Bundoran
beach and has a difficult par of 69. Designed by Harry
Vardon, it offers a challenging game of golf in beautiful
surroundings and has been the venue for a number of
Irish golf championships.
18 holes, 5599mtrs, Par 69, SSS 70, Course record 66.
Club membership 560.

Visitors	must contact in advance.
Societies	must contact in advance.
Green Fees	IR£14 (IR£16 weekends & bank holidays) + VAT.
Facilities	ⅼ ♥ ♀ ⅄ 🏠 ⅌ ℓ David T Robinson.
Leisure	trolley for hire, putting green, practice area.
Hotel	★★★ 73% Sand House Hotel, ROSSNOWLAGH ☎ 072 51777 46 ⇆ 🏌

CRUIT ISLAND
Map 01 B5

Cruit Island Kincasslagh ☎ 075 43296
A links course on a small island. It is perched along the cliffs
overlooking the Atlantic. The course is short but always
challenging as the wind blows 90% of the time. It is
crowned by a magnificent 6th hole which is played across a
cove to an island green. With the prevailing wind in your face
and the Atlantic waves crashing in front, it is not for the
fainthearted.
9 holes, 4833mtrs, Par 68, SSS 66, Course record 62.
Club membership 200.

Visitors	restricted Sun & Thu mornings for Club competitions.
Societies	apply in writing to secretary.
Green Fees	not confirmed.
Facilities	♀ (all day in summer) ⅄
Hotel	★★ 70% Arnold's Hotel, DUNFANAGHY ☎ 074 36208 & 36142 34 ⇆ 🏌

DUNFANAGHY

Map 01 C6

Dunfanaghy Kill ☎ 074 36335 & 36488
Overlooking Sheephaven Bay, the course has a flat central
area with three difficult streams to negotiate. At the Port-na-
Blagh end there are five marvellous holes, including one
across the beach, while at the Horn Head end, the last five
holes are a test for any golfer.
18 holes, 5066mtrs, Par 68, SSS 66, Course record 64.
Club membership 395.
Visitors must book in advance, Jun-Aug time sheet in operation.
Societies must telephone in advance.
Green Fees IR£12.50 per round (IR£14.50 weekends).
Facilities ⬛ 🍷 ♀ ⚑ 🏐 ⚐
Leisure motorised carts for hire, buggies for hire, trolley for hire, putting green, practice area.
Location On N56
Hotel ★★ 70% Arnold's Hotel, DUNFANAGHY
☎ 074 36208 & 36142 34 ⇔ ⋒

GREENCASTLE

Map 01 C6

Greencastle Moville ☎ 077 81013
A typical links course along the shores of Lough Foyle,
surrounded by rocky headlands and sandy beaches. In 1992 to
celebrate its centenary, the club increased its size from 9 to
18 holes.
18 holes, 5118mtrs, Par 69, SSS 67.
Club membership 600.
Visitors no restrictions.
Societies telephone in advance.
Green Fees not confirmed.
Facilities ♀ ⚐
Leisure putting green.
Hotel ★★★ 65% Everglades Hotel, Prehen Rd,
LONDONDERRY
☎ 01504 46722 52 ⇔ ⋒

GWEEDORE

Map 01 B6

Gweedore Derrybeg ☎ 075 31140
This 9-hole links course provides plenty of challenge with
two subtle Par 3s and the Par 5 5th/14th at 556yards into the
prevailing west wind is a monster.
9 holes, 6201yds, Par 71, SSS 69.
Club membership 150.
Visitors no restrictions.
Societies telephone in advance.
Green Fees not confirmed.
Facilities ⚐
Hotel ★★ 65% Carrig Rua Hotel, DUNFANAGHY
☎ 074 36133 22 ⇔ ⋒

LETTERKENNY

Map 01 C5

Letterkenny Barnhill ☎ 074 21150
The fairways are wide and generous, but the rough, when you
find it, is short, tough and mean. The flat and untiring terrain
on the shores of Lough Swilly provides good holiday golf.
Many interesting holes include the intimidating 1st with its
high tee through trees and the tricky dog-leg of the 2nd hole.
18 holes, 6239yds, Par 70, SSS 71, Course record 67.
Club membership 500.

Visitors preferred Mon-Fri. Advisable to contact in advance for weekends and bank holidays.
Societies apply by writing or telephone.
Green Fees not confirmed.
Facilities ♀ ⚐ ⚐
Leisure table tennis.
Location 2m from town on Rathmelton road
Hotel ★★★ 62% Kee's Hotel, Stranolar,
BALLYBOFEY
☎ 074 31018 36 ⇔ ⋒

NARIN

Map 01 B5

Narin & Portnoo ☎ 075 45107
Seaside links with every hole presenting its own special
feature. The Par 4 5th, for instance, demands a perfectly
placed drive to get a narrow sight of the narrow entrance to
the elevated green. Cross winds from the sea can make some
of the Par 4s difficult to reach with two woods.
18 holes, 5322mtrs, Par 69, SSS 68, Course record 63.
Club membership 420.
Visitors weekends by arrangement.
Societies telephone in advance.
Green Fees IR£12 per day (IR£15 weekends & bank holidays).
Facilities ⬛ 🍷 ♀ ⚑ ⚐
Leisure trolley for hire, putting green.
Location 6m from Ardara
Hotel ★★★ 63% Abbey Hotel, The Diamond,
DONEGAL
☎ 073 21014 49 ⇔ ⋒

PORTSALON

Map 01 C6

Portsalon ☎ 074 59459
Another course blessed by nature. The three golden beaches
of Ballymastocker Bay lie at one end, while the beauty of
Lough Swilly and the Inishowen Peninsula beyond is a
distracting but pleasant feature to the west. Situated on the
Fanad Peninsula, this lovely links course provides untiring
holiday golf at its best.
18 holes, 5878yards, Par 69, SSS 68, Course record 66.
Club membership 400.
Visitors telephone in advance.
Societies telephone in advance.
Green Fees IR£12 (IR£14 weekends).
Facilities ⊗ 🍴 ⬛ 🍷 ♀ ⚑
Leisure trolley for hire, putting green.
Hotel ★ 61% Pier Hotel, RATHMULLAN
☎ 074 58178 & 58115 10 ⇔ ⋒

RATHMULLAN

Map 01 C6

Otway Saltpans ☎ 074 58319
9 holes, 4234yds, Par 64, SSS 60.
Visitors welcome.
Societies contact for details.
Green Fees not confirmed.
Location W shore of Loch Swilly
Hotel ★★★⚜ 69% Fort Royal Hotel, Fort Royal,
RATHMULLAN
☎ 074 58100 11 ⇔ ⋒Annexe4 ⇔

ROSAPENNA · · · · · · · · · · · Map 01 C6

Rosapenna Downings ☎ 074 55301
Dramatic links course offering a challenging round.
Originally designed by Tom Morris and later modified by
James Braid and Harry Vardon, it includes such features as
bunkers in mid fairway. The best part of the links runs in the
low valley along the ocean.
18 holes, 6271yds, Par 70, SSS 71.
Club membership 200.
Visitors no restrictions.
Societies must contact in advance.
Green Fees not confirmed.
Facilities ♀ ♨ 🏠 ♟ 🛏 ℓ Simon Byrne.
Leisure hard tennis courts.
Hotel ★★ 70% Arnold's Hotel, DUNFANAGHY
☎ 074 36208 & 36142 34 ⇆ 🐾

CO DUBLIN

BALBRIGGAN · · · · · · · · · · · Map 01 D4

Balbriggan Blackhall ☎ 01 8412229 & 01 8412173
A parkland course with great variations and good views of
the Mourne and Cooley mountains.
18 holes, 5881mtrs, Par 71, SSS 71.
Club membership 650.
Visitors must contact in advance. With member only at
weekends.
Societies must apply in writing.
Green Fees IR£14 per round. Early bird before 10am IR£8
(ex Tue).
Facilities ⊗ ℳ ♨ ♭ ♥ ♀ ♨
Leisure trolley for hire, putting green, practice area.
Hotel ★★★ 65% Boyne Valley Hotel, DROGHEDA
☎ 041 37737 35 ⇆ 🐾

BRITTAS · · · · · · · · · · · Map 01 D4

Slade Valley Lynch Park ☎ 01 4582183 & 4582739
This is a course for a relaxing game, being fairly easy and in
pleasant surroundings.
18 holes, 5388mtrs, Par 69, SSS 68, Course record 65.
Club membership 800.
Visitors must contact in advance.
Societies telephone in advance.
Green Fees IR£17 per round (afternoons); IR£15 (before
noon).
Facilities ⊗ ℳ ♨ ♭ ♥ ♀ ♨ 🏠 ♟ ℓ John Dignam.
Leisure trolley for hire, putting green.
Location 9m SW of Dublin on N81
Hotel ★★★ 56% Downshire House Hotel,
BLESSINGTON
☎ 045 865199 14 ⇆ 🐾Annexe11 ⇆ 🐾

CLOGHRAN · · · · · · · · · · · Map 01 D4

Forrest Little ☎ 01 8401183
Testing parkland course.
18 holes, 5865mtrs, Par 70, SSS 70.

Visitors preferred weekday mornings.
Green Fees not confirmed.
Facilities ♀ 🏠 ♟ ℓ Tony Judd.
Location 6m N of Dublin on N1
Hotel ★★★ 68% Marine Hotel, Sutton Cross,
DUBLIN ☎ 01 8390000 26 ⇆ 🐾

CLONSILLA · · · · · · · · · · · Map 01 D4

Luttrellstown Castle ☎ 01 8208210
18 holes, 6032mtrs, Par 72, SSS 73, Course record 66.
Club membership 400.
Visitors welcome.
Societies must phone in advance.
Green Fees IR£34 per 18 holes (IR£39 weekends).
Facilities ⊗ ℳ ♨ ♭ ♥ ♀ 🏠 ♟ 🛏 ℓ Graham Campbell.
Leisure hard tennis courts, heated outdoor swimming
pool, fishing, sauna, buggies for hire, trolley for
hire, driving range, putting green, practice area,.
Location Porterstown rd
Hotel ★★★ 66% Finnstown Country House Hotel &
Golf Course, Newcastle Rd, LUCAN
☎ 01 6280644 25 ⇆ 🐾Annexe20 ⇆ 🐾

DONABATE · · · · · · · · · · · Map 01 D4

Balcarrick Corballis
☎ 01 8436228 & 8436957
Splendid 18-hole parkland course located close to the sea. A
strong prevailing wind often plays a big part on every hole.
Many challenging holes, notably the 7th - nicknamed 'Amen
Corner'.
18 holes, 6273mtrs, Par 73, SSS 71.
Club membership 480.
Visitors advisable to contact for weekend play.
Societies telephone in advance.
Green Fees IR£10 (IR£15 weekends & bank holidays).
Facilities ♭ ♥ ♀ ♨ 🏠
Leisure putting green.
Hotel B Forte Posthouse Dublin, Cloghran, DUBLIN
☎ 01 8444211 188 ⇆ 🐾

Beaverstown Beaverstown
☎ 01 8436439 & 8436721
Well wooded course with water hazards at more than half of
the holes.
18 holes, 5855mtrs, Par 71, SSS 71, Course record 69.
Club membership 800.
Visitors may not play 12.30-1.30pm daily & must contact
in advance to play on Wed, Sat or Sun.
Societies must contact in writing.
Green Fees not confirmed.
Facilities ♀ ♨
Leisure caddy cars.
Location 5m from Dublin Airport
Hotel B Forte Posthouse Dublin, Cloghran, DUBLIN
☎ 01 8444211 188 ⇆ 🐾

Corballis Public Corballis ☎ 01 8436583
Well maintained coastal course with excellent greens.
18 holes, 4971yds, Par 65, SSS 64.
Visitors no restrictions.
Societies apply in writing or telephone.
Green Fees IR£7 per round (IR£8 weekends).
Facilities ♥ ♨ 🏠 ♟ ▶

Leisure   buggies for hire, trolley for hire, putting green.
Hotel   B Forte Posthouse Dublin, Cloghran, DUBLIN
            ☎ 01 8444211 188 ⇄ ↑

Donabate Balcarrick ☎ 01 8436346 & 8436001
Level parkland course.
18 holes, 5704yds, Par 70, SSS 69, Course record 67.
Club membership 900.
Visitors   welcome, weekdays & late Sunday afternoon.
Societies   must apply in writing.
Green Fees IR£18 (IR£24 Sunday).
Facilities   ⊗ ⅋ ⅃ ⅃ ⅀ ⅃ ⅃ ↑ ⅃ Hugh Jackson.
Leisure   buggies for hire, trolley for hire, practice green,
            putting green.
Hotel   B Forte Posthouse Dublin, Cloghran, DUBLIN
            ☎ 01 8444211 188 ⇄ ↑

The Island Corballis ☎ (01) 8436104 & 8436205
Links course on a promontory, with sea inlets separating
some of the fairways. Accuracy as well as length of shots
are required on some holes and sand hills provide an
additional challenge.
18 holes, 6078mtrs, Par 71, SSS 72.
Club membership 800.
Visitors   preferred on Mon, Tue & Fri.
Societies   must apply in advance.
Green Fees   not confirmed.
Facilities   ⅀ ⅃
Leisure   putting green,practice area,trolley hire.
Hotel   B Forte Posthouse Dublin, Cloghran,
            DUBLIN ☎ 01 8444211 188 ⇄ ↑

DUBLIN   Map 01 D4

Carrickmines Carrickmines ☎ 01 2955972
Meadowland course.
9 holes, 6100yds, Par 71, SSS 69.
Club membership 500.
Visitors   with member only Sat, Sun & bank holidays.
Societies   contact for details.
Green Fees not confirmed.
Location   7m S of Dublin
Hotel   ★★★ 61% Royal Marine Hotel, Marine Rd,
            DUN LAOGHAIRE ☎ 01 2801911 104 ⇄ ↑

Castle Woodside Dr, Rathfarnham
☎ 01 4904207 & 4905835
A tight, tree-lined parkland course which is very highly
regarded by all who play there.
18 holes, 5732mtrs, Par 70, SSS 68, Course record 63.
Club membership 1200.
Visitors   welcome but may not play at weekends.
Societies   must apply in writing 6 months in advance.
Green Fees IR£27 per round.
Facilities   ⊗ ⅋ ⅃ ⅃ ⅀ ⅃ ⅃ David Kinsella.
Leisure   trolley for hire, putting green, practice area.
Hotel   ★★★★ 70% Jurys Hotel, Pembroke Rd,
            Ballsbridge, DUBLIN 4 ☎ 01 6605000 292 ⇄ ↑

Clontarf Donnycarney House, Malahide Rd
☎ 01 8331892 & 8331520
The nearest golf course to Dublin city, with a historic
building as a clubhouse, Clontarf is a parkland type course
bordered on one side by a railway line. There are several
testing and challenging holes including the 12th, which
involves playing over a pond and a quarry.

18 holes, 5459mtrs, Par 69, SSS 68, Course record 66.
Club membership 1100.
Visitors   welcome daily but advisable to contact in
            advance.
Societies   Tue & Fri. Must contact in advance.
Green Fees Apr-Oct IR£23 per round. Nov-Mar IR£15..
Facilities   ⊗ ⅋ ⅃ ⅃ ⅀ ⅃ ⅃ ↑ ⅃ Joe Craddock.
Leisure   buggies for hire, trolley for hire, practice area,
            putting green, bowling green.
Location   2.5m N via Fairview
Hotel   ★★★ 65% Doyle Skylon Hotel, Drumcondra
            Rd, DUBLIN 9 ☎ 01 8379121 92 ⇄ ↑

Corrstown Kilsallaghan ☎ 01 8640533
A new course with the first 9 holes in play - a pleasant
parkland setting well sheltered by mature trees. An additional
18-hole championship standard course is due to open in
Spring 1995. It has been designed by Eddie B. Connaughton
to test the best golfers.
River: 18 holes, 6885yds, Par 72, SSS 73.
Orchard: 9 holes, 3053yds, Par 70, SSS 69.
Club membership 900.
Visitors   welcome to play 9 hole course but with member
            only on weekdays. Further 18 Holes open by
            mid Sep 1995.
Societies   by arrangement.
Green Fees not confirmed.
Facilities   ⅃ ⅃ ↑ ⅃ Pat Gittens.
Leisure   motorised carts, practice area, buggy & trolley
            hire.
Location   W of Dublin Airport via St Margarets
Hotel   ★★★ 65% Doyle Skylon Hotel, Drumcondra
            Rd, DUBLIN 9 ☎ 01 8379121 92 ⇄ ↑

Deer Park Hotel & Golf Course Howth ☎ 01 8322624
Claiming to be Irelands largest golf/hotel complex, be warned
that its popularity makes it extremely busy at times and only
hotel residents can book tee-off times.
St Fintans: 9 holes, 3373yds, Par 37.
Deer Park: 18 holes, 6678yds, Par 72.
Grace O'Malley: 9 holes, 3105yds, Par 35.
Short Course: 12 holes, 1810yds, Par 36.
Club membership 200.
Visitors   no restrictions. There may be delays especially
            Sun mornings.
Societies   must contact by telephone.
Green Fees not confirmed.
Facilities   ⅀ ⅃ ↑ ⅃
Leisure   putting green,practice area,trolley hire.
Location   On right 0.5m before Howth Harbour
Hotel   ★★★ 66% Howth Lodge Hotel, HOWTH
            ☎ 01 8321010 46 ⇄ ↑

Edmonstown Edmondstown Rd, Edmondstown
☎ 01 4931082
A popular and testing parkland course situated at the foot of
the Dublin Mountains in the suburbs of the city. An attractive
stream flows in front of the 4th and 6th greens calling for an
accurate approach shot.
18 holes, 5663mtrs, Par 70, SSS 69.
Club membership 750.
Visitors   must contact in advance as there are daily times
            reserved for members.
Societies   must contact in advance.
Green Fees IR£24 per round (IR£28 weekends) summer.
            IR£18 per round (IR£24 weekends) winter.

Facilities ⊗ ⅲ ⅬⅬ ♥ ♀ ♣ ⚑ ⚑ ℓ Andrew Crofton.
Leisure trolley for hire, putting green, practice area.
Hotel ★★★ 68% Doyle Montrose Hotel, Stillorgan Rd, DUBLIN ☎ 01 2693311 179 ⇔ ⋒

Elm Park Golf & Sports Club Nutley House, Nutley Ln, Dennybrook ☎ 01 2693438
Interesting parkland course requiring a degree of accuracy, particularly as half of the holes involve crossing the stream.
18 holes, 5355mtrs, Par 69, SSS 68, Course record 64.
Club membership 1750.
Visitors must contact in advance.
Societies apply in advance.
Green Fees IR£40 per round (IR£45 weekends).
Facilities ⊗ ⅲ ⅬⅬ ♥ ♀ ♣ ⚑ ⚑ ℓ Seamus Green.
Leisure grass tennis courts, trolley for hire, putting green.
Location 3m from city centre
Hotel ★★★★ 70% Jurys Hotel, Pembroke Rd, Ballsbridge, DUBLIN 4 ☎ 01 6605000 292 ⇔ ⋒

Foxrock Torquay Rd, Foxrock
☎ 01 2895668 & 2893992
A well-treed parkland course.
9 holes, 5667mtrs, Par 70, SSS 69.
Club membership 650.
Visitors welcome but contact in advance, no green fees Tue & weekends.
Societies apply in writing to William Daly.
Green Fees not confirmed.
Facilities ♀ ♣ ⚑ ⚑ ℓ David Walker.
Leisure practice area,trolley hire.
Hotel ★★★ 61% Royal Marine Hotel, Marine Rd, DUN LAOGHAIRE ☎ 01 2801911 104 ⇔ ⋒

Grange Rathfarnham ☎ 01 932889
Wooded parkland course which provides both interest and challenge.
18 holes, 5517mtrs, Par 68, SSS 69.
Visitors preferred on weekdays.
Green Fees not confirmed.
Facilities ♀ ⚑ ℓ W Sullivan.
Location 6m from city centre
Hotel ★★★ 68% Doyle Montrose Hotel, Stillorgan Rd, DUBLIN ☎ 01 2693311 179 ⇔ ⋒

Hollywood Lakes Hollywood ☎ 01 8433406 & 8433407
A parkland course opened in 1992 with large USGA-type, sand-based greens and tees. There are water features on seven holes. The front nine requires accuracy while the second nine includes a 636yard Par 5.
18 holes, 6246mtrs, Par 72, SSS 72, Course record 67.
Club membership 380.
Visitors welcome but may not play weekends & bank holidays.
Societies telephone then write in advance.
Green Fees IR£16 per day (IR£20 weekends).
Facilities ⊗ ⅲ ⅬⅬ ♥ ♀ ♣
Leisure trolley for hire, practice area.
Location 3m off main Dublin/Belfast road
Hotel ★★★ 68% Marine Hotel, Sutton Cross, DUBLIN ☎ 01 8390000 26 ⇔ ⋒

Howth St Fintan's, Carrickbrack Rd, Sutton ☎ 01 8323055
A moorland course with scenic views of Dublin Bay. It is very hilly and presents a good challenge for the athletic golfer.
18 holes, 5618mtrs, Par 71, SSS 69.
Club membership 1200.
Visitors contact in advance.
Societies must contact in advance.
Green Fees not confirmed.
Facilities ⊗ ⅲ ⅬⅬ ♥ ♀ ♣ ⚑ ℓ John McGuirk.
Leisure trolley for hire, practice area.
Hotel ★★★ 68% Marine Hotel, Sutton Cross, DUBLIN ☎ 01 8390000 26 ⇔ ⋒

Milltown Lower Churchtown Rd ☎ 01 4976090
Level parkland course on the outskirts of the city.
18 holes, 5638mtrs, Par 71, SSS 69, Course record 64.
Club membership 1400.
Visitors must contact in advance but may not play weekends.
Societies apply in writing.
Green Fees IR£30 Mon-Fri.
Facilities ⊗ ⅲ ⅬⅬ ♥ ♀ ♣ ⚑ ℓ John Harnett.
Leisure trolley for hire, putting green, practice area.
Hotel ★★★★ 70% Jurys Hotel, Pembroke Rd, Ballsbridge, DUBLIN 4 ☎ 01 6605000 292 ⇔ ⋒

Newlands Clondalkin 22 ☎ 01 4593157
Mature parkland course offering a testing game.
18 holes, 5714mtrs, Par 71, SSS 70.
Club membership 1000.
Visitors must contact in advance and may play Mon, Thu, Fri and Wed mornings only.
Societies must contact in writing.
Green Fees not confirmed.
Facilities ♀ ♣ ⚑ ⚑ ℓ Karl O'Donnell.
Leisure putting green,practice area,trolley hire.
Hotel ★★★ 61% Doyle Green Isle Hotel, Naas Rd, DUBLIN 12 ☎ 01 4593406 48 ⇔ ⋒Annexe35 ⇔ ⋒

The Open Golf Centre Newton House, St Margaret's ☎ 01 8640324
A 27-hole Pay and Play parkland course that is testing for the low handicap golfer but not too intimidating for high handicapper.
18 holes, 5973yds, Par 71, SSS 71, Course record 66.
Visitors no restrictions. Booking essential.
Societies telephone for booking form.
Green Fees IR£7.60 per 18 holes (IR£11.50 weekends & bank holidays).
Facilities ♥ ♣ ⚑ ⚑ ℓ Roger Yates.
Leisure trolley for hire, indoor driving range, video tuition, putting green.
Location Adjacent to Dublin airport
Hotel ★★★ 68% Marine Hotel, Sutton Cross, DUBLIN ☎ 01 8390000 26 ⇔ ⋒

Rathfarnham Newtown ☎ 01 4931201 & 4931561
Parkland course designed by John Jacobs in 1962.
9 holes, 2921mtrs, Par 36, SSS 70, Course record 69.
Club membership 624.
Visitors must contact in advance but may not play weekends.
Societies restricted to Mon, Wed & Fri. ▶

Green Fees IR£20 per round.
Facilities ![icons] Brian O'Hara.
Leisure buggies for hire, putting green, practice area.
Hotel ★★★★ 70% Jurys Hotel, Pembroke Rd, Ballsbridge, DUBLIN 4
☎ 01 6605000 292 ⇔ ↰

Royal Dublin North Bull Island, Dollymount
☎ 01 8336346
A popular course with visitors, for its design subtleties, for the condition of the links and the friendly atmosphere. Founded in 1885, the club moved to its present site in 1889 and received its Royal designation in 1891. A notable former club professional was Christie O'Connor, who was appointed in 1959 and immediately made his name. Along with its many notable holes, Royal Dublin has a fine and testing finish. The 18th is a sharply dog-legged par 4, with out of bounds along the right-hand side. The decision to try the long carry over the 'garden' is one many visitors have regretted.
18 holes, 6030mtrs, Par 72, SSS 71, Course record 65.
Club membership 800.
Visitors must contact in advance & have handicap certificate.
Societies must book one year in advance.
Green Fees IR£45 per round (IR£55 weekends).
Facilities ⊗ ⅲ ![icons] Leonard Owens.
Leisure practice ground & nets, putting green.
Hotel ★★★ 66% Howth Lodge Hotel, HOWTH
☎ 01 8321010 46 ⇔ ↰

St Anne's North Bull Island, Dollymount ☎ 01 8336471
Links course, recently extended from 9 holes to 18.
18 holes, 5652mtrs, Par 70, SSS 69.
Club membership 500.
Visitors telephone for restrictions.
Societies must apply in writing.
Green Fees not confirmed.
Facilities ![icons]
Leisure putting green,trolley hire,practice area.
Hotel ★★★ 66% Howth Lodge Hotel, HOWTH
☎ 01 8321010 46 ⇔ ↰

St Margaret's Golf & Country Club St Margaret's
☎ 01 8640400
A championship standard course which measures nearly 7,000 yards off the back tees, but flexible teeing offers a fairer challenge to the middle and high handicap golfer. The modern design makes wide use of water hazards and mounding. The Par 5 8th hole is set to become notorious - featuring lakes to the left and right of the tee and a third lake in front of the green. Ryder Cup player,Sam Torrance, has described the 18th as 'possibly the strongest and most exciting in the world'.
18 holes, 6917yds, Par 73, SSS 73, Course record 69.
Club membership 200.
Visitors telephone in advance.
Societies apply in writing.
Green Fees IR£40 per round.
Facilities ⊗ ⅲ ![icons]
![icon] Ciaran Monaghan.
Leisure buggies for hire, trolley for hire, driving range, putting green, practice area.
Location 3m NW
Hotel ★★★ 68% Marine Hotel, Sutton Cross, DUBLIN ☎ 01 8390000 26 ⇔ ↰

Finnstown Country House Hotel & Golf Course ★★★

Newcastle Road, Lucan, Co Dublin
Tel: 00 3531 628044   Fax: 00 3531 6281088
Finnstown Country House is only eight miles from Dublin city centre. Situated off the main road and on 50 acres of mature woodlands, guests may relax and enjoy the friendly atmosphere and service of a small grade A country house hotel together with the amenities of today and a fine Restaurant. The hotel has its own wooded walks, 9 hole golf course, hard tennis courts, outdoor pool, gymnasium, saunas and Turkish bath.
A beautiful place in a great location.

Stackstown Kellystown Rd, Rathfarnham
☎ 01 4942338 & 4941993
Pleasant course in scenic surroundings.
18 holes, 5925mtrs, Par 72, SSS 72, Course record 70.
Club membership 1042.
Visitors preferred Mon-Fri.
Societies telephone in advance and confirm in writing.
Green Fees not confirmed.
Facilities ![icons] Michael Kavanach.
Leisure sauna.
Location 9m S of city centre
Hotel ★★★ 68% Doyle Montrose Hotel, Stillorgan Rd, DUBLIN ☎ 01 2693311 179 ⇔ ↰

Sutton Cush Point, Burrow Rd, Sutton
☎ 01 8324875
Founded in 1890.
9 holes, 5226mtrs, Par 70, SSS 67.
Visitors welcome except for competition days, contact for further details.
Societies by prior arrangement.
Green Fees not confirmed.
Facilities ![icon] Nicky Lynch.
Leisure lessons can be arranged.
Location Approx 7m NE of city
Hotel ★★★ 66% Howth Lodge Hotel, HOWTH
☎ 01 8321010 46 ⇔ ↰

DUN LAOGHAIRE   Map 01 D4

Dun Laoghaire Eglinton Park, Tivoli Rd
☎ 01 2803916 & 2805116
This is a well wooded parkland course, not long, but

requiring accurate club selection and placing of shots. The course was designed by Harry Colt in 1918.
18 holes, 5197mtrs, Par 69, SSS 67, Course record 63.
Club membership 1040.

Visitors	may not play Sat.
Societies	must apply in writing.
Green Fees	IR£26 per day.
Facilities	⊗ ⅢⅢ ⅃ 🍴 ♀ ▲ 📦 ⛳ ♂ Owen Mulhall.
Leisure	trolley for hire, putting green.
Hotel	★★★ 61% Royal Marine Hotel, Marine Rd, DUN LAOGHAIRE ☎ 01 2801911 104 ⇥ ℟

KILLINEY
Map 01 D4

Killiney Ballinclea Rd ☎ 01 2852823 & 2851983
The course is on the side of Killiney Hill with picturesque views over south Dublin and the Wicklow Mountains.
9 holes, 5430mtrs, Par 70, SSS 68.
Club membership 450.

Visitors	welcome Mon, Wed, Fri & Sun afternoons.
Green Fees	IR£20.
Facilities	⊗ ⅢⅢ ⅃ 🍴 ♀ ▲ 📦 ⛳ ♂ P O'Boyle.
Leisure	buggies for hire, trolley for hire, putting green, practice area.
Hotel	★★★ 66% Fitzpatrick Castle Hotel, KILLINEY ☎ 01 2840700 90 ⇥ ℟

KILTERNAN
Map 01 D4

Kilternan Golf & Country Club Hotel ☎ 01 2955559
Interesting and testing course overlooking Dublin Bay.
18 holes, 4914mtrs, Par 68, SSS 67, Course record 69.
Club membership 789.

Visitors	may not play before 1.30pm at weekends.
Societies	apply in writing/telephone in advance.
Green Fees	not confirmed.
Facilities	♀ ▲ 📦 ⛳ ♂ ♂
Leisure	hard tennis courts, heated indoor swimming pool, fishing, sauna, solarium, gymnasium, dry ski slope, indoor tennis, night club.
Hotel	★★★ 66% Fitzpatrick Castle Hotel, KILLINEY ☎ 01 2840700 90 ⇥ ℟

LUCAN
Map 01 D4

Finnstown Fairways Newcastle Rd
☎ 01 6280644
A flat parkland 9-hole course based in grounds originally laid out in the 18th century. Very challenging 6th and 7th holes among many mature trees.
9 holes, 2695yds, Par 66, SSS 66.
Club membership 200.

Visitors	time sheet in use, must reserve in advance.
Societies	must reserve in advance.
Green Fees	IR£10 per day (IR£12 weekends).
Facilities	⊗ ⅢⅢ ⅃ 🍴 ♀ ▲ ⛳ ♂
Leisure	hard tennis courts, heated outdoor swimming pool, sauna, solarium, gymnasium, buggies for hire, trolley for hire, driving range, practice area, turkish bath.
Location	Off N4
Hotel	★★★ 66% Finnstown Country House Hotel & Golf Course, Newcastle Rd, LUCAN ☎ 01 6280644 25 ⇥ ℟ Annexe20 ⇥ ℟

Hermitage Ballydowd
☎ 01 6265049 & 6268491
Part level, part undulating course bordered by the River Liffey and offering some surprises.
18 holes, 6034mtrs, Par 71, SSS 70.
Club membership 1100.

Visitors	contact for details
Societies	must telephone well in advance.
Green Fees	not confirmed.
Facilities	♀ ▲ 📦 ⛳ ♂ Ciaran Carroll.
Leisure	putting green, trolley hire.
Hotel	★★★ 66% Finnstown Country House Hotel & Golf Course, Newcastle Rd, LUCAN ☎ 01 6280644 25 ⇥ ℟ Annexe20 ⇥ ℟

Lucan Celbridge Rd ☎ 01 6282106
Founded in 1902 as a 9-hole course and only recently extended to 18 holes, Lucan involves playing across both the main road and a lane which bisects the course.
18 holes, 5958mtrs, Par 71, SSS 71.
Club membership 780.

Visitors	with member only Sat & Sun, after 1pm Wed.
Societies	must apply in writing.
Green Fees	not confirmed.
Facilities	♀ ▲
Leisure	putting green, trolley hire, practice area.
Hotel	★★★ 55% Lucan Spa Hotel, LUCAN ☎ 01 6280494 50 ⇥ ℟

MALAHIDE
Map 01 D4

Malahide Beechwood, The Grange
☎ 01 8461611
Splendid parkland course with raised greens and water hazards affecting many of the holes, demanding accuracy from tee to green.
Blue Course: 18 holes, 5372mtrs, Par 69, SSS 68.
Red Course: 18 holes, 5708mtrs, Par 71, SSS 71, Course record 67.
Yellow Course: 18 holes, 5304mtrs, Par 69, SSS 68.
Club membership 1100.

Visitors	must contact in advance.
Societies	must contact in advance.
Green Fees	IR£25 per 18 holes (IR£35 weekends & bank holidays).
Facilities	⊗ ⅢⅢ ⅃ 🍴 ♀ ▲ 📦 ⛳ ♂ David Barton.
Leisure	trolley for hire, putting green, practice area.
Location	1m from coast road at Portmarnock
Hotel	★★★ 66% Howth Lodge Hotel, HOWTH ☎ 01 8321010 46 ⇥ ℟

PORTMARNOCK
Map 01 D4

PORTMARNOCK See page 387

RATHCOOLE
Map 01 D4

Beech Park Johnstown
☎ 01 580100
Relatively flat parkland with heavily wooded fairways.
18 holes, 5730mtrs, Par 72, SSS 70, Course record 67.
Club membership 750.

Visitors	restricted on some days, telephone in advance. ▶

Societies apply in writing.
Green Fees not confirmed.
Facilities ♀ ⏶
Hotel ★★★ 66% Finnstown Country House Hotel & Golf Course, Newcastle Rd, LUCAN
☎ 01 6280644 25 ⇥ 🐾Annexe20 ⇥ 🐾

RUSH

Map 01 D4

Rush ☎ 01 8438177
Seaside borders three fairways on this links course. There are 28 bunkers and undulating fairways to add to the challenge of the variable and strong winds that blow at all times and change with the tides. There are no easy holes!
9 holes, 5598mtrs, Par 70, SSS 69.
Club membership 350.
Visitors restricted Wed, Thu, weekends & bankholidays.
Societies apply in writing.
Green Fees not confirmed.
Facilities ♀ ⏶
Hotel B Forte Posthouse Dublin, Cloghran, DUBLIN
☎ 01 8444211 188 ⇥ 🐾

SKERRIES

Map 01 D4

Skerries Hacketstown
☎ 01 8491567
Tree-lined parkland course on gently rolling countryside, with sea views from some holes. The 1st and 18th are particularly challenging. The club can be busy on some days, but is always friendly.
18 holes, 6081mtrs, Par 73, SSS 72.
Club membership 800.
Visitors must contact in advance but may not play at weekends.
Societies must contact well in advance in writing.
Green Fees IR£18 per round (IR£22.50 weekends).
Facilities ⊗ ⫼ ⃦ ⃦ ♀ ⏶ 🏨 🕪 ʃ Jimmy Kinsella.
Leisure buggies for hire, trolley for hire, putting green, practice area.
Hotel ★★★ 65% Boyne Valley Hotel, DROGHEDA
☎ 041 37737 35 ⇥ 🐾

TALLAGHT

Map 01 D4

Ballinascorney Ballinascorney
☎ 01 4516430
A meadowland course founded in 1971.
18 holes, 5465yds, Par 71, SSS 67.
Club membership 500.
Visitors welcome weekdays. Weekends after 4pm.
Societies contact for details.
Green Fees not confirmed.
Facilities ♀ ⏶
Leisure putting green,practice area,trolley hire.
Location 10m SW of Dublin
Hotel ★★★ 61% Doyle Green Isle Hotel, Naas Rd, DUBLIN 12
☎ 01 4593406 48 ⇥ 🐾Annexe35 ⇥ 🐾

> Entries with a shaded background identify courses that are considered to be particularly interesting

CO GALWAY

BALLINASLOE

Map 01 B4

Ballinasloe Rosglos ☎ 0905 42126
Well maintained parkland course, recently extended from a par 68 to a par 72.
18 holes, 5868metres, Par 72, SSS 70.
Club membership 840.
Visitors contact in advance.
Societies contact in advance.
Green Fees IR£14 daily.
Facilities ⊗ ⫼ ⃦ ⃦ ♀ ⏶
Leisure trolley for hire, putting green, practice area.
Hotel ★★★ 67% Hayden's Hotel, BALLINASLOE
☎ 0905 42347 50 ⇥ 🐾

BALLYCONNEELY

Map 01 A4

Connemara ☎ 095 23502 & 23602
This championship links course is situated on the verge of the Atlantic Ocean in a most spectacular setting, with the Twelve Bens Mountains in the background. Established as recently as 1973, it is a tough challenge, due in no small part to its exposed location, with the back 9 the equal of any in the world. The last six holes are exceptionally long.
18 holes, 6173mtrs, Par 72, SSS 73, Course record 68.
Club membership 700.
Visitors advisable to book in advance.
Societies telephone in advance.
Green Fees May-Sep IR£25 (other times IR£16).
Facilities ⊗ ⫼ ⃦ ⃦ ♀ ⏶ 🏨 🕪
Leisure motorised carts for hire, buggies for hire, trolley for hire, putting green, practice area.
Location 9m SW of Clifton
Hotel ★★★ 69% Abbeyglen Castle Hotel, Sky Rd, CLIFDEN ☎ 095 21201 40 ⇥ 🐾

GALWAY

Map 01 B4

Galway Blackrock, Salthill ☎ 091 22033
Designed by Dr Alister MacKenzie, this course is inland by nature, although some of the fairways run close to the ocean. The terrain is of gently sloping hillocks with plenty of trees and furze bushes to catch out the unwary. Although not a long course, it provided a worthy challenge as the venue of the Celtic International Tournament in 1984 and continues to delight the visiting golfer.
18 holes, 6376yds, Par 70, SSS 70.
Club membership 1050.
Visitors preferred on weekdays, except Tue.
Societies must apply in writing.
Green Fees not confirmed.
Facilities ♀ ⏶ 🏨 🕪 ʃ Don Wallace.
Leisure trolley hire.
Location 2m W in Salthill
Hotel ★★ 58% Lochlurgain Hotel, 22 Monksfield, Upper Salthill, GALWAY
☎ 091 22122 due to change to 529595 13 ⇥ 🐾
Additional hotel ★★★★ 64% Ardilaun House Hotel, Taylor's Hill, GALWAY ☎ 091 21433 90 ⇥ 🐾
See advertisement on page 388.

PORTMARNOCK

PORTMARNOCK *Co Dublin* ☎ 01 8462968   Map 01 D4

John Ingham writes: The night before our fourball tackled
Portmarnock was spent, as I recall, in Dublin. Guinness in that city
seems smoother, while the conversation with locals, ranged from why
no southern Irish player ever won the Open to how such a small nation
can boast so many great writers, wits and actors.

I can thoroughly recommend this preparation, prior to facing one
of the world's great golfing challenges - providing you only intend
playing eighteen holes in one day! Frankly, you will have to reach into
the base of your golf bag to pull out every shot if you want to play to
your handicap on this superb links.

An opening birdie, downwind, made me wonder what the fuss was
about. Two hours later, with a backswing too fast and the breeze now
something near a gale, I decided that a test of 7182 yards off the back
tees was too man-size for me. Maybe it would be more enjoyable on a
calm, summer evening!

I remember the course not for the way it humiliated me, but for
the 1960 Canada Cup where I watched Sam Snead and Arnold Palmer
winning with such skillful play. Even so, both took 75 in one round
while scores by the mighty Gary Player ranged from 65 to 78.

There are no blind shots, unless you drive into sandhills. This is
natural golf with no unfair carries off the tee and the only damage to
your card is self-inflicted. True, there are a couple of holes of 560 yards
and the 522-yard 16th is frightening as you tee up in a fierce wind.

It's incredible to think that Portmarnock was 'discovered' almost
by accident in 1893 by a Mr Pickeman and the course architect, Ross.
They had rowed a boat from Sutton to the peninsula where they came
across a wilderness of bracken, duneland and natural-looking bunkers
made by God. They were inspired to create the course, built a shack for
a clubhouse and talked about the only real hazard left - a cow that
devoured golf balls.

Today it's so very different - with a modern clubhouse filled with
members delighted to belong to such an internationally well-known
establishment.

Visitors	contact in advance and confirm in writing. Restricted Saturday, Sunday and public holidays. Handicap certificate required
Societies	must contact in advance
Green fees	Monday-Friday (excluding public holidays) £IR60: Saturday, Sunday & public holidays – Men only £IR70 per day
Facilities	⊗ ⅷ ⅃ ⅄ (all day) ⚒ 📧 🍴 (Joey Purcell)
Location	12m from Dublin. 1m from village down Golf Rd

27 holes. Old Course: 18 holes,
7182 yds, Par 72, SSS 75, course
record 64 (Sandy Lyle)
New Course: 9 holes, 3478yds,
Par 37

WHERE TO STAY AND EAT NEARBY

HOTELS:
HOWTH
★★★ 66% Howth Lodge.
☎ 01 8321010. 46 (5 ⌂ 3 ⇄
38 ⇄ ⌂)

Ardilaun House Hotel

Taylors Hill, Galway
Telephone: 00 353 91 521433 Fax: 0035 91 521546

Originally a country mansion located in it's own 5 acres of Private grounds, 5 minutes from Galway city. The hotel has luxurious accommodation with 89 bedrooms, an award winning restaurant and leisure centre. Choose from six superb golf courses within close proximity, including the renowned Galway Bay Golf and Country Club. *Discounted group and midweek rates available.* Ample car parking.

Internet http://www.iol.ie/ardilaun   Email ardilaun@iol.ie

Glenlo Abbey Bushy Park ☎ 091 26666
A championship course overlooking the magnificent Lough Corrib but only 10 minutes from the centre of Galway city. Nine fairways but large double green with two flags and four tee postions allows 18 diffent holes. The Par 3, 4th hole is on an island-like green extending into the lough.
9 holes, Par 72, SSS 72.
Visitors   no restrictions.
Societies   telephone in advance.
Green Fees not confirmed.
Facilities   ♀ ♨ 🏠 ⛳ ⊨
Leisure   fishing, sauna, gymnasium.
Location   On N59 Galway/Clifden rd
Hotel   ★★★★♨♨ 69% Glenlo Abbey, Bushypark, GALWAY
                  ☎ 091 526666 45 ⇄ 🐾

GORT   Map 01 B3

Gort Laughtyshaughnessy ☎ 091 31336
Replacing the original 9-hole course, this new 18-hole course, opened in June 1996, offers golfers a real challenge. The 564yd 9th and the 516yd 17th are played into a prevailing wind and the par 4 gog-leg 7th will test the best.
18 holes, 6538yds, Par 71.
Club membership 350.
Visitors   telephone in advance.
Societies   must contact in advance.
Green Fees £10 per day.
Facilities   ♨ ♥ ♀ ♨
Leisure   putting green, practice area.
Hotel   ★★★ 67% Galway Ryan Hotel, Dublin Rd, GALWAY
                  ☎ 091 753181 96 ⇄ 🐾

LOUGHREA   Map 01 B3

Loughrea Bullaun Rd, Graigue ☎ 091 841049
An excellent parkland course with good greens and extended in 1992 to 18-holes. The course has an unusual feature in that it incorporates a historic souterrain (underground shelter/food store).
9 holes, 5261metres, Par 69, SSS 67, Course record 68.
Club membership 615.
Visitors   contact in advance, may not generally play Sun.
Societies   written application required. Anytime weekdays, 9-11.30 Sat, no play Sun.
Green Fees IR£10 per day (IR£12 weekends and bank holidays).
Facilities   ♨ ♥ ♀ ♨
Leisure   trolley for hire, putting green, practice area.
Hotel   ★★★ 67% Hayden's Hotel, BALLINASLOE
                  ☎ 0905 42347 50 ⇄ 🐾

MOUNTBELLEW   Map 01 B4

Mountbellew Ballinasloe ☎ 0905 79259
A 9-hole wooded parkland course with 2 quarries and penalty drains to provide hazards.
9 holes, 5143mtrs, Par 69, SSS 66.
Visitors   welcome.
Societies   by prior arrangement.
Green Fees not confirmed.
Facilities
Location   Of N63 midway between Roscommon/Galway
Hotel   ★★★ 67% Hayden's Hotel, BALLINASLOE
                  ☎ 0905 42347 50 ⇄ 🐾

ORANMORE   Map 01 B3

Athenry Palmerstown ☎ 091 794466
Wooded parkland course, recently extended to 18 holes.
18 holes, 5552metres, Par 70, SSS 69, Course record 70.
Club membership 800.
Visitors   advisable to telephone in advance, may not play Sun.
Societies   must apply in writing for booking to the secretary.
Green Fees IR£15 per day.
Facilities   ⊗ ⋔ ♨ ♥ ♀ ♨ 🏠 ⛳ ⛳ Declan Cummingham.
Leisure   buggies for hire, trolley for hire, putting green, practice area.
Hotel   ★★★ 67% Galway Ryan Hotel, Dublin Rd, GALWAY
                  ☎ 091 753181 96 ⇄ 🐾

Galway Bay Golf & Country Club Renville
☎ 091 790500
A championship golf course surrounded on three sides by the Atlantic Ocean and featuring water hazards on a number of holes. Each hole has its own characteristics made more obvious by the everchanging seaside winds.
18 holes, 6091mtrs, Par 72, SSS 71.
Club membership 400.
Visitors   contact in advance.
Societies   contact in advance.
Green Fees IR£25 per round (IR£30 weekends & bank holidays).
Facilities   ⊗ ⋔ ♨ ♥ ♀ ♨ 🏠 ⛳
                  ⛳ Eugene O'Connor.
Leisure   sauna, motorised carts for hire, buggies for hire, trolley for hire, driving range, putting green, practice area.
Hotel   ★★★★♨♨ 69% Glenlo Abbey, Bushypark, GALWAY
                  ☎ 091 526666 45 ⇄ 🐾

OUGHTERARD
Map 01 B4

Oughterard ☎ 091 82131
Well maintained parkland course with mature trees and shrubs. Some very challenging holes.
18 holes, 6150yds, Par 70, SSS 69, Course record 67.
Club membership 630.
Visitors contact secretary in advance.
Societies must apply in writing, 12 mths notice required for weekend play
Green Fees IR£15 per day; married couple IR£25.
Facilities ⊗ ⅢⅢ ⅃ ⅃ ⅃ ⅃ ⅃ Michael Ryan.
Leisure motorised carts for hire, buggies for hire, trolley for hire, driving range, putting green, practice area.
Location 1m from town on Galway road
Hotel ★★★ 65% Connemara Gateway Hotel, OUGHTERARD ☎ 091 82328 62 ⇥ ♞

PORTUMNA
Map 01 B3

Portumna ☎ 0509 41059
Parkland course with mature trees.
18 holes, 5474mtrs, Par 68, SSS 67, Course record 68.
Club membership 650.
Visitors restricted Sun & public holidays.
Societies must contact in writing.
Green Fees IR£12 per day.
Facilities ⊗ by prior arrangement ⅢⅢ by prior arrangement ⅃ ⅃ ⅃ ⅃ ⅃
Leisure trolley for hire, putting green, practice area.
Location 2.5m from town on Woodford/Ennis road
Hotel ★★ 66% County Arms Hotel, BIRR ☎ 0509 20791 & 20193 18 ⇥ ♞

RENVYLE
Map 01 A4

Renvyle House Hotel ☎ 095 43511
Pebble Beach course at Renvyle House is an exceptionally demanding Par 3. Exposed to Atlantic winds, crosswinds are a regular feature. A lake comes into play on 3 holes on one of which is a drive over water. On 4 holes pebble beach and the sea demand precision.
9 holes, 2000yds, Par 32.
Visitors must contact in advance.
Societies contact in advance.
Green Fees IR£10 per day.
Facilities ⊗ ⅢⅢ ⅃ ⅃ ⅃ ⅃ ⅃ ⅃ Gus Murphy.
Leisure hard tennis courts, heated outdoor swimming pool, fishing, trolley for hire, putting green, croquet, bowling.
Hotel ★★★ 68% Renvyle House Hotel, RENVYLE ☎ 095 43511 65 ⇥ ♞

TUAM
Map 01 B4

Tuam Barnacurragh ☎ 093 28993
Interesting course with plenty of trees and bunkers.
18 holes, 6377yds, Par 73, SSS 70.
Visitors preferred Mon-Fri.
Green Fees not confirmed.
Facilities ⅃ ⅃ ⅃
Location 0.5m from town on Athenry road
Hotel ★★★★ 64% Ardilaun House Hotel, Taylor's Hill, GALWAY ☎ 091 21433 90 ⇥ ♞

CO KERRY

BALLYBUNION
Map 01 A3

BALLYBUNION See page 391

BALLYFERRITER
Map 01 A2

Ceann Sibeal ☎ 066 56255 & 56408
This most westerly golf course in Europe has a magnificent scenic location. It is a traditional links course with beautiful turf, many bunkers, a stream that comes into play on 14 holes and, usually, a prevailing wind.
18 holes, 6700yds, Par 72, SSS 71, Course record 72.
Club membership 432.
Visitors telephone in advance.
Societies must contact in advance.
Green Fees IR£27 per day; IR£21 per round.
Facilities ⊗ ⅢⅢ ⅃ ⅃ ⅃ ⅃ ⅃ ⅃ Dermot O'Connor.
Leisure trolley for hire, putting green, practice area.
Hotel ★★★ 70% Skellig Hotel, DINGLE ☎ 066 51144 115 ⇥ ♞

CASTLEGREGORY
Map 01 A2

Castlegregory Stradbally
☎ 066 39444
A links course sandwiched between the sea and a freshwater lake and mountains on two sides. The 3rd hole is visually superb with a 365yard drive into the wind.
9 holes, 2569mtrs, Par 68, SSS 68, Course record 67.
Club membership 200.
Visitors advisable to contact in advance.
Societies apply in advance.
Green Fees IR£12 per 18 holes.
Facilities ⊗ ⅢⅢ ⅃ ⅃ ⅃ ⅃
Leisure fishing, trolley for hire, putting green.
Hotel ★★★ 64% The Brandon Hotel, TRALEE ☎ 066 23333 160 ⇥ ♞

GLENBEIGH
Map 01 A2

Dooks ☎ 066 68205
Old-established course on the sea shore between the Kerry mountains and Dingle Bay. Sand dunes are a feature (the name Dooks is a derivation of the Gaelic word for sand bank) and the course offers a fine challenge in a superb Ring of Kerry location.
18 holes, 6010yds, Par 70, SSS 68.
Club membership 750.
Visitors must contact in advance.
Societies contact in advance.
Green Fees IR£18 per day.
Facilities ⊗ ⅢⅢ ⅃ ⅃ ⅃ ⅃ ⅃
Leisure trolley for hire, putting green.
Hotel ★★★ 64% Gleneagle Hotel, KILLARNEY ☎ 064 31870 177 ⇥ ♞

KENMARE

Map 01 B2

Kenmare Kilgarvan Rd ☎ 064 41291
Extended to a championship 18-hole course in 1993 this
challenging parkland course enjoys a magnificent setting
where the cascading waters of the Sheen and Roughty rivers
join the Atlantic. Although it can be exacting on a good
golfer, it is never unfair to the weak or the novice golfer.
18 holes, 5615yds, Par 71.
Club membership 400.
Visitors   enquire for weekends.
Societies   contact in advance.
Green Fees IR£12.50 per 18 holes.
Facilities ⓑ ☰ ♀ ♨ ☞
Leisure   trolley for hire, putting green, practice area.
Hotel   ★★★★(red)♨ Park Hotel Kenmore,
                KENMARE ☎ 064 41200 49 ➪ ☏

KILLARNEY

Map 01 B2

Beaufort Churchtown, Beauford
☎ 064 44440
A championship standard Par 71 parkland course designed by
Dr Arthur Spring. This relatively new course is in the centre
of south-west Ireland's golfing mecca. Old ruins of an 11th
century castle dominate the back nine and the whole course is
overlooked by the MacGillycuddy Reeks. The Par 3 8th and
Par 4 11th are two of the most memorable holes.
18 holes, 6149yds, Par 71, SSS 72.
Club membership 150.
Visitors   booking advisable for weekends.
Societies   advance booking essential.

Green Fees IR£25 per round,IR£10 second round (IR£28,
                IR£12 weekends).
Facilities ⊗ ☰ ⓑ ☰ ♀ ♨ ☞
Leisure   motorised carts for hire, buggies for hire, trolley
                for hire, putting green, practice area.
Location   7m W of Killarney, off R562
Hotel   ★★★ 64% Castlerosse Hotel, KILLARNEY
                ☎ 064 31144 110 ➪ ☏

Killarney Golf & Fishing Club Mahony's Point
☎ 064 31034
Both of the courses are parkland with tree-lined fairways,
many bunkers and small lakes which provide no mean
challenge. Mahoney's Point Course has a particularly
testing par 5, 4, 3 finish and both courses call for great
skill from the tee. Killarney has been the venue for many
important events, including the Irish Open in 1991, and is
a favourite of many famous golfers
*Mahony's Point: 18 holes, 5826mtrs, Par 72, SSS 72,
Course record 68.*
*Killeen: 18 holes, 6474mtrs, Par 72, SSS 73, Course
record 65.*
Club membership 1300.
Visitors   must contact in advance & have a handicap
                certificate.
Societies   must telephone in advance.
Green Fees IR£33 per round.
Facilities ⊗ ☰ ⓑ ☰ ♀ ♨ ☰ ☞ ☏ Tony Coveney.
Leisure   sauna, gymnasium, trolley for hire, putting
                green, practice area.
Location   On Ring of Kerry road
Hotel   ★★★★ 76% Aghadoe Heights Hotel,
                KILLARNEY
                ☎ 064 31766 60 ➪ ☏
Additional ★★★ 64% Gleneagle Hotel,
hotel   KILLARNEY
                ☎ 064 31870 177 ➪ ☏

KILLORGLIN

Map 01 A2

Killorglin Stealroe ☎ 066 61979
A parkland course designed by Eddie Hackett as a
challenging but fair test of golf.
18 holes, 6497yds, Par 72, SSS 71, Course record 68.
Club membership 200.
Visitors   pre booking of tee time advisable.
Societies   apply in writing.
Green Fees IR£12 per 18 holes (IR£14 weekends & bank
                holidays).
Facilities ⊗ ☰ ⓑ ☰ ♀ ♨ ☰ ☞
Leisure   fishing, trolley for hire.
Location   3km from Killorglin, on N70 to Tralee
Hotel   ★★★ 64% The Brandon Hotel, TRALEE
                ☎ 066 23333 160 ➪ ☏

PARKNASILLA

Map 01 A2

Parknasilla ☎ 064 45122
Short, tricky 9-hole course, with 18·different tees which make
the second 9 more interesting.
9 holes, 2447yds, Par 70, SSS 65.
Club membership 90.
Visitors   may not play on competition days.
Societies   must contact in advance.
Green Fees not confirmed.

▶

BALLYBUNION

BALLYBUNION *Co Kerry* ☎ 068 27146   **Map 01 A3**

*J*ohn Ingham writes: Since golf is a state of mind over muscle and a great day on the links is exhilarating, it is my view that memorable fairways tend not to be decorated with artificial lakes that are fun only for ducks and golf ball manufacturers.

Some of the best courses look natural, even though they may have been helped along by skilful architects such as Colt, Hawtree or Mackenzie. And in the Emerald Isle, it is entirely appropriate that, back in 1906, a Mr Murphy built Ballybunion on the West Coast of Ireland. Believe me, there are few greater adventures waiting to be tackled and not to play this old course is a crime.

In an American list of the world's top 100 courses, Ballybunion is in there at number eight and the reason is simple: it probably represents the ultimate links on as wild a stretch as you will find. The Atlantic waves crash into the shore and no golfer will ever feel closer to nature as he hunts his ball and flights it through crosswinds and breathtaking views. This course is a star even in a part of Ireland that is wall-to-wall golf courses of the highest calibre. The experience of taking on this classic will be remembered as long as you live.

There are now two courses at Ballybunion, separated only by a 19th hole that has heard all the wondrous stories before, as well as hosting such great names as Tom Watson, five times winner of the Open. Likeable Tom can't speak highly enough of the place and claims that before anyone builds a golf course, they should play Ballybunion.

Visitors	must contact in advance, preferred Mon-Fri
Societies	must book in advance
Green fees	Old Course: £IR45 per round; Cashen Course: £IR30 per round. Both courses IR£65
Facilities	⊗ ⪥ ⅄ ⏴ ♨ ⅋ ⏏ ☋ ⅃ caddy cars, putting green, practice area, trolleys
Leisure	private fishing, sauna
Location	Sandhill Rd

36 holes. Old Course: 18 holes, 6603 yds, Par 71, SSS 72
Carshen Course: 18 holes, 6477 yds, Par 72

WHERE TO STAY AND EAT NEARBY

HOTELS:
BALLYHEIGE

★★★⊛ 58% The White Sands
☎: 066 33102 75. ⊶ ⋔

Facilities ♀️⛳🏌️‍♂️🏇♣ Charles McCarthy.
Leisure hard tennis courts, heated indoor swimming pool, sauna, trolley hire,clay pigeon shooting.
Hotel ★★★★ 74% Great Southern Hotel, PARKNASILLA
   ☎ 064 45122 25 ⇄ ♣Annexe59 ⇄ ♣

TRALEE   Map 01 A2

Tralee West Barrow ☎ 066 36379
The first Arnold Palmer designed course in Europe, the magnificent 18-hole links are set in spectacular scenery on the Barrow peninsula. Perhaps the most memorable hole is the par four 17th which plays from a high tee, across a deep gorge to a green perched high against a backdrop of mountains.
18 holes, 5961mtrs, Par 73.
Club membership 1000.
Visitors may play before 4.30pm on weekdays but only 10.30am-12.15pm on Wed & 11am-12.30pm at weekends & bank holidays. Must have a handicap certificate.
Societies weekdays only; must contact in writing.
Green Fees not confirmed.
Facilities ♀️⛳📶
Leisure buggy/trolley hire.
Location 8m W of Tralee on Spa-Fenit road
Hotel ★★★ 64% The Brandon Hotel, TRALEE
   ☎ 066 23333 160 ⇄ ♣

WATERVILLE   Map 01 A2

Waterville House & Golf Links ☎ 066 74102
On the western tip of the Ring of Kerry, this course is highly regarded by many top golfers. The feature holes are the par five 11th, which runs along a rugged valley between towering dunes, and the par three 17th, which features an exceptionally elevated tee. Needless to say, the surroundings are beautiful.
18 holes, 6549yds, Par 72.
Visitors must contact in advance.
Societies must contact secretary/manager in advance.
Green Fees IR£40 per round.
Facilities ⊗ ♍ ▙ ☕ ♀️⛳📶🏌️‍♂️🏇♣ Liam Higgins.
Leisure heated outdoor swimming pool, fishing, sauna, motorised carts for hire, buggies for hire, trolley for hire, driving range, putting green, practice area.
Hotel ★★★ 57% Derrynane Hotel, CAHERDANIEL ☎ 066 75136 75 ⇄

● CO KILDARE ●

ATHY   Map 01 C3

Athy Geraldine ☎ 0507 31729
A meadowland course approaching its centenary year having been founded in 1906.
18 holes, 5500mtrs, Par 72, SSS 69, Course record 69.
Club membership 400.

Visitors welcome weekdays.
Societies contact for infromation.
Green Fees not confirmed.
Facilities ♀️⛳
Leisure putting,trolley hire,practice area.
Location 2m N of Athy
Hotel ★★ 60% Hotel Montague, Portlaoise, EMO
   ☎ 0502 26154 75 ⇄ ♣

CARBURY   Map 01 C4

Highfield Highfield House ☎ 0405 31021
A relatively flat parkland course but with interesting undulations, especially by the fast flowing stream which runs through many holes. The 7th doglegs over the lake, the 10th is a great Par 5 with a challenging green, the 14th Par 3 over rushes onto a plateau green (out of bounds on lift) and the 18th Par 3 green is tucked between bunkers and a huge chestnut tree.
18 holes, 5707mtrs, Par 72, SSS 69.
Club membership 400.
Visitors welcome, must contact in advance for weekend play.
Societies telephone or apply in writing.
Green Fees IR£7 per day (IR£10 weekends & bank holidays).
Facilities ▙ ⛳🏌️‍♂️
Leisure trolley for hire, driving range, practice area, putting green.
Location 9m from Enfield
Hotel ★★ 59% Curryhills House Hotel, PROSPEROUS
   ☎ 045 868150 10 ⇄ ♣

CASTLEDERMOT   Map 01 C3

Kilkea Castle ☎ 0503 45156
A beautiful new course opened in the summer of 1994 in the grounds of a 12th-century castle - visible from all over the course. The River Griese and two lakes create numerous water hazards.
18 holes, 6200mtrs, Par 71.
Visitors welcome contact for details.
Societies welcome, contact for details.
Green Fees not confirmed.
Facilities ♀️⛳📶

DONADEA   Map 01 C4

Knockanally Golf & Country Club ☎ 045 69322
Home of the Irish International Professional Matchplay championship, this parkland course is set in a former estate, with a Palladian-style clubhouse.
18 holes, 6485yds, Par 72, SSS 72.
Club membership 500.
Visitors may not play on Sun 8.30am-noon.
Societies must contact in writing or telephone.
Green Fees not confirmed.
Facilities ♀️⛳📶🏌️‍♂️♣ Peter Hickey.
Leisure fishing, putting green,practice area,trolley hire.
Location 3m off main Dublin-Galway road
Hotel ★★ 59% Curryhills House Hotel, PROSPEROUS
   ☎ 045 868150 10 ⇄ ♣

KILDARE

Map 01 C3

Cill Dara Cill Dara, Little Curragh
☎ 045 21295
Only 1 mile from the famous Curragh racecourse, this 9-hole parkland course is unusual in having links type soil as well as plenty of trees.
9 holes, 5738mtrs, Par 71, SSS 70, Course record 64.
Club membership 450.
Visitors   welcome.
Societies   apply in writing to Mr J Commins, Society
                 Secretary.
Green Fees not confirmed.
Facilities   ♀ ♨ 🏠 ⌇ J Bulger.
Leisure   putting green,trolley hire.
Location   1m E of Kildare
Hotel   ★★ 60% Hotel Montague, Portlaoise, EMO
                 ☎ 0502 26154 75 ➡ 🐾

Curragh Curragh ☎ 045 41238
A particularly challenging course, well wooded and with lovely scenery all around.
18 holes, 6003mtrs, Par 72, SSS 71.
Club membership 900.
Visitors   preferred on Mon, Thu & Fri.
Societies   apply in writing.
Green Fees not confirmed.
Facilities   ♀ ♨ 🏠 � ⌇ Phil Lawlor.
Leisure   putting green,practice area,trolley hire.
Location   Off N7 between Newbridge & Kildare
Hotel   ★★ 59% Curryhills House Hotel,
                 PROSPEROUS ☎ 045 868150 10 ➡ 🐾

KILL

Map 01 D4

Killeen ☎ 045 866003 & 866045
Set in pleasant countryside, the attractive course is characterised by its many lakes. It provides a challenge to test the skills of the moderate enthusiast and the more experienced golfer.
18 holes, 5561mtrs, Par 71, SSS 70.
Visitors   please ring for tee-times
Societies   must contact in advance.
Green Fees IR£13 per round (IR£15 weekends & bank
                 holidays).
Facilities   ⊗ ⵗ ♨ 🐟 ♀ ♨ 🏠 ⵟ
Leisure   trolley for hire, putting green, practice area.
Location   Off N7 at Kill signposted
Hotel   ★★★ 75% Barberstown Castle, STRAFFAN
                 ☎ 01 6288157 & 6288206 10 ➡ 🐾

NAAS

Map 01 D4

Bodenstown Sallins ☎ 045 897096
The old course in Bodenstown has ample fairways and large greens, some of which are raised, providing more than a fair test of golf. The Ladyhill course is a little shorter and tighter, but still affords a fair challenge.
Bodenstown: 18 holes, 6132mtrs, Par 71, SSS 71.
Ladyhill: 18 holes, 5428mtrs, Par 71, SSS 68.
Club membership 700.
Visitors   may not play on Bodenstown course at
                 weekends.
Societies   must contact by telephone.

Green Fees £10 per round; £8 weekends (Ladyhill Course).
Facilities   ⊗ ⵗ 🐟 ♨ 🐟 ♀ ♨
Leisure   trolley for hire, putting green, practice area.
Location   4m from town near Bodenstown graveyard
Hotel   ★★★ 56% Downshire House Hotel,
                 BLESSINGTON ☎ 045 865199 14 ➡
                 🐾Annexe11 ➡ 🐾

Naas Kerdiffstown ☎ 045 897509
Scenic parkland course with different tees for the return 9.
9 holes, 3000mtrs, Par 36, SSS 70, Course record 68.
Club membership 800.
Visitors   may not play on Sun, Tue or Thu.
Societies   must contact in advance.
Green Fees not confirmed.
Facilities   ♀ ♨
Location   1m from town on Sallins-Johnstown road
Hotel   ★★★ 56% Downshire House Hotel,
                 BLESSINGTON
                 ☎ 045 865199 14 ➡ 🐾Annexe11 ➡ 🐾

Woodlands Cooleragh, Coill Dubh ☎ 045 860777
Interesting 9-hole course currently undergoing reconstruction. The orientation of play will change to clockwise from its present anti-clockwise direction, with new greens, tees and additional ground coming into play, making it a more challenging round in 1997.
9 holes, 5292yds, Par 68, SSS 66, Course record 71.
Club membership 325.
Visitors   must contact in advance.
Societies   telephone in advance for details.
Green Fees IR£6 per 18 holes (IR£7 weekends).
Facilities   ⊗ 🐟 ♨ ♀ ♨
Leisure   trolley for hire, putting green, practice area.
Location   Off the Clane/Edenderry road
Hotel   ★★★ 68% Keadeen Hotel, NEWBRIDGE
                 ☎ 045 431666 37 ➡ 🐾

STRAFFAN

Map 01 D4

Castlewarden ☎ 01 4588218 & 4589254
Founded in 1990, Castlewarden is maturing into a delightful parkland course.
18 holes, 6452ydss, Par 72, SSS 70.
Club membership 646.
Visitors   welcome contact for details.
Societies   by prior application.
Green Fees IR£12 (IR£16 weekends).
Facilities   ⊗ ⵗ 🐟 ♨ ♀ ♨ 🏠 ⌇ Gerry Egan.
Leisure   trolley for hire, putting green, practice area.
Location   Between Naas/Newlands Cross
Hotel   ★★★★★(red)♨ The Kildare Hotel & Country
                 Club, STRAFFAN
                 ☎ 01 6273333 36 ➡ 🐾Annexe7 ➡ 🐾

Kildare Hotel & Country Club ☎ 01 6273333
Known as The K-Club, this course is growing in reputation. Designed by Arnold Palmer, its 6,456 metre length is a challenge to even the best golfers. Covering 177 acres of prime Kildare woodland there are 14 man-made lakes as well as the River Liffey to create water hazards. There is the promise of a watery grave at the monster 7th (Par 5, 520 metres) and at the 17th the tee shot is to the green on the water's edge. There is also a practise area and driving range.
                                              ▶

18 holes, 6163mtrs, Par 72, SSS 72, Course record 68.
Club membership 390.
Visitors contact in advance, restricted at members times.
Societies telephone & write in advance, societies not allowed on weekends & Wed afternoon.
Green Fees IR£100.
Facilities ⊗ ⅏ ⅃ ⅂ ♀ ♨ 🏠 ⚑ ⛳ ℓ Ernie Jones.
Leisure hard tennis courts, heated indoor swimming pool, squash, fishing, sauna, solarium, gymnasium, buggies for hire, trolley for hire, driving range, practice area, driving range, tuition, horseriding,.
Hotel ★★★★★(red)⚐ The Kildare Hotel & Country Club, STRAFFAN ☎ 01 6273333 36 ⇥ ℟Annexe7 ⇥ ℟

18 holes, 5857mtrs, Par 71, SSS 70, Course record 65.
Club membership 1000.
Visitors must contact in advance.
Societies must contact in advance.
Green Fees IR£20 per day (IR£22 weekends & bank holidays).
Facilities ⊗ ⅏ ⅃ ⅂ ♀ ♨ 🏠 ⚑ ⛳ ℓ Noel Leahy.
Leisure buggies for hire, trolley for hire, driving range, putting green, practice area.
Location 1m from centre on Castlecomer road
Hotel ★★★ 68% Hotel Kilkenny, College Rd, KILKENNY ☎ 056 62000 80 ⇥ ℟

THOMASTOWN
Map 01 C3

MOUNT JULIET HOTEL GOLF COURSE See page 395

CO KILKENNY

CALLAN
Map 01 C3

Callan Geraldine ☎ 056 25136 & 25949
Meadowland.
9 holes, 5722mtrs, Par 72, SSS 70, Course record 67.
Club membership 500.
Visitors welcome. Weekend play by prior arrangement.
Societies must apply in writing.
Green Fees IR£11 per round.
Facilities ⊗ ⅏ ⅃ ⅂ ♀ ♨ 🏠 ⚑
Leisure fishing, trolley for hire, putting green.
Hotel ★★★ 68% Hotel Kilkenny, College Rd, KILKENNY ☎ 056 62000 80 ⇥ ℟

CASTLECOMER
Map 01 C3

Castlecomer Drumgoole ☎ 056 41139
9 holes, 5923mtrs, Par 71, SSS 71, Course record 65.
Club membership 500.
Visitors welcome Mon-Sat book in advance.
Societies welcome Mon-Sat.
Green Fees not confirmed.
Facilities ♀ ♨
Leisure practice area.
Location 10m N of Kilkenny
Hotel ★★★ 68% Newpark Hotel, KILKENNY ☎ 056 22122 84 ⇥ ℟

KILKENNY
Map 01 C3

Kilkenny Glendine ☎ 056 65400 & 22125
One of Ireland's most pleasant inland courses, noted for its tricky finishing holes and its par threes. Features of the course are its long 11th and 13th holes and the challenge increases year by year as thousands of trees planted over the last 30 years or so are maturing. As host of the Kilkenny Scratch Cup annually, the course is permanently maintained in championship condition. The Irish Dunlop Tournament and the Irish Professional Matchplay Championship have also been held here.

CO LAOIS

ABBEYLEIX
Map 01 C3

Abbeyleix Rathmoyle ☎ 0502 31450 & 31229
9 holes, 5626mtrs, Par 70, SSS 68.
Club membership 300.
Visitors welcome.
Societies apply in writing.
Green Fees not confirmed.
Facilities ⊗ by prior arrangement ⅏ ⅃ ⅂ ♀ ♨
Leisure putting green, practice area.
Hotel ★★★ 62% Killeshin Hotel, Dublin Rd, PORTLAOISE ☎ 0502 21663 44 ⇥ ℟

MOUNTRATH
Map 01 C3

Mountrath Knockanina ☎ 0502 32558
Small picturesque course at the foot of the Slieve Bloom Mountains in central Ireland. The course is in the process of being extended to 18 holes, due to be completed by summer 1994.
9 holes, 4634mtrs, Par 68, SSS 66.
Club membership 300.
Visitors no restrictions.
Societies must contact in advance.
Green Fees not confirmed.
Facilities ♀ ♨
Location 1.5m from town on Dublin-Limerick road
Hotel ★★★ 62% Killeshin Hotel, Dublin Rd, PORTLAOISE ☎ 0502 21663 44 ⇥ ℟

PORTARLINGTON
Map 01 C3

Portarlington Garryhinch ☎ 0502 23115
Lovely parkland course designed around a pine forest. It is bounded on the 16th and 17th by the River Barrow which makes the back 9 very challenging.
18 holes, 5673mtrs, Par 71, SSS 69.
Club membership 562.
▶

MOUNT JULIET

THOMASTOWN *Co Kilkenny*

☎ **056 24455**   **Map 01 C3**

Charlie Mulqueen writes: Nick Faldo and David Leadbetter are just two of the game's luminaries to have fallen in love with Mount Juliet, the only Jack Nicklaus designed golf course in Ireland. Faldo, perhaps, is somewhat biased given that he completed a hat-trick of Irish Open successes there in 1993.

Mount Juliet stands as a monument to the architectural ability of Nicklaus. The estate was acquired in the late '80s by Tim Mahony, who gave the Golden Bear a free hand. In return, Nicklaus delivered a 7100 yards, par 72 course of great quality and considerable charm. The hundreds of mature trees help to give the impression that the course has been here for centuries rather than just since 1991 - an occasion marked by a memorable exhibition between Nicklaus and Ireland's own great Christy O'Connor Senior. Since 1993 it has hosted the Murphy's Irish Open.

Mount Juliet's 'signature hole' arrives as early as the third, played from an elevated tee across an awesome lake to an island green. The golfer confronts a lot more water as the round progresses, especially at the perilous 13th, which has certainly proved unlucky for many of the contestants in each of the last three Irish Opens. Nor can even the best relax until they have completed the 470 yards, par four 18th. Again a lake comes into play all the way down the left and very frequently it requires two full woods to reach the long, narrow green. South African David Frost took 10 here in the opening round of the 1993 Irish Open and still hit back to finish third!

When the golf is over, the 1500 acres of the Mount Juliet estate offers many more attractions; horse riding, clay pigeon shooting or archery, fishing in the delightful River Nore or dinner in the superb 18th-century mansion transformed into a luxury hotel. And if the golf hasn't been up to requirements, up you get bright and early the following morning for a lesson on the magnificent David Leadbetter academy. Mount Juliet has it all - it's a must!

Visitors	no restrictions
Societies	book in advance by telephone
Green fees	Week days £IR65 (residents £IR35). Weekends £IR70 (residents £IR45)
Facilities	⊗ ⅻ ⅃ ⅃ ♀ ⌂ ♨ ☖ ⅂ ↑ ↿ (David Leadbetter Golf Academy) driving range, putting green, motor carts, practice area, trollies, caddy cars, caddies
Leisure	tennis, indoor swimming pool, private fishing, clay target shooting, archery, full leisure centre
Location	Dublin/Waterford rd Off the N9

18 holes, 7100yds, Par72 SSS 74
Course record 65 (Nick Faldo/John Daly)

WHERE TO STAY AND EAT NEARBY

HOTELS:

THOMASTOWN
★★★★ (Red) ✿✿ ⏣ Mount Juliet Hotel, ☎ 056 24455. 32 ⇆ ↾ Annexe 21 ⇆ ↾

KILKENNY
★★★ 68% Newpark Hotel ☎ 056 22122. 84 (25 ⇆ 59 ⇆ ↾)

★★★ 68% Hotel Kilkenny, College Rd ☎ 056 62000. 80 ⇆ ↾

Visitors welcome but restricted Tue-Ladies Day, Sat & Sun societies and club competitions.
Societies must apply in writing.
Green Fees IR£12 per round (IR£14 weekends & bank holidays).
Facilities ⊗ ⅷ ⅃ ⅃ ⅃ ⅃ ⅃
Leisure trolley for hire, putting green, practice area.
Location 4m from town on Mountmellick road
Hotel ★★ 60% Hotel Montague, Portlaoise, EMO
☎ 0502 26154 75 ⇆ ⟋

PORTLAOISE Map 01 C3

The Heath ☎ 0502 46533 & 46622 (Pro shop)
One of the oldest clubs in Ireland. The course is set in pretty countryside and offers a good challenge.
18 holes, 5736mtrs, Par 71, SSS 69, Course record 69.
Club membership 800.
Visitors contact in advance, preferred on weekdays.
Societies apply in advance.
Green Fees IR£16 per round (IR£10 weekends and bank holidays).
Facilities ⊗ ⅷ ⅃ ⅃ ⅃ ⅃ ⅃ ⅋ ⟋ ⟋ Eddie Doyle.
Leisure trolley for hire, driving range, putting green, practice area.
Location 3m N on N7
Hotel ★★★ 62% Killeshin Hotel, Dublin Rd, PORTLAOISE ☎ 0502 21663 44 ⇆ ⟋

RATHDOWNEY Map 01 C3

Rathdowney ☎ 0505 46170
A pleasant 9-hole course. 1st is difficult with out-of-bounds along the right. 5th, Par 3 has out-of-bounds very close to left. Plans are in hand for conversion to 18-holes.
9 holes, 6196yds, Par 70, SSS 69, Course record 70.
Club membership 230.
Visitors welcome. Ladies have priority on Wed, Sat & Sun mornings are reserved for member & societies.
Societies must apply in writing and pay deposit to confirm booking.
Green Fees IR£6 per day.
Facilities ⊗ by prior arrangement ⅷ by prior arrangement ⅃ by prior arrangement ⅃ by prior arrangement ⅃ ⅃
Location 0.5m SE
Hotel ★★★ 68% Hotel Kilkenny, College Rd, KILKENNY ☎ 056 62000 80 ⇆ ⟋

CO LEITRIM

BALLINAMORE Map 01 C4

Ballinamore ☎ 078 44346
A very dry and very testing 9-hole parkland course along the Ballinamore/Ballyconnell Canal.
9 holes, 5680yds, Par 68, SSS 66, Course record 66.
Club membership 100.
Visitors restricted occasionally.
Societies must contact in writing.

Green Fees not confirmed.
Facilities ⅃ ⅃
Leisure fishing.
Hotel ★★ 64% Royal Hotel, BOYLE
☎ 079 62016 16 ⇆ ⟋

CO LIMERICK

ADARE Map 01 B3

Adare Manor ☎ 061 396204
An 18-hole parkland course, Par 69, in an unusual setting. In the grounds of an ancient monastery, the course surrounds the ruins of a castle, a friary and an abbey.
18 holes, 5800yds, Par 69, SSS 69.
Club membership 600.
Visitors for weekends it is adviable to contact in advance.
Societies by prior arrangement, preferably in writing.
Green Fees not confirmed.
Facilities ⅃ ⅃ ⅋
Leisure caddy cars & caddies available.
Hotel ★★★★(red)⚇ Adare Manor, ADARE
☎ 061 396566 28 ⇆ ⟋Annexe36 ⇆ ⟋

LIMERICK Map 01 B3

Castletroy Castletroy
☎ 061 335753 & 335261
Parkland course with out of bounds on the left of the first two holes. The long par five 10th features a narrow entrance to a green guarded by a stream. The par three 13th has a panoramic view of the course and surrounding countryside from the tee and the 18th is a daunting finish, with the drive played towards a valley with the ground rising towards the green which is protected on both sides by bunkers. In recent years the club has hosted the finals of the Irish Mixed Foursomes and the Senior Championships.
18 holes, 5793mtrs, Par 69, SSS 71.
Club membership 1066.
Visitors must contact in advance & have handicap certificate but may not play Sun or 1-2.30pm weekdays.
Societies must contact in advance.
Green Fees not confirmed.
Facilities ⅃ ⅃ ⅋ ⟋ ⟋ Noel Cassidy.
Leisure caddy cars & motorised buggy for hire.
Location 3m from city on Dublin road
Hotel ★★★★ 68% Castletroy Park Hotel, Dublin Rd, LIMERICK
☎ 061 335566 107 ⇆ ⟋

Limerick Ballyclough ☎ 061 415146 & 414083
Tree-lined parkland course which hosted the 1991 Ladies Senior Interprovincial matches. The club are the only Irish winners of the European Cup Winners Team Championship.
18 holes, 5938mtrs, Par 72, SSS 71, Course record 67.
Club membership 1300.
Visitors may not play after 4pm or on Tue & weekends.
Societies must contact in writing.
Green Fees IR£22.50 per round.
Facilities ⊗ ⅷ ⅃ ⅃ ⅃ ⅃ ⅃ ⅋ ⟋ ⟋ John Cassidy.

Leisure	trolley for hire, putting green, practice area.
Location	3m S on Fedamore Road
Hotel	★★★ 69% Jurys Hotel, Ennis Rd, LIMERICK ☎ 061 327777 94 ⇆ ♙

Limerick County Golf & Country Club Ballyneety
☎ 61 351881
Limerick County was designed by Des Smyth and presents beautifully because of the strategic locaton of the main features. It stretches over undulating terrain with one elevated section providing views of the surrounding countryside. It features over 70 bunkers with six lakes and several unique design features.
18 holes, 6712yds, Par 72, SSS 74, Course record 70.
Club membership 300.

Visitors	welcome but prebooking essential.
Societies	book by telephone or in writing.
Green Fees	IR£20 per round; IR£12.50 before 9.30am Mon-Fri..
Facilities	⊗ ⅲ ⅱ ⅱ ♀ ⚲ 🏠 ⟍ ⟊ ♩ Philip Murphy.
Leisure	sauna, buggies for hire, trolley for hire, driving range, golf school, jacuzzi.
Location	5m SE of Limerick on R512
Hotel	★★★ 66% Limerick Inn Hotel, Ennis Rd, LIMERICK ☎ 061 326666 153 ⇆

NEWCASTLE WEST   Map 01 B3

Killeline Cork Rd
☎ 069 61600
Set in 160 acres of gently contoured parkland in the heart of the Golden Vale with views to the Galtee Mountains. Because of its design and many mature trees, accuracy in playing is the key to good scoring.
18 holes, 5800yds, Par 70.
Club membership 400.

Visitors	welcome weekdays, by arrangement weekends.
Societies	telephone in advance.
Green Fees	IR£11 per 18 holes.
Facilities	⊗ ⅱ ⅱ ♀ ⚲ 🏠 ⟍
Leisure	trolley for hire, practice area.
Location	0.25m off main Limerick/Killarney route
Hotel	★★★ 76% Dunraven Arms Hotel, ADARE ☎ 061 396633 66 ⇆ ♙

Newcastle West Ardagh
☎ 069 76500
A new course set in 150 acres of unspoilt countryside, built to the highest standards on sandy free draining soil. A practice ground and driving range are included. Hazards on the course include lakes, bunkers, streams and trees. A signature hole is likely to be the Par 3 6th playing 185 yards over a lake.
18 holes, 6041yds, Par 71, SSS 73.
Club membership 620.

Visitors	advisable to contact in advance.
Societies	contact in advance.
Green Fees	IR£15 per day.
Facilities	⊗ ⅲ ⅱ ⅱ ♀ ⚲ 🏠 ⟍
Leisure	trolley for hire, driving range, putting green, practice area.
Location	2m off N21 between Limerick & Killarney
Hotel	★★★★(red)⚶ Adare Manor, ADARE ☎ 061 396566 28 ⇆ ♙Annexe36 ⇆ ♙

CO LONGFORD

LONGFORD   Map 01 C4

County Longford Glack, Dublin Rd ☎ 043 46310
A lovely 18-hole parkland course with lots of trees.
18 holes, 6044yds, Par 70, SSS 69, Course record 69.
Club membership 739.

Visitors	very welcome, but advisable to telephone in advance for Tue and Sun play.
Societies	by prior arrangement.
Green Fees	not confirmed.
Facilities	♀ ⚲
Leisure	buggy/trolley hire.
Location	E of town
Hotel	★★★ 58% Abbey Hotel, Galway Rd, ROSCOMMON ☎ 0903 26240 & 26505 25 ⇆ ♙

CO LOUTH

ARDEE   Map 01 D4

Ardee Townparks ☎ 041 53227
Pleasant parkland course with mature trees and a stream.
18 holes, 6100yds, Par 69, SSS 69.

Visitors	may normally play on weekdays (except Wed).
Green Fees	not confirmed.
Facilities	♀
Hotel	★★★ 65% Ballymascanlon House Hotel, DUNDALK ☎ 042 71124 36 ⇆

BALTRAY   Map 01 D4

County Louth ☎ 041 22329
Generally held to have the best greens in Ireland, this links course was designed by Tom Simpson to have well guarded and attractive greens without being overly dependant on bunkers. It provides a good test for the modern champion, notably as the annual venue for the East of Ireland Amateur Open.
18 holes, 6613yds, Par 73, SSS 71.
Club membership 1100.

Visitors	must contact in advance.
Societies	by prior arrangement.
Green Fees	IR£35 (IR£40 weekends).
Facilities	⊗ ⅲ ⅱ ⅱ ♀ ⚲ 🏠 ⟍ ⟊ ♩ Paddy McGuirk.
Leisure	hard tennis courts, buggies for hire, trolley for hire.
Location	5m NE of Drogheda
Hotel	★★ 60% Conyngham Arms Hotel, SLANE ☎ 041 24155 16rm(15 ⇆ ♙)

DUNDALK   Map 01 D4

Ballymascanlon House Hotel ☎ 042 71124
Now a testing 18-hole parkland course with numerous water hazards and two difficult holes through woodland, this very scenic course is set at the edge of the Cooley Mountains. ▶

18 holes, 5512yds, Par 68.
Visitors must telephone in advance to check availability.
Societies booking by telephone or letter.
Green Fees IR£10 per 18 holes (IR£14 weekends & bank holidays).
Facilities ⊗ ⅏ ⅃ ⅂ ♆ ⅄ ⅌ ⊷
Leisure a complete new complex is due to open October 1996.
Location 3m N of Dundalk on the Carlingford road
Hotel ★★★ 65% Ballymascanlon House Hotel, DUNDALK ☎ 042 71124 36 ⊷

Dundalk Blackrock ☎ 042 21731
A tricky course with extensive views.
18 holes, 6115mtrs, Par 72, SSS 72.
Club membership 1000.
Visitors must contact in advance and may not play Tue or Sun.
Societies must apply in writing in advance.
Green Fees not confirmed.
Facilities ⅂ ⅄ ⅌ ⅓ ⅟ James Cassidy.
Leisure sauna, putting green, practice area, trolley hire.
Location 2.5m S on coast road
Hotel ★★★ 65% Ballymascanlon House Hotel, DUNDALK ☎ 042 71124 36 ⊷

Killinbeg Killin Park ☎ 042 39303
Opened in 1991 and designed by Eddie Hackett, this undulating 12-hole parkland course has mature woodland and river features.
12 holes, 3322yds, Par 72, SSS 69.
Club membership 100.
Visitors no restrictions.
Societies apply by telephone or in writing in advance.
Green Fees not confirmed.
Facilities ⅂ ⅄ ⅟
Location Bridge-a-Crinn
Hotel ★★★ 65% Ballymascanlon House Hotel, DUNDALK ☎ 042 71124 36 ⊷

GREENORE   Map 01 D4

Greenore ☎ 042 73212 & 73678
Situated amidst beautiful scenery on the shores of Carlingford Lough, the trees here are an unusual feature on a links course. There are quite a number of water facilities, tight fairways and very good greens.
18 holes, 6506mtrs, Par 71, SSS 71.
Club membership 500.
Visitors must contact in advance at weekends. A letter of introduction is desirable, but not essential.
Societies must contact well in advance.

Green Fees not confirmed.
Facilities ⅂ ⅄
Leisure trolley hire.
Hotel ★★★ 65% Ballymascanlon House Hotel, DUNDALK ☎ 042 71124 36 ⊷

TERMONFECKIN   Map 01 D4

Seapoint ☎ 041 22333
A very long championship links course of 7,000 yards with a particularly interesting 17th hole.
18 holes, 5904yds, Par 72, SSS 71.
Club membership 330.
Visitors phone in advance for restrictions.
Societies apply in writing or telephone in advance.
Green Fees IR£22.50 per 18 holes (IR£27.50 weekends & bank holidays).
Facilities ⊗ ⅏ ⅃ ⅂ ♆ ⅄ ⅓ ⊷ ⅟ David Carroll.
Leisure trolley for hire, putting green, practice area.
Hotel ★★ 60% Conyngham Arms Hotel, SLANE ☎ 041 24155 16rm(15 ⊷ ⅟)

CO MAYO

BALLINA   Map 01 B4

Ballina Mossgrove, Shanaghy ☎ 096 21050
Undulating but mostly flat inland course. Planned to be extended to 18 holes during 1995.
18 holes, 5700yds, Par 70, SSS 68 or 5933yds.
Club membership 478.
Visitors welcome but may not play Sun before 3.30pm. Restrictions apply depending on competitions/society visits.
Societies apply in writing or telephone in advance.
Green Fees IR£16 per day.
Facilities ⅃ ♆ ⅂ ⅄ ⅟
Leisure trolley for hire, putting green.
Location 1m outside town on Bonnocolon Rd
Hotel ★★★ 57% Downhill Hotel, BALLINA ☎ 096 21033 50 ⊷ ⅟

BALLINROBE   Map 01 B4

Ballinrobe Cloonagashel ☎ 092 41118
Mainly flat terrain with some very interesting features. Although no other club plays on the course, its landlords, The Ballinrobe Race Company, hold races there five or six times a year.

18 holes, 4300mtrs, Par 73, SSS 73, Course record 69 or 60 holes.
9 holes, 5540yds, Par 72, SSS 68.
Club membership 420.

Visitors	welcome daily, telephone to reserve Tee-time.
Societies	must telephone or write to Secretary in advance.
Green Fees	IR£17.50 per day; 9-hole course IR£10.
Facilities	⊗ ⓑ ♨ ♀ ⚒ ⛳
Leisure	buggies for hire, trolley for hire, driving range, putting green, practice area.
Hotel	★★★ 62% Breaffy House Hotel, CASTLEBAR ☎ 094 22033 38 ⇋ ☏

BALLYHAUNIS
Map 01 B4

Ballyhaunis Coolnaha ☎ 0907 30014
Undulating parkland course with 9 holes, 10 greens and 18 tees.
18 holes, 5413mtrs, Par 70, SSS 68.
Club membership 340.

Visitors	welcome all times but must avoid members competitions on Sun & Thu.
Societies	must apply in writing or telephone.
Green Fees	IR£10 per day.
Facilities	by prior arrangement by prior arrangement ⓑ ♨ ♀ ⚒
Leisure	trolley for hire, putting green.
Hotel	★★★ 62% Breaffy House Hotel, CASTLEBAR ☎ 094 22033 38 ⇋ ☏

BELMULLET
Map 01 A5

Carne Carne ☎ 097 82292 & 81051
18 holes, 6042mtrs, Par 72.
Club membership 350.

Visitors	welcome, booking essential to guarantee tee-time.
Societies	booking advisable.
Green Fees	IR£17 per day (Mar-Oct); IR£11.50 (Nov-Feb).
Facilities	⊗ �𝄡 ⓑ ♨ ♀ ⚒ ⛳
Leisure	buggies for hire, trolley for hire.
Hotel	★★★ 57% Downhill Hotel, BALLINA ☎ 096 21033 50 ⇋ ☏

CASTLEBAR
Map 01 B4

Castlebar Hawthorn, Rocklands ☎ 094 21649
Pleasant parkland course with a particularly interesting 9th hole.
18 holes, 5698mtrs, Par 71, SSS 70, Course record 67.
Club membership 800.

Visitors	very welcome weekdays, must contact in advance for weekend play.
Societies	must contact in advance.
Green Fees	IR£12 per day (IR£15 weekends).
Facilities	⊗ ⓑ ♨ ♀ ⚒ ⛳ 🏠 ⛳
Leisure	trolley for hire, putting green, practice area.
Location	1m from town on Belcarra road
Hotel	★★★ 62% Breaffy House Hotel, CASTLEBAR ☎ 094 22033 38 ⇋ ☏

CLAREMORRIS
Map 01 B4

Claremorris Castlemagarrett ☎ 094 71527
A 9-hole parkland course on hilly terrain. There are plenty of trees and a drain across the course.
9 holes, 5600mtrs, Par 70, SSS 69, Course record 66.
Club membership 300.

Visitors	no restrictions.
Societies	welcome weekdays, contact 094 71868 for details.
Green Fees	not confirmed.
Facilities	♀ ⚒
Leisure	putting green,practice area.
Location	1.5m from town
Hotel	★★★ 62% Breaffy House Hotel, CASTLEBAR ☎ 094 22033 38 ⇋ ☏

KEEL
Map 01 A4

Achill Achill Island, Westport ☎ 098 43456
Seaside links in a scenic location on the edge of the Atlantic Ocean.
9 holes, 2723yds, Par 70, SSS 66, Course record 69.
Club membership 170.

Visitors	welcome but cannot play on some Sundays
Societies	must write or telephone in advance.
Green Fees	IR£5 per round.
Facilities	⛳
Leisure	trolley for hire, practice area.
Hotel	★★★ 59% Hotel Westport, The Demesne, Newport Rd, WESTPORT ☎ 098 25122 49 ⇋ ☏

SWINFORD
Map 01 B4

Swinford Brabazon Park ☎ 094 51378
A pleasant parkland course with good views of the beautiful surrounding countryside.
9 holes, 5542mtrs, Par 70, SSS 68.
Club membership 420.

Visitors	must contact in advance in peak season.
Societies	must apply in writing or telephone in advance.
Green Fees	IR£7 per day.
Facilities	ⓑ ♨ ♀ ⚒
Leisure	squash, fishing, trolley for hire, putting green, practice area.
Hotel	★★★ 62% Breaffy House Hotel, CASTLEBAR ☎ 094 22033 38 ⇋ ☏

WESTPORT
Map 01 B4

Westport Carrowholly ☎ 098 28262 & 27070
This is a beautiful course with wonderful views of Clew Bay, with its 365 islands, and the holy mountain called Croagh Patrick, famous for the annual pilgrimage to its summit. Golfers indulge in a different kind of penance on this challenging course with many memorable holes. Perhaps the most exciting is the par five 15th, 580 yards long and featuring a long carry from the tee over an inlet of Clew Bay.
18 holes, 6667yds, Par 73, SSS 71, Course record 65.
Club membership 750.

Visitors	must contact in advance. ▶

Societies	apply in writing or telephone well in advance.
Green Fees	IR£15-IR£18 (IR£15-IR£22.50 weekends & bank holidays).
Facilities	⊗ ℳ ᒡ ☕ ♀ ♨ 🏠 ⭐ ৳ Alex Mealia.
Leisure	buggies for hire, trolley for hire, putting, practice area.
Location	2.5m from town
Hotel	★★★ 59% Hotel Westport, The Demesne, Newport Rd, WESTPORT ☎ 098 25122 49 ⇆ 🐾

CO MEATH

BETTYSTOWN
Map 01 D4

Laytown & Bettystown ☎ 041 27170
A very competitive and trying links course, home of famous golfer, Des Smyth.
18 holes, 5652mtrs.
Club membership 950.

Visitors	may not play 1-2pm. Must contact in advance.
Societies	must contact in writing.
Green Fees	not confirmed.
Facilities	ᒡ 🏠 ⭐ ৳
Leisure	tennis courts.
Hotel	★★ 60% Conyngham Arms Hotel, SLANE ☎ 041 24155 16rm(15 ⇆ 🐾)

DUNSHAUGHLIN
Map 01 D4

Black Bush Thomastown ☎ 01 8250021
Three 9-hole courses, giving three possible 18-hole combinations, set in lovely parkland, with a lake providing a hazard at the 1st. Recently added creeks, trees and bunkers make for challenging and accurate shot-making.
Course 1: 18 holes, 6930yds, Par 73, SSS 72.
Course 2: 18 holes, 6559yds, Par 71, SSS 71.
Course 3: 18 holes, 6647yds, Par 72, SSS 71.
Club membership 900.

Visitors	must contact in advance but cannot play 1-2pm weekdays.
Societies	advance booking by letter.
Green Fees	IR£13 per round (IR£15 weekends).
Facilities	⊗ by prior arrangement ℳ by prior arrangement ᒡ ☕ ♀ ♨ 🏠 ⭐ ৳ Shane O'Grady.
Leisure	trolley for hire, driving range, putting green, practice area.
Location	1.5m from village on Dublin-Navan road
Hotel	★★★ 66% Finnstown Country House Hotel & Golf Course, Newcastle Rd, LUCAN ☎ 01 6280644 25 ⇆ 🐾Annexe20 ⇆ 🐾

KELLS
Map 01 C4

Headfort ☎ 046 40857 & 40639
A delightful parkland course which is regarded as one of the best of its kind in Ireland. There are ample opportunities for birdies, but even if these are not achieved, Headfort provides for a most pleasant game.

18 holes, 6007mtrs, Par 72, SSS 71, Course record 67.
Club membership 680.

Visitors	restricted Tues Ladies Day. Must contact in advance.
Societies	must apply in writing.
Green Fees	IR£17 (IR£20 weekends and bank holidays).
Facilities	⊗ ℳ ᒡ ☕ ♀ ♨ 🏠 ⭐ ৳ Brendan McGovern.
Leisure	trolley for hire, putting green, practice area.
Hotel	★★ 62% Headfort Arms Hotel, Ceanannus, KELLS ☎ 046 40063 & 40121 18 ⇆ 🐾

NAVAN
Map 01 C4

Royal Tara Bellinter ☎ 046 25508 & 25244
Pleasant parkland course offering plenty of variety. Situated close to the Hill of Tara, the ancient seat of the Kings of Ireland.
New Course: 18 holes, 5757mtrs, Par 71, SSS 70.
Old Course: 9 holes, 3184yds, Par 35, SSS 35.
Club membership 1000.

Visitors	prior arrangement is advisable. Tue is ladies day.
Societies	apply in writing or telephone.
Green Fees	IR£15 per round (IR£20 weekends & bank holidays).
Facilities	⊗ ℳ ᒡ ☕ ♀ ♨ 🏠 ⭐ ৳ Adam Whiston.
Leisure	trolley for hire, putting green, practice area.
Location	6m from town on N3
Hotel	★★ 60% Conyngham Arms Hotel, SLANE ☎ 041 24155 16rm(15 ⇆ 🐾)

TRIM
Map 01 C4

Trim Mewtownmoynagh ☎ 046 31463
Extended in 1990 to form a big 18-hole parkland course. The new part blends well with the old and is only distinguished by a plentiful planting of young trees. Four very challenging Par 5's.
18 holes, 6720mtrs, Par 73, SSS 72.

Visitors	welcome some restrictions telephone for details.
Societies	not Sun, enquiries welcome.
Green Fees	not confirmed.
Facilities	♀
Location	3m outside Trim on Trim/Longwood rd
Hotel	★★ 60% Conyngham Arms Hotel, SLANE ☎ 041 24155 16rm(15 ⇆ 🐾)

CO MONAGHAN

CARRICKMACROSS
Map 01 C4

Mannan Castle Donaghmoyne ☎ 042 63308
Parkland and picturesque, the course starts with a dogleg, then a Par 4 Index 1, next a Par 5 with majestic cypress trees as a back drop to the green. The 4th needs a good tee shot to the green. The long Par 5 5th requires a straight hitter; the 6th doglegs left and the 7th overlook the whole course. Downhill to the 8th with trouble on the right and straight and long into the 9th.
9 holes, 5900mtr, Par 72, SSS 70.
Club membership 340.

Visitors	may play anytime except competition times Sat, Sun & Mon from 2-2.30pm.
Societies	apply in writing to the secretary.
Green Fees	IR£8 per day.
Facilities	ⓑ ▮ ♥ ♀ ♨
Location	4m N
Hotel	★★★ 65% Ballymascanlon House Hotel, DUNDALK ☎ 042 71124 36 ⇆

Nuremore ☎ 042 61438 & 64016
Picturesque parkland course of championship length incorporating the drumlins and lakes which are a natural feature of the Monaghan countryside. Precision is required on the 10th to drive over a large lake and between a narrow avenue of trees.
18 holes, 6400yds, Par 72, SSS 70, Course record 67.
Club membership 150.

Visitors	welcome all times but must contact Maurice Cassidy in advance.
Societies	must contact in advance.
Green Fees	IR£16 per day (IR£20 weekends & bank holidays).
Facilities	⊗ ⌇ ▮ ▮ ♥ ♀ ♨ ⌂ ↑ ⌁ ⒧ Maurice Cassidy.
Leisure	hard tennis courts, heated indoor swimming pool, squash, fishing, sauna, gymnasium, buggies for hire, trolley for hire, putting green, practice area.
Location	S on Dublin road N7
Hotel	★★★★ 69% Nuremore Hotel, CARRICKMACROSS ☎ 042 61438 69rm

---

CASTLEBLAYNEY   Map 01 C4

Castleblayney Onomy ☎ 042 46356
Scenic course on Muckno Park estate, adjacent to Muckno Lake and Blayney Castle.
9 holes, 5378yds, Par 68, SSS 66, Course record 68.
Club membership 275.

Visitors	may not play during competitions.
Societies	must contact in advance.
Green Fees	not confirmed.
Facilities	♀ ♨
Leisure	hard tennis courts, fishing.
Hotel	★★★ 65% Ballymascanlon House Hotel, DUNDALK ☎ 042 71124 36 ⇆

CLONES   Map 01 C5

Clones Hilton Park ☎ 047 56017
Parkland course set in Drumlin country. Due to limestone belt, the course is very dry and playable all year round. There is a timesheet in operation on Sundays.
9 holes, 5880yds, Par 68, SSS 67.
Club membership 329.

Visitors	must contact in advance.
Societies	apply in writing.
Green Fees	IR£6 per day (IR£10 weekends).
Facilities	⊗ ▮ ▮ ♥ ♀ ♨
Leisure	putting green, practice area.
Location	3m from Clones on Scotshouse rd
Hotel	★★★ 65% Ballymascanlon House Hotel, DUNDALK ☎ 042 71124 36 ⇆

MONAGHAN   Map 01 C5

Rossmore Rossmore Park, Cootehill Rd ☎ 047 81316
An undulating 18-hole parkland course amidst beautiful countryside.
18 holes, 5534mtrs, Par 70, SSS 68.
Club membership 700.

Visitors	must contact in advance.
Societies	must apply in writing.
Green Fees	IR£13 per day.
Facilities	⊗ ▮ ▮ ♥ ♀ ♨ ⌂
Leisure	driving range, putting green.
Location	2m S on Cootehill road
Hotel	★★★ 65% Ballymascanlon House Hotel, DUNDALK ☎ 042 71124 36 ⇆

CO OFFALY

BIRR   Map 01 C3

Birr The Glenns ☎ 0509 20082
The course has been laid out over undulating parkland utilising the natural contours of the land, which were created during the ice age. The sandy subsoil means that the course is playable all year round.
18 holes, 5700mtrs, Par 70, SSS 70, Course record 64.
Club membership 750.

Visitors	contact in advance,
Societies	advance contact to secretary.
Green Fees	IR£12 per round (IR£14 weekends).
Facilities	⊗ ⌇ ▮ ▮ ♥ ♀ ♨ ⌂ ↑
Leisure	motorised carts for hire, trolley for hire, driving range, putting green, practice area.
Hotel	★★ 66% County Arms Hotel, BIRR ☎ 0509 20791 & 20193 18 ⇆ ⒧

EDENDERRY   Map 01 C4

Edenderry ☎ 0405 31072
A most friendly club which offers a relaxing game in pleasant surroundings. In 1992 the course was extended to 18 holes.
18 holes, 6121mtrs, Par 73, SSS 72.
Club membership 700.

Visitors	restricted Thu & weekends.
Societies	may not play on Thu & Sun; must contact the secretary in writing.
Green Fees	not confirmed.
Facilities	♀ ♨
Leisure	putting, trolley hire, practice area.
Hotel	★★ 59% Curryhills House Hotel, PROSPEROUS ☎ 045 868150 10 ⇆ ⒧

TULLAMORE   Map 01 C4

Tullamore Brookfield ☎ 0506 21439
Well wooded parkland course.
18 holes, 6322yds, Par 71, SSS 70, Course record 65.
Club membership 989.

Visitors	must contact in advance, restricted on Tue & at weekends.

▶

Societies must contact in writing.
Green Fees not confirmed.
Facilities ♀ ♨ 🏠 ⛳ 🏌 Donagh McArdle.
Leisure putting green,practice area,trolley hire.
Location 2.5m SW on Kinnitty road
Hotel ★★★ 64% Prince Of Wales Hotel, ATHLONE
☎ 0902 72626 73 ➟ ♞

CO ROSCOMMON

ATHLONE
Map 01 C4

Athlone Hodson Bay
☎ 0902 92073
A picturesque course with a panoramic view of Lough Ree.
Overall, it is a tight, difficult course with some outstanding
holes and is noted for its magnificent greens.
18 holes, 5935mtrs, Par 71, SSS 70.
Club membership 1000.
Visitors must contact in advance.
Societies apply in writing.
Green Fees IR£15 (IR£18 weekends).
Facilities ⊗ ♨ ♨ ♨ ♀ ♨ 🏠 ⛳ 🏌 Martin Quinn.
Leisure trolley for hire, driving range, putting green,
practice area.
Location 4m from town beside Lough Ree
Hotel ★★★ 69% Hodson Bay Hotel, Hodson Bay,
Kiltoom, ATHLONE
☎ 0902 92444 46 ➟ ♞

BALLAGHADERREEN
Map 01 B4

Ballaghaderreen ☎ 0907 60295
Mature 9-hole course with an abundance of trees. Accuracy
off the tee is vital for a good score. Small protected greens
require a good short-iron plan. The Par 3, 2nd hole at 178
yards has ruined many a good score.
9 holes, 5727yds, Par 70, SSS 66.
Club membership 150.
Visitors no restrictions.
Societies apply in writing or telephone Sec 0907 60029
during office hours.
Green Fees not confirmed.
Facilities ♀ ♨
Leisure putting,practice area,trolley hire.
Location 3m W of town
Hotel ★★ 64% Royal Hotel, BOYLE
☎ 079 62016 16 ➟ ♞

BOYLE
Map 01 B4

Boyle Roscommon Rd ☎ 079 62594
Situated on a low hill and surrounded by beautiful scenery,
this is an undemanding course where, due to the generous
fairways and semi-rough, the leisure golfer is likely to finish
the round with the same golf ball.
9 holes, 5324yds, Par 67, SSS 66, Course record 65.
Club membership 260.
Visitors no restrictions.

Societies must contact in writing.
Green Fees not confirmed.
Facilities ♀ ♨ 🏌
Leisure putting green,practice area.
Hotel ★★ 64% Royal Hotel, BOYLE
☎ 079 62016 16 ➟ ♞

CARRICK-ON-SHANNON
Map 01 C4

Carrick-on-Shannon Woodbrook
☎ 079 67015
A pleasant 9-hole course overlooking the River Shannon.
9 holes, 5571mtrs, Par 70, SSS 68.
Club membership 500.
Visitors contact in advance.
Societies must contact in advance.
Green Fees IR£10 per day.
Facilities ⊗ ♨ ♨ ♀ ♨ 🏌
Leisure trolley for hire, driving range, putting green,
practice area.
Location 4m W beside N4
Hotel ★★ 64% Royal Hotel, BOYLE
☎ 079 62016 16 ➟ ♞

CASTLEREA
Map 01 B4

Castlerea Clonalis ☎ 0907 20068
The clubhouse is virtually at the centre of Castlerea course
with 7 tees visible. A pleasant parkland very near the centre
of town.
9 holes, 4974mtrs, Par 68, SSS 66.
Club membership 200.
Visitors welcome.
Societies contact for details.
Green Fees not confirmed.
Facilities ♀ ♨
Leisure putting,driving range,practice area.
Location On Dublin/Castlebar road
Hotel ★★★ 58% Abbey Hotel, Galway Rd,
ROSCOMMON
☎ 0903 26240 & 26505 25 ➟ ♞

ROSCOMMON
Map 01 B4

Roscommon Mote Park
☎ 0903 26382 & 26927
Located on the rolling pastures of the old Mote Park estate,
this recently extended 18-hole course successfully blends the
old established nine holes with an exciting and equally
demanding new 9-hole lay-out. Numerous water hazards,
notably on the tricky 13th, multi-tiered greens and an
excellent irrigation to give an all-weather surface.
18 holes, 6290mtrs, Par 72, SSS 70, Course record 64.
Club membership 500.
Visitors contact in advance.
Societies apply in writing.
Green Fees IR£15 per day.
Facilities ⊗ ♨ ♨ ♨ ♀ ♨
Leisure trolley for hire, putting green, practice ground.
Location 0.5m S of Roscommon town
Hotel ★★★ 58% Abbey Hotel, Galway Rd,
ROSCOMMON
☎ 0903 26240 & 26505 25 ➟ ♞

CO SLIGO

BALLYMOTE
Map 01 B4

Ballymote Ballinascarrow ☎ 071 83158 & 83089
Although Ballymote was founded in 1940, it has a new
course only opened in July 1993. This is a 9-hole parkland
course with some trees.
9 holes, 5302mtrs, Par 68, SSS 67.
Club membership 250.

Visitors welcome except for club competitions.
Societies telephone in advance.
Green Fees IR£5 per day.
Facilities ⌣
Location 1m N
Hotel ★★ 64% Royal Hotel, BOYLE
☎ 079 62016 16 ⇥ ☝

ENNISCRONE
Map 01 B5

Enniscrone ☎ 096 36297
In a magnificent situation with breathtaking views of
mountain, sea and rolling countryside, this course offers
some unforgettable golf. It has been designated by the
Golfing Union of Ireland as suitable for major national
and provincial championships and offers an exciting
challenge among its splendid sandhills. A particularly
favourite hole is the tenth, with a marvellous view from
the elevated tee and the chance of a birdie with an
accurate drive.
18 holes, 6620yds, Par 72, SSS 72.
Club membership 900.

Visitors may not play before 10.30am or between
1.30 & 3pm on Sun.
Societies must telephone in advance.
Green Fees not confirmed.
Facilities ♀⌣☺☝☂
Leisure driving range, putting green, practice area,
trolley & buggy hire.
Location 0.5m S on Ballina road
Hotel ★★★ 57% Downhill Hotel, BALLINA
☎ 096 21033 50 ⇥ ☝

SLIGO
Map 01 B5

County Sligo Rosses Point ☎ 071 77134 or 77186
Now considered to be one of the top links courses in
Ireland, County Sligo is host to a number of
competitions, including the West of Ireland

Championships and internationals. Set in an elevated
position on cliffs above three large beaches, the
prevailing winds provide an additional challenge.
18 holes, 6003mtrs, Par 71, SSS 72.
Club membership 1069.

Visitors must contact in advance. Must play on
medal course (white tee markers).
Societies must contact in writing & pay a deposit.
Green Fees not confirmed.
Facilities ♀⌣☺☂☝ Leslie Robinson.
Leisure putting,practice area,buggy/trolley hire.
Location Off N15 to Donegal
Hotel ★★ 60% Ballincar House Hotel, Rosses
Point Rd, Ballincar, SLIGO
☎ 071 45361 25 ⇥ ☝

Strandhill Strandhill ☎ 071 68188
This scenic course is situated between Knocknarea Mountain
and the Atlantic, offering golf in its most natural form amid
the sand dunes of the West of Ireland. The 1st, 16th and 18th
are Par 4 holes over 364 metres in length; the 2nd and 17th
are testing Par 3s which vary according to the prevailing
wind; the Par 4 13th is a testing dogleg right. This is a course
where accuracy will be rewarded.
18 holes, 5516mtrs, Par 69, SSS 68.
Club membership 450.

Visitors must contact in advance.
Societies apply in advance.
Green Fees IR£14 (IR£17 weekends).
Facilities ⊗∭☺☂♀⌣☺☂
Leisure motorised carts for hire, buggies for hire, trolley
for hire, putting green, practice area.
Location 5m from town
Hotel ★★ 60% Ballincar House Hotel, Rosses Point
Rd, Ballincar, SLIGO ☎ 071 45361 25 ⇥ ☝

TOBERCURRY
Map 01 B4

Tobercurry ☎ 071 85849
A 9-hole parkland course designed by Edward Hackett. The
8th hole, a Par 3, is regarded as being one of the most testing
in the west of Ireland.
9 holes, 2745mtrs, Par 35, SSS 35.
Club membership 300.

Visitors restricted on Sun.
Societies telephone in advance on 071 85770.
Green Fees IR£10 per day.
Facilities ⊗☺☂♀⌣
Leisure trolley for hire, putting green.
Location 0.25m from Tobercurry
Hotel ★★★ 57% Downhill Hotel, BALLINA
☎ 096 21033 50 ⇥ ☝

CO TIPPERARY

CAHIR   Map 01 C3

Cahir Kilcommon ☎ 052 41474
Parkland course dissected by the River Suir which adds a
challenge to the par 4 8th and par 3 16th.
18 holes, 5740mtrs, Par 71, SSS 71.
Club membership 350.
Visitors   may play any time except during competitions.
Societies   by prior arrangement, apply in writing.
Green Fees IR£12 per round or part of round..
Facilities   ⊗ by prior arrangement ✕ by prior arrangement
                  ⮞ ⬛ ♀ ⬥ ℓ Dominic Foran.
Leisure   trolley for hire, putting green, practice area.
Location   1m from Cahir on the Clogheen road
Hotel   ★★★ 63% Clonmel Arms, Sarsfield Rd,
                  CLONMEL ☎ 052 21233 31 ⇄ ⬧

CARRICK-ON-SUIR   Map 01 C2

Carrick-on-Suir Garvonne ☎ 051 40047
9 holes, 5948yds, Par 70, SSS 68.
Visitors   may not play on Sun.
Societies   contact for details.
Green Fees not confirmed.
Facilities
Location   2m SW
Hotel   ★★★ 72% Minella Hotel, CLONMEL
                  ☎ 052 22388 70 ⇄ ⬧

CLONMEL   Map 01 C2

Clonmel Lyreanearla, Mountain Rd
☎ 052 24050
Set in the scenic, wooded slopes of the Comeragh
Mountains, this is a testing course with lots of open space
and plenty of interesting features. It provides an
enjoyable round in exceptionally tranquil surroundings.
18 holes, 5785mtrs, Par 71, SSS 70.
Club membership 850.
Visitors   may not play at weekends & bank holidays.
                  Must contact in advance.
Societies   must contact in writing.
Green Fees not confirmed.
Facilities   ♀ ⬥ ☎ ⬧ ℓ Robert Hayes.
Leisure   bowls, pool table, table tennis.
Hotel   ★★★ 72% Minella Hotel, CLONMEL
                  ☎ 052 22388 70 ⇄ ⬧

NENAGH   Map 01 B3

Nenagh Beechwood ☎ 067 31476
Interesting gradients call for some careful approach shots.
Some magnificent views.
18 holes, 5491mtrs, Par 69, SSS 68, Course record 64.
Club membership 820.
Visitors   must contact in advance.
Societies   must apply in writing.
Green Fees IR£15 per day.
Facilities   ⊗ ✕ ⮞ ⬛ ♀ ⬥ ☎ ⬧
Leisure   trolley for hire, driving range, putting green,

practice area.
Location   3m from town on old Birr rd
Hotel   ★★★ 65% Castle Oaks House Hotel,
                  CASTLECONNELL
                  ☎ 061 377666 11 ⇄ ⬧

ROSCREA   Map 01 C3

Roscrea Golf Club Derryvale ☎ 0505 21130
An 18-hole parkland course.
18 holes, 5750mtrs, Par 71, SSS 70, Course record 69.
Club membership 420.
Visitors   on Sun by arrangement.
Societies   apply in writing to Hon Secretary.
Green Fees not confirmed.
Facilities   ♀ ⬥ ⬧
Leisure   caddy car/trolley hire,practice area.
Location   N7, Dublin side of Roscrea
Hotel   ★★ 66% County Arms Hotel, BIRR
                  ☎ 0509 20791 & 20193 18 ⇄ ⬧

TEMPLEMORE   Map 01 C3

Templemore Manna South ☎ 0504 31400
Parkland course with newly planted trees which offers a
pleasant test to visitors without being too difficult. Walking is
level too.
9 holes, Par 68, SSS 67, Course record 68.
Club membership 220.
Visitors   may not play on Sun during Special Events &
                  Open weeks.
Societies   must contact in advance.
Green Fees not confirmed.
Facilities   ♀ ⬥
Location   0.5m S
Hotel   ★★ 66% County Arms Hotel, BIRR
                  ☎ 0509 20791 & 20193 18 ⇄ ⬧

THURLES   Map 01 C3

Thurles Turtulla ☎ 0504 21983 & 22466
Superb parkland course with a difficult finish at the 18th.
18 holes, 5904mtrs, Par 72, SSS 71, Course record 65.
Club membership 800.
Visitors   welcome, limited availability at weekends,
                  Tuesday is Ladies day.
Societies   apply in writing to Hon Secretary.
Green Fees IR£16 per round.
Facilities   ⊗ ✕ ⮞ ⬛ ♀ ⬥ ☎ ⬧ ℓ Sean Hunt.
Leisure   squash, sauna, gymnasium, trolley for hire,
                  driving range, putting green, practice area.
Location   1m from town on Cork road
Hotel   ★ 57% Royal Hotel, Bridge St, TIPPERARY
                  ☎ 062 33244 16 ⇄ ⬧

TIPPERARY   Map 01 C3

County Tipperary Dundrum House Hotel, Dundrum
☎ 062 71116
The course had been built into a mature Georgian estate using
the features of woodland and parkland adorned by the
Multeen River. Designed by Philip Walton. The 4th hole is
one of the most testing Par 5's in Ireland.
18 holes, 6709yds, Par 72, SSS 72, Course record 70.

Club membership 190.

Visitors	booking is advisable especially at weekends.
Societies	apply in writing.
Green Fees	IR£18 per round (IR£20-IR£22 weekends).
Facilities	⊗ ⅢⅢ ⅃ ⅃ ♀ ⅄ ⅏ ⅌
Leisure	hard tennis courts, fishing, buggies for hire, trolley for hire, driving range, putting green, practice area.
Location	7m W of Cashel off N8
Hotel	★ 57% Royal Hotel, Bridge St, TIPPERARY ☎ 062 33244 16 ⇥ ⋔

Tipperary Rathanny ☎ 062 51119
Recently extended to 18-holes, this parkland course has plenty of trees and bunkers and water at three holes to provide additional hazards.
18 holes, 5761mtrs, Par 71, SSS 71, Course record 69.
Club membership 700.

Visitors	advisable to contact by phone, weekend play available but limited on Sun.
Societies	apply in writing.
Green Fees	IR£12 per day.
Facilities	⊗ ⅃ ⅃ ♀ ⅄ ⅏ ⅌
Leisure	buggies for hire, trolley for hire, putting green.
Location	1m S
Hotel	★ 57% Royal Hotel, Bridge St, TIPPERARY ☎ 062 33244 16 ⇥ ⋔

CO WATERFORD

DUNGARVAN   Map 01 C2

Dungarvan Knocknagrannagh ☎ 058 41605 & 43310
Opened in June 1993. A championship-standard course beside Dungarvan Bay, with seven lakes and hazards placed to challenge all levels of golfer.
18 holes, 6487yds, Par 72, SSS 71, Course record 66.
Club membership 575.

Visitors	welcome weekdays, booking advisable weekends.
Societies	telephone then write to confim booking.
Green Fees	IR£14 per round (IR£18 weekends & bank holidays).
Facilities	⊗ ⅢⅢ ⅃ ⅃ ♀ ⅄ ⅏ ⅌ ⅃ David Hayes.
Leisure	trolley for hire, driving range, putting green, practice area.
Location	Off N25 between Waterford & Youghal
Hotel	★★★ 59% Lawlors Hotel, DUNGARVAN ☎ 058 41122 & 41056 89 ⇥ ⋔

Gold Coast Golf & Leisure Ballinacourty ☎ 058 42249
A parkland course bordered by the Atlantic Ocean.
9 holes, 5659mtrs, Par 72, SSS 69, Course record 67.
Club membership 400.

Visitors	book in advance, times available throughout the week.
Societies	apply by telephone in advance.
Green Fees	IR£12 per day.
Facilities	⊗ ⅢⅢ ⅃ ⅃ ♀ ⅄ ⅌ ⅏
Leisure	hard tennis courts, heated indoor swimming pool, sauna, gymnasium, trolley for hire, driving range, putting green, practice area.

Hotel	★★★ 59% Lawlors Hotel, DUNGARVAN ☎ 058 41122 & 41056 89 ⇥ ⋔

West Waterford Coolcormack ☎ 058 43216 & 41475
Designed by Eddie Hackett, the course is on 150 acres of rolling parkland by the Brickey River with a backdrop of the Comeragh Mountains, Knockmealdowns and Drum Hills. The first nine holes are laid out on a large plateau featuring a stream which comes into play at the 3rd and 4th holes. The river at the southern boundary affects several later holes.
18 holes, 6004mtrs, Par 72, SSS 74, Course record 70.
Club membership 175.

Visitors	pre book for tee times.
Societies	telephone or write in advance.
Green Fees	IR£15 per 18 holes (IR£20 weekends & bank holidays).
Facilities	⊗ ⅢⅢ ⅃ ⅃ ♀ ⅄ ⅏ ⅌
Leisure	buggies for hire, 5 acre practice area.
Location	Approx 3m W of Dungarvan, off N25
Hotel	★★★ 59% Lawlors Hotel, DUNGARVAN ☎ 058 41122 & 41056 89 ⇥ ⋔

DUNMORE EAST   Map 01 C2

Dunmore East ☎ 051 383151
Challenging golf for low and high handicappers. The 6th hole requires a tee shot that carries 150yards over the sea. The course overlooks the village of Dunmore East and the sea so many holes are affected by crosswinds.
18 holes, 6655yds, Par 72, SSS 70.
Club membership 300.

Visitors	welcome, no restrictions.
Societies	telephone in advance.
Green Fees	IR£10 per day (IR£12 weekends & bank holidays).
Facilities	⊗ ⅢⅢ ⅃ ⅃ ♀ ⅄ ⅏ ⅌
Leisure	trolley for hire, putting green, practice area.
Hotel	★★ 66% Dooley's Hotel, 30 The Quay, WATERFORD ☎ 051 73531 35rm(34 ⇥ ⋔)

LISMORE   Map 01 C2

Lismore Ballyin ☎ 058 54026
Picturesque tree-dotted sloping course on the banks of the Blackwater River. Rothwell's is a diffiuclt hole with a sloping green and trees to either side.
9 holes, 5790yds, Par 69, SSS 67, Course record 67.
Club membership 350.

Visitors	may not play Sun before noon. Restricted Wed, Thu & weekends.
Societies	must apply in writing.
Green Fees	IR£8 per day (IR£10 weekends & bank holidays).
Facilities	⅃ ⅃ ♀ ⅄
Leisure	trolley for hire, putting green, practice area.
Hotel	★★★ 59% Lawlors Hotel, DUNGARVAN ☎ 058 41122 & 41056 89 ⇥ ⋔

TRAMORE   Map 01 C2

Tramore Newtown Hill ☎ 051 386170
This course has matured nicely over the years to become a true championship test and has been chosen as the venue for the Irish Professional Matchplay Championship and the Irish Amateur Championship. Most of the fairways are lined by evergreen trees, calling for accurate placing of shots, and the course is continuing to develop. ▶

18 holes, 5918mtrs, Par 72, SSS 72, Course record 65.
Club membership 1200.

Visitors	pre-booking required.
Societies	apply in writing.
Green Fees	IR£22 per round (IR£25 weekends & bank holidays).
Facilities	⊗ ⅲ ⅼ ⚑ ♀ ♨ 🏠 ⅱ 🏌 Derry Kiely.
Leisure	squash, trolley for hire, putting green, practice area.
Hotel	★★★★ 75% Waterford Castle Hotel, The Island, WATERFORD ☎ 051 78203 19 ⇔ 🐾

WATERFORD
Map 01 C2

Faithlegg House Dunmore East ☎ 051 382241
Some wicked slopes and borrows on the immaculate greens, a huge 432yard 17th what has a host of problems and a doglegged approach to the two-tier 18th green are just some of the novel features on this course. Set on the banks of the River Suir, the course has been integrated into a landscape textured with mature trees,flowing parkland and five lakes.
18 holes, 6057mtrs, Par 72, SSS 72, Course record 69.
Club membership 65.

Visitors	no restrictions.
Societies	apply in writing or telephone at least a month in advance.
Green Fees	not confirmed.
Facilities	♀ ♨ 🏠 ⅱ 🏌 Ted Higgins.
Hotel	★★★ 66% Jurys Hotel, Ferrybank, WATERFORD ☎ 051 32111 98 ⇔ 🐾

Waterford Newrath ☎ 051 76748 & 74182
Undulating parkland course in pleasant surroundings.
18 holes, 5722mtrs, Par 71, SSS 70, Course record 66.
Club membership 931.

Visitors	must contact in advance.
Societies	must apply in writing.
Green Fees	IR£20 (IR£22 weekdays & bank holidays).
Facilities	⊗ ⅲ ⅼ ⚑ ♀ ♨ 🏠 ⅱ 🏌 Eamonn Condon.
Location	1m N
Hotel	★★★ 66% Jurys Hotel, Ferrybank, WATERFORD ☎ 051 32111 98 ⇔ 🐾

Waterford Castle The Island, Ballinakill ☎ 051 71633
18 holes, 5810mtrs, Par 72, SSS 71.
Club membership 300.

Visitors	must contact in advance.
Societies	apply in advance.
Green Fees	IR£20 (IR£22 weekends).
Facilities	ⅼ ⚑ ♀ ♨ 🏠 ⅱ
Location	2m E on Island approached by private ferry
Hotel	★★★★ 75% Waterford Castle Hotel, The Island, WATERFORD ☎ 051 78203 19 ⇔ 🐾

CO WESTMEATH

ATHLONE
Map 01 C4

Glasson Golf & Country Club Glasson ☎ 0902 85120
An 18-hole championship standard course designed by Christy O'Connor Jnr. There are a number of outstanding holes including the Par 3 15th which has both tee and green

situated in Killiure Bay. As Christy said 'Although only 185 yards off the back tee there is no room for error whatsoever'.
18 holes, 6653yds, Par 72, Course record 65.
Club membership 240.

Visitors	no restrictions.
Societies	telephone in advance.
Green Fees	not confirmed.
Facilities	♀ ♨ 🏠 ⅱ 🏌
Leisure	caddy cars & buggies, caddies available.
Location	6m N of Athlone on N55
Hotel	★★★ 64% Prince Of Wales Hotel, ATHLONE ☎ 0902 72626 73 ⇔ 🐾

DELVIN
Map 01 C4

Delvin Castle Clonyn ☎ 044 64315
Only opened in 1991, Delvin is a developing course. The design of the course is built around the prevailing wind.
18 holes, 5800mtrs, Par 70, SSS 68.
Club membership 400.

Visitors	no restrictions.
Societies	apply in writing in advance.
Green Fees	not confirmed.
Facilities	♨ 🏠 ⅱ 🏌 David Keenaghan.
Leisure	trolleys for hire.
Hotel	★★ 62% Headfort Arms Hotel, Ceanannus, KELLS ☎ 046 40063 & 40121 18 ⇔ 🐾

MOATE
Map 01 C4

Moate ☎ 0902 81271
Extended in 1994 to 18 holes, the course is parkland with trees. Although the original 9-holes did not have water hazards the new section has a lake.
18 holes, 5642mtrs, Par 72, SSS 70, Course record 67.
Club membership 550.

Visitors	welcome, advisable to telephone in advance.
Societies	welcome, prior arrangement not needed.
Green Fees	IR£10 (IR£13 weekends).
Facilities	ⅼ ⚑ ♀ ♨
Leisure	buggies for hire, trolley for hire, putting green, practice area.
Location	1m N
Hotel	★★★ 64% Prince Of Wales Hotel, ATHLONE ☎ 0902 72626 73 ⇔ 🐾

Mount Temple Mount Temple Village
☎ 0902 81841 & 81545
A traditionally built, highly-rated, all year round course with parkland and unique links-type greens and natural undulating fairways.A challenge for all levels of golfers as the wind plays a major part in the scoring on this course.
18 holes, 5950mtrs, Par 71, SSS 71, Course record 73.
Club membership 150.

Visitors	welcome but must book for weekends.
Societies	telephone in advance.
Green Fees	IR£10 per round (IR£14 weekends & bank holidays).
Facilities	⊗ ⅼ ⚑ ♀ ♨ 🏠 ⅱ
Leisure	putting green.
Hotel	★★★ 64% Prince Of Wales Hotel, ATHLONE ☎ 0902 72626 73 ⇔ 🐾

MULLINGAR
Map 01 C4

Mullingar ☎ 044 48366
The wide rolling fairways between mature trees provide parkland golf at its very best. The course, designed by the great James Braid, offers a tough challenge and annually hosts one of the most important amateur events in the British Isles - the Mullingar Scratch Cup. It has also been the venue of the Irish Professional Championship. One advantage of the layout is that the clubhouse is never far away.
18 holes, 6406yds, Par 72, SSS 71, Course record 63.
Club membership 1000.
Visitors preferred if booked in advance, Sundays are Medal days, Wednesday Ladies day.
Societies apply in writing.
Green Fees IR£18 per round (IR£26 weekends & bank holidays).
Facilities ⊗ ⅏ ⅃ ▦ ♀ ⚑ 🏠 ⚑ 𝄃 John Burns.
Leisure buggies for hire, trolley for hire, driving range, putting green, practice area.
Location 3m S
Hotel ★★★ 64% Prince Of Wales Hotel, ATHLONE ☎ 0902 72626 73 🛏 🐾

● CO WEXFORD ●

COURTOWN HARBOUR
Map 01 D3

Courtown Kiltennel, Gorey ☎ 055 25166
Treelined fairways and views of the sea make this 18-hole parkland course attractive. There are 4 excellent Par 3's, one of which is the 18th played over a large pond.
18 holes, 5852mtrs, Par 71, SSS 70.
Visitors may not play on competition days.
Societies contact for details.
Green Fees not confirmed.
Facilities ♀ 𝄃 John Coone.
Hotel ★★ 69% Courtown Hotel, COURTOWN HARBOUR
☎ 055 25210 & 25108 21 🛏 🐾

ENNISCORTHY
Map 01 D3

Enniscorthy Knockmarshall ☎ 054 33191
A pleasant course suitable for all levels of ability.
18 holes, 5697mtrs, Par 70, SSS 68.
Club membership 800.
Visitors must telephone for booking.
Societies must book in advance.
Green Fees IR£14 per day (IR£16 weekends & bank holidays).
Facilities ⊗ ⅏ ⅃ ▦ ♀ ⚑
Leisure trolley for hire, putting green, practice area.
Location 1m from town on New Ross road
Hotel ★ 56% Murphy-Flood's Hotel, Market Square, ENNISCORTHY
☎ 054 33413 21rm(5 🛏 13 🐾)

GOREY
Map 01 D3

Courtown Kiltennel ☎ 055 25166
A pleasant parkland course which is well wooded and enjoys views across the Irish Sea near Courtown Harbour.
18 holes, 5898mtrs, Par 71, SSS 71, Course record 65.
Club membership 1200.
Visitors must contact in advance.
Societies advisable to contact in advance.
Green Fees IR£14-IR£18 (IR£18-IR£23 weekends).
Facilities ⊗ ⅏ ⅃ ▦ ♀ ⚑ 🏠 ⚑ 𝄃 John Coone.
Leisure trolley for hire, putting green, practice area.
Location 3m from town, off Courtown Road
Hotel ★★★(red)🏵 Marlfield House Hotel, GOREY
☎ 055 21124 19 🛏 🐾

NEW ROSS
Map 01 C3

New Ross Tinneranny ☎ 051 21433
Recently extended to 18-holes, this well kept parkland course has an attractive backdrop of hills and mountains. Straight hitting and careful placing of shots is very important, especially on the 2nd, 6th, 10th and 15th, all of which are challenging holes.
18 holes, 5751yds, Par 71, SSS 70.
Club membership 700.
Visitors welcome, booking required for weekend play.
Societies apply to secretary/manager.
Green Fees IR£13 (IR£16 weekends & bank holidays).
Facilities ⅃ ▦ ♀ ⚑
Leisure trolley for hire, putting green, practice area.
Location 3m from town centre
Hotel ★★ 59% The Old Rectory Hotel, Rosbercon, NEW ROSS
☎ 051 21719 12 🛏 🐾

ROSSLARE
Map 01 D2

Rosslare Rosslare Strand
☎ 053 32203 & 32238
This traditional links course is within minutes of the ferry terminal at Rosslare, but its popularity is not confined to visitors from Fishguard or Le Havre. It is a great favourite with the Irish too. Many of the greens are sunken and are always in beautiful condition, but the semi-blind approaches are among features of this course which provide a healthy challenge.
Old Course: 18 holes, 6577yds, Par 72, SSS 71, Course record 68.
New Course: 9 holes, 3153yds, Par 70, SSS 70.
Club membership 900.
Visitors book in advance.
Societies apply in writing/telephone.
Green Fees not confirmed.
Facilities ♀ ⚑ 🏠 ⚑ 𝄃 Austin Skerritt.
Leisure putting,buggy/trolley hire,practice area.
Location 6m N of Rosslare Ferry Terminal
Hotel ★★★★ 76% Kelly's Resort Hotel, ROSSLARE
☎ 053 32114 Annexe99 🛏 🐾

St Helen's Bay Golf & Country Club St Helens, Kilrane
☎ 053 33234 & 33669
A championship-standard golf course designed by Philip
Walton. Parkland with water hazards, bunkers and trees
incorporated generously.
18 holes, 5813mtrs, Par 72, SSS 72, Course record 69.
Club membership 180.
Visitors   contact in advance.
Societies   telephone in advance.
Green Fees IR£15-IR£18 per 18 holes (IR£19-IR£20
           weekends). IR£10-IR£12 per 9 holes (IR£12-
           IR£14 weekends).
Facilities ⊗ ⅧⅠ ⅢⅠ 戼 ♀ 夲 値 ⫪ ⋈
Leisure   hard tennis courts, sauna, gymnasium, buggies
           for hire, trolley for hire, driving range, putting
           green, practice area.
Hotel   ★★★ 58% Hotel Rosslare, ROSSLARE
           HARBOUR
           ☎ 053 33110 25rm(22 ⇌ ℝ)

WEXFORD   Map 01 D3

Wexford Mulgannon ☎ 053 42238
Parkland course with panoramic view of the Wexford
coastline and mountains.
18 holes, 6100yds, Par 71, SSS 69.
Club membership 800.
Visitors   must contact in advance but may not play Thu &
           weekends.
Societies   must contact in writing.
Green Fees not confirmed.
Facilities ♀ 夲 値 ⫪ G Ronayne.
Leisure   pool table.
Hotel   ★★★ 72% Talbot Hotel, Trinity St,
           WEXFORD
           ☎ 053 22566 100 ⇌ ℝ

CO WICKLOW

ARKLOW   Map 01 D3

Arklow Abbeylands ☎ 0402 32492
Scenic links course.
18 holes, 5404mtrs, Par 68, SSS 67, Course record 66.
Club membership 450.
Visitors   may play Mon-Fri.
Societies   must apply in writing.
Green Fees not confirmed.
Facilities ♀ 夲 値
Location   0.5m from town centre
Hotel   ★★★(red)⚘ Marlfield House Hotel, GOREY
           ☎ 055 21124 19 ⇌ ℝ

BALTINGLASS   Map 01 D3

Baltinglass Dublin Rd
☎ 0508 81350
On the banks of the River Slaney, the 9-hole course has 4
Par-4s over 400 yards which have to be played twice.
Reputed to be one of the hardest 9-hole courses in the

Republic.
9 holes, 5554mtrs, Par 68, SSS 69, Course record 68.
Club membership 400.
Visitors   advisable to check availability for weekends.
Societies   apply in writing.
Green Fees IR£10 (IR£12 weekends & bank holidays).
Facilities ⊗ ⅧⅠ ⅢⅠ 戼 ♀ 夲
Leisure   putting green, practice area.

Rathsallagh ☎ 045 403316
Designed by Peter McEvoy and Christy O'Connor Jnr, this is
a spectacular course which will test the pro's without
intimidating the club golfer. Set in 252 acres of lush parkland
with thousands of mature treesn naturalwater hazards and
gently rolling landscape.
18 holes, 6916yds, Par 72, SSS 74.
Club membership 180.
Visitors   must have appropriate attire & book in advance.
           Restricted weekends.
Societies   telephone in advance.
Green Fees IR£25 Sun pm/Mon; Tue-Fri am IR£29; Fri pm-
           Sun am & holidays IR£35. Early Bird before
           9.30am Mon-Fri.
Facilities ⊗ ⅧⅠ ⅢⅠ 戼 ♀ 夲 値 ⫪ ⋈
Leisure   hard tennis courts, heated indoor swimming
           pool, sauna, motorised carts for hire, buggies for
           hire, trolley for hire, driving range, putting
           green, practice area, riding.
Location   15m SE of Naas
Hotel   ★★★ 56% Downshire House Hotel,
           BLESSINGTON
           ☎ 045 865199 14 ⇌ ℝAnnexe11 ⇌ ℝ

BLAINROE   Map 01 D3

Blainroe ☎ 0404 68168
Parkland course overlooking the sea on the east coast,
offering a challenging round to golfers of all abilities.
18 holes, 6068mtrs, Par 72, SSS 72, Course record 71.
Club membership 868.
Visitors   must contact in advance.
Societies   must telephone in advance.
Green Fees IR£20 (IR£28 weekends and bank holidays).
Facilities ⊗ ⅧⅠ ⅢⅠ 戼 ♀ 夲 値 ⫪ ⫯ John McDonald.
Leisure   trolley for hire, putting green, practice area.
Location   S of Wicklow, on coast road
Hotel   ★★★(red)⚘ Tinakilly Country House &
           Restaurant, RATHNEW
           ☎ 0404 69274 29 ⇌ ℝ

BLESSINGTON   Map 01 D3

Tulfarris Hotel & Country Club
☎ 045 64574 & 51219
Designed by Eddie Hachett, this course is on the Blessington
lakeshore with the Wicklow Mountains as a backdrop.
9 holes, 2806mtrs, Par 36, SSS 69, Course record 74.
Club membership 150.
Visitors   tee booking advisable; may not play Sun 8-
           12.30pm.
Societies   must contact in writing or telephone in advance.
Green Fees not confirmed.
Facilities ♀ 夲 値 ⫪ ⋈
Leisure   hard tennis courts, heated indoor swimming
           pool, fishing, sauna, gymnasium, caddy cars.

Location	Via N81, 2m from Blessington village
Hotel	★★★ 56% Downshire House Hotel, BLESSINGTON
	☎ 045 865199 14 ➡ ⮀Annexe11 ➡ ⮀

BRAY

Map 01 D4

Bray Ravenswell Rd ☎ 01 2862484
A 9-hole parkland course with plenty of trees and bunkers.
9 holes, 5761mtrs, Par 70, SSS 70, Course record 65.
Club membership 500.

Visitors	restricted Mon, Sat & Sun.
Societies	contact in advance.
Green Fees	IR£17 per day.
Facilities	⬤ ♀ ⬥ ⬤ ⟙ ⟨ Michael Walby.
Leisure	trolley for hire, putting green, practice area.
Hotel	★★★ 58% Royal Hotel, Main St, BRAY
	☎ 01 2862935 91 ➡ ⮀

Old Conna Ferndale Rd ☎ 01 2826055 & 2826766
Fairly young but interesting course with a number of shots across water.
18 holes, 6550yds, Par 72, SSS 71, Course record 70.
Club membership 900.

Visitors	advisable to contact in advance but may not play weekends. Smart dress essential on course & in clubhouse.
Societies	must telephone well in advance.
Green Fees	IR£22.50 per round. Early bird before 9.30am IR£13.50.
Facilities	⊗ ⫿ ⬛ ⬤ ♀ ⬥ ⬤ ⟙ ⟨ Paul McDaid.
Leisure	trolley for hire, putting green, practice area.
Hotel	★★★ 58% Royal Hotel, Main St, BRAY
	☎ 01 2862935 91 ➡ ⮀

Woodbrook Dublin Rd ☎ 01 2824799
Pleasant parkland with magnificent views and bracing sea breezes which has hosted a number of events, including the Irish Close and the Irish Open Championships. A testing finish is provided by an 18th hole with out of bounds on both sides.
18 holes, 5996mtrs, Par 72, SSS 71, Course record 65.
Club membership 960.

Visitors	must contact in advance and have a handicap certificate.
Societies	must contact in advance.
Green Fees	not confirmed.
Facilities	♀ ⬥ ⬤ ⟙ ⟨ Billy Kinsella.
Location	11m S of Dublin on N11
Hotel	★★★ 58% Royal Hotel, Main St, BRAY
	☎ 01 2862935 91 ➡ ⮀

BRITTAS BAY

Map 01 D3

The European Club ☎ 0404 47415
A major new links course 30 miles south of Dublin, the course runs through a large dunes system with great views of Arklow Bay. It was ranked no 7 in Ireland's 30 greatest golf courses by the Irish Golf Institute in 1994.
18 holes, 6800yds, Par 71, SSS 71.
Club membership 100.

Visitors	pre-booking advised especially for weekends.
Societies	must book in advance.
Green Fees	IR£25 (IR£30 weekends). Oct-Feb: £20/£25.
Facilities	⊗ ⫿ ⬛ ⬤ ⬥ ⟙

Leisure	trolley for hire, putting green, practice area.
Hotel	★★★(red)⬥⬥ Tinakilly Country House & Restaurant, RATHNEW
	☎ 0404 69274 29 ➡ ⮀

DELGANY

Map 01 D3

Delgany ☎ 01 2874536
An undulating parkland course amidst beautiful scenery.
18 holes, 5474mtrs, Par 69, SSS 68, Course record 63.
Club membership 850.

Visitors	may play Mon, Wed (until 11am), Thu & Fri. Contact in advance.
Societies	contact in advance.
Green Fees	IR£20 weekdays (IR£24 weekends & bank holidays).
Facilities	⊗ ⫿ ⬛ ⬤ ♀ ⬥ ⬤ ⟙ ⟨ Gavin Kavanagh.
Leisure	motorised carts for hire, buggies for hire, trolley for hire, putting green, practice area.
Location	0.75m from village
Hotel	★★★ 58% Royal Hotel, Main St, BRAY
	☎ 01 2862935 91 ➡ ⮀

GREYSTONES

Map 01 D3

Charlesland Golf & Country Club Hotel ☎ 01 2876764
Championship lenght, Par 72 course with a double dog-leg at the 9th and 18th. Water hazards at the 3rd and 11th.
18 holes, 5907mtrs, Par 72, SSS 72.
Club membership 744.

Visitors	must contact in advance.
Societies	must apply in advance.
Green Fees	IR£23 per round (IR£28 weekends & bank holidays).
Facilities	⬥ ⬛ ⬤ ♀ ⬥ ⬤ ⟙ ⟨ Paul Heeney.
Leisure	sauna, motorised carts for hire, buggies for hire, driving range, putting green.
Hotel	★★★(red)⬥⬥ Tinakilly Country House & Restaurant, RATHNEW
	☎ 0404 69274 29 ➡ ⮀

Greystones ☎ 01 2876624 & 2874136
A part level and part hilly parkland course.
18 holes, 5401mtrs, Par 69, SSS 68.
Club membership 941.

Visitors	may only play Mon, Tue & Fri morning. Must contact in advance.
Societies	must contact in writing.
Green Fees	not confirmed.
Facilities	♀ ⬥ ⬤ ⟙ ⟨
Hotel	★★★(red)⬥⬥ Tinakilly Country House & Restaurant, RATHNEW ☎ 0404 69274 29 ➡ ⮀

KILCOOLE

Map 01 D3

Kilcoole Ballyfillop ☎ 01 2872066
9 holes, 5506mtrs, Par 70, SSS 69.
Club membership 250.

Visitors	restricted Sat & Sun 8-10am.
Societies	apply in writing or telephone.
Green Fees	not confirmed.
Facilities	♀ ⬥ ⬤
Leisure	caddy cars.
Location	N11 Kilcoole/Newcastle ▶

Hotel ★★ 65% Hunter's Hotel, RATHNEW
☎ 0404 40106 16 ⇥ ⋔

RATHDRUM

Map 01 D3

Glenmalure Greenane ☎ 0404 46679
A moorland course with elevated tees and greens. The 12th, known as the Helicopter Pad, is difficult.
18 holes, 5300yds, Par 71, SSS 67, Course record 73.
Club membership 200.
Visitors no restrictions.
Societies telephone at least 3 days in advance..
Green Fees IR£12 per day (IR£18 weekends & bank holidays).
Facilities ⊗ ⍟ ⓑ ⚑ ♀ ⚲ ⋔
Leisure buggies for hire, trolley for hire, putting green.
Hotel ★★ 64% Woodenbridge Hotel, WOODEN BRIDGE ☎ 0402 35146 12 ⇥ ⋔

SHILLELAGH

Map 01 D3

Coollattin Coollattin ☎ 055 26302
Plenty of trees provide features on this 9-hole parkland course.
9 holes, 5672mtrs, Par 70, SSS 70.
Visitors may not play weekends.
Societies contact for details.
Green Fees not confirmed.
Facilities ♀
Hotel ★★★(red)♨ Marlfield House Hotel, GOREY ☎ 055 21124 19 ⇥ ⋔

WICKLOW

Map 01 D3

Wicklow Dunbur Rd ☎ 0404 67379
Partly links, partly meadow, the Wicklow course does not have any trees. It was extended to 18-holes in spring 1994 by adding 11 new holes.
18 holes, 5556mtrs, Par 71.
Club membership 475.
Visitors welcome, no restrictions.
Societies contact for details.
Green Fees IR£15 (IR£18 weekends).
Facilities ⊗ ⍟ ⓑ ⚑ ⚲ ⚑ ⓒ David Daly.
Leisure trolley for hire, putting green, practice area.
Hotel ★★★(red)♨ Tinakilly Country House & Restaurant, RATHNEW ☎ 0404 69274 29 ⇥ ⋔

WOODENBRIDGE

Map 01 D3

Woodenbridge Arklow ☎ 0402 35202
Expanded to 18 holes in summer of 1994, this course is in a lovely wooded valley - the Vale of Avoca.
9 holes, 5582mtrs, Par 70, SSS 68.
Visitors welcome.
Societies no details given.
Green Fees not confirmed.
Facilities
Hotel ★★ 64% Woodenbridge Hotel, WOODEN BRIDGE ☎ 0402 35146 12 ⇥ ⋔

GOLF DRIVING RANGES

ENGLAND

BEDFORDSHIRE

Bedford, Mowsbury Driving Range (01234 216374) 14 bays covered floodlit 9am-9pm

Ivinghoe, Ivinghoe Driving Range (01296 662720) 30 bays open floodlit 9.30am-9.30pmWD 7.30pmWE

Leighton Buzzard, Aylesbury Vale (01525 240196) 10 bays covered floodlit 8am-9pm

Luton, Stockwood Park Golf Centre (01582 413704) 20 bays covered floodlit 6am-9.30pmWD5.30pm-8pmWE

Tilsworth, Tilsworth Golf Centre (01525 210721/2) 30 bays covered floodlit 10am-10pm

Wyboston, Wyboston Lakes Range (01480 223004) 14 bays covered floodlit 7am-10pm

BERKSHIRE

Ascot, Lavender Park Golf Centre (01344 884074 / 886096) 29 bays floodlit 9am-10.30pmWD 9am-10pmSUN

Binfield, Blue Mountain Golf Centre (01344 300200) 33 bays covered floodlit 7.15am-9pm

Maidenhead, Bird Hill Golf Range (01628 771030 / 75588) 38 bays covered floodlit 8am-10pm

Wokingham, Downshire Golf Range (01344 422708) 30 bays covered floodlit 7.30am-10pmWD 6am- 10pmWE

BUCKINGHAMSHIRE

Bletchley, Windmill Hill Golf Complex (01908 378623) 23 bays covered floodlit + 5 bays open 8am-9pmWD 8am-8pmWE

Colnbrook, Colnbrook Driving Range (01753 682670/685127) 15 bays covered floodlit + 10 bays open 9.am-10.30pm

Loudwater, Wycombe Heights Golf Range (01494 812862) 24 bays covered floodlit 10am-10pm

Wavendon, Wavendon Golf Centre (01908 281811) 36 bays covered floodlit 7am(Mon.10am) - 10pm

CAMBRIDGESHIRE

Hemingford Abbots, Hemingford Golf Centre (01480 492939) 30 bays floodlit 10am-9.30pmWD(Fri.10am-8.30pm) 9am-8.30pmWE

Thorney, Thorney Golf Centre (01733 270570) 13 bays covered floodlit 8am-dusk

Pidley, Lakeside Lodge (01487 740540) 6 bays covered floodlit + 17 bays open 7am-11pm

Ramsey, Edrich Golf Driving Range (01487 813519) 12 bays covered floodlit + 12 bays open 7am-9pmWD 7am-7pmWE

St Neots, Abbotsley Golf & Squash Club (01480 215153) 22 bays floodlit covered 7.30am-10pm

CHESHIRE

Hartford, Hartford Golf Range(01606 871162) 30 bays covered floodlit 10am-9pm exc. Sat 10am-7pm

Heaton Mersey, Cranford Golf Driving Range (0161 432 8242) 43 bays covered floodlit 10.am-11pm

Knutsford, Mere Golf & Country Club (01565 830219) 6 bays open (floating ball) 8am-7pm

Warrington, Drive Time Golf Range (01925 234800) 60 bays covered floodlit 9am-10pm

CORNWALL

Lostwithiel, Lostwithiel Golf & Country Club (01208 873822 / 873550) 6 bays floodlit 7.30am-9pm

St. Austell, Porthpean (01726 64613) 9 bays covered floodlit 9am-9pm

Redruth, Treleigh, Radnor Golf Centre (01209 211059) 12 bays covered floodlit + 6 bays open 8.30am-8.30pmWD 8.30am-6pmWE

Truro, Killiow Park (01872 70246) 8 bays indoor floodlit + 4 bays open 9.30am-9pmWD 9.30am-6pmWE

CUMBRIA

Crosby-on-Eden, Eden (01228 573003) 16 bays floodlit 8am-8.30pmWD 8am-6pmWE

DERBYSHIRE

Chesterfield, Grassmoor Golf Centre (01246 856044) 26 bays floodlit covered 8am-9pm

Horsley, Horsley Lodge Golf Range (01332 780838) 10 bays covered floodlit Dawn-10.pm

Long Eaton, Trent Lock (0115 9464398/9461184) 24 bays covered floodlit 8am-10pm

DEVON

High Bicklington, Libbaton (01769 560269) 7 bays covered floodlit 8.am-10pm

Ilfracombe, Ilfracombe & Woolacombe Golf Range (01271 866222) 12 bays covered (not floodlit) + 6 open tees 8am-8pm summer 6pm winter

Ivybridge, Dinnaton (01752 892512/892452) 6 tee driving net 10am-9pm

Tedburn St. Mary, Fingle Glen Golf Range (01647 61817) 12-bays covered floodlit 9am- 9.pmWD 9am-8.30pmWE

DORSET

Christchurch, Iford Bridge Golf Range (01202 473817) 14 bays open 8am-6pm

Wareham, Hyde, East Dorset Golf Centre (01929 472272) 22 bays floodlit (12 indoor) 8am-9pmWD 8am-6pmWE (Sum. 7.30am WD/WE)

Verwood, Crane Valley Golf Range (01202 814088) 10 bays covered + 2 bays open floodlit 7.30am-9pmWD 5pmWE)

Weymouth, Wessex Golf Centre (01305 784737) 20 bays open 9am-7pm

CO. DURHAM

Chester-le-Street, Roseberry Grange (0191 370 0660) 17 bays covered floodlit 8am-9pmWD 7am-9pm Sat 7pm Sun

Durham, Ramside Hall (0191 386 9514) 16 bays covered floodlit 8am-8.45pm

Newton Aycliffe, Aycliffe Driving Range (01325 310820) 18 bays covered floodlit 7am-8.30pmWD-8pmWE

Stockton-on-Tees, Knotty Hill Golf Centre (01740 620320) 14 bays covered floodlit +12 bays open 8am-9pm

ESSEX

Bulphan, Langdon Hills Driving Range (01268 548444) 22 bays covered floodlit 7am-9.30pmWD/9pmWE

Canvey Island, Castle Point (01268 510830) 21 bays covered floodlit 7am-9pmWD 8pmWE

Colchester, Colchester Golf Range (01206 230974) 12 bays covered floodlit + 2 open bays 10am-9pmWD 10am-6pmWE

Chelmsford, Chanels (01245 361100) 13 bays covered floodlit 7am-10pmWD 6.30am-10pmWEr

Earls Colne, Earls Colne (01787 224466) 20 bays covered floodlit 9am-10pmWD 8am-9pmWE

Epping, Nazeing Golf Club (01992 893798) 16 mats open air driving area (buckets of balls available) 7.30am-8pm

Leigh-on-Sea, Leigh Driving Range (01702 710586) 18 bays covered floodlit 9am-9.30pmWD/ 9pmWE

Maldon, Woodham Mortimer (01245 222276) 15 ·bays covered floodlit + 6 open tees 10am-9pm

GLOUCESTERSHIRE

Gloucester, Gloucester Hotel & CC (01452 525653) 12 bays covered floodlit 10am-8.45pm

GREATER LONDON

Addiscombe, Croydon Golf Centre (0181 656 1690) 24 bays covered floodlit 9am-10pmWD 9am-8pmWE

Arkley, A1 Golf Range (0181 447 1411) 47 bays covered floodlit (10 open) 8am-10pm

Bushey, Bushey Golf Range (0181 950 2215) 27 bays covered floodlit 9am-10pm

Carshalton, Oaks Sports Centre (0181 643 8363) 16 bays covered floodlit 9am-10pm

Chadwell Heath, Warren Park (0181 597 1120) 30 bays covered floodlit 9am-10pmWD/Sun. 9am-9pmSat.

Chessington, Chessington Golf Centre (0181 391 0948) 17 bays covered floodlit 9am-10pmWD 9am-9pmWE

Elstree, Elstree Golf Range (0181 953 6115) 62 bays covered floodlit 7am-10pm

Greenford, Lime Trees Park (0181 842 0442) 24 bays covered floodlit 8am-10pm

Hounslow, Airlinks (0181 561 1418) 36 bays covered floodlit 10am-10.30pm

Ilford, Barkingside, Fairlop Waters (0181 500 9911) 36 bays covered floodlit 9am-10pm

Kingston, Beverley Park (0181 949 9200) 60 bays covered floodlit summer 8.am-10pmWD9pmWE winter 9am-10pmWD 8am-9pmWE

Northolt, Ealing Golf Range (0181 845 4967) 36 bays covered floodlit + 4 bays open floodlit 10am-10pm

Northolt, London Golf Centre (0181 845 3180) 19 bays covered floodlit 9am-10pm

Orpington, Lullingstone Park (01959 533793) 15 bays covered 7am-darkWD 5am-darkWE

Orpington, Ruxley Park Golf Centre (01689 871490) 28 bays covered floodlit summer5am-10pm winter7.30am-10pm

Richmond, Richmond Driving Range (0181 332 9200) 23 bays covered floodlit 9.30am-9.30pm

Ruislip, Ruislip Driving Range (01895 638081) 40 bays covered floodlit 10am-10pm

Twickenham, Twickenham (0181 783 1748) 12 bays covered floodlit 9.30am-10pm

GREATER MANCHESTER

Altrincham, Altrincham (0161 927 7504) 27 bays covered floodlit 9am-9.30WD/-7pmWE

Bardsley, Bardsley Park Golf Centre (0161 627 2463) 18 bays covered floodlit 10am-9pmWD 9.30am-6pmWE

Castleton, Castle Hawk Golf Range (01706 59995) 20 bays covered floodlit 9.am-8pmWD 9.am-6pmWE

Wigan, Up Holland, Beacon Park Driving Range (01695 622700) 24 bays covered floodlit 9am-9pm

HAMPSHIRE

Alton, Worldham Park (01420 543151) 6 bays covered + 7 bays open 9am-8pmWD 8am-7pmWE

Basingstoke, Basingstoke Golf Centre (01256 50054) 24 bays covered floodlit 8.30amWD/8amWE-9.30pm

Botley, Botley Park Hotel & Country Club (01489 780888) 7bays open +6 bays covered daylight hours

Crondall, Oak Park (01252 8500660) 16 bays floodlit covered summer 6.30am-9pm winter7am-7pm

Dibden, Dibden Golf Centre (01703 845596) 20 bays floodlit 8am-8pm

Ower, Paulton's Golf Centre(01703 813992) 24 covered floodlit 8am-8,30pmWD 7am-6.30pmWE

Liphook, Old Thorns (01428 724555) 7 bays covered 8am-6pm

Portsmouth, Portsmouth Golf Centre (01705 664549) 22 bays covered floodlit 8am-9pmWD 7am-8pmWE

Southampton,Chilworth, Southampton Golf Range (01703 733166) 24 bays covered + 10 bays open floodlit 7.30am-9pmWD 6pmWE

Tadley, Tadley Driving Range (01734 815213) 12 bays covered floodlit summer8am-9pmWD 7.30am-6WE winter 8am-8pmWD 6pmWE

HEREFORD & WORCESTER

Bishampton, The Vale Driving Range (01386 462781) 20 bays floodlit 8am-10pm

Bransford, Bank House Hotel (Pine Lakes) (01886 833551) 20 bays (5covered) summer8am-dark winter8am-4pm 9pmTuie & Thu

Ombersley, Ombersley Golf Range (01905 620747) 30 bays open daylight hours

Redditch, Abbey Park (01527 63918) 10 bays covered summer 7am-9pm winter7am-dark

Worcester, Worcester Golf Range (01905 421213) 26 bays covered floodlit 9.30am-9.45WD 5.30pmWE/BH

HERTFORDSHIRE

Berkhamsted, Shooters Golf Centre (01442 872048) 25 bays covered floodlit 9am-10pm

Bishop's Stortford, Great Hadham (01279 843558) 15 bays covered floodlit 7.30am-dusk

Graveley, Chesfield Downs (01462 482929) 21-bays covered floodlit + 3 open 7am-10pm (9am-10pm Tue & Thu)

Hemel Hempstead, Little Hay Golf Range (01442 833798) 23 bays covered floodlit 10am-8pmWD 7.30pmWE/BH

Royston, Kingsway (01763 262727/262943) 36 bays covered floodlit 8.30am-10pmWD 7.30am-9.30pmWE

Royston, Whaddon Golf Centre (01223 207325) 14 bays covered floodlit 8am-dusk

Stevenage, Stevenage Golf Range (01438 880424) 24 bays covered floodlit 7.30am-10pm

Ware, Whitehill Golf Centre (01920 438495) 25 bays covered floodlit + open range 7am-9.30Mon Wed Thu Fri 10am-9.30pm Tue 7am-duskWE

Welwyn Garden City, Gosling Sports Park (01707 331056) 22bays covered floodlit 10am-10pm(Mon-Thu)10am-9pm(Fri.) 9am-8pmWE

KENT

Ashford, Homelands Bettergolf Centre (01233 661620) 15 bays covered floodlit 8am-10pm

Biddenden, Chart Hills (01580 292148 pro shop)Chatham, Chatham Golf Centre practice area 30 bays summer 8am-8pm winter 8am-1hr before dusk

Chelmsfield, Chelmsfield LakesGolf Centre (01689 896266) 40 bays covered floodlit 6.30am-9.30pm

Dartford, Birchwood Park (01322 660554) 38 bays covered floodlit 7.30am-10pm

Dartford, Swanley, Olympic Golf Centre (01322 669201) 18 bays covered +9 bays open floodlit 10am-10pm

Edenbridge, Edenbridge Golf Range (01732 865202) 16 bays floodlit 8am-10pm

Folkestone, Etchinghill Golf Course (01303 863863) 11 bays covered floodlit 8am-9pmWD 7pmWE

Herne Bay, Herne Bay Golf Range (01227 742742) 15 bays covered floodlit 9am-10pm

Maidstone, Langley Park Driving Range (01622 863163) 25 bays covered floodlit 10am-10pmWD 10am-9pmWE

Orpington, St. Paul's Cray, Ruxley Park Golf Centre(see under Greater London)

Sittingbourne, The Oast Golf Centre (01795 473527) 17 bays covered floodlit 9am-9.30pm

Sittingbourne, Upchurch, RiverValley Golf Range (01634 379592) 16 bays covered floodlit 7am-9pmWD 6am-8pmWE

LANCASHIRE

Blackburn, Blackburn Driving Range (01254 581996) 27 bays covered floodlit 9am-9pmWD /7pmWE

Blackpool, Heron's Reach, de Vere Hotel (01253 838866) 18 open7am-9pm

Blackpool, Phoenix Driving Range (01253 854846) 27 bays covered floodlit 9.30am-10pmWD 9am-10pmWE

Bolton, Kearsley Golf Range (01204 575726) 10 covered floodlit +30 grass tees 11am-10pmWD 11am-5pmWE

Chorley, Euxton Park Golf Centre (012572 61601) 11 bays covered floodlit + grass tees 11am-10pmWD 11am-5pmWE

Preston, Preston Driving Range (01772 861827) 23 bays covered floodlit 9.30am-9pmWD 9am-6pmWE (Sun. 1.30pm 6pm Winter)

Tarleton, Leisure Lakes Golf Range (01772 815842) 20 bays covered floodlit 9am-8.30pmWD 6pmOWE

Upholland, Beacon Park (01695 622700) 24 bays covered floodlit 9am-9pm

LEICESTERSHIRE

Botcheston, Leicestershire Forest (01455 824800) 20 covered 7am-dusk

Greetham, Greetham Valley (01780 460666) 16 bays covered floodlit +5 open 8am-9pmWD 7.30am-7amWE/Bank Hols.

Leicester, Humberstone Heights (0116 2764674) 25 bays covered floodlit 8.30am-9.30pmWD 7am-7pmWE

Leicester, Whetstone Golf Range (0116 2861424) 20 bays open 8am-dusk

Loughborough, Charnwood Golf Centre (01509 610022) 24 bays covered floodlit 8.30am-10.30pm

Wilson, Breedon Priory Golf Course (01332 863081) 2 bays covered 20 bays open summer 8am-8pm approx. winter 8am-dusk

LINCOLNSHIRE

Belton, DeVere Belton Woods (01476 593200) 24 bays covered floodlit 8am-10pm(Summer) 8am-9pm(Winter)

Gainsborough, Thonock Driving Range (01427 613088) 25 bays covered floodlit 9am-8pmWD 8am-duskWE

Holbeach, Gedney Hill (01406 330922) 10 bays covered floodlit

Horncastle, Horncastle (01507 526800) 25 bays covered floodlit 9am-9.30pm

Lincoln, Lincoln Bowls (01522 522059) 20 bays covered floodlit 9am-late

Scunthorpe, Messingham, Grange Park (01724 764478) 20 bays covered floodlit 9am-9.30pmWD /8.30pmWE

Skegness, The Elms Golf Centre (01754 881230) 20 bays covered floodlit 10am-10pm

LONDON SEE ALSO GREATER LONDON

N9 Edmonton, Lea Valley Leisure Centre (0181 345 6666) 20 bays covered floodlit 8am-9.30pmWD/-8.30pmWE

N14 Southgate, Trent Park (0181 366 7432) 24 bays floodlit 9am-10pmWD 7.30am-9.30pmWE

E4 Chingford, Chingford Golf Range (0181 529 2409) 18 covered floodlit 9.30am-10pm

MERSEYSIDE

Formby, Formby Golf Centre (017048 75952) 14 bays covered floodlit + 7bays open summer9.30am-9.30pm winter8.30pm

Moreton, Wirral Golf & Drive Centre (0151 677 6606) 20 bays covered floodlit +10 bays open 8am-9pm

NORFOLK

Norwich, Bawburgh, Norwich Golf Centre (01603 742323) 14 bays covered floodlit 8am-8.30pmWD 5pmWE

King's Lynn, Eagles Golf Centre (01553 827147) 20 bays covered floodlit 8am-9pmWD/-8pmWE

King's Lynn, Middleton Hall (01553 841800) 6 bays covered floodlit 8am-10pm

Norwich, Sprowston Park (01603 410657) 27 bays covered floodlit 7.30am-8.30pmWD 6.30WE

Norwich, Wensum Valley (01603 261012) 4 bays covered + 2 bays open floodlit 7.30am-dusk

NORTHAMPTONSHIRE

Daventry, Staverton Park (01327 302000) 16 bays covered floodlit 7.30am-10pm

Northampton, Collingtree Park (01604 700000) 16 bays covered floodlit 8am-9pm

Northampton, Delapre Golf Complex (01604 764036) 40 bays covered floodlit 9am-10pm

NOTTINGHAMSHIRE

Newark, John Lee Golf Centre (01636 702161) 24 bays covered floodlit 9.am-10pmWD/-6pmWE

Nottingham, Richard Harrod Leisure Centre (0115 961 2949) 28 bays covered floodlit 9.30am-10pm exc. Mon 12-10pm

Nottingham, Cotgrave Place Golf Range(0115 933 4686) 10 bays covered floodlit 8am-8.45pm

Nottingham, Ramsdale Park Golf Centre (0115 965 5600) 25 bays covered floodlit + 1 video training bay 7.30am-10pmWD 6am-10pmWE

Nottingham, Riverside Golf Centre (0115 986 2179) 24 bays closed floodlit 9.30am-9.30pm

Oxton, Oakmere Park (0115 965 3545) 33 bays covered floodlit 7.30am-9.30pmWD 7am-7pmWE

OXFORDSHIRE

Abingdon, Drayton Park (01235 550607) 21 bays covered floodlit 8am-8.30pmWD 7am-8.30pmWE

Oxford, Oxford Golf Centre (01865 721592) 19 bays covered floodlit + 8 bays open 10am-9pmWD 8pmWE.

SHROPSHIRE

Oswestry, Mile End (01691 670580) 12 bays covered floodlit 8.30am-dusk(Summer) 8.30am-6pm(Winter)

Telford, Telford Hotel Golf & Country Club (01952 586052) 8 bays covered floodlit dawn-10pm

SOMERSET

Congresbury, Mendip Spring (01934 852322) 11 bays covered floodlit 8am-9pm

Farrington Gurney, Farrington Golf Range (01761 241274) 18 bays floodlit +10 open grass 8am-9am

Langport, Long Sutton Golf Range (01458 241017) 10 bays covered floodlit 8am-9.30pm(Sun-9pm)

Monkton Combe, Combe Grove Manor Golf Range (01225 835533) 19 bays (9 covered) 10am-7.45pmWD 6.30pmWE

Taunton, Swingrite Golf Range, Holway (01823 442600) 12 bays covered + 7 bays open floodlit 9am-9pmWD/-7pmWE

Taunton, Oake Manor (01823 461993) 11-bays covered dawn-dusk

Taunton, Taunton Vale, West Monkton (01823 412220) 8 bays floodlit 80am-9pm

Tickenham, Golf Drive-In (01275 856626) 24 covered floodlit 8.30am-8.30pmWD 8am-6.30pmWE

Yeovil, Halstock Driving Range (01935 891689) 12 bays covered floodlit 8.30am-7.30pm(-7pm Winter)

STAFFORDSHIRE

Burton-upon-Trent, Craythorne (01283 564329) 13 bays covered floodlit 8am-9.30pm

Litchfield, Seedy Mill Golf Range (01543 417333) 27 bays covered floodlit 7am-10pm

Newcastle-under-Lyme, Keele Golf Centre (01782 717417) 26 bays covered floodlit 9am-10pm

SUFFOLK

Halesworth, St. Helena (01986 875567) 10 bays covered floodlit + 8 bays open 8.30am-9.30pm

Ipswich, Fynn Valley (01473 785463) 10 bays covered floodlit + 13 bays open 8am-8.30pmWD -7pmWE

Ipswich, Ipswich Golf Centre (01473 726821) 15 bays open + 2 bay covered 9am-7pmWD 6.30pmWE

SURREY

Camberly, Pine Ridge (01276 20770) 36 bays covered floodlit 8am-10pm

Cobham, Silvermere Driving Range (01932 867275) 34 bays covered floodlit 8am-9.30pmWD 8pmWE

Esher, Sandown Golf Centre (01372 461234) 33 bays floodlit 10am-10pmWD/-9pmWE (closed during race meetings)

Farnham, Blacknest Golf Club (01420 22888) 24 bays covered 7.30am-9pm

Godalming, Broadwater Park (01483 429955) 16 bays covered floodlit 8am-10pm

Old Woking, Hoebridge Golf Centre (01483 722611) 25 bays covered floodlit 7.30am-10pmWD dawn-10pmWE

Woking, Windlemere Golf Range (01276 858727) 12 bays covered floodlit 9am-10pm

SUSSEX (EAST)

Ditchling, Mid Sussex Golf Course (01273 846567) 20 bays open summer 7.30am-9.30pm winter 9am-4/5pm

Eastbourne, Eastbourne Golfing Park (01323 520400) 24 bays covered floodlit 10amm-10pm

Hellingly, Wellshurst Golf Range (01435 813456) 16 bays covered floodlit 7.30am-9.30pm

Horam, Horam Park (01435 813477) 16 bays covered floodlit 10am-9pm (approx.)

Ticehurst, Dale Hill (01580 200112) 10 open bays 7.30am-7pm

SUSSEX (WEST)

Chichester, Chichester Golf Range (01243 533833) 27 bays covered floodlit 8.30am-8.830pm

Crawley, Pease Pottage Driving Range(01293 521706) 30 bays covered floodlit 8am-10pm

Crawley, Tilgate Driving Centre (01293 530103) 35 bays covered floodlit 7am-10pmWD/-8.30pmWE

Horsham, Horsham Golf Park (01403 271525) 30 bays open 7.30am-dusk

Petworth, Osiers Farm (01798 344097) 6 bays open 8am-dusk

Pulborough,West Chiltington Driving Range (01798 812115) 8 bays covered floodlit + 8 bays ope 7.30am-dusk

Rustington, Rustington Golf Centre (01903 850790) 30 bays covered floodlit +10 bays open 9am-9pm

Slinfold, Slinfold Park (01403 791555) 14 bays covered + 5 bays open floodlit 8am-9pmWD/-7pmWE

TYNE & WEAR

Newcastle-upon-Tyne, Parklands (0191 236 4480) 45 bays two-tier covered floodlit 8am-10pm

Washington, Washington Moat House (0191 4029988) 21 bays covered floodlit 9am-9pm

WARWICKSHIRE

Coventry, Brandon Wood (01203 543141) 11 bays covered + 8 bays open floodlit 9am-8.30pmWD 8am-9pmWE

Lea Marston, Lea Marston Driving Range (01675 470707) 30 bays covered floodlit 9am-10pmWD 8.30am-10pmWE

Nuneaton, Purley Chase (01203 395348) 13 bays covered floodlit 8am-9.30pm

Stratford on-Avon, Stratford Oaks Golf Range (01789 731571) 23 bays covered floodlit 8am-9pm

Warwick, Warwick Golf Centre (01926 494316) 24 bays covered floodlit 8am-9pmWD 6pmWE

WEST MIDLANDS

Bromsgrove, Bromsgrove Golf Centre (01527 575886) 41 bays covered floodlit 9am-10pmWD 6pmSat.10am-6pmSun

Coventry, John Reay Golf Centre (01 203 333920 /333405) 30 bays covered floodlit 9am-10pm

Dudley, Sedgley Driving Range (01902 880503) 16 bays covered floodlit 9.30am-9pmWD 9am-6pmWE

Dudley, Swindon Ridge (01902 896191) 23 bays covered + 5 bays open floodlit 9am-9.30pmWD 10am-6pmWE

Halesowen, Halesowen Golf Range (0121 550 2920) 4 bays closed + 11 bays open 9.30am-dusk 7.30pmWE

Solihull, Four Ashes Golf Centre (01564 779055) 28 bays covered floodlit 10am-10pmWD 10am-6pmWE

Wishaw, The Belfry (01675 470301) 16 bays covered floodlit 7.30am-9.30pm

Wolverhampton, Three Hammers (01902 790940) 23 bays covered floodlit 9.30am-10pmWD 9am-9pmWE

Wolverhampton, Perton Park Golf Range (01902 380103) 12 bays covered + 6 bays open 7am-dusk

WILTSHIRE

Calne, Bowood (01249 822228) 10 bays covered floodlit 7.30am-10pm

Westbury, Thoulstone Park (01373 832825) 24 bays covered floodlit 8am-7.30pmMon.-Thu. 8am-6.30pmSun.

Swindon, Broome Manor Golf Complex (01793 532403) 34 bays covered + 6 bays open floodlit 8am-9.30pmWD 7am-9pmWE

Swindon, Wrag Barn Golf Range (01793 766027) 12 bays covered floodlit 8am-7.30pm

Trowbridge, Wingfield Golf Range (01225 776365) 28 bays covered floodlit 9.30am-9.30pm-6pm Sun

YORKSHIRE EAST RIDING

Hull, Hull Golf Centre (01482 492720) 24 bays covered floodlit 9am-9pmWD 8pmWE

YORKSHIRE (NORTH)

Middlesborough, Middlesborough Driving Range (01642 300720) 20 bays covered floodlit 9am-9pmWD 9am-6pmWE

York, York Driving Range (01904 690421) 20 bays floodlit 10am-5pmWD 7am-10pmWE

YORKSHIRE (SOUTH)

Bawtry, Austerfield Park (01302 710841) 10 bays covered floodlit 9am-10pm

Barnsley, Sandhill Golf Range (01226 751775) 18 bays covered floodlit 9am-9.WD 9am-6.pmWE

YORKSHIRE (WEST)

Huddersfield, Bradley Park (01484 223772) 14 bays covered floodlit 9am-9.30pm

Knaresborough, Scotton Golf Range (01423 868943) 12 bays covered + 6 bays open 10am-dusk

Leeds, Leeds Golf Centre (0113 288 6000) 21 covered floodlit 7am-9.30pm

Leeds, Oulton Park (01132 823152) 22 bays covered floodlit 9am-9pm

Pontefract, Mid Yorkshire (01977 704522) 28 bays covered floodlit 8am-dusk

CHANNEL ISLANDS
GUERNSEY

L'Ancresse Vale, Royal Guernsey (01481 45070) 12 bays open dawn-dusk

JERSEY

St. Ouens Bays, Les Mielles Golf & Country Club (01534 482787) 20 bays covered + 10 open 7am-dark

ISLE OF MAN

Douglas, Mount Murray (01624 661111) 20 bays covered + 4 bays open floodlit 8am-10pmWD 9am-10pmWE

SCOTLAND

HIGHLANDS & ISLANDS

Inverness, Fairways Golf Range (01463 713334) 22 bays covered floodlit 8am-10pm

Spey Bays, Spey Bays Hotel (01343 820424) 16 bays covered floodlit 10am-10.30pm

CENTRAL

Bathgate, Whitburn, Polkemmet Country Park (01501 743905) 15 bays covered floodlit 9am-9pm

Edinburgh, Port Royal (0131 333 4377) 24 bays covered + 13 bays open floodlit 10am- 10.pm

Edinburgh, Lasswade, Melville (0131 663 8038) 22 bays covered + 12 bays open floodlit 9am-10pmWD 9am-8pmWE

Errol, Middlebank Golf Range (01821 670320) 7 bays covered + 21 bays open floodlit 9am-9pm

Glenrothes, Glenrothes Golf Range (01592 775374) 20 bays covered floodlit 10am-8.30pmWD 5.30pmWE

Perth, Murrayshall Country House Hotel (01738 551171) 10 bays covered + 8 open floodlit + indoor facility 7.30am-dusk

SOUTHERN LOWLANDS & BORDERS

Cumbernauld, Cumbernauld Golf Range (01236 737000) 20 bays covered floodlit 9am-10.30pm (Summer) 9.30am-9.30pm(Winter)

Cumbernauld, Westerwood (01236 457171) 8 bays open 7.30am-dusk

Glasgow, Bishopbriggs Golf Range (0141 762 4883) 20 bays covered + 2 bays open floodlit 10am-10pm(closed5pm-6pm)

Glasgow, Renfrew, Normandy Golf Range (0141886 7477) 20 bays covered + 5 bays open floodlit 9.30am-10pm

Glasgow, Uddingston, Clydeway Golf Centre (0141 641 8899) 25 bays covered floodlit 9am-9pmWD 10am-6.30pmWE

Stevenston, Auchenharvie Driving Range (01294 603103) 18 bays covered floodlit 8am-3pm 4pm-8.30pmWD 8am-5pmWE

WALES

NORTH

Penymynydd, Bannel Golf Range (01244 544639) 10 bays closed floodlit + 3 bays open 10am-9pmWD 10am-6pmWE

Bodelwyddan, Kinmel Park Golf Complex (01745 833548) 24 bays covered floodlit 10am-10pmWD 6pmSat 8pmSun(

St. Asaph, North Wales Golf Range (01745 730805) 14 bays covered floodlit 10am-9pm (close earlier Winter)

Wrexham, Clays Farm Golf Centre ((01978 661406/661416) 16 bays covered floodlit 8am-9pmWD 6pmWE

CENTRAL

Caersws, Mid-Wales (01686 688303) 12 bays covered floodlit 8.30am-9.30pm (8.30-6pmWE Winter)

Haverfordwest, Mayfield Golf Range (01437 890308) 12 bays covered floodlit 10am-9.pmWD 10am-9pmWE

Middletown, Welsh Border Golf Range (01743 884247) 10 bays covered floodlit 9am-8.30pm winter 6pmWE

Newport, Parc (01633 680933) 30 bays covered + 8 open floodlit 7.30am-10pmWD 8pmWE

SOUTH

Abergavenny, Wernddu Golf Centre (01873 856223) 26 bays covered floodlit 8am-9.30pm

Barry, South Wales Golf Range (01446 742434) 16 bays covered floodlit 9am-8pmWD 9am-5pmWE

Bridgend, Pencoed, St. Mary's Driving Range (01656 860280) 15 bays covered floodlit 8am-9pm

Caerleon, Carleon Driving Range (01633 420342) 12 bays covered floddlit+ 3 open 7.30-8am-9pm

Caerphilly, Mountain Lakes (01222 861128) 20 bays covered floodlit 8am-9pm

Caerwent, Dewstow (01291 430444) 20 bays covered floodlit 9am-9pm

Cwmbran, Green Meadow (01633 862626) 26 bays covered floodlit 8am-10pm

NORTHERN IRELAND

CO ANTRIM

Whitehead, Whitehead Driving Range (01960 353159) 18 bays covered 18 bays open floodlit 10am-9pmWD 6pmWE

CO ARMAGH

Lurgan, Craigavon Golf Centre (01762 326606) 10 bays covered + 10 bays open all floodlit 9am-9.30pmWD 9am-8pmWE

CO BELFAST

Belfast, Knockbracken Golf Centre (01232 792108) 30 bays covered + 60 grass baysopen 9am-11pm

Belfast, Newtonabbey, Ballyearl Golf Centre (01232 848287) 27 bays covered floodlit 9am-10pm

CO DOWN

Bangor, Blackwood (01247 852706) 20 bays covered floodlit 8am-10pm

Warrenpoint, Newry & Mourne Golf Centre (016937 73247) 10 bays closed floodlit 10am-10pmWD 10am-8pmWE

CO TYRONE

Omagh, Clanabogan Driving Range (01662 245409) 10 covered floodlit 9am-9.30pm 10am-10pmSun.

REPUBLIC OF IRELAND

(From UK dial 00353 and ignore first digit of numbers below)

CO CORK

Little Island, Harbour Point (021 353094) 21 bays covered floodlit 9.30am-9.30pm

CO DUBLIN

Dublin, Leopardstown Golf Centre (01 289 5341 / 895671) 40 bays covered floodlit + 50(approx.) bays open 9am-9.30pmWD 7.30am-9.30pmWE

Dublin, Ward Golf Centre (01 834 8711) 30 bays covered + 20 bays open floodlit 10am-10pm

CO GALWAY

Galway, Galway Range (091 526737 / 26753) 24 bays floodlit 10am-10pmWD 10am-9pmWE

9.30pmWD WE Summer only-call first

CO KILDARE

Celbridge, Celbridge Golf Centre (01 628 8833) 40 bays covered floodlit + 20 bays open 8.30am-10pm summer 10am-10pm winter

CO LAIOS

Portlaiose, The Heath (0502 46533) 10 bays covered floodlit 10.30am-10.30pm

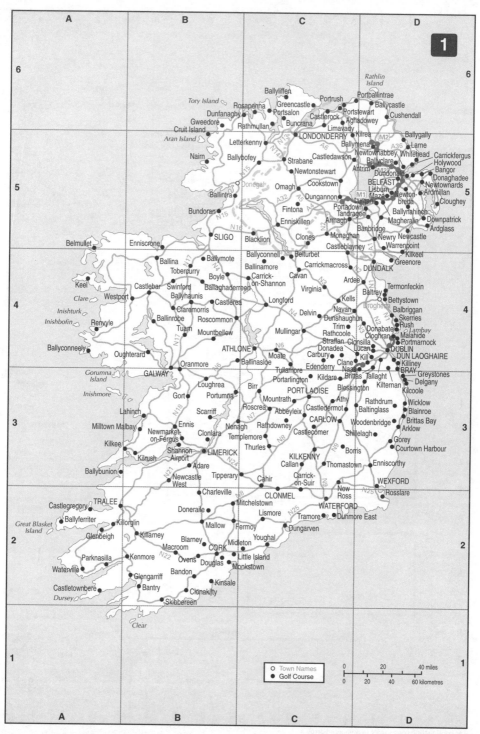

© The Automobile Association 1996

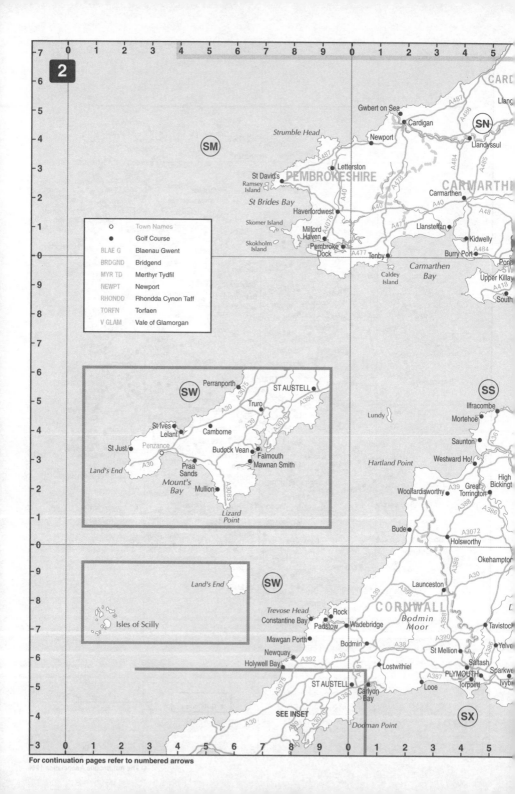

2

○	Town Names
●	Golf Course
BLAE G	Blaenau Gwent
BRDGND	Bridgend
MYR TD	Merthyr Tydfil
NEWPT	Newport
RHONDD	Rhondda Cynon Taff
TORFN	Torfaen
V GLAM	Vale of Glamorgan

(SM)

Strumble Head

(SN)

Gwbert on Sea
Cardigan
Llandyssul
Newport
Llang

CARD

St David's
PEMBROKESHIRE
Letterston
Ramsey
Island
CARMARTHE
St Brides Bay
Carmarthen
Skomer Island
Haverfordwest
Llansteffan
Skokholm
Island
Milford
Haven
Kidwelly
Pembroke
Dock
Burry Port
Tenby
Ponthe
Caldey
Island
Carmarthen
Bay
SW
Upper Killay
South

(SW)

Perranporth
ST AUSTELL
Lundy
Ilfracombe
(SS)
Truro
Mortehoe
St Ives
Lelant
Camborne
Saunton
St Just
Penzance
Budock Vean
Falmouth
Westward Ho!
Land's End
Praa
Sands
Mawnan Smith
Hartland Point
High
Bickingt
Mount's
Bay
Mullion
Woolfardisworthy
Great
Torrington
Lizard
Point
Bude
Holsworthy
Okehampton

Land's End
(SW)

Isles of Scilly
CORNWALL
Launceston
Trevose Head
Rock
Bodmin
Moor
Tavistock
Constantine Bay
Padstow
Wadebridge
Mawgan Porth
Bodmin
St Mellion
Yelve
Newquay
Lostwithiel
Saltash
Holywell Bay
PLYMOUTH
Sparkwe
Torpoint
Ivybr
ST AUSTELL
Looe
Carlyon
Bay
(SX)
SEE INSET
Dodman Point

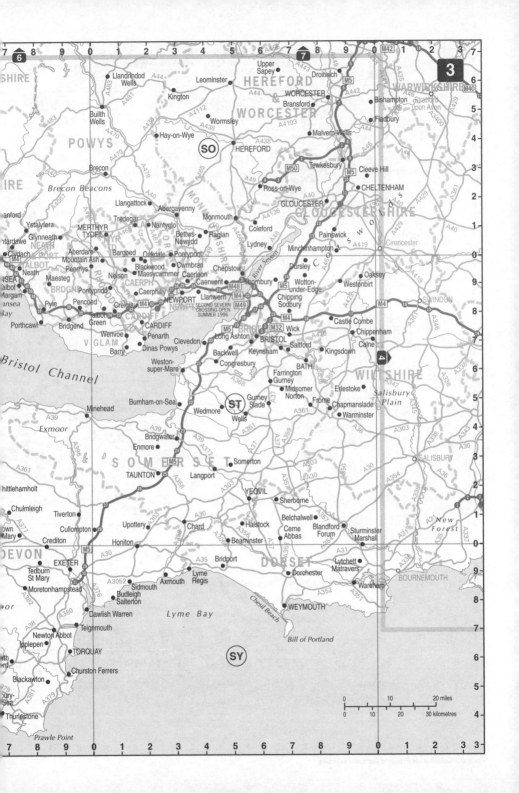

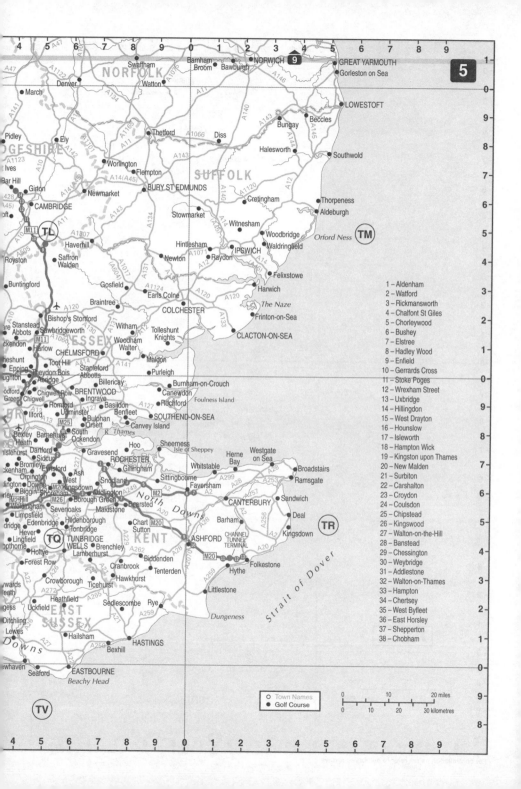

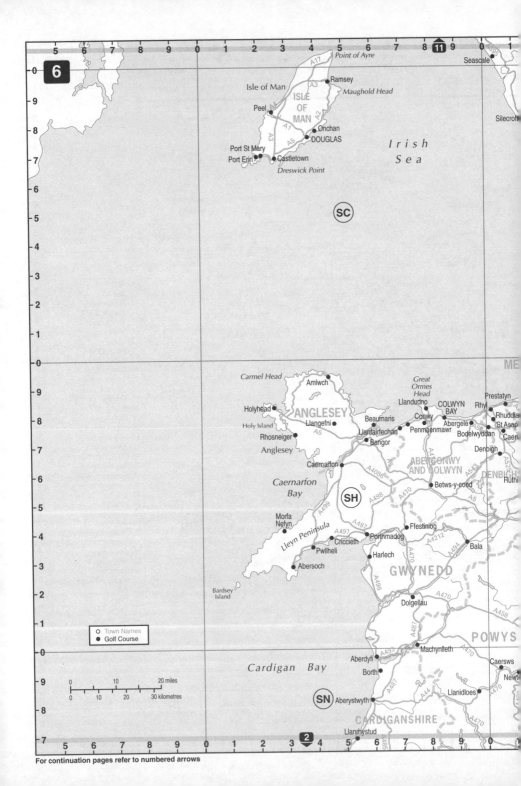

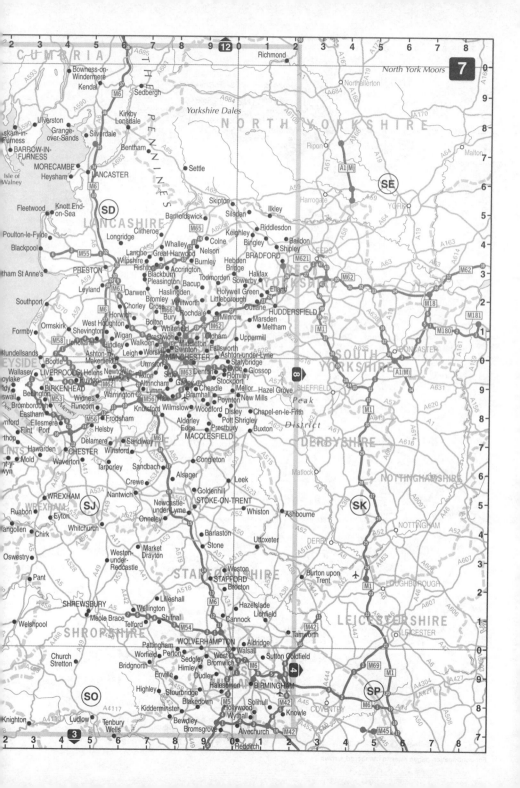

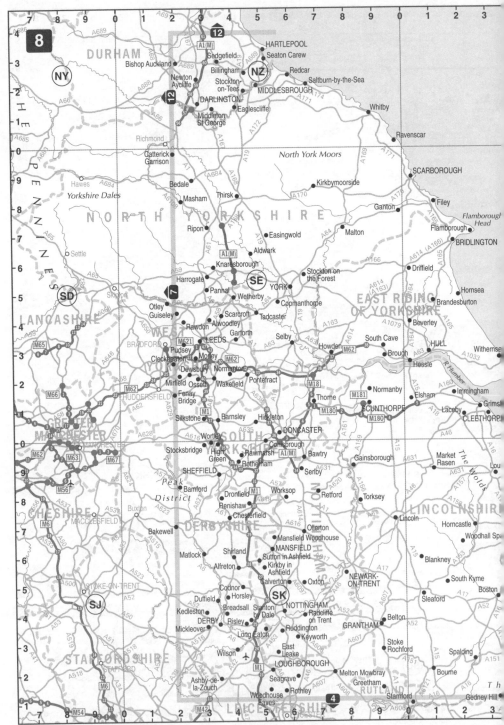

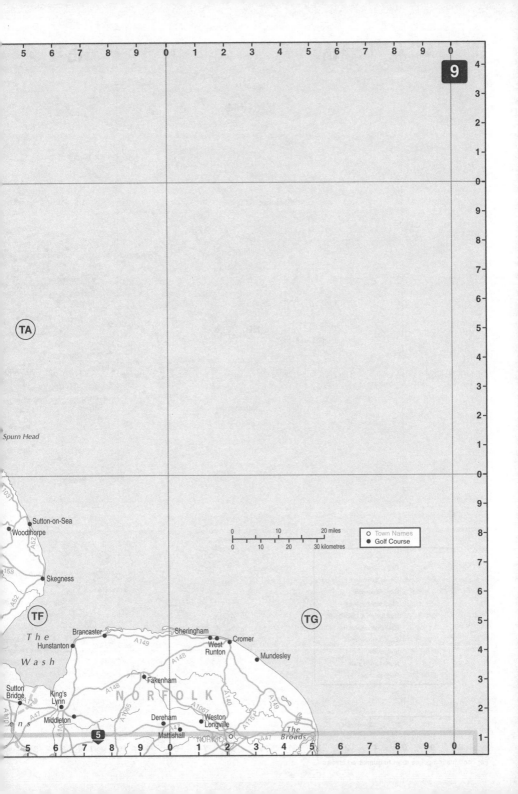

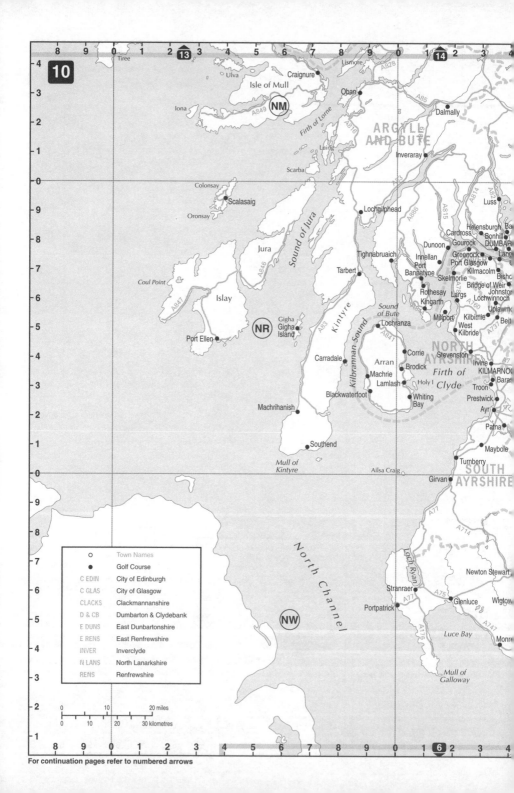

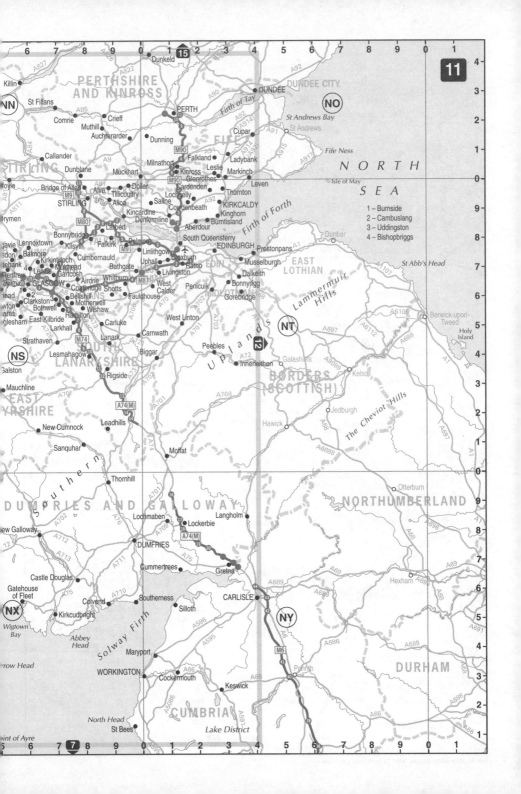

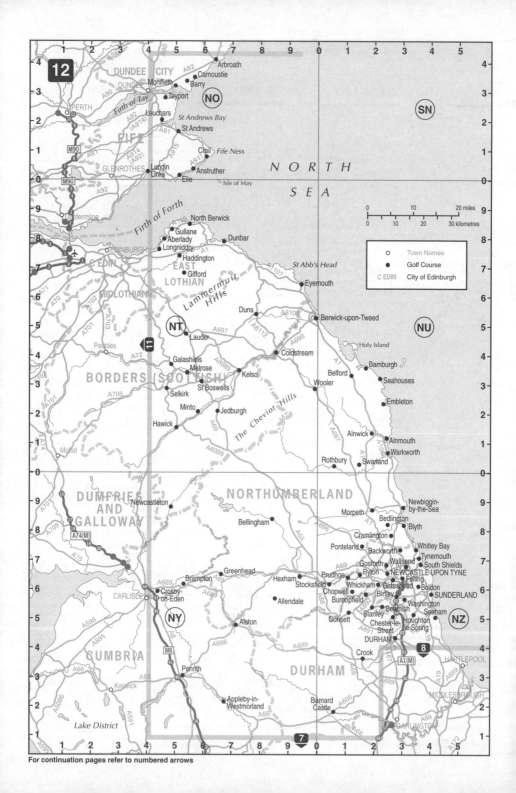

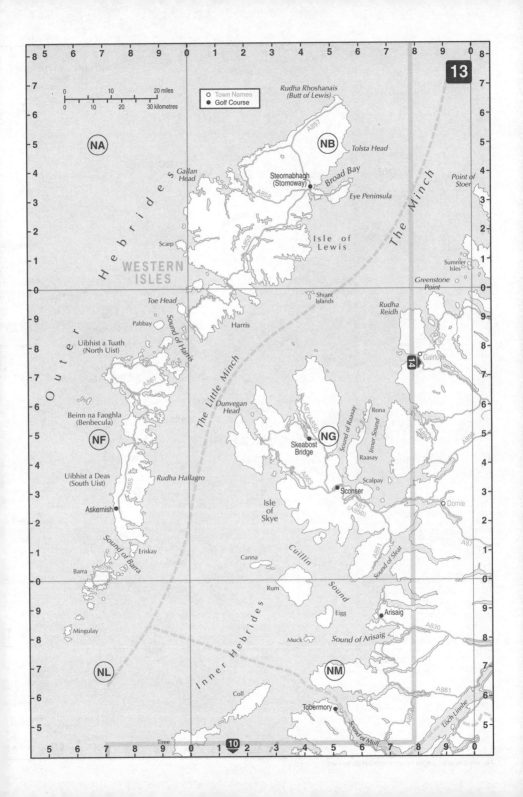

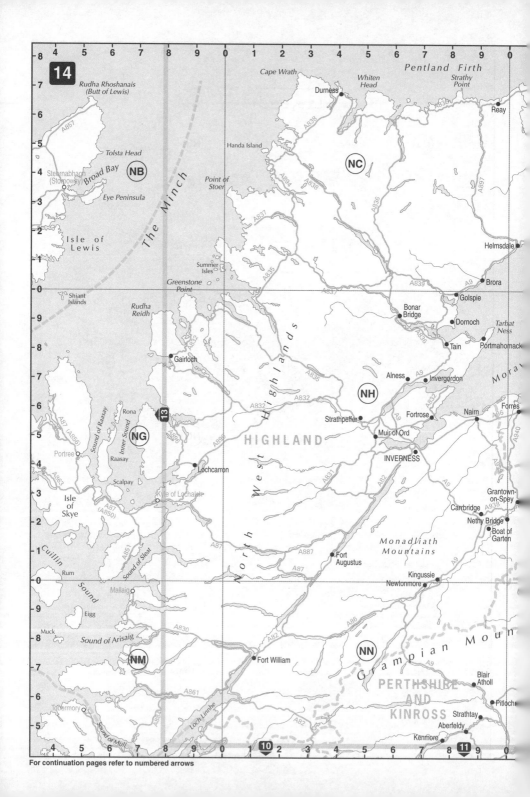

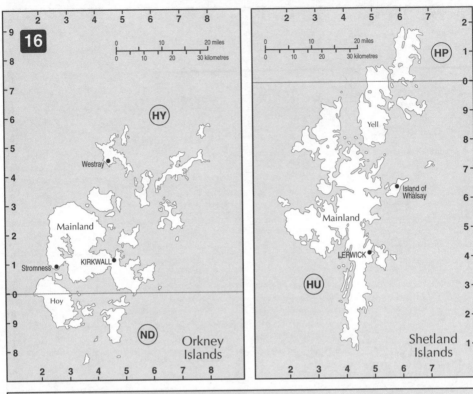

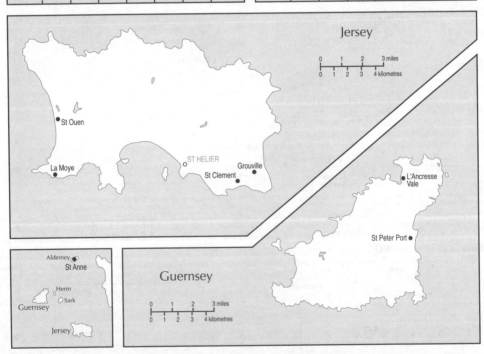

16

0   10   20 miles
0   10   20   30 kilometres

Orkney Islands

HY

ND

Westray

Mainland

KIRKWALL

Stromness

Hoy

Shetland Islands

HP

HU

Yell

Island of Whalsay

Mainland

LERWICK

0   10   20 miles
0   10   20   30 kilometres

Jersey

St Ouen

La Moye

ST HELIER

St Clement

Grouville

0   1   2   3 miles
0   1   2   3   4 kilometres

L'Ancresse Vale

St Peter Port

Alderney
St Anne

Herm

Guernsey

Sark

Jersey

Guernsey

0   1   2   3 miles
0   1   2   3   4 kilometres

INDEX